INTERNATIONAL DICTIONARY OF

FOOD & COOKING

INTERNATIONAL DICTIONARY OF

FOOD & COOKING

Ingredients, additives, techniques, equipment, menu terms, catering terms, food science, and outline domestic and production recipes

compiled by
Charles G. Sinclair

FITZROY DEARBORN PUBLISHERS
CHICAGO • LONDON

Published in Great Britain by
Peter Collin Publishing Ltd
1 Cambridge Road, Teddington, Middlesex, TW11 8DT

Published in the United States of America by
Fitzroy Dearborn, Publishers
70 East Walton Street, Chicago, Illinois 60611

Text computer typeset by Tradespools, Frome, Somerset
Printed and bound by WSOY in Finland

A Cataloging-in-Publication record for this book is available from the Library of Congress

ISBN 1-57958-057-2

First Published in the USA and UK 1998

Preface

The language of English cuisine is unusual in that it uses many words of foreign origin often in their original spelling. The purpose of this dictionary is to give short definitions of these words so that both the practising chef and the amateur enthusiast, the gastronome or the student may quickly determine the meaning. It is not a recipe book or repertoire, but the ingredients of classic and well-known dishes together with a brief summary of the cooking processes are given. With this information any professional or amateur cook could, after a little experimentation, roughly reproduce the dish.

As in all dictionaries, the compiler has had to be selective in the words chosen for inclusion. Even so, the dictionary lists over 24,000 words of which very few are not in current use somewhere in the English-speaking world. Some entries have been included for historical reasons and the browser will find much of interest. Classical dishes, ingredients, cooking processes, cooking implements and equipment, descriptions of function and details of service are included as well as scientific, botanical, medical, technological, hygienic and nutritional terms. Many single words appertaining to the catering industry from the countries of the European Union are translated, and the dictionary is of use in translating menu items not included. Drinks, wines and spirits are not included except where they are used as flavourings in food and food preparation.

Sorting and ordering of entries

All entries are sorted in numerical and alphabetical order, numerical coming first. Accented characters are assumed to follow the unaccented characters which they resemble. Thus ø follows õ, ö, ô, ò, ó and o in that order. The rules for the treatment of spaces and hyphens are as follows:

For all European languages, European derived (American, South American, Australasian and some Filipino) plus Russian, Turkish and Iranian, the space and hyphen are considered as the first letter in the alphabet. Prepositions, articles, abbreviations, and small linking words such as **con**, and **à la, po**, are ignored except where they are at the beginning of a phrase as for example in **à point, al dente, S-Gebäck**. Where such words occur at the beginning of a phrase, the following space or hyphen is assumed not to be present. Thus **à point** comes after **apog** and **S-Gebäck** after **sformata**.

For all other languages, mainly Asian and Indian, spaces and hyphens are assumed not to exist, so that, for example, **nam katee** *(Th)* comes before **na mool** *(Ko)*, i.e. in the order **namkatee, namool**, where with the European convention, **na mool** would come before **nam katee** in the order **na, nam**.

The names of many items in the French repertoire have been taken over wholesale into the English language. For example, 'sauce béchamel' is known as 'béchamel sauce', often retaining the French acute accent and for this reason and to avoid making the entries too repetitious this type is listed in reverse order of the words in the dictionary.Thus **Sauce béchamel** would appear under the heading **béchamel, sauce**. The comma in the phrase indicates that the following words precede the words before the comma. Other examples are **suprême, sauce**, and **aurore, sauce**. Similar examples occur with whole classes of French names such as **garniture** (garnish), **salade, potage** (soup), **consommé, soufflé,** etc. Such entries occur before the root word in alphabetical order. Thus **anchois, beurre de** and **anchois, sauce** occur after **anchois** but before **anchois frais marinée**.

Verbs are indicated by the prefix 'to', e.g. 'to blend, to roast' and listed as **blend, to** and **roast, to**.

Language, origins, gender

The language of words or phrases, if important or not obvious from the definition, is given in brackets immediately after the entry. Thus for example, **'Arroz** *(Sp)* **Rice'** indicates that the word 'arroz' is Spanish, but the dish **'Arroz con frijoles** *(Me)* **Rice with beans'** shows that the dish is of Mexican origin. Where a dish is of some regional origin within a country, the region will usually be indicated in the text whereas the abbreviation for the country will be given in brackets after the entry. For example, the entry **'Athol brose** *(UK)* **A Scottish dish....'** indicates that the dish is from the Scottish region of the United Kingdom. The list of abbreviations is given later. The gender is only indicated for French words, since in general there is no way of ascertaining the gender from the spelling and because of the importance of the French language in the language of gastronomy.

Recipes

In some of the entries, outline recipes are given together with quantities of key ingredients. The usual method of giving quantities is to give the relative proportions by weight in brackets after the list of ingredients. Thus for example, **genoise paste** is defined as 'Flour, butter, caster sugar and eggs (2:1:3:5) made up....' This could be 4oz of flour, 1oz of butter, 6oz of caster sugar and 5 eggs (recalling that a standard egg weight 2oz or 60g), or alternatively in metric measure, 24g of flour, 12g of butter, 36g of caster sugar to each egg.

All cooking temperatures are given in °C (degrees centigrade or Celsius). Equivalents in other units (°F or gas mark) can be found in any reasonable recipe book.

Transliteration

The transliterations used from the Greek, Russian, South-East Asian, Chinese, etc. languages are those adopted in the English translations of the original dishes and terms. Different authorities give different transliterations and where several are in common use for the same dish they are all given in their correct alphabetical order referring back or forwards to the master entry. Chinese terms are transliterated in a variety of ways from either Cantonese or Mandarin according to the source of the entry. Accents are not shown for Chinese transliterations hence they give only a very rough approximation of the spoken word.

Acknowledgements

Every compiler of a dictionary is indebted to so many written sources that it would be impossible to list them all. Most of the extant dictionaries and encyclopaedias of food have been consulted and many hundreds of cookbooks trawled. Quite a few errors in the published literature have been spotted and corrected but it is inevitable that some will not have been detected and it is hoped that correspondents will point these out.

I am eternally indebted to those persons who first inspired me to undertake this work and to those who have given so freely of their time to correct the spellings and definitions of foreign terms. In chronological order, these are Gareth Burgess, at that time Head of the Catering and Hospitality department of City College, Manchester, whose encouragement and practical help were given freely when it was most needed, and my agent, Chelsea Fox, whose efforts on my behalf were most welcome. My publisher, Peter Collin, has been a tower of strength and his continuous guidance, help and assistance eased the long path from first to last draft. Lecturing staff and former lecturing staff at the City College, Manchester, in particular Gordon Hetherington, Mary Cork and Anthony Fallon have been unstinting in giving me the benefit of their knowledge and experience.

I wish to pay tribute to those students and friends at UMIST and from all over the world who have corrected the entries in their respective mother tongues. Without their help the errors in this dictionary would have been legion; as it is, the ones that remain are solely my responsibility.

In alphabetical order of surname, they are:

Norhafizah Abdullah, Cornelia Allen, Christine Biermann, Bao-Dong Chen, Jan Cilliers, George Devarkos, Rosa Maria Dominguez, Tom Dyskowska, Amer El-Hamouz, Claudia Aguilar Garcia, Vipa Jayranaiwachira, Brahim and Mrs H. Khalfaoui, Jiri Klemes, Claudia Konscaq, Joan and Bjorn Kristiansen, Asher Kyperstock, Gen Larssen, Emma Marigliano, Ferda Mavituna, David Miller, Gunnar Munksgaard, Mehdi Nemati, Ma Prem Nitayamo, Claire O'Beirne, Severino Pandiella, Megan Sinclair, Amita Sitomurni (Adji), David Webb

And finally to my good lady bed companion, Pamela Davis, for whose tolerance and support over the many years that it took to compile, check and type this dictionary I owe an irredeemable debt of gratitude.

Abbreviations

adj.	adjective
Af	Africa
Ar	Argentina
Au	Austria
Ba	Balkans (former Yugoslavia)
Be	Belgium
BG	Bouquet garni
Bm	Burma, Burmese (Myanmar)
Bot.	Botanical name of
Br	Brazil
Bu	Bulgaria, Bulgarian
° deg	Degree centigrade (Celsius)
Ca	Caribbean
CA	Central America
CE	Central Europe
Ch	China
cm	centimetre
Cm	Cambodia
Cn	Canada
coll.	colloquial
Cu	Cuba
Cy	Cyprus
Cz	Czech Republic, Slovakia
De	Denmark, Danish
dia.	diameter
EA	East Africa
e.g.	for example
En	English language
esp.	especially
Eu	Europe
EU	European Union
Ey	Egypt
f	form (Bot.)
deg	Degree Fahrenheit
fem.	feminine
Fi	Finland, Finnish
Fr	France, French
g	gram
Ge	Germany, German
GM	Gas mark
Gr	Greece, Greek
He	Switzerland
Ho	Holland, Dutch
Hu	Hungary, Hungarian
Ic	Iceland, Icelandic
Id	Indonesia, Indonesian
i.e.	that is to say
In	India, Indian subcontinent, including Pakistan and Bangladesh
Ir	Ireland (Republic)
Ja	Japan, Japanese
kg	kilogram
Ko	Korea, Korean
La	Laos, Laotian
lb	pound weight
Li	Lithuania, Lithuanian
Lit.	Literal meaning
Lu	Luxembourg
m	metre
mm	millimetre
Ma	Malaysia, Malaysian
masc.	masculine
Me	Mexico
ME	Middle East
Ml	Malta, Maltese
No	Norway, Norwegian
NZ	New Zealand
o.e.	Old English
oz	ounce
pl.	plural
Pe	Iran
Ph	Philippines, Filipino
Pl	Poland, Polish
Po	Portugal, Portuguese
q.v.	which see
Ro	Romania, Romanian
Ru	Russian Federation, Russian
Sa	Scandinavia
SA	South America
Saf	South Africa
SEA	South-East Asia
Sp	Spain, Spanish
spp.	species
Sr	Sri Lanka (Ceylon)
subsp.	subspecies (Bot.)
Sw	Sweden, Swedish
Th	Thailand, Thai
Tu	Turkey, Turkish
UK	United Kingdom
USA	United States of America
var.	variety (Bot.)
Ve	Venezuela
Vi	Vietnam, Vietnamese
WA	West Africa
Yu	former Yugoslavia
x	Botanical cross
>	Greater than
<	Less than

Aa

à la *(Fr)* In the style of-, in the manner of-, with-, used before feminine French nouns

AA *see* arachidonic acid

aachar *see* acar

aahaar *(Ne)* Food

Aal *(Ge & Ho)* Eel

Aalquappe *(Ge)* Eel pout

Aalsuppe *(Ge)* Eel soup

aam *(In)* Ripe mango

aamchur *see* amchoor

aam ka achar *(In)* Mango pickle made with halved unripe mangoes, mixed with fenugreek, turmeric, asafoetida, dried red chillis and salt, allowed to rest then covered with warm mustard oil and kept warm until matured

aara *(In)* Wholewheat flour

aardappel *(Ho)* Potato

aardbei *(Ho)* Strawberry

aarey A semi-hard, scalded curd, rindless cheese similar to Gouda, made in India from buffalo milk

abacate *(Po)* Avocado

abacaxi *(Po)* Pineapple

abadejo *(Sp)* Fresh codfish

abaissage *(Fr)* The process of rolling out pastry, etc.

abaisse *(Fr) fem.* Thinly rolled out pastry used as a base for other foods

abaisser *(Fr)* To roll out

abalone A bivalve mollusc *Haliotis tuberculata* and other *Haliotis* spp. found in warm sea water worldwide. It is larger than the oyster (to 13 cm). The edible part is the foot which it uses to move and attach itself to rocks, the frilly mantle is discarded. The foot may be eaten raw if very young but normally must be tenderized before being braised or lightly sautéed (less than 1 minute); *see also* blacklip abalone, greenlip abalone, paua, ormer and mutton fish [also called **sea ormer, sea ear, earshell**]

abalone mushroom *see* oyster mushroom

abats *(Fr) masc.* Offal, internal organs and other edible parts of an animal from its extremities, e.g. heads, hearts, liver, kidneys, tripe, sweetbreads, thymus gland, etc.

abatte *(Fr) masc.* A thick, broad, double-edged knife used to flatten meat

abattis *(Fr) masc.* Poultry offal or giblets

abattis à la bourguignonne *(Fr) masc.* Giblets, excluding livers, and chopped onions fried in butter, flour added, cooked with red wine, stock, BG and garlic in the oven, before completion, drained, placed in a clean pan with fried diced bacon, cooked button onions, raw sliced livers and strained reduced cooking liquor and finished

abattis de volaille aux champignons *(Fr) masc.* Poultry giblets cut in pieces, browned in butter, cooked in a moderate oven with flour, stock, seasoning, skinned tomatoes and BG for 1 hour, mushrooms added and cooking continued until all tender, cooking liquor thickened and all served with chopped parsley

abattis chipolata *(Fr) masc.* As abattis à la bourguignonne, but with white wine replacing red and grilled chipolata sausage, cooked chestnuts and fried diced salt belly of pork added at the final stage

abattis aux navets *(Fr) masc.* As abattis à la bourguignonne but without red wine and with cooked button onions, small turned pieces of turnip sautéed in butter and fried diced bacon added at the final stage with the raw livers

abattis printanier *(Fr) masc.* As abattis à la bourguignonne but with a printanier garnish with the raw livers replacing the diced bacon and button onions

abattoir A slaughter house, a place where live food animals are killed, desanguinated, gutted, skinned and prepared for sale to the trade

abba *(Sr)* Black mustard seed

abbacchio *(It)* Milk fed lamb

abbacchio *(It)* Young unweaned lamb

abboccato *(It)* Slightly sweet, e.g. of wine

abborre *(Sw)* Perch

abbrühen *(Ge)* To scald

abbrustolito *(It)* Toasted

Abelmoschus esculentus *Bot.* Okra

abelmosk *see* abelmusk

abelmusk A seed of a plant of the marrow family, *Hibiscus abelmoschus,* which has a musk-like flavour [also called **abelmosk**]

Abendessen *(Ge)* A light evening meal or supper

Aberdeen Angus *(UK)* Prime, Scottish beef cattle renowned for the flavour, texture and tenderness of its meat. Because of lax English law, far more is sold than is raised for slaughter

Aberdeen crulla *(UK)* A sweet, Scottish, deep fried cake made from a stiff dough of creamed butter and sugar, eggs and flour, rolled into rectangles, each rectangle partially cut into three lengths, these plaited, deep fried, drained and sprinkled with sugar

Aberdeen fillet *(UK)* A single, lightly smoked, unskinned fillet of haddock noted for its use in omelette Arnold Bennett

Aberdeen nips *(UK)* Cooked smoked haddock and egg yolk, blended into a hot Béchamel sauce, served on fried bread or toast and garnished with parsley and paprika

Aberdeen rowies *(UK)* A type of croissant made from a yeast-raised strong dough in the manner of puff pastry interleaved with butter mixed with a little lard using two triple folds, made into rounds, proven a second time and baked at 200°C

Aberdeen sausage *(UK)* A Scottish slicing sausage made from 2 parts minced beef, 1 part fat bacon and 1 part fine oatmeal with spices and seasoning, wrapped in a cloth and boiled. After unwrapping it is cooled and glazed or breadcrumbed. About 30 cm long by 10 cm diameter. Some sources give it as being made from minced mutton

Aberdeen sole The Scottish name for witch sole, a flat fish similar to the lemon sole

Aberffrau cakes *(UK)* Small Welsh cakes made from Victoria sponge mix, baked for 15 minutes at 190°C in greased deep scallop shells and sprinkled with sugar

Abernethy biscuit *(UK)* A Scottish caraway-flavoured sweet biscuit

Abgesottener *(Au)* An acid curdled cheese made from skimmed cow's milk, cooked to produce a soft, golden yellow, round cheese weighing between 0.2 and 1 kg. Contains 70% water, 10% fat and 16% protein

A.B. Goods *(USA)* A term used to describe gum, jelly and marshmallow types of sweets, origin unknown

abi *see* abiu

abiu A bright yellow round fruit with a white sweet caramel-flavoured flesh from a South American tree, *Pouteria caimito,* now grown commercially in Florida and Australia. It can only be used when fully ripe

abji l'amid *(Tu)* Potato soup flavoured with lemon juice

abklären *(Ge)* To clarify, to clear

abkochen *(Ge)* To blanch

abóbora *(Po)* Pumpkin

abodabo *(Ph)* A method of cooking meat by frying pieces with garlic until browned then adding a little stock and vinegar to make a sauce

abon *(Id)* Meat flesh, cooked in water until tender and all the water evaporated, flesh shredded and deep fried until crisp. Used as a method of preserving meat

aborinha *(Po)* Courgette

aboyeur *(Fr) masc.* The person responsible for shouting out the customer's order to the various kitchen departments. Lit. barker

abricot *(Fr) masc.* Apricot.

abricot, sauce *(Fr) see* apricot sauce

abricots Bourdaloue *(Fr) masc.* Halves of apricots poached in vanilla-flavoured syrup, placed on frangipane cream, covered with same, sprinkled with crushed macaroons and glazed quickly. The dish may be made up in a baked pastry flan, a timbale or contained in a ring of dessert rice or genoise coated with apricot jam

abricots Colbert *(Fr) masc.* Poached apricots with stone removed, filled with dessert rice, panéed and deep fried. Served with apricot sauce

abricots Condé *(Fr) masc.* Apricots poached in sugar syrup, arranged on a ring of dessert rice mixed with diced crystallized fruits macerated in kirsch, the whole decorated with crystallized fruits and coated with a kirsch-flavoured apricot syrup

abricots Cussy *(Fr) masc.* The flat side of a soft macaroon covered with a finely cut salpicon of fruit mixed with apricot purée, half a poached apricot placed on top, the whole coated with Italian meringue, dried in the oven without colour and served with kirsch-flavoured apricot sauce

abricots gratinés *(Fr) masc.* Halves of apricots poached in sugar syrup, placed on a 2 cm. thick layer of sweetened apple purée or dessert semolina, covered with royal icing praline, dredged with icing sugar and placed in a moderate oven to colour the praline

abricots meringués *(Fr) masc.* Halves of poached apricot placed on top of a layer of dessert rice, covered with meringue and decorated with same, dredged with icing sugar, coloured in a warm oven and served with a garnish of redcurrant and apricot jams

abricots mireille *(Fr) masc.* Peeled and halved ripe apricots, mixed with skinned apricot kernels, sprinkled with sugar and cooled to 0°C. Prior to serving sprinkled with kirsch, covered with vanilla-flavoured whipped cream and decorated with crystallized flowers

abricots à la parisienne *(Fr) masc.* Halved apricots poached in vanilla-flavoured syrup, cooled, reformed around vanilla ice cream, placed on a large flat macaroon, covered in a cone shape with vanilla-flavoured crème chantilly and sprinkled with fine hazelnut praline

abricots à la royale *(Fr) masc.* Apricot halves poached in vanilla-flavoured syrup, placed in tartlet moulds, filled with kirsch-flavoured jelly, cooled to set, demoulded, placed around top of a genoise ring glazed with red currant jelly cooked to the soft ball stage, centre of ring filled with chopped anisette-flavoured jelly

abricots sultane *(Fr) masc.* A ring baked genoise stuck to a base of short pastry with apricot jam, outside coated and top decorated with meringue, baked to a colour, centre filled with dessert rice mixed with frangipane cream and chopped pistachios, filling covered with poached apricots and sprinkled with chopped pistachios

abrikoos *(Ho)* Apricot

abrikosi *(Ru)* Apricot

Abruzzese, all' *(It)* In the style of Abruzzo, i.e. with green or red peppers

abschäumen *(Ge)* To skim

absorption method The method of cooking rice by adding the exact proportions of rice and water needed to cook the rice without leaving free water, to a heavy pan with a tight fitting lid, placing this on a heat source for some time then allowing the rice to dry out by leaving off the heat. Proportions and times depend on the rice type. Rice cooked in this way is also known as steamed rice

abulón *(Sp)* Abalone

aburage *(Ja)* Soya bean pouches made by deep frying slices of strained and pressed bean curd and splitting them open from one side to form pouches which may be stuffed

abura-kiri *(Ja)* A type of colander which fits in to a receptacle. Used for draining oil from fried food

abutilon A plant of the marrow family, *Abutilon esculentum,* whose leaves are used in the same way as spinach [also called **raughi** (In)]

acacia flower fritters *see* flower fritters

acacia gum *see* gum arabic

açafrão *(Po)* Saffron

açafrão-da-índia *(Po)* Turmeric

acajou *see* cashew nuts

Acanthosicyos horrida *Bot.* Nara nut

acar *(Id & In)* Shredded cabbage, carrots, cauliflower and other vegetables parboiled in spiced vinegar with turmeric and left to mature for a week [also called **achar, atjar, aachar, achard**]

acar bening *(Id)* A mixed vegetable, sweet pickle containing an assortment of cucumber, onion, pineapple, green pepper and tomato in vinegar, water, brown sugar and salt

acar ikan *(SEA)* The Malaysian version is a sweet and sour cold dish made from suitable whole fish, fried in oil until brown, then cooking in vinegar, water, brown sugar and a fried pounded spice mixture *(chillis, ginger, onions, garlic, turmeric and macadamia nuts),* decorated with slices of onion and chicken and served cold. The Indonesian version is similar but with the addition of lemon grass, laos, bay leaves and lime leaves to the pounded spice mixture and with shallots, spring onions and tomatoes added towards the end

acarje *(Bm)* An appetizer made from a processed mixture of blackeyed beans and dried shrimps, made into balls, fried in oil and served with a spicy shrimp sauce

acar kuning *(SEA)* A highly spiced mixed vegetable dish which can be served hot or cold. Onions, carrots, french beans, cauliflower, sweet peppers and cucumber, all cut to the size of a quartered french bean, are fried progressively in oil in the order given, with a fried spice mixture of pounded shallots, garlic, candlenuts, turmeric, ginger and red chillis, with water and vinegar added progressively and sugar, mustard and cucumber last of all, cooked until al dente

acar timun *(Ma)* A vegetable pickle made from salted and drained cucumber heated gently in vinegar, water, brown sugar and tomato sauce and mixed with a fried pounded spice mixture of garlic, chillis, turmeric and ginger

accartocciato *(It)* Twisted or wrapped, e.g. in spirals

accelerated freeze drying Freeze drying in which the rate of temperature drop between 0 and −5°C is very rapid, thus preventing the growth of ice crystals which would disrupt the cells and destroy the texture of the food and in which heat is supplied to the food whilst under high vacuum and at a low temperature to remove the free and combined water

acciughe *(It)* Salted anchovies, singular is acciuga. Fresh anchovies are alici

acciughe alla carabiniera *(It)* Anchovies with potato salad

acciughe contadina *(It)* Anchovy salad with capers, onions and olives

acciughe marinate *(It)* Cleaned and filleted fresh anchovies marinated in olive oil, lemon juice, garlic, parsley, red chillis and seasoning for at least 4 hours

acciughe ripiene al forno *(It)* Cleaned fresh anchovies with heads and tails off, back bone removed leaving two fillets joined kipper style, two anchovies made into a sandwich skin side out, with a filling of chopped herbs, garlic, pinenuts or walnuts and olive oil, sprinkled with breadcrumbs and olive oil and baked for 10 minutes in a 220°C oven

acciughe in salsa verde *(It)* Anchovies in green sauce made by alternating in a jar, layers of drained anchovies with a mixture of chopped parsley, garlic, red chillis and white of bread soaked in vinegar, covering the layers with olive oil and refrigerating until required

accompaniments Items offered separately with a main dish of food

accra *(Ca)* A yeasted doughnut mixture containing pounded salt cod and chillis, deep fried and eaten hot with floats

acedera *(Sp)* Sorrel

aceite *(Sp)* Oil

aceitunas *(Sp)* Olives

aceitunas rellenas *(Sp)* Stuffed olives (e.g. with anchovy)

acelga *(Sp)* Spinach beet

acepipes variados *(Po)* Assorted hors d'oeuvres

Acer saccharum *Bot.* Sugar maple tree

acerola The large dark cherry-like fruit of a tree *Malpighia glabra,* originating in Brazil but now grown in the Caribbean and Australia. It is the richest natural source of vitamin C, primarily used as a health food [also called **Brazilian cherry, Barbados cherry, West Indian cherry**]

acescence The slight vinegar smell of wine and fortified wines that has undergone some acetification particularly for those aged in wood. Not necessarily unpleasant

acesulfame K *see* acesulfame potassium

acesulfame potassium An artificial sweetener roughly 150 times as sweet as sucrose, used in canned foods, soft drinks and table top sugar substitutes [also called **acesulfame K**]

acetic acid E260, the acid contained in vinegar which at 3.5% concentration will ensure the stability of pickles, etc. Obtained by biological oxidation of alcohol in wine, ale and other fermented beverages. Very cheap vinegars are made from a chemically produced acetic acid

acetini *(It)* Pickles

aceto *(It)* Vinegar

Acetobacter spp. A group of microorganisms associated with rot and browning in apples, but more importantly used for the production of vinegar from wines and ales by oxidation of alcohol to acetic acid.

aceto balsamico *(It)* Balsamic vinegar

aceto-dolce *(It)* Sweetened vinegar (sometimes with honey), also used of pickles prepared with same

acetoglyceride A fat containing one or more acetic acid side chains instead of the normal longer chain fatty acids thus giving a much lower melting point. It is used in the compounding of shortenings

acetosa *(It)* Garden sorrel

acetosella *(It)* Wood sorrel

achar *see* acar

achards *(In & Fr) masc.* A macedoine of vegetables preserved in vinegar with spices. Escoffier gives mustard, Alexander Dumas suggested salt, saffron, chilli pepper and ginger root; *see also* acar

achee *see* akee

achiar *(SEA)* A bamboo pickle made from vinegar and young green bamboo shoots

Achillea millefolium *Bot.* Yarrow

achiote *see* Annatto seed

Achras sapota *Bot.* Sapodilla

achtarmige poliep *(Ho)* Octopus

achtfüssiger Tintenfisch *(Ge)* Octopus

acid A substance containing an excess of hydrogen ions when compared with pure water which contains equal amounts of hydrogen ions *(acid forming)* and hydroxyl ions *(alkali forming)*. This excess causes the characteristic sour taste response; *see also* acidity, alkali, alkalinity

acid brilliant green BS E142, a synthetic green food colouring which maintains its colour in acid conditions

acid calcium phosphate The acid ingredient in some baking powders

acid cherry A much smaller cherry *Prunus*

cerasus than the sweet cherry, and prized for jam making and culinary use. The two well known varieties are the Morello and the Montmorency [also called **sour cherry, pie cherry**]

acid potassium tartrate *see* cream of tartar

acidification The process of adding acids to, or causing acids to be produced in, foods for preservation as in pickles, sauerkraut, soused herrings. mayonnaise, etc. The usual acids are acetic, citric and lactic. Benzoic acid is effective at low concentrations

acidify, to To add an acid (e.g. lemon juice, vinegar or permitted additive) to a mixture to reduce its pH to below 7 [also called **to acidulate**]

acidity Acidity is a measure of the strength of an acid measured on the scale of pH which goes from 1 *(very acid)* through 2 *(acidity of lemon juice),* 3 *(apple juice)* to 7 *(neither acid nor alkaline),* the pH of pure water. pH values greater than 7 refer to alkalis. Very few food spoiling organisms will grow at a pH equal to or less than 2

acidless orange A type of sweet orange rarely found in Europe or North America. Grown mainly in Egypt *(Succari)* and Brazil *(Lima),* they have very low acid levels and are highly appreciated where grown. Some believe them to have special therapeutic and prophylactic properties. They are not suitable for processing [also called **sugar orange**]

acido *(It)* Acid, pickled, sour, sharp

acidophilus milk Milk soured with a pure culture of *Lactobacillus acidophilus* at 37°C to give a lactic acid content of 0.6 to 0.8%. It is refreshing and easily digested and considered to be a health food

acidulate, to *see* to acidify

acidulated cream Cream to which lemon juice is added in the proportions of 1 to 8

acini *(It)* Tiny pasta shapes similar to rice, used for soups [also called **acini di pepe**]

acini de pepe *see* acini

acitron A candied cactus *Echino cactus grandis* from Mexico. Used as an ingredient of a meat stuffing

ackara *(WA)* A Gambian christening food made of ground white beans mixed to a stiff paste with water, shaped into balls, deep fried and served with a tomato, sweet pepper and onion sauce flavoured with garlic and chillis

ackee *see* akee

Ackersalat *(Ge)* Lamb's lettuce

ackra fritters *(Ca)* Jamaican deep fried fritters made from a mixture of cooked and mashed blackeyed beans with chopped chillis

açorda *(Po)* Bread soup made from pounded herbs, salt, garlic and water mixed with olive oil and cubed stale bread onto which boiling water is poured until the bread softens. It can be garnished with poached egg

açorda de mariscos *(Po)* An açorda flavoured with shellfish and coriander

acorn squash *(USA) see* table queen squash

Acorus calamus *Bot.* Calamus

acqua *(It)* Water

acqua cotta *(It)* A mushroom soup made from a mixture of varieties of fresh and soaked dried fungi, sautéed with chopped garlic for 15 minutes, boiled with canned plum tomatoes and their juice, stock, and any available mushroom steeping liquor, finished with chopped basil and served over toast with grated Parmesan cheese. Also used of many vegetable soups. Lit. cooked water

acra lamori *(Ca)* Fried salt cod fish cakes

acrolein The acrid smelling chemical produced from the thermal decomposition of overheated fat which causes eye and throat irritation

Actinidia deliciosa *Bot.* The kiwi fruit or Chinese gooseberry

activated dough development A method of speeding up the primary proving of dough by adding small quantities of chemicals such as ascorbic acid, cysteine, bromates, etc. which modify the properties of the gluten

açúcar *(Po)* Sugar

açúcar granulado *(Po)* Granulated sugar

adam's fig *see* plantain

Adam's needle *(USA) see* yucca (2)

Adamsapfel *(Ge)* Pummelo

adaptation The process by which the senses become less sensitive to and less stimulated by particular odours or flavours with repeated contact, thus accounting for acquired tastes and the tolerance of high levels of spices, garlic and chillis, etc. in some cultures

adas *(Id & Ma)* Fennel seed

adas cina *(Id)* Dill

adas manis *(Id)* Dill seed

addition *(Fr) fem.* The bill (in a restaurant)

additive A substance added to food to improve its properties such as keeping quality, health value, flavour, texture, colour, acidity, stability, tendency to oxidize or dry out, sweetness, cooking properties, viscosity, stickiness and the like. All must be listed on packaging either by an E number q.v. in the European Union or by name or both unless they are natural materials not required to be listed by any law, regulation or directive. See under letter E for most additives. Some without numbers are included elsewhere

Adelaide cake A cake made from a Victoria sponge mixture with added cornflour (1:2 ratio to flour), chopped glacé cherries and chopped almonds

Ädelost A soft to semi-hard Swedish blue cheese made from whole cow's milk and cast in large rounds. Contains 44% water, 28% fat and 25% protein

aderezo *(Sp)* Salad dressing

adianto *(It)* Maidenhair fern

Adiantum capillus-veneris *Bot.* Maidenhair fern

adipic acid *see* (E)355

adley *(Ph)* Job's tears

adobada sauce *(Me)* A Mexican sauce used in making tamales, consisting of pounded or liquidized garlic, onion and cinnamon, fried in oil until dry then simmered with tomato purée. chicken stock, chocolate, sugar and powdered dry chillis or chilli powder [also called **adobo**]

adobo 1 *(Me) see* adobada sauce **2** *(Ph)* A pork, poultry or fish stew with sweet peppers, garlic, soya sauce, vinegar and coconut milk. The pieces of meat are first crisp fried before combining with to the sauce

adrak *(In)* Ginger

adriatico, alla modo dell' *(It)* In the Adriatic style, i.e. fish grilled over wood or charcoal

adschempilavi *(NA)* Pickled meat stewed with rice

aduki bean *see* adzuki bean

adulterant A cheaper substance added to food in order to increase its weight without changing its appearance and thus increase the profit margin. Some are legal such as water and phosphates in chickens, or extenders added to chilli powder

adulterate, to To add adulterants to food

adzuki bean A type of small flattened oval-shaped reddish brown bean with a white hilum *Phaseolus angularis,* from Japan and China, used as a pulse or ground into flour. They contain more sugar than most beans and are sometimes used as confectionery. They can be sprouted [also called **aduki bean, azuki bean**]

æbleflæsk *(De)* Fried diced bacon and chopped apples

æblekage *(De)* An individual dessert made from layers of sweetened apple purée and breadcrumbs which have been fried in butter and mixed with sugar, the whole decorated appropriately

æbler *(De)* Apples

æbleskiver *(De)* A non-yeasted type of doughnut with a light texture filled with apple purée and cooked in a special pan with indentations

æg *(De)* Egg

æggekage *(De)* A thick omelette topped with fried bacon and served in wedges

aegletree fruit *see* wood apple

aemono *(Ja)* A highly decorative mixed salad usually of chicken, seafood or vegetables dressed with various sauces one of which is made from miso, mashed tofu or egg yolk, vinegar and seasoning [also called **sakizuke, tsuki dashi, zenzai**]

aerate, to To incorporate finely divided air into a liquid or powder mixture, by for example sieving flour, whisking or beating eggs, or beating air into a cake mixture

aerated bread Bread made from dough which has been mechanically mixed with carbon dioxide without using yeast

aerial yam An orange coloured yam plant *Dioscorea bulbifer,* which grows several bulbils about the size of a large thumb above ground. These resemble small tubers and are very tasty. The underground tuber is edible but not used. It is cultivated in Africa, Asia and the Caribbean [also called **air potato, potato yam**]

Aerobacter spp. Bacteria used to oxidize alcohol to acetic acid in vinegar production

aerobe The term is applied to microorganisms which require oxygen from the air in order to grow and reproduce; *see also* anaerobe

Aeromonas hydrophilia A food poisoning bacterium which will grow at temperatures below 10°C

ærter *(De)* Peas

afelia *(Gr)* Tender pork, cubed and browned in olive oil, then simmered in white wine with coriander seeds and seasoning until the meat is tender

affettato *(It)* Sliced e.g. of ham or sausage

affogato *(It)* Poached, steamed or plunged

affumicare *(It)* To smoke

affumicato *(It)* Smoked

afiorata *(It)* The finest grade of olive oil made

from the cream which rises to the top of the first cold pressing. It is skimmed off and bottled separately and contains a maximum of 1% free oleic acid

aflatoxin A toxin produced by certain moulds which grow on stored grains and nuts in tropical areas. The toxin tends to cause low-grade illness and reduced food absorption and growth and is thus not easily noticed unless specially tested for. It is most serious in animal feeds

áfonya *(Hu)* Blueberries

Aframomum korarima *Bot.* Ethiopian cardamom

Aframomum melegueta *Bot.* Grains of paradise

africaine, à l' *(Fr)* In the African style, i.e. garnished with aubergines, tomatoes, mushrooms and potatoes

africains *(Fr) masc.* Small dessert biscuits

African horned melon *see* kiwano

African spinach *see* amaranths

afronchemoyle *(UK)* A form of haggis consisting of whole eggs, white breadcrumbs, finely diced soft interior fat of lamb, pepper and saffron, mixed and stuffed into a sheep's stomach (honeycomb tripe stomach) and steamed or boiled. The first written record is from 1390 A.D.

afternoon tea *(UK)* Cakes, biscuits, scones and dainty sandwiches served with tea in the mid-afternoon

afters *(UK) coll.* The sweet or dessert course of a meal. Compare starters

agachadiza *(Sp)* Snipe

agami *(SA)* A popular game bird, *Guiana agami,* used in soups, stews and braised dishes [also called **trumpeter**]

agar-agar *(SEA)* E406, a natural gelling agent made from seaweed of the Gelidum, Eucheuma or Gracilaria spp., sometimes used instead of gelatine. The gel has a very high melting point and it will only dissolve in boiling water. Suitable for vegetarians [also called **seaweed gelatine, seaweed jelly, Japanese gelatine**]

agar-agar dengan serikaya *(SEA)* A sweet sugar and agar-agar jelly served with a type of sweetened egg custard made with eggs beaten with brown sugar (e.g. muscovado) and coconut cream until fluffy then cooked over a bain-marie until thick

agar-agar noodles Fine strips of agar-agar soaked in boiling water until just tender and appropriately flavoured. They are used to bulk out cold appetizers. Not to be confused with cellophane noodles

agaric A family of fungus, some edible, some deadly poisonous

Agaricus arvensis *Bot.* Horse mushroom

Agaricus bisporus *Bot.* Cultivated mushroom

Agaricus campestris *Bot.* Common field mushroom

agate ware Enamel-lined metal kitchen ware

age *(Ja)* Deep fried tofu, cut into pouches, used to make inari by stuffing with sushi rice and flavourings prior to braising in a mixture of dashi, sugar, soya sauce and sake

agedofu *(Ja)* Fried bean curd

agemono *(Ja)* Deep fried food, also the coating, batter or pané used. Always done in vegetable oil, vegetables at 160°C and meat and fish at 170°C. Abbreviated to age in recipes

agemono-nane *(Ja)* Pan for deep-frying

agemono no dogu *(Ja) see* agemono-nane

agerhøne *(De)* Partridge

ägg *(Sw)* Egg

ägg à la Lena *(Sw)* A cocotte dish with a little liver paté on the base, a trimmed poached egg on top and all surrounded with a sherry-flavoured setting consommé, garnished with a ring of sweet pepper and cooled until set

aggiada *(It)* A garlic soup from the north west Mediterranean region

äggkulor *(Sw)* Egg balls made from hard boiled egg yolks, seasoned, mashed with soft butter and paprika, cooled, formed into small balls and rolled in diced truffles, truffle oil or chopped wild mushrooms. Used as garnish for soup

aigre *(Fr)* Sour, sharp, acid

agliata, all *(It)* With garlic sauce

aglio *(It)* Garlic

aglio e olio *(It)* Sauce or dressing composed of garlic and oil pounded together

agliota *(It)* A sauce made by pounding garlic with bread and vinegar

aglycone One of the antibacterial agents in olives which inhibit lactic acid fermentation and which is removed by treatment with lye (caustic soda solution)

agneau *(Fr) masc.* Lamb

agneau à la Hongroise *(Fr) masc.* Hungarian style lamb made from breast of lamb, defatted and cut into small pieces, browned, added to a roux made from sliced onions browned in butter and flour, paprika added and stock as required, simmered for 1 to 1½ hours

agneau de lait *(Fr) masc.* Unweaned milk-fed lamb

agneau pascal *(Fr) masc.* Spring lamb

agneau de Pauillac *(Fr) masc.* A small milk-fed lamb usually roasted

agneau de pré-salé *(Fr) masc.* Young lamb fed on sea-washed pastures (salt marshes or meadows)

agnelet *(Fr) masc.* Milk-fed lamb

agnello *(It)* Lamb

agnello con cicoria *(It)* Pieces of boned leg of lamb, casseroled with sliced onions, olive oil, tomatoes, salt and red chillis in the oven at 200°C for 1 hour, chicory, endive or blanched dandelion leaves placed over the lamb and cooked for a further 30 minutes

agnello al forno *(It)* A saddle of lamb larded with onions and garlic, sprinkled with salt and chopped rosemary, roasted in lard and served with potatoes roasted in the same dish

agnello in fricassea *(It)* Lamb chops browned in lard with chopped onions and strips of pancetta (or smoked bacon), nutmeg, seasoning and brown stock added and evaporated, braised in white wine, pan juices defatted and mixed off heat with beaten egg yolks and lemon juice which is served as a coating on the chops

agnello di latte *(It)* Milk-fed lamb

agnello con olive all'abbruzzo *(It)* Floured steaks of boned leg of lamb, browned in olive oil, salted, defatted and heated briefly with stoned black olives (4:1 ratio), oregano, chopped green peppers and finally dressed with lemon juice

agneshka kebab *(Bu)* A casserole of lamb, including its kidneys and sweetbreads with onions, wine, lemon juice, chillis, herbs and seasoning, thickened with eggs and accompanied with boiled rice

agnolini *(It)* Stuffed pasta from Lombardy similar to tortellini

agnolotti *(It)* A half moon shaped ravioli stuffed with minced lamb and onion sautéed in butter mixed with boiled rice or spinach, cheese and seasoning. Served after cooking in standard fashion, sometimes tossed in meat pan juices [also called **pazlache (It)**]

agnostinele *(It)* Tiny red mullet passed through seasoned flour and fried

Agnès Sorel, garnish Chopped fried mushrooms, small rounds of cooked tongue and chicken mousse or pâté

agoni *(It)* Small flat freshwater fish found in the Italian lakes, often salted and dried; *see also* misoltini

Agostano *(It) see* Parmigiano Reggiano

agourtsi *(Ru)* Small cucumbers pickled in salt

Agrafa *(Gr)* A hard, scalded curd, ewes' milk cheese similar to Gruyère with a few holes and a dry rind

agrazada *(Sp)* Verjuice

agresto *(It)* Verjuice from grapes

agridulce *(Sp)* Sweet and sour sauce

agrini A small, soft, acid curdled Swiss cheese made from cow's or goat's milk with a slightly sour fresh taste, 40 to 60 g in weight

agrio *(Sp)* Sour

agriões *(Po)* Watercress

agro, all' *(It)* Dressed with oil and lemon, also soured with lemon juice

agrodolce *(It)* Sour and sweet, bitter sweet, with a sugar and vinegar sauce

agua *(Po & Sp)* Water

aguacate *(Sp)* Avocado pear

aguacates rellenos de atun *(Me)* Halved avocado pears filled with a mixture of tuna, tomato sauce, soured cream, Worcestershire sauce and seasoning. Garnished with chiffonade of lettuce and radish, used as a hors d'oeuvre

aguado *(Sp)* Liquid

aguaturma *(Sp)* Jerusalem artichoke

aguglia *(It)* Garfish

aguinaldo honey *(Me)* A very pale honey from Mexico

aguja *(Sp)* Garfish

agulat *(Sp)* Rock salmon

agurk *(De & No)* Cucumber

agurksalat *(De & No)* Cucumber salad. Generally slices of cucumber, salted and drained for an hour, dried, dressed with pepper, sugar and vinegar, chilled, drained and garnished with chopped parsley or dill

ah moi's mee *(Ma)* A Malaysian dish of stir fried noodles with soaked Chinese mushrooms, prawns, cooked chicken, greens, garlic, onion, ginger, egg and soya sauce, garnished with crabmeat, shredded omelette and spring onion

ah moi's rendang *(Ma)* A chicken curry made with sugared chicken pieces, onions, garlic, ginger, laos, lemon grass, coconut milk, desiccated coconut and pandan leaves

Ahornsaft *(Ge)* Maple syrup

ahumado *(Sp)* Smoked

ahumar *(Sp)* To smoke

ahven *(Fi)* Perch

aiglefin *(Fr) masc.* Haddock

aïgo bouïdo *(Fr)* A simple soup of garlic and sage, possibly thyme and bay, boiled in water with olive oil, strained and poured over dried French bread

aïgo bouïdo à la ménagère *(Fr)* A Provençale soup made from sliced onions and leeks fried in olive oil, crushed garlic, potatoes, fennel and mixed herbs boiled in saffron-flavoured water with orange zest. The strained soup is served over French bread and the potatoes served separately with poached egg and chopped parsley

aïgo saou *(Fr)* A fish and garlic soup made from pieces of fish, sliced onions, potatoes, BG, seasoning and garlic boiled in water. The soup is eaten with French bread dressed with olive oil and the fish is eaten separately

aigre doux *(Fr)* Bitter sweet

aigrette *(En & Fr) fem.* A savoury fritter made from cheese-flavoured choux pastry, served as an appetizer

aïgroissade *(Fr) fem.* Cooked solid vegetables, e.g. roots, tubers, sweet peppers, aubergine, courgettes and the like, served warm with a mayonnaise and garlic sauce

aiguillat *(Fr) masc.* Rock salmon

aiguille *(Fr) fem.* Needlefish or garfish q.v. from the Mediterranean with green bones which become mauve when cooked [also called **orphie**]

aiguille à brider *(Fr) fem.* Trussing needle

aiguille à piquer *(Fr) fem.* Larding needle used for small cuts, e.g. filet mignon or rack of hare

aiguillette *(Fr) fem.* A long thin cut of beef from the extreme top of the rump extending from the sirloin to the tail stump and about one quarter way down the animal. Used for braising and boeuf à la mode

aiguillettes *(Fr) fem.* Long thin slices usually of duck breast

ai gwa *(Ch)* Aubergine

ail *(Fr) masc.* Garlic. The rarely used plural is aulx

ail, à l' Flavoured with garlic

aile *(Fr) fem.* Wing e.g. of poultry or of a game bird

aileron *(Fr) masc.* Wing, strictly wing tip, of a bird, fin of a fish

ailerons de poulet carmelite *(Fr) masc.* Breasts and wing bones of poached chicken removed as two pieces, skinned, coated in aspic, placed on a layer of crayfish mousse in a timbale, interspersed with cooked and shelled crayfish tails, covered in aspic jelly, refrigerated and served cold.

ailerons de volaille dorés *(Fr) masc.* Large chicken or turkey winglets fried in butter to a colour and reserved. Sliced carrots and onions browned in same butter, placed in oven dish with seasoning and herbs, winglets placed on top and cooked in a slow oven, winglets removed, remainder cooked with white stock for 10 minutes, reduced, strained and poured over winglets

ailerons de volaille farcis chipolata *(Fr) masc.* Boned winglets of large chicken or turkey stuffed with sausage meat, braised and decorated with chipolata garnish 15 minutes before finishing

ailerons de volaille farcis grillés *(Fr) masc.* Boned winglets of large chicken or turkey stuffed with sausage meat, braised, coated with sausage meat, covered with caul fat, dipped in melted butter and breadcrumbs, grilled and served with sauce périgueux

ailerons de volaille Lady Winter *(Fr) masc.* Breasts and wing bones of poached chicken removed as two pieces, skinned, coated in aspic placed with the points uppermost around a cone of set mousse made from the flesh of the chicken legs and decorated with chopped truffle and red ox tongue

aillade *(Fr) fem.* A garlic and nut emulsion sauce made with skinned hazel nuts, pounded with garlic and egg yolk to which a mixed nut and olive or sunflower oil is added as for mayonnaise

aillade toulousaine As aillade but with walnuts

ailloli *(Fr) masc.* An emulsion sauce made from white crustless bread soaked in milk, squeezed and mixed with pounded garlic (and possibly egg yolk) to which olive oil is added as in making mayonnaise. The final mixture is let down with lemon juice or wine vinegar to taste. Sometimes ground almonds are added [also called **beurre de Provence**]

ailloli garni *(Fr) masc.* A Provençal dish of salt cod and vegetables garnished with snails

aioli 1 *(It)* Garlic pounded with egg yolk and salt then made into a mayonnaise in standard fashion **2** An alternative French spelling for ailloli

aipo *(Po)* Celery

air dry, to To hang foodstuffs on hangers or racks in sheds or cages or in open sunlight in cold climates where there is a reasonable flow of fresh air over them. Used for hams, fish, etc.

air potato *see* aerial yam

airelle *(Fr) fem.* Bilberry, whortleberry, blueberry

airelle rouge *(Fr) fem.* Cranberry

airelles, sauce *(Fr) fem.* Cranberry sauce

ajam panggang *(Ho)* Grilled chicken flavoured with ginger, garlic, chilli peppers and saffron. From Indonesia *(Dutch East Indies)*

ají 1 *(Sp)* Chilli peppers **2** *(Ja)* Horse mackerel, used in sushi

aji li mojili A sour garlic sauce from Puerto Rico

ajiaceite *(Sp) see* alioli

ajiaco *(SA)* A thick soup or thin stew from Columbia of chicken cooked in stock with sweetcorn and sausages, each serving garnished with sliced hard boiled eggs and cream

ajiaco cubano *(Cu)* A soup made from salt pork, pickled pork and pork flesh with chick peas, garlic, aubergine, sweet corn, pumpkin and potatoes, seasoned and flavoured with saffron

ajiaco de papas *(SA)* A potato stew from Peru made from cubed boiled potatoes mixed with chopped and fried garlic, onion and jalapeno chillis all fried to a colour, milk or cream, chopped hard boiled eggs and crumbled cheese

ajillo, al *(Me)* Fried with ajillo chilli

aji-mirin *(Ja)* A mixture of mirin, sugar syrup and salt used in the same way as mirin

aji-no-moto *(Ja) see* monosodium glutamate. The name comes from the Japanese company which manufactures it

ajo *(Sp)* Garlic

ajo blanco *(Sp)* **1** A basic bread, garlic, oil and vinegar gazpacho with added pounded or liquidized skinned almonds, garnished with peeled and deseeded grapes **2** A cold soup made from garlic and almonds pounded with olive oil to a thick paste, mixed with water and seasoning and served with sippets

ajonjoli *(Sp)* Sesame seeds

ajowan A plant of the caroway family *Carum ajowan,* whose seeds are used as a spice and as a source of ajowan oil and thymol. It has a strong thyme-like flavour. Used in Indian cooking often in conjuction with starch foods and pulses [also called **lovage, ajwain, carom, bishop's weed**]

ajula *(It)* Striped sea bream, northern Italy

ajwain *see* ajowan

akadashi-miso *(Ja)* A miso similar to hatcho-miso [also called **aka-miso**]

akagai *(Ja)* Ark shell, a type of clam about 10 cm in diameter. This is one of the few shellfish which use haemoglobin to transport oxygen and is thus red in colour. Usually available cooked and used in preparing sushi

akami *(Ja)* A dark red meat from around the spine of the tuna fish, used as a separate cut in sushi

aka-miso *(Ja) see* akadashi-miso

akee The fruit of a small African tree, *Blighia sapida,* introduced to the Caribbean by Captain Bligh and now extensively grown there. The soft creamy flesh of the ripe fruit is used as a vegetable e.g. in saltfish and akee. The outer pink skin is poisonous [also called **achee, ackee**]

åkerärter *(Sw)* Field peas which are yellow when dried. Used in the Swedish national soup gula ärter med fläsk

akni *(In)* A court bouillon used in Indian cooking made by simmering herbs, spices and other flavourings in water to aromatize it. Used for steaming rice and vegetables. Typical flavourings are fried onion, coriander seed, fennel seed, chopped sweet pepper, garlic and fresh ginger

akureyri *(Ic)* A blue cheese made from ewes' milk

ak yaw *(Bm)* A crisp accompaniment made from a batter of rice flour, turmeric and water, shallow fried in spoonfuls in oil and scattered with yellow and green split peas before the fritters are turned over in the oil

ål *(De, No & Sw)* Eel

al'-, all'-, alla- *(It)* In the style of

al macc *(It)* A northern soup of milk with chestnuts and rice [also called **mach** in Lombardy]

alaccia *(It)* **1** A large variety of sardine **2** Celery *(Naples)*

alalonga *(It)* Albacore

alamang *(Ph)* The tiny shrimp (to 1 cm) used to make bagoong (shrimp paste)

alanine A non-essential amino acid

alaria A seaweed *Alaria esculenta* found in the North Atlantic; similar to the Japanese wakame q.v [also called **murlins, brown ribweed, ribweed, wing kelp**]

Alaska *see* Baked alaska

Alaska black cod *see* black cod

Alaska Dungeness crab *see* Dungeness crab

Alaska pollack A variety of the seawater fish pollack *Theragra chalcogramma* found in the north west Pacific. It is of the cod family, weighs around 1 kg and has an olive green to brown upper skin and the the lean white flesh may be cooked in any way. Usually salted and dried or pickled. The roe is also salted for the Japanese market. Also known as walleye pollack because of its distinctive appearance [also called **Alaska pollock**]

Alaska pollock *see* Alaska pollack

Alaskan king crab A very large crab, *Paralithodes camtschatica,* weighing to 10 kg and with a leg span of 3 m from the northern Pacific. It excellent meat is usually processed or canned

Alba, alla moda d' *(It)* In the Alban style, i.e. with truffles

albacore A small variety of tuna, *Thunnus alalunga,* up to 1 m in length with a soft white flesh, not recommended for poaching, but can be eaten raw e.g. for sashimi or baked or grilled [also called **long fin tuna**]

albagore *(Ja)* Tuna

albahaca *(Sp)* Basil

albaricoque *(Sp)* Apricot

albedo *(USA)* The white inner pith of the citrus fruit skin

Albert oranges *(Cn)* Rose hips

Albert, sauce *(En & Fr) fem.* Grated horseradish simmered in white bouillon for 20 minutes, butter sauce, cream and breadcrumbs added, thickened by reduction, sieved, thickened again with egg yolks and finished with seasoning, English mustard, vinegar and chopped parsley

albicocca *(It)* Apricot

albillos *(Sp)* White grapes

albóndigas *(Sp & Me)* Meatballs or meat patties made from finely chopped tenderloin of pork and fat bacon combined with chopped garlic and red pepper, seasoning and bound with whole egg, fried, then braised in a suitable sauce

albóndigas con chilpotle *(Me)* Minced pork, beef, bread, vinegar, sugar and seasoning, formed into balls, shallow fried in oil until brown then baked in the oven with salsa de chile chilpotle. Garnished with flaked almonds

albóndigas con guisantes *(Sp)* Meat patties made from chopped beef, onions and seasoning, formed, browned on both sides in butter, simmered in demi-glace with tomato purée and garlic paste and served with the sauce and green peas

albondiguillas *(Sp)* Small patties made from minced cooked meat mixed with breadcrumbs, egg, white wine, chopped parsley, seasoning and herbs, panéed, shallow fried in oil and served with tomato sauce

albondiguillas a la criolla *(Sp)* Albondiguillas served with a tomato sauce mixed with chopped sweet pepper sweated in butter and a separate saffron-flavoured and coloured rice pilaff

albondiguitas *(Me)* Small fried meatballs made from pork. beef, bread, vinegar, sugar and seasoning, usually served on sticks as a cocktail snack

albricoque *(Po)* Apricot

albufera, sauce *(En & Fr) fem.* Sauce suprême mixed with meat glaze and pimento butter

albumen The white of egg, the nutritive material surrounding the yolk of the eggs of higher animals, which also contains various anti-bacterial substances. Hen's egg albumen consists of the protein albumin (9 - 12%) and water (84 - 87%), in total about 58% of the weight of the egg. It forms a very stable emulsion with air and hence is used in a variety of air-raised dishes. It may be dried to a powder for reconstituting or deep frozen

albumen index A measure of egg quality equal to the ratio of the height of a mass of egg white to its diameter as it sits on a flat surface. A higher index indicates higher quality

albumin A mixture of water soluble proteins found in egg white, blood and other foods. Like all proteins they denature and coagulate when heated or treated with various chemicals e.g. alcohol; *see also* ovalbumin

alcachofa *(Sp)* Globe artichoke

alcachôfra *(Po)* Globe artichoke

alcahual *(Me)* A delicately flavoured amber coloured honey from Mexico

alcaparras *(Sp)* Capers

alcaravea *(Sp)* Caraway

alcaravia *(Po)* Caraway

alce *(It)* Elk

Alchemilla vulgaris *Bot.* Lady's mantle

Alcobaça *(Po)* A semi-hard cheese made from ewe's milk with a white smooth paste and thin dry rind, cast in small rounds (about 220 g). Contains 45% water, 30% fat and 20% protein

alcohol The generic name for a class of chemical

compounds which includes ethanol, the commonest mood altering substance used in all cultures. Most are toxic, particularly methanol which is found in methylated and surgical spirits and many household liquids. Propanol and butanol, the other common alcohols, are used as solvents and in cleaning agents

al cuarto de hora *(Sp)* Mussel soup made from chopped onions, parsley, diced ham and rice all sweated in butter, mixed with water and the liquor from the cooking of the mussels, seasoned and cooked, served with the mussels and garnished with chopped hard boiled eggs. The name indicates that it can be made in 15 minutes

al dente *(It)* Literally 'to the tooth', used to describe pasta or vegetables which are cooked to be firm to the bite. Dried commercial pasta is al dente when the whitish centre of the paste just disappears

aldoxime An artificial zero calorie sweetener 450 times sweeter than sucrose

ale An alcoholic drink made from top fermented extract of malted grains. Generally nowadays applied only to crystal (lightly coloured) malts. May be flavoured e.g. with hops

ale berry *see* ale gruel

ale flip *(UK)* Beer heated with mace, cloves and butter, poured into separately beaten egg yolk let down with cold beer and egg white (1 egg per litre)

ale gruel *(UK)* A Yorkshire drink made from a very thin gruel of porridge oats and water mixed when hot with an equal part of beer to which is added grated ginger root, nutmeg, cinnamon and sugar to taste

ale jelly *(UK)* A jelly made from ale, sugar, cinnamon and lemon juice boiled together, clarified with egg white and set with gelatine

alecost *see* Costmary

alecrim *(Po)* Rosemary

alegar Ale vinegar

alemtejo *(Po)* A soft, round cheese made from ewe's milk with added thistle type flowers

alentejana, à *(Po)* In the style of Alentejo, i.e. with garlic, olive oil and paprika

Aleppo nuts *see* pistachio nuts

alesandre salami A variety of Italian salami

aletria *(Po)* Vermicelli

aletta *(It)* Wing of a bird, fin of a fish

Aleurites moluccana *Bot.* Candlenut tree

Aleurobius acaras A mite sometimes found in old, poorly stored flour. If serious infested the flour has a purplish tinge

alewife *(USA)* A member of the herring family *Alosa pseudoharengus,* similar to the true herring but with a deeper body. It is found off the east coast of North America and may be baked, fried or grilled

alewife caviar *(USA)* The female roe of the alewife, processed to resemble caviar

alexanders A hardy biennial herb *Smyrnium olusatrum*, with a celery type flavour resembling lovage and angelica, whose roots can be boiled or candied, young stems braised, leaves and flower buds used in salad or as a pot herb and seeds used for flavouring [also called **black lovage**]

alface *(Po)* Lettuce

alfalfa A variety of lucerne *Medicago sativa,* a leguminous plant normally used as cattle fodder. The seeds are sprouted to give a crisp plant stem about 4 cm long used in salads or for stir frying as a vegetable

alfredo, all' *(It)* Tossed in cream and butter, e.g. pasta

alfóncigo *(Sp)* Pistachio nut

alfóstigo *(Po)* Pistachio nut

alga *(It & Sp)* Seaweed, algae

alga mar An edible seaweed *Durvillea antarctica* exported to the USA from Chile

algae Non self-supporting vegetable-like organisms which flourish in fresh to salt water, generally greenish in colour, ranging in size from the microscopic to 100 metre long fronds. Of culinary importance are the microscopic Chlorella and Spirulina which are used as health foods, and the larger seaweeds used either as a vegetable or as a source of various food thickening agents. See agar-agar, alginic acid, carrageen, laver bread, nori

algarroba *(Sp)* Carob

Alge *(Ge)* Seaweed, algae

Algerian clementine *(USA) see* fina

algin *(USA)* Alginates used for thickening. See alginic acid

alginates Salts and esters of alginic acid q.v

alginic acid A carbohydrate acid, E400, obtained from various seaweeds used as a thickening and gelling agent in commercial ice cream and convenience foods. Also supplied as the sodium salt, sodium alginate, E401, used mainly in ice cream, the potassium salt, E402, and the calcium salt, E404, which forms a much stiffer gel than the other salts. It is also available as an ester, propane 2-diol alginate, E405

algue *(Fr) fem.* Seaweed, algae

algue rouge *(Fr) fem. see* dulse

algérienne, à l' *(Fr)* In the Algerian style, i.e. garnished with small croquettes of sweet potato and small empty tomatoes, seasoned and braised in oil

alheira *(Po)* A sausage made with smoked ham, garlic and nuts

alho *(Po)* Garlic

alho-porro *(Po)* Leek

alholva *(Sp)* Fenugreek

alhos franceses *(Po)* Leeks [also called **alho-porras**]

Alicante *(Sp)* A fresh, white, rindless cheese made from goat's milk, curdled with rennet and stored in weak brine or water. Contains 60% water, 15% fat and 20% protein

alice *(It)* Fresh anchovy

aligi *(Ph)* Tomalley

aligot de marinette *(Fr)* A purée of potatoes beaten vigorously with crushed garlic, bacon fat and half its weight of Laguiole cheese in a bain-marie until just smooth and elastic

alimentação *(Po)* Food, nourishment

alimentari *(It)* Groceries or grocery shop

aliñado *(Sp)* Seasoned

aliño *(Sp)* Seasoning, salad dressing

alioli *(Sp)* Garlic-flavoured mayonnaise [also called **ajiaceite**]

alitán *(Sp)* Larger spotted dogfish

alkali An alkali is a substance containing a deficiency of hydrogen ions (or an excess of hydroxyl ions) compared with pure water. An alkali (e.g. sodium hydroxide) will combine with an acid (e.g. alginic acid) to form a neutral salt (e.g. sodium alginate). The most common culinary alkalis are sodium bicarbonate and ammonium carbonate both of which liberate carbon dioxide gas when heated or combined with an acid such as tartaric acid

alkalinity A measure of the strength of an alkali on the scale of pH which goes from 7 (neutral) through 7.7 to 9.2 (egg white), 8.4 (sodium bicarbonate or baking soda), 11.9 (household ammonia) to 14 (highest value of alkalinity). Strong alkalis such as sodium hydroxide react with fat in the skin to form soaps which give the characteristic slimy feel

alkaioids The components of plants responsible in most cases for their bitter taste and therapeutic effects. Typical examples are quinine used in tonic water and caffeine and theobromine found in coffee beans. Other well known alkaloids are cocaine, strychnine, atropine and morphine

alkanet A Mediterranean plant of the borage family *Anchusa tinctora,* whose roots provide a red or blue (depending on pH) food dye similar to henna [also called **alkanna**]

alkanna *see* alkanet

all-purpose flour *(USA)* Plain white flour blended from hard and soft wheat flours

allache *(Fr) fem.* A large sardine

allemande *(Fr)* The term applied to dishes garnished with German specialities such as sauerkraut, smoked sausage, pickled pork, potato dumpling, etc.

allemande, à l' *(Fr)* In the German style, i.e. garnished with noodles and mashed potatoes

allemande, sauce *(En & Fr) fem.* White velouté sauce thickened with egg yolks [also called **sauce parisienne**]

allergens Compounds, either proteins or smaller chemicals which react with the proteins of the skin and mucous membranes (eyes, nose, lungs, gut, etc.) of some persons to form compounds, both types of which elicit the immune response of the body causing rashes, irritation, asthma, etc. Typical food allergies occur with strawberries, eggs, milk, cereal, fish, peas, and nuts. The response should not be confused with that produced by enzyme deficiencies as for example with the inability to metabolize lactose found in most Chinese and the inability to metabolize gluten which is fairly common in the west

Allgäuer Bergkäse *(Ge)* A hard cow's milk cheese similar to Emmental

Allgäuer Rahmkäse *(Ge)* A soft, mild, Limburger type cheese

Allgewürz *(Ge)* Allspice

Alliaria petiolata *Bot.* Garlic mustard

allicin The chemical compound in garlic which gives it its characteristic smell and taste

alligator A large carnivorous amphibian found in the swamps and rives of the southern USA and the Yangtze river in China. The meat, especially the tail meat, is eaten during the hunting season and is a speciality of Cajun cuisine

alligator pear *see* avocado

allioli *(Sp)* A thick emulsion of garlic, salt and olive oil either pounded together or prepared in a mechanical blender. Served cold as an accompaniment to fish, meat or vegetables. From the Catalan, alli = garlic

allis shad *see* shad

Allium ascalonicum *Bot.* Now superseded, see *Allium cepa* Aggregatum Group

Allium cepa *Bot.* Onion and spring onion

***Allium cepa* Aggregatum Group** *Bot.* Shallot

Allium cepa* var. *proliferum *Bot.* Egyptian onion

Allium fistulosum *Bot.* Welsh onion

Allium porrum *Bot.* Leek

Allium ramosum *Bot.* Asian leek

Allium sativum *Bot.* Garlic

Allium schoenoprasum *Bot.* Chives

Allium scorodoprasum *Bot.* Giant garlic

Allium spp. The botanical name for the important onion family of plants, including onions and spring onions *Allium cepa,* shallots *Allium cepa* Aggregatum group, Welsh or bunching onions (ciboule) *Allium fistulosum,* Egyptian onion or tree onion *Allium cepa* var. *proliferum,* leeks *Allium porum,* garlic *Allium sativum,* giant garlic (rocambole) *Allium scorodoprasum,* chives *Allium schoenoprasum* and Chinese chives *Allium tuberosum*

Allium tuberosum *Bot.* Chinese chives

allodolla *(It)* Lark (bird)

alloro *(It)* Bay tree, (foglie di alloro, bay leaves)

allspice The dried, green, unripe berry of a tree *Pimenta dioca or P. officinalis* which grows exclusively in the Caribbean and South America. It has a flavour of cinnamon, nutmeg, and cloves combined. Used in cakes, in food manufacture and extensively in Jamaican meat dishes [also called **Jamaican pepper, pimento, myrtle pepper**]

allumettes *(Fr) fem.* Matchsticks e.g. pommes allumettes = straw potatoes; allumettes au fromage = cheese straws

allumettes aux anchois *(Fr) fem.* Rectangles of puff pastry coated with a thin layer of fish forcemeat flavoured with anchovy essence and garnished with fillets of anchovy prior to baking

allumettes caprice *(Fr) fem.* As allumettes aux anchois but with a forcemeat of chicken and cream with chopped ox tongue and truffle

allumettes aux crevettes *(Fr) fem.* As allumettes aux anchois but with a forcemeat of whiting and shrimp butter containing cooked and sliced shrimps

allumettes pour hors d'oeuvres *(Fr) fem.* Rectangles of 8 mm. puff pastry used as a base for hors d'oeuvres, generally covered with a thin layer of forcemeat flavoured with cayenne pepper and cut into 7 cm by 2.5 cm rectangles prior to baking. They are decorated as appropriate

alma-ata plov *(Ru)* A Central Asian rice pilaf made with chicken stock and containing cubed lamb, julienned carrots, sliced onions, chopped apples, dried raisins, dried apricots and almonds, flavoured with orange juice and zest

almaciga *(Sp)* Mastic

almamártás *(Hu)* Apple sauce

almás palacsintas *(Hu)* Pancake with chopped apples

almavica *(It)* A dessert similar to semolina pudding

almeja *(Sp)* Clam, carpet shell and similar bivalve molluscs

almejas marineras *(Sp)* Clams in a garlic and olive oil based sauce

almejas palourdes *(Sp)* Carpet shell clams

almejón brillante *(Sp)* Venus shell clam

almendra *(Sp)* Almond

almendrado *(Sp)* Macaroon

almendras garapiñadas *(Sp)* Sugared almonds

almôço *(Po)* Lunch (taken 13.30 to 15.00 hours)

almond The kernel (nut) of the fruit of the almond tree. The sweet variety *Prunus dulcis* var. *dulcis* is used whole, split, flaked, chopped or ground in cookery. The bitter variety *Prunus dulcis* var. *amara* is used for the production of almond essence and almond oil and very occasionally in cooking

almond biscuits Ground almonds and castor sugar folded into stiffly beaten egg white, piped onto rice paper, decorated and baked at 180°C

almond butter A compound butter made from freshly shelled sweet almonds pounded to a fine paste with twice their weight of butter and passed through a fine sieve [also called **amandine butter**]

almond cream A sweet made from a mixture of ground almonds with egg yolks and orange flower water, thickened in a bain-marie and garnished with almond praline

almond essence An alcoholic extract of fermented bitter almonds, used to give an almond flavour to cakes, etc. Some almond essences are made from apricot kernels

almond flakes Dehusked almonds separated into two halves [also called **flaked almonds**]

almond flavouring A synthetic chemical product with an almond flavour and smell, much cheaper than almond essence and commonly used as a substitute

almond milk *(UK)* A medieval substitute for milk during lent made by pounding sweet almonds together with a few bitter almonds with water then mixing with barley water and sugar and boiling to a creamy consistency

almond nibs Evenly chopped blanched almonds about 2 to 3 mm diameter used as a decoration

almond oil An oil with a very delicate flavour obtained by pressing or solvent extraction from bitter almonds. Used in confectionery and for oiling dessert moulds

almond paste *see* marzipan

almond potatoes *see* pommes amandine

almond powder *(USA)* Very finely ground almonds used in desserts

almond sauce Sweetened milk, thickened with cornflour and flavoured with almond essence

almond slice An individual cake made from a rectangle of pastry covered with a thick almond topping similar to frangipane and decorated with flaked almonds

almôndêga *(Po)* Meat ball

almuerzo 1 *(Me)* Brunch **2** *(Sp)* Lunch

Alnwick stew *(UK)* A casserole from Northumberland of cubed bacon layered with onions and potatoes, seasoned with pepper and mustard and simmered with water and bay leaf for about 2 hours

aloo *(In)* Potato

aloo bokhara *(In)* Sour prunes

aloo chat *(In)* A spiced potato dish made from large diced potatoes, fried in ghee until coloured, mixed with minced onions and garlic, chat masala, chilli powder, seasoning, crumbled bay leaf, chopped red chilli and chopped fresh coriander leaves, then cooked until tender in a covered pan with a little water if necessary

alootikka *(In)* A potato and chickpea rissole served with yoghurt and tamarind sauce [also called **alutikka**]

alosa *(It)* Shad

alose *(Fr) fem.* Shad

alose farcie *(Fr) fem.* Whole shad stuffed with a forcemeat of soft roes, white bread moistened with milk, seasoning, nutmeg, chives, parsley, chervil, egg and egg yolks, incised, wrapped in oiled paper, baked for 35-40 minutes and accompanied by sauce Bercy

alose feinte *(Fr)* Fem. Twaite shad

alose grillée *(Fr) fem.* Shad incised whole or cut into darnes, marinated in oil, lemon juice and herbs, grilled over moderate heat until cooked through, served with lemon slices and either parsley or anchovy butter and sauce bercy

alose grillée à l'oseille *(Fr) fem.* Grilled shad *(see alose grillée)* accompanied by sorrel stewed in butter then braised and the whole presented in a deep dish and served with melted butter presented separately

alose de la Loire à l'oseille *(Fr) fem.* Incised and seasoned whole shad, oiled and grilled for 2.5 minutes per side, finished in the oven on a bed of sorrel purée mixed with butter and lemon juice and served with the purée, wedges of hard boiled egg and slices of lemon

alose à la provençale *(Fr) fem.* Alternate layers of sorrel mixed with chopped onions and slices of shad finishing with a sorrel layer placed in a garlic-flavoured pan or casserole with a tight fitting lid, the top sprinkled with thyme, oil, seasoning and marc or brandy, the lid sealed on and the whole cooked over a very low heat or in a slow oven for 7 hours

alose à la tomate et au vin *(Fr) fem.* A whole shad placed on a bed of tomato concassé, butter and chopped garlic in a flame proof casserole, covered with tomato concassé, chopped onions, chopped mushrooms, white wine and melted butter, covered, cooked on top of the stove for 3 minutes and finished in a moderate oven for 20 to 25 minutes

alouette *(Fr) fem.* Lark, a small bird. Once used in cooking now protected in the EU

alouette sans tête *(Fr) fem.* A beef olive, also made with veal

aloyau de boeuf *(Fr) masc.* Sirloin of beef on the bone, usually including the fillet and prepared especially for top class roasting

aloyau de boeuf froid *(Fr) masc.* Cold roast sirloin of beef including the fillet, on the bone and coated with aspic jelly

Aloysia triphylla *Bot.* Lemon verbena

alp cheese *see* Berg

Alpbergkäse A cooked curd, dense German cheese made from whole cow's milk with a dense dry rind and a few holes, cast into large rounds weighing 20 to 30 kg. Contains 40% water, 27% fat and 25% protein

Alpenkäse *see* Berg

Alpenklüber *(He)* A rohwurst made of lean pork, beef and pork fat, air dried and eaten raw

Alpenschneehuhn *(Ge)* Ptarmigan

alpha-linolenic acid A fatty acid found in ester form in high proportion in walnut oil, purslane and soya oil. Said to be the reason why

Cretans and Japanese have a low incidence of heart attacks due to its protective effects esp. against repeat heart attacks

Alpin *(Fr)* A soft rindless cheese made from cow's milk curdled with rennet and made into small rounds similar to Vacherin Mont d'Or. It is dry salted and ripened for a week or more. Contains 55% water, 21% fat and 21% protein

Alpine cheese *see* Berg

alpine hare *see* Scottish hare

alpine strawberry A small, delicately flavoured strawberry *Fragaria vesca sempiflorens, F. alpina* which fruits constantly from June to October in the UK

Alpinia galanga *Bot.* Greater galangal

Alpinia officinarum *Bot.* Lesser galangal

alpino *(USA)* A variety of salami

alsacien(ne) *(Fr) adj.* From Alsace, usually garnished with sauerkraut and/or ham, smoked sausage, peas

alsacienne, à l' In the Alsacian style, i.e. garnished with small tartlet cases filled with braised sauerkraut and topped with a round slice of lean ham

Alse *(Ge)* Shad

ålsoppa *(Sw)* A thick soup or thin stew made from pieces of skinned eel boiled in salted water with some mixed peppercorns for 25 minutes, eel removed and replaced with floury potatoes and leeks which are cooked until the potatoes fall and the whole is like thin mashed potatoes, eel added back, seasoned and consistency adjusted with milk

alt Kuhkäse *(Ge)* Hard cheese

Altaiski *see* Altay

Altay *(Ru)* A hard cheese with a dry rind and medium sized holes cast into large rounds weighing about 12 to 20 kg. Contains 42% water, 30% fat and 24% protein [also called **Altaiski, Altaysky**]

Altaysky *see* Altay

altea *(It)* Marshmallow

Altenburger (Ziegenkäse) A variable fat content small, round, soft cheese made in eastern Germany from goat's and cow's milk, similar to Camembert. Contains 66 to 56% water, 7 to 20% fat and 25 to 20% protein for the half fat to full fat versions

Althaea officinalis *Bot.* Marshmallow

altitude effects The temperature at which water boils depends upon the pressure to which it is subjected, which in an open vessel depends upon the altitude. The boiling point of water drops by approximately 1°C for every 900 feet (290 m) rise, hence the need for pressure cookers at high altitudes

alto-zukuri *(Ja)* A type of cut for fish used in sashimi, in which very narrow slivers are cut from thin fillets and piled in small mounds

alubias *(Sp)* Kidney beans

alum *see* aluminium potassium sulphate

alumbeberas *(Ph)* Pomfret, the fish

aluminium E173, an extremely thin aluminium foil which may be used as food decoration. No nutritional value and may be harmful

aluminium calcium silicate *see* (E)556

aluminium foil Aluminium metal rolled until very thin and flexible. Because it is relatively inert and does not easily corrode it is useful as a wrapping for food or for cooking [also called **cooking foil**]

aluminium potassium sulphate A firming agent used in for example chocolate coated cherries. Used as a preservative and firming agent for pickles in SEA cooking [also called **alum**]

aluminium sodium silicate *see* (E)554

alutikka *(In) see* alootikka

alveograph The instrument which measures the strength of dough prior to baking by injecting air into the dough at a fixed depth and flow rate through a specific nozzle and recording the pressure at which the resulting bubble bursts

Alvorca *(Po)* A hard, dense, grating cheese made with ewe's milk in 200 to 300g rounds with a dry brown rind. Contains 25% water, 37% fat and 33% protein

alya *(ME)* Fat from the tails of lamb and mutton much used in Iraq

amahong *(Ph)* Asian mussel

amai *(Ja)* Sweet

Amalfi lemon *(It)* A prized variety of lemon from the south of Naples which is allowed to ripen on the tree and is thus less acid. It is larger than normal with a rough knobbly skin and a very fine flavour and aroma

Amalfi salad Cleaned and prepared mussels and small clams boiled to open with dry white wine and chopped shallots, sound meat reserved, meat from opened scallops sliced and sautéed in butter for a few second and the clam and mussel liquor reduced by half and finished with single cream to form a sauce. The salad is assembled from sliced cold waxy potatoes topped with the cooked shell fish, the sauce poured over and garnished with chopped parsley. Served warm

amalgamer *(Fr)* To mix, amalgamate or blend

amande *(Fr) fem.* Almond

amandel *(Ho)* Almond

amandes, fish aux Fish meunière with coarsely chopped almonds added to the beurre noisette [also called **poisson meunière aux amandes (Fr)**]

amandine *(Fr) fem.* Name given to certain almond-flavoured French pastries and sponges

amandine butter *see* almond butter

amaranth **1** A widely distributed tropical and sub-tropical plant species *Amaranthus* spp. whose leaves are used as a vegetable, supplied fresh or canned. Often attributed with magical powers. There are two popular types, one is green and mild and the other is red. Generally lightly cooked by steaming. A variety of names are used for the local species viz. callaloo, bhaji, elephant's ear, sag, sagaloo, African spinach, Chinese spinach, Indian spinach, Surinam amaranth **2** E123, a synthetic yellow food colouring banned in the USA

Amaranthus caudatus *Bot.* One of the amaranths with pale green leaves and vivid red tassel-like flowers. Often grown as an ornamental plant

Amaranthus cruentus *Bot.* The most commonly grown amaranth with oval, light green leaves and long spiky flowers

Amaranthus spp. *Bot.* Amaranths

Amaranthus tricolor *Bot.* Chinese spinach

amardine *(ME)* Sheets of dried apricot paste used for flavouring drinks or desserts or as a constituent of certain Middle East lamb stews

amarelle *(USA)* A sour red variety of cherry with a colourless juice, used for cherry pie and liqueurs

amarena *(It)* Morello cherry

amaretti *(It)* Small sweet meringue-like macaroons made from ground almonds, sugar and stiffly whipped egg whites (3:5:1), alternatively (2:3:1), blended to a stiff paste, possibly with almond essence, piped onto parchment paper and baked at 175°C. They may be decorated with almond flakes before baking. Usually shop bought; *see also* almond biscuits

amasar *(Sp)* To knead

amassada *(Po)* Mashed

amatriciana, all' *(It)* In the style of Amatrice, i.e. used of dishes with a sauce made of tomatoes, onions and salt pork or bacon

amayuela *(Sp)* Golden carpet shell clam

amazu shoga *(Ja) see* beni-shoga

amberjack A large round brightly coloured fish *Seriola dumerili* and other *Seriola* spp. found in tropical and sub-tropical waters

amb halad *(In)* Zedoary

ambrosia *(It)* A dessert made from layers of thinly sliced oranges, sliced bananas, fresh pineapple, desiccated coconut and caster sugar

ambrosía *(Me)* A very sweet scented herb whose leaves are used in cold drinks in the same way as mint

amchar *see* amchoor

amchoor *(In)* A flavouring similar to tamarind made by drying slices of unripe mango *Magnifera indica.* It is also supplied in powdered form and is used for souring and tenderizing [also called **aamchur, amchar, amchor, amchur, mango powder**]

amchor *see* amchoor

amchur *see* amchoor

ame *(Ja)* A sweet jelly made from boiled millet used to flavour fish dishes

ame hnat *(Bm)* A dish of braised beef with fried chopped onions, garlic, ginger, chilli powder, lemon zest, etc. garnished with crisp fried onions

amêijoas *(Po)* Small, thin shelled and very sweet clams

ameixa *(Po)* Plum or prune

Amelanchier canadensis *Bot.* Juneberry

amêndoa *(Po)* Almond

amendoim *(Po)* Peanut

américaine, garnish à l' Slices of lobster tails which have been fried then cooked in white wine, fish stock, brandy, meat glaze, demi-glace sauce, chopped shallots, tomato concassée, chopped parsley and cayenne pepper

américaine, sauce *(Fr) fem.* The cooking liquor from garnish or homard à l'américaine, reduced, mixed with the lobster coral and cream from its head plus butter, strained and finished with chopped parsley

American broccoli *see* calabrese

American brown shrimp *see* American shrimp

American burbot A freshwater non-oily relative of the cod *Lota maculosa* found in the Great Lakes of Canada and North America. Cooked like cod

American crayfish The small common

crayfish *Procambarus clarkii* of North American rivers

American cress *see* land cress

American frosting *(USA)* A cake icing, hard on the outside but soft inside made from sugar and water boiled to 120°C with a little cream of tartar, slightly cooled and whisked into stiffly beaten egg white [also called **boiled frosting, boiled icing, frosting**]

American fudge cake *see* fudge cake

American grape A more cold-tolerant grape *Vitus labrusca and V. rotundifolia* which has been hybridized with the European grape *Vitus vinifera* to produce a wide range of cooler climate cultivars. They are considered to be inferior to the European varieties, *V. rotundifolia* having a foxy flavour

American long-grain rice A long thin white rice from which the husk, bran and germ have been removed. Stays separate when cooked [also called **regular-milled white rice**]

American meringue *(USA)* The type of meringue used for a Pavlova, made by mixing cornflour and acid with meringue Suisse and baking at a higher temperature than normal for a shorter period to give a crisp outside with a soft sticky centre

American mustard A sweet, mild variety of mustard made from ground, dehusked white mustard seeds coloured with turmeric and mixed with vinegar, etc. Used as a condiment particularly with hot dogs and hamburgers

American navy bean *see* navy bean

American oyster A variety of oyster *Crassostrea virginica* reaching 17 cm in length and found on the American side of the Atlantic. Usually cooked [also called **eastern oyster**]

American persimmon A variety of persimmon *Diospyros virginiana* about 4 cm in dia. and with redder skin and flesh

American pink shrimp *see* American shrimp

American plaice A large flat fish *Hippoglossoides platesoides* similar to, but with less definite markings than, the European plaice [also called **Canadian plaice, sand dab**]

American relishes Hors d'oeuvres consisting of aceto-dolce pickles flavoured with cinnamon and cayenne and accompanied by small cinnamon biscuits

American service Method of serving food in a restaurant by dividing it amongst individual plates in the kitchen rather than serving from a platter at the table

American shad A variety of shad *Alosa sapidissima,* more popular in the USA than shad is in Europe

American shrimp Large shrimps *Penaeus* spp. (to 15 cm) fished south of the Carolinas and closely related to the king prawn. They are the brown *P. aztecus aztecus,* the pink *P. duorarum duorarum* and the white *P. setiferus*

American veal cuts *(USA)* *see* veal cuts (USA)

American whelk A variety of whelk *Busycon carica* which can reach 30 cm in length

American white shrimp *see* American shrimp

a-mer-tha-hin *(Bm)* A mild beef curry made from fried pieces of stewing beef and a fried, pounded spice mixture (onions, garlic, fresh ginger, salt, turmeric and chilli powder) cooked in beef stock and thick soy sauce. Other recipes include vinegar, bay leaves, fish sauce and cinnamon [also called **amé-thà-hin**]

amé-thà-hin *(Bm)* *see* a-mer-tha-hin

amido *(It)* Starch

amigdala alatismena *(Gr)* Salted almonds made by baking for 30 minutes at 180°C, salted (45 g per kg), unskinned, shelled almonds which have been marinated in lemon juice or citric acid solution and drained. Eaten as an appetizer

amilbar de arce *(Sp)* Maple syrup

amino acid An organic acid which is the building block of proteins. The sequence of amino acids in a protein determines its properties. 20 amino acids are incorporated in human tissue. Of these 12, or 11 in the case of rapidly growing infants, can be synthesized in the body, the remaining 8 or 9 (essential amino acids) must be obtained from food. High class proteins contain the essential amino acids. They are in alphabetical order: alanine, arginine, aspartic acid, cysteine, cystine, glutamic acid, glycine, histidine, isoleucine, leucine, lysine, methionine, norleucine, ornithine, phenylalanine, serine, threonine, tryptophan, tyrosine and valine

amiral, à l' *(Fr)* In the style of the admiral, i.e. garnished with a mixture of sliced truffles, mussels, lobster meat, oysters and crayfish tails

ami-shakushi *(Ja)* A fine wire mesh skimmer for cleaning deep fat frying oil

ammantato *(It)* Covered with another ingredients such as cheese, sauce, etc., napped

ammiraglia, all' *(It)* In the admiral's style i.e. containing fish or shellfish

ammollicato *(It)* Soaked and softened

ammonia A pungent irritating gas used in water solution as a cleaner and bleach. Often smelled on rotting fish and overripe cheese

ammonium bicarbonate (E)503, an old-fashioned raising agent which releases carbon dioxide on heating or reaction with acid. Not in general use [also called **salts of hartshorn**]

ammonium carbonate *see* (E)503

ammonium chloride *see* (E)510

ammonium ferric citrate *see* (E)381

ammonium phosphatides Food additives used as emulsifiers and stabilizers for cocoa and chocolate products

ammonium polyphosphate *see* (E)545

ammonium sulphate The ammonium salt of sulphuric acid used as a yeast food

Amomum globosum *Bot.* Chinese cardamom

Amomum melegueta *Bot.* Grains of paradise

Amomum subulatum *Bot.* Nepal cardamom

amoras *(Po)* Berries

Amorphophallus campanulatus *Bot.* Elephant's foot

Amorphophallus konjac *Bot.* Devil's taro, used for preparing black bean curd

amorphous sugar *(USA)* Non-crystalline sugar made by melting sucrose and cooling rapidly to form a transparent glass-like material

amouille *(Fr)* Beestings

amourettes *(Fr) fem.* The spinal marrow of veal and lamb. Prepared by thorough cleaning followed by poaching for 30 minutes in a boiling vinegar court-bouillon. Literally, passing fancies

amourettes de veau Tosca *(Fr) fem.* Short lengths of cooked amourettes of veal mixed with macaroni, butter, grated Parmesan cheese, coulis of crayfish tails, carefully heated in a timbale, covered with coulis d'écrivisses (crayfish coulis) and garnished with amourettes

ampalaya *(Ph)* Bitter gourd

ampil khui *(Cm)* Tamarind

ampil tum *(Cm)* Unripe tamarind

amsamgelugor *see* tamarind

amsoh galbi kui *(Ko)* Marinated and grilled short ribs of beef

amsterdamse korstjes *(Ho)* Spice cake

amuse gueule *(Fr) masc.* Small appetizers usually served before or while the menu choice is being made. Literally mouth pleasers

amydated pectin E440(b), a synthetic derivative of pectin which is more stable than the parent product

amyl acetate An ester formed from amyl alcohol and acetic acid used to flavour the confectionary item, pear drops. Some say it has a banana flavour

amyl butyrate An ester formed from amyl alcohol and butyric acid used as an artificial flavouring

amyl valeriate An ester formed from amyl alcohol and valerianic acid with an apple-like flavour

amylase An enzyme (naturally occurring catalyst of chemical reactions) found in saliva and gastric juices which breaks down starch (a polysaccharide) into smaller subunits which are further broken down by other enzymes or which can be directly absorbed, usually as glucose, into the blood stream. Strains obtained commercially by fermentation from *Aspergillus niger* and *Bacillus subtilis* are used in the manufacture of syrups, in the brewing industry and generally in food manufacturing [also called **diastase**]

amylopectin The main and more easily digested component of starch

amylose The minor and less easily digested constituent of starch

an *(Ja)* A sweetened smooth or crunchy paste of ground adzuki beans

Anacardium occidentale *Bot.* The cashew nut tree

anadama bread *(USA)* A yeast-raised bread containing cornmeal and molasses or black treacle

anadromous A term describing fish which are born in a river, migrate to the sea to grow and return to their birth river to spawn. The salmon is a common example. The opposite is catadromous

anaerobe The term applied to describe microorganisms which will grow and reproduce in the absence of air. Facultative anaerobes will grow with or without air. Strict (i.e. non-facultative) anaerobes are poisoned by the oxygen in the air

anago *(Ja)* Conger or seawater eel, thin slices are used raw in sushi

anaheim chilli A fairly hot, long, green to yellow chilli pepper which is never dried [also called **guero, Californian chilli, California pepper**]

analcolico *(It)* Non-alcoholic drink

ananá *(Sa & Sp)* Pineapple

ananas *(De, Ge, Ho, No, Ru, Sw & Fr) masc.* Pineapple

ananâs *(Po)* Pineapple

Ananas comosus *Bot.* Pineapple

ananas Condé *(Fr) masc.* Pineapple poached and served on dessert rice with a fruit syrup

ananas à la créole *(Fr) masc.* Peeled and cored pineapple cooked in kirsch-flavoured sugar syrup, cut into thin semicircles, these used to line a dome shaped mould, the centre filled with a layer of vanilla dessert rice followed by diced custard apple, pineapple and banana cooked in syrup to complete, chilled until set, demoulded, decorated with angelica and surrounded with poached bananas

ananas georgette *(Fr) masc.* A large whole pineapple with top removed and reserved, centre scooped out, chopped finely and mixed with an iced fruit mousse mixture made from cold syrup (35°Be, 1.86 kg per litre of water), pineapple purée and crème chantilly, replaced in the pineapple, covered with the top and allowed to set in the refrigerator

Ananas Kaltschale *(Ge)* A cold pineapple soup made from crushed pineapple boiled in a light sugar syrup, allowed to cool and stand, pushed through a strainer, mixed with white wine, chilled and garnished with a macedoine of pineapple steeped in sugar and lemon juice

ananas Ninon *(Fr) masc.* A vanilla ice cream filled soufflée mould with a conical depression from the centre to the outer edges, lined with overlapping slices of pineapple, the centre heaped with wild strawberries covered with a purée of raspberries and sprinkled with chopped pistachios.

ananas à la royale *(Fr) masc.* Pineapple prepared as for ananas georgette, but filled with fresh fruit salad flavoured with kirsch. The base of the pineapple is surrounded with alternate poached peaches and strawberries macerated in kirsch

ananas Virginie *(Fr) masc.* Pineapple prepared as for ananas georgette but with a strawberry mousse mixed with the diced flesh of the pineapple as filling

ananasso *(It)* Pineapple

ananász *(Hu)* Pineapple

anar *(In)* Pomegranate

anara *(It)* Duck [also called **anatra**]

anardana *(In)* The ground dried seeds of sour pomegranates used in North India as a souring agent in chutneys and curries, in fillings for bread and savoury pasties, and with braised vegetables and pulses

Anari A soft, white, unripened curd, Cypriot cheese made from ewe's milk, with a slightly sweetish flavour and moist texture similar to the Greek mizithra or Italian ricotta and eaten as a dessert

anatra *(It)* Duck [also called **anara**]

anatra arrosto *(It)* Duck, blanched for 5 minutes, dried with paper then hot air (paint stripper or hair dryer), rubbed with ground rosemary, sage, salt and black pepper, stuffed with the same herbs mixed with chopped liver, roasted and served with sauce made from pan juices and the stuffing

anatra col pien *(It)* Duck braised with a stuffing of meat, sausage, mushrooms and pistachio nuts

anatrino *(It)* Duckling

anatto *see* annatto

anchoa *(Sp)* Anchovy

anchoïade *(Fr) fem.* An anchovy paste made with anchovies pounded or processed with olive oil and possibly garlic to make a dip for canapés. From Provence

anchois *(Fr) masc.* Anchovy

anchois, beurre d' masc. See anchovy butter

anchois, canapé d' *(Fr) masc.* Canapé with anchovy butter

anchois, sauce *(Fr) fem.* Anchovy sauce

anchois frais marinés *(Fr) masc.* A hors d'oeuvre made from fresh anchovies salted for 2 hours, drained, plunged into hot fat to stiffen, then marinaded in oil with a little acid (lemon or vinegar) for 2 days. Served with a little of the marinade

anchois de Norvège *(Fr) masc.* Norwegian anchovies, preserved in brine

anchois à la parisienne *(Fr) masc.* Fillets of desalted anchovies arranged in a multi diamond pattern in the centre of a plate covered with a little vinaigrette mixed with soy sauce. The centre of the diamonds and the border filled with separately chopped hard boiled egg yolk, hard boiled egg white and green herbs to give a pleasing pattern

anchois aux poivrons *(Fr) masc.* A hors d'oeuvre of anchovy fillets marinated in oil, alternating with strips of sweet pepper and decorated with chopped hard boiled egg, parsley and capers

anchois des tamarins *(Fr) masc.* A hors d'oeuvre composed of anchovy paupiettes, each topped with a black olive, arranged around a centre of grated warm potatoes seasoned with oil and vinegar and sprinkled with chopped fines herbes

ancho pepper A mild, richly flavoured variety

of pepper *Capsicum frutescens*, usually dried and used in Latin American cooking

anchouiada *(Fr)* Anchovy fillets pounded with garlic, shallots, thyme and olive oil with a little vinegar, used as a flavouring or dip. Similar to bagna cauda

anchovas *(Po)* Anchovies [also called **enchovas**]

Anchovis *(Ge)* Anchovy

anchovy A small Mediterranean fish of the herring family *Engraulis encrasicolus*, up to 20 cm in length and fished in the Mediterranean and the bay of Biscay between January and September. Usually salted whole and used as a garnish or for flavouring. Similar fish *Stolephorus heterolobus* are found throughout SEA and used fresh, salted or dried and are one of the fish fermented to produce fish pastes and sauces

anchovy butter A compound butter made from butter and anchovy fillets pounded together and sieved

anchovy essence A liquid extract of cured and salted anchovies used for flavouring

anchovy fingers *see* allumettes aux anchois

anchovy paste Salted anchovies, vinegar, spices and water pounded together

anchovy paupiettes A hors d'oeuvre of flattened anchovy fillets spread with a purée of cooked fish mixed with mayonnaise seasoned with cayenne, rolled into a paupiette and decorated with anchovy butter

anchovy sauce A rich fish velouté thickened with egg yolk and cream or sauce Normande without the butter and flavoured with anchovy butter; alternatively, Béchamel sauce with 2 tablespoons of anchovy essence per litre. May be finished with diced, dried and desalted anchovy fillets. Used with fish

anchovy toast *(UK)* A savoury or appetizer made from rounds of bread fried to a pale straw, covered with anchovies and topped with chilled Devonshire or whipped cream and served immediately

an chun *(Ch)* Quail

an chun dan *(Ch)* Quail egg

Anchusa tinctora *Bot.* Alkanet

ancidda *(It)* Eel *(Sardinia)*

ancien impérial *(Fr)* A soft mild cheese cast in squares. May be eaten fresh or ripened

ancienne, à l' *(Fr)* In the old style, i.e. with boiled rice, Béchamel sauce and mushrooms

ancient egg *see* Chinese preserved eggs

ancono *(It)* A soup made with fish, shellfish and tomatoes

and *(De & No)* Duck

andaa *(Ne)* Egg

andalouse, à l' *(Fr)* In the Andalusian style, i.e. garnished with halves of grilled red pepper filled with rice cooked à la Grecque and slices of aubergine, 4 cm thick, with the centre hollowed out and filled with tomatoes sautéed in oil

andalouse mayonnaise Mayonnaise mixed with tomato purée and the finely chopped flesh of skinned and cooked sweet red peppers. Served with roast veal, poultry and hard boiled eggs

andalouse, sauce *(En & Fr) fem.* Mayonnaise mixed with tomato purée and garnished with julienned red sweet pepper

Andalusian sauce *see* sauce andalouse

ande *(In)* egg

andijvie *(Ho)* Endive

andouille *(Fr) fem.* Large, black, pig based sausage boiled in water then grilled, may be served hot or cold usually in thin slices and garnished with mashed potato. Generally made from pork, tripe, pork chitterlings, calf mesentery, pepper, wine, onions and spices, depending on region. May be white through various shades of brown to black and may be dried (sechée) or smoked (fumée)

andouille bretonne *(Fr) fem.* Pig tripe and chitterlings, cut into strips a little shorter than the sausage, dry cured in salt, pepper and spices or marinated in wine and herbs, mixed with half their combined weight of similar strips of hard pork fat, placed regularly or jumbled up in beef runners, tied, salted for a week, smoked for 3 days over apple wood, brushed off, floured and boiled in water for 2 hours before serving.

andouille de Cambrai *(Fr) fem.* Tripe sausage dating from 1767

andouille de campagne *(Fr) fem.* The typical andouille containing about 50% pork shoulder meat, the remainder being chitterlings, tripe and seasonings

andouille de Nancy *(Fr) fem.* Equal parts of calf mesentery and belly pork cut in 20 cm long strips, treated with salt, pepper and spice or marinated in wine and herbs, drained, seasoned, possibly mixed with chopped onions and mushrooms sweated in lard, moistened with Madeira or white wine, stuffed into beef runners and tied. Cooked by pricking and simmering in water with aromatic vegetables and a BG then left to cool in the cooking liquor

andouille pur porc *(Fr) fem.* Andouilles made with seasoned pork shoulder meat and fat

andouille vigneronne *(Fr) fem.* Soaked

haricot beans put in a casserole with diced fat bacon and pork rind, carrots, onions, a BG and seasoning, covered with water and boiled with some wine for an hour, a previously cooked pork andouille added and the whole braised in the oven for 2 hours. The meat and beans are served separately

andouille de Vire *(Fr) fem.* As andouille bretonne but with fat bacon replacing the pork fat, chopped onion, shallots and parsley added and the whole seasoned and moistened with white wine. The strips are formed in bundles and placed neatly in beef runners tying each bundle in place. The andouille may be salted in brine and/or smoked but in all cases finally simmered in a bouillon for 3 hours

andouillette *(Fr) fem.* A small version of the andouille but usually containing only coarsely chopped chitterlings and tripe and purchased in the cooked state. Generally lightly slashed and grilled or fried and served hot with fried potatoes, mustard and onions

andouillette (à la) bourguignonne *(Fr) fem.* Andouillettes cut into 1 cm. slices sautéed in hot butter and lard until browned, fat drained off and andouillettes served with melted well seasoned snail butter

andouillette fine de porc *(Fr) fem.* Calf mesentery and lean bacon cut in pieces, simmered in stock with herbs and an onion clouté for 2 hours, removed, coarsely chopped and combined with the strained reduced cooking liquor, egg yolks and chopped shallots, mushrooms and parsley, sweated in lard, filled into casings and tied to form small sausages. May be brined and/or smoked before simmering in a bouillon

andouillette à la lyonnaise *(Fr) fem.* Andouillettes cut into 1 cm. slices, sautéed in very hot butter until browned, sliced onion added and coloured, seasoned, mixed well and finished with chopped parsley and a little vinegar.

andouillette de Savoie *(Fr) fem.* Andouillettes containing pork chitterlings, tripe and calf mesentery flavoured with cumin

andouillette à la strasbourgeoise *(Fr) fem.* Grilled or fried andouillette served on a bed of sauerkraut accompanied by boiled potatoes

andouillette de Troyes *(Fr) fem.* Andouillettes containing calf mesentery, udder, egg yolks, shallots, parsley, seasoning and nutmeg, moistened with white wine

añejo 1 *(Me)* A cheese made from cow's or goat's milk, well matured with a strong salty flavour **2** *(Sp)* Meat from 14 to 15 month old beef cattle

anelli *(It)* Rings of pasta cut from a tube about 1 cm. in diameter

anellini *(It)* Tiny pasta rings used for soup, a smaller version of anelli

anémona de mar *(Sp)* Sea anemone

anemone di mare *(It)* Sea anemone

anémone de mer *(Fr) fem.* Sea anemone

aneth *(Fr) fem.* Dill

Anethum graveolens *Bot.* Dill

Anethum sowa *Bot.* Indian dill

aneto *(It)* Dill

aneurin *see* vitamin B1

ange de mer *(Fr) masc.* Angel fish

angel cake *(Po & USA)* A fat and egg yolk free light sponge made by folding very low gluten cake flour sieved with cream of tartar and caster sugar into stiffly beaten egg whites. Usually baked in a ring mould [also called **angel food cake**]

angel fish A type of shark *Squatina squatina* with large pectoral fins which can be treated as skate wings. The tail is also thick and meaty with a few soft flexible bones [also called **angel shark, fiddle fish**]

angel flake coconut A much wider cut of desiccated coconut like large flakes

angel food cake *see* angel cake

angel shark *see* angel fish

Angelica archangelica *Bot.* Angelica

angelica A tall parsley-like plant *Angelica archangelica, A. officinalis.* The blanched, peeled and boiled stalks and leaf ribs are candied for use as a decoration

Angelica officinalis *Bot.* Angelica

Angelica sinensis *Bot.* Dang gui *(Chinese angelica)*

angélique *(Fr) fem.* Angelica

angelitter Schnüss *(Ge)* A soup made from bacon, young beans and milk

angelot *(Fr) masc.* Angel fish

angelote *(Sp)* Angel fish

angel's farts *see* fritole di lino

angel's hair A very fine and thin noodle wrapped in skeins like wool [also called **vermicellini**]

angels on horseback A savoury consisting of oysters wrapped in streaky bacon, grilled and served on buttered toast

anges à cheval *(Fr) masc.* Angels on horseback

angevine, à l' *(Fr)* In the style of Anjou, i.e. with the addition of local wine

anghiti *(In)* A charcoal burning brazier rather like a modern barbecue

angkak *(Ph)* Dried and ground rice which has been coloured red/purple by fermentation with *Monascus purpureus.* Used to colour and flavour foods prepared from fish and cheese and to produce red rice wine

anglaise, à l' *(Fr)* In the English style, meaning plain cooked or if deep fried, coated with flour, egg and breadcrumbs *(panéed)*

anglaise, fish à l' Fillets of fish, panéed, deep fried at 185°C, drained and garnished with lemon wedges and a sprig of parsley and served with tartare sauce

anglaise, sauce *(En & Fr) see* crème à l'anglaise

anglaise, sauce à l' *(Fr) fem. see* egg custard sauce

angled loofah The fruit of a climbing vine *Luffa acutangula* which grows to 3 m. It has a dull green skin with 10 longitudinal ridges and is harvested at up to 50 cm. It is slightly bitter and has a similar taste and texture to okra. It is peeled before use and may be steamed, fried or braised; *see also* loofah and club gourd [also called **Chinese okra, ridged gourd, ridged melon, pleated squash, angled luffa**]

angler fish *(USA)* Monkfish

angola *(Sp)* Sour milk

anguele in salsa *(It)* Small fried fish marinated in vinegar

anguidda *(It)* Eel *(Sicily)*

anguila *(Sp)* Eel

anguila ahumada *(Sp)* Smoked eel

anguilla *(It)* Eel

anguilla argentina *(It)* A silvery coloured eel *Anguilla anguilla*

anguilla in carpione *(It)* A hors d'oeuvre of pieces of eel. salted and oiled, grilled over charcoal until cooked and marinated in a mixture of oil, vinegar, bay leaves, garlic and seasoning for a minimum of 24 hours

anguilla alla fiorentina *(It)* Eels rolled in seasoned breadcrumbs and baked

anguilla gialla *(It)* The common eel

anguilla alla griglia *(It)* Boned eels, cut in 10 cm pieces, seasoned, floured, oiled and grilled over charcoal until slightly charred

anguilla alla marinara *(It)* Eel in vinegar sauce

anguilla in tiella al pisello *(It)* Fried eel with tomato sauce and peas

anguilla alla veneziana *(It)* Eel with tuna and lemon sauce

anguille *(Fr) fem.* Eel

anguille à la Beaucaire *(Fr) fem.* Skinned boned eel stuffed with whiting and chopped mushroom forcemeat, sewn up, formed into an oval then braised in white wine with chopped shallots, mushrooms, glazed button onions and brandy. Served from the cooking dish

anguille benoîton *(Fr) fem.* Boned, skinned and filleted eel, cut into 10 cm. thin slices, twisted into spirals, passed through seasoned flour, deep fried and piled up with fried parsley. Accompanied with a strained reduced red wine sauce made with shallots, parsley stalks and eel trimmings, thickened with butter

anguille à l'escabèche *(Fr) fem.* Pickled eel, fried in oil then cooled in aspic jelly

anguille frite *(Fr) fem.* Fried eel. Small skinned eels, incised both sides, folded into figures of eight and skewered, deep fried and garnished with fried parsley

anguille frite à l'anglaise *(Fr) fem.* Cleaned, skinned, boned and filleted eel cut into thin slices, marinated with seasoning, chopped parsley, oil and lemon juice, panéed and deep fried, finished with anchovy butter and served immediately accompanied with sauce bâtarde

anguille fumée *(Fr) fem.* Smoked eel, served with skin and bone removed and cut into sections

anguille en matelote *(Fr) fem.* Cleaned skinned eel cut in pieces, boiled with red or white wine, sliced onions, BG, garlic, and seasoning, flamed with brandy and cooking finished in a tightly closed pan. Strained cooking liquor, if white, reduced and thickened with a fish velouté and garnished with button onions, crayfish and croûtons *(marinière)* or if red, thickened with beurre manié and garnished with crayfish and croûtons *(à la meunière)*

anguille à la ménagère *(Fr) fem.* Cleaned and skinned eel cut into 8 cm. pieces, incised on each side, seasoned, grilled and served with a border of gherkins, accompanied with softened parsley butter mixed with a small amount of prepared mustard

anguille de mer *(Fr) fem.* Conger eel [also called **congre**]

anguille à la meunière *(Fr) fem.* Cleaned and skinned eels, cut in pieces, passed through seasoned flour and shallow fried in butter, finished with beurre noisette

anguille pompadour *(Fr) fem.* Cleaned and skinned eel, incised both sides, formed into a ring cooked in white wine court-bouillon and cooled in the cooking liquor, drained, dried, coated with a mixture of sauce villeroy and soubise, panéed and deep fried until heated through and browned. Served with fried parsley and croquettes of pommes dauphine, accompanied with tomato-flavoured Béarnaise sauce

anguille à la romaine *(Fr) fem.* Cleaned and skinned eels cut into 5 cm pieces, stiffened in hot butter then stewed gently with peas, shredded lettuce and white wine, thickened with beurre manié and served immediately

anguille à la rouennaise *(Fr) fem.* Cleaned and skinned eel, incised both sides, formed into a ring and poached with a mirepoix of aromatic vegetables. When cooked, glazed whilst basting with the cooking liquor. Served with a centre garnish of mushrooms, poached oysters and poached soft roe. Garnish coated with strained cooking liquor thickened with sauce espagnol, the whole surrounded with shallow fried smelts

anguille à la tartare *(Fr) fem.* Cleaned and skinned eel either whole or in portions, poached in white wine court-bouillon, drained, panéed, deep fried, garnished with fried parsley and gherkins and served with tartare sauce

anguille au vert *(Fr) fem.* Cleaned and skinned eels cut into 5 cm. pieces, placed on a bed of garden herbs (sorrel, nettle tops, parsley, salad burnet, sage, savory, chervil and tarragon and butter), cooked until the flesh stiffens, then white wine, seasoning, and sage added, cooking finished and liquor thickened with egg yolk and finished with lemon juice. Usually served cold

anguille au vert à la flamande *(Fr) fem.* Cleaned and skinned eels cut into 5 cm pieces, cooked in butter until flesh stiffens, further cooked in beer and seasoning and towards end of cooking chopped garden herbs (as in anguille au vert) added, thickened with arrowroot. Usually served cold

anguille au vin blanc et paprika *(Fr) fem.* Cleaned eels cut into 8 cm. pieces, cooked in a shallow pan with sliced onions, BG, garlic, seasoning, white wine and paprika, boiled, flamed with brandy, covered and cooked, cooled in cooking liquor, skinned, fillet detached and covered with defatted and thickened cooking liquor

anguillette *(Fr) fem.* Small eel, a speciality of the Basque country

anguria *(It)* Water melon

Angus fish soup *(UK)* A Scottish soup made from fresh haddock heads, boiled, skinned then simmered with aromatic vegetables, turnips, parsley and seasoning for 20 minutes, strained onto a white roux and finished with milk, thyme, chopped parsley and a liaison of eggs and cream

Angus potatoes *(UK)* A Scottish dish of baked potatoes from which the cooked interior has been removed, mixed with flaked Arbroath smokie flesh, butter, milk, seasoning, returned to the case and heated through in the oven

anho *(Po)* Lamb

anhydrate, to *(USA)* To dehydrate

anice *(It)* Anice; semi di anice is aniseed

Anice stellato *(It)* Star anise

anicini *(It)* Aniseed biscuits from Sardinia

anijs *(Ho)* Anise

animelle *(It) fem.* Sweetbreads

animelle con limone e capperi *(It)* Poached calf's sweetbreads, sliced, seasoned and floured, sautéed in butter until golden, mixed with capers and lemon juice and served with the pan juices and chopped parsley

animelles *(Fr)* Testicles, usually of oxen or sheep, the latter also known as sheep's fry. Prepared by scalding, skinning and soaking in running water, then marinated and deep fried or treated as kidneys [also called **frivolités**]

anis *(Ph & Fr) masc.* Aniseed

anise A half-hardy annual umbelliferous plant *Pimpinella anisum* related to the plants which produce cumin, dill and fennel. It grows erect or prostrate to about 45 cm. The seeds are known as aniseed. The flowers and fresh leaves may be used in salads and as a garnish. The plant is sometimes known as aniseed

anise fern *see* sweet cicely

anise pepper A Chinese spice made from the ground dried red berries of the feathery-leaved prickly ash tree *Xanthoxylum piperitum.* It has a pronounced spicy-woody smell and a numbing taste and is one of the constituents of five spice powder much used in Chinese cooking; *see also* sansho [also called **Sichuan pepper, Szechuan pepper, Chinese pepper, Chinese aromatic pepper, Japanese pepper, xanthoxylum, fagara**]

aniseed The aromatic, oval seeds of the anise plant with a sweet liquorice like flavour. Used in cakes, for liqueurs and in Indian cookery and as a general flavouring. First mentioned in the written literature in 1500 BC by the Egyptians [also called **anise**]

anithi *(In)* Dill seed

anitra *(It)* Duck

anka *(Sw)* Duck

ankerias *(Fi)* Eel

anko *(Ja)* A sweet bean paste made from adzuki beans, blanched and simmered for 1 to 1.5 hours until soft and passed though a sieve into a little water. This water is removed by squeezing in muslin and the paste combined with sugar equal in weight to the original dried beans and a little salt is worked over a low heat until glossy and thick

annanas *(In)* Pineapple

annatto A bright orange permitted food colour, E160(b) made from the fruit pulp of a South American tree *Bixa orellana* together with bixin and norbixin. Must be acidified before use [also called **anatto**]

annatto lard Red coloured lard used in Filipino cooking. Made by frying annatto seeds in the lard then discarding them

annatto seed The seeds of the annatto fruits *Bixa orellana,* usually fried in oil or lard to impart a subtle flavour and red colour to food. After cooking the seeds are discarded

annegato *(It)* Simmered in wine

annona *see* custard apple

Annot *(Fr)* A ewes' or goats' milk cheese from Provence

anolini *(It)* Small, half circle shaped, stuffed pasta similar to ravioli. The stuffing always contains meat and is often a well reduced and sieved meat stew

anona *see* custard apple

Anona cherimolia *Bot.* Cherimoya

Anona diversifolia *Bot.* Ilama

Anona muricata *Bot.* Soursop

Anona purpurea *Bot.* Soncoya

Anona reticulata *Bot.* Bullock's heart

Anona spp. *Bot.* Custard apples and related fruits

Anona squamosa *Bot.* Sweet sop

anone *(Fr) fem.* Custard apple

ansarino *(Sp)* Gosling

Anschovis *(Ge)* Anchovy

Ansgar *(Ge)* A milder variety of Tilsit cheese made in the west of Germany

ansjos *(No)* Anchovy

ansjovis *(Ho & Sw)* Anchovy

anthocyan(in) E163, a glucoside plant pigment extracted from grape skins which is red in acid and blue in alkaline conditions. It forms coloured complexes with metals e.g. grey with iron, green with aluminium and blue with tin, hence the off colours in e.g. canned pears where its reaction with tin gives the pears a pink colour

anthoxanthan A colouring compound in potatoes and onions which is colourless in acid and yellow in alkaline conditions

Anthriscus cerefolium *Bot.* Chervil

antibiotics Chemicals produced by various moulds which can kill or prevent the growth of microorganisms. Often incorporated in animal feeds, residues may occur in the milk or flesh of the animal. The limits of these residues are strictly controlled as continuous ingestion could develop antibiotic resistant microorganisms in the human gut

antiboise, à l' *(Fr)* In the style of Antibes, i.e. garnished with garlic, cheese and sometimes sardines

antica, all' *(It)* In the old fashioned, classical style

anticaking agent A compound added to powdered foods to prevent their particles sticking together. E numbers 530 to 578

anticuchos *(SA)* Kebabs made from marinated ox hearts brushed with a hot chilli sauce and grilled. Common in Peru

antimycotic Referring to the action of compounds which kill, slow down or prevent the growth of moulds. e.g. calcium propionate

antin, fish d' *see* fish bréval

antioxidant A chemical compound of synthetic or natural origin which retards the rate of reaction of the oxygen in the air with foods, thus slowing down the development of off flavours in fats and the colouring of cut fruit, etc. E numbers 300 to 321. Typical examples are vitamin E (from soya beans), vitamin C (from citrus fruit or made synthetically), BHT *(butylated hydroxytoluene)*, BHA *(butylated hydroxyanisole)* and propyl gallate. The last three are synthetic

antipasti almagro *(It)* Seafood salad

antipasti assortiti *(It)* Mixed antipasti of ham, salami, anchovies, olives, fruit, etc.

antipasto *(It)* Starter(s), hors d'oeuvre(s), first course of a meal, usually various cooked vegetables or fish preserved in oil or marinated in oil, vinegar, herbs and spices - plural is antipasti

antipasto alla genovese *(It)* Young broad beans with sausage

antispattering agent A compound such as lecithin which, when added to fat, prevents spattering due to water droplets

antistaling agent A compound such as sucrose stearate or glycerol which apparently slows down the staling of baked goods by softening the crumb of the bread

antojitos *(Me)* Appetizers or starters, literally

'what you fancy'. The Mexican name for small portions of classical Mexican dishes served as snack food for street eating or as starters

añu *see* ysaño

anversoise, à l' *(Fr)* In the style of Antwerp (Anvers), i.e. garnished with hop shoots in cream

AOC *see* appellation d'origine controlée

ao-jiso *(Ja) see* green shiso

aole *(It)* A fresh water fish

aonegi *(Ja)* Spring onions

ao-nori *(Ja)* Flaked or shredded nori used as a seasoning. Nori is the chopped, compressed and dried sheets of purple laver seaweed used for wrapping Japanese sushi

ao-togarashi *(Ja)* A small green sweet pepper the size and shape of a chilli pepper but with a mild sweet flavour

aoyagi *(Ja)* A round clam used raw or lightly cooked for sushi.

ao-yose *(Ja)* A natural green food colouring extracted from spinach leaves

apaz onion *(USA)* An edible, small wild onion

apee *(USA)* A biscuit (cookie) created by Ann Page (AP), its distinguishing feature being the use of sour cream in the batter

apelsin *(Sw)* Orange, the fruit

Apfel *(Ge)* Apple

Apfel Kaltschale *(Ge)* As ananas kaltschale but with cooked apples rubbed through the strainer and garnished with diced apples and sultanas simmered in a light syrup

Apfelbettelmann *(Ge)* Chopped, peeled and cored apples, well sprinkled with sugar, layered alternately in an ovenproof dish with a mixture of fine pumpernickel crumbs, sugar, butter and chopped nuts (3:3:2:1) flavoured with cinnamon and lemon zest, starting and finishing with a breadcrumb mixture layer, topped with butter and baked at 175°C until apples are soft

Apfelbröisi *(Ge)* A bread pudding containing apples. See Apfelbettelman

Apfelkren *(Au)* Apple and horseradish sauce made from cooking apples simmered with sugar and lemon juice, mashed and mixed with shredded horseradish from the outer part of the root, served with Viennese boiled beef *(Tafelspitz)*

Apfelkuchen *(Ge)* An open apple tart made with a slightly sweetened pastry flavoured with lemon zest and brought together with egg yolks. The base is coated with breadcrumbs mixed with melted butter, followed by sliced cooking apples and topped with currants soaked in rum. It is baked at 175°C for 10 minutes, then filled with a sweetened egg custard made with cream, sprinkled with sugar and butter and baked until the custard is set and browned

Apfelmus *(Ge)* Stewed apple

Apfelpfannkuchen *(Ge)* A pancake with an apple filling

Apfelschmarren *(Au)* Pancake batter mixed with diced apple, cooked (about 1 cm thick) until brown on both sides, broken up and sprinkled with caster sugar

Apfelschnitze *(Ge)* Apple fritter

Apfelsine *(Ge)* Orange, the fruit

Apfelstrudel *(Au)* Strudel (filo) pastry rolled around a mixture of chopped raw cooking apples, sultanas, caster sugar and chopped nuts, sealed and baked. The pastry may be covered on the inside with grated nuts or fried dry white breadcrumbs [also called **apple strudel** (En)]

Apfeltorte *(Ge)* Apple cake

apio 1 *see* arracacha **2** *(Po & Sp)* Celery

apio-nabo *(Sp)* Celeriac

Apios tuberosa *Bot.* Arracacha

Apium graveolens *Bot.* Wild celery

Apium graveolens* var. *dulce *Bot.* Celery

Apium graveolens* var. *rapaceum *Bot.* Celeriac

apog *(Ph)* Lime (calcium hydroxide)

à point *(Fr)* Medium rare, a degree of cooking meat or fish so that protein at the centre of the piece is coagulated but not discoloured or hardened

appa *(In & Sr)* Soft spongy breads made from a ground rice, rice flour and coconut milk batter or dough raised using the fermenting sap of the coconut palm (although yeast may be substituted) and cooked in small, greased and covered wok-like pans. Eaten for breakfast; *see also* string hopper

apparecchiato *(It)* Prepared, referring to food, laid, referring to the table

appareil *(Fr) masc.* Food mixture or items for preparing a dish, e.g. appareil à crêpes means pancake batter

appel *(Ho)* Apple

äppel-fläsk *(Sw)* Panéed strips of derinded pork belly, fried until brown, layered in a casserole with sweated sliced onions and raw, cored but unpeeled, slices of apple, seasoned, moistened with pan juices and water, and simmered with a lid on for 30 minutes. Served with boiled potatoes

appelbeignet *(Ho)* Apple fritter

appellation d'origine *(Fr) fem.* The French certificate of origin for foodstuff, esp. wine and cheese *(see cheese certification)*. There are only 27 French cheeses entitled to this certificate. Lit. label of origin

appellation d'origine contrôlée *(Fr) fem.* The French designation that a wine or cheese has an appellation d'origine which guarantees the origin of the grapes and the yield [also called **AOC**]

appelmoes *(Ho)* Apple sauce

äppelmos *(Sw)* Apple sauce

appelsin *(De & No)* Orange, the fruit

appeltaart *(Ho)* Apple cake

Appenzell *(He) see* Appenzeller

Appenzeller *(He)* A strong, slightly bitter, semi-hard, scalded curd cheese made from whole cow's milk cast in large rounds (6 to 8 kg), matured in brine with wine and spices for 3 to 6 months to give it its characteristic flavour. Contains 43% water, 28% fat and 26% protein [also called **Appenzell**]

Appenzellerli *(He) see* Knackerli

appertization The term for heat processing of foods at temperatures above 120°C, in particular, retorting and high temperature short time (HTST) processing. This process does not guarantee complete sterility but any spores present should be non pathogenic and unable to grow in the processed food environment

appertize, to The general term for heat treatment by retorting (121°C) or high temperature short time (HTST) (132°C and above) hence appertization

appetite The desire for food evoked by hunger and the taste, smell or appearance of various foodstuffs

appetitost *(De)* A sour buttermilk cheese

appetizer A general name given to small items of food served before or at the beginning of a meal or at cocktail parties

apple The fruit of the apple tree *Malus sylvestris* var. *domestica* which requires cool winters to fruit. There are thousands of varieties but only about fifty are commercially available. Dessert varieties are sweetish, sometimes combined with acid, used for eating raw, and, since they keep their shape on cooking, are used for tarts and in other cases where the shape of the cut fruit is important. Cooking varieties are generally acid and become soft and mushy when boiled, stewed or baked

äpple *(Sw)* Apple

apple amber *(UK)* An 18th century dish consisting of peeled chopped apples boiled in water with sugar, lemon juice and lemon zest. After cooking mixed with whole beaten eggs and baked in the oven with a puff pastry cover

apple amber pudding *(UK)* A shortcrust pastry case filled with a sweetened apple purée mixed with lemon juice and lemon zest, topped with meringue and baked

apple banana The small sweet fruit of a tropical herb of the *Musa* spp. with a flavour similar to a mixture of pineapple and apple

apple bread *(UK)* A Derbyshire bread made from dough kneaded with sweetened apple purée prior to proving

apple brown Betty *(USA)* Stewed apple layered with toasted butter-soaked cake crumbs

apple butter *see* apple cheese

apple cake *see* Norfolk apple cake

apple charlotte A sweet made from apples cooked in butter and sugar flavoured with grated lemon zest and ground cinnamon, placed in a mould lined with stale bread soaked in melted butter or browned bread crumbs, covered in same, baked in the oven and served with apricot or custard sauce

apple cheese *(UK)* Whole apples cut so as to break open the pips, cooked until soft in cider, passed through a coarse sieve to allow the pip kernels to pass through, then cooked with an equal amount of sugar and a clove until of coating consistency [also called **apple butter**]

apple corer The tube shaped implement used to remove the core from apples

apple cream bun *(UK)* A large choux pastry spherical bun filled with whipped cream into which slices of apple poached in syrup have been folded

apple crumble Apples, prepared as for apple charlotte, with a crumble topping baked in the oven

apple cucumber A distinctive variety of almost spherical cucumber up to the size of an orange

apple curd A fruit curd flavoured with puréed unsweetened apples, lemon juice and lemon zest

apple dumpling Cored apples filled with a mixture of butter, caster sugar and possibly dried fruit, cinnamon, etc., enclosed in short pastry, top decorated and egg washed, pierced and baked in a hot oven for 15 minutes

apple flan The base of a cooked flan case covered with apples cooked as for apple charlotte and finished in a variety of ways e.g. with other fruits, nuts or a purée or mousse of candied chestnuts and either glazed with apricot syrup or melted red currant jelly or covered with meringue or dredged with icing sugar, the latter two cooked in the oven to brown

apple fritters As for apricot fritters but substituting peeled, cored and sliced apple

apple mayonnaise *(Sa)* Equal quantities of mayonnaise and slightly sweetened apple purée flavoured with horseradish sauce

apple of the Orient *see* persimmon

apple pandowdy *(USA)* An apple pie made in a dish with spiced sliced apples, covered in a pastry crust

apple pudding A suet pastry lined basin filled with sliced apples mixed with sugar, ground cinnamon, grated lemon zest, sealed with more suet pastry, covered with a cloth or lid and steamed or boiled for approximately 2 hours

apple sauce Peeled, cored and chopped apples, sweated in butter and a little water, possibly with ground cinnamon and then sieved, liquidized or whisked to a smooth sauce

apple sauce cake **1** *(UK)* A Somerset cake made from a spiced cake mixture using brown sugar to which unsweetened apple sauce is added prior to folding in the flour, spices, salt and dried fruit. Topped with vanilla butter icing [also called **Somerset apple cake**) **2** *(USA)* A cake containing mixed dried fruit, nuts and apple sauce.

apple schnitz *(USA)* Dried apple slices used in the Pennsylvania cooking originated by German immigrants

apple slim *(Ir)* A griddle-cooked double crust apple tart

apple snow Apple pulp or purée mixed with meringue

apple soup *(UK)* Chopped whole apples simmered in mutton broth passed through a strainer and seasoned with ginger and salt. May be reheated with pearl barley until the barley is soft

apple strudel *see* Apfelstrudel

apple turnover Rounds of 3 mm puff pastry, egg washed, one half of each round heaped with a mixture of finely sliced apples, sugar and cinnamon, other half folded over and sealed, egg washed, baked and glazed with icing sugar just before finishing

applemint One of the common culinary varieties of mint *Mentha suaveolens,* with hairy apple-scented bright green leaves, used for making mint sauce, mint jelly, stuffings, salads, etc. and as a general flavouring herb [also called **Egyptian mint**]

äpplen *(Sw)* Apples

appelsiini *(Fi)* Orange, the fruit

Applewood *(UK)* A medium-flavoured Cheddar cheese from Somerset, flavoured with an extract of applewood smoke or smoked over applewood and coated with paprika

apricot A round, orange coloured fruit from a tree *Prunus armeniaca* of the plum family, with a rich aromatic flavour. Suitable for stewing, for sorbets and for jam making, often preserved by drying

apricot flan Flan ring lined with sugar paste, pierced, sugared, filled with neatly arranged half apricots, sugared, baked at 210°C, ring removed, rebaked and glazed as for apple flan

apricot fritters Firm but not overripe halved apricots, sprinkled with sugar and macerated with kirsch, brandy or rum, dried, dipped in batter and deep fried, drained, dredged with icing sugar and glazed

apricot glaze Sugar syrup boiled to 115°C, mixed with approximately half its quantity of apricot purée, reboiled to 110°C and sieved

apricot ice cream *see* bombe andalouse

apricot kernel The small flat kernels of the apricot stone which must be blanched in boiling water and dried in a warm oven to detoxify them. Used in Chinese cooking [also called **Chinese almond**]

apricot marmalade *see* apricot glaze

apricot sauce Apricot jam boiled with water and lemon juice, thickened as required with cornflour and strained, alternatively very ripe or drained stewed apricots sieved and thinned with sugar syrup (28°Be, 1.1 kg sugar per litre water) and reduced to a coating consistency

apricot stuffing *(UK)* Roughly chopped destoned apricots mixed with an equal quantity of fine white breadcrumbs seasoned and moistened with water if required. Used for stuffing hams before they are covered in pastry

aprikos *(Sw)* Apricot

aprikos och appel soppa *(Sa)* Apricot and apple soup consisting of apricots (fresh or reconstituted dried), cooking apples, celery, parsley and bay leaf, simmered in a light stock, celery and herbs discarded, the whole then liquidized or passed through a sieve, cream added and garnished with toasted almonds

Aprikose *(Ge)* Apricot

aprikose *(De & No)* Apricot

Aprikosen Kaltschale *(Ge)* As Ananas Kaltschale but with ripe apricots and ground, skinned apricot kernels pushed through the strainer and garnished with slices of skinned destoned apricots

apu lapu *(Ph)* Garoupa, the fish

apulid *(Ph)* Water chestnut

apyelsiny v romye z pryanostyami *(Ru)* Oranges with spiced rum. Peeled, depithed and sliced oranges, marinated and served in a sugar syrup flavoured with cloves and rum

ap yeung cheung *(Ch)* A sausage from Hong Kong containing lean and fat pork, preserved duck livers, sugar, soya sauce and rice wine

Arabica coffee A type of coffee from the bush *Coffea arabica* with a finer flavour than the higher yielding robusta varieties

arachide *(It & Fr) fem.* Peanut, groundnut

arachidonic acid A polyunsaturated fatty acid which cannot be synthesized by the human body and is therefore one of the essential fatty acids (EFA's). It is found in egg yolks and fish oils. Its lack in infant milk formulae is thought to cause retarded brain development in new born infants [also called **AA**]

Arachis hypogaea *Bot.* The groundnut plant whose seed pods, which grow underground, are the source of peanuts

arachis oil *see* peanut oil

Aragackij A round, scalded curd, semi-hard, slicing cheese from Armenia made with ewe's and goat's milk matured for 2 months and with a thin dark bluish rind. Contains 40% water, 30% fat and 25% water

Aragón *(Sp)* A semi-hard, firm cheese made with goat's and/or ewe's milk curdled with rennet, shaped into cones, dry salted and the firm paste containing a few holes ripened for 1 week [also called **tronchon**]

aragosta *(It)* Lobster, also used of langouste, rock lobster, spiny lobster, crayfish and most *Palinurus* spp.

aragosta americana *(It)* Florida lobster

aragosta atlantica *(It)* Large pink spiny lobster *Palinurus* spp.

aragosta bollita *(It)* Cold boiled lobster served with a vegetable salad

aragosta fra diavolo *(It)* Lobster baked with a spicy tomato sauce

aragosta alla griglia con burro *(It)* Grilled lobster with melted butter

aragosta mediterranea *(It)* Spiny lobster.

araignée de mer *(Fr) fem.* Spider crab

Aralar *see* Idiazabal

arame *(Ja)* A brown variety of seaweed similar to wakame *Eisenia bicyclis* from Japan which is dried, cut into strips and used as a vegetable, in soup or for flavouring [also called **sea oak**]

arance caramellate *(It)* A dessert of peeled, depithed and sliced oranges coated with sugar syrup and decorated with caramelized orange peel

arancia *(It)* Orange, the fruit

arancia cardinale *(It)* Peeled and segmented oranges dressed with salt and olive oil

arancini *(It)* Croquettes made of savoury rice with butter and saffron wrapped around a filling e.g. meat and tomatoes, chicken liver and tomatoes, mozarella cheese and tomatoes or ham and peas, and then fried

arancio amaro *(It)* Seville orange

arándano *(Sp)* Bilberry

arándano agrio *(Sp)* Cranberry

aranygaluska *(Hu)* A sweet dumpling

araruta *see* arrowroot

Araucaria spp. Various pine trees which are the source of pine nuts q.v.

arbi *(In & Ma)* Yam

arborio rice A medium grain, superfino, pearly rice grown in northern Italy, used in Italian cooking and for making risotto. Cooks in 20 minutes and absorbs five times its weight of liquid. Starch is released during cooking and makes the grains creamy

Arbroath fillet *see* Arbroath smokie

Arbroath smokie *(UK)* The original gutted, deheaded haddock or whiting from Scotland salted for 2 hours, hot smoked in less than an hour over oak and about 250 g in weight. Can be eaten cold or hot and does not need recooking [also called **Arbroath fillet**]

Arbroath style lobster *(UK)* A Scottish dish of sliced, precooked lobster flesh, mussels and shrimps cooked in butter, served bound with a reduced wine and velouté based sauce, seasoned, flavoured with lemon juice, placed in lobster shells lined with fried mushroom slices, covered with sauce and grated cheese, glazed and garnished with parsley, anchovies and poached, turned mushrooms

arbutus The fruit of the strawberry tree *Arbutus unedo* used in preserves and to make an alcoholic drink. Not suitable for dessert purposes

Arbutus unedo *Bot.* Arbutus

arbuz *(Ru)* Watermelon

arca di noe *(It)* A small shell fish

archangels on horseback *(UK)* As angels on horseback but substituting scallops for oysters

Archestratus The Greek author of the oldest surviving cookbook 'The life of luxury' dating from 300 BC

archiduc, à l' *(Fr)* In the style of the Archduke, i.e. coated with a paprika-flavoured white sauce

archimede A pasta shape, see fusilli

arctic char A type of trout *Salvelinus alpinus* found in both fresh and sea water in the northern hemisphere. It is better tasting than trout and is best simply baked and served with butter; *see also* potted char

Arctium lappa *Bot.* Burdock

Arctostaphylos uva-ursi *Bot.* Bearberry

ardennaise, à l' *(Fr)* In the style of the Ardennes, i.e. including juniper berries

Ardennes ham A high quality cured Belgian ham ranked alongside Parma, York and Bayonne hams. Eaten raw

ardilla *(Sp)* Squirrel

ardisone rice *(It)* A moderately priced semi-fino oval and slightly sticky rice suitable for minestrone

Areca catechu *Bot.* Betel nut palm

areca nut *see* betel nut

areganato *(It)* With oregano

Arekanuss *(Ge)* Betel nut

Arenga pinnata *Bot.* Sugar palm

Arenga sacchifera *Bot.* Sugar palm

arenque *(Sp)* Herring

arenque en escabeche *(Sp)* Pickled herring

arequipe *(SA)* A dessert made from a caramelized milk and sugar mixture, best made by boiling a tin of sweetened condensed milk for 2 hours. Quite common in the UK during the second world war. Name derived either from the Peruvian town Arequepeno or from arequipa, the Andalusian word for rice pudding [also called **dulce de leche, cajeta de celaya, manjar blanco, natillas pluranas, doce de leite**]

arête *(Fr) fem.* Fish bone

argenine A non-essential amino acid

argenteuil, à l' *(Fr)* In the style of Argenteuil, i.e. garnished with asparagus

argentina *(It)* Argentine, a small fish similar to a sardine

argentine A small silvery fish similar in appearance to a sardine or a smelt but from a different family. The three varieties of commerce are the lesser, the larger and the deep sea argentine, which latter comes from Japan. They may be grilled or fried

Argentinian jujube A species of jujube which is used for the Bolivian drink chicha [also called **mistol jujube**]

argraz *(Sp)* Verjuice

arhar *(In)* Pigeon peas

arhrot *(In)* Walnut

ariégeoise, à l' *(Fr)* In the style of Ariège, i.e. containing salt pork, kidney beans, cabbage and potatoes

arigusta *(It)* Crawfish, crayfish

aringa *(It)* Herring, plural aringhe

aringa alla casalinga *(It)* A hors d'oeuvre of sliced pickled herrings mixed with slices of salad onions, cooking apples and boiled waxy potatoes bound with cream and chopped parsley

aringhe *(It)* Herrings

arista *(It)* Loin of pork

arkshell *see* cockle

Arles salami A variety of French salami

arlésienne, à l' *(Fr)* In the style of Arles, i.e. garnished with 1 cm thick aubergine slices seasoned, floured and fried in oil, onion rings floured and deep fried and peeled tomatoes sautéed in butter

Armada *(Sp)* A semi-hard, sharp tasting cheese made from cow's colostrum and matured for two months [also called **Calostro, Sobado**]

armadillo sausage *(USA)* A Texan speciality sausage made from 4 parts armadillo meat to 1 part breadcrumbs flavoured with allspice, sage, crushed black peppercorns and salt

armagnac *(Fr) masc.* A brandy from the Southern Bordeaux region, used for flavouring

arme Ritter *(Ge)* French toast, pain perdue

Armenian bole E172, very finely powdered ferric oxide (iron oxide) (orange/red) used to colour food

Armenian bread A standard bread containing sesame and toasted sunflower seeds made into flat loaves and spread with a paste of grated Parmesan cheese, eggs, cumin, chopped walnuts and pepper before baking but after proving

Armenian cucumber *(USA)* A sweetish cucumber which grows in a coiled shape 25 to 50 cm long

Armenian wax pepper chilli *(USA)* A long waxy-skinned yellow chilli pepper with a relatively mild sweet taste

Armillaria edodes *Bot.* Matsutake *(mushroom)*

Armillaria mellea *Bot.* Honey fungus

armleti *(It)* Savoury dumplings from Tuscany

Armoracia rusticana *Bot.* Horseradish

armoricaine, à l' *(Fr)* In the Armorican (old name for Brittany) style, i.e. with brandy, white wine, onions and tomatoes

armotte *(Fr)* Maize flour cooked and mixed with goose fat, similar to polenta and eaten as a staple carbohydrate in Gascony

armyanski manny pudding *(Ru)* An Armenian pudding made from semolina boiled in white wine and water (2:3, 120 g semolina per litre of liquid)) sweetened and flavoured with sugar, orange juice and zest and lemon zest until cooked. Egg yolks mixed in off the heat followed by stiffly beaten egg whites folded in. Baked in a mould in a bain-marie at 170°C for 1 hour, cooled slightly, demoulded and served with lemon juice flavoured syrup and chopped pistachio nuts

arni se lathoharto *(Gr)* Small steaks from boned leg of lamb, larded with garlic and cooked en papillote for 3 hours in the oven with olive oil, red wine, seasoning, chopped fresh marjoram and dried oregano

arni palikari *(Gr)* Fried lamb chump chops, cooked en papillote with fried chopped onions and garlic, layered with tomato slices and oregano, potato slices, seasoning and Faseri or Gruyère cheese slices before wrapping, brushed with oil and baked for 1.5 hours at 180°C

arni yiouvetsi *(Gr)* A trimmed leg of lamb, piquéed with sliced garlic, rubbed with lemon juice, oregano and seasoning, roasted with chopped onion, lamb reserved, defatted pan juices mixed with tomato purée, seasoning and cooked pasta, sprinkled with grated Parmesan or Kefalotiri cheese, reheated in the oven and served around the roast lamb

Arnold Bennett omelette An omelette named after the author Arnold Bennett and created for him at the Savoy, covered with flaked smoked haddock mixed with grated Parmesan cheese, cooked one side, top side dressed with cream and grilled, served unfolded

aroma The pleasant fragrance of food caused by a complex mixture of volatile chemicals released from the food during, or produced by, the cooking process, but lost by evaporation and steam distillation; hence the necessity for careful control of the time and temperature of the cooking process. The aroma of food has important effects on both the feeling of well-being and on the digestive system.

aromate *(Fr) masc.* Aromatic material, e.g. herbs, spices, etc.

aromatic With a fragrant, slightly spicy and slightly pungent smell. Used of herbs, spices and vegetables which impart flavour and aroma to a dish

aromatic sauce White bouillon, boiled and infused with thyme, savory, marjoram, chives, chopped shallots, peppercorns and grated nutmeg for 10 minutes, strained, thickened with a blond roux, cooked out and finished with lemon juice and chopped and blanched tarragon and chervil

aromatic vegetables Carrots, leeks, onions and celery. Used for flavouring stocks, sauces, soups, etc.

Aromes de Lyon *(Fr) masc.* A strong tasting cheese made from goats and/or cows' milk, ripened in white wine for a month, dried for a month and wrapped in chestnut or plane leaves

aromi *(It)* Culinary herbs

Aroserli *(He) see* saucisses d'Arosa

arpajonnaise, à l' *(Fr)* In the style of Arpajon, i.e. including haricot beans

arracacha **1** A leguminous plant *Apios tuberosa* from North America whose roots can be cooked liked potatoes and also used in desserts [also called **apio**] **2** The Peruvian carrot *Arracacia xanthorrhiza*, a native of Columbia whose roots are use like potatoes or turned into a flour used for bread and pancakes

Arracacia xanthorrhiza *Bot.* Arracacha, the Peruvian carrot

arracanato *(It)* With oregano

arragosta *(It)* Spiny lobster, rather like a very large prawn and with no claws like a true lobster

arraia *(Po)* Skate

Arran cheese *(UK)* A hard, moist, close-textured, rindless cheese made on the Scottish island of Arran from whole cow's milk. The usual size is just less than 1 kg

arrayán *(Sp)* Myrtle, bog myrtle

arricchito *(It)* Enriched, e.g. with cream

arroser *(Fr)* To baste, to sprinkle with a liquid

arrosticini all'abruzzese *(It)* Skewers of lamb, marinated in olive oil with seasoning, marjoram and garlic and grilled over charcoal

arrostino annegato alla milanese *(It)*

Boned loin of veal, rolled around calves liver, strung or skewered, cut into thick slices, slices sprinkled with chopped sage, rosemary and salt, floured, fried both sides in oil, stewed in the oven in white wine, lemon juice and brown stock, glazed to finish and served with risotto and the reduced, thickened and strained cooking liquor

arrostire *(It)* To roast

arrostiti *(It)* Roasted

arrosto *(It)* Roasted, also roast meat or anything baked in the oven. arrosto-di bue, roast beef; arrosto-di castrato, roast mutton; arrosto-d'agnello, roast lamb; anguilla-arrosta, grilled eels

arrosto di maiale *(It)* Scored leg of pork, salted, oiled, sealed in the oven at 220°C for 25 minutes, then basted with a mixture of white wine, finely chopped carrots, garlic and pepper and cooking continued in this basting liquor at 190°C until done. Served with red cabbage and mashed potatoes

arrosto di maiale ubriaco *(It)* A tied, boned pork loin larded with carrots, floured, browned in butter, braised slowly in grappa (or brandy), red wine, nutmeg, bay leaves and seasoning until tender and served sliced with the cooking liquor. Lit. tipsy pork

arrotolato *(It)* Rolled up

arrowhead A water plant *Sagittaria sagittifolia* with arrow shaped leaves. Both the leaves and roots are used in Chinese cooking

arrowroot *(En & Fr) masc.* A starch powder obtained from the root of a West Indian plant *Maranta arundinacea,* used for thickening where a clear, glossy glaze is required. Loses its thickening power if overcooked [also called **araruta**]

arroz *(Sp, Po & Ph)* Rice

arroz abanda *(Sp)* Fish stew served on rice

arroz a la alicantina *(Sp)* A fish stew made with additions of pepper, garlic, artichoke hearts and saffron, served on rice

arroz blanco 1 *(Sp)* White rice **2** *(Me)* Long grain rice fried in garlic-flavoured oil until white, cooked slowly with 2.5 times its weight of water or chicken stock and finely chopped onion, carrot, chilli and parsley or coriander

arroz con camaron seco *(Me)* Rice with dried fish. Same as arroz con pollo but with dried shrimps reconstituted in boiling water and tinned tuna fish substituted for the poached chicken

arroz con frijoles *(Me)* Rice with beans, the staple dish of Mexicans. Long grain rice fried in garlic-flavoured oil until golden, the oil discarded and the rice simmered with a green chilli, chicken stock, chopped onion and parsley, tomato purée and cooked beans plus the bean cooking liquor until all the liquid is absorbed

arroz con leche *(Sp)* Rice pudding

arroz de grano largo *(Sp)* Long grained rice

arroz doce *(Po)* Rice pudding

arroz parillada *(Sp)* Chicken, sausage, pork, onions, tomatoes, string beans and artichoke hearts fried together and served in a mould with rice

arroz con pimenton *(Me)* Rice with sweet red pepper. As arroz con frijoles but with liquidized sweet red peppers and julienned peppers substituted for the beans and their cooking liquor

arroz con pollo *(Me)* A Mexican variant of paella made with rice fried until pale yellow in garlic-flavoured oil and simmered with a whole onion and chilli which are later discarded, sealed and poached chicken meat, tomato purée, a macedoine of carrots and potatoes, peas, shredded cabbage, runner beans and red sweet pepper in chicken stock until all the liquid is absorbed. Garnished with chopped parsley

arroz con rajas *(Me)* An oven baked dish of layers of arroz blanco, sliced sweet peppers, sour and single cream, sliced Cheddar type cheese and seasoning, topped with cheese

arroz refogado *(Po)* Savoury rice with an onion and tomato sauce

arroz Valencia *(Sp)* Rice pilaff made with chopped chicken meat, ham, red and green sweet peppers and boletus funghi, served with a tomato-flavoured demi-glace sauce

arroz con verduras *(Me)* Arroz blanco with sweet corn, peas and macedoine of carrots added prior to cooking in water or stock

arrurruz *(Sp)* Arrowroot

arsekka *(It) coll.* Mussel

arselle *(It)* Scallop

arsuma *(It)* An uncooked custard similar to zabaglione made with whole eggs whipped with sugar and dry white wine

Artemisia dracunculoides *Bot.* Russian tarragon

Artemisia dracunculus *Bot.* Tarragon

Artemisia lactiflora *Bot.* White mugwort

Artemisia vulgaris *Bot.* Mugwort

ärter *(Sw)* Peas [also called **ärtor**]

ärter med fläsk *(Sw)* The Swedish national soup of split yellow peas and pork; *see also* gula ärter med fläsk [also called **ärter och fläsk**]

ärter och fläsk *(Sw) see* ärter med fläsk

artichaut *(Fr) masc.* Artichoke

artichauts à la barigoule *(Fr) masc.* Trimmed and blanched globe artichokes from which the choke has been removed, filled with a duxelle enriched with chopped ham and herbs, wrapped in salt pork fat, braised in white wine or brown stock, fat discarded and served with a reduced brown sauce made with the cooking liquor

artichauts Cavour *(Fr) masc.* Small tender artichokes, trimmed to egg shape, cooked in white bouillon, drained, dipped in melted butter and coated with a mixture of grated Parmesan and Gruyère cheeses, coloured in the oven and served with chopped hard boiled egg fried in butter and mixed with anchovy essence and chopped parsley

artichauts Clamart *(Fr) masc.* Trimmed and divided artichokes with choke removed cooked slowly in the oven in water with diced carrots, fresh peas, BG and salt, when cooked, BG removed, cooking liquor thickened with beurre manié and the whole served in same dish. A simpler alternative has cooked artichoke bottoms filled with a sieved pureé of the bases of the sepals and piled with cooked young new peas *(petits pois)*

artichauts Grand Duc *(Fr) masc.* Trimmed medium sized artichokes cooked in salt water, drained, arranged in a circle on a dish coated with cream sauce, napped with same, sprinkled with grated Parmesan cheese and melted butter and glazed. Served with buttered asparagus tips in the centre, and a slice of warm truffle and melted meat glaze on each artichoke

artichauts à la grecque *(Fr) masc.* Globe artichoke hearts cooked à la grecque q.v

artichauts grosse horloge *(Fr) masc.* Cooked artichoke bottoms covered with mussels and cockles and topped with a Béarnaise sauce flavoured with reduced shellfish cooking liquor

artichauts de Jerusalem *(Fr) masc. see under* Jerusalem artichokes; *and some dishes under* topinambours

artichauts à la provençale *(Fr) masc.* Small trimmed artichokes placed in hot oil, seasoned, covered and cooked for 10 minutes, fresh peas and shredded lettuce added and the whole tightly sealed and cooked slowly in the juices from the vegetables

artichauts, purée d' *(Fr) fem. see* artichoke soup

artichauts Stanley *(Fr) masc.* Small trimmed artichokes or artichoke bottoms cooked over a layer of sliced, blanched onions and raw ham with white wine and thin Béchamel sauce, cooking liquor reduced, sieved and finished with butter, poured over the cooked artichokes and sprinkled with a brunoise of ham

artichoke Also known as the globe artichoke. A plant of the thistle family *Cynara scolymus,* whose unopened flower buds are used, particularly the base of the bracts and the base of the immature flower. The choke consisting of the immature petals and stamens, etc. is removed [also called **globe artichoke, French artichoke**] *see also* Jerusalem artichoke, Chinese artichoke, Japanese artichoke

artichoke bottom The flower base of the globe artichoke after the choke and bracts have been removed. Often use to hold garnishes

artichoke heart A small immature globe artichoke with the tips of the bracts cut off. The choke has not formed at this stage

artichoke, Jerusalem *see* Jerusalem artichoke

artichoke soup Basic soup with artichokes [also called **purée d'artichauts**]

artichokes Greek style *see* artichauts à la grecque

artificial sweeteners Chemical and natural products other than those containing sugars used to sweeten food and drink

Artischocke *(Ge)* Globe artichoke

artisjok *(Ho)* Globe artichoke

Artocarpus communis *Bot.* Breadfruit tree

Artocarpus heterophyllus *Bot.* Jackfruit tree

ärtor *(Sw)* Peas [also called **ärter**]

ärtsoppa *(Sw) see* gula ärter med fläsk

arugula *see* rocket

arum root *see* snake palm plant

Arundel mullets *(UK)* A 17th century Sussex dish made from small, cleaned and washed mullets, simmered in a court bouillon for 10-15 minutes, served with a reduced sauce made from the cooking liquor, sweated onions, lemon juice, white wine, herbs, chopped anchovies, seasoning and nutmeg

arval cake Cake given to mourners at funerals in the north of England. Derived from the old English word 'arfwol' (inheritance ale) used to designate the feast given by the heir of a deceased king

arvi *(Id)* Yam

arvi leaf *see* dasheen leaf

arwa chawal *(In)* Long grain rice

asadero *(Me)* A cooking cheese made from cows' milk. Lit. good for roasting

asado 1 *(Sp & Me)* Grilled or roasted, often with garlic, ham, red pepper and saffron **2** *(Ar)* An outdoor barbecue **3** *(Ph)* A method of cooking meat by simmering in soya sauce with bay, onion, tomato and peppercorns

asados *(SA)* Spit-roasted meat from Uruguay

asadura *(Sp)* Offal

asafoetida A rather unpleasant hard resin obtained from the root or stem latex of some species of Ferula *F. asafoetida, F. narthex* which grow in Afghanistan and Iran. The powdered form is used sparingly in Indian cookery, and the taste improves when it is briefly fried in hot oil. Also known as devil's dung for obvious reasons. The related garden plant is highly poisonous [also called **hing** (In)]

asam *(Id)* Tamarind

asam gelugor *(Ma)* Dried slices of tamarind

asam java *(Ma)* Tamarind

asam jawa *(Id & Ma)* Dried slices of tamarind pulp

asam koh *(Ch)* Tamarind

asam pedas *(Id)* A description of fish or meat cooked in a hot (chilli hot) and sour sauce or cooking liquor

asar *(Me & Sp)* To roast, broil or grill

asar a la parrilla *(Sp)* To grill

asarijiru *(Ja)* Cleaned and debearded mussels, simmered in dashi until open, unopened mussels discarded, mirin added and all simmered for a further 5 minutes, mussels removed and kept warm whilst the soup is seasoned and flavoured with soya sauce and shichimi togarishi. Mussels served in their shells with the soup

asciutto *(It)* Dry or drained. This applies only to items such as pasta, gnocchi, rice, etc. which could otherwise be served in stock

ascorbates Salts and esters of L-ascorbic acid (vitamin C) used as antioxidants. Sodium, E301, calcium, E302 and 6 ortho-palmitoyl, E304 are used in the food industry

ascorbic acid E300, vitamin C *(strictly L-ascorbic acid, the biologically active laevo-form)* used to prevent oxidation and thus browning reactions and colour changes in foods. Also used as a flour improver

ascorbyl palmitate A chemical compound derived from ascorbic and palmitic acids used as an antistaling agent

ascorbyl stearate A chemical compound derived from ascorbic and stearic acids used as an antioxidant

a-sein thanat sohn *(Bm)* A hors d'oeuvre consisting of blanched vegetables and spring onion pieces with a sauce of tomato concassée mixed with finely chopped green chillis, salt and sugar

asepsis The prevention of contamination of a sterile or appertized food with organisms that can cause spoilage

aseptic packaging Packaging of food to ensure asepsis either by filling into unsterilized containers at 124°C, closing and leaving at temperature until all contaminants are inactivated, or by filling the food into sterilized containers in an apparatus which is itself sterilized where they can be sealed. The second method is generally used only where large numbers of containers are to be packed

ash gourd *see* wax gourd

Ashburton open pastie *(UK)* A Derbyshire pastie made from a large rectangle of puff pastry 1 cm thick, covered with stewed fruit, soaked dried fruit, mincemeat or jam to 3 cm. from edges, edges turned to centre and baked at 220°C for 20 minutes

Ashdown partridge pudding *(UK)* A Sussex dish consisting of a savoury suet pastry pudding filled with joints of old partridge, sliced rump steak, mushrooms, herbs, seasoning, moistened with red wine and stock. Steamed for 3 hours.

ashe reste *(Pe)* Meat balls possibly flavoured with cinnamon, boiled in water or stock with kidney beans, lentils, fine noodles, seasoning, chopped parsley, spinach and Persian leek, finished with dried mint and fried garlic

Ashley bread *(USA)* A type of bread from the south made from a rice flour bread mix and cooked in a casserole

Asiago d'allevo *(It)* A hard, granular, semi-fat, sharp, grating cheese from the north west, made from a mixture of skimmed and full cream milk, curdled with lactobacillus and scalded, cast into large rounds (8 to 12 kg). It can be aged up to 2 years and becomes sharper with aging. The minimum fat content is 24% of dry matter

Asiago grasso di monte *(It)* A semi-soft cooked curd, mellow summer cheese made in the north west from raw whole cow's milk with numerous holes and a delicate flavour

Asiago pressato *(It)* A white, scalded curd, mild tasting cheese from the north west, cast in large rounds (11 to 15 kg) with a white to pale straw paste containing a few irregular holes and a thin elastic rind. it is matured for 20 to 40 days. Contains 37% water, 23% fat and 33% protein

Asian leek A variety of small thin leek *Allium ramosum* grown in China and Japan. The central white part is used in cooked dishes and the green leaves are used as a garnish

Asian mussel A greenish-black shelled mussel

Perna virides commonly found and cooked in SEA. The flesh is sometimes dried or deep fried as a snack food

Asian pear The crisp, white, pear-flavoured fruit of a Japanese tree *Pyrus pyrofolia and P. ussuriensis,* now also cultivated in New Zealand. The shape varies from apple to pear. The juicy semi-sweet flesh has a fragrant flavour and is enclosed in a golden skin rather like a russet apple. It is eaten raw or as a garnish e.g. with game [also called **Japanese pear, Beijing pear, Peking pear, snow pear, nashi**]

Asiatic yam A very heavy yam *Dioscorea alata* (to 10 kg) grown in SEA. The plant is distinguished by the winged petioles of the leaves [also called **winged yam, greater yam**]

asier *(De)* Sweet pickled cucumber used as a garnish

Asimina triloba *Bot.* Papaw

asino *(It)* Donkey

asparagi alla Fiorentina *(It)* Boiled asparagus browned in butter and garnished with a fried egg

asparagi e funghi al burro *(It)* Diagonally cut 25 mm pieces of asparagus and similar sized pieces of mushrooms, sautéed (asparagus first) in butter with seasoning until dry and al dente, served immediately

asparagi al Parmigiano *(It)* Tender, cooked asparagus with grated Parmesan cheese and melted butter

asparagi pasticciati con uova *(It)* Peeled asparagus stalks cut into 5 cm lengths, boiled until tender, drained and mixed with sliced onion cooked to transparency in butter, beaten eggs with seasoning and grated Parmesan cheese added while the mixture is hot and stirred until scrambled, cream added and the whole served immediately with the cooked asparagus tips as a garnish.

asparago *(It)* Asparagus

asparagus A perennial plant of the lily family *Asparagus officinalis.* The young shoots are removed in spring. White asparagus is cut below ground when the tips protrude about 5 cm above ground. Green asparagus is cut at ground level when the shoots are about 15cm long. Asparagus should be used as fresh as possible, scraped, carefully washed and cooked in plenty of boiling salted water; *see also* sprue

asparagus bean A long (to 40 cm) green bean *Dolichos sesquipedalis* with a frill down four sides, which can be cooked whole when young in the same way as French beans. The dried, ripe beans of some varieties are sold as black-eyed beans [also called **yard long bean, long bean, yard bean**]

Asparagus officinalis *Bot.* Asparagus

asparagus pea A leguminous plant *Lotus tetragonolobus or Psophocarpus tetragonolobus* from southern Europe, with a flower rather like a small sweet pea with smooth brown seeds and grown extensively in SEA. The pods can be eaten like a mange-tout when not longer than 6 cm and preferably 3 cm. Not to be confused with asparagus bean [also called **Goa bean, winged pea**]

asparagus royale Half cooked asparagus tips, cold Béchamel sauce, cream, green spinach for colouring and egg yolk, mixed, sieved and poached as a royale q.v

asparagus sauce Cooked asparagus, liquidized with white stock and white wine, strained, seasoned and cream added

asparagus soup Basic soup without leek and using chicken stock and fresh asparagus trimmings or a tin of asparagus, finished with cream or milk [also called **crème d'asperges**]

asparagus tip omelette *see* omelette aux points d'asperge

asperges *(De & No)* Asparagus

aspargesbønner *(No)* French beans (pods)

aspartame A dipeptide made from the two amino acids, aspartic acid and the methyl ester of phenylalanine used as an artificial sweetener with roughly 180 times the sweetening power of sucrose. It is a risk to persons suffering from phenylketonuria (1 in 15000 Europeans), and a warning to this effect should be on all containers. Used in soft drinks, yoghurts, drink mixes and sweetening tablets

aspartic acid A non-essential amino acid

asperge *(Ho & Fr) fem.* Asparagus.

asperges à la flamande *(Fr) fem.* Cooked asparagus served with a sauce made from hard boiled yolk of egg combined with melted butter. The sauce may be made at the table by each guest from individually served portions of hot hard boiled egg and melted butter

asperges au gratin *(Fr) fem.* Cooked asparagus arranged in rows, tips and one third of remaining stalk coated in mornay sauce, uncoated stalk protected with buttered paper, sauce sprinkled with grated Parmesan cheese and the whole glazed [also called **asperges mornay**]

asperges à l'italienne *(Fr) fem. see* asperges à la milanaise

asperges à la milanaise *(Fr) fem.* Cooked asparagus laid in rows on a buttered dish which has been sprinkled with grated Parmesan cheese, points sprinkled with same, coated with brown butter and the whole glazed lightly [also called **asperges à l'Italienne**]

asperges mornay *(Fr) fem. see* asperges au gratin

asperges à la polonaise *(Fr) fem.* Cooked asparagus arranged in rows, tips sprinkled with a mixture of chopped hard boiled yolk of egg and parsley, coated with brown butter and fine white breadcrumbs which have been fried to a golden brown in butter

aspergesoep *(Ho)* Asparagus soup

Aspergillus flavus The mould which produces aflotoxin. It is a strict aerobe

Aspergillus niger One of the principal moulds used in the production of food grade citric acid, and for the production of enzymes such as glucose oxidase and pectinase

Aspergillus oryzae A fungus or mould used to ferment rice in the first stage of soya sauce and miso production

Aspergillus parasiticus A mould which grows on cereals, potatoes and onions and produces aflotoxin

Aspergillus sojae One of the moulds used to ferment soybeans and rice to make miso

asperula *(It)* Sweet woodruff

aspérula olorosa *(Sp)* Sweet woodruff

aspic *(En, It, Sp & Fr) masc.* A savoury jelly made with the appropriate clarified stock (meat, chicken or fish) flavoured with vegetables, herbs, sherry, etc. with added gelatine if required, mainly used for decorative larder work. Nowadays instant aspic granules at 70 g per litre of water are usually used

aspic de bécasses *(Fr) masc.* The leg flesh and intestines of roast woodcock pounded together with brandy and aspic jelly and sieved, piled onto slices of breast, cooled, covered with a brown chaud-froid sauce, placed breast uppermost in an aspic lined mould, filled with aspic jelly and demoulded when set

aspic of fillets of sole A fish aspic lined mould, decorated and filled with either cooled and aspic coated poached and trimmed fillets of sole or paupiettes of sole stuffed with a fish forcemeat and truffle and cut in slices, the whole filled with aspic jelly and demoulded when set

aspic of foie gras An aspic lined mould decorated with truffle and cooked egg white, filled with slices or scoops of cooked foie gras each coated with cool aspic, the whole filled with aspic and demoulded when set

aspic d'ortolans *(Fr) masc.* Cold roast whole buntings (not boned out) placed breast side down in a border mould coated with aspic, filled with aspic jelly and demoulded when set. (Unlikely to be offered in the EU)

aspic de volaille gauloise *(Fr) masc.* An aspic lined mould decorated with slices of truffle, filled with alternate layers of slices of chicken, cockscombs coated with brown chaud-froid sauce, chicken kidneys coated with white chaud-froid sauce and slices of ox tongue, all cooked, each layer being separated with aspic jelly, demoulded when set

aspic de volaille à l'italienne *(Fr) masc.* An aspic lined mould decorated with slices of truffle, filled with alternate layers of julienne of cooked chicken breast, slices of cooked red ox tongue and truffle, each layer separated by cool aspic jelly, the whole filled with aspic jelly and served with salade italienne and sauce remoulade

Aspik *(Ge)* Aspic

assad *(In)* Cubed pork shoulder, coated with a paste of ginger, garlic, turmeric and seasoning, fried in ghee until coloured, then simmered with water, cinnamon stick, cloves, dried chillis and mace until tender

assadeiro *(Po)* A large, shallow roasting pan

assado *(Po)* Roasted

assaisoner *(Fr)* To season

assam jawa *(SEA)* Tamarind

assam tea A high quality tea from Assam in north east India

assiette *(Fr) fem.* Plate

assiette anglaise *(Fr) fem.* A plate of assorted sliced cold meats and sausages

assiette de charcuterie *(Fr) fem.* A plate of assorted sliced sausages

assonza *(It)* Lard flavoured with hot pepper and fennel seeds, spread on toast

assorted hors d'oeuvres A variety of hors d'oeuvres served separately in raviers or similar dishes, e.g. potato salad, niçoise salad, egg mayonnaise, rice salad, anchovies, cauliflower à la grecque, tomato salad, Russian salad. The assortment should have contrast of colour, taste and texture

assorti *(Fr)* Past participle of assortir, assorted

assortito *(It)* Assorted

astaco *(It)* The crayfish *Astacus fluviatilis*, also the popular name for lobster

astaco americano *(It)* True lobster

astakos me latholemono *(Gr)* Lobster flesh, dressed with a mixture of olive oil, lemon juice, chopped marjoram and seasoning, piled in the pregrilled half lobster shells, brushed with more dressing, grilled for 8 minutes and served immediately

astaxanthin The pink colouring in a small shrimp like creature which gives the pink colour to the flesh of salmon. Now fed to farmed salmon which are generally pinker than wild

astice *(It)* Plural of astaco

astringent A description of a liquid such as lemon juice or a solution of tannin which tightens up the skin or mucous membranes of the mouth

asukal *(Ph)* Sugar

asupara *(Ja)* Asparagus

ata *see* atta

atap chee *(Ma)* Palm nut

atasuki *(Ja)* Scallion

atemoya A hybrid variety of custard apple *Anona* spp. derived from the cherimoya and the sweet sop. See custard apple

athénienne, à l' *(Fr)* In the Athenian style, i.e. garnished with onion, aubergine, tomato and sweet red pepper, all fried in oil

atherine A small silvery fish similar in appearance to the lesser argentine, grilled or fried

athol brose *(UK)* A Scottish dish consisting of a gruel made by pouring boiling water over oatmeal with whisky and honey added for flavour. Sometimes most of the oatmeal is omitted

atis *(Ph)* Rose apple

atjar *see* acar

Atlantic blue crab *see* blue crab

Atlantic butterfish *see* butterfish

Atlantic catfish *see* catfish

Atlantic cod The name given in North America to cod caught in the North Atlantic ocean

Atlantic croaker A seawater fish *Micropogonia undulatus* found off the North American coast, up to 1 kg in weight and with lean delicately flavoured flesh

Atlantic deep sea scallop A large North Atlantic scallop *Placopecten magellanicus* fished off the American coast

Atlantic mackerel *see* mackerel

Atlantic salmon The wild salmon of the Atlantic *Salmo salar*, with medium oily pink flesh and a mild flavour, which can weigh up to 18 kg. It can be distinguished from farmed salmon by signs of wear esp. on the tail fin. Cooked in any way and often smoked

Atlantic silverside A slender round oily seawater fish *Menidia menidia* 13 to 15 cm long with a translucent green back and silver bands lengthways along the sides, caught on the Atlantic coast and estuaries of North America. Fried or grilled

Atlantic squid A slightly larger variety *Loligo forbesi* of squid than the Mediterranean but otherwise similar

Atlantic sturgeon *see* common sturgeon

Atlantic thread herring *see* thread herring

atmospheric steamer A device used to cook foods in live steam at atmospheric pressure, Condensation of steam on the surface of the food or its container gives the highest rate of heat transfer available with the exception of high temperature radiant heat. The food temperature is limited to 100°C

atole *(Me)* A thin porridge or thick gruel of masa harina (maize flour) or cornflour, boiled with water, milk, cinnamon, sugar and puréed fresh fruit. Served hot for breakfast

atole de arroz *(Me)* As atole but made with rice or rice flour and flavoured with cinnamon

Atriplex hortensis *Bot.* Orach

atsu-age *(Ja)* Lightly fried bean curd

atta *(In)* A wholemeal flour used for making unleavened breads such as chapatis, puri and paratha [also called **ata**]

attar *(ME)* Spice shop in Arab countries

attelette *(Fr) fem.* The small silver skewer used to present attereaux after cooking or for certain garnishes.

atterato *(It)* A method of serving vermicelli with butter, pinenuts and chocolate

attereaux *(Fr) masc.* Hors d'oeuvres consisting of thin slices of various cooked (e.g. meats) or raw (e.g. vegetables) ingredients on a skewer, coated in a reduced sauce, panéed and deep fried just before serving, garnished with fried parsley and possibly presented on a socle or mound of rice or on fried bread

attereaux à la florentine *(Fr) masc. see* attereaux au parmesan

attereaux à la genevoise *(Fr) masc.* Attereaux of chicken livers, lambs sweetbreads, brains, mushrooms, truffles, artichoke hearts coated with a well reduced duxelle sauce, when cool covered with a forcemeat mixed with beaten egg, panéed, deep fried and served immediately

attereaux d'huitres à la Villeroy *(Fr) masc.* Attereaux of oysters alternating with slices of cooked mushrooms on a skewer coated with sauce Villeroy reduced with juices from the oysters, panéed, deep fried and served immediately

attereaux au Parmesan *(Fr) masc.*

Semolina cooked in just sufficient white bouillon, mixed with grated Parmesan cheese and butter, spread out 0.5 cm thick to cool into a stiff paste, cut into 2.5 cm rounds and alternated with similar slices of Gruyère cheese on a skewer, panéed, deep fried and served immediately [also called **attereaux à la florentine, attereaux à la princesse, attereaux à la royale**]

attereaux à la princesse *(Fr) masc. see* attereaux au Parmesan

attereaux à la royale *(Fr) masc. see* attereaux au Parmesan

attereaux Villeroy *(Fr) masc.* Attereaux coated with sauce Villeroy

ättika *(Sw)* Vinegar [also called **vinättika**]

attorta *(It)* An S-shaped cake from Umbria made from flour, ground almonds, sugar and lemon zest

atum *(Po)* Tuna fish

atún *(Sp)* Tuna fish

au *(Fr)* In the style of, used before masculine French nouns, also means, with, in

aubergine *(En, It & Fr) fem.* The purple fruit of an East Indian annual plant *Solanum melongena* of the same family as the tomato and deadly nightshade, now also called aubergine in English. Generally violet to deep purple in Europe and North America and up to 30 cm long, but can be white or deep yellow streaked with purple and the size of a hen's egg. The bitter taste of some varieties is removed by sprinkling with salt and allowing to drain [also called **eggplant, garden egg, Guinea squash**]

aubergines à la bordelaise *(Fr) fem.* Salted and drained slices of aubergine, seasoned, floured and sautéed in olive oil with finely chopped shallots, white breadcrumbs used to absorb the excess oil, the whole served with lemon juice and chopped parsley or grilled with olive oil and coated with bordelaise sauce

aubergines à la crème *(Fr) fem.* Aubergines cut in 0.5 cm slices, salted and drained for 1 hour, dried, cooked in butter and mixed with cream sauce

aubergines à l'égyptienne *(Fr) fem.* Aubergines cut in half lengthwise, flesh cut away from edges and scored, deep fried, flesh removed from skins. Skins arranged in a buttered dish, filled with a mixture of chopped flesh and chopped onions cooked in oil, oiled, baked for 15 minutes and served topped with sautéed sliced tomato and chopped parsley

aubergines frites *(Fr) fem.* Aubergines cut in thin round slices, seasoned, battered or panéed, deep fried and served immediately

aubergines au gratin *(Fr) fem.* As for aubergines à l'égyptienne but filled with a mixture of chopped aubergine flesh and duxelles, arranged in a dish, sprinkled with white breadcrumbs and oil, baked and served with tomato sauce

aubergines à la napolitaine *(Fr) fem.* Peeled aubergines, cut lengthwise in slices, seasoned, floured, deep fried, reformed with tomato purée flavoured with Parmesan cheese between the slices, arranged in a dish coated with tomato sauce, sprinkled with grated Parmesan cheese, oiled and buttered and baked

aubergines à l'orientale *(Fr) fem.* Peeled aubergines cut lengthwise into slices, seasoned, floured, deep fried, made into sandwiches with a filling of chopped fried aubergine and tomato flesh, white breadcrumbs, seasoning and garlic flavouring, placed in an oiled dish, sprinkled with oil and baked for 30 minutes. Served hot or cold.

aubergines à la parisienne *(Fr) fem.* As for aubergine à l'égyptienne but filled with a mixture of chopped aubergine flesh, white meat, marrow or bacon fat, egg yolks, stale breadcrumbs, nutmeg and seasoning then baked in the oven

aubergines à la provençale *(Fr) fem.* As for aubergines à l'égyptienne but filled with a mixture of aubergine flesh, onions and tomato flesh, all coarsely chopped and cooked in oil, fresh breadcrumbs, chopped parsley, seasoning and flavoured with garlic, gratinated and served with tomato sauce

aubergines à la serbe *(Fr) fem.* As for aubergines à l'égyptienne but filled with a mixture of chopped cooked mutton, tomato flesh and onions chopped and cooked in butter, plain boiled rice, crumbed and gratinated and served with tomato sauce and chopped parsley [also called **aubergines à la Turque**]

aubergines à la turque *(Fr) fem. see* aubergines à la serbe

Auflauf *(Ge)* Omelette or baked soufflé

Aufschnitt *(Ge)* Cold meat

Aufschnittwurst *(He)* A Brühwurst (scalded sausage) made with pork and beef

Augsburgerwurst *(Ge)* A lightly smoked cooking sausage made with chopped lean pork and back fat, flavoured with cinnamon, cloves, nutmeg, seasoning and a little saltpetre, filled into beef runners and air dried for 4 days before being smoked

augurk *(Ho)* Gherkin

augurken *(Ho)* Pickles

Auld Reekie plum cake *(UK)* A Scottish rich fruit cake flavoured with whisky (added at the flour folding stage) and chopped preserved ginger

aumônières surprise *(Fr) fem.* A dessert

made from thin sweet pancakes or crêpes with a centre filling of fruit salad, ice cream, etc., pulled up into a bag or purse shape and tied with a blanched strip of angelica or liquorice, served on a coulis of fruits

Aunus *(Fr)* A small triangular shaped cheese from Charente made with ewes' milk

Aura *(Fi)* A semi-soft, blue veined cheese made from whole cow's milk, cast in 2.5 kg rounds. Contains 45% water, 28% fat and 24% protein

Auricularia auricula *Bot.* Jew's ear

Auricularia polytricha *Bot.* Chinese mushroom

aurin *(Fr) masc.* Grey mullet

aurore maigre, sauce *(Fr) fem.* As sauce aurore but using fish stock to make the velouté base. Used for fish

aurore, sauce *(En & Fr) fem.* Suprême sauce, lightly flavoured with either tomato purée or sieved tomato concassée and finished with butter. Used for boiled chicken, poached eggs, etc.

Ausbackteig *(Ge)* Dough or flour based paste or pâte

Auster *(Ge)* Oyster, originally the European flat oyster

Austerpilz *(Ge)* Oyster mushroom

Australian barracuda *see* snoek

Australian fondant icing *see* plastic icing

Australian oyster An oyster *Crassostrea commercialis* grown off the coasts of Australia and New Zealand

australique *(Aus) see* ortanique

Austrian pancakes *see* Salzburger Nockerln

autoclave A high pressure steamed and steam heated chamber which cooks food very rapidly and which is also used to sterilize canned and bottled food

autocondimentor A person who seasons any meal placed in front of them whatever it is and regardless of how much seasoning it has already had and of how it tastes

autolysed yeast Yeast cells which have been subjected to limited and controlled autolysis to liberate cell contents and change their flavour. The result which looks like thick molasses in appearance is used in vegetarian cooking and as a sandwich spread

autolysis The process by which cells are broken down by their own enzymes or acid products when dead. In the early stages cell contents are released adding to flavour but later the material becomes putrid. The process occurs when meat is hung or when fish goes bad

automatic boiler A boiler with an automatic water feed designed to produce fresh boiling water on demand

autrichienne, à l' In the Austrian style, i.e. including soured cream, paprika, onions and fennel

autumn partridge pot *(UK)* A Norfolk dish of jointed older partridges passed through seasoned oatmeal and slowly casseroled between diced bacon and mushrooms, onions and tomatoes with stock and red wine flavoured with cloves, bay, thyme and seasoning

autumn pudding *(UK)* As summer pudding but using stewed autumn fruits such as apples, plums and blackberries, etc.

autumn vegetable soup *(UK)* A variety of diced vegetables, sweated in butter and cooked in vegetable stock with a BG until just tender

avaisances *(Be)* Meat filled pastries

avanzi *(It)* Leftovers

avdrakla *(Gr)* Purslane

ave maria *see* cannolicchi

aveia *(Po)* Oatmeal

aveline *(Fr) fem.* Filbert

avella *(It)* Hazel nut

avellanas *(Sp)* Hazel nuts

avena a medio moler *(Sp)* Oat grits, coarse oatmeal

avena *(It & Sp)* Oats

aves *(Sp & Po)* Poultry

aves de corral *(Me)* Poultry

avgolemono *(Gr)* A sauce made by combining egg yolks or whole eggs with lemon juice and stock then cooking in a double boiler until thick. Alternatively a reduced velouté sauce thickened with a mixture of egg yolks and lemon juice [also called **saltsa avgolemono**]

avgolemono soupa *(Gr)* A soup made with chicken stock and rice with eggs, lemon juice and seasoning

avgotarabo The salted and dried roe of grey mullet used as an appetizer and for making taramasalata *(Eaten by Samuel Pepys on the 5th June 1661)* [also called **Botargo**]

avidin A component of egg white which impairs the uptake and utilization of the vitamin biotin in the body. One of a number of protective chemicals in the white whose function is to prevent bacterial attack of the yolk. It is inactivated by heat

avocado 1 The pear shaped fruit of a species of sub-tropical laurel *Persea americana* with a rough, thick, green to dark brown skin, a creamy yellow flesh and a large single stone, usually eaten as a starter or salad. Used as an ingredient of guacamole. The flesh mixed wih grated nutmeg is said to be a male aphrodisiac [also called **avocado pear, alligator pear**] **2** *(It)* Avocado

avocado mousse Purée of avocado flesh, mixed with lemon juice, icing sugar, and hot gelatine solution, cooled, whipped cream folded in, moulded, set and demoulded

avocado oil Cooking oil extracted from the pulp of damaged avocados. Contains about 20% saturated, 65% monounsaturated and 15% polyunsaturated fats

avocado pear *see* avocado

avocado soup *see* sopa de aguacate

avocat *(Fr) masc.* Avocado

avocat épicure *(Fr) masc.* The diced flesh of halved avocados, mixed with diced gherkins, walnuts, mayonnaise and paprika, replaced in the empty half skins, garnished with pickled walnut and served on crisp lettuce

avocat Singapour *(Fr) masc.* The diced flesh of halved avocados sprinkled with vinegar, mixed with crab meat, mayonnaise, cream and lemon juice, replaced in the empty half skins and served on crushed ice with crisp lettuce and lemon slices

avoine *(Fr) fem.* Oats

awabi *(Ja)* Abalone

awayuki kan *(Ja)* A dessert made from agar-agar and caster sugar dissolved in boiling water (1:50:60) cooled to less than 60°C, beaten into stiffly beaten egg whites (one fifth of the weight of the sugar) and poured into a mould or dish and decorated

awenda bread *(USA)* A bread of Amerindian origin made from hominy grits

ayam *(Id & Ma)* Chicken

ayam bakar *(Ma)* Chicken pieces coated with a paste of pounded garlic, lemon grass, laos, turmeric and salt, left for 50 minutes, boiled in water with bay leaves, soya sauce and butter for 30 minutes until the cooking liquor is reduced to coating consistency then grilled to finish

ayam goreng jawa *(Id)* A dish of chicken cut in pieces, simmered until tender in water, with chopped shallots, garlic, coriander powder, laos powder, lemon grass, grated nutmeg, cinnamon, bay leaves, brown sugar and salt until most of the liquid is absorbed, drained, cooled and deep fried until golden brown

ayam kecap *(Id)* A dish of poached chicken pieces, tossed with a fried pounded spice mixture of onion, garlic and deseeded red chillis, simmered with chicken stock, nutmeg, cloves, strained tamarind purée and soya sauce until tender

ayam opor *(Id)* A dish of chicken pieces fried in a pounded spice mixture (garlic, onion, macadamia nuts and coriander seeds), stewed with coconut milk, laos, lemon grass, lime leaves, bay leaves, salt and sugar until tender and garnished with crisp fried onions

ayam panggang kecap *(SEA)* Roasted chicken cut into four pieces, flattened, marinated with dark soya sauce, chopped shallots, garlic, chilli powder, lemon or lime juice and sesame seed oil for 1 hour then reheated under the grill

Aylesbury duck *(UK)* One of the 2 standard duck breeds, the other being Pekin. It matures in about 7 weeks and contains a lot of fat

Aylesbury game pie *(UK)* A Buckinghamshire terrine made in a dish lined with bacon from alternating layers of seasoned forcemeat (pork fat, leg meat, liver, etc.) and diced meat from hare, chicken and pheasant previously marinated in brandy, thyme, bay and seasoning, covered with marinade and bacon, sealed and oven cooked in a bain-marie for 3 hours. May be served hot or cold and demoulded

ayran *(ME)* A yoghurt based drink similar to lassi but flavoured with cardamom seeds (2 pods per 100 ml yoghurt)

Ayrshire bacon *(UK)* Bacon from Ayrshire in Scotland which has its rind removed after curing and is tightly rolled and secured with string

Ayrshire galantine *(UK)* A Scottish galantine of minced bacon and beef shoulder steak mixed with breadcrumbs, nutmeg, mace and seasoning, bound with egg and stock, rolled in a cloth, simmered in water with aromatic vegetables, removed from the cloth, pressed until set, glazed with aspic jelly and served cold

Ayrshire gigot *(UK)* A boned, rolled and tied gammon joint from Scotland

Ayrshire meat roll *(UK)* A mixture of minced Ayrshire bacon, minced stewing steak, finely chopped onions, eggs, white breadcrumbs, nutmeg and pepper, rolled and wrapped in a floured cloth, simmered for two hours, removed from the cloth and coated with toasted breadcrumbs

Ayrshire roll Back bacon, skinned, rolled and tied. Available in Scotland

Ayrshire shortbread *(UK)* A Scottish shortbread using less butter than the standard recipe but enriched with egg and cream

ayu *(Ja)* Freshwater trout

ayurveda *(In)* A science of living which offers

guidance on food, menus, cooking techniques and conditions in which food should be eaten. In brief it recommends fresh vegetarian food but definitely not red meat and that a balanced meal should contain a little of each taste and quality. Six tastes are distinguished, sweet, salt, sour, bitter, pungent and astringent and six qualities, light, heavy, oily, dry, hot and cold. Eating should be a leisurely activity and a period of quiet after a meal should also be observed. Steaming is considered the best method of cooking and the attitude of the cook, who should be serene and tranquil, is important

azafrán *(Sp)* Saffron

azarole The Naples medlar *Crataegus azarolus*, a native of the Mediterranean with a crisp fruit the size of a crab apple containing 3 or 4 hard seeds. It is eaten fresh or used for jam making [also called **Naples medlar, Mediterranean medlar**]

azêda *(Po)* Sorrel

azêdo *(Po)* Sour

azeite *(Po)* Olive oil

azeitão *(Po)* A soft, mild, ewe's milk cheese made in cylinders (to 250 g) with a creamy fine textured tangy flavoured paste and a yellow rind. Eaten with a spoon

azeitonas *(Po)* Olives

azijn *(Ho)* Vinegar

azodicarbonamide *see* (E)927

azorubine *see* carmoisine

azúcar *(Sp)* Sugar

azúcar en cortadillo *(Sp)* Cube sugar

azúcar en cuadrillo *(Sp)* Sugar lump

azúcar de pilón *(Sp)* Sugar lump

azúcar en polvo *(Sp)* Granulated or caster sugar

azuki bean *see* adzuki bean

azul A nondescript, dense, strong tasting blue cheese made in Latin America from pasteurized and homogenized cow's milk, similar to the equally nondescript Danish blue. Contains 43% water, 31% fat, 22% protein

azyme *(Fr) adj.* Unleavened, as a description of bread

Bb

baak dau gok *(Ch)* The light green variety of long bean

baak guo *(Ch)* Ginkgo nut

baars *(Ho)* Perch, bass, the fish

baba 1 *(Pl)* A Polish cake resembling a long gathered skirt. Lit. an old woman **2** *(Fr) masc.* A light textured cake made from a sweetened yeast-raised dough, often baked in small or large ring moulds or in dariole moulds. May be soaked in syrup flavoured with rum or liqueur and/or filled with cream. Served hot or cold

baba au kirsch *(Fr) masc.* A baked baba cake soaked in kirsch-flavoured sugar syrup

baba au rhum *(Fr) masc.* A baba cake baked in a small ring mould, soaked in rum-flavoured syrup and the centre filled with whipped cream

babaco A hybrid of the paw paw *Carica papaya,* which when cut across resembles a five pointed star. The soft pulp has a pleasant mixed fruit taste. Originally from Ecuador but now grown in New Zealand [also called **star fruit**]

baba ganouje *(ME)* A cold salad from northern Syria made from a mixture of diced, grilled aubergine flesh, thinly sliced green sweet pepper and onion, all seasoned and dressed with an olive oil and lemon juice mixture flavoured with chilli powder, ground cumin seed and chopped parsley. Served with bread or as an accompaniment to grilled or roast meat [also called **imam bayaldi**]

babaghanouji *(Ru)* An Armenian aubergine paté the same as baklazhannya ikra except that parsley is substituted for coriander and pomegranate seeds are added at the same time as the parsley

babao fan *(Ch)* Glutinous rice pudding

babassu The Brazilian palm *Orbignija speciosa or O. martiana* whose nuts yield a valuable oil

babbelaar *(Ho)* Butter cake

babelutten *(Be)* A caramel biscuit

babeurre *(Fr) masc.* Buttermilk

babi guling *(Id)* Roast pork

babi lemak *(SEA)* A pork stew from Singapore made with coconut milk, onions, blachan, herbs and spices

baboy letsonin *(Ph)* Roast sucking pig

baby beef *(USA)* Meat from a calf younger than 12 months

baby bel *(Fr) masc.* A small, soft, whole cows' milk cheese similar to Edam and covered in red wax

baby corn *see* miniature corn

baby's head *(UK) coll. (navy)* Steak and kidney pudding

bacalao *(Sp)* Dried cod, salt cod, cod or ling

bacalao a la ajo arriero *(Sp)* Cod cooked in a garlicy sauce with parsley and pepper

bacalao al pil-pil *(Sp)* Cod cooked in olive oil, from the Basque region

bacalao seco *(Sp)* Stockfish

bacalao a la vizcaína *(Sp)* Poached salt cod, boned, floured and browned in oil, bread cubes, raw ham, garlic, chopped onions, bay leaf and ñoras added and sweated until tender, pimenton and poaching liquor added and cooked 10 minutes, fish reserved, cooking liquor liquidized, sieved, seasoned and sugared, consistency adjusted and poured over salt cod and all heated through

bacalhau *(Po)* Dried salt cod used as a staple protein food in Portugal

bacalhau cozido *(Po)* Salt cod boiled with vegetables

bacalhau fresco à portuguêsa *(Po)* Cod steaks fried in oil with aubergines, tomatoes, onions and garlic. Served with rice

bacalhau à portuguêsa *(Po)* Casseroled salt cod with tomatoes, onions, potatoes and sweet peppers

bacca *(It)* Berry pl. bacche

baccalà *(It)* Salt cod

baccalà alla bolognese *(It)* Salt cod cooked in butter and oil with garlic and pepper

baccalà alla cappuccina *(It)* Salt cod cooked with oil, vinegar, parsley and garlic

baccalà alla genovese *(It)* Salt cod grilled and served with oil, lemon juice and boiled potatoes

baccalà alla napoletana *(It)* Salt cod, fried

in oil then stewed in a sauce of tomatoes, garlic, oil and capers

baccalà alla veneziana *(It)* Salt cod browned in oil with onion and stewed in a thick anchovy sauce

bacche *(It)* Berries

bac cua *(Vi)* Ginkgo nut

bachelor's button *(USA)* A round sweet biscuit with a cherry in the centre

Bachforelle *(Ge)* River trout

bacile *(Fr)* Samphire *C. maritimum*

Bacillus cereus Bacteria which grows on rice, usually found in temperate countries in spore form. The spore will germinate after cooking and lead to growth of the vegetative form which can cause food poisoning. There are 2 strains, one has an incubation period of 1 - 5 hours, a duration of 6 - 24 hours and the symptoms are nausea and vomiting and occasionally diarrhoea, the other has an incubation period of 8 - 16 hours, a duration of 12 - 24 hours and the symptoms are abdominal pain, diarrhoea and occasionally nausea

Bacillus licheniformis Bacteria which can produce a toxin causing diarrhoea and vomiting. The incubation period is 4 - 8 hours

Bacillus subtilis Bacteria which can produce a toxin causing vomiting, abdominal pain and diarrhoea. The incubation period is 2 - 18 hours

back bacon That part of the side of bacon which if uncured would be pork loin or shoulder chop

back fat Hard fat from the back of the pig, usually specified for high quality sausage making

backen *(Ge)* To bake

Backerei *(Ge)* **1** Pastries **2** Patisserie

Backhendl *(Au)* Panéed chicken fried in lard or oil

Backhuhn *(Ge)* Panéed and fried chicken

Backobst *(Ge)* Dried fruit

Backobstkompott *(Ge)* Mixed dried fruit, soaked overnight then simmered in a sugar water syrup (4:5) with a cinnamon stick and lemon rind until the fruit is all tender, drained and covered with the reduced cooking liquor. Served hot or cold and possibly flavoured with liqueur or spirits

Backpflaume *(Ge)* Prune

Backpulver *(Ge)* Baking powder

Backstein *(Ge)* The Bavarian version of Limburger cheese

Backteig *(Ge)* Batter for deep frying

Backwerk *(Ge)* Cakes, pastries

bacon *(En, Sp & Fr) masc.* The flesh of pork, divided in two halves along the backbone, which has been dried and preserved by treatment with salt, saltpetre and spices. These remove water from the meat and have some antibacterial action. Commercial curing methods leave more water in the flesh by including polyphosphates and do not give a bacon which keeps as well as the traditionally or dry cured variety. May be smoked after curing to enhance the flavour. Usually sold after boning

bacon froise *(UK)* A plain flour, egg and milk batter into which whisked egg white is folded, half added to a buttered fry pan and cooked until set, crisp bacon pieces added, the remaining batter added, cooked and turned to brown both sides

bacon omelette *see* omelette au lard

bacon rasher A thin slice cut at right angles to the backbone from a side of bacon [also called **rasher**]

bacon strip *(USA)* Bacon rasher

baconer A pig bred for bacon to give a high yield of back bacon, generally long with little fat and small head and legs

bacoreta *(Sp)* Little tunny

bacteria *Plural of* bacterium. Important in the food industries are *Salmonella, Bacillus cereus, Campylobacter, Staphylococcus, Listeria,* all of which are food poisoning organisms and *Lactobacillus* spp. and *Streptococcus* spp., etc. which are used in the production of various foodstuffs. See under each heading; *see also* food poisoning organisms

bacterium A singled celled micro-organism which replicates by growth and then division. Some are beneficial some harmful. The plural form is bacteria. See examples under entry 'bacteria'

badaam *(In)* Almond

badasco *(Fr)* The Provençal name for the fish, rascasse, used in fish soups and bouillabaisse

badèche *(Fr)* Sea bass *(bar)*

badischer Hecht *(Ge)* Pike fillets with button onions, covered in sour cream half baked in the oven then finished by gratinating with breadcrumbs and grated cheese

baecheoffe *(He)* Baked potato

baechu *(Ko)* Chinese leaves

baeckoffe *(Fr)* A meat and potato hot pot from the Alsace region of France made from boneless stewing meat marinaded in Alsace riesling wine with chopped onions, garlic and herbs, layered with potatoes and onions, covered in the marinade, the pot sealed and cooked in the oven for up to 4 hours at 175°C. Literally baking oven

bagaceira *(Po)* The Portuguese equivalent of marc or grappa, a type of rum made with sugar cane residues

bagel A Jewish bread roll made by forming the dough into a ring, then briefly boiling after proving and prior to baking

baggiana *(It)* A bean, tomato and basil soup from Umbria

baghar *(In)* A mixture of sliced onions and possibly other vegetables, flavoured with chopped garlic, chillis and whole spices, fried in ghee or clarified butter and used as a topping for dhal

baghlava *(Pe)* Baklava

bagna 1 *(Fr) coll. (Provence)* A small Niçoise salad served on a round bun with the centre scooped out. Street food **2** *(It)* Sauce *(regional)*

bagna calda *(It)* A mixture of melted butter or olive oil, chopped anchovies, garlic, and basil, served hot with raw or cooked vegetables

Bagnes et conches *(He)* A hard delicately flavoured cheese

bagnet *(It)* Sauce *(Piedmont)*

bagnomaria *(It)* Bain marie

bagolan *(Ph)* Cuttlefish

bagoong *(Ph)* Salted shrimps or small fish fermented in a closed jar for several weeks and used as a flavouring or condiment. The liquid which is drawn off is used as a fish sauce *(known as patis)*

Bagozzo *(It)* A cooked curd, grana type cheese with a very hard yellow paste containing fine holes, a sharp flavour and a red rind. Often sliced and grilled

Bagration *(Ru)* A veal and chicken consommé flavoured with bay, thyme and dill and served hot over cooked asparagus tips and garnished with sour cream. Named after General Bagration killed at the battle of Borodino. Various dishes are named after him

baguette *(Fr) fem.* Long, thin, crusty French bread, about 250 g weight and formed on a cloth. Not baked in a tin. The top is slashed in a characteristic diagonal pattern before baking. The form originated in Paris in the middle of the 19th century where it was introduced from Vienna by the Austrian embassy. It rapidly became popular throughout France

baharat *(ME)* A spice mix from the Persian Gulf consisting of nutmeg, black peppercorns, coriander seeds, cumin seeds, cloves, green cardamom, paprika and cayenne pepper and used with meat and vegetables

bahia orange *see* Washington orange

bai cai *(Ch)* Pak choy

baie *(Fr) fem.* Berry

baie de ronce *(Fr) fem.* Wild blackberry

baigan *(In)* A long thin aubergine

bai horapa *(Th)* Sweet basil [also called **horapa**]

bai karee *(Th)* Curry leaf

bai krapow *(Th)* Purple basil

bai magrut *(Th)* Makrut lime leaves

bai mak nao *(Cm)* Lemon grass

bain-marie *(En & Fr) masc.* Dish to contain boiling or hot water in which other dishes are stood for cooking or to keep them warm at temperatures below boiling. May be specially made with appropriate containers

bain-marie, au *(Fr)* Method of cooking an item in a container placed in a pan of water so as to prevent it reaching too high a temperature

baingan *(In)* Aubergine

bainiko *(Ja)* Puréed umeboshi plums added to dips and sauces to give a tart flavour

bai sa ra neh *(Th)* Mint

baiser *(Fr) masc.* Two meringue shells sandwiched together with whipped cream. Lit. a kiss

bai toey hom *(Th)* Screwpine

bajai halászlé *(Hu)* A fish and potato soup from Baja

bajoue *(Fr) fem.* Pig's cheek

bajra *(In)* Bulrush millet

bake *(USA)* A North American term for a social gathering at which baked or barbecued food is served. See e.g. clam bake

bake, to To cook in an oven with dry heat. Heat is transferred by radiation from the hot metal surfaces or by convection from natural or forced circulation of hot air or gas combustion products. Sometimes steam may be added to increase the relative humidity and reduce the loss of weight by evaporation of water. Baked goods are usually brown on the outside

bake blind, to To bake an unfilled pastry case

in a tin by lining the inside with foil or greaseproof paper and filling this with dried beans or grain so as to prevent the case losing its shape. After the pastry has set, the filling is removed and the pastry case is finished in the oven.

bakeapples *see* cloudberries

Baked Alaska Very cold ice cream placed on a sponge cake, covered with meringue and baked in a hot oven so that the meringue is browned whilst the ice cream remains solid [also called **Norwegian omelette, omelette soufflée surprise (Fr), omelette norvégienne (Fr)**]

baked apple *(UK)* A cored apple with skin on, stuffed with sultanas, brown sugar and cinnamon powder and baked in the oven as a dessert

baked bananas Peeled bananas, halved, baked with rum, brown sugar, lemon juice and butter and served with whipped cream or ice cream

baked batter pudding *(UK)* A Yorkshire pudding batter baked in the oven with sweet or savoury solid additions.

baked beans Cooked navy beans *(from the USA)* in a tomato sauce. The tinned variety are an important source of protein and fibre in Europe and North America, especially for children. The navy bean is now being replaced in some brands by European varieties of the haricot bean

baked custard *(USA)* Crème renversée

baked egg custard An egg custard mix of eggs, sugar, milk and flavourings, baked in the oven until set and browned, sometimes in a pastry case (4 to 5 eggs per litre)

baked pudding *(UK)* As steamed pudding but cooked uncovered at 180°C in an oven for about an hour until well risen

bakelse *(Sw)* A sweet pastry or small cake

baker's cheese *(USA)* A soft, smooth type of cottage cheese made from a pasteurized skimmed milk with a lactic starter culture. Extensively used in the bakery trade. Contains 74% water, 0.2% fat and 19% protein

baker's yeast A particular strain of the yeast *Saccharomyces cerevisiae,* suitable for bread making. Sold as a beige, crumbly, solid cake, usually containing about 75 to 80% free water. Must be used fresh

bakery An establishment where cakes and bread are baked, often with a shop attached

Bakewell pudding *(UK)* A thickish irregular puff pastry case lined with jam and filled with an almond-flavoured egg, butter and sugar mixture, eaten hot or cold. So called from the town of Bakewell in Derbyshire. Originally the filling was a flavoured egg and butter mix said to have been made to rectify a mistake when the pastry for a jam tart was not enriched with butter and eggs as instructed. The forerunner of the Bakewell tart. At least 3 establishments in Bakewell claim to have been handed down the original secret recipe - all different

Bakewell tart *(UK)* A shortcrust pastry case lined with jam and filled with an almond cake mixture, baked and finished with icing. So called from the town of Bakewell in Derbyshire

baking chocolate Unsweetened or bitter chocolate used in cooking

baking powder A chemical raising agent made from a finely ground mixture of two parts cream of tartar to one part bicarbonate of soda which liberates carbon dioxide gas on heating. Domestic baking powders replace some of the cream of tartar with an acid phosphate which is slower to act and gives more time for preparation and cooking

baking sheet A heavy steel sheet, usually rectangular with raised edges on 3 sides, on which rolls, biscuits, etc. are cooked in the oven. The unraised edge is to facilitate sliding the baked goods onto a cooling rack; *see also* baking tray

baking soda Sodium bicarbonate

baking tray A steel sheet with a raised edge all around or on three sides for use in an oven. Various shapes are available for pizzas, tarts, etc. or the rectangular tray can be used as a base for flan rings and smaller containers [also called **baking sheet**]

baklava A Middle Eastern, Armenian and Greek sweet made from layers of filo pastry interspersed with chopped nuts, ground almonds, breadcrumbs, sugar, spice, butter, etc. soaked in sugar syrup or honey after baking at 170°C for 50 minutes, cooled and cut into squares or diamonds. The Armenian version is usually baked in a round pan and prescored in a diamond pattern and cut into diamonds after baking [also called **baklaoua** (NA)]

baklazhannya ikra *(Ru)* A Georgian paté made from the flesh of roasted aubergines, simmered with chopped and sweated spring onions and green sweet peppers, skinned tomatoes and cayenne pepper until all cooked and thick, mixed with chopped coriander and lemon juice and cooled

bakonyi betyárleves *(Hu)* A thick soup of chicken, beef, noodles, mushrooms and vegetables [also called **outlaw soup**]

bakonyi gombamártás *(Hu)* A mushroom sauce from Bakony

bakudai *(Ja)* A type of pea used as a garnish for sashimi and salads. The pods are steeped in tepid tea to make them open and the seeds are removed and washed prior to use

balabusky *(Ru)* A yeast-raised Ukrainian

bread made from rye flour, wheat flour and sour cream (1:2:1). Water, sugar and yeast are used to form the slightly sticky dough which is mixed with caraway seeds, shaped into rolls, sprinkled with more caraway seeds, proved and baked at 200°C

balacan *(Ma)* Blachan

balachaung *(Bm)* Chopped garlic, spring onion and ginger root fried in oil until golden, reserved, finely chopped dried shrimps fried with turmeric in the same oil, mixed with the garlic, etc. softened shrimp paste added and all cooked over a low heat to form a smelly but tasty concoction. Used as a side dish

balachong *(In)* A South Indian relish of minced prawns fried with minced onion, mango and tomatoes or similar plus spices then pounded with salt and vinegar to an acceptable taste and consistency [also called **balachow, balichow**]

balachow *(In) see* balachong

balantier *(Fr)* Wild pomegranate

Balaton *(Hu)* A semi-hard, scalded curd, cows' milk cheese with a buttery, aromatic flavoured paste with holes. Contains 42% water, 20% fat and 25% protein

balcalhao di kismur *(In)* A seafood salad from Goa made of salt cod soaked in diluted palm vinegar, flaked and mixed with fried sliced onions, green and red chillis, sweet green peppers, ginger, garlic and spices and finished with dried shrimp powder and lemon juice

baleron *(Pl)* A popular smoked pork sausage

balichow *(In) see* balachong

balik *(Tu)* Fish

ball garlic *see* bulb garlic

baller A food preparation implement consisting of half a hollow sphere with sharp edges on the end of a handle. Used for cutting out balls from melons, cucumbers, root vegetables, ice cream, cheese, cooked gizzards, etc. Made in various sizes

ballon *(Fr) masc.* A boned joint of meat tied into a ball shape prior to cooking

balloon whisk The professional chef's whisk which consists of about 12 tear drop shaped pieces of stainless steel wire, the two ends of each secured around the circumference of a stout circular handle about 2 cm dia. by 15 cm long. The whole forms a 3 dimensional tear drop shape which fits easily the contours of a basin. They come in various sizes

ballottine *(Fr) fem.* **1** A roll of boned and stuffed poultry, meat or fish **2** Meat loaf

ballottine de volaille *(Fr) fem.* A chicken boned from the inside, lined with pâté, stuffed with forcemeat made from the leg meat, cooked, cooled and coated with aspic jelly

balm *see* lemon balm

balmain bug *(Aus) see* sand lobster

balmoral loaf tin A corrugated cylindrical metal loaf tin somewhat like a bellows, which produces a ridged loaf or cake easily cut into slices [also called **ribbed loaf tin, toast rack tin**]

balnamoon skink *(Ir)* Chicken broth finished with egg yolks and milk and garnished with green peas, shredded lettuce and diced celeriac

baloney *(USA)* Bologna sausage

balsam apple *see* kantola

balsam pear *see* bitter gourd

balsamella *(It)* Béchamel sauce

balsamic vinegar A highly fragrant, sweetish vinegar from Italy, made from concentrated grape juice and aged in wood for at least 10 years

Balsamita major *Bot.* Costmary

balti A style of cheap Indian fast food which originated in Birmingham, UK, in the 1970's, consisting of marinated and spiced ingredients stir fried and served in a karahi. Balti is Hindi for bucket and there is no suggestion that there is an authentic Indian balti cooking style

Baltic herring A small species of herring *Opisthonema oglinum* found in the Baltic sea

balut *(Ph)* Fertilized duck eggs containing an intact embryo duck. Thought to increase male potency when eaten

bamboo A large tropical woody grass *Bambusa* spp., normally used as a construction material. The leaves and shoots of some species are used in cooking

bamboo fungus A very expensive fungus fruiting body *Dictyophora phalloidea* which grows in China on a certain kind of bamboo. It is light in colour, looks like a small lacy purse and has a musty earthy taste and crunchy texture [also called **staghorn fungus**]

bamboo leaf The blanched and softened leaves of certain species of bamboo used as a food wrapping for grilling, steaming, boiling, etc.

bamboo mustard cabbage *see* chuk gaai choy

bamboo shoots The immature shoots of the bamboo *Bambusa* and other spp. used either fresh, salted, pickled, dried or canned in Chinese and SEA cooking. Fresh shoots must be parboiled to remove toxins. Dried shoots are the most tasty but require long soaking and cooking. Tinned are the most convenient

bambú *(It & Sp)* Bamboo

***Bambusa* spp.** Bot Bamboo

Bambusa vulgaris *Bot.* Cultivated bamboo shoots

Bambussprosse *(Ge)* Bamboo shoot

bamee *(Ma)* A thin white noodle made from wheat flour

ba mee *(Th)* Egg noodle

bami *(Ho)* A spicy dish of noodles with all or some of pork, shrimp, eggs, onions and various vegetables. Brought from Indonesia *(Dutch East Indies)*

bamieh *(ME) see* okra

bamiya *(ME) see* okra

bamya *(Tu)* A stew of minced lamb, okra, tomato, onion, green pepper, lemon juice, and herbs

bana caldo *(It)* Olive oil mixed with chopped anchovies, chopped garlic and seasoning simmered in butter for 10 minutes. Used as a dip

banaan *(Ho)* Banana

banak *(Ph)* Grey mullet

banán *(Hu)* Banana

banana *(It, Ja, Po & En)* The fruit of a giant herb genus *Musa*, (all sterile hybrids without exact species names, but sometimes named *M.sapientum)*, grown in hot climates throughout the world. The individual fruits 7 - 24 cm long grow in bunches from a central stalk and are usually picked green for transportation and ripened to yellow prior to sale. The flesh is soft and cream coloured and when underripe a source of useful low digestibility starch said to reduce the chance of bowel cancer. The skin is thick and easily removed. Dessert bananas when ripe have a sugar content of 17 to 19%. Unripe bananas and some which would never reach a high sugar content are eaten as a staple food and known as plantain. After fruiting the stem of the plant dies back and new suckers grow from the base

banana chilli A yellow and rather mild sweet chilli pepper

banana fig *(USA)* Sun dried slices of banana which are dark and sticky and resemble figs

banana flour A flour made from plantains which have been dried and ground [also called **pisang starch, plantain flour**]

banana flower The fat red to purple pointed group of male flowers which forms in the initial stages at the tip of a bunch of bananas. Used like the globe artichoke in Indian and SEA cooking

banana fritter *see* fruit fritter

banana heart The pith at the centre of the trunk of a banana plant. It is sliced and soaked in salted water for several hours and used in Burmese cooking. The sap must not be allowed to contact the clothes or body

banana leaf The leaves of bananas sometimes used as disposable table cloths or plates in Indian and SEA restaurants or as a substitute for greaseproof paper when cooking en papillote

banana pepper *(USA)* A mild yellow-green pepper up to 10 cm long used in salads and as a stuffed vegetable

banana prawn A yellowish beige variety of king prawn *Penaeus merguiensis*

banana shoot The shoots which grow from the base of the banana plant are forced by excluding light and become long thick white spikes rather like asparagus. Cooked in hot ashes or baked

banana split A longitudinally split banana filled with ice cream and finished with whipped cream and chopped nuts

banana squash A winter squash shaped like a banana

bananas Foster *(USA)* A New Orleans speciality of fried bananas, spiced, sugared, flamed with rum and served with whipped cream

banane *(Ge & Fr) fem.* Banana

banane des antilles *(Fr) fem.* Plantain [also called **banane plantain**]

banane plantain *(Fr) fem.* Plantain

bananer *(De, No & Sw)* Bananas

bananes baronnet *(Fr) fem.* Bananas served with cream and Kirsch

bananes Beauharnais *(Fr) fem.* Bananas served with sugar, rum and macaroons

Banbury cakes *(UK)* An oval-shaped Oxfordshire cake made from puff pastry filled with dried vine fruits, sugar, butter, spices, flour and rum, prior to baking, finished with an egg white and caster sugar glaze just before removing from the oven

banda *(Id)* Yam

bandal *(In)* A rich cream cheese made from cows' or buffaloes' milk

bandeng *(Id)* Bangus, or milkfish

bangers *(UK) coll.* Cooked English sausages

bangers and mash *(UK) coll.* A simple meal of fried English sausages, mashed potatoes and gravy

bangkwang *(Ma)* Yam bean

bangus A farmed round fish *Chanos chanos* and *C. Salmoneus,* which is very popular in the Phillipines and Indonesia. It grows up to 1.5 m and has a greenish grey skin and delicate flesh [also called **milkfish**]

banh hoi *(Vi)* Rice vermicelli

banh pho *(Vi)* White rice noodles about 3 mm wide. They cook very quickly and are used with the popular Hanoi soup called pho [also called **nu tieu**]

banh phong tom *(Vi)* Prawn crackers

banh trang *(Vi)* Dried thin and almost transparent pancakes made from rice flour, water and salt. Moistened to soften before use in wrapping food prior to cooking as in e.g. spring rolls

banh uot *(Vi)* Freshly made thin pancake wrappers similar to banh trang but made with a mixture of wheat, tapioca and corn flours with peanut oil, water and salt

banira *(Ja)* Vanilla

banitza susu sirene *(Bu)* A pie made of layers of pastry interlayered with a mixture of egg, cheese and yoghurt

bankebiff *(No)* Beef, browned in butter and simmered in stock

bankekød *(De)* Stewed beef

banket letter *(Ho)* Flaky pastry *(millefeuille)* cakes filled with almond paste

bannock *UK* **1** A Scottish circular scone made from barley flour, oatmeal or barley meal and cooked on a griddle. Various types are produced for breakfast and high tea **2** A Scottish biscuit resembling shortbread but containing chopped mixed peel and almonds [also called **Pithcaithley bannock**]

bannock fluke *see* turbot

banon *(Fr)* A small Provençal cream cheese sprinkled with savory, wrapped in vine leaves and presented on a slice of wood

banquet A formal meal with many courses served to a large gathering of people

bantam A small, more primitive type of domestic fowl or chicken usually with brightly coloured feathers producing small eggs

bantam eggs Eggs from the bantam fowl, sometimes used of the very small eggs first laid by chickens; *see also* pullet eggs

banteng A small cow-like animal from SEA and domesticated in Indonesia. The flesh is reputed to be very tasty

bao *(Ch)* **1** Blanching and refreshing **2** Aubergine

baobab The fruit of the African baobab tree *Adansonia digitata.* The fruit is large and pulpy [also called **monkey bread**]

bap *(UK)* A small, flat round white bread with a soft crust and generally dusted with flour

baptist cake *(USA)* A deep fried enriched yeast dough bun from New England [also called **hustlers, holy pokes, huff juffs**]

bar 1 *(Fr) masc.* Bass [also called **badèche, bézuche, cernier, loup de mer**] **2** *(En & Fr) masc.* An establishment which serves drinks and light snacks **3** A unit of pressure, 1 bar roughly equals the pressure exerted by the atmosphere

bär *(Sw)* Berry

bar clam *see* surf clam

bara brith *(UK)* A Welsh sweet bread made from a yeasted dough with caraway seeds and a high proportion of dried vine fruits. Lit. speckled bread

bara jheenga *(In)* Lobster

bara lawr *(UK)* Welsh for laver bread

baranina *(Ru)* Lamb

bárányhús *(Hu)* Lamb

báránypaprikás *(Hu)* Diced lamb fried in lard with diced lean bacon, chopped onions and paprika then all simmered with water, tomato purée, thinly sliced sweet green peppers and seasoning until cooked and finished with sour cream. Served with rice, tarhonya or dumplings

bárány pörkölt *(Hu)* Diced lamb fried in lard with chopped onions, diced bacon and paprika and all simmered in seasoned brown stock and tomato purée until cooked. Served with tarhonya

bara sem *(In)* Jack bean and sword bean

barbabietola *(It)* Beetroot

barbada *(Sp)* Brill

barbadine *(Fr) fem.* Passion fruit [also called **fruit de la passiflore**]

Barbados cherry *see* acerola

Barbados sugar *see* muscovado sugar

Barbarakraut *(Ge)* Land cress

Barbarea verna *Bot.* Land cress

Barbarea vulgaris *Bot.* Winter cress

barbary duck A fleshy, well-flavoured, slightly gamey lean duck *Cairina moschata,* with musky flavoured flesh, originally from South America but now bred in France and elsewhere and very popular in Australia. It is slaughtered at up to 3 months old and should be cooked more slowly than duckling and barded and basted [also called **muscovy duck**]

barbary pear *see* prickly pear

Barbe *(Ge)* Barbel, the fish

barbeau *(Fr) masc.* Barbel, the fish

barbecue A method of cooking food similar to grilling, generally in the open air over smouldering charcoal or some other form of radiant heat. The meats are often treated with spice mixture for examples see barbecue-, paprika-, juniper- and fennel spice mix. Alternatively the equipment used for the same. Derived from the French barbe à queue *(beard to tail)* referring to the barbecueing of the whole animal [also called **barbeque**]

barbecue sauce The general term for any spicy sauce served with barbecued food. e.g. a mixture of soya sauce, rice wine or vinegar, spring onions, garlic, chilli sauce and ground toasted sesame seeds or peanuts blended in a food processor

barbecue spice mix A medium hot blend of ground spices rubbed on to meat before grilling, made from black peppercorns, celery seeds, cayenne pepper, dried thyme, dried marjoram, paprika, mustard powder, salt and soft brown sugar

barbeel *(Ho)* Barbel, the fish

barbel The coarse European freshwater fish *Barbus barbus* related to the carp. Can grow up to 45 cm in length

barbeque *see* barbecue

Barberey *(Fr)* A soft cheese made from partially skimmed cows' milk formed into a disc (250 g), covered with wood ash and ripened for a month [also called **Troyes**]

barberon *(Fr) masc.* The Provençal name for salsify

barberry The fruit of the bush *Berberis vulgaris,* generally used for preserves if at all

barbo *(It, No, Po & Sp)* Barbel, the fish

barbot *see* eel pout

barbotine *(Fr)* Tansy

barbounia *(Gr)* Red mullet

barbue *(Fr) fem.* Brill

barbue Brancas *(Fr)* Brill baked with vegetables in a tomato sauce

Barcelona nut *see* hazelnut

barchetta *(It)* Barquette, small boat shaped tartlet

bard, to To cover meat with thin layers of fat or fatty bacon to prevent it drying out during roasting whilst other parts of the meat are cooking. Often used to protect the breast meat of birds and chicken

bardatte *(Fr)* Cabbage stuffed with hare

barde *(Fr) fem.* A layer of fat or fatty bacon used to bard meat

bardé *(Fr)* Past participle of barder, i.e. wrapped or covered in a thin solid sheet of fat or fat bacon, used in roasting to protect parts from the heat

barder *(Fr)* To bard

barfi *see* burfi

barista *(In)* Sliced onions fried until crisp. Used to finish savoury dishes

bark gor *(Ch)* Ginkgo nut

barley One of the oldest cultivated cereals *Hordeum vulgare,* with a seed of similar size to rice. Not suitable on its own for making leavened bread since it contains little gluten. Sometimes used in soups (as an addition to broth), occasionally to make a flour or meal, but predominantly either as animal feed or for conversion to malt (by sprouting) for fermentation in the beer and spirit industries; *see also* pot barley, pearl barley

barley flakes Partially cooked barley, flattened and dried. Used as one constituent of muesli, also for puddings and toppings

barley flour Ground barley used as a thickening agent, for making unleavened bread, or as a substitute for some of the wheat flour in leavened bread

barley meal Coarsely ground pot barley used to make a kind of porridge or gruel and bannocks

barley sugar A transparent, caramel-coloured and lemon-flavoured brittle sweet now made from sugar and water, originally from sugar and barley water

barley syrup *see* malt

barley water A drink made from the water in which pearl barley has been cooked. Once thought to have medicinal properties

barm *see* yeast

barm brack *(Ir)* A sweet bread made from yeasted dough mixed with dried vine fruits and chopped candied peel, possibly previously soaked in tea to rehydrate, and caraway seeds, popular at Christmas and Hallowe'en

barm cake *(UK)* A soft bread roll in the shape of a circle often split and filled for use as a sandwich

Bärme *(Ge)* Yeast *(North Germany)*

barnacle A cylindrical stalk-like crustacean *Pollicipes cornucopia,* up to 15 cm long which is found on sea-washed rocks around the Atlantic coast. The foot with which it attaches itself to the rock and the tough papery skin covered in small scales are discarded. May be eaten raw or cooked. Popular in Spain and Portugal [also called **goose barnacle, goose-necked barnacle**]

barnacle goose *see* Brent goose

Barnstaple fair pears *(UK)* Large Comice pears, peeled with the stalk on, piquéed with blanched halved almonds, poached in red wine with sugar and cloves for 15 minutes and served with the strained reduced cooking liquor and clotted cream.

barnyard millet A type of millet *Echinochloa crusgalli,* grown mainly as a fodder crop in the east and now an escaped wild plant in the UK and the USA

baron d'agneau *(Fr) masc.* Fillet end (top half) of a leg of lamb used for roasting

baron of beef *(UK)* A large beef joint consisting of two sirloins, connected by the backbone. Roasted for celebratory occasions

barquette *(Fr) fem.* **1** Small boat shaped tartlet **2** The small tin in which a barquette is baked

barquillo *(Sp)* Wafer

barracouta *see* snoek

barracuda A group of slender round bodied ferocious seawater game fish *Sphyraena* spp. found in warm water worldwide. They are generally eaten at around 2.5 kg and have lean firm flesh. Very large Caribbean barracudas over 1 m long have poisonous flesh which causes joint pains, trembling and vomiting

barramunda *(Aus)* Freshwater river fish of various types [also called **lungfish**]

barrel 1 A wooden cask with specially shaped wooden staves forming the sides which are held together with iron hoops which when knocked down from either end compress all the staves together to make the sides watertight. Used for wine, beer, salted herrings, olives and the like **2** A liquid measure equivalent to 159 litres, 42 US gallons or 35 imperial gallons

barrel bread A cylindrical loaf baked in a ridged tin so that it can easily be cut into uniform slices [also called **crinkled musket, landlady's loaf, lodger's loaf, pistol, piston, rasp**]

barrinaire *(It)* Sand eel

barrogog bis basela *(NA)* A lamb stew with prunes

Barsch *(Ge)* Perch or bass

barszcz *(Pl)* A Polish version of borscht made from fermented sour beet juice, traditionally served on Easter day

barszcz zimny *(Pl)* Cold soup made from the juice of pickled beetroot and cucumbers, thickened with semolina, finished with egg yolks and sour cream, seasoned, chilled and served with slices of hard boiled egg

barya a jagnjetinom *(Bk)* A lamb and okra casserole from Serbia

barzotte *(It)* Soft boiled, as of eggs

bas de carré *(Fr) masc.* The top part of the shoulder of veal equivalent to scrag end of lamb

base 1 The chemical term for a substance which reacts with an acid to form a salt **2** The major component of a dish which is the main determinant of its properties as e.g. stock is the base of soups and sauces [also called **fond** (Fr)]

Basella alba *Bot.* Ceylon spinach

bashan *(ME)* A smoked cheese from Israel made with ewes' and goats' milk. The rind is a glossy red and the paste has a sharp flavour

bashit *(UK) coll. (Scotland)* Mashed, as in bashit neeps

basic cake mixture Flour, butter, castor sugar and eggs in the proportions by weight of 8:5:5:5 with 1 level teaspoon of baking powder per 8 oz of flour (16 g per kg flour)

basic soup A mirepoix of onions, leek and celery plus twice the quantity of the vegetable after which the soup is named, sweated in butter, flour added and cooked out without colour, a BG and white stock added, simmered and skimmed for 1 hour, BG removed, liquidized, seasoned and consistency adjusted, creamed if required *(see cream soup)* and garnished as appropriate

basil A tender annual herb *Ocimum basilicum* with an aromatic flavour reminiscent of mint and cloves used in salads, pesto and Italian cooking, and added at the last minute to cooked dishes [also called **sweet basil**]; *see also* bush basil, holy basil, lemon basil, hairy basil, purple basil, kermangi

basilic *(Fr) masc.* Basil

basilico *(It)* Basil

Basilienkraut *(Ge)* Basil

basin A wide flattish dish

basket A steel mesh (about 8 to 12 mm pitch) utensil with a handle which fits in a deep fat fryer and is used to lower damp foods, esp. potato chips into the fat slowly so that the boiling off of the water does not cause the fat or oil to boil over or for blanching vegetables in boiling water

Basler Leckerli *(He)* A Christmas biscuit

containing candied peel, almonds, honey, hazelnuts, cinnamon and kirsch baked in relief-carved wooden moulds depicting traditional scenes; *see also* Tirggel, Züritirggel

basmati rice A dense thin long grain rice with an aromatic and nutty flavour, more expensive than American long grain rice, used in Indian cooking for biryani and pilau. Best boiled without salt for about 10 minutes, or in lots of boiling water for 8 minutes then drained, covered and finished on a very low heat for a further 10 minutes. The name means fragrant and the rice is grown in the foothills of the Himalayas

basquaise, à la *(Fr)* In the Basque manner, i.e. with ham, tomatoes and red peppers

bass A prized silvery grey round non-oily fish *Dicentrarchus labrax* up to 1 m in length which lives in saltwater lakes, estuaries and around some European coasts. The flesh is white and is cooked in any way [also called **salmon dace, salmon bass, common bass**]

bassia fat *(In) see* mowra butter

bastani *(Pe)* Ice cream

bastard saffron *see* safflower

baste to To spoon melted fat over food during cooking either to prevent drying out or to aid heat transfer

bastilla *(NA)* Layers of crisp fried warkha pastry interleaved in the savoury version with pigeon meat, chicken or fish, almonds, spices and lemon-flavoured eggs, or in the sweet version with a milky almond sauce to make a kind of pie. Both types are liberally dusted with icing sugar [also called **b'stilla, pastilla, bisteeya**]

bastoncini *(It)* Small stick shaped biscuits

bat out, to To flatten pieces of raw meat with a cutlet bat and thus reduce cooking time

batagur *(Ma)* A species of turtle now endangered due to excessive exploitation. Even though local consumption is forbidden by the Muslim religion they have been exported in quantity

batakh *(In)* Duck

batangas *(Ph)* Ponkan mandarin

bâtarde, sauce *(Fr) fem.* Salted water thickened with a white roux then reheated with a liaison of egg yolks and cream and a little lemon juice, strained and about 30% of its weight in butter added just before service. Served with asparagus or poached fish [also called **sauce au beurre** (Fr)]

batata 1 *(Po)* Potato, usually firm waxy types **2** *(Sp)* Sweet potato

batata frita *(Po)* Potato chips

Batate *(Ge)* Sweet potato

batavia *(Fr) fem.* Batavian endive [also called **scarole**]. Also used for curly lettuce, e.g. Webb's

batavian endive A variety of winter endive *Cichorium endivia* with larger flatter leaves than true endive. Used as a salad green [also called **plain leaved escarole**]

batch loaf *(UK)* A loaf which has been baked close to others on a tray so that the dough touches and partially joins. After baking they are split apart to reveal soft sides

batelière, à la *(Fr)* In the boatman's style, i.e. garnished with some or all of fried eggs, mushrooms, button onions, and crayfish, or, with small pastry shells with a rich fish filling

Bath bun *(UK)* A sweet, yeast-raised bun containing mixed peel and sultanas originating in Bath, Wiltshire, egg-washed and topped with coarse white sugar crystals before baking.

Bath chap *see* pig's cheek

Bath Oliver A plain flat biscuit invented by Dr Oliver of Bath in the 1700's, at that time supposed to have slimming properties

batir *(Sp)* To whip or whisk

bâton 1 *(En & Fr) masc.* A long baguette type French loaf or bread roll tapering at either end and baked on a flat tray **2** A type of cut for root vegetables roughly 6mm x 6mm x 25mm

bâtons royaux *(Fr) masc.* Small patties of minced chicken and game

batsoa *(It) see* piedini de maiale alla piemontese

Battelmatt *(He, It & Au)* A soft cooked-curd cheese made from cows' milk with a springy tender texture and delicate taste and numerous small holes. The curd is pressed in variously sized cylindrical moulds, salted in brine or dry salt and ripened for 3 to 4 months

Battenberg A rectangular long oblong sponge made in two different colours arranged lengthwise in a 2x2 checkerboard pattern and covered all round with a marzipan coating

batter 1 A basic mixture of flour, milk and eggs with possible added flavourings, either pouring consistency for pancakes, drop scones, Yorkshire pudding, etc. or coating (i.e. more viscous) consistency for fritters, cromeskis, bhajis, etc. From the French battre, to beat **2** *(USA)* A general term used in North America for any soft mixture made from flour including cake and scone mixes, etc. as well as batter proper

batter, to To coat with batter

batter bread *(USA)* An unsweetened bread or pudding made with white cornmeal from dent corn raised with well beaten eggs. From the southern states [also called **spoon bread**]

batter dip *(USA)* Frying batter

battre *(Fr)* To whip, esp. eggs

battuto *(It)* A mixture of chopped onion, garlic, celery and herbs, sweated in oil and used as a base or flavouring ingredient for soups and stews

batu giling *(Id)* A granite slab and rolling pin used for grinding spices or crushing flavourings such as ginger, onions, garlic, chillis, etc. [also called **batu lesong**]

batu lesong *(Id & Ma) see* batu giling

bau dau gok *(Ch)* A light coloured variety of long bean

baudroie *(Fr) fem.* Monkfish [also called **lotte de mer, diable du mer**]

bauern *(Ge)* Country style

Bauernbratwurst *(He)* A country style scalded sausage made for grilling or frying

Bauernbrot *(Ge)* Peasant bread, rye bread

Bauernfrühstuck *(Ge)* Fried potatoes topped with scrambled eggs, ham and cucumber. Served at lunch. Lit. country breakfast

Bauernomelett *(Ge)* A bacon and onion filled omelette

Bauernschmaus *(Au)* A dish of sauerkraut, pork sausages and dumplings

Bauernsuppe *(Ge)* A country soup of beans, bacon and vegetables

bauletti *(It)* Paupiettes of veal

Baumé scale A complicated scale of density originally based on brine and equivalent to the percentage by weight of salt in a salt and water solution at 15.5°C. Also used for sugar syrups but this has no simple relationship to sugar concentration. Written °B or °Bé. The relationship between °Bé and specific gravity is °Bé = 145 - (145/specific gravity), e.g. a 50% sugar solution, specific gravity 1.23, is 27°Bé

Baumkuchen *(Ge)* A Christmas cake shaped like a tree and iced with chocolate to resemble bark

Baumwollöl *(Ge)* Cottonseed oil

baunilha *(Po)* Vanilla

Bavarian cream *see* bavarois

Bavarian sausage Very well trimmed lean pork and veal, finely minced with back fat, shallots and garlic, mixed with a little coriander, sugar, seasoning and saltpetre, packed in sheep casings, linked, air dried and smoked until golden brown

bavarois *(Fr) masc.* A dessert made from either a vanilla-flavoured egg custard or a fruit purée let down with sugar syrup both containing gelatine, combined when beginning to thicken, with whipped cream and sugar. Cooled in a mould which is either oiled or lined with caramel, demoulded when fully set and decorated if required [also called **crème bavaroise, Bavarian cream**]

bavarois au marasquin *(Fr) masc.* A cherry-flavoured bavarois

bavaroise *(Fr) fem.* Not to be confused with bavarois, a hot drink made with milk, tea, eggs and sugar, flavoured with vanilla or liqueur

bavaroise, sauce *(En & Fr) fem.* Hollandaise sauce flavoured with grated horseradish

bavette 1 *(Fr) fem.* Flank or skirt of beef **2** *(It)* Long thin strips of pasta noodles with an oval cross section, available fresh or dried

baveuse *(Fr) adj.* Moist or runny, the French term used to describe the just runny top of an omelette which becomes the interior when it is folded

bavosa *(It)* Soft in the centre, as of omelettes and frittatas; *see also* baveuse

bavose *(It)* Blenny, the fish

bawal puteh *(Ma)* White pomfret, the fish

bawal putih *(Id)* Pomfret, the fish

bawang bakung *(Ma)* Asian leek

bawang besar *(Ma)* Onion

bawang bombay *(Id)* Onion

bawang daun *(Id & Ma)* Spring onion

bawang merah *(Id & Ma)* Shallots

bawang putih *(Id & Ma)* Garlic

bawd *(UK) coll. (Scotland)* Hare, rabbit

ba-wel *(Bm)* Squid

bay An evergreen laurel-like shrub *Laurus nobilis* whose fresh or dried leaves are used for flavouring, esp. in a BG, marinades, Béchamel sauce, milk puddings and fish [also called **sweet bay, laurel**]

bay boletus An edible mushroom *Boletus badius* with a 5 to 15 cm dia. smooth brown cap and a short slender stem and with pores rather than gills under the cap. It grows profusely under spruce and pine trees and occasionally on the wood or pine cones

bay bug *see* sand lobster

bay lobster *see* sand lobster

bay salt Salt produced by the natural solar evaporation of seawater. usually in large crystals to 5 mm; *see also* sea salt

bay scallop A small bivalve scallop *Argopecten irradians* up to 7.5 cm dia. with an off-white to black shell. Found off the east coast of North America. It has a very delicate flavour and can be eaten raw when fresh

bayam *(Id & Ma)* Amaranth

Bayerische Leberknödel *(Ge)* Liver dumplings made with raw chopped calves' liver, sieved and mixed with egg, chopped bacon fat, onions, fried bread crumbs, seasoning and flour to stiffen, formed into tangerine sized dumplings, poached and served with beurre noisette and sauerkraut

bayonnaise, à la *(Fr)* In the style of Bayonne, i.e. containing Bayonne ham

Bayonne ham *(Fr)* A dry cured lightly smoked ham similar to Parma and eaten raw

bazilik *(Ru)* Basil

BBB *see* bleu-blanc Belge

beadlet A sea anemone q.v. *Actinia equina,* eaten in France, generally brown to green in colour but occasionally red. [also called **tomate de mer** (Fr)]

bean A leguminous plant characterized by a long pod containing a string of separated seeds. Both the young immature pods and seeds and fresh or dried mature seeds are used for a variety of culinary purposes. The principal vegetable varieties in Europe and north America are broad, dwarf French, climbing French and runner, but many others e.g. mung, soya, lima, etc. are in widespread use

bean clam A small American clam *Donax* spp. similar to the wedge shell clam

bean curd A rather flavourless, textureless but nutritious coagulated soya bean protein made by treating boiled soya milk with various coagulants such as nigari (flaked sea salt), Epsom salts, vinegar, etc. and separating off the curd as for cheese. It can be soft and jelly-like or have the water content progressively reduced to form finally a cheese-like substance. It may be boiled, fried, etc. and is a most important source of first class protein, minerals and vitamins in Chinese and Japanese cuisine and for vegans [also called **tofu, soya bean curd, bean custard, soya bean cake**]

bean curd brains A cream coloured lightly coagulated bean curd which has a soft lumpy appearance

bean curd cheese Bean curd fermented with brine or rice wine and spices and mixed with red food colouring and sometimes cereal extenders. It has a strong cheesy flavour and is served as a side dish or condiment, or used as flavouring [also called **Chinese cheese, pickled bean curd, red bean curd, soya bean cheese, fermented bean curd**]

bean curd noodles Thin strips of dried bean curd used in the same way as noodles but not normally fried after boiling. More nutritious than starch based noodles [also called **soya noodles, soya vermicelli**]

bean curd sheets *see* bean curd skin

bean curd skin The skin which forms on the surface of hot soya bean milk if allowed to stand. It is lifted off and dried. When softened it is used for wrapping food prior to cooking [also called **bean curd sheets**]

bean curd sticks Bean curd skins rolled into stick-like quills before drying. After softening they are cut in pieces and used in cooked dishes as is or after deep frying [also called **rolled bean curd, second bamboo**]

bean paste A variety of seasonings made from yellow or black dried soya beans, softened, fermented with an added culture, salted and dried or mixed with brine. Sometimes other grains or pulses are added. They keep well, are strongly flavoured and are used in Japanese, Chinese and SEA cuisines. The important ones are yellow bean sauce, black bean sauce, chilli bean paste, Hoisin sauce, hot black bean sauce, Dhwen-jang, soya bean paste, sweet bean paste and miso

bean sauce A bean paste let down with brine or oil to give a softer consistency

bean sprouts The young shoots of the mung bean *Phaseolus aureus* or adzuki bean, used as a vegetable in Chinese and Japanese cooking. Other seeds that may be sprouted include soya beans, lentils, wheat, rye, mustard seed and cress [also called **green gram, moyashi, tu ya ts'ai**]

bean thread noodles *see* cellophane noodles

bean threads *(USA)* Cellophane noodles

bear **1** A large omnivorous animal *Ursidae* family. Black bears and polar bears are confined to the Northern Hemisphere and brown bears are found worldwide. The meat which tastes like strong flavoured beef is very rare as the species is becoming endangered **2** *see* bere

bear grass *(USA) see* yucca (2)

bearberry The red fruit of a plant from northern moors *Arctostaphylos uva-ursi* similar to the cranberry and picked from the wild

beard The gills of an oyster or the fibrous threads by which mussels attach themselves to rocks

beard, to To remove the frilly gill parts or beards of certain shellfish such as oysters and the threads from mussels which attach them to the rocks

béarnaise, sauce *(En & Fr) fem.* As Hollandaise sauce but with chopped tarragon stalks in the initial reduction and finished after straining with chopped tarragon and chervil. More egg yolks are used than for Hollandaise to give a thicker sauce. Served warm with grilled meat and fish

béarnaise tomatée, sauce *(Fr) fem. see* sauce choron

bearnässås *(Sw)* Béarnaise sauce

bearss lime *see* Persian lime

beastlyns *see* beestings

beat, to To incorporate air into a mixture and to intimately combine the ingredients by vigorous agitation with a spoon, whisk, fork or mechanical or electric mixer

beater A general term for any implement used for beating

Beaufort *(Fr)* A hard cooked-curd cows' milk cheese from Haute Savoie with AOC status. It is ripened for 3 months and has a firm springy paste with a thin rind. It is similar to Gruyère but with higher fat content and fruitier aroma [also called **Gruyère de Beaufort**]

Beaumont *(Fr)* A semi-hard cheese made with cows' milk in the Haute Savoie using the same techniques as Toma. It has a springy texture without holes and is cast in 20 cm dia. thin rounds

bebek *(Id)* Duck

becado *(Sp)* Woodcock

bécasse *(Fr) fem.* Woodcock

becasseau *(Fr) masc.* Young woodcock

bécassine *(Fr) fem.* Snipe

beccaccia *(It)* Woodcock

beccaccia alla norcina *(It)* Woodcock stuffed with a mixture of its entrails, herbs and truffle

beccacino *(It)* Snipe

beccafico *(It)* Game bird

beccute *(It)* Maize flour cakes containing pine nuts and sultanas.

bêche-de-mer *(Fr) fem.* Sea cucumber. Lit. spade of the sea

béchamel, sauce *(En & Fr) fem.* A basic white sauce made from a white roux and seasoned milk flavoured with an onion clouté using 100g of flour per litre. The onion is removed and the sauce strained after simmering for at least 30 minutes. A very important base and often referred to simply as béchamel

beckasin *(Sw)* Snipe

bécsi heringsaláta *(Hu)* Herring salad with vinegar

Beda *(Ey)* A soft scalded-curd cheese made from buffalos' or cows' milk. The unbroken salted curd is drained in cheese cloth and may be eaten fresh or ripened for up to 3 months. Contains 53% water, 21% fat and 19% protein [also called **Domiati**]

bedeu *(Fr)* The Provençal word for tripe

bee balm *see* bergamot

beech nut A small nut from the beech tree *Fagus* and *Nothofagus* spp. similar in flavour to a hazel nut but not commonly used. A flavoursome oil can be extracted from them [also called **beechmast**]

beechmast *see* beech nut

beechwheat *see* buckwheat

beef The meat of the animal known as cattle *(pl.)*, cow *(fem.)*, bull (entire male), bullock (young bull), steer (castrated male 2 to 4 years old). The animal has no generic name in the English language. The Anglosaxon ox is still used for some of what were once the less desirable parts e.g. ox tail, ox liver

beef bourguignonne *see* boeuf bourguignonne

beef cervelat *(UK)* A variety of smoked red dyed sausages made with lean beef, possibly bullock heart, fat pork, seasoning and a little saltpetre, sometimes with ground spices. The mixture is left to cure then sometimes packed in beef middles, tied and smoked for 12 hours at 50°C, or, dried for eight days and cool smoked for 6 days

beef cotto *(USA)* A low fat coarse cut beef salami containing whole peppercorns

beef dripping The fat collected after roasting beef or rendered from beef suet. A less flavoursome variety is made by boiling up beef scraps and separating off the fat which collects on the surface

beef hare *(UK)* Strips of chuck steak passed through seasoned flour flavoured with nutmeg, packed in an ovenproof dish with celery seeds, topped with onion and parsnip, moistened with red wine, stood for 2 hours and baked with a tight fitting lid at 170°C until tender

beef herbs The principal herbs used with beef are basil, bay, caraway, chervil, lovage, marjoram, mint, oregano, parsley, peppermint, rosemary, sage, savory, tarragon and thyme

beef middles Beef casings for salami, knackwurst, cervelat and similar sausages about 4.5 to 5.5 cm dia. taken from the middle of the beef intestine

beef olive A thin slice of topside of beef rolled around a savoury stuffing, tied and braised in the oven

beef runners Beef casings for black puddings, Bolognese sausage, etc. about 3.5 to 4.5 cm in dia., made from the first part of the beef intestine

beef sausage *(UK)* A Scottish sausage of lean beef, bullock heart, suet, chopped onions and seasoning chopped very fine (cheaper varieties adulterated with bread and meal) packed into pig casings and possibly smoked.

beef Stroganoff Strips of fillet steak or other tender cut of beef, shallow fried in butter and mixed with sweated chopped shallots, reduced white wine, cream, lemon juice and seasoning, possibly finished with soured cream

beef suet The hard granular fat interspersed with membranes from around the kidneys of cattle

beef tea A clear consommé of beef

beef tenderloin *(USA)* Fillet of beef

beef tomato A very large fleshy tomato up to 10 cm in dia. often stuffed as an individual dish

beef Wellington A part roasted fillet of beef spread with a duxelle and liver pâté, wrapped in puff pastry, egg washed and baked in the oven. The meat and pastry should finish cooking simultaneously. Served sliced

beefburger A mixture of lean minced beef, chopped onions and seasoning formed into a thin patty. Usually grilled and served as fast food on a soft white bread bun with a variety of garnishes [also called **hamburger**]

beefsteak *(USA)* Steak, as in beefsteak and kidney pie

beefsteak fungus *(UK)* A bright red edible fungus *Fistulina hepatica* shaped rather like a thick tongue which grows on trees. Treat as mushroom [also called **poor man's beefsteak**]

beefsteak plant *see* shiso

beefsteak tagalog *(Ph)* Trimmed rump steaks marinated with sliced onion, soya sauce, lime juice and pepper for 2 hours, removed, dried, fried in oil with sliced onion and bacon and served with a sauce made from the deglazed pan juices and the marinade accompanied by garlic-flavoured rice

Beenleigh blue *(UK)* A ewe's milk cheese made in Devon similar to Roquefort

beer Fermented malt extract flavoured with hops, sometimes used as a cooking liquor

beer sausage *see* Bierwurst

bees sting *see* Bienenstich

beesting pudding Colostrum from the cow and sugar baked slowly in the oven

beestings The first milk *(colostrum)* from the cow after giving birth. It is very rich and creamy and is used for puddings and sweets. (Also frozen to preserve it for use as a restorative for newly born lambs)

beestings curd A curd made by mixing cow's colostrum with fresh milk and water, heating to 37°C, cooking and straining

beeswax (E)901, the wax excreted by bees to construct honeycomb. Used as a glazing agent in sugar and chocolate confectionery

beet 1 The generic name for members of the *Beta* family including beetroot, Swiss chard, spinach beet and sugar beet, which latter is the main source of sugar in Europe **2** *(USA)* Beetroot

beet sugar Sugar produced from sugar beet. Chemically it is identical to cane sugar *(sucrose)*

Beetensuppe *(Ge)* Borsch

beetroot A biennial plant *Beta vulgaris* subsp. *vulgaris,* grown as an annual for the swollen root which grows at ground level. Most are deep red but there are pink and yellow varieties. The roots contain a high proportion of sugar and as the red colour easily leaches out they are boiled in their skins as a vegetable. They are also used for soup *(Borsch)* and pickled in vinegar. The young leaves may be used as a vegetable

beetroot consommé Grated beetroot, onion and carrot simmered with a bay leaf and chicken stock for 40 minutes, strained, simmered with egg white for 15 minutes to clarify, strained and finished with lemon juice and sour cream

beetroot red E162, a red food colouring extracted from beetroot [also called **betanin**]

beetroot soup Shredded beetroot and onion sweated in butter, flour added and cooked out, stock added, simmered and skimmed for 30 minutes, seasoned, consistency adjusted and finished with lemon juice and cream or sour cream

beetwortel *(Ho)* Beetroot

bef stroganov *(Ru)* Beef Stroganoff traditionally made with sliced onions sweated for at least 30 minutes with sliced mushrooms added towards the end, combined in the pan with sautéed strips of fillet steak, English mustard, sugar and sour cream, all warmed through and served with straw potatoes and chopped parsley

begendi *(Tu)* A smooth paste made from a

mixture of thick Béchamel and a purée of cooked aubergine flesh. Used as a starter

begiessen *(Ge)* To baste or sprinkle with liquid

beid hamine *(ME)* Hard boiled eggs, the shells coloured with onion skins or ground coffee. They are simmered for 5 to 6 hours in water with the colourant and are served as an appetizer with salt and ground cumin

beid mahshi *(ME)* Hard boiled eggs, halved lengthways, yolks mashed with finely chopped onion and parsley, olive oil, cinnamon and seasoning, made into balls and replaced in the egg whites, laid on lettuce leaves, sprinkled with paprika or chilli powder, dressed with vinaigrette or yoghurt sauce and garnished with chopped parsley

beigel *see* bagel

beignet *(Fr) masc.* **1** Fritter, a food item coated in batter and deep fried [also called **French fritter**] **2** A ball of yeast-raised sweetened dough or flavoured choux pastry, deep fried and served hot with a dusting of sugar and possibly jam or fruit sauce. Rather like a doughnut [also called **French puff**]

beignet de fleurs *(Fr) masc.* Flower fritters, see e.g. acacia flower fritters

beignet soufflé *(Fr) masc. see* pet-de-nonne

Beijing cabbage *see* Chinese leaves

Beijing duck *see* Peking duck

beijing kao ya *(Ch)* Peking duck

Beijing pear *see* Asian pear

Beilagen *(Ge)* Accompaniments to a meal

Bein *(Ge)* Leg; of an animal, etc.

Beinfleisch *(Au)* Boiled beef

Beja *(Po)* A ewes' milk cheese from the Alentajo weighing about 2 kg. It can be eaten fresh or after ripening into a semi-hard cheese for from 1 to 2 years

bejel *(Sp)* Tub gurnard

Bekassine *(Ge)* Snipe

bekon *(Ja & Ru)* Bacon

bekutak *(Id)* Cuttlefish

bel *(Ne)* Wood apple

Bel Paese *(It)* A rich, mild, quick-ripened creamy cheese made on an industrial scale since 1906 from whole cows' milk, weighing about 2.5 kg and coated with a yellow wax rind. Lit. beautiful country

beladi *(ME)* The common orange

belan *(In)* Rolling pin

belangah *(Ma)* A terracotta cooking pot similar to an Indian chatty [also called **blangah**]

belarno *(It)* A hard, rich cheese

belegte Brote *(Ge)* An open sandwich on rye bread

Belfast ham *(UK)* A dry salted ham smoked over peat. Also found on the West coast of Scotland

Belfermière *(Lu)* A semi-hard cows' milk cheese cast in squat cylinders *(1.8 kg)*. Similar to Port-Salut

Belgian chicory A perennial dandelion-like plant *Cichorium intybus* with bitter green leaves. The conical roots are trimmed and have the leaves cut off 2 cm above the crown and are then forced to produce white, yellow tipped, compact, leafy shoots up to 15 cm long by 5 cm dia, known as chicons, which are in season from January to March. They can be cooked as a vegetable or eaten raw in salads. The roots have been used as a coffee substitute and when young can be boiled as a root vegetable. The flowers and seedlings of the unforced plant can be used in salads [also called **Witloof chicory, succory, Belgian endive** (USA), **endive** (Fr)]

Belgium endive *(USA) see* Belgian chicory

beliashi *(Ru)* A shallow fried pastry made with a wheat flour unleavened dough containing a variety of fillings

belimbing *(Ma)* The fruit of a relative of the carambola *Averrhoa bilimbi,* about 8 cm long, light green and acidic. Used for souring food [also called **sour finger carambola, cucumber tree fruit**]

belimbing manis *(Id)* Carambola

belimbing wuluh *(Id)* Belimbing, the fruit

belinjo *(Id) see* melinjo

bell pepper *(USA)* Sweet pepper

belle dijonnaise, à la *(Fr)* With blackcurrants

Belle-Hélène *(Fr)* Description of fruit served with ice cream and chocolate sauce as in pear Belle-Hélène

belle meunière, fish Fish meunière dressed with one grilled mushroom, one slice of peeled tomato and one floured and shallow fried soft herring roe

Bellelay *(Fr) see* Tête de Moine

bellevue, à la *(Fr)* In full view, i.e. a

description of food, decorated or not, but coated in transparent aspic jelly

Bellos *(Sp)* A hard cheese made from ewes' and/or goats' milk with a strong pungent close-textured paste and a dry rind. Usually cast in smallish cylinders (700 g). Contains 27% water, 36% fat and 27% protein [also called **Queso de Los Bellos, Bellusco**]

Bellusco *(Sp) see* Bellos

belly fat Soft fat from the belly of a pig with specific uses in sausage, pâté and pastry making

belly of pork *see* pork belly

belly pork *see* pork belly

belon *(Fr) masc. or fem.* A particular size of oyster from Brittany

beluga caviar *(Ru)* The light grey caviar from the roe of the female beluga, the largest of the sturgeon family. Usually served as a hors d'oeuvre

beluga sturgeon One of the largest fish *Acipenser huso or Huso huso* in the sturgeon family from the Black Sea, the Caspian Sea and the rivers that flow into them. It can live up to 100 years and weigh up to 1600 kg but is normally caught much younger and produces up to 20 kg of caviar of the same name. It should not be confused with the beluga whale

beluge *(Pe)* Beluga caviar

Belval *(Fr)* A firm mild cheese from Picardy with a shiny rind

belyashi *(Ru)* A deep fried meat pasty

bem passado *(Po)* Well done, e.g. of meat

ben cotta *(It)* Well done, as of steaks

ben tree *see* drumstick pod

benfri gädda *(Sw)* Boneless pike. A whole pike, head on, cleaned but not scaled, boiled in salted water then allowed to cool before gently easing the flesh from the skin and bones. The flesh is ideal for filling vol-au-vents when combined with a Béchamel and/or velouté sauce. Often served with an egg or horseradish sauce

Bengal gram *(In) see* channa (1)

Bengal rice A small-grain white rice with a fine flavour from Bengal in the east of India

Benicasa hispida *Bot.* Fuzzy melon

beni-shoga *(Ja)* Red coloured wafer thin slices of pickled ginger rhizome used as an accompaniment to Japanese dishes esp. sushi [also called **gari, amazu shoga**]

benløse fugler *(No)* Beef olives *(paupiettes)* stuffed with pork and onion and served with a spiced gravy

benne seed Sesame seed

benoil tree *see* drumstick pod

benoiton, à la *(Fr)* Fish served with a reduced red wine sauce flavoured with shallots

bento box *(Ja)* The partitioned lacquered lunch box used by Japanese office workers to hold their midday meal

bentonite *see* (E)558

bentoo no tomo *(Ja)* A seasoning made from a mixture of dried fish, salt, soya sauce, seaweed and MSG pounded or processed to a paste

benzoates Salts of benzoic acid used as food preservatives, those used in the food industry are, sodium E211, potassium E212 and calcium benzoate E213

benzoic acid A naturally occurring acid found in most berries and in large concentrations in gum benzoin, now made synthetically for use as the food preservative E210

berawecka *(Fr)* A spiced bread roll from Alsace containing dried vine fruits and flavoured with Kirsch [also called **bireweck**]

berbere A ground spice mix from Ethiopia used in stews and in panés. Made from dry fried deseeded red chillis, coriander seeds, cloves, green cardamom, ajowan, allspice, black peppercorns, fenugreek seeds, cinnamon and dry ginger

berberecho *(Sp)* Cockle

Berberis vulgaris *Bot.* Barberry

berbigão *(Po)* Cockle or mussel

Bercy *(Fr)* With sauce Bercy or beurre Bercy

Bercy butter *see* beurre Bercy

Bercy, fish White fish, shallow poached in fish stock, white wine, lemon juice, chopped parsley and sweated chopped shallots. The cooking liquor is strained, mixed with fish velouté. seasoned, consistency adjusted, finished with butter, lightly whipped cream and a sabayon. The reserved and dried fish is coated with this sauce, glazed under the grill and garnished with chopped parsley, e.g. filets de sole bercy

Bercy, sauce *(En & Fr) fem.* Chopped shallots sweated in butter, white wine and fish stock added and reduced, fish velouté added, seasoning and consistency adjusted and the sauce finished with butter and chopped parsley

bere A type of primitive barley first recorded in 4000 BC, still grown in the Orkneys and said to be an acquired taste [also called **bear**]

bere bannock *(UK)* A brown round scone-like cake made in the Orkneys with the flour ground from bere

berenjena *(Sp)* Aubergine

Beresford pudding *(UK)* A steamed pudding made from a Victoria sponge mixture flavoured with grated orange zest

Berg *(Ge)* A hard, pale yellow mountain cheese made from full fat cow's milk resembling Emmental but cast in smaller rounds [also called **Alp cheese, Alpenkäse, Alpine cheese, mountain cheese**]

Bergader *(Ge)* A soft blue-green veined cows' milk cheese with a cracked but smooth strong flavoured paste and a wrinkled light brown rind

bergamot **1** A citrus hybrid probably of Seville orange and sweet lime *Citrus bergamia* used only for its highly perfumed rind oil which amongst other uses is sprayed on tea to produce Earl Grey **2** A perennial lemon-scented herb *Monarda didyma* used in salads, summer drinks and with pork [also called **bee balm**]

bergère, à la *(Fr)* In the style of the shepherdess, i.e. garnished with fried sliced mushrooms and straw potatoes

Bergkäse A generic name for many different typed of cooked-curd, pressed semi-hard cows' milk cheeses from the Alps such as Berg, Gruyère, Fontina, Montasio, Walliser and the like [also called **mountain cheese**]

Bergues *(Fr)* A soft cows' milk cheese similar to Saint-Paulin made near Dunkirk. It has a dense supple paste with a thin washed rind covered in blue-black mould and is cast in thin rounds (2 kg)

berinjela *(Po)* Aubergine

Berliner *(Ge)* A jam filled doughnut from Berlin. Made famous by President Kennedy who when visiting Berlin and speaking near the Berlin wall said 'Ich bin ein Berliner' He should have said 'Ich bin Berliner' or 'Ich komme aus Berlin'

Berliner Hühnerfrikasse *(Ge)* Diced chicken flesh, diced calf's tongue, sweetbreads, prawns, sliced asparagus and diced mushrooms (8:2:2:2:2:1), all previously cooked mixed with a chicken velouté with added egg yolks (2 per litre) and lemon juice, heated to boiling and served. The velouté is normally made with the chicken cooking liquor

Berliner Luft *(Ge)* A light mousse of egg yolks, creamed with sugar and lemon juice, flavoured with lemon zest, mixed with softened gelatine leaves and strained, stiffly beaten egg whites folded in, all placed in a mould to set, demoulded and served with a border of raspberry syrup

Berliner Pfannküchen *(Ge)* A thick puffy pancake with jam

Berliner Riesen Bratwurst *(Ge)* A very large bratwurst

Berliner Rotwurst *(Ge)* A type of black pudding made with pig's blood, coarsely chopped meat and diced bacon with salt and black pepper, coloured dark red

Berliner Torte *(Ge)* Short pastry flavoured with cinnamon and lemon zest, mixed with finely chopped hazelnuts and baked in 4 circles which are filled when cool with 3 layers of red currant jelly and covered with vanilla-flavoured fondant

berlingozzo *(It)* Cream cake

Bermuda onion *(USA)* Spanish onion

bernard-l'ermite *(Fr) masc. see* hermit crab

bernard-l'hermite *(Fr) masc. see* hermit crab

Berner Platte *(He)* A dish of smoked pork ribs, beef, tongue or sausage, lean bacon, ham, salted tongue and roasted marrow bone arranged on a bed of sauerkraut or beans

berrichonne, à la *(Fr)* With a garnish of cabbage, bacon, onions and chestnuts for large joints of meat

berro *(Sp)* Watercress

berry A small fruit with pulpy flesh enclosing one or more seeds or an assembly of small sacs of juice each enclosing one seed within it or on its surface

berry sugar *(USA)* Sugar finer than granulated similar to caster sugar

Bertholletia excelsa *Bot.* Brazil nut tree

bertorella *(Sp)* Three-bearded rockling, the fish

berza *(Sp)* A pork stew made with chopped aromatic vegetables and garlic browned in olive oil, 5 cm cubes of floured and browned pork, soaked haricot beans and chick peas and stock added and all simmered until almost cooked, French beans and sliced roasted sweet red peppers added and cooked 15 minutes followed by sliced black pudding and seasoning for a further 10 minutes

berza marina *(Sp)* Sea kale

besan *(In)* Ground chick pea flour, more aromatic and less starchy than wheat flour, excellent for batter and for coating fish. Used extensively in Indian cookery [also called **besan flour, gram flour, bessan**]

besan flour *see* besan

beschuit *(Ho)* A well toasted dry rusk

beschuittaart *(Ho)* A cake made with rusks

besciamella *(It)* Béchamel sauce

beskidzka *(Pl)* A very common hard sausage made from pork and beef

bessan *see* besan

bessara *(NA)* A Moroccan dip made from cooked broad beans and red sweet peppers, ground cumin seeds, oil and lemon juice all processed to a smooth paste

best-before date Date mark used on packaged food which has a shelf life of 6 weeks to 3 months after packing. Under UK regulations this date can be changed by the manufacturer after the first date has expired. Such relabelled foods tend to enter the market and discount shop trade

best-before-end date Date mark giving only the month and year. Used on packaged food which will stay in good condition for longer than 3 months (usually not more than 18 months). Under UK regulations this date can be changed by the manufacturer after the first date has expired. Such relabelled foods tend to enter the market and discount shop trade

best end of lamb The vertebrae and first six rib bones counting from the rear of the lamb, cut down the centre of the back bone. The ribs are shortened to about 10 cm. Usually skinned and chined and the ends of the ribs scraped before cooking

best end of veal *(UK)* The ribs of the animal extending about half way down its side from the backbone and from the loin to the shoulder. Corresponds to the best end of lamb. Roasted, fried or grilled

besugo *(Sp)* Bream (1)

beta-apo-8'-carotenal (C30) E160(e), an orange carotene compound extracted from fruit and vegetables used as a food colouring. The more fat soluble ethyl ester, E160(f), is also available

***Beta vulgaris* Cicla group** *Bot.* Swiss chard, spinach beet

Beta vulgaris* subsp. *maritima *Bot.* Sea beet

Beta vulgaris* subsp. *vulgaris *Bot.* Beetroot

betacyanin One of the red colours in beetroot, less susceptible to colour change than anthocyanin

beta-jio *(Ja)* A method of salting food by sprinkling it with salt for an hour then rinsing off the salt. This leaves the surface layer lightly salted. Used for fatty fish

betanin *see* beetroot red

betasuppe *(No)* Mutton broth

betel leaf The leaf of the betel pepper *Piper betle* used in Indian cooking and as a wrapping for pan

betel nut The hard nut of a palm tree *Areca catechu* with stimulating properties, ground and mixed with lime and other spices and wrapped in a betel leaf to make pan. The green unripe nuts are known as chikni and are shelled and boiled before drying. The orange to scarlet ripe nuts are known as chali and are dried in the husk and shelled [also called **areca nut**]

beterraba *(Po)* Beetroot

bethmale *(Fr)* A hard cows' milk cheese from Tourraine with a spicy flavour

Bethmännchen *(Ge)* A marzipan biscuit from Frankfurt

bette *(Fr) fem.* Chinese cabbage or Chinese leaves. Sometime used for Swiss chard

betterave rouge *(Fr) fem.* Beetroot

beurre *(Fr) masc.* Butter

beurre, au *(Fr)* Used of dishes cooked in or served with butter

beurre d'ail *(Fr) masc.* A compound butter made from equal quantities of blanched peeled cloves of garlic and butter, processed and passed through a sieve

beurre d'amandes *(Fr) masc.* Almond butter

beurre d'anchois *(Fr) masc.* Anchovy butter

beurre d'aveline *(Fr) masc.* Hazelnut butter

beurre Bercy *(Fr) masc.* White wine reduced by one half with chopped shallots, cooled, mixed with softened butter, diced, poached and drained bone marrow, chopped parsley, seasoning and lemon juice. Used as a garnish with steaks and chops

beurre blanc *(Fr) masc.* Reduced white wine and vinegar flavoured with shallots, strained, sufficient cold butter beaten in in stages over a low heat until the sauce is of coating consistency. Served warm with fish and vegetables

beurre de caviar Caviar butter

beurre chivry *(Fr) masc.* Ravigote butter

beurre Colbert *(Fr) masc.* Maître d'hôtel butter mixed with melted meat glaze and chopped tarragon

beurre composé *(Fr) masc.* Compound butter

beurre de crevettes *(Fr) masc.* A compound butter made from equal quantities of cooked shrimps and butter, pounded together and sieved, alternatively it can be made by pounding together butter and shrimp remains, shells, etc. and sieving

beurre d'échalotes *(Fr) masc.* A compound butter made of equal quantities of chopped shallots and butter, the shallots blanched, refreshed and squeezed dry through a cloth, then all pounded together and sieved

beurre d'écrevisses *(Fr) masc.* A compound butter made from the remains of crayfish cooked for some other purpose, pounded with an equal quantity of butter and sieved

beurre d'estragon *(Fr) masc.* Tarragon butter

beurre fondu *(Fr) masc.* Butter and a small amount of water or wine, boiled until combined then strained through double muslin or a tammy cloth. Served hot with boiled fish and some vegetables [also called **melted butter sauce**]

beurre de hareng Fr) *masc.* Herring butter

beurre de laitance *(Fr) masc.* A compound butter made with poached soft roes pounded with twice their weight in butter, flavoured with mustard and sieved

beurre (à la) maître d'hôtel *(Fr) masc.* A compound butter made with lemon juice, seasoning and finely chopped parsley. Formed into rolls, refrigerated and cut into 0.5 cm thick slices. Served with grilled meat and grilled or fried fish

beurre manié *(Fr) masc.* A well kneaded mixture of equal quantities of flour and butter, small quantities of which are used to progressively thicken liquids and sauces

beurre marchand de vins *(Fr) masc.* Red wine reduced with chopped shallots, seasoned, then mixed with a little melted meat glaze and softened butter equal in weight to the original wine, lemon juice and chopped parsley. Used with grilled sirloin steaks

beurre à la meunière *see* beurre noisette

beurre monté *(Fr) masc. see* monter au beurre

beurre de Montpellier *(Fr) masc.* A mixture of blanched, refreshed and drained watercress, parsley, chervil, tarragon, chives and spinach leaves with blanched chopped shallots, gherkins, capers, garlic and anchovy fillets processed to a fine paste, mixed with three times its weight of butter, raw and hard boiled egg yolks mixed in and one fifth the combined weight of olive oil whisked in, seasoned and finished with a little cayenne pepper. Used to coat fish for cold buffets

beurre de moutarde *(Fr) masc.* Mustard butter

beurre noir *(Fr) masc.* Butter browned in the frying pan, passed through a fine strainer and mixed when lukewarm with a reduction of vinegar and coarsely ground pepper. This may be kept molten until used when fried chopped parsley and chopped capers are sprinkled over the food to be coated with the butter

beurre noisette *(Fr) masc.* Nut brown butter prepared by melting butter over heat and adding lemon juice after it has melted and foamed and just before it burns, used with fish meunière [also called **beurre à la meunière**]

beurre de noisettes *(Fr) masc.* Hazelnut butter

beurre de paprika A compound butter made from softened butter mixed with chopped onions and paprika powder which have been sweated in butter, and all sieved

beurre de piments *(Fr) masc.* A compound butter made from braised sweet red pepper pounded with twice its weight in butter and sieved

beurre à la polonaise *(Fr) masc.* Butter cooked until nut brown, one quarter its weight of very fine fresh white breadcrumbs added and cooked until golden brown

beurre printanier *(Fr) masc.* A compound butter made from vegetables appropriate to the dish being garnished, cooked, pounded with an equal weight of butter and sieved

beurre de Provence *(Fr) masc. see* allioli

beurre de raifort *(Fr) masc.* Horseradish butter

beurre ravigote *(Fr) masc.* Ravigote butter

beurre, sauce au *(Fr) fem. see* sauce bâtarde

beurre de saumon fumé *(Fr) masc.* Smoked salmon butter

beurre de truffes *(Fr) masc.* Truffle butter

beurre vert *(Fr) masc.* Ravigote butter

Beuschel *(Au & Ge)* Stewed calves' lungs with vinegar and sugar. Served with dumplings

Beutelmelone *(Ge)* Melon

beyaz peynir *(Tu)* A soft white freshly eaten cheese made from ewes' milk, possibly mixed with goats' milk. It may be ripened in brine

bézuque *(Fr)* Bar, the fish

BG *see* bouquet garni

BHA E320, butylated hydroxyanisole, a controversial antioxidant allowed only for use in fats, oils and essential oils

bhaatmas *(Ne)* Soya beans

bhagoni *(In) see* degchi

bhaji **1** *see* amaranths **2** *see* bhajia

bhajia An Indian vegetable fritter, usually onion, served as a starter or as an accompaniment to a meal; *see also* pakora [also called **bhaji**]

bharta *(In)* A description of cooked and puréed food esp. vegetables

bharti *(In)* Barnyard millet

bhat *(Ne)* Rice

bhatoora *(In) see* puri

bhatura *(In) see* puri

bhedaa *(Ne)* Lamb, sheep

bhel puri *(In)* Puffed rice and peanuts mixed with cooked and dried lentils, chopped onion and coriander leaves. Served with a spicy sauce as a snack

bhindi *(In)* Okra

bhojia *(In)* Spiced stir-fried vegetables

bhoona Indian frying which covers sautéing - sukha bhoona, pot roasting - dumned bhoona *(see dum, to)* and a type of braising in ghee in a closed container - ard bhoona [also called **bhuna**]

bhorji *(In)* Scrambled, as of eggs

BHT E321, butylated hydroxytoluene, a controversial antioxidant allowed only for use in fats, oils and essential oils

bhuna 1 *see* bhoona **2** A dry curry dish made with fried meat

bhuni khichhari *(In)* A dry version of khichhari q.v

bianchetti *(It)* Very tiny fish fry so small that they are transparent. Generally mixed with egg and made into an omelette or used in soup [also called **gianchetti**]

bianco, in *(It)* A description of boiled fish served with oil, melted butter and lemon juice

bianco di Spagna *(It)* A large tender and commonly used white bean

bianco d'uovo *(It)* White of egg

bian dou *(Ch)* Beans

biarrotte, à la *(Fr)* In the style of Biarritz, i.e. garnished with ceps and potato cakes

bias cut An oblique cut or one at an angle to the grain of the food

bibb lettuce *(USA)* A variety of butterhead lettuce considered to be one of the finest

biber *(Tu)* Sweet peppers

biber dolmasi *(Tu)* Sweet peppers stuffed with a mixture of chopped onions, raisins, pine nuts, cooked rice, herbs and seasoning, baked in the oven and served cold

bibliothèque internationale de gastronomie *see* international library of gastronomy

bicarbonate of potash *see* (E)501

bicarbonate of soda (E)500, sodium bicarbonate, a mild alkali which gives off carbon dioxide when heated or mixed with acid. One of the ingredients of baking powder also used as a mild cleansing agent [also called **sodium bicarbonate, baking soda**]

bicchiere *(It)* A glass or tumbler, also a measuring cup

biefstuk *(Ho)* A cut of beef equivalent to sirloin or round steak (USA)

biefstuk van de haas *(Ho)* Filet mignon of beef

bien cuit *(Fr)* Well done, in the case of meat, all pinkness gone

bien padado *(Sp)* Well done, as of meat

Bienenstich *(Ge & Au)* A yeasted pastry with an almond topping similar to an almond slice [also called **bee sting** (UK)]

bier *(Ge)* Beer

Bierkaltschale *(Ge)* Cold beer soup

Bierkäse *(Ge) see* Wiesslacher

Bierplinsen *(Ge)* Cooked meat or sausages, coated in frying batter made with beer and deep fried

Bierschinken *(Ge)* A brühwurst made with 2 parts lean shoulder pork, 1 part belly pork, minced very fine with seasoning, spices and containing chunks of cooked ham fat and sometimes pistachio nuts. Usually eaten cold

Biersuppe *(Ge)* Lager, boiled and thickened with a brown roux, flavoured with cinnamon stick, cardomom seeds and lemon zest plus salt and sugar, strained and served with croûtons

Bierwurst *(Ge)* A coarse textured dried slicing sausage made from spiced pork or pork and beef, and garlic. Once made from ham marinated in beer hence the name [also called **beer sausage**]

Biestmilch *(Ge)* Beestings

biet *(Ho)* Beetroot

biete *(It)* Swiss chard

bietola *(It)* Swiss chard or spinach beet

bietola da coste *(It)* Spinach beet

bietoline *(It) see* erbette

bière *(Fr) fem.* Beer

bife *(Po)* Steak of beef, pork, lamb, fish, etc.

biff *(No & Sw)* Beef

biff à la Lindstrom *(Sw)* Raw minced fillet steak mixed with diced cold boiled potatoes, double cream, diced pickled beetroot, grated onion, capers, egg yolk and seasoning, formed into egg sized balls and shallow fried so as to remain pink in the middle. Served hot with fried onions

biff med lök *(Sw)* Fried rump steak served with fried onions and boiled potatoes

biffstek *(Sw)* Beef steak

Bifidobacterium plantarum One of the microorganisms used as starter culture for fermented milk products esp. in Japan

***Bifidobacterium* spp.** Bacteria used for the fermentation of milk

bifsteks *(Ru)* Steak

bifteck *(Fr) masc.* General name for steak suitable for frying or grilling

bifteck américaine *(Be)* Chopped raw beef with mayonnaise, seasoning and spices

bifteck Bercy au père François *(Fr) masc.* Beefsteak with a sauce based on red wine, shallots and parsley

bifteck haché *(Fr) masc.* Minced beef, hamburger or beefburger

bifteck tartare *(Fr) masc. see* steak tartare

biftek *(Sp)* Beef steak [also called **bistec**]

bifuteki *(Ja)* Beef steak

biga *(It)* A starter for bread made from plain flour, water and fresh yeast (32:12:1) mixed to a slack dough and left to work for at least 12 hours

bigarade *(Fr) fem.* Seville orange [also called **orange amère**]

bigarade, à la *(Fr)* Used as a description of dishes served with orange or an orange based sauce using Seville oranges if available

bigarade, sauce *(Fr) fem.* Sauce made from the cooking liquor or deglazed pan residues of duck with Seville orange if available and lemon juice and finished with a julienne of blanched lemon and orange zest [also called **orange sauce**]

bigarro *(Sp)* Winkle

bigatan *(Ph)* Ridged sand clam

bigoli *(It)* Thick home-made spaghetti from Venice

bigorneau *(Fr) masc.* A small gastropod mollusc *Nassa mutabilis* similar in shape to a winkle and treated in the same way. Very common in Brittany

bigos *(Pl)* A typical winter stew made from cabbage, sauerkraut, chopped pork, gammon, smoked sausage, dried mushrooms, onions, lard, tomato purée, garlic, paprika and seasoning, cooked in advance and reheated. Sometimes prunes, plum tomatoes and red wine are added

bigoudine, à la *(Fr)* In the style of Bigouden in the region of Pont l'Âbbé, i.e. with baked slices of scrubbed potatoes with the skin left on

bihun *(Id & Ma)* Rice vermicelli

bijan *(Ma)* Sesame seed

bijane *(Fr)* A cold soup made from sweetened red wine thickened with fresh breadcrumbs

bijeni sir *(Gr & Bk)* A soft cooked-curd cheese with holes from Macedonia. It is made from ewes' or a mixture of ewes' and cows' milk

biji sawi *(Ma)* Black mustard seed

biko *(Ph)* A dessert made from glutinous rice, sugar and coconut milk. Served with latik

biksemad *(De)* Beef hash, served with a fried egg

bilberry The dark blue-bloomed berry of a low-growing wild bush *Vaccinium myrtillus* that grows on acid moorland. Harvested with a large-toothed curved comb. Slightly acid and used for pies or jam [also called **whortleberry, huckleberry, blaeberry, whimberry, windberry**]

billeri *(It)* Lady's smock

billy bi *(Fr)* A mussel soup made from fish stock, mussel liquor and a little cream, flavoured with lemon zest or lemon grass and garnished with shelled mussels

biltong *(Saf)* Dried strips of game meat or beef which will keep for years. Very tough and leather like, requires cutting into very thin strips before eating raw or cooking [also called **jerky, jerked beef, jerked meat**]

bind, to To bring together dry or crumbly ingredients with a binding agent such as egg, flour paste, thick sauces or even water, etc. so as to make a cohesive mass which can be shaped prior to, and which will hold its shape during, cooking

bindae duk *(Ko)* Fritters made with a mung bean flour batter

bindi *(In)* Okra

bing cherry *(USA)* A round plump red to purple and very juicy cherry

bing-ji-ling *(Ch)* Ice cream

bingleberry A variety of dewberry

bin tong *(Ch)* Lump sugar (3)

biocoli *(It)* Toasted sweet bread

bioflavonoids A complex family of chemicals including rutin and hesperidin which are widely distributed in fresh raw fruits and vegetables. It is thought that they have protective effects on vitamin C stores in the body and are involved in the strength of capillaries. They have no known toxicity

biotin A very stable vitamin necessary for yeast and bacterial reproduction. Its presence in bread dough is essential. Its absence, in an active form, in egg white is responsible for the preservation of the egg against bacterial attack. It is widely distributed in all animal and plant tissues with high concentrations in yeast, liver and kidney. It is also synthesized by intestinal bacteria and easily absorbed in the gut. It is required for the metabolism of carbohydrates and has no known toxicity. Raw egg white taken in excessive quantities whilst under antibiotic treatment could lead to a deficiency state which would appear as skin disease. Currently this affects only a few babies and is easily cured [also called **vitamin H**]

biphenyl *see* E230, diphenyl

bird A feathered and winged animal, not necessarily having the ability to fly. Either domesticated e.g. chicken, duck, goose, turkey, guinea fowl, etc. or wild e.g. duck, pheasant, partridge, etc.

bird cherry *(USA)* A native cherry *Prunus pennsylvanica* used to make a jelly type conserve [also called **pin cherry**]

bird's nest **1** The nest of a small species of swallow found on the coasts of SEA. The birds, which consume a lot of seaweed, secrete a gelatinous saliva which they use to construct the nest. This is used to make a soup which is more renowned for its texture than its flavour but is regarded as a health food by the Chinese (to prevent brittle bones in old age. There may be some scientific justification for this) **2** *(USA)* A nest made from raw straw potatoes deep fried between nesting frying baskets

bird's nest soup A delicately flavoured soup made by cooking cleaned birds' nests in a sweet or savoury consommé

birdseye chilli A small (max. 2 cm long) chilli from Thailand, blisteringly hot and varying in colour from green to red

bireweck *(Fr) see* berawecka

Birkhuhn *(Ge)* Grouse

Birne *(Ge)* Pear

Birnenbrot *(Ge)* A sweetened fruit loaf

biroldo *(It)* A Tuscan blood pudding containing pinenuts and raisins or cheese

birthday cake An iced and decorated cake to celebrate a birthday. Often baked in special tins to give shapes appropriate to the occasion and recipient. Usually with as many candles as the age and some piped greeting

biryani *(In)* A vividly coloured and aromatic pilau-type dish of rice and fish or meat. The meat or fish, precooked with spices, is mixed with uncooked, parboiled or cooked rice previously fried with spices as for risotto, caramelized onions, possibly almonds and steamed in a tightly sealed container. The colour is derived from saffron or turmeric. Spices and herbs are selected from parsley, bay, mint, lovage, coriander leaves, garlic, fresh ginger root, chillis, cardamom, cloves, coriander seed, peppercorns, cumin, fennel, anise, cinnamon or cayenne pepper. Vegetables incorporated include carrots, green peppers and onions. Additional ingredients include butter and yoghurt

bis(e) *(Fr) adj.* Greyish brown, or brownish grey, wholemeal, as a description of flour or bread

Bischofsbrot *(Ge)* A Christmas cake containing dried vine fruits, nuts and chocolate drops. Lit. bishop's bread

biscocho *(Ph)* Crumbled dried toast used for thickening sauces and stews

biscoito *(Po)* Biscuit

biscote *(Sp)* Rusk

biscotte *(Fr) fem.* Rusk or melba toast

biscotti *(It)* Biscuits, rusks

biscotti da tè *(It)* Tea cakes, petits fours

biscotti di prato *(It)* A hard sweet biscuit containing almond pieces

biscuit **1** A crisp, dry, small, flat, baked, sweet or savoury cake. Lit. twice cooked. See biscuit production methods **2** *(USA)* English scone [also called **hot biscuit**] **3** *(Fr) masc.* Sponge cake

biscuit crust pastry *see* flan pastry

biscuit à la cuiller *(Fr) masc.* Lady finger (USA), sponge finger (UK)

biscuit production methods The five methods are sugar batter, flour batter, blending, foaming and rubbing in. See under each name for method

biscuit de Reims *(Fr) masc.* A type of macaroon

biscuit sec *(Fr) masc.* Cookie (USA), plain biscuit (UK)

biscuit tortini *(USA)* A frozen dessert made with cream, eggs and crushed macaroons

bishop's cake *(USA)* A light sponge cake with raisins and almonds

bishop's weed *see* ajowan

Biskotte *(Ge)* Langue de chat

biskvit *(Ru)* Sponge cake

bismalva *(It)* Marshmallow

Bismark herrings Flat fillets of herring interspersed with sliced onion and marinated in spiced vinegar

bisque *(En & Fr) fem.* A soup made from shellfish or crustaceans in a way similar to lobster sauce but using a white meat stock instead of fish stock, omitting the garlic and finishing with diced shellfish or crustacean flesh and cream

bisque de homard *(Fr) fem.* A bisque q.v., made either with live lobster, halved, cleaned and claws cracked, or, cooked lobster shell excluding the claws [also called **lobster bisque**]

bisquit tortoni *(It)* A frozen dessert of cream, nuts and fruit sprinkled with crushed macaroons

bistec *(Sp) see* biftek

bistecca *(It)* Beef steak

bistecca fiorentina *(It)* Beef steak grilled over charcoal and served rare with a little olive oil

bistecca alla pizzaiola *(It)* Beef steak with a sauce of sweet peppers, tomatoes and garlic flavoured with oregano and spices

bistecchina *(It)* A thin steak

bisteeya *see* bastilla

bistro *(En & Fr) masc.* A small restaurant, with a bar, serving snacks and full meals. The Russian word was taken over by Napoleon's troops during the invasion of Russia. Means quick and was used jocularly of the slow service in that country's inns

biswa tulsi *(In)* Sweet basil

bitki *(Ru)* Minced pork or beef patties with breadcrumbs and sweated chopped onions bound with egg, panéed, fried in chicken fat or lard and served with ligonberry or cranberry sauce or the pan residues deglazed with sour cream

bitochki *(Ru)* Small meat balls, fried and served with a piquant sauce enriched with soured cream [also called **bitok**]

bitok 1 *(Fr)* The French term for a Russian meat loaf served with soured cream **2** *see* bitochki

bittara appa *(In & Sr)* A popular breakast food made from appa batter or string hoppers, cooked very slowly with a whole shelled egg in the centre

bitter almond The kernel of the nut of the bitter almond tree *Prunus dulcis* var. *amara* used for the production of almond essence and almond oil. Toxic if the kernel is consumed in quantity. Used occasionally as a flavouring in some classic European dishes. The oil is not available in the USA

bitter cucumber *see* bitter gourd

bitter gourd An Indian vegetable *Momordica charantia,* but found also in China and SEA, which looks like a small green warty cucumber, usually sliced, seeds discarded and soaked in salt water to remove the bitter taste. It is usually braised or steamed and combined with strong flavours. It can be pickled and in Indonesia it is eaten raw in salads [also called **balsam pear, bitter cucumber, bitter melon**]

bitter melon *see* bitter gourd

bitter orange *see* Seville orange

bitterballen *(Ho)* Minced ham bound with a thick white sauce containing gelatine. Formed into balls, panéed and deep fried. Eaten as an appetizer. Probably derived from the old nautical term, bitter, meaning the end of a cable

bitterkoekjes *(Ho)* Macaroons

bitto *(It)* A hard cooked-curd cheese cast and pressed in cylinders weighing 15 to 25 kg. After moulding, the cheese is repeatedly dry salted and then ripened and dried for 2 to 6 months for the table version and 2 to 3 years for the grating version. The paste of the young cheese has a buttery texture with a few holes and a delicate taste. It becomes denser and more crumbly with age. Used esp. in polenta, taragna and sciatti

bivalve Any shellfish of the mollusc family with two shells hinged together enclosing the animal. Examples are mussels, oysters, cockles, clams and scallops

biwa *(Ja)* Loquats

Bixa orellana *Bot.* Achiote

bixin *see* annatto

bizcocho *(Sp)* Biscuit or sponge cake

bizcochos borrachos *(Sp)* Sponge cake dredged with sugar and cinnamon and splashed with wine

bjano sirene *(Bu)* A soft ewes' milk cheese cast like a small brick (1 kg). The salty, acid paste is dense and covered with a thin rind. Contains 50% water, 25% fat and 20% protein

björnbär *(Sw)* Blackberry

björnebær *(No)* Blackberry

blåbær *(No)* Blueberry or huckleberry

blåbär *(Sw)* Blueberry

blacan *see* blachan

blachan A strong smelling dried paste from the

Far East made from salted and fermented small crustaceans and sold in small blocks. Used for flavouring [also called **blacan, blakhan, kapi, terasi, balachan, trasi**]

black bass *(USA)* A small freshwater fish *Micropterus* spp. with a firm delicate white flesh found in North American rivers. The skin must be removed before cooking to avoid off flavours

black bean 1 A type of French bean *Phaseolus vulgaris* widely cultivated in South America and the Far East. The dried bean has a black skin and white flesh and can be used as kidney beans. Must be boiled vigorously for 15 minutes [also called **black kidney bean, Mexican black bean, Mexican bean**] **2** Fermented soya beans made by cooking, salting and fermenting when they become almost black. Used as flavouring in made up dishes or to produce various pastes and sauces. See e.g. black bean sauce

black bean curd A dirty grey, spongy curd made from the tuber of a taro-like snake palm *Amorphophallus konjac* by peeling, pounding, boiling then precipitating the curd with lime. Can be flavoured or deep frozen *(snowed)* to give it a different texture. Added to soups, braised dishes and the like; *see also* konnyaku (Ja) [also called **devil's taro, devils' tongue**]

black bean sauce Black fermented soya beans flavoured with garlic and star anise and let down with brine. Used as flavouring, dressing or dip

black bottom pie *(USA)* A custard pie with a layer of dark chocolate custard on the bottom

black bread *see* pumpernickel

black bream One of the seawater bream *Spondiyliosona cantharus* with an excellent flavour found from the Mediterranean to the North Sea [also called **old wife**]

black bun *(UK)* A rich, spiced, dark fruit cake encased in pastry and eaten in Scotland on New Year's eve. Often well matured [also called **Scotch bun, Scotch black bun**]

black butter *see* beurre noisette

black cap pudding *(UK)* A pudding made from basic steamed pudding mixture, poured into a greased basin whose base is covered with currants or blackcurrant jam. When turned out it has a black cap. Served with a sweet jam or syrup sauce

black cod A round bodied fish *Anoplopoma fimbria* from the North Pacific which has a grey-black to black upper surface and weighs about 2.5 kg. It is not a member of the cod family and has a rich oily flesh. Available fresh or preserved [also called **blue cod, Alaska black cod**]

black crowdie *(UK)* Crowdie cheese combined with cream and coated with oatmeal and crushed black pepper

black cumin A variety of cumin q.v. with a very dark seed and a sweeter smell than ordinary cumin found in Northern India and Iran. Used in North Indian and Moghul cooking. Sometimes the name is used incorrectly for nigella [also called **sweet cumin** (Ma)]

black drum *see* sea drum

black duck *(USA)* A highly prized wild duck *Anas rupripes* shot for the table. The domesticated version is the cayuga duck

black-eyed bean 1 *see* black-eyed pea (1) **2** *(UK)* Cow pea

black-eyed pea 1 A legume *Vigna catjang* related to the other *Vigna* spp. *(cow pea and long bean)* from South America but now grown also in India and SEA. The pods grow up to 60 cm long and the beans when mature are yellow-brown to red in colour with a dark eye and similar in size and and shape to a kidney bean. To confuse matters it is sometimes referred to as asparagus bean which is a completely different species [also called **black-eyed bean, catjang bean**] **2** *(USA)* Cow pea

black-eyed susan *(USA)* Cow pea

Black Forest cherry cake *see* black forest gateau

Black Forest gateau A layered chocolate sponge partially soaked in kirsch-flavoured sugar syrup, with whipped cream and black cherries between the layers, the whole decorated with whipped cream, cherries and grated chocolate or caraque [also called **Black forest cherry cake**]

Black Forest ham A smoked and air dried ham from southern Germany with a strong flavour. Served with potato salad

black forest mushroom *see* shiitake

black fungus Cloud ear fungus

black game *see* black grouse

black gram A legume *Phaseolus mungo* grown mainly for its dry seeds but the young pods can be eaten as a vegetable, and found in India and the Caribbean. The plant and pods are very hairy and look somewhat like the dwarf French bean. The small seeds are black or dark green with a white interior and prominent white hilum. They require long boiling and are very important in Indian cooking. It is one of the most expensive pulses but widely used. The ground bean is used in idlis, dosas and poppadoms [also called **urd bean, urad dal, black lentil, mash, woolly pyrol** (Ca)**, uluthan**]

black grouse A game bird *(Lyrurus tetrix)*. Shooting season in the UK 20th August (1st of September in parts of the south) to the 10th of December. Hanging time 3 to 10 days. Drawn and trussed and roasted like chicken for about 1 hour. Sometimes called moorfowl, moorgame and moorcock in England adding to the confusion [also called **black game, blackcock, greyhen (female)**]

black halibut *see* Greenland halibut

black kidney bean *see* black bean

black leg chicken A traditional French breed of chicken with firm flesh, superior in quality to the normal roasting chicken. Needs slightly slower cooking

black lentil *see* black gram

black lovage *see* alexanders

black Mike *(USA) coll. (Forestry workers)* A meat and vegetable stew

black moss *see* hair vegetable

black mustard seed A strong, pungent variety of mustard *Brassica nigra* from Southern Europe and India not grown for international trade and only available locally. Used in curries

black olive *see* olive

black pepper Made from whole green unripe berries of the vine *Piper nigrum* dried in the sun. Usually freshly ground, it has a hot pungent flavour; *see also* peppercorn

black PN E151, a synthetic black food colouring

black pomfret A grayish-brown skinned variety of pomfret q.v. with not as fine a flavour as white pomfret

black pots *(UK)* A Cornish speciality of gerty meat pudding with added pig's blood

black pudding *(UK)* Groats boiled in muslin until cooked, mixed with diced pork leaf or back fat, a little finely chopped onion, seasoning, herbs and spices and mancu. Pig's blood is added to the warm mixture (roughly 2/3rds the dry weight of the groats), the whole thickened with fine oatmeal. Filled into beef runners or wide hog casings tied in smallish links, platted and boiled gently for 20 minutes. Preservative is added to commercial varieties. The spices and herbs added vary according to region. See under Bury, North Staffordshire, Stretford, Yorkshire and Welsh blood pudding; *see also* Scottish blood pudding [also called **blood pudding, blood sausage**]

black rice 1 A type of glutinous rice from Indonesia and the Phillipines. It resemble wild rice in appearance but is a true rice. Its nutty flavour is appreciated in puddings and cakes **2** *(Me)* Rice cooked in the cooking liquor obtained after boiling black beans

black salsify *see* scorzonera

black sea bass (A deep-bodied seawater game fish *Centropistes striatus* also caught commercially. It has a grey to black upper skin surmounted by a very sharp fin and weighs between 0.5 and 2 kg. It has firm white flesh and may be cooked in any way. Found in deep water off the eastern coast of the USA

black sesame seeds A black coloured sesame seed used as a garnish in desserts and puddings and, when ground, in soup or to make gomasio q.v.

black soya bean A smaller variety of soya bean than the yellow. Served as a salad or, when puréed and sweetened, as a cake and bun filling

black treacle A mixture of molasses and invert sugar syrup used as a general sweetener but particularly for treacle toffee and treacle tart

black tree fungus Cloud ear fungus

black trumpet *see* horn of plenty

black turnip A large black skinned turnip from Italy with a sharp, pungent, white and crisp flesh

black vinegar A dark, mild and sweetish vinegar similar to balsamic vinegar but made from fermented glutinous rice or sorghum. Presumably made in a similar way. Commonly added to many dishes as a flavouring in north and central China

black walnut *(USA)* A variety of walnut tree with black coloured walnuts

blackberry A dark red to black soft fruit *Rubus fruticosus* which grows on long rambling canes in late summer. The berries consist of a large number of individual sacs of juice each containing a seed and all gathered in an elongated sphere. Available wild or cultivated they are used for pies, jam or stewed fruit, often teamed with apples [also called **bramble**]

blackcurrant The fruit of a low growing bush *Ribes nigrum* looking like small black grapes. The berries can be combed off the stalks with a fork. They have a rich slightly sour flavour and are used to flavour liqueurs, in pies, to make jam and occasionally to make a sauce similar to redcurrant sauce.

blackcock *see* black grouse

blackened *(USA)* A term used in cajun cooking for searing meat or fish in a very hot cast iron skillet to give the aroma of barbecued or charcoal grilled meat or fish

blacklip abalone One of the main species of abalone *Haliotis ruber* with a red corrugated shell which lives in crevices in rocks and reefs. So called because of its black mantle

blackstrap molasses The darkest variety of molasses being that black mixture of invert sugars and other compounds remaining after crystallization of raw sugar from sugar cane juice

bladder cherry *see* Chinese lantern

blade bone *(UK)* A large beef joint from the top of the forequarter between the ribs and the neck and clod. Usually boned and sold as blade steak or chuck steak

blade mace The one piece outer covering or aril of the nutmeg; *see also* mace

blade of pork *(UK)* The shoulder blade and surrounding muscle. Can be roasted or boned out and roasted or cut up for braising or stewing

blade steak *(UK) see* blade bone

blaeberry *see* bilberry

blakhan *(In) see* blachan

blanc 1 *(Fr) adj.* White **2** *(Fr) masc.* A cooking liquor consisting of water, lemon juice, flour and salt **3** *see* blanc de poulet

blanc, au *(Fr)* Description of a dish that is white in colour e.g. chicken or veal or which is cooked in white stock

blanc d'oeuf *(Fr) masc.* White of egg

blanc de poulet *(Fr) masc.* White meat or breast of chicken

blanc de volaille *(Fr) masc.* Breast of chicken

blanch, to 1 To plunge items into boiling (salted) water or to bring to the boil in same and cook for 2 to 5 minutes, in order to part cook, retain colour and nutrients, to inactivate enzymes that cause changes in colour, flavour or nutritive properties during storage or, for a shorter time, to loosen tomato, almond and other skins prior to removing. Usually followed by refresh **2** To partially cook chipped potatoes in the deep fryer, in order to prevent discolouring and to improve the texture, also to have them prepared ready for quick cooking

blanchaille *(Fr) fem.* Young fish similar to whitebait but of sardines with possibly a few anchovies. Cooked as whitebait

blanched almonds Almond kernels with the skin removed

blanchir *(Fr)* To blanch or scald

blancmange *(UK)* A sweet, semi-solid dessert made with milk, sugar, flavourings and colour thickened with cornflour, poured into a mould and demoulded when set. Originally a medieval dish made with almonds. Lit. white eats

blancmange mould Same as jelly mould q.v

blanco *(SA)* A cows' milk cheese similar to Ricotta

blandad frukt *(Sw)* Mixed fruit

blandade grönsaker *(Sw)* A large white cauliflower cooked al dente and cored, placed at the centre of a dish, decoratively surrounded by small carrots, young beetroot, mange-tout peas, spinach, petit pois and spring onions all cooked al dente plus hard boiled eggs, sliced tomatoes and sliced cucumber, all sprinkled with chopped parsley. Served with mousseline sauce or melted butter

blangah *(Ma) see* belangah

blanket tripe A smooth tripe from the first stomach of the cow or ox. Considered to be the finest [also called **plain tripe**]

blanquette *(Fr) fem.* A white stew of meat cooked in stock with onions and mushrooms, the cooking liquor then made into a sauce with a liaison of egg yolks and cream

blanquette de veau *(Fr) fem.* Veal stewed in a lemon-flavoured white sauce

Blarney *(Ir)* A firm, semi-hard pale coloured mild cows' milk cheese with a few scattered large holes which resembles the Danish Samsø. The yellow paste is enclosed in a red rind. Contains 39% water, 29% fat and 24% protein [also called **Irish Swiss cheese**]

Blätterteigpastete *(Ge)* Vol-au-vent

blau *(Ge)* Very rare, of meat; *see also* bleu (Fr)

Blaubeere *(Ge)* Blueberry

Blaufelchen *(Ge)* Pollan, the fish

blé *(Fr) masc.* Wheat, corn

blé noir *(Fr) masc.* Buckwheat flour

bleaching agent Any compound used to whiten flour or other food commodity, such as chlorine or chlorine dioxide.

bleak A small freshwater fish of the carp family found in European rivers. Cooked like sprats

blend to To mix into a homogeneous mass

blended flour *(USA)* Two or more types of flour blended for making specific items, e.g. pretzels, cookies

blender 1 An electric machine consisting of a glass or plastic vessel with a fast rotating steel blade directly coupled to an electric motor below. This pulverizes, mixes, blends or emulsifies the contents of the vessel which can be wet or dry **2** A hand held electric machine with a fast rotating shrouded metal blade at the end of an extension on the motor, used for wet mixtures e.g. for making purées or emulsions such as mayonnaise [also called **liquidizer**]

blending method for biscuits A method of making biscuits by simply blending or mixing all the ingredients together, e.g. brandy snaps

blenny A small slimy fish found both in the sea

and in rivers in Europe and North America, treated like whitebait

blette *(Fr) fem. see* bette

bletted The term used to describe a fruit which is very over-ripe, soft and almost disintegrating

bleu *(Fr)* **1** Of meat, very underdone, the surface only of the meat being quickly browned **2** Of cheese, blue veined with penicillium moulds grown within the paste usually along cracks or needle holes. Lit. blue

bleu, au *(Fr)* A method of cooking fish or shellfish by plunging them alive into boiling water or court bouillon

Bleu d'Auvergne *(Fr) masc.* A soft blue-veined unpressed cows' milk cheese made in small (to 1 kg) and larger (to 3 kg) cylinders. The starter is a spore suspension of *Penicillium glaucum* and the moulded cheese is dry salted for 5 to 6 days and ripened at high humidity for 2 to 4 weeks. The paste is white and creamy with evenly distributed veining and a pleasant but distinctive taste. Used as a dessert cheese. Made in the Massif Central and has Appellation d'Origine status

bleu-blanc Belge *(Be)* A breed of cattle with a high yield of hindquarter, bred for its beef [also called **BBB**]

Bleu de Bresse *(Fr)* A heavily promoted, modern French semi-hard, blue veined cheese made from pasteurized cows' milk and sold in small short cylinders [also called **Bresse Bleu**]

Bleu des Causses *(Fr)* A soft blue-veined cheese made from the milk of cows pastured on Les Causses (high limestone pastures) in southern France. The paste is firm, rich and evenly veined. It has Appellation d'Origine status

Bleu de Corse *(Fr)* A soft ewes' milk cheese with a firm buttery texture, a strong flavour and a few blue-veined cracks. The best are ripened in the Rochefort caves

Bleu de Gex *(Fr)* A semi-hard blue veined cheese with AOC status, made from cows' milk, cast into 7 to 8 kg rounds, pressed, dry salted and ripened for 3 to 4 months. Contains 31% water, 33% fat and 30 % protein

Bleu de Haut-Jura *(Fr)* The official name for cheese made in this region. The most well known are Bleu de Gex and Bleu de Septmoncel, both of which have AOC status

Bleu de Laqueuille *(Fr)* A cheese similar to Bleu d'Auvergne but with a milder taste and dryer rind

Bleu de Quercy *(Fr)* A soft blue cheese made in Aquitaine from cows' milk. It has a strong flavour and a greyish green natural rind. It has Appellation d'Origine status

Bleu de Sainte Foy *(Fr)* A strong tasting blue-veined cows' milk cheese from Savoie

Bleu de Sassenage *(Fr)* A semi-hard blue cheese from near Grenoble, similar to Bleu de Gex with slightly more water and less fat [also called **Sassenage**]

Bleu de Septmoncel A blue cheese similar to Bleu de Gex but with a slightly smoother rind. It has AOC status

Bleu de Thiézac *(Fr)* A blue-veined cows' milk cheese very similar to bleu d'Auvergne

Bleu de Tigne *(Fr)* A blue-veined cows' milk cheese from Savoie

blewit A variety of edible fungus *Tricholoma saevum* with a short stem with a blueish appearance thickening at the base and a 6 to 15 cm dia. dirty yellow to greyish ochre smooth cap rather like a field mushroom. The flesh has a pleasant scent but should be thoroughly cooked. It grows in grass and pasture land along the edges of woods esp. in warm areas

Blighia sapida *Bot.* Akee

blind scouse Lobscouse without meat, eaten in very hard times

blinde vinken *(Ho)* A stuffed piece of veal or beef, a beef olive

Blindhuhn *(Ge)* A bean and bacon casserole with dried apples and vegetables from Hanover

blindjo *(Id) see* melinjo

blini *(Ru)* Small pancakes made from a yeast-raised batter of buckwheat flour and milk rested overnight, mixed with milk, plain flour, melted butter, egg yolks and salt, proved, stiffly beaten egg whites folded in and then browned either side in 10 cm circles on a buttered griddle. May be kept for up to 2 days. Traditionally served with melted butter but may be garnished with various fillings [also called **bliny**]

blintzes A Jewish speciality of small pancakes made into turnovers with a sweetened cream cheese filling, sealed and fried in butter, sprinkled with cinnamon and served with soured cream

bliny *see* blini

bloater A whole herring still containing the gut which is lightly salted and cold smoked. Has a gamey flavour. Sometimes gutted herring that have been similarly treated are sold as bloaters. Grilled or fried.

block roux Roux made in large quantities, cast into blocks and portioned for use as required

block sausage Diced streaky pork mixed with finely chopped garlic, cardamom and seasoning, moistened with rum, packed into ox casings, air dried, salted and cold smoked

blodfersk *(No)* Blood fresh, referring to very fresh fish or meat

blødkogt *(De)* Soft boiled, as of eggs

blodkorv *(Sw)* Swedish blood sausage

blóðmor *(Ic)* Blood sausage

blodpudding *(Sw)* Black pudding

bloedpens *(Be)* Boudin noir

bloedworst *(Ho)* A blood sausage containing raisins, oat bran and pork fat

bloemkool *(Ho)* Cauliflower

blomkål *(De, No & Sw)* Cauliflower

blomkålsgratang *(Sw)* Cauliflower au gratin

blommer *(De)* Plums

blond roux A mixture of equal parts of fat (dripping, clarified butter, etc.) and flour cooked to a sandy texture for slightly longer than a white roux with no more than a hint of colour. Used for thickening liquids, soups, veloutés, sauces, etc. [also called **roux blond** (Fr)]

blondir *(Fr)* To sweat in fat or oil (esp. onions) until they start to take a hint of colour

blood The red oxygenating liquid that circulates around the body of animals, usually drained after killing and used as a commercial raw material. Pig's blood is used for making black puddings, hare' blood in jugged hare and chicken's blood in coq au vin. It adds flavour and can be used in the same way as and with the same precautions as egg for thickening sauces. It is often sold in a coagulated cooked state for use in various dishes When not drained from the animal the meat is very dark.

blood heat *see* lukewarm

blood orange *see* pigmented orange

blood pudding *see* black pudding

blood sausage *see* black pudding

bloom 1 The white coating on some fruits such as plums, grapes and peaches which is said to consist of wild yeasts **2** A white coating which appears on the surface of chocolate after variations in temperature over some time. Probably recrystallized fat and sugar

bloomer A large loaf made from a roll of proven dough baked on a flat tray, diagonally slashed and glazed with beaten egg or salt water

bløtkake *(No)* A cream filled sandwich sponge sometimes coated with marzipan

bløtkokt *(No)* Soft boiled, as of egg

blu, al *(It)* *see* au bleu

blubber The subcutaneous fat of the whale, seal and other marine mammals

blue 1 When applied to meat means the surface just seared brown whilst the interior is still raw **2** When applied to cheese means inoculated with various *Penicillium* spp. using needles to encourage the growth of the blue green fungus within the cheese

blue cheese dressing Soured cream, blue cheese, vinegar, pepper and crushed garlic combined with mayonnaise

blue Cheshire *(UK)* A blue veined Cheshire cheese made in 8 kg cylinders and ripened for up to 6 months. It has a strong flavoured warm yellow paste

blue cod *see* black cod

blue crab A mottled blue crab *Callinectes sapidus,* up to 20 cm across, with blue claws and a very fine flavour often eaten just after it has shed its shell. Very popular in North America and caught off the south eastern coast of the USA mainly in Chesapeake Bay and in the eastern Mediterranean where it has been recently introduced [also called **Atlantic blue crab, blue manna crab, sand crab**]

blue Dorset *(UK)* A white, crumbly, blue cheese from Dorset with a brown, crusty rind made with skimmed cow's milk. It has a strong flavour similar to Stilton. The blue mould is evenly distributed through the paste and is not in veins [also called **Dorset blue, blue vinny, blue vinney**]

blue garoupa *see* garoupa, the fish

blue ginger *see* ginger shoots

blue hare *see* Scottish hare

blue manna crab *see* blue crab

blue meat *(USA)* The meat of a suckling calf

blue melilot A Turkish melilot *Melilotus coeruleus* with blue flowers, now predominantly used to flavour the curds used for Sapsago cheese

blue mould *Penicillium* spp. which grow as surface moulds on e.g. bread and jam; *see also* mould

blue mussel The European mussel *Mytilus galloprovincialis* very similar to the common mussel

blue sausage *(He)* Sausages containing horsemeat which are dyed blue

blue shark A common European shark *Prionace glauca* sometimes passed off as tuna

blue Shropshire *(UK)* A blue veined cheese similar to Stilton but with a milder flavour and made in Leicestershire [also called **Shropshire blue**]

blue Stilton *see* Stilton

blue trout *see* Forelle blau

blue velvet swimming crab A gourmet crab from Spain

blue vinney *see* Blue Dorset

blue vinny *see* Blue Dorset

blue Wensleydale *(UK)* A blue-veined version of Wensleydale cheese. Very rare

blueberry **1** Highbush blueberries *Vaccinium corymbosum* have been bred from the American wild blueberry. The purple fruits with a grey bloom are produced in clusters on 1.5 to 2 m high bushes and are similar to bilberries **2** Rabbit-eye blueberries *Vaccinia ashei* are smaller and grittier than the highbush varieties. Both cultivated and wild varieties are used to make the well known American blueberry pie

blueberry muffin *(USA)* A slightly sweetened muffin mixture containing blueberries which have been washed, drained and added to the other dry ingredients. Baked at 200°C in muffin tins for 18 minutes

bluebonnet rice A type of long grain rice

bluefin tuna The tasty but very rare variety of tuna *Thunnus thynnus* growing to 2 m long and 150 kg. It migrates over wide reaches of the southern oceans and was once very common in the Mediterranean. Now a threatened species

bluefish A medium sized (to 3 kg), oily seawater fish *Pomatomus saltarix* with a grey to greenish blue upper skin with firm, white flesh found in the warmer waters of the Atlantic and in the Mediterranean. It leaves the deep water for the coast during summer and is sometimes fished for sport. Poach, bake or grill

bluegill A freshwater fish *Leponis macrochirus* found in North America and farmed in the USA and Japan. Generally blue with dark blue gill covers and a firm moist flesh, weighing up to 0.5 kg. Usually shallow fried or partly poached, skinned, battered and deep fried

bluemouth A type of deepwater scorpion fish *Sebastes dactylipterus* with red skin mottled with black and with a blue flash on the gill covers. Used in bouillabaisse

bluepoint *(USA)* A popular type of oyster found and farmed off the coast of Long Island

Blumenkohl *(Ge)* Cauliflower

Blumenkohlsuppe *(Ge)* Cream of cauliflower soup

Blut *(Ge)* Blood

Blut Schwartenmagen *(Fr)* *see* Schwartenmagen

Blutwurst *(Ge)* A raw sausage made from pig's blood with a variety of meat, bacon or offal additions, possibly onions, together with herbs and spices. May be poached or fried and eaten hot or cold

boar A species of wild pig *Sus scrofa and others* still hunted in parts of Europe and Asia. It is not bled after killing so has a very dark meat [also called **wild boar**]

boar's head The head of a boar, almost exclusively used for decoration in the same way as a pig's head

bo bay mon *(Vi)* An elaborate and costly meal of seven different beef dishes *(Lit. beef in seven dishes)* starting with a beef fondue with vinegar *(see fondue Chinoise)* and ending with chao thit bo, a kind of gruel

bobe *(It)* A type of sea bream

bobi *(Ru)* Beans

bobotee *(USA)* A pudding-like dish of almonds, onions and breadcrumbs in a seasoned white sauce.

bobotie *(Saf)* Cooked minced beef or lamb, mixed with milk-soaked bread, raisins, almonds, sweated chopped onions, vinegar or lemon juice, spices and seasonings, placed in a dish, covered in an egg custard and baked until set.

bocas de la isla *(Sp)* A speciality of Cadiz made from the claw of the fiddler crab

bocca di dama *(It)* Fruit and nut cake

bocca negro *(It)* Dogfish

bocconcino *(It)* Thin slices of ham, veal and cheese, panéed and fried

böckling *(Sw)* Buckling

böckling-låda *(Sw)* Buckling pie made with cleaned and filleted buckling placed in a dish and covered with a rich seasoned egg custard mix sprinkled with chopped chives and cooked in the oven until set

böckling och purjolökslåda *(Sw)* Cleaned and filleted buckling laid in the base of a greased oven proof dish, covered with alternate stripes of chopped hard boiled egg yolk, egg white and raw leeks, seasoned, dotted with butter and baked in a moderate oven for 15 minutes adding double cream half way through

Bocksbart *(Ge)* Salsify

Bockshornklee *(Ge)* Fenugreek

Bockwurst *(Ge)* Similar in appearance to a long frankfurter but made from finely minced veal or beef together with pork, back fat, and seasoning, flavoured with nutmeg, coriander, ginger and garlic, packed into sheep casings, smoked and scalded. Served hot

bockwurst *(USA)* As the German variety of Bockwurst but with the addition of eggs and sometimes milk and flavoured with leeks or chives

boczek *(Pl)* Hard, smoked pork meat

body mass index A measure of obesity in human beings equal to a person's weight in kilograms divided by the square of their height in metres. If between 25 and 30, then the person is considered overweight, if over 30 they are obese. (Example weight 75 kg (168 lb), height 1.7 m (5 ft 7 in), body mass index = 75/(1.7 x 1.7) = 25.95, hence overweight)

body skirt *(UK)* The less muscular part of the diaphragm of beef cattle

boeren *(Ho)* Farm. Printed on the rind of genuine Dutch farmhouse cheeses

boerenkool *(Ho)* Kale or broccoli

boerenkool met worst *(Ho)* Broccoli or kale and mashed potatoes with sausage

boerewors *(Saf)* Pork or lamb sausages made from the principal meat mixed with other meats and bacon or pork fat, seasoned, flavoured with coriander and other spices and herbs, moistened with vinegar or wine and packed after standing into hog casings. Usually grilled

boeuf *(Fr) masc.* Beef or ox

boeuf à la bourguinonne *(Fr) masc.* A piece of beef, usually topside, larded and marinated in red wine and brandy for 12 hours, drained, sealed, browned and braised in the marinade and brown stock to half cover. Served with a sauce made from the degreased, strained and reduced cooking liquor and garnished with glazed button mushrooms and onions, fried diced bacon and heart shaped croûtons

boeuf de Constance *(Fr) masc.* Specially selected beef carcases from animals finished on yeasty beer with their fodder without exercise for the last three months to make their muscles tender and massaged daily during this period to push surface fat into the back muscles. The technique was copied from the Japanese

boeuf en daube *(Fr) masc.* Marinated and larded beef braised with the marinade and a BG in a daubière lined with salt pork for at least 4 hours and served as is. Sometimes used incorrectly of beef braised with wine, onion, vegetables and garlic; *see also* daube

boeuf, estouffade de *(Fr) masc.* Similar to boeuf en daube and enriched with pigs' trotters

boeuf à la ficelle *(Fr) masc.* A fine, trimmed boneless piece of fillet, rump or sirloin of beef, suspended in seasoned and boiling water with a mirepoix of aromatic vegetables, a BG and an onion clouté so that it does not touch the base of the pan and simmered very slowly at 35 minutes per kg. Served sliced with watercress, mustard, horseradish and pickles

boeuf miroton *(Fr) masc. see* miroton

boeuf à la mode *(Fr) masc.* Aiguillette of beef, larded, marinated and braised in red wine, served with vegetables

boeuf salé *(Fr) masc.* Smoked brisket of beef [also called **pikefleisch**]

bøf *(De)* Beef

bofu *(Ja)* The thin red stems from parsnips, split in four lengthwise using a skewer, curled in ice water and used as a garnish for sushi and sashimi

bog myrtle An aromatic bush *Myrica gale*, with a flavour like bay which grows wild on boggy moors. The oil is said to be the best repellent for the ferocious Scottish midges [also called **sweet gale**]

boga *(It & Sp)* Bogue, the fish

bogavante *(Sp)* Large clawed lobster

boghe *(It)* Bogue, the fish

bogue *(En & Fr) masc.* A small (to 1 kg) round seawater fish *Boops boops* with a silvery yellow skin, interchangeable with bream

Bohemian pheasant *see* guinea fowl

bohémienne *(Fr) fem.* A very simple ratatouille made from tomatoes and aubergines, separately cooked in olive oil before combining

bohémienne, à la *(Fr)* In the gypsy style, i.e. garnished with tomatoes, rice, fried onions and possibly sweet red peppers and paprika

bohémienne, sauce A cold sauce made like mayonnaise using a base of thick cold Béchamel, egg yolks, seasoning and a little vinegar into which olive oil and tarragon vinegar are whipped. Finished with mustard.

Böhmische Dalken *(Au)* An egg yolk and sugar enriched yeast-raised dough mixed with stiffly beaten egg whites before proving, made into a circular shape which has the centre indented after proving and served hot with red jam in the centre after baking

Bohnen *(Ge)* Beans

Bohnenkraut *(Ge)* Savory

boil, to To cook in water or a water based liquid at its boiling point and with sufficient heat input to generate bubbles of steam which agitate and stir the mixture

boiled beef and carrots *(UK)* A famous traditional London dish, the subject of a popular song. Made from soaked salted silverside or brisket simmered with an onion clouté, turnips, celery, leeks and small carrots until tender and served with the defatted and reduced cooking liquor.

boiled custard *(USA)* Custard made on top of the stove

boiled egg Soft boiled see oeuf mollet, hard boiled see oeuf dur

boiled frosting *(USA) see* American frosting

boiled icing *(USA) see* American frosting

boiled sweets Hard translucent sweets made by boiling sugar, glucose, acid and flavourings to 149°C

boiler onions *(USA)* Small white mild onions used whole in soups, stews, etc. or may be puréed

boiling fowl Chickens older than 18 months weighing between 2 to 3.5 kg not suitable for roasting, grilling or frying. Usually a hen which has had 1 or 2 laying seasons. Used to produce a highly flavoured stock

boissons *(Fr) fem.* Drinks, e.g. boissons incluses means drinks included

bok choi *see* pak choy

bok-choy *see* pak choy

bokking *(Ho)* Bloater

bokko ko maasu *(Ne)* Goat

bolacha *(Po)* Crackers *(biscuits)*

bolet bronze *(Fr) masc. see* cèpe de vendage

Boletaceae A family or sub group genus of the funghi of which *Boletus edulis* or cep is the most well known. All varieties are characterized by close packed tubular structures under the cap in place of the more common gills and only one variety, the bitter boletus, is poisonous and is distinguished from the cep by its bitter taste. Of the others, the white boletus *B. albidus,* the devil's boletus *B. satanus,* the red stalked boletus *B. erthropus* and the yellow boletus *B. calopus* are inedible. All the other 23 varieties are edible. However all pickers should be trained by an expert

Boletus badius *Bot.* Bay boletus

Boletus edulis *Bot.* Cep

bolinhos *(Po)* Small balls (of meat, fish, etc.)

boller *(De)* Balls, as in fish or meat balls

bollicina *(It)* Whelk

bollito *(It)* Boiled

bollito misto *(It)* A rich stew made by simmering in water for 4 hours, boned pig's head, flank of beef with bones in, shin beef, boiling fowl, tongue, sausage and sweated carrots, onions and celery, and seasoning, adding the boiling fowl and sausage towards the end. It is usually served from a special trolley with the meats carved at the table and presented with a sharp sauce. Used as a test of a good restaurant

bollo *(Sp)* A small loaf or a bread roll

bõlo *(Po)* Ball, cake or pie

bõlo de anjo *(Po)* Angel cake

bolognaise, sauce *(Fr) fem. see* Bolognese sauce

Bologna sausage *(It)* A smoked slicing sausage from Bologna, made from various ingredients mainly finely ground pork with spices and seasonings but also veal, beef, tripe, pistachio nuts, onion, tongue, etc. cooked in wine and stuffed into beef bungs then simmered. Similar to Mortadella. Some are smoked [also called **polony** (UK), **bolony** (USA), **poloney**]

Bolognese sauce A sauce made from fine minced beef fried in olive oil with chopped onions, garlic and skinned tomatoes, mixed with herbs and seasonings and simmered with stock or wine and/or tomato juice and possibly thickened with flour. Served with spaghetti [also called **sauce bolognaise** (Fr)]

bolony *(USA) see* Bologna sausage

bomba di riso *(It)* A dish of cooked rice moulded around a filling of cooked minced meat, herbs and seasoning, chopped mushrooms and diced cheese or ham

Bombay duck *(In)* Sun dried pieces of the bummaloe fish *Harpodon nehereus* found in Indian waters. It has a very strong smell and a not particularly pleasant taste. Served with curry [also called **bombil**]

bombe 1 *(Fr) fem.* An ice cream speciality of different flavours in a near spherical or conical shape, often made by lining a bombe mould with one ice cream and filling the centre with another, possibly mixed with nuts, glacé fruits or liqueurs **2** *(It)* A breakfast roll

bombe glacée *(Fr) fem.* A mixture of ice creams and flavoured ices

bombe mould A special mould for making ice cream bombes

bombil *(In)* Bombay duck

bombolette *(It)* Fritters

bomeloe *see* bummaloe, the fish

bonalay *see* ale flip

bonavist bean *see* hyacinth bean

bonbon *(Fr) masc.* Sweet, confectionery

bondail A bondon type cheese flavoured with garlic

Bondard *see* Bondon

Bondart *see* Bondon

bondas *(In)* Spiced balls of mashed potatoes coated in a besan batter and deep fried

Bonde *see* Bondon

bondelle *(Fr) fem.* Houting, the fish

bondepige med slør *(De)* A traditional dessert made from layers of crumbled rye bread, sweetened apple purée and molten red jam, finished with a whipped cream and red jam topping

Bondon *(Fr) fem.* A small bun shaped, soft, whole cows' milk cheese made in Normandy [also called **Bondard, Bondart, Bonde**]

bone, to To remove bones from animal carcases and fish, generally with as little damage to the flesh as possible

bone marrow *see* marrow

bone marrow sauce *see* sauce moelle

bone taint A fault which can occur in meat on the bone preserved by surface salting due to growth of *Clostridium* spp. and *Streptococcus* spp. around the bone which is furthest from the salt and the last part to become salted. Particularly noticeable if the meat is not correctly chilled. But see also cold shortening

boneless steak *(USA)* A steak without bone cut from the sirloin. See sirloin steak (USA)

bonen *(Ho)* Beans

bones The skeleton of animals and fishes together with connective tissue, gristle, etc. Used to make stock by long simmering (4 hours plus) with water, aromatic vegetables and a BG to release flavour and gelatine. The simmering stock is repeatedly skimmed to remove fat and scum (coagulated protein and dirt). Bones are either browned or blanched before simmering. They are sometimes put in the bottom of a pan to prevent food sticking to the base and to add flavour to the dish

boniatos *(Ca & Sp)* Sweet potatoes

boning knife A thick, non-pliable, sharp knife used for boning animals or a thin, pliable sharp knife for boning fish

bonita *(It)* Bonito

bonite *(Fr)* Bonito

bonito 1 A fish *Katsuwonus pelamis,* more correctly called Pacific bonito, whose dried flesh is used as a base for all Japanese broths and stocks. The dried flesh is gray black with a light gray coating of mould and is sold either in blocks *(katsuo-kesuriki)* or as very thin shavings *(hana-katsico* or *kezuri-bushi).* It is also ground and agglomerated into granules for making dashi [also called **frigate mackerel**] **2** *see* little tunny and skipjack tuna

bonito flakes Dried shavings or flakes of Pacific bonito used in Japanese cooking esp. for making dashi. Removed from the dish after the flavour has been extracted

Bonitol *(Ge)* Little tunny, the fish

boniton *(Fr)* Little tunny, the fish

bonnachen *(UK)* A sausage from the Highland region of Scotland made from 2 parts lean beef to 1 part suet with seasoning, saltpetre, sugar, ground ginger and cloves

bonne bouchée *(Fr) fem.* A canapé or savoury food item served as an appetizer or at the end of a meal. Lit. a good mouthful

bonne femme *(Fr) fem.* Used to describe simple or home cooking involving little or no complication

bonne femme, à la *(Fr)* In the housewife's style, i.e. cooked with mushrooms, potatoes, onions and sometimes fried bacon

bonne femme, fish As for fish Bercy with the addition of sliced button mushrooms to the cooking liquor. The mushrooms are separated after poaching and used as a garnish

bonnefoy, sauce *(Fr) fem.* A white bordelaise sauce made with dry white instead of red wine and a white velouté instead of espagnole sauce. Finished with a little chopped tarragon [also called **sauce bordelaise au vin blanc**]

bønner *(De)* Beans

bönor *(Sw)* Beans

Boodles' orange fool *(UK)* A type of syllabub made with filtered orange juice replacing the alcoholic liquid. Alternatively a bowl lined with slices of trifle sponge and filled with a type of fool made from sweetened orange and lemon juice with grated zest and whipped cream, allowed to soak, refrigerated and decorated with orange slices. Named after Boodle's club

Boodles' stuffing Mashed ripe bananas mixed with an equal volume of wholemeal breadcrumbs, finely chopped onion, chopped tarragon and seasoning. Used to stuff quails, small birds or chicken breasts

bookmaker sandwich An underdone minute steak between two slices of hot buttered toast

bookweeten janhinnerk *(Ho)* Buckwheat pancake with bacon

boomla *(In)* Bummaloe, the fish

boontjie sop *(Saf)* Bean soup made from

stock and dry beans (3 or 4:1), the beans soaked overnight and simmered in the stock with a chilli until soft, then all passed through a sieve

boova shenkel *(USA)* A meat stew with dumplings, originating with the Dutch immigrants to Pennsylvania

boquerones *(Sp)* Fresh anchovy fillets, pickled in salt and vinegar or crisp fried.

borage A hardy annual herb *Borago officinalis* with hairy, cucumber-flavoured leaves and intense blue flowers. Used to flavour drinks and rarely in salads and the leaves can be cooked as spinach. The flowers may be crystallized for decoration

Borago officinalis *Bot.* Borage

borassus palm *see* palmyra palm

borda *(Hu)* Chop

Bordeaux mustard A dark coloured, slightly sweet, prepared mustard often flavoured with herbs and milder than Dijon mustard

bordelaise, à la *(Fr)* Used of dishes incorporating wine sauce, bone marrow, ceps or a garnish of artichokes and potatoes

bordelaise, sauce *(En & Fr) fem.* A brown sauce made from a reduction of red wine, shallots, thyme, bay leaf and mignonette pepper, simmered with demi-glace for 30 minutes and strained. Finished with meat glaze and lemon juice and garnished with diced poached bone marrow if available. Used with steak

bordelaise au vin blanc, sauce *(Fr) fem. see* sauce bonnefoy

border *see* bordure

border mould *see* ring mould

bordetto *(It)* A fish stew in tomato sauce from the north of Italy

bordure *(Fr) fem.* Ring or border, usually of cooked rice or vegetables around the edge of a plate, used to contain other foods in the centre

borecole A flat leaved variety of kale

boreg *see* borek

börek *(Tu)* A puff pastry or filo pastry pastie sometimes filled with honey and nuts and soaked in a sugar syrup or alternatively with a meat or cheese filling. The sweet variety is similar to the Greek bourekakia [also called **boreg**]

boretto *(It) see* brodetto

borgmästarfläta *(Sw)* Rectangles of Danish pastry 40 cm by 8 cm, spread with cinnamon-flavoured butter cream followed by almond paste, rolled into long cylinders, 3 cylinders plaited, proved for 45 minutes, egg washed, sprinkled with flaked almonds and baked at 230°C for 15 to 20 minutes

borgrács gulyás *(Hu) see* Hungarian goulash

borjú *(Hu)* Veal

borjúpaprikas *(Hu)* As paprikas csirke but substituting veal for chicken

borjúpörkölt *(Hu)* Diced veal fried in lard with chopped onions, paprika and garlic then simmered with water, tomatoes or tomato purée and seasoning until cooked

borlotto bean An Italian bean of the same family as French beans with a pinkish skin when dried [also called **rose cocoa bean, rosecoco bean**]

bornholmeræggekage *(De)* An omelette filled with smoked herring, radish and chives

bornholmere *(De)* Buckling

borowik szachetny *(Pl)* Boletus edulis or cep

borragine *(It)* Borage

borrêgo *(Po)* Lamb

borride *see* bourride

bors *(Hu)* Pepper

bors de fasole *(Ro)* A broth made with haricot beans, raw beetroot, onions, celery, spinach, tomatoes, oil, vinegar and seasoning

borscht *(Pl)* Borshch

borshch *(Ru)* A generic name for various Russian and Central European soups based on beetroot. See e.g. beetroot soup, beetroot consommé, borszcz, borshchock [also called **bortsch**]

borshchock *(Ru)* A clear beetroot soup often made with or containing game birds. Served with croûtons [also called **bortschchock**]

borststuk *(Ho)* Brisket of beef

bortsch *see* borshch

bortschchock *(Ru) see* borshchock

bosanske cufte *(Bk)* A Bosnian speciality of meat balls made from seasoned minced lamb or beef, bound with egg and flour, baked in the oven and served reheated with an egg and yoghurt sauce flavoured with caraway seeds

bosanske lonac *(Bk)* A rich casserole from Bosnia based on diced pork, lamb and beef cooked in wine with vegetables and seasoning, given body with a calf's foot and flavoured with vinegar

bosbessen *(Ho)* Blueberries, bilberries, whortleberries

boscaiolo, al' (It) In the style of the forester, i.e. with mushrooms

bosega *(It)* Grey mullet

bossons macérés *(Fr)* *masc.* A strong tasting goats' milk cheese from Languedoc soaked in olive oil, white wine and brandy

Boston baked beans *(USA)* White beans casseroled with salt pork, an onion clouté, mustard, sugar or treacle and salt for a long time until tender. Served with Boston brown bread

Boston bean *see* navy bean

Boston blue fish *see* coley

Boston brown bread *(USA)* A steamed, yeast-raised bread containing white and brown flour, fine cornmeal or semolina and treacle

Boston cracker *(USA)* A large, thin and slightly sweet cracker

Boston cream pie *(USA)* A sandwich sponge filled with crème patissière and coated with chocolate icing

Boston lettuce *(USA)* A small variety of butterhead lettuce

bot *(Ho)* Flounder, the fish

botargo *(En & It)* The salted, pressed and dried roe of the female tuna fish or grey mullet, which latter is often coated with a preservative wax. A popular delicacy or hors d'oeuvre in Italy, Greece and Egypt [also called **bottarga**]

boter *(Ho)* Butter

boterham *(Ho)* A slice, cold sliced meats, assiette Anglaise

boterhammenworst *(Ho)* A boiled sausage made from minced fatty veal and pork back fat cured with a mixture of salt, sugar and saltpetre (6:2:1) for 2 days using 1 part of the curing mixture per 30 parts of meat mixture, this then mixed with flour, ground pepper, ginger, nutmeg and mace, packed into ox bungs, hot smoked and simmered in water

boterhammetje *(Ho)* Sandwich

boterkoek *(Ho)* Butter cake, similar to Scottish shortbread

bot gao *(Vi)* Rice flour

botifarra *(Sp)* *see* butifarra

boti kabab *(In)* Small pieces of very tender meat, marinated for several hours, skewered and grilled under intense heat whilst being basted with ghee

bot nep *(Vi)* Glutinous rice flour

bot ngot *(Vi)* Monosodium glutamate

bottagio *(It)* Pork stew

bottarga *(En & It)* Botargo

bottatrice *(It)* Eel pout

bottle, to To preserve food, usually fruit but sometimes vegetables, in sealed sterilized bottles. Prevention of bacterial spoilage is by heating to 130°C for 30 minutes, or addition of acid, salt or sugar, all of which inhibit bacterial growth. Apart from fruit, most food is too difficult to bottle under domestic conditions

bottle gourd Although often scooped out and dried for ornamental use, this fruit of the plant *Lageneria siceraria* is used when young as a somewhat bland vegetable after removing the large seeds. It looks like a smooth cucumber with a bulge at the flower end. Used to make kampyo q.v. [also called **trumpet gourd**, and **calabash** when inedible or **dudhi** when edible]

bottom round *(USA)* The bottom of the hindquarter of beef adjacent to shin beef

Botton *(UK)* A semi-hard Cheddar like cheese made from unpasteurized cows' milk in Danby, Yorkshire

botulism Food poisoning caused by the toxin excreted by *Clostridium botulinum* which is a strict spore-forming anaerobe. It can therefore only grow in sealed cans and jars from which air is excluded or rarely in the centre of cooked food. Used to be responsible for deaths when home bottling of vegetables was common. The toxin is destroyed and made harmless by boiling for a few minutes; *see also* *Clostridium botulinum*

botvinia *(Ru)* A celebratory summer soup from the Ukraine made with white wine mixed with pickled beetroot juice, spinach and sorrel leaves, beetroot tops, pickled cucumber, shrimps, sturgeon, herbs, vinegar and seasoning, all cooled with crushed ice

bot xa xiu *(Vi)* Roast pork spices

bou de Fagne *(Be)* A small soft brick-shaped cheese made from cows' milk. The paste has a pleasant taste and aroma with a few holes. The rind is orange-yellow with a slight bloom

bouchée *(Fr)* *fem.* A small filled vol-au-vent or puff pastry shell made by cutting virgin puff pastry in a round and half cutting the centre, cooking and scooping out the middle prior to filling. When half risen in the oven it should be pressed down flat to give an even rise. Lit. a mouthful

bouchées de fruits de mer *(Fr)* *fem.* Bouchées filled with diced mushrooms cooked in butter, which have been sweated with mixed shellfish, bound with sauce vin blanc and garnished with picked parsley

bouchées à la reine *(Fr) fem.* Chicken filled bouchées

boudin 1 *(Fr) masc.* Sausage or pudding as in black or white pudding, boudin noir or boudin blanc **2** *(USA)* A Creole sausage mixture made from pork liver, cooked pork and rice, spring onions and seasoning

boudin Asturien *(Fr) masc. see* Morcilla

boudin d'Auvergne *(Fr) masc.* A boudin noir mix with added milk and hard pork back fat and flare fat

boudin blanc *(Fr) masc.* A white cooked sausage made from finely ground white meat (chicken, rabbit, veal, pork), cream, egg, onions, starchy material, spices, herbs and seasoning. It is then boiled and may be eaten cold or cooked in the usual manner. Popular at French Christmas celebrations

boudin blanc à l'ancienne *(Fr) masc.* A boudin blanc made from raw fish, chicken breast, sweetbreads, carp roes pounded one by one with bread boiled in milk, butter, cooked cows' udder, boiled rice, onion purée and egg yolks, seasoned and flavoured with nutmeg and mixed with cream before being filled into casings and simmered in milk

boudin blanc d'Ourville *(Fr) masc.* A panada made with milk, mixed with chopped pork fat, sweated chopped onions, butter, cream, egg yolks, seasoning and quatre-épices, packed into pieces of casing tied either end leaving room for expansion, simmered in water then grilled

boudin blanc de Paris *(Fr) masc.* A mixture of finely processed raw poultry breast meat, pork loin, flare and back fat, sweated chopped onions, softened breadcrumbs, eggs, cream, seasoning and quatre-épices filled loosely into beef runners, linked and simmered in milk and water for 20 minutes, cooled and grilled or fried.

boudin blanc rennais *(Fr) masc.* A mixture of chopped poultry breast meat and fat pork with onions boiled in milk flavoured with cloves and chervil, fine breadcrumbs, eggs and seasoning, filled loosely into beef runners, linked and simmered for 45 minutes, cooled then fried

boudin de Brest *(Fr) masc.* A boudin noir mix with higher proportions of blood and cream and boiled onion instead of sweated chopped onion. Made into long 20 cm links

boudin Breton *(Fr) masc.* A boudin noir mix using a mixture of pigs' and calf's blood

boudin à la crème *(Fr & Be)* masc. A simple boudin noir mix of 2 parts pigs blood to 1 part cream with egg, butter, chopped onion and seasoning

boudin creole *(USA)* A boudin noir mix of blood, milk-soaked bread, pork back fat, garlic, parsley, chives, seasoning, quatre-épices and rum

boudin à la Flamande *(Be)* masc. A boudin noir mix with a large amount of onion, dried vine fruits and chopped parsley instead of spices

boudin du Languedoc *(Fr) masc.* A boudin noir mix including lean neck and spare rib of pork, flavoured with caraway seeds or aniseed

boudin de Lyon *(Fr) masc.* A boudin noir mix flavoured with paprika, chives, thyme, parsley and brandy

boudin noir *(Fr) masc.* A black pudding made with pigs' blood, pork, kidney fat, cream, onions, salt and spices. The chopped pork fat and onions are sweated in lard, mixed with the other ingredients, poured into casings, linked, and simmered at 90°C until the blood solidifies and they rise in the water. There are many variations

boudin noir à l'ail *(Fr) masc.* A boudin noir mix with chopped garlic instead of spice

boudin noir alsacien *(Fr) masc.* A boudin noir mix with chopped apple

boudin noir à l'anglaise *(Fr) masc.* A boudin noir mix with the addition of boiled rice or pearl barley

boudin noir à la normande *(Fr) masc.* Sliced boudin noir and peeled and sliced dessert apples sautéed in butter until slightly browned. Served as is or with a reduction of cider and pan juices or flamed with calvados

boudin du Poitou aux épinards *(Fr) masc.* A boudin noir mixture of blood, chopped spinach, pork flare fat and gin, flavoured with orange flower water, thyme, quatre-épices and salt. Cooked as boudin noir

boudins entre ciel et terre *(Fr) masc.* A dish of mashed potatoes, enriched with egg yolks and butter, and apple purée placed in a serving dish, warmed, well grilled boudins placed on top and all napped with melted butter

bouffi *(Fr) masc.* A type of bloater lightly salted and smoked, eaten cooked or raw [also called **craquelots, demi-doux**]

bouillabaisse *(Fr) fem.* A Mediterranean soup made with firm white fish and shellfish, with tomatoes, garlic, saffron, herbs and olive oil boiled 10 minutes before adding soft fish. Served with slices of French bread

bouilli 1 *(Fr)* Boiled, past participle of bouillir to boil **2** *(USA)* A classic cajun soup made with beef offal

bouillie *(Fr) fem.* **1** A thick porridge from Brittany made with buckwheat flour and resembling polenta **2** Baby cereal, gruel, porridge, pulp

bouillinade *(Fr) fem.* A fish stew with onions, potatoes, garlic and sweet peppers from Roussillon

bouillir *(Fr)* To boil

bouillir à petit feu *(Fr)* To simmer

bouillon 1 *(Fr) masc.* A stock specifically made for soup, not especially clarified **2** *(En)* A pasty mixture of salt, MSG, vegetable and/or meat extracts and flavourings sold commercially in large tubs for making convenience stocks

bouillon cube *see* stock cube

boula *(USA)* A green turtle soup with green peas, flavoured with sherry, garnished with grated cheese and sometimes with whipped cream

boulangère, à la *(Fr)* In the style of the baker's wife, i.e. cooked in the oven with sliced onions, potatoes and stock

boule *(Fr) fem.* The flat ball-shaped traditional bread loaf with a rough crust, weighing up to 12 kg. Sometimes made by the sourdough method. It is the origin of the word boulangerie

boule de Bâle *(He)* fem. A pork meat, beef and fat pork sausage, smoked over beech wood, scalded and cooled. Served hot

boule de macreuse *(Fr) fem.* A forequarter cut of beef extending down from the middle of the shoulder to the top of the leg including parts of English chuck, leg of mutton cut and brisket. Used for braising and stewing

boule de neige *(Fr) fem.* A sponge or ice cream dessert topped with whipped cream

boulette *(Fr) fem.* **1** Rissole, meatball or meat croquette **2** A small shortcrust or puff pastry pasty with a cooked meat or poultry filling, panéed and deep fried **3** *(Be)* A small strong-flavoured cheese made in a variety of shapes, often flavoured with herbs

boulette d'Avesnes *(Fr)* A soft, cooked and kneaded-curd cheese made from buttermilk in northern France. It is seasoned with salt, herbs and spices and ripened for 3 months

boulettes creole *(WA)* Highly spiced minced meatballs from Gambia simmered with onions, green sweet peppers, tomatoes, ginger and chillis in oil and stock

bounceberry *see* cranberry

bouquet *(Fr) masc.* Common prawn

bouquet garni *(Fr) masc.* Herbs tied in a bundle, or wrapped in muslin or a blanched leek leaf, usually consisting of thyme, parsley stalks, celery leaves, bayleaf and possibly peppercorns. Abbreviated to BG

bouquet de Moines *(Be)* A soft cows' milk cheese with a smooth even-textured delicately flavoured paste covered in a brown rind and made in 400 g cylinders

bouquetière, à la *(Fr)* In the style of the florist, i.e. a method of presentation of hot cooked food, usually steaks or chops or the like on a platter surrounded by alternating small piles of individual servings of vegetables. The number of each variety corresponding to the number of servings of meat, etc.

bouquette *(Be)* A pancake made with a buckwheat batter containing raisins

bourani esfenaj *(Pe)* A mixture of cooked spinach, yoghurt and chopped garlic, served as a starter

Bourbon biscuit Two rectangular chocolate-flavoured biscuits, sandwiched together with a chocolate cream filling

bourdaine *(Fr) fem.* A dessert from Anjou consisting of an apple dumpling with jam

bourdaloue *(Fr)* Poached fruit served in a vanilla syrup

bourekakia *(Gr)* A small sweet cake made from nuts and honey surrounded by layers of filo pastry or puff pastry like a sausage roll, baked, cooled and soaked in sugar syrup. Similar cakes are common throughout the Middle East. Also used of a savoury pasty made with filo pastry filled with cheese, poultry, vegetables or meat, fried or baked and eaten hot or cold

bourgeoise, à la *(Fr)* Description of dishes that are domestic in nature and usually without a set recipe, often garnished with carrots, onions and bacon

bourgouri *see* bulgar

bourguignonne, à la *(Fr)* In the style of Burgundy, i.e. with red Burgundy wine, shallots, mushrooms and bacon

bourguignonne, sauce *(En & Fr) fem.* Red wine flavoured with chopped shallots or onions, mushrooms, parsley, thyme and bay leaf, reduced, strained and thickened with beurre manié. Served with grilled or roast beef [also called **Burgundy sauce**]

bouride *(Fr)* Strongly garlic-flavoured

bourride *(Fr) fem.* A Provençal fish soup made with small pieces of sea fish sautéed with onions, celery, and garlic, boiled in white wine, water, herbs and seasoning and garnished with diced boiled potatoes. Served with mayonnaise and bread

boursin *(Fr)* A commercial fresh cream cheese flavoured with garlic and herbs or rolled in crushed peppercorns

boursotto *(Fr)* A rice, anchovy, vegetable and cheese pasty from Nice

boutefas *(He)* A large smoked sausage from the Vaudois made of 4 parts pork to 1 part beef

bovine somatotrophin A genetically

engineered growth hormone given to cows to increase their milk production but leading to their discomfort and an increased incidence of udder troubles. Banned in the EU until 2000 AD at the earliest

bovine spongiform encephalopathy The so-called mad cow disease caused by an infective agent *(prion)* which causes scrapie in sheep and which has been passed on to cattle by feeding them with sheep offal. It has now been shown that the agent can be transmitted to other animals and there is a strong presumption that it can cause a new type of Creutzfeldt-Jacob disease in humans especially amongst those who consumed the cheaper types of manufactured beef products in the 1980's. There is considerable evidence that the incubation period depends on the amount of the agent ingested. It has led to a decrease in the consumption of beef and the banning of the sale of certain parts of the beef carcase. Many scientists in the UK will not eat manufactured beef products or beef offal for fear they may contain some of the BSE agent [also called **BSE**]

Bovril *(UK)* A proprietary meat extract made from hydrolysed meat protein and extractives used for flavouring or as a drink when diluted with hot water

bowl A vessel of roughly hemispherical shape, sometimes with a flat base, used in the kitchen to mix, weigh and prepare the mis en place

Bowles' mint The common mint type *Mentha x villosa 'Alopecuroides'* with large roundish hairy leaves, mid green in colour and with a mixed apple/spearmint aroma

box crab A small pink crab *Calappa granulata* with red claws which fit over its face and jaw parts so that it looks like an irregular ball. Found off Spanish coasts

boxthorn A plant *Lycium chinese* of the tomato family with small deep-green, oval leaves used in Cantonese cooking to flavour soup

boxty *(Ir)* Mashed cooked potatoes mixed with grated raw potatoes, flour, baking powder, fat and seasoning, formed into cakes, baked, split and eaten hot with butter

boxty bread *(UK)* A potato bread from Northern Ireland made of equal parts of mashed potatoes, grated raw potatoes and self raising flour with a little extra baking powder, brought together into a stiff dough and baked at 200°C

boysenberry A hybrid of raspberry, strawberry, dewberry and blackberry, similar to a blackberry but dark red and with a rather acid taste

bra *(It)* A soft or hard cows' milk cheese from Piedmont cast in wheel shapes (6 to 8 kg). The cheese is moulded, pressed, salted and ripened 45 days for the soft version or 6 months for the hard version. The paste is pale cream changing to a dense yellow with minute holes as it ages

braadkip *(Ho)* Chicken, broiler

braai *(Saf)* Barbecue

braaivleis *(Saf)* Barbecue

brabançonne, à la *(Fr)* In the style of Brabant, Belgium, i.e. garnished with Brussels sprouts, hops or chicory

bracchiolini *(It)* A giant beef olive from Sicily made with a stuffing of hard boiled eggs, pork fat, parsley, cheese and chopped onions. This is then fried in oil and brandy, stewed in a tomato sauce flavoured with cinnamon and herbs and cut in slices for serving

brace of pheasants Two pheasants, one the brightly plumaged cock and the other the hen, the better eater

Brachsenmakrelle *(Ge)* Pomfret, the fish

bracia, alla *(It)* Charcoal grilled

braciola *(It)* Cutlet, chop

braciola di maiale *(It)* Pork chop

braciolette ripiene *(It)* Veal olives *(paupiettes)*

bracioline *(It)* Small cutlets of lamb

bräckkorv *(Sw)* A sausage made from finely minced beef, lean pork and fat bacon, mixed with mashed potatoes, milk, seasoning, sugar, saltpetre and allspice, diced bacon added, the whole filled into casings, linked, dry salted for 1 day and possibly smoked

Bradenham ham *(UK)* A west country ham cured with dry salt or brined for a month, pickled in molasses, salt and saltpetre for a month and smoked over applewood and oak. This turns the skin black and the meat red and sweet. To cook, it is soaked in water to remove salt and then boiled

brændende kærlighed *(De)* Mashed potato and bacon. Lit. burning love!

bragance, à la *(Fr)* In the style of Braganza, Portugal, i.e. garnished with stuffed tomatoes and potato croquettes

Braganza cabbage *see* Portuguese cabbage

Brägenwurst *(Ge)* A lightly smoked thin sausage made from pigs' brains, oats and flour

braid cheese *see* string cheese

brains The brains of animals are classed as offal and are a delicacy in Italy, France and other countries. Their use is falling out of favour due to problems with the agent responsible for scrapie and BSE which affects the brains of sheep and cows. If used they should be plump, fresh and covered with an easily removed membrane. They are soaked in salted water, the membrane and blood vessels removed and the brains poached in acidulated water

brains sausage *(USA)* Casings filled with a mixture of chopped brains, pork and pork fat with grated onions and seasoning, linked, boiled for a few minutes and cooled. Served fried in butter

braisé(e) *(Fr)* Braised, past participle of braiser, to braise

braise to To cook previously browned food in just enough liquid to cover it in a pan with a very tight fitting lid which reduces evaporation. The cooking is very slow and the meat is usually placed on a mirepoix of vegetables. Braising is often finished in the oven after bringing to the boil on top of the stove

braised rice *see* rice pilaff

braiser *(Fr)* To braise

bramble *see* blackberry

bramble jelly 1 *(UK)* Wild blackberry jelly **2** *(USA)* Crab apple and blackberry jelly (a clear jam without seeds)

bramborová polévka *(Cz)* Beef stock, thickened with a brown roux and simmered with garlic, marjoram and seasoning, strained and garnished with diced carrots and celeriac and shredded cabbage previously sweated in butter plus diced boiled potatoes, mushrooms and fried salt pork

Bramley's seedling *(UK)* A large green sour cooking apple, ideal for purées, sauces, baking and most culinary uses. Available all year round

bran The outer layer of cereal grains composed mainly of cellulose, which is left in wholemeal flour. When removed by sifting the flour it is used as an animal feed or for high fibre breakfast cereals

bran flour *(USA)* Wheat bran finely ground

branche, en *(Fr)* Served whole, esp. of vegetables, (e.g. celery, spinach)

branco *(Po)* White

Brand *(Ge)* A hard cheese made from naturally soured milk mixed with beer

brandade de morue *(Fr) fem.* Poached salt cod, skinned, boned and fried in oil with garlic, then pounded with oil, milk and seasonings to a fine paste, put in a baking dish and glazed

brandade de thon *(Fr) fem.* A dish from Brittany of canned or cooked tuna chunks mixed with cooked haricot beans and dressed

brandon puff *(USA)* A muffin made with a mixture of cornmeal and flour

brandy A high alcohol spirit distilled from wine and matured. Used for flavouring and flambéeing or flaming food. Similar spirits are grappa and marc [also called **cognac, armagnac**]

brandy butter A mixture of softened butter, caster sugar, brandy and possibly spice, served when cool with hot puddings or mince pies usually at Christmas [also called **hard sauce**]

brandy sauce *(UK)* A sweetened Béchamel sauce flavoured with brandy. Served with Christmas pudding or mince pies

brandy snap A crisp biscuit made with a thin mixture of butter, icing sugar, egg whites, soft flour and flavouring dropped in spoonfuls onto a baking tray, cooked at 240°C until lacy and brown, immediately rolled into a tube and left to cool. Generally filled with whipped cream

Brandza *see* Brynza

brank *see* buckwheat

Brânză de burduf *(Ro)* A ewes' milk cheese stronger than Brynza which is matured in a special leather bag *(a burduf)*. Sometimes flavoured by bringing into contact with fir tree bark

Branzi *(It)* A semi-hard scalded-curd slicing cheese from Bergamo cast in wheel shapes (to 15 kg). The moulded and pressed curd is salted in brine and ripened for 3 to 5 months. The paste has a soft supple texture with small evenly distributed holes. If kept, it will harden and may be used as a grating cheese

branzino *(It)* Bass

brasare *(It)* To braise

brasas, nas *(Po)* Charcoal grilled

brasato *(It)* Braised

braskartofler *(De)* Fried potatoes

brasserie 1 *(Fr) fem.* Brewery **2** *(En & Fr) fem.* An informal eating house or pub which supplies à la carte cooked dishes at all hours. They tend to be rather pretentious and expensive in the UK

Brassica hirta *Bot.* Mustard (for sprouting and salads)

Brassica juncea *Bot.* Brown mustard and oriental mustard

Brassica napus *Bot.* Rape and salad rape

***Brassica napus* Napobrassica Group** *Bot.* Swede

Brassica nigra *Bot.* Black mustard

***Brassica oleracea* Acephala Group** *Bot.* Kale

***Brassica oleracea* Botrytis Group** *Bot.* Cauliflower

***Brassica oleracea* Capitata Group** *Bot.* Cabbage

***Brassica oleracea* Gemmifera Group** *Bot.* Brussels sprouts

***Brassica oleracea* Gongylodes Group** *Bot.* Kohl rabi

***Brassica oleracea* Italica Group** *Bot.* Calabrese and sprouting broccoli

Brassica oleracea* var. *tronchuda *Bot.* Portuguese cabbage

***Brassica rapa* Rapifera Group** *Bot.* Turnip and turnip tops

***Brassica rapa* Utilis Group** *Bot.* Broccoli raab

Brassica rapa* var. *alboglabra *Bot.* Chinese broccoli

Brassica rapa* var. *chinensis *Bot.* Pak choy

Brassica rapa* var. *nipposinica *Bot.* Mizuna greens

Brassica rapa* var. *parachinensis *Bot.* Choy sum

Brassica rapa* var. *pekinensis *Bot.* Chinese leaves

Brassica rapa* var. *perviridis *Bot.* Komatsuna

Brassica rapa* var. *rosularis *Bot.* Chinese flat cabbage

***Brassica* spp.** The most important class of leafy vegetables grown throughout the world in a variety of forms. See individual items for details. Generally classified as western brassicas such as kale, cauliflower, cabbage, Brussels sprouts, calabrese, broccoli raab, kohl rabi, swedes and turnips, and oriental brassicas such as mizuna greens, komatsuna, Chinese cabbage, pak choy and Chinese broccoli. The oriental brassicas are mainly cultivated for the leaves and leafy stems

Brat *(He)* A grilling cheese made from cows' milk

Bratapfel *(Ge)* Baked apple

Braten *(Ge)* Roast meat

braten *(Ge)* To roast

Bratenbrühe *(Ge)* Gravy

Bratenfett *(Ge)* Dripping

Bratfisch *(Ge)* Fried fish

Brathendl *(Au)* Roast chicken

Bratheringe *(Ge)* A type of escabeche made from filleted herrings, floured and fried then marinated in vinegar with onion, bay leaf, peppercorns and mustard seed. Served cold

Brathuhn *(Ge)* Roast chicken

Bratkartoffeln *(Ge)* Fried potatoes

Bratrollmops *(Ge)* Rollmop herrings made up and fried before pickling

bratt pan A large versatile rectangular tilting pan used in commercial kitchens, heated by gas or electricity and mainly used for shallow or deep frying, boiling, braising and stewing. A typical installation can process 200 portions per hour

Bratwurst *(Ge)* A pale coloured raw sausage, made from finely ground pork or veal, sweated chopped onion, seasoning and ground mace. Sometimes smoked and/or lightly scalded and grilled or fried before serving

Braudost *(Ic)* A cows' milk cheese similar to Edam. Lit. bread cheese

braune Ecke *(Ge)* A crisp and crusty rye bread roll

braune Tunke *(Ge)* Brown sauce

Braunschweiger Cervelat *(Ge)* A cervelat q.v. mix containing sugar, packed into beef middles, air dried for 3 weeks and cool smoked over oak and beech with juniper berries

Braunschweiger Kohl *(Ge)* Common cabbage

Braunschweiger Kuchen *(Ge)* Brunswick cake

Braunschweiger Mettwurst *(Ge)* A Mettwurst speciality from Brunswick. See Mettwurst

Braunschweigerwurst *(Ge)* Speciality sausages from Brunswick known by their type, e.g. Braunschweiger Mettwurst or Schlackwurst, etc. See under type names

brawn Meat from the head, generally of pigs but sometimes veal, sheep or cow, etc. stewed on the bone with the usual flavourings, deboned, defatted, put in a mould and covered with reduced, defatted and strained cooking liquor, demoulded when set and served thinly sliced [also called **head cheese**]

brazil nut A large hard shelled nut from the fruit of a tall tropical tree *Bertholletia excelsa.* The nuts in their shells are shaped liked the segments of an orange and are grouped together inside the round fruit. Usually sold shelled except at Christmas [also called **cream nut, para nut**]

Brazilian cherry *see* acerola

Brazilian guava *see* feijoa

Brazilian santos *see* santos

brazo de gitano *(Sp) see* gypsy's arm

bread A staple food made from a mixture of ground grains or seeds (flour), salt and water, baked grilled of fried to a solid mass. Now usually refers to wheat or rye flours but other grains are used in small quantities and ground legumes in India. Bread is either unleavened, i.e. no raising agent is used, or leavened, i.e. raised by the action of a chemical raising agent or a yeast fermentation of part of the flour. Leavening introduces small bubbles of gas into the flour water matrix giving the bread a lighter texture

bread, to *(USA)* To pané

bread and butter pudding *(UK)* A dessert made from slices of white crustless bread well soaked in an egg custard mixture, layered or arranged in an oven-proof dish with dried vine fruits and spices and baked in the oven until crisp and brown on top

bread and butter sausage *(UK)* Finely chopped veal and pork, mixed with ground cloves, ginger, saltpetre, seasoning and small pieces of scalded lean bacon, packed into ox casings, smoked until red, boiled and cooled. Possibly eaten with bread and butter

bread flour The type of flour made from hard wheat used in the West for making bread. It generally, though not necessarily, contains a high proportion of protein (greater than 12%), the gluten content of which aids, after kneading, the rising of the dough and the stabilization of the texture on baking

bread herbs The principal herbs used in bread are aniseed, basil, caraway, chives, dill, fennel, lovage seed, poppy seed, rosemary, sunflower seed and thyme

bread knife A long non-tapering knife with a serrated edge used for cutting bread, cakes and other friable dryish foods [also called **serrated knife**]

bread pudding *(UK)* A baked pudding made from white crustless bread mixed with milk, eggs, sugar, dried vine fruits, flour, butter, jam or marmalade and spices and baked in the oven. Eaten hot or cold

bread sauce A thick sauce made from white crustless bread mixed with milk which has been simmered with an onion clouté, chopped sweated onions, butter, spices and seasoning. Served with roast poultry and game

bread saw A knife with a serrated edge used to cut cleanly bread, cakes and other dry crumbly goods

bread sticks *see* grissini

breadcrumbs Crustless bread reduced to a fine particle size generally less than 3 mm in diameter. Used either fresh, dried, fried or toasted in various dishes and coatings

breadfruit A large, heavy, 20 cm diameter fruit *Artocarpus communis,* mostly starch with a thick yellow to green and brown rind. Introduced into the Carribean from the Pacific islands by Captain Bligh of mutiny fame. Used as a staple food, baked, boiled or fried like yam

breadnut A variety of breadfruit which contains large 2.5 cm long seeds which may be roasted or boiled and eaten as nuts

breakfast The first meal of the day. See English breakfast, continental breakfast

breakfast cereals Breakfast food other than bread or cake made from cereal grains, principally, maize, rice, wheat, or oats. Some are cooked as needed such as porridge, boiled rice and congé, others are commercially processed by precooking, pressing, drying and coating exemplified by cornflakes and rice crispies, yet others use only a part of the cereal e.g. bran flakes and others are used raw such as rolled oats in muesli. Generally eaten with milk and sugar, possibly fruit and other flavourings

breakfast cream *(USA)* Light cream

breakfast sausage Equal parts of finely chopped beef and lean pork, mixed with breadcrumbs, 1 cm dice of pork back fat, ground mace, nutmeg and seasoning, packed into weasands, smoked, then boiled. May be eaten cold or heated using any cooking method

bream 1 A round, red backed, deep bodied seawater fish *Pagellus* and *Spondyliosoma* spp. with a silver underside and red fins weighing up to 1 kg and with a firm, mild tasting, white flesh. Found in the North East Atlantic [also called **red bream**] **2** A yellowish similarly shaped freshwater fish *Abramis brama* of the carp family of little importance

breast of lamb A cheap cut of lamb consisting of the rib cage and belly, composed of layers of fat, connective tissue and muscle. Usually boned, stuffed, rolled and braised or roasted but can be chopped on the bone and stewed or barbecued

breast of veal The rib cage of the calf cooked like breast of lamb

brécol *(Sp)* Broccoli

brecoli *(Sp)* Broccoli

bredie *(Saf)* A meat and vegetable stew

bree *(UK) coll. (Scotland)* Soup

Breitling *(Ge)* Sprat

breka *(Sp)* Pandora, the fish

brème *(Fr) fem.* Bream

brème de mer *(Fr) fem.* Pomfret, the fish

Bremer Klaben *(Ge)* A raisin and citron cake

Bremer Kükenragout *(Ge)* Stewed chicken and vegetables in a cream sauce

Brennsuppe *(Ge)* A brown soup in which the flour is browned by dry roasting or frying. Usually contains onions and wine

Brent goose A small, dark, wild goose *Branta bernicla* and other *Branta* spp. that breeds in the Arctic [also called **barnacle goose**]

Brenten *(Ge)* Almond pastry from Frankfurt, flavoured with rosewater and rum

bresaola *(It)* Cured air-dried beef matured for several months, cut in wafer thin slices, marinated and served as a hors d'oeuvre

bresi Air dried beef from the Haute Savoie on the French Italian border similar to bresaola from the contiguous Italian region

Bressan *(Fr)* A mild goats' milk cheese from Bresse

bressane, à la *(Fr)* In the style of Bresse in eastern France. See e.g. Potage à la Bressane

Bresse bleu *(Fr) see* bleu de Bresse

Bresse chicken A famous free range chicken from the north of Lyon, France. It is considered to have the finest flavoured flesh of any chicken and is correspondingly expensive. It is the only poultry with an Appelation d'Origine

Breton sauce Sauce bretonne

bretonne, à la *(Fr)* In the style of Brittany, i.e. with whole or puréed white beans, also use of eggs or fish coated in Breton sauce

bretonne, fish Fish meunière dressed with a few picked shrimps and sweated sliced mushrooms

bretonne, garnish Shrimps, capers and gherkins for fish and haricot beans for meat

bretonne, sauce *(Fr) fem.* For cooked haricot beans: chopped onions fried in butter until light brown, white wine added and reduced by half, Espagnole sauce, a little tomato sauce and chopped garlic added, simmered 8 minutes and finished with chopped parsley. For fish: fish velouté mixed with a fine julienne of leek, celery, onion and mushrooms sweated in butter, simmered and skimmed and finished with cream and butter

bretonneau *(Fr) masc.* Turbot

brettone *(Sp)* Brussel sprouts

bretzel *(Fr) masc.* Pretzel

bréval, fish As for fish Bercy with the addition of sliced button mushrooms and tomato concassée to the cooking liquor. These are reserved after poaching and used as a garnish [also called **fish d'Antin**]

Brevibacterium linens A microorganism associated with the ripening of Brick cheeses

brewer's yeast *see* yeast

Brezel *(Ge)* Pretzel

briciola *(It)* Crumb, of bread, etc.

briciolone *(It)* Lit. broken bits, e.g. of dried porcini

Brick *(USA)* A brick shaped, yellow, medium soft, slicing cheese with a lot of small holes, created in Wisconsin. It has a lactic starter and is surface ripened with *Brevibacterium linens*. It is ripened for 15 days at high humidity and then under cooler conditions whilst the rind which develops a red colour is washed at intervals until the cheese is ready to be wrapped. The paste has a sweet and spicy nutty flavour, similar to Münster, Saint Paulin and Tilsit

brider *(Fr)* To truss

bridge rolls Small finger rolls of soft white bread about 8 by 3 cm, the dough often enriched with egg, usually filled and served as open or closed sandwiches at buffets and functions

bridie *(UK)* A meat pasty from Scotland and Northumberland

Brie *(En & Fr) masc.* A soft, smooth, full fat cow's milk cheese, formed into a large wheel shape with a surface fungus used to develop its flavour. It matures in about 6-8 weeks when the centre should be soft but not runny with a faint mushroom aroma and a mild piquant, aromatic and slightly acid taste. Usually sold in wedges, sometimes flavoured with herbs, etc. and now available in a blue veined version. Contains 46% water, 30% fat and 22% protein.

Brie de Coulommiers *(Fr)* A milder and smaller version of Brie [also called **Coulommiers**]

Brie de Meaux *(Fr)* A Brie cheese with AOC status, produced from unpasteurized cow's milk in the area surrounding Paris

Brie de Melun *(Fr)* The original Brie (13th century) made from unpasteurized cow's milk with an orange-red rind and a strong flavour. It is sold on straw mats and has AOC status

brigade A team of people working in a restaurant generally divided into the kitchen brigade and the restaurant brigade

brigidini *(It)* Aniseed-flavoured biscuits

brik *(Tu)* A large deep fried pasty made from filo pastry with a filling of raw egg, vegetables and tuna fish, served hot

brill A firm-fleshed flat fish *Schopthalmus rhombus and Rhombus laevis* from the shallow waters of the North Atlantic and Mediterranean. About 30-40 cm long with a freckled grey or brown upper surface. At best in autumn and winter, and cooked on the bone.

Brillat-Savarin **1** A 19th century French epicure who had an important influence on classic French cooking **2** *(Fr)* A triple cream, cow's milk cheese from Normandy similar to Brie **3** A garnish of small tartlets filled with foie gras, asparagus tips, truffles, etc.

brilliant black PN E151, a synthetic black food colouring

brilliant blue FCF E133, a synthetic blue food dye licensed for use in the UK but not in the EU generally. Used in canned vegetables

brin *(Fr) masc.* Sprig, of a herb

Brin d'amour *(Fr) masc.* A soft goats' milk cheese from Corsica, flavoured with and the grey surface coated with, herbs. Presented in small squares which have been matured for three months [also called **Fleur de Maquis**]

brine A solution of salt in water used to preserve food. Preservation occurs by diffusion of salt from the brine into the food and of water from the food into the brine. On a small scale this can make the brine too dilute. Brines should be between 80 and 100% saturation i.e. between 290 and 360g of salt per litre of water. Eggs and potatoes will float in such a brine. However 200g of salt per litre of water is sufficient to inhibit bacterial growth

brine, to To soak a foodstuff in brine

brine, pickling A solution of salt, saltpetre and herbs and spices in water used to preserve raw meats and sometimes vegetables by soaking

bringa *(Sw)* Brisket *(of beef)* or breast *(of lamb)*

bringebær *(No)* Raspberry

brinjal *(In)* A long thin aubergine extensively used in Indian cuisine

brinjal kassaundi *(In)* A hot spicy pickle made from brinjal aubergines

brinjela *(Po)* Aubergine

Brinza 1 *(ME)* A soft rindless ewes' milk cheese with irregular holes made in Israel. Contains 60% water. 18% fat and 20% protein **2** *see* Brynza

brioche *(Fr) fem.* A yeast-raised bread enriched with eggs and butter, often eaten warm, and sometimes filled

brioche loaf A large brioche which is sliced like bread

brioche à tête *(Fr) fem.* Small brioche made with a ball of the same dough on top

Briol *(Be)* A Limburger-type cheese

brionne *see* choko

brioscia *(It)* Brioche

briouats *(NA)* A type of sweet triangular samosa from Morocco filled with date or almond paste

brique à l'oeuf *(NA)* An egg deep fried in a filo pastry packet, from Morocco and Algeria

Briquette *see* Neufchâtel

briser *(Fr)* To break, of bones

brisket *(UK & USA)* A coarse fatty cut of beef from the lower part of the shoulder. Usually boned and rolled for boiling, braising or pot roasting. May be salted or pickled and sold cold

brisler *(De)* Sweetbreads

brisling Small sprats similar to sardines, usually canned in oil [also called **Swedish anchovies**]

brit *(USA)* Young herring or mackerel

brittle *see* praline

Brix scale A scale of density based on sugar syrups and measured in degrees. The degree Brix, °Brix, is the percentage by weight of sugar in a sugar water solution at 20°C. Thus 100°Brix is pure sugar, 50°Brix is equal weights of sugar and water i.e. 1 kg of sugar per litre of water. Some hydrometers are calibrated in °Brix

broa 1 *(Po)* A very popular yeast-raised large flat bread from Minho made with various flours **2** *(Sp)* Cornmeal bread

broach A spit, for roasting of meats, etc.

broad bean The seed of a legume *Vicia faba* eaten as the whole pod when very young (to 8 cm) or as green unripe oval shaped beans from more mature pods (to 30 cm). Usually boiled but uncooked beans are eaten as a snack food in the Eastern Mediterranean. The dried bean which is creamy in colour is used as a pulse or canned. It is one of the first legumes to be harvested in Europe. It is a direct descendant of the field bean or horse bean which has been cultivated in Europe since the Stone Age [also called **fava bean, flava bean, Windsor bean, shell bean, Scotch bean**]

broad bean sauce A thick brown sauce made from fermented ground broad beans and flavoured with garlic, chillis and spices. Used in Szechuan, China instead of soya bean sauces

broad leaf sage *see* sage

broad leaf sorrel *see* sorrel

broad leaf thyme A bushy shrub *Thymus pulegioides* growing to 40 cm. with large leaves and a stronger flavour than garden thyme

Broccio *(Fr)* A ewes' or goats' milk unsalted curd cheese from Corsica, similar to the Italian Ricotta. Eaten as soon as made [also called **Brocciu cheese**]

Brocciu cheese *see* Broccio

broccoletti *(It)* Broccoli raab

broccoli *(En & It)* A brassica related to the cauliflower which exists in two forms, the calabrese q.v. and the sprouting varieties *Brassica oleraceae* Italica Group. The sprouting variety are harvested in spring after overwintering and consist of small immature purple or green tight clusters of miniature flowers which branch from a thick 1 m tall main stem. They are cut repeatedly for use as a vegetable or salad item until they become too small to be of use. Eaten raw, boiled, steamed, cold or hot

broccoli raab The leaves of a turnip type plant *Brassica rapa* Utilis Group used in the same way as turnip tops q.v.

broccoli rabe *(It)* Broccoli

broccoli rape *see* rape

broccolo *(It)* Broccoli

brochan *(UK)* Porridge or gruel from Scotland

broche *(Fr) fem.* Spit, for roasting of meats, etc.

broché(e) *(Fr)* Trussed, past participle of brocher, to truss

broche à la *(Fr)* Spit roasted

brochet *(Fr) masc.* Pike

brochet de mer *(Fr) masc.* Barracuda

brocheta *(Me & Sp)* Skewer or brochette

brochette *(Fr) fem.* **1** Skewer, used for kebabs **2** pieces of meat, etc. on a skewer and cooked

brochette of lamb *see* shish kebab

brochettes *(NA)* Kebabs of marinated offal, lamb or mutton and fat

brochettes de Parme *(Fr) fem. see* attereaux au Parmesan

brocoli *(Fr) masc.* Broccoli

bróculi *(Sp)* Broccoli

brød *(De & No)* Bread

bröd *(Sw)* Bread

brodettato, a *(It)* Finished with egg yolks and lemon juice, esp. of lamb stews

brodetto *(It)* **1** A sauce made from broth with beaten eggs and lemon juice **2** A saffron-flavoured fish stew similar to bouilabaiise. It has many local variations [also called **boreta, broeta**]

brodetto alla romana *(It)* An easter stew of beef and lamb finished with egg yolks, lemon juice and grated Parmesan

brodo *(It)* Broth, stock

brodo di manzo *(It)* A clear beef broth, usually containing pastini

brodo ristretto *(It)* Consommé

broeto *(It) see* brodetto (2)

broil, to *see* grill, to

broiler *(USA)* A young chicken weighing just over 1 kg

brokkoli *(No)* Broccoli

Brombeere *(Ge)* Blackberry

bromelain *see* bromelin

bromelin A protease used in beer production to remove protein haze and also to solubilize soya protein. Can be used to convert topside into a much softer meat resembling fillet steak [also called **bromelain**]

bronze turkey A breed of turkey usually hung to improve its flavour. It has an excellent taste and a plump breast. It is more slow growing than the whiter breeds and the white meat is darker [also called **Cambridge bronze**]

bronzino *(It)* Sea bass

brood 1 *(Ho)* Bread **2** *(Be)* A cows' milk cheese similar to Edam, shaped like a loaf and coated with a yellow wax

broodje *(Ho)* A longish bread roll used to make a sandwich

broodpap *(Ho)* Bread pudding

broom corn *see* common millet

Bröschen *(Ge)* Sweetbreads

brose *see* Athol brose

Brot *(Ge)* Bread

brotchan *(Ir)* A broth made with leeks, potatoes and onions

Brötchen *(Ge)* Small bread roll

broth 1 The liquid in which meat or fish had been boiled together with herbs, vegetables and spices *(original meaning)* **2** Stock, brunoise vegetables and either barley or rice simmered with a BG and seasoning and finished with chopped parsley

Brotkock *(Ge)* Bread pudding

Brotkrümmel *(Ge)* Breadcrumbs

Brotsuppe *(Ge)* Bread soup made with meat stock and bread and flavoured with nutmeg

Brotwurzel *(Ge)* Cassava

broufado *(Fr)* A Provençal beef stew with vinegar, anchovies and capers

brouillade *(Fr) fem.* A stew using oil. Lit. a fog

brouillade périgourdine *(Fr) fem.* Scrambled eggs flavoured with truffles

brouillée *(Fr)* Scrambled, as in oeufs brouillés, scrambled eggs

brousse du Rõve *(Fr)* A ewes' milk curd cheese from Provence similar to Ricotta

brown *adj.* Used to describe foods that are partially or wholly untreated. e.g. brown rice, brown sugar

brown, to To bake grill or roast in the oven so that the outer surface of the food turns a golden brown due to caramelization or Maillard reactions

brown bean sauce *see* yellow bean sauce

brown beef stock Chopped beef bones, roasted in the oven until brown and the fat poured off. The bones, deglazed pan juices, chopped aromatic vegetables browned in fat and a BG are added to water, simmered for 8 hours, skimmed continuously and strained (proportions: bones 4, vegetables 1, water 10) [also called **fond brun** (Fr), **estouffade** (En & Fr)]

brown betty *(USA)* A pudding made from layers of sugar, breadcrumbs, butter, sliced apples, spices and lemon zest baked until brown

brown braising Refers to sealing of meat in oil by browning on all sides prior to braising on a bed of chopped root vegetables

brown bread A general term for bread made from a brown low extraction flour such as wholemeal. Now also applied to artificially coloured white breads

brown bread ice cream *(UK)* A vanilla-flavoured ice cream containing brown breadcrumbs

brown butter sauce *see* beurre noisette

brown cap mushroom A derivative of the cultivated white mushroom more like its wild counterpart with a lightly feathered effect above the rim. They have a lower water content than the white mushroom and keep their shape better when cooked. They do not need peeling.

brown chaud-froid sauce Demi-glace thickened with 75 g of gelatine per litre

brown chicken stock As for brown beef stock but with chicken bones substituted for beef bones [also called **fond brun de volaille** (Fr)]

brown FK E154, a synthetic brown food dye, licensed for use in the UK but not in the EU generally. Used to dye kippers

brown flour Wheat flour contains between 80 and 90% of the dehusked grain. Part of the bran is removed but the wheatgerm remains [also called **wheatmeal flour**]

brown fungus *see* cloud ear fungus

brown hare *see* common hare

brown lamb stew *see* navarin d'agneau

brown long grain rice An unpolished long grain rice which when boiled has a nutty flavour with a chewy texture. Requires about 30 minutes boiling; *see also* brown rice

brown mustard seed The hot and bitter brown seed of an annual *Brassica juncea* native to India. Used whole in Indian cooking or ground and mixed with white mustard in the various mustard based condiments and flavourings available [also called **Indian mustard**]

brown mutton stock As for brown beef stock but with mutton or lamb bones substituted for beef bones [also called **fond brun de mouton** (Fr)]

brown onion sauce *see* Lyonnaise, sauce

brown onion soup Finely sliced onion and garlic well browned in butter, flour added and cooked to a brown roux, brown stock added, simmered for 15 minutes, strained and seasoned. The soup is served in bowls with the top covered with toasted French bread slices and the whole sprinkled with cheese and browned under a fierce heat [also called **French onion soup**]

brown oyster sauce Any of the European oyster sauces with the milk and cream replaced with brown stock. Used for grills and meat puddings

brown ribweed *see* alaria

brown rice Unprocessed rice *Oryza sativa* from which only the husk is removed. More flavoured and chewy than polished rice

brown roux Four parts of fat (clarified butter, dripping or vegetable oil) cooked slowly but not overcooked with 5 parts of soft plain flour until the flour is light brown in colour. Used for Espagnole sauce and soups and as a general thickening agent

brown sauce *see* Espagnole, sauce

brown and serve *(USA)* Convenience food, usually bread, cooked to a state where it just needs to be browned before serving

brown shrimp One of the common European varieties *Crangon crangon* of shallow water shrimp up to 6 cm long found on sandy shores. It has the ability to vary its colour for camouflage

brown sugar Unrefined or partially refined

sugar, dark brown to fawn in colour with varying crystal sizes and varying amounts of entrapped molasses. See demerara sugar, muscovado sugar

brown trout A golden brown game fish *Salmo trutta* with white flesh found in the upper reaches of unpolluted rivers. It has a better flavour than rainbow trout. Best shallow fried but may be grilled, poached or baked en papillote [also called **river trout**]

brown veal stock As for brown beef stock but substituting veal bone for beef bones [also called **fond brun de veau** (Fr)]

brown vegetable stock Chopped aromatic vegetables browned in oil, simmered with water, tomatoes, mushroom trimmings, peppercorns and yeast extract for 1 hour and strained (proportions vegetables 1, water 3 and 4 g yeast extract per litre)

browned flour *(USA)* Flour which has been browned or dry roasted to give it a nutty baked flavour. Used for thickening stews and sauces

brownie *(USA)* A slightly underbaked rich chocolate sponge, soft in the middle, possibly with nuts and/or iced with chocolate, made in a square tin and cut into square or rectangular individual pieces

broyé(e) *(Fr)* Bruised or ground

Brucialepre *(It)* A soft surface ripened cows' milk cheese from Piedmont with a white creamy mild paste and a thin soft rind. Made in thin circles (300 g)

brugnon *(Fr) masc.* Nectarine

Brühe *(Ge)* Broth, gravy

Brühne *(Ge)* Consommé

Brühwurst *(Ge)* A group of German/Austrian sausages including Frankfurters, Bockwurst and Bierschinken made from finely minced pork or beef with spices and bacon, filled into casings and generally lightly smoked before being scalded at 80°C to seal in the flavour. Not suitable for keeping

bruin brood *(Ho)* Wholewheat bread

bruine bonen *(Ho)* Kidney beans

bruinkaalssupe *(Ho)* Brown cabbage soup

bruiss *(USA)* Pobs *(boiled milk and bread)*

brûlé(e) *(Fr)* Caramelized, browned, usually applied to dishes with a crisp caramelized sugar topping as in crème brûlée

brûler *(Fr)* **1** To burn **2** To brown or caramelize

brun fisksuppe *(No)* Fish soup thickened with a brown roux

bruna bönor *(Sw)* Brown beans, also a national dish of soaked brown beans, simmered until tender, drained and mixed with salt, vinegar and dark brown sugar. Eaten with fried pork

brunch A combination of breakfast and lunch eaten any time between 10.00 and 15.00 hours

brune kager *(De)* Brown spiced biscuits

brunede kartofler *(De)* New potatoes fried in butter and sugar until golden brown and tender

Brunnenkresse *(Ge)* Watercress

brunoise *(Fr)* (fem) Small 2mm cubed dice of vegetables, etc. Method of cutting same

brunoster *(No)* A sweet cheese, the colour of brown sugar, from the north of Norway

Brunswick cake A rich cake with dried fruit and almonds

Brunswick salad Strips of slicing sausage mixed with finely chopped pickled cucumber, sliced tomato, grated apple and cooked French green beans all dressed with a vinaigrette made from the cucumber pickle juice and finished with chopped parsley

Brunswick stew *(USA)* A stew made from chicken and/or squirrels, vegetables, garlic, tomatoes, sweetcorn and seasoning, sometimes thickened with okra

bruschetta *(It)* Lightly toasted thick slices of bread rubbed with cut garlic cloves and cut ripe tomatoes, sprinkled with olive oil and salt and eaten as an accompaniment to a meal or as a snack [also called **fettunta, fett'unta, fregolotta**]

bruscion *(He)* A soft goats' milk cheese eaten very fresh

brusco *(It)* Sharp, sour

brush, to To cover or coat foods before, during or after cooking with milk, fat, oil, beaten egg, sieved jam or sugar syrup or the like using a small brush

brush roast *(USA)* Oysters cooked over a barbecue or wood fire, served with mustard pickle, butter and cornbread

brusselkaas *(Be) see* fromage de Bruxelles

Brussels lof *(Ho)* Endive, also cooked endive rolled in ham with cheese

Brussels mosaic A sausage attributed to Belgium consisting of finely minced pickled pork and veal flavoured with ground pepper, ginger and cardamom, this paste mixed with largish chunks of ox tongue, liver sausage, bacon fat and frankfurter to give a mosaic appearance when cut, packed into middles or bungs, smoked, simmered and resmoked

brussels sprouts A member of the *Brassica*

family *Brassica oleraceae* Gemmifera Group consisting of small (to 4 cm diameter), usually tight, basal leaf buds distributed evenly along a thick vertical stalk, harvested in autumn and winter and said to taste better after being frosted. Usually boiled or steamed but may be braised

Brust *(Ge)* Breast (of meat)

brut(e) *(Fr)* Raw

Bruxelles *(Be)* A soft fermented skimmed cows' milk cheese

bruxelloise, à la *(Fr)* In the Brussels style, i.e. with a garnish of brussels sprouts, braised chicory and chateau potatoes

brylépudding *(Sw)* Crème caramel

Bryndza *see* Brynza

brynt smör *(Sw)* Beurre noisette

Brynza A Central European and Balkan semi-hard ewes' and goat's milk white cheese similar to Feta [also called **Brandza, Brinza, Bryndza**]

brysselkål *(Sw)* Brussel sprouts

BSE *see* bovine spongiform encephalopathy

B'soffner Kapuziner *(Au)* An almond and raisin pastry. Lit. drunk monk

BST *see* bovine somatotrophin

b'stilla *(NA) see* bastilla

buab *(Th)* Angled loofah

buah keloh *(Ma)* Drumstick vegetable

buah keras *(Ma)* Candlenut

buah pala *(Ma)* Nutmeg

buah pelaga *(Ma)* Cardamom

bubble and squeak *(UK)* A South Eastern dish of leftover mashed potatoes and chopped cooked cabbage, fried in dripping or lard and stirred until the crisp brown bits are well distributed throughout the mixture. May have chopped cooked beef, fish or other protein source added. Once a dish of the poor

bubbly jock *(UK) coll. (Scotland)* Turkey

bucaniere, al' *(It)* In the style of the pirate, i.e. with seafood and tomato sauce

bucati *(It)* A type of macaroni. From bucare, to pierce

bucatini *(It)* A smaller version of bucati [also called **perciatelli, perciatelloni**]

buccellato *(It)* Aniseed-flavoured cake containing currants

buccin *(Fr) masc.* Whelk

buccino *(It & Sp)* Whelk

bûche de chèvre *(Fr) fem.* A soft goat's milk cheese rather like Saint Maure. Made in a log shape (900 g)

bûche de Noël *(Fr) fem.* Yule log. The traditional French Christmas cake made like a Swiss roll and decorated with a chocolate cream to simulate the bark of a tree and dusted with icing sugar to simulate snow

Buchweizen *(Ge)* Buckwheat

buck rarebit Welsh rarebit topped with a poached egg

buck venison *see* venison

buckler leaf sorrel A hardy perennial *Rumex scutulatus* of the sorrel family. It has light green silver-patched leaves with a mild lemony flavour and is less acid than sorrel. Preferred by the French for sorrel soup

buckling Whole hot smoked herrings ready for eating. Traditionally smoked over juniper twigs, esp. in Scandinavia

buckwheat The seed of a plant *Fagopyrum esculentum* of the dock family native to Russia. After dehusking the grain may be toasted and/or ground to a flour and used in the same way as other cereal grains. Has a pleasant nutty flavour [also called **beechwheat, saracen corn, kasha, brank**]

buckwheat flour A flour made from buckwheat, used in making kasha, Russian blinis, Breton galettes and pancakes of various kinds

buckwheat noodles *see* soba and cha-soba

Buddha's hand citron A type of citron in which the fruit is split down its length into many finger-like section each with its own skin. Mainly used for perfuming rooms and clothing in Japan and China [also called **fingered citron**]

budding *(De)* Pudding

budduzze *(It)* A Sicilian dish of meat balls simmered in tomato sauce

budelli *(It)* Intestines, entrails, guts

budelline *(It)* Giblets

bu ding *(Ch)* Pudding

budino *(It)* Pudding, also a small black pudding or boudin noir from Aosta

budino di ricotta *(It)* Cheese pudding

budino torinese *(It)* Chestnut pudding

bue *(It)* Old beef

buey *(Sp)* Meat from old bulls, rather tough

buey del mar *(Sp)* The common crab of Northern Europe. Lit. ox of the sea

bufala *(It)* Buffalo

buffalo The meat of the draught animal, the water buffalo, used in SEA in place of beef

buffalo wings *(USA)* Deep fried chicken wings brushed with a hot chilli sauce

buffet A meal consisting of large tables laid out with a selection of hot and/or cold foods and drinks from which guests make a selection. May be self service or served. Usually for large formal or small informal gatherings

buglosa *(Sp)* Sweet violet

bugloss *(Sp)* Viper's bugloss

bugne lyonnaise *(Fr) fem.* A sweet fritter from Lyon

buisson *(Fr) masc.* A cluster, of small fish, langoustines, etc. Lit. a bush

buko *(Ph)* Young coconut, see kelapa

bulavesa *(Sp)* A fish soup similar to bouillabaisse

bulb garlic A rounded mild garlic resembling a button onion from Szechuan province in China [also called **ball garlic**]

bulgar *see* burghul

bulgogi *(Ko)* A circular metal hotplate over a heat source used to grill or cook food at the table

bulgogi wa sajeog gui *(Ko)* Slices of beef marinated in soy sauce, rice wine, onions, garlic, ginger, sesame oil, spices and seasoning, then grilled or barbecued

bulgur *see* bulgar

buljong *(No)* Beef broth

bull An uncastrated male of the bovine species usually used as a source of semen for impregnating cows

bullabesa *(Sp)* The Spanish corruption of the word bouillabaisse

bullace A small wild blue-black plum *Prunus insititia* with a tart flavour used for jam making

bullock A young bull less than a year old

bullock's heart A type of custard apple *Anona reticulata* with a more solid granular flesh than usual. It is heart shaped with a reddish brown skin. [also called **ramphal**]

bully beef *see* corned beef

bul'on *(Ru)* Broth

bulrush millet An important staple millet *Pennisetum typhoideum* from Africa and India which grows quickly, will stand drought and is used for making flour and unleavened bread [also called **reedmace, cat tail**]

bulviv desros *(Li)* A cheap peasant sausage made from grated potatoes, a little sweated diced bacon and chopped onion, bound together with eggs and water, filled into casings, linked and baked for 2 hours, basting as necessary with water. Served with sauerkraut

bummaloe A predatory fish with easily perishable flesh *Harpodon nehereus* up to 40 cm long and found off the west coast of India. When salted and dried it is known as Bombay duck, because of the ease of catching it during the monsoon [also called **bomeloe, bummalow**]

bummalow *see* bummaloe

bun 1 A small round, oval or cylindrical baked shape made from sweetened, yeast-raised dough with flavourings and spices usually containing dried vine fruits **2** *(Vi)* Rice vermicelli

bun loaf A sweet, yeast-raised loaf with flavourings and spices possibly containing dried vine fruits

bun tin Individual round tins either in trays or single, used for baking small cakes, buns, tartlets, yorkshire puddings, popovers, etc.; *see also* barquettes [also called **patty tins**]

Bundenfleisch *see* Bünderfleisch

Bünderfleisch *(He)* Cured and dried beef similar to bresaola [also called **Bundenfleisch, Bündnerfleisch**]

Bundkuchen *(Ge) see* Gugelhupf

Bündnerfleisch *(He) see* Bünderfleisch

Bündnerplat *(He)* A dish of cured and dried beef

Bündnerwurst *(He)* Minced pork and diced pork fat, seasoned and flavoured with ground cloves, packed into a pig's bladder, smoked then boiled. Served hot or cold

bung The sausage casing made from the large intestine being about 50 mm dia. from a pig *(hog bung)* or 75 to 100 mm dia. from beef *(ox bung)*. Used for large diameter sausages, e.g. Bologna, liver sausage, haggis, etc. [also called **fat end**]

bunga *(Ph)* Pigeon pea

bunga cingkeh *(Ma)* Cloves

bunga kantan *(Ma)* Ginger buds

bunga lawang *(Id & Ma)* Star anise

bunga pala *(Ma)* Mace

bunga siantan *(Ma)* Ginger buds

buntan *(Ja)* Pummelo

bun tau *(Vi)* Cellophane noodles

Bunter Hans *(Ge)* A large bread based dumpling, cooked in a cloth then cut up and served with cooked vegetables or stewed fruit

buñuelos *(Sp & Me)* Light and puffed up fritters made from a biscuit dough, sprinkled with icing sugar and cinnamon and served as soon as cooked

buost *(Sw)* A firm, low fat, slightly pungent cow's milk cheese rather like Tilsit

burbot *see* eel pout

burdock The widely distributed, dock-like plant *Arctium lappa* popular in China and Japan whose young spade-like leaves are eaten like spinach and whose long thin roots are used as a vegetable. Once used in the UK to flavour the drink dandelion and burdock [also called **gobo**]

Burenwurst *(Ge)* A Brunswick sausage containing beef and bacon fat bound with a little fécule

burfi *(In)* A sweetmeat made from a mixture of sugar syrup and ground almonds or pistachios resembling fudge [also called **barfi**]

Burgenländisch Hauswürstel *(Au)* A famous sausage from Burgenland adjacent to the Hungarian border containing roughly 2 parts lean pork to 1 part pork back fat and 1 part beef

burger *see* beefburger

burghul *(ME)* Wheat which has been dehusked, parboiled, dried then cracked into a coarse powder prior to sale. It is easily reconstituted with boiling water and may be used for made up dishes or to accompany a main dish [also called **bulgur, bulgar, bourgouri, pourgouri**]

burgonya *see* krumpli

burgonyakrémleves *(Hu)* Cream of potato soup

burgonyát *(Hu)* Potatoes

burgoo *(USA)* A meat and vegetable stew thickened with okra [also called **Mulligan stew**]

Burgos *(Sp)* A soft mild scalded-curd cheese made from ewes' milk around the town of the same name. It has an even textured paste without holes and is cast in 1 to 2 kg discs. Often sweetened and used as a dessert. Contains 65% water

Burgundy beef *see* boeuf à la bourguignonne

Burgundy sauce *see* sauce bourguignonne

buri *((Ja)* Yellowtail, the fish

burida *(It)* Fish stew with garlic, oil, tomatoes, dried mushrooms, onions, celery and saffron

Burmeister *(USA)* A cows' milk cheese from Winsconsin similar to Brick

burnet *see* salad burnet

burnt cream *(UK)* A version of crème brûlée as served at Trinity college, Cambridge [also called **Cambridge burnt cream**]

buro *(Ph)* Salt

burong dalag *(Ph)* Mudfish cured by layering it in an earthenware dish with salt, soft boiled rice and angkak colouring

burong mustasa *(Ph)* Pickled mustard greens which are red in colour

burpless cucumber *(USA)* Long cucumber [also called **hot house cucumber**]

burrida *(It)* A fish soup made from available seafood in Sardinia

burrie *(Po)* Winkle

burrino *(It)* A small, mild, spun curd pear shaped cheese made from a cow's milk and moulded around a centre of butter, Eaten young (3-4-weeks) and sometimes waxed [also called **Butirro, Burro, Manteca**]

burritos *(Sp & Me)* Rolled pancakes filled with pork, ham and melted cheese or other savoury filling possibly coated with cheese sauce, gratinated with cheese and browned in the oven, or served with guacamole and a sour cream topping

burro *(It)* **1** Butter **2** *see* Burrino

burro, al *(It)* With butter only, usually of pasta

burro banana *(USA)* A flat, square-shaped banana with a lemony flavour from Texas [also called **chunky banana**]

burro e formaggio *(It)* A sauce or dressing of melted butter and grated cheese

burro fuso *(It)* Melted butter

burro nero *(It)* Beurre noisette

burro nocciola *(It)* Beurre noisette

burro e parmigiano *(It)* A sauce or dressing of melted butter and grated Parmesan cheese used with pasta

Bury black pudding *(UK)* The most famous of the UK black puddings, flavoured with marjoram, thyme, mint, penny royal and celery seed [also called **Bury pudding**]

Bury pudding *see* Bury black pudding

busecca *(It & Sw)* A thick tripe soup made with onions and usually with beans

bush basil A compact, tiny-leaved and very hardy variety of basil *Occimum basilicum* var. *minimum* with a medium flavour which originated in South America [also called **Greek basil**]

bushel A volume measure equal to 8 gallons in either imperial or USA measure

bushukan *(Ja)* Citron, the fruit

Busserl *(Ge)* Small pastries. Lit. kisses

bustard A large game bird of the family *Otididae* from Asia, Africa and Australasia.

bustard plover *see* plover

buster *(USA)* The name for a crab which has just shed its shell

buta *(Ja)* Pork

butaniku *(Ja)* Pork

butarega *(It)* Botargo

butcher A person who prepares slaughtered and dressed meat for sale. Sometimes also slaughters the animals and dresses the carcases

buterbrod *(Ru)* Open sandwich

butifarra *(Sp)* A small firm sausage from Catalonia made with minced pork loin and belly, moistened with white wine, seasoned and flavoured with garlic, cinnamon and powdered cloves, air dried for 2 days, boiled in salted water and air dried again [also called **botifarra**]

butifarra negra *(Sp)* Butifarra with added pigs' blood and chopped mint

butifarrón sabroso *(Ca)* A meat loaf or giant rissole containing minced beef and salt pork, chillis, sweet pepper, onion, coriander and oregano and cooked in a large heavy frying pan

butirro *(It) see* Burrino

buttariga *(It)* Botargo

Butter *(Ge)* Butter

butter 1 The emulsion of milk in fat produced by churning (i.e. mechanically mixing) cream and containing about 80% fat and 17% water. There are roughly 1 billion separate liquid globules per gram. A variety of types of butter are produced depending on, the type of animal, the method of production, the season, added salt or acidification of the cream prior to churning **2** A name given to various soft butter-like preserves made from fruits. Similar to fruit cheeses

butter basted poultry Ready basted poultry q.v. in which the fat part of the injected material contains butterfat

butter bean The butter coloured, kidney shaped seed of the legume *Phaseolus lunatus* and *P. limensis,* grown worldwide in warm climates. May be eaten like broad beans in the country of cultivation but usually ripened and dried for export. Must be boiled for 15 minutes to destroy protease inhibitors [also called **lima bean** (USA), **Madagascar bean**]

butter clam *(USA)* Two varieties of clam of the *Saxidomus* spp. found on the Pacific coast

butter cream A cake filling or coating made by whisking butter with an equal part of icing or caster sugar. It can be made less rich by replacing some of the butter with milk or coffee

butter pat A small pat of butter

butter pit *see* nara nut

butter sauce Sauce bâtarde thickened with white roux only and with no egg yolks

butter swirls *(USA)* The process known as monté au beurre, i.e. adding cold butter to a sauce or soup at the last moment before service to give it a sheen

buttercrunch lettuce *(USA)* A variety of butterhead lettuce

buttercup squash A winter squash common in the USA with a deep green striped skin and a medium-sweet creamy and mild orange flesh. It is in the shape of a turban surmounted with a pale cap

butterfat The fat found in milk which forms the main part (82 percent) of butter. It contains about 40% saturated, and less than 4% unsaturated fats

butterfish 1 A small oily seaweater fish *Peprillus tricanthus* with white tender flesh, a bluish upper surface, weighing up to 200 g and found on the Atlantic coast of the USA. May be baked or fried **2** A small eel-like seawater fish *Pholis gunnellus* [also called **gunnel**] **3** A deep bodied freshwater fish *Eupomotis gibbosus* with greyish skin changing to golden yellow on the underside

butterfly cakes Small sponge cakes from the top of which a hemispherical section is removed, cut in half and replaced like wings on top of the depression which is filled with cream, butter cream, mashed fruit or the like

butterfly chop A thick chop cut through until almost separated, opened out and flattened to look like a pair of butterfly wings prior to cooking

butterfly cut A type of cut in which any piece of meat, chop, prawn or the like is cut through until almost separated then flattened out to look like a butterfly

butterhead lettuce A type of lettuce with smooth soft leaves forming a rounded compact head [also called **flat lettuce, round lettuce, cabbage lettuce**]

Butterkäse *(Ge)* A soft rich, cow's milk cheese

with a close textured elastic paste with no holes and a delicate buttery taste and smell. The thin rind is covered with mould. Sometimes flavoured with carroway seeds. Contains about 60% water, 18% fat and 17% protein [also called **Damenkäse, ladies cheese**]

Buttermilch *(Ge)* Buttermilk

Buttermilchquark *(Ge)* A quark q.v. made from a mixture of buttermilk and skimmed milk

buttermilk The liquid remaining after the conversion of cream into butter. If made from raw cream it will thicken naturally from the naturally present lactobacillus. Used as a drink or for scones and soda bread

butternut **1** The edible oily nuts of the tree *Juglans cinerea* a member of the walnut family found in the USA **2** *see* nara nut

butternut squash A bulbous, pear shaped, pale yellow, winter squash *Cucurbita maxima* with orange flesh, common in the USA; the flesh is used as a vegetable or for savoury dishes

Butterschmalz *(Ge)* Melted butter

Butterteig *(Ge)* Puff pastry

buttock steak *(UK) see* topside

button mushroom A small immature mushroom in which the gills are not visible

button onion Small onions less than 2.5 cm dia. used for pickling and in boeuf Bourguignon. Best peeled after blanching [also called **pickling onion, pearl onion**]

button quail A small ground living bird of the *Turnicidae* family from the warmer parts of Africa, Europe and Asia

butty *(UK) coll.* The slang name for a sandwich, mainly used in the North esp. Liverpool

butyl stearate The ester formed from butanol and stearic acid used as a release agent

butylated hydroxyanisole *see* BHA

butylated hydroxytoluene *see* BHT

butyric acid A fatty acid which when in ester form is a constituent of butter fat. The free fatty acid is liberated by oxidation of the butter and is responsible for the rancid flavour and smell

Butyrospermum parkii *Bot.* Shea tree *(shea nut)*

buz *(Tu)* Ice

byssus The beard of tough fibres with which a mussel attaches itself to solid objects

Cc

cabai *(Id)* Pepper *Piper nigrum*

cabai hijau *(Id)* Green chilli

cabai merah *(Id)* Red chilli

cabai rawit *(Id)* Bird's eye chilli

caballa *(Sp)* Mackerel

cabanos *(Pl) see* Kabanosy

cabassol(les) *(Fr)* A dish of lamb offal cooked with ham and vegetables from Languedoc

cabbage The most common member of the *Brassica* family *Brassica oleracea* Capitata Group which consists of green, white or reddish leaves springing from a central stalk either loosely as in spring cabbage or in a tight pointed or round mass of layered leaves with some open outer leaves. The white varieties are often eaten raw or fermented but all may be pickled, fermented, boiled, stewed, braised or fried. The coarser outer green leaves are a major source of folic acid essential to prevent some birth defects.

cabbage lettuce *see* butterhead lettuce

cabbage palm *see* palmetto

cabbage rolls A very common North and Eastern European dish made from blanched and trimmed cabbage leaves made into a parcel-like roll with the sides tucked in using a variety of fillings and baked generally in a tomato sauce. Taken to North America by immigrants [also called **pigs in blankets** (UK)]

cabbage turnip Kohlrabi

Cabeça de velha *(Po)* One of the finest of the Quiejo da Serra cheeses Lit. Old lady's head

cabécou *(Fr)* A small highly-flavoured cheese made from ewe or goat's milk in Aquitaine

cabello de ángel *(Sp)* A dessert made from a squash

cabeza *(Sp)* Head, of an animal or of e.g. garlic

cabichou *see* chabichou

cabidela *(Po)* A blood-thickened sauce

cabillaud *(Fr) masc.* Cod [also called **cabliaud**]

cabillaud à la boulangère *(Fr) masc.* Fresh cod baked in butter with potatoes and chopped parsley

cabillaud à la flamande *(Fr) masc.* Cod, poached in white wine with chopped shallots and served with lemon wedges

cabillaud à la portugaise *(Fr) masc.* Sliced cod, cooked with wine, tomatoes and garlic and served with rice

cabinet pudding A simple moulded pudding made from bread and butter or sponge cake with chopped glacé cherries and dried vine fruits soaked in egg custard (6 to 8 eggs per litre of milk) cooked in the oven in a bain-marie and served hot accompanied with egg custard sauce or apricot sauce [also called **pouding de cabinet** (Fr)]

cabliaud *(Fr) masc.* Cod [also called **cabillaud**]

caboc *(UK)* A mild, smooth, Scottish cheese made from full cream cow's milk with added cream, coated with fine oatmeal

cabot *(Fr) masc.* Chub, the fish. Lit. dog, cur

ca bo uang *(Cm)* Yellowfin tuna

caboul sauce Mayonnaise flavoured with curry powder. Used with cold meats

cabra *(Po & Sp)* Goat

cabracho *(Sp)* Scorpion fish

Cabrales *(Sp)* A distinctive, strong-flavoured, smooth, semi-hard cheese made from cow's milk in Asturia, sometimes blue veined and sometimes wrapped in leaves. Ripened for 5 to 6 months in limestone caverns. Contains 30 to 35% water, 31% fat and 28 to 30% protein [also called **Cabraliego, Picon**]

Cabraliego *(Sp) see* Cabrales

Cabreiro *(Po)* A white, strong-flavoured cheese made from a mixture of goat's and ewe's milk eaten either young or after maturing in brine

cabrichiu *(Fr) see* chabichou

cabrito *(Po)* Kid or young goat

cabrito asado *(Me)* Roast baby kid flavoured with garlic and chillis

cabrón *(Sp)* Goat

cabus *(Fr) masc. see* chou cabus

caça *(Po)* Game

cacahouette *(Fr) fem. see* cacah(o)uète

cacah(o)uète *(Fr) fem.* Peanut [also called **cacahouette**]

cacahué *(Sp)* Peanut

cacahuete *(Sp)* Peanut

cacao *(It, Sp & Fr) masc.* Cocoa

cacao butter *see* cocoa butter

cacao bean *see* cocoa bean

cacau *(Po)* Cocoa

caccia Torino Small salami, weighing about 200 g, made of pork and beef and being small, mature quicker than the normal size

cacciagione *(It)* Wild game

cacciucco *(It)* A fish and shellfish stew

cacerola *(Me)* Casserole

cachalot *(Fr) masc.* Sperm whale

cachat *(Fr)* A strong-flavoured ewes' milk cheese from Provence, often ripened in vinegar

cachet *(Fr) masc.* A soft, white, creamy farm cheese made from ewe's milk in Provence. Lit. tablet

ca chim den *(Vi)* Black pomfret, the fish

ca chim mi *(Vi)* White pomfret, the fish

ca chim trang *(Vi)* White pomfret, the fish

Cacietto *(It)* A smaller version of Cacio Cavallo

cacik *(Tu)* A mixture of chopped cucumber, garlic and lettuce in yoghurt, similar to tsatsiki

cacio *(It)* Cheese

Cacio Cavallo *(It)* A semi-hard, mild-flavoured, pale yellow, pear shaped cheese from Sicily with a shiny yellow rind and made from spun curd similar to Provolone. It is ripened 2 to 3 months for slicing and 6 to 12 months for grating

Caciofiore *(It)* A hard ewes' milk cheese with a high fat content, a tender paste and no rind, suitable for the table or for cooking

Cacioricotta *(It)* A ewes' milk cheese from central and southern Italy and Sardinia made in 2 versions. The soft version is made by a lactic coagulation and may be eaten fresh or salted and ripened for 2 to 3 months for use as a dessert or grating cheese. The hard version is coagulated with rennet or fig juice and the curd is moulded, salted and ripened for 3 to 4 months

Caciotta *(It)* A small soft slicing mild cheese made from a variety of pateurized milks with a lactic starter. usually contains 50% water, 32% fat and 22% protein

Caciotta di Pecora *(It)* A soft ewes' milk cheese shaped like a small drum 14 cm dia. by 7 cm with a mild tasting dense paste and a smooth soft rind. Contains 50% water, 26% fat and 23% protein

caciucco *(It)* A highly seasoned fish soup served with pieces of garlic-flavoured toast

ca com *(Vi)* A small fish similar to an anchovy prepared like ikan bilis

cactus leaf *see* nopales

cactus pear *see* prickly pear

Cádiz *(Sp)* A soft goats' milk cheese made in 1.5 kg discs and eaten afer a few day's ripening

cadju *(Sr)* Cashew nut

caecum A blind, sac-like extension to the intestine of an animal which after cleaning is used as a type of sausage skin

Caerphilly *(UK)* A moist, mild, crumbly cheese made from cow's milk, originating in Wales it is now made generally in the UK. It is slightly acidic from the lactic starter and matured for less than 2 weeks. May be substituted for feta cheese [also called **new cheese**]

Caesar salad *(USA)* A mixture of crisp lettuce, anchovies, garlic-flavoured croutons and grated Parmesan cheese, tossed with a dressing of raw or coddled egg, seasoning, oil and vinegar

caesar's mushrooms *see* ovoli

café *(Fr) masc.* **1** Coffee **2** *(En & Fr) masc.* The name given to a place selling drinks and snacks but not formal meals

café brûlot *(Fr) masc.* Hot black coffee, sometimes with added spices (e.g. cardamom), flamed with brandy

Café Konditorei *(Au)* A coffee shop which sells cakes and sweets for consumption both on and off the premises

café au lait *(Fr) masc.* Coffee mixed with hot milk

café liégeoise *(Fr) masc.* Iced coffee served in a glass with whipped cream or ice cream

café renversé *(He)* masc. Café au lait

cafetière A straight sided glass pot with a lip into which a tight fitting plunger with a fine wire mesh is fitted. Ground coffee and boiling water are put in the pot, the plunger is placed on top and when the coffee has infused, the plunger is depressed to filter the coffee extract which is then poured out

caffeine The alkaloid found in tea (2-4% by weight) and coffee (1-2% by weight) and in cola drinks, responsible for some of their stimulating properties

caglio *(It)* Rennet

cai juan *(Ch)* Spring roll

caille *(Fr) fem.* Quail

caillé *(Fr) masc.* Curds

caillebotte *(Fr) fem.* A white, soft, creamy curd cheese made from a variety of milks usually sold in small wickerwork baskets or earthenware pots. Lit. curdled bale or bunch.

cailleteau *(Fr) fem.* Young quail

caillette *(Fr) fem.* **1** The fourth stomach of the calf used as a source of rennet **2** A package of flavoured chopped meat and offal wrapped in pig's caul or wafer thin sheets of pork fat **3** The Provençale for crépinette, but the crépinette does not usually contain offal

caillettes de foie de porc *(Fr) fem.* Strips of pigs' liver and bacon and chopped pigs' sweetbreads marinated for 24 hours with chopped garlic, parsley and seasoning, formed into thin cylinders and wrapped in pig's caul, tied, roasted in a medium oven for 1 to 2 hours, cooled in the pan juices and served cold in slices

caillettes provençales *(Fr) fem.* Chopped lean pork, pork belly and liver mixed with chopped cooked spinach, sweated chopped shallots, garlic, parsley, thyme and seasoning, the whole lightly fried, bound with egg, made into balls, each ball wrapped in pig's caul and all baked in a moderate oven with skinned and deseeded tomatoes, chopped parsley and garlic. Served hot

caimo *see* abiu

Caithness cheese *(UK)* A mild, pale yellow, creamy cheese from Scotland made from cow's milk

cajan pea *see* pigeon pea

Cajanus cajan *Bot.* The pigeon pea plant

cajeta de celaya *see* arequipe

caju *(Po)* Cashew nut

cajun A style of cooking based on rice, okra and crayfish, developed by the French Canadians who settled during the 18th century in Southern USA *(Louisiana)*; *see also* Créole cuisine

Cajun blacken, to To sear on an extremely hot cast iron frying pan or griddle, batted out or thin tender cuts of meat, fish or poultry which have been dipped in molten butter and sprinkled with cajun spice mix.

Cajun spice mix A mixture of ground spices from Louisiana used in Cajun and Créole cooking consisting of paprika, black pepper, cumin seeds, mustard seeds, cayenne pepper, dried thyme, dried oregano and salt. Usually blended with garlic and onion and rubbed on meat or fish prior to cooking

cake 1 A baked or fried mixture of generally fat, flour, eggs and sugar with flavourings and raising agents to lighten and aerate the mixture. May also incorporate root vegetables, principally carrot **2** *(Ho)* Cake

cake flour *(USA)* A very high extraction low protein white flour used for making very light textured cakes such as angel cake

cake mixtures The five important cake mixtures are basic, Victoria sponge, Genoese, pound and fatless. The first two use a chemical raising agent, the last three rely on air beaten into the egg for raising. See under the name for proportions; *see also* cake production methods

cake production methods The five methods are:- rubbing in, creaming, fatless whisking, whisking and melting. See under each name for details

ca khoai *(Vi)* Bummaloe, the fish

calabacin *(Sp)* Marrow, courgette

calabacita *(Sp)* Courgette

calabash Bottle gourd

calabaza A member of the squash family found in Spain and popular in the Carribean. Very large with yellow flesh and used in savoury dishes

calabrese A variety of broccoli *Brassica oleracea* Italica Group originally from Calabria in Sicily but now widely grown. The immature compact central flower heads, about 10 cm across, and their stems, and young side shoots are harvested in summer and cooked as a vegetable; *see also* broccoli [also called **American broccoli, Italian broccoli**]

calaloo *see* callaloo soup

calamar *(Sp)* Squid

calamares en su tinta *(Sp)* Squid, stuffed and fried, served with a sauce made from their ink

calamaretti *(It)* Small squid

calamari *(It)* pl. Squid

calamaro *(It)* Squid

calamento *(Sp)* Catmint

calaminta *(Sp)* Catmint

calamondin A small mandarin x kumquat hybrid *Citrofortunella microcarpa,* up to 4 cm dia., rather like a small thin skinned orange. Used for marmalade and pickles [also called **China orange, Panama orange**]

calamus A wild marsh plant *Acorus calamus*

whose roots used to be candied. Used as a flavouring, mostly in liqueurs [also called **sweet flag**]

Calamus rotang *Bot.* Rattan palm

calas *(USA)* A breakfast dish from New Orleans consisting of a mixture of cooked rice, flour, spices and sugar, spoonfuls of which are deep fried

calawissa onion *see* Egyptian onion

Calcagno *(It)* A hard ewes' milk cheese aged for at least 6 months and moulded in wicker baskets so that it has an uneven rind

calciferol *see* vitamin D

calcionetti *(It)* Apple and almond fritters

calcium An essential element for health used in the formation of bones and for the transmission of nerve impulses as well as in other metabolic processes. Requires vitamin D for absorption. Available from milk products, pulses and cereals as well as from inorganic sources such as hard water, chalk and lime

calcium acetate E263, the calcium salt of acetic acid (vinegar) used as a preservative and firming agent

calcium carbonate E170, a natural mineral source of calcium produced from limestone. Used in a very finely ground form as an acidity regulator and as a source of calcium in processed foods, esp. manufactured bread in the UK [also called **chalk, ground chalk, precipitated chalk**]

calcium chloride *see* (E)509

calcium dihydrogen di-L-glutamate *see* (E)623

calcium disodium EDTA *see* (E)385

calcium formate E238, the calcium salt of formic acid used in the same way as the acid

calcium gluconate *see* (E)578

calcium glutamate *see* (E)623

calcium heptonate A food additive used as a firming agent and sequestering agent in prepared food and vegetables

calcium hydrogen malate *see* (E)352

calcium hydroxide *see* (E)529

calcium lactate *see* E327

calcium malate *see* (E)352

calcium phytate A sequestering agent used in wine

calcium polyphosphate *see* (E)544

calcium saccharin The calcium salt of saccharin used as saccharin

calcium silicate *see* (E)552

calcium stearoyl-2-lactate E482, the calcium salt corresponding to the sodium salt and with the same uses

calcium sulphate *see* (E)516

caldeirada de peixe *(Po)* A fish and/or shellfish stew similar to bouillabaisse. The ingredients depend on what is available locally and may include potatoes

caldereta *(Sp)* A thick fish stew

caldereta asturiana *(Sp)* Fish stewed with onions, pepper and spices

caldillo de congrio *(SA)* A fish soup from Chile made from the local fish, congrio

caldo 1 *(It & Sp)* Hot **2** *(Po & Sp)* A clear soup or broth

caldo de carne *(Po)* Meat stock

caldo gallego *(Sp)* A stew of beans, ham, chicken, beef, cabbage, potatoes, turnips and onions

caldo de gallina *(Sp)* Chicken broth

caldo de perro gaditano *(Sp)* A fish stew made from sliced white fish salted for 1 hour, drained, added to fried onions and garlic, water, seasoning and Seville orange juice and cooked until tender

caldo de pescado *(Sp)* Fish soup

caldo de pimentón *(Sp)* A fish stew with potatoes, tomatoes, garlic and paprika

caldo verde *(Po)* Potato and cabbage soup. The national soup of Portugal, made with potatoes, olive oil and finely shredded green Portuguese cabbage

calendola *(It)* Marigold

caléndula *(Sp)* Marigold

Calendula officinalis *Bot.* Marigold

calf The young of some of the larger herbivores, principally used of young cows or beef cattle *(pl. calves)*

calf's foot The foot of the calf which when boiled is a useful source of gelatine for aspic and other jellies or to give body to a stew

calf's foot jelly The jelly made by boiling a calf's foot with aromatic vegetables and herbs, straining and clarifying then cooling. Once thought to be beneficial for invalids

calf's head The head of a calf usually boiled

and the flesh used for brawn or pies. Not generally available during the BSE scare because of the danger of infection from brain tissue

calf's tongue The tongue of a calf usually boiled, skinned and then either eaten hot or pressed in a mould with a setting jelly, cooled, demoulded and sliced

caliente *(Sp)* Hot

California bonito *see* skipjack tuna

California dry chilli *(USA)* A long red chilli pepper that has been left to dry on the bush

California pepper *(USA) see* Anaheim chilli

California roll *(USA)* A cone of nori filled with sushi rice and pieces of crab meat and avocado pear

California whiting *(USA)* A similar fish *Merluccius undulatus* to North Atlantic whiting

Californian chilli *(USA) see* Anaheim chilli

Californian halibut A sinistral flat fish *Paralichthys californicus* related to the brill and turbot but not to the halibut

Californian mussel *(USA)* A mussel *Mytilus californianus* found along the west coast and very similar to the common mussel

Calimyrna fig *(USA)* A small sweet nutty-flavoured fig with an amber skin. Used fresh, in fruit salads and chutney and in cooked meat dishes

calipash The fatty, gelatinous, dull-green, edible lining of the upper shell of a turtle

calissons *(Fr) masc.* Lozenge shaped almond biscuits or confections

callaloo 1 *see* amaranths **2** *(Ca)* In spite of its name, a stew made with dasheen leaves, okra, aubergines, tomatoes, onions and garlic with meat or crab, all cooked in coconut milk and flavoured with herbs and spices

callaloo soup *(Ca)* In spite of its name, a soup made from dasheen leaves, okra, crabmeat, salt pork, onions, garlic and sometimes coconut [also called **kallaloo, calaloo, callau, callilu**]

callau *see* callaloo soup

callilu *see* callaloo soup

callos *(Sp)* Tripe, usually served in a stew with chick peas

calmar *(Fr) masc.* Squid and flying squid

Calocarpum mammosum *Bot.* Sapote

Calocarpum viride *Bot.* Green sapote

calorie The outdated measure of the energy content of foods still used in popular parlance to estimate the fattening potentiality of food (since if not used for energy, food is usually stored as fat). The Calorie *(capital C)* or kilocalorie used in nutrition has 1000 times the value of the calorie *(small c)* used in science and is the energy required to heat 1 kg of water by 1°C; *see also* Joule

calorific value The amount of heat produced when 1 g (small calorie) or 1 kg (large Calorie or kilocalorie) of food is completely burned or metabolized to carbon dioxide and water by oxygen

calostro *(Sp)* **1** *see* Armada, the cheese **2** Beestings

calrose rice A type of slightly glutinous white rice with a higher starch content than normal making it easier to eat with chopsticks

caltrops A very similar fruit to water caltrop from the related species *Trapa natans.* It too has been used as a food source since Neolithic times and is still grown and eaten in central Europe and Asia. It has a floury texture and an agreeable flavour and may be eaten raw, roasted or boiled like a chestnut. Unfortunately it also is often called a water chestnut, but it is not the canned water chestnut familiar in the west [also called **Jesuit's nut**]

calvados *(Fr) masc.* An alcoholic spirit made by distilling cider, much used for flavouring dishes from Normandy

calves' kidneys Light coloured, tender and delicately flavoured kidney of young cattle, grilled or fried

calves' liver A golden brown, smooth and delicate liver much used in Italian cooking. Requires very little cooking

calzenglide *(It) see* calzone

calzociedde *(It) see* calzone

calzone *(It)* A yeasted, white bread dough, rolled out thinly, formed into a pocket and filled with cheese or salami and cheese *(Naples)* or with onions, olives, anchovies, capers and cheese, rather like a large pizza. Baked in the oven or if small sometimes fried [also called **calzengliede, calzuncieddi**]

ca mang *(Vi)* Bangus, the fish

camarão *(Po)* Common prawn

Camargue *(Fr) fem.* A soft, creamy cheese made from ewes' milk and flavoured with fresh thyme and bay

Camargue red rice A natural hybrid between short grain rice and the wild red rice of the Camargue discovered in 1980. It has the red colour and subtle taste of its wild parent but does not shed its grain on ripening

camarón *(Sp)* Common prawn

camaroon *(Ph)* Large shrimp or prawn

Cambazola A dull, fat, soft, blue veined German cheese with a white Camembert type rind

Cambridge bronze *see* bronze turkey

Cambridge burnt cream *(UK)* *see* burnt cream

Cambridge cheese *see* York cheese

Cambridge sauce *(UK)* A processed mixture of hard boiled egg yolks, anchovy fillets, capers, mustard, tarragon, chervil and chives, made into a thick emulsion sauce with oil and vinegar and finished with chopped parsley. Served with cold meat

Cambridge sausage *(UK)* A lean, English pork frying sausage flavoured with sage, cayenne pepper, ground mace, nutmeg and seasoning

camel A large domesticated animal from arid regions with either one hump *Camelus dromedarius* or two *C. bactrianus,* used both as a draught animal and as a source of meat and milk. The fat in the milk is very finely dispersed and cream cannot be separated from it

Camembert *(Fr) masc.* A soft, small, wheel-shaped cheese about 250 g in weight made from full cream cow's milk, dry salted to 3% salt, surface ripened for 10 to 14 days with *Penicillium candidum* and *P.camembertii,* which forms a white fungus on the rind then wrapped in paper and boxed. Contains 57% water, 21% fat and 20% protein a half of which is hydrolysed by the fungus. Originating in Normandy but now widely produced

Camembert de Normandie *(Fr) masc.* The traditional Camembert cheese from Normandy made with unpasteurized milk and specially licensed with Appellation d'Origine status

Camerano *(Sp)* A soft goats' milk cheese, moulded in wicker baskets and eaten within one day of draining and salting

camicia, in *(It)* Poached *(of eggs),* baked in their jackets *(of potatoes).* Lit. in a shirt, en chemise

camoscio *(It)* Chamois, a small goat-like mammal *Rupicapra rupicapra,* famous for its leather but the meat is eaten in Italy, usually marinated and stewed

camotes *(Ph & Sp)* Sweet potatoes

camp coffee A liquid extract of coffee and chicory once used as an instant coffee

campagnola, alla *(It)* Country style

campden tablets A mixture of sodium metabisulphite, E223, and potassium benzoate, E212, used as a food and wine preservative

campo, di *(It)* Wild e.g. mushrooms, asparagus, etc. Lit. of the field

Campylobacter jejuni A food poisoning bacteria found in chicken and milk which is a major cause of gastroenteritis. The incubation period is 2 to 10 days and the duration of the often severe illness which is flu like with abdominal pain and fever followed by diarrhoea is 5 to 10 days

***Campylobacter* spp.** Food poisoning bacteria found in raw meat and poultry which cause diarrhoea, vomiting and fever

ca muc *(Cm)* Cuttlefish

ca mu cham *(Vi)* Garoupa, the fish

can *(USA)* Any metal container used for keeping or preserving food, hermetically sealed if used for preservation

can, to To preserve food in a sealed, tin plated steel or aluminium can by heating after sealing to cook and sterilize the contents

can measure *(USA)* North American recipes sometimes use USA can sizes as a volume measure. They are approximately: buffet, 236 ml; picnic, 295 ml; no. 300, 413 ml; no. 1 tall and no. 303, 472 ml; no. 2, 590 ml; no. 2½, 826 ml; no. 3 cylinder, 1375 ml and no. 10, 2830 to 3060 ml

can opener An implement for removing the tops from sealed cans of food

caña medular *(Sp)* Marrow bone

Canadian bacon *see* Canadian-style bacon

Canadian Cheddar A Cheddar type cheese made in Canada

Canadian plaice *see* American plaice

Canadian-style bacon A quick cured, mild bacon with more sugar and less salt than normal in the curing liquid

canapé *(En & Fr) masc.* Small biscuits or pieces of toast covered with various savoury items and decorated. Served at buffets, cocktail parties and with drinks. Lit. couch, settee

canard *(Fr) masc.* Duck

canard à l'orange *(Fr) masc.* Duck with orange. Roast mallard (200°C, 40 min.) or widgeon or teal (220°C, 25 min.) previously seasoned and flavoured, served with sauce made from defatted pan residues, red wine, stock and Seville orange juice thickened with fécule or arrowroot. Garnished with wedges of sweet orange and watercress

canard à la presse *(Fr) masc.* Breasts of lightly roasted (20 minutes) Rouen duck sliced and warmed at the table in a mixture of brandy and the blood and juices obtained by crushing in a press the remainder of the carcase less the legs.

Sometimes flambéed with brandy [also called **canard rouennais à la presse**]

canard rouennais *(Fr) masc.* A specially bred duck from the Rouen district, usually filled with a stuffing made from its own liver, roasted and served with a red wine sauce

canard sauvage *(Fr) masc.* Wild duck, usually mallard duck

canardeau *(Fr) masc.* Duckling (slightly older than a caneton)

Canary pudding *(UK)* A basic steamed pudding mixture with half the flour replaced with fresh breadcrumbs, a third to a half of the milk with Madeira and flavoured with grated lemon zest

Canavalia ensiformis *Bot.* Jack bean

Canavalia gladiata *Bot.* Sword bean

cancalaise, à la *(Fr)* In the style of Cancale, Brittany, i.e. with a fish sauce made from white wine with mussels, prawns and oysters

canch mexicana *(Me)* A chicken broth containing chopped onions and tomatoes sweated in butter, rice, diced chicken meat and chopped mint

candied fruit Pieces of fruit soaked in a heavy sugar syrup until all the water is replaced with the syrup, then dried so that the surface is covered with crystalline sugar unlike glacé fruit. Used as a confectionery item and for decoration [also called **crystallized fruit, preserved fruit**]

candied peel Citrons, halved, pulp removed, immersed in brine or sea water for 1 month to ferment then washed, dried and candied with sugar syrup. Usually candied in the country where used. Sometimes used as a confectionery item but more usually chopped and used in cakes

canditi *(It)* Candied fruit

candle fruit A North African variety of aubergine shaped like a small banana with ivory coloured skin

candlenut The macadamia-shaped nut of a tree *Aleurites moluccana* grown in SEA. When ground, used as a thickening agent in Malaysian cooking. It must be cooked before consumption to detoxify it. The kernel is removed by charring the outer shell so that it can be cracked. So called because the nuts were once ground to a paste with copra and cotton to make candles

cane *(Fr)* Female duck

cane syrup *(USA)* The concentrated juice from sugar cane used in place of golden syrup or molasses

canel *(Ca)* Cinnamon

canela *(Ca, Po & Sp)* Cinnamon, the most important spice used in Portugal

canela em pau *(Po)* Cinnamon quill

canelle knife A small knife shaped so that thin narrow strips of skin may be cut from the skin of citrus fruit, cucumbers, etc.

canellini *(It)* A generic name for all types of white beans

canelones *(Sp)* Minced meat

canesca *(It)* A variety of shark

Canestrato *(It)* A semi-hard scalded curd Sicilian cheese made from ewe's milk and matured in a wicker basket to give it a distinctive surface pattern [also called **Incanestrato, Pecorino, Pecorino canestrato, Siciliano, Rigato**]

canestrelli *(It)* **1** Small scallops **2** Sweet scallop-shaped pastries from the north west

caneton *(Fr) masc.* Small duck or duckling

caneton rouennais *(Fr) masc.* A specially bred duckling from the Rouen district, generally pot roasted or roasted but may be braised if to be served cold

caneton à la rouennaise *(Fr) masc.* Rouen duck strangled, plucked whilst warm, liver less gall bladder returned to the cavity, spit roasted for 15 to 30 minutes and skinned. Legs removed and thigh bones excised, brushed with butter, grilled and salted, wing removed, panéed and grilled and all, together with the sliced breast served with a sauce made with juices pressed from the carcase, red wine, shallots and the sieved liver

cangrejo *(Sp)* Crab

cangrejo de mar *(Sp)* Shore crab

cangrejo moruno *(Sp)* A small furry crab *Eriphia verrucosa* found in the Mediterranean used particularly in the paella of the Balearic islands

cangrejo de rio *(Sp)* Freshwater crayfish

canistel *(USA)* An egg shaped fruit *Pucheria campechiana* with a thin glossy skin and a yellowish, creamy and slightly sweet flesh. Used in fruit salads

canja *(Po)* A clear chicken soup with rice, shreds of chicken breast, mint and lemon juice

canja de galinha *(Po)* Chicken broth with chicken livers and rice

canneberge *(Fr) fem.* Cranberry

canned food Food preserved in cans or tins

cannella *(It)* Cinnamon

cannelle *(Fr) fem.* Cinnamon

cannellino bean A variety of haricot bean

Phaseolus vulgaris, slightly larger than normal, now extensively grown and used in Italy [also called **fazolia bean**]

cannelloni *(It)* Large squares of thin pasta which are first poached, then rolled around a stuffing to form tubes which are placed in a dish, covered in a sauce, possible gratinated with cheese and baked in the oven

cannelon *(Fr) masc.* A small puff pastry roll, filled with meat, fish, poultry or game

cannocchia *(It)* Mantis shrimp

cannoli *(It)* Horn shaped pastries filled with cream cheese, whipped cream, custard, chocolate cream or similar

cannolicchi *(It)* Short and fairly thick tubes of pasta used in soups [also called **ave maria**]

cannolichio *(It)* Razor shell, mollusc

canola *see* rapeseed

canotière, à la *(Fr)* In the style of the boatman, i.e. freshwater fish cooked with shallots, mushrooms and white wine

canotière, sauce *(Fr) fem.* The lightly salted cooking liquor from poached freshwater fish reduced by two thirds, thickened with beurre manié, simmered 5 minutes, strained and finished with butter and a little cayenne pepper

Cantal *(Fr)* A large (to 50 kg) semi-hard cheese made from cow's milk and matured from 3 to 5 months. The rind is grey with red streaks and has a powdery surface and the paste is firm, full of bite and has a nutty flavour. It has been made for at least 2000 years and is protected by an Appellation d'Origine. Contains 44% water, 26% fat and 23% protein [also called **Fourme de Cantal, Fourme de Salers, Salers**]

Cantalon *(Fr)* A smaller version of Cantal cheese

cantaloup *(En & Fr) masc.* Cantaloupe melon

cantaloupe melon 1 A variety of sweet melon *Cucumis melo* developed in Cantelupo, central Italy. It has a grey-green rough skin with deep longitudinal grooves, the flesh is orange-yellow, very sweet and fragrant and individual fruits weigh up to 750 g. It is ripe when there is a slight give at the stalk end under gentle pressure. The principle types in Europe are the charentais, ogen, tiger and sweetheart [also called **rock melon**] **2** *(USA) see* musk melon

canterellen *(Ho)* Chanterelles

canthaxanthin *see* E161(g)

Cantonese cooking The style of cooking from South East China, including, stir frying of meat and vegetables with the addition of cornflour thickened chicken stock, sweet and sour dishes, and steamed sweet and savoury delicacies known as dim sum

Cantonese onion *see* Chinese chive

cantucci *(It)* Small hard, sweet biscuits containing almond pieces. Traditionally dunked in Vino Santo, a rich sherry like wine from Tuscany [also called **biscotti di Prato, cantuccini**]

cantuccini *(It) see* cantucci

canvas back *(USA)* A wild duck *Aythya valisineria* with a distinctly flavoured flesh due to its diet of wild celery shoots

cao gu *(Ch)* Straw mushroom

cao mi *(Ch)* Strawberries

capão *(Po)* Capon

caparon *(It)* Shellfish

cape gooseberry A cherry-sized, yellow-fleshed, slightly sour fruit of a plant *Physalis peruviana* originally from Peru but now grown in Egypt, Colombia and South Africa. It is loosely enclosed in a segmented, papery, fawn husk which looks like a Chinese lantern. Used in fruit salads and for decoration [also called **physalis, goldenberry**]

capeado *(Sp)* Battered and deep fried

capelan *see* capelin

capelin *(USA)* A medium oily fish *Mallotus villosus* similar to smelt and up to 25 cm in length. It is greenish on top and white underneath and found in the North Atlantic [also called **capelan, caplin**]

capelli d'angelo *(It) see* Angel's hair

capellini *(It)* A very thin spaghetti

capelvenere *(It)* Maidenhead fern

caper The flower bud of a small Mediterranean bush *Capparis spinosa* and *C. inermis* which is pickled in brine for use in sauces and on pizzas

caper mayonnaise Chopped capers, chopped sweet red peppers and tarragon vinegar mixed with mayonnaise

caper sauce A velouté sauce made from mutton stock flavoured with chopped capers, served with boiled leg of mutton; *see also* sauce aux câpres

capercaillie A large game bird *Tetrao urogallus* about the size of a turkey, common in Scandinavia, northern Russia and the alps and recently reintroduced to Scotland. In season 1st October to 31st January, hanging time 7 to 14 days [also called **capercailzie, wood grouse**]

capercailze *see* capercaillie

caperzzoli *(It)* Molluscs

capillaire commun *(Fr) masc.* Maidenhair fern

capillaire syrup A thick mucilaginous liquid extracted from the maidenhead fern and flavoured with orange flower water or other

capillari *(It)* Tiny eels

capilotade *(Fr) fem.* Boned out leftovers of chicken or game birds sliced and reheated in sauce italienne with some sweated sliced mushrooms, garnished with chopped parsley and accompanied by heart shaped croûtons

capilotade, en *(Fr)* In crumbs *(of a cake)*; squashed to a pulp or to bits

capirotada *(Me)* Bread pudding

capitone *(It)* Conger eel

caplin *see* capelin

capocollo *(It)* Boned out, skinned, cured and cooked pork shank, rolled in ground spices and pepper and served in thin slices

capon A castrated male domestic fowl which grows larger and is more tender than the intact bird

capone gallinella *(It)* Tub gurnard

caponata *(It)* A salad of fried aubergines and onions with tomatoes, anchovies, capers and olives served on a large dry biscuit or toasted bread. Other fruits and vegetables may be included together with some sugar and vinegar and the whole mixture may be reduced to a thick chutney-like consistency

caponatine *(It)* A salad of pickled vegetables

capozzella *(It)* Roasted lamb's head

cappa *(It)* Razor shell, mussel, various shellfish generally

cappa ai ferri *(It)* Grilled scallops

cappa liscia *(It)* Venus shell clam [also called **fasolaro**]

cappalletti *(It)* Small ravioli made in the shape of a three cornered hat, usually stuffed with a mousseline of fish or shellfish

Capparis inermis *Bot.* Caper bush, spineless variety

Capparis spinosa *Bot.* Caper bush, spiny variety

cappelle di fungo *(It)* Mushroom caps

cappello *(It)* Hat, used of foods shaped like a hat, either conical or like an Italian priest's, e.g. pies or boned out hams, etc.

capperi *(It)* Capers

cappon magro *(It)* A mixed salad of cooked vegetables, anchovies, fish, lobster and garlic-flavoured rusks

cappone *(It)* **1** Capon **2** Gurnard, the fish

cappone in galera *(It)* A salad of anchovies and capers

capponi *(It)* Small red mullet

cappuccino *(It)* **1** Espresso coffee mixed with milk that has been boiled and foamed by steam injection, served with a sprinkling of ground spice such as cinnamon, nutmeg or cocoa **2** Nasturtium leaves

cappuccio, a *(It)* Round, as in round lettuce Lit. like a hood or cap

cappucina *(It)* Lettuce

capra *(It)* **1** Goat **2** A freshwater lake fish similar to trout

capra di mare *(It)* Spider crab

câpre *(Fr) fem.* Caper

câpres, sauce aux *(Fr) fem.* Butter sauce with the addition of 120 g of capers per litre at the last moment. Served with boiled fish

capretto *(It)* Kid, young goat

Caprice des Dieux *(Fr) masc.* An oval shaped, mild, soft cheese from the Champagne region made from cow's milk with added cream and sold in a small box

caprice, fish As fish St. Germain but topped with a lengthways slice of banana passed through seasoned flour and shallow fried. Served with Robert sauce

capricorn *(UK)* A goats' milk cheese from Somerset with a relatively mild flavour and cast in cylinders

caprini *(It)* Small goats' milk cheeses

caprino a pasta cruda *(It)* A soft cheese made from unpasteurized goats' milk and ripened for 3 months

caprino semicotto *(It)* A hard scalded-curd goats' milk cheese from Sardinia made in a drum shape. The cheese is brined, dry salted and ripened for at least 3 months

capriolo *(It)* Deer, roebuck

caprylic acid A fatty acid which when esterified is a constituent of goat's milk fat, butter fat and coconut oil. When liberated by oxidation it has a rancid goaty smell

capsaicin The hot flavouring component of chilli peppers and cayenne peppers

capsanthin E160(c), a peppery flavouring and pink food colouring obtained from paprika [also called **capsorubin**]

Capsella bursa-pastoris *Bot.* Shepherd's purse

capsicum The general name for the hollow seed pods of *Capsicum* spp. which are relatives of the tomato. They range from green, yellow or red sweet peppers to the very hot chilli and cayenne peppers, not to be confused with the spice pepper *Piper nigrum*; *see also* under sweet peppers, chilli peppers and cayenne peppers

***Capsicum annuum* Grossum Group** *Bot.* Sweet peppers

***Capsicum annuum* Longum Group** *Bot.* Chilli peppers

Capsicum frutescens *Bot.* Cayenne peppers

capsorubin *see* capsanthin

capuchina *(Sp)* Nasturtium

capucine *(Fr) fem.* Nasturtium

Caquelon *(He)* A wide based pot with a short stubby handle to one side in which cheese fondue is prepared and kept hot and molten over a spirit lamp or candle

carabinero *(Sp)* Crevette rouge (Fr)

caracóis *(Po)* Snails

caracol gris *(Sp)* Winkle

caracoles *(Sp)* Snails

carafe An open topped glass container with a bulbous or conical shape, a narrow neck and a wide rim used for serving wine or water at meals

carajay *(Ph)* Wok

carambola The fruit of a small evergreen tree *Averrhoa carambola* from SEA which when cut across its axis has the appearance of a five pointed star. The crisp yellow flesh has an acid, sweet and aromatic flavour and it is often used for decoration. The flavour and colour are improved by poaching it in a little light syrup. It can also be used for jam and chutney [also called **star fruit**]

caramel *(En & Fr) masc.* The golden brown distinctly flavoured compound formed when sugar is heated to 182°C. Used for colouring, as an ingredient in its own right and to flavour the confectionery called caramel. In its darker form it is the permitted food colouring E150

caramel cream *see* crème caramel

caramel stage *see* sugar cooking

caramelize, to To cause sugars to break down into brown flavoured compounds by heating to around 180-185°C. Responsible for some of the brown colour developed by baking, frying, roasting or grilling sugar containing foods

caramelized potatoes *see* brunede kartofler

caramella *(It)* Caramel

caramellato *(It)* Caramelized, candied or glazed

caramelo *(Sp)* Caramel

caramote *(Fr)* A transverse striped king prawn *Penaeus kerathurus* from the Mediterranean. It is brown with reddish tints becoming pink when cooked and is up to 22 cm long. It is considered to be the finest crustacean flesh in the world. [also called **crevette royale, grosse crevette**]

caramujo *(Sp)* Winkle

caranguejo *(Po)* Crab

carapace The hard upper shell of crustaceans, tortoises or turtles

carapau *(Po)* A small seawater fish between a sardine and smelt in size

carapulca *(SA)* A Peruvian stew made from meat, papa seca, tomatoes, onions and garlic

caraque A form of flaked chocolate made by coating a thin layer of chocolate on marble or on a steel tray, allowing it to set and cool, then removing it with a scraper as though stripping paint

caraway The plant from which caraway seeds q.v. are obtained. The young leaves may be used in salads and soups and the roots can be cooked as a vegetable

caraway mint Sprouted caraway seeds used as a herb in Vietnamese cooking

caraway seeds The small brown seeds of a biennial European plant *Carvum carvi* with a sweet aromatic flavour. Used to flavour rye bread, cakes, cheese and other foods and is the principal flavouring in Kümmel liqueur

carbohydrates The principal energy sources in human food which are simple sugars *(monosaccharides)* or chains of repeated sugar units *(disaccharides, trisaccharides and polysaccharides)*. The polysaccharides have many repeated sugar units and are starches or various types of cellulose. They are all with the exception of cellulose and a few starches broken down in the gut into absorbable monosaccharides either by acids and enzymes in the gastric juices or by the action of microorganisms; *see also* monosaccharides, cellulose and dietary fibre.

carbon black E153, a very finely divided form of carbon used as a food colouring [also called **vegetable carbon**]

carbon dioxide E290, the gas produced when

the carbon in foods is oxidized either by the action of yeasts and other microorganisms, by combustion or by cellular processes in the body, or when chemical raising agents are heated or react in water. The gas is responsible for the raising of bread, cakes, etc.

carbonade *(Fr) fem.* Meat grilled over charcoal but now often used of very dark coloured braised beef [also called **carbonnade**]

carbonade of beef *see* carbonnade à la flamande

carbonado *(Ar)* Beef stew with apples, pears, potatoes, tomatoes and onions

carbonara *(It)* The sauce or dressing used with spaghetti alla carbonara q.v

carbonata *(It)* A dish from the north west of beef or salt beef stewed in red wine. Often served with polenta

carbonate, to To dissolve carbon dioxide gas in a liquid as in the production of soft drinks or some sparkling wines

carbonated water Water in which carbon dioxide has been dissolved. Sometimes stored under pressure. The gas is released when the pressure is reduced or when the water is warmed up on contact with the mouth [also called **soda water, mineral water**]

carbonnade *(Fr) fem. see* carbonade

carbonnade à la flamande *(Be)* fem. A stew made from beef, onions, garlic and dark beer, thickened with slices of bread coated in French mustard. So called because of its dark colour

carborundum stone A hard stone made from finely powdered silicon carbide fused together used for sharpening knives, often shaped like a steel and used in the same way. Causes more wear than a conventional steel

carcase of chicken The remains of plucked and dressed chicken after the legs, breasts and wings have been removed. Cut into 3 pieces for chicken sauté so as to add flavour to the pan residues or used for stock

carcasse *(Fr) fem.* Carcase, e.g. of chicken

carciofi alla romana *(It)* Artichokes boiled in oil with herbs

carciofini *(It)* Artichoke hearts

carciofo *(It)* Artichoke

carciofo di giudea *(It)* Jerusalem artichoke

cardamine *(It, Sp & Fr) fem.* Lady's smock

Cardamine pratensis *Bot.* Lady's smock

cardamom The dried fruit of a perennial bush *Elettaria cardamomum* belonging to the ginger family, consisting of green or bleached pods (5 to 10 mm long) containing loose black seeds with an aromatic flavour and smell. Larger pods are in general brown to black and their seeds are of a lower quality and used in pickles and chutneys. Cardamom is used to flavour coffee in the Middle East as well as being common in Indian, Eastern and Scandinavian cuisines. Young cardamom leaves are used as a food wrapping and to flavour food in SEA cuisines. Cheap cardamom substitutes are Nepal cardamom, Chinese cardamom, Javanese winged cardamom and Ethiopian cardamom [also called **cardamon, cardamum**]

cardamome *(Fr) fem.* Cardamom

cardamomo *(It & Sp)* Cardamom

cardamon *see* cardamom

cardamum *see* cardamom

cardeau *(Fr)* Sardine

cardi *(It)* Cardoon

cardinal *(Fr) masc.* A term used to describe the pinky red colour of food by analogy with the colour of a cardinal's robes

cardinal fish The large red mullet of the Mediterranean. Considered to be the finest quality

cardinal, sauce *(Fr) fem.* A pink sauce based on lobster and truffles, served with fish

cardinal suppe *(No)* A cream soup containing chopped ham and noodles

cardine *(Fr) fem.* Megrim, the fish

cardo silvestre *(Sp)* Cardoon

cardon *(Fr) masc.* Cardoon

cardone *(It)* Cardoon

cardoni *(USA)* A thistle like plant resembling celery with an artichoke flavour. Used cooked or raw in salads

cardoon A relative of the globe artichoke (*Scolymus cardunculus*), which can grow to a height of 2 or more metres. The thick celery-like stems are blanched whilst growing in the autumn to reduce bitterness and used as a vegetable. They need long slow cooking. The leaves, roots and buds can also be used

Carême, Antonin 1784 - 1833. A famous French chef who worked for George IV, Napoleon and Czar Alexander amongst others, originated the classic French repertoire of cooking 'La Grande Cuisine' and developed the organisation of the brigade of chefs into specialities

cargo rice A dark rice which has only been dehusked, rich in bran, protein, vitamins, etc.

cari *(Sp & Fr) masc.* Curry

Caribbean banana bread *(Ca) see* pain fig banane

Caribbean black pudding *(Ca)* An exotic black pudding made with chopped spring onions, sweet red peppers, grated sweet potato or boiled rice, pig's blood, butter, seasoning and marjoram, well mixed, packed into hog casings leaving room for expansion, tied in circles, simmered for 20 minutes, pricked, cooked for a further 30 minutes and served hot

caribou *see* moose

Carica papaya *Bot.* The papaya tree *(pawpaw or papaya fruit)*

caril *(Po)* Curry powder

Carlsbad prune A large dessert prune meant to be eaten at the end of a meal

Carlton salad dressing Pineapple juice thickened with a sabayon whilst whisking vigorously, cooled, a well rubbed mixture of hard boiled yolk of egg, raw yolk of egg, French mustard and vinegar whisked in and all finished with slightly whipped double cream.

carmarguaise, à la *(Fr)* In the style of the Carmargue, i.e. cooked with tomatoes, garlic, orange peel, olives, herbs and wine or brandy

carmine *see* cochineal

carmoisine E122, a synthetic red food colouring [also called **azorubine**]

cârnăcior *(Ro)* A grilling sausage made with ground lamb, garlic and spices

carnaroli rice The best superfino Italian risotto rice from Piedmont, well rounded and extremely absorbent

carnauba A Brazilian palm *Copernicia cerifera* with an edible starchy root. Also the source of carnauba wax [also called **wax palm**]

carnauba wax (E)903, the wax from the Brazilian palm used in the food industry as a glazing agent in sugar and chocolate confectionery

carne *(It, Po & Sp)* Meat, e.g. carne de porco is pork in Portuguese, carne di maiale is the same in Italian and so on

carne asada al horno *(Sp)* Baked or roasted meat

carne asada a la parilla *(Sp)* Boiled meat

carne de boi *(Po)* Beef

carne a la castellana *(Sp)* Meat served with tomatoes, potato croquettes and onion rings

carne de cerdo *(Sp)* Pork

carne de cordero *((Sp)* Lamb

carne ensopada *(Br)* A pot roast of beef, bacon, ham, garlic, onions, butter and seasoning

carne lessa *(It)* Boiled beef

carne di maiale *(It)* Pork

carne mechada *(CA)* A stuffed beef roll, boiled and served sliced with its puréed cooking liquor

carne de membrillo *(Sp)* Quince jelly, reduced to a thick paste, usually eaten with cheese

carne picada *(Po)* Chopped or minced meat

carne picardo *(Sp)* Minced meat

carne de porco à algarvia *(Po)* Fried pork and clams

carne seca *(It)* Bacon *(Tuscany)*

carne de ternera *(Sp)* Veal

carne tritata *(It)* Minced meat

carne in umido *(It)* Stewed beef

carne de vaca 1 *(Po)* Cow beef **2** *(Sp)* Beef

carne de veado *(Po)* Venison

carne de venado *(Sp)* Venison

carne de vinha de alhos *(Po)* Pickled pork

carneiro *(Po)* Mutton

carnero *(Sp)* Mutton

carnes frias *(Po)* Cold meats sliced and presented as in assiette anglaise

Carnia *(It)* A semi-hard scalded-curd cows' milk cheese similar to Montasio from Friuli

carnitine A chemical widely distributed in plant and animal tissues and in particularly high amounts in muscle. No vitamin function has been ascribed to it but it may be involved in fatty acid transport in muscle cells and has been suggested for the medical condition myalgic encephalopathy (ME, muscle fatigue syndrome)

carob The fruit of a leguminous evergreen tree *Ceratonia siliqua* from the Mediterranean. The brown, ripe seed pods (20 by 2.5 cm) contain an edible sweet pulp and hard inedible seeds. The pulp is dried and ground into a powder resembling and used as a substitute for cocoa and chocolate powder especially by those who required stimulant-free confectionery and drinks [also called **locust bean**]

carob flour *see* carob powder

carob powder The powdered dried inner pulp

of the carob bean, used in place of cocoa powder in cakes and drinks [also called **carob flour, St John's bread**]

Carolina duck *(USA)* A highly prized wild duck *Aix sponsa* shot for the table [also called **wood duck**]

Carolina rice A round short grain rice from South Carolina which, when cooked, is sticky, but not as sticky as Italian rice. Used for puddings, Italian style risotto and as a staple carbohydrate in China and Japan. The seed was originally introduced into the USA from Italy by Thomas Jefferson

Carolina whiting *(USA)* A similar fish *Merluccius americanis* to the North Atlantic whiting

caroline *(Fr) fem.* **1** A small eclair made from choux pastry, often filled with a savoury stuffing as a hors d'oeuvres **2** Chicken consommé with rice and chervil

carom *see* ajowan

carota *(It)* Carrot

carotenes Various yellow/orange pigments in carrots and other yellow and green vegetables and fruit. It is converted into the antioxidant vitamin A in the body and used as a permitted orange food colouring E160(a). Lycopene in tomatoes and beta-carotene in carrots are two well known examples [also called **carotenoids, provitamin A**]

carotenoids *see* carotenes

carotte *(Fr) fem.* Carrot

carottes, purée de *(Fr) fem. see* carrot soup

carottes vichy *(Fr) fem. see* Vichy carrots

caroube *(Fr) fem.* Carob

carp A medium oily, variously coloured, freshwater fish *Cyprinus carpio* which is found worldwide both in the wild and farmed, harvested at 30 - 60 cm long (1.5 - 2.5 kg) but can grow much bigger. A common feast dish in Central Europe and highly regarded in Asia

carp caviar *(USA)* Female carp roe, treated to resemble and used as a substitute for caviar

carpa *(It & Sp)* Carp

carpaccio *(It)* Raw fillet of beef, sliced paper thin and served with a mustard sauce or oil and lemon juice

carpe *(Fr) fem.* Carp

carpe à la juive *(Fr)* Baked carp stuffed with raisins, chopped almonds, herbs and spices originating in the Alsace region of France

carpeau *(Fr) masc.* Young carp

carpet bag steak A thick beef steak *(sirloin or fillet)* into which a pocket is cut and filled with oysters, then grilled. Popular in Australia and North America, but originated in the UK when oysters were very cheap

carpet shell A small European bivalve mollusc, *Tapes decussatus,* with a dark grey shell, similar to various small clams

carpet shell clam A white to light brown clam *Venerupis decussata,* with dark brown radial markings and up to 8 cm in diameter. It is found around Britain and in the Mediterranean and can be eaten raw like an oyster

carpion *(Fr) masc.* A type of trout

carpione *(It)* Carp [also called **carpa**]

carragahen *(Sp)* carragheen

carrageen *see* carragheen

carragheen *(Ir & Fr) masc.* E407, an extract of the seaweeds *Chondrus crispus* and *Gigantina stellata,* which are rinsed, kept damp and bleached in the open air until creamy white, dried and used as a thickening agent. Used in Jamaica as the basis of a punch called Irish moss [also called **Irish moss, sea moss, pearl moss, carrageen**]

carré *(Fr) masc.* Best end *(of lamb, carré d'agneau or of veal, carré de veau)*

carré de Bray *(Fr) masc.* A small, square, soft, creamy cow's milk cheese from Normandy sold on rush mats

carré de l'est *(Fr) masc.* A small, square, soft and rather salty Camembert type cheese made in Lorraine and Champagne from cow's milk. Contains 52% water, 25% fat and 20% protein

carré de porc *(Fr) masc.* The equivalent of the best end of lamb cut from the front of the loin of pork

carrelet *(Fr) masc.* Plaice

carrello *(It)* Sweet or hors'd'oeuvre trolley brought to the table in a restaurant

carrettes *(USA)* Small immature carrots [also called **French carrots**]

carrot An orange-coloured, tubular root vegetable from a biennial plant, *Daucus carota,* common all over the world. One of the aromatic vegetables used for its flavour but also eaten raw when young or cooked as a vegetable

carrot cake 1 *(USA)* A cake made with grated raw carrots, oil, sometimes crushed pineapple, flour, sugar, etc. with a cream cheese based topping [also called **paradise cake, passion cake**] **2** Various cake recipes found in many countries containing grated young raw carrots in part substitution for or in addition to the the flour

carrot soup Basic soup with carrots and a small amount of tomato purée Served accompanied with croûtons [also called **purée de carottes**]

carruba *(It)* Carob

carry *(Fr) masc.* Curry

çarsi kebabi *(Tu)* Cubes of lamb or mutton marinated in vinegar with chopped onions and seasoning, skewered and grilled. Served with a sprinkling of roasted almond slivers and sour cream

carta cinese *(It)* Rice paper

carta de musica *(It)* A paper thin crisp bread [also called **fresa pistocco**]

cártamo *(It & Sp)* Safflower

carte *(Fr) fem.* Menu in a restaurant

carte, à la *(Fr)* Dishes prepared to order and individually priced on the menu usually more expensive than a fixed menu *(formule)* or a plat du jour

carte du jour *(Fr) fem.* The menu of the day, usually cheaper than the à la carte menu, similar to table d'hôte in more prestigious restaurants

carthame *(Fr) masc.* Safflower

Carthamus tinctorus *Bot.* Safflower

cartoccio, al *(It)* En papillote

cartouche *(En & Fr) fem.* A circle of buttered greaseproof paper place over the liquid contents in a dish to exclude air and to prevent a skin forming whilst it is cooking or being kept hot

Carum carvi *Bot.* Caraway

carve, to To cut slices of cooked meat from a large joint for serving or any similar operation. Meat that is roasted is usually left to rest for 10 - 20 minutes to improve its texture for carving

carvery A restaurant or section of a restaurant where roast or baked joints of meat or poultry are sliced to order and served. Sometimes self service or at least with customer participation

carvi *(It & Fr) masc.* Caraway seed

Carya illionensis *Bot.* The hickory tree which produces pecan nuts

casa, di *(It)* Home made

casaba melon *see* winter melon

casalinga *(It)* Home made

Casanova *(Ge)* A soft surface ripened cows' milk cheese which is creamy and delicate when young but becomes sharper with age. Contains 55% water, 22% fat and 19% protein

casatella *(It)* A soft fresh rindless cows' milk cheese from Lombardy

cascabel *(Me) see* chilli cascabel

cascia, alla maniera di *(It)* In the style of Cascia, i.e. with anchovies, tomatoes and truffles, esp. of pasta

casein The main protein found in milk and in cheese

casein mark A mark placed on the rind of a cheese which usually gives the date of manufacture, the geographical source of the cheese and other special quality designations

caseiro *(Po)* Home made

caserta *(It)* A pepperoni sausage containing chilli

Cashel blue *(Ir)* A semi soft, sharp flavoured, blue veined cheese made from unpasteurized milk

cashew apple The fruit associated with the cashew nut. It is eaten raw in Indonesia but generally is only suitable for making jam

cashew leaves The young leaves of the cashew are used to flavour rice in Java (Indonesia)

cashew nut The slightly curved nut from the fruit of a tropical tree *Anacardium occidentale* originally from SA but now grown worldwide. The nut and shell hang below the fruit and the shells contain a skin irritant and are removed before exporting the nuts; *see also* cashew leaves, cashew apple [also called **acajou**]

casia *(Sp)* Cassia

casings The name given to all parts of the alimentary canal from the gullet to the rectum used, after cleaning and treatment, to enclose meat mixtures as in sausages, salamis, puddings, etc. Nowadays casings are often made of plastic. See ox casings, hog casings, sheep casings, bung, middle, runner and weasand

casow *(Ph)* Cashew nut

cassaba The variety of melon *Cucumis melo inodorus* from which various sweet melons e.g. honeydew have been bred

cassareep The reduced sweetened spicy juice made from a bitter variety of cassava. Used as a condiment in Caribbean cooking

cassata *(It)* A compound ice cream made from layers of at least three different flavours and colours containing chopped nuts and chopped glacé fruits [also called **Neapolitan ice cream**]

cassata alla siciliana *(It)* A many layered chocolate cake from Sicily, soaked in liqueur, filled with Ricotta cheese and decorated with nuts and glacé fruits. Sometimes layered with ice cream

cassatedde di Ricotta A deep fried, crescent shaped pasty filled with chocolate and sweetened Ricotta cheese, the baking powder raised pastry for which is made with flour, wine, butter, lard and sugar

cassava *(En & It)* A tropical, virtually pure starch tuber up to 30 cm long of a plant *Manihot utilissima,* which is grown in hot countries and used as a major carbohydrate source in South America, Africa and other countries. The roots of some varieties have to be grated and boiled in several changes of water or partially fermented to remove toxic cyanide compounds which are in the plant cells and are broken down by enzymes in the sap. The leaves are also edible and do not contain toxic compounds and are cooked as a vegetable or used as a food wrapping. Many people are permanently crippled by the poison esp. in Africa [also called **manioc, tapioca, yuca, yucca**]

casse *(Fr) fem.* Cassia

casse croûte *(Fr) masc.* A sandwich made by slicing a small crusty French bread *(pistolet, flute or baguette)* lengthways, then buttering and filling

casser *(Fr)* To break, e.g bones, eggs

casser la croûte *(Fr)* To eat

casserole *(En & Fr) fem.* **1** A heavy metal, glass or earthenware dish with a tightly fitting lid used for slow cooking of meat, vegetables, etc. **2** Any food cooked in a casserole **3** The trade description for one-dish, in-flight meals prepared by commercial companies for airlines

casserole, en *(Fr)* Cooked in a saucepan on top of the stove

casserole, to To cook slowly a selection of ingredients, meat, vegetables, etc., usually in the oven but possibly on the stove in a dish with a tightly closed lid. The food is normally served from the casserole dish

casserolette A small casserole dish in which food may be heated and/or served

casseruola *(It)* Casserole

Cassette *(Be)* fem. A soft, pale, creamy, rectangular cow's milk cheese, seasoned, wrapped in walnut leaves and sold in small willow baskets

cassettine siciliane *(It)* Sweet almond pastries

cassia *(En & It)* A spice which is the inner bark of a tropical evergreen tree *Cinnamomum cassia* grown in China and the East. It has a similar aroma to cinnamon but is not as delicate. One of the constituents of five spice powder

cassia buds The dried unripe fruits of the cassia tree used as a flavouring and as a substitute for curry leaves. The fresh buds and leaves are used as a vegetable

cassis *(Fr) masc.* Blackcurrant, also a liqueur flavoured with blackcurrant = crème de cassis

cassol *(Fr)* The clay cooking pot from Languedoc in which Cassoulet is traditionally made

cassola *(It)* Fish soup from Sardinia with chillis and tomatoes. Served with a garlic toast

cassolette *(Fr)* A small portion-sized dish or casserole used for presenting small entrées, hors d'oeuvres or entremets, made of pleated paper, silver or china

cassonade *(Fr) fem.* Soft brown sugar

cassoni *(It)* Pasties filled with green vegetables and fried

cassoulet *(Fr) masc.* A rich stew from Languedoc consisting of haricot beans which have been simmered in a flavoured bouillon, layered in an earthenware pot with lamb or fresh and smoked pork, smoked sausages, possibly confit d'oie, onions, carrots and a pig's foot for its gelatine content. Cooked slowly in a casserole in the oven, the lid being removed towards the end to develop a crust on the surface

castagna *(It)* Chestnut

castagnaccio *(It)* A sort of cake made from a chestnut flour/water paste mixed with pine nuts, fennel seeds and plumped and dried currants or sultanas, placed in a greased baking tray dribbled with olive oil and baked until a crust forms

castagnaci *(It)* Fritters or waffles made with a chestnut flour batter

castagne all'ubriaco *(It)* Peeled roasted chestnuts covered with a cloth soaked in red wine and kept warm for 30 minutes. Eaten as is or with honey

castaña *(Sp)* Chestnut

castañas con mantequilla *(Sp)* Peeled chestnuts simmered in water with celery, salt and sugar for 40 minutes, celery removed, drained and served very hot with butter

Castanea crenata *Bot.* Japanese chestnut

Castanea sativa *Bot.* Sweet chestnut

castanha *(Po)* Chestnut, cashew nut

Castelmagno *(It)* A soft blue veined cows' milk cheese from Cuneo which is ripened in cool damp conditions. It resembles a milder version of Gorgonzola

Castelo Branco *(Po)* A smooth, white, semi-hard cheese from the town of the same name, made with a mixture of cows' milk and ewes' or goats' milk. and cast in a disc shape. The paste has no holes and no rind. It is delicately flavoured when young but develops a strong flavour after 3-4 weeks

caster sugar Refined white sugar *(sucrose)* intermediate in size between granulated and icing sugar, used in cake and dessert making because it dissolves easily without forming lumps [also called **castor sugar**]

Castigliano *(Sp)* A hard ewes' milk cheese with a strong flavour, a pale cream paste and brown rind shaped in a thin disc

castle cheese *see* Schlosskäse

castle pudding A small steamed or baked pudding made from a Victoria sponge mixture flavoured with vanilla and lemon zest cooked in individual dariole moulds and served with jam sauce

castor sugar *see* caster sugar

castradina *(It)* **1** Mutton **2** Smoked and dried mutton from Venice. Usually boiled with rice

castrato *(It)* Mutton

cat tail *see* bulrush millet

cata *(Fr)* Dogfish

catadromous A term describing fish which are born at sea, migrate to brackish or fresh water to grow and then return to the estuaries or the sea to spawn. The eel is a common example. The opposite of anadromous

cataire *(Fr) fem.* Catmint [also called **herbe aux chats**]

catalane, à la *(Fr)* In the Catalan *(North East Spain)* style, i.e. with tomatoes and rice and possibly olives and aubergine

cataplana *(Po)* A hinged metal cooking container shaped like a giant clam, or two woks, which has a very good seal for use on top of the stove

catchup *see* ketchup

cater to To provide prepared food for large or small groups usually as part of a business or public enterprise

catfish A medium-oily, white-fleshed, blunt-headed seawater fish *Anarchis lupus* with a long dorsal fin and whiskers. It is greenish grey with darker stripes and is found in the North Atlantic [also called **Atlantic catfish, wolf fish, sea cat, sea wolf**]

catjang bean *see* blackeyed pea

catmint A sprawling aromatic hardy perennial plant *Nepeta cataria* which may be used as a flavouring for meat or as a tea and the young shoots may be used in salads. If grown in the open the plant will be destroyed by cats who are inordinately attracted to it [also called **catnip**]

catnip *see* catmint

cat's tongues *see* langues de chat

catsup *(USA)* Ketchup (usually tomato)

cattle The plural collective English term for all ages and sexes of the bovine species

cattley *see* strawberry guava

Caucasian pilaff A rice pilaff containing chopped lamb and onion which is first fried in lard then simmered in stock with bay and seasoning

cauchoise, à la *(Fr)* In the style of Caux, Normandy, i.e. cooked with apples, cream and calvados, usually refers to meat

caudière *(Fr) see* caudrée

caudle *(UK) coll. (Cornwall)* A mixture of freshly soured cream and beaten eggs added to pies and casseroles about 15 minutes before the end of the cooking period

caudrée *(Fr) fem.* A one pot meal of vegetables and fish from the north rather like a potée, i.e. the liquor is used as the soup course followed by fish plus vegetables as the main course [also called **caudière**]

caul The lace-like fatty membrane which lines the abdominal cavity of sheep, pigs, etc. Used for covering joints of meat, wrapping stuffed meats, faggots and other foods, where string or casing could be used, to hold their shape during cooking. It has the advantage of adding fat to baste the food and being edible [also called **lard net**]

cauliflower A vegetable *Brassica olereacea* Botrytis Group consisting of a short thick central stalk topped with a white hemispherical head of closely packed immature flowers, 10-15 cm in diameter surrounded with long green leaves. Usually eaten raw, steamed, boiled or pickled

cauliflower bellevue A steamed whole head of cored cauliflower presented on a plate which has been covered with chopped cooked spinach sautéed in butter with garlic until fairly dry and the cauliflower surrounded decoratively with steamed carrot slices which have been sautéed in butter

cauliflower cheese *(UK)* Cooked sprigs of cauliflower coated with a cheese sauce, gratinated with cheese and browned under the grill [also called **cauliflower au gratin**]

cauliflower au gratin *(UK) see* cauliflower cheese

cauliflower soup Basic soup with cauliflower, garnished with small cooked florets of cauliflower [also called **purée de chou-fleur**]

caustic soda *see* sodium hydroxide

cavallucci di Siena *(It)* Small honey cakes containing candied fruit peel and nuts shaped in the form of a horse

cavatieddi *(It)* Pasta curls served with sauces or cheese. [also called **mignuic, mignule**]

caveach A method of preserving fish by first frying it then pickling it in vinegar; *see also* escabèche [also called **pickled fish**]

cavedano *(It)* Chub

caviale *(It)* Caviar or substitutes

caviar 1 *(En, Sp & Fr) masc.* The very expensive prepared roe of the female sturgeon q.v. found in the wild in Russia, the Mediterranean, the eastern Atlantic and the western Pacific but now being farmed. The main varieties are beluga, sevruga and osciotre caviar. The colour can vary from white to black and gold to orange brown, but different colours are not mixed. It is prepared from freshly caught fish within 2 hours. The roes are removed carefully and rubbed through a string sieve to removed membranes and then drained. The eggs are mixed with 50 to 80 g of fine salt per kg and preservative according to destination. It is not sterilized and must therefore be kept under refrigeration. It is at its best after 3 days and thereafter develops a fish flavour **2** A general term used for prepared fish roe where the eggs are separated so as to resemble sturgeon caviar, e.g. lumpfish roe; *see also* imitation caviar

caviar d'aubergine *(Fr) masc.* Poor man's caviar

caviar blanc *(Fr) masc.* Mullet roe

caviar butter Butter and caviar (4:1) pounded together and passed through a fine sieve

caviar niçois *(Fr) masc.* A paste made from anchovies, olives and herbs processed with olive oil

caviar pearls *see* ikura

caviar rouge *(Fr) masc.* Salmon roe [also called **caviar de saumon**]

caviar de saumon *(Fr) masc.* Salmon roe

caviglione *(It)* Small gurnard

cavolata *(It)* A pork, cabbage and potato soup from Sardinia

cavolfiore *(It)* Cauliflower

cavolfiore indorato e fritto *(It)* Cauliflower panéed and fried

cavolfiore alla romana *(It)* Cauliflower browned in oil and served with a tomato sauce gratinated with cheese

cavolfiore a vastedda *(It)* Cauliflower florets dipped in anchovy butter and deep fried

cavolfiore alla villeroy *(It)* Cauliflower with lemon sauce

cavolini di Bruselle *(It)* Brussel sprouts

cavolo *(It)* Cabbage

cavolo broccoluto *(It)* Broccoli

cavolo marino Sea kale

cavolo nero *(It)* Black cabbage, a type of kale

cavolo rapa *(It)* Kohlrabi

cavolo riccio *(It)* Kale

cavolo verza *(It)* Savoy cabbage

cavroman *(It)* A mutton or lamb stew with potatoes, sweet peppers and onions

cawl cennin *(UK)* A Welsh leek, onion and celery purée soup made with chicken stock. Garnished with chopped chives

çay *(Tu)* Strong tea usually served in glasses with sugar but without milk

cayenne chilli A long, thin, red chilli pepper which is extremely hot-flavoured and used to make cayenne pepper

cayenne pepper The dried and finely ground spice made from a variety of cayenne peppers used sparingly as a seasoning in Europe and the USA

cayenne peppers The very pungent fruit of a branching perennial bush *Capsicum frutescens* which may be yellow, orange or red and are similar in shape to chilli peppers. May be used sparingly as a flavouring and in sauces [also called **hot peppers**]

cay hoy *(Vi)* Star anise

Cayuga duck The domesticated version of the wild black duck of North America

cay vi *(Vi)* Aniseed

caza *(Sp)* Game

cazón *(Sp)* **1** Smooth hound, the fish **2** Brown sugar

cazuela *(Sp)* An earthenware casserole glazed on the inside

cazuela a la catalana *(Sp)* Minced meat browned in olive oil and reserved, carrots and onions fried until golden in same oil, flour, tomatoes, stock and reserved mincemeat added back, simmered 45 minutes, topped with slices of butifarra and baked or grilled until piping hot

cazuela de cordero *(SA)* A lamb and vegetable stew from Chile, containing pumpkin and thickened with beaten egg

cazuela de habas verdes a la granadilla *(Sp)* French green beans and artichokes with poached eggs.

cebada *(Sp)* Barley

cebada perlada *(Sp)* Pearl barley

cebiche *see* ceviche

cebola *(Po)* Onion

cebolado *(Po)* A soft brown paste made by first frying onions and possibly garlic in olive oil until golden brown then covering and sweating until soft and able to be mashed

cebolinha verde *(Po)* Spring onions

cebolinho *(Po)* Chives

cebolla *(Sp)* Onion

cebolleta *(Sp)* Shallot

cebollino *(Sp)* Chive

Cebrero *(Sp)* A hard, cooked-curd, full-flavoured, firm, mountain cheese made from cow's milk and shaped like a malformed mushroom [also called **Piedrafita**]

cece *(It)* Chick pea

cecenielli *(It)* Deep fried tiny anchovies and sardines

ceche *(It)* Elvers, fried with garlic and sage, bound with egg and flour and refried as small loose pancakes

Cecil A spun curd cows' and/or ewes' milk cheese with no rind from Armenia in which the curd is twisted into a spiral shape to give a 4 kg cheese. Eaten fresh

cedioli *(It)* Tiny eels

cedoaria *(Sp)* Zedoary

cédrat *(Fr) masc.* Citron, the fruit

cédrat de corse *(Fr) masc.* Corsican citron

cedro *(It)* Citron, the fruit

cedro di diamante *(It)* Diamante citron

cedrone *(It)* Capercaillie, the bird

cefalo *(It)* Grey mullet

celan *(Fr) masc.* Sardine

céleri *(Fr) masc.* celery

céleri, purée de *(Fr) fem. see* celery soup

céleri-rave *(Fr) masc.* Celeriac

céleri remoulade *(Fr) masc.* Grated celeriac in mayonnaise sauce

celeriac The thickened globular upper root of a plant *Apium graveolens* var. *rapaceum* with a pronounced celery flavour much used as a winter root vegetable in central Europe [also called **knob celery**]

celery One of the aromatic vegetables *Apium graveolens* var. *dulce* used for flavouring and also eaten braised or raw. It grows as a cluster of green, ridged crisp stalks about 30 cm long, closely packed and white in the centre with feathery leaves. The whole may be grown in a paper collar to whiten all the stalks. The leaves are used in a BG. There are other strong-flavoured varieties grown for their seeds or for drying and grinding; *see also* wild celery

celery cabbage *see* Chinese leaves

celery salt A mixture of table salt and dried and ground celery from a strong tasting variety or a mixture of salt and the essential oil of celery, both used for flavouring

celery sauce Celery hearts simmered with white bouillon, a BG and an onion clouté until tender, the celery passed through a fine sieve and mixed with an equal quantity of cream sauce and a little of the reduced celery cooking liquor

celery seeds The small brown seeds of a wild celery plant *Apium graveolens* native to southern Europe, used as a flavouring in pickles, tomato ketchup and tomato juice. Used by Scandinavians and Russians in soups and sauces

celery soup Basic soup with celery, garnished with a fine julienne of celery cooked in salted water [also called **purée de céleri** (Fr)]

celestine *(Fr)* A garnish for consommé of strips of fried pancake

cellentani *(It)* Pasta made from short pieces of ridged macaroni shaped in a helix

cellophane noodles Thin dried noodles made from seaweed and mung bean flour which are translucent. Used in Chinese and Japanese cooking. They can be boiled and become soft, slippery and gelatinous, cooked as a stir-fry or deep fried [also called **bean thread noodles, transparent noodles, jelly noodles, transparent vermicelli**]

cellulose Long chain polysaccharides grouped into bundles cemented together with other compounds which form the structural support of all plants and plant parts. Not digested by humans but provides roughage or fibre which swells in the gut and is a necessary component of a healthy diet for correct operation of the bowels

cellulose derivatives Various derivatives made by adding side chains to cellulose used as bulking and thickening agents. The principal ones used in food manufacture are methyl cellulose, E461, hydroxypropyl-, E463, hydroxypropyl methyl-, E464 and ethyl methyl cellulose, E465

Celsius scale The scale of temperature in which the freezing point of water is 0 and the boiling point 100, written 0°C and 100°C [also called **Centigrade scale**]

celtuce *(USA)* A lettuce grown for the stalk only which is eaten raw or sliced and braised [also called **stem lettuce**]

cenci *(It) see* Galani

cendawan *(Ma)* Shiitake mushroom

cendré(e) *(Fr)* General term for small, strong-flavoured, cow's milk cheeses in a variety of shapes which have been matured in wood ash. Lit. ashen, ash coloured, covered with ash

cengkeh *(Id)* Cloves

cenouras *(Po)* Carrots

centeio *(Po)* Rye

centeno *(Sp)* Rye

centigrade scale *see* Celsius scale

centilitre One hundredth of a litre, 10 millilitres

centola *(Sp)* Spider crab

century egg *see* Chinese preserved egg

cep An edible group of the *boletaceae*, the most common of which is *Boletus edulis.* All are characterized by very fat stems, a round sometimes shiny cap and spongy flesh with tiny pinholes. The edible varieties are fawn to brown with white to brown flesh. They are common in Europe under beech, oak and pine and are slightly phosphorescent at night. They can grow to 1 kg in weight, have a meaty taste and dry well. Used in all mushroom dishes [also called **penny bun** (UK)]

cèpe *(Fr) masc.* cep

cèpe de chêne *(Fr) masc.* A variety of cep which grows under oak trees and is said to have a finer flavour than the cèpe de pin

cèpe de pin *(Fr) masc.* A variety of cep which grows under pine trees

cèpe de vendage *(Fr) masc.* A darker variety of cep which grows in vineyards [also called **tête-de-nègre, bolet bronzé**]

cèpes à la bordelaise Sliced ceps fried in butter with chopped shallots and parsley or in oil with garlic

cephalopod The sub-group of molluscs such as squid, octopus, cuttle fish with a soft body, tentacles growing from around the the head and gut parts and in some a hard internal shell. All have a sac of dark brown or black ink in their body cavity which they can squirt out to provide a protective screen. Lit. head-footed

cepumi *(Lv)* Biscuits made from creamed butter and sugar with caraway seeds, orange juice and orange zest, made into a dough with self-raising flour and salt, rolled to a dia. of 5 cm, chilled, sliced and baked at 180°C until browned

cerdo *(Sp)* Pork [also called **puerco**]

cereal The edible grains of monocotyledons such as wheat, rice, barley, maize, oats, etc. which may be eaten whole or ground into flour. Together with starchy roots they are the main source of energy carbohydrates for humans

cereal cream *(USA) see* half and half

céréale *(Sp & Fr) fem.* Cereal

cereali *(It)* Cereal

cerebro *(Sp)* Brains

cereja *(Po)* Cherry, ripe coffee bean

cerezas *(Sp)* Cherries

cerf *(Fr) masc.* Stag, male deer

cerfeuil *(Fr) masc.* Chervil

cerfeuil musqué *(Fr) masc.* Sweet cicely

cerfoglio *(It)* Chervil

ceriman *see* monstera deliciosa

cerise *(Fr) fem.* Cherry

cerises jubilées *(Fr) fem.* Hot cherries flambéed with Kirsch

cerises, sauce aux *(Fr) fem. see* cherry sauce

çerkez tavugu *(Tu)* Chicken poached in water with sliced onion browned in oil, drained, cooled and disjointed and served covered with a sauce made from soaked bread crusts pounded with hazelnuts, let down with seasoned chicken stock and flavoured with paprika. The dish is sprinkled with a mixture of hot oil and paprika

cerneau *(Fr) masc.* Unripe or half shelled walnut

cernia *(It)* Mediterranean grouper

cernier *(Fr) see* bar, the fish

certosa *(It)* A mild and creamy Stracchino type cheese made from cow's milk

certosino *(It)* A small version of Certosa

cervelas *(Fr) masc.* A large, thick, smooth sausage usually made from pork flavoured with garlic and in a red casing. It is boiled then smoked before sale. So called because originally made from brains [also called **saveloy**]

cervelas maigre à la bénédictine *(Fr) masc.* A sausage made from eel and carp flesh, minced together with onions, garlic and shallots sweated in butter, spices and seasoning, bound with egg and packed in cleaned fish intestines. Smoked for 3 days before poaching in white wine.

Used by the monks as a substitute for pork sausages during Lent

cervelas de poisson *(Fr) masc.* A fish loaf from Champagne made with pike flesh

cervelat *(Eu)* The general European name for a large thick linked sausage made of various meats, mainly lean pork and beef and pork fat, usually packed in beef middles, dried, smoked and dyed red or yellow. The meat is chopped or minced finely and incorporates saltpetre, seasoning and flavourings but not garlic. Served cold in slices

cervellata *(It)* A pork sausage from Northern Italy flavoured with Parmesan cheese, saffron and spices

cervelle *(Fr) fem.* Brains

cervello *(It)* Brains

cervo *(It)* Venison

Cetraria islandica *Bot.* Iceland moss

cetriolini *(It)* Gherkins

cetriolo *(It)* Cucumber

ceun chai *(Ch)* Chinese celery

cevada *(Po)* Barley

cevapcici *(Bk)* Grilled mincemeat balls from Serbia

cévenole, à la *(Fr)* In the style of the Cevennes, i.e. with chestnuts and mushrooms

ceviche *(SA)* A dish of cubed, raw, white fish marinated in lime juice, lemon juice, garlic, onions, chillis, chopped coriander leaves and seasoning, and served with chopped skinned tomatoes and avocado. Originally from Peru, now widely available. Does not need further cooking [also called **seviche, cebiche**]

Ceylon moss Agar-agar

Ceylon spinach A short lived tropical and sub-tropical twining perennial *Basella alba* with large green or red leaves which can grow to 4 m. The leaves are grown as a vegetable [also called **Indian spinach, vine spinach**]

Ceylon tea A black tea produced in Sri Lanka

cha *see* char

chá *(Po)* Tea

chã *(Po)* Round of beef

chaamal *(Ne)* Uncooked rice

chaat *(In) see* chat

chaat masala *(In) see* chat masala

chaat murgh *(In) see* chat murgh

chabai *(Ma)* Bird's eye chilli

chabi *see* chabichou

chabichou *(Fr)* A small, white, firm, soft cone-shaped goat's milk cheese from Poitou with a strong goaty flavour ripened for 15 to 20 days [also called **cabichou, cabrichiu, chabi**]

chablisienne, à la *(Fr)* In the style of Chablis, i.e. cooked in the white wine chablis or served with a sauce based on the same

chabyor *(Ru)* Savory, the herb

chado *see* cha no yu

Chaenomeles speciosa *Bot.* Japonica

chafing dish 1 A dish with a spirit lamp beneath placed on the table in front of the guests and used to keep food warm or to cook it **2** A small portable bain-marie for use at the table

chagga coffee A full bodied coffee from the slopes of Mount Kilimanjaro in Tanzania, named after the Wachagga people who grow and process it

cha gio *(Vi)* Rice paper rolls filled with pork, fish, vegetables and noodles which are deep fried until crisp

cha gwa *(Ch)* Cucumber

cha gwoo *(Ch) see* tso gwoo

chahr ziu *(Ch) see* char siu

chai *(Ru)* Tea

chair blanche *(Fr)* Fem. White meat, as of breast of chicken

chair noire *(Fr) fem.* Dark meat, as of chicken

chakchouka 1 *(Tu)* Seasoned sweet peppers, onions and skinned tomatoes sliced and sautéed in olive oil with harissa until soft and blended. Formed into patties, a hollow made in each and a raw egg put in and cooked until set **2** *(NA)* A vegetable stew similar to ratatouille

chakhokbili *(Ru)* A Georgian meat and potato stew made with lamb or chicken pieces browned in oil, chopped onions and tomatoes added and softened, cubed potatoes and seasoning added and all simmered or braised until tender. Chopped garlic, coriander leaves, parsley and basil added, simmered 10 minutes with stirring then rested a few minutes before serving

chakla *(In)* A wooden board with a smooth side for rolling out dough and a recessed side for kneading dough

chal *(Ru)* A fermented camel's milk from central Asia rather like a strong smelling yoghurt

chali *(In)* The orange to scarlet ripe nuts of betel

chalk *see* calcium carbonate

challa A plaited bread covered in poppy seeds made from yeast-raised dough enriched with eggs and used on the Jewish sabbath [also called **challah, cholla**]

challah *see* challa

chalota *(Po)* Shallot

chalote *(Sp)* Shallot

chalupa *(Me)* A filled oval piece of tortilla dough, raised at the edges and cooked and garnished with black beans, diced fresh cheese and nopales

chamak *(In) see* tarka

Chambarand *(Fr)* A small, creamy, delicately flavoured cheese with a pink/orange rind made from cow's milk by Trappist monks [also called **Trappiste de Chambarand**]

Chamberat *(Fr)* A cow's milk cheese similar to Saint Paulin

chambourcy *(Fr)* A commercial version of cream cheese

chamois d'or *(Fr)* A soft cheese made with cows' milk enriched with cream and shaped rather like a thick Brie

champ *(Ir)* Rich mashed potatoes mixed with chopped spring onions. Served with melted butter for dipping

champignon *(De, Ge, Ho & Fr) masc.* Mushroom

champignons, aux *(Fr)* Description of dishes cooked or garnished with mushrooms or coated with a mushroom sauce

champignons, crème de *(Fr) fem. see* mushroom soup

champignons marinés *(Fr) masc.* Pickled mushrooms

champignons, sauce aux *(Fr) fem.* **1** For meat see mushroom sauce **2** For fish, fish velouté, consistency adjusted with fish stock or cream, seasoned, strained and finished with sliced button mushrooms sweated in butter and lemon juice. Served with boiled or poached fish

champinjoner *(Sw)* Mushrooms [also called **svamp**]

champiñón *(Me)* Mushroom

champorado *(Ph)* Chocolate-flavoured glutinous rice eaten as a snack

chamsur *(In & Ne)* Watercress

chana *(In) see* chana

chandagar *(Bm)* Lump sugar (3)

chandi ka barakh *(In)* Silver leaf. See varaq

chandi ka warq *(In)* Silver leaf. See varaq

chane jar garam *(In)* Dry roasted chick peas, seasoned with amchoor, chilli and cumin. Eaten as a snack

chanfaina *(Sp)* A liver and giblets stew

chanfana *(Po)* A leg of lamb or goat browned in oil with sliced onion and garlic, seasoned and floured, covered with red wine, flavoured with cloves and bay and simmered or braised in the oven in a closed dish for 3 to 4 hours topping up with wine as required

chang *(Ch) see* cheung

chang hau *(Ch)* Asian mussel

channa *(In)* **1** A small variety of chick pea and the most common pulse used in India. When dehusked and split into dal it is oval and yellow as opposed to the split pea which is round. [also called **Bengal gram, chana, gram**] **2** *see* paneer

channa ki dal *(In)* Dehusked, split and polished chick pea

channel catfish A freshwater catfish *Ictaluris natalis* with the usual whiskers around the mouth and a very black skin, white on the underside

Channel Islands milk *(UK)* Milk from Jersey, Guernsey or South Devon cow's with a minimum butterfat content of 4%. but averaging 4.8% [also called **Jersey milk, gold top**]

cha no yu *(Ja)* The traditional Japanese tea ceremony [also called **chado**]

chanquetes *(Sp)* Young fish similar to whitebait but of sardines and other local fish varieties. Cooked as whitebait

chantelle *(USA)* A cow's milk cheese similar to Bel Paese

chanterelle *(Fr) fem.* An edible mushroom *Cantharellus cibarius,* deep yellow and smelling of apricots, shaped like the upturned horn of a trumpet with wavy edges on a short stalk. Much prized in French cuisine [also called **girolle**]

chantilly cream A sweetened whipped cream flavoured with vanilla or brandy which is often substituted for plain whipped cream

chantilly, crème *(Fr) fem. see* crème chantilly

chantilly mayonnaise A mixture of mayonnaise and whipped cream served with cold foods

chantilly, sauce *(Fr) fem.* A mayonnaise made very thick and using lemon juice instead of vinegar. Stiffly whipped cream added at the last moment. Sometimes used for sauce mousseline which is a warm butter emulsion sauce [also called **mayonnaise chantilly**]

chao **1** *(Ch)* To stir fry or sauté **2** *(Vi)* A type of wok but smaller and shallower than the Chinese type

chao fan *(Ch)* Fried rice

chao ji dan *(Ch)* Scrambled eggs

chao mian *(Ch) see* chow mein

chao pai *(Vi)* Dried and possibly salted fish

chao thit bo *(Vi)* A thin stew or thick soup based on rice, diced beef, fried noodles and peanuts

Chaource *(Fr)* A soft, cows' milk cheese shaped like a small drum (600 g) which can be eaten fresh or after ripening for a month when the rind becomes covered in a mould and the interior breaks up into small cracks. Contains 63% water, 19% fat and 15% protein. It has AOC status

chao yulapian donggu *(Ch)* Sliced hoshi-shiitake mushrooms sautéed with sliced bamboo shoots

chap The lower part of a pig's cheek; *see also* pig's cheek

chapan *(Fr) masc.* A crust of bread rubbed with raw cut garlic to absorb the flavour. This is then tossed with a salad to give it a garlic flavour

chapathi *see* chapati

chapati *(In)* An unleavened bread made from a wholemeal dough shaped like a pancake and dry cooked on a hot griddle or flat slightly dished pan [also called **chapathi, chapatti, phulka**]

chapatti *see* chapati

chapelure *(Fr) fem.* Sieved breadcrumbs made from crushed oven dried bread

chapon *(Fr) masc.* **1** Capon **2** The end of a loaf of bread rubbed with garlic and dressed with oil and vinegar. Eaten with or added to salad

char **1** A fresh water fish of the salmon family with firm white to pink flesh found in unpolluted rivers and lakes in Europe **2** *see* arctic char **3** Colloquial name for tea from the Cantonese word chai, e.g. char and a wad - tea and bun. The name tea comes from the Chinese province of Amoy, where it is called t'e

charbon de bois, au *(Fr)* Grilled over charcoal

charcuterie *(Fr) fem.* **1** Cooked and ready prepared pork products, e.g. sausages, hams, rillettes **2** A shop which makes and sells charcuterie and other delicatessen items

charcutier, -ière *(Fr)* pork butcher, delicatessen dealer. From chair cuitier, flesh cooker

charcutière, sauce *(En & Fr) fem.* As for Robert sauce but finished with a julienne of gherkins

chard *see* Swiss chard

chard cabbage *(USA)* Chinese leaves

char dou fu *(Ch)* Fried bean curd

charentais melon A French variety of cantaloupe melon with a greenish yellow skin and a sweet, juicy, orange and highly scented flesh.

charlotte *(En & Fr) fem.* **1** *see* apple charlotte but can also be used of other fruits substituted for the apple. The original French word and dish moved to the UK in the 18th century. The French version is usually lined with lady fingers, meringue, etc. **2** A variety of salad potato

charlotte moscovite A charlotte russe but with the base of the mould filled with red jelly

charlotte mould A straight or sloping sided round mould used for making charlottes and charlotte Russe

charlotte royale *(Fr) fem.* A charlotte mould lined with slices of jam-filled swiss rolls and filled with a charlotte mixture or bavarois

charlotte russe *(Fr) fem.* A charlotte mould, sides lined with sponge finger biscuits, base layered with fan shaped pieces of finger biscuit and filled with a vanilla bavarois. When set, demoulded and decorated

charlotte sibérienne *(Fr) fem.* A cake with the centre removed to form a bowl and filled with fruit and cream

char masala A simple spice mix from Afghanistan used to flavour rice dishes. Made from equal parts of cinnamon, cloves, cumin seed and black cardamom seed

charn *(Ch)* The curved spoon shaped spatula which fits the curve of a wok and is used to manipulate the food in the wok

charni *(In)* Chutney

Charnwood *(UK)* A smoked Cheddar cheese coated with paprika

charolais *(Fr) masc.* **1** A very large breed of French cattle famous for its meat **2** A small, soft, strong-flavoured, hard, cylindrical cheese made from cow's and/or goat's milk which is ripened for 2 to 3 weeks. The paste has a delicate texture with a few small cracks and the greyish blue rind is thin and unblemished. Contains 58% water, 24% fat and 21% protein

charoli nut Small round nuts about the size of

pine nuts used to garnish Indian sweatmeats [also called **chironju**]

charoset A condiment made from chopped apples and walnuts flavoured with cinnamon and moistened with a sweet dessert wine. Used at the Jewish passover feast [also called **charoseth**]

charoseth *see* charoset

charqui *(USA)* Smoked and sun dried strips of beef or venison [also called **jerked beef, chipped beef, jerky, jerked meat**]

char siu *(Ch)* Chinese honey roast pork made from skinned and deboned pork shoulder or fillet, marinaded in salt, sugar, hoisin sauce, yellow bean sauce, red bean curd, chopped garlic, light soy sauce and dry sherry, roasted and basted with the marinade until a rich dark brown, removed from the oven and brushed with honey. Excess marinade can be reduced for use as a dipping sauce [also called **chahr ziu, cha siew, red pork**]

char siu bow *(Ch)* Bread dough formed into small balls around a filling of finely chopped stir fried char siu, reconstituted black mushrooms and spring onion mixed with hoisin sauce, oyster sauce and a little sugar and thickened with cornflour and stock. The balls are allowed to rise then cooked by steaming for 15 minutes

char siu jeung *(Ch)* Roast pork spices

char siu powder *see* roast pork spices

chartreuse ragoût *(De)* A decoratively arranged casserole of meat or poultry with colourful vegetables

cha shao bao *(Ch)* A steamed bun filled with roast pork

cha siew *(Ch)* *see* char siu

chasni *(In)* A sweet and sometimes sour syrup used to glaze food which is being grilled or roasted. Usually for meat or poultry

chasnidarh *(In)* A style of Indian dish made with young meat or fish in a sweet and sour sauce, possibly with fruits and vegetables

cha-soba *(Ja)* Buckwheat noodles containing powdered green tea. They have a distinctive colour and smell

chasseur, (à la) *(Fr)* In the hunter's style, i.e. with a selection of onions, shallots, sliced mushrooms, tomatoes and white wine and/or brandy

chasseur, sauce Chopped shallots, garlic and mushrooms sweated in butter, fat removed, reduced with red wine, skimmed, deseeded tomatoes and demi-glace added, simmered, seasoned and finished with parsley and tarragon

chat *(In)* Description of a mixture of diced fruit, vegetables, possibly with meat and shrimps and with a spicy, sour dressing. See e.g. fruit chat

châtaigne *(Fr) fem.* Sweet chestnut

châtaigne d'eau *(Fr) fem.* Water chestnut

château potatoes **1** *(UK)* Roast turned potatoes **2** *(USA)* Long thin strips of potatoes cooked in butter

chateaubriand *(En & Fr) masc.* A large steak cut from the thickest part of a fillet of beef. Generally grilled to serve two persons or the whole thick end roasted

chateaubriand cheese A cream cheese from Normandy made with cow's milk and added cream

chateaubriand, sauce *(En & Fr) fem.* White wine with chopped shallots, thyme, bayleaf and mushroom trimmings reduced by two thirds, an amount of brown veal stock equal to the original wine added and all reduced by half, strained and finished with maître d'hôtel butter and chopped tarragon. Used with red meat

châtelaine, à la *(Fr)* Garnished with artichoke hearts, chestnuts and puréed onions and served with a cream sauce

chat masala *(In)* An Indian spice and herb mixture for fruit and vegetable salads with a fresh sour taste containing cumin seeds, black peppercorns, ajowan seeds, anardana seeds, salt, asafoetida, chilli powder, amchoor, dried mint and dried ginger [also called **chaat masala**]

chat murgh *(In)* Lettuce, topped with a mixture of sliced tomatoes, eggs and onion, deseeded and finely chopped green chillis and shredded chicken, sprinkled with salt, sugar and chat masala and dressed with lemon juice. Allowed to stand for 10 minutes before serving

chattak *(In)* A unit of weight equal to 5 tolas approximately 56 g, 2 oz [also called **chitak**]

chatti *(Sr)* A terracotta cooking pot similar to an Indian chatty

chatty *(In)* An unglazed clay cooking pot. Because the clay absorbs flavours from the food, separate pots are used for different classes of food, e.g. fish, meat, vegetables, etc.

chatui *(In)* Sambal-like side dishes

chaud(e) *(Fr) adj.* Hot

chaud-froid, sauce A coating sauce made from equal parts of warmed Béchamel or velouté sauce and aspic jelly, or either sauce thickened with gelatine. Used to coat salmon, chicken, turkey, hams, etc. for cold buffets; *see also* brown chaud-froid sauce

chaudeau *(Fr) masc.* Sweet pudding sauce

chaudeu *(Fr)* An orange-flavoured tart from Nice in Provence

chaudin *(Fr) masc.* The large intestine (colon) used in sausage making

chaudrée *(Fr) fem.* A dish from Bordeaux of conger eel and other white fish cooked with potatoes, garlic and white wine, a type of chowder or fish soup

chaudron *(Fr) masc.* Cauldron

chauna *see* chhana

chaunk gobhi *(In)* Brussel sprouts

chaurice *(USA)* A Creole version of chorizo containing chopped onions and parsley, thyme, bay leaves and allspice

chausson *(Fr) masc.* A round flat light pastry turnover usually filled

chaussons aux pommes *(Fr) masc.* Literally apple slippers, see apple turnover

chaussons aux queues de langoustines *(Fr) masc.* A pastry turnover filled with lobster meat from the tail

chávena *(Po)* Teacup, used as a fluid measure

Chavignol *(Fr) see* Crottin de Chavignol

chawal *(In)* Rice

chawan *(Ja)* A straight sided porcelain or glazed pot dish about the size of a teacup with a conical lid. Used for steaming egg custards

chawan mushi *(Ja)* A savoury steamed custard made with 7 eggs per litre of ichiban dashi, flavoured with mirin and salt and contains a few pieces of chicken breast meat, prawn and mushroom marinaded in soya sauce and sake. It is steamed for 15 minutes, garnished and served in the chawan

cha wara *(Ch)* Date

chayote *see* Choko

checkerberry *(USA) see* wintergreen

cheddar *(UK)* The renowned English cheese from the Cheddar Gorge area now made all over the world. It is a hard, scalded curd, full fat cows' milk cheese made with a lactic starter and traditionally cloth bound. The paste is firm and yellow with a very pleasant flavour ranging from mild to sharp (tasty) depending on maturity (3-12 months). It is available in farmhouse (5-12 kg rounds) and commercial versions of indeterminate size. An excellent dessert and cooking cheese. Contains 36% water, 34% fat and 29% protein

cheddar, to To repeatedly cut and stack blocks of milk curd turning between operations so as to drain off as much whey as possible

Cheedham *(Aus)* A cow's milk cheese similar to Cheddar and Edam

cheegay *(Ko)* A thin stew or thick soup of various ingredients. Crabs, fish and bean curd are often cooked in this way

chee mah *(Ch)* Sesame seed

chee mah jee mah *(Ch)* White sesame seeds

cheena chatti *(Sr)* A slightly dished circular pan like a shallow wok used for cooking bread esp. atta

cheese 1 A solid derivative of milk made by coagulating most of the protein matter *(casein)* in the milk into curds and draining off the remaining watery constituents of the milk *(whey)*. The processing combines a variety of the following processes: separating or adding cream, souring the milk with a lactobacillus, heating or boiling it, coagulating the protein content with rennet or other coagulant, breaking up the curd and draining off the whey, salting the curd, heating the curd, milling the curd, adding cultures of microorganisms, pressing the curd to a paste, needling the paste and maturing it. The type of cheese depends on the source of the milk, the treatment, the amount of water removed from the curd, the butterfat left in the curd, the microorganisms that grow in it or on the surface and the length of time and the conditions under which it matures. Cheese is a major source of protein and fat for humans **2** *see* fruit cheese

cheese cake *(CE & USA)* A crushed biscuit or pastry base covered with a processed mixture of cream, cottage or curd cheese mixed with eggs, sugar, butter and/or cream, lemon juice, grated lemon zest, vanilla and cornflour and baked in the oven

cheese certification Cheeses may be certified by type or by origin as detailed in the 1951 Stresa convention. Typical type certifications are Cheddar, Camembert, Brie, Gruyère, Gouda, Fynbo and Adelost. Typical origin certifications are Gorgonzola, Parmesan, Pont l'Evêque, Roquefort and Bleu d'Auvergne. Type certified cheeses may be made in any country, e.g. Canadian Cheddar, but origin certified may only be made in designated geographical areas

cheese fondue *(He)* A coating consistency mixture of Emmental or Gruyère cheese melted with garlic, white wine, cornflour and kirsch in a caquelon, kept hot on the centre of the table and immediately eaten by guests who use it to coat cubes of bread impaled on fondue forks

cheese herbs The principal herbs used in cheese are basil, caraway, chervil, chives, dill, fennel, marjoram, mint, rosemary, sage, savory, tarragon and thyme

cheese layer cake *(USA)* A three layered cheese made from a white cheddar, one layer of which is flavoured with pistachios and one with pink champagne, the whole coated with almonds

cheese pastry Shortcrust pastry flavoured with cheese and seasoning used as a basis for savouries and sometimes in the UK for apple pie

cheese plate Several varieties of cheese arranged on a plate and shown to customers or guests who make a selection from them

cheese sauce A boiling Béchamel sauce into which grated melting cheese (Cheddar, Gruyére, Emmental, etc.) and egg yolks are incorporated off the heat, the whole strained and reheated but not boiled. Used for fish or vegetables [also called **Mornay, sauce**]

cheese spread A rather nondescript cheese preparation made by combining mild cheese with milk and emulsifiers, used for spreading on bread or biscuits and appreciated by children

cheese straws Cheese pastry cut into narrow finger length strips and baked. Used as a snack food

chef *(En & Fr) masc.* A generic name for a restaurant cook, see e.g. chef de partie, sous chef, etc.

chef de cuisine *(En & Fr) masc.* Head chef in the kitchen

chef entremétier *(Fr) masc.* Vegetable chef

chef écailler *(Fr) masc.* Oyster opener

chef garde-manger *(Fr) masc.* Larder chef who is concerned with cold dishes, salads and preparation of meat and fish for cooking by others

chef de partie *(En & Fr) masc.* Chef in charge of a section of the kitchen e.g. vegetables, sauces, meat cooking, larder, etc., usually given the name of the section

chef pâtissier *(Fr) masc.* Pastry chef

chef poissonier *(Fr) masc.* Fish chef

chef potager *(Fr) masc.* Soup chef

chef restaurateur *(Fr) masc.* Chef in charge of the à la carte menu

chef rôtisseur *(Fr) masc.* Roast chef

chef saucier *(Fr) masc.* Sauce chef

chef de station *(Fr) masc.* Waiter who serves a particular group of tables [also called **station waiter**]

chef tournant *((Fr) masc.* A chef who helps out in any section of the kitchen. Lit. rotating chef

chef traiteur *(Fr) masc.* Chef in charge of outside functions, buffets, etc.

chefe de mesa *(Po)* Head waiter, maître d'hôtel

chef's salad An over the top, large salad combining vegetables, salad vegetables, meats, cheeses, eggs, etc.

che hau sauce *(Ch)* A spicier version of hoisin sauce

chelou *(Pe)* Cooked rice

chelou kabab *(Pe)* A kebab of lamb fillet, marinated in lemon juice with chopped onion and spearmint, grilled over charcoal and served with rice

Chelsea bun *(UK)* A bun made by taking a rectangle of egg-enriched yeast-raised dough, covering it with melted butter, currants and sugar, rolling it up, slicing it, then packing these into a buttered tray so that the spiral is visible prior to baking and glazing. Much liked by King George III and Queen Charlotte in the 18th century

chemise, en *(Fr)* Used of food wrapped or left in its natural skin prior to cooking. Wrappings include pastry, pané, batter, vine leaves, etc. Lit. in a shirt

chemiser *(Fr)* The verb meaning to coat the inside of a mould with aspic or other coating so that when the whole is demoulded it is 'en chemise'

chenelline *(It)* Tiny dumplings used to garnish soup

cheng mein *(Ch)* Wheat starch

chenna *(In) see* paneer

Chenopodium album *Bot.* Fat hen

Chenopodium bonus-henricus *Bot.* Good King Henry

Chenopodium quinoa *Bot.* Quinoa

cheong *(Ch) see* cheung

cheppia *(It)* Twaite shad, the fish

cherimoya *(SA)* One of the most common custard apples *Anona cherimolia* with a pineapple type flavour, from Peru, now grown in Spain and Israel. See custard apple [also called **cherimoyer**]

cherimoyer *see* cherimoya

cherries jubilee *(USA)* Vanilla ice cream topped with a sweet cherry sauce and flambéed at the table

cherry The fruits of various members of *Prunus* spp., 1 - 2.5 cm in dia., generally spherical with a slight depression where they are attached to the stalk, with a central stone (to 5mm dia.) surrounded by a plum-like flesh and a smooth shiny outer skin. The colours range from white to deep purple/black and the flavours from sweet to acid. Used in sweet and savoury dishes and the kernels are used to flavour some liqueurs. Classified as sweet cherries and acid or sour cherries

cherry cake A rich sponge cake containing glacé cherries

cherry plum A small variety of plum *Prunus cerasifera* from western Asia, common in China. It is sometimes used as a windbreak in the UK. The rather tasteless flesh improves with cooking

cherry salmon A Pacific salmon *Oncorhynchus masu* found off the coast of Japan

cherry sauce Port wine reduced with a little mixed spice and grated orange zest, redcurrant jelly and orange juice added and dissolved then finished with stoned cherries which have been poached in syrup. Used with venison and duck

cherry tomato A very small (to 2 cm dia.) tomato used principally for decoration

cherrystone *(USA) see* quahog clam

chervil A herb of the carrot family *Anthriscus cerefolium* with flat parsley-like leaves and a slightly pungent mild parsley flavour. It loses its flavour on boiling and is usually added to hot dishes just before serving

Cheshire black pudding *(UK)* Black pudding flavoured with coriander, pimento and caraway seeds

Cheshire cheese *(UK)* A crumbly, mellow, slightly salty cow's milk cheese which is matured from 1 to 15 months *(farmhouse types usually over 9 months)* suitable for dessert or culinary use, manufactured in a similar way to Cheddar. There is a white variety and a red one coloured with annatto. It is the oldest known English cheese dating from at least Roman times

Cheshire potted cheese *(UK)* Grated Cheshire cheese, mixed with softened butter, ground mace and sweet sherry or Madeira into a smooth paste, placed in pots and covered with melted butter. Used as a spread with celery or for canapés, etc.

chesnock *(Ru)* Garlic

chess pie *(USA)* A pastry case filled with a mixture of walnuts or pecans, fruit juice or sweet sherry, butter, eggs and cream

chessel A vat or mould used in cheese making [also called **chessit**]

chessit *see* chessel

Chester *(Fr)* A hard, scalded-curd cows' milk cheese made with a lactic starter on a large commercial scale in blocks or rounds of 30 kg. It has a mild tasting smooth paste and a thin rind. Contains 39% water, 31% fat and 24% protein

chestnut The edible fruit (to 4 cm dia.) of the sweet chestnut tree *Castanea sativa,* a native of southern Europe. They have a hard woody skin and a cream coloured interior containing more starch and less protein and fat than most nuts [also called **Spanish chestnut, sweet chestnut**]

chestnut purée Chestnuts incised with a cross at the top, boiled for 15 minutes and the outer and inner skin removed. Boiled in stock with a sprig of celery for 45 minutes, rubbed through a sieve, warmed and mixed with cream, butter, salt and sugar to taste

chetha si biyan *(Bm)* A chicken stew flavoured with onions, garlic, turmeric, fresh ginger, coriander leaves, lemon and salt

cheung *(Ch)* Sausage [also called **cheong, chang**]

cheu yuan *(Ch)* Citron, the fruit

chevaine *(Fr) masc.* Chub, the fish

chevesne *(Fr) masc.* Chub, the fish.

cheveu d'ange *(Fr) masc.* Angel's hair

cheveux de vénus adiante *(Fr) masc.* Maidenhair fern

Cheviot cheese *(UK)* A Cheddar cheese flavoured with chopped chives

chèvre *(Fr) fem.* **1** Goat **2** The generic name for goat's milk cheese *(fromage de chèvre or mi-chèvre)*

chevreau *(Fr) masc.* Kid, the young of the goat

chevrette *(Fr) fem.* **1** Kid, a young goat **2** Doe, female deer **3** A metal tripod

chevreuil *(Fr) masc.* **1** Male deer **2** Venison

chevreuil, sauce *(En & Fr) fem.* As sauce poivrade but with bacon or game trimmings added to the mirepoix and with red wine added after straining. Finished with a little sugar and cayenne pepper. Served with game.

chevreuse *(Fr) fem.* A small goose liver tart

chevron *(USA)* A young goat

Chevrotin des Aravis *(Fr)* A semi-hard goats' or goats' and cows' milk cheese from Savoie with a typical goaty smell and taste

Chevru *(Fr)* A cow's milk cheese from the region surrounding Paris, similar to Brie des Coulommiers

chewing betel *see* pan

chezzarella *(USA)* A coarse mixture of Cheddar and Mozzarella cheeses to give a marbled effect

chhana *(In)* A sour cow's milk cheese [also called **chauna**]

chhanna *(In)* Pomfret, the fish

chhas *(In)* Buttermilk

chhena *(In) see* paneer

chi *(Ch)* Chicken

chiarificare *(It)* To clarify

chícharo *(Me)* Pea

chicharro *(Sp)* Mackerel

chicharrón *(Me & Sp)* Pork crackling

chichinda *(In)* Snake gourd

chick pea A legume *Cicer arietinum* with 2 or 3 brown or yellow peas per pod, usually used as a dried pulse or ground to make besan, but may be used like broad beans. Common around the Mediterranean in the Middle East and India; *see also* channa [also called **garbanzo, garbanzo pea. ram's-head pea**]

chicken The common domestic fowl *Gallus gallus,* bred for its meat and eggs. Generally known as poultry

chicken breasts Bellinger *(Aus)* Suprêmes of chicken stuffed with a salpicon of avocado and banana, sautéed and served in a sauce of the same ingredients as the stuffing flavoured with orange zest and garnished with orange segments

chicken brick An unglazed terracotta dish in two halves shaped to take a whole chicken and used to cook a chicken in the oven without added fat. Dates back to Roman times [also called **roman pot, Römertopf**]

chicken broth Blanched boiling fowl simmered in water with constant skimming for 1 hour, brunoise of celery, turnip, carrot and leek and a BG added, simmered until almost cooked, washed rice added, cooked chicken and BG removed, diced lean chicken meat returned, the whole skimmed, seasoned and served with chopped parsley

chicken cacciatora *see* pollo alla cacciatora

chicken demi-deuil Chicken stuffed with truffle and poached with aromatic vegetables, jointed, slices of truffle inserted between the skin and flesh and served with the vegetables and strained reduced cooking liquor. Lit. chicken half mourning, because of the black and white contrast

chicken fat A soft fat used as a substitute for butter in Jewish cooking, since meat and milk products cannot be used together. It contains about 35% saturated, 50% monounsaturated and 15% polyunsaturated fat [also called **schmalz,** various spellings in yiddish]

chicken feet The feet of chickens, not usually sold with the carcase, are blanched, descaled and used to add flavour and gelatine to stocks and sauces

chicken fried steak *(USA)* Good quality frying steak, floured, coated with an egg based batter, floured again then deep fried and served with a white gravy

chicken gumbo Portioned chicken and diced smoked ham (2.5 mm cubes) browned in oil, sliced onion, tomato concassée and sliced okra added and fried for 5 minutes then all simmered in water with salt, cayenne pepper, dried red chilli and a faggot of herbs for 1.5 hours skimming as necessary, faggot removed, shelled oysters added and cooked 2 minutes, seasoning adjusted and finished with a little filé powder. Served with rice

chicken halibut A small immature halibut

chicken Kiev *(Ru)* A pocketed chicken suprême filled with a pounded mixture of garlic butter and chopped parsley, opening secured, panéed and shallow fried and cooked through until golden

chicken à la king *(USA)* Diced cooked chicken, fried chopped onions, mushrooms and green and red peppers in a Béchamel sauce. Sometime flavoured with sherry. Served with rice

chicken liver Small delicately-flavoured and very tender livers used for patés, terrines, etc.

chicken Marengo *see* poulet sauté Marengo

chicken Maryland *(USA)* Panéed chicken portions deep fried in oil, served with corn fritters, fried bananas and gravy

chicken paprika *see* paprikás csirke

chicken piri-piri Charcoal grilled chicken basted with a mixture of piri-piri sauce, olive oil, garlic, tomato purée, Worcestershire sauce and salt both before and during cooking

chicken soup A mirepoix of onion, leek and celery sweated in butter, flour added and cooked out without colour, chicken stock and a BG added, simmered and skimmed for 1 hour, BG removed, liquidized, strained and finished with cream. Garnished with diced cooked chicken meat [also called **crème reine** (Fr), **crème de volaille** (Fr)]

chicken spatchcock *see* spatchcock

chicken steak *(USA)* Thin small portions of chuck steak with the characteristic line of white connective tissue down the middles

chicken stock *(Ch)* A most important stock in Chinese cooking made by simmering chicken carcases with onions and ginger; *see also* white chicken stock and brown chicken stock

chicken tetrazzini *(USA)* Cooked chicken pieces in a velouté sauce over cooked pasta, gratinated with breadcrumbs and Parmesan cheese and browned under the grill. Served with broccoli

chicken turbot A small immature turbot

chicken of the woods A rare fan shaped fungus which grows on old oak trees often in inaccessible places. The flesh is white to salmon and the surface skin is orange to yellow. It must always be cooked

chickling vetch *see* lath

chickweed A vigorous creeping annual *Stellaria media* usually classed as a weed but may be eaten raw in salads or boiled as a vegetable

chicle The coagulated sap or latex of the sapodilla tree used in the production of chewing gum

chico *see* sapodilla

chicon *(En & Fr) masc.* The white, yellow-tipped, compact and pointed rosette of leaves produced by forcing the trimmed roots of Belgian chicory q.v

chicorée *(Fr) fem.* Endive

chicorée frisée *(Fr) fem.* Endive

chicorées au jambon *(Be)* fem. A Belgium dish of cooked heads of chicory, wrapped in ham, reheated in cheese sauce and served with boiled potatoes

chicory A group of plants *Cichorium intybus* grown for their leaves which all have a distinctive slightly bitter flavour. They include Belgian chicory whose roots are forced to produce the well known white compact chicons commonly known as chicory, red chicory also known as radicchio and sugar loaf chicory

chicory escarole *(USA)* Batavian endive

chieh *(Ch)* Mandarin orange

chifferoni *(It)* Curved pasta tubes, elbow macaroni

chiffon cake A cake similar to angel cake but enriched with oil

chiffon pie *(USA)* A baked pastry case filled with a fruit-based mousse and decorated

chiffonade *(Fr) fem.* **1** A garnish or base for other foods made from a very finely sliced roll of lettuce or sorrel leaves (not chopped) **2** A soup of finely shredded herb leaves

chiftele *(Ro)* Croquettes of minced cooked beef mixed with minced lean pork, seasoned, flavoured with paprika and marjoram, panéed and deep fried. Served with a tomato sauce

chih mah *(Ch)* Sesame seeds of either colour

chikhirtma *(Ru)* A sour chicken soup from Georgia made by simmering a whole chicken with onion, celery, saffron, peppercorns and cayenne pepper for 90 minutes, skimming as necessary and straining. The stock thickened with a roux made with onions fried until coloured and finished with beaten eggs, egg yolks, lemon juice and chopped fresh mint, parsley and coriander.

chikku *see* sapodilla

chikni *(In)* The green unripe nuts of betel

chiko *see* sapodilla

chikosapote *(Sp)* Sapodilla

chiku *see* sapodilla

chikuwa *(Ja)* A fish cake *(see kamaboko)* formed in a cylindrical shape around a sliver of bamboo. After steaming it is usually grilled

chila *(Po)* A gourd with long thin stranded flesh similar to vegetable spaghetti [also called **gila**]

chilaquiles *(Me)* Strips of cornmeal tortilla, fried until crisp and reheated with tomato sauce. may have cooked meat added. Garnished with grated cheese, chopped onions, chillis and cream

chile *see* chilli pepper

chile guajillo *(Me)* A long thin reddish brown and very hot chilli, smooth with a pointed end and often dried

chile pasilla *(Me)* A round flat chilli pepper with a mild to medium hot rich sweet taste

chile peppers *see* chilli peppers

Chile saltpetre Sodium nitrate which can be used instead of saltpetre. As it contains more nitrate radical per gram than saltpetre it is roughly one sixth more effective in weight terms

chiles en nagada *(Me)* As chiles rellenos but stuffed with minced beef, fruits (apricots, apples, plums), napped with a sweet sauce made of nuts and cream and garnished with grenadine seeds to resemble the Mexican flag

chiles rellenos *(Me)* Sweet peppers stuffed with a cheese filling, deep fried and topped with cheese

chili *(USA)* The term used for the fruit of all capsicum species whether hot or sweet

chili con carne *(USA)* As chilli con carne, but need not include beans

chili con queso *(USA)* Molten cheese flavoured with minced or finely chopped chillis and served hot with tortilla chips

chilienne, à la *(Fr)* In the Chilean manner, i.e. with rice and red peppers

chilindron *(Sp)* A meat casserole from Aragon made without water from either split game birds, chicken, pork chops or lamb chops, sautéed in olive oil until brown, added to a mixture of sweated chopped onion and garlic with diced ham, saffron, paprika, red peppers and skinned tomatoes, and simmered in a covered pan until cooked

chill, to To reduce the temperature of cooked

food to between 0 and 5°C in a refrigerator or cold room. An initial cooling may be done in cold water if suitable and will be quicker

chill storage A method of preserving foods by storing at temperatures between −1°C and +4°C. Not suitable for all foods

chilled food Food, usually cooked, kept at a temperature between 0 and 5°C so that it only needs reheating prior to serving

chilli *see* chilli pepper

chilli arbol Very small hot chilli peppers used in Mexico and the East

chilli bean *see* red kidney bean

chilli bean paste Yellow or black bean sauce left thick and mixed with chopped dried chillis and other spices. Recipes vary with the manufacturer [also called **hot bean paste, Sichuan hot bean paste**]

chilli California A variety of chilli pepper grown in California. It is large, fairly mild and deep red, and resembles the Kashmiri chilli. Roasting intensifies the flavour.

chilli cascabel A round dried variety of hot chilli pepper whose seeds rattle inside, from the Spanish for rattle.

chilli con carne A dish adapted from Mexico and the southern United States and now adopted in many countries. It contains stewed minced beef and cooked red kidney beans in a sauce made of onions, garlic, chilli powder, tomatoes, spices, seasonings and stock

chilli flakes Dried and crushed chillis used as a flavouring

chilli flower A garnish made by slicing a long chilli into 7 or 8 segments from the base to the tip leaving them attached at the base and not disturbing the inner pith and seeds. It is then placed in iced water to make the petals curl back on themselves

chilli oil A red coloured, hot tasting oil made by infusing crushed dried chillis in hot vegetable oil. Used as a flavouring or condiment.

chilli peppers The fruit of the annual bush *Capsicum annuum* Longum Group, related to the sweet pepper but thinner and and up to 9 cm long. They mature from green to red becoming hotter as they mature. The main sources of the capsaicin and other hot flavouring compounds are the seeds and internal white pith which can be discarded. They are used for flavouring and as an appetizer. If eaten raw or cooked they can be intensely irritating to the mucous membranes unless the person is habituated to them, and hands should be thoroughly washed after handling. Much used in Indian, Mexican and other highly spiced cuisines. See under individual names, Anaheim chilli, banana chilli, chilli arbol, chilli California, chilli cascabel, chilli pequin, chilli poblano, Fresno chilli, guajillo, guero chilli, habanero chilli, jalapeno chilli, New Mexico chilli, serrano chilli, etc. [also called **chile peppers, chillis**]

chilli pequin A very small hot green chilli pepper used in Mexico and the Far East

chilli poblano A chocolate brown variety of the hot chilli pepper used in Mexico to make a sauce, mole poblano, with unsweetened chocolate, as well as for general cooking

chilli powder The name of various mixtures of dried ground chillis with other dried herbs and spices. The pure chilli powder is very hot but milder blends contain ground, dried sweet red peppers, oregano, and garlic amongst other things. Some are quite mild but all should be tested by adding to a known quantity of the cooked food and tasting before use

chilli sauce A hot, commercially prepared, cold sauce or ketchup made from chilli peppers and used for flavouring other dishes

chillies The plural form of the fruits of *Capsicum* spp., but usually confined to the hot varieties

chilogrammo *(It)* Kilogram, unit of weight, abbreviated kg

chimichangas *(Me)* Fried stuffed tacos made from wheat flour tortillas, filled with cooked minced beef, accompanied by shredded lettuce, grated cheese, radishes and spring onions. From Sonora state

chimichurri *(Ar)* A sauce for meat and poultry made from, oil, vinegar, garlic, chopped onions, cayenne pepper and seasonings blended together

China orange *see* calamondin

chine, to To cut through the ribs of a joint of meat close to the back bone so as to make the meat easier to carve or preparatory to removing the backbone. Usually done with lamb and pork

chine of beef *see* forerib of beef

chine bone A joint of meat consisting of the vertebrae (backbone) of an animal with some of the surrounding muscle. Usually stewed or braised

chine of pork The term used for a saddle, i.e. two undivided loins from a small pig

Chinese anise *(USA)* Star anise

Chinese apple *see* pomegranate

Chinese aromatic pepper *see* anise pepper

Chinese artichoke The pale, short, tapering tuber of a plant *Stachys sieboldii* which has concentric segments and resembles Jerusalem artichokes although more regular in shape [also called **chorogi, crosnes, Japanese artichoke, stachys**]

Chinese bean *see* cowpea

Chinese black bean A fermented and salted soya bean used for flavouring and for making sauces

Chinese broccoli *see* Chinese kale

Chinese cabbage *see* Chinese leaves

Chinese cardamom A dark brown, rather hairy cardamom substitute from the plant *Amomum globosum*. Usually available in Chinese food stores

Chinese celery A variety of celery with narrow deep green stems and a strong flavour

Chinese cheese *see* bean curd cheese

Chinese cherry *see* lychee

Chinese chive A vegetable of the onion family *Allium tuberosum* like a very large chive. Sold in three forms, dark green leaves, blanched leaves known as yellow chives and the round fairly stiff flowering stem with a pointed flower bud at the tip known as flowering chive. The taste varies from mild to strong according to the variety; *see also* garlic chive [also called **Chinese onion, Chinese leek, Cantonese onion**]

Chinese cinnabar melon *(USA)* A deep red coloured melon with sweet smooth textured flesh

Chinese date *see* Mauritanian jujube

Chinese dried black mushroom *see* shiitake mushroom

Chinese egg roll *see* spring roll

Chinese flat cabbage A low growing brassica *Brassica rapa* var. *rosularis* with white stems and small rounded white-veined deep green leaves. Resistant to frost [also called **flat cabbage**]

Chinese gooseberry *see* kiwi fruit

Chinese green cabbage *see* jiu la choy

Chinese honey orange *see* ponkan mandarin

Chinese kale An annual leaf vegetable *Brassica rapa* var. *alboglabra* growing to 45 cm. The soft green leaves, green stems and white flower buds are used like broccoli [also called **Chinese broccoli**]

Chinese keys A reddish brown root vegetable from the ginger family that looks like a misshapen bunch of keys. Used in Thai and Indonesian curries and pickles

Chinese lantern A type of physalis *Physalis alkekengi* grown mainly for its decorative red papery husk. Edible varieties are light brown; *see also* cape gooseberry [also called **bladder cherry**]

Chinese leaves The large, generally close packed, very pale green heads of an oriental brassica *Brassica rapa* var. *pekinensis* but loose-leaved varieties are available. Grown widely, they originated in China, have a mild flavour and are often pickled. Used in stir fries [also called **Chinese cabbage, Nappa cabbage, Shantung cabbage, Korean cabbage, celery cabbage, Beijing cabbage**]

Chinese leek *see* Chinese chive

Chinese mushrooms Whole dried mushrooms from China which when reconstituted are used to flavour Chinese dishes

Chinese mustard cabbage A leaf vegetable with long stalks and small leaves with a strong mustard flavour used in soup or salads, cooked like spinach, or pickled like sauerkraut

Chinese nuts Dried lychees

Chinese okra A large (to 30 cm) variety of okra grown in the USA, originally by Chinese market gardeners

Chinese olive seed Kernels of the small Chinese kanari fruit *Canarium album* similar in size to a pine nut and used in the same way

Chinese onion *see* Chinese chive

Chinese parsley *see* coriander

Chinese pea *see* mange-tout

Chinese pepper *see* anise pepper

Chinese plum A variety of red-gold apricot *Prunus armeniaca* grown in China and Japan since records were kept. They are dried and candied or salted

Chinese plum sauce *see* plum sauce

Chinese preserved eggs Hen and duck eggs preserved by coating them in a mixture of lime, wood ash, salt and rice husks and packing them into earthenware tubs for 3 to 4 months. The yolk becomes a grayish green and the white a pale amber and translucent. They are served shelled as an appetizer. Variously known with characteristic modesty as 1000 year old eggs, 100 year old eggs, century eggs, Ming dynasty eggs and ancient eggs; *see also* salted duck eggs

Chinese red date *see* jujube

Chinese red stew *(USA)* Red cooked meat, see red cooking

Chinese sausage *see* lap cheong

Chinese spinach One of the amaranths

Amaranthus tricolor with red, yellow and green leaves [also called **spineless amaranth**]

Chinese truffle A truffle *Tuber himalayense* indistinguishable from the French black truffle except by taste and smell, but being imported into Europe and, since it is much cheaper than the French truffle, in some cases being substituted for the genuine article

Chinese vegetable marrow *see* wax gourd

Chinese water chestnut *see* water chestnut

Chinese water lily *see* lotus

Chinese water spinach *see* swamp cabbage

Chinese yam A scaly skinned variety of yam with white flesh *Dioscorea esculenta*. The plant produces several small tubers instead of the more usual single tuber

ching chao ming zia *(Ch)* Sautéed prawns

ch'ing ts'ai *(Ch)* Pak choy

chini *(In)* Sugar

chinois *(Fr) masc.* **1** A conical metal strainer with one handle usually about 15 cm deep and 12 cm across either of perforated metal or fine wire mesh. So called because of its resemblance to a Chinese coolie hat **2** A candied small green kumquat

chinonaise, à la *(Fr)* In the style of Chinon, i.e. with a garnish of potatoes and cabbage filled with sausage

chinook salmon The largest of the Pacific salmon *Oncorhynchus tshawytscha* weighing between 4 and 22 kg with a flaky, oily flesh [also called **king salmon, royal chinook, spring salmon**]

chinquapin *(USA)* Pine nut

chiocciola di mare *(It)* Winkle

chiocciole *(It)* **1** Snails **2** Small pasta shells used in soup

chiodi di garofano *(It)* Cloves

chip *see* chips

chip basket A wide, 1 cm mesh, woven wire metal basket used to hold food for deep frying or blanching [also called **frying basket**]

chip butty *(UK) coll.* A sandwich containing fried potato chips popularized in Liverpool humour

chi po *(Th)* Preserved finely chopped turnip used in Thai cooking

chipolata garnish A garnish of brown glazed button onions, chipolata sausages, chestnuts poached in white stock, glazed turned carrots (olive size) and diced belly of salt pork fried to a light brown colour

chipolata sausages Small pork or beef sausages cooked and served whole. From the Italian for onion, cipolla, but contains no onion. A typical recipe might contain seasoned lean and fat pork, a little rusk and ground rice, coriander, paprika, nutmeg, cayenne pepper and thyme, all packed in sheep casings and made into small links

chipotle chilli A dried and smoked chilli widely used in Mexican cooking

chipped beef Flakes of charqui used as a flavouring

chips **1** Batons of potato deep fried until brown and soft (UK) or golden and crisp (USA, Fr and elsewhere) **2** A generic name for thin slices of potato or other starchy product or mixture, deep fried until crisp and brown. See game chips

chiqueter *(Fr)* To flute the edge *(of pastry)*

chirashi-zushi *(Ja)* A plate or lacquered box of sushi-meshi rice scattered with various fillings

chirongi nut A round nut the size of a small pea with a musky flavour. Used in the Hyderabad state of India.

chironju *(In)* Charoli nut

chitak *(In) see* chattak

chitcharon *(Ph) see* sitsaron

chitterlings **1** The cleaned middle portion of pig gut about 18 m from the stomach generally boiled before sale. May be fried. Often chopped and incorporated into sausage fillings **2** *(USA)* Odd pieces of newly killed pigs, cut into squares and simmered in broth

chive A small invasive perennial plant of the onion family, *Allium schoenoprasim,* with thin tubular leaves and purple flowers. The chopped leaves have a mild onion flavour and are used as a garnish or for flavouring but not with prolonged cooking. The flowers are used for decorating dishes

Chivry, sauce *(Fr) fem.* White wine boiled and infused with chervil, parsley, tarragon, chopped shallots and fresh young salad burnet for 10 minutes, squeezed out, mixed with 5 times its volume of velouté sauce and finished with beurre à la Chivry. Served with boiled and poached chicken

chi yu *(Ch)* Chicken fat

chi zhi *(Ch)* Black bean sauce

chlorine (E)925, a highly irritant gas liberated when bleach reacts with organic matter and acids. Can be dangerous if some cleaning agents are used improperly. Used as a flour improver

chlorine dioxide *see* (E)926

chlorophyll The green colouring matter in plants which is a part of the system which turns carbon dioxide into carbohydrates using the energy from the sun. Also used as a permitted green food colouring E140, together with its copper complex E141

chnang phleung *(Cm)* Steamboat

chocart *(Fr) masc.* A Breton pastry tart filled with a spice and lemon mixture [also called **choquart**]

chochon rouci *(Ca)* A meat stew from St Lucia containing pork, onions, leeks, celery, cabbage, carrots, tomatoes, cucumber, garlic and seasonings

chocola *(Ho)* Chocolate

chocolade *(Ho)* Chocolate

chocolat *(Fr) masc.* Chocolate

chocolat liégois *(Fr) masc.* As café liégois but with chocolate

chocolate 1 *(En & Sp)* A bitter dark brown solid mixture of cocoa butter and cocoa bean solids made from the fermented pods of the cacao tree from which the seeds are removed, dehusked, roasted and shelled, then ground into a paste which is worked between rollers until the correct smooth physical form is achieved. This chocolate is then further processed to make cocoa solids, cocoa butter, cocoa powder, chocolates *(confectionery)*, cooking chocolate, couverture, etc. **2** A confectionery item made by mixing chocolate and cocoa butter to give about 35% fat content then flavouring with almond, vanilla and/or other spices and sweetening to taste. In the UK, chocolates are adulterated with vegetable fat, butter fat and milk solids

chocolate cake A cake flavoured and coloured with chocolate or cocoa powder

chocolate chip cookies *(USA)* Biscuits containing small recognizeable pieces of chocolate and possibly chopped nuts [also called **Maryland cookies**]

chocolate fudge sauce A thick pouring sauce made from melted chocolate, brown sugar, butter, vanilla essence and milk, served hot with ice cream

chocolate log A cake consisting of a Swiss roll coated with chocolate or chocolate butter cream, the coating made to resemble bark using a fork or other implement [also called **yule log**]

chocolate pudding *(UK)* Basic steamed pudding flavoured with cocoa or grated chocolate

chocolate sauce 1 A sweetened white sauce flavoured with chocolate or cocoa powder used with baked or steamed puddings **2** Molten chocolate mixed with sugar, butter and vanilla essence used to coat profiteroles, cakes, ice cream, etc. Solid when cold

chocolate vermicelli Short fine strands of extruded chocolate 1mm by 3 mm approx. Used for decoration

chodnik litewski *(Pl)* A chilled summer soup originating in Lithuania, made from beetroot, cucumber, dill, chives, milk or yoghurt, lemon juice and soured cream processed with water or chicken stock. Served with quartered hard boiled eggs and sliced radishes

choice *(UK)* A rump and sirloin of beef not disjointed

choice beef *(USA)* A high quality tender and well flavoured beef with less marbling than prime quality

choix, au *(Fr)* At the choice of the customer, choose at will

cho kanjang *(Ko)* Tahini

choke The central hairy part of an artichoke consisting of immature petals and stamens which is removed when cooked before serving or using

choke cherry *(USA)* A small astringent native cherry *Prunus virginiana* used to make a jelly-type conserve

choklad *(Sw)* Chocolate

chokladglass *(Sw)* Chocolate ice cream

choko A green pear-shaped squash similar in size to the avocado which grows on a rampant vine *Sechium edule.* Originally from South America, it is now grown in Australia, the Caribbean and the USA. The flesh is fairly tasteless and must be cooked before eating. The central seed may be eaten when very young and the young leaves and shoots and fleshy roots are also edible [also called **brionne, christophine, custard marrow, mango squash, chayote, mirliton, pepinello, vegetable pear, xoxo, chow-chow**]

chokolade *(De)* Chocolate

chokoreto *(Ja)* Chocolate flavour

cholecalciferol *see* vitamin D3

cholent A Jewish casserole made from beef brisket, beans, vegetables and barley which is cooked slowly for 24 hours in flavoured stock so that it can be prepared and started the day before the sabbath

cholent simmes A cholent based on a mixture of minced turkey meat and onions bound with egg and matzo meal, used in one piece instead of brisket, together with beans and possibly dried fruits, casseroled in a lemon, honey and chicken stock

cholesterol A complex alcohol *(sterol)* found

in most body tissues and many foods. It is a high molecular weight alcohol normally synthesized by the liver, a constituent of cell membranes and a precursor of steroid hormones. There is a total of about 140 g in the body most of which is synthesized in the body. There is no evidence that dietary cholesterol influences the amount of body cholesterol. The concentration in blood is thought to be an indicator of other problems predisposing to heart and vascular system disease

choline A water soluble compound which is needed for B vitamin action and is important for brain function and fat metabolism. It can be synthesized in the body by healthy humans when adequate methionine is present in the diet and is not strictly a vitamin. It is found in high concentration in most animal tissues and egg yolk is the richest source. Deficiency may cause fatty liver and a predisposition to cirrhosis of the liver. It has no known toxicity

cholla 1 *see* challa **2** *see* chickpea

cholodyetz *see* petcha

chompoo *(Th)* Rose apple

chongos *(Sp)* A lemon and cinnamon-flavoured custard

chop A slice of meat cut across the back about 1 to 3 cm thick consisting of a part of the the spinal column, the muscles surrounding it and part of the rib cage or belly extending to at most 15 cm. either side. Usually halved through the spinal chord but sometimes complete e.g. Barnsley chop. Usually from a lamb, pig or goat

chop, to To divide food into pieces of varying size using a knife or cleaver on a chopping board

chop kebab *(Bu)* Cubes of lamb and peeled marrow, threaded on skewers, marinated in tomato juice, seasoned and grilled

chop sticks Two slender tapering wood, plastic or ivory sticks about 30 cm long used in the East for eating solid food. The technique for use requires some practice

chop suey A Western version of Chinese food invented to use up scraps of meat, consisting of shredded meat or poultry, chopped or sliced mushrooms, onions and bamboo shoots, bean sprouts, seasoning, etc. in a cornflour thickened chicken stock laced with MSG. Served with rice and soya sauce

chop suey greens *see* garland chrysanthemum

chopa *(Sp)* Black bream

chopped egg and onion A Jewish appetizer made with chopped hard boiled eggs, onions and seasoning bound together with molten chicken fat

chopped herring A Jewish appetizer of chopped salted herring fillets mixed with white bread, grated sour apples, chopped onion and hard boiled egg white, vinegar and seasonings. Served on lettuce and garnished with sieved hard boiled egg yolk

chopped liver A Jewish appetizer made from cooked liver, onions and hard boiled egg yolks all chopped, seasoned, bound with molten chicken fat, served on lettuce and garnished with chopped hard boiled egg white

chopping board A thick board of hard wood or plastic used to protect the edge of a knife and the surface of the table when chopping food. Different coloured plastics are now recommended for different types of food in commercial establishments to reduce cross contamination: red - raw meat, blue - fish, brown - vegetables, green - salads and fruit, yellow - cooked meats, white - dairy products

choquart *(Fr)* *see* chocart

choriceros chilli A mild and piquant hot chilli from Spain

chorizo *(Me & Sp)* A type of sausage made from pork, beef, olive oil, red peppers, garlic and seasoning, stuffed in hog casings. Often scalded, dried and left to mature for 2 to 3 months when it develops a surface mould. Sometimes cold smoked. Served as an appetizer or with chick peas as a main course

chorizo basquais *(Fr & Sp)* masc. A softer and less highly spiced version of chorizo

chorizo canton *(Ph)* Lap cheong, Chinese sausage

chorizo de Catimpalos *(Sp)* A chorizo containing large chunks of ham

chorizo combinados *(Sp)* Mixed sliced sausages

chorizo d'Estramadura *(Sp)* A highly spiced expensive chorizo made with finely processed pork fillet and pig's liver flavoured with the usual sweet red pepper, but including crushed juniper berries, tomato purée, cayenne pepper and other spices, packed in beef casings and cold smoked for a week or more with juniper berries added to the fire.

chorizo de lomo *(Sp)* A chorizo sausage made with large pieces of pork loin

chorizo picante *(Me)* A pork chorizo made without fat, seasoned, flavoured with garlic, chilli powder and ground cumin seed and preserved with added vinegar. When dried will keep for several weeks

chorizo de Salamanca *(Sp)* A coarse textured chorizo

Chorley cake *(UK)* A parcel of shortcrust pastry with a filling of currants, brown sugar and melted butter in the centre, rolled flat until the currants show through the pastry, egg washed, slit and baked at 190°C

Chorleywood process *(UK)* A method of making bread developed at the British Baking Industries Research Association, Chorleywood, (now the Flour Milling and Baking Research Association) which cuts down on the time necessary to knead and prove the dough. In essence it uses intensive mixing of the flour, water, salt, yeast, vitamin C and fat for from 3 to 5 minutes imparting 11 watt-hours of energy per kg of the dough in that time and raising its temperature to 30°C. Double the normal amounts of yeast and improvers are also added. The dough can then be immediately divided into tins. The whole bread-making process takes less than 3.5 hours from flour to bread and produces a very cheap loaf without character suitable only for use as a loss leader and for feeding ducks

chorlito *(Sp)* Plover

chorogi *see* Chinese artichoke

choron, sauce *(En & Fr)* A béarnaise sauce combined with tomato purée [also called **sauce béarnaise tomatée**]

chota piaz *(In)* Shallot

chotenn bigoudenn *(Fr)* A pig's head roasted with garlic

choti elaichi *(In)* Bleached or green cardamom

chotodziec *(Pl)* A cold soup made from the juice of pickled cucumbers blended with sour milk, strained and garnished with diced beetroot, slices of hard boiled egg, crayfish tails, chopped chives and chopped dill. Served on a plate with an ice cube

chou *(Fr) masc.* Cabbage

chou blanc *(Fr) masc.* White cabbage [also called **chou pomme**]

chou brocoli *(Fr) masc.* Broccoli

chou cabus *(Fr) masc.* White cabbage

chou à la crème *(Fr) masc.* Cream puff

chou farci *(Fr) masc.* Stuffed cabbage

chou-fleur *(Fr) masc.* Cauliflower

chou frisé *(Fr) masc.* Kale

chou marin *(Fr) masc.* Seakale

chou de mer *(Fr) masc.* Seakale

chou navet *(Fr) masc.* Swede

chou palmiste *(Fr) masc.* Heart of palm

chou pomme *(Fr) masc.* White cabbage

chou-rave *(Fr) masc.* Kohlrabi

chou rouge *(Fr) masc.* Red cabbage

chou vert *(Fr) masc.* Green cabbage

choucroute *(Fr) fem.* Sauerkraut or pickled cabbage

choucroute garnie à l'alsacienne *(Fr) fem.* Pickled cabbage topped with sausages, pork chops and knuckles of ham. Served with mustard and horseradish sauce

choucroute aux poissons *(Fr) fem.* Poached fresh water fish served on a bed of pickled cabbage with a wine based cream sauce

chouriço *(Po)* A chorizo type sausage made with pork cured in brine, seasoned, flavoured with garlic and paprika and moistened with red wine, packed into casings, smoked and preserved in olive oil

chouriço de sangue *(Po)* Black pudding, boudin noir

choux de Bruxelles *(Fr) masc.* Brussels sprouts

choux pastry Pastry made by melting 4 parts butter and 10 parts water, beating in 5 parts strong flour and 8 parts of egg over heat until the paste leaves the side of the pan, piping onto baking trays and baking until dry

chow chow 1 *see* choko **2** *see* chow chow preserve

chow chow preserve 1 A Chinese preserve of ginger, fruits and peel in a heavy syrup **2** Chopped mixed vegetables in a mustard flavoured pickle sauce

chowder *(USA)* The name for fish soups generally based on a mixture of fish stock and milk with sweated chopped vegetables usually including potatoes and sweet corn, pieces of fish and/or shellfish added towards the end so as not to overcook and occasionally thickened with cornflour, a similar starch or beurre manié. In the USA, meat, salt pork and bread or crackers may be included

chow fun *(Ch)* Wide flat rice noodles

chow mein As chop suey but served with boiled or fried noodles [also called **chao mian**]

choy pin *(Ch)* Turnip

choy sum *(Ch)* A leaf vegetable *Brassica rapa* var. *parachinensis* resembling pak choy but with slightly bitter stems which are the part usually eaten. It occasionally shows small yellow flowers [also called **flowering white cabbage**]

chrain A Jewish relish made from grated horseradish mixed with chopped beetroot. Served with gefilte fish or cold fried fish

christening cake A rich fruit cake covered with marsipan and white icing with appropriate decorations to be served after a christening

Christmas cake A very rich moist cake with a high proportion of dried vine fruits, chopped nuts and candied peel, often with added brandy or rum, covered with almond paste and icing and appropriately decorated. The cake itself before covering is often matured for several months

Christmas melon *(USA)* A small smooth melon with a mottled green and yellow rind and pale green flesh. it is similar in taste to the honeydew [also called **Santa Claus melon**]

Christmas pudding A steamed or boiled pudding made from flour, suet, sugar, dried vine fruits, spices, milk and sometimes breadcrumbs, cooked, matured and reheated for serving. Traditionally a small coin was inserted into the pudding as a token of good fortune for the receiver [also called **plum pudding**]

christophine *see* choko

Christstollen *(Ge)* An enriched sweetened Christmas bread. See Dresdener Christstollen

christstollen A yeasted, egg enriched and sweetened fruit bread incorporating almond flakes, rum soaked dried vine fruits, candied peel, glacé cherries and chopped angelica and flavoured with lemon zest and almond essence

chromium A trace element required by the body for health, found in fish, nuts, whole grains, yeast and seaweed

chrysanthemum Particular types of chrysanthemum plants grown for their edible flowers, petals and leaves in China and Japan. There are two types grown for leaves and one for flowers. See garland chrysanthemum

Chrysanthemum coronarium *Bot.* Garland chrysanthemum

chrysanthemum cut *(Ja)* A method of cutting turnip or other root vegetables by standing the piece between 2 parallel chopsticks, cutting down at right angles to the chopsticks in very thin slices joined at the base, rotating the piece through 90 degrees and repeating. This gives fine strands springing from a solid base like the centre of any Compositae *(daisy-like flowers)*

chrysanthemum greens *see* garland chrysanthemum

chtapothi *(Gr)* Octopus

chtodnik *(Pl)* A cold soup similar to chotodziec but containing blanched young beetroot tops and an additional garnish of diced fresh cucumber, lemon slices and occasionally cold sturgeon

chub A freshwater fish *Leuciscus cephalus* which is a relative of the carp. Rarely used for food on account of the numerous small bones and the somewhat muddy flavour. Braised chub's head is a popular dish in China

chuck *(USA)* The name of a large part of the forequarter of beef extending to the brisket and excluding only the foreribs and part of the middle ribs. It is cut in a number of different ways which depend on the locality but are mainly self explanatory such as chuck roll, chuck steak, blade steak, chuck tender, shoulder steak, chuck short ribs, arm steak, etc.

chuck ribs of beef *(UK)* The first two ribs of beef counting from the head end, the meat of which is generally used off the bone for stewing and braising

chuck roll *(USA)* A rolled joint of beef from the ribs of the chuck

chuck steak 1 *(UK) see* blade bone **2** *(USA)* A cut of beef from between the neck and shoulder used for stewing

chuck wagon stew *(Cn)* A stew from Alberta made from beef fried in fat, water, potatoes, carrots, apples, small onions, herbs and seasonings thickened with cornflour

chucruta *(Sp)* Sauerkraut

chufa *(Sp)* Tiger nut

chui kan *(Ch)* Kumquat

chu ju *(Ch)* Mandarin orange

chuka-nabe *(Ja)* Wok

chukandar *(In)* Beetroot

chuk gaai choy *(Ch)* One of the oriental mustards with ribbed green stalks and serrated leaves growing to 30 cm. The strong flavour is reduced by parboiling [also called **bamboo mustard cabbage**]

chuk surn *(Ch)* Bamboo shoot

chuleta de cordero *(Sp)* Lamb chop

chuleta de ternera *(Sp)* Veal cutlet

chuleta a la vienasa *(Sp)* Veal cutlet

chum salmon *see* Siberian salmon

chump chops *(UK)* Chops cut from the top of a leg of lamb and the rear of the loin including parts of the pelvis but not any vertebrae except the coccyx

chump end of loin of lamb *(UK)* The end of the loin nearest the tail or pelvis

chump of pork *(UK)* The top of the pork leg and the rear of the loin including parts of the pelvis but not any vertebrae except the coccyx, usually sold as a piece and not as chops

chung *(Ch)* Scallion

chung choy *(Ch)* Turnip

chung tau *(Ch)* Shallots

chun juan *(Ch)* Spring roll

chunky banana *(USA) see* burro banana

chuño blanco *(SA)* A preserved form of bitter potato from the Andean region of Peru made by freezing raw potatoes, removing the skins, squeezing out the released liquid, washing in running water and drying. Used as a basis of stews, soups and cheese dishes and with fruit and molasses as a dessert *(mazamorra)*

chuño negro *(SA)* A preserved form of potato similarly processed to chuño blanco but with the skins left on and not washed in running water. Dark brown in colour it is usually soaked in water for one to two days before cooking to remove strong flavours

chuoi *(Vi)* Banana

chupe de camarones *(SA)* A thick soup from Peru containing prawns, fried onions, garlic, tomatoes, peppers, potatoes, peas, sweet corn, eggs, cream, parsley or coriander and seasoning

churek *(Ru)* A yeast-raised bread from the Caucasus enriched with milk and melted butter, flavoured with ground anise (aniseed), glazed with egg and sprinkled with sesame seeds

churn **1** A tall almost cylindrical metal vessel with a deep rimmed lid used in the olden days to keep milk for sale or further processing **2** A vessel of moderate size, often made of wood in which cream was converted to butter by agitation, now superceded by machinery

churn, to To agitate cream with a regular motion to convert it into butter and buttermilk

churrasco *(Po)* Charcoal grilled meat or chicken, usually on a skewer

churrasco a gaucha *(Br)* A barbecue usually featuring beef or chicken

churros *(Sp)* Banana shaped fritters squeezed through a nozzle into deep fat, fried, sprinkled with sugar and eaten for breakfast often by dunking in a hot cinnamon drink

chutney A mixture of chopped apples, onion and garlic with possibly other vegetables and/or fruits cooked in a vinegar, sugar and spice mixture to a thick consistency, used as a relish [also called **sweet pickle**]

chyet-thon-phew *(Bm)* Garlic

chymosin A protease used in cheese making

chymotripsin One of the proteases found in the human digestive system. The seeds of some legumes contain chymotrypsin inhibitors which prevent its digestive action. For this reason these seeds must be well cooked before consumption

ciabatta *(It)* An oval shaped bread made from a very slack dough of flour, water and fresh yeast (20:14:1) with dried milk powder, salt and olive oil and some sour dough or biga. The batter is beaten then kneaded until silky (1000 movements suggested), proved 2 to 3 hours at 26 to 30°C, shaped on a flat tray, proved again until doubled in volume and baked 20 to 25 minutes at 230°C. Lit. slipper

ciafotta *(It) see* ciambotta

cialda *(It)* Waffle, wafer

cialledda del massaro *(It)* A country soup made with slices of bread covered with vegetables

ciambelle *(It)* **1** Ring-shaped cakes or pastries with nuts and candied fruit [also called **panafracchi**] **2** Bread loaves *(Tuscany and Sardinia)*

ciambotta *(It)* A type of Spanish omelette made with potatoes, sweet green peppers, tomatoes and aubergines cooked in olive oil [also called **ciamotta, cianfotta**]

ciammotte ammuccate *(It)* Snails seasoned with pepper, mint and herbs

ciamotta *(It) see* ciambotta

cianfotta *(It) see* ciambotta

ciaronciedi moena *(It)* A potato based ravioli from the Dolomite region of Italy, stuffed with a filling based on figs or dried pears and finished with melted butter and poppy seeds

ciasto *(Pl)* Cake

ciboule *(Fr) fem.* Spring onion, chive

ciboulette *(Fr) fem.* Chives

cibreo *(It)* Cooked cockscombs and sweetbreads served with a vegetable timbale. The dish is said to date from Roman times

cicala *(It) see* cigarra (Sp)

ciccioli *(It)* Pork scratchings, crackling

cicely *see* sweet cicely

Cicer arietinum *Bot.* Chick pea

cicerchia *(It)* A large pebble-like pea

cicerelle *(Fr) fem.* Sand eel

cicerello *(It)* Sand eel

cichorel *(Ho)* Chicory, endive

Cichorium endivia *Bot.* Endive

Cichorium intybus *Bot.* Chicory *(in French called endive)*

Cichorium intybus* var. *foliosum *Bot.* Red chicory

cicoria *(It)* Chicory, the leaf

cicoria spadona *(It)* Sword leaved green chicory

cicoriella *(It)* Wild chicory

cider The fermented juice of apples, often used as a cooking liquor in Southern England and Northern France. Can be distilled to a strong spirit sometimes used for flavouring

cider cake A chemically raised basic cake mixture made by the creaming method containing sultanas equal in weight to the flour which have been soaked in dry cider (8:5) for at least 12 hours. Baked at 180°C until cooked

cider vinegar A vinegar made by the oxidation of the alcohol in cider to acetic acid

cidra *(Sp)* Citron, the fruit

cidre *(Fr) masc.* Cider

ciernikis *(Pl)* An appetizer made from a cottage cheese, butter and flour dough, seasoned and flavoured with nutmeg, rolled out, cut in squares, boiled, drained and served sprinkled with grated cheese and breadcrumbs which have been browned in butter

ciervo *(Sp)* Venison

cigala *(Sp)* Dublin bay prawn

cigalle *(Sp)* Dublin bay prawn

cigarra *(Sp)* A flat Mediterranean lobster-like creature, *Scyllarides latus,* very similar to the slipper lobster and with small claws. Large ones are treated like lobster, small ones are used in paella

cilantro 1 *(Sp & USA)* Coriander leaves **2** A herb, *Geringium foetidum,* from Costa Rica, Dominica and Mexico with a similar flavour to coriander

ciliegia *(It)* Cherry

cili padi *(Ma)* Bird's eye chilli

cima ripiena *(It)* Breast of veal with a pocket cut into it and filled with various stuffings

cima di vitello *(It)* Veal in aspic

cimbopogone *(It)* Lemon grass

cime di rapa *(It)* Broccoli raab

cincho *(SA)* A ewe's milk cheese from Venezuela similar to Villalon

cinghiale *(It)* Wild boar

Cinnamomum cassia *Bot.* Cassia

Cinnamomum zeylanicum *Bot.* Cinnamon

cinnamon A very popular spice made from the dried bark of a tree of the laurel family, *Cinnamomum zeylanicum,* which is either ground or rolled into quills rather like small cigarillos. Extensively used for sweet and savoury items

cinnamon basil *(It)* A variety of basil with a cinnamon aroma

cinnamon sugar A mixture of caster sugar and ground cinnamon used for baking, principally in Central and Northern Europe

cioccolata *(It)* Chocolate

cioppino *(USA)* A mixed seafood stew from the west coast similar to bouillabaisse, i.e. with wine, olive oil, garlic, onions, tomatoes, green sweet peppers, spices, herbs and seasoning

cipolette *(It)* Spring onions

cipolla *(It)* Onion

cipolline *(It)* Small silverskin onions, pearl onions

Circassian sauce *see* satsivi

ciriole *(It)* **1** Tiny eels **2** Crusty round bread rolls *(Rome)*

ciruela pasa *(Sp)* Prune

ciruelas *(Sp)* Plums

ciruelas damascenas *(Sp)* Damsons

ciruelas pasas *(Sp)* Prunes

ciruelas secas *(Sp)* Prunes

cisco *see* lake herring

ciseler *(Fr)* To shred or cut in julienne strips, to incise

citrange A hybrid of the sweet orange and a poncirus citrus, developed in the USA to withstand cool climates. The flesh is sharp tasting

citrates and dihydrogen citrates Salts of citric acid used for the same purposes as citric acid, see E330. The ones used are sodium, E331, potassium, E332 and calcium, E333

citric acid The commonest food acid originally extracted from citrus fruits where it is in high concentration but now made by a fungal fermentation. Also found in gooseberries, raspberries, etc. See E330 for uses

citroen *(Ho)* Lemon

citrom *(Hu)* Lemon

citron 1 A citrus fruit from an evergreen tree *Citrus medica,* native to the Far East. It is shaped like a lemon up to 20 cm long by 13 cm dia. with a knobbly skin. It is grown for its skin which is used to make candied peel, as a flavouring and after carving as a garnish. The flesh is very sour **2** *(De, Sw & Fr) masc.* Lemon

citron fromage *(De)* A lemon-flavoured dessert

citron peel The peel, including the zest and pith, of the citron which is brined, dried, soaked in a strong sugar syrup, then dried and chopped

citron vert *(Fr) masc.* Lime, the fruit [also called **lime** (Fr)]

citronella *see* lemon grass

Citronella microcarpa *Bot.* Calamondin

citronkräm *(Sw)* A lemon-flavoured dessert

citronnat *(Fr) masc.* Candied lemon peel

citrouille *(Fr) fem.* Pumpkin

Citrullus lanatus *Bot.* Watermelon

Citrullus vulgaris *Bot.* Watermelon

Citrullus vulgaris* var. *fistulosus *Bot.* Tinda

citrus The most important tree fruit crop in the world (around 70% of all fruit grown) which will grow within 40 degrees of latitude on either side of the equator, There are 6 genera of which 3 are of commercial importance viz. Poncirus *(trifoliate orange),* Fortunella *(kumquat)* and Citrus (8 important species). For the latter see under *Citrus* spp. All three will hybridize with each other and most *Citrus* spp. are cross fertile, hence the increasing number of varieties

Citrus aurantifolia *Bot.* West Indian lime

Citrus aurantium *Bot.* Seville orange

Citrus bergamia *Bot.* Bergamot, the fruit

Citrus deliciosa *Bot.* Mediterranean mandarin

citrus fruits Fruits of the species Citrus which have been cultivated for 2000 years and known in Europe since the 16th century. They all have a two layered separable green, yellow or orange skin, the outer layer (zest) being rich in essential oils, the inner (pith or albedo) being white and soft, all enclosing a segmented fruit containing juice sacs and seeds (pips). The juices contain sugar, flavours, aromas and citric acid. The relative proportions of these determine the palatability and uses of the fruit. For examples see orange, lemon, lime, cumquat, grapefruit, mandarin, tangerine, clementine, etc.

Citrus grandis *Bot.* Pummelo

Citrus hystrix *Bot.* Makrut lime

Citrus junos *Bot.* Yuzu

Citrus latifolia *Bot.* Persian lime

Citrus limettiodes *Bot.* Sweet lime

Citrus limon *Bot.* Lemon

Citrus medica *Bot.* Citron

Citrus nobilis *Bot.* King mandarin

Citrus paradisi *Bot.* Grapefruit

Citrus reticulata *Bot.* Common mandarin

Citrus sinensis *Bot.* Sweet orange

Citrus sphaerocarpa *Bot.* Kabosa

***Citrus* spp.** The 8 most important Citrus species are sweet orange *C. sinensis,* mandarin *C. reticulata,* grapefruit *C. paradisi,* pummelo *C. grandis,* lemon *C. limon,* lime *C. aurantifolia,* citron *C. medica* and sour orange *C. aurantium.* All of these varieties will cross fertilize and it is thought that the sweet orange may be a pummelo x mandarin cross, the grapefruit a pummelo x sweet orange cross and the lemon a lime x citron x pummelo cross. For more detail see under citrus fruits

Citrus sudachi *Bot.* Sudachi

Citrus unshui *Bot.* Satsuma mandarin

city chicken *(USA)* Diced veal from the lean part of the shoulder cooked on a skewer

ciuppin *(It)* A fish stew

cive *(Fr) fem.* Chives

civet *(En & Fr) masc.* A dark brown stew made from wild rabbit, hare or other game animal, thickened with its blood

civet de lièvre *(Fr) masc.* Jugged hare

civette *(Fr) fem.* Chives

clabber *(USA)* Sour curdled milk which has not separated into curds and whey, something like junket

clafoutis *(Fr) masc.* Black cherries baked in a thick creamy batter until golden brown, sprinkled with sugar and served warm with cream, often at harvest time

claire *(Fr) fem.* A fattened oyster [also called **huître de clair**]

clam A bivalve shellfish found worldwide with lean flesh which can be eaten raw, poached, steamed, baked or fried. All must be live when purchased and consumed as soon as possible after being allowed to clean themselves in water with a little oatmeal for 24 hours and subsequently well scrubbed. There is considerable confusion in the naming and classification of clams for culinary purposes. See amongst others, bean, carpet shell, golden carpet shell, little neck, quahog, sand, soft shell, surf, venus shell, warty venus shell and wedge shell

clam bake *(USA)* A social gathering at the beach in which food (clams, chicken, corn on the cob, potatoes, etc.) is steamed in a pit in the beach by means of heated rocks using damp seaweed to provide the steam

clam chowder *(USA)* A famous USA soup made from small clams cooked over a high heat with dry white wine and water until all open. The sound clams are reserved and the cooking liquor is strained off to make a broth with fried diced bacon, leeks and celery and chopped potatoes. Towards the end of the cooking period, milk, cream, seasoning and the reserved clams are added, simmered for 5 minutes, finished with chopped parsley and served with croûtons

clamart *(En & Fr) masc.* A garnish of globe artichoke hearts filled with petit pois

clapper cut *see* hyoshi-giri

clapshot *(UK)* A Scottish vegetable accompaniment of potatoes and swedes boiled in salted water until soft and mashed with seasoning, butter and chopped chives

claquebitou *(Fr)* A goats' milk cheese flavoured with herbs from Burgundy

clara *(Po)* Egg white

clarificar *(Sp)* To clarify

clarified butter Pure butter fat without any solids, liquid or foam. It should be transparent when molten

clarifier *(Fr)* To clarify, e.g. butter, consommé

clarify, to To remove all solids and immiscible fluids from a liquid by skimming, filtering, by entrapping the impurities in coagulated egg whites or isinglass, by solubilizing with enzymes, etc. to leave a perfectly clear liquid e.g. for bouillon

clary sage A biennial herb *Salvia sclarea* belonging to the mint family with a flavour similar to sage. Famous for its very expensive essential oil [also called **clear eye**]

clavelado *(Fr)* Skate, the fish

claviari *(It)* A type of fungus

clavo *(Me)* Clove

claytonia *see* winter purslane

clear, to **1** The description of what happens during the later phases of kneading dough when it becomes elastic, smooth and silky, e.g. to clear the dough **2** To clarify

clear eye *see* clary

clear oxtail soup As thick oxtail soup but omitting the flour and slightly thickening before garnishing using arrowroot and cooking until clear [also called **queue de boeuf clair**]

clear soup *see* consommé

clementine A hybrid citrus fruit of the mandarin and Seville orange, one of the common mandarins *Citrus reticulata* said to have been grown accidentally in 1902 by a Father Clément. It is small, sweet, round and juicy with a thin skin and few pips. See common mandarin

clipfish *see* klipfish

clod *(UK)* A cut of beef from the neck between the head and the blade bone suitable only for mincing or long slow stewing or braising

clonorchis A species of fluke with a similar mode of transmission, prevalence and effects as opistharchis q.v

cloot *(UK)* A large square of muslin or linen used in Scotland to contain boiled puddings

clootie dumpling *(UK)* A spiced pudding from Scotland similar to Christmas pudding and boiled in a cloot. Sometimes eaten cold like cake [also called **cloutie dumpling**]

Clostridium botulinum The bacterium found in home canned and bottled vegetables which causes botulism q.v. The spores of this organism are not killed by cooking at normal temperatures. The incubation period is 18 to 36 hours and death occurs in 1 to 8 days or there is a slow recovery lasting 6 to 8 months. The symptoms are disturbance of vision, dry mucous membranes of the mouth, tongue and pharynx which cause difficulty in speaking and swallowing, and progressive weakness and respiratory failure. Immediate medical attention should be sought if there is any suspicion of the condition

Clostridium perfringens A food poisoning bacteria found in cooked and reheated meats and meat products. The incubation period is 8 to 12 hours, the duration 12 to 24 hours and the symptoms are diarrhoea, abdominal pain and nausea. There is rarely vomiting and no fever

clot, to *see* to coagulate

clotted cream *(UK)* A thick, yellow, pasteurized cream with a minimum fat content of 48% from Devon or Cornwall, made by heating full cream milk slowly and skimming off the cream from the surface. Used with jam as a spread on scones for the traditional Devon cream tea [also called **clouted cream**]

clou de girofle *(Fr) masc.* Clove

cloud ear fungus An edible fungus *Auricularia polytricha* grown in China on oak logs and available as small, black, brittle dried pieces which expand 5 times in volume when reconstituted. Used in Chinese dishes [also called **wood ear, wood fungus, tree fungus, brown fungus, black fungus, black tree fungus, rat's ear, tree ear**]

cloudberry A wild berry from a creeping plant *Rubus chamaemorus* similar to a blackberry and found in Northern Europe and North America. It is a deep golden colour with a baked apple/honey taste. Used to flavour a liqueur

clouté(e) *(Fr)* Studded, as in onion clouté; *see also* piquer

clouted cream *see* clotted cream

cloutie dumpling *see* clootie dumpling

clovas de comer *(Ph)* Cloves

clove basil A variety of basil with a slight clove aroma and flavour

cloverleaf roll *(USA)* Three balls of yeasted and proven dough placed on a baking tin so that when risen and baked they stick together and resemble a cloverleaf

cloves The dried unopened flower buds of an evergreen tree *Eugenia caryophyllus* with a strong, sweet, aromatic smell and flavour; a native of Indonesia but now grown in East Africa. Used whole or ground in desserts and savoury dishes. Ground cloves are mixed with tobacco to make the Indonesian kretek cigarette which has a soporific effect on the smoker

clovisse *(Fr) fem.* Carpet shell and golden carpet shell clam

club gourd *see* angled loofah

club sandwich A sandwich made from two slices of toasted bread filled with lettuce, sliced chicken, sliced tomatoes, crisp fried bacon and mayonnaise, garnished with chutney, pickles or olives

club steak *(USA)* A beef steak cut from the small end (rib end) of the short loin with no fillet

cluck and grunt *(USA) coll. (Wild West)* Eggs and bacon

cluster bean *see* guar bean

coagulate, to The process by which liquids or some of the soluble components of liquids, usually proteins, become solid, e.g. when white of egg or blood solidifies or milk curdles [also called **to clot**]

coalfish *see* coley

coarse salt *(USA)* Sea salt

coat, to To cover pieces of cooked or uncooked food with a liquid which sticks to the surface, e.g. sauce, batter, melted butter or a glaze, or a combination of liquid and solid, e.g. egg and breadcrumbs, either to seal in flavour, to add flavour or to improve the appearance

coating batter A thick, viscous mixture of flour, water or milk, with possibly egg, cream or sugar, and seasoning used to coat items of food, generally prior to frying, deep frying, or baking

coating consistency The description of a liquid mixture with sufficient body or viscosity such that when it coats a solid it will not drain off. Tested by inverting a spoonful of the mixture which should not leave the spoon

coating sauce A thick sauce of coating consistency used to cover foods to improve their appearance and flavour

cob A round, hemispherical, white or brown loaf baked on a flat tray, sometimes with a cross incised on the top before baking

cobalamin *see* vitamin B12

cobalt A trace element necessary for health which is a constituent of vitamin B12 (cobalamin). Found in meat, eggs, dairy products and yeast extract

cobbler *(UK)* Any sweet or savoury cooked food mixture covered or part covered with uncooked scones (sweet or savoury as appropriate), egg or milk washed, possibly cheese gratinated and baked at 220°C until the scones rise and are browned. See e.g. fish cobbler, cobbler pudding

cobbler pudding A cold stewed fruit mixture covered with round scones, brushed with beaten egg and baked until brown

cobek *(Id)* A ceramic mortar used with a ceramic pestle *(uleg-uleg)* [also called **tjobek**]

Coblenz sausage *see* Koblenz sausage

cobnut *see* hazelnut

Coburg cake A small, spiced sponge cake soaked in flavoured sugar syrup

coca The American shrub *Erythroxylon coca* from whose leaves an extract is obtained which was once used used in cola drinks

cocada *(Sp)* A coconut-flavoured custard

cocciole *(It)* Cockles, shellfish

cocer en cazuela con poco agua *(Sp)* To braise

cocer al vapor *(Sp)* To steam

cochineal A deep red food colouring extracted from and contained in the fat and egg yolks of an insect *Coccus cacti* found in Mexico and Brazil but now made synthetically [also called **carmine**]

cochineal red *see* ponceau 4R

cochinillo *(Sp)* Sucking pig

cochinillo asado *(Sp)* Spit roasted sucking pig

cochinita pibil *(Me)* Minced pork mixed with annatto seeds ground to an oily paste and pork fat, wrapped in banana leaves and baked in the oven. Served with black beans, tortillas and chopped onions in vinegar [also called **pibil pork**]

cochino *(Sp)* Pig

cochon *(Fr) masc.* Pig

cochon de lait *(Fr) masc.* Sucking pig

cocido *(Sp)* **1** A stew; *see also* olla podrida **2** Cooked

cocido a la madrilena *(Sp)* A slowly cooked casserole containing meat, fowl, sausages, vegetables and chickpeas

cock The adult uncastrated male of the domestic fowl *Gallus gallus.* Also used of other males e.g. crabs, fish, wild birds

cock-a-leekie *(UK)* A Scottish soup made with equal parts of chicken and veal stock garnished with a julienne of prunes, cooked white chicken meat and leeks

cock paddle *see* lumpfish

cockle A bivalve shellfish *Cerastaderma edule* (UK), *C. glaucum* (Mediterranean) *and Cardium edule* with ribbed, grey to brown, pink or even dark blue, almost circular shell from 2.5 to 10 cm dia. found on most sea coasts and with over 200 varieties worldwide. May be eaten raw or cooked for 6 minutes, but usually sold cooked. Treat like mussels; *see also* cuore rossa, dog cockle, prickly cockle and spiny cockle [also called **arkshell**]

cocktail avocado *(USA)* A small seedless fruit of the Fuerte avocado with the characteristic buttery flavour and used in the same way

cocktail sauce Mayonnaise flavoured with tomato purée, horseradish sauce, Worcestershire sauce and Tabasco, used with prawns, crab and lobster

coco *(Me, Po & Fr) masc.* Coconut

cocoa bean The seed of a tree *Theobroma cacao* originally from South America but now grown in West Africa. Used as the source of chocolate and cocoa

cocoa butter The highly saturated white or yellow fat pressed out of cocoa beans, mainly used for chocolate manufacture

cocoa powder Defatted cocoa beans treated with an alkali, further processed, dried and ground to a fine powder for use as a flavouring or to make drinks

cocomero *(It)* Watermelon

coconut **1** The oval fruit (to 20 cm long) of a tropical palm *Cocus nucifera* with an outer fibrous covering, an inner hard shell lined with a white crisp flesh about 6 mm thick and containing a white, sweet, translucent liquid **2** The inner lining of the coconut often shredded, grated and/or dried; *see also* desiccated coconut, makapuno

coconut crab A large edible land crab *Birgus latro* which lives in burrows and is found on islands in the Indian and Pacific oceans

coconut cream A thick creamy liquid made either by mixing coconut milk with sufficient dried coconut milk powder or puréeing coconut flesh with coconut milk. Used to add body and flavour to stews, etc.

coconut grater A hemispherical grater with a handle used for removing the flesh from fresh coconuts

coconut milk **1** The liquid obtained by soaking grated or desiccated coconut in water and straining off the solid particles. Used in Indian and Eastern dishes. Available as a dried powder for reconstituting **2** The white translucent liquid inside a coconut used as a refreshing drink or as flavouring [also called **coconut water**]

coconut oil The highly saturated oil extracted from dried coconut *(copra)* used in the food manufacturing industry and in Asian cooking as well as for soap and cosmetics. It contains about 75% saturated fat and is solid at ambient temperatures in temperate climates

coconut pudding *(UK)* Basic steamed pudding mixture with 1 part in 6 of the flour replaced by desiccated coconut

coconut sugar *see* palm sugar

coconut syrup A clear viscous sweet syrupy sap extracted from the trunk of the coconut palm

coconut vinegar A mild vinegar made from coconut wine; *see also* suka

coconut water *see* coconut milk (2)

coconut wine The fermented sap of the coconut palm from India. Used as a beverage and as the ferment for appa bread [also called **toddy**]

cocotte *(Fr) fem.* A shallow earthenware, cast iron or porcelain dish with a lid, a casserole

cocotte, en *(Fr)* A method of cooking eggs in a small cocotte, ramekin or soufflé dish which is placed in rapidly boiling water. Various food items may be put under the egg before cooking or over it after cooking

cocotte minute *(Fr) fem.* A domestic pressure cooker

cocoyam *see* taro

cocozelle squash *(USA)* A small summer squash resembling the courgette

cocum *see* kokum

cod A round, non-oily sea water fish *Gadus morrhua* from the Northern oceans up to 40 kg in weight with a white flaky flesh and a grey green skin. Used to be cheap and common in the Northern hemisphere. Dried and salted it is a major item in international trade as a protein source

cod liver oil Oil extracted from cod livers used as a major natural source of vitamins A and D and EFA's

cod roe The eggs of the cod fish, available fresh, canned or smoked. It has a mild fishy flavour and a creamy grainy texture. Used to make cheaper versions of taramasalata instead of grey mullet roe.

coda di bue *(It)* Oxtail

coddes *(USA)* A Maryland speciality of codfish fish cakes panéed and deep fried

coddle, to A way of cooking eggs by putting them into boiling water which is then covered and removed from the source of heat. The white is usually just set

coddled eggs Eggs cooked by coddling, i.e. by being placed in boiling water which is not further heated

codling A young, immature cod

codorniz *(Po & Sp)* Quail

coelho *(Po)* Domesticated rabbit

coelho bravo *(Po)* Wild rabbit

coeliac disease A metabolic disease in which the sufferer must not eat foods containing gluten

coentro *(Po)* Coriander leaves

coeur *(Fr) masc.* **1** Heart **2** *see* Neufchâtel

coeur d'artichaut *(Fr) masc.* Artichoke heart

coeur à la crème *(Fr) masc.* A dessert made from a curd or cream cheese allowed to drain in a perforated heart shaped mould, turned out onto a plate and decorated with summer fruits and sprinkled with sugar [also called **fromage à la crème**]

coeur de filet *(Fr) masc.* The trimmed eye of the fillet of beef

coeur de palmier *(Fr) masc.* Heart of palm

coeurs d'artichauts *(Fr) masc.* Artichoke hearts, small, tender and trimmed artichokes; *see also* under artichauts Clamart or artichaut Grand-Duc

coffee The water extract of ground, roasted coffee beans used as a beverage and for flavouring

coffee bean The fruit of an evergreen bush *Coffea arabica* and *C. canephora* native to Ethiopia but now widely grown in high altitude tropical regions. The red fruit which contains two almost hemispherical green seeds is first fermented, the pulp removed and the seeds dried prior to roasting at or near their point of sale. After roasting they contain about 50% water soluble material including caffein and flavours. The two main varieties are robusta and arabica but they are often identified by their place of origin

coffee cake *(USA)* A plain sponge cake usually served warm with coffee

coffee cream *(USA)* Pasteurized cream from cow's milk containing 18 to 30% butterfat for adding to coffee [also called **light cream, table cream**]

coffee grinder A mechanically, electrically or hand operated grinder for roasted coffee beans with an arrangement for adjusting the particle size, very fine for espresso, fine for filters, Turkish and cona, medium for cafetières and percolators and coarse for jug infusion

coffee kisses Small drop cakes or biscuits containing ground nuts, sandwiched together with coffee flavoured butter cream

coffee sugar Coarse crystals, to 3 mm, of translucent, usually amber coloured sugar but these may be mixed with other colours

cognac *(Fr) masc.* Brandy from the Cognac region of France used as a flavouring and for flambéing

cogumelos *(Po)* Mushrooms

coho salmon An important commercial variety *Oncorhynchus kisutch* of Pacific salmon up to 4.5 kg in weight with an oily, deep pink to red flesh. Now in danger of extinction due to degradation of the coastal streams where the salmon spawn [also called **silver salmon**]

cohombrillo *(Sp)* Gherkin

coiled wire whisk The normal domestic whisk consisting of a loose coil of stainless steel wire wrapped around a single loop of stiff wire held in a suitable handle

coing *(Fr) masc.* Quince

Coix lachryma-jobi *Bot.* Job's tears

col *(Sp)* Cabbage

col de Bruselas *(Sp)* Brussel sprouts

col fermentada *(Sp)* Sauerkraut

col rizado *(Sp)* Kale

cola bean The nut of a West African tree *Cola acuminata* and *C. nitida* now also grown in the Caribbean and South America, which yields a red extract containing caffeine and other stimulants and flavours used to make cola type drinks [also called **cola nut, kola nut**]

cola nut *see* cola bean

colache *(Me)* Diced squash mixed with chopped onions fried in butter, tomato conacassée, sweet corn kernels and seasoning and baked in a slow oven in a covered dish without added water

colander A perforated bowl used to drain liquids from solid food. Usually with handles and sometimes with a flat base

colazione *(It)* Lunch

colbert, (à la) *(Fr)* Description of a clear soup containing small pieces of vegetables and poached egg; *see also* sole colbert

colbert butter A compound butter containing parsley, lemon juice, tarragon and meat extract, refrigerated in the shape of a cylinder and cut into 5 mm thick rounds to garnish grilled fish, steaks and rare roast beef

colbert sauce A sauce flavoured with parsley, spices, lemon and Madeira wine, served with vegetables

Colbi *(ME)* An Israeli cow's milk cheese resembling Gouda cheese [also called **kol-bee**]

Colby *(USA)* An orange-coloured scalded-curd hard Cheddar-like cheese but slightly softer and with a more open texture from Colby, Wisconsin. Made from whole cow's milk. It has a dark brown rind and is not cheddared

colcannon *(Ir)* Potato mashed with onion flavoured milk and butter to which are added chopped and poached spring onions and (savoy) cabbage seasoned with nutmeg. Sometimes topped with grilled bacon rashers [also called **Kolcannon**]

colcasia *(Id)* Yam

Colchester *(UK)* A famous oyster from the town of the same name

cold collation A meal consisting of a selection of cold foods

cold pressed A term used of oil which has been produced by direct pressure on the cold untreated fruit, nut or seed. This usually gives a more distinctive flavour than hot pressing or solvent extraction

cold shortening The process by which carcase meat becomes tough if chilled too rapidly after slaughter, esp. with beef and sheep. The chilling rate should not lead to temperatures in any part of the carcase below 10°C in 10 hours or less after slaughter

cold smoke, to To lightly smoke food at a temperature not greater than 33°C so as not to cook the flesh but usually in the range 20°C to 30°C. Used mainly for salmon, kippers, gammon and some sausages. The weight loss should be about 18% for salmon, 12 to 14% for haddock and 25% for cod roes. With the exception of things like cheese and hard boiled eggs, the goods are first lightly brined

cold soufflé A gelatine based mousse put in a soufflé dish with a paper collar extending about 8 cm vertically above the rim, this being removed when the mousse has set so as to resemble a soufflé

cold table *see* smörgåsbord

cole An old English word used for members of the cabbage family, now only surviving in borecole, coleslaw and the corrupted forms kale and cauliflower, but see also rape

colère, fish en Long round fish, skinned, degutted, gills and eyes removed, tails fixed in mouth, panéed and deep fried, stuffed olives put in eye sockets and served with remoulade or tartare sauce

coleseed Rape

coleslaw Finely shredded white hearts of cabbage bound together with various dressings such as mayonnaise, soured cream, yoghurt, French dressing, possibly in combination, and with other possible additions such as nuts, grated carrots, chopped and vinegared onions, celery, apples, etc. A very popular salad item [also called **slaw**]

coleweed *see* rape

coley A cheap fish *Pollachius virens* of the cod family up to 6.5 kg in weight but with a darker skin and a brownish flesh which whitens on cooking. Found in the North Atlantic [also called **saithe, coalfish, pollock, Boston bluefish**]

coliflor *(Sp)* Cauliflower

colimaçon *(Fr) masc.* A variety of snail

colin *(Fr) masc.* Hake, also coley

colin mayonnaise *(Fr) masc.* Cold poached hake, served with mayonnaise

colinabo *(Sp)* Turnip

colineau *(Fr) masc.* Codling

colinot *(Fr) masc.* Codling

collagen One of the constituents of connective tissue (the supporting structure of the body). It is a fairly soft protein which breaks down into gelatine on prolonged boiling or cooking at low temperatures

collar bacon The top front section of a side of bacon cut into bacon joints or sliced into rather rectangular shaped rashers

collard *see* collard greens

collard greens The edible green leaves from non-hearting brassicas including root vegetables

collé(e) *(Fr)* With added gelatine. From coller, to glue

college cake A spiced fruit cake containing caraway seeds

college pudding *(UK)* A steamed or baked pudding made from fresh breadcrumbs, shredded beef suet or softened butter, caster sugar and eggs (4:3:2:2) with 15 g (4.5 teaspoons) of baking powder per kg of breadcrumbs, the same weight of mixed sultanas and raisins as breadcrumbs and generously flavoured with ground cinnamon, cloves and nutmeg. Baked in dariole moulds at 180°C for 45 minutes

coller, to To add body to a mixture by dissolving gelatine in it

collet *(Fr) masc.* Neck of lamb or veal [also called **collier**]

colli di polli ripieni *(It)* The skin of a chicken's neck stuffed loosely with a mixture of finely processed lean beef, egg, cheese, lemon zest, lemon juice and breadcrumbs, tied either end and poached in stock until cooked. Served cold and sliced

collier *(Fr) masc. see* collet

collo *(It)* Neck (of lamb, etc.)

collop 1 *(UK) coll. (Scotland)* A small slice of meat like an escalope **2** *(UK)* A minced beef stew from Scotland **3** Egg fried with bacon

collop, to To cut into small pieces

colmenilla *(Sp)* Morel

colo de castra *(It)* A Venetian dish of mutton, stewed with celery and onions and served with rice and peas

Colocasia esculenta *Bot.* The taro plant

colocassa A Mediterranean tuber of the *Colocasia* spp., similar in size to a small pointed swede up to 2 kg in weight with a rough, light brown skin and a starchy, bland, white flesh similar to the eddoe. Used in stews or fried [also called **cologassi, kolocassi**]

cologassi *see* colocassa

colomba *(It)* Dove-shaped Easter cake

colombaccio *(It)* Wood pigeon

colombian coffee A smooth strong coffee from Colombia

colombière *(Fr)* A soft cows' milk cheese from Savoie cast in the shape of a dish with a mild smooth paste

colombo *(It)* Wood pigeon

colon The large intestine of an animal used as a casing for sausages

colorau *(Po)* Dried and powdered red pepper made from a reasonably hot variety of capsicum

colorau-doce *(Po)* Paprika

colostro *(It)* Colostrum, beestings

colostrum The first liquid obtained from the mammary gland after an animal has given birth. It is extremely nutritious and health promoting and is used by farmers as a miracle cure for new born animals in difficulty. See beestings

colour, to To give colour to food by the addtion of natural or artificial food colourings or by heating to produce a brown colour by caramelization or Maillard reactions

coltsfoot The green stalks of the coltsfoot plant *Tussilago farfara* are rinsed, dry salted for 10 minutes to draw out the juices, rinsed, the outer fibrous covering stripped off and eaten as rhubarb, generally only in the east [also called **bog rhubarb**]

Colwick *(UK)* A soft, white, creamy, slightly acid cow's milk cheese from England

colza *(It, Sp & Fr) masc.* Rape *Brassica napus* used for its leaves and young shoots or for its oil seeds

colza oil *see* rapeseed oil

com *(Vi)* Cooked rice

comal *(Me)* The terracotta griddle on which tortillas are baked

combavas *(Fr)* Makrut lime, the fruit

comber 1 A seawater fish of the perch family *Serranus cabrilla* [also called **sea perch**] **2** *(Ir)* A very sweet, fine potato from Ireland which when new can be eaten as a dish in its own right

combination oven A standard fan-assisted electric oven combined with a microwave energy source to give very fast cooking together with the surface browning and hardening of a conventional oven

combine, to To mix ingredients together

comfrey A hardy herbaceous perennial herb *Symphytum officinale* rarely used nowadays. The young leaves can be used in salads and the stems blanched and cooked like asparagus. The leaves contain more protein than any other known member of the vegetable kingdom and are commonly used as an organic fertilizer

comida *(Sp)* Lunch

comino *(It, Me & Sp)* Cumin

comino dei prati *(It)* Caraway seed

çömlek kebabi *(Tu)* A lamb and mixed vegetable casserole served with boiled potatoes or rice pilaf

commercial beef *(USA)* Beef from old animal used for manufacturing, more flavoursome than standard grade [also called **utility beef**]

commis chef A junior chef, assistant to the chef de partie

commis waiter An assistant to a station waiter

common crab The common decapod crustacean *Cancer pagurus* found from Norway to Spain in the North Atlantic. It has a generally mottled brownish red shell with ten legs, two of which have developed into muscular claws, a tail which is tucked underneath the body; it is up to 20 cm. in diameter. The shell is shed periodically to allow the animal to grow. The edible parts, which must be cooked in salted water (35 g salt per litre), consist of white muscular tissue and a soft brown tissue. The grey feather-like gills (dead man's fingers), the mouth and the stomach bag and all its green to grey-white contents are discarded. Often served in the shell. It is illegal to sell juvenile crabs (less than 13 cm across) or gravid females in the UK [also called **edible crab**]

common eel *see* eel

common flounder *see* winter flounder

common hare A hare *Lepus europaeus* distributed across the whole of Europe through to eastern Asia [also called **brown hare**]

common jack *see* crevalle jack

common ling *see* ling

common mandarin An extensive group of mandarins *Citrus reticulata* of which the clementine is perhaps the best known. The fanciful origin *(see clementine)* is not thought to be correct and it is probably the same fruit as the mandarin grown in southern China. It is grown extensively in Spain and Morocco and seedless varieties have been developed in Spain

common marjoram *see* oregano

common millet A temperate climate millet *Panicum miliaceum* mainly used as birdseed and animal feed in the west but can be made into an unleavened bread [also called **broom corn, hog millet, proso, Indian millet**]

common morel *see* morel

common mushroom The most common cultivated mushroom *Agaricus bisporus* , also found in the wild. It has a light creamy coloured top with a definite skin and brown gills underneath the cap. Sold as button (completely closed cap with no gills showing), cup (half open cap) and flat (fully mature open cap)

common mussel The usually dark blue to black crescent-shaped bivalve *Mytilus edulis* with orange flesh grown extensively around the Atlantic coast in unpolluted seawater. They are also found in the wild but these are suspect because of pollution. If purchased live the shells should be tightly closed or close when tapped and only those which open when heated should be used

common orange A type of sweet orange which comprises a large and diverse group with a wide range of qualities but generally paler than navels and with many seeds. Usually suitable for processing into juice. The best known of this group is the Valencia although the Shamouti *(Jaffa or Cyprus)* is quite common and there are at least 20 varieties traded widely

common otter shell clam A white to light yellow clam with a long shell up to 12.5 cm

common prawn The main British and Western European prawn *Palaemon serratus* fished extensively from Norway down to Spain. It reaches a maximum length of 9 cm and is translucent when alive

common puffball The edible pear-shaped or pestle-like fruiting body of a fungus *Lycoperdon perlatum* which when young is densely covered with spines or loose cone shaped warts which leave their marks on the older fungus. Grows profusely up to 8 cm tall and 5 cm dia. Eaten when young before the centre becomes full of spores

common purslane *see* summer purslane

common skate A European skate *Raja batis* with a long pointed snout and smooth greenish brown skin with spots. The eyes are on the upper side with the mouth and gills on the lower. The medium oily white flesh which is taken from the wings has a good flavour and may be cooked in any way [also called **tinker skate**]

common snook A pike-like game fish *Centropus undecimalis* caught off the coast of Florida, USA

common sturgeon A large sturgeon *Acipenser sturio* which can grow to 60 kg and is found in the Caspian sea, Black sea, Mediterranean and the western Atlantic. It has a firm white to pink flesh which may be baked, grilled or smoked. The roe, which may amount to up to 22 kg from a single female, is processed into caviar mainly in Russia and Iran. The Atlantic sturgeon is now only found in the Gironde estuary and is currently an endangered species. Captive breeding is being attempted

composé(e) *(Fr)* Arranged with several elements as for e.g. in salade composée

composta *(It)* Compote of fruit, stewed fruit

composto *(It)* Composed, compound (of a salad, etc.)

compota *(Po & Sp)* Jam and stewed fruits.

compote *(En & Fr) fem.* **1** Stewed fruit **2** A stew made from game birds such as pigeon or partridge, cooked until the meat is very tender

compote d'abricots à la minute *(Fr) fem.* Halved apricots boiled in sugar syrup for 3 minutes, skimmed and orange juice added

compotier *(Fr) masc.* A large shallow glass dish on a raised stem and base, used to serve fruit compotes and other desserts

compound butter Butter flavoured by pounding it with herbs, shells, spices, etc. then sieving out any inedible or unwanted bits. Usually formed into a roll, refrigerated and cut in slices to finish hot dishes for presentation. usually written as beurre followed by the name of the flavouring e.g. beurre d'amande, beurre de paprika. All are listed under beurre and/or the English name of the flavouring

compressed yeast *(USA)* Small greyish cakes of compressed live yeast weighing about 18 g, used in baking

Comté *(Fr) masc.* A hard, cooked-curd Gruyère type cheese produced from cow's milk in Franche-Comté, with AOC status. It has an aromatic nutty-flavoured soft paste with medium sized holes. Used as a cooking cheese or for dessert [also called **Gruyère de Comté**]

comuna *(Sp)* Common orange

comune *(It)* Common orange

concas peregrina *(Sp)* Coquille Saint-Jacques (scallop)

concassé(e) *(Fr)* Chopped or crushed as in tomates concassées; past participle of concasser, to crush or to grind

conch A large sea snail with a spirally coiled shell found on the Central American and Florida coast. The tough flesh requires tenderizing

concha *(Sp)* Mussel, scallop

concha de peregrino *(Sp)* Scallop

conchiglia *(It)* **1** Shellfish **2** Shell-shaped pasta

conchiglia di San Giacomo *(It)* Coquille Saint-Jacques (scallop)

conchiglie *(It)* **1** Shells, esp. scallop shells used as containers for hot dishes **2** Pasta shaped like a half shell (not the conch shell) **3** Small shell-shaped citron-flavoured cakes from Sicily

conchigliette *(It)* Small pasta shells used in soup

con chom chom *(Vi)* Sea urchin

concombre *(Fr) masc.* Cucumber

concombre salé *(Fr) masc.* Pickled cucumber

Condé *(Fr) masc.* A dessert made from individual portions of dessert rice or pastry topped with canned or poached fruit, glazed with jam and decorated with whipped cream; *see also* condés au fromage

condensed milk Milk from which about 85 to 90% of the water has been removed to leave an evaporated milk containing 45 to 50% water, to this is added about 70 g of sugar per 100 g of evaporated milk to give a thick sticky liquid containing about 55% sugar including lactose, and 28% water which is thus resistant to bacterial contamination. Available in both full cream and skimmed versions. the skimmed version containing about 60% sugar in the resulting mixture

condés au fromage *(Fr) masc.* Puff pastry rectangles, covered with an egg-enriched Béchamel sauce, seasoned with Cayenne pepper and mixed with finely diced cheese and baked in a hot oven

condiment *(En & Fr) masc.* Seasoning, usually salt, pepper, nutmeg, various pasty or dry mixtures of herbs and/or spices, sometimes pickles, individually added to food by the eater after it is served

condimento *(It & Sp)* Seasoning, condiment

condito *(It)* Seasoned or dressed

cone *see* cornet

conejo *(Sp)* Rabbit

conejo frito a la Catalina *(Sp)* Rabbit, marinated in vinegar and white wine then fried

conejo a la Gallega *(Sp)* Rabbit fried with onions and tomatoes

coney **1** *(UK) coll.* Rabbit **2** *(USA)* A hot dog

confectioner's custard *see* crème pâtissière

confectioner's sugar *(USA)* Icing sugar containing a little cornstarch [also called **powdered sugar**]

confeitado *(Po)* Candied [also called **conservado**]

confettura *(It)* Jam

confit(e) *(Fr) masc.* **1** Well cooked meat, particularly duck, goose or pork, preserved in its own fat **2** Fruits cooked and preserved in brandy or a sweetened liquor; vegetables preserved in vinegar or pickled

confit d'oie *(Fr) masc.* Slices of cooked goose breast preserved in goose fat

confiture *(Fr) fem.* Jam or marmalade

confiture d'abricots *(Fr) fem.* Apricot jam

confiture d'oranges *(Fr) fem.* Orange marmalade

cong *(Ch)* Scallion or spring onion.

cong bao yan grou *(Ch)* Stir fried lamb and spring onions

congeal, to To become stiff or jelly-like owing to a drop in temperature

congee The standard breakfast dish of the Chinese consisting of a gruel of well soaked rice boiled with salt and water, flavoured by sprinkling sweet or savoury ingredients over the surface [also called **rice gruel, rice soup**]

congelato *(It)* Frozen

congeler *(Fr)* To freeze or deep freeze

conger eel A seawater eel *Conger conger* which grows up to 2 metres long with an oily, coarse, well-flavoured firm flesh, usually sold in steaks

conger pie *(UK)* Conger eel poached in a seasoned stock and red wine, skinned, deboned and laid in a buttered ovenproof dish over a bed of sweated onions and garlic, and covered with the poaching liquor, thickened if required. It is then topped with potatoes creamed with milk and egg yolks and lightened with stiffly beaten white of egg, the whole gratinated with grated Cheddar cheese and baked in a 200°C oven for 20 minutes

congou Black tea from China sometimes used in blended tea

congre *(Fr) masc.* Conger eel [also called **anguille de mer**]

congress tart A small pastry tart spread with jam and filled with a mixture of ground almonds, sugar and egg prior to baking

congrio *(Sp)* Conger eel

congro *(Po)* Conger eel

cong tou *(Ch)* Onion

coniglio *(It)* Rabbit

coniglio alla reggiana *(It)* Jointed rabbit browned in oil and lard or bacon fat, reserved, chopped onion browned in the same fat, chopped and crushed garlic, chopped celery and tomato concassée added and simmered followed by dry white wine and the reserved rabbit, seasoned and all simmered until the rabbit is tender. Finished with chopped chervil or parsley

conkies A sweet or savoury cornmeal and grated coconut mixture from the Caribbean, wrapped in a banana leaf and steamed [also called **paimi**]

connective tissue The structural material of the animal body normally seen as cartilage, sinew or gristle in meat but also present in bone and as the inner layer of skin, etc. It consists mainly of proteins principally collagen fibres interlaced with elastin fibres embedded in a gel. The more elastin the less soluble is the tissue

con poy *(Ch)* Dried slices of a type of scallop with a distinctive flavour. Very expensive and used like truffles in western cooking

conserva *(It)* **1** Preserve or jam made from fruit or vegetables **2** Tinned

conserva de fruta *(Po)* Jam

conserva di frutta *(It)* Jam

conservado *(Po) see* confeitado

conservare in iscatola *(It)* To can

conserve Fruits preserved in sugar, usually as a jellied mixture which may or may not contain distinct pieces of fruit. The jelling properties come from pectin, the vegetable equivalent of gelatine. Jam and marmalade are examples

conserve, en *(Fr)* In a tin, canned

conserve, petit-pois en *(Fr)* Tinned peas

conserves *(USA)* Elaborate jams with additions such as nuts, raisins, liqueurs, etc.

conserves au vinaigre *(Fr) fem.* Pickles

consistency The property of a mixture which determines its flow or cutting properties. The word is usually qualified as e.g. coating consistency, dropping consistency, thick consistency, jam-like consistency, buttery consistency, etc.

consistency of cheese Cheeses are classified as soft, semi-hard or hard according to their consistency

consommé *(En & Fr) masc.* A transparent clear soup made from a well-flavoured meat, fish, chicken or vegetable stock, simmered without stirring or disturbance with the appropriate minced flesh and/or vegetables mixed with egg whites for 2 hours and carefully strained. Will usually set when cold and as such is sometimes chopped and used as a garnish [also called **clear soup**]

consommé brunoise *(En &Fr) masc.* As consommé julienne with the same vegetables cut as a brunoise

consommé celestine *(En & Fr) masc.* Hot consommé with the addition at the last moment of a julienne of pancake, the pancake seasoned and flavoured with chopped parsley, tarragon and chervil

consommé julienne *(En & Fr) masc.* A hot consommé garnished at the last moment with a julienne of carrot, turnip and leek previously cooked in salted water and refreshed

consommé madrilène *(En & Fr) masc.* A basic consommé well-flavoured with tomato and celery and garnished with a brunoise of skinned and deseeded tomato flesh just before serving

consommé aux profiteroles *(En & Fr) masc.* A hot consommé with unsweetened choux paste piped into pea sized pieces, baked and added to it at the last moment

consommé à la royale *(En & Fr) masc.* A hot consommé garnished with royale shapes

consommé en tasse *(En & Fr) masc.* Cold consommé served lightly jellied in a cup. If there is not sufficient natural gelatine, more may be added

consommé vermicelle *(En & Fr) masc.* Hot consommé with cooked and refreshed vermicelli added at the last moment

consommé des viveurs *(Fr) masc. see* viveur-en-tasse

conta *(Po)* The bill in a restaurant

conti, à la *(Fr)* Garnished with a bacon and lentil purée, usually used of joints of meat

continental breakfast A small breakfast consisting of bread rolls, croissants or toast with butter and jam or marmalade plus a hot drink of coffee, chocolate or tea

continental sausage Sausages usually made from 100% meat which are traditionally preserved by the addition of small amounts of glucose on which *Lactobacillus* spp. grow and reduce the pH by producing lactic acid. They are also ripened by the surface growth of aspergillus and penicillium moulds

continuous phase That phase in a two or more phase mixture which is continuously interconnected, e.g. vinegar is the continuous phase in mayonnaise and hollandaise sauces, butterfat in butter and milk in cream; *see also* dispersed phase, emulsion

contiser *(Fr)* To make small incisions in food in which to insert small pieces of solid flavouring as e.g. garlic slivers, truffle, tongue, etc.; *see also* piquer

conto *(It)* The bill in a restaurant

contorno *(It)* Vegetable dish or side dish, vegetable garnish

contre-filet *(Fr) masc.* Sirloin off the bone [also called **faux-filet**]

controfiletto di bue *(It)* Sirloin of beef

convenience food Food which allegedly needs little preparation prior to serving. It may be a chilled, non-sterile cooked meal or a vacuum-packed fully cooked meal. Other forms require the addition of eggs, milk, water, etc. or elaborate mixing, heating and stirring, often taking as long to prepare as the same dish cooked with fresh ingredients purchased in semi-processed form

converted rice Rice which has been soaked and steamed before being hulled. This preserves more of the nutrients from the outer coat in the polished grain which is yellow but whitens on cooking. The process does not shorten the cooking time [also called **parboiled rice**]

con vich *(Vi)* Turtle

coo-coo *(Ca)* A cooked paste of cornmeal or breadfruit, okra and water, served with fish esp. in Barbados [also called **cou-cou**]

cook A person who prepares food for eating

cook, to To make food flavoursome, edible and digestible usually, but not necessarily, by subjecting it to heat

cook out, to To completely finish the cooking process so that no suggestion of the uncooked food remains. Used esp. of starch-thickened sauces, soups, etc.

cooked cheese Cheese made from curdled milk which has been cooked before the whey is separated from the curds

cooked curd Curd for cheese which has been heated to temperatures greater than 48°C; *see also* scalded curd

cooker An appliance for cooking food by the application of heat or other type of energy, usually self contained

cookie 1 *(USA)* A biscuit **2** *(UK)* A Scottish name for a glazed bread roll made from enriched yeast dough containing dried vine fruits

cooking apple *(UK)* A variety of apple, usually large, as e.g. the Bramley, which usually goes soft when cooked, particularly suitable for stewing and baking, generally with a tart flavour

cooking chocolate Unsweetened chocolate available in block form or as chips. Not to be confused with the cheap, brown chocolate-flavoured substance often sold as such

cooking fat Normally a white, hard and tasteless unsalted fat made by hydrogenation of deodorized vegetable or fish oils

cooking foil *see* aluminium foil

cook's knife A heavy, easily sharpened, well balanced, steel bladed knife with a substantial handle, sharpened on one edge, broad near the handle and tapering to a point and with a convex curve to the blade so that it can be used for chopping with a rocking motion

cool, to To reduce the temperature of food by a variety of means e.g. placing in a refrigerator, plunging in cold water, adding ice cubes, standing a container in cold water, etc.

coon *(USA)* A strong tasting Cheddar type cheese made from cow's milk

copeau *(Fr) masc.* Pastry twist. Lit. shaving

copeaux de chocolat *(Fr) masc.* Chocolate shavings used for decoration

coperto *(It)* **1** Cover charge in a restaurant **2** Covered with some ingredient e.g. a slice of cheese

copha *(Aus)* A white shortening made from hardened vegetable oils

copocolla *(It)* A sausage made from chunks of mildly cured shoulder pork, sometimes air dried before being mixed with finely minced fat pork, red sweet peppers, seasoning and spices and packed in beef casings

copollotto The boiled bulbs of grape hyacinth served in a sweet and sour sauce [also called **labascione**]

copos de avena *(Sp)* Rolled oats

coppa 1 A salted pork slicing sausage, dried and smoked with herbs; from Corsica **2** *(It)* A rather fatty ham cut from the shoulder **3** A large sausage containing distinct pieces of shoulder pork and pork fat obtained from pigs fed on chestnuts **4** *(It)* Bowl or cup

coppa di Corse *(It)* Smoked ham produced in Corsica

coppa cotta *(It)* A type of brawn made from the meat of pig's heads and tongues, pressed until set into a solid mass

coppa gelata *(It)* Mixed ice creams

copper A trace element necessary for health. Sufficient is usually obtained from water that has been delivered via copper pipes

copper pan The type of pan generally used in high class kitchens made of thick copper with a tin lining. The copper makes for even and quick distribution of heat and uniformity of temperature

copra The white inner meat of the coconut. Used fresh or grated and dried in cooking. The dried copra is traded internationally as a source of oil and animal feed

Coprinus comatus *Bot.* Shaggy ink cap

coq *(Fr) masc.* Male of a bird, esp. of a chicken, cockerel

coq à la bière *(Fr) masc.* As coq au vin but cooked in beer and flavoured with juniper berries. From the north

coq de bruyère *(Fr) masc.* Grand *(large)* capercaillie or petit *(small)* black grouse

coq en pâte *(Fr) masc.* Chicken pie

coq au vin *(Fr) masc.* Chicken, possibly previously marinated, simmered in red wine with brandy, onions, carrots, garlic and BG and sometimes bacon, garnished with glazed button onions, glazed button mushrooms and croûtons

coq au vin jaune *(Fr) masc.* Chicken stewed with fungi, cream and the local white wine from Arbois

coque *(Fr) fem.* **1** Shell of an egg **2** Cockle **3** An Easter cake made from a brioche dough flavoured with citron

coque, à la *(Fr)* Cooked in its shell, esp. of an egg

coquelet *(Fr) masc.* A young cock chicken around 1 kg

coquillage *(Fr) masc.* Shellfish

coquille *(Fr) fem.* Shell of an egg, nut, mollusc, etc.

coquille, en *(Fr)* Cooked in a scallop shell

coquille Saint Jacques 1 *(En & Fr) fem.* The commonest European scallop *Pecten jacobaeus* [also called **pilgrim scallop**] **2** *(En & Fr) fem.* Halved scallops, poached in seasoned milk, reserved, a thick velouté sauce made with sliced mushrooms and the cooking liquor, cooked out, scallops and sherry added and the mixture spooned onto scallop shells and gratinated with a mixture of breadcrumbs, grated cheese and dry mustard. Garnished with lemon twists and picked parsley

coquina 1 *(Sp)* Wedge shell clam **2** *(USA)* Winkle, the shellfish

coquito nut *(SA)* Small immature coconuts which are eaten whole

corail *(Fr) masc.* Coral, eggs of shellfish and crustaceans. See entry under coral

coral The ovaries and eggs of the female lobster which turn a brilliant red when cooked and are used in the sauce to accompany lobster dishes

corallo *(It)* Lobster coral

coratella *(It)* Offal, also a stew of lambs' lungs, liver and heart

coratella de agnello alla sarda *(It)* Lamb offal interspersed with slices of ham, threaded on a skewer, wrapped in pig's caul or intestine and grilled

corazón *(Sp)* Heart

çorba *(Tu)* Soup

corbeille de fruits *(Fr) fem.* Basket of fruit

corbina *(USA)* A fish of the drum family [also called **corvina**]

Corchorus olitorius *Bot.* The meloukhia plant

cordeiro *(Po)* Lamb

cordero *(Sp)* Lamb

cordero en ájillo *(Sp)* Lamb fried with garlic, pepper and saffron

cordero asado *(Sp)* Roast lamb

cordero lechazo *(Sp)* Suckling lamb

cordero a la manchego *(Sp)* Lamb casseroled in wine and garlic, served with fried sweet peppers and garnished with chopped parsley

cordon *(En & Fr) masc.* A line of sauce or gravy poured around an item of food on a dish

cordon bleu 1 *(Fr) masc.* A style of cooking based on classic French cooking taught by some French and English cookery schools or a description of a person so trained. Often part of the 'finishing' education of children of the wealthy **2** *see* escalope cordon bleu

core, to 1 To remove the inedible centre of fruits which contain seeds and seed capsules where there isn't a distinct stone, using a cylindrical corer and without damaging the edible part of the fruit **2** To remove the central blood vessels and tubes from a kidney

coregone bondella *(It)* Houting, the fish

coregone laverello *(It)* Pollan, the fish

coriander An annual plant *Coriandrum sativum* cultivated worldwide for its leaves, seeds and roots. The leaves look like flat parsley and have a slightly soapy herb-like flavour and are used as a herb. The small, brown, round seeds (3 to 4 mm dia.) have a mild sweet spicy flavour quite different to the leaves with a hint of pepper and aniseed and are used extensively throughout the world as a whole or ground spice. The roots are used as a vegetable and also as a flavouring in Thai cooking [also called **Chinese parsley** *(leaves only)*, **cilantro**]

coriandre *(Fr) fem.* Coriander

coriandro *(Sp)* Coriander

Coriandrum sativum *Bot.* Coriander

corindolo *(It)* Coriander

corkscrew greens *see* fiddlehead fern

corn A general term once used of all grains such as wheat, oats, barley, rye, maize, etc. but now used only of wheat in Europe and of maize in the USA

corn bread *(USA)* A deep yellow coloured bread made with a mixture of cornmeal from flint corn and flour

corn chips *see* tortilla chips

corn on the cob A complete cob of sweet corn, (a variety of maize), boiled, leaves removed and kernels eaten with salt and butter [also called **sweet corn**]

corn dog *(USA)* A Frankfurter dipped in a cornmeal batter, deep fried until crisp and presented on a stick

corn-fed chicken Chicken fed principally on yellow maize which gives its skin and flesh a yellow colour

corn flakes A popular breakfast cereal made from small blobs of cooked and flavoured maize porridge, flattened, crisped and toasted to a golden colour

corn flour 1 *(UK)* Pure starch powder extracted from maize kernels. It blends easily with water without forming lumps and thickens into a translucent paste. Used for blancmange, English custard, for thickening sauces and gravies and to give a lighter shorter texture to some cakes and biscuits. It is a common thickening agent and source of starch in Chinese cooking [also called **cornstarch** (USA)] **2** *(USA)* Ground corn which can be white or yellow. When used in baking it must be used with gluten-rich flours

corn fritter *(USA)* Sweet corn kernels bound in batter and deep fried. Served hot with chicken Maryland

corn oil A light delicately flavoured vegetable oil extracted from the germ of maize kernels. Contains 15% saturated, 35% monounsaturated and 50% polyunsaturated fat. [also called **maize oil**]

corn pone *(USA)* An unleavened cornmeal bread made from dent corn, fried or baked

corn salad *see* lamb's lettuce

corn starch *(USA)* Cornflour

corn sugar *(USA)* Sugar, principally glucose, crystallized from acid hydrolysed cornstarch. Less sweet than sucrose

corn syrup 1 Hydrolysed maize starch consisting mainly of glucose. Used as a general liquid sweetener in drinks and manufactured foods **2** *(USA)* Golden syrup [also called **light syrup, light corn syrup**]

corncrake A small game bird *Crex crex* which migrates from Northern Europe to Africa during the winter

corne *(Fr) fem.* A horn shaped brioche from Nantes

corne grecque *(Fr) fem.* Okra

corned beef Beef that has been cooked and preserved in salt together with some sodium nitrite to give it a pink colour. Usually sold in tins. So called from the corns (small crystals) of salt used in the curing [also called **bully beef**]

corned beef hash *(USA)* A mixture of coarsely mashed potatoes, chopped corned beef and cooked chopped onion formed into a cake and shallow fried on each side until browned. Topped with a poached egg and served with toast and chilli sauce

corned bief *(Ho)* Corned beef

Corneli bread *(USA)* A high protein bread developed at Cornell university containing soya bean flour, wheat germ and dried skimmed milk solids

corner of gammon A triangular piece of meat cut from a gammon

cornes de gazelle *(NA)* Croissant-like pastries filled with honey and almonds

cornet A large cone shape (to 12 cm by 4 cm dia.) made with a wafer mixture in which ice cream is served so that it can be eaten as a snack [also called **cone**]

cornetti *(It)* **1** Sweet breakfast bread rolls **2** Pastry horns usually filled with cream

cornichon *(Fr) masc.* Gherkin

Cornish fairings *(UK)* Crisp and spicy biscuits from Cornwall enriched with butter and sweetened with brown sugar and golden syrup

Cornish heavy cake *(UK)* A cake from Cornwall made from a lard based puff pastry containing currants [also called **heavy cake**]

Cornish hog pudding *(UK) see* hog pudding

Cornish pasty *(UK)* A pasty made from a rolled out circle of short pastry, preferably made with strong flour filled with diced raw skirt steak and vegetables (turnips, potatoes and onions), the opposite edges of the circle brought together over the filling, sealed, fluted and the whole then baked. Originally used by Cornish miners as a complete meal. It is said that a genuine Cornish pasty can be dropped down a mine shaft and not break

Cornish saffron cake *(UK)* A fruited yeast-raised cake flavoured with saffron, baked in a deep round tin, sliced and buttered when cold [also called **saffron cake**]

Cornish sly cake *(UK)* Currants, chopped mixed peel, spices and sugar sandwiched between layers of flaky pastry, the whole rolled out until the currants just show, sprinkled with caster sugar, cut into fancy shapes and baked [also called **sly cake, fig sly cake**]

Cornish yarg *(UK)* A creamy mild flavoured cheese made from cow's milk and generally covered with nettles

cornmeal *(USA)* White, yellow or rarely blue, dried maize kernels ground to varying degrees of fineness

corona, alla *(It)* Ring-shaped

coronation chicken A cold dish made from diced, cooked chicken meat mixed with mayonnaise, chopped tomatoes, onions and apricots, whipped cream and flavoured with curry powder, lemon and bay

corps, qui a du *(Fr)* With body, as applied to sauces and soups

correlet *(Fr) masc.* Dab, the fish

Corsican citron A citron lacking acidity with a very rough and bumpy ridged skin

Corsican mint A type of mint *Mentha requiena* with tiny peppermint-scented bright green leaves and tiny flowers. Grows only to 3 cm

corvina *(USA) see* corbina

corvino *(Po)* Croaker, the fish

Corylus avellina *Bot.* Hazelnut

Corylus colurna *Bot.* Turkish hazelnut

Corylus maxima *Bot.* Filbert

cos lettuce A type of lettuce with long, substantial and well-flavoured leaves and with a fairly loose heart [also called **romaine lettuce** (USA)]

coscetta *(It)* Leg of lamb or poultry

coscia *(It)* Haunch (of venison), leg (of lamb, goat, etc.)

coscia di montone *(It)* Leg of lamb

cosciotto *(It)* Leg of lamb

costalame di bue *(It)* Ribs of beef

costata *(It)* Rib chop

costeleta *(Po)* Cutlet or boned out chop

costeleta de carne *(Po)* Chop, of an animal

costeletas de carneiro *(Po)* Mutton chops

costeletas de porco *(Po)* Pork chops

costillas *(Sp)* Chops, ribs

costmary A bitter mint-flavoured herb *Tanacetum balsamita* resembling tansy, once used in beer making. Can be used sparingly as a culinary herb [also called **alecost**]

costole *(It)* Ribs

costoletta *(It)* Cutlet

côte *(Fr) fem.* Rib (beef), cutlet (veal, lamb), chop (mutton, pork)

côte d'agneau *(Fr) fem.* Lamb chop

côte de boeuf *(Fr) fem.* Rib of beef

côte de porc bruxelloise *(Be)* Pork chop served with a large amount of endive

côte de porc fumée *(Fr) fem.* Smoked bacon

côte première *(Fr) fem.* Loin chop

cotechino *(It)* A large cooking sausage made with lean and fat pork, white wine, spices and seasoning, usually simmered and served with polenta, mashed potatoes or lentils. Used in bollito misto

coteghino *(It)* A stew made with pork skin

côtelette *(Fr) fem.* Chop or cutlet

côtelettes decouvertes *(Fr) fem.* The ribs between the best end of lamb or veal and the neck which are hidden behind the shoulder blade cut into cutlets. Equivalent of scrag end

côtelettes premières *(Fr)* Fem. The first four ribs of lamb or veal counting from the rear of the animal equivalent to the best end, divided into cutlets

côtes couvertes *(Fr) fem.* Rolled rib of beef from the middle and chuck rib end. Usually slow roasted or braised

côtes premières *(Fr) fem.* Best end of lamb or veal used for roasting in the piece

côtes secondes *(Fr) fem.* The four ribs next to the best end of lamb or veal used for roasting in the piece

Cotherstone *(UK)* A white loose-textured cheese with a clean fresh flavour, made in Yorkshire from unpasteurized cow's milk

cotiche *(It)* Pork rind

cotignac *(Fr) masc.* A thick quince and apple jelly eaten as a confectionery item

cotochinjos *(Br)* Parboiled chicken legs, coated in a paste of tapioca cooked in stock, deep fried and served with a tomato sauce

cotogno *(It)* Quince

cotolette *(It)* Chops, cutlets

cotriade *(Fr) fem.* A fish stew from Brittany using a fish stock made from wine, water, sweated finely chopped onions, a BG and the fish heads and trimmings, all strained through a coarse colander, sliced or whole potatoes simmered in the stock for 30 minutes, pieces of various fish added and simmered a further 12 minutes, the broth then separated, finished with cream and served over toasted bread, the fish and potatoes served as a separate course

Cotswold cheese *(UK)* A type of double Gloucester cheese flavoured with chopped chives and/or onions

cottage cheese A low fat, very loose textured, soft mild cheese made of small white curds which have been repeatedly washed and drained and not pressed or matured. Popular in the USA and Europe. Contains 75 to 80% water, 3 to 5% fat and 15 to 16% protein

cottage loaf A white yeasted bread made from a large sphere of dough on which is placed and secured a small sphere, the whole proven and baked on a flat baking tray

cottage pie Stewed minced beef and onions in a thick gravy placed in a basin, topped with a layer of mashed potatoes whose surface is roughened with a fork, the whole then baked in the oven until browned

cottage potatoes *(USA)* Cold cooked potatoes, diced or sliced, fried in butter without stirring until brown on one side, then turned over and browned on the other side [also called **country fried potatoes**]

cottage pudding *(USA)* Plain cake covered with a hot sweet pudding sauce

cotto 1 *(USA)* A type of salami containing pork and peppercorns. Abbreviated from salame cotto *(cooked salami)* **2** *(It)* Cooked

cotton bean curd *see* momen tofu

cotton thistle The true Scottish thistle, a hardy biennial *Onopordum acanthium* which can grow to 2.5 m. The young stems may be blanched, peeled and used like asparagus. The large flower heads may be cooked like globe artichokes

cottonseed flour A high protein flour (about 40%) often used to enrich bread

cottonseed oil Oil extracted from cotton seeds used in the fish canning industry

cotufa *(Sp)* Jerusalem artichoke

coturnice *(It)* Partridge, quail

cou *(Fr) masc.* **1** Neck, of chicken, etc. **2** Scrag end of lamb or veal, not the neck

cou-cou *see* coo-coo

cou nu *(Fr)* A breed of chicken with a well-flavoured flesh not suitable for factory farming. Usually free range and maize fed. Lit. bare neck

cou d'oie *(Fr) masc.* A boned neck of goose with intact skin stuffed with a mixture of goose flesh, goose liver and truffles, cooked and preserved in goose fat. Eaten cold as a hors d'oeuvres

couche-couche *(USA)* A Cajun dish of fried corn dough served with jam and milk or cane syrup

coudenac *(Fr)* A pork sausage from the Basque country. Eaten hot

Couhé Vérac *(Fr)* A goats' milk cheese from Poitou which is wrapped in leaves

coulibiac *(Fr) masc.* A fish pie, originally from Russia, of brioche or puff pastry filled with salmon or sturgeon, butter, mushrooms, rice or buckwheat and cream and possibly chopped hard boiled eggs [also called **koulibiac**]

coulis *(En & Fr) masc.* A purée or strongly flavoured thick sauce prepared without starch, of vegetables, tomatoes, meat, fish, etc. but more often of liquidized and sieved fruit, possibly with added sugar, acid or liqueur, consistency adjusted with fruit juice

coulis of shellfish The pounded remains of prawn or crawfish shells, eggs, coral and other remains of lobster or crawfish, mixed with cream and passed through a very fine sieve

Coulommiers *(Fr)* A mild soft creamy cheese made from cow's milk, similar to Brie but cast in smaller (500 g) rounds [also called **Brie de Coulommiers**]

country captain **1** *(In)* A west Bengal Anglo-Indian dish of skinned chicken pieces, browned in oil with sweated onion slices and mixed with a paste blended from fresh ginger, onion, garlic and water together with cayenne pepper, salt, sugar and white vinegar and all cooked until tender **2** *(USA)* A chicken stew adapted from the Indian version with green pepper, onion, garlic, curry powder, herbs, raisins, tomatoes, almonds and seasoning

country fried potatoes *(USA) see* cottage potatoes

country ham *(USA)* Dry cured and highly salted ham

coupe *(En & Fr) fem.* An individual dish of ice cream, decorated and garnished with fruit sauces, fresh and preserved fruit, nuts, whipped cream, crystallized flowers, chopped jelly, etc.

coupe dish A small, goblet shaped glass or metal dish in which cold desserts are assembled and served

coupe glacée *(Fr) fem.* Ice cream sundae

coupe Jacques *(En & Fr) fem.* Strawberry and lemon ice cream topped with Kirsch-soaked fruit and decorated

coupe-oursin *(Fr) masc.* A special tool for cutting sea urchins in half

coupe St-Jacques *(Fr) fem.* Fruit salad topped with vanilla ice cream

couques *(Be)* A heavy, very sweet gingerbread

courge *(Fr) fem.* Squash or gourd

courge à la moelle *(Fr) fem.* Vegetable marrow

courgette *(En & Fr) fem.* The small juvenile version of the vegetable marrow (summer squash, *Cucurbita pepo*) up to 15 cm in length, usually green but yellow cultivars exist. Cooked whole or sliced, boiled, stewed, roasted or fried, used as a raw salad vegetable when very young [also called **zucchini**]

courgette flowers The large, yellow, male flowers of pumpkins, squash and marrows. Must be used very fresh and are often stuffed with flavoured meat or served as fritters [also called **squash blossoms, zucchini flowers**]

couronne *(Fr) fem.* A baguette formed into a circle or torus

couronne, en *(Fr)* In the shape of a ring or torus

couronne de côtelettes d'agneau rôties *(Fr) fem.* Crown roast of lamb made from two best ends

course An individual stage in a meal, particularly in the West, where different classes of food, e.g. soup, meat, desserts, hors d'oeuvres, savouries, cheese, fruit, etc. are served separately

court bouillon *(En & Fr) masc.* A cooking liquor for deep poaching fish consisting of water, vinegar, lemon juice, white wine, a BG and seasoning for the white variety, and malt vinegar, a BG and aromatic vegetables for the brown variety. Brown court bouillon should be cooked and strained before use. Other types are available, see plain court bouillon, white wine court bouillon, red wine court bouillon and salted water. Fish served cold are allowed to cool in the CB

courting cake *(UK)* A Victoria sponge cake in three layers with strawberries and whipped cream filling and sprinkled with icing sugar. Once made in the north of England as evidence of the bride-to-be's pastry skills

couscous *(NA)* **1** A cereal made from fine semolina agglomerated with a little water to form grains about 3 mm across which are coated with fine wheat flour and dried **2** The name of the dish made from couscous which has been moistened with water to make it swell, then steamed, heaped on a plate and covered with steamed vegetables, mutton or chicken, with possibly chickpeas and/or onions glazed in honey

couscous royale *(NA)* Couscous with vegetables and grilled meats or kebabs, all served in separate dishes accompanied with harissa and individually self served by guests

couscousière *(Fr) fem.* An open steamer used for cooking couscous over a pan of stew as it simmers

couteau *(Fr) masc.* **1** Knife, as e.g. couteau de cuisine, kitchen knife **2** Razor shell (UK), Razor shell clam (USA)

couve *(Po)* Cabbage and various *Brassica* spp.

couve de bruxelas *(Po)* Brussel sprouts

couve-flor *(Po)* Cauliflower

couve gallego *see* Portuguese cabbage

couve lombarda *(Po)* Collard greens, kale

couve tronchuda *see* Portuguese cabbage

couvert *(Fr) masc.* Cover, place setting

couverture A high quality chocolate with added cocoa butter to give a high gloss and various proportions of sugar, used for coating confectionery items and cakes and for making caraque. Milk solids are added to milk chocolate couverture

Coventry cakes *(UK)* Oven baked pastry triangles filled with jam and glazed with sugar

Coventry god cakes *(UK)* Oven baked puff pastry triangles filled with fruit mincemeat and glazed with sugar. Eaten at Christmas

cover **1** A place setting for one person in a dining area. Capacities or quantities are often measured in covers **2** A lid of a dish or pan, etc.

cover charge A charge made in a restaurant on a per-capita basis, supposedly to cover the cost of preparing the table for the customer

cow A female of the bovine species usually used for milking and reproduction and then for cheap beef or manufactured beef products

cow heel The foot of a cow which, because of the large amount of collagen in the connective tissue is used to add gelatine to stocks or stews when boiled with them

cow pea An important erect legume *Vigna unguiculata* with pods to 15 cm which originated in Africa where it is grown for the dried seeds which can be black through to white or coloured. Now also grown in the Caribbean and the USA. It can be sprouted or, rarely, cooked in the pod when young. The leaves are sometimes eaten as a vegetable. The long bean q.v. which is common in southern China and SEA has been bred from it [also called **black-eyed bean** (UK), **black-eyed pea** (USA), **black-eyed susie** (USA), **Chinese bean, southern pea** (USA)]

cowberry Large, tart, dark red berries similar to the cranberry, from a shrub *Vaccinium vitisidaea* which grows in the colder high altitude regions of Europe and North America. Popular in Germany and Scandinavia [also called **lingonberry, mountain cranberry**]

cow's udder *see* elder

cowslip A hardy herbaceous perennial *Primula veris* with yellow flowers and a rosette of primrose type leaves. The flowers may be used in jams, pickles or for flavouring desserts. The leaves may be used in salads or for meat stuffings

cozido **1** A Brazilian meat stew **2** *(Po)* Boiled

cozido à portuguesa *(Po)* A Portuguese national dish, being a stew made from brisket or similar cut of beef, bacon, sausage, yams, vegetables, cabbage, haricot beans and rice. The cooking liquor serves as both soup and sauce. The sausage is usually bland e.g. farinheira, but white or black pudding may be substituted. Pigs' ears, tails and trotters are sometimes included [also called **Portuguese boiled dinner**]

cozinha *(Po)* Kitchen

cozze *(It) coll. (southern Italy)* Mussels

cozzula *(It)* A type of bread from Sardinia

crab A short tailed decapod (10 legged) crustacean which yields 38 to 50% of its weight in edible meat. For a detailed description see under common crab; *see also* blue crab, common crab, jonah crab, mud crab, red crab, rock crab, shore crab, snow crab, southern stone crab, spanner crab and spider crab

crab apple The wild version of the apple *Malus pumila* with generally small (to 3 cm dia.) tart and crisp fruits. Used for making jams and preserves

crab backs *(Ca)* A dish of cooked crab meat mixed with fried onions, fried skinned tomatoes, Worcestershire sauce, vinegar and seasoning, served on a crab shell, sprinkled with breadcrumbs and butter and browned in the oven

crab bisque *(USA)* A Louisiana bisque made from a white roux thickened milk base with fried onions, cooked crab meat, sweet corn kernels, Tabasco and Worcestershire sauces and seasoning

crab boil *(USA)* A social occasion at which crabs are boiled in water flavoured with the following whole spices in a BG, black peppercorns, mustard seed, dill seed, coriander seed, cloves, allspice, dried ginger and bay leaf, and then served with accompaniments

crab butter The yellow-white fat which lines the upper shell of the crab. Used in dressings and sauces

crab claws The two large pincer-like claws on either side of the mouth parts. The meat is considered to be the best from the crab

crab au gratin *(USA)* A Louisiana dish of cooked crab meat bound together with a Béchamel sauce mixed with sour cream and seasoning, gratinated with cheese and browned in the oven

crab legs. *(USA)* The legs of the Alaskan king crab which are large enough to be eaten on their own. They do not include the claws

crab Louis *(USA)* A Californian salad of crab meat on a chiffonade of lettuce, coated with Louis sauce and garnished with hard boiled egg and black olives

crab yolk Tomalley

crabe *(Fr) masc.* Crab

crabe froid à l'anglaise *(Fr) masc.* Dressed crab

crabe vert *(Fr) masc.* Shore crab

cracked wheat Coarsely crushed grains of wheat, dry cooked for 25 minutes. Served hot as a breakfast cereal, served as an accompaniment to other dishes or sprinkled on rolls or bread prior to baking [also called **kibbled wheat**]

cracked wheat flour *(USA)* A coarse flour rather like oatmeal which has been cut from the wheat rather than ground and hence does not release starch very readily

cracker *(USA)* The general name given to any type of plain or salted hard biscuit

cracker flour *(USA)* A soft wheat flour with a low water absorption ability

crackling The skin of a pork, bacon or ham joint which has been scored to 3 or 4 mm with a sharp knife in strips or a diamond pattern prior to roasting and which becomes crisp and golden brown if basted with water; it is served as an accompaniment to the roast

cracklins *(USA)* Crackling

cracknel *(USA)* A type of hard crisp plain biscuit made of a paste which is boiled before being baked causing it to puff up

crackseed *(USA)* The bruised and squashed seeds of various fruits which are preserved in salt and sugar. From Hawaii

crakeberry *see* crowberry

Crambe maritima *Bot.* Seakale

cranberry The hard ripe fruits (dia. to 2 cm) of a wild or cultivated evergreen shrub *Vaccinium macrocarpum* which grows in cool regions of the Northern hemisphere. They are deep red in colour, very tart and used in sweet and savoury dishes, the most famous of which is as a sauce accompaniment to turkey [also called **bounceberry, craneberry**]

cranberry sauce Cranberries stewed with water and sugar, liquidized and sieved. Traditionally served with turkey [also called **sauce airelles** (Fr)]

craneberry *see* cranberry

crannokan *(UK)* A Scottish dessert made from raspberries, cream, toasted oatmeal, whisky liqueur and heather honey

cranshaw melon *(USA)* A hybrid of the Persian and the winter melon

crapaud *(Ca)* An edible toad found in Dominica and Montserrat [also called **mountain chicken**]

crapaudine, à la *(Fr)* Refers to a chicken, or other bird, cut horizontally from below the point of the breast over the top of the legs to the wing joints, back bone broken and the whole flattened so that the breast points forward, the legs back and the wings are folded in the centre. It is then grilled and with imagination resembles a toad. Lit toad-like [also called **spatchcock**]

craquelet *(He)* Seasoned pork and beef, processed to a very fine creamy paste, packed into casings, smoked and cooked. Eaten hot or cold

craquelot *(Fr) masc. see* bouffi

Crataegus azarolus *Bot.* Azarole

Craterellus cornucopioides *Bot.* Horn of plenty

crauti *(It)* Sauerkraut

cravo *(Po)* Clove

cravo-de-india *(Po)* Clove

crawfish 1 Spiny lobster **2** *(USA)* Créole term for freshwater crayfish

crayfish 1 Freshwater crustacean resembling lobsters found in unpolluted streams and lakes but now generally farmed. They breed in autumn and are best caught in summer. Cooked as lobster. The European variety *Astacus fluviatilis* is about the size of a Dublin Bay prawn. Some Australian varieties can weigh up to 6 kg. Most make excellent eating. For Australian varieties see Tasmanian crayfish, Murray river crayfish, yabbie and marron; *see also* signal crayfish [also called **crawfish** (USA)] **2** The name often used indiscriminately for crayfish, crawfish and similar crustaceans with or without claws, esp. in the USA

crayfish butter Beurre d'écrivisse

crayfish sauce Hollandaise sauce or sauce vin blanc mixed with beurre d'écrivisse

crayfish, Scandinavian cooking Cleaned live crayfish immersed in just sufficient salted boiling water flavoured with dill flowers to completely cover them, the water brought back to the boil and the crayfish boiled for exactly 3 minutes, drained, refreshed and then left in the cooled cooking liquor for 24 hours

cream The globules of butter fat which rise to the top of milk entrapping larger or smaller amounts of milk. The type is determined by the butterfat content. See half cream, single cream, whipping cream, double cream, extra thick double cream, clotted cream, Jersey cream, etc.

cream, to To beat one or a mixture of ingredients vigorously so as to give it or them the consistency of whipped cream and incorporate air, esp. fat and sugar in cake making

cream of artichoke soup *see* crème Palestine

cream bun *see* cream puff

cream caramel *see* crème caramel

cream cheese A soft, acid curdled spreading cheese made from a mixture of cows' milk and cream. The curds are spun off and milled with stabilizers and preservatives prior to packaging for immediate sale and consumption. Contains between 45% and 65% butter fat [also called **Philadelphia cream cheese**]

cream crackers Light, fawn-coloured, square unsweetened biscuits made from flour, fat, water and salt. Usually eaten with cheese. Nothing to do with cream

cream of green pea soup *see* St Germain, crème

cream horns Cones made from overlapping strips of puff pastry wrapped around conical metal moulds, baked in the oven, cooled, removed from the mould and filled with jam and whipped cream

cream nut *see* Brazil nut

cream puff 1 A round bun of cooked choux pastry, split, centre scooped out if soft, the halves filled with whipped cream or crème pâtissière and sandwiched together then dusted with icing sugar or coated with coffee or chocolate-flavoured soft icing [also called **cream buns**] **2** *(USA)* Profiterole

cream puff pastry *(USA)* Choux pastry

cream sauce Béchamel sauce with the addition of cream, natural yoghurt or fromage blanc. Used for poached fish and boiled vegetables [also called **sauce crème** (Fr)]

cream slices Baked rectangles of puff pastry divided into two rectangles of the same area which are sandwiched together with jam and whipped cream or crème pâtissière and the top covered with soft icing [also called **millefeuilles**]

cream soup A soup made from (a) a vegetable purée soup with added cream, milk or yoghurt, (b) a vegetable purée type of soup mixed with Béchamel sauce or (c) a velouté soup with added cream, milk or yoghurt

cream of tartar Acid potassium tartrate (potassium hydrogen tartrate), a crystalline substance which is precipitated from wine as it ages. Now made synthetically and combined with sodium bicarbonate to make the raising agent baking powder

cream tea *(UK)* An afternoon snack or meal consisting of scones, whipped or clotted cream and jam served with tea. Popular in Devon and Cornwall and country district tourist areas

cream of tomato soup *see* crème de tomates

cream of vegetable soup Vegetable soup with added cream, milk or Béchamel sauce

creamed cakes Cakes made by the creaming method with high proportions of fat, sugar and eggs to flour. Usually require little if any raising agent due to the amounts of air incorporated during preparation. Examples are Madeira cake, rich fruit cake, Victoria sponge [also called **rich cakes**]

creamed coconut *see* coconut cream

creamer 1 A dry white powder made from glucose and vegetable fats used as a substitute for cream or milk in coffee **2** An implement for separating cream from milk

creaming method of making cakes The method of making cakes by vigorously beating together fat and sugar to incorporate air and give a soft, light, fluffy texture, incorporating well beaten eggs slowly with continuous beating to form a stable emulsion, then gently folding in flour and other dry ingredients to avoid losing air. The trapped air expands with steam during the baking and setting process. e.g. Victoria sandwich, fruit cake

crecchietto *(It)* A type of pasta from Apulia

crècy, (à la) *(Fr)* In the style of Crècy, i.e. garnished with or containing carrots

crédioux aux noix *(Fr)* A soft, cooked-curd cows' milk cheese coated with walnut pieces

cree'd wheat *see* frumenty wheat

crema 1 *(It & Sp)* Cream **2** *(It)* Custard, custard cream, dessert **3** *(It)* Cream soup

crema batida *(Sp)* Whipped cream

crema catalana *(Sp)* Crème brûlée

crema española *(Sp)* A dessert made with flavoured and sweetened milk and eggs set with gelatine

crema fritta *(It)* Fried sweet or savoury egg custard cut in diamond shapes

crema pasticceria *(It)* Crème pâtissière, confectioner's custard

crema di pollo *(It)* Cream of chicken soup

crema rovesciata *(It)* Baked egg custard

crema de verdura *(It)* Puréed vegetables possibly including potatoes or cooked rice and finished with cream

creme *(Po)* Cream soup, cream

crème *(Fr) fem.* Cream

crème, à la *(Fr)* With or containing cream

crème Agnés Sorel *(Fr) fem.* A cream of chicken soup garnished with mushroom slices and julienne of tongue

crème aigre *(Fr) fem.* Sour cream

crème d'amandes *(Fr) fem.* Almond cream

crème anglaise *(Fr) fem. see* crème à l'anglaise

crème à l'Anglaise *(Fr) fem.* A thick egg custard made with 16 egg yolks and 500 g of sugar per litre of milk, flavoured as required with vanilla, lemon zest or, after cooling, with liqueur. The sugar and egg are whisked to the ribbon stage and boiling milk added, whisked, and heated to a coating consistency. Must not be boiled. Strained and served hot or cold [also called **sauce anglaise, crème anglaise, English egg custard**]

crème bachique *(Fr) fem.* Cinnamon and sauternes flavoured custard

crème bavaroise *(Fr) fem. see* bavarois

crème beurre *(Fr) fem.* A butter cream for filling or covering cakes made by combining hot sugar syrup with egg yolks, cooling the mixture then whisking it into well creamed butter with flavourings such as chocolate, coffee, vanilla and fruit purée [also called **crème au beurre**]

crème au beurre *(Fr) fem. see* crème beurre

crème brûlée *(Fr) fem.* A thick, rich egg custard baked in individual portions in ramekins, cooled, sprinkled with brown sugar and caramelized under the grill or with a blow torch until crisp

crème caramel *(Fr) fem.* Individual sized ramekins, with a base layer of, or lined with, caramel, filled with egg custard, baked in a bain-marie in the oven, cooled, demoulded on to a plate so that the caramel is on top and decorated or left plain. Sometimes made in a large dish and portioned [also called **cream caramel, caramel cream, French flan, flan** (Po & Sp)]

crème chantilly *(Fr) fem.* Sweetened whipped cream

crème crécy *(Fr) fem.* Creamed carrot soup garnished with plain boiled rice

crème fleurette *(Fr) fem.* Unsweetened whipping cream

crème fouettée *(Fr) fem.* Whipped cream

crème fraîche *(Fr) fem.* A lactobacillus culture of cream with a fresh sour taste, may be used as cream, keeps better and does not separate on boiling

crème frite *(Fr) fem.* A thick flour and egg yolk stiffened, flavoured and sweetened custard, spread 1.5 cm thick, cooled and chilled, cut in shapes, battered or panéed and deep fried. If panéed sprinkled with caster sugar, if battered dredged with icing sugar and glazed under the grill

crème glacée *(Fr) fem.* Ice cream or ice cream sundae

crème moulée *(Fr) fem.* Baked egg custard served cold either in a dish or demoulded

crème d'orge *(Fr) fem.* Soup made with fine barley

crème patisserie *see* crème pâtissière

crème pâtissière *(En & Fr) fem.* Confectioners custard. An egg and flour thickened custard made with sweetened milk flavoured with vanilla (4 eggs and 200 g flour per litre). Used as a filling for flans, cakes, pastries, tarts, etc. The flour prevents the egg from curdling

crème pralinée *(Fr) fem.* Crème pâtissière flavoured with powdered praline

crème renversée *(Fr) fem.* A demoulded crème caramel [also called **cup custard** (USA)]

crème de riz *(Fr) fem.* White soup coloured and thickened with powdered rice

crème à la vanille *(Fr) fem.* A vanilla-flavoured baked egg custard

Crémet Nantais *(Fr)* A soft white unsalted cream cheese from Brittany made with cow's milk

crémeux (euse) *(Fr)* Creamy

cremona mustard *see* mostarda di Cremona

crenata *(USA)* Pine nut

créole *(USA)* A style of cooking developed by the settlers of part French descent from Louisiana using tomatoes, peppers, onions and spices, but see also créole cuisine

créole, à la *(Fr)* In the Creole style, i.e. with rice and possibly tomatoes and sweet peppers

Créole cheese *(USA)* A New Orleans speciality cheese consisting of cottage cheese with double cream

Créole Christmas cake *(Ca)* A dark, rich fruit cake from Trinidad well-flavoured with rum, brandy, port and liqueur [also called **gateau noir**]

Créole crab *(USA)* The meat from freshly boiled crab (10 minutes) fried gently in olive oil, a little water, chopped onion and garlic, lemon juice, seasoning, thyme, bay leaf and a chilli pepper added, then simmered slowly for 30 minutes. Served with boiled rice after discarding the bay, thyme, BG and chilli pepper

Créole cuisine *(USA)* A cooking style developed in the Southern USA combining Caribbean, French, African and Spanish cooking based on shellfish, rice, okra and filé powder

Créole mustard *(USA)* A hot whole grain mustard seed macerated in vinegar

crepe *(It & Po)* Pancake

crêpe *(Fr) fem.* A large thin pancake made with white flour

crêpe dentelle *(Fr) fem.* A very thin pancake from Brittany

crêperie *(Fr) fem.* A restaurant or shop usually with a connection with Brittany which specializes in filled sweet and savoury crêpes and pancakes

crepes do céu *(Po)* Pancakes filled with whipped cream and candied fruit. Lit. Heavenly crêpes

crêpes Parmentier *(Fr) fem.* Potato based pancakes

crêpes Suzette *(Fr) fem.* Small pancakes folded in quarters, simmered in a buttery orange sauce, flamed with brandy and served as a dessert

crépine *(Fr) fem.* Pig's caul

crépinette *(Fr) fem.* **1** A grilled or fried bacon wrapped croquette **2** A ball of seasoned and flavoured minced meat, wrapped in pig's caul or very thin slices of salt pork fat, possibly coated with melted butter and breadcrumbs and baked, grilled or fried [also called **caillette** (Provence)]

crépinettes d'agneau *(Fr) fem.* Crépinettes filled with a mixture of chopped lamb and duxelle bound with espagnole sauce

crépinettes d'agneau à la liégeoise *(Be) fem.* Crépinettes filled with a mixture of chopped lamb, breadcrumbs moistened with milk, sweated chopped onions, seasoning and crushed juniper berries

crépinettes de foie de porc à la vauclusienne *(Fr) fem.* Crépinettes filled with a seasoned mixture of chopped pig's liver, bacon, spinach, onion and stoned black olives, flavoured with chopped parsley and nutmeg, tied and baked in the oven

crépinettes Reine Jeanne *(Fr) fem.* Crépinettes filled with chopped blanched sheep's or calves' brains, duxelle and truffles, bound with a thick Béchamel sauce, panéed with egg white and breadcrumbs, fried and served hot with lemon wedges

crépinettes de volaille *(Fr) fem.* Crepinettes filled with chopped chicken and mushroom, possibly with truffles, bound in a chicken velouté sauce

crèque *(Fr)* Bullace, the fruit

crescent *(USA)* Croissant

crescente *(It)* Dough made with flour, sodium bicarbonate raising agent, salt and milk, rested, rolled into very thin discs which are fried both sides in hot olive oil until they bubble, drained and served hot with a savoury topping

crescentina *(It)* Flat bread made from dough containing pieces of bacon

crescenza *(It)* A soft cow's milk cheese with a buttery texture and no rind from Northern Italy and similar to Stracchino. Contains 57% water, 22% fat and 20% protein

crescione *(It)* Deep fried pasta triangles filled with spinach and cream

crescione di fonte *(It)* Watercress

crescione di giardino *(It)* Cress

crescione dei prati *(It)* Lady's smock

crespella *(It)* A thin stuffed crêpe

crespone *(It)* A salami from Milan made with approximately equal amounts of lean pork, lean beef and pork fat, seasoned and flavoured with garlic and moistened with white wine, packed in fat ends or beef middles, dry salted and air dried

cress A small plant *Lepidium sativum* from Iran. The seeds are grown to the two leaf stage on a 6 cm stalk, generally together with mustard and used in salads or for garnishing. It may be grown for the the young true leaves which are harvested continuously [also called **garden cress, curly cress, peppercress, peppergrass**]

cresson alénois *(Fr) masc.* Land cress

cresson cultivé *(Fr) masc.* Cress

cresson de fontaine *(Fr) masc.* Watercress

cresson d'Inde *(Fr) masc.* Nasturtium

cresson de prés *(Fr) masc.* Lady's smock

cresson de ruisseau *(Fr) masc.* Watercress

cressonnière, purée *(Fr) fem.* A purée parmentier with watercress added with the potatoes, and garnished with blanched and refreshed watercress leaves

cretons 1 *(Fr) masc.* Crackling 2 *(Cn)* A type of rillette from Quebec made from crisped bacon rind simmered with pork, onions, spices and seasoning until soft, thickened with bread crumbs and allowed to set in a mould. Usually served on bread

crevalle *see* crevalle jack

crevalle jack An oily tropical and warm water sea fish *Caranx* spp. with a deep body, bluish green on top, silver underneath, weighing 1 to 3 kg [also called **crevalle, jack, common jack**]

crevette *(Fr) fem.* Brown shrimp

crevette grise *(Fr) fem.* Shrimp

crevette nordique *(Fr) fem.* Deepwater prawn

crevette rose *(Fr) fem.* Common prawn [also called **bouquet**]

crevette rose du large *(Fr) fem.* A large pink king prawn *Parapenaeus longirostris*, caught off Spain, Portugal and in the Mediterranean and up to 16 cm long [also called **red prawn**]

crevette rouge *(Fr) fem.* A large king prawn found in the Mediterranean which is either *Aristeus antennatus* up to 20 cm long with a light red body and a mauve head or *Aristeomorphia foliacea* up to 30 cm and blood red in colour

crevette royale *(Fr) fem. see* caramote

crevettes, sauce aux *(Fr) fem.* Boiling fish velouté, consistency adjusted using fish stock or cream, seasoned, strained and finished with picked shrimps

criadilla de tierra *(Sp)* Truffle, the fungus

criadillas *(Sp)* Sweetbreads, testicles

crimp, to To pinch together, successively along the edges of pastry where two layers meet, as in a covered pie or pasty, so as to seal the pastry and for decoration; *see also* to scallop

crinkled musket *see* barrel bread

criolla, a la *(Sp)* In the South American style

crisp, to To make food brittle and firm e.g. by chilling vegetables, by drying off biscuits or bread in the oven, by soaking in water or commercially with a variety of firming agents

crispbread A, usually rectangular, crisp, light biscuit made from crushed rye or wheat, salt and water, often with a pattern of depressions. Thought to be non-fattening but if buttered, the depressions hold more butter that the equivalent flat biscuit

crisphead lettuce A type of lettuce with very crisp leaves forming a tight solid ball. Called iceberg when the outer leaves are removed

crispito *(Me)* A tightly rolled tortilla, fried or deep fried and eaten with dipping sauces

crisps Thin slices of raw potato deep fried in hot oil until brown and crisp. Nowadays often made with processed potatoes so as to have a regular shape. May be flavoured and seasoned [also called **potato crisps, game chips**]

Crithmum maritimum *Bot.* Samphire

critmo *(It)* Samphire *Crithmum maritimum*

croaker The general term for any of over 200 species of fish which make croaking noises. See e.g. Atlantic croaker

croccante *(It)* Praline

crocche *(It)* Croquette

crocchetta *(It)* Croquette

crocette *(It)* Small cone shaped shellfish

crockery Plates, dishes, cups, etc. and all types of domestic pots, usually of ceramic materials, used at meals

Crocus sativus *Bot.* Saffron

croissant *(Fr) masc.* A light, flaky, crescent shaped breakfast roll made from white, yeast-raised dough interleaved with butter in the same way as puff pastry. Cut in triangular shape, rolled with a point on the outside and bent into a croissant shape before baking

cromesquis *(Fr) masc.* A small cylindrical croquette of minced meat bound with a thick sauce, wrapped in bacon or pig's caul, coated with fritter batter and deep fried. Served as a hors d'oeuvre or light main course [also called **kromeski, kromesky**]

crookneck squash A yellow or orange summer squash with a neck bent into a hook, common in the USA [also called **yellow squash**]

crop A chamber at the bottom of a bird's throat in which food is stored prior to it being passed on to the gizzard for processing

croquant 1 *adj. (Fr)* Crunchy 2 *masc.* A type of crisp biscuit

croque-madame *(Fr) masc.* As croque monsieur but with cooked chicken replacing the ham

croque-monsieur *(Fr) masc.* Popular French fast food consisting of a sandwich filled with ham and Gruyère cheese, crust removed, cut into decorative shapes, dipped in beaten egg and shallow fried until golden. Sometimes only toasted. Eaten hot

croque au sel, à la *(Fr)* With salt and nothing else, with a sprinkling of salt

croquembouche *(Fr) masc.* A tall pyramid

made of cream-filled choux pastry spheres coated with caramel and decorated. Traditionally served at French weddings

croquesignole *(USA)* A round or square holeless Cajun doughnut

croqueta *(Sp)* Croquette or meat ball

croquetes *(Po)* Croquettes

croquetes de camarão *(Po)* Shrimp croquettes eaten as an appetizer or hors d'oeuvres

croquetjes *(Ho)* Croquettes

croquette *(En & Fr) fem.* Any mixture of minced cooked meat, etc. combined with mashed potatoes and/or breadcrumbs, herbs, onions, seasonings and egg or stock to form a stiff paste which is shaped into cylinders, spheres, rounds, ovals etc., panéed and deep fried

crosnes *(Fr) masc.* Chinese artichoke, so called from the French town where they were first introduced

crosnes du Japon *(Fr) masc.* Japanese artichoke

crosse de boeuf *(Fr) fem.* Knuckle of beef, also used of calf's foot

crosta *(It)* Crust, e.g. of bread

crostacei *(It)* Crustaceans

crostata *(It)* Pie

crostata di fragole *(It)* Strawberry pie

crostatina *(It)* Tart

crostato *(It)* Browned, with a crust

crostini *(It)* **1** A piece of good bread, toasted over charcoal or on a griddle, rubbed with a cut clove of fresh garlic, spread with olive oil or butter and topped with a variety of savoury items such as sliced tomatoes, capers, olives, anchovies, cheese, avocado or prawns, i.e. bruschetta with a topping. Eaten as a starter [also called **crostoncini**] **2** Croûtons or toasted bread

crostini alla fiorentina *(It)* A crostini spread witha chicken liver pâté

crostini di mare *(It)* A crostini spread with minced shellfish

crostini alla napoletana *(It)* A crostini spread with tomatoes and anchovies

crostini alla parmigiana *(It)* A crostini spread with grated Parmesan and anchovies

crostoncini *(It) see* crostini

crostoni *(It)* A large crostini eaten as a light meal

crostoni, sul *(It)* On toast

Crotonese *(It)* A hard, scalded-curd, ewes' milk cheese cast in wicker basket moulds in 2 kg discs. It has a dry rough orange/yellow rind with a cream coloured paste and the odd hole or crack. Used for slicing or grating depending upon age

Crottin *(Fr) masc. see* Crottin de Chavignol

Crottin de Chavignol *(Fr) masc.* A small, hard, goat's milk cheese with a strong flavour from the Berry region.I has AOC status. Often deep fried or grilled and served with lettuce as a starter. Lit. droppings, because of its appearance [also called **Crottin, Chavignol**]

croupion *(Fr) masc.* Parson's nose

croustade *(Fr) fem.* A hollowed out piece of bread, deep fried until crisp, or a baked pastry case used to serve cooked meats, vegetables, etc. bound in a savoury sauce

croustade d'oeufs de caille Maintenon *(Fr) fem.* Poached quails' eggs laid on a bed of duxelle and Hollandaise sauce in a pastry barquette

croustillant *(Fr) adj.* Crunchy, crisp, crusty

croustilles *(Fr) fem.* Potato crisps

croûte *(Fr) fem.* **1** Crust, rind or toast **2** A circle or rectangle of fried or toasted bread on which game or other dishes and savouries are served **3** A small pastry crust usually crescent shaped served with savoury dishes

croûte, en *(Fr)* Enclosed in pastry then baked e.g. of fish or meat

croûte anchois *(Fr) fem.* Anchovy toast

croûte aux morilles *(Fr) masc.* Morels on toast

croûte au pot *(Fr) masc.* A beef and vegetable soup each serving topped with toasted bread and cheese

croûtons *(En & Fr) masc.* Small (8mm) cubes of bread fried until crisp and golden in clarified butter and served as an accompaniment to purée soups

crow *(UK) see* mesentery

crowberry The black skinned fruit of a shrub *Empetrum nigrum* which grows in hilly areas of Northern Europe, similar to and can be substituted for the cranberry [also called **crakeberry**]

crowdie *(UK)* **1** A gruel made from oatmeal once used as a staple food in Scotland **2** A mild-flavoured cottage cheese from Scotland made from rennet-curdled, skimmed, unpasteurized cow's milk. Eaten fresh usually with an admixture of cream [also called **crowdy**]

crowdy *see* crowdie

crown roast of lamb Two best ends of lamb, chined and with scraped ribs, joined in a circle so that the ribs curve outwards like a crown. Roasted and served with cutlet frills on the ends of the ribs. The centre may be filled with stuffing before cooking

cru *(Po)* Raw

cru(e) *(Fr)* Raw

crubeens *(Ir)* Pigs' trotters

crucetta *(It)* A Calabrian dish of roasted figs stuffed with nuts

cruchade *(Fr)* fem A sweet cornmeal fritter

crucian carp A silver coloured type of carp similar to bream in appearance

crudités *(Fr) fem.* A selection of crisp vegetables suitable for eating raw, cut into long strips or batons and often served with a dipping sauce such as mayonnaise, soured cream or other cold sauce, usually as a hors d'oeuvre or appetizers

crudo *(It & Sp)* Raw, fresh

cruet A set of pots, shakers and grinders for serving condiments, usually on a small tray

crullers *(USA)* A sweetened egg enriched pastry made with butter, cut into strips, deep fried and dusted with icing sugar. Eaten warm. Also a popular snack in China and often sliced and served with congee or soup

crumb, to *(USA)* To pané or cover with crumbs

crumb crust A mixture of crushed biscuits combined with sugar and melted butter which is often substituted for pastry, e.g. in cheese cakes and in the USA for tarts and flans where Graham crackers are the biscuit of choice

crumble A compote of fruit topped with a mixture of fat, flour and sugar, sometimes with oatflakes and/or white of egg, baked in the oven until the topping is crisp and crumbly

crumble, to To rub a dry solid between the fingers or otherwise so as to reduce it to crumbs

crumbs Small irregularly shaped particles made from large friable pieces, e.g. of cake, bread, biscuits

crumpets A yeasted flour liquid batter (3:4) made with equal parts of milk and water and a little oil, allowed to froth, baking powder added at the rate of 5 g per kg of flour, left 40 minutes to rest then cooked in rings on a greased griddle to form small, circular, flat buns with a honeycombed top surface. Usually served toasted with butter

crusca *(It)* Bran

crush, to To squeeze or press a solid so as to extract liquid, to turn it into a semi-solid or to reduce it to smaller particles

crust 1 The outer hard golden brown surface of bread or cakes or other mixtures which are baked or fried **2** The pastry top on a filled sweet or savoury pie or dish not necessarily having a pastry base

crustacean A class of aquatic animals with a hard external segmented shell *(exoskeleton)* containing a soft body, usually with muscular legs, tail and possibly claws, such as lobster, prawn, crab, etc.

crustacés *(Fr) masc.* Shellfish, seafood, crustaceans

crustáceos *(Sp)* Crustaceans

cryptoxanthin *see* E161(c)

crystallized flowers Small flowers or flower petals soaked in sugar syrup and dried, often artificially coloured, used for decoration. Traditionally violets

crystallized fruit *see* candied fruit

Csaba *(Hu)* A well-flavoured spicy sausage containing chilli pepper and paprika

császárkörte *(Hu)* A type of pear, white butter pear

csemege *(Hu)* Dessert

cseresznye *(Hu)* Cherries

csipetke *(Hu)* Tiny dumplings made by cooking pieces of egg noodle dough in simmering water until al dente, draining and tossing in lard. Served with soups and stews

csirke *(Hu)* Chicken

csuka *(Hu)* Pike, the fish

cu *(Ch)* Vinegar

cuajada 1 *(Sp)* Curds **2** *(SA)* A soft, creamy, cow's milk cheese from Venezuela often wrapped in banana leaf

cuajo *(Sp)* Rennet

cuan *(Ch)* Simmering of meat or vegetables e.g in a steamboat

cuaresmeño *(Me)* A dark green round chilli

cube sugar White or brown crystals of sugar compressed into small cubes (about 15 mm edge) [also called **sugar lump, loaf sugar** (USA)]

cubeb The dried, dark brown, unripe fruits of a plant *Piper cubeba* native to Indonesia and about the size of a peppercorn with a stalk. They have a warm, somewhat bitter, flavour close to allspice with a hint of turpentine and were one of the spices used to flavour hippocras. Used in Indonesian cooking [also called **tailed pepper**]

cu cai tau *(Vi)* Mooli

cucchiaino *(It)* Teaspoon, also used as a volume measure equal to 5 ml

cucchiaio da tavola *(It)* Tablespoon, also used as a volume measure equal to 15 ml

cuchara *(Sp)* Spoon, ladle

cucharada *(Sp)* Tablespoonful used as a volume measure equal to 15 ml

cucharadita *(Sp)* Teaspoonful used as a volume measure equal to 5 ml

cuchay *see* Chinese chive

cucina *(It)* Cooking, cuisine, kitchen

cuckoo flower *see* lady's smock

cucumber A fruit of a member of the *Cucurbitaceae* family, *Cucumis sativus*, introduced to the UK from India in 1573 and harvested in the unripe green stage between 5 and 35 cm in length and 1.5 to 5 cm in diameter. The smaller ones are usually pickled in flavoured brine or vinegar, the larger are generally eaten raw as a salad vegetable or deseeded, salted, drained and diced combined with herbs and yoghurt or used as a bulking agent in various mixtures; *see also* dill pickles, gherkins, Japanese cucumber, yellow cucumber, ridge cucumber, long cucumber

cucumber mayonnaise Finely chopped cucumber and salt mixed with mayonnaise

cucumber sauce *see* doria, sauce

cucumber tree fruit *see* belimbing (1)

***Cucumeropsis* spp.** *Bot.* Egusi melon

Cucumis anguria *Bot.* Gherkin

Cucumis melo *Bot.* The vine from which the sweet melons, mush melon, canteloupe and honeydew melon are obtained.

Cucumis sativus *Bot.* Cucumber

Cucurbitaceae The botanical family name for a group of fruiting vine plants whose fruits include cucumbers and melons, watermelons, summer squash including marrows and courgettes, winter squash, pumpkins, chokos, etc.

Cucurbita maxima The botanical name of the American vine from which some varieties of winter squash are obtained. Distinguished by soft hairs on the stems, a swollen almost smooth stem and leaves which are not deeply lobed

Cucurbita moschata The botanical name of the American vine from which some varieties of winter squash are obtained esp. the cushaw and crookneck

Cucurbita pepo The botanical name of the vine from which pumpkins, marrows and summer squash are obtained. Distinguished by roughly bristled stems, short ridged fruit stalks and deeply lobed leaves

cuiller à bouche *(Fr) fem.* Tablespoon, also used as a volume measure equal to 15 ml

cuiller à café *(Fr) fem.* Coffee spoon = teaspoon, also used as a volume measure equal to 5 ml

cuiller à dessert *(Fr) fem.* Dessertspoon

cuillerée à café *(Fr) fem.* Teaspoonful

cuillerée à soupe *(Fr) fem.* Tablespoonful

cuipi ji *(Ch)* Chicken cooked so that the skin is crisp

cuire *(Fr)* To cook

cuire à la vapeur *(Fr)* To steam

cuisine *(Fr) fem.* **1** Kitchen **2** Cooking, cookery, the art of cookery **3** Kitchen or catering staff

cuisine bourgeoise *(Fr) fem.* Plain cooking

cuisine épicée *(Fr) fem.* Hot or spicy dishes or food

cuisine au jus *(Fr) fem.* A style of cooking avoiding cream, butter and flour for sauces but instead relying on the natural cooking juices

cuisine ménagère *(Fr) fem.* The cooking of the ordinary household

cuisine minceur *(Fr) fem.* A low calorie style of cooking with little or no fat or starch

cuisine du soleil *(Fr) fem.* The modern haute cuisine of the French Riviera based on fresh fruit and vegetables, olive oil, garlic and the herbs of Provence such as thyme, fennel, sage, etc.

cuisine de terroir *(Fr) fem.* Regional cooking

cuisse *(Fr) fem.* Thigh

cuisse de mouton *(Fr) fem.* Leg of mutton

cuisse de poulet *(Fr) fem.* Chicken leg, divided into pilon de cuisse *(drumstick)* and gras de cuisse *(thigh)*

cuisseau *(Fr) masc.* Haunch (of veal)

cuisses de grenouilles *(Fr) fem.* Frogs' legs, usually sautéed with butter, chopped garlic and parsley or served in a cream sauce

cuisson *(Fr) fem.* Cooking

cuissot *(Fr) masc.* Haunch of venison or wild boar

cuit(e) *(Fr)* Cooked, past participle of cuire, as in bien cuit, well cooked

cuka *(Ma)* Rice vinegar

cukor *(Hu)* Sugar

cul de veau *(Fr) masc.* Chump chop

culaccio *(It)* Rump of beef

culantrillo *(Sp)* Maidenhair fern

culatella *(It)* A smoked raw ham made from lean pork cut from the leg, similar to Parma ham. Sometimes soaked in wine before maturing. Very expensive, used for hors d'oeuvres [also called **culatella di Parma, culatella di Zibello**]

culatella di Parma *see* culatella

culatella di Zibello *see* culatello

culinaire *(Fr)* Culinary, appertaining to cookery

cullen skink *(UK)* A Scottish fish stew or soup made from onions sweated in butter, mixed with flour to make a roux, chopped potatoes and milk added, simmered, then 10 minutes before serving flaked smoked haddock or smoked cod added and the whole diluted with stock to the right consistency

cullis A misspelling or bastardized English translation of the French word coulis

culotte de boeuf *(Fr) fem.* Rump steak of beef

cultivated mushroom *see* common mushroom

cultivateur, à la *(Fr)* In the farmer's style, i.e. with mixed vegetables and pork or bacon

culture A large quantity of bacteria, yeast, fungal mycelium or fungal spores grown in a nutrient medium and used to start fermentation as in the production of wine, cheese, yoghurt, etc. [also called **ferment**]

cultured buttermilk Buttermilk which has been fermented with a *Lactobacillus* spp. May be sweetened and flavoured for use as a drink or may be substituted for milk or buttermilk in recipes

cultured milk Milk soured with various *Lactobacillus* spp. at 20°C to give 0.45 to 0.6% lactic acid concentrations It has a refreshing acid taste

Cumberland ham *(UK)* A large, traditional, strong tasting ham, cured with salt, saltpetre and brown sugar, matured in air for 3 months. Usually boiled or baked

Cumberland rum nicky *(UK)* A rich double crust tart filled with a sticky mixture of chopped stoned dates, soft brown sugar and stem ginger soaked in rum

Cumberland sauce *(UK)* A mixture of warmed red currant jelly, blanched and refreshed chopped shallots, lemon juice, orange juice, port and a little English mustard, finished with a blanched and refreshed fine julienne of orange zest. Served with cold ham

Cumberland sausage *(UK)* A sausage made of coarsely chopped pork with seasoning and nutmeg in a natural casing. Not linked but sold from a large coil. Now often modified with the addition of rusk and cereal

cumi-cumi *(Id)* Squid

cumin 1 *(En & Fr) masc.* The seeds of an annual plant *Cuminum cyminum* grown around the Mediterranean and through to the Far East. It has a strong pungent flavour and is much used in Arab, Indian and Spanish cooking [also called **white cumin**] **2** *(Fr) masc.* Caraway

cumin des prés *(Fr) masc.* Caraway seed

cumino *(It)* Cumin

Cuminum cyminum *Bot.* Cumin

cumquat *see* kumquat

cu nang *(Vi)* Water chestnut

cuoccio *(It)* Gurnard, the fish

cuocere a vapore *(It)* To steam

cuocere alla graticola *(It)* To grill

cuocere in umido *(It)* To stew

cuore *(It)* Heart

cuore edule *(It)* Cockle

cuore rossa *(It)* A cockle used in Italian cooking with bright red flesh when alive

cuoriccini *(It)* Sicilian heart-shaped biscuits traditionally served at weddings

cup cakes Small sponge cakes cooked in individual bun tins or paper cases. So called because originally baked in cups

cup custard *(USA) see* crème renversée

cup leaf *see* daun mangkok

cup measure A volumetric method of measuring out ingredients now only used in the US and Australia, but once used in the UK. 1 US standard cup = 236 ml volume (8 US fluid oz.) and will hold 145 grams of plain flour, 200 grams of dry rice and 220 grams of caster sugar. The British standard cup was 285 ml (10 fluid oz.) [also called **liquid measure, volume measure, dry measure**]

curaçao The generic name for various orange-flavoured liqueurs used to flavour cakes and desserts

curcuma *(Fr) masc.* Turmeric

cúrcuma *(Sp)* Turmeric

Curcuma longa *Bot.* Turmeric

Curcuma zedoaria *Bot.* Zedoary

Curcuma zerumbet *Bot.* Zedoary

Curcumin E100, a natural yellow food colouring obtained from turmeric

curcumina *(It)* Turmeric

curd the solid which separates from milk or soya milk which has been coagulated and cut or stirred. Used to make curds and whey, cheese, or soya bean curd

curd cheese A soft, white cheese made from the curds which separate from a lactic acid fementation and coagulation of milk. It is not pressed and is slightly sour tasting. often used for making cheesecake

curd cheese pastry *(CE)* Pastry made from equal parts of curd cheese, butter and flour. It resembles flaky pastry when cooked

curd, fruit Mixtures of sugar and butter thickened with egg yolks over a double boiler and flavoured with various fruits. The most common is lemon curd

curdle, to To separate into visible immiscible solid and/or liquid phases as in the production of curds and whey from coagulated milk, or when mayonnaise breaks down into oil droplets and vinegar or when a cooked egg mixture separates

cure, to To preserve meat, game, poultry, fish or any flesh by smoking, salting or treating with salt, saltpetre, sodium nitrite or sugar or with brine or any combination of these. The purpose is to remove water from the flesh and to inhibit bacterial action. The nitrite accentuates the pink colour of haemoglobin; *see also* to dry salt, pickling brine

curled octopus A species of octopus *Eledone cirrosa* with a maximum length of 40 cm and curled tentacles with a single row of suckers. Not as fine a quality as the common octopus but often served braised in tomato sauce and sometimes canned [also called **white octopus**]

curly algae *see* wakame

curly cress *see* cress

curly endive *see* endive

curly kale *see* kale

curly parsley *see* parsley *Petroselinum crispum*

curly seaweed *see* wakame

currant pasty A mixture of currants, brown sugar, spices, apple and pork scratchings sandwiched between 2 layers of pastry, baked and cut into squares

currant raisin *(USA)* currant

currant tomato A tiny tomato *Lycopersicon pimpinelli folium* 1 cm in dia. and used for decoration

currants **1** Dried grapes of the small black Corinth variety from Greece now grown elsewhere. More tart and with less sugar than sultanas and raisins [also called **currant raisins** (USA)] **2** The small, round berries of a variety of shrubs from Northern Europe and North Africa. See under blackcurrant, redcurrant and white currant

currie, sauce *(Fr) fem.* Curry sauce made with white bouillon

currie à l'indienne, sauce *(Fr) fem.* Finely sliced onion sweated in butter with a BG, mace and a cinnamon stick, sprinkled with curry powder, fried, then a mixture of equal parts of coconut milk and veal or fish stock added, simmered, strained and finished with cream and lemon juice [also called **sauce indienne**]

curry **1** *(En & Fr) masc.* A general term for highly spiced cooked dishes of meat, vegetables, fish, pulses, etc. originating from India and SEA, popular in the West, often containing varying proportions of hot chillis. Curry means mixture in Hindi and the dish got its name when foreigners asked what was being cooked and were told a mixture **2** *(In)* A stew with a pungent aromatic sauce made by browning onion in ghee, separating, adding meat which has been defatted and degristled to the fat, searing this, adding aromatics and frying over medium heat until the fat separates, then adding salt, water and chillis or sweet peppers, simmering for a long period adding water as necessary and finally adding onions and other vegetables towards the end [also called **turrcarri** (In)]

curry butter A compound butter flavoured with curry powder, cayenne pepper, ginger and lemon juice, refrigerated as a roll and cut into 5 mm slices for use as a garnish

curry-flavoured oil Peanut oil flavoured with curry powder

curry leaf The leaves of a small tree *Murraya koenigii* from hilly regions of India which give off a spicy odour when bruised. Fresh leaves are used to add flavour to many Indian dishes. The dried leaves lose much of their flavour

curry mayonnaise *see* caboul sauce

curry paste Ground spices and flavouring agents processed with garlic, chilli peppers and fresh ginger to a thick paste and fried in oil until the oil separates (about 10 minutes) and then mixed with a little salt. This will keep for a considerable time. Vinegar is added for vindaloo curry paste

curry plant A shrub *Helichrysum angustifolium* of the daisy family from Southern Europe with silvery needle-like leaves which impart a mild curry (Indian spice mix) flavour to cooked dishes. Use like rosemary. Not to be confused with curry leaves

curry powder A mixture of ground spices used for making curry esp. in the West, from a selection of coriander seeds, cumin seeds, mustard seeds, black peppercorns, fenugreek seeds and chillis to produce varying degrees of hotness, all of which are dry roasted, together with unroasted dried ginger, turmeric, cinnamon and cloves. There are many variations, see e.g. Madras and West Indian curry powder. Rarely used in Indian cooking but useful for those not wishing to stock individual spices

curry sauce Chopped onions and garlic cooked in fat without colour, flour and curry powder added and the roux cooked without browning the flour, tomato purée and stock added to form a smooth sauce, chopped apples, chutney, desiccated coconut, sultanas, grated fresh ginger and salt added, simmered and skimmed for 30 minutes. Served with meat, fish, eggs, etc.

currysill *(Sw)* A typical smörgåsbord dish of sliced matjes herring, diced cold boiled potatoes and chopped hard boiled eggs mixed and bound with a curry-flavoured mayonnaise and served cold

curuba A type of elongated passion fruit *Passiflora maliformis* from South America with a yellow green skin and a taste similar to, but slightly more acid, than passion fruit

Curworthy *(UK)* A semi-hard cheese made with unpasteurized cow's milk from Devon and Cornwall. It is matured for 6 weeks and has a creamy buttery taste

cuscinetti *(It)* Fried cheese sandwich. Lit. small cushion

cush *(USA)* A cornmeal pancake

cush cush yam A red skinned yam from a plant *Dioscorea trifida* native to SA which produces several small tubers instead of the more normal single large tuber

cushaw *(USA)* A large variety of crookneck squash

cushion A cut of lamb, veal or beef from the inside top of the rear leg

cushion of veal *(UK)* The thick longitudinal muscle at the rear inside of the leg of veal, equivalent to topside of beef. Used for escalopes, roasting, braising and sautéing [also called **nut**]

cusk *see* tusk

cussy, à la *(Fr)* Garnished with large mushrooms, chestnuts, cock's kidneys and truffles, usually of steaks and roast chicken

custard 1 A general term for various sweetened milk based sauces, flavoured with vanilla and thickened with flour and/or eggs **2** *(UK) see* English custard

custard apple The general name for a group of tropical fruits *Anona* spp. including atemoyas, cherimoyas, sweet sops and sour sops which generally have a scaly skin and a soft custard like flesh tasting variously of combinations of pineapple, strawberry, banana, etc. [also called **annona, anona**]

custard banana The fruit of a tree *Asimina tribloa* from the South East of the USA and Mexico. It looks and tastes something like a small vanilla-flavoured banana but has a thin skin and numerous seeds in the flesh

custard cream *see* crème patissière

custard fritters Crème frites q.v. which have been battered

custard marrow 1 *see* patty pan squash **2** *see* choko

custard powder *(UK)* A mixture of cornflour, sometimes yellow colouring, and artificial vanilla flavouring very popular in England for thickening sweetened milk to make English custard

custard sauce *see* English custard

cut, to To use a knife or scissors to divide solid foods into smaller pieces

cut and fold, to To mix dry ingredients into a batter or foamed mixture by gently sprinkling them on the surface and very carefully incorporating them by slowly turning over the mixture with a metal spoon, spatula or knife

cut in, to To combine hard fat with dry ingredients by repeatedly cutting the fat with one or two knives beneath the surface of the the dry ingredients until it is reduced to small uniform pieces each coated with dry ingredients

cutlet A transverse section from the rib cage of an animal containing part of the vertebrae and ribs with accompanying flesh. Usually of lamb, veal or pork

cutlet bat A heavy metal implement with a flat face about 10 cm by 7 cm and a handle used to thin out pieces of meat, fish, etc. by striking the food, usually contained between two pieces of polythene, on a solid work surface; *see also* to bat out

cutlet frill A small piece of frilled white paper shaped like a chef's hat which is used to cover the end of the bare, scraped rib bone on a cutlet or roast joint after it has been cooked [also called **frill, paper frill**]

cutters *see* pastry cutters

cuttle fish A cephalopod *Sepia officinalis* from the Mediterranean and Eastern Atlantic with an oval body and head from which two long and eight short tentacles spring, in all about 25 cm long. It has one internal stiffening bone (cuttle bone). The guts which together with the parrot like beak must be removed before cooking include the ink sac, the contents of which can be used in an accompanying sauce. Cooked like squid or octopus. Sometimes eaten in the Far East as a snack food when in its dried form; *see also* little cuttlefish

cwt Abbreviation for hundredweight, a unit of weight still used in the USA

Cyamopsis psoraloides *Bot.* Guar bean

cyanocobalamin Vitamin B12

cyclamate An artificial sweetener about 30 times as sweet as sugar, now banned in many countries

Cydonia oblonga *Bot.* Quince

cygne *(Fr) masc.* A swan shaped pastry filled with chantilly cream

Cymbopogan citratus *Bot.* Lemon grass

cymling *see* patty pan squash

Cynara scolymus *Bot.* The globe artichoke

Cyperus esculentus *Bot.* Tiger nut

Cyphomandra betacea *Bot.* Tamarillo

cyprus oval *see* shamouti

cysteine hydrochloride *see* (E)920

Cystophyllum fusiforme *Bot.* Hiziki

czirkegulyás szegedi módra *(Hu)* Jointed chicken simmered in white stock with thinly sliced green sweet peppers, diced potatoes, tomatoes, sweated celeriac, onions, carrots and Hamburg parsley and served with boiled czipetke tossed in butter

Dd

daai dau nga choy *(Ch)* Soya bean sprouts

daai gaai choy *(Ch)* One of the oriental mustards with a rounded lettuce-type head, curly pale green leaves and thick grooved stems. It has a slightly astringent taste and is usually pickled or salted [also called **Swatow mustard cabbage**]

daam *(Ch)* Sea urchin

daanti *(In)* A ceramic pestle used with a matching mortar *(imamdusta)* for grinding soft grains and spices

daarim *(Ne)* Pomegranate

dab A small flatfish *Limanda limanda* up to 25 cm long, from North West European coastal waters, white below and brown with greenish spots above. Cooked as plaice

da bai cai *(Ch)* Chinese cabbage

Dacca *(In)* A cheese made from cow or buffalo milk, ripened for 2 to 3 weeks in wicker baskets, then smoked

dace A bony freshwater fish *Leuciscus leuciscus* resembling in shape a small haddock. Steamed, baked or fried [also called **dare, dart**]

dacquoise *(Fr) fem.* A speciality of Dax consisting of layers of meringue containing toasted and coarsely ground nuts interspersed with whipped cream and soft fruits such as raspberries and strawberries, the whole decorated and circular in shape. Cut in wedges for serving

dadarisi *(Ho)* An omelette stuffed with a spicy Indonesian filling

dadels *(Ho)* Dates

dadi *(It)* Dice, of vegetables, etc.

dadlar *(Sw)* Dates

dadler *(De & No)* Dates

da dou *(Ch)* Soya beans

daging kambing *(Id & Ma)* Lamb

daging kerbau *(Id)* Buffalo meat

daging smor *(Ho)* Stewed meat, Indonesian style

dagwood sandwich *(USA)* A multi-layered sandwich with a variety of fillings in between each layer

dahchini *(In)* Cinnamon or cassia

dahi *(In & Ne)* Yoghurt

dahi balle *(In)* Fried bean cakes served in a herb and spice-flavoured yoghurt sauce

dahl *see* dhal

dahorpt *(Bk)* Diced mutton simmered with onions and herbs until tender, reserved, rice cooked in the strained cooking liquor with chopped sweet green peppers, mixed with the meat and lightly vinegared; *see also* kissella dahorp

dai *(Ja) see* red sea bream

dai choy goh *(Ch)* Agar agar

daidai *(Ja)* Seville orange

daikon *(Ja)* A shorter and rounder variety of mooli q.v. used in the same way

daikon nimono *(Ja)* 4 cm pieces of daikon boiled in salted water until tender and simmered in dashi with a little soya sauce and mirin and covered with an otoshi-buta for about 30 minutes

daikon oroshi *(Ja)* Finely grated daikon or mooli used as a marinade esp. for octopus and to mask or remove strong fishy smells

daikon shreds *(Ja)* Very fine almost hair-like shreds of mooli made by cutting a long thin ribbon like a wide potato peeling, rolling it up and cutting it across in very thin slices. Used as a garnish for sushi

daing *(Ph)* Cleaned fish which have been salted and dried in the sun

dai rau song *(Vi)* A platter of mixed herbs, salad leaves, raw vegetables cut in strips and cooked rice or noodles served with meals as a side dish

dairy The buildings in which milk is removed from the animals and further processed into cream, butter, cheese and other milk products. Nowadays removal and processing are usually carried out at different locations

dairy products Milk and all other products derived directly from it such as cheese, butter, cream, yoghurt, etc.

dai suen *(Ch)* Asian leek

daizu *(Ja)* Dried soya beans

daktyla *(Gr)* A long loaf of bread, topped with sesame seeds and made up of several sections easily pulled apart

dal *see* dhal

dalchini *(In)* Cinnamon and cassia bark

Dalia *(Ro)* A cow's milk cheese similar to Kashkaval

dalle *(Fr) fem.* A thin slice or escalope of round fish cut across the bone. Lit. slab

damaschina *(It)* Damson

damascos *(Po)* Apricots

damask cream *(UK)* A junket made with sweetened single cream flavoured with nutmeg and brandy, set with rennet at 37°C for 2 to 3 hours, and carefully decorated with a mixture of clotted cream and rosewater [also called **Devonshire junket**]

Damaszenerpflaume *(Ge)* Damson

dame *(It)* Small raisin cakes

dame blanche *(Fr) fem.* A common Belgian and Northern French dessert of white ice cream, whipped cream and chocolate sauce

Damenkäse *(Ge) see* Butterkäse

damper *(Aus)* Unleavened bread made from flour, salt and water cooked on a griddle, barbecue or in hot wood fire ashes

Dampfbraten *(Ge)* Beef stew

Dampfnudeln *(Ge)* Sweetened yeast-raised, flour based dumplings or noodles, steamed or poached in milk and served with custard, stewed fruit or jam

Dampfwürstel *(Au)* A mild sausage containing beef and bacon fat bound with a little fécule, lightly scalded and possibly smoked

damson A small blue black plum with a yellow green flesh from a Middle Eastern tree *Prunus damascena* or *P. insititia* with a greyish yeast bloom. Rather acid but excellent in preserves and cooked dishes

damson and apple tansy *(UK)* Cooked apples and stoned damsons fried in butter with sugar until soft, mixed with ground cloves and cinnamon followed by stiffly beaten egg whites. Cooked over a low heat until set, sprinkled with sugar and browned under the grill. Originally flavoured with tansy

dan *(Ch)* Egg

dana *(Tu)* Veal

Danablu *see* Danish blue

Danbo *(De)* A hard cows' milk cheese which is salted in brine and matured for 5 months, often waxed and with internal holes like Emmental. Fairly mild in flavour and often contains caraway seeds. Contains 45% water, 24% fat and 29% protein

Dancy tangerine *(USA)* The traditional Christmas tangerine is an old (1867) variety of mandarin grown from seed by Colonel Dancy. It has a deep orange-red thin skin with a tender well-flavoured flesh. They tend to decay rapidly [also called **obeni-mikan** (Ja)]

dandelion A common European wild plant *Taraxacum officinale.* The young and/or garden blanched leaves are used in salads and the ground and roasted roots are used to make a coffee substitute

dan gao *(Ch)* Cake

dang gui *(Ch)* The dried root of a relative of angelica *Angelica sinensis* used to flavour soup and reputed to have medicinal properties

dang noi *(Th)* Cassava

dango *(Ja)* Dumpling

Danish *(USA)* A Danish pastry

Danish blue *(De)* A blue veined white and crumbly cooked-curd cows' milk cheese made commercially in large quantities. It is inoculated with *Penicillium roquefortii* spores to produce the blue veining. It is dry salted, ripened for 3 months and held in a cold store for a further 2 months. The flavour is sharp and somewhat salty. Marketed aggressively [also called **danablu**]

Danish blue brie *(De)* A Danish version of a blue veined Brie cheese

Danish mellow blue *(De)* A more mellow and creamier textured version of Danish blue cheese

Danish open sandwich *see* smørrebrød

Danish pastries Sweet cakes and buns made with Danish pastry q.v. usually filled with fruit, custard, jam or the like. Examples are spandauer, wienerlangd, kammar and borgmästarfläta, all strangely enough from Sweden.

Danish pastry A yeasted egg and sugar enriched strong flour dough (2 eggs per kg of flour) brought together with cold milk, layered with 0.6 times the weight of flour in butter, using the English puff pastry method with 3 threefold turns, resting between turns as usual. The pastry is rolled out to the appropriate thickness, garnished appropriately, proved and then baked at 230°C

Danish salami A type of salami made with a mixture of pork, beef or veal and a high proportion of pork fat coloured red to resemble meat, dry salted or brined, air dried and possibly smoked. Eaten raw in thin slices and not suitable for cooking

dansk fläskkotlett *(Sw)* Danish pork chops made from seasoned chops rubbed with curry powder, fried quickly in butter, soured cream added and all simmered for 10 minutes. Garnished with diced ham and apple and sliced onion sweated in butter

dansk leverpostej *(De)* A pâté made from calf's liver, flour, cream, butter, eggs, onions, spices and seasoning served warm with boiled potatoes or cold with open sandwiches, etc.

dansk potatis *(Sw)* Large potatoes baked with the skin on at 200°C for 45 minutes, rolled between the hand and a board to soften the inside, opened and topped with chopped prawns in creamed butter

dansk wienerbrød *(De) see* Danish pastry. Lit. Danish Vienna bread

darang *(Ph)* Dried smoked fish which develop a characteristic deep red colour

darchini *(In)* Cinnamon

dare *see* dace

dare oh *(Bm)* A rounded deep pan similar to a wok made of brass or cast iron with a handle at either side

dariole *(Fr) fem.* A small pastry with custard cooked in a dariole mould

dariole mould A small bucket shaped mould used to make individual desserts such as crème caramel, madeleines, etc.

Dariworld *(USA)* A semi-hard cooked-curd cows' milk cheese, salted in brine then ripened in plastic packs. Contains 45% water, 27% fat and 23% protein

darjeeling An expensive unblended black tea with a very fine flavour from the foothills of the Himalayas. Often drunk without milk or sugar

dark brown sugar *(USA)* Muscovado sugar

dark soya sauce A less salty version of soya sauce used to colour food as well as for its full bodied flavour

dark sugar General term for the various brown sugars q.v.

darn *(Ch)* Hen egg

darne *(Fr) fem.* A thick slice or steak of fish cut across the backbone and including the bone; *see also* fish steak

dart *see* dace

dartois *(Fr) masc.* **1** A garnish of celery, carrots, turnips and potatoes used with meat dishes **2** Two pieces of sweet or savoury puff pastry sandwiched together with a sweet or savoury filling and baked

dasheen *see* taro

dasheen leaf The fan like leaf of taro and similar tubers of the *Colocasia* spp. used as a vegetable and in callaloo soup q.v. [also called **arvi leaf, patra**]

dashi *(Ja)* A fish stock used in Japanese cooking made from dried seaweed *(kelp* or *kombu),* dried Pacific bonito flakes and other flavourings. The first infusion of the raw materials is called ichiban dashi and is used for soups, whilst the second, niban dashi, is used as a stock or cooking liquor; *see also* katsuo dashi and hon dashi

date The fruit of the date palm *Phoenix dactylifera* with a yellow skin and brown sweet flesh enclosing a single elongated stone, the whole about 4 cm by 2 cm, which grow in clusters arranged in two rows along a central stalk. Usually traded in the dried form which is sweet and sticky. Popular at Christmas in Europe as a snack and also used to sweeten and flavour cakes

date mark A date stamped on a packaged food item indicating either the use-by date, best-before date, best-before-end date or display-until date q.v.

date mussel *see* sea date

date shell *see* sea date

dátil de mar *(Sp)* Sea date

dátiles *(Sp)* Dates

datolya *(Hu)* Dates

datte *(Fr) fem.* Date

datte de mer *(Fr) fem.* Sea date

Datteln *(Ge)* Dates

datteri *(It)* Dates

datteri farciti *(It)* Stuffed dates

dattero di mare *(It)* Sea date

daub, to *see* lard, to

daube *(Fr) fem.* A rich casserole made from previously marinated meat with a selection of vegetables, wine, garlic, onions and seasonings according to region. Cooked slowly in a sealed pot. Traditionally served with boiled potatoes or pasta

daube disef An egg stew from Mauritius made with hard boiled eggs and new potatoes boiled in their skins, both fried until brown, mixed with a sauce made from chopped onions, garlic, green chillis, ginger, parsley and thyme all sweated in oil, chopped skinned tomatoes, tomato purée, sugar, seasoning and water and finished with chopped coriander and petit pois

daubière *(Fr) fem.* An earthenware casserole

with a tight fitting lid used to cook daubes. Originally they had a deep lid in which burning charcoal could be put

Daucus carota *Bot.* Carrot

dau gok *(Ch)* A dark green variety of long bean

dau hao *(Vi)* Oyster sauce

dau hu *(Vi)* Bean curd

dau hu chien *(Vi)* Fried bean curd

dau hu chung *(Vi)* Bean curd

dau hu ki *(Vi)* Dried bean curd

dau me *(Vi)* Sesame seed oil

dau mil *(Ch)* Pea leaf or shoot

dau miu *(Ch)* Pea leaf or shoot

daum kesom *(Id & Ma)* Polygonum

daumont, à la *(Fr)* Garnished with mushrooms, soft fish roe, crayfish tails and sometimes fish quenelles. Used for fish

daun bawang *(Id & Ma)* Scallion or spring onion

daun jeruk purut *(Id)* Makrut lime leaves

daun kari *(Id)* Curry leaf

daun kari pla *(Ma)* Curry leaf

daun kemangi *(Id)* The most commonly used basil

daun ketumbar *(Id & Ma)* Coriander leaves

daun limau purut *(Ma)* Kaffir lime

daun mangkok *(In)* A shrub *Polyscias scutellarium* whose aromatic young leaves are used as a green vegetable, usually shredded. The whole leaves are also used to hold food

daun pandan *(Id & Ma)* Screwpine

daun pudina *(Ma)* Mint

Dauphin *(Fr) masc.* **1** Dolphin **2** A cow's milk cheese from the near the Belgian border, flavoured with herbs and spices and formed into decorative shapes. The cheese itself is similar to Maroilles

dauphine, à la *(Fr)* With pommes dauphine

dau phong *(Vi)* Peanut

dau phong rang *(Vi)* Roasted peanuts used as a garnish and for flavouring

daurade *(Fr) fem.* Gilt-head bream

daurade commune *(Fr)* Bream (1)

dau see *(Ch)* Black bean (2)

dau xanth *(Vi)* Mung bean or bean sprout

da xia *(Ch)* Prawn

dayap *(Ph)* A small lime (to 1.5 cm dia.) used as a souring agent

DeArbol chilli A small long and thin, very hot dried chilli pepper with a bright shiny skin. Should be used with care

deauvillaise, à la *(Fr)* In the style of Deauville (Normandy), esp. of sole poached with cream and chopped onions

debowiecka *(Pl)* A firm medium-sized slicing sausage from Poznan, made with pork contining only a little fat

debrecen *(Hu)* A spicy sausage made of 2 parts lean pork, 1 part pork fat and 1 part beef, seasoned and flavoured with spices. Used in various stews

debrecener rohwurst *(Hu)* A hard Rohwurst made entirely of pork

debrecziner *(Hu)* A spicy coarse textured sausage similar in size to the Frankfurter

decaffeinated coffee Coffee made in the usual way from green beans which have been solvent treated to selectively remove the caffein. It has a similar flavour to, but is not as stimulating as coffee

decant, to To gently pour off the clear liquid from the top of a mixture of liquid and heavier particles where the latter have settled to the bottom. Usually applied to wine to separate it from the crystals of tartaric acid which are precipitated on long standing

decanter A glass container with a stopper, often decorated, in which decanted wine or other drinks are kept for serving

dechi *(In & Ne) see* degchi

decilitre One tenth of a litre, 100 millilitres

decompose, to The process of bacterial, fungal or enzymic attack on food which causes it to break down into usually strong smelling and often toxic components. Some decomposition enhances flavour and texture e.g. in game, cheese and many fermented foods, but these can easily go bad as the process of decomposition has started

decorate, to To make pleasing to the eye by adding shapes, colours and textures to a dish, e.g. to cakes, desserts, cold buffet items, sandwiches, salads, etc.

decorated eggs Painted and decorated hard boiled eggs in their shells. Often used at Easter as symbols of resurrection or of fertility

découper *(Fr)* To carve, joint or cut in pieces

dee la *(Th)* Sesame seed

deem sum *(Ch) see* dim sum

deep dish pizza *(USA)* A North American style pizza made in a dish with sides like a flan or tart tin. Used so that more filling than is usual with a traditional pizza may be cooked with the dough [also called **deep pan pizza**]

deep fat Hot fat or oil of sufficient depth to completely cover the item being fried. Usually held in a special cooking utensil designed to prevent accidents

deep freeze An insulated and refrigerated cabinet or chest for freezing and storing frozen food at temperatures below −20°C

deep freeze, to To cool food below −20°C so as to prevent deterioration

deep freezing A method of preserving food by storing at temperatures below −10°C, usually around −18°C to −20°C

deep fry, to To cook food by immersing it in and covering it with hot fat or oil at a temperature between 175 and 195°C. The food is quickly sealed, crisped and cooked if not too thick

deep fryer The cooking utensil which contains sufficient depth of fat and a means of heating it, used for deep frying. It should have a cool zone below the heating element and hot fat, to collect burnt fragments of food, and a thermometer and/or thermostat to control the temperature

deep poaching, fish Large cuts of fish or whole fish cooked in simmering court bouillon or acidulated and salted water until cooked. Cooking is finished when the flesh leaves the bone. Usually garnished with picked parsley, plain boiled potatoes, slices of blanched aromatic vegetables and a little cooking liquor and served separately with a suitable sauce

deep sea argentine *see* argentine

deepwater prawn A large prawn *Pandalus borealis* up to 13 cm long, red when live and found from Greenland to the UK, large quantities being fished in Norwegian waters [also called **northern prawn, deepwater shrimp**]

deepwater shrimp *see* deepwater prawn

deer A family of herbivores, *Cervidae*, found throughout the world. Most of the males have bony antlers which are shed and regrow annually throughout life. They range in size from 55 cm high at the shoulder to 2.4 m. The important meat varieties are red, fallow and roe deer in Europe, the white-tailed mule deer and moose in North America and the caribou and reindeer of Arctic regions. The meat is known as venison

defrost, to 1 To thaw or warm up deep frozen food to room temperature in readiness for cooking or eating. Usually done by slow application of heat to avoid cooking part of the food, often in a microwave oven **2** To warm up a refrigerator or deep freeze so as to remove ice and snow encrusted on the internal surfaces

degchi *(In)* A tinned brass cooking pot with a heavy base, straight sides and no handles used for cooking over charcoal or wood [also called **bhagoni, dechi, patila**]

deghi mirch *(In)* Kashmiri chilli [also called **degi mirich**]

déglaçage *(Fr) masc.* The process of deglazing or defrosting

déglacer *(Fr)* To deglaze or to defrost

deglaze, to To dissolve and loosen coagulated meat juices which stick to the bottom of a roasting dish or frying pan using water, stock or wine. The resulting solution or suspension is sometimes reduced in volume by boiling and is used to add flavour to sauce or stock

degorge, to *see* dégorger

dégorger, faire *(Fr)* **1** To soak in water to remove impurities before cooking e.g with fish, offal, meat, etc. **2** To remove water and sometimes bitter flavours from a food by chopping, covering with salt, allowing to drain for some time then rinsing and drying. Used with cucumbers, aubergines, courgettes, kantolas and karellas

dégraisser *(Fr)* To skim off fat and scum from the top of a simmering liquid as in the preparation of stocks and sauces, also to remove fat from meat

degrease, to To remove fat from the surface of a liquid, either by skimming, decanting or soaking it into paper

degree Celsius The divisions of the Celsius scale of temperature of which there are 100 between the freezing point and the boiling point of water, 0°C and 100°C respectively. Written °C [also called **degree centigrade**]

degree Centigrade *see* degree Celsius

degree Fahrenheit The divisions of the Fahrenheit scale of temperature of which there are 180 between the freezing point and the boiling point of water, 32°F and 212°F respectively. Written °F

dégustation *(Fr) fem.* Tasting or sampling e.g of wine, oysters, etc.

dehydrate, to To remove water from a food product generally to improve its keeping quality. Food may be dehydrated by sun or air drying, heating, salting or applying a vacuum whilst adding heat

deipnon The first part of a formal meal in

ancient Greece when the food was served; *see also* symposium

déjeuner *(Fr) masc.* Lunch

deli *(USA)* A delicatessen where food can also be eaten on the premises

delicatessen A shop or area within a shop selling ready-to-eat savoury items such as preserved meats and fish, cheese, slicing sausages, salads, pâtés, dips, etc.

délice *(En & Fr) masc.* A thin fillet of fish with the two ends folded underneath to form a rectangular parcel. Usually poached. Lit. a delight

Délice de Saint Cyr *(Fr) fem.* A rich, triple cream cheese made from cow's milk in the area surrounding Paris

Delikatessaufschnitt *(Ge)* Assorted cold meats, assiette anglaise

delizie *(It)* Appetizers, delicacies

della rice A type of long grain rice

Delmonico potatoes *(USA)* Potato balls, boiled then dressed with butter, lemon juice, chopped parsley and seasoning

Delmonico steak *(USA)* A boneless beef steak 2.5 to 5 cm thick, cut from the wing and fore rib with all bone fat and coarse meat removed. Treat like fillet steak [also called **spencer steak**]

Demeltorte *(Au)* A pastry filled with candied fruit

demerara sugar A light brown sugar with coarse crystals originally from Demerara in British Guiana but now produced widely from raw cane sugar. Used for coffee and various desserts. Less moist than muscovado

demersal A term used to describe fishes such as flat fish which live near or on the sea bed

demi *(Fr)* Half

demi-deuil *(Fr)* A description of a dish with black and white ingredients, usually poached chicken, sweetbreads, eggs, shellfish, etc. for white and truffles for black and served with suprême sauce. Lit. half mourning

demi-deuil salad A salad of sliced boiled waxy potatoes, seasoned, mixed with real truffle shavings and dressed with a mixture of olive oil, vinegar, French mustard and single cream. Lit. half mourning salad

demi-doux *(Fr) see* bouffi

demi-glace, sauce *(En & Fr) fem.* A mixture of equal parts of espagnole sauce and brown stock reduced by simmering to a half quantity, skimming as necessary, and finally strained. Used as a basis for other sauces

demi-loaf *(USA)* A small individual sized loaf

demi-sel *(Fr)* **1** Slightly salted, as of butter, cheese, etc. **2** A moist, white, salted curd cheese made from cow's milk and with 40% butterfat content. It has a mild, slightly sour flavour

demi-suisse *(Fr & He)* A 30 g Suisse cheese [also called **petit-suisse**]

demi-tasse *(USA & Fr) fem.* A half cup or a small cup usually used to serve coffee

demoiselles de Cherbourg *(Fr) fem.* Small lobsters

dendang *(Id)* Surf clam

dénerver *(Fr)* To remove tendons, gristle, arteries, veins and membranes from meat and muscle

dengaku *(Ja)* A description of grilled skewered food which has been coated with a sweetened miso

dénoyauter *(Fr)* To stone or pit a fruit

density **1** Mass or weight per unit volume. e.g. water has a density of 1 kg per litre, saturated brine about 1.22 kg per litre and vegetable oil about 0.8 kg per litre **2** A description of the quality of hardness, thickness, opacity, etc. of something; *see also* specific gravity

dent corn *(USA)* A common tall form of maize *Zea mays* var. *indentata* with yellow or white kernels in which the hard coat covers only the sides so that they are indented at the top

dent-de-lion *(Fr) fem.* Dandelion

denté *(Fr) masc.* Dentex, the fish. Lit. toothed

dente, al *(It) see* al dente

dentex The general species name of a group of Mediterranean fish (*Dentex dentex*) similar to sea bream with a firm flesh and up to 1 m in length. Baked or grilled

dentice *(It)* Dentex, the fish

dentón *(Sp)* Dentex, the fish

Denver sandwich *(USA) see* western sandwich

dépecer *(Fr)* To joint, to carve

dépouiller *(Fr)* **1** To skim fat, scum and similar from the surface of stock, soup, sauce and the like **2** To remove the skin of an animal

Derby *(UK)* A pale yellow, hard but flaky textured, English cheese made from cows' milk. Mild when young but matures over 6 months to develop a fuller flavour

Derby sauce *(UK)* A proprietary sauce

invented by Escoffier. Worcestershire sauce is used as a substitute

dés, en *(Fr)* Diced

desayuno *(Me & Sp)* Breakfast

Desenchildkröte *(Ge)* Terrapin

deshebrar *(Sp)* To shred

déshydrater *(Fr)* To dehydrate

desiccate, to To dry or dehydrate

desiccated coconut The grated or shredded white inner lining of the coconut vacuum dried at 70°C and used as an ingredient in sweet and savoury dishes and as a decoration

desnatar *(Sp)* To skim

désossé Boned, without bones

dessaler *(Fr)* To desalt by soaking in water

dessert *(De, En, No & Fr) masc.* The pudding, ice cream, fruit or other sweet item served at or towards the end of meal

dessert apple A normally sweet apple suitable for eating raw and because they do not lose their shape on cooking are used to make uncovered decorative apple tarts

dessert cream Mixtures of cream with custard and/or fruit purée, often set with gelatine and with a smooth creamy texture. Used as the basis of many desserts

dessert grape Special grape varieties selected for eating raw. Classed as sweetwater - the earliest ripening, muscat - the second to ripen and having the finest flavour, and vinous which have less flavour but are strong growing and mature late in the season

dessert herbs The principal herbs used in desserts, custards, fruit salads, compôtes and the like are angelica, aniseed, bay (custard only), bergamot, dill, elderflower, lemon balm, lemon thyme (custard only), lemon verbena, mint, rosemary, rose petals, scented geraniums and sweet cicely

dessert rice Rice prepared for compounded sweets, puddings and desserts, etc. using long grain rice, washed and blanched twice, cooked with boiling milk, sugar, butter, salt, and vanilla or orange zest flavouring in the oven without stirring, when cooked removed from the oven and enriched with egg yolks. Nowadays more often made with short grain rice cooked in sweetened milk, drained and sweetening adjusted

destone, to *see* to stone

détrempe *(Fr) fem.* A slack mixture of flour and water

devein, to To remove the large vein which runs along the back of the tail meat of a shrimp or prawn

Deventer koek *(Ho)* Deventer cake, a spice cake from Deventer

devil butter A compound butter flavoured with cayenne pepper, vinegar, Worcestershire and Tabasco sauces, refrigerated in a roll and cut into 5 mm slices for garnishing meat and fish dishes

devilled *see* diable, à la

devilled kidneys Peeled, cored and chopped kidneys, sautéed in butter, drained and mixed off the heat with boiling sauce diable. Usually served on toast

devilled sauce *see* sauce diable

devilled sausages Sausages baked in the oven, basted at intervals with a mixture of mustard, chutney, anchovy essence, oil and cayenne pepper. Served with mashed potatoes

devilling Application of a selection from Worcestershire sauce, Tabasco sauce, mustard, cayenne pepper, vinegar and other highly-flavoured condiments to the surface of meat, fish, etc. prior to panéing and frying; *see also* à la diable

devil's dung *see* asafoetida

devil's food cake *(USA)* A rich, sweet and dark brown chocolate cake

devils on horseback As angels on horseback but with prunes instead of oysters

devil's taro *see* black bean curd

devil's tongue **1** *see* snake palm plant **2** Black bean curd

Devon flat *(UK)* A flat biscuit made with self raising flour, caster sugar, clotted cream and egg (4:2:2:1), brought together with a little milk and baked at 220°C

Devon garland *(UK)* A cow's milk cheese from North Devon flavoured with fresh herbs

Devonshire cream Clotted cream

Devonshire hog pudding *(UK) see* hog pudding

Devonshire junket *(UK) see* damask cream

Devonshire split *(UK)* A sweet yeasted bun, split open and filled with jam and whipped cream

Devonshire squab pie *(UK)* A deep pie filled with lamb, apples, onions and seasoning and covered in a pastry crust prior to baking

dewberry An early ripening soft fruit hybrid of the blackberry *Rubus* spp. similar to, but larger and juicier that a blackberry and with a more trailing habit. Cook or use as blackberry

dewcup *see* lady's mantle

dextral Term used of a flat fish in which the eye on the left of the juvenile form moves to join that on the right which becomes the uppermost side of the adult fish

dextrin A polysaccharide made by reducing the number of repeating glucose units in starch. Used in commercial food preparations and when dissolved in water as a glaze for bread and rolls

dextrose *see* glucose

d-glucono-1,5-lactone *see* (E)575.

DHA *see* docosohexanoic acid

dhal *(In)* **1** Term used for dehusked and split pigeon peas, lentils or similar small pulses from the Hindi to split **2** A thin gruel-like dish of cooked dehusked split pulses with aromatic flavourings and spice, onions and other vegetables, very commonly served at Indian meals [also called **dal, dahl, dholl**]

dhania *(In)* Coriander seed

dhania-jeera *(In)* Mixed coriander and cumin seeds (2:1), dry roasted to bring out the flavour and ground

dhania-jira *(In) see* dhania-jeera

dhaniya *(In)* Coriander seed

dhansak *(In)* A mild lamb or chicken stew with vegetables, lentils and spices topped with fried onion rings. Originally brought from Iran to India by the Parsees

dhansak masala *(In)* A mixture of ground coriander and cumin seeds

dholl *see* dhal

dhuli urd *(In)* Dehusked black gram from which all traces of black have been washed out

dhwen-jang *(Ko)* A strong-flavoured salty bean paste similar to hatcho-miso q.v.

diabetic food Food with reduced sugar and carbohydrate suitable for diabetic persons, esp. jams, marmalades, soft drinks, biscuits, cakes and confectionery items

diable *(Fr) masc.* **1** An unglazed earthenware cooking pot in two symmetrical halves which when put together resembles a ball with two flat sides and a long handle. Used for cooking chestnuts and vegetables without water either in the oven or on top of the stove. Can be shaken and turned over for even cooking **2** Kidneys or poussins, split, flattened, grilled and served with sauce diable

diable, à la *(Fr)* Used of food strongly-flavoured with a selection of Worcestershire and Tabasco sauces, mustard, cayenne pepper and vinegar [also called **devilled**]

diable de mer *(Fr) masc.* Monkfish

diable, sauce *(En & Fr) fem.* A reduction of chopped shallots, white wine, vinegar, cayenne pepper and mignonette pepper simmered with demi-glace, strained and seasoned. Served with fried or grilled fish or meat [also called **devilled sauce**]

diablo, en *(Me & Sp)* Devilled, hot and spicy

diablotins *(Fr) masc.* **1** Cheese-flavoured croûtons **2** Christmas crackers

diacetin *see* glycerol diacetate

diamant noir *(Fr) masc. see* French black truffle

diamante citron The principal Italian citron grown in Calabria with a very thick, yellow smooth and slightly ridged skin.

diane, sauce *(En & Fr) fem.* A poivrade sauce enriched with cream

diaphragm The muscular partition separating the lung and abdominal cavity in mammals. Not usually traded separately except in beef cattle

diastase *see* amylase

diavola, alla *(It)* Devilled, served with a spicy sauce, often of a chicken, split, flattened and grilled

diavolini *(It)* Small fried spicy rice cakes

dibs *(ME)* A sugar syrup made from the sugar in sweet grapes, raisins or carob beans by expression, extraction and concentration. Used as a sweetener

dicalcium diphosphate *see* (E)540

dice, to To cut into small cubes with sides between 5 and 15 mm

di centro *(It) see* Parmigiano Reggiano

dick *(Ge)* Thick

Dictyophoria phalloidea *Bot.* Bamboo fungus

dienone A breakdown product of ptaquiloside found in bracken and a potent carcinogen

diente *(Sp)* Clove, e.g. of garlic, not the spice

dieppoise, à la *(Fr)* In the style of Dieppe. Used of any dish containing or garnished with shrimps or served with a shrimp sauce

diepvries *(Ho)* Deep frozen

diet, to To control the intake of food in general or of particular types of food usually with a view to losing weight but sometimes for other medical or health reasons e.g. for coeliac disease and diabetes

dietary fibre Long chain carbohydrates which are not digested in the gut but which add to the bulk of bowel contents, reducing constipation and decreasing the transit time of waste matter thus thought to reduce the incidence of bowel cancer [also called **roughage**]

dietetics The science and study of nutrition and diet

diethyl ether An organic solvent used in some flavourings and food colours

dietician A person trained in dietetics, nutrition and food related illness who advises on these topics usually in relation to illness and health

digester The original name of the pressure cooker.

digestion The processes which take place in the stomach and bowels whereby food is broken down into small molecules which can be absorbed into the blood and transported round the body for use. The process makes use of acid, enzymes and emulsifying agents secreted into the mouth, stomach and bowel and of microorganisms in the gut which convert food into other compounds necessary for health

dill pickles Small cucumbers *(gherkins)* pickled in vinegar flavoured with dill seed or dill weed as well as garlic, spices and salt. The best undergo a lactic fermentation

digestive Any item of food or drink thought to aid digestion

digestive biscuit *(UK)* A crumbly slightly sweet biscuit made from wholemeal flour

Digitaria exilis *Bot.* Hungry rice

dihydrogen citrates *see* citrates

Dijon mustard A pale, smooth and clean tasting prepared French mustard made with brown mustard seed, salt, spices, water and white wine or, more traditionally, verjuice. The most common mustard used in cooking

dijonnaise, à la *(Fr)* In the style of Dijon, i.e. with mustard or blackcurrants and blackcurrant liqueur

dilaw *(Ph)* Turmeric

dilis *(Ph)* A small fish similar to anchovy prepared like ikan bilis

Dill *(Ge)* Dill

dill A tall, hardy annual *Anethum graveolens* from the Mediterranean amd Southern Russia with feathery leaves and clusters of tiny brown seeds reminiscent of aniseed and carroway. Used in bread and cakes, with fish and in pickled cucumbers. From the Norse 'dilla' to lull or induce sleep; *see also* Indian dill

dill sauce *(Sw)* A white velouté sauce flavoured with white wine vinegar, sugar and dried dill, finished with a liaison of egg and cream and garnished with fresh dill

dill weed The leaves of the dill plant used in salads and to flavour pickled cucumbers and fish [also called **Laotian coriander**]

dillilammas *(Fi)* Boiled mutton in dill sauce

dillkött *(Sw)* Best end or scrag end of lamb, blanched and simmered in stock with dill weed, parsley, salt and peppercorns until tender (about 1 hour). Served with dill sauce

dillsås *(Sw)* Dill sauce

dilute, to To make less concentrated by adding e.g. water to sugar syrup or vinegar to prepared mustard

dimbula *(Sr)* A mellow and smooth unblended black tea from Sri Lanka

dimethylpolysiloxane *see* (E)900

dim sum *(Ch)* Steamed or deep fried sweet or savoury snacks served at lunch or in the afternoon before a Chinese meal or with Chinese tea. If steamed often served in characteristic woven split cane baskets. Lit. heart warmers [also called **deem sum**]

dinde *(Fr) fem.* Hen turkey

dindon *(Fr) masc.* Cock turkey

dindonneau *(Fr) masc.* Young turkey, poult

diner *(Ho & Fr) masc.* Dinner

dinner The main meal of the day usually of two or more courses containing meat, fish, cheese or other high protein foods as well as carbohydrates. Served in the evening or around noon, depending on working patterns, region or country, or social class

dió *(Hu)* Walnuts

Dioscorea alata *Bot.* Asiatic yam

Dioscorea bulbifera *Bot.* Aerial yam

Dioscorea cayenensis *Bot.* Guinea yam

Dioscorea elephantipes *Bot.* Elephant's foot (2)

Dioscorea esculenta *Bot.* Chinese yam

Dioscorea japonica *Bot.* Mountain yam

Dioscorea rotundata *Bot.* White yam

***Dioscorea* spp.** The group of plants from which the starchy tuber yam is obtained. See under yam for varieties

Dioscorea trifida *Bot.* Cush-cush yam

diosmetélt *(Hu)* Freshly cooked egg noodles mixed with lard, finely chopped walnuts and sugar, served as a dessert

Diospyros discolor *Bot.* Mabalo

Diospyros kaki *Bot.* Kaki fruit, persimmon

***Diospyros* spp.** *Bot.* Persimmon, American persimmon, kaki, sharon fruit

Diospyros virginiana *Bot.* American persimmon

diot *(Fr)* A fresh sausage containing root vegetables, turnips, beetroot and carrots according to season

dip A soft savoury, usually cold, sauce into which pieces of food such as raw vegetables, crisps, biscuits, etc. are dipped prior to eating

dip, to To fully or partially immerse a solid material or food into liquid or semi-liquid, either to coat the solid or to absorb some of the liquid into it

diphenyl E230, a potent fungicide permitted for use in the wrappings of and in packing cases for oranges and tomatoes [also called **biphenyl, phenylbenzene**]

diphenylamine A food additive with no E number or UK number used as an antioxidant

diplomat pudding As cabinet pudding but served cold with redcurrant, raspberry, apricot or vanilla sauce [also called **pouding diplomate** (Fr)]

diplomat sauce *see* sauce diplomate

diplomate, sauce *(Fr) fem.* Sauce normande with 75 g per litre of lobster butter, garnished with truffles and diced lobster meat. Served with whole large fish

diplomatico *(It)* A chocolate cake flavoured with rum and coffee

dipper A large ladle with a long handle used for transferring small quantities of liquid from a large container

dirty rice *(USA)* A Louisiana dish consisting of a mixture of fried chopped onions, celery, sweet peppers, garlic and minced beef cooked with long grain rice in a seasoned stock. So called because of its appearance

disaccharide A sugar consisting of two simple sugars such as glucose, fructose or galactose chemically bonded together. The most common is sucrose, ordinary beet or cane sugar which consists of glucose and fructose

disjoint To cut carcase meat, game or poultry into pieces by severing the joints between bones

disodium dihydrogen EDTA *see* disodium dihydrogen ethylene diamine-NNN'N'-tetra acetate

disodium dihydrogen ethylenediamine-NNN'N'-tetra acetate A salt of EDTA used as a sequestering agent [also called **disodium dihydrogen EDTA**]

disossato *(It)* Boned, without bones

dispersed phase That phase in a two or more phase mixture which consists of separate and unconnected globules, droplets, particles or bubbles, e.g. oil is the dispersed phase in mayonnaise and hollandaise sauce, buttermilk in butter and air is the dispersed phase in whipped white of egg; *see also* continuous phase

display-until date A date mark used on packaged food for stock control purposes and not an indication of shelf life

dissolve, to To mix a solid with a liquid so that the individual molecules of the solid are separately dispersed in the liquid and cannot be seen. The colour but not the transparency of the liquid may be changed. Not all solids dissolve in all or any liquids

disznóhús *(Hu)* Pork

ditali *(It)* Thimble sized tubes of pasta

ditalini *(It)* A small version of ditali used in soup

di testa *(It) see* Parmigiano Reggiano

ditini *(It)* Cinnamon biscuits from Sicily

divinity A type of fudge made with egg whites, sugar and ground nuts

djej *(NA)* Chicken

djej bil loz *(NA)* A Moroccan dish of chicken stewed with blanched almonds and spices, the sauce thickened with mashed chicken liver

djej mqualli *(NA)* A Moroccan dish of chicken stewed with preserved lemons and olives, the sauce thickened with mashed chicken liver

djuvec *(Bk)* A casserole of meat and rice with tomatoes, aubergines, peppers, courgettes, celery, onions and garlic

djuvec od praziluka *(Bk)* A vegetarian casserole of leeks, tomatoes, chillis and rice from Macedonia

doan gwa *(Ch)* Wax gourd

Döbel *(Ge)* Chub

Dobosch Torte *(Ge)* A tall 10 layer sponge cake with a mocha filling

dobostorta *(Hu)* A layered cake filled with and sides coated with chocolate cream, top covered with caramel which is divided before it sets to facilitate serving

dobrada *(Po)* Tripe

dobrada com feijão branco *(Po)* Stewed tripe, sausages and white beans

dobrada a modo de porto *(Po)* Cooked chick peas, pieces of honeycomb tripe cooked in water, black pepper, bay leaf, cumin parsley, onions and garlic browned in oil and cooked tomatoes all combined in a casserole and simmered or baked for 1 hour

dobrogea *see* peneteleu

doce *(Po)* Sweet

doce de amendos *(Po)* A sweet almond-flavoured dessert with almonds

doce de chila *(Po)* The tough threads of chila or vegetable spaghetti, separated, refrigerated in water overnight, drained, blanched, drained and cooked over medium heat with an equal weight of sugar, drained, the syrup boiled with a cinnamon stick to 116°C and added back to the strands off the heat. Cooled and bottled. Used in sweets and in place of marmalade or jam

doce de leite *(Po & Br)* Arequipe

dock, to To make a number of closely spaced holes in rolled out pastry either with a fork, a hand roller with many short spines or an industrial scale machine. The purpose is to allow any air bubbles in the pastry to collapse and thus prevent irregularities when baked

docosahexanoic acid A polyunsaturated essential fatty acid (EFA) found in egg yolk and fish oils. Its lack in the food of newborn children raised on breast milk substitutes is thought to cause retarded brain development [also called **DHA**]

doddy *see* bottle gourd

dodine *(Fr)* Boned poultry stuffed with pâté, simmered in wine and served with deglazed pan juices

dodol *(Ma)* A dark sweet dessert made from cooked rice and mangosteen

doe Female deer

dog cockle A variety of cockle *Glycmeris glycmeris* found throughout the Mediterranean. They have a distinctive patterned shell, yellow with red to brown circles which appear as though feathered

dog rose *see* rose

dog salmon *see* Siberian salmon

dogfish White fleshed, slightly oily, round bodied fish comprising various species of the shark family with a flexible cartilaginous skeleton up to 1 m in length and usually bought skinned. Common in European waters. See e.g. larger spotted dogfish, lesser spotted dogfish, rock salmon and smooth hound [also called **huss, rock eel, flake, rigg**]

dogh *(Pe)* A type of lassi made from yoghurt, dried peppermint or spearmint, salt and water

doh peeazah A variation of korma *(Indian braising)* in which two additions of onions are made (2 parts onion to 1 part meat). The first half are browned and then cooked with the meat, the second half are grated or processed and added to the meat near the end of the cooking process [also called **do piaaza, dopiaza**]

dok jun *(Th)* Mace

dok mali *(Th)* Jasmine essence

dolce *(It)* Sweet, mild, soft, fresh

Dolce Latte *(It)* A soft creamy and mild blue veined cheese made from cow's milk. Lit. sweet milk

dolceforte *(It)* Sweet and strong as applied to dishes with these characteristics

dolci *(It)* Sweets or desserts, usually eaten in a pastry shop, not with a meal

dolichos bean *see* hyacinth bean

Dolichos biflorus *Bot.* Horse gram

Dolichos sesquipedalis *Bot.* The asparagus bean. Also named *Vigna sesquipedalis*

dolma 1 *(Tu)* Blanched vine, fig, cabbage or other edible leaves wrapped around a filling of minced lamb and rice or other savoury mixture then braised. Served hot or cold **2** *(ME)* Stuffed aubergines or courgettes

dolmades *(Gr)* Vine leaves, wrapped around a filling of fried onions, rice, parsley, seasonings and either currants and nuts, or, fried minced beef or veal, the parcels simmered in water and lemon juice and served cold as an appetizer; *see also* dolmas [also called **dolmathes**]

dolmathes *see* dolmades

Dolmeh *(Pe)* Dolmades

dolphin fish A warm seawater round fish *Coryphaena* spp. found worldwide with a bright silvery gold colour and very tender flesh. Up to 7.5 kg in weight. Poached, baked, fried or grilled [also called **dorado**]

domasni nadenizi-na furna *(Bu)* A mixture of chopped onions, minced meat, fat and a little raw rice, seasoned and flavoured with paprika, packed into sheep's casings and baked in the oven in water and fat with frequent basting

domates dolmasi *(Tu)* Tomatoes stuffed with a mixture of fried onions, raisins, pine nuts, rice, herbs and seasoning, baked in the oven and served cold

domiati *(Ey)* *see* Beda

Dominican masked duck *(USA)* A highly

prized wild duck *Nomonyx dominicus* from the south, shot for the table

domsiah *(Pe)* The finest quality rice

domuz *(Tu)* Pork

donabe *(Ja)* An earthenware casserole used for one pot meals *(nabemono)* cooked at the table

Donaukarpfen *(Ge)* Carp from the river Danube

donburi *(Ja)* A dish of cooked rice topped with some or all of meat, fish, egg, vegetables and garnishes all arranged in a decorative manner and served with spicy sauces

dondurma *(Tu)* Ice cream

doner kebab Thin slices of raw lamb meat with fat and seasoning built up on a spit to make a cylinder 20 cm dia. and 60 - 80 cm long, spit roasted while rotating in front of a source of radiant heat and thin slices carved from the surface as it is cooked. Served with a meal or as takeaway food in a pocketed hot pitta bread with salad. A cheaper version made from minced lamb, fat and other ingredients is common in the UK [also called **döner kebabi**]

döner kebabi *(Tu)* The authentic Turkish version of doner kebab q.v

dong *(Th)* Pickle

dong de *(Ch)* Frozen

dong gu *(Ch)* Hoshi-shiitake mushroom harvested in winter

dong guei *(Ch) see* dang gui

dong gwa *(Ch)* Wax gourd

dong gwa jong *(Ch)* A rich broth served in the elaborately carved skin of a wax gourd

do'nut *(USA)* The American spelling of the doughnut, a version of the similar European bun which is made in the form of a torus after its inventor observed that the centre of the European version was sometimes not cooked

donzella *(It)* Wrasse, the fish

doodh *(In)* Milk

doodhi *see* bottle gourd

dooren *(Ma)* Durian

doperwtjes *(Ho)* Green peas

do piaaza *(In) see* doh peeazah

dopiaza *see* doh peeazah

Doppelrahmstufe *(Ge)* An official category of double cream cheeses with a fat content of 60 to 85% (based on dry matter)

doppio *(It)* Strong, concentrated

doppskov *(De)* Diced leftovers of meat, fried in butter with chopped onion, simmered in cream sauce until heated though, mixed with diced boiled potatoes and served topped with a fried egg

dorada *(Sp)* Gilt-head bream

dorade *(Fr) fem.* Gilt-head bream

dorado 1 *see* dolphin fish **2** A freshwater fish from South American rivers

dorata *(It)* Gilt-head bream

dorato *(It)* Dipped in an egg batter and fried to a light golden colour

doré *(Fr) adj.* **1** Egg washed with beaten egg yolks **2** Golden brown

dorée *(Fr) fem.* John Dory, the fish

dorer, faire *(Fr)* To brown slightly

doreshingu *(Ja)* A salad dressing

doria *(Fr)* Description of a dish containing cooked cucumber

doria, fish Fish meunière dressed with small turned pieces of cucumber sweated in butter or blanched

doria, sauce *(En & Fr) fem.* A Béchamel sauce enriched with cream and flavoured with cooked, chopped cucumber and grated nutmeg. Served with fish

dormeur *(Fr) masc.* Common crab

dorogobouski *(Ru)* A strong-flavoured cow's milk cheese matured for 6 weeks with an orange red rind. Sold in small squares

Dorsch *(Ge)* Cod

Dorset blue *see* blue Dorset

dorso *(It)* Back, of a rabbit, hare, etc.

dorure *(Fr) fem.* Beaten egg for egg washing and glazing

dory A seawater fish *Zeus taber* from the Mediterranean and the Bay of Biscay, famous for St Peter's thumbprint (a large black spot ringed with yellow) behind both gill covers. The head takes up nearly half its length (up to 60 cm female, 45 cm male). The fish is a sandy colour tinged with yellow and blue and has a very fine-flavoured white flesh [also called **John Dory**]

dosa *(In)* A South Indian dish of fried pancakes for which the partially fermented thick pouring batter is made from ground rice and ground urad dal in water. Often stuffed with cooked vegetables e.g. mashed potato

dot, to To put small pieces of butter, etc. over the surface of food so that when grilled or heated it will cover it

Dotterkäse *(Ge)* A cheese made from skimmed cows' milk and egg yolks

dou *(Ch)* Bean

douara *(NA)* A casserole of marinated lamb's tripe, liver and heart

double boiler Two saucepans which fit together one on the other. The top one contains the food to be cooked and the lower one which is directly on the heat contains boiling or hot water. Used to limit the temperature of the food being cooked and to prevent burning esp. when melting chocolate, thickening with egg yolk, etc. [also called **double saucepan**]

double cream **1** A thick cream with a minimum butterfat content of 55%. Sometimes used for whipping but should be diluted with 10% milk **2** *(USA)* Soft cream cheese made from milk enriched with extra cream

double cream cheese A cream cheese with a high fat content made from cream. Generally used for spreading on bread or as a constituent of desserts

double-crème *(Fr) masc.* Soft cream cheese

double crust The term used for tarts and pies with a pastry base and top and any filling

double crust pie A pie with both a pastry base and top

double-decker sandwich *(USA)* A sandwich made with 3 slices of bread and 2 fillings

double Gloucester *(UK)* A hard orange-coloured cow's milk cheese with a rich mellow flavour suitable for cooking and as a dessert. Double refers to its size

double saucepan *see* double boiler

douce *(Fr)* Sweet or mild, before feminine words

douce-amère *(Fr)* Sweet and sour

dou fu *(Ch)* Bean curd [also called **tofu**]

dou fu nao *(Ch) see* bean curd brains

dou fu pok *(Ch)* Fried bean curd

dough A mixture of flour, liquid and possibly yeast and other ingredients which after kneading has a firm, pliable and sometimes elastic consistency rather like putty. Used for making bread, buns, scones, etc.

dough cake *(UK)* A white bread dough enriched with eggs and butter containing sugar, spices and dried vine fruits and baked in a cake or loaf tin

doughboy *(USA)* Dumpling

doughnut A ball of slightly sweetened yeasted or chemically raised dough, deep fried, drained and coated with caster sugar often with jam in the middle. The ring doughnut was the original form made by wrapping the dough around a stick which was suspended in hot oil, the ball form followed but was in turn generally superceded by a ring formed by extrusion because of the difficulty of cooking the centre of the ball without overcooking the surface

douille *(Fr) fem.* Piping nozzle or tube

dou sha bao *(Ch)* Sweet buns made from bean flour

doux *(Fr)* Sweet or mild, before masculine words

dou zhi *(Ch)* Black soya beans

Dover sole One of the finest seawater flatfish *Solea solea* and *S. vulgaris* up to 50 cm long and caught around North West Europe and in the Mediterranean. It is much prized for its lean white flesh. The upper surface is a mud colour and the lower is white. It is very slimy when fresh [also called **sole**]

dow foo *(Ch)* Bean curd

dow ghok *(Ch)* Asparagus bean

dow see *(Ch)* Fermented and salted black soya beans

drabantost *(Sw)* A semi-hard scalded-curd cows' milk cheese. The paste has a bland flavour and is springy with occasional holes

Drachenkopf *(Ge)* Bluemouth, the fish

dragées *(Fr) fem. pl.* **1** Sugared almonds **2** Small silver coloured sugar balls and small chocolate hemispheres used for cake decoration

dragoncello *(It)* Tarragon

dragon's eye *see* longan

drain, to To allow liquid to fall away from a solid by holding it in a colander, chinois or similar item or by laying the solid on absorbent paper. The liquid is usually either water, fat or cooking liquor

dranken *(Ho)* Drinks, beverages

draw, to To remove the innards (heart, lungs, intestines, etc.) of birds and poultry, and sometimes the leg sinews

drawn butter **1** *(USA)* Clarified butter **2** Melted butter used as a dressing for vegetables, sometimes emulsified with water or vinegar

drawn butter sauce *(UK)* A sauce made from a white roux and flavoured water, traditionally served with vegetables or, with the addition of lemon juice, with steamed or poached fish

dredge, to To lightly sprinkle with flour or sugar or other fine powder using a dredger or sieve

dredger A cylindrical metal can with either a removable perforated top or a mesh base used for sprinkling flour, sugar or other fine powders on food items prior to or whilst cooking

Dresden dressing *(USA)* A condiment sauce made from hard boiled egg, onions, mustard and other flavourings and seasonings. Used with meat

Dresdener Stollen *(Ge)* A variety of stollen q.v. from Dresden

dress, to 1 To add a dressing, e.g. of oil and vinegar, to a salad prior to tossing the salad **2** To garnish a dish **3** To arrange a food item which has been cooked as in to dress a crab **4** To prepare poultry or game for cooking by plucking, drawing and trussing

dressé(e) *(Fr)* Garnished

dressed crab Seasoned white and dark crab meat, the latter mixed with breadcrumbs, placed in the upturned cleaned crab shell and garnished or decorated with sieved egg yolk, chopped egg white and chopped parsley arranged in rows across the surface

dressed tripe Bleached and partially cooked tripe

dressieren *(Ge)* To truss

dressing 1 A mixture of oil and vinegar with various flavourings used to dress salads **2** *(USA)* Stuffing or forcemeat

dreux *see* Feuille de Dreux

dried The adjective applied to any edible material from which all or most of the water has been removed so as to improve its keeping quality and inhibit bacterial, fungal and insect attack as e.g applied to fruit, milk, mushrooms, pasta, yeast, egg, tomatoes, peas, pulses, etc.

dried beef *(USA)* Round beef cured with salt and sugar, sliced paper thin, then smoked and pressed [also called **smoked beef, sliced beef**]

dried duck *see* pressed duck

dried fruit Fruit that has had the water content reduced by solar or other drying methods to give a hard almost leathery texture and to reduce the water activity so that it is not degraded by microorganisms. Apricots, peaches, apples, bananas, grapes, tomatoes, plums and similar are all dried

dried gourd strips *see* kampyo

dried grapes *see* dried vine fruits

dried lychees The dried fruit which looks like a raisin and is eaten as a confection or added to desserts

dried mushrooms Completely dehydrated fungi of various types, used extensively in Chinese and Japanese cooking

dried shrimp Whole or ground dried shrimps used extensively in SEA cooking [also called **shrimp floss**]

dried vine fruits Dried grapes esp. currants, sultanas and raisins

drikker *(No)* Drinks, beverages

drinde Dehydrated pork rind, ground and formed into granules for incorporation in cheap English sausages. Up to 10% of the required meat content of sausages may be drinde under UK law

dripping The fat which is extracted from fatty animal tissue and bones by heating or boiling. Originally referred only to the fat from roast meat or bird which had a fine flavour

dripping cake *(UK)* A spiced fruit cake with beef dripping substituted for butter

drisheen *(Ir)* A black pudding made with 2 parts blood to 1 part cream and 1 part breadcrumbs, seasoned and flavoured with tansy and other chopped herbs, filled into 4 cm casings, knotted and boiled for 20 or so minutes. The blood used depends on the supply. Sheep, pig, goose, turkey and hare blood have all been used. The original from Limerick uses sheep's blood

drizzle, to A vogue word for to sprinkle or perhaps with the connotation of a thin stream rather than individual droplets of a liquid

dronningsuppe *(No)* Chicken broth finished with sherry and a liaison of egg yolks and cream and garnished with small forcemeat balls

drop lid A floating wooden pan lid. See otoshi buta

drop scone *(UK)* A flat cake made from a thick coating batter of flour, water, sugar, eggs and cream or butter and a raising agent, dropped on to a hot greased griddle and cooked on both sides. Served with butter and jam [also called **dropped scone, Scottish pancake, Scotch pancake, flapjack scone, griddle cake**]

dropped scone *see* drop scone

dropping consistency The consistency of a cake or pudding mixture such that a spoonful of the mixture held upside down should drop off the spoon in more than 1 and less than 5 seconds

druer *(No)* Grapes

druif *(Ho)* Grape

druiven *(Ho)* Grapes

drum The general class of fish which make drumming noises using their air bladders. Similar to croaker

drumstick The lower part of a chicken or other fowl's leg below the thigh

drumstick bean *see* drumstick pod

drumstick pod The green-skinned slightly peppery tasting seed pod of a tree *Moringa oleifera* which is very thin and up to 40 cm long with small cream coloured seeds. The young pods can be used as a vegetable or when older, boiled and the centre scooped out for use in soup. The mature beans only are used in Indian cooking. Originally from India it is now grown in the Caribbean, Africa and Southern USA [also called **drumstick bean, benoil tree, bentree, susumber**]

drumstick vegetable The pods of a relative of the drumstick tree *Moringa pterygosperma* which grows in India and has the taste and texture of a vegetable marrow. Cut in lengths and cooked like asparagus. The roots of the tree can be grated as a substitute for horseradish

drunken chicken Boiled chicken pieces drained and marinated for 12 to 24 hours with a mixture of salt, sugar and yellow rice wine or dry sherry, drained and garnished with chopped coriander leaf

drupe The name for any fleshy or pulpy fruit enclosing a single stone

druvor *(Sw)* Grapes

dry, to **1** To remove superficial or surface moisture from food **2** To remove superficial and bound water from edible products to produce e.g. dried fruit, dried beans, etc.

dry fry, to To heat and cook food in a frying pan without oil or fat. Suitable for fatty foods or for non fatty foods using, with care, a non stick frying pan. Often used to prepare spices

dry jack *(USA)* A 6 month old Monterey Jack with a distinctive flavour. Suitable for grating

dry measure *see* cup measure

dry mustard *(UK)* Ground dried yellow mustard seeds used as a spice and flavouring agent or when mixed with water as an English condiment

dry roast, to A method of bringing out the flavours of spices and other flavouring agents by subjecting them to dry heat (180°C) in an oven for a few minutes. Pastes, etc. should be wrapped in foil prior to dry roasting

dry-salt, to To preserve food by covering with, immersing in or rubbing on a mixture of coarse dry salt, saltpetre and sugar and possibly spices in the absence of light and leaving it until the food is dehydrated and brine runs off, the first 3 usually in the proportions 50:2:1. Can be used for meat, fish, vegetables, nuts, etc.

dry shell bean *(USA)* Haricot bean

dua nao *(Vi)* Freshly grated young coconut. See kelapa

dua nao kho *(Vi)* Desiccated coconut

Dubarry, à la *(Fr)* Used of a dish containing, or garnished with, cauliflower

Dubarry, crème *(Fr) fem.* Creamed cauliflower soup garnished with small, cooked florets of cauliflower

dubbele boterham *(Ho)* An English type sandwich with two pieces of buttered bread and a filling

dubbelsmörgås *(Sw)* An English type sandwich with two pieces of buttered bread and a filling

Dublin bay prawn A type of lobster *Nephrops norvegicus* up to 25 cm long (excluding the claws) and rose grey to pink in colour, fished from the Western Mediterranean through to Iceland. It is not a prawn. The shelled tail meat is known in the UK as scampi, although monk fish is a cheaper version often substituted for it [also called **scampi, Norway lobster**]

Dublin coddle *(Ir)* A casserole of onions, bacon, potatoes and pork sausage traditionally served with soda bread

duchesse, à la *(Fr)* **1** A description of any dish garnished or served with duchesse potatoes **2** A dish of tongue and mushrooms in a Béchamel sauce **3** A description of pastries containing an almond mixture

duchesse potatoes Seasoned, riced or mashed potatoes mixed with butter and egg yolks and piped into assorted shapes then baked in the oven until browned. Often egg glazed after an initial drying period in the oven [also called **pommes duchesse** (Fr)]

duchesse, sauce *(En & Fr) fem.* Tomato and Hollandaise sauces combined with chopped ham and white wine

duck The general name for a family of swimming birds *Anatidae* with webbed feet and a broad flat beak, some wild, others domesticated, common in French and Chinese cuisines. See e.g. Peking duck and entries under canard

duck eggs The eggs of ducks which are about twice the weight of a hen's egg and are usually pale blue in colour with an almost translucent white when set; *see also* salted duck egg, preserved egg, thousand year egg

duck feet A Chinese delicacy. They are

deboned and softened by slow braising. Sometimes stuffed [also called **duck webs**]

duck sauce 1 *see* Hoisin sauce **2** The sauce used with Peking duck consisting of sweet bean paste, sugar and sesame seed oil processed together, let down with water and simmered until thick

duck skin When cooked to a crisp texture, the most prized part of a roast duck in Chinese cuisine

duck webs *see* duck feet

duckling A young duck

dudhi *see* bottle gourd

dudi *see* bottle gourd

due *(De)* Pigeon or squab

Dugléré, fish As for fish Bercy with tomato concassée added to the cooking liquor. Cooking liquor strained, reduced, mixed with fish velouté and butter, consistency adjusted, seasoned and served over the fish with some of the strained shallots and tomatoes

dügün çorbasi *(Tu)* A beef broth thickened with flour and garnished with diced beef, Paprika butter is added just before serving

dügün eti *(Tu)* A dish of cubed mutton fried in mutton fat with quartered onions, then stewed in tomato purée and water flavoured with lemon juice

duhay *(Ph)* Pomfret, the fish

duja *(It)* *see* salamin d'la duja

duke cherry A hybrid of sweet and acid cherries originating in France where they are known as royale

dukka *(Ey)* A ground spice mix used as a condiment esp. to flavour bread dipped in olive oil. It is made from sesame seeds, skinned hazel nuts or chick peas, coriander seeds, cumin seeds, all dry roasted, with salt, black pepper and dried thyme or mint

dukkah *(Ey)* *see* zahtar (2)

dulce *(Me & Sp)* Sweet

dulce de leche *see* arequipe

dulces *(Sp)* Sweets, desserts

dulse A seaweed *Palmaria palmata* or *Rhodymenia palmata* from the intertidal zone in Ireland and the coastal regions of the North Atlantic, eaten raw or cooked and then dried for use as a snack food or health food

dum, to To steam in the Indian way, for meat usually on a trivet standing clear of the liquid in a pan with a tight fitting lid, for vegetables by chopping them and browning in a little ghee then heating in a closed pan with a little water or akni

dumned Steamed Indian fashion. See to dum

dumpling 1 A round ball of sweet or savoury dough or pastry sometimes made with suet or dripping or other fat, cooked in soups and stews to accompany them, or if sweet, steamed, boiled or baked as a pudding. Sometimes used to coat a piece of fruit as in apple dumpling **2** In Asia a dumpling is often a savoury or sweet filling surrounded with a thin dough sheet similar to ravioli and steamed or boiled

dumpling wrappers *(SEA)* Wrappers for filled dumplings consisting of a wheat flour dough made with egg yolks and warm water, salt and baking powder, kneaded until silky, rested and rolled out thinly and cut in squares or circles. They are normally filled and the edges brought together like a purse

dun *(Ch)* Braising of food in its own juices in a tightly sealed casserole [also called **wei**]

Dundee biscuit *(UK)* A rich short biscuit from Scotland made with plain flour, caster sugar and butter (4:2:1) bound with egg yolk, glazed with egg white and sprinkled with chopped almonds

Dundee cake *(UK)* A Scottish fruit cake made by the creaming method from pound cake mixture containing about 25% more flour than normal and using soft brown sugar with an equal amount of dried vine fruits, candied peel and chopped almonds flavoured with grated lemon and orange zest and topped with rings of split blanched almonds before baking

dun dun *(Af)* Slices of yam or sweet potato, floured, egged and deep fried. Served hot with omelettes [also called **dundu**]

dundu *see* dun dun

Dungeness crab *(USA)* The most popular crab *Cancer magister* caught off the shores of the North Pacific ocean weighing up to 1 kg. The legs are often as meaty as the claws [also called **market crab, Alaska Dungeness crab**]

dunk, to To dip a solid cake or biscuit into a hot drink before eating it

Dunlop *(UK)* A mild, hard cows' milk cheese from Scotland made in the same way as Cheddar except that the curd is not cheddared and the cheese is consequently moister. Developed independently of Cheddar. Contains 43% water, 27% fat and 23% water

Dunmow flitch *(UK)* The name given to the flitch which is awarded annually in Great Dunmow to any married couple who can prove that they have not quarrelled during the preceding year

dünsten *(Ge)* To steam or stew

duo *(USA)* A pasteurized and processed Emmental type cheese filled with walnuts, herbs, spices, black pepper and a salami or smoked salmon forcemeat

duong cuc vang *(Vi)* Palm sugar

dur *(Fr)* Hard, as in oeuf dur, hard boiled egg

durchgebraten *(Ge)* Well done

durian *(En Id & Ma)* The fruit of a Malaysian tree *Durio zibethinus* cultivated all over SEA which has an offensive odour but pleasant taste. It has a green to yellow spiky thick rind, is shaped like a rugby ball and weighs up to 4.5 kg. The segmented flesh is a yellowy soft pulp containing brown inedible seeds. Eaten raw or in both sweet and savoury dishes. The flesh may be canned and the peel is used to smoke fish

duro *(It)* Hard as in a hard crust

durra *see* great millet

Dürrerund *(Au)* A medium sized brown skinned sausage similar to Brunswick sausage

durum wheat A hard, high protein wheat *Triticum durum* used for the production of semolina and pasta. Grown in Italy, Spain and North and South America

Durvillea antarctica *Bot.* Alga mar

Duse, à la *(Fr)* Garnished with tomatoes, French beans and potatoes, particularly of joints of meat

dust, to To sprinkle lightly with finely ground powder such as icing sugar, cocoa, flour, ground nuts, etc.

Dutch cabbage *see* savoy cabbage

Dutch cheese *(USA)* Cottage cheese

Dutch sauce Béchamel sauce enriched with egg yolks and cream and flavoured with lemon juice. Served with fish, chicken and vegetables

duva *(Sw)* Pigeon

duvor i kompott *(Sw)* Braised pigeons made by frying a little diced pork in pork fat, adding pigeons to brown followed by mushroom and covering with seasoned stock flavoured with parsley, chives and tarragon. This is then simmered with a lid on until the pigeons are tender and served with thickened cooking liquor and garnished with the pork and mushrooms

duxelles Chopped shallots or onions and mushrooms, sautéed in butter until quite dry. Used in many other dishes for flavour and bulk

duxelles, sauce *(En & Fr) fem.* Equal volumes of white wine and mushroom cooking liquor with chopped shallots reduced by two thirds then simmered with demi-glace sauce, tomato purée and duxelles for 5 minutes and finished with chopped parsley. Used for gratinated dishes

D value The number of minutes of heat required to reduce the number of viable organisms in a sample of food by a factor of 10. This depends on the temperature and the microorganisms, e.g. 12D minutes of heat treatment are required for canning where D is determined at the treatment temperature and conditions for *Clostridium botulinum*

dwaeji galbi kui *(Ko)* Marinated and grilled pork spare ribs

dwarf bean *see* French bean

dwarf cape gooseberry A smaller version of the cape gooseberry *Physalis pruinosa* with a similar structure and found in the USA. It grows wild in Hawaii [also called **ground cherry, strawberry tomato, poha**]

dybfrossen *(De)* Deep frozen

dynya *(Ru)* Melon

dyrerya *(De)* Saddle of venison

dyrerygg *(No)* Previously marinated venison cooked in sour cream

dyrestek *(No)* Roast venison

dyrlægens natmad *(De)* A Danish open sandwich spread with spiced lard, liver pâté, veal and jellied consommé. Lit. vet's midnight snack

Ee

E numbers All numbers prefixed with E are food additives which are legal in the whole of the EU. Those prefixed with (E) are licensed for use in the UK and possibly other countries but not throughout the EU generally. There are some additives which for reasons of long history are not controlled. These are listed in the general text. A few examples of use are given, These are not exhaustive

E100 Curcumin, the natural colouring obtained from turmeric, used in cakes and margarine

E101 Riboflavin and riboflavin-5'phosphate, vitamin B2 used as a food colouring

E102 Tartrazine, a synthetic dye used as a food colouring in soft drinks but suspected of possibly causing allergies and hyperactivity in children

E104 Quinoline yellow, a synthetic food colouring

E110 Sunset yellow FCF or orange yellow S, synthetic food colourings used in biscuits

E120 Cochineal, the red food colouring extracted from an insect

E122 Carmoisine or azorubine, synthetic red food colourings

E123 Amaranth, a synthetic yellow food colouring banned in the USA, used in alcoholic drinks

E124 Ponceau 4R a synthetic red food colouring used in dessert mixes

E127 Erythrosine BS, a synthetic red food colouring used in glacé cherries

(E)128 *(UK)* Red 2G, a synthetic dye. Used to colour sausages

E131 Patent blue V, a synthetic food colouring

E132 Indigo carmine or indigotine, a synthetic blue food colouring

(E)133 *(UK)* Brilliant blue FCF, a a synthetic food dye used in conjunction with yellows to colour canned vegetables

E140 Chlorophyll, the green food colour made from plants

E141 Copper complexes of chlorophyll used as food colourings

E142 Green S, acid brilliant green BS and lissamine green, synthetic green food colourings

E150 Caramel, the dark brown food colouring made from sugar. Used in beer, soft drinks, sauces and gravy browning

E151 Black PN or brilliant black PN, synthetic black food colourings

E153 Carbon black or vegetable carbon, very finely divided carbon used as a food colouring in e.g. liquorice

(E)154 *(UK)* Brown FK, a synthetic food dye used on kippers

(E)155 *(UK)* Brown HT, a synthetic food dye used for chocolate cake

E160(a) Carotenes, orange food colourings from plants, also precursors of vitamin A

E160(b) Annatto, bixin and norbixin, golden yellow food colourings obtained from the seeds of achiote. Used on crisps

E160(c) Capsanthin or capsorubin, peppery flavoured and pink food colouring obtained from paprika

E160(d) Lycopene, a natural red food colour, one of the carotenoids extracted from ripe fruit esp. tomatoes

E160(e) Beta-apo-8'-carotenal (C30), an orange carotene compound extracted from fruit and vegetables

E160(f) The ethyl ester of E160(e), an orange food colouring.

E161(a) Flavoxanthin, a natural carotenoid yellow food colouring

E161(b) Lutein, a natural carotenoid yellow/red food colouring extracted from flower petals [also called **xanthophyll**]

E161(c) Cryptoxanthin, a natural yellow carotenoid food colouring with some vitamin A activity extracted from petals and berries of *Physalis* spp.

E161(d) Rubixanthin, a natural carotenoid yellow food colouring, isomeric with E161(c) extracted from rose hips

E161(e) Violaxanthin, a natural carotenoid yellow/brown food colouring

E161(f) Rhodoxanthin, a natural carotenoid violet food colouring

E161(g) Canthaxanthin, a natural orange food

colouring extracted from shellfish and used in fish food to give colour to farmed salmon

E162 Beetroot red or betanin, a red food colouring extracted from beetroot. Used for ice cream and liquorice

E163 Anthocyanins, red, violet or blue vegetable food colours extracted from grape skins. Used in yoghurt

E170 Calcium carbonate used as an acidity regulator, obtained from limestone. Used as a firming agent, release agent and diluent

E171 Titanium dioxide, an inert white pigment, usually used in high quality white paints, but also in sweets

E172 Iron oxide and hydroxides, natural red, brown, yellow and black food colourings and pigments

E173 Aluminium, a silvery metal sometimes used in very thin films as a food decoration

E174 Silver, sometimes used in very thin films or layers as a food decoration

E175 Gold, sometimes used as gold leaf, a very thin film for decoration of cakes and dragees

E180 Pigment rubine or lithol rubine BK, a synthetic red colour restricted to colouring the rind of hard cheeses

E200 Sorbic acid, used as a preservative in baked and fruit products, soft drinks and processed cheese slices

E201 Sodium sorbate, the sodium salt of sorbic acid used as a preservative in frozen pizzas and flour confectionery

E202 Potassium sorbate, the potassium salt of sorbic acid used as E201

E203 Calcium sorbate, the calcium salt of sorbic acid used as E201

E210 Benzoic acid, a naturally occurring organic acid also made synthetically, used as a preservative in beer, jam, salad cream, soft drinks, fruit products and marinated fish

E211 Sodium benzoate, the sodium salt of benzoic acid used as E210

E212 Potassium benzoate, the potassium salt of benzoic acid used as E210

E213 Calcium benzoate, the calcium salt of benzoic acid used as E210

E214 Ethyl 4-hydroxybenzoate, a synthetic derivative of benzoic acid used as a food preservative

E215 Sodium ethyl 4-hydroxybenzoate, the sodium salt of E214 used as E210

E216 Propyl 4-hydroxybenzoate, a synthetic derivative of benzoic acid used as E210

E217 Sodium propyl 4-hydroxybenzoate, the sodium salt of E216 used as E210

E218 Methyl 4-hydroxybenzoate, a synthetic derivative of benzoic acid used as E210

E219 Sodium methyl 4-hydroxybenzoate, the sodium salt of E218 used as E210

E220 Sulphur dioxide, a pungent and irritating gas which is one of the most common preservatives used in food. Used in dried fruit, dehydrated vegetables, fruit products, juices and syrups, sausages, cider, beer and wine, to prevent the browning of peeled potatoes and to condition biscuit doughs

E221 Sodium sulphite, a compound formed from caustic soda and sulphur dioxide used as E220

E222 Sodium hydrogen sulphite, a similar food preservative to E221, but containing a higher proportion of sulphur dioxide

E223 Sodium metabisulphite, a compound which contains twice as much sulphur dioxide as E221

E224 Potassium metabisulphite, a similar compound to E223

E226 Calcium sulphite, a food preservative similar to E221

E227 Calcium hydrogen sulphite, a food preservative similar to E222

E228 Potassium bisulphite, a food preservative used in wines

E230 Diphenyl, a fungicide which may be used on the wrappings of oranges and bananas or in their packing cases [also called **biphenyl, phenyl benzene**]

E231 2-hydroxy diphenol, a synthetic compound used in the same way as E230 [also called **orthophenylphenol**]

E232 Sodium diphenyl-2-yl oxide, a synthetic compound used in the same way as E230 [also called **sodium orthophenylphenate**]

E233 2-(thiazol-4-yl) benzimidazole, a synthetic compound used in the same way as E230 [also called **thiabendazole**]

(E)234 *(UK)* Nisin, a food preservative licensed for use in the UK but not generally in the EU. Used in cheese and clotted cream

E236 Formic acid, a natural chemical found in some fruit but made synthetically for use as a flavour enhancer

E237 Sodium formate, the sodium salt of formic acid used as a flavour enhancer

E238 Calcium formate, the calcium salt of formic acid used as a flavour enhancer

E239 Hexamine, a synthetic chemical used as a preservative, restricted to preserved fish and Provolone cheese

E249 Potassium nitrite, the potassium salt of nitrous acid used to maintain the pink colour of cured meats and in some cheeses

E250 Sodium nitrite, the sodium salt of nitrous acid used to maintain the pink colour of cured meat by reacting with the haemoglobin

E251 Sodium nitrate, the sodium salt of nitric acid used for curing and preserving meat

E252 Potassium nitrate the potassium salt of nitric acid used for curing and preserving meat [also called **saltpetre**]

E260 Acetic acid, the acid component of vinegar used as an acidity regulator, as a flavouring and to prevent mould growth

E261 Potassium acetate, the potassium salt of acetic acid used as a preservative and firming agent

E262 Sodium hydrogen diacetate, a sodium salt similar in effect to E261, used as a preservative and firming agent

(E)262 *(UK)* Sodium acetate used in the same way as potassium acetate, E261. Licensed for use in the UK but not generally in the EU

E263 Calcium acetate, the calcium salt of acetic acid used as a firming agent and as a calcium source in quick-setting jelly mixes

E270 Lactic acid, one of the products of anaerobic metabolism of some microorganisms and animal muscle, widely used as an acidifying agent, flavouring and as a protection against mould growth in e.g. salad dressings and soft margarine

E280 Proprionic acid, a simple fatty acid naturally occurring in dairy products but also synthesized for use as a flour improver and preservative

E281 Sodium proprionate, the sodium salt of proprionic acid used as a flour improver and preservative

E282 Calcium proprionate, the calcium salt of proprionic acid used as a flour improver and preservative

E283 Potassium proprionate, the potassium salt of proprionic acid used as a flour improver and preservative

E290 Carbon dioxide, the gas produced when sugar and many other food items are metabolized in the body and by microorganisms. Provides the gas for raising yeasted goods, for use as a propellant, as the gas in sealed packs where oxygen must be excluded and in fizzy drinks

(E)296 *(UK)* Malic acid, an acid found in fruit and also produced synthetically, used as a flavouring in soft drinks, biscuits, dessert mixes and pie fillings

(E)297 *(UK)* Fumaric acid used as (E)296

E300 L-ascorbic acid, vitamin C used to prevent oxidation and thus browning reactions and colour changes in food. Also used as a flour improver

E301 Sodium L-ascorbate, the sodium salt of ascorbic acid used for the same purposes as E300

E302 Calcium L-ascorbate, the calcium salt of L-ascorbic acid used for the same purposes as E300

E304 6-o-palmitoyl L-ascorbic acid, an oil soluble ester of ascorbic acid used for the same purposes as E300 and esp. in Scotch eggs

E306 Extracts of natural substances rich in tocopherols, i.e. vitamin E, used as vitamin additive to foods and as an anti-oxidant esp. in vegetable oils

E307 Synthetic alpha-tocopherol, one of the tocopherols, used an anti-oxidant in cereal based baby foods

E308 Synthetic gamma-tocopherol, one of the tocopherols, used as E306

E309 Synthetic delta-tocopherol, one of the tocopherols, used as E306

E310 Propyl gallate, the propyl ester of gallic acid allowed for use as an anti-oxidant in oils, fats and essential oils only

E311 Octyl gallate, the octyl ester of gallic acid allowed for use as an anti-oxidant in oils, fats and essential oils only

E312 Dodecyl gallate, the dodecyl ester of gallic acid allowed for use as an anti-oxidant in oils, fats and essential oils only

E320 BHA, butylated hydroxyanisole, a controversial anti-oxidant allowed for used in fats, oils and essential oils only

E321 BHT, butylated hydroxytoluene, a controversial anti-oxidant allowed for use in fats, oil, essential oils and chewing gum

E322 Lecithin, a natural substance found in egg yolk, used as an emulsifier and anti-oxidant, for example in low fat spreads

E325 Sodium lactate, the sodium salt of lactic acid used as a buffer i.e. to maintain near constant pH in foods and as a humectant in jams, preserves and flour confectionery

E326 Potassium lactate, the potassium salt of

lactic acid used as a buffer in foods such as jams, preserves and jellies

E327 Calcium lactate, the calcium salt of lactic acid used as a buffer and as a firming agent in canned fruits and pie fillings

E330 Citric acid, the acid present in citrus and other fruit and in animals, used as an acidifying agent, as an emulsifier, as a flavour enhancer, to increase the effects of preservatives, to inhibit bacterial action, as a buffer and as a sequestrant to protect foods from reaction with metals in for example soft drinks, biscuit fillings, jams, dessert mixes and processed cheeses

E331 Sodium dihydrogen citrate, disodium citrate, trisodium citrate, sodium salts of citric acid with the same uses as E330

E332 Potassium dihydrogen citrate, tripotassium citrate, potassium salts of citric acid with the same uses as E330

E333 Calcium citrate, dicalcium citrate, tricalcium citrate, calcium salts of citric acid used in the same way as E330 and also as a firming agent

E334 Tartaric acid, an acid naturally present in many fruits with the same uses as citric aid, E330

E335 Monosodium and disodium tartrate, sodium salts of tartaric acid, used as E334

E336 Potassium tartrate and potassium hydrogen tartrate, potassium salts of tartaric acid used in the same way as E334, the latter is the cream of tartar used as a constituent of baking powder

E337 Potassium sodium tartrate, a mixed salt of tartaric acid used in the same way as E334

E338 Orthophosphoric acid, an inorganic acid used as an acidity regulator in soft drinks and cocoa

E339(a) Sodium dihydrogen orthophosphate, a sodium salt of orthophosphoric acid used as a buffer, sequestrant and emulsifying agent

E339(b) Disodium hydrogen orthophosphate, used as E339(a)

E339(c) Trisodium orthophosphate, used as E339(a) but not as a buffer

E340(a) Potassium dihydrogen orthophosphate, a potassium salt of orthophosphoric acid with the same uses as E339(a)

E340(b) Dipotassium hydrogen orthophosphate with the same uses as E339(a)

E340(c) Tripotassium orthophosphate with the same uses as E339(a) but not as a buffer

E341(a) Calcium tetrahydrogen diorthophosphate, a calcium salt of orthophosphoric acid used as a firming agent, anti-caking agent and raising agent

E341(b) Calcium hydrogen orthophosphate with the same uses as E341(a)

E341(c) Tricalcium orthophosphate with the same uses as E341(a)

(E)350 *(UK)* Sodium malate and sodium hydrogen malate, sodium salts of malic acid used as buffers and humectants in sweets, cakes and biscuits

(E)351 *(UK)* Potassium malate used as (E)350

(E)352 Calcium malate and calcium hydrogen malate, calcium salts of malic acid (E)296, used as firming agents in processed fruit and vegetables

(E)353 Metatartaric acid, a sequestering agent used in wine

(E)355 Adipic acid, an organic acid used as a buffer and flavouring in sweets and synthetic cream desserts

(E)363 Succinic acid, an organic acid used as a buffer and flavouring in dry foods and beverage mixes

(E)370 1,4-heptanolactone, used as an acid and sequestering agent in dried soups and instant desserts

(E)375 Nicotinic acid used as a colour stabilizer in bread, flour and breakfast cereals [also called **vitamin B3**]

(E)380 Triammonium citrate, an ammonium salt of citric acid used as a buffer and emulsifier in processed cheese

(E)381 Ammonium ferric citrate, used as an iron supplement in bread

(E)385 Calcium disodium EDTA, used as a sequestering agent in canned shellfish

E400 Alginic acid, a water-loving carbohydrate acid extracted from seaweeds in the form of mixed sodium, potassium and magnesium salts, capable of absorbing 200 to 300 times its weight in water. Used for thickening and gelling, e.g. in ice cream and soft cheeses

E401 Sodium alginate, the sodium salt of alginic acid used as an emulsifier and stabilizer in cake mixes and in ice cream to provide a creamy texture and to prevent the formation of ice crystals

E402 Potassium alginate, the potassium salt of alginic acid used as a thickener and stabilizer

E403 Ammonium alginate, the ammonium salt of alginic acid used as a more soluble thickener and stabilizer

E404 Calcium alginate, the calcium salt of

alginic acid which gives a much more solid gel than the other alginates.

E405 Propane-1, 2-diol alginate, an ester of alginic acid which is more miscible with fats and oils than simple salts. Used in salad dressings and cottage cheese

E406 Agar-agar, a polysaccharide extracted from certain seaweeds used for thickening, gelling and stabilizing purposes. Soluble only in hot water. Used in ice cream and vegetarian jellies

E407 Carrageenan, a polysaccharide extracted from certain seaweeds consisting of galactose units several of which are sulphated. Used as an emulsifier for oil water mixtures and for gelling and thickening. Used in quick setting jelly mixes and in milk shakes

E410 Locust bean gum, a plant gum used as a thickener or gelling agent, e.g. in salad cream

E412 Guar gum, a plant gum used as a thickener or gelling agent in packet soups and meringue mixes

E413 Gum tragacanth, a plant gum used as a thickener or gelling agent in e.g. salad dressings and processed cheese

E414 Gum arabic, a plant gum used as a thickener or gelling agent esp. in confectionery [also called **acacia gum**]

E415 Xanthan gum, a thickener and gelling agent used in sweet pickles and coleslaw

(E)416 *(UK)* Karaya gum used as an emulsifier and stabilizer in e.g. soft cheeses and brown condiment sauce

E420(i) Sorbitol, a compound found in many berries and fruits, generally synthesized from glucose. Used as a humectant and as a sweetening agent for diabetics.

E420(ii) Sorbitol syrup, a water solution of sorbitol

E421 Mannitol, found in many plants and plant exudates, now synthesized from sucrose. Used as a humectant and in sugar free confectionery

E422 Glycerol, the alcohol which occurs in nature as the other component of fatty acid esters in fats and oils. Used as a humectant in cake icing and confectionery

(E)432 - 436 A group of polyoxyethylene (20) sorbitan esters of fatty acids, used as emulsifiers and stabilizers in bakery products and confectionery creams. They are polyoxyethylene (20) sorbitan monolaurate (432), monooleate (433) monopalmitate (434), monostearate (435) and tristearate (436)

E440(i) Pectin, a natural plant polysaccharide used as a gelling agent or thickener

E440(ii) Amydated pectin, a synthetic derivative of pectin more stable than the parent product

E450(a) Disodium dihydrogen diphosphate, tetrasodium diphosphate, tetrapotassium diphosphate, trisodium diphosphate, salts of phosphoric acid used for flavouring, as stabilizers, buffers, sequestrants, emulsifiers, texturizers and raising agents in fish and meat products, whipping cream, bread, canned vegetables, processed cheese and the like

E450(b) Pentasodium triphosphate and pentapotassium triphosphate, used as E450(a)

E450(c) Sodium polyphosphates and potassium polyphosphates, mixtures of phosphoric acid salts used as E450(a) and to stabilize added water in poultry, ham, bacon and other similar meat products where it appears as a white exudate on cooking

E460(i) Microcrystalline cellulose, a bulking agent used to add bulk and to stabilize slimming foods, convenience foods, desserts and the like and also in grated cheese

E460(ii) Powdered cellulose, as E460(i)

E461 Methyl cellulose, a methyl derivative of cellulose used as a thickener, e.g. in low fat spreads

E463 Hydroxypropyl cellulose, a derivative of cellulose used as E461

E464 Hydroxypropylmethyl cellulose, a mixed derivative of cellulose used as a thickener in ice cream

E465 Ethylmethyl cellulose, a mixed derivative of cellulose used as a thickener in gateaux

E466 Sodium carboxymethyl cellulose, the sodium salt of a derivative of cellulose used as a thickener and bulking agent in jellies and gateaux but mainly used for wallpaper paste

E470 Sodium, potassium and calcium salts of fatty acids, edible soaps used for emulsification of cake mixes

E471 Mono and di-glycerides of fatty acids, manufactured synthetic fats used in place of fats and oils in baked goods, desserts, etc. to improve keeping qualities and to soften and stabilize them

E472(a) Acetic acid esters of mono and di-glycerides of fatty acids, manufactured synthetic fats and oils used as E471

E472(b) Lactic acid esters of mono and di-glycerides of fatty acids, manufactured synthetic fats and oils used as E471 and in convenience toppings

E472(c) Citric acid esters of mono and di-glycerides of fatty acids, manufactured synthetic fats and oils used as E471 and in continental sausages

E472(d) Tartaric acid esters of mono and di-glycerides of fatty acids, manufactured synthetic fats and oils used as E471

E472(e) Diacetyl tartaric acid esters of mono and di-glycerides of fatty acids, manufactured synthetic fats and oils used as E471, esp. in bread and frozen pizzas

E472(f) Mixed acetic and tartaric esters of mono and di-glycerides of fatty acids used as E471

E473 Sucrose esters of fatty acids, manufactured synthetic fats and oils used as E471

E474 Sucroglycerides, manufactured synthetic fats and oils used as E471, esp. in ice creams

E475 Polyglycerol esters of fatty acids, manufactured synthetic fats and oils used as E471, esp. in cakes and gateaux

E476 Polyglycerol esters of polycondensed fatty acids of castor oil used in chocolate flavoured coatings for cakes

E477 Propane-1, 2-diol esters of fatty acids, manufactured synthetic fats and oils used as E471, esp. for instant desserts

E481 Sodium stearoyl-2-lactylate, the sodium salt of a derivative of lactic and stearic acids used to stabilize doughs, emulsions and whipped products

E482 Calcium stearoyl-2-lactylate, the calcium salt corresponding to E481. Used in gravy granules

E483 Stearyl tartrate, a derivative of stearic and tartaric acids used in cake mixes

(E)491 - 495 *(UK)* Sorbitan monostearate (491), tristearate (492), monolaurate (493), monooleate (494) and monopalmitate (495), fatty acid esters of sorbitol used in cake mixes

(E)500 Sodium carbonate, sodium hydrogen carbonate *(bicarbonate of soda)* and sodium sesquicarbonate, used as bases, aerating agents and diluents in jams, jellies, self-raising flour, wine, cocoa and the like

(E)501 Potassium carbonate and potassium hydrogen carbonate *(bicarbonate of potash)* used as (E)500

(E)503 Ammonium carbonate and ammonium hydrogen carbonate, used as buffers and aerating agents in cocoa and biscuits

(E)504 Magnesium carbonate, used as a base and anti-caking agent in wafer biscuits and icing sugar

(E)507 Hydrochloric acid

(E)508 Potassium chloride, used as a gelling agent and as a substitute for salt *(sodium chloride)*

(E)509 Calcium chloride, used as a firming agent in canned fruit and vegetables

(E)510 Ammonium chloride, used as a yeast nutrient in bread making

(E)513 Sulphuric acid, a common industrial acid used for neutralizing alkaline mixes. It produces sulphates on reaction which are mostly harmless

(E)514 Sodium sulphate, used as a diluent for food colours

(E)515 Potassium sulphate, used as a substitute for salt *(sodium chloride)*

(E)516 Calcium sulphate, used as a firming agent and as a yeast food in bread making

(E)518 Magnesium sulphate, used as a firming agent [also called **Epsom salts**]

(E)524 Sodium hydroxide, a very strong base used to adjust acidity in cocoa, jams and sweets

(E)525 Potassium hydroxide, a very strong base used to adjust acidity in sweets

(E)526 Calcium hydroxide, a weak base used as a firming agent in sweets

(E)527 Ammonium hydroxide, a weak base used as a diluent and solvent for food colours and as an acidity regulator for cocoa

(E)528 Magnesium hydroxide, a weak base used to regulate acidity in sweets

(E)529 Calcium oxide, a weak base used to regulate acidity in sweets

(E)530 Magnesium oxide, a fine white powder used as an anti-caking agent in cocoa products

(E)535 Sodium ferrocyanide, used as an anti-caking agent in salt and used in winemaking

(E)536 Potassium ferrocyanide, used as an anti-caking agent in salt and used in winemaking

(E)540 Dicalcium diphosphate, a calcium salt of phosphoric acid, used as a buffer and neutralizing agent in cheese

(E)541 Sodium aluminium phosphate, used as an acid and raising agent in cake mixes, self-raising flour and biscuits

(E)542 Edible bone phosphate, a fine powder made from boiled dried and ground bones, used as an anti-caking agent

(E)544 Calcium polyphosphate, used as an emulsifier in processed cheese

(E)545 Ammonium polyphosphate, used as an emulsifier, a texturizer and to help retain water in frozen chickens without drip on thawing

(E)551 Silicon dioxide, very finely powdered

purified sand, used as an anti-caking agent in skimmed milk powder and sweeteners

(E)552 Calcium silicate, used as an anti-caking agent in icing sugar and as a release agent in sweets

(E)553(a) Magnesium silicate and magnesium trisilicate, used as anti-caking agents and in sugar confectionery

(E)553(b) Talc, a very finely ground natural mineral with a slippery feel, used as a releasing agent in tabletted confectionery

(E)554 Aluminium sodium silicate, used as an anti-caking agent

(E)556 Aluminium calcium silicate, used as an anti-caking agent

(E)558 Bentonite, a very fine white clay-like mineral used as an anti-caking agent

(E)559 Kaolin, a very fine white clay used in dry powder form as an anti-caking agent

(E)572 Magnesium stearate, a type of soap used as an emulsifier and releasing agent

(E)575 D-glucono-1,5-lactone, an acid and sequestering agent used in cake mixes and continental style sausages [also called **glucono delta-lactone**]

(E)576 Sodium gluconate, used as a sequestering agent

(E)577 Potassium gluconate, used as a sequestering agent

(E)578 Calcium gluconate, used as a buffer, firming agent and sequestering agent in jams and dessert mixes

(E)621 Sodium hydrogen L-glutamate, the sodium salt of glutamic acid, used as a flavour enhancer [also called **monosodium glutamate, MSG**]

(E)622 Potassium hydrogen L-glutamate, similar to (E)621 [also called **monopotassium glutamate**]

(E)623 Calcium dihydrogen di-L-glutamate, similar to (E)621 [also called **calcium glutamate**]

(E)627 Guanosine 5'-disodium phosphate, a breakdown product of the nucleus *(genetic material)* of cells, used as a flavour enhancer in savoury foods, snacks, soups, sauces and meat products [also called **sodium guanylate**]

(E)631 Inosine 5'-disodium phosphate, a flavour enhancer similar to (E)627 [also called **sodium inosinate**]

(E)635 Sodium 5'-ribonucleotide, a flavour enhancer similar to (E)627

(E)900 Dimethylpolysiloxane, used as and anti-foaming agent in liquid foodstuffs and ingredients

(E)901 *see* beeswax

(E)903 *see* carnauba wax

(E)904 *see* shellac

(E)905 Mineral hydrocarbons, highly purified mineral oils used to prevent dried vine fruits sticking together and as a glazing and release agent

(E)907 Refined microcrystalline wax derived from crude oil, a soft amorphous looking wax used as a release agent and in chewing gum

(E)920 Cysteine hydrochloride, the acid salt of the amino acid cysteine used as a flour improver [also called **L-cysteine hydrochloride**]

(E)925 *see* chlorine

(E)926 Chlorine dioxide, used as a flour improver

(E)927 Azodicarbonamide, used as a flour improver

ear A tight cluster of seeds or grains at the top of a stalk as in wheat, rye, etc.

early flowering yellow rocket *see* land cress

earshell *see* abalone

earth almond *see* tiger nut

earth nut *see* tiger nut

earthenware Dishes and pots made from baked and vitrified clay, sometimes porous and sometimes glazed, i.e. coated with a glass-like substance to avoid absorption of water and flavours. Sometimes heat resistant; *see also* ceramic and stoneware

Easter biscuit *(UK)* A rich biscuit from the West Country once eaten at Easter. It is made with plain flour, caster sugar, butter and egg yolk (7:3:4:0.6) by the creaming method and flavoured with mixed spice, cinnamon, currants and chopped peel. Glazed with egg white and sugar

Easter cake *see* simnel cake

Easter egg **1** A hollow egg-shaped chocolate confection given as a gift at Easter **2** Hard boiled eggs with the shell painted and decorated, regarded as a symbol of fertility or resurrection according to beliefs and given as a gift at Easter. In the UK, rolled down hills by children until broken

eastern king prawn A variety of king prawn *Penaeus plebegus* found in the East

eastern oyster *see* American oyster

eastern rock lobster *(Aus)* A type of spiny lobster *Jasus verreausci* coloured olive green and found in Eastern Australia. [also called **crayfish** (seawater)]

eastern surf clam *see* surf clam

easternola *(USA)* A mild pork sausage seasoned and flavoured with garlic

eau *(Fr) fem.* Water

eau-de-Cologne mint A herb of the mint family *Mentha piperata* var. *citrata* with smooth bergamot-scented purple tinged dark green leaves and a distinct eau de Cologne smell, suitable for drinks but not used in cooking

eba *(WA)* A thick porridge made from gari and served with soups and stews as the carbohydrate component

ébarber *(Fr)* To remove the beard from shellfish, to trim

Eberesche *(Ge)* Rowanberry

ebi *(Ja)* Shrimp or prawn, often eaten raw in sushi

ebi suimono *(Ja)* A clear soup with shrimps

écarlate, à l' *(Fr)* Salted and pickled meat, usually tongue. Lit. scarlet

Ecclefechan tart *(UK)* A Scottish tart filled with a mixture of butter, dried vine fruits and walnuts

Eccles cake *(UK)* A filled puff pastry case similar to the Banbury cake q.v. Originated in Eccles, now a suburb of Manchester

ecet *(Hu)* Vinegar

ecetestorma *(Hu)* Horseradish sauce

échalote *(Fr) fem.* Shallot

échauder *(Fr)* To heat a liquid such as milk to just below its boiling point, or to heat by pouring boiling water over

échine *(Fr) fem.* The top part of the forequarter of pork, the spare rib joint. Lit. backbone

Echinochloa colona *Bot.* Shama millet

Echinochloa crusgalli *Bot.* Barnyard millet

Echinochloa frumentacea *Bot.* Japanese millet

Echium vulgare *Bot.* Viper's bugloss

Echourgnac *(Fr)* A small, pale yellow, delicately flavoured cow's milk cheese from Aquitaine. It has brown rind and the cheese contains small holes

Echtermainzkäse *(Ge)* A soft Handkäse-type cows' milk cheese with a yellow rind and white paste. The flavour varies from mild to sharp depending on age

éclair *(En & Fr) masc.* A finger length of choux pastry piped on a tray, baked, cooled, split in half lengthways and filled with Chantilly cream or crème patissière, the top coated with coffee or chocolate glacé icing

éclanche *(Fr) fem.* Shoulder of mutton

Ecole Supérieure de Cuisine Française de Paris A prestigious private cookery school for grands chefs cuisiniers

écossaise, à l' In the Scottish style, i.e. with barley and root vegetables

écossaise, sauce Cream sauce mixed with a brunoise of carrot, celery, onion and french beans which have been stewed in butter and white bouillon until almost dry. Served with eggs and poultry

écrevisse *(Fr) fem.* Crayfish

écrevisse à pattes rouges *(Fr) fem.* Freshwater crayfish

écumer *(Fr)* To skim

écureuil *(Fr) masc.* Squirrel

Edam *(Ho)* A semi-hard, ball-shaped, yellow cheese made from partially skimmed cows' milk using a lactic starter. It dates from at least the 8th century. After shaping, it is dry salted or brined, ripened for a few weeks and coated with a red wax. Rather mild and bland but easily sliced. Contains 45% water, 25% fat and 28% protein [also called **Manbollen, Katzenkopt, Moor's head**]

edamame *(Ja)* Fresh soya beans

Edamer *(Ge)* The German version of Edam cheese [also called **loaf cheese**]

eddik *(No)* Vinegar

eddike *(De)* Vinegar

eddo *see* eddoe

eddoe A roundish scaly African tuber from a plant *Colocassia esculenta* var. *antiquorum*, similar to but smaller than taro and used as a starchy staple food in African and Caribbean cuisine [also called **malanga**]

Edelblankkäse *(Ge)* A soft surface ripened cow' milk cheese with white veining. The flavour is mild when young but becomes sharper with age

Edelkastanie *(Ge)* Chestnut

Edelpilzkäse *(Ge) see* Pilz

édeskömény *(Hu)* Caraway seeds

edesseget *(Hu)* Sweet things

edible bone phosphate *see* (E)542

edible chrysanthemum *see* garland chrysanthemum

edible crab *see* common crab

edible sea urchin A large sea urchin *Echinus esculentus* up to 8 cm across but not as flavoursome as the small varieties. Found from Norway to Portugal

Edinburgh fog *(UK)* Sweetened whipped cream flavoured with vanilla and mixed with chopped almonds and crushed macaroons

EDTA *see* ethylenediamine-NNN'N'-tetra-acetate

eel A long, smooth, round, catadromous fish *Anguilla* spp. up to 130 cm long and weighing to 8 kg, usually without scales and with no pelvic fins. The flesh is dense and fatty and the bones are a good source of gelatine. Usually killed immediately before cooking. Often smoked and served with horseradish. Popular in Japan and Chinese coastal regions; *see also* elver

eel pie island pie *(UK)* A pie of skinned and boned eel pieces brought to the boil in water with nutmeg, sherry, chopped parsley and sweated chopped onions and immediately removed. Placed in a pie dish with some coarsely chopped hard boiled eggs, the cooking liquor thickened with beurre manié, seasoned and acidulated with lemon juice poured over the eel, the top covered with puff pastry, egg washed and the whole baked at 220°C for 15 minutes then at 190°C for a further 30 minutes. Named after Eel Pie Island in the Thames at Twickenham

eel pout A freshwater, non-oily relative *Lota lota* of the cod, found in Northern Europe. Resembles and is cooked like eel [also called **barbot, burbot, lote**]

een choy *(Ch)* Chinese spinach

eend *(Ho)* Duck

EFA Essential fatty acid

effervesce To bubble vigorously or foam, not by boiling

efterrätt *(Sw)* Dessert

e-fu noodles Flat yellow coloured egg noodles from China which have been fried until crisp before sale. They can be eaten as is or softened by blanching

egg *(En & No)* A most important food item both for its nutritive and texturizing properties. Most eggs have a hard shell made of calcium carbonate, an inner membrane, an air pocket at one end between the membrane and the shell, a central yellow to orange yolk supported by two filaments and a surrounding transparent white. In fertilized eggs the embryo is seen as a small blood spot at the edge of the yolk. Hen's eggs are the most common food item, but duck eggs and quail's eggs are available; *see also* egg white, egg yolk and egg sizes

egg and butter sauce Melted butter, seasoned, flavoured with lemon juice and chopped parsley and mixed with diced hard boiled eggs at the rate of 12 per kg of butter. Used for whole poached fish

egg coagulation Separated white of egg coagulates between 60 and 65°C and the yolk between 62 and 70°C. These temperatures are raised when eggs are mixed into liquids with other additions. Coagulation and thickening of an egg, milk and sugar mixture, as in custard, will take place between 80 and 85°C and it will start to curdle at 88 to 90°C [also called **egg setting**]

egg and crumb, to *(USA)* To pané

egg cup A small container shaped like a goblet used to hold a soft boiled egg in its shell for ease of opening and eating

egg custard A mixture of egg (whole or yolk), sweetened milk and flavouring cooked over a bain marie or in a double boiler until the egg has set (80 to 85°C). The consistency depends on the proportions of egg to milk

egg custard sauce A thin pouring sauce similar to crème à l'anglaise but with only 8 to 10 egg yolks per litre of milk [also called **fresh egg custard sauce, sauce à l'anglaise**]

egg herbs The principal herbs used with eggs are basil, chervil, chives, dill, marjoram, oregano and rosemary

egg mayonnaise A hors d'oeuvre consisting of shelled, hard-boiled eggs, halved lengthwise, placed on a plate, cut side down, coated with mayonnaise and garnished

egg noodles Narrow ribbons of pasta containing eggs, sometimes made from eggs, flour and salt only. Available fresh or dried. Common in Italy, SEA, Japan and China. Chinese egg noodles are sometimes flavoured to suit the dish they will be served with

egg pasta *see* pasta all'uovo

egg poacher A type of miniature bain marie with an upper dish containing hemispherical indentations each sized to hold an egg. Used to poach eggs

egg roll *see* spring roll

egg sauce Béchamel sauce flavoured with nutmeg with the addition of diced hard boiled eggs (6 eggs per litre). Used for poached or boiled fish and smoked haddock; *see also* Scottish egg sauce

egg separator An implement shaped like a large spoon or small ladle with a slot or holes to allow the white of an egg to pass through leaving the yolk in the spoon

egg setting *see* egg coagulation

egg sizes A numerical system for sizing eggs ranging from size 1 greater than 70 g to size 7 less than 45 g. The standard egg used in recipes is size 3 weighing 60 to 65 g (2oz). The system in the UK has recently been changed to small, minimum weight 45 g; medium, minimum weight 55 g; large, minimum weight 65 g and extra large minimum weight 90 g. The standard 2 oz egg size in this system is medium

egg slicer A small implement rather like a cheese slice but with a hollow base to hold a hard boiled and shelled egg, and multiple wires on a hinged frame which cut through the egg and into slots in the base

egg thread net A lacy crêpe made by allowing beaten and strained eggs to drip off the fingers into hot fat in an omelette pan to form a lacy pattern which is cooked until firm enough to handle. Used as a food wrapping or garnish in SEA

egg wash, to To brush beaten egg over bread rolls, pastry, duchesse potatoes and similar foods prior to cooking in order to glaze them and give them a pleasant brown colour. They may be partially baked to harden the surface prior to egg washing

egg wedger As egg slicer but with the wires arranged to cut the egg into wedges

egg white The transparent gel surrounding the yolk of an egg which amounts to about 60% of the weight of a hen's egg. (See albumen for its composition). When fresh the egg white is viscous and stands high on a plate, as it ages it becomes thinner and is better for whisking

egg yolk The central part of the egg usually light yellow to orange, semi-liquid and held separate within a fragile membrane. It contains about 16% protein mainly lecithin, 33% fat including cholesterol plus vitamins, trace elements and water. It represents about 30% of the total weight of a hen's egg

eggah *see* eggeh

eggeh *(ME)* The Arabic version of the omelette in which precooked vegetables together with seasonings, herbs and spices are bound into a stiff mixture with the egg prior to cooking by frying on both sides. May be cooked as one large circle or in tablespoonfuls. Probably the origin of the Spanish tortilla

eggeh beythat *(ME)* Hard boiled eggs with the shell removed, pricked through to the yolk in several places, deep fried in olive oil until brown, then rolled in a mixture of cinnamon, turmeric, ground cumin and coriander and seasoning. Served hot or cold

eggerøre *(No)* Scrambled egg

egg foo yung *(Ch)* An omelette filled with a mixture of shredded cooked meat, shellfish and cooked vegetables flavoured with soya sauce, garlic, chopped spring onions and sherry or rice wine

eggkake *(No)* Omelette

eggplant *see* aubergine

eggs Benedict *(USA)* A muffin or slice of toast covered with grilled Canadian-style bacon, topped with a poached egg, coated with Hollandaise sauce and garnished with a slice of truffle

eggs Sardou *(USA)* Poached eggs served with artichoke hearts, anchovies, chopped ham and truffle and accompanied with Hollandaise sauce

eggy bread *(UK)* Unsweetened and unflavoured pain perdu topped with grated Caerphilly cheese and chopped pickled onion mixture and grilled until brown. Served immediately

eglantine *see* rose

églefin *(Fr) masc.* Haddock [also called **aiglefin**]

eglefino *(It)* Haddock

Egon Ronay's Guide *(UK)* One of the restaurant guides to which complaints or experiences may be sent. Address: 73 Ulverdale Rd. London SW10 0SW. Others are Good Food and Michelin

egres *(Hu)* Gooseberries

egusi melon A melon *Cucumeropsis* spp. esp. *C. edulis* grown in west Africa for its oil-bearing seeds

Egyptian bean *see* hyacinth bean

Egyptian lentils *see* masoor

Egyptian lotus The Nile plant *Nymphaea lotus*, used in the same way as the true lotus

Egyptian mint *see* applemint

Egyptian onion A member of the onion family *Allium cepa* var. *proliferum* which produces a cluster of small bulbs at the flower instead of seeds. These are often too small to be of culinary interest [also called **tree onion, calawissa onion**]

égyptienne, à l' *(Fr)* In the Egyptian style, i.e. with lentils

égyptienne, purée *(Fr) fem.* As purée St Germain, but substituting yellow split peas for the peas and leaving out the carrot [also called **yellow pea soup**]

Ei *(Ge)* Egg

ei *(Ho)* Egg

ei gebakken *(Ho)* Fried egg

Eichhörnchen *(Ge)* Squirrel

Eidotter *(Ge)* Yolk of egg

eierenpannekoeken *(Ho)* Pancakes

Eierfrucht *(Ge)* Aubergine

Eierhaber *(He)* A type of omelette made with eggs, milk, seasoning and a little flour, cooked then cut in small pieces

Eierkuchen *(Ge)* Pancake

Eierpflanze *(Ge)* Aubergine

Eierrösti *(He)* Diced bread soaked in milk then mixed with beaten eggs and cooked in butter with continuous stirring

Eierteigwaren *(Ge)* Egg noodles and egg based pasta

eindosen *(Ge)* To can

eingemacht *(Ge)* Preserved, as of fruits, etc.

Eingemachte *(Ge)* Jam. marmalade, preserves

Eingepökelte *(Ge)* Pickles

Einkorn A variety of wheat *Triticum monococcum* grown on poor soil in Central Europe, containing a single column of grains along the ear

Einsiedlerkrebs *(Ge)* Hermit crab

Eintopf *(Ge)* A meat and vegetable stew from the mining areas using fairly tender cuts of meat served with the unthickened cooking liquor. Lit. one pot

Eis *(Ge)* Ice cream, ice

Eisbein *(Ge)* Boiled pickled pig's knuckles, usually served with sauerkraut, puréed peas and potatoes

Eisenia bicyclis *Bot.* Arame

Eiweiss *(Ge)* White of egg

ejotes *(Me)* Green beans

ekmek *(Tu)* Bread

ekmek kadayifi *(Tu)* Honey-soaked bread or cake topped with buffalo milk cream

eksili çorba *(Tu)* Mutton broth thickened with a mixture of flour, eggs, lemon juice and water and garnished with diced fatty mutton

eksili köfte *(Tu)* Meat balls made from a mixture of chopped raw beef, eggs, chopped parsley, moistened breadcrumbs and seasoning, cooked in a sauce of water, tomato purée and sweated chopped onions, finished just before service with crushed garlic, cinnamon and vinegar

ekte mysöst Real mysöst, i.e. made from pure goat's milk

Elaeis guineensis *Bot.* Oil palm from which palm oil and palm kernel oil are extracted

elaichi *(In)* Cardamom

elastin One of the proteins which make up connective tissue, predominating in sinews and gristle. It does not break down into gelatine on cooking

Elbo *(De)* A hard, mild, slightly acidic tasting cheese similar to Danbo, made from cow's milk and cast in bricks to 5 kg. The slightly acid-tasting paste contains a few holes and the smooth brown rind is usually covered in red wax

elbow macaroni *(USA)* Short pieces of macaroni curved into a right angle bend

elder *(UK)* Cooked and pressed cows' udder. Now rare

elderberry The fruit of a tree *Sambucus niger (EU & USA), S. canadensis (Eastern USA)* and *S. caerula (Western USA)* which consist of clusters of spherical shiny black fruits to 5 mm in dia. each containing a single seed. The Eastern and Western USA varieties are larger than the European, may be red or golden and are commercially cultivated as a fruit

elderflower The white creamy flowers of the elderberry tree which grow in clusters. Used for decoration and sometimes deep fried as fritters

élédone *(Fr)* Curled octopus

eleesh *(In)* A rather oily river fish from the Hooghly

elefante di mare *(It)* Lobster

Elefantenlaus *(Ge)* Cashew nut

elenolic acid One of the antibacterial agents in olives which inhibit lactic acid fermentation. It is removed by treatment with dilute caustic soda solution (lye) or by daily soaking in fresh water for 2 to 3 weeks

Eleocharis dulcis *Bot.* Water chestnut

Eleocharis tuberosa *Bot.* Water chestnut

elephant apple *see* wood apple

elephant garlic *(USA)* A very large garlic-looking vegetable with a very mild garlic flavour. The cloves may be cooked as any tuber, or may be used raw in salads

elephant's ears *see* amaranths

elephant's foot 1 A member of the arum

family *Amorphophallus campanulatus* from India grown for its white to pink fleshed tubers which keep extremely well. The higher yielding type is rather acrid and requires long boiling [also called **suram**] **2** An African species of yam *Dioscorea elephantipes* with clusters of tubers which grow above ground

Elettaria cardamomum *Bot.* Cardamom

Eleusine caracana *Bot.* Ragi

elevenses *(UK) coll.* A mid-morning drink and possibly snack

elft *(Ho)* Shad

el ful *(Ey) see* ful medames (2)

elg *(No)* Elk

eliche *(It)* Pasta twists rather like fusilli

Ellendale *(Aus)* An important mandarin from Australia with a very juicy high quality flesh which is sweet and tasty. Now also grown in South America

elmo *(USA)* A semi-soft creamy textured cow's milk cheese with a hickory nut flavour

elöétel *(Hu)* Hors d'oeuvres

elöételek *(Hu)* Appetizers

elote *(Me)* Fresh corn

elver A young eel considered a delicacy in France and Spain, usually stewed in garlic, sautéed or deep fried

emblanquecer *(Sp)* To blanch

embuchado de lomo *(Sp)* A cured loin of pork (eye of loin only) enclosed in a skin like a long straight sausage and kept in olive oil. Eaten raw

embutidos *(Sp)* Pork sausage and cured meat

emek *(ME)* A popular Israeli cheese resembling Edam

émincé *(Fr)* A description of food cut into thin slices or shredded with a knife or mandolin or in a food processor

émincer *(Fr)* To slice thinly, to cut into slivers or thin slices

émissole lisse *(Fr)* Smooth hound, the fish

Emmental *(He)* A hard cooked-curd cow's milk cheese from the Emmental valley with a sweet, nutty flavoured glossy paste containing random holes. Both lactic and propionic acid starters are used and after forming into a large wheel (to 80 kg) wrapped in cheesecloth it is salted in brine and ripened for 5 to 7 months. Copied worldwide. Used to make fondue. Contains 35% water, 37% fat and 27% protein [also called **Emmenthal, Emmentaler**]

Emmental grand cru de l'Est *(Fr)* A French Emmental cheese with a regionally administered appellation d'origine

Emmentaler *(He)* **1** *see* Emmental **2** A regional Brühwurst type sausage

Emmenthal *(He) see* Emmental

émoudre *(Fr)* To grind

empada *(Po)* Pie, patty

empadinha *(Po)* Small pie or tart

empadinhas de camarão *(Po)* Small shrimp pies

empanadas *(Me & SA)* Pasties made from a yeast-raised dough containing sweet or savoury fillings, baked or shallow fried and eaten hot

empanadillas *(SA & Sp)* Small semicircular pasties made with a well rested flour and butter pastry (8:5), rolled very thin, filled with a savoury mixture and deep fried until golden

empanaditas *(Me & SA)* Small empanadas eaten as snacks or appetizers

empanado *(Sp)* Coated in breadcrumbs

emperor's omelette *see* Kaiserschmarren

Empetrum nigrum *Bot.* Crowberry

emping melinjo *(Id)* The kernel and horny covering around the fruit of the melinjo tree. It is rolled flat and sun dried for use as a snack or garnish

emulsifier A compound which aids the dispersion of one liquid or semi-solid in another with which it is immiscible, e.g. oil and vinegar to make mayonnaise, butter with milk and sugar in cake mixes. The emulsifier is usually a long chain molecule one end of which dissolves in water and the other end in fat. Egg yolk and French mustard are culinary emulsifiers but many others, synthetic as well as natural, are used in commercial made up dishes and mixes

emulsion **1** A mixture of two or more immiscible liquids or semi-solids in which one is divided into very small droplets (less than 0.01 mm dia.) dispersed in the other(s). Mayonnaise, Hollandaise sauce and cake batters are typical examples; *see also* emulsifier, homogenize, dispersed phase and continuous phase **2** Butter whisked into salted boiling water, used for reheating vegetables just before service to give a pleasing sheen

en *(Fr)* In, as in en croûte, in a crust; en papillote, in paper or foil

enamel A glass like covering for steel sometimes

used for trays, saucepans, casseroles, etc. The enamel can be chipped, crazed by temperature shock or scratched with harsh cleansers or metal spoons, etc.

enasal *(Sr)* Cardamom

encarnada *(Po)* Red

enchaud *(Fr) masc.* A dish from Périgord of pork and pigs' trotters piquéed with garlic, baked and flavoured with truffles

enchilado *(Me)* A white, salty and crumbly cow's milk cheese made in a block and sometimes coloured on the outside with chilli powder or annato. Used for cooking esp. enchillada

enchillada *(Me)* A thin masa harina tortilla fried both sides, brushed with chilli or tomato sauce, rolled around a filling of cooked meat or poultry or grated cheese, coated with more sauce and eaten hot with guacamole and/or refried beans

enchovas *(Po)* Anchovies [also called **anchovas**]

encornet *(Fr) masc.* Squid

encre *(Fr) fem.* The black ink from squid or octopus used in sauces for same

encurtidos *(Sp)* Pickles

endive 1 A bitter salad plant *Cichorium endivia* with curly ragged leaves all springing from the base without a heart. Originally from SEA and introduced by the Dutch in the 16th century and subsequently developed. It can be blanched by excluding light when growing to remove the bitterness. Known as chicorée in France and escarole in the USA. Unfortunately (Belgian) chicory is known as 'endive' in France causing much confusion; *see also* escarole, Batavian endive [also called **moss curled endive, staghorn endive, curly endive, winter frisée**] **2** *(Fr) fem.* Belgian chicory

endiver *(Sw)* Chicory or chicon

endives à l'étuvée *(Fr) fem.* Braised chicons of Belgian chicory

endives au jambon *(Fr) fem.* Braised chicons of Belgian chicory wrapped in a slice of ham

Endiviensalat *(Ge)* Endive salad

endomame *(Ja)* Peas

endosperm The white 80% to 90% inner portion of the wheat grain consisting of spherical starch granules surrounded by a protein matrix and some cell wall material which remain after the bran and wheatgerm have been removed

endrina *(Sp)* Sloe, the fruit

endrina grande *(Sp)* Bullace, the fruit

endura *(Sr)* Dill seed

enebro *(Sp)* Juniper

eneldo *(Sp)* Dill

engelsk bøf *(De)* Fillet steak. Lit. English beef

English breakfast *(UK)* A substantial meal of fruit juice, fruit and/or cereals followed by a selection of bacon, sausages, kidneys, eggs, tomatoes, mushrooms and bread, all grilled or fried, or kedgeree or kippers followed by toast, butter, jam and/or marmalade and tea or coffee

English custard *(UK)* Sweetened milk thickened with custard powder (cornflour and vanilla flavouring) and served as a sweet pouring sauce. Sometimes coloured yellow [also called **custard, custard sauce**]

English egg custard *(UK) see* crème à l'anglaise

English muffin *(USA) see* muffin (1)

English mustard A mixture of dehusked and ground brown and white mustard seeds mixed with wheat flour and turmeric, sold dry or mixed with water and preservatives. Used for flavouring or as a condiment

English puff pastry method Roll out dough into a rectangle 20 cm x 30 cm, cover two thirds (20 x 20) with an even layer of the remaining fat, fold in three to give three layers of dough interleaved with two layers of fat, roll out to the original size repeat the fold, rest the dough then proceed as for puff pastry q.v.

English sausage *(UK)* Apart from regional and speciality sausages a rather revolting mixture of ground meat (which includes fat, drinde, MRM and other parts of the animal not generally considered to be meat) with rusk, extenders, binders and flavourings packed in casings. By law, pork sausage must contain 65% meat (of which 10% may be drinde), whilst pork and beef sausage need only contain 50% meat

English truffle A truffle *Tuber aestivum* found in Wiltshire, UK, growing in the root area of beech trees, but not generally available

enguia *(Po)* Eel

enlatar *(Sp)* To can

enlever *(Fr)* To remove

enoki *(Ja) see* enokitake

enokitake *(Ja)* A small delicately flavoured mushroom *Flammulina velutipes* which grows in clumps at the base of the Chinese hackberry tree. They have slender stalks (to 8 cm long) with a white gold cap. Sold in clumps for use as a garnish or in Japanese salads such as aemono and sunomono. Available fresh or dried [also called **enoki**]

enrich, to 1 To add some or all of butter, milk, sugar and eggs to a bread dough to produce buns, etc. or to add butter or cream to a batter or sauce, or similar additions **2** To add back vitamins, trace elements or minerals to processed foods such as white flour, cereals, margarine, fruit juice, etc., sometimes to replace losses in processing, sometimes as a matter of public health policy

enriched rice *(USA)* Rice, enriched with vitamins and minerals to make up for some of the losses in milling

enrollado *(Me)* Rolled

ensaimada *(Sp)* A stuffed savoury or sweet bread similar to an empanada

ensalada *(Sp)* Salad

ensalada andaluza *(Sp)* A salad of sweet peppers, tomatoes, olives, rice and garlic

ensalada de arroz *(Sp)* Rice salad

ensalada de pepino *(Sp)* Cucumber salad

ensalada de San Isidro *(Sp)* Lettuce and tuna salad

ensalada de verano *(Sp)* A salad of baked aubergine, tomatoes, sweet peppers and onions with an oil and lemon juice dressing

ensalada variada *(Sp)* Mixed green salad

ensaladilla *(Sp)* Salad

enset A relative *Ensete ventricosum* of the banana whose corms and stems are used as a food and fibre source in Ethiopia. The tree is very resistant to drought and supports some of the densest populations in Africa. It could be grown in western and southern Africa

ensopada *(Po)* A meat or fish and vegetable soup thickened with bread

Ente *(Ge)* Duck

Entenbrüstchen *(Ge)* Duck breast

Entenmuschel *(Ge)* Barnacle

Entenweissauer *(Ge)* Duck in aspic

entosensal *(Ph)* Caul

entrahmte Milch *(Ge)* Skimmed milk

Entrammes *(Fr)* The cheese from Entrammes in Brittany made by the monks who originally made Port-Salut but who sold the name to commercial interests. Very similar to Port-Salut

entrecot *(Sp)* Entrecôte steak

entrecôte 1 A steak cut from the middle part of a sirloin of beef **2** *(It & Fr) fem.* A thick juicy well marbled beef steak cut from the wing ribs

entrecôte al ferri *(It)* Grilled fillet or entrecôte steak of beef

entrée 1 *(En & Fr) fem.* The main course or courses of a dinner consisting usually of a proteinaceous part such as meat, game, fish or pulses with or without accompaniments but complete with one of the classic white or brown sauces and garnish. Served hot or cold but if there are two dishes, the hot is served first **2** Traditionally, a dish forming a complete course in itself without accompaniments served between the fish course and the roast

entrée, en *(Fr)* A method of trussing a bird in which the drumstick is put through an incision in the skin

entremeses *(Sp)* Hors d'oeuvres

entremets *(Fr) masc.* Sweet or dessert, the course following the cheese at a French dinner. Originally any dish served after the main course

entremétier *(En & Fr) masc.* Vegetable cook

entrocosta *(Po)* Entrecôte steak

E number A three figure number currently in the range 100 to 500 prefixed by a capital E which is used on packaging to identify all food additives which are accepted as safe throughout the EU. These do not cover all the additives allowed in the UK or other countries of the EU. Many of these have numbers and those legal in the UK but not generally throughout the EU are given in numerical order with the E numbers at the beginning of this section. They are distinguished by the prefix (E)

enzyme A natural protein which speeds up the rate of chemical reaction under moderate conditions of temperature, such as oxidation, browning of apples, decolourizing of vegetables, etc. They are easily inactivated by extremes of pH, high concentrations of salt, addition of alcohol or most importantly by temperatures of 80°C or above

épaule *(Fr) fem.* Shoulder, usually of lamb or veal, épaule d'agneau, épaule de veau

epazote A strong flavoured herb used in Mexican cooking and to make an infused tea [also called **Mexican tea, wormseed**]

eper *(Hu)* Strawberries

éperlan *(Fr) masc.* Smelt

épice *(Fr) fem.* Spice

épices composées *(Fr) fem.* A classic spice mix of dried and ground thyme, basil, bay and sage plus coriander seeds, mace and black peppercorns all ground [also called **spice Parisienne** (USA)]

epicure A person who appreciates fine food

épicurienne, sauce *(Fr) fem.* Mayonnaise

flavoured with gherkins and smooth chutney. Served with cold meat, eggs, poultry and fish

épigramme *(Fr) fem.* Slices of boiled breast of lamb, panéed and fried in butter

épinard *(Fr) masc.* Spinach

épine *(Fr) fem.* Loin of meat. Lit. backbone

épis de maïs *(Fr) masc.* Sweet corn

eple *(No)* Apple

eplesnø *(No)* Apple snow

éplucher *(Fr)* To peel

Epoisses *(Fr)* A soft strong flavoured cows' milk cheese from Burgundy, formed into 300 to 400 g discs and washed in brine or local eau-de-vie. Sometimes wrapped in vine leaves or flavoured with spices. Normally has a scored orange crust

éponger *(Fr)* To dry using an absorbent material as e.g. using kitchen paper

Epping sausage *(UK)* A skinless frying sausage made of equal parts of pork meat and beef suet, finely minced, seasoned, flavoured with nutmeg, sage and a little bacon and bound with egg

Epsom salts *see* (E)518

équille *(Fr) fem.* Sand eel

erba *(It)* Herb

erba cipollina *(It)* Chive

erba dei gatti *(It)* Catmint

erba riccia *(It)* Lamb's lettuce

erbaggi *(It)* Pot herbs, green vegetables, salads

erbette *(It)* A spinach or beet-like leaf vegetable [also called **bietoline**]

Erbsen *(Ge)* Peas

Erbsenbrei *(Ge)* Puréed peas

Erbsensuppe *(Ge)* Pea soup

Erdapfel *(Au)* Potato

Erdapfelnudeln *(Au)* Very small potato dumplings rolled in fried breadcrumbs

Erdartischocke *(Ge)* Jerusalem artichoke

Erdbeere *(Ge)* Strawberry

Erdbeerkaltschale *(Ge)* A cold strawberry soup made from pulped wild strawberries mixed with sugar and white wine, passed though a sieve and garnished with whole wild strawberries dipped in sugar

Erdnuss *(Ge)* Peanut

ergocalciferol *see* vitamin D2

Erimis peynir *(Tu)* A semi-hard spun curd cheese made from ewes' or goats' milk and eaten fresh

Eriobotrya japonica *Bot.* Loquat

eriphie *(Fr) see* cangrejo moruno (Sp)

erizo de mar *(Sp)* Sea urchin

Erkentaler *(Ge)* An Emmental-type cheese

ermek kaimaksi *(Ru)* A bread pudding from Armenia made from slices of crustless heavy bread toasted in the oven at 170°C until golden, overlapped in a shallow dish, moistened with a little milk and then soaked in a sugar syrup (2 kg per litre) and baked at 180°C until brown and puffy. Served covered with kaimak, a type of clotted cream

ermitaño *(Sp)* Hermit crab

Ermite *(Cn)* A semi-hard blue veined cows' milk cheese from Quebec

erter *(No)* Peas

ertersuppe *(No)* Pea soup

Eruca vesicaria *Bot.* Rocket

erucic acid A fatty acid once a significant constituent of rapeseed oil and considered a potential danger to health in large quantities. Varieties of rape which contain only low concentrations have now been developed for oil production

erugala *see* rocket

ervanço *(Po)* Chick peas

ervilhas *(Po)* Peas

erwentensoep *(Ho)* A thick puréed soup made from split green peas and vegetables in a meat stock. It is refrigerated after cooking then reheated with Frankfurter sausages. A national dish of Holland

erwten *(Ho)* Peas

erythrosine BS E127, a synthetic red food colouring, used for glacé cherries

ésaü *(Fr) masc.* Description of any dish containing lentils. (From the Bible story)

escabeche *(Sp)* **1** Pickled **2** Cooked small whole fish marinated in a spiced oil and vinegar mixture and served cold in the marinade **3** The marinade used in 2 above

escalfado *(Po)* Poached

escalfados Poached eggs

escalfar *(Sp)* To poach

escalivada *(Sp)* A Catalan dish of vegetables grilled over charcoal or on a barbecue

escalopado *(Me)* Made into escalopes

escalope *(En & Fr) fem.* A thin slice of meat cut from a large muscle without bone, gristle or sinews, often from the top of the leg or the fillet, beaten out until very thin prior to frying

escalope cordon bleu Two escalopes of pork or veal, made into a sandwich with 1 slice of Gruyère cheese and 1 slice of ham, edges dampened to seal, panéed, marked with a diamond pattern on the presentation side, shallow fried and served with a rondel of lemon and chopped parsley

escalope normande, vallée d'Auge *(Fr) fem.* An escalope of veal or chicken breast served with a calvados flavoured cream sauce and sautéed apples

escalope de veau *(Fr) fem.* A veal escalope usually panéed and fried or coated with flour, seared and simmered in stock or wine

escargot *(Fr) masc.* Edible snail

escargot de mer *(Fr) masc.* Whelk. Lit. sea snail

escargotière *(Fr) fem.* Dish on which snails are served

escargots à la bourguignonne *(Fr) masc.* Snails with garlic butter and chopped parsley

escarola *(Sp)* Endive

escarole *(It & USA)* A variety of slightly bitter broad-leaved endive *Cichorium endivia* used in salads. Usually blanched in the garden [also called **scarola** (It)]

Escherichia coli A human gut bacteria whose presence in food indicates poor food hygiene. Some strains found in meat can cause food poisoning. The incubation period in 12 to 72 hours, the duration is 1 to 7 days and the symptoms are either cholera-like illness with watery diarrhoea and pain or prolonged diarrhoea with blood and mucous

***Escherichia coli* strain 0157:H7** A strain of the gut bacteria *Escherichia coli* found in hamburger-type ground beef which has picked up toxin-producing genes from *Shigella* spp. These toxins can destroy gut and kidney cells leading to diarrhoea and kidney failure. The incubation period is 3 to 4 days. Common in the USA, and has occurred in Europe, Africa, Australia and Japan. The organism is killed by a temperature of 70°C for 2 minutes

Escoffier Auguste Escoffier 1846 - 1935, apprentice chef at age 13, worked until 1920, took charge of the Savoy Hotel (London) kitchens in 1890, opened the Carlton and the Paris Ritz in the late 1890's, wrote and published Le Guide Culinaire in 1903 which contains over 5000 recipes and is still a classic reference book. Famous for his instruction to chefs - 'faites simple' - keep it simple

escovitch *(Ca)* Escabeche

escupina gravada *(Sp)* Warty venus clam

Eskdale *(UK)* A Camembert type cheese from Yorkshire

espadín *(Sp)* Sprat

espadon *(Fr) masc.* Swordfish

espagnole, à l' *(Fr)* In the Spanish style, i.e. with sweet peppers, tomatoes, garlic and onions

espagnole, sauce *(En & Fr) fem.* Brown sauce, one of the three classic basic sauces made from a brown roux mixed with tomato purée and brown stock flavoured with defatted browned aromatic vegetables and simmered from 4 to 6 hours skimming as necessary, finally strained [also called **brown sauce, Spanish sauce**]

espaguetis *(It)* Spaghetti

espargo bravo *(Po)* Wild asparagus

espargos *(Po)* Asparagus

espárrago *(Sp)* Asparagus

especia *(Sp)* Spice

espetar *(Sp)* To truss

espinaca *(Sp)* Spinach

espinafre *(Po)* Spinach

espresso *(En & It)* Coffee made with dark roasted finely ground coffee through which superheated water (water under pressure at a temperature greater than 100°C) is forced. This extracts a high proportion of coffee solubles plus bitter components not normally found in conventionally brewed coffee

esprot *(Fr) masc.* Sprat

esqueixada *(Sp)* Fish salad from Galicia

esquinade *(Fr)* Spider crab

Esrom *(De)* A semi-hard soft cheese with irregularly shaped holes ripened for 1 to 3 weeks. It is cast in 500 g to 1 kg bricks and has a mild piquant flavour and a thin yellow to orange coloured rind. Contains 50% water, 23% fat and 22% protein

essbare Muschel *(Ge)* Clam

essence An extract of flavouring compounds usually from fruit or vegetable matter but occasionally from meat. The extractant is usually alcohol

essential amino acids Amino acids which are necessary for health and cannot be synthesized in the body and must therefore be obtained from food. They are:- isoleucine, leucine, lysine, methionine, phenylalanine, threonine, tryptophan and valine plus histidine which is required by growing infants and may be required by adults

essential fatty acids Fatty acids which cannot be synthesized in the body and must be obtained from food sources. The important ones are linolenic, linoleic, arachidonic (AA), gammalinolenic (GLA) and eicosopentanoic acid (EPA). All are involved in the synthesis of prostaglandins which have a variety of important bodily functions and in the construction of the myelin sheaths around nerve fibres and the synthesis of cell walls [also called **vitamin F, EFA**]

essential oil The oily compounds secreted by or extracted from plants, flowers and fruit which have a concentrated aroma. Used in flavourings

essenza *(It)* A meat or fish glaze

Essig *(Ge)* Vinegar

Essiggurke *(Ge)* Pickled gherkins

Essigkren *(Ge)* Horseradish sauce, grated horseradish in vinegar with sugar and spices

Essigpilze *(Ge)* Pickled mushroom

ester The general name for the compound produced by reacting an alcohol with an acid. Most esters have pleasant fruity flavours and aromas. Some are extracted from fruits but many are now made synthetically.

Esterhazy Rostbraten *(Au)* Roast stuffed fillet of beef basted with Madeira wine

Esterházy rostélyos *(Hu)* Thin slices of seasoned sirloin steak browned in lard and casseroled with sliced onion, carrots, Hamburg parsley and flour, browned in the same fat, seasoned stock, slices of lemon and capers until cooked. The steak is removed and transferred to a dish on a bed of julienned carrots and Hamburg parsley previously fried in butter and simmered in stock. The strained juices from the casserole are poured over, sour cream added and all simmered for a few minutes. Served with rice or noodles

estofado *(Sp)* Beef or veal pieces simmered with sliced onions, strips of green pepper, chopped tomatoes, the flesh of charred garlic, olive oil, lemon juice, wine, paprika, bay, parsley and thyme for about 2 hours or until cooked adding a minimum of water as required; *see also* humba (Ph)]

estofado de rabo *(Sp)* Oxtail stew with garlic, tomato and anchovy paste

estofar *(Sp)* To stew

estomac *(Fr) masc.* Stomach

Estonkij *see* Estonski

Estonski A semi-hard cows' milk cheese from Estonia which uses a complex mixed culture as a starter to give it a mildly acid aromatic flavour. Contains 45% water, 25% fat and 23% protein [also called **Estonkij**]

estouffade 1 *(En & Fr) fem. see* brown beef stock **2** *(Fr) fem.* A beef or pork pot roast with vegetables or beans, herbs, seasoning and stock or wine [also called **etouffat**]

Estragon *(Ge)* Tarragon

estragon *(Ru & Fr) masc.* Tarragon

estragón *(Sp)* Tarragon

estragon, à l' *(Fr)* Flavoured with tarragon

estragon, sauce *(En & Fr) fem.* A velouté sauce based on fish stock flavoured with tarragon. Served with fish

estrella *(Sp) see* Oropesa

estrellado *(Sp)* Fried (egg)

esturgeon *(Fr) masc.* Sturgeon

esturión *(Sp)* Sturgeon

et *(Tu)* Meat

étamine *(Fr) fem.* Muslin, cheese cloth or tammy cloth for straining

ethanol The alcohol produced by the fermentation of sugars which is responsible for the intoxicating effects of alcoholic drinks. It disappears from boiling liquid after some time. Used as a solvent for food colourings and flavourings [also called **ethyl alcohol**]

Ethiopian cardamom The seed pods of a bush *Aframomum korarima* from Ethiopia used as a cheap substitute for green cardomom. Has a more camphor like flavour than the true cardamom

ethoxyquin A chemical used to prevent discolouration (scald) on apples and pears

ethrog *see* etrog (citron)

ethyl acetate An ester of ethanol and acetic acid used as a solvent for food colours and flavourings

ethyl alcohol *see* ethanol

ethylenediamine-NNN'N'-tetra-acetate A very common and powerful sequestering agent both as is and as its salts. Abbreviated to EDTA

etikkasilli *(Fi)* Pickled herring

etolaj *(Hu)* Cooking oil

Eton mess *(UK)* Chopped strawberries macerated in Kirsch (5:1 by weight) then mixed with cream whipped to a trail and crushed meringue and served immediately in individual dishes decorated with strawberies and mint leaves

étouffat *(Fr)* *see* estouffade

étouffe of beef *(USA)* A Creole pot roast from Louisiana containing beef, onions, green peppers, tomatoes, garlic and seasonings [also called **smothered beef**]

étouffée *(Fr) fem.* A pot with a very tight fitting lid used for steaming or braising

étouffée, à l' *(Fr)* Cooked in a pot with a tight fitting lid and with very little liquid over a low heat

étrille *(Fr) fem.* Velvet swimming crab

etrog A citron smaller than most varieties with a smooth firm and yellow to yellow orange skin with deep ridges. Used in the Jewish feast of the tabernacles. [also called **ethrog**]

etto *(It)* Hectogram equal to one tenth of a kilogram, 100 g

étuvée, à l' *(Fr)* Braised

Euda *(USA)* A low fat semi-hard cows' milk cheese which is salted, moulded and ripened for 3 months

Eugenia caryophyllus *Bot.* Cloves

Eugenia uniflora *Bot.* Surinam cherry

europäischer Flusskrebs *(Ge)* Freshwater crayfish

European edible frog *see* frog

European flat oyster The original oyster of European waters *Ostrea edulis.* Considered to have the best flavour with the English native being the most prized. They are found from Norway down to Morocco and the Mediterranean and are best served raw with a squeeze of lemon; *see also* oyster

European grape The original European grape variety (*Vitis vinifera*); *see* grape

European sand smelt *see* sand smelt

European Welsh onion *see* Welsh onion

eustis A variety of limequat q.v.

Euter *(Ge)* Udder

evaporated milk Homogenized cow's milk from which 60 to 65% of the water has been removed under a vacuum at not more than 66°C. Sold sterilized in cans. Use as a cream substitute

evening primrose A hardy biennial plant *Oenothera biennis* growing to 2 m with large yellow flowers. The seeds are the source of evening primrose oil which contains a high proportion of gamma linoleic acid, a precursor of many important body chemicals and used as a health supplement and prophylactic. The leaves and stems were once used as a popular food by North American Indians. The root may be boiled and eaten either pickled or as a salad vegetable

Eve's darning needle *(USA)* *see* yucca (2)

Eve's pudding *(UK)* A pudding made in a dish with alternating layers of sliced apples and sugar, topped with a basic steamed pudding mix or Victoria sponge mixture and baked

Evora *(Po)* A pale yellow mountain cheese made from a mixture of ewe's and cow's milk. It is well salted with a full flavour and has a crumbly texture. Eaten either fresh when creamy and piquant or fully ripe when firm and biting

ewe A female sheep

Excelsior *(Fr)* A mild double cream cow's milk cheese from Normandy shaped like a small cylinder

Exeter stew *(UK)* A beef, onion and dumpling stew

exocet *(Fr) masc.* Flying fish [also called **poisson volant**]

explorateur *(Fr)* A small cylindrical shaped triple cream cow's milk cheese from the Paris region with a delicate flavour and a Camembert type rind

extended life *see* ultra-heat treated

extender A substance added to food to increase its bulk as e.g. flour with ground spices or gelatine, water and sugar with whipped cream

extra vergine *(It)* *see* extra virgin olive oil

extra virgin olive oil The first cold pressing of stoned and skinned ripe olives with a free oleic acid content of less than 1% The term has nothing to do with quality and there is no regulation to prevent manufacturers reducing the acidity by chemical means

extract, to To extract flavour, colour or aroma from a foodstuff by a variety of means, e.g. simmering in water, macerating in alcohol, with oil, steam distillation, squeezing, pressing or absorbing onto a solid or fat

extraction 1 The process of extracting one component from a mixture **2** The percentage of flour which is obtained from the original dehusked wheat grain. For white flours this is normally around 80%. Above this figure the bran content starts to increase giving a brown appearance

extractives The flavouring components in meat and browned vegetables which dissolve in the cooking liquor to give it flavour

extracts Flavourings, aromas and colours in concentrated form produced by extraction

Extrawurst *(Au & Ge)* A moist, light coloured Bruhwurst made from a well spiced mixture of beef and pork or bacon fat. Used for slicing and sandwiches, in salads, or cooked in stews and casseroles [also called **Fleischwurst**]

extrude, to To force a paste or semi-solid through variously shaped holes under high pressure as e.g. in the production of sphaghetti, macaroni and the like

eye 1 The term for the circular or oval shape formed from the cross section of a single muscle cut out from a chop or slice of meat **2** The dark spot on a potato from which the next year's shoots would sprout

eye of round *(USA)* The round muscle in the centre of the top of the hindquarter (rear leg) of beef. Part of the topside in the English cuts

eyeballs Eyeballs of sheep removed from the head after cooking are eaten as a delicacy in some Middle Eastern countries

Ff

faa jiu *(Ch)* Anise pepper

faan *(Ch)* Rice

faan sue *(Ch)* Sweet potato

faarn woon *(Ch)* The small individual rice bowl from which Chinese meals are eaten

faat sau gwa *(Ch)* Choko

fabada *(Sp)* A Spanish cassoulet from Asturia made with butter beans, sausage and smoked ham

façon de, à la *(Fr)* In the style or manner of

fadge *see* Irish potato cakes

fagara *see* anise pepper

fågel *(Sw)* Poultry or game

fågelbo *(Sw)* As solöga but with a ring of chopped cold boiled potatoes added. Lit. bird's nest

fågelsås *(Sw)* Game sauce made from game bones browned with aromatic vegetables, simmered in stock for 20 minutes, skimmed, strained, thickened with beurre manié and finished with cream

faggot 1 The name applied to a bunch of herbs tied with string and used as a BG **2** *(UK)* A pâté of liver, salt pork or bacon, herbs, spices, seasoning, minced onion and extender such as breadcrumbs, oatmeal or mashed potato, formed into a tennis ball size and covered with pig's caul. Traditionally made with liver, lungs, spleen, pork scraps and fat. Simmered or baked [also called **savoury duck, poor man's goose, Welsh faggot**]

fagianella *(It)* Pheasant [also called **fagiano**]

fagiano *(It)* Pheasant [also called **fagianella**]

fagioli *(It)* Dried beans

fagioli asciaboli *(It)* Butter beans

fagioli assoluti *(It)* Cooked bean fried with garlic in oil

fagioli di lima *(It)* Butter beans

fagiolini *(It)* French green beans

fagiolini all'aretina *(It)* French beans stewed with oil, tomatoes and sage

fa goo *(Ch)* Shiitake mushroom

fagot *(USA)* Faggot (of herbs)

fagottino *(It)* Pastry

fagylaltot *(Hu)* Ice cream

fah chiu *(Ch)* Hot seasoning pepper

Fahrenheit scale The scale of temperature in which the freezing point of water is 32 and the boiling point 212 written 32°F and 212°F. Once used in the UK and found in old recipes, still in use in the USA

faht choy *(Ch)* A marine algae made up of fine hair-like strands, probably the same as nori

fai chee *(Ch)* Chopsticks

fai gee *(Ch)* Large chopsticks (30 to 50 cm), used in cooking

fair maids *coll. (Cornwall)* Smoked pilchards

faire lever *(Fr)* To leaven or raise with yeast or chemical raising agent

faire revenir *(Fr)* To brown (vegetables, meat, etc.)

fairy cakes Small individual cakes made from a sponge mixture with currants, baked in a bun tin or paper case and decorated

fairy ring mushroom An edible mushroom *Marasmius oreades* which grows in circular rings on grass land, the rings becoming larger each year. It has a small fawn hump backed cap on a slender stem

faisan *(Fr) masc.* Cock pheasant

faisán *(Sp)* Cock pheasant

faisandeau *(Fr) masc.* Young pheasant

faisander *(Fr)* To hang game

faisane *(Fr) fem.* Hen pheasant

faisão *(Po)* Pheasant

faisinjan *see* fesejan

fajita *(Me)* A soft tortilla filled and rolled with some or all of grilled meat, grated cheese, chopped lettuce, tomatoes and spring onions. Served warm with sour cream

fak *(Th)* Wax gourd

falafel *(ME)* A common street food made from

soaked chick peas, onions, garlic, fresh parsley or coriander leaves, ground cumin and coriander seed, cayenne pepper, salt and baking powder processed to a fine cohering paste, formed into small flattened balls and deep fried for 3 to 4 minutes; *see also* ta'amia [also called **felafel**]

faloode *(Pe)* An Iranian version of ice cream made from starch noodles, herb extract, rosewater and sugar

falscher Hase *(Ge)* Mock hare made with chopped beef, pork and veal mixed with sweated chopped onions, capers, lemon juice and seasoning, bound with eggs, formed into a roll, panéed and roasted in butter. Served with pan residues deglazed with cream

falscher Wildschweinbraten *(Ge)* Mock boar made from a skinned and trimmed leg of pork, marinated in red wine and vinegar (4:1) with grated onions, juniper berries, lemon zest, bay leaves, tarragon, ground cloves, allspice, ginger and black pepper for 2 days then roasted at 160°C in the usual way

falsk hollandäs *(Sw)* Mock Hollandaise sauce, not based on Béchamel as is Dutch sauce but on a fish velouté enriched with egg yolks into which butter and lemon juice are whisked over a low heat until thick and creamy

falukorv *(Sw)* A sausage from Falun made of beef, lean pork and pork back fat, hot smoked and eaten hot either as is or as a made up dish

familiario *(It)* In a simple, homely style

fan *(Ch)* Rice

fan mussel One of the largest British mussels *Pinna fragilis, P. pectinata* up to 35 cm long with a yellow brown shell which it buries in the sand. Cooked like a scallop [also called **pen shell, sea wing**]

fanchette *(Fr) fem.* A tiny tart made of puff pastry filled with crème patissière and covered with meringue [also called **fanchonnette**]

fanchonnette *see* fanchette

fanesca A lenten soup from Ecuador made from salt cod, vegetables, peanuts, cheese, milk, cream, stock and seasonings

fan kua *(Ch)* A heavy metal pan used for cooking rice by the absorption method

far *(Fr) masc.* A rum flavoured tart or flan from Brittany

får *(Sw)* Mutton

får i kål *(Sw)* A lamb and cabbage casserole consisting of blanched and possibly parboiled breast of lamb or shoulder of lamb, trimmed, defatted and cut in pieces, layered with cabbage in a large pan with a few peppercorns, salt and flour between each layer, covered in stock and simmered 1.5 to 2 hours. Served garnished with chopped parsley. It may be reheated

faraona *(It)* Guinea fowl, often covered in damp clay before roasting

Färberbaum *(Ge)* Sumac

farce *(En & Fr) fem.* A stuffing or forcemeat

farce, to To stuff

farce de gibier *(Fr) fem.* Game livers quickly browned with chopped onion in butter (4:1:1), plus thyme and bay leaf, the centre of the livers must be underdone, then sieved, seasoned and mixed with butter equal in quantity to that used for frying

farci(e) *(Fr) adj.* A description of any food filled with a savoury stuffing or forcemeat

farci niçois *(Fr) masc.* Stuffed courgettes, aubergines, tomatoes and onions braised slowly in olive oil.

farcima A type of ancient Roman sausage thought to be the origin of the words farce and forcemeat

farcir *(Fr)* To stuff

farcito *(It)* Stuffed

farçon au cerfeuil *(Fr)* Riced potatoes, mixed with beaten eggs, milk, fried diced bacon, onions and shallots, raisins, grated cheese, seasoning and chervil and baked in a greased dish at 220°C until golden

fare bollire *(It)* To boil

fåre frikassée *(No)* Fricassée of lamb or mutton

fåre kød *(De)* Mutton

fårekjøtt *(No)* Mutton

fårekotelett *(No)* Mutton chop

fårestek *(No)* Roast leg of lamb or mutton

fårepølse *(No)* A sausage made with a mixture of mutton, beef, goats' meat and sugar, seasoned and moistened with alcohol of some kind

farfalle *(It)* Small pasta pieces made in the shape of a bow tie or butterfly

farfallini A small version of farfalle

farfel A small diamond or pellet shaped Jewish pasta

fårgryta med linser *(Sw)* A casserole of middle neck of lamb browned in dripping, laid in a heavy pot on a bed of sweated onions, covered with water or stock plus a BG and seasoning, simmered and skimmed for an hour, soaked lentils added and simmered until cooked, BG removed and the whole finished with a little soya sauce and chopped parsley

farina *(En & It)* The name given to various types of flours made from wheat, nuts or root vegetables

farina di granturco *(It)* Cornflour

farinaceous Containing a high proportion of starch

farinata alla contadina *(It)* Polenta, wheat flour and milk boiled to a gruel with poppy seeds and sweetened [also called **mus**]

farinata alla ligure *(It)* A fried cake of chick pea flour

farine *(Fr) fem.* Flour

farine de blé *(Fr) fem.* Wheat flour

farine de froment *(Fr) fem.* Wheat flour

farine de maïs *(Fr) fem.* Cornflour

farinha de avêa *(Po)* Oatmeal

farinha de mandioca *(Po)* A flour made from cassava much used in Brazil

fårkött *(Sw)* Mutton

farl *(UK)* Small thin triangular shaped biscuits or cakes from Scotland and Northern Ireland made with wheat flour or oatmeal. Usually baked in the round and scored for quarters. Lit. fourth part

farmed salmon Salmon grown in cages in sea lochs or inlets in Scotland, Norway and other suitable locations. Distinguishable from wild salmon by their pinker flesh and perfect tail fins

Farmers' *(USA)* Cottage cheese made from cultured cow's milk with added cream, salted and sold in tubs

farmhouse Cheddar *(UK)* The traditional Cheddar cheese made in small dairies, always matured in cloths for 1 to 2 years and having a superb flavour

farmhouse loaf A white bread dough raised in an oblong loaf tin, dusted with flour and the top slit or slashed lengthwise so that the slit opens out as it bakes

farofa *(Br)* A bland mealy flour made from cassava, often toasted before use

farricello *(It)* Barley

far sang *(Ch)* Peanut

farsh *(Ru)* Stuffing

farshi *(Ne)* Winter squash

farshirovannye pertsy *(Ru)* Stuffed sweet peppers, usually with a cooked spicy mixture of minced lamb, onions, rice and sultanas with tomato purée, eggs and honey and all baked at 190°C for 40 minutes [also called **perets farshirovanny**]

Färsk getost *(Sw)* A semi-hard goats' milk cheese made in a brick shape (to 1.2 kg) and ripened for up to 1 week

färsk sill *(Sw)* Fresh herring

fårstek *(Sw)* Leg of mutton

far sung yau *(Ch)* Peanut oil

Fasan *(Ge)* Pheasant

fasan *(De, No & Sw)* Pheasant

faschierter Braten *(Ge)* Meat loaf

fasciola A species of fluke infecting cattle and sheep worldwide, transmitted to humans by watercress and other aquatic plants which act as host to the larvae, and causes liver damage for which no satisfactory cure yet exists

faséole *(Fr) fem. see* haricot rouge

fasnacht *(USA)* A yeast-raised potato dough, rolled out, cut in diamond shapes, proved and fried. Traditionally eaten on Shrove Tuesday by the descendants of Pennsylvania Dutch immigrants

fasol *(Ru)* French beans in the pod, flageolet beans or haricot beans

fasolaro *(It)* Venus shell clam [also called **cappa liscia**]

fassolatha *(Gr)* A meatless soup made with parboiled (15 minutes) haricot beans drained then fried with chopped onions and garlic in olive oil, all boiled in water with tomato purée, tomato concassée, bay and origano until the beans are tender, seasoned and finished with chopped parsley

fast food Food which can be cooked very quickly while the customers wait, e.g. fish and chips, hamburgers, doner and shish kebabs and Chinese stir fry dishes

fast freeze, to To freeze food very rapidly so as to prevent the formation of large ice crystals within the cell which would disrupt them and cause the contents to leak out on thawing, thus destroying the structure of the food

fasulya *(Tu)* Beans

fasulya plâki *(Tu)* A salad made from cooked haricot beans, chopped onions, tomatoes and sweet peppers, dressed with olive oil, flavoured with seasonings and chopped parsley or dill

fat An ester of fatty acids and glycerol formed in

the bodies of animals or plants as a long term energy store, and in the case of animals as a source of energy for their young prior to weaning and as an essential component of cell walls. May be heated to high temperatures without decomposition and generally adds flavour, texture and succulence to most foods and dishes. Oils are fats with low melting points [also called **lipid**]

fat content of cheese The fat content is expressed as a percent by weight of the dry matter, so that a soft high fat cheese could contain a lower overall percentage of fat than a hard low fat cheese

fat end *see* bung

fat hen A hardy perennial herb *Chenopodium album* similar to good King Henry whose seeds, which are rich in fat and protein, have been used since Neolithic times and may be ground into a flour

fat mouse Various varieties of short-tailed mice *genus Steatomys* which are eaten as a delicacy in South America

fatányéros *(Hu)* A mixed grill of 3 or 4 kinds of meat and offal, served on a wooden platter and accompanied by chips and pickles

fat choy *(Ch)* Hair vegetable

fathead *see* sheepshead fish

fatia *(Po)* Slice

fatias frias *(Po)* Sliced meats, assiette anglaise

fatless cake mixture Equal parts by weight of flour, caster sugar and eggs without raising agent, made up using the fatless whisking method

fatless sponge A light sponge cake made without fat and which goes dry and stale very quickly. Angel food cake is an example

fatless whisking method A method of making cakes by combining eggs and sugar with a balloon whisk over hot water until light, creamy and doubled in volume and at the ribbon stage, removing from the heat and continuing to whisk until cool, then carefully folding in the dry ingredients. The job may be done in a mechanical mixer without heat

fa ts'ai *(Ch)* Hair vegetable

fattiga riddare *(Sw)* Pain perdu, French toast

fatto in casa *(It)* Made on the premises, home made

fattoosh *(ME)* *see* fattoush

fattore, alla moda del *(It)* In farmhouse style, i.e. crisply fried with gherkins and mustard sauce

fattoush *(ME)* A Syrian and Lebanese salad of chopped cucumber, tomatoes, spring onions and sweet green peppers with shredded lettuce heart, chopped mint, parsley and coriander leaves, all seasoned and dressed with olive oil and lemon juice. The salad is chilled and just before serving, cubes of thin crisply toasted bread are added [also called **fattoosh**]

fatty acid A long chain hydrocarbon with an acid group at one end. This combines with an alcohol such as glycerine by the esterification reaction to form natural fats and oils, or with a metal such as sodium to form a soap. They are also esterified with a variety of higher alcohols for use in convenience foods. Generally produced from natural fats and oils, and they are the initial breakdown product of fats in the body

fatty acid salts E470, sodium, potassium and calcium salts of fatty acids which form edible soaps used as emulsifying agents

Faubonne *(Fr)* A puréed vegetable soup flavoured with herbs

fausse limande *(Fr) fem.* Scald, the fish

fausse tortue *(Fr) fem.* Mock turtle

faux-filet *(Fr) masc.* A cut of beef steak from the top of the sirloin [also called **contre-filet**]

fava *(It)* Broad bean

fava bean *see* broad bean

favas *(Po)* Broad beans

favata *(It)* A rich stew of dried beans, pork, fennel, cabbage and tomatoes

fave *(It)* Broad beans

fave dei morti *(It)* Almond and pine nut biscuits, traditionally baked in Lombardy for All Soul's day

faverolles *(Fr) fem. (Provence)* Haricot beans

favollo *(It)* Cangrejo moruno (Sp)

favorite, à la *(Fr)* Garnished with asparagus tips, pâté de foie gras and truffles (steaks), or artichoke hearts, potatoes and celery (roasts)

fazan *(Ru)* Pheasant

fazan po-gruzinsky *(Ru)* Georgian style pheasant braised in green tea, grape juice, orange juice and zest, chopped walnuts and sweet fortified wine for 50 minutes. The drained pheasant is portioned, browned in the oven at 220°C and served with the strained cooking liquor reduced to a syrupy consistency and accompanied with quince jelly

fazolia bean *see* cannellino bean

feather beef steak A frying or braising steak cut from between the neck and fore rib of beef. It is oval in shape with a feathery line of gristle running down the centre

febras de porco *(Po)* A boned-out leg of pork cooked in red wine and flavoured with brandy, cloves, garlic and cumin

fechun *(Fr)* Cabbage rolls stuffed with pork from Franche-Comté

fécula *(Sp)* Starch

fécule **1** Starch, particularly potato starch which is made by grinding raw potatoes and washing away the solubles with water leaving a pure starch similar in properties to cornflour and arrowroot [also called **potato starch, potato flour**] **2** *(Fr) fem.* Starch

fedelini *(It)* Very thin pasta noodles used in soup

Federwild *(Ge)* Game birds

fegatelli *(It)* Small cubes or slices of pig's liver threaded on skewers then grilled or baked in various ways

fegatini *(It)* Chicken livers

fegato *(It)* Liver

fegato di maiale *(It)* Pork liver

fegato d'oca *(It)* Goose liver

fegato alla Veneziana *(It)* Liver and onions

fehérhagyma mártás *(Hu)* Onion sauce

Feige *(Ge)* Fig

feijão **1** *(Po)* Bean **2** *(Br)* Butter bean, lima bean

feijão branco *(Po)* White bean

feijão encarnado *(Po)* Red bean

feijão de frade *(Po)* Black-eyed pea

feijão manteiga *(Po)* Butter bean

feijão preto *(Po)* Black bean

feijão de vaca *(Po)* Black-eyed pea or cow pea

feijão de vagem *(Po) see* feijão verde

feijão verde *(Po)* Green beans, runner or French [also called **feijão de vagem, vagem**]

feijoa The fruit of an evergreen shrub *Feijoa sellowiana* a native of SA but now grown in Australia and Southern USA. It is about 5 cm long with a reddish green inedible skin and whitish to green flesh which surrounds a core of soft seed-filled pulp. Tastes like guava with a hint of pineapple [also called **Brazilian guava, pineapple guava**]

Feijoa sellowiana *Bot.* Feijoa

feijoada completa *(Br & Po)* A stew of black beans, dried and salted beef, fresh beef, tongue, bacon, sausage, pig's trotters, ears and tails, onions, garlic, tomatoes, parsley, bay leaves chillis and seasoning. A national dish of Brazil accompanied with white rice, farofa, orange and green vegetables

feine Extrawurst *(Au)* Extrawurst in which the filling is very finely minced

feine (Extrawurst) in Stangen *(Ge & Au)* Feine Extrawurst sold in short lengths rather than linked

feine Mettwurst *(Ge)* Fine textured Mettwurst

feiner Zucker *(Ge)* Granulated or castor sugar

Feingebäck *(Ge)* Pastry

feingemischter Aufschnitt *(Ge)* Mixed sliced sausages

fejessaláta *(Hu)* Lettuce

felafel *see* falafel

Felchen *(Ge)* A type of freshwater trout

felisówka *(Pl)* Soured buttermilk which has been allowed to ferment slightly and is slightly alcoholic

fenalår *(No)* Smoked leg of mutton

Fenchel *(Ge)* Fennel

fen chiew *(Ch)* Shaohsing rice wine

fennel **1** *see* Florence fennel **2** A herb *Foeniculum vulgare* indigenous to the Mediterranean with an aniseed flavour. The dried seeds are used as a spice or may be sprouted for winter salads and the feathery leaves are used to flavour fish dishes or in salads [also called **sweet cumin**]

fennel sauce Butter sauce, mixed with blanched chopped fennel at the rate of 20 ml per litre

fennel spice mix A blend of flavours suitable for coating fish prior to barbecueing. Made from fresh garlic, grated lemon zest and ground black peppercorns, coriander seeds, fennel seeds and dried thyme pounded together

fenogreco *(Sp)* Fenugreek

fenouil *(Fr) masc.* Florence fennel

fenouil de mer *(Fr) masc.* Samphire *Crithmum maritimum*

fen si *(Ch)* Cellophane noodles

fenugrec *(Fr) masc.* Fenugreek

fenugreek A herb *Trigonella foenum-graecum* with 10 cm long seed pods containing irregular yellow seeds about 4 mm long. The seeds are cooked or roasted (but not too much), before use, to develop the flavour, and they have an aromatic smell. They are ground for use as a spice esp. in commercial curry powders and other spice mixtures and can be sprouted for salad purposes. The leaves known as methis are used as a vegetable and lose their bitterness on cooking. Dried fenugreek leaves are used as a flavouring and in marinades

ferchuse *(Fr) fem.* A Burgundian dish of pig's heart and lights possibly with other offal cooked in red wine with onions and potatoes

ferment *see* culture

ferment, to To carry out the process of fermentation

fermentation The process whereby a microorganism such as a yeast, fungi, lactobacillus, etc. breaks down an energy source (starch, sugar, protein, etc.) in the absence of air, into smaller molecules such as alcohol, acetic acid, lactic acid, etc. thus gaining the energy necessary for growth and reproduction. The process is important in the production of many foods such as yoghurt, cheese, soya sauce, tempeh, vinegar, sauerkraut, etc.

fermented Description of a food that has been subjected to the process of fermentation

fermented bean curd *see* bean curd cheese

fermented black bean *see* black bean (2) (fermented soya bean)

fermented red rice The yeasty rice grains (brewer's grains) left after making rice wine, coloured red. Alternatively cooked rice fermented with *Monascus purpureus*. This latter is sold in Chinese stores as a mixed culture called wine balls or cubes. Used mainly in northern China [also called **red rice, red mash**]

Fermier *(Fr) masc.* Farmhouse cheese, usually made from unpasteurized milk. Lit. farmer

fermière, à la *(Fr)* In the style of a farmer's wife, i.e. with carrots, onions, celery and turnips

ferri, ai *(It)* Grilled over a barbecue or open fire

ferritu *(It)* An instrument used for making pasta cylinders

fersk røget laks *(De)* Freshly smoked salmon

fersken *(De & No)* Peach

Ferula asafoetida *Bot.* Asafoetida

Ferula narthex *Bot.* Asafoetida

ferulic acid An acid which concentrates in the bran fraction of wheat and can be used to measure the bran content of flour

fesa *(It)* Leg of veal

fesenjan *(Pe)* Fried chicken or duck cooked in a pomegranate and crushed walnut sauce and served with rice [also called **faisinjan**]

festen Preisen, zu *(Ge)* Fixed price (meal)

feta *(Gr)* A white, dry, crumbly cheese made from cow, ewe or goat's milk, cut in blocks ('fetes' is the word for block or slice) and matured in brine to give it a sharp acidic and salty taste. Widely used throughout the Balkans and now made in Western Europe. Contains 46% water, 27% fat and 21% protein [also called **fetta**]

fetta 1 *(Gr) see* feta **2** *(It)* A slice

Fettsuppe *(Ge)* A rich soup

fettuccine *(It)* Flat narrow ribbon noodles made from an egg based pasta dough, available fresh or dried

fettuccine al burro *(It)* Fettuccine with butter and grated Parmesan cheese

fettuccine alla papolina *(It)* Fettuccini with ham and butter

fettuccine alla trota *(It)* Fettucine pasta cooked al dente and mixed with sweated chopped onions and garlic, flaked smoked trout, seasoning, mace and cream, heated for 1 minute and garnished with chopped parsley and red lumpfish roe

fettunta *(It) see* bruschetta

feuille de chêne *(Fr) fem.* Oak leaf lettuce

feuille de Dreux *(Fr) fem.* A soft surface ripened cheese made in Normandy from partially skimmed cows' milk and cast in 300 to 500 g discs. Contains 55% water, 14% fat and 26% protein

feuille de vigne *(Fr) fem.* Vine leaf

feuilletage *(Fr) masc.* Puff pastry

feuilleté(e) *(Fr)* **1** *adj.* Flaky as in pâte feuilletée, meaning flaky pastry, puff pastry **2** *masc.* Danish pastry

feuilleté de poularde riviera *(Fr)* Chicken pie

feuilleter de la pâte *(Fr)* To turn and roll flaky or puff pastry

fève *(Fr) fem.* Broad bean

fèves d'Espagne *(Fr) fem.* Runner beans

ffagod sir benfro *(UK)* A type of faggot from Pembrokeshire made with minced pigs' liver and onions mixed with suet and breadcrumbs, seasoned and flavoured with chopped sage

fiambre *(Po)* Ham, cold cooked meat

fiambre de bonito *(Sp)* Tuna fish balls cooked in a white wine sauce

fiambres *(Sp)* Cold cooked meats

fiamma, alla *(It)* Flamed, flambéed

fiasco, al *(It)* Cooked in a sealed flask, esp. beans

fibre Non-digestible carbohydrates of vegetable origin which add bulk to the bowel contents causing a more rapid transit through the body, curing constipation and reducing the incidence of bowel cancer. Available from most whole unprocessed natural vegetables, seeds and fruit and in processed form from the bran by-products of grain milling

fica *(It)* Pomfret, the fish

ficelle *(Fr) fem.* A short very thin French bread similar in construction to the baguette

fichi *(It)* Figs

fichi indiani *(It)* Prickly pears

fichi secchi *(It)* Dried figs

fico *(It)* Fig

fico d'India *(It)* Prickly pear

Ficus carica *Bot.* Fig

fiddle fish *see* angel fish

fiddlehead fern *(USA)* The tightly curled young fronds of the oyster fern *Matteuccia struthiopteris,* used either as a salad vegetable or cooked like spinach. Grown in the north east of the USA, it becomes toxic when the fronds begin to open [also called **corkscrew greens**]

fidegela *(He)* A sausage made with pigs' liver and rind flavoured with fennel

fideos *(Sp)* Noodles, spaghetti

fideos gordos *(Sp)* Thick spaghetti

fidget pie *(UK)* A pie made in a dish from chopped back bacon, onion, cooking apples and chopped parsley combined with cider and flour (for thickening) covered with short pastry and baked at 190°C until brown. Originally used as a food for the harvest workers

field bean A hardy legume *Vicia faba* related to, but a more primitive form of, the broad bean. It is grown all over Europe and Asia often on poor soils. The beans may be used fresh or dried but must be boiled before eating to destroy toxic compounds. In Western Europe used for animal food and as the principal component in the production of quorn [also called **horse bean**]

field lettuce *(USA)* Lamb's lettuce

field mushroom An edible wild mushroom *Agaricus campestris* with a white cap and pink to brown gills found in late summer on rough grassland

fieno greco *(It)* Fenugreek

fieto *(It)* Pomfret, the fish

fig The fruit of a tree *Ficus carica* which grows in warm and semi-tropical regions. The fruit which varies from round to pear shape has a soft skin varying from green to purple filled with a red to purple sticky seed filled pulp. They may be eaten raw for dessert, are easily skinned if required, but are commonly dried or canned and used for desserts, snacks, in cakes and biscuits and sometimes with meat and game

fig sly cake *(UK)* A sugar pastry brought together with water instead of egg and made into a sandwich with a filling of chopped dried figs, currants, raisins and walnut pieces all cooked in water and reduced to a thick paste. Baked at 190°C until brown and cut in squares; *see also* Cornish sly cake

figa *(It)* **1** Pomfret, the fish **2** Liver *(Venice)*

figa garbo e dolce *(It)* Panéed and fried calves' liver with vinegar and sugar

figadini con l'uva *(It)* Sautéed chicken livers with grapes

figado *(Po)* Liver

figatelli *(Fr)* A pigs' or lambs' liver sausage from Corsica

figgy pudding *(UK)* A steamed suet pudding filled with minced apples and figs. Served at Christmas

figner *(De)* Figs

figos *(Po)* Figs

figue *(Fr) fem.* Fig

figue de barbarie *(Fr) fem.* Prickly pear

figue de mer *(Fr) fem.* Violet (2)

fijn brood *(Ho)* Fine bread

fikener *(No)* Figs

fikon *(Sw)* Figs

filato *(It)* In strands or threads

filbert The fruit of a small deciduous tree *Corylus maxima* very similar to the hazelnut but with a husk that is longer than the nut and often completely encloses it [also called **Kentish cob**]

filbunke *(Sw)* Soured milk or junket

filé *(Hu & Po)* Fillet of beef, pork, etc.

filé powder Dried and ground sassafras leaves used as a flavouring in Creole cooking [also called **gumbo filé, filet powder**]

filet de boeuf *(Fr) masc.* **1** The whole fillet of beef often roasted whole **2** A boneless piece of tender frying or grilling quality beef

filet mignon *(En & Fr) masc.* A steak cut from the thin end of a fillet of beef. Grilled, fried or used for beef stroganoff, stir fries, steak tartare or the like. Lit. dainty fillet

filet de porc *(Fr) masc.* The centre part of the pork loin to which the kidney is attached, a prime roasting joint which may or may not included the pointe de filet (pork fillet)

filet powder *see* filé powder

filete *(Sp)* Fillet of beef, pork or lamb; *see also* tenderloin

filete de vaca *(Sp)* Fillet of beef

filetto *(It)* Fillet (of pork, beef, etc.)

filfil soodani *(ME)* Sudanese pepper

filhó *(Po)* Fritter or pancake

Filipendula ulmaria *Bot.* Meadowsweet

filipino red A thin sausage made of dried raw pork minced with garlic and mixed with saltpetre, brown sugar, MSG, seasoning and a red dye and packed into narrow hog casings

fillet 1 A piece of fish removed from the bone and running the whole length of the fish **2** Various cuts of meat and poultry

fillet, to To cut away from the bone the flesh of fish, meat or poultry

fillet of beef The muscle which runs along the lower portion of the backbone on the inside of the ribs. As it is very little used by the animal it is very tender and is the most expensive cut of beef. It is cut into fillet steak, filet mignon, chateaubriand and tournedos

fillet end of leg of lamb The upper half of a hind leg of lamb

fillet of fish The flesh of fish free from skin and bone. Two fillets are usually obtained from a round fish and four from a flat fish

fillet of lamb *(UK)* The top half of a leg of lamb

fillet of pork *(UK)* The top half of a leg of pork

fillet steak A transverse slice through the centre part of a fillet of beef

fillet of veal *(UK)* The equivalent of sirloin and rump in beef usually cut into thin slices for escalopes

filling 1 A food item contained within a case as e.g. jam in a doughnut, cream in an eclair, stuffing in a chicken **2** Term describing a food which leaves the consumer feeling satiated

filmjölk *(Sw)* A sour tasting yoghurt

filo pastry A pastry rolled out so thin that it is translucent, usually sold ready prepared in layers of several rectangular sheets. It originated in Turkey and travelled into central Europe during the spread of the Ottoman empire. Used for many Balkan and ME specialities [also called **phyllo pastry**]

filosoof *(Ho)* A type of cottage pie Lit. philosopher

filter, to To strain through fine muslin, paper or a tammy cloth so as to remove suspended solids from a liquid

filter coffee Coffee made by letting near boiling water flow through ground coffee held in a filter paper supported on a metal or plastic mesh or perforated container

filtrate The liquid that flows through a filter

Fin de siècle *(Fr) fem.* A double cream cows' milk cheese from Normandy

fina A variety of clementine or common mandarin originating in Algeria and widely grown in Spain. It has a very pleasant flesh but the fruit tend to be small [also called **Algerian clementine** (USA)]

financière, à la *(Fr)* In the style of the financier, i.e. garnished with cockscombs, kidneys, slices of truffle, mushrooms and olives

financière, sauce *(Fr) fem.* Madeira sauce reduced by 25%, a little truffle essence added and all strained. Served with dishes garnished à la financière

finanziere *(It) see* cibreo

findik köftesi *(Tu)* Small meat balls made from a mixture of chopped mutton, chopped and sweated onions, flour, eggs, butter and seasoning, fried in butter then simmered in mutton stock with chopped fresh mint

Findon haddock *(UK) see* finnan haddock

fine marineret sild *(De)* Fine quality pickled herrings

fine olive oil Oil pressed from the olive pulp after the second cold pressing and after heating the pulp with water. The free oleic acid content must not be more than 3.3%. This oil is also referred to as refined olive oil

fines herbes *(Fr) fem.* A classic herb mixture usually chopped chervil, chives, parsley and tarragon although other similar herbs may be substituted. Used particularly in omelettes

fines herbes, sauce aux *(Fr) fem.* Boiling white wine infused with fines herbes for 20 minutes, strained, mixed with twice its amount of demi-glace sauce if required brown or with white velouté sauce if white and finished with chopped fines herbes and lemon juice just before serving

finger A strip of food usually a rectangular piece of toast or a white bread roll about 10 cm by 2-3 cm

finger buffet A buffet consisting of only those items which can be eaten with the fingers and do not require the use of a knife, fork or spoon

finger food Food served at a buffet or stand-up meal which can be eaten with the fingers

finger kombu *(USA) see* sea girdle

finger millet *see* ragi

fingered citron *see* Buddha's hand citron

fingerling A small fish of any species under 1 year old

finik *(Ru)* Dates

finlabong *(Ph)* Bamboo shoot

finnan haddie *(UK) see* finnan haddock

finnan haddock *(UK)* Haddock which has been split, soaked briefly in brine and cold smoked for 6 hours over oak to a pale straw colour. Originally from Findon near Aberdeen [also called **finnan haddie, Findon haddock**]

finnisk far-stuvning *(Fi)* Breast of lamb cut in pieces, fried in butter and stewed with stock, carrots, turnips and potatoes

finnlandskaia *(Fi)* A strong flavoured beef broth served with slices of sour cream pancakes mixed with Hamburg parsley on toast topped with cheese and grilled until brown

fino *(It)* **1** *see* fine olive oil **2** A grade of rice which is long and tapering and requires about 16 minutes to cook but will stand long cooking without losing structure. used for risotto. See e.g. vialone

finocchio *(It)* Fennel

finocchio marino *(It)* Samphire *Crithmum maritimum*

finocchiona *(It)* A type of salami flavoured with fennel which cannot be kept for any length of time

Finte *(Ge)* Twaite shad

fiocchi d'avena *(It)* Oatmeal

fiocchi di granturco *(It)* Cornflakes

fiochetti *(It)* Small bow shaped pieces of pasta

Fior di latte *(It)* A soft, spun-curd cows' milk cheese made in the same way as Mozzarella using a lactic starter or citric acid addition before coagulation and formed into various shapes. Contains 61% water, 18% fat and 17% protein. Used as a cheaper substitute for Mozzarella in the pizza trade

fiore di sambuco *(It)* Small pasta stars used in soup. Lit. elder flowers

Fiore Sardo *(It)* A hard ewes' milk cheese from Sardinia made in the shape of two cones joined at their bases. It is salted in brine, dry salted and may be ripened for 3 to 4 months. It has a sharp tasting paste with a dry brown rind. Eaten when young as a dessert cheese, when mature after 6 months, it is used for grating and cooking. Contains 26% water, 35% fat and 30% protein

fiore di zucchine ripiene *(It)* Stuffed courgette flowers

fiorentina *(It)* A grilled fillet steak with no sauce

fiorentine, alla *(It)* In the Florentine style, i.e. with oil, garlic, ham, parsley and pepper

fiori di zucca *(It)* Pumpkin or squash flowers

firm ball stage *(USA) see* sugar cooking

firming agent A chemical compound used to maintain crispness in canned and bottled vegetables

firni *(In)* A milk pudding made with ground rice and almonds

firstings *see* beestings

Fisch *(Ge)* Fish

Fischbeuschlsuppe *(Au)* A thick well flavoured soup made with the gills of freshwater fish

Fischbrut *(Ge)* Fish fry, small fish, whitebait

Fischcrouton *(Ge)* Fish balls

Fisch mit feinen Kräuten *(Au)* Fish with chopped mixed herbs

Fischhackbraten *(Ge)* Baked fish loaf

Fischlaich *(Ge)* Soft fish roe

Fischrogen *(Ge)* Hard fish roe

Fischschüssel *(Ge)* Fish and bacon terrine

fish Cold blooded, free swimming vertebrate animals with flat or spindle shaped streamlined bodies which live either in fresh or seawater and obtain oxygen for respiration by circulating water over gills from which mammalian vertebrate lungs evolved. They have fins instead of limbs and their skin is usually covered with scales. Classified as freshwater, seawater, anadromous or catadromous, flat or round, oily or white and if flat, dextral or sinistral

fish cake A circular patty made from a mixture of mashed potato, cooked fish and seasoning, panéed and usually fried

fish and chips *(UK)* A national dish consisting of deep fried battered fish fillet and potato chips usually served with salt and vinegar. Reputedly invented in the 17th century in the Meuse valley when the newly arrived potato, which was viewed with some suspicion, was cut to resemble small fishes and deep fried with them

fish cobbler *(UK)* A savoury cobbler, q.v. made with sweated chopped onion and garlic with sliced carrots, courgettes and celery, cooked for 10 minutes, chopped tomatoes, fresh herbs and stock added, simmered, seasoned and small pieces of white fish added and cooked for a maximum of 2 minutes then finished as a cobbler

fish cooking methods The principal methods are shallow poaching, deep poaching, grilling, shallow frying, steaming and baking en papillote. Stewing is only used for fish soups. See under each name for details

fish cutlet A slice of fish cut across the backbone anywhere from the head to the vent so that a cross section of the gut space is shown

fish fillet *see* fillet of fish

fish finger A rectangular piece of compressed white fish flesh with a breadcrumb coating. Usually sold frozen. The fish flesh is usually mechanically recovered from all the bones and skin and there is no waste and often little taste. Popular with children

fish glaze Fish stock reduced by boiling until a sticky consistency. Used as a base for sauces and to improve their flavour [also called **glace de poisson** (Fr)]

fish gravy *see* nuoc-mam

fish herbs The principal herbs used with fish are alexanders, basil, bay, caraway, chervil, chives, dill, fennel, lemon balm, lemon thyme, lovage, marjoram, mint, parsley, rosemary, sage and savory

fish kettle A long (to 60 cm) deep and narrow pan especially made for poaching a large whole round fish. It has an internal perforated plate with handles on which the fish rests and with which it is lifted out without damage

fish maw The buoyancy bladder of a fish similar in appearance to the mammalian lung. The maw of the conger pike is used in Chinese cooking and is usually sold in dried form which needs reconstituting for about 3 hours and treating with vinegar. It has little flavour of its own but absorbs flavours and is prized for its spongy texture

fish muddle *(USA)* Fish stew

fish oil Oil obtained from fish, principally from the livers of cod and halibut, which contains essential fatty acids (EFAs) as well as vitamins A and D which are all necessary for health. Often sold in gelatine capsules as a vitamin supplement, but the required amounts can be obtained by eating oily fish once a week. Oily fish can contain up to 30% fat of which about 20% is saturated

fish paste Fish preserved either by salting or fermenting or both, sometimes with added grain, and processed to make a paste of variable consistency with a fishy salty flavour. The liquid which drains off is fish sauce. It is made all over Asia, esp. in SEA

fish pie *(UK)* Sliced parboiled potatoes layered in the base of a greased casserole, covered with a mixture of flaked smoked haddock, sliced mushrooms, chopped tomatoes and soured cream, covered with another layer of sliced potatoes, gratinated with grated Cheddar cheese and butter and baked at 180°C for 30 minutes

fish pudding *(Sc)* White fish fillets, minced twice and flavoured with allspice and seasoning, combined with thin cream, butter, eggs and flour (8:10:2:2:1), adding the cream last of all in a food processor. Tested by dropping a teaspoonful into boiling water and adjusting the consistency with milk or egg white. The mixture is put in a cake tin which has been buttered and sprinkled with breadcrumbs and this is cooked in a slow oven in a bain-marie for 1 to 1.5 hours. Allowed to rest then demoulded and served with a sauce

fish sauce The salty fishy tasting liquid which drains off fermented and/or salted fish. It is a popular flavouring agent in SEA and is used in the same way as soya sauce. Nuoc-mam is the commonest example in the west

fish sausage A sausage made with 80% fish flesh, free of skin and bone, blended to a fine paste with suet and fécule or cornflour, seasoned, flavoured with mace and cayenne pepper, filled into narrow casings and linked

fish slice A flat oblong slatted sheet of metal on a long handle used in the domestic kitchen for handling flat items of food such as fish fillets, fried eggs, rissoles and hamburgers in shallow frying or poaching pans. Professional chefs use a palette knife for fish fillets

fish soup *(UK)* Strained fish stock thickened with a white roux and enriched with cream or milk, flaked cooked fish added and chopped parsley sprinkled on the surface

fish steak A slice of fish cut across the back bone anywhere from the vent to the tail of a round fish

fish stew *see* bouillabaisse, bourride, chaudrée, cotriade, matelote, meurette, pochouse and waterzoie

fish stick *(USA)* Fish finger

fish stock Stock made from the bones of white fish sweated with onions and lemon juice in butter, simmered for 30 minutes with water (0.4 kg bones, per litre), skimmed continuously then strained [also called **fond de poisson** (Fr), **fumet de poisson** (Fr)]

fish velouté A velouté sauce made with fish stock and used as a base for many fish sauces

fisk *(De, No & Sw)* Fish

fisk på fat *(No)* Fish fried then baked in a sauce. Lit. fish on a platter

fisk med fyllning *(Sw)* Stuffed fish

fisk og skalldyr *(No)* Seafood

fiskbullar *(Sw)* Fish balls

fiskeballer *(No)* Fish balls made with processed fish and cooked potatoes

fiskeboller *(No)* A mixture of minced raw cod and/or haddock, bread crumbs, egg, cream and seasonings formed into balls, poached in fish stock and served with a wine or cheese sauce

fiskefärs *(De)* Minced fish

fiskefrikadellar *(De)* Fish balls

fiskegrateng *(No)* Skinned and flaked boiled cod covered with a cream and egg yolk enriched white sauce, gratinated with cheese and baked in the oven until brown

fiskekaker *(No)* Fishcakes made from chilled raw haddock, cornflour, cream and milk processed in a blender then fried in butter and oil

fiskepudding *(No)* Fish pudding

fiskesuppe *(No)* A strong fish stock made with bones, fins, cleaned fish heads, a BG and an onion clouté just covered with water, simmered for 30 minutes, skimmed and strained, mixed with half its volume of milk thickened with a blond roux, cooked out, seasoned, finished with sour cream and lemon juice and garnished with chopped parsley

fiskfärs *(Sw)* Fish pudding

fiskgryta *(Sw)* Paupiettes made from plaice or sole fillets rubbed with salt and filled with a mixture of chopped onion, grated cheese and tomato concassé, packed tightly and poached in a dish moistened with lemon juice or wine, dotted with butter and baked in a moderate oven for 30 minutes. Served from the dish

fiskkaggen *(No)* A fish loaf made with boiled white fish processed with butter, egg yolks, breadcrumbs, nutmeg and seasoning, stiffly beaten egg whites folded in and all baked in a mould as a soufflé, cooled, demoulded and eaten cold

fiskkroketter *(Sw)* Fish cakes or croquettes

fisksoppa *(Sw)* Fish soup. First a stock is made from roughly chopped small cleaned fish with their gills removed, covered with roughly 2 to 3 times their weight in water with salt, sliced onion and white peppercorns and simmered for 30 minutes. The skimmed and strained stock is then mixed with sweated chopped onions, sliced leek and mushrooms, skinned and cored tomatoes, saffron, rosemary, basil, garlic and seasoning, simmered until all cooked, then prawns and mussels added for the last minute.

fisnoga *see* petcha

Fistulina hepatica *Bot.* Beefsteak fungus

five spice powder *(Ch)* A blend of five spices, star anise, anise pepper, cassia or cinnamon, fennel seed and cloves ground together. May include two from cardamom, dried ginger or dried liquorice root. Used to flavour marinades and to season roast meat and poultry [also called **Chinese five spices**]

fjærkre *(No)* Poultry

fjordland *(No)* A semi-skimmed cows' milk cheese resembling Emmental or Jarlsberg

Fladen *(He)* A flat fruit cake made with pears, nuts and marzipan

fläderbär *(Sw)* Elderberries

flæsk *(De)* Pork, bacon [also called **svinekød**]

flæskesteg *(De)* Roast pork

flageolet *(Fr) masc.* Flageolet bean

flageolet bean An 8 to 10 mm long, light green oval bean from semi-mature French bean pods after the pod has become stringy but before it dries off. Eaten fresh or dried [also called **green shell bean** (USA)]

Flageolett *(Ge)* Flageolet bean

flake 1 Thin slivers or slices of food such as is obtained when a cooked fish is gently broken with a fork or as in corn flakes, almond flakes, etc. **2** The flesh of certain small Australian sharks **3** *see* dogfish

flake, to To form or make into flakes

flake salt *(USA)* A flaked form of salt used for pickling

flaked almonds *see* almond flakes

flaked rice *see* rice flakes

flaky pastry A pastry similar to puff pastry made with a lower ratio of fat to flour (3 to 4) and folded, rolled and turned only three times. The lift is not as great as with puff pastry

flamande, à la *(Fr)* In the Flemish style, i.e. with a garnish of braised vegetables and bacon or small pork sausages, usually for joints of meat

flambé, to To add an alcoholic spirit to a dish and set it alight either before (in the ladle or spoon) or after adding it. This may be done in the kitchen during cooking or when presenting the dish to the customer. Used to add the flavour of brandy, whisky or rum to a dish and for the visual effect [also called **to flame**]

flamber *(Fr)* To flambé

flame, to *see* flambé, to

flameado *(Sp)* Flamed, flambéed

flamiche *(Be)* A deep shell or case of bread dough baked with a filling of egg and cheese

Flammulina velutipes *Bot.* Enokitake mushroom

flan 1 An open, cylindrical and straight sided tart either sweet or savoury and either in a blind prebaked pastry case or with a sponge or biscuit crumb base with fillings that require little if any cooking **2** *(Fr) masc.* Custard tart **3** *(Sp & Po)* Crème caramel

flan brioche aux fruits confits *(Fr) masc.* A dessert similar to bread and butter pudding

flan pastry A rather brittle shortcrust pastry q.v. in which beaten egg instead of water is used to bind the fat and flour. Caster sugar (4 g per 100 g of flour) may be used for sweet tarts and flans [also called **biscuit crust pastry, sweet crust pastry**]

flan ring A plain or fluted ring of metal placed on a flat baking tray and used to form flan pastry cases for blind or other baking

flanchet *(Fr) masc.* Breast of veal

flank A cut of beef or veal. See thick flank, thin flank

flank of lamb *see* lamb flank

flank steak *(USA)* A narrow flat cut of beef from below the short loin, fried or grilled [also called **London broil**]

flapjack 1 *(UK)* a type of biscuit made from fat, sugar, rolled oats and golden syrup, baked in a shallow tray and cut into rectangles or squares **2** *(USA)* A thick pancake cooked on a griddle

flapjack scone *see* drop scone

flare fat A sheet of soft fat from the inner lower part of a pig's abdominal cavity

flash, to To brown the surface of a cooked dish very quickly under a very hot grill (salamander) or in a very hot oven

flash-fry steak *see* minute steak

fläsk *(Sw)* Pork

fläsk i form *(Sw)* A type of pork pie made from alternate layers of seasoned sliced potatoes and onions covered in milk and topped with slices of rindless salted pork belly, sprinkled with powdered rosemary and baked in a hot oven until the pork is crisp and all cooked

fläskgryta med jordärtscockor *(Sw)* Cubed pork fillet browned and seasoned, sprinkled with flour, then stock, tomato purée and cream added, simmered until cooked, mixed with cooked Jerusalem artichokes and finished with sherry

fläskkorv *(Sw)* A sausage made from lean pork and fat bacon (3:1), minced twice, bound with fécule and ham stock, seasoned, flavoured with ginger, loosely filled into casings, linked, dried and dry salted for a day. May be stored in brine

fläskkorvsstuvning *(Sw)* Thick slices of pork sausage cooked in pork stock with sliced onions and diced potatoes

flat A flat dish, usually oval, on which food is presented to the customer in a restaurant

flat bread Unleavened bread made without yeast such as chapati, paratha, tortilla, matzo and crispbread

flat fish A fish which, as it matures, changes shape so that both eyes and the mouth are on on one side which becomes the upper part when swimming or lying on the sea bottom; *see also* dextral and sinistral

flat leaved parsley *see* parsley and flat parsley *P. crispum Neapolitanum*

flat lettuce *see* butterhead lettuce

flat lobster *see* slipper lobster

flat mushroom A fully mature mushroom in which the cap is fully open so that all the gills are exposed on one side

flat parsley A variety of parsley *P. crispum Neapolitanum* in which the leaves are flat rather than curled. It is said to have a superior flavour. It is the commonest form in continental Europe

flatbone steak *(USA)* A steak cut from the sirloin. See sirloin steak (USA)

flattbrød *(No)* A thin crisp flat biscuit made of wheat, rye and barley flours. See crispbread

flauta *(Me)* A large tortilla filled and rolled. Lit. a flute, the instrument

flava bean *see* broad bean

flavour The blend of taste and smell sensation experienced when food and drink are placed in the mouth. Taste is a direct nervous transmission from the tongue and is the same for all humans comprising salt, sweet, sour and bitter. Smell is far more complex, involves the nose and a large area of the cerebral cortex and is to some extent culturally determined

flavour enhancer A substance which having little or no flavour of its own intensifies other flavours with which it is combined. MSG is the most common and is used to enhance the flavour of vegetables and meat, esp. in Chinese cooking. Flavour enhancers are common in processed and convenience foods

flavoured crisps Crisps with added flavour usually artificial and sprayed on as they are being cooled, e.g. cheese and onion, smoky bacon, salt and vinegar, etc.

flavourings Ingredients in cookery which add flavour to a dish made principally from other ingredients. They can be of natural origin and add little bulk such as herbs, spices, seasoning, extracts, essences, etc. and those which also add bulk such as aromatic vegetables and meats. Others, particularly fruit flavours, are purely synthetic in origin. Processed and convenience foods generally contain mixtures of natural and synthetic flavours.

flavoxanthin E161(a), a natural carotenoid yellow food colouring

Flavr Savr *(USA)* A genetically engineered tomato designed to maintain its flavour over an extended shelf life now on sale in the USA. It contains anti-ripening genes and does not need to be labelled under current UK rules

flead *(UK)* Mesenteric fat from veal or beef

Flecke *(Ge)* Tripe

Fleisch *(Ge)* Meat

Fleischbrühe *(Ge)* A consommé based on meat stock

Fleischgerichte *(Ge)* Meat dishes

Fleischkäse *(Ge)* Meat loaf

Fleischklösse *(Ge)* Meat balls

Fleischkuchen *(Ge)* Meat pies

Fleischschnitte *(Ge)* Slice of meat

Fleischwurst *(Ge) see* Extrawurst

flensje *(Ho)* Thin pancakes

flesh The name for edible muscular parts of animals, for some other tissues of shellfish and crustaceans and for the edible parts of fruits

fleshy Succulent and slightly resistant to the bite

fleske pannekaker *(No)* Pancakes filled with a pork stuffing

fleskepølse *(No)* Very fatty pork sausages

flet *(Fr) masc.* Flounder, the fish

flétan *(Fr) masc.* Halibut

fleur de maquis *(Fr) fem. see* Brin d'amour

fleur de muscade *(Fr) fem.* Mace

fleuriste, à la *(Fr)* In the style of the florist, i.e. with a garnish of potatoes and tomatoes stuffed with mixed vegetables

fleuron *(En & Fr) masc.* A small crescent shaped piece of flaky or puff pastry which after cooking is used as a garnish

Flieder Kaltschale *(Ge)* A cold soup made from hot milk infused with elder blossoms, vanilla and cinnamon, strained, sweetened and thickened with egg yolks, cooled and served sprinkled with crushed macaroons

flies' cemeteries *(UK) coll.* Eccles cakes or similar currant cakes and biscuits

flint corn *(USA)* An early maturing variety of maize *Zea mays* var. *indurata* in which the small kernels are completely covered by a flinty hard skin. Not as widely grown as dent

flipper pie *(Cn)* A pie from Newfoundland made from the flippers of young harp seals together with vegetables during the annual cull (April/May)

flippit *(UK)* A small pancake made from a seasoned self-raising flour and egg (2:1) batter with just enough water to make it a thick dropping consistency, cooked in oil for 2 minutes then flipped over and cooked until it bubbles and rises slightly. Served immediately with a savoury topping

flitch A complete side of pork (half a pig), salted and cured

floating islands *see* îles flottantes

floats *(Ca)* Yeasted bread from Trinidad, cut into thin rounds and fried. Served hot with accra

fløde *(De)* Cream

flødekage *(De)* A layered cream sponge cake

flødeost *(De)* Cream cheese

flødeskum *(De)* Whipped cream

Flohkraut *(Ge)* Pennyroyal, the herb

flondre *(Fr) masc.* Flounder, the fish

flor de Jamaica *see* Jamaica flower

Florence fennel The swollen bases of the leaves of a variety of plant *Foeniculum vulgare* var. *dulce* which form a tight bulb-like crisp vegetable with a pleasant mild aniseed flavour. Eaten raw or cooked [also called **fennel, sweet anise** (USA)]

florentine A biscuit containing a high proportion of chopped dried vine fruits, candied peel and nuts and coated with chocolate on one side

florentine, à la *(Fr)* In the Florentine style i.e. served with spinach, usually fish or eggs, sometimes napped with cheese sauce

florentine, fish As for fish mornay but with the fish placed on a bed of cooked spinach prior to coating with sauce

florid lobster *(USA)* A large spiny lobster (crawfish) *Palinurus argus* with a purple/brown shell and a yellow band across the tail

fløte *(No)* Cream

fløtekaker *(No)* Cream cakes

fløtekarameller *(No)* Crème caramel

fløtemysost *(No)* A semi-hard cooked-curd cheese made with a mixture of cows' milk and cream. It has no rind and a smooth texture. Contains 20% water, 25% fat and 50% protein

fløtesuppe *(No)* Cream soup

fløtevafler *(No)* Cream based waffles

flounder **1** A flat sea fish *Platichthys flesus* similar to plaice but with an inferior taste and texture. Found in all coastal regions of the Atlantic ocean. Some varieties are found in the Pacific ocean **2** *(USA)* The general term for any flatfish

flour Finely ground cereal grains, dried pulses and dried starchy tubers, consisting mainly of starch, often treated to remove fibre and oils or modified to change its cooking or baking properties. The term is most commonly used of wheat flour

flour, to To cover the surface of a food or cooking implement or preparation surface with flour, usually to absorb surface moisture and to prevent sticking

flour batter biscuit method A method of making biscuits by creaming half the flour with the fat, beating in the sugar and eggs previously mixed, then blending in the other dry ingredients. An example is the cookie

flour corn *see* squaw corn

flour dredger A dredger filled with flour used to flour

floury **1** The description of potatoes which have an open soft texture when cooked as opposed to the waxy variety. See entry under potato for the common varieties **2** The taste of food containing flour which is undercooked

flower fu *see* kohana fu

flower pepper *see* anise pepper

flowering chive The flower stem and bud of the Chinese chive used as a garnish or vegetable

flowering white cabbage *see* choy sum

flowers for salads *see* salad flowers

fluid ounce A subdivision of the pint. There are 20 in the imperial pint equal in volume to 28.4 ml and 16 in the US pint equal to 29.6 ml. Abbreviated to fl oz

flukes Long lived parasitic flatworms which infect vertebrate (including human) livers, lungs and brains, causing a variety of diseases. The eggs are shed in fæces. The larval stages first infect snails, then pass to aquatic plants, shellfish and fish from whence they reinfect the vertebrates. Freezing kills the larvæ but raw freshwater fish, shellfish and unwashed aquatic plants represent the greatest danger to both tourists and the more affluent countries which import them unfrozen

flummery **1** *(UK)* An old Welsh dessert made of sweetened and flavoured milk thickened by boiling with oatmeal, and set in a mould prior to turning out when cold. Originally a fermented and soured oatmeal gruel **2** *(USA)* Any of several sweet puddings thickened with cornflour. Usually milk or fruit based

Flunder *(Ge)* Flounder

flundra *(Sw)* Flounder

flute An indentation pressed into the edge of pie or pasty for decoration or to help seal two edges of pastry together

flûte **1** *(Fr)* A small French bread stick smaller than a baguette but bigger than a ficelle **2** A transverse slice of French bread, toasted and cut in quarters and served as an accompaniment to soup esp. minestrone **3** A type of glass for drinking champagne

flute, to *see* to scallop

Flügel *(Ge)* Wing *(of poultry)*

flying fish The name given to various species of seawater fish which have enlarged pectoral fins allowing them to glide above the surface of the water for considerable distances so as to avoid predators. Found in tropical and semi-tropical waters where they are prized as a food

flying flusk *see* flying squid

flying lamb slices *(Ch)* A pot of flavoured stock at the table kept boiling over a heater, into which guests dip very thin slices of raw, possibly marinated, leg of lamb using chopsticks or a fondue fork. When cooked in a few seconds, they are eaten with a variety of dips and relishes. The cooking liquor remaining may have eggs and soya sauce, etc. added and is consumed by the diners

flying squid A relative *Todarodes sagittatus* of the common squid up to 120 cm long and with two broad, flat swimming fins which allow it to glide above the surface for short distances. Fished commercially but rather tough and needs long slow cooking [also called **flying flusk**]

flyndre *(No)* Sole, the fish

foaming biscuit method A method of making biscuits by whisking egg whites with some sugar to a light meringue, then folding in the dry ingredients being extra careful with ground nuts

focaccia *(It)* **1** A bun or cake **2** A flour, salt and water yeast-raised dough rolled out thinly and formed into a sandwich with a cream cheese filling, sealed at the edges and baked at 230°C for 20 minutes [also called **focacetta**]

focaccia ligure *(It)* A baked round of yeasted dough with many toppings including herbs, coarse salt, diced ham, onions, artichokes and cheese

focaccia del Venerdí Santo *(It)* A tart filled with a mixture of fennel, endive, anchovies, olives and capers [also called **scalcione**]

focaccia di vitello *(It)* Focaccia with a veal filling

focacetta *(It) see* focaccia (2)

foderare *(It)* To line a dish or pan, e.g. with sponge fingers, sponge cake slices, biscuits, bacon, dough, etc.

Foeniculum vulgare *Bot.* Fennel

Foeniculum vulgare* var. *dulce *Bot.* Florence fennel

fofas de bacalhau *(Po)* Cod fish balls

fogas *(Hu)* A type of pike-perch

foglia *(It)* Leaf

foglia di vite *(It)* Vine leaf

Fogosch *(Au & Ge)* A freshwater fish similar to a trout

foie *(Fr) masc.* Liver

foie gras *(En & Fr) masc.* The grotesquely enlarged liver of goose or duck achieved by force feeding with cooked maize gruel using a tube inserted down the throat of the bird. Used for savoury dishes and pâté de foie gras

foie gras de canard *(Fr) masc.* A pâté of duck liver made in the Dordogne. Some think it better than the goose liver foie gras

foie gras en croûte *(Fr) masc.* Prepared goose liver cooked in a pastry case and very expensive

foie de poulet *(Fr) masc.* Chicken livers

foie de veau *(Fr) masc.* Calf's liver

foie de veau moissonnière *(Fr) masc.* Calf's liver fried with onions and herbs and deglazed with red wine

foie de volaille *(Fr) masc.* Chicken livers

foil *see* aluminium foil

foiolo alla milanese *(It)* Tripe and onion stew with cheese

foi thong *(Th)* A dessert made by pouring beaten egg in a thin stream into hot sugar syrup. A type of roti jala cup is used called a foi tong cone

fokhagymásmártás *(Hu)* Garlic sauce

folares *(Po)* An Easter gift of eggs baked in scooped out bread rolls

fold in, to The procedure of combining one ingredient with a liquid or semi-solid either of which contains entrapped air bubbles, so as not to break down or release the air, usually by very gentle cutting and turning with a metal spoon or spatula as e.g. icing sugar into whisked egg white, flour into an egg/fat/sugar batter, whisked egg white into an egg milk mixture

folic acid One of the B group of vitamins found in green leaves (hence the name) and other foods. Essential for health and esp. to prevent foetuses developing neural cord defects (e.g. spina bifida) and cleft palates during pregnancy. Deficiency can cause a form of anæmia *(megaloblastic anæmia)* but excess can mask the signs of pernicious anæmia caused by vitamin B12 deficiency [also called **vitamin Bc**]

Folie de béguines *(Be)* A large loaf-shaped cows' milk cheese (to 8 kg). The paste is strong flavoured with many small holes

foncer *(Fr)* To line the base of a pan or dish with slices of ham or bacon

fond *(Fr) masc.* Foundation or basis, meaning the foundation of all cooking i.e. the stocks which are converted into soups and sauces and are used as cooking liquors. Generally reserved for meat and vegetable stocks, e.g fond de veau meaning veal stock and so on; *see also* fumet

fond blanc *(Fr) masc. see* white beef stock

fond blanc de veau *((Fr) masc. see* white veal stock

fond blanc de volaille *(Fr) masc. see* white chicken stock

fond brun *(Fr) masc. see* brown beef stock

fond brun de veau *(Fr) masc. see* brown veal stock

fond brun de volaille *(Fr) masc. see* brown chicken stock

fond d'artichaut *(Fr) masc.* Artichoke bottom

fond de gibier *(Fr) masc. see* game stock

fond de marmite *(Fr) masc. see* white beef stock

fond de tarte *(Fr) masc.* **1** Pastry base **2** The crème patissière base of a French tart

fondant Sugar syrup boiled to 116 to 118°C, i.e. between the soft and hard ball stage, used when cooled as a basis for cake icing. It must be diluted with water and used at a precise temperature. If mixed with glycerine and gums it remains temporarily malleable at room temperature and may be rolled out for covering cakes and used to mould decorations

fondant potatoes Thick sliced or turned potatoes, buttered and seasoned, half covered in white stock and cooked in the oven at 240°C until tender and all stock absorbed

fondanti *(It)* Small savoury croquettes

fondo *(It)* **1** Stock **2** bottom or heart, e.g. of an artichoke

fondre *(Fr)* To melt

fondre, faire *(Fr)* To sweat

fonds d'artichauts aux points d'asperge *(Fr) masc.* Artichoke bottoms cooked in butter filled with creamed asparagus tips coated with mornay sauce and glazed

fondue 1 *(En, He & Fr) fem.* Cheese melted with wine and flavourings and kept hot at the table over a heater. Guests dip cubes of bread impaled on fondue forks into the molten mixture prior to consuming them [also called **Swiss fondue**] **2** Any type of food preparation and cooking in which guests dip small or thin pieces of food into a hot liquid (oil, boiling stock or the like), which is kept hot at the table, and then consume the pieces individually **3** *(Fr) fem.* A vegetable cooked until it is reduced to a pulp e.g tomatoes

fondue bourguignonne *(Fr) fem.* Oil kept hot at the table and into which guests dip pieces of raw lean meat impaled on fondue forks to cook the meat prior to consuming it with various sauces and condiments

fondue chinoise *(Fr & He)* fem. As flying lamb slices but with rolls of wafer thin slices of lean beef

fondue fork A long fork, usually with two barbed prongs at the end of a thin metal rod with a handle. Used for dipping food into hot oil, boiling stock or molten cheese at the table; *see also* fondue

fondue au marc *(Fr) fem. see* Tomme au raisin

fondue neufchâteloise *(He)* Gruyère and Emmental cheese dissolved in hot white wine with butter, pepper, cayenne pepper, kirsch and flavoured with garlic rubbed around the bowl. Eaten on cubes of bread in the usual way

fondue au raisin *(Fr) fem. see* Tomme au raisin

fonduta *(It)* Fontina cheese, soaked in milk for half an hour, warmed while stirring, beaten egg and butter added, whisked until thick and finished with grated truffle. Served with bread

fong toa hu *(Th)* Bean curd sticks

Fontainebleau *(Fr)* A cheese with a soft creamy texture made from cows' milk in the area around Paris. It is usually mixed with cream and served as a dessert with fruit

Fontal *(It & Fr)* A smooth, semi-hard mild flavoured cow's milk cheese similar to Fontina made in both Italy and France. It is cast in large 20 kg wheels and has a tender, buttery, mild tasting paste with occasional holes and is waxed or wrapped in plastic. Suitable for melting. Contains 43% water, 27% fat and 27% protein

Fontina *(It)* A semi-hard scalded-curd mild-flavoured slightly rubbery textured dark yellow cheese with numerous small holes and a tough brown rind made from very fresh unpasteurized cows' milk in the Aosta valley. It is dry salted or brine washed intermittently for 2 months whilst being ripened in caves. Used for fondue, fonduta and as a dessert cheese. Contains in summer 38% water, 31% fat and 26% protein. The winter cheese has about 2 percentage points less fat and 2 percentage points more water

food colourings Permitted dyes either of natural or synthetic origin used to colour food esp. by manufacturers of processed food

food fibre *see* fibre

food hygiene That science and/or craft which determines how food should be grown, picked or harvested, slaughtered if appropriate, transported, stored, handled, cooked and served to avoid contamination or deterioration which could be harmful to health, and also the design and cleaning of premises, vehicles, implements and equipment with which food is associated

food hygiene certificate A certificate of competence in food hygiene issued after appropriate training. Required for all food handlers in the EU

food labelling Under EU rules packaged food must be labelled with the name, the list of ingredients in descending order of weight, the net quantity, a best-before or best-before-end date, special conditions of storage or use, the name and address of the packager or seller and, under certain conditions, the particulars of the place of origin. The location of the factory or packaging centre is required in some countries

food laws The legislation which lays down requirements for food hygiene, for the purity of food, for the description of food and for the weights and measures associated with it

food poisoning Any disease of an infectious

or toxic nature caused by or thought to be caused by consumption of food or water regardless of presenting symptoms and signs (i.e. not necessarily gastrointestinal) and including illness caused by toxic chemicals associated with food but excluding illness due to known allergies or food intolerances

food poisoning bacteria The main bacteria responsible for food poisoning are, in alphabetical order: *Bacillus cereus, Campylobacter* spp., *Clostridium botulinum, Clostridium perfringens, Escherichia coli, Salmonella* spp., *Staphylococcus aureus, Vibrio parahæmolyticus* and *Yersinia enterocolitica.* See under each heading

food poisoning by bacteria, causes The principal causes are in descending order of importance: inadequate cooling; more than 24 hours between preparation and consumption of a meal; inadequate thermal processing; inadequate hot storage; inadequate reheating; eating contaminated raw food; cross contamination; inadequate cleaning of equipment; food from unsafe sources; use of leftovers

food poisoning causative agents These are: added during preparation, e.g. lead; synthesized by the commodity during growth and storage e.g. poisons in potatoes and red beans; formed by processing or storage under poorly controlled conditions e.g. some kinds of fish poisoning; stored by a commodity e.g. paralytic shellfish poisoning caused by a poison in some of the plankton or algæ that they consume; allergens, e.g. strawberries; bacteria, see food poisoning bacteria; and unidentified agents, probably viruses

food preservation science The study of the means used to destroy or inhibit the growth of those microorganisms with the potential to cause deterioration in food. The means involve intrinsic properties of the food, extrinsic properties of the environment and physiological properties of the microorganisms which enable them to flourish because of the interaction of the intrinsic and extrinsic properties

food processor A kitchen appliance consisting of a cylindrical bowl with cover through which projects a vertical shaft onto which various circular cutting, slicing and beating implements may be attached. The shaft is rotated by an electric motor at varying speeds but generally lower than a blender q.v. Used for chopping, slicing, mixing, purèeing and pulverizing tasks for all kinds of ingredients and mixes

food safe *see* meat safe

food store A room or cabinet set aside for storing foods, generally with good ventilation, vermin proof and with easy clean slotted or mesh shelving

foo gwa *(Ch)* Bitter gourd

fool A purée of fruit into which whipped cream or custard is mixed. May be sieved and sometimes thickened with gelatine

foon tiu meen *(Ch)* Wide flat noodles

foo yu *(Ch)* Bean curd cheese

foo yung *(Ch)* Omelette, often filled with cooked meat, vegetables and/or shellfish

forcemeat A gristle, bone and fat free meat, game or fish flesh ground finely and mixed with a panada of flour, rice, potato or bread, possibly cream, eggs, egg yolks or egg whites, fat or suet, etc., together with seasonings and butter to a piping consistency. Used as a basis of stuffings, quenelles, mousselines, borders and bases, pies, terrines and galantines.

forcing bag *see* piping bag

fore rib of beef *(UK)* The joint of beef consisting of the 7th to the 10th rib counting from the head of the beast with the attached muscles and the half vertebræ from a side of beef but excluding the breast end of the ribs. Used for roasting on or off the bone and first class braising [also called **standing rib roast**]

forel *(Ho & Ru)* Trout

foreleg of beef *see* shin beef

forell *(Sw)* Trout

Forelle *(Ge)* Trout

Forelle blau *(Au)* Freshly caught trout, possibly knocked on the head and gutted, plunged into a gently boiling white fish court bouillon. The skin turns a characteristic blue if the fish is absolutely fresh. When cooked, it is served with melted butter and boiled potatoes [also called **blue trout**]

Forellenbarsch *(Ge)* Largemouth black bass

foreloin of pork *(UK)* The rib end of the loin, equivalent to the best end of lamb. Roasted on or off the bone or cut into chops

forequarter The front half of a meat animal usually extending to the last rib

foreshank *(USA)* Shank of beef

forest mushroom *see* hoshi-shiitake mushroom

forestière, (à la) *(Fr)* In the style of the forester, i.e. garnished with mushrooms, ham or bacon and fried potatoes. Usually meat or poultry

Forfar bridie *(UK)* A Scottish pastry turnover containing beef, suet and onions

fork An implement with 2 or more prongs and a handle conveniently grasped in the hand used for eating solid foods, carving or cooking. Carving forks usually have 2 large prongs

fork luncheon A buffet type meal served on a plate and eaten with a fork usually while standing up

förlorade *(Sw)* Poached

forloren skildpadde *(De)* A dish supposed to resemble turtle made from the meat, tongue and brains of a calf's head, with meat balls, fish balls and hard boiled eggs

forlorent *(No)* Poached

Formagella Ticinese A soft cows' milk cheese with an even textured, delicately flavoured paste from Ticino cast in 2 kg rounds

Formagella della Val Bavona *(He)* A soft cows' milk cheese with an even textured, delicately flavoured paste and a thin smooth rind

formagelle *(It)* Small farmhouse cheeses from North Italy made with any type of milk

formaggini *(It)* Small cheeses, see Robiolini

formaggio *(It)* Cheese

formaggio bianco *(It)* The general term for soft unripened lightly salted cows' milk cheeses

formaggio di crema *(It)* Cream cheese

formic acid E236, the simplest organic acid found in some fruits and in the poison of ants, now made synthetically for use as a flavour enhancer

forno, al *(It)* Cooked in the oven

forrett *(No)* Appetizer, hors d'oeuvre

fortuné *(Fr) masc.* A miniature cake similar to a macaroon, baked and served in a small paper case, sprinkled with icing sugar and topped with half a glacé cherry. Lit. fortunate

fortune cookie *(USA)* A small cake or biscuit originated by Chinese Americans containing a slip of paper on which a horoscope, proverb or joke is printed

Fortunella One of the three important genera of citrus fruit of which the kumquat and the calamondin are the most common examples

Fortunella japonica *Bot.* Kumquat

Fortunella margarita *Bot.* Kumquat

fouasse *(Fr) fem.* A sweet bun

foudjou *(Fr)* A dish from Languedoc consisting of strong flavoured pungent goats' milk cheese flavoured with garlic and brandy and served with potatoes

fouet *(Fr) masc.* Whisk

fouetter *(Fr)* To whip or whisk, esp. cream

fougasse *(Fr) fem.* A type of bread or pastry made from yeast-raised dough, oval or ring shaped with a variety of fillings put between two layers of raised and knocked-back dough, proved, then baked at 200°C

fougassettes *(Fr) fem.* A bread made with olive oil and flavoured with orange flower water

foule medames *see* ful medames

four *(Fr) masc.* Oven

four, au *(Fr)* Cooked in the oven

four spices *see* quatre-épices

Fourme d'Ambert *(Fr) fem.* A semi-hard blue veined cows' milk cheese from the Auvergne ripened for 2 to 3 months and with a creamy texture and full bodied flavour. It is cast in a tall cylinder shape and has a dark rind rather like Stilton. It has AOC status [also called **Fourme de Montbrison, Fourme de Pierre-sur-Haute**]

Fourme de Cantal *(Fr) fem. see* Cantal

Fourme de Laguiole *(Fr) fem. see* Laguiole

Fourme de Montbrison *(Fr) fem. see* Fourme d'Ambert

Fourme de Pierre-sur-Haute *see* Fourme d'Ambert

Fourme de Salers *(Fr) fem. see* Cantal

fourrage *(Fr) masc.* Stuffing or filling

fourré(e) *(Fr) adj.* Filled

fourré à la crème *(Fr)* Filled with cream e.g. a cake

fowl An edible bird, usually applied to older or tougher poultry suitable for boiling, casseroling or making soup

fox noodles *(Ja) see* kitsume donburi

fox tail millet A temperate climate millet *Setaria italica* certainly grown in China in 2700 BC, now grown in the USA for animal feed and in Russia for beer [also called **German millet, Hungarian millet, Siberian millet, Italian millet**]

foyot, sauce *(Fr) fem.* Béarnaise sauce with added melted meat glaze whisked in slowly [also called **sauce valois**]

főzeléket *(Hu)* Vegetables

fracassata *(It)* Meat stew with an egg sauce

Fragaria alpina *Bot.* Alpine strawberry

Fragaria x ananassa *Bot.* Cultivated strawberry. Originally a cross between *F. virginiana* (arrived 1556 from the USA) and *F. chiloensis* (arrived 18th century)

Fragaria vesca *Bot.* Wild strawberry

Fragaria vesca sempiflorens *Bot.* Alpine strawberry

fragole *(It)* Strawberries

fragole di bosco *(It)* Wild strawberries

fragolini *(It)* Wild strawberries

fragolini di mare *(It)* Curled octopus

fragolino *(It)* Sea bream [also called **pagello**]

fragrant mushroom *see* shiitake mushroom

fraîche *(Fr)* Fresh or cool, the feminine form of frais

frais *(Fr)* Fresh or cool, usually applied to fresh cheeses and vegetables

fraisage *(Fr) masc.* A method of kneading dough by spreading it across the board with the heel of the hand, gathering it up into a ball and repeating the process

fraise *(Fr) fem.* 1. Strawberry. 2. Caul, the inner fatty membrane of the abdominal cavity

fraise de bois *(Fr) fem.* Wild strawberry

fraises Romanoff *(Fr) fem.* Fresh strawberries macerated in liqueur and orange juice and served with a topping of whipped cream

framboesas *(Po)* Raspberries

framboise *(Fr) fem.* Raspberry, also raspberry liqueur (liqueur de framboise)

frambozen *(Ho)* Raspberries

frambuesas *(Sp)* Raspberries

française, à la *(Fr)* In the French style i.e. with a garnish of spinach and potatoes, sometimes also cooked lettuce and asparagus

française, fish à la Fillets of fish dipped in milk and passed through seasoned flour, deep fried at 195°C, drained, garnished with lemon wedges and picked parsley and served with sauce diable

frangipane 1 *(Fr) fem.* Almond paste **2** *(UK)* An almond flavoured cake mixture made from butter, sugar, eggs, ground almonds and flour, used for Bakewell tarts q.v. and other similar items **3** *(Fr) fem.* A thickening agent or panada made rather like choux pastry from flour, egg yolks, butter and milk with seasonings for use in the manufacture of chicken and fish forcemeats **4** *(Fr) fem.* Confectioner's custard containing chopped or ground almonds used as crème patissière

frangipane flan *see* frangipane tart

frangipane tart A 16th century Italian tart introduced to France at that time, consisting of a blind baked pastry case lined with jam, filled with cooked cream containing crushed ratafia biscuits, lightly browned butter, rum and lemon zest, decorated with whipped cream and chopped pistachios [also called **frangipane flan**]

frango *(Po)* A young chicken

frango com ervilhas *(Po)* Chicken cooked in olive oil and butter and served with petit pois, onions and the pan residues deglazed with port

frango guisado *(Po)* A chicken, onion and tomato stew

frank *(USA) coll.* Frankfurter

Frankfurt tongue sausage *(Ge)* Cured pork leg meat finely minced, seasoned and flavoured with mace and cardamom, diced pork tongue and pistachio nuts added, the mixture packed into thin bullock casings, boiled until cooked then smoked over oak and juniper berries

Frankfurter *(Ge)* A yellowish-brown, smooth textured, scalded and cold smoked sausage made from finely ground pork and bacon fat. Usually poached in water to heat it up. Called bockwurst in Frankfurt

frankfurter *(USA)* A cheap imitation of the German Frankfurter made from the cheapest pig and beef meat and offal, finely ground with water and emulsifiers, mixed with flour, onion, seasoning, spices, saltpetre, colouring and so on, packed into narrow casings and linked. Made in various lengths. Used for hot dogs

Frankfurter Bohnensuppe *(Ge)* Kidney beans previously rehydrated, boiled in water or stock with herbs until tender, finished with butter and garnished with sliced frankfurters

Frankfurter Kranz *(Ge)* A rich cake made by the creaming method from sugar, cornflour, plain flour, butter and eggs (4:3:2:3:3) with 8 teaspoonfuls of baking powder (6 g) per kg of total flour and flavoured with lemon zest and rum, baked at 160°C, cut in 3 horizontal slices, filled with a rum flavoured and egg yolk enriched butter cream and the top and sides covered with crushed almond praline

Frankfurter Würtschen *(Ge)* A pale boiled sausage for which Frankfurt is famous, containing finely ground meat products

Frankische Butterplätzchen *(Ge)* Biscuits made by the creaming method from half and half butter and clarified butter, sugar, eggs, and flour (4:4:3:9), flavoured with vanilla and baked at 200°C

franskbröd *(Sw)* French bread, i.e. baguette, petit pain, bread roll or the like

franskbrød *(De)* French bread, i.e. baguette, petit pain, bread roll or the like [also called **rundstycke**]

franske kartofler *(De)* Potato chips

franske poteter *(No)* Potato chips

frappe *(It)* Galani q.v., but the strips of pastry knotted

frappé(e) *(Fr)* Frozen or chilled. Used to describe dishes served on crushed ice

frappo *(Fr)* A strong tasting casserole of ox tripe from Languedoc

frassino di montagna *(It)* Rowanberry

Frauenhaar *(Ge)* Maidenhair fern

freak coconut *see* makapuno

fréchure *(Fr)* A casserole of pig's lights from Vivarais

freddo *(It)* Cold

free range eggs Eggs laid by hens which nominally have free access to open pasture. Often theoretical since the birds have only limited openings from the barn to the outside and are not bred to freedom from hatching

freeze, to To reduce the temperature of food to below 0°C so that any free water solidifies and other materials become stiff or glass like. Mixtures are frozen to make ice cream, sorbet, etc. At even lower temperatures below −20°C food is preserved from deterioration; *see also* to deep freeze

freeze dried bean curd Bean curd which has been freeze dried. When reconstituted it retains the porous texture of the dried product

freeze dry, to A method of dehydrating food by subjecting it to a vacuum whilst it is frozen. This causes the frozen water to evaporate whilst preserving an open structure in the food which facilitates rehydration. Freeze dried vegetables are used in instant soups and the technique is most widely used for instant coffee

freezer A chest, upright cabinet or walk-in room which is kept at a temperature of −20°C in which deep frozen foods may be stored. Also used to deep freeze foods

freezer burn The discolouration which occurs on the surface of food where it comes into direct contact with a cold surface because of inadequate packaging

freezer knife A strong bladed knife with a serrated or saw like edge used for cutting up frozen food

fregolatta *(It) see* bruschetta

fregula *(It)* Saffron flavoured semolina dumplings cooked in broth and served with cheese [also called **succu tundu**]

Freiburger Vacherin *(Ge & He) see* Vacherin Fribourgeoise

frejoles *(Sp)* Beans

French artichoke *see* artichoke

French bean A South American, half hardy annual legume *Phaseolus vulgaris* usually a dwarf bush but occasionally climbing, which carries 10 to 15 cm long thin fleshy pods, usually green but some yellow or purple. When immature the whole pod is eaten as a vegetable. At a later stage when the pods become stringy the fresh green beans are known as flageolet beans and can be treated as peas, i.e.used as is or dried. When fully mature, cream or fawn coloured and completely dry the beans are known as haricot beans. Grown extensively all over the world [also called **dwarf bean. kidney bean, string bean** (USA), **snap bean** (USA), **haricot vert** (Fr)]

French black truffle The famous and expensive truffle *Tuber melanosporum* from Périgord which grows in the root area of oak and hazelnut trees. In appearance it is wrinkled and warty, dark brown to black with a strong distinctive fragrance and mild flavour. Now grown in California, New Zealand and Australia [also called **diamant noir (Fr), Périgord truffle**]

French bread Any of the varieties of long thin bread with a crisp brown crust and the characteristic diagonal slashes which imitate the traditional French daily bread [also called **French stick**] *see also* the French varieties, flute, baguette, grand pain, etc.

French carrots *(USA) see* carrettes

French dressing *see* vinaigrette

French flan *see* crème caramel

French fries *(USA)* Potato chips

French fritters *see* beignet

French frying *(USA)* Deep fat frying

French icing *(USA)* A cooked cake covering made from icing sugar, butter, eggs and flavouring

French marjoram *see* pot marjoram

French meringue 1 part egg white beaten until stiff with 2 parts of icing sugar, vanilla essence and a pinch of salt over a bain marie for up to 30 minutes. Piped to form various shapes

French mustard A mild flavoured mustard made from dehusked and ground, brown and black mustard seeds mixed with vinegar and water

French onion soup *see* brown onion soup

French parsley *see* parsley *Petroselinum crispum 'Neapolitanum'*

French puff *see* beignet

French puff pastry method Dough formed

into a ball, cross cut on the top, corners pulled out and rolled out to a square with a thick centre and thin corners. Fat of the same consistency as the dough placed on the centre, the corners pulled over the fat and rolled out to a rectangle to give 2 layers of dough sandwiching 1 layer of fat, folded, rolled out and rested, then turned and rolled as for puff pastry q.v.

French service **1** A style of laying the table with a plate (not necessarily used), cutlery, glasses and a napkin on the plate **2** A method of serving food in which guests help themselves from food offered on a dish or flat from the left by a waiter

French sorrel A name used indiscriminately for both sorrel and buckler leaf sorrel

French stick *see* French bread

French tarragon *see* tarragon

French toast *see* pain perdu. The sweet version is served as a dessert in France and as a breakfast dish in the USA topped with maple syrup, fruit or jam or sprinkled with cinnamon and sugar

Freneuse, crème *(Fr) fem.* Purée freneuse creamed with cream, milk or thin Béchamel sauce

Freneuse, purée *(Fr) fem.* Basic soup with potatoes and turnips [also called **potato and turnip soup**]

fresa **1** *(Sp)* Strawberry **2** *(It) see* carta di musica

fresca *(Me)* **1** *adj.* Fresh, cool **2** *fem.* A cocktail made with tequila, grapefruit juice and soda water

fresco *(It, Po & Sp)* Fresh, cool

fresh egg custard sauce *see* egg custard sauce

fresh fruit salad As fruit salad but restricted to fresh fruits

fresh ham *(USA)* An uncured hind leg of pork

fresh pasta Freshly made soft pasta which cooks in 3 to 5 minutes. Cannot be formed into elaborate shapes like dried pasta

freshwater bream A fish *Abramis brama* related to the carp family with a lot of bones and a muddy flavour. Generally caught for sport only

freshwater drum The only member of the drum family of fish *Alpodinotus grunniens* which lives all its life in fresh water. It is 30 to 40 cm long weighs to 500 g and is from the lakes and rivers of the Northern USA. The flesh is light coloured and mild in flavour

freshwater shark *see* pike

Fresno chilli *(Me)* A small conical fairly hot chilli pepper with a green or greenish yellow colour

fresones *(Sp)* Large strawberries

fresse alla cunese *(It)* Minced pork liver and beef wrapped in pig's caul and fried

fressure *(Fr) fem.* Offal from pigs or calves

friand sanflorain *(Fr) masc.* A herb flavoured pork pie from Saint Flour in the Auvergne

friandises *(Fr) fem.* Titbit, delicacy, sweetmeat. A selection of small sweets, preserved fruits, etc. served with petit fours and tea or coffee

friar's chicken *(UK)* Soup made by cooking a small chicken cut in four pieces in veal stock until tender. The seasoned cooking liquor is thickened with egg yolks, finished with chopped parsley and served with the chicken meat

friar's omelette A baked omelette with stewed apples

fricadelle **1** *see* frikadeller **2** *(Fr) fem.* Croquette

fricandeau *(En & Fr) masc.* A slice of meat, usually cushion veal, or large fish, cut along the fibres to 4 cm thick, beaten with a cutlet bat, larded with thin strips of salt pork fat and braised slowly until tender so that it may be cut with a spoon. Served dressed with the braising liquor and suitable garnishes

fricassea *(It)* Fricassée, usually finished with eggs and lemon juice

fricassee *(USA)* A veal or poultry stew in which the meat is first lightly browned so as to give a light brown colour to the stew

fricassée *(En & Fr) fem.* A stew of sealed white meat and/or vegetable in a velouté sauce, cooked in the oven and finished with a liaison of egg yolks and cream

fricaude *(Fr) fem.* A rich Lyonnaise stew of pigs' offal

Fridatten *(Au)* Thin strips of pancake used as a garnish

fried bean curd Cubes of bean curd deep fried to give a golden outer skin if lightly fried, or a crisp outer skin with just a little soft bean curd in the centre

fried cream *(USA)* As crèmes frites but panéed with crushed cake crumbs and sprinkled with sugar and rum

fried creams Crèmes frites

fried eggs Shelled eggs shallow fried in hot fat. The white on the top of the egg is coloured either by basting with hot fat or by turning the egg over when almost finished. Tastes differ as to the amount of cooking required

fried rice Cooked rice stir fried in oil with

chopped vegetables usually containing spring onions, and beaten egg which is dribbled into the mix as it is being stirred and fried. Often served in place of boiled rice in western Chinese restaurants or as a dish on its own

fries Plural of fry q.v.

friese *(Ho) see* Nagelkaas

friese Kanterkaas *(Ho) see* Kanterkaas

friese Nagelkaas *(Ho) see* Nagelkaas

frigate mackerel *see* bonito (1)

friggere *(It)* To fry

frijolada *(Sp)* A stew made with black beans, ham shank and sausage with fried onion and sweet peppers in a chicken or beef stock flavoured with herbs and served with rice.

frijoles *(Sp)* Beans

frijoles blancos *(Sp)* Haricot beans

frijoles negros *(Sp) see* black beans (1)

frijoles con puerco *(Me)* Black beans cooked until soft in water, drained and cooked in the oven with cubes of pork. The beans and pork are served on top of rice cooked in the bean cooking liquor (black rice) and garnished with coriander, chopped onions, chopped radish and a well spiced tomato and garlic sauce

frijoles refritos *(Me)* Refried beans made from various beans boiled until tender with onions, garlic, chillis, seasoning and sometimes skinned tomatoes, drained, mashed, mixed with fried onions, reheated and served as an accompaniment or as a dip

frijoles rojos *(Sp)* Kidney beans

Frikadeller *(Ge)* Small meat balls of minced pork, deep or shallow fried, served in a tomato sauce and popular in northern Europe

frikadeller *(De & Sw)* Small meat balls of minced beef and pork with grated onion, allspice, egg, seasoning and milk, deep or shallow fried, served in tomato sauce with potatoes and cooked red cabbage or salad. Popular in Northern Europe [also called **fricadelle**]

frikkadels *(Sr)* An adaptation of the European frikadeller made with minced beef, desiccated coconut, garlic, etc. and flavoured with dill or mint

frill 1 *see* cutlet frill **2** *see* mesentery

frío *(Po & Sp)* Cold

frire *(Fr)* To fry

Frisch *see* Frischkäse

frische Leberwurst *(Ge)* Fresh linked sausages made from pork meat and pigs' liver

frischer Hering *(Ge)* Fresh herring

frisches Obst *(Ge)* Fresh fruit

frischgemachte *(Ge)* Freshly cooked, cooked to order

Frischkäse Fresh cheese, refers to products such as quark and cream cheese which are not left to mature [also called **Frisch**]

frise kaas *(Ho)* Soft cheese

frisée *(Fr) fem.* Endive. Lit. curly

frit(e) *(Fr)* Fried

fritella *(It)* A thick, yeast-raised flour and water batter mixed with chopped vegetables, etc. and deep fried

frites *(Fr) fem.* Potato chips, chips, usually cut thinner than the UK version

friteuse *(En & Fr) fem.* Chip pan, deep fryer

fritieren *(Ge)* To deep fry

frito *(Sp)* Fried

frito de cordero *(Sp)* A lamb stew made with cubed lamb, onions, bay, paprika, white wine and hot chilli pepper, thickened with machado

frito de verduras *(Sp) see* pisto

fritole di lino *(It)* A choux pastry, teaspoonfuls of which are fried in a 2 cm depth of olive oil until the expanding ball turns itself over to complete browning taking about 2 minutes in all. When cooled filled with any thickened cream mixture and served warm

frittata *(It)* An omelette made in the same way as the Spanish tortilla but incorporating a variety of ingredients such as cheese, prosciutto, precooked vegetables and pasta shapes

frittatine *(It)* Pancakes

frittella *(It)* Fritter, pancake

frittelli di Venezia *(It)* Balls of yeast-raised flour dough, flavoured with white wine, grated lemon zest and raisins soaked in wine, deep fried in oil, drained and dusted with icing sugar

fritter The general name for a portion of sweet or savoury food coated with batter and deep fried

fritter batter A thick coating batter made from a smooth mixture of flour, oil and warm water into which stiffly beaten egg whites are blended. Alternatively yeast and sugar may be used to raise the batter

fritto *(It)* Fried

fritto composto *(It)* A mixture of fried croquettes each made from a different meat

fritto misto *(It)* Various items of boned meat and poultry, offal and vegetables, panéed or coated in batter and deep fried

fritto misto di mare *(It)* As fritto misto but with fish or shellfish. Served with lemon wedges

frittura *(It)* Fried food

fritura *(Sp)* Fried food

friture *(Fr) fem.* **1** The process of frying **2** Fried food **3** Deep fat for frying **4** *(En)* A large oval pan fitted with a wire basket used for deep frying. Usually placed on top of the stove

frituurvet *(Ho)* Oil, deep fat for frying

Friulano *(It)* A semi-hard scalded-curd cheese from Friuli rather like a young Montasio with a yellow/brown rind enclosing a firm paste containing a few small holes

frivolité *(Fr) fem.* Small savouries served at the beginning of a formal meal or banquet

frivolités *(Fr) fem. coll. see* animelles

frizzes *(USA)* Dried sausages made from coarsely chopped pork and beef flavoured with peppercorns and garlic and filled into hog casings

frizzle, to To fry until very crisp and brown

frog One of a group of amphibian animals most of which are edible. The European edible frog *Rana esculenta* grows to 12 cm long in the body, is green and does not have black marks behind the eyes. It is generally farmed for the back legs only, although it may be stuffed and eaten whole

frog's legs The hind legs of frogs which when fried or stewed resemble chicken. Popular in France and the USA

froid(e) *(Fr)* cold

froise An old English word for fritter, still in use when qualified, e.g. apple froise

frokost 1 *(No)* Breakfast **2** *(De)* Lunch

frollo *(It)* **1** Short (of pastry) **2** Tender or high (of meat or game)

fromage *(Fr) masc.* Cheese

fromage affiné *(Fr) masc.* Cheese which is fully matured and ripened

fromage blanc *(Fr) masc.* A very smooth textured low fat soft cheese with a fresh clean taste. Made from cows' milk with medium to low butterfat content, sometimes flavoured. Often served for dessert in place of whipped cream

fromage de Bruxelles *(Be)* masc. A low fat tangy rindless cheese made from pasteurized cow's milk [also called **Brusselkaas, Hettekees**]

fromage à la crème *(Fr) masc.* Cream cheese; *see also* coeur à la crème

fromage à la croûte *(Fr) masc.* Welsh rarebit

fromage du curé *(Fr) masc.* A strong smelling cows' milk cheese from Normandy cast in squares

fromage fondu *(Fr) masc.* **1** Cheese spread **2** *see* Tommes au raisin

fromage fort *(Fr) masc.* A mixture of overripe dessert cheese mixed with herbs, spices, oil and spirits, sealed in pots and left to mature to the strength required. Very strong tasting and piquant

fromage frais *(Fr) masc.* A soft young cultured cheese with a pleasant fresh flavour, often enriched with cream. Used as a dessert mixed or flavoured with fruit and since it does not curdle when boiled, used as a cream substitute

fromage glacé *(Fr) masc.* Cheese shaped ice cream

fromage d'Italie *(Fr) masc.* A dish made from pigs' liver

fromage de monsieur *(Fr) masc.* A soft cows' milk cheese similar to, but milder than, Camembert

fromage du pays *(Fr) masc. see* fromage des Pyrénées

fromage à la pie *(Fr) masc.* A white cheese prepared with full cream milk mixed with herbs. Said to resemble the black and white plumage of the magpie

fromage des Pyrénées *(Fr) masc.* A semi-hard ewes' milk cheese made in cylinders (to 7 kg). The paste is yellowish with a strong taste and the dry rind is sometimes coloured black [also called **fromage du pays**]

fromage de tête (de porc) *(Fr) masc.* Brawn. Lit. head cheese

fromage de trappiste *(Be)* masc. A semi-soft cheese made from cows' milk. Similar to Port-Salut

fromager *(Fr)* To add grated cheese

fromaget *(Fr)* Cheesecake

fromez *(ME)* A mild goat's milk cheese from Israel

Froschschenkel *(Ge)* Frogs' legs

frossen fløde *(De)* Frozen whipped cream, used for decoration

frost, to 1 To give items esp. soft fruits and the rims of glasses or coupes a frosty appearance by dipping in lightly whipped egg white then in caster sugar and leaving to dry **2** *(USA)* To ice a cake

frosting *(USA) see* American frosting

frozen food Particular foods, made-up or partially made-up dishes which have been frozen to −20°C and which can be stored for a least 6 weeks and generally much longer. It is generally stated that once defrosted, frozen foods cannot be refrozen but there is no justification for this rule providing the period at greater than 0°C is less than an hour. Frozen foods have generally been prepared for use prior to freezing

frozen yoghurt A dessert similar to ice cream made from a mixture of yoghurt, sugar and flavourings

Frucht *(Ge)* Fruit

Frucht des Brotbaumes *(Ge)* Breadfruit

Fruchteis *(Ge)* Fruit ice

Fruchtpastete *(Ge)* Fruit pie or tart

Fruchtsalat *(Ge)* Fruit salad

fructe coapte le flamă *(Ro)* Fruit fritters dusted with icing sugar, sprinkled with spirits or alcohol and flamed at the table

fructose One of the three common monosaccharides found in fruit and with a sweetening power greater than glucose or sucrose (cane or beet sugar). One of the sugars in corn syrup [also called **fruit sugar, laevulose, levulose**]

frugt *(De)* Fruit

frugt kage *(De)* Fruit pie

Frühlingskäse *(Au)* Cottage cheese mixed with cream, caraway seeds and chopped chives and parsley

Frühlingsuppe *(Ge)* Spring vegetable soup based on a meat stock

Frühstück *(Ge)* Breakfast

Frühstückkäse *(Ge)* A cheese similar to Limburger used as a breakfast cheese

fruit *(En, Ho & Fr) masc.* The seed-bearing part of any growing plant but generally restricted to those fruits in which the seeds are unimportant and the flesh or juice sac surrounding the seeds contains, when ripe, a high proportion of sugar plus various esters which give the fruit its distinctive flavour. The natural function of such fruits is to be eaten by animals who as a result diperse the seeds. Some fruit trees and bushes have been bred to have infertile seeds with no or only vestigial seeds

fruit and almond tartlets *(Ir)* Equal quantities of butter, caster sugar and ground almonds mixed and baked in tartlet moulds at 180°C till straw coloured. Filled before serving with fruit and whipped cream

fruit batter pudding *(UK)* A baked pudding mixture from Yorkshire containing pieces of fresh fruit

fruit bread Bread made from a sweetened and possibly egg and butter enriched yeast dough, containing dried vine fruits and sometimes spices, candied peel and citrus zest [also called **fruit loaf**]

fruit butter *see* fruit cheese

fruit cake **1** A generic term for cake mixes containing various amounts of dried vine fruits, glacé cherries and chopped candied peel **2** *(USA)* Candied fruits, dried vine fruits and nuts, bound together with just sufficient cake mixture to hold the fruit together when baking

fruit chat *(In)* A fruit and vegetable salad served on lettuce made from boiled waxy potato, deseeded and peeled cucumber, banana, papaya, mango, pineapple and apple all cubed, and orange segments, sprinkled with chat masala and lemon juice

fruit cheese A solid preserve made by boiling a purée of fruit with sugar to form a mixture which when cooled and set can be sliced like cheese. (But not lemon cheese q.v.)

fruit cocktail A mixture of various diced, possibly parboiled fruits, with cherries and other whole small fruit, in a sugar syrup. Used in desserts, pies, tarts, etc.

fruit crumble *(UK)* A dessert or pudding made from fruit and sugar in an oven proof dish, topped with a crumble mixture q.v., baked in the oven and eaten hot with cream, custard or ice cream [also called **fruit streusel** (USA)]

fruit essences *see* essences

fruit flavoured yoghurt Yoghurt mixed with fruit juice, fruit flavouring or essences, usually sweetened, often coloured and thickened with starch

fruit fritters Largish slices or pieces of raw fruit, coated in fritter batter, deep fried until golden brown, drained, dusted with icing sugar and eaten hot

fruit jelly **1** A gelatine-set dessert made from sweetened fruit juice or fruit flavoured water, also used in trifles **2** A jam or preserve made from strained and clear fruit juice boiled with sugar and set with fruit pectin if necessary

fruit juice Liquid extracted from raw or cooked fruit used for flavouring, as a starter or appetizer or as a drink

fruit leather *(USA)* An early method of preserving fruit by mixing fruit purée with brown sugar or honey, spreading on a baking sheet and drying in a slow oven. It was then cut in strips and dusted with sugar [also called **leather**]

fruit loaf *see* fruit bread

fruit à pain *(Fr)* Breadfruit

fruit de la passiflore *(Fr) masc.* Passion fruit [also called **fruit de la passion**]

fruit pie A pie with a base and top of pastry filled with fruit, sweetened if necessary before baking

fruit pudding *(UK)* Basic steamed pudding mixture with soaked dried vine fruits equal to half the weight of flour added in

fruit salad A mixture of sliced, or whole if small, fresh fruit and presoaked dried fruits in fruit juice or a plain or flavoured sugar syrup, served as a dessert often with cream, custard, yoghurt or crème fraiche

fruit snow Lightly sweetened fruit purée combined with egg whites which have been beaten with icing sugar

fruit soup *(CE & Sa)* A popular soup made from sweetened stewed fruit thickened with fécule, arrowroot, cornflour or fine semolina and flavoured with wine, lemon juice or vanilla

fruit sponge pudding A baked pudding rather like a fruit crumble but with a topping of Victoria sponge mixture

fruit streusel *(USA) see* fruit crumble

fruit sugar *see* fructose

fruit syrup Fruit flavoured sugar syrup made from fruit juices and water, used for flavouring and as a drink base

fruit turnover As apple turnover but with various fruits

fruit yoghurt Yoghurt to which has been added a sterilized mixture of suitably sized fruit pieces in a sugar syrup

fruits cuits *(Fr) masc.* Stewed fruit

fruits glacés *(Fr) masc.* Candied fruit

fruits de mer *(Fr) masc.* Lit. fruits of the sea, i.e. shellfish, crustaceans, etc. but excluding oysters

fruits rafraîchis *(Fr) fem.* Fruit salad

frukost *(Sw)* Breakfast

frukt *(No & Sw)* Fruit

frukt-kräm *(Sw)* Puréed fruit

frukti *(Ru)* Fruit

fruktpai *(No)* Fruit pie

fruktpaj *(Sw)* Fruit pie

frullato *(It)* Whisked or whipped

frumento *(It)* Wheat

frumenty *(UK)* A medieval pudding made from frumenty wheat boiled with milk and presoftened dried vine fruits, thickened if necessary with flour, sweetened and spiced with cinnamon, allspice or nutmeg. Traditionally eaten at Christmas, Easter and in Lent. Served with butter, cream or rum [also called **furmenty, fumenty, thrumenty**]

frumenty wheat Hulled or pearled wheat, soaked in excess water and a pinch of salt for 24 hours, excess water poured off and the remaining softened wheat stirred over heat until it boils, cooled and used to make frumenty [also called **cree'd wheat**]

fruta *(Po & Sp)* Fruit

fruta del arbol del pan *(Sp)* Breadfruit

fruta azucarada *(Sp)* Candied fruit

frutas doces *(Po)* Sugar plums, plums preserved by soaking in sugar syrup then draining

frutas del mar *(Sp)* Fruits of the sea, shellfish, crustaceans, etc.

frutta *(It)* Fruit

frutta candita *(It)* Candied fruit

frutti di mare *(It)* Shellfish

frutto del albero del pane *(It)* Breadfruit

fry The collective noun for the pair of testicles of a lamb or calf (thus lamb's fry), skinned then fried, braised or stewed. Sometimes used of other offal. *(pl. fries)*

fry, to To cook food in hot fat or oil at temperatures which seal the surface rapidly. May be in shallow or deep fat or oil

fry-up *(UK)* An informal dish of fried assorted fresh or, more generally, leftover food

fryer **1** *(USA)* A young chicken suitable for frying **2** The pan used for deep frying

frying basket *see* chip basket

frying batter. A batter of flour and water (4:5), plus salt and/or oil and/or whole egg or stiffly beaten egg white (4 eggs per kg of flour)

frying pan A shallow circular pan with outwardly sloping sides, a heavy base and a long handle. Used for shallow frying

fu *(Ja)* Wheat gluten

fudge cake *(USA)* A rich, moist chocolate cake which has a fudge like texture [also called **American fudge cake**]

fudge icing *(USA)* A thick fudge like icing usually containing chocolate or cocoa powder

fufu *(WA)* A purée of yams, sweet potatoes or plantains served as the carbohydrate source with stews

fugath *(In)* A style of cooking in which vegetables are fried with onions and spices

fugu *(Ja)* The puffer fish *Fugu rubripes* whose liver and blood contain a deadly nerve poison. The flesh is used in sashimi and this contains just enough of the poison to give a tingling sensation in the lips. Only licensed chefs may prepare the fish. Several deaths occur yearly in Japan from consuming incorrectly prepared fugu

fu jook pin *(Ch)* Bean curd sticks

fukasa-zushi *(Ja)* A sushi rolled in a thin pancake or crêpe instead of nori

fuki *(Ja)* Coltsfoot stalks

Fukien cooking The cooking of the Eastern coast province of China between Shanghai and Canton. It includes delicate soups, sucking pig, seafood, egg rolls and makes extensive use of soya sauce

ful *(Ey)* Brown beans [also called **ful medames**]

ful medames *(Ey)* **1** A brown dried bean similar to a broad bean [also called **ful**] **2** A dish of ful medames which have been soaked and drained then casseroled for 4 to 7 hours to soften, cooking liquor discarded and the beans dressed with lemon juice, olive oil, crushed garlic and seasoning without breaking them up then garnished with chopped hard boiled eggs and parsley [also called **el ful, foule medames**]

ful nabed *(Ey)* Broad beans

full cream milk Pasteurized unskimmed milk with a minimum 3% butterfat content (average 3.8%) [also called **whole milk, silver top**]

full fat soft cheese A soft white cheese with a butterfat content between 20 and 45% made from cow's milk. Used for dessert or cooking

Füllung *(Ge)* Stuffing

fumaric acid *see* (E)297

fumé(e) *(Fr)* smoked

fumenty *see* frumenty

fumer *(Fr)* To smoke

fumet *(Fr) masc.* **1** aroma **2** A concentrated fish or mushroom stock used for flavouring. Made by boiling the stock with additional fish or mushrooms and aromatic vegetables, straining off the liquid and reducing it to a syrupy consistency

fumetto *(It)* Fumet, concentrated stock

funchi *(Ca)* A pudding from the Dutch West Indies made from cornmeal or cornflour [also called **fungee**]

fungee *(Ca)* *see* funchi

funghi *(It)* Mushrooms, fungi

funghi porcini *(It)* *see* porcini

fungi The plural of fungus, in cooking generally refers only to the fruiting bodies of various fungi. For details see blewitt, boletus, cep, chanterelle, chestnut mushroom, common mushroom, field mushroom, girolle, honey fungus, horn of plenty, horse mushroom, Jew's ear, matsutake, morel, orange peel fungus, oyster mushroom, parasol mushroom, pine mushroom, puffball, shiitake, truffle, wood ear, etc. In the UK many of these fungi are referred to as mushrooms or wild mushrooms

fungo *(It)* Mushroom

fun gor *(Ch)* Ground pork and shrimp mixed with chopped chives or spring onions and light soya sauce. Made into small turnovers with wheat starch dough circles and steamed for 12 to 15 minutes

fungus The name given in cookery to the fruiting body of a fungus *(plural fungi)* which arises from the long branching thread-like strands of mycelium which grow on decaying organic matter and is usually the only visible part of the fungus. The fruiting bodies grow extremely rapidly and carry the spores by which the fungi are dispersed. They grow in the wild or are cultivated and are generally eaten before they mature. They do not require sunlight to grow and are most colours except green

funnel cake *(USA)* A cake made by running batter through a funnel into hot fat in a spiral pattern. When cooked it is served with sugar or maple syrup. Introduced by Dutch immigrants to Pennsylvania; *see also* furtaies

furi-jio *(Ja)* Hand sprinkled salt used for salting vegetables, meats and fish. The food is laid on a salt sprinkled board and sprinkled with salt from above. It is usually left about 40 to 60 minutes then rinsed and dried

furmenty *see* frumenty

furtaies *(It)* A fried pastry dessert from the Dolomite region made from a batter of milk, flour, salt, egg yolks beaten with grappa into which is folded stiffly whipped egg whites. The batter is dribbled through a funnel into hot butter to make a spiral, fried on both sides and sugared

fu-ru *(Ch)* Bean curd cheese

furutsu jusu *(Ja)* Fruit juice

fusilli *(It)* Pasta made into the shape of a corkscrew, hence the alternative name archimede (from Archimedes' screw pump) [also called **rotelle, tortiglione, tortiglioni, archimede**]

fuso *(It)* Melted or clarified (of butter), processed (of cheese)

fuzzy melon A Chinese vegetable like a

dumbbell shaped courgette but covered with a fine down which grows on a vine *Benincasa hispida*. It is used in its immature state as a vegetable and must be peeled before use. Steamed, stir fried or added to soup. The mature version is known as Chinese vegetable marrow [also called **hairy melon, summer melon, hairy brinjal**]

fyldt *(De)* Filled or stuffed

fyll *(No)* Stuffing

fyllda svamphattar *(Sw)* A dish served at smörgåsbord consisting of parboiled mushroom caps marinated in French dressing and filled with a mixture of cleaned sardines, grated onion, hard boiled egg yolk. Worcestershire sauce and mayonnaise

Fynbo *(De)* A semi-hard scalded-curd cows' milk cheese similar to Samsø from the island of Fyn. It has a lactic starter and the paste is smooth and creamy with a few large holes. The brown dry rind is usually waxed

fytt kålhode *(No)* Stuffed cabbage

Gg

gaai laan *(Ch) see* Chinese kale

gaau sun *(Ch)* Wild rice shoots

Gabelfrühstück *(Ge)* Fork breakfast, i.e. a substantial breakfast similar to an English breakfast or brunch

gabi *(Ph)* Taro

gacha *(Sp)* A soft pudding

gad *(ME)* A cows' milk cheese similar to the Danish Danbo with fairly large holes

gädda *(Sw)* Pike. See benfri-gädda for boneless pike

gado gado *(Id)* A salad made from a mixture of bean sprouts and shredded or julienned vegetables, steamed until al dente, dressed with a thick spicy sauce based on onions, garlic, dry roasted trassi, brown sugar, tamarind juice, peanut butter, coconut milk, ground cumin, dark soya sauce and ground lemon grass processed together, the whole garnished with chopped hard boiled eggs

gaelic *see* galic

gaeng *(Th)* Indicates liquid in the description of a dish. Used therefore as a prefix for stews, soups, etc. [also called **kaeng, keng**]

gaeng dang *(Th)* Red curry paste

gaeng jued *(Th)* Clear soup

gaeng kaee *(Th)* A thick, slightly sweet and sour, shrimp soup flavoured with turmeric, citrus (peel, lemon grass or leaves) and a variety of aromatic spices. Sometimes meat or chicken are substituted for shrimps

gaeng khiao wann *(Th)* Curry

gaeng mussaman *(Th)* A heavily spiced beef curry with coconut and peanuts said to have been introduced by Muslim civil servants from British India [also called **Muslim curry, musaman curry**]

gaffel *(De, No & Sw)* Fork

gaffelbitar *(Sw)* Small pieces of herring

gage A group of smaller plums *Prunus domestica* or *P. insititia,* noted for their sweet flavour and pleasant smell. The two common varieties are the greengage and the golden mirabelle

Gagel *(Ge)* Bog myrtle

gai *(Th)* Chicken [also called **kai**]

gai choy *see* Chinese mustard cabbage

gai hoot *(Ch)* Steamed coagulated chicken blood used in soups and stews

gaika *(Ru)* Nut

gai larn *(Ch)* Chinese kale

gai larn tau *(Ch)* Kohl rabi

Gaisburger Marsch *(Ge)* A beef and vegetable broth made from cubed chuck steak (1:4 on water) and pieces of marrow bone simmered with a BG and onion clouté for 2 hours, skimmed, BG, marrow bone and onion clouté removed, marrow from bone added back and simmered with diced root vegetables and leeks for 30 minutes and garnished with small Spätzle dumplings

Gaiskali *(Ge)* A soft goats' milk cheese

gai ts'ai *(Ch) see* Chinese mustard cabbage

gai yau *(Ch)* Chicken fat

gajar *(In)* Carrot

gaji jijim *(Ko)* Thin slices of roast beef sandwiched between fried aubergine slices. Served with a mixture of soya sauce and vinegar

gajjar *(In)* Carrot

gajjar halwa *(In)* A sweetmeat made from dried milk, carrots and spices rather like fudge [also called **gajjar ka halva**]

gajjar ka halva *see* gajjar halwa

gajus *(Ma)* Cashew nut

gal Abbreviation for gallon

galactose One of the common monosaccharides which in combination with glucose forms lactose, the sugar in milk. It is this monosaccharide liberated in the body which is responsible for lactose intolerance.

galamb *(Hu)* Pigeon

galangal The roots of plants of the ginger family respectively greater galangal, lesser galangal and kempferia galangal q.v. Greater galangal has a flavour like a mixture of ginger and pepper with a sour overtone, lesser galangal is more pungent with a hint of cardamom and eucalyptus, whilst kempferia galangal has a stronger taste and is the variety found dried and sliced in the West

galani *(It)* A Venetian snack of crisp, wafer-thin, deep fried strips of pastry, dusted with icing sugar [also called **cenci, frappe**]

galantina 1 *(It)* Galantine (of meat) **2** *(Po)* Aspic

galantine *(En & Fr) fem.* Boned white meat, possibly stuffed and rolled, cooked and pressed into a symmetrical shape and glazed with aspic

galapong *(Ph)* A dough made with ground rice and left standing overnight to partially ferment. Used for making sweet snacks

galego lime *see* West Indian lime

galera *(Sp)* Mantis shrimp

galette *(Fr) fem.* **1** A round flat sweet or savoury cake or biscuit made from a variety of foods, e.g. puff pastry, shortbread, batter, almond paste, potatoes, etc. **2** A buckwheat or brown flour pancake very popular in Brittany as a lunch dish with a sweet or savoury filling

galette de la chaise-dieu *(Fr) fem.* A sweetish goats' milk cheese from the Auvergne

galette des Rois *(Fr) fem.* A galette made from puff pastry for the twelfth night after Christmas. A single bean is baked in the galette which brings luck to the person finding it

Galia melon A variety of musk melon with green flesh and a green to yellow skin. It is sweet, juicy and fragrant

Galic *(UK)* A rich full cream soft cows' milk cheese from Scotland. It is flavoured with the chopped leaves of wild garlic *(ransoms)* and covered with rolled oats and chopped nuts [also called **gaelic**]

Galician cabbage *see* Portuguese cabbage

gali foto *(Af)* Cooked cassava flour served with fried lobster or shrimp and a sauce of fried onions, tomatoes, eggs, spices and corned beef

galil *(ME)* A blue veined ewe's milk cheese from Israel, similar to Roquefort

galingale 1 *see* tiger nut **2** The original European name for greater galangal, once considered to be an aphrodisiac

galinha *(Po)* Chicken

galinha recheada *(Po)* Chicken stuffed with eggs and olives

galinha salteada *(Po)* Sautéed chicken

galinhola *(Po)* Woodcock, moorhen

galit *see* na'ama

Galium odoratum *Bot.* Sweet woodruff

Galium verum *Bot.* Lady's bedstraw

gallates Esters of gallic acid used as antioxidants in oils, fats and essential oils only. Those available are propyl gallate, E310, octyl gallate, E311 and dodecyl gallate, E312

gallera, in *(It)* Wrapped in a beef and/or ham slice

Gallert *(Ge)* Gelatine, jelly

galleta *(Sp)* Biscuit

galletta *(It)* Wafer, biscuit, hard tack, ship's biscuit

galletto *(It)* Cockerel, young cock chicken

gallina *(It & Sp)* Hen

gallina di faraone *(It)* Guinea fowl

gallina de Guinea *(Sp)* Guinea fowl

gallina pepitoria *(Sp)* Fried chicken served with a sauce of pounded garlic, almonds and hard boiled egg yolks

gallinaccio *(It)* **1** Turkey, turkey cock **2** Chanterelle, the fungus

gallinaceous The generic description of an order of heavy-bodied ground-living birds *galliformes* which include the domestic fowl, turkey, pheasant and grouse

gallinella *(It)* **1** Hen, boiling fowl **2** Woodcock

gallinella d'acqua *(It)* Moorhen

gallineta 1 *(Sp)* Bluemouth, the fish **2** *(SA)* Guinea fowl

gallino rennet A type of rennet extracted from the gizzard lining of chickens or turkeys which produces a delicate curd

gallo *(It)* Cock, rooster, male chicken

gallo di bosque *(It)* Grouse

gallo cedrone *(It)* Grouse

gallon 1 *(UK)* The old imperial liquid measure still found in recipes. 1 imperial gallon equals 4.54 litre, 160 fluid oz, 8 pints or 32 gills **2** *(USA)* The liquid measure still in use in the USA. 1 US gallon equals 3.78 litres. Both are abbreviated gal

galupe *(It)* Grey mullet

galuptzes *see* holishkes

Galway oyster festival *(Ir)* An annual festival in celebration of the oyster held annually at the end of September in this attractive Irish town

gamat *(Ph)* Nori

gamba *(Sp)* Prawn esp. the crevette rose du large q.v.

gambas *(Sp & Fr) fem.* Large Mediterranean prawns, esp. the crevette rose du large, q.v.

gambas a la plancha *(Sp)* Grilled prawns

gamberello *(It)* Common prawn

gamberetti *(It)* Small shrimps

gamberetti di mare *(It)* Prawns

gamberettino *(It)* Shrimp

gamberetto grigio *(It)* Brown shrimp

gambero *(It)* Crayfish

gambero di acqua dolce *(It)* Freshwater crayfish

gambero imperiale *(It)* Caramote (Fr)

gambero di mare *(It)* Lobster

gambero rosa *(It)* Crevette rose du large (Fr)

gambero rosso *(It)* Crevette rouge (Fr)

gambrel The hock of an animal

game Wild birds and animals hunted for food, generally only in season at certain times of the year. Some animals and birds such as quail, rabbit and deer which are now reared for the table in captivity are still classed as game. The flavour of true game is supposed to be related to the intermittancy of its food and its more stressful life than a domestic animal or bird. See under individual types: boar, capercaillie, deer, duck, goose, grouse, partridge, pheasant, wood pigeon, ptarmigan, quail, rabbit, snipe, teal, widgeon and woodcock

game chips *see* crisps

game farce *see* farce de gibier

game fish Fish which are caught by rod or line for sport as well as for food, e.g. wild salmon, trout, shark, etc.

game herbs The principal herbs used with game are basil, bay, juniper, lovage, marjoram, rosemary, sage, savory and thyme

game pie *(UK)* A traditional raised pie with a pastry top made with hot water pastry and filled with pieces of boned game, rump steak, lean ham, pork sausage meat and seasonings, baked in a hinged oval mould and filled when cool with aspic jelly

game pie mould An oval metal mould consisting of two side pieces and a base which all clip together, often fluted. Used for raised game and pork pies

game pudding *(UK)* The cooked flesh of game pounded with liver of the same animal together with bread and game stock or mashed potatoes and butter and packed into suitable casings

game sausage Trimmed flesh of game minced with lean ham, then processed with butter, seasoning, sweet red peppers and mace and packed into suitable casings

game stock As for brown beef stock but substituting game bones for beef bones [also called **fond de gibier** (Fr)]

gamecock The male of the wild fowl

gamey The smell and flavour of meat and game which has been hung. In meat such a smell would indicate that it had hung too long. In game this is the smell and flavour required to indicate that the meat has been sufficiently tenderized

gamma-linoleic acid A fatty acid obtained from the seeds of the evening primrose q.v., used as a medicine

Gammelost *(No)* A soft, cooked-curd, blue veined cheese made from unpasteurized skimmed cows' milk. The natural *Streptococcus lactis* acts as a starter and the curd is inoculated with *Penicillium roquefortii* and ripened for 4 weeks at high humidity to give the blue veining and a heavy growth on the rind which give it its strong flavour

gammiris *(Sr)* Peppercorn

gammon The name given to a whole hind leg cut from a side of bacon after curing. It has a lighter cure than ham and is either used as bacon or cut into thick (1 cm) gammon rashers or steaks

gammon corner A large triangular joint of meat cut from a boned gammon

gammon hock The knuckle (foot) end of gammon containing more sinews and connective tissue than usual. Suitable for boiling, stewing and braising. The meat is often used in pies [also called **gammon knuckle**]

gammon knuckle *see* gammon hock

gammon slipper A triangular piece of lean meat cut from a gammon. It is smaller than a gammon corner and is used for boiling

gammon steak A thick slice of bacon cut from across a boned gammon

Gamonedo *(Sp)* A strong, smoked, blue vein cheese made in Asturia from a mixture of cow, goat and ewe's milk and similar to Cabrales. After smoking it is wrapped in fern leaves and matured for 2 months

ganache *(Fr) fem.* A chocolate-flavoured cream mixture used as a filling or topping for cakes pastries, etc., made from cream and melted chocolate with flavourings and sometimes butter.

The quality depends on the quality of the chocolate

gan bian siji dou *(Ch)* Stir fried sliced French beans

gander The male goose

gandhmul *(In)* Zedoary

gan dia fen *(Ch)* Cornflour

gan modoki *(Ja)* Patties of bean curd mixed with vegetables and spices

Gans *(Ge)* Goose

gans *(Ho)* Goose

Gänschen *(Ge)* Gosling

Gänsebraten *(Ge)* Roast goose

Gänsebrust *(Ge)* Breast of goose

Gänseleberpastate *(Ge)* Goose live pâté, pâté de foie gras

Gänseleberwurst *(Ge)* A fine goose liver kochwurst

Gänseweisssauer *(Ge)* Goose cut into small pieces, simmered in water with vinegar, seasoning and herbs until tender, reserved, cooled and served covered with the strained and clarified cooking liquor cooled over ice until viscous but not set, extra gelatine added if necessary

ganso *(Po & Sp)* Goose

ganth gobhi *(In)* Kohl rabi

gan zi *(Ch)* Orange

gao *(Vi)* Uncooked rice

gao yang rou *(Ch)* Lamb

Gaperon *see* Gapron

Gapron A dome-shaped low fat, soft and supple cheese made in the Auvergne from skimmed cows' milk or buttermilk and flavoured with garlic [also called **Gaperon**]

gar *see* garfish

garam *(Id)* Salt

garam masala *(In)* A blend of ground spices with many variants meant either to be sprinkled on food just before it is served, to be added towards the end of cooking, or to be used to form an aromatic crust on foods which are bland and simple. Typically it will contain black pepper, black cumin, cinnamon, cloves, mace, cardamom, coriander seed and bay leaf all dry fried or roasted then dried and ground. For particular blends see Moghul masala, Gujerati masala, Kashmiri masala, parsi dhansak masala, chat masala, char masala and green masala

garbanzo *(Sp)* Chick pea

garbanzo pea *see* chick pea

garbure *(Fr) fem.* A thick vegetable soup from Béarn containing beans, garlic, herbs, seasoning, preserved meats (duck, goose, turkey or ham), and sometimes chestnuts. Served over slices of bread

Garcinia indica *Bot.* Kokum

Garcinia mangostana *Bot.* Mangosteen

garde manger *(En & Fr) masc.* The larder area of a kitchen used for preparing cold buffets, canapés, hors d'oeuvre and the like and for preparing meat, fish and shellfish ready for cooking by others

garden cress *see* cress

garden egg *see* aubergine

garden orach *see* orach

garden pea *see* pea

garden rue *see* rue

garden thyme *see* thyme

Gardinia schomburgiana *Bot.* Madun (2)

gardon *(Fr) masc.* Roach, the freshwater fish

garfish A long (up to 60 cm) slender seawater fish *Belone belone* with green bones and a firm flesh, greeny blue in colour with a silver underside and found on most European coasts. Usually skinned before cooking [also called **gar, garpike, longnose**]

garganelli *(It)* Home made macaroni

garhi yakhni *(In)* A highly reduced meat stock similar to glace de viande; *see also* yakhni

gari 1 A coarse flour or meal rather like coarse semolina made from dried cassava. Used as a source of carbohydrate [also called **garri**] **2** *(Ja) see* beni-shoga

garibaldi A soft, thin, rectangular biscuit consisting of a layer of minced currants between two layers of soft sweet biscuit

garithes *(Gr)* Prawns

garland chrysanthemum A hardy perennial *Chrysanthemum coronarium* whose flowers are used in Chinese cooking. The seed may also be sewn thickly like cress and the young leaves used in salads or stir fried [also called **chop suey greens, chrysanthemum greens, edible chrysanthemum**]

garlic The cluster of bulblets that grow at the base of a plant *Allium sativum* after the first season of growth. Each bulblet is called a clove and the whole cluster a head of garlic. Each clove gives rise to a new head after one season. The clove consists of a white pungent, peppery flesh in a relatively tough skin. This is easily removed by squashing the clove. When raw the smell and taste are very strong and a cut clove run around a bowl will flavour anything contained within it. When cooked it loses most of its pungency. Very widely used in cookery throughout the world. It has been considered as an aid to good health since antiquity and is now thought to have anti-cancer properties

garlic bread A long thin French loaf cut almost through transversely at 2 to 4 cm intervals, a pat of garlic butter put in each cut and the whole, wrapped loosely in aluminium foil and baked in the oven until the butter has melted, and the outside become crisp (180°C for 15 minutes.)

garlic butter A compound butter made by processing butter, garlic, salt and chopped parsley to a smooth paste

garlic chive A type of Chinese chive with a pronounced garlic taste used as a flavouring.

garlic clove An individual bulblet of garlic covered in a thin layer of papery skin

garlic dressing A salad dressing (French or vinaigrette), flavoured with crushed garlic

garlic head The cluster of garlic cloves that grows beneath the soil

garlic mustard An early flowering perennial or biennial wild herb *Alliaria petiolata* growing to 1 m. The heart shaped indented leaves have a slight garlic flavour and may be included in salads or boiled as a vegetable [also called **jack-by-the-hedge**]

garlic powder Finely ground dried garlic flesh

garlic press A small implement rather like a lever type nut cracker with a receptacle with a perforated base on one arm to hold the clove of garlic and a piston on the other which when pressed into the receptacle pushes the flesh of the garlic though the perforations thus effectively chopping and crushing it

garlic purée Puréed garlic flesh with preservative, and possibly oil and salt. Available in tubes or jars to use for flavouring in the same way as tomato purée

garlic salt Dried and ground garlic mixed with salt used for flavouring

garlic sausage *(UK)* A smooth pale coloured slicing sausage made from pork and beef coarsely minced, cured separately (4% curing salt) in the refrigerator for 36 hours, finely minced with garlic, mixed with extenders, packed into weasands or large casings and hot smoked

garmeroug *see* muhamarah

garmucia *(It)* A mixed vegetable soup from Tuscany

garmugia *(It)* Beef stewed with peas and artichokes

garnacha *(Me)* A turnover made with tortilla dough, filled with a savoury stuffing and cooked. Used as an appetizer or snack [also called **picada, sope**]

garnalen *(Ho)* Very small shrimps

Garnelen *(Ge)* Brown shrimps

garni Past participle of garnir meaning garnished with vegetables

garnir *(Fr)* To garnish

garnish A decoration, always edible, added to a savoury dish to enhance its appearance, ranging from the simple sprig of a herb, to very elaborate garnishes which are often more difficult to prepare than the main dish

garniture *(Fr) fem.* Garnish

garofano di mare *(It)* Sea anenome

garofolato *(It)* **1** With cloves **2** A pot roast of beef with tomatoes and wine, flavoured with cloves

garoupa One of the grouper family of fish *Plectropomous leopardus* which is found around the coasts of China and SEA. It is up to 1 m in length and comes in two types. Red garoupa is pink with orange red spots and blue garoupa is red with blue spots. Prized in Chinese cooking.

garpike *see* garfish

garretto *(It)* Shin beef, knuckle or hock

garri *see* gari

Gartenkresse *(Ge)* Cress

Gartenraute *(Ge)* Rue, the herb

Gartensalat *(Ge)* Lettuce

garum Fermented fish made into a paste used by the ancient Romans as a flavouring. Probably like some of the Far Eastern fish pastes

gås *(De, No & Sw)* Goose

gas mark A scale of temperature, written as GM, peculiar to gas ovens and based on an arbitrary scaling of the first oven thermostat when °F were in use. The relationship to temperature is as follows:- GM1/4 110°C, 225°F; GM1/2 130°C, 250°F; GM1 140°C, 275°F; and thereafter 25°F per unit until GM9 240°C, 475°F [also called **regulo**]

gåsestak *(No)* Roast goose

gåsesteg *(De)* Roast goose

gäsleverkorv *(Sw)* A goose liver sausage

made with minced goose liver mixed with boiled rice, sweated chopped onions, raisins, corn syrup, seasoning and chopped marjoram, loosely packed in the unbroken neck skin of the goose, tied and simmered until cooked. Served cold or in made up dishes

gåsleverpastej *(Sw)* One goose liver finely minced with one third of it weight of lean pork and one third its weight of suet, passed through a coarse sieve, mixed with ground cloves, bayleaf and nutmeg, seasoned, placed in a covered greased mould and cooked in a bain-marie in a medium oven for 30 to 40 minutes

gåsöga *(Sw)* As solöga but with rings of anchovy, onion and dill

gaspereau *see* alewife

gastaurello *(It)* Skipper, the fish

gastronome A connoisseur of fine food and wine

gastronomy The study and knowledge of fine food and wine

gastropod The name given to any mollusc (soft bodied invertebrates without segments or limbs) with a hard, one piece outer shell, sometimes coiled such as the abalone, snail, whelk, winkle, etc. [also called **univalve**]

gata *(Ph)* Coconut

gâteau 1 *(Fr) masc.* Cake, gateau **2** *(En & Fr)* An elaborate cake sliced for a dessert made from layers of sponge, biscuit or pastry or a mixture of these interspersed with sweet fillings and decorated

gâteau aux amandes *(Fr) masc.* Almond cake

gâteau d'anniversaire *(Fr) masc.* Birthday cake

gâteau au fromage *(Fr) masc.* Cheesecake

gâteau noir *(Fr) masc. see* Créole christmas cake

gâteau Pithiviers *(Fr) masc.* Two layers of puff pastry with a rich cream filling containing almonds and rum. From Pithiviers

gâteau de riz *(Fr) masc.* Rice pudding

gâteau Saint Honoré *(Fr) masc.* A circle of cooked shortcrust or sugar pastry, biscuit or sponge, with a circle of choux pastry piped around the edge, topped with choux buns filled with whipped cream and coated with caramel, the centre filled with crème patissière and the whole decorated

gâteau de semoule *(Fr) masc.* Semolina pudding

gâteaux à apéritif *(Fr) masc.* Small savoury biscuits

gato marino *(Sp)* Lesser spotted dogfish [also called **pintarroja**]

gato pardo *(Sp)* larger spotted dogfish

gatto *(It)* Seasoned mashed potatoes enriched with eggs, milk and Parmesan cheese, half of the mixture spread in a flat oven-proof dish, covered with Mozzarella and/or other cheeses or fillings, covered with the remainder of the mixture, gratinated with breadcrumbs and baked until crisp on top [also called **gatto di patate**]

gatto di patate *(It) see* gatto

gattuccio *(It)* Lesser spotted dogfish

Gätupgelter *(Ge)* Channel catfish

gaucho *(Ar)* A rich tasting firm cheese made from skimmed cows' milk resembling Port-Salut

gau choy *(Ch)* Chinese chive or garlic chive

gau choy fa Flowering chive with a mild flavour

gau choy sum *(Ch)* Flowering chive with a strong flavour

gaufres *(Be & Fr) fem.* Rectangular waffles made by cooking a pancake mixture with raising agent between two hot indented metal plates *(gaufrier)* to give a large surface to volume ratio. Served with butter or sugar syrup

gaufrette *(Fr) fem.* Wafer

Gaultheria procumbens *Bot.* Wintergreen

gaur *see* guar

gaur bean *see* guar bean

gau wong *(Ch)* Yellow chives, i.e. Chinese chives which have been blanched by growing them in the dark

gayette *(Fr) fem.* A small Provençal crepinette made with pigs' liver, fat bacon and possibly pork, diced, finely seasoned and flavoured with garlic and spice, wrapped in pig's caul and tied, baked in the oven in lard or stock. Served hot or cold

gazpacho *(Sp)* A cold soup based on stale bread, garlic, oil and vinegar pounded to a paste and mixed with water, nowadays incorporating various salad ingredients such as tomatoes, sweet peppers, cucumbers, leaves and herbs. The bread is often omitted

ge *(Ch)* Pigeon

Gebäck *(Ge)* Fancy pastries, tortes, rolls, biscuits, generally eaten in the afternoons

gebacken *(Ge)* Fried or baked

gebackene Eier *(Ge)* Fried egg [also called **Spiegeleier**]

gebackene Kartoffel *(Ge)* Baked potato

gebakjes *(Ho)* Pastries, tartlets

gebakken *(Ho)* Fried

gebonden soep *(Ho)* Cream soup, thick soup

gebraden *(Ho)* Roasted

gebraden kip *(Ho)* Roast or fried chicken

gebraten *(Ge)* Roasted

gebraten Kalbskopf *(Ge)* Roasted calf's head

gebunden *(Ge)* Thickened (as of sauces)

gedämpfte Ente *(Ge)* Steamed duck

gedämpfte Rinderbrust *(Ge)* Beef, marinated in wine and slowly braised with onions and carrots

ge dan *(Ch)* Pigeon egg

gedünstete Gurke *(Ge)* Stewed cucumbers in a sour cream sauce

gedünstete Ochsenschlepp *(Ge)* Braised oxtail

gee choy *(Ch)* Nori sheets

gee jook *(Ch)* Bean curd sticks

gefilte fish Fish balls of ground raw fish with seasonings or fish cutlets stuffed with the same mixture, simmered in a court bouillon with sliced carrots and saffron. A Jewish speciality served hot or cold

Geflügel *(Ge)* Poultry, fowl

Geflügelklein *(Ge)* Chicken giblets

Geflügelleber *(Ge)* Chicken livers

Geflügelragout *(Au)* A chicken and chicken giblet stew

gefüllt *(Ge)* Stuffed

gefüllte Kartoffeln *(Ge)* Stuffed baked potatoes

gefüllter Gansenhals *(Ge)* A goose liver sausage made from chopped goose liver and pork, mixed with breadcrumbs and seasoning, bound with egg, stuffed into the intact skin of the goose's neck, tied and fried in goose fat. Eaten cold

gefüllter Rinderbraten *(Ge)* Rib roast of beef stuffed with onions, celery, carrots and hard boiled eggs

gefüllter Schöpsenrücken *(Ge)* Roast and stuffed saddle of mutton

gegrillt *(Ge)* Grilled

gehakt *(Ho)* Chopped

gehaktballetjes *(Ho)* Meat balls

Geheimratskäse *(Ge & Au)* A semi-hard, scalded-curd close textured cheese produced in Southern Germany. The paste has small holes and a delicate taste and is enclosed in a tender rind

Gehirn *(Ge)* Brains

Gehirnwurst *(Ge)* A sausage made from a mixture of 2 parts pigs' brain, 1 part lean pork and 1 part pork fat, chopped, seasoned and flavoured with mace, filled into hog casings, linked in pairs, boiled for 5 minutes then cooled. Served fried in butter

gekocht *(Ge)* Boiled, cooked

gekookt *(Ho)* Boiled

gekristalliseerde gember *(Ho)* Crystallized ginger

gel Jelly. Technically any liquid which is in a solid state by virtue of the network of strands of protein or carbohydrate which gives it a solid structure

gel, to To set into a jelly

gelatin *(USA)* Gelatine

gelatina *(It & Sp)* Gelatine, jelly

Gelatine *(Ge)* Gelatine

gelatine The soluble protein obtained by boiling bones and connective tissues in water and purifying it by fractional precipitation. Produced in powder form and as a purer sheet or leaf. Used extensively for gelling and setting jellies, aspic, mousses, etc. and adding body to sauces and soups. Since proteases break down the protein and destroy the gelling action it cannot be used with raw pineapple or paw paw or other fruits used to tenderize meat; *see also* leaf gelatine

gélatine *(Fr) fem.* Gelatine

gelato *(It)* Ice cream, iced, frozen, chilled

Gelbe Rübe *(Ge)* Carrot

Gelbwurz *(Ge)* Turmeric

gelé *(Sw)* Jelly

gelée *(Fr) fem.* Jelly, aspic

gelée, en *(Fr)* Garnished with chopped jelly or coated in aspic jelly

geléia *(Po)* Jelly

gelinotte *(Fr) fem.* Hazel hen

gelling agent Any substance which when dissolved in a liquid will enable it to set into a gel

gelo *(It)* Ice

gelo di melone *(It)* The diced and sieved pulp of watermelon, sweetened, thickened with arrowroot or fécule, flavoured with vanilla and mixed when cool with chopped bitter chocolate, candied fruit and pistachio nuts, allowed to set in moulds, demoulded and sprinkled with cinnamon

gelsomino *(It)* Jasmine

gemas *(Po)* Egg yolks

gember *(Ho)* Ginger

gemeine Sepie *(Ge)* Cuttlefish

gemeiner Dornhai *(Ge)* Rock salmon

gemeiner Krake *(Ge)* Octopus

gemelli *(It)* Short lengths of spaghetti twisted together

gemischt *(Ge)* Mixed

gemischter kalter Braten *(Ge)* A plate of assorted sliced cold roast meats

gemischter Salat *(Ge)* Mixed salad

gemsenfleish *(It)* A dish of chamois cooked in vinegar and served with polenta. From the alpine region

Gemüse *(Ge)* Vegetables

Gemüsesuppe *(Ge)* Vegetable soup

gendarme 1 *(Fr) masc.* Popular name for hareng saur (red herring), often served as a hors d'oeuvre **2** *(Fr & He)* A small flat rectangular spicy smoked sausage made with beef, pork fat, pork rind and wine [also called **Ländjäger**]

genevoise, sauce *(Fr) fem.* A fine mirepoix of vegetables browned in butter with parsley, thyme and bayleaf, a chopped salmon head and pepper added and stewed, fat drained off, red wine added and reduced by half, fish stock based espagnole sauce added, simmered 1 hour, strained, skimmed and finished with anchovy essence and butter. Served with salmon and trout

gen furay *(WA)* A snack from the Gambia consisting of small fried fish, coated with a mixture of fried onions, tomatoes, garlic and chilli

Genghis Khan griddle Mongolian barbecue

gengibre *(Po)* Ginger

genièvre *(Fr) masc.* Juniper berry

genip *(Ca)* A small round fruit like a grape, eaten raw by removing the skin and sucking the pulp off the seed [also called **Spanish lime**]

gen mai *(Ja)* Brown rice

genoa cake A fruit cake decorated with almonds or brazil nuts

genoese A light sponge cake made from creamed eggs and sugar into which molten butter is rapidly whisked to form a stable emulsion. Sifted flour is then folded in prior to baking [also called **génoise** (Fr), **genoese cake, genoese sponge**]

genoese cake *see* genoese

genoese sponge *see* genoese

genoese sponge mixture Flour, butter, castor sugar and eggs (2:1:2:4) without raising agent. Made up by the whisking method

génoise *(Fr) fem.* Genoese sponge

génoise, à la *(Fr)* In the Genoese style, i.e. including tomato sauce

genoise paste Flour, butter, caster sugar and eggs (2:1:3:5), made up using the whisking method and used for baked desserts. Not to be confused with genoese, which is a cake

génoise, sauce *(Fr) fem.* A purée of skinned pistachios, pinenuts and a little cold Béchamel, strained then made into a mayonnaise type sauce with egg yolk, lemon juice and oil

genovese, alla *(It)* In the Genoese style, i.e. with olive oil and garlic

gen stew *(WA)* A fish stew from the Gambia containing onions, green sweet peppers, tomatoes, garlic and chilli

gentleman's relish *(UK)* A paste made from salted anchovies, tomatoes and extenders used as a relish and to spread on fingers of hot buttered toast as a savoury

geoduck A large Pacific clam *Panope generosa* weighing up to 1.5 kg. The flesh is usually fried

George's bank flounder *see* winter flounder

gepökeltes Rindfleish *(It)* Ham, from the alpine region

geranium *see* scented geranium

Gerardmer *see* Lorraine

geräuchert *(Ge)* Smoked

geräucherte Bratwurst *(Ge)* A smoked bratwurst containing 6 parts of lean pork chopped fine to 1 part of fat bacon chopped coarsely

Geringium foetidum *Bot.* Cilantro (2)

germ That part of a seed, grain or nut from which the new plant starts to grow, equivalent to an embryo. The remainder of the seed is the food supply for the growing plant

German chocolate *(USA)* A milk chocolate for cooking, flavoured with vanilla and containing additives which make it stable when heated

German coffee A mixture of kirsch and hot sweetened coffee topped with whipped cream and drunk through the cream

German garlic sausage *see* Jagdwurst

German lentils The original brown lentils used in British cooking since the Victorian era

German millet *see* foxtail millet

German mustard A prepared, sweetish mustard from Dusseldorf, often flavoured with herbs and spices

German pound cake A cake similar to genoa cake but with less fruit and no almonds or brazil nuts

German salami A hard, preserved and highly seasoned slicing sausage about 5 cm in diameter made from finely minced pork and beef, normally flavoured with garlic and peppercorns and contained in a casing. Sometimes smoked

German sausage **1** A generic name for all sausages originating in Germany usually made from 100% meat products with spices, flavourings, garlic and seasoning, often smoked. There are three principal types: Brühwurst, Röhwurst and Kochwurst **2** *(UK) see* luncheon sausage

germano reale *(It)* Mallard, the wild duck

Géromé *(Fr)* A cow's milk cheese from Lorraine similar to Munster

Géromé anisé *(Fr)* Géromé cheese flavoured with aniseed

gerookt *(Ho)* Smoked

gerookte paling *(Ho)* Smoked eel eaten as a snack or hors d'oeuvres, garnished with lemon and gherkin slices

geroosterd brood *(Ho)* Toast

geröstete *(Ge)* Grilled

geröstete Kartoffeln *(Ge)* Fried potatoes

gerst *(Ho)* Barley

Gerste *(Ge)* Barley

Gerstensuppe *(Ge & It)* Barley soup containing bacon, onions and celery from the alps

gerty meat pudding *(UK)* A type of haggis from Cornwall made from boiled pigs' offal including lungs and spleen, minced with the scallops from the fat and with groats, boiled in the cooking liquor from the offal, seasoned, packed into large casings, tied and boiled

Gervais *(Fr)* A branded soft cream cheese generally sold in 6 individually wrapped segments of a circle, but the name is also used to denote the general types of fresh cows' milk cheeses sold in small tubs

geschabt *(Ge)* Scraped, grated or ground

geschmort *(Ge)* Braised or stewed

Geschnetzeltes *(He)* Fried pieces of veal and fried chopped onions simmered in a sauce made from wine, stock, seasoning and cream. Usually accompanied by Rösti

geselchtes *(Au)* Smoked pork or bacon

gesinka *(Pl)* A soup made from chopped carrots, onions, celeriac and mushrooms sweated in butter until tender, passed through a sieve and mixed with beef broth, seasoned, thickened with sour cream and egg yolks and finished with lemon juice and a little cooked pearl barley

gesottenes Rindfleisch *(Ge)* Boiled beef and vegetables, served with horseradish sauce

gestoofd *(Ho)* Stewed

Gestreifte *(Ge)* Red mullet *Mullus surmuletus*

getmesost *(Sw)* A Swedish version of gjetost cheese made with the whey from goats' milk cheese

getost *(Sw)* A hard goats' milk cheese, dry salted and ripened for 2 to 4 months and with a dry rind

Getreide *(Ge)* Cereal

getrüffelte *(Ge)* Flavoured with truffles *(used as an adjective before a food item)*

geung *(Ch)* Ginger root

gevogelte *(Ho)* Poultry

gevuld *(Ho)* Stuffed

gevulde boterkoek *(Ho)* Buttercake with a marzipan filling

gevulde broodje *(Ho)* Filled bap or bread roll

gevulde kalfsborst *(Ho)* Stuffed breast of veal

gevulde kool *(Ho)* Cabbage rolls stuffed with a meat filling

gewöhnliche Herzmuschel *(Ge)* Common cockle

Gewürz *(Ge)* Spice

Gewürzegurke *(Ge)* Pickled gherkin

Gewürzgurkensosse *(Ge)* A seasoned meat

stock slightly thickened with roux, mixed with sweated chopped onions and finely chopped dill pickles (300 g per litre) and simmered 10 minutes

Gewürzkuchen *(Ge)* Spice cake

Gewürznelke *(Ge)* Clove, the spice

ghaw-be-thot *(Bm)* Fried cabbage flavoured with blachan

ghee *(In)* Clarified unsalted butter used in Indian cooking because of its high smoke point in comparison with other oils and fats [also called **ghi, usli ghee**]

gherigli *(It)* Kernels of nuts, etc.

gherkin A small (to 8 cm long) variety of prickly cucumber which grows in damp sub-tropical and tropical climates. The immature fruits are soaked in brine and treated with boiling vinegar. Some varieties of small ridge cucumbers are occasionally sold as gherkins

ghi *see* ghee

ghiaccio *(It)* Ice or iced

ghiandole *(It)* Glands (thyroid, lymph, etc.) of pork

ghiotta *(It)* Dripping pan used under spit roasts

ghiotta, al *(It)* In a delicious style, nowadays with tasty vegetables and accompaniments such as onions, tomatoes, sweet peppers, olives, capers or raisins

ghiotto *(It)* Greedy, delicious, appetizing

ghiottone *(It)* A gourmand

ghiozzo *(It)* Goby, the fish

ghisau *(It)* A beef stew from Sardinia made with red wine, tomatoes and potatoes [also called **stuffau**]

ghiu *(Ne)* Ghee

ghiveci călugăresc *(Ro)* Fried onions stewed with potatoes, carrots, celery, aubergines, courgettes, French beans, garlic and salt. Served with roast meat and bread [also called **monk's hotchpotch**]

ghivetch 1 *(Ru)* An Armenian vegetable stew made from garlic-flavoured olive oil and beef stock (3:8), seasoned, flavoured with bay, dried tarragon and oregano, brought to the boil, whatever mixed vegetables are available added and the whole baked in a closed dish at 180°C for about 1 hour until all tender. Quick cooking vegetables may be added towards the end **2** *(Bu)* As the Armenian version but with and egg and yoghurt topping and baked without a lid

ghormehsabzi *(Pe)* Lamb chops and kidney beans in a thick sauce flavoured with parsley, Persian leek, coriander and sun-dried lemon, served with rice

ghuiyan *(In & Ne)* Yam

gia *(Vi)* Bean sprouts

giallo *(It)* Yellow

giambonetto *(It)* A boned leg of chicken shaped and tied to resemble a ham

gianchetti *(It) see* bianchetti

gianfottere *(It)* A vegetable stew from Calabria made with aubergines, courgettes, sweet peppers and herbs

giant garlic A mild garlic-flavoured bulb *Allium scorodoprasum* of the onion family with mauve flowers which develop edible aerial bulbs like the tree onion [also called **rocambole, Spanish garlic**]

giant granadilla A large tropical passion fruit *Passiflora quadrangularis* with an indifferent tasting greenish yellow fruit. Immature fruits are sometimes baked as a vegetable

giant puffball A spherical fruit body of a fungus *Langermannia gigantea* which can grow up to 30 cm in dia. but is eaten when young before the spores, which are made within the outer flesh, have formed. Normally sliced, panéed and fried

giant saxidome A large clam *Saxidomus gigantus* found along the west coast of North America down to San Diego

giant shells *(USA)* Conchiglie, pasta shells

giant west coast clam A large clam *Schizothaerus nuttalli* from the west coast of the USA which lives 60 cm deep in the mud. It makes excellent chowder [also called **Washington clam**]

giant white radish *see* mooli

giardiniera, alla *(It)* In the gardener's style, i.e. with assorted fresh or pickled vegetables

gia vi pha lau *(Vi)* Five spice powder

gibelotte *(Fr) fem.* A fricassée of rabbit in wine usually with onions and potatoes

gibier (à poil, à plume) *(Fr) masc.* Game (animals, birds)

gibier d'eau *(Fr) masc.* Waterfowl

giblets The entrails and neck of poultry and birds comprising the neck, gizzard, liver, heart and sometimes kidneys. Used for stock or gravy, but livers and gizzards often used as the basis of separate dishes

Gien *(Fr)* A soft creamy but firm cheese with a fine flavour made around Orleans from a mixture of goats' and cows' milk, matured in leaves or wood ash for about 3 weeks

Gigha *(UK)* A firm cheese made from cows' milk on the island of Gigha in Scotland

gigoret *(Fr)* Pig's head cooked in blood and red wine. A dish from Poitou-Charentes

gigot *(Fr) masc.* Leg of lamb or deer

gigot d'agneau à la couronne d'ail *(Fr) masc.* Sealed and browned leg of lamb, pot roasted with 50 to 60 cloves of garlic, sweet white wine, brandy and seasoning. Served with defatted pot juices and a fresh green salad

gigot boulangère *(Fr) masc.* A garlic piquéed leg of lamb, roasted with butter at 200°C over a thick bed of preroasted sliced potatoes flavoured with chopped onions and herbs until the lamb is cooked, the dish then covered with foil and rested 10 minutes before serving

gigot of lamb *(UK)* The Scottish term for a full leg of lamb

gigot lamb chops *(UK)* Term used in the North of England for chump chops of lamb

gigot pourri *(Fr) masc.* A leg of lamb roasted with a large number of garlic cloves

gigue *(Fr) fem.* Haunch (of venison, etc.)

gila *(Po) see* chila

Gilboa *(ME)* A cows' milk cheese from Israel similar to Edam

gild, to 1 To glaze with beaten egg before baking. Gives a rich golden colour to the goods **2** To coat the surface of some hard food with gold leaf for decorative purposes and to exhibit the wealth of the person serving it

gildeneh yoich Jewish chicken soup

gilead *(ME)* A ewes' milk cheese from Israel resembling Kashkaval

gili khichhari *(In)* A moist version of khichhari q.v. for children and invalids

gill *(UK)* A fluid measure equal to one quarter of an imperial pint in the standard British and USA system,i.e. 142 ml and 118 ml respectively, and one eighth of a pint in Scotland. To confuse matter further a gill of beer in England is half a pint

gilt A young sow, female pig

gilt-head bream A silvery seawater bream *Sparus aurata* and *Chrysophrys aurata* from the Northern Mediterranean with a gold tinged head and fine tasting flesh, very similar to the sea bream and easily confused with it. Weighs approximately 1 kg. A related species *Chrysophrys major* is used in Japan for sashimi

gin *(Bm)* Ginger

ginepro *(It)* Juniper berry

ginestrata *(It)* A light mildly spiced soup from Tuscany made with chicken stock, egg yolks, butter and white wine

gingelly *(In)* Light sesame seed oil

gingembre *(Fr) masc.* Ginger

ginger The knobbly, buff coloured, branching rhizome (creeping fleshy root) of a tropical plant *Zingiber officinale* with a warm aroma and hot burning taste. Available fresh, dried, preserved in sugar syrup and as a ground dried powder. Used extensively in all forms in all cuisines

ginger buds The pink buds of various types of ginger plant which are sliced and used as a garnish or eaten raw in salads [also called **pink ginger buds, torch ginger**]

ginger mint A mint type *Mentha x gentilis 'variegata'* with smooth, gold splashed leaves and a spicy flavour. Used for flavouring

ginger nut A small round biscuit strongly flavoured with ginger

ginger pudding *(UK)* Basic steamed pudding mixture flavoured with ground ginger and chopped stem ginger

ginger shoots Long thin pinkish stalks of the ginger plant which are harvested in spring. They are pickled in vinegar in Japan where they are known as hajikama shoga [also called **blushing ginger**]

ginger snap A round sweet biscuit flavoured with ginger and very crisp and crunchy

gingerbread 1 *(UK)* A moist fawn to dark brown cake made by the melting method, sweetened with golden syrup or treacle and flavoured with powdered ginger root. May be decorated with slices of preserved ginger **2** *(USA)* A ginger-flavoured biscuit

gingerbread man *(UK)* A ginger biscuit mixture rolled and cut in the shape of a man (the traditional shape) and decorated with currants to represent eyes and buttons. Baked at 190°C until brown

gingko *see* ginkgo nut

ginitan *(Ph) see* guinataan

Ginkgo biloba *Bot.* Maidenhair tree

ginkgo leaf cut *see* icho giri

ginkgo nut The kernel of the fruit of the maidenhair tree *Ginkgo biloba* from the Far East but now grown around the Mediterranean. The flesh of the fruit is not edible but the nuts are used in Japanese cooking. May be roasted, used in sweet or savoury dishes or as a garnish or snack food

ginnan *(Ja)* Ginkgo nut

ginseng The roots of various members of the *Panax* spp. found in East Asia and North America. Besides its medicinal uses it is used to flavour soups and stews

giorno, del *(It)* Of the day, as in dish of the day

giovane *(It)* Young, new, of vegetables, etc. [also called **giovine**]

giovine *(It) see* giovane

girasol *(Sp & Fr) masc.* Sunflower

girasole *(It)* Sunflower

girdle *see* griddle

girdle cake *see* griddle cake

giri *(Ja)* A cutting stroke of the knife

girofle *(Fr) masc.* Cloves [also called **clou de girofle**]

girolle 1 *(Fr) fem.* Chanterelle **2** A special knife used to cut very thin slices of cheese and butter

gist *(Ho)* Yeast

gîte *(Fr) masc.* Lamb shank and foot

gîte-gîte *(Fr) masc.* Shin beef

gîte à la noix *(Fr) masc.* Thick flank of veal, topside of beef (UK), bottom round of beef (USA) [also called **noix pâtissière**]

giuncata *(It)* **1** A soft curd cheese retaining some whey, made from cows' or ewes' milk and named after the rush container in which the curds are drained **2** Curds and whey, junket

givre The powdery white crystals of vanillin found on the best quality vanilla pods

gizzard A thick muscular organ in a bird, often the second stomach, used to grind food

gizzard shad *see* shad

Gjetöst *(Sa)* A sort of cheese which is an aquired taste. It is made with the whey from cheese made with goats' and cows' milk. This is reduced by boiling to a paste of caramelized lactose and whey proteins and is made in both soft, for spreading, and hard consistencies. The hard variety is eaten as shavings made with a special knife

gjuwetch *(Bu)* Diced mutton simmered in oil with chopped onions, sweet green peppers, aubergines, green beans, squash, okra and potatoes until cooked, most oil drained off the mixture, seasoned, covered with slices of tomatoes, oiled and baked in the oven

glaçage *(Fr) masc.* Icing or glazing with an egg wash

glace *(Fr) fem.* **1** Ice **2** Ice cream **3** Glaze, i.e. reduced clear meat stock **4** Royal icing

glace de poisson *(Fr) fem. see* fish glaze

glace portative *(Fr) fem.* Ice cream to take away as e.g. ice cream cone

glace de viande *(Fr) fem.* A reduction of clarified meat stock which is shiny and syrupy. Used to add flavour and body to other dishes [also called **glaze**]

glacé(e) *(Fr)* **1** Ice cold, iced **2** Glossy

glacé cherry Candied cherries, not dried and with a glossy appearance, coloured with red or various other colours of food dye, used for decoration of cakes and desserts or sometimes in cake mixtures

glacé fruit Candied fruit which has not been dried so as to retain a glossy appearance

glacé icing A simple mixture of sugar and water or strained fruit juice (100:15) of coating consistency which has a glossy appearance when spread on cakes, biscuits, etc. Possibly coloured and flavoured [also called **water icing**]

glacer *(Fr)* To glaze

glacière *(Fr) fem.* Ice box

gladde haai *(Ho)* Smooth hound, the fish [also called **toonhaai**]

Glamorgan cheese sausage *(UK)* A skinless sausage from Wales made with a mixture of grated cheese, breadcrumbs, chopped onion, parsley, thyme or rosemary, seasoning and possibly mustard, bound with egg, shaped into cylinders and fried [also called **Glamorgan sausage**]

Glamorgan sausage *see* Glamorgan cheese sausage

Glarnerschabziger *see* sapsago

glas *(De & Sw)* Glass, tumbler

Glasgow pale *(UK)* A small haddock prepared as finnan haddock but smoked more. From Scotland

glasmästarsill *(Sw)* Pieces of herring, marinated in vinegar and sugar for 2 days, the marinade drained off, heated and poured over the herring pieces which have been packed in a jar interspersed with slices of carrot and onion, grated horseradish, bay leaves and pickling spices. Refrigerated until eaten [also called **glass blower's herring**]

glass 1 *(Sw)* Ice cream **2** *(No)* Glass, tumbler

glass blower's herring *see* glasmästarsill

glassato *(It)* Glazed, iced

glasswort *see* samphire *Salicornia europaea*

Glasur *(Ge)* Icing

Glattbutt *(Ge)* Brill

Glatthai *(Ge)* Smooth hound, the fish

Glattrochen *(Ge)* Common skate

glaze *see* glace de viande

glaze, to 1 To give a glossy coating to sweet and savoury dishes so as to produce a decorative finish. Beaten egg, milk, and lard are used with bread or buns. Sugar and fruit syrups are used with sweetened doughs and cakes. Arrowroot and sugar thickened fruit juices are used with fruit tarts, butter with vegetables, and aspic jelly is used with savoury items, canapés, etc. **2** To brown food under a very hot grill e.g. crème brulée and sauces containing a liaison of eggs and cream used on fish

glazuur *(Ho)* Glazed

gliadin One of the types of protein in gluten which is soluble in dilute salt solutions. This affects the plasticity of dough

globe artichoke *see* artichoke

globe onion The common variety of spherical onion with a brown papery skin and concentric layers of white translucent crisp flesh springing from the root end. Fairly strong flavoured and esp. pungent when raw

Glomzda *(Pl)* Cottage cheese, quark

Gloucester cheese *(UK)* Cheese originally made from morning milk (lower fat) of the Gloucester cow. It is a hard cheese with a mild and pale coloured paste and cast in squat cylinders. Now very rare; *see also* single and double Gloucester cheese

Gloucester pudding *(UK)* A steamed suet pudding containing chopped raw apple and chopped candied mixed peel

Gloucester sauce *(UK)* Very thick mayonnaise mixed with sour cream, lemon juice, chopped fennel and a little Worcester sauce. Served with cold meat

Gloucester sausage *(UK)* A pork sausage made with meat from the Gloucester old spot, a traditional breed of pig with plenty of fat

Gloucester squab pie *(UK)* The same as Devonshire squab pie q.v.

glucono delta-lactone *see* (E)575

glucose A monosaccharide which forms the building block of many starch and cellulose carbohydrates and is one of the constituents of the disaccharides sucrose (with fructose), maltose (with itself) and lactose (with galactose). It inhibits the oxidation of foods and facilitates browning in fried sausages. Often added to continental sausages to act as the substrate for a lactic acid fermentation which improves their keeping qualities [also called **dextrose**]

glucose oxidase An enzyme obtained from *Aspergillus niger*, used to remove traces of glucose from egg white that is to be dried

gluea *(Th)* Salt

Glumse *(Ge)* Cottage cheese

glutamate de sodium *(Fr)* MSG

glutamato de sodio *(Sp)* MSG

glutamic acid (E)620 one of the amino acids used by animals and humans

gluten The general name given to the proteins in common wheat consisting mainly of glutenin and gliadin. These are responsible for the visco-elastic behaviour of and the baking properties of dough made from wheat flours and for the ability of the dough to entrap bubbles of carbon dioxide. It is extracted from wheat, esp. in the Far East and when cooked forms a spongy soft mass which absorbs flavours and is used rather like bean curd and for making cakes

gluten flour Dry powdered gluten made by washing the starch from high protein flour, drying and grinding

gluten free food Food which contains no gluten. Necessary for the small fraction of people who are allergic to gluten

glutenin One of the protein types in gluten insoluble in water or salt solution. It contains many cross linkages which are broken or rearranged during the kneading of dough and is responsible for its elasticity

glutiminato di soda *(It)* MSG

glutinous rice Black or white, short or long grain rice which is particularly sticky when boiled and easy to handle with chopsticks. Used in Chinese and Japanese dishes esp. boiled and sweetened in sushi. It should be soaked in cold water for 8 hours then cooked with an equal weight of water for about 12 minutes and left to stand covered for a further 10 minutes; *see also* black rice, mochi-gome and pinipig [also called **sticky rice**]

glutinous rice flour A fine white flour made from glutinous rice and used to make soft cakes, buns and dumplings esp. in Asian and SEA cooking

glycérie *(Fr) fem.* Sweet woodruff

glycerine E422, a sweetish colourless oily liquid, completely miscible with water, which when esterified with fatty acids forms natural fats and oils. Used as a humectant to prevent foodstuffs drying out, esp. royal icing [also called **glycerol**]

glycerol *see* glycerine

glycerol di-acetate An ester of glycerol and

acetic acid used as a solvent for food colours and flavourings [also called **diacetin**]

glycerol monoacetate An ester of glycerol and acetic acid used as a solvent for food colours and flavourings [also called **monoacetin**]

glycerol tri-acetate An ester of glycerol and acetic acid used as a solvent for food colours and flavourings [also called **triacetin**]

glycine An amino acid used as a sequestering agent and buffer

Glycine max *Bot.* Soya bean

glycogen A polysaccharide produced in the animal body from glucose and stored in the liver and muscles. Very quickly broken down into glucose and thus a very important quickly available energy store. Animals that are killed after stress e.g of the hunt or from poor handling have little or no glycogen in their muscles which are thus less flavoursome than otherwise

Glycyrrhiza glabra *Bot.* Liquorice

GMP Good manufacturing practice

gnocchetti *(It)* Tiny gnocchi used for garnishing soup

gnocchi *(It)* Small dumplings made in the form of balls, cylinders or circular slices which are poached and used as a garnish or served with a sauce. Made from semolina, choux paste or potatoes

gnocchi alla bava *(It)* Gnocchi made with buckwheat flour, fresh cheese and cream

gnocchi dolce *(It)* Sweet dumplings

gnocculi *(It)* Potato gnocchi from Sicily served with cheese and broth or meat sauce

goa *(Ph)* Goa bean

goa bean A legume *Psophocarpus tetragonolobus* which is a native of southern Europe but grown extensively in SEA. It has winged four angled pods similar to the asparagus pea which are cooked whole in the same way. The roots are also edible

goak sung *(Ch)* Bamboo fungus,

goat A horned animal, slightly bigger than a sheep, which can metabolize almost any carbohydrate source. Bred mainly for their milk in the West, they are an important source of meat in Africa, the Eastern Mediterranean, the Middle East, the Caribbean and parts of Asia. Young goats' meat is eaten in France and Italy esp. in the spring

goat fish *see* red mullet

goat milk Goat's milk has a higher fat and protein content and a stronger flavour than cow's milk and is often made into cheese. It has something of a health food reputation in the West

goat pepper A very small chilli pepper from Indonesia dried and sold worldwide for pickling

gobhi *(In)* Cauliflower

gobo *(Ja)* Burdock root used in sauces, stocks and braised dishes

goby A small seawater fish *Gobidae* family with a sucker, similar to the freshwater gudgeon. Treated as a whitebait

gochian *(In)* A type of black mushroom from Kashmir similar to the morel

gochujang *(Ko)* A chilli paste similar to sambal oelek

gochu jeon *(Ko)* Green sweet pepper rings and halved chilli peppers stuffed with a meat mixture, floured, dipped in beaten egg and deep fried in sesame seed oil

godard, sauce *(Fr) fem.* White wine reduced with a fine mirepoix of vegetables and ham, demi-glace sauce and mushroom essence added, simmered, strained and reduced

godaste färsen *(Sw)* Finely minced beef and pork mixed with softened rusk, egg yolk, seasoning and a little paprika. Half of this placed in a greased oblong mould, slices of skinned tomatoes placed on top followed by the remainder of the forcemeat, topped with a mixture of French mustard, chopped onion and parsley and butter and baked in a 200°C oven for 1 hour to give a crisp crusty surface. Served from the dish. Lit. the finest forcemeat

godiveau *(Fr) masc.* A forcemeat made with cushion of veal, beef kidney suet and eggs (4:4:1) with all skin, tissue, sinew, etc. removed, processed, seasoned and flavoured with nutmeg, sieved and, after resting on ice, blended with ice water or cream over ice until of the correct consistency as checked by poaching a small amount

goed doorbakken *(Ho)* Well done (of meat, steak, etc.)

goetberg *(USA)* A cardamom-flavoured sausage originating in Sweden and resembling the German cervelat

Goetta *(Ge)* As scrapple but thickened with oats

goettinger *(USA)* A German style hard sausage similar to cervelat

gofio *(Sp)* A flour with a nutty flavour made by grinding a variety of toasted cereal grains such as wheat, maize and barley. Originating in the Canary islands it is sold as a health food in Spain

gogi jeon-gol *(Ko)* Stir-fried strips of beef

with sliced onion, mushrooms and mooli, strips of fresh pear and egg

gogue *(Fr) masc.* A boudin noir made with pigs blood, cream, eggs, chopped onions sweated in lard, breadcrumbs moistened in milk, beet leaves and seasoning, poached in casings and air dried for 5 to 7 days

gohan *(Ja)* Cooked rice served on a plate, Western style

gohanmono *(Ja)* The generic Japanese term for all types of cooked rice and rice dishes

Golan *(ME)* A ewe's milk cheese from Israel similar to Provolone

gold beet *(USA)* A golden yellow and sweeter variety of beetroot which may be eaten raw or cooked

gold leaf E175, gold beaten out until it is extremely thin. Occasionally used for decoration

gold top *(UK)* Channel Islands milk q.v. So called because in the UK the bottles have a gold coloured foil top

Goldbrassen *(Ge)* Gilt-head bream

golden buck cheese *(USA)* Buck rarebit

golden carpet shell A small European bivalve mollusc *Venus gallina* similar to various small clams with a greyish brown shell

golden carpet shell clam Smaller versions *Venerupis aurea* (yellow) and *V. geographica* (grey) of the carpet shell clam, without radial markings

golden cutlets Small decapitated haddocks split, boned and smoked. A smaller version of the Arbroath smokie

golden fillets *(UK)* Thin fillets of haddock or cod, lightly smoked and artificially coloured golden yellow [also called **smoked fillets**]

golden gage *see* mirabelle

golden gram *see* mung bean

golden grey mullet A variety of grey mullet *Mugil auratus* with golden spots on its gill covers

golden mountain oyster *(USA)* A light brown fan-shaped mushroom

golden mullet *see* red mullet

golden needles *see* lily buds

golden nugget A variety of squash which may be used as a potato substitute, i.e. chipped or mashed

golden oak mushroom *(USA)* Shiitake mushroom

golden passion fruit *see* yellow passion fruit

golden plover *see* plover

golden sweetie *see* sweetie

golden syrup An invert sugar mixture (i.e. one which will not crystallize) made either by clarifying and decolourizing the remaining uncrystallizeable portion of the sugar after production of sugar crystals or by treatment of sugar syrup with acids or the enzyme invertase. Contains sucrose, glucose and fructose and is used as a sweetening agent

golden threads Beaten and strained egg yolks piped using a very fine nozzle in a piping bag onto the surface of hot sugar syrup to form a lacy pattern. Removed and rolled up and repeated as required; *see also* yemas de San Leandro

goldenberry *see* cape gooseberry

Goldkarpfen *(Ge)* Gilt-head bream

gold'n'rich *(USA)* A cow's milk cheese from Illinois similar to Port-Salut

goliath *(ME)* A variety of pummelo from Israel with a pebbly greenish-yellow rind and white seedless juicy flesh. Unfortunately it is being marketed as a pomelo (Spanish for grapefruit)

gol mirich *(In)* Peppercorns

golonka w piwie *(Pl)* Pork knuckle cooked in beer

golubtsy *(Ru)* Cabbage rolls made from blanched and trimmed cabbage leaves wrapped in neat parcels around a mixture of minced beef and veal, chopped onion sautéed in butter, cooked rice and seasonings, the parcels placed seam side down in a deep oven dish and covered with a thickened sauce of concassée tomatoes, beef stock and sour cream, topped with bacon and baked open-topped at 180°C for 1 hour until the rolls are slightly browned. Rested for 10 minutes before serving

goma *(Ja)* Sesame seed

goma abura *(Ja)* Sesame seed oil

goma arábiga *(Sp)* Gum arabic

gomashio *see* gomasio

gomasio 1 *(Ja)* A mixture of black sesame seeds and coarse salt ground together and used as a condiment on rice, raw vegetables and salads [also called **gomashio, sesame salt**] **2** A mixture of toasted celery seeds and salt

gombaleves *(Hu)* Mushroom soup

gombás *(Hu)* Mushrooms

gombo *see* okra

gomma arabica *(It)* Gum arabic

gomme adragante *(Fr) fem.* Gum tragacanth

gomme arabique *(Fr) fem.* Gum arabic

Gomolya *(Cz & Hu)* A ewes' milk cheese very similar to Lipto. Also used to make Brynza [also called **Homolky, Hrudka**]

Gomost *(Sc)* A cheese made in the same way as gjetost but with whole milk curds and whey

gong bao rou ding *(Ch)* Chopped pork cooked with hot peppers

gong bao xiaren *(Ch)* Shrimps cooked with hot peppers

gong jao lei *(Ch)* A large perforated metal skimmer used for retrieving deep fried food from a wok and draining it

gong yiu chee *(Ch)* Conpoy

Gonterser Bok *(He)* Hard boiled egg, dipped in batter and fried in butter

good beef *(USA)* A relatively tender grade of beef with little fat but less juicy or flavoursome than choice grade beef

Good Food Guide *(UK)* One of the restaurant guides to whom complaints or experiences may be sent. Address: Freepost, 2 Marylebone Road, London NW1 1YN. Others are Egon Ronay and Michelin

Good King Henry A hardy perennial herb *Chenopodium bonus-henricus* whose leaves have been used as a vegetable from Neolithic times. The flower spikes may be cooked like broccoli and the young shoots like asparagus. The water should be changed during cooking

good manufacturing practice Methods used in the food industry to control contamination with food poisoning organisms, their toxins or food spoilage enzymes; *see also* HACCP [also called **GMP**]

goose A large migratory game bird of various species from the *Anser* genus. Pink footed and greylag are the common varieties. The domestic goose was bred from the greylag. Wild geese are cooked as game. Domestic geese are generally eaten when less than a year old. The points to look out for are a yellow hairless beak, yellow supple feet (red indicates an older bird) and pale yellow fat. Usually roasted. It is one of the few domesticated birds which cannot be reared intensively

goose barnacle *see* barnacle and percebes

goose blood pudding *(UK)* A Scottish pudding made with goose blood mixed with seasoned barley meal, stuffed into the unbroken skin of the goose's neck, tied and simmered in broth until cooked

goose egg A large egg with a taste similar to a hen's egg and cooked in the same way. It requires 7 minutes for soft boiling

goose liver *see* foie gras

goose liver sausage *(Sw) see* gåsleverkorv

goose sausage *(UK)* A sausage made with 2 parts of lean beef chopped with a little suet and mixed with 1 part of chopped roast lean goose meat, moistened with garlic-flavoured Madeira wine, seasoned and packed into hog casings

goose skirt *(UK) see* thick skirt

gooseberry The fruit of a bush *Ribes uva-crispa* of the same family as the blackcurrant. Generally picked when immature and around 1 to 4 cm in length. They have a firm yellowish green flesh containing several embedded seeds and a hairy, occasionally smooth, green striated skin. In this state they are used for pies, tarts and preserves. Dessert gooseberries are green to light brown and are eaten raw when ripe

gooseberry sauce A purée of gooseberries, water or white wine and a little sugar, boiled 5 to 10 minutes, sieved and mixed with a little butter sauce. Served with mackerel, duck and goose

goosefish *(USA) see* monkfish

goosenecked barnacle *see* barnacle

gorchitsa *(Ru)* Mustard

gorda *(Me)* A cornmeal dough enriched with lard and cooked as a thick cake

gordita *(Me)* A cornmeal and potato dough mixed with cheese and fried in lard. Served with minced pork and guacamole

Gorgonzola *(It)* The famous soft, blue-veined, creamy textured, sharp flavoured cheese made from pasteurized cows' milk in the Lombardy region since at least the 11th century and legally protected with a certificate of origin. A lactic starter is used and after draining and turning, it is dry salted, drained for a further 3 to 4 days, ripened at high humidity, salted, wiped and turned then needled with *Penicillium glaucum* and ripened for 50 to 60 days in natural caves. It is well veined and internally cracked. Wrapped in foil before sale. Used as a dessert cheese or in cooking

Gorgonzola bianco *(It) see* Pannerone

Gorgonzola a due paste *(It)* A Gorgonzola made from curd from an evening milking which has been exposed to mould spores. This is moulded in the shape of a cone and surrounded in a cylindrical mould by lightly drained curds made from the next morning's warm milk

Gornoaltaysky *(Ru)* A hard pungent cheese made from cows' or ewes' milk. Sometimes smoked

goroka *(Sr)* A tart orange fruit used for souring in the same way as tamarind e.g. in fish dishes

gorokh *(Ru)* Peas

gorokha *(Ru)* Lentils

goshi *(In)* Goat or lamb

gosht *(In)* Meat

gosling A young goose up to 6 months old

gospel green *(UK)* A semi-hard, milled, slightly crumbly cheese made from the unpasteurized milk of Friesian cows in Sussex

gota *(In)* A mixture of seeds, sometimes dyed. e.g. aniseed, fennel and similar served at the end of a meal as a digestive

gothaer *(USA)* An air dried German sausage similar to cervelat

Götterspeise *(Ge)* Chantilly cream mixed with grated chocolate and pumpernickel crumbs

Gouda *(Ho)* A large (5 kg) wheel shaped semi-hard mild and creamy cows' milk cheese with a small number of irregular holes and a wax coating made in the same way as Edam. If matured for a year its colour darkens and the flavour becomes strong and piquant. Small Gouda cheeses are also supplied. Suitable for slicing and cooking. Very popular as a part of Dutch breakfast

Gouds kaas *(Ho)* Gouda cheese

Gougelhopf *see* Kugelhopf

gougère *(Fr) fem.* A savoury dish made by piping choux pastry, sometimes cheese-flavoured, in a large or small circular tart shape on a baking tray, baking it and filling the centre with fish, chicken, mushrooms, kidneys, etc. bound in a savoury sauce. Served cold or warm as a main course or as hors d'oeuvres

gougnette *(Fr) fem.* A type of doughnut dredged with sugar

goujon **1** *(Fr) masc.* Gudgeon **2** *(En & Fr) masc.* A strip of skinned white fish, usually sole, cut on the diagonal 8 cm by 6 mm, possibly marinated, rolled in the hand, panéed or battered and deep fried, now also used of similar sized strips of chicken. So called from the resemblance to gudgeons which are cooked whole in the same way

goujonette *(En & Fr) fem.* A small goujon of fish 5 cm by 6 mm cooked in the same way as a goujon

goulash A rich beef stew flavoured with paprika and originally based on Hungarian gulyás, a meat and vegetable soup. Served with sour cream

gourd The name used for members of the squash family the skins of whose fruits can be used as containers or for decoration. Several of the over 500 varieties are useful as edible vegetables e.g. bottle gourd, turk's cap gourd turban gourd, towel gourd, snake gourd

gourmandise *(Fr) fem.* Sweetmeat, delicacy

gourmet A person who appreciates good food and drink

gourmet powder *see* monosodium glutamate

Gournay *(Fr)* A mild, somewhat acidic, slightly salty and rindless, soft Camembert type cheese from Normandy

Gournay affiné *(Fr)* Gournay cheese, surface ripened for up to 8 days in damp cellars to develop the mild flavour

gousse d'ail *(Fr) fem.* Clove of garlic

goûter *(Fr)* To taste

govyadina *(Ru)* Beef

Goya *(Ar)* A cheese similar to Asiago

goyave *(Fr) fem.* Guava

Graçay *(Fr)* A dense, soft, white goats' milk cheese from Berry, matured for 6 weeks and coated with charcoal powder. Formed into stubby cones

Gracillaria verrucosa *Bot.* Hair vegetable

Grádaost *(Ic)* A blue cheese made from cows' milk

grädde *(Sw)* Cream

Gräddost *(Sw)* A semi-hard, scalded-curd cows' milk slicing cheese with a pale yellow, close textured paste containing numerous small holes

gräddvåfflor *(Sw)* Waffles made with sour cream

Graham bread *(USA)* Wholemeal bread

Graham cracker *(USA)* A biscuit made from Graham flour, similar to the UK digestive biscuit

Graham flour *(USA)* A wholemeal flour developed by the nutritionist Sylvester Graham in the early 19th century. Used to make Graham bread and Graham crackers. Graham is now added to the name of any food made from wholemeal or wholewheat flour

Graham rusk *(USA)* A bread roll made from Graham flour, split in half after baking and dried slowly

grain The edible seeds of various cultivated plants usually but not always monocotyledons (grasses). The most common are wheat, rice, maize, barley, oats, rye and millet. Sold as whole, kibbled, cracked, ground into flour, flattened into flakes or partially cooked

grain de cassis *(Fr) masc.* Blackcurrant

grain de groseille *(Fr) masc.* Redcurrant

grains of paradise A spice with a hot peppery taste made from the dried seeds of a perennial reed-like plant *Amomum melegueta* or *Aframomum melegueta* indigenous to West Africa and used in its cookery [also called **Guinea pepper, Guinea grains, melegueta pepper**]

graisse *(Fr) fem.* Fat, grease

graisse de porc *(Fr) fem.* Lard

graisse de rognon *(Fr) fem.* Suet

graisse de rôti *(Fr) fem.* Dripping

gram 1 Subdivision of the kilogram unit of weight, 1 kilogram equals 1000 grams. Abbreviated g **2** *(In)* Channa, unless qualified as in black gram or green gram, etc.

gram flour *see* besan

gramme *(Fr) masc.* Gram (1), unit of weight

grammi *(It)* Gram (1), unit of weight

gramugia *(It)* An artichoke, asparagus, bean and bacon soup from Tuscany

grana 1 *(It)* A hard, cooked-curd cows' milk cheese with a granular texture made with partially skimmed (2% butterfat) cows' milk. A lactic starter is used and the curd moulded and drained for 2 days, brined for 28 days and ripened under controlled conditions for up to 18 months. Used for cooking, grating and dessert and very popular in Italy. They are usually stamped with the type and the name of the producer when soft and have the same information printed on the rind **2** *(Ph)* A red food colouring obtained from a local plant

grana Bagozzo *(It)* A grana cheese from Brescia where it is referred to as the 'cheese of love'

grana Emiliano *(It)* A grana cheese similar to Grana Lodigiano with a very black rind

grana Lodigiano *(It)* A grana cheese produced near Milan. The hard smooth rind encloses a more crumbly paste than most grana cheeses and tiny scattered holes each of which may contain a drop of clear liquid. The paste tends to turn green when cut

grana Padano *(It)* A hard grana cheese which easily melts and dissolves in the mouth with a mellow but intense flavour which strengthens with age (of the cheese). Used both for grating and dessert

grana Parmigiano *(It)* *see* Parmigiano Reggiano

granada *(Ph & Sp)* Pomegranate

granadilla *(Sp)* Purple passion fruit

granadillo *see* passion fruit

granary bread Bread made from granary flour

granary flour A strong brown flour to which malted wheat flakes have been added

granata *(It)* Pomegranate

Granatapfel *(Ge)* Pomegranate

granatina *(It)* Pomegranate syrup

granceole *(It)* Large crabs served in their shells and dressed with oil and vinegar

grancevola *(It)* Spider crab

granchio *(It)* Crab

granchio comune *(It)* Shore crab [also called **moleche**]

granchio di sabbia *(It)* A small crab *Portunus holsatus* with a dark body and pink claws and legs. The two rear legs have spade-like ends to assist it in moving over sand. Lit. sand crab

granciporro *(It)* Common crab

grand-duc, au *(Fr)* In the style of the Grand Duke, i.e. garnished with asparagus, truffle, crayfish tails and Mornay sauce, esp. of chicken

grand marnier *(Fr) masc.* An orange-flavoured liqueur used to flavour desserts esp. crèpes Suzette

grand-mère, à la *(Fr)* In the style of grandmother, i.e. with onions or shallots, bacon, mushrooms and diced potatoes. Also used to denote croûtons in scrambled egg and pasta in vegetable soup

grand tétras *(Fr) masc.* Capercaillie

grand-veneur, sauce *(Fr) fem.* A poivrade sauce prepared with game stock, game blood added and cooked then all strained. Served with game

grande *(It)* Large, big

grande cigale *(Fr) fem. see* cigarra *(Sp)*

grande roussette *(Fr) fem.* Larger spotted dogfish

granelli *(It)* **1** Grains, seeds, pips **2** Lambs' or calves' testicles

granelli alla maremmano *(It)* Lambs' testicles floured, egged and fried. Served with lemon wedges

granita *(It)* A partially and slowly frozen flavoured sugar syrup which consists of an ice crystal (to 3 mm) mush in a syrupy substrate. Used as a dessert

granité *(Fr) masc.* Granita

grano *(It & Sp)* Wheat, corn, grain

grano saraceno *(It)* Buckwheat

granola *(USA)* A breakfast cereal mix similar to muesli. The composition varies but is taken from rolled oats, wheat and rye flakes, seeds, nuts, wheat germ, bran, raisins, desiccated coconut and similar. Usually lightly toasted or baked with butter and served with milk, yoghurt, fresh fruit, etc.

granoturco *(It)* Maize, corn

granoturco dolce *(It)* Sweet corn

granseola *(It)* Spider crab

granseola alla triestina *(It)* Spider crab baked with breadcrumbs and garlic

granulate, to To form into small particles or granules by crystallization or agglomeration

granulated sugar Standard refined white sugar (sucrose) with crystals from 0.5 mm to 1 mm across

granzeola alla veneziana *(It)* Boiled crayfish or spidercrab served on the shell with lemon juice and oil

grape The fruit of a vine *Vitis vinifera, V. labrusca* or *V. rotundifolia* and hybrids, grown worldwide where the winters are cool and summers long and hot. The berries normally grow in clusters and range from green to dark purple and from 5 to 30 mm in diameter. The flesh varies from sour to sweet and succulent and is usually relatively firm but juicy and may contain up to 3 inedible seeds. Used for wine making, as a dessert fruit for decoration and garnishing and when dried for use as dried vine fruits (raisins, currants and sultanas)

grape cheese *see* tomme au raisin

grape hyacinth A type of lily *Muscari comosum* whose bulbs are boiled and eaten as a vegetable esp. in Italy. See capollotto

grape leaves *(USA)* Vine leaves

grapefrugt *(De)* Grapefruit

grapefruit Large spherical fruits of a citrus tree *Citrus paradisis* which grow in clusters and are cultivated in the USA, South America and some Mediterranean countries. They are probably a cross between sweet orange and pummelo, the latter's seeds were taken to Barbados by the British. The two main types are Marsh seedless and pigmented varieties. They have a thick yellow skin, with red pigmentation in some cases, with somewhat astringent typical citrus flesh. Halved grapefruits with the flesh loosened and membranes removed are often used as a breakfast dish or starter to clear the palette. Used for marmalade and supplied as skinned segments in cans

grapefrukt *(No & Sw)* Grapefruit

grapeseed oil A delicately flavoured oil extracted from grape seeds used in the manufacture of margarine and for salad dressings

grappa *(It)* A clear alcoholic spirit distilled from the fermented remains of the grapes after they have been pressed for winemaking

grappe de raisin *(Fr) fem.* Bunch of grapes

gras (grasse) *(Fr)* **1** *adj.* Fat **2** *masc.* Fat

gras, au *(Fr)* Richly cooked

gras de cuisse *(Fr) masc.* Chicken thigh

gras-double *(Fr) masc.* Tripe

gräslök *(Sw)* Chive

Grasmere gingerbread *see* Grasmere shortbread

Grasmere shortbread *(UK)* Shortbread from Grasmere in the Lake District containing chopped mixed candied peel, sweetened with brown sugar and flavoured with ginger. Normally dusted with its own crumbs before baking [also called **Grasmere gingerbread**]

grass carp A carp with a long round body rather like a mullet

grass mushroom *see* straw mushroom

grass pea *see* lath

grassato *(It)* A goat or lamb stew from Sicily containing potatoes, cheese and wine

grasso *(It)* **1** Fat, grease **2** Fatty, rich, with meat

grasso d'arrosto *(It)* Dripping

grasso di bue *(It)* Suet

grate, to To shred or convert to a powder, firm textured foods such as carrots, cheese, apples, nutmegs, etc. using either a hand operated or food processor type of grater

grater 1 A round or rectangular shaped thin metal tube with a handle at one end, in the sides of which are pressed arrays of hole of differing sizes with sharp projections. Food rubbed against the projections is cut into fine slivers or raspings depending on the size of the holes and projections. Slivers accumulate on the inside of the tube, powder or raspings on the outside **2** A hand operated version of the above in which the cylinder rotates while the food is pressed against it **3** A food processor attachment consisting of a rotating circular disc containing the sharpened holes

graticola *(It)* Grill, gridiron

gratin *(De)* Soufflé

gratin, au 1 *(Fr)* Sprinkled with grated cheese and/or breadcrumbs and browned under the grill **2** *(USA)* Covered with cheese sauce or grated cheese and baked

gratin dauphinois *(Fr) masc.* Thin slices of potato, layered with garlic, cheese, seasoning and cream/milk, then baked slowly until the top is golden brown and the potatoes cooked

gratin dish An oval dish used for the cooking and presentation of gratinated food

gratin, sauce *(Fr) fem.* White wine, fish stock and chopped shallots reduced by half, duxelles and fish based demi-glace sauce added and simmered, then finished with chopped parsley. Used for the preparation of gratinated fish

gratin savoyard *(Fr) masc. see* pommes savoyard

gratinate, to To bake food so as to form a crust on the surface, now usually done by sprinkling the surface of a prepared dish of food with grated cheese and/or breadcrumbs and then browning it under the grill or in the oven

gratinato *(It)* Gratinated

gratiné(e) *(Fr)* A description of food gratinated or napped with a glazing sauce and browned in the oven or under the grill

gratiniert *(Ge)* Gratinated

gratter *(Fr)* To scratch or scrape

gratterons *(Fr) masc.* Fried diced pork and pork fat; *see also* pork scratchings

grattugiato *(It)* Grated

Gratz *(Au) see* Graz

Graupensuppe *(Ge)* Barley soup

gravad lax *(Sw) see* gravlax

gravad makrill *(Sw)* Pickled mackerel prepared in the same way as gravlax, except that the skin is not used. Very fresh mackerel is essential

Graviera *(Gr)* A cheese made from cows' milk and resembling Gruyère

gravlax Two scaled, boned and surface dried salmon fillets sandwiched skin side out with a mixture of 2 parts salt, 2 parts sugar, 1 part saltpetre (if available), and crushed white peppercorns with a layer of dill weed also in the sandwich and laid beneath and on top. The thick part of each fillet is opposite the thin part of the other. They are then pressed together in a bowl with a board and weight and left in the refrigerator for 24 hours, turning the package a couple of times. Wash, dry and cut thin slices of the flesh for use as a hors d'oeuvre. The skin is cut in strips and dry fried until crisp and served as a garnish with dill and lemon. Traditionally salmon blood was also rubbed into the flesh to give it a scarlet colour. Lit. grave salmon referring to the underground chambers where it was prepared. Gravadlax means buried salmon [also called **gravadlax**]

gravlax sauce *(Sa)* A sauce made from French mustard mixed with oil, vinegar, sugar, chopped dill and seasoning. Served with gravlax and other marinated fish [also called **Scandinavian sweet mustard sauce**]

gravy 1 A sauce made from the fat free juices, extracts and scrapings from the pan in which meat, fowl or game has been roasted, mixed with wine or stock, reduced, seasoned and possibly cream added; *see also* jus roti and jus lié **2** *(UK)* Juices, extracts and scrapings plus some of the fat from the pan in which meat, fowl or game has been roasted, mixed with flour to make a roux, briefly cooked, stock or water added to give the consistency required, sometimes coloured with gravy browning

gravy browning A solution of dark caramel with salt used to colour gravies, etc. Sometimes other permitted brown colouring agents are used

grayling A silvery freshwater fish *Thymallus* spp. belonging to the salmon family with firm white flesh and a scent of thyme, weighing between 0.5 and 1.5 kg. Different varieties are found in Northern and Central Europe, the USA and New Zealand. Cooked like trout

Graz *(Au)* A firm and full-flavoured cheese made from cows' milk

Grazalema *(Sp)* A ewes' milk cheese from the Cadiz area which resembles Manchego. Contains 35% water, 33% fat and 25% protein

grease, to To coat the surface of a tin, dish, baking sheet, paper or aluminium foil, etc. which comes into contact with food with fat or oil so as to prevent the food sticking to it during the cooking or preparation process

greasyback prawn *see* greentail prawn

great lakes trout *see* lake trout

great millet The principal type of sorghum *Sorghum vulgare* which is a staple throughout the underdeveloped world. It comes in two varieties, white grain sorghum used for bread and the red bitter grain used for brewing beer

great northern bean *see* navy bean

great scallop One of the larger scallops *Pecten maximus* with a pink to brown shell up to 15 cm across. The flesh weighs about 60 g [also called **king scallop**]

greater galangal The root of an Indonesian

lily-like plant *Langusa galanga or Alpinia galanga* somewhat similar to ginger in appearance and with a sour gingery/peppery taste used extensively in South East Asian cooking. The flowers, buds and young shoots may also be used as a garnish or vegetable [also called **galingale, Laos ginger, Siamese ginger, Thai ginger**]

greater yam *see* Asiatic yam

greaves *see* scallops

greca, alla *(It) see* grecque, à la

grecque, à la *(Fr)* **1** A method of cooking vegetables e.g. artichokes, button onions, cauliflower sprigs, celery, leeks, etc. for use as a cold hors d'oeuvres, in a liquor consisting of water, olive oil, lemon juice, bay, thyme, coriander seeds and seasoning **2** In the Greek style, i.e. with olive oil, lemon, herbs and spices

Greek basil *see* bush basil

green almond *see* pistachio nut

green bacon *(UK)* Bacon which has not been smoked; *see also* Wiltshire cure [also called **plain bacon**]

green banana *see* plantain

green bean The immature pod of the French bean q.v.

green butter *see* ravigote butter

green cheese *see* sapsago

green cod *see* pollack

green coffee bean Coffee beans which are ready to be roasted. These will keep indefinitely and some will improve with age

green curry paste *(Th)* A paste used for curry made from dry fried shallots, garlic, lemon grass, coriander seeds and cumin seeds blended with fresh green chillis, black peppercorns, coriander root and leaves, galangal, lime peel, trassi and salt

green dressing *see* salsa verde

green fig A fresh as opposed to a dried fig

green goddess dressing *(USA)* Thick mayonnaise thinned with soured cream and flavoured with garlic, anchovy, minced spring onions, parsley and lemon juice. Served with fish and shellfish

green goddess salad *(USA)* An elaborate salad of chopped cos lettuce, endive and chicory, mixed with chopped anchovies, spring onion, parsley, tarragon and cloves, served in a bowl rubbed with raw garlic, dressed with mayonnaise let down with tarragon vinegar and topped with chicken, crab meat or shrimps

green goose *(UK)* A young goose up to 3 months old which has been fed on pasture. Generally eaten at Michaelmas (September 29th) and less fatty than the Christmas goose

green gram *see* bean sprouts and mung bean

green laver *see* nori or sea lettuce

green leaf lettuce *(USA)* Loose leaf lettuce

green lipped mussel A large variety of mussel *Perna canalicula* from New Zealand with a green blue shell and a particularly rich flavour. Reputed to have medicinal and prophylactic properties

green lollo lettuce *see* lollo biondo

green masala *(In)* A mixture of fresh ginger, garlic, green chillis and fresh coriander leaves pounded together with water into a paste. Used with fish or chicken

green mayonnaise *see* sauce verte

green olive The unripe fruit of the olive tree which are treated with dilute caustic soda solution (1.5%) to remove glycosides, then repeatedly washed with water prior to placing in brine (8%) in which they are left to ferment for 1 to 6 months prior to storing in 7.5% brine

green onion Spring onion

green oriental radish One of the large radishes *Raphanus sativa* with green flesh and skin, about 20 cm by 5 cm dia

green pea soup *see* purée St Germain

green peppercorns Soft dark green and underripe peppercorns with a mild subtle flavour, usually pickled in brine or vinegar. Also sold fresh or dried, but the flavour is less piquant. Used for flavouring esp. beef, game and marinades or in the ground dried version as a condiment [also called **Madagascar green peppercorns**]

green peppers *(USA)* Underripe sweet peppers

green plantain *(USA)* Plantain

green plover *see* plover

green purslane *see* summer purslane

green S E142, a synthetic green food colouring

green salad A salad of mixed raw green leaves. Occasionally sliced raw green vegetables or fruits might be added

green sapote A fruit similar to the sapote from a deciduous tree *Calocarpum viride* which grows in cooler climates. It is round, green skinned and more sweet and juicy than the true sapote

green sauce Blanched and refreshed leaves of spinach, tarragon, chervil, chives and watercress, squeezed dry, passed through a fine sieve and combined with mayonnaise [also called **sauce verte** (Fr), **salsa verde** (It)]

green sea urchin A 5 cm sea urchin *Strongylocentrus droebachiensis* which is found on both sides of the North Atlantic

green shell bean *(USA) see* flageolet bean

green shiso A variety of shiso with wide flat deep green leaves with serrated edges. It is used as a garnish, added to sushi, battered and fried as tempura and sometimes pickled

green snap bean *(USA)* The immature pod of the French bean q.v.

green sprouting broccoli *see* calabrese

green swimming crab *see* shore crab

green tomatoes Underripe tomatoes sometimes used to make chutney

green turtle A large edible sea turtle *Chelonia mydas* found in warm seas. Now very rare and possibly an endangered species

green walnuts Young immature walnuts picked before the shell develops. Usually pickled which causes them to turn black, but also made into jam

greengage A sweet amber coloured plum (*Prunus domestica* or *P. insititia*) about 25 to 4 cm in diameter and with a fine flavour, introduced to England from France by Sir William Gage as an unlabelled specimen in 1724 [also called **gage**]

Greenland halibut A sinistral flat fish *Reinhardtius hippoglossoides* found in Arctic and sub-Arctic deep water of the North Atlantic ocean at depths of 200 to 2000 m. The skin is dark grey or brown on both sides and the flesh is dense and oily. Often smoked. Known as turbot by Canadians who control some of its habitat. Rapidly being fished out by Canadian and EU fishing fleets [also called **Greenland turbot** (USA), **black halibut, turbot** (USA)]

Greenland turbot *see* Greenland halibut.

greenlip abalone One of the most tender of the abalone *Haliotis laevigata* with a corrugated red shell streaked with light green. Found on open rock faces

greens A generic term for all types of leaf that are cooked and used as a vegetable. See e.g. spring greens

greentail prawn A type of prawn *Metapenaeus bennettae* intermediate in size between the deep water and the king prawn. Found in river estuaries [also called **greasyback prawn**]

greeter *(USA)* The male person who greets guests in a restaurant, the female is called a hostess

grelhado *(Po)* Grilled

grelos *(Po)* Buds, sprouts

gremolada *(It)* A mixture of chopped parsley, chopped garlic and grated lemon zest; *see also* alla gremolata [also called **gremolata**]

gremolata, alla *(It)* Sprinkled with a mixture of chopped garlic, grated lemon zest and grated nutmeg

grenade *(Fr) fem.* Pomegranate

grenadier An ugly fish found on the Hatton bank to the west of Rockall. Now being fished commercially. The name was changed from rat fish to aid marketing

grenadilla *see* purple passion fruit

grenadin *(En & Fr) masc.* A small slice or fillet of veal, usually larded and braised

grenadin de veau fermier Prince Orloff *(Fr) masc.* A grenadin of veal stuffed with a duxelle of mushrooms and foie gras

grenadine 1 *(En & Fr) fem.* A sweet tart red fruit syrup made from pomegranate juice. Used as a flavouring **2** *(It)* Grenadin of veal

grenobloise, à la *(Fr)* In the style of Grenoble, i.e. fish which is floured, fried and served with a garnish of lemon, capers and chopped parsley

grenobloise, fish Fish meunière dressed with peeled segments of lemon and a few capers

grenouille *(Fr) fem.* Frog

gressin *(Fr) masc.* A long baguette like French loaf

Gressingham duck *(UK)* A cross between a mallard and domestic duck with lean dark and tender meat combining the advantages of both

gretski orekhi *(Ru)* Walnuts

Grevéost *(Sw)* A commercially produced semi-hard scalded-curd cows' milk cheese with a mild flavoured paste containing very large holes

grey gurnard *see* gurnard

grey legged partridge An English native bird *Perdrix perdrix* which is leaner and tastier than the red legged partridge found in France. It weighs about 450 g and is suitable for 1 serving. Roasted at 190°C for 20 to 25 minutes

grey mullet A round seawater weed eating fish *Liza auratus* and various *Mugil* spp. 30 to 70 cm long and 0.5 to 1 kg in weight, some of which are farmed. It has a small head with vestigial teeth and is found worldwide in many varieties in warm waters. The skin is silvery grey and the flesh is firm, white and oily but bruises easily. The skin requires thorough scaling. Suitable for all cooking methods. The roe is traditionally used to make taramasalata. The dried and salted roe is known as botargo; *see also* golden grey mullet [also called **striped mullet** (USA), **black mullet** (USA)]

grey mullet roe *see* botargo

grey plover *see* plover

grey squirrel A tree living American squirrel *Sciurus carolinensis* once an important item of food, now used only in Brunswick stew. Introduced into Europe in the 19th century

Greyerzer *(He) see* Gruyère

greyhen Black grouse

greylag goose A variety of wild goose from which most of the domesticated varieties have been developed

gribiche, sauce *(En & Fr) fem.* Mashed hard boiled egg yolks blended with oil and vinegar or lemon juice, flavoured with chopped capers and gherkins, tarragon, chervil and parsley, seasoned and finished with a julienne of egg white. Served with fish

griblette *(Fr) fem.* Pork chop

gribnaya ikra *(Ru)* A paté made from minced mushrooms and onions, sweated in butter and mixed with cream, curd cheese, dry sherry and chopped fresh herbs. Lit. mushroom caviar

gribouis A variety of cep common in Russia and often dried

griby *(Ru)* Mushrooms

grid iron A stout metal rack used inside a grill pan or over an open fire or barbecue

griddle A thick heavy flat metal plate which is heated either continuously or intermittently and on which drop scones, pancakes, crumpets and any item which does not need to be contained in a pan may be cooked by conduction of heat [also called **girdle**]

griddle cakes Drop scones made on a griddle [also called **girdle cake**]

griddle pan cake *(UK)* Drop scone

griddle scone A traditional scone mix cooked on a griddle instead of in the oven

griechisches Heu *(Ge)* Fenugreek

Grièges *(Fr) see* Pipo crèm'

Griesbrie *(Ge & He)* Semolina pudding

griesmeelpap *(Ho)* Semolina pudding

Griessklössche *(Ge)* Dumplings made from semolina boiled in milk and seasoned water with butter until thick, eggs (3:4 based on dry semolina) beaten in off the heat and small balls poached in simmering water for 20 minutes. Served with a sweet sauce as a dessert, with butter as an accompaniment to meat or made very small as a soup garnish

Griessmehl *(Ge)* Semolina

Griessnockerl *(Ge)* Semolina dumplings made with a seasoned semolina, egg and butter dough, simmered in beef stock

Griessnockerlsuppe *(Au)* A clear meat or chicken stock or consommé garnished with tiny Griessnockerl

Griesstorte *(Ge)* A layer cake similar to Mandeltorte but using a mixture of semolina and ground almonds (5:3) instead of ground almonds

griet *(Ho)* Brill

grifole *(It)* A type of fungus which grows on trees

griglia, alla *(It)* Cooked on the grill

grigliate *(It)* Grilled

grignaudes *(Fr)* Pieces of shredded pork fried until crisp. Eaten cold as a snack in the same way as pork scratchings

gril, sur le *(Fr)* Grilled

grill A metal box like structure with an open front and a rack on which to place food to be grilled. Elements on the underside of the top surface are heated to a red glow with either gas or electricity [also called **salamander**]

grill, to To cook food by direct radiant heat over or under a heat source, e.g. barbeque or grill. A quick method of cooking to a crisp brown finish without added fat or oil [also called **to broil**]

grill pan A shallow metal pan with a handle and removable metal rack used for grilling food

grillad *(Sw)* Grilled

grillade *(Fr) fem.* A mixed grill or any food which has been grilled or a grilled slice of meat or fish

grillade à la champagneules *(Fr) fem.* Fried ham on toast coated with a cheese and beef fondu. From Lorraine

grillades *(USA)* A Creole light stew from Louisiana of thinly sliced veal cooked with green sweet pepper, celery, onion, tomatoes and seasoning. Served with rice

grillé(e) *(Fr)* Grilled

grilled grapefruit Half a grapefruit prepared for eating, covered with brown sugar and butter and browned under the grill. Served hot as a starter

grilleret lammehoved *(De)* Grilled lamb's head

grillettato *(It)* Simmered or braised, a braised dish

grilling fish Small whole fish diagonally slashed, fillets, darnes, tronçons and suprêmes of fish, passed through seasoned flour and melted butter, possibly breadcrumbs, then grilled both sides until the flesh leaves the bone or is cooked through. See e.g. fish St Germain and fish caprice.

grilling sauce *see* barbecue sauce

grilse A small 3 year old salmon (1 to 4 kg) which returns to its birthplace to spawn after its first year at sea

grind, to 1 To reduce hard substances such as coffee beans, nuts. spices, dried roots and cereals to a fine powder using either a pestle and mortar, a food processor, an electric or hand operated rotary grinder or a food mill **2** *(USA)* to mince meat (as in 'ground beef')

grinder *(USA) see* hoagie

griotte *(Fr) fem.* Morello cherry

gris de Lille *(Fr) masc.* A strong smelling salty cows' milk cheese from the north, cast in squares

griset *(Fr) masc.* Black bream

grisette An edible mushroom *Amanita vaginata* of the generally toxic *Amanita* spp. It has a grey cap and a white stem and does not travel well. Should only be picked by experts

grisfötter *(Sw)* Pig's feet

griskin 1 The oval shaped lean part of a a loin of bacon **2** The meat left attached to the spine of a pig when it is separated from the sides which are to be made into bacon

grisköttt *(Sw)* Pork [also called **fläsk**]

Grisoni *(He)* Thin square sectioned salami made with salted air dried beef

grissini *(It)* Long thin (to 30 cm by 1 cm) dried bread sticks served as an appetizer, snack or accompaniment to a meal [also called **Italian bread sticks, torinese**]

gristle Tough inedible connective tissue which forms tendons, the covering of individual muscles and the structures which hold joints together. It is composed of varying proportions of collagen and elastin according to function. The collagen is broken down into gelatine on prolonged boiling

grits 1 *(USA)* Coarsely ground dried maize kernels, usually boiled in water until soft, traditionally served with bacon and eggs for breakfast [also called **hominy grits**] **2** Any coarsely ground dehusked grain [also called **semolina**]

grive *(Fr) fem.* Thrush, the songbird. Like the lark can no longer be hunted in the EU. Once made into pâté

grive del langhe *(It)* A mixture of chopped pork, liver and spices, wrapped in pigs' caul and simmered in oil

groaning cake *(UK)* A light fruit cake given to women in labour

groats Dehusked whole oat grains. Can be used to make a coarse textured porridge preferred by some

grød *(De)* Porridge

grødaertesuppe *(De)* Green pea soup

groen haring *(Ho)* Matjes herring

groente *(Ho)* Vegetables, greens

groentesoep *(Ho)* A mixed vegetable soup containing vermicelli

grönar bönar *(Sw)* Green beans

grondin *(Fr) masc.* Gurnard

grondin galinette *(Fr) masc.* Gurnard

grongo *(It)* Conger eel

grønlangkål *(De)* Creamed cabbage

grønnsaker *(No)* Vegetables

grønsagsfromage *(De)* A vegetable soufflé

grönsaker *(Sw)* Vegetables

grönsakpuré *(Sw)* Thick puréed mixed vegetable soup

grönsakssoppa *(Sw)* Vegetable soup

grönsallad *(Sw)* Lettuce salad

grøntsager *(De)* Vegetables

groppa *(It)* Back or rump of an animal

gros Lorraine *(Fr) masc. see* Lorraine

gros mollet *(Fr) masc.* Lumpfish

gros pain *(Fr) masc.* A large crusty French loaf similar in construction to the baguette [also called **pain Parisien)**

gros sel *(Fr) masc.* Cooking salt

groseille blanche *(Fr) fem.* White currant

groseille à maquereau *(Fr) fem.* Gooseberry

groseille noire *(Fr) fem.* Black currant

groseille rouge *(Fr) fem.* Red currant

groseille verte *(Fr) fem.* Gooseberry [also called **groseille à maquereau**]

groseilles, sauce *(Fr) fem. see* gooseberry sauce

groselhas *(Po)* Berry fruits such as red or blackcurrants, gooseberries

groselheira *(Po)* Gooseberry

grosella blanca o verde *(Sp)* Gooseberry

grosella colorada *(Sp)* Red currant

grosella negra *(Sp)* Black currant

grosse Bohne *(Ge)* Broad bean

grosse crevette *(Fr) fem. see* caramote

grosse Mettwurst *(Ge)* Coarse textured Mettwurst

grosse palourde *(Fr) fem.* Venus shell clam

grosse pièce *(Fr) fem.* A joint of meat

grosser Weisenkopf *(Ge)* Salad burnet

grossetana, alla *(It)* In the style of Grosseto, Tuscany, i.e. with mushrooms and tomato sauce, or of pasta, with butter and cheese

grossköpfige Meeräsche *(Ge)* Grey mullet

grosso rombo *(It)* Halibut

grösti *(It)* A meat loaf with potatoes and onions from the alpine region

Gröstl *(Au)* Cubes of beef fried with onion in pork fat, seasoned and served mixed with slices of fried waxy potatoes

grotebonen *(Ho)* Broad beans

ground almonds Dried sweet almonds, dehusked and ground to a soft meal

ground beef *(USA)* Minced beef

ground chalk *see* calcium carbonate

ground cherry *see* dwarf cape gooseberry

ground meat *(USA)* Minced meat

ground rice Rice flour or meal available in a range of particle sizes. Used for milk puddings, as a thickener and to give a crisp texture to biscuits, shortbread and batters

ground tomato *see* tomate verde

groundhog *(USA) see* woodchuck

groundnut *see* peanut

groundnut oil *see* peanut oil

grouper A variety of warm seawater fish of various spp. but all with firm white flesh. Found in the Caribbean, Mediterranean, SEA and similar warm waters. Colours vary from gray green through blue to red and brown, often with contrasting coloured spots. Lengths are usually in the range 30 cm to 1 m and weights from 2 to 10 kg; *see also* Garoupa, Mediterranean grouper

grouse *(En & Fr) fem.* A small single portion wild game bird which is found on heather moors in Northern Europe, the finest of which is the red grouse found only in the UK and Ireland. The young birds which have downy feathers under their perfectly fledged wings are the best eating. The shooting season in the UK is 12th August to the 10th of December. The birds should be hung for 2 to 4 days before drawing and plucking. Barded and roasted on toast in the roasting pan at 200°C for 40 minutes, or at 230°C for 20 minutes and rested for 10. Garnished with watercress and served with jus rôti, bread sauce, fried breadcrumbs and pommes allumettes; *see also* black grouse, red grouse, sage grouse, moorcock [also called **moor fowl, moor game**]

grouse family A family of game birds from cold regions with feathered legs and feet including grouse, ptarmigan, capercaillie and hazelhen

grovbrød *(No)* A coarse dark rye bread

gruau d'avoine *(Fr) masc.* Oat grits, coarse oatmeal

gruel A thin porridge made by boiling fine oatmeal or barley meal in water, milk or stock. Once believed to be suitable for invalids and convalescents

grün *(Ge)* Green

grüne Bohnen *(Ge)* Green beans

grüne Bohnen auf norddeutsche Art *(Ge)* Blanched French beans simmered in a thin velouté sauce with chopped parsley

grüne Erbsen *(Ge)* Green peas, garden peas

grüne Fisolen *(Au)* Green beans flavoured with fennel

grüne Gurke *(Ge)* Cucumber

grüne Pflaume *(Ge)* Greengage

grüne Sosse *(Ge)* Sauce verte mixed with finely chopped hard boiled eggs, additional green herbs and flavourings as available, e.g. parsley, sorrel, savory, dill, onion and leek. A speciality of Frankfurt served with meat

grüner Salat *(Ge)* A green leaf salad dressed with a herb and garlic-flavoured vinaigrette

Grünkohl *(Ge)* Kale

grunt *(USA)* An early settlers' dessert of steamed dough mixed with berries, probably an adaptation of the English spotted dick

grusha *(Ru)* Pear

gruth dhu *see* black crowdie

Grütze *(Ge)* Groats, grits

Grützewurst *(Ge)* A sausage made from strips of chitterling mixed with groats or wheatmeal which have been boiled in a flavoured stock, the mixture seasoned and flavoured with grated lemon zest, packed into casings, linked, boiled for a few minutes, dried, then fried in butter [also called **saucisson au gruau** (Fr)]

Gruyère *(He)* A sweetish, nutty-flavoured large (to 45 kg), hard cooked-curd cheese made in Switzerland from the milk of cows grazed on Alpine pastures but now copied throughout the world. It is dry salted or brined for 8 days and ripened for up to 3 months and eaten between 3 and 10 months old. The paste is pale yellow and contains scattered small holes. Served as a dessert or slicing cheese and used to make fondue

Gruyère de Beaufort *(Fr)* A Gruyère type cheese from Beaufort, sometimes without holes and weighing up to 65 kg [also called **Beaufort**]

Gruyère de Comté *(Fr) see* Comté

gruzinskaya granatovaya podlivka *(Ru)* A Georgian chutney made from pomegranate seeds, depithed orange segments cut in pieces, chopped spring onions and chopped chilli peppers combined with lemon or lime juice, paprika, cayenne pepper and chopped coriander leaf and matured for 12 hours

grystek *(Sw)* Pot roasted beef or reindeer with a cream enriched thickened sauce, served for Sunday lunch with boiled potatoes, vegetables and red currant jelly

gryta *(Sw)* Stew

grzyby *(Pl)* Mushrooms

gua *(Ch)* Melon

guacamole *(Me)* A purée of ripe avocado flesh, skinned and deseeded tomatoes, deseeded chillis, lime juice and parsley used as a dip or as a filling for tacos and tortillas

guaiva *(It)* Guava

guai wei ji *(Ch)* Sliced chicken marinated in soya sauce and garlic. Lit. strange tasting chicken

guajolote *(Me)* Wild turkey

guanbano *(Ph)* Soursop

guanciale *(It)* A cured bacon made from the jaw and cheek of the pig. Traditionally used for spaghetti alla carbonara

guanosine 5' disodium phosphate *see* (E)627

guar bean A variety of green bean *Cyamopsis psoraloides* with long thin pods that grow in clusters. Used in India as a vegetable and in the USA as cattle fodder. The dried beans are not eaten. The beans are a source of guar gum (E412) used as a thickener and stabilizer in processed foods [also called **gaur bean, cluster bean)**

guar gum A gum (E412) extracted from guar, used as a thickener and stabilizer in processed food

guard of honour Roast lamb consisting of two best ends or racks of lamb, rib bones scraped as for a crown roast and interlinked, with the vertebrae at the base and the skin side outwards so as to look like a guard of honour. The space between two joints may be filled with stuffing. The bone ends are fitted with cutlet frills before presentation

guarnecido *(Po)* garnished

guarnito *(It)* Garnished

guava A round or pear shaped tropical fruit from a tree *Psidium guajava* related to the myrtle and eucalyptus. It is the size of an orange, has a musky smelling white to pink flesh containing a lot of edible seeds, and an inedible red skin which is removed before the fruit is used. It can only be eaten when ripe and does not travel well except by air freight. Made into a jelly or available tinned in the west

guayaba *(Sp)* Guava

guaymas sauce Mayonnaise flavoured with fresh tomato purée and chopped stuffed olives. Served with cold meat and poultry

gubbins sauce *(UK)* A cold condiment sauce made by blending butter, made up English mustard, wine vinegar and Devonshire cream (1:1:1:2) with a little tarragon vinegar and seasoning

guchalpan *(Ko)* Stuffed pancakes. Traditionally there are 9 different stuffing ingredients

guchi *(In)* Cloud ear fungus

gudbrandsdalsost *(No)* A hard, cooked-curd cheese made from a mixture of the whey from cows' milk, cream and goats' milk which is coagulated by heating

gudgeon A European freshwater fish *Gobio gobio* of the carp family up to 20 cm long with whiskers at the corners of the mouth. Generally fried, grilled or panéed or battered and deep fried

guéridon *(Fr) masc.* The pedestal table use by a waiter when he cooks food at the customer's table e.g. crêpes suzette, tournedos

güero *(Me)* Anaheim chilli (USA)

gueyteow *(Th)* Noodles

guey teow sen lek *(Th)* Rice ribbon noodles

Gugelhopf *(He)* A fatless sponge mixture containing lemon zest, chopped almonds, seedless raisins and milk, either yeast or baking powder raised, baked in a deep fluted ring mould and iced when cold; *see also* Kugelhopf which is a different cake [also called **Gugelhupf** (Ge)]

Gugelhupf *(Ge) see* Gugelhopf

gui choy *(Ch)* Mustard greens

guimauve *(Fr) fem.* Marshmallow

guinataan *(Ph)* A cooking method in which the ingredients are simmered in coconut milk [also called **ginitan**]

guindilla chilli A long and thin mildly piquant red coloured hot chilli from Spain, usually dried

guinea corn *see* sorghum

guinea fowl A recently domesticated game bird *Numida meleagris* related to the pheasant, between 1 and 2 kg in weight with white spotted grey plumage and rather dry flesh. Cooked as chicken or pheasant but barded or larded [also called **Bohemian pheasant**]

guinea fowl eggs Small eggs hard boiled for 5 minutes and used as a garnish

guinea grains *see* grains of paradise

guinea pepper *see* grains of paradise

guinea pig A large rodent *Cavia porcellus* widely used in Europe as a pet or laboratory animal but an important source of animal protein in South America where large varieties are bred. The flesh is rather like pork

guinea squash *see* aubergine

guinea yam A largish yam (to 5kg) with distinctive yellow flesh from a plant *Dioscorea cayenensis* grown in the USA, Africa and the Caribbean [also called **yellow yam**]

guisado *(Ph, Po & Sp)* A method of cooking in which meat is first sautéed then braised or simmered until done, also stew or stewed

guisantes *(Sp)* Green peas

guiso de dorado *(SA)* A fish stew from Paraguay containing dorado, a famous river fish of that country

guiso de repollo *(SA)* A Bolivian dish consisting of cooked cabbage mixed with tomato sauce containing onion, potatoes, chillis, coriander and seasonings. Served with grilled or fried meat and poultry

guitar fish A type of skate *Rhinobatus rhinobatus* which looks a little like an angel fish and is found in the southern Mediterranean. Moderately good to eat

guitare *(Fr) fem.* Guitar fish

guitarra *(Sp)* Guitar fish

gui yu *(Ch)* Crucian carp

Guizotia abyssinica *Bot.* The plant from which niger oil is extracted

Gujerat masala *(In)* A hot spice mix containing in addition to those listed under garam masala, sesame seeds, fennel seeds, ajowan seeds and chillis

gujjia *(In)* A crescent shaped sweet pasty filled with chopped nuts and grated coconut

gula *(Id & Ma)* Sugar

gula ärter med fläsk *(Sw)* A substantial national soup served traditionally on winter Thursdays. Made from dried yellow peas soaked overnight and cooked in the soaking water, as many pea skins as possible removed, a piece of boned pork, sliced onion or leek, marjoram or ginger and seasoning added and the whole simmered for 2 hours until peas and pork are tender. The pork is removed and served separately with mustard. The soup is served very hot [also called **ärter med flask, ärtsoppa**]

gulab *(In)* Rosewater

gulab jamon *(In)* A Bengali speciality of dumplings made from dried milk and syrup, deep fried, soaked in a sugar syrup and flavoured with rose essence and cardamom [also called **gulab jamun**]

gulab jamun *see* gulab jamon

gulai *(Ma & Id)* A type of curry in which the ingredients are simmered in an excess of coconut milk or soured stock with rempah and spices and with a little jaggery

gula jawa *(Id)* Palm sugar

gulaman *(Ph)* Agar-agar

gula melaka *(Ma)* Palm sugar

gula merah *(Id & Ma)* Brown sugar

Gulasch *(Ge)* Goulash

gule ærter *(De)* A winter soup made from pork belly, mixed vegetables and yellow split peas similar to the Swedish gula ärter med fläsk

gulerødder *(De)* Carrots

gull's eggs Eggs of various species of gulls, usually sold hard boiled for hors d'oeuvres. Examples are turquoise blue and speckled; fawn with dark brown speckling from the common gull, brownish olive green with dark brown spots from the black-headed gull and off white with brown and blue-grey spots from the herring gull. The latter is about twice the size of a hen egg

gullet of beef *(UK)* A western Scottish term for clod of beef

gully bean *see* pea aubergine

gulrøtter *(No)* Carrots

Gulyas *(Au)* Goulash

gulyás *(Hu)* A thicker more stew-like version of gulyás le leves

gulyás lé leves *(Hu)* A rich meat and vegetable soup made from shin beef, onion, tomatoes, green sweet peppers and potatoes flavoured with paprika. The original goulash

Gulyassuppe *(Au)* Soup with diced meat and vegetables

gum A polysaccharide, usually obtained from plants in water solution with sticky and gelling properties. The common types of vegetable origin are gum arabic, gum tragacanth, guar gum, locust bean gum and xanthan gum

gum arabic E414b, a polysaccharide vegetable gum obtained from the dried exudate of a Middle Eastern and Indian tree *Acacia senegal,* used as a thickener, emulsifier and stabilizer, in the manufacture of chewing gum, marshmallows and fruit gums and as a glaze on cake decorations [also called **gum acacia, acacia gum**]

gum tragacanth E413, a vegetable gum obtained from a shrub *Astralagus gummifer* grown in Western Asia. Used for thickening creams and jellies, to prevent crystallization of sugars in jam and ice creams and to make pastillage, a particularly stiff royal icing used with wedding cakes

gumbo 1 *see* okra **2** *(USA)* A thick soup or thin stew from Louisiana made with chicken or prawns, tomatoes, rice, sweet peppers, spices, herbs and seasonings and thickened with okra. See e.g. chicken gumbo

gumbo filé *see* filé powder

gum jum *(Ch)* Lily bulb

gum kum *(In)* Lily bulb

Gummiarabicum *(Ge)* Gum arabic

Gundel palacsinta *(Hu)* A pancake filled with a creamed nut and raisin filling, flambéed at the table

gung 1 *(Th)* Crustaceans **2** *(Vi)* Ginger

gunga pea *see* pigeon pea

gung foi *(Th)* Shrimp or prawn

gung nang *(Th)* Shrimp or prawn

gunnel *see* butterfish (2)

guo jiang *(Ch)* Jam

guo tieh *(Ch)* Fried dumpling

gur *see* jaggery

gurdakupura turrcarri *(In)* A kidney curry made with lamb or veal kidneys which have been soaked in vinegared water for 24 hours, then skinned and cored. Chopped onions are fried in a large amount of ghee until brown, sesame seeds, turmeric, cumin seed and cayenne pepper added and fried, kidneys added and fried 5 minutes until butter fat separates, tomato concassée, powdered bay leaf and mace with a little water added, cooked until dry, more water added and cooked until dry then fried until dark red with constant stirring, simmered with water *(see turcarri)* until kidneys are tender, and kept warm for 10 minutes until served.

gurepufuruto *(Ja)* Grapefruit

gurka *(Sw)* Cucumber

Gurke *(Ge)* Cucumber

Gurkensalat *(Ge)* Cucumber salad

gurnard A small round seawater fish *Friglidae* spp. with an ugly oversized head and enormous spiny fins, highly coloured with glittering scales and found in the Mediterranean and the North East Atlantic. There are three types, grey, red and yellow. Poached or steamed, popular in France [also called **gurnet, sea robin, tub gurnard**]

gurnet *see* gurnard

gus *(Ru)* Goose

gus prigotovlyenny v marinadye *(Ru)* An Estonian dish of goose rubbed with lemon juice, salt and saltpetre, rested 1 day, then marinated in a boiled water, salt and sugar brine (120:10:3) with raw onion, carrot, garlic, peppercorns and bay for 3 days, drained, then simmered in water with the pickling vegetables, herbs and spices until cooked (100 minutes). Served with ligonberry or cranberry sauce

guscio *(It)* Shell, husk, pod

guscio, al *(It) (of eggs)* Boiled in the shell

gush halav *(ME)* A cows' milk cheese from Israel similar to Edam

Güssing *(Au)* A cheese similar to Brick made from semi-skimmed cows' milk

gut, to To remove the entrails from an animal or fish including the gills in a fish and to clean out the abdominal cavity

gutap *(Ru)* Deep fried pasties made with a

wheat flour unleavened dough enriched with butter and filled with e.g. meat mixture, vegetables or set egg custards with vegetables

gutdurchgebraten *(Ge) (of steaks, meat, etc.)* Well done

guts *see* innards

Gutsleberwurst *(Ge)* A mild-flavoured, coarse-textured liver sausage *(kochwurst)* containing recognizable pieces of liver, pork and fat

güveç *(Tu)* A casserole very similar to agneshka guvetch

guvetch *(CE)* A type of ratatouille made from various colours of sweet pepper, onion, garlic, green beans, tomatoes, chillis and seasoning all stewed in sunflower oil. Served with rice or pasta

gwaar ki phalli *(In)* Guar bean

gyin sein *(Bm)* Ginger

gypsy herring *(UK) coll. (Cornwall)* Pilchard

gypsy's arm *(Sp)* A type of Swiss roll filled with jam or strawberries and cream [also called **brazo de gitano**]

gyudon *(Ja)* Rice with stir-fried beef and onions and a sauce served with green tea as fast food

gyulai *(Hu)* A smoked pork sausage flavoured with paprika

gyümölcslé *(Hu)* Fruit juice

gyümölcsöt *(Hu)* Fruit

gyuniku *(Ja)* Beef

Hh

Haagse bluf *(Ho)* A light sorbet of whipped egg whites and red currant juice Lit. Hague swank

haam *(Ch)* Salt

haam daan *(Ch)* Salted duck egg

haar chee meen *(Ch)* Brown noodles flavoured with shrimp

haas *(Ho)* Hare

haas ko phul *(Ne)* Duck egg

habanero chilli An extremely hot, lantern-shaped chilli from the Caribbean, with a colour varying from green to red looking rather like a small sweet pepper

habas *(Sp)* Broad beans, fava beans

habas al horno *(Sp)* Baked beans

habas a la montañesa *(Sp)* Beans baked with ham

habichuelas *(Sp)* Kidney beans

habichuelas verdes *(Sp)* Green beans

habitant pea soup *(Cn)* A thick soup from Quebec using dried yellow and green peas with onions, salt pork, herbs and seasonings

HACCP Hazard analysis critical control point system A system developed by NASA to ensure safe food for astronauts, now applied in industry. It consists of applying checks to possible contamination points at all stages of food processing from primary producer through slaughter houses, packers, processors, retailers and restaurants or canteens. However the adoption of this system should not be an excuse for abandoning end product testing

haché(e) *(Fr)* Finely chopped or minced

hachee *(Ho)* Minced meat

hachée, sauce *(Fr) fem.* Vinegar with finely chopped onion and shallot reduced by half, court bouillon from the fish being poached added, thickened with beurre manié, simmered 10 minutes and finished with chopped fines herbes, capers and duxelles

hacher *(Fr)* To chop up or mince

hachis 1 *(De)* Minced meat **2** *(Fr) masc.* Finely chopped cooked meat reheated in a sauce **3** *(Fr) masc.* Chopped vegetables

hachis Parmentier *(Fr) masc.* Shepherd's pie

hachoir *(Fr) masc.* A rocking chopper consisting of a curved blade with a vertical handle at each end which is used with a rocking motion. Several blades can be paralleled together for a faster chopping action

hackad *(Sw)* Chopped

hackad biff med lök *(Sw)* Chopped beef and onions

Hackbraten *(Ge)* Meat loaf

hacken *(Ge)* Minced or chopped

Hackfleisch *(Ge)* Minced meat

haddock A common round fish *Melanogrammus aeglefinus* of the cod family found in the Atlantic ocean. It is up to 60 cm long and 4 kg in weight with a greyish brown upper surface and with a dark spot behind each of the gill covers. The flesh is softer and less flaky than cod and may be cooked in any way. Often smoked

haddock à la russe *(Sw)* A large cleaned haddock with head and fins, simmered in salted water with onion, bayleaf and mixed peppercorns for 15 minutes. Flesh removed and reserved, cooking liquor strained and made into a velouté with an equal amount of thin cream, finished with butter and egg yolk and poured over the fish, reheated and garnished with crisp fried onion and chopped hard boiled egg

haemagglutinin *see* lectin

haemoglobin The red cells in blood responsible for the transport of oxygen from the lungs to the tissues

haew *(Th)* Water chestnut

Hafer *(Ge)* Oats

Haferbrei *(Ge)* Porridge

Hagebuttensuppe *(Ge)* A warm soup made from blanched rose hips simmered with breadcrumbs, cinnamon, lemon zest, sugar, a little salt and white wine, sieved, let down with white wine, thickened with egg yolks and finished with butter. Served with croûtons

haggamuggie *(UK)* Haggis made with fish liver instead of sheep offal

haggis *(UK)* A Scottish sausage made from the minced heart, liver and lungs of a sheep mixed with oatmeal, suet, minced onion, spices, herbs and seasoning, all encased in a sheep's stomach and boiled prior to being served hot. Nowadays more commonly stuffed in a plastic casing. Traditionally served at Burns' night suppers with tatties, bashit neeps and an excess of whisky, whilst Burns' Ode to the Haggis is recited with due ceremony

hagyma *(Hu)* Onions

Hahn *(Ge)* Rooster, mature male chicken

Hähnchen *(Ge)* Spring chicken

hahni *(Fi)* Goose

haiga-mai rice *(Ja)* An incompletely polished rice leaving the germ attached so that it has a nutty flavour

hair vegetable A black algae *Gracillaria verrucosa* which grows in very fine hair-like strands off the south coast of China. It is steamed as a vegetable, braised with bacon for Chinese New Year and used as a garnish or decoration [also called **black moss**]

hairy aubergine A Thai variety of aubergine with a bitter tart taste and an orange skin covered in fine hairs. It is sliced and used raw in salads or finely chopped for use in sauces

hairy basil *(SEA)* One of the South East Asian basils *Ocimum* spp. with lemony-peppery-flavoured narrow pale leaves and red tinged seed pods, similar to the Italian dwarf basil. The flavourless seeds are used as a thickening agent

hairy brinjal *see* fuzzy melon

hairy gourd A variant of the bottle gourd *Lageneria siceraria* with not such a pronounced bottle shape. It is light green, covered in fine hairs and grows up to 75 cm in length

hairy lychee *see* rambutan

hairy melon *see* fuzzy melon

hai shen *(Ch)* Sea cucumber. Lit. ginseng of the sea

hai wei *(Ch)* Sea food

hai zhe *(Ch)* Jellyfish

hai zhe pi *(Ch)* Jelly fish

hajdú *(Hu)* A cheese made from cows' milk and resembling kashkaval

hajikama shoga *(Ja)* Pickled ginger shoots. See ginger shoots

hákarl *(Ic)* Shark, alternatively, strips of shark flesh, tenderized by being left to ripen under stones in the open air for several weeks, then washed and air dried. Has rather a pungent odour

hak chih ma *(Ch)* Black sesame seeds

hake A superior tasting fish *Merluccius merluccius* of the cod family with a grey to bluish skin and lean white flesh. The lower jaw protrudes beyond the upper. Caught in the western part of the North Atlantic. Cooked in any manner

hakkebøf *(De)* Minced or chopped beef

hakket æg og sild *(De)* Smoked herring and hard boiled eggs minced together and used as a topping on open sandwiches

hakusai *(Ja)* Chinese leaves

halal A description of meat slaughtered according to the rules of the Muslim religion or of a butcher who sells such meat

halászlé *(Hu)* A fish stew made with a mixture of freshwater fish cut in pieces, simmered in water and sour cream with paprika and tomato purée, strained and the fish pieces served with cooking liquor thickened with egg yolks and lemon juice

halawch *(ME)* *see* halva

hal *(Hu)* Fish

halb durchgebraten *(Ge)* Medium rare (as of steak, meat, etc.)

halb roh *(Ge)* Rare (as of meat steaks, etc.), al dente

halba *(Ma)* Fenugreek

halber Hahn *(Ge)* A dark bread roll spread with ripe cheese and mustard

halbran *(USA)* A very young duckling

haldi *(In)* Turmeric

half cream A thin cream with a minimum butterfat content of 12% used as a pouring cream

half-and-half *(USA)* Cream containing 10.5 to 18% butterfat [also called **cereal cream**]

half moon cut *see* hangetsu giri

half-mourning *(USA)* Poularde demi-deuil

half pound cake *(UK)* Pound cake made with half quantities (225 g) sufficient to make one 20 cm round cake

halfatányéros *(Hu)* A mixture of a variety of panéed and plain fried fish served with tartare sauce

halia *(Ma)* Ginger

halibut *(En)* A large (to 3 m) fine-flavoured seawater fish *Hippoglossus hippoglossus* found in Northern waters. It has dark green to brown upper side and the flesh is firm, white and medium oily. Cooked in any way. The liver is an important source of fish oils used as a vitamin (A & D) supplement

hälle-flundra *(Sw)* Halibut

hallon *(Sw)* Raspberry

halmajonéz *(Hu)* Fish with mayonnaise served as a hors d'oeuvre

Haloumi *(Gr & ME)* A soft or semi-hard cheese with a salty lactic flavour made from ewes' or goats' milk. It is heated in whey to boiling point, drained, salted and preserved in salted whey for up to 40 days. Known as jubna in Arabic

Hals und Innereien *(Ge)* Giblets

halstra *(Sw)* Roast

halstrad *(Sw)* Grilled

halva *(NA & ME)* A sweetmeat made from crushed sesame seeds or almonds combined with boiled sugar syrup. Made in block form and sold in slices [also called **halawch**]

halwa *(In)* A type of pudding made from vegetables, lentils, nuts and fruit, cooked with sugar and ghee to a sticky consistency

ham 1 *(En & Ho)* The hind leg and thigh of a pig cut from the carcase and matured separately. Sometimes incorrectly used for the hind leg and thigh cut from a side of bacon. If to be cooked it should be soaked in water until the soaking water is not salty and boiled at a temperature around 80°C or baked until the final centre temperature is 65°C **2** *(USA)* Leg of pork either cured or uncured

ham sausage 1 *(Ge)* A scalded sausage made from finely ground pork and beef mixed with spices and garlic and interspersed with chunks of ham and lean bacon (minimum 50%) to give a marbled appearance. Used for slicing and grilling or frying or as an addition to stews, etc. **2** *(UK)* A sausage made from finely chopped ham mixed with 20% coarsely chopped pork fat, moistened with stock and flavoured with white pepper, cayenne pepper, mace and ginger, packed into weasands, tied, simmered for an hour and cold smoked for 10 days

hamaguri *(Ja)* Clams

hamaguri sumashi-jiru *(Ja)* Clam and mushroom soup made from sound clean clams soaked in salt water for 3 hours, boiled in water until the shells open, unopened ones discarded, mushroom caps and watercress added to the cooking liquor, cooked 1 minute, a little soya sauce and some sake added, heated to boiling point, garnished and served

Haman's ears *(ME) see* hamantaschen

hamantaschen The Yiddish name for small sweet triangular pastries filled with a mixture of poppy seeds, chopped walnuts, syrup, raisins, butter and milk. Eaten at the Jewish festivals of Purim and Lots [also called **Haman's ears**]

Hamburg parsley A type of parsley *Petroselinum crispum 'tuberosam'* whose root, which has a strong celery-like flavour, is used as a vegetable in Central Europe [also called **parsley root, turnip rooted parsley**]

hamburger *see* beefburger

Hamburger Aalsuppe *(Ge)* Eel pieces poached in fish stock and reserved. Peeled and quartered pears poached in white wine with a little sugar and lemon zest and reserved. The strained cooking liquors mixed with a strong beef broth, slightly thickened with a brown roux and garnished with green peas and a brunoise of carrots, leeks and Hamburg parsley and served over dumplings, the eel pieces and the pears

Hamburger Apfelsuppe *(Ge)* As Hagebuttensuppe with apples instead of rose hips and cider instead of white wine. Served warm

hamburger bun A soft flat round yeast-raised bun which is used to make a sandwich with a hamburger. Standardized by some fast food chains to a tasteless uniformity

Hamburger Krebssuppe *(Ge)* Crayfish soup made from crayfish sautéed in butter and flamed with brandy, cooked in white stock and white wine until tender, tail meat reserved, the shells pounded, sweated in butter, flour added and cooked, cooking liquor added, simmered, seasoned and strained over the crayfish tails, small dumplings and green peas

Hamburger Rauchfleisch *(Ge)* Very thin slices of cold smoked brisket of beef served with horseradish sauce

hamburgerkött *(Sw)* Smoked ox breast

hamburgerryg *(De)* Smoked loin of pork served with a sauce made from red currant jelly, mustard and grated onion

Hämchen *(Ge)* Pigs' knuckles and sauerkraut

ha mei *(Ch)* Dried shrimp

Hammel *(Ge)* Mutton

Hammelfleisch *(Ge)* Mutton

Hammelkeule *(Ge)* Leg of mutton

Hammelkotelett *(Ge)* Mutton chop

Hammelschulter *(Ge)* Shoulder of mutton

Hammelwürste *(Ge)* A sausage made of minced pork, mutton and garlic

hammerhead shark One of the better edible sharks *Sphyrna zygaena* found in the Atlantic and Mediterranean. Palatable when young

hampe *(Fr) fem.* Thin flank of beef; breast of venison

hamperilainen *(Fi)* Hamburger

hamu *(Ja)* Ham

hana gatsuo *(Ja)* *see* hana katsuo

hana giri *(Ja)* The flower cut of root vegetables made by trimming cylinders lengthways so that when sliced transversally, they make a 5 petalled shape

hana hojiso *(Ja)* Small stems of the shiso plant with seed pods, used as a garnish. The seeds are also scraped from the stem into the soya dipping sauce used with sashimi [also called **hijiso, hojiso**]

hana katsuo *(Ja)* Pacific bonito flakes or shavings [also called **hana gatsuo**]

hanatsuki kyuri *(Ja)* Very small cucumbers with intact flowers still attached, used as a garnish

Hand *(Ge)* *see* Handkäse

hand *(UK)* *see* hand of pork

hand of pork *(UK)* *see* hand and spring of pork

hand and spring of pork *(UK)* Name used in London and the south west for a foreleg and shoulder of pork excluding the blade [also called **hand of pork**]

Handkäse *(Ge)* A variety of soft hand moulded cheeses (25 to 125 g) made from naturally soured and curdled skimmed or semi-skimmed cows' milk. Sometimes flavoured with herbs or spices and widely variable in colour, texture and flavour. Contains 50 to 55% water, 2% fat and 27 to 35% protein [also called **Hand, Harzkäse, Sauermilchkäse**]

hang, to To leave meat or game birds, esp. the tougher old birds, to hang in a cool dry airy store for sufficient time to allow the meat fibres to be broken down by the acid conditions which develop. Animal meat is hung as complete or half carcases for up to 2 weeks or more. Game birds with the exception of wild duck which may be drawn, are hung by the neck without being drawn or plucked

hangetsu giri *(Ja)* Half round cuts of vegetables esp. carrots, bamboo shoots, radishes, etc. [also called **half moon cut**]

hangibjúga *(Ic)* Smoked sausage

hangikjöt *(Ic)* Smoked lamb

hangop *(Ho)* Cottage cheese, curds, alternatively a thick buttermilk and sugar dessert

hangtown fry *(USA)* An omelette served with fried bacon and panéed and fried oysters

hanhea *(Fi)* Goose

hanh la *(Vi)* Spring onions

hanh tay *(Vi)* Onion

hanjuku tamago *(Ja)* Soft boiled eggs

Hanoi beef soup *(Vi)* *see* pho

hanpen *(Ja)* A soft fish cake made from ground fish flesh and starch formed into squares or triangles and steamed. Eaten as is or grilled, poached or deep fried and dipped in soya sauce

hao you gai lan *(Ch)* Broccoli in oyster sauce

hao you niu rou *(Ch)* Beef with oyster sauce

hapankaali *(Fi)* Sauerkraut

har *(Ch)* Shrimp or prawn

hara dhania *(In)* Coriander leaves

harak mas *(Sr)* A beef curry flavoured with onions, garlic, ginger, vinegar, spices and coconut

hara mirich *(In)* Green chilli

häränfile *(Fi)* Fillet steak

häränhäntäliemi *(Fi)* Oxtail soup

hara piaz *(In)* Spring onions

harcsa *(Hu)* Wels, the fish

hard Hard to the bite as applied to wheat, difficult to cut as applied to cheese, resisting penetration by a sharp object

hard ball stage *see* sugar cooking

hard boil, to To boil something until it hardens, usually used of whole eggs boiled for 10 minutes until the yolk is solid

hard cheese A cheese which is difficult to cut, normally with a water content less than 40%

hard clam *see* quahog clam

hard crack stage A stage in sugar cooking when the sugar temperature rises to 157°C in the UK and 149°C in the USA; *see also* sugar cooking

hard dumpling *see* Sussex dumpling

hard-neck clam *see* quahog clam

hard red spring wheat flour *(USA)* A high gluten bread flour

hard red winter wheat flour *(USA)* A good bread flour made from a more flaky and thinner seed than the equivalent spring wheat flour

hard roe The eggs of female fish usually floured and fried

hard sauce *see* rum or brandy butter

hard smoked herring *see* red herring

hard wheat A tough wheat which resists

cracking and with the starch grains tightly bound. It contains no triabolin and it fractures across the starch grains. Durum wheat is one of the hardest

hardal *(Tu)* Mustard

hardfiskur *(Ic)* Fish cleaned and split along the abdominal cavity, sometimes with bone removed, to make a triangular shape. In this form hung up to air dry in freezing conditions. When dry will keep almost indefinitely. Eaten raw

hårdkogt *(De)* Hard boiled

hårdkokt *(No & Sw)* Hard boiled

hardshell clam *see* quahog clam

hardtack A hard biscuit made of flour, salt and water only [also called **ship biscuit, sea biscuit, pilot biscuit**]

Harduf *(ME)* An Israeli semi-soft spreading cheese made from ewes' milk to resemble Lipto

hare *(En & No)* A wild game animal resembling a large rabbit but which does not hop nor live in burrows. There are several varieties, the common, Scottish and the Mediterranean all distinguished from rabbit by their dark flesh and powerful back legs. The blood which is collected for jugged hare q.v. is prevented from coagulating by adding 5 ml of vinegar. Hares are usually hung by the legs for 5 to 10 days before being paunched. May be roasted, braised or stewed. Shooting season in the UK is from the 1st of August to the last day of February although it is not a law. Hare is not sold from March to July

hare channa *(In)* Fresh or dried, green immature chick peas

hareng *(Fr) masc.* herring

hareng fumé *(Fr) masc.* Kipper

hareng mariné *(Fr) masc.* Pickled herring

hareng salé *(Fr) masc.* Bloater

hareng saur *(Fr) masc.* The French version of the red herring often served as a hors d'oeuvre

hareragu *(No)* Jugged hare

haresteg *(De)* Roast hare

har gow *(Ch)* Small purses of minced shrimp made by placing the filling in the centre of a rolled out circle of wheat starch dough and pulling the edges to the centre to make it look like a string purse or bag

harhardal *(In)* Yellow dahl

haricot bean The shelled and dried mature French bean usually white, about 8 to 10 mm long and oval shaped. Sometimes coloured. Used extensively in Western cooking. The name is derived from the Aztec ayecotl; *see also* French bean [also called **dry shell bean** (USA)]

haricot bean soup *see* purée soissonnaise

haricot beurre *(Fr) masc.* Butter bean or a type of yellow French bean

haricot grimpant *(Fr) masc.* Runner bean

haricot lamb *(UK)* A lamb stew with haricot beans, onions and turnips

haricot de mouton *(Fr) masc.* Stewed mutton with root vegetables

haricot à rame *(Fr) masc.* Runner bean

haricot rouge *(Fr) masc.* Kidney bean

haricot sec *(Fr) masc.* Haricot bean

haricot de Soissons *(Fr) masc.* Kidney bean

haricot vert *(Fr) masc.* The immature pod of the French bean q.v. or green beans

hari gobhi *(In)* Broccoli

hari mirch *(In)* Sweet green pepper

harina *(Sp)* Flour

harina de maiz *(Sp)* Cornflour

haring *(Ho)* Herring

haringsla *(Ho)* Herring salad

harira *(NA)* A thick purée type soup of chick peas, lentils and haricot beans in a mutton or chicken stock with eggs, lemon, sometimes tomatoes and various herbs such as coriander, parsley or tarragon. Often served as a starter

harissa *(NA)* A hot chilli sauce made from softened, deseeded red chillis, garlic, salt, caraway seeds, cumin seeds, coriander seeds and dried mint leaves blended to a paste with olive oil. Some versions contain many more spices

harrar A top quality Ethiopian arabica coffee bean used for Turkish coffee

harslet *(UK) see* haslet

hart *(Ho)* Heart

hartgekocht *(Ge)* Hard boiled

harusame *(Ja) see* cellophane noodles. Lit. spring rain

Harvard beets *(USA)* Sliced, diced or julienned beetroot cooked in vinegar and sugar then thickened with cornflour

Harz *(Ge) see* Harzerkäse

Harzer *(Ge) see* Harzerkäse

Harzerkäse *(Ge)* A small, round, firm, pungent cheese made by hand from cows' milk in the Harz mountains. Often eaten with goose fat on black bread [also called **harz, harzer**]

Hase *(Ge)* Hare

Hase im Topf *(Ge)* Hare casseroled with wine and spices

Hasehendl *(Ge) coll. (Frankfurt)* Chicken

Haselhühner *(Ge)* Hazel hen

Haselnuss *(Ge)* Hazelnut

Haselnusscreme *(Ge)* A sweetened custard made with milk, sugar and egg yolks (10:4:1), heated to coating consistency, softened gelatine (2 g per 100 ml) and ground blanched hazelnuts (40 g per 100 ml) added, cooled but not set, then a third of its volume of cream whipped to a soft peak folded into the mixture which is poured into moulds to set

Haselnussmakronen *(Ge)* Hazelnut macaroons made in the same way as ordinary macaroons using ground skinned hazelnuts and flavouring them with cocoa powder and lemon zest

Hasenbraten *(Ge)* Roast hare

Hasenklein *(Ge)* Hare, floured and browned with bacon dice then all braised in red wine and stock with with pepper, spices, herbs, redcurrant jelly and lemon juice

hash *(UK & USA)* Pieces of leftover meat served in a well seasoned gravy or brown sauce with mashed potatoes and cooked vegetables

hash, to To cut or chop food into small pieces

hash brown potatoes *(USA)* A southern dish of grated raw potatoes fried like a pancake in bacon fat, often served for breakfast with bacon and egg, also, diced potatoes fried with onions [also called **hash browns, hashed brown potatoes**]

hash browns *see* hash brown potatoes

hashed brown potatoes *see* hash brown potatoes

hashi *(Ja)* Chopsticks

ha shoga *(Ja)* Ginger shoots

haslet *(UK)* An old English meat loaf, or faggot if wrapped in pig's caul, based either on pigs heart, liver, lungs and sweetbreads or pork mixed with finely chopped onion, dried bread crumbs, herbs and seasonings, cooked, sliced and served hot or cold. Sometimes wrapped in a pig's caul. Similar ingredients may also be stewed or casseroled under the same name. A more expensive version uses lean pork [also called **harslet, pig's fry**]

hassaku *(Ja)* A naturally occurring hybrid of *Citrus* spp. relatively unknown outside Japan

hasselback potatoes *see* hasselbackspotatis

hasselbackspotatis *(Sw)* Medium potatoes, peeled, cut with thin parallel cuts without completely severing each slice, each slice brushed with butter and sprinkled with dried white breadcrumbs, half baked in the oven, sprinkled with cheese and baking completed. Lit. hazel hill potatoes

hasselnöt *(Sw)* Hazelnut

hasty pudding 1 *(UK)* A thick Béchamel sauce enriched with egg, placed in a flameproof dish, covered with butter, brown sugar and cinnamon and browned under the grill **2** *(USA)* Cornmeal thickened and spiced milk sweetened with molasses. [also called **Indian pudding**]

hasu *(Ja)* Lotus root

hatcho-miso *(Ja)* A very dark, salty, thick and strong-flavoured miso made mainly of soya beans and used in soups

hauki *(Fi)* Pike

haunch The rear leg of an animal with part of the loin attached

Hauptelsalat *(Au)* Lettuce

Hausfrauenart *(Ge)* In the style of the housewife, i.e. with sour cream and pickles

hausgemacht *(Ge)* Home-made

Hausmachernodeln *(Ge)* Home-made noodles

haute cuisine *(Fr) fem.* Top grade cooking

havande gädda *(Sw)* A whole pike, scaled and opened up from the back and cleaned so as not to break the abdominal skin and leaving in the backbone. A salt herring is placed in the abdominal cavity and the pike is reformed, seasoned, panéed and baked, basting with milk. Served with the juices which have been thickened with crushed ginger biscuits. Lit. pregnant pike

Havarti *(De)* A semi-hard scalded-curd cows' milk cheese with a pungently-flavoured paste containing numerous holes. The rind may be dry or washed in which case the cheese has a better flavour. Either 45% or 60% butterfat content

havermout *(Ho)* Oatmeal, rolled oats

Haxe *(Ge)* Knuckle (of veal, etc.)

haybox cooking A method of slow cooking in which the food is brought to the boil in a container which is then put inside an insulated container with an insulated lid to complete cooking without further heating. Originally the insulation was hay packed in a wooden box or hole in the ground

haymaking cheese *see* single Gloucester

haze peper *(Ho)* A thick hare stew made from the hindquarter or the legs

hazel grouse *see* hazel hen

hazel hen A European woodland grouse *Tetrastes bonasia,* mainly from Scandinavia and Russia with a white excellently flavoured and tender flesh [also called **hazel grouse**]

hazelnut A thick-shelled nut from the European or North American hazel tree *Corylus avellana* with an outer husk that does not completely cover the nut. The nuts are small (to 1 cm) and pointed, with a firmly attached skin which is loosened by roasting or blanching. Grown in the UK, Italy and Spain. They have a distinctive flavour and are used in cooking, confectionery and as a dessert nut. The oil is prized for its flavour; *see also* filbert [also called **cobnut, Barcelona nut**]

hazelnut butter A compound butter made from skinned and roasted hazelnuts pounded with a few drops of water, mixed with softened butter and passed through a sieve

HDL High density lipoprotein

head cheese *see* brawn

heart The muscular organ which continually pumps blood around the body. From a young animal they are reasonably tender, but older hearts being tough require long braising or stewing

heart cockle *see* heart shell

heart of palm The hearts, i.e. terminal buds or young shoots of various types of palm, an important leek-like vegetable grown in Brazil and Florida, now common in canned form throughout the USA and France [also called **cabbage palm, palm heart**]

heart of rape *see* rape

heart shell A bivalve mollusc *Glossus humanus* similar to but not a true cockle; it is heart-shaped when viewed side on. Found in the Eastern Atlantic from Iceland to the Mediterranean [also called **heart cockle**]

heat, to To warm through without boiling

heat treatment of curds Curds for cheese may be uncooked, i.e. not subjected to a temperature greater than 39°C, scalded, i.e. subjected to temperatures between 40 and 48°C or cooked i.e. subjected to temperatures in excess of 48°C

heavenly hash *(USA)* The name given to various sweet desserts

heavy cake *see* Cornish heavy cake

heavy cream *(USA)* A cow's milk cream with a butterfat content of 36 to 40%. Used for whipping [also called **heavy whipping cream**]

heavy syrup *see* syrup

heavy whipping cream *(USA) see* heavy cream

hechima *(Ja)* Loofah

hechos, muy *(Sp)* Well done (of meat, steak, etc.)

Hecht *(Ge)* Pike

Hecht mit Sauerkraut *(Ge)* Flaked pike flesh mixed with sauerkraut, covered with cream and baked in the oven

Hechtdorsch *(Ge)* Hake

hedelma *(Fi)* Fruit

hedelmäkakku *(Fi)* Fruit cake

hedelmäkeitto *(Fi)* Cold fruit soup

hedelmäslaatti *(Fi)* Fruit salad

hed fang *(Th)* Straw mushroom

hedgehog A small rodent like animal with a covering of sharp retractable quills. Traditionally baked in a clay covering by country folk. The clay enables the skin and quills to be easily removed

hedgehog mushroom *(USA)* A type of mushroom with a fawn-orange cap and white tooth-like projections below.

hed hom *(Th)* Shiitake mushroom, Chinese mushroom

hed hunu *(Th)* Cloud ear fungus

heet bliksem *(Ho)* A spiced mixture of pork chops, potatoes and apples. Lit. hot lightning

Hefe *(Ge)* Yeast

Hefeklosse *(Ge)* Yeast-raised dumplings made with an egg and butter enriched flour dough (1:1:7) made with milk flavoured with nutmeg, kneaded and proved as bread and finally steamed. Served with sweet or savoury dishes

Hefekranz *(Ge)* A savarin usually decorated with almonds and candied fruit

Heidelbeere *(Ge)* Blueberry, bilberry

Heidesand *(Ge)* Biscuits made from self raising flour, butter and sugar (4:3:2) mixed by the blending method, flavoured with vanilla, cut into rounds as in refrigerator cookies and baked at 175°C until firm and light brown

heiko *(Ma)* A smooth dark brown shrimp paste used in Thailand and Malaysia

heilbot *(Ho)* Halibut

Heilbutt (Ge) Halibut

Heilbutt unterm Sahneberg *(Ge)* Fillets of halibut laid in a buttered baking dish, sprinkled with onions sweated in bacon fat and covered with parcooked lean bacon rashers, covered with a white wine court bouillon and baked at 165°C until the fish is firm. Served topped with a velouté sauce made with the cooking liquor into which whipped double cream has been folded, sprinkled with grated cheese and browned under a very hot grill. Lit. halibut under a mountain of cream

heimische *(Yiddish)* Home-made

heiss *(Ge)* Hot

heisse Biersuppe *(Ge)* Lager and sugar (9:1) boiled then thickened off the heat to avoid curdling, with a liaison of egg yolks and sour cream (1:7 on lager), seasoned and flavoured with a little cinnamon

heko *(Ph)* The sediment from the fermented fish or shrimp paste bagoong, boiled with 3 times its weight in water for 30 minutes and then allowed to settle. Used as a mild fishy seasoning.

helado *(Sp)* Ice cream, frozen

heldersoep *(Ho)* Clear soup, consommé

helgeflundra *(Sw)* Halibut

Helianthus annuus *Bot.* Sunflower

Helianthus tuberosus *Bot.* The Jerusalem artichoke plant

Helichrysum angustifolium *Bot.* Curry plant

hellefisk *(No)* Halibut

helleflynder *(De)* Halibut

helstekt *(No)* Fried

Hemerocallis fulva *Bot.* The day lily from which lily buds are obtained

hemicellulose A polysaccharide carbohydrate found in fruit and vegetables. Some forms known as pectin are responsible for the setting of jams

hen The female of a bird, usually the female chicken which has been bred to lay eggs

Hendel *(Au)* Chicken

Henne *(Ge)* Hen

hennepot *(Be)* Chicken hot pot

herb A generic name for low growing plants and shrubs but more generally reserved for those plants with flavouring and medicinal properties. See culinary herb

herb salts *(USA)* A mixture of pure ground salt and ground dried herbs, Used as a flavouring

herbe aux chats *(Fr) fem.* Catmint

herbes de Provence *(Fr) fem.* A mixture of culinary herbs usually containing thyme, marjoram, basil and oregano. Used fresh or dried

herbs for particular food items *see* under food items, beef, bread, cheese, desserts, eggs, fish, game, lamb, liver, pork, poultry, salads, soup, turtle soup, vinegars. e.g. herbs for beef are listed under beef herbs

hergma *(NA)* Calves' feet

Hering *(Ge)* Herring

Hering Rollmop *(Ge)* Rollmop herring, often served with mustard, horseradish sauce or tomato sauce

Heringshai *(Ge)* Porbeagle shark

Heringskartoffeln *(Ge)* A casserole of alternate layers of herring and sliced potatoes

Herkimer *(USA)* A Cheddar-like factory produced cows' milk cheese from New York

herkkusienikastike *(Fi)* Mushroom sauce

herkkusienikeitto *(Fi)* Cream of mushroom soup

hermit crab An edible crab normally found in France [also called **bernard l'hermite** (Fr)]

herneet *(Fi)* Peas

hernekeito *(Fi)* Green pea soup

hero *(USA) see* hoagie

herrera *(Sp)* Striped bream

Herrgårdsost *(Sw)* A hard scalded-curd factory-produced cheese made from pasteurized cows' milk using a lactic starter and resembling Emmental. The pressed cheese is salted in brine, coated in wax and ripened for 3 to 4 months. Available in skimmed milk (30% butterfat) and whole milk (45% butterfat) versions

herring A round oily fish *Clupea harengus* with a wide distribution. The upper surface is steel blue and the underside silvery white. Sizes range from 20 to 40 cm in length. It has rather a lot of fine bones and may be cooked whole or filleted and is also sweet and/or sour pickled (see rollmop), salted and smoked (see kipper). Very popular in Northern Europe and an important source of EFA's. The name is from the old German 'heer', meaning an army, referring to its habit of once congregating in very large shoals

herring butter A compound butter made from filleted, smoked salt herrings, diced and pounded with half their weight of butter and sieved

herring caviar *(USA)* The roe of the female alewife herring processed to resemble caviar

herring flippits *(UK)* Freshly cooked flippits q.v. spread with a little mustard, topped with a grilled herring fillet, sprinkled with black pepper and served with lemon wedges

hertebout *(Ho)* Haunch of venison

hertevlees *(Ho)* Venison

Herve *(Be)* A soft, washed rind cows' milk cheese from north of Liège with a very strong pungent smell formed into squat 7.5 cm cubes with the typical red brown rind. Contains 51% water, 24% fat and 22% protein

hervir *(Sp)* To boil

hervir a fuego lento *(Sp)* To simmer

Herzmuschel *(Ge)* Cockle

Herzogin Kartoffeln *(Ge)* Mashed potatoes browned in the oven, duchesse potatoes

Herzwurst *(Ge)* A sausage made from coarsely chopped pigs' hearts mixed with finely minced pork shoulder and belly, seasoned, flavoured with nutmeg and allspice and filled into hog casings

hesperidin One of the bioflavonoids found in high concentration in citrus fruit

Hesperis matronalis *Bot.* Sweet rocket

hetao ren *(Ch)* Walnut

hetao zha ji pian *(Ch)* Deep fried chicken with walnuts

hettekees *see* Fromage de Bruxelles

heuk bone of beef *(UK)* The eastern Scottish term for rump of beef

heung mao tso *(Ch)* Lemon grass

heung nu fun *(Ch)* Five spice powder

hexamethylene tetramine *see* E239

hexamine E239, a preservative permitted only for fish and Provolone cheese

hibachi *(Ja)* A cast iron barbecue with a slatted iron grid

Hibiscus sabdariffa *Bot.* Jamaica flower

hickory *(USA & Fr) masc.* A hardwood tree *Carya* spp. commonly used for smoking food

hickory nut *(USA)* The sweet edible nut of the hickory tree related to the pecan and similar to the walnut

hielo *(Sp)* Ice

hierbabuena *(Sp)* Mint, the herb

hierbas finas *(Sp)* Fine herbs, a mixture of herbs

higadillos *(Sp)* Livers of small animals, particularly birds

higaditos de pollo *(Sp)* Chicken livers

hígado *(Sp)* Liver

higashi *(Ja)* Hard cakes mainly made of sugar and always purchased. They keep well

high density lipoprotein A specific complex of fat and protein that transports cholesterol in the blood. High levels appear to protect against heart and vascular disease; *see also* cholesterol and low density lipoprotein. [also called **HDL**]

High Moisture Jack A young Monterey Jack with a mild flavour matured up to 6 weeks

high tea *(UK)* A substantial afternoon meal once popular in Scotland and the north of England, now usually found only in more traditional hotels and boarding houses. Usually an assortment of cold meats and fish, salads, sandwiches, sweets, cakes and buns with tea or coffee

highbush blueberry *see* blueberry

Highland Crowdie *(UK)* A smooth cottage type cows' or goats' milk cheese from Scotland with a light fresh flavour

higo chumbo *(Sp)* Prickly pear

hiilillä paistettus silakkaa *(Fi)* Grilled herring

hijiki *see* hiziki

hijiso *(Ja) see* hana hojiso

hikiniku *(Ja)* Minced beef

hildersheimer Streichleberwurst *(Ge)* A spreading paste-like sausage made with pigs' liver and pork

hilloa *(Fi)* Jam

hilum The scar on a seed or bean where it joined its stalk

him *(Ch)* Ridged sand clam

Himbeere *(Ge)* Raspberry

Himbeerkaltschale *(Ge)* Raspberries, macerated in sugar syrup, sieved, mixed with white wine and a little lemon juice and served cold garnished with whole raspberries dipped in sugar

Himmel und Erde *(Ge)* Creamed potatoes and apple purée mixed with fried chopped onions and topped with fried liver. Lit. heaven and earth: which is which is unknown

himmelsk lapskaus *(No)* Fresh fruit and nuts sometimes served with a brandy-flavoured egg sauce. Lit. heavenly potpourri

himmeri *(Fi)* Lobster

hina *(Ja)* A 3 to 4 month old chicken [also called **hinadori**]

hinadori *(Ja)* *see* hina

hind loin of pork The rear of the loin containing the kidneys and pork fillet (tenderloin). Roasted or cut into loin chops and chump chops (rear end)

hindbær *(De)* Raspberry

hindi *(Tu)* Turkey

hing *(In)* Asafoetida

hinojo *(Sp)* Fennel

hinojo marino *(Sp)* Samphire *Crithmum maritimum*

hin sui *(Ch)* Squid

hip The seed capsule of a flower, used esp. of the rose

hip bone of beef *(UK)* A Midlands term for beef rump

hipogloso *(Sp)* Halibut

Hippen *(Ge)* Almonds pounded with egg whites, caster sugar, a little flour and cinnamon, stiffly beaten egg whites folded in, the batter spread thinly on oiled baking sheets, baked at 220°C, taken off the sheet when hot and rolled around a thin cylinder like a brandy snap. Used for garnishing desserts [also called **Hohlhippen**]

hirame *(Ja)* Flounder or halibut, used raw in sushi

Hirams Söndagshöna *(Sw)* Sunday chicken. A large chicken stuffed with a mixture of minced gammon and giblets, fresh white breadcrumbs, chopped and crushed garlic, seasoning and chopped parsley, stitched up, brought to the boil in water or stock flavoured with cloves, skimmed then simmered with parsnip, onions and leeks until tender. Served with a roux-thickened, strained cooking liquor finished with a cream and egg yolk liaison

hiratake *(Ja)* Oyster mushroom

hira-zukuri *(Ja)* A type of cut for fish such as snapper or sea bass used in sashimi in which the fillets are skinned and cut across the grain in slices

hirino *(Gr)* Pork

Hirn *(Ge)* Brains

hirn-profesen *(It)* Bread slices spread with brains, dipped in batter and deep fried. From the alpine region of Italy

Hirsch *(Ge)* Stag, deer

Hirschbraten Roast venison

Hirse *(Ge)* Millet, sorghum

hirvi *(Fi)* Elk

hisopo *(Sp)* Hyssop

hiyamugi *(Ja)* A somen type noodle but even thinner. Generally served cold with a dipping sauce

hiyashi somen *(Ja)* Cooked, refreshed, drained and chilled somen noodles served on a bed of ice with a platter of decoratively arranged hard boiled eggs, cucumber and ham sprinkled with strips of mint leaves and served with a dipping sauce made with chopped reconstituted shiitake mushrooms, dashi, soya sauce, sugar and sake, all boiled together then cooled. Lit. ice noodles

hiyu *(Ja)* Amaranth

hiziki *(Ja)* A sun dried and coarsely shredded brown seaweed *Cystophyllum fusiforme* or *Hisikia fusiforme* found in shallow coastal waters of the Far East and rich in iron and calcium. May be eaten on its own, as a garnish or in soups and stews [also called **hijiki**]

hjärta *(Sw)* Heart

hjerte *(De & No)* Heart

hjort *(Sw)* Deer, roebuck

hjortetakk *(No)* A special doughnut made at Christmas

hjortron *(Sw)* Cloudberry

hjortstek *(Sw)* Venison steak. [also called **rådjursstek**]

hmo *(Bm)* Straw mushroom

hoagie *(USA)* A sandwich made with a split hoagie roll filled with an assortment of meats, cheeses, salad vegetables, pickles, onions, etc. [also called **grinder, Italian sandwich, sub and submarine**]

hoagie roll A flat oblong bread roll about 15 to 20 cm long, used for a hoagie

hoan jo *(Ch)* Date

hob 1 The flat metal framework on top of a cooker on which pans are placed in order to be heated or a similar surface above or beside an open fire on which food containers are put to keep hot **2** A set of gas or electric rings set in a metal plate with controls, usually mounted in a work surface separate from the oven

hochepot *(Fr) masc.* A soup made with salt pork, pigs' tails and ears, beef, mutton, cabbage and root vegetables. Lit. shaking pot

hochepot flamand *(Be)* As hochepot, but

the meat and most of the vegetables served separately from the soup with small boiled sausages

Hochwild *(Ge)* Game

hock The part of an animal between the foot and lower limb corresponding to the ankle and part of the lower calf of a human. It consists mainly of gristle and connective tissue with a little flesh. Used to provide gelatine by prolonged boiling

hodesalat *(No)* Lettuce

hodge-podge *see* hotch-potch

hoe cake *(USA)* A dent corn cornmeal batter pancake originally cooked on the blade of a hoe [also called **johnny cake**]

hoen kwe *(Id & Ma)* Mung bean flour

hog 1 *(USA)* A general term for pig **2** *(UK)* A castrated male pig reared for slaughter

hog casings The cleaned and scraped intestines of pigs, being the first 18 m of pig gut measuring from the stomach with a diameter between 32 and 46 mm, classed as narrow, medium, wide and extra wide. Used for sausages and bratwursts

hog millet *see* common millet

hog plum The plum or egg shaped fruit (to 7.5 cm) of trees *Spondias* spp. similar to the mango. Cultivated in South East Asia and South America. A large stone is surrounded by yellow and flavoursome flesh and a yellow to red skin [also called **Jamaica plum, otaheite apple**]

hog pudding *(UK)* A type of haggis from the south west made with finely chopped pigs' pluck or fatty pig meat for the more expensive versions, mixed with boiled groats, seasoning and flavourings, packed into wide hog casings and boiled until cooked. The Devonshire variety is flavoured with mace, nutmeg, thyme and cayenne pepper, the Cornish one with mace, nutmeg, parsley and thyme [also called **hog's pudding**]

hogget A sheep between 12 months and 24 months old, popular in Australia

hog's pudding *(UK)* *see* hog pudding

hoh laan dau *(Ch)* Mangetout pea

hoh laan dow *(Ch)* Mangetout pea

hohle Schokoladenhippen *(Ge)* Tubes made ot of thin chocolate, filled with whipped cream

Hohlhippen *(Ge)* *see* Hippen

hoh yow *(Ch)* Oyster sauce

hoi git *((Ch)* Jellyfish

hoi sin cheung *(Ch)* Hoisin sauce

hoisin sauce *(Ch)* A sweet thick red-brown sauce made from fermented soya beans, sugar, garlic, five spices and a little chilli and coloured with annatto. Used with roast pork and poultry as a condiment or to glaze the meat as it is being roasted so as to give it a rich red chestnut colour [also called **duck sauce, suan mei jiang**]

hoja *(Sp)* Leaf

hoja de laurel *(Sp)* Bay leaf

hojaldre *(Sp)* Puff pastry

hojiso *(Ja)* *see* hana hojiso

hökarepanna *(Sw)* Grocer's stew made from sliced pork fillet and calves' kidney alternated in a casserole dish with seasoned sliced raw potatoes and onions, finishing with potatoes, covered with lager and dotted with butter, boiled, skimmed then simmered with a lid for 1 hour or more

hoki An important deep water commercial fish from New Zealand. Exported to Europe as fillets

hokkaido *(Ja)* A Cheddar-type cheese made from cows' milk

hokkien mee noodles *(Ch)* Egg noodles

holipce *see* holishkes

holishkes A Jewish speciality consisting of blanched cabbage leaves wrapped around a filling of meat and rice and simmered in a sweet and sour tomato sauce [also called **gluptzes, holipce, praakes**]

hollandaise, à la *(Fr)* In the Dutch style, i.e. served with Hollandaise sauce, or sometimes used of poached fish coated with melted butter and served with boiled potatoes

hollandaise, sauce *(En & Fr) fem.* A reduction of crushed peppercorns and vinegar, cooled, a small amount of cold water added, egg yolks whisked in and the whole cooked to a thread over a bain marie whilst continuing to whisk, removed from the heat and molten clarified butter poured in slowly with vigorous whisking to form a stable emulsion, seasoned and strained. Served warm with hot fish and some vegetables

hollandse palingsoep *(Ho)* A soup made from sweated skinned eels poached in a stock made from the eel trimmings and white wine, eel flesh reserved, poaching liquor strained, seasoned and thickened with egg yolks and butter and poured over the eel pieces and toast and garnished with a julienne of sweated leek, celery and Hamburg parsley.

holländische Sosse *(Ge)* Hollandaise sauce

holodny sup-salat *(Ru)* A cold soup made from chopped red onion, radishes, tomatoes, cucumbers and garlic seasoned and dressed with a little Tabasco sauce plus oil and lemon juice, mixed with chilled chicken consommé just before serving accompanied by garlic-flavoured croûtons

Holsteiner schnitzel A panéed and fried veal escalope topped with a fried egg and garnished with various items, usually anchovy fillets. The German is Holsteinschnitzel

Holsteinerwurst *(Ge & USA)* A sausage consisting of equal parts of cured pork and fresh beef minced finely with sugar, seasoned and strongly spiced with coriander, nutmeg and cardamom, filled into casings, linked or made into rings and smoked for a considerable time

holubsti *(Ru)* Cabbage rolls *(golubtsy)* from the Ukraine often containing chopped mushrooms instead of minced meat

holy basil An oriental variety of basil with a darker leaf than sweet basil and a sharper, slightly aniseed flavour

holy pokes *(USA) see* Baptist cake

homard *(Fr) masc.* Lobster

homard à l'américaine *(Fr) masc.* Lobster killed with a knife, chopped lobster tail and cracked claws seasoned, lightly fried with chopped shallots and garlic in oil and butter, flamed with brandy, then white wine, fish stock, meat glaze, demi-glace sauce, chopped tomato flesh, parsley and cayenne pepper added, cooked 15 minutes, lobster removed and meat reserved, coral and creamy parts of head added to cooking liquor, this reduced, butter added, the sauce strained and poured over the reserved lobster meat prior to serving; *see also* note next entry

homard à l'armoricaine *(Fr) masc.* Lobster cooked in oil with shallots, tomatoes, white wine and brandy. From Brittany. There is controversy over the attribution of the name américaine or armoricaine to these lobster dishes which are essentially the same

homard à la bordelaise *(Fr) masc.* Lobster prepared as for homard à l'américaine, up to and including flaming, reduced white wine, fish stock, tomato sauce, a BG and seasoning added, cooked 15 minutes, meat removed and sauce prepared in the same way and finished with butter, lemon juice and chopped tarragon and chervil

homard cardinal *(Fr) masc.* Cooked lobster flesh arranged with a salpicon of chopped lobster flesh, cooked mushrooms, the creamy parts from the head and chopped truffle mixed with a little sauce cardinal, either in a dish or a halved lobster shell supported by the lobster claws, coated with sauce cardinal, sprinkled with grated cheese and butter and glazed under the grill

homard, sauce *(Fr) fem.* A lobster-flavoured sauce made by sweating lobster flesh in the shell or well crushed cooked lobster shell with a mirepoix of onion, carrot and celery in butter, flaming with brandy, adding flour and tomato purée to make a cooked out roux, adding fish stock, white wine, a BG and garlic, simmering, removing lobster flesh if used, returning crushed shell to the sauce, simmering and straining. Coral if any should be added before straining

homard thermidor The sliced flesh from a grilled half lobster laid on cream sauce mixed with a little English mustard, coated with the same and glazed lightly in the oven or under the grill [also called **lobster thermidor**]

hom horm *(Th)* Good smell sometimes used for the shiitake mushroom

hominy Dehusked whole dried maize kernels with the germ removed. Usually boiled in water with 1 teaspoonful of bicarbonate of soda per litre to dehusk and soften it, prior to drying or using in cooking [also called **hulled corn**]

hominy grits *(USA)* Coarsely ground dehusked maize kernels used to make a kind of porridge

homity pie *(UK)* A short crust pastry pie filled with potato, onion, cheese, garlic, herbs and seasoning then baked

hom lek *(Th)* Shallots

homo *(USA) see* homogenized milk

homogenize, to To break down the dispersed phase of a two-phase mixture into such small droplets that they cannot separate out under gravity and thus form a stable emulsion. Fat globules in milk are treated in this way to give homogenized milk

homogenized milk **1** *(UK)* Milk which has been homogenized so that the cream does not separate out. Sold in red topped bottles **2** *(USA)* As the UK type but with 3.25% butterfat and 8.25% other milk solids

Homolky *see* Gomolya

homos *see* hummus

höna *(Sw)* A boiling or large older chicken

Honan cooking A style of Chinese cooking from the inland province of Honan which is north east of Szechuan. It is highly spiced and often contains wine. Yellow river carp is a speciality of the region. [also called **Hunan cooking**]

hon dashi *(Ja)* Instant dashi granules

høne *(De)* Chicken

høne bryst *(De)* Chicken breast, the white meat of chicken

hønekødsuppe *(De)* Chicken and vegetable soup

honey Flower nectar partially digested and regurgitated by the honey bee *Apis mellifera* as a thick sugary syrup with a distinctive flavour. Used by bees as a convenient food source and food storage medium. Its flavour and aroma depend to some extent on the types of flower from which the nectar was obtained. Strict vegans should not eat honey

honey baked ham *(UK)* Ham baked in the oven whilst basting with honey and possibly brown sugar

honey fungus A fungus *Armillaria mellea* which is a garden pest and grows on live trees causing them to wilt and die. The cap is golden brown when young becoming lighter as it ages. The slender stem curls out from a swollen base attached to the tree trunk. Although edible it has a bitter taste and unpleasant smell and is not recommended

honey tangerine *(USA)* A mandarin/orange cross developed in Florida in 1913 and propagated by C Murcott Smith and J Ward Smith. It has a rather leathery peel and tough segment walls but the juice content is very high and it is sweet and well-flavoured. It is grown in Florida and Brazil and commands a premium price [also called **Murcott, Smith tangerine**]

honeybun *(USA)* A flat yeast-raised bread roll glazed with honey before baking

honeycomb The hexagonal wax storage chambers of the honey bee which are formed in stacked tiers and in which which honey is stored. Honey can still be purchased in this form

honeycomb mould A light dessert made by folding stiffly whisked egg white into a mixture of jelly and cold egg custard sauce. If the mixture of egg custard and jelly is warm prior to folding in the egg white, then it separates into a jelly layer topped by a fluffy mousse

honeycomb tripe Tripe from the second stomach of an ox which has a honeycomb appearance

honeydew melon A slow ripening oval, i.e. rugby ball shaped, variety of winter melon with a thick yellow to green ridged skin and firm pale green, sweet and delicately-flavoured flesh. Not as sweet as some varieties but a good keeper

hong chee *(Ch)* Persimmon

hong dow *(Ch)* Adzuki bean

hong dow sar *(Ch)* Sweet red bean paste

hong mei *(Ch)* Red rice

hongos *(Sp)* Funghi

hongroise, à la *(Fr)* In the Hungarian style, i.e. in a sauce flavoured with paprika or with onions, tomatoes, paprika and soured cream

hongroise, sauce *(Fr) fem.* A velouté sauce flavoured with lightly fried onions and paprika. Served with freshwater fish, poultry and roast veal [also called **Hungarian sauce**]

hong-shao *(Ch)* Red cooking

hong yu *(Ch)* Red snapper

hong zao *(Ch)* Red rice

Honig *(Ge)* Honey

Honigkuchen *(Ge)* Honey cake made by the melting method from self raising flour, honey, sugar and ground almonds (5:3:2:1) flavoured with lemon zest, cocoa powder, ground spices, candied peel and almond essence, thinned with a little water to a moderately stiff dough and baked at 175°C. The top is covered with almond flakes when it is removed from the oven. Best after maturing for several days

honiglekach *see* lekach

honing *(Ho)* Honey

honingkoek *(Ho)* Honey cake

honje *(Id)* Torch ginger

hon mirin *(Ja)* Mirin

honning *(No)* Honey

honningkake *(No)* Honey cake

hønsekødsuppe *(De)* Chicken and vegetable soup

hønsesuppe *(De & No)* Chicken soup

hon shimeji *(Ja)* Oyster mushroom

hönssoppa *(Sw)* Chicken soup

hon tarako *(Ja) see* tarako

honung *(Sw)* Honey

hoo pla chalarm *(Th)* Shark's fin

hop A plant *Humulus lupulus* of the mulberry family with long twining stems bearing catkin-like flower clusters which when dried are used to give the bitter flavour to beer. The young shoots may be used as a vegetable

hop shoots The tender shoots of the hop plant used as a vegetable in France and Belgium

Hopfen *(Ge)* Hops

Hopfenkäse *(Ge) see* Nieheimer

hop jeung gwa *(Ch)* Choko

Hoppel-Poppel *(Ge)* Scrambled eggs with bacon and/or sausages and potatoes

hopper *(Sr)* A type of flat bread or pancake made with rice flour and coconut milk and deep fried until crisp; *see also* string hoppers

hopping John *(USA)* A mixture of cooked rice and black-eyed peas

horapa *(Th)* *see* bai horapa

horchata *(Sp)* A summer drink made from the ground tiger nuts called chufa in Spanish

Hordeum vulgare *Bot.* Barley

horenso no sarada *(Ja)* Spinach leaves washed and cooked for 5 minutes until tender, wrung out, cut into shreds and dressed with pasty mixture of soya sauce, rice vinegar, toasted and crushed sesame seeds, a little dry mustard, minced spring onions, grated fresh ginger and schichimi togarishu

horenzo *(Ja)* A delicate mild-flavoured variety of spinach with pink stems

hor fun *(Ch)* Rice ribbon noodles

horiatiki *(Gr)* A Greek salad of cucumber, tomato, olives, onions and feta cheese with an olive oil and vinegar dressing

horn of plenty A funnel shaped mushroom *Craterellus cornucopioides* with a grey exterior and browny black gills. Grows in beech woods [also called **black trumpet**]

Hörnchen *(Ge)* Slightly sweet crescent shaped-rolls similar to croissants

horned melon *see* kiwano

horno, al *(Me & Sp)* Baked or roasted in the oven

horoku *(Ja)* A large earthenware plate with a fitted lid used for baking

hors-d'oeuvre *(En, Ho & Fr) masc.* Single cold food items, a selection of well seasoned cold dishes or well seasoned hot dishes usually served at the beginning of a meal but sometimes as snacks or with a buffet or cold table

horse An animal *Equus caballus* whose sweet-flavoured meat is eaten in many countries and used as a substitute for beef in many recipes. Not eaten in the UK and the USA

horse bean *see* field bean and jack bean

horse clam A large (to 1.5 kg) clam *Thesus nuttalli* from the Pacific ocean with lean light coloured meat generally fried but in Japan eaten raw

horse gram The reddish brown, white, black or mottled seed of a legume *Dolichos biflorus* from India, which is rather wrinkled in appearance, similar to a chick pea, and rarely split. Eaten if there is nothing else but usually the whole plant is used as green manure or animal fodder [also called **Madras gram, kulthi bean**]

horse mackerel Various large fish of the mackerel family *Trachurus trachurus, Decapterus punctatus* and others found in tropical and sub-tropical seas; with elongated bodies and large spiky scales. They do not have so good a flavour as mackerel [also called **scad**]

horse mushroom A wild edible mushroom *Agaricus arvensis* similar to the field mushroom. It has a cream to yellow cap and greyish gills and turns yellow when cut or broken giving off an aniseed smell

horse mussel A large mussel *Modiolus modiolus* found throughout the North Atlantic. It has a purplish yellow shell and orange flesh which is not as well-flavoured as that of the common mussel

horseradish A hardy invasive perennial plant *Armoracia rusticana* whose thick roots have a hot pungent white flesh which is grated for use in horseradish sauce. The young leaves have a similar but milder flavour and may be used in salads

horseradish butter A compound butter made from grated horseradish pounded with 5 times its weight of butter and sieved

horseradish sauce Peeled and grated horseradish, mixed with vinegar, seasoning and lightly whipped cream. Served with roast beef, smoked trout and smoked eel; *see also* Albert sauce [also called **sauce raifort** (Fr)]

hortalizas *(Sp)* Green leaves cooked as a vegetable

hortelã pimenta *(Po)* Peppermint

hortobágyi rostélyos *(Hu)* Beef steak braised with stock and bacon bits and served with a large semolina dumpling

ho see *(Ch)* Dried oysters

hoshi-shiitake *(Ja)* A close relative of the shiitake mushroom *Cortinellus shiitake* fawn to black in colour and available fresh or dried [also called **winter mushroom, forest mushroom, Japanese black mushroom**]

hostess *(USA)* The female person who greets guests when they enter a restaurant. The male equivalent is called a greeter

hot bean paste *see* chilli bean paste

hot biscuit *(USA)* Scone

hot black bean sauce A sauce made from cooked black soya beans mashed with chillis, sesame oil, garlic, salt and sugar. Used as a flavouring

hot cross bun Originally called a cross bun and could be eaten on Good Friday without breaking the fast; now consisting of a yeast-raised enriched sweet bun flavoured with spices, currants and chopped candied peel, well glazed and with a cross formed on the top using a slack flour water mixture, pastry or by cutting a cross prior to proving. Eaten at Easter

hot dog *(USA)* A hot poached or steamed North American frankfurter served in a long soft white bread roll with American mustard or other relish

hot fudge *(USA)* A hot topping for ice cream and desserts made with chocolate, butter and sugar

hot house cucumber *(USA)* Long cucumber [also called **burpless cucumber**]

hot peppers *see* cayenne peppers

hot smoke, to To smoke food at a temperature between 40 and 105°C thus cooking it at the same time. Food is usually cold smoked first and fish is restricted to 80°C

hot and sour soup *(Ch)* A Pekinese soup or broth with vegetables, mushrooms, threads of egg, soya sauce, vinegar and spices including hot chillis. Thickened with cornflour to a runny consistency

hot water pastry A strong dense pastry used for hand raised meat pies made from flour, fat and water and/or milk (2:1:1) boiled together. Moulded whilst warm

hotategai *(Ja)* Scallop, served raw in sushi or fried

hotchpotch A thin stew of lamb or mutton and vegetables similar to Irish stew

hotel rolls White crusty rolls, the tops of which are slashed after proving so that when baked the crust opens in a cross

hôtelière, à l' *(Fr)* In the style of a hotelier, i.e. garnished with maître d'hôtel butter and chopped fried mushrooms, esp. of fish

hotpot A casserole of meat or fish and vegetables baked in the oven with a topping of either sliced potatoes which become brown and crisp when done or a pastry crust; *see also* Lancashire hotpot

houblon *(Fr) masc.* Hops

hough of beef *see* skink of beef

hough of pork *(UK) coll. (Scotland)* The knuckle half of a leg of pork

hou goo *(Ch)* Oyster mushroom

houmous *see* hummus

houmus *see* hummus

house lamb *(UK)* Milk fed lamb

house leek A hardy evergreen perennial succulent *Sempervivum tectorum* which grows in clusters of rosettes on walls and roofs. The leaves are used in salads by the Dutch

household flour *see* plain flour

houtic *(Ho)* Houting, the fish

houting A freshwater white fish *Coregonus oxyrhynchus* and *C. lavaretus* from the northern rivers of Europe and Asia

hovdessert *(Sw)* Meringues with chocolate sauce and whipped cream, sometimes with chopped bananas and/or whipped cream

Hovis The name of bread made with Hovis flour

Hovis flour Flour milled by a process which preserves the wheat germ from degredation. The name was derived from the latin 'homines vis', i.e. strength of man

howtowdie *(UK)* A Scottish dish of boiled chicken with poached eggs and spinach

hoy kwai *(Ch)* Turtle

hoy lai *(Th)* Surf clam

hoy meng phu *(Th)* Asian mussel

hoy nangrom *(Th)* Oyster

ho yo jeung *(Ch)* Oyster

hrachová polevká *(Cz)* Beef stock thickened with a white roux, simmered with onions, garlic and marjoram, mixed with a purée of yellow split peas, strained and garnished with diced fried pigs' ears, potatoes, croûtons and chopped parsley

hramsa *(UK)* A mixture of Scottish Cabroc cheese and double cream flavoured with chopped wild garlic (ransoms) leaves, served as a dessert or a dip

Hrudka *see* Gomolya

hsien ts'ai *(Ch)* Chinese spinach

htamin *(Bm)* Rice

htamin lethoke *(Bm)* A platter or platters of cold, cooked long grain rice, various types of noodles and vegetables served to guests who pick up a selection with their fingers and mix them in their own bowl with small amounts of sauces, condiments and other spicy or pungent accompaniments always using their fingers. Lit. finger mixed rice

huachinango *(Me)* Red snapper

hua daio *(Ch)* Shaohsing rice wine

hua hom *(Th)* Onion

hua jiao *(Ch)* Sichuan peppercorn

hua jiao you *(Ch)* Sichuan pepper oil

hua juan *(Ch)* Steamed bread rolls

huang chiu *(Ch)* Shaohsing rice wine

huang gwa *(Ch)* Cucumber

huang you *(Ch)* Butter

huang yu *(Ch)* Croaker, the fish

hua pak had *(Th)* Mooli

hua sheng *(Ch)* Peanuts

hua sheng you *(Ch)* Peanut oil

hua tiao *(Ch)* Shaohsing rice wine

hubbard squash A very warty-skinned winter squash, eaten at the green unripe stage as well as in the orange mature stage. Common in the USA

hu chiao *(Ch)* Anise pepper

huchiao *(Ch)* Peppercorn

hucho A freshwater fish found in the rivers of northern Europe. Prepared like salmon [also called **huck**]

huck *see* hucho

huckleberry 1 *see* bilberry **2** *(USA)* The fruit of a small bush *Garlussacia frondosa* related to the blueberry. It is up to 1 cm in diameter and has a sweet and juicy flesh

hueso *(Sp)* Bone

hueso medular *(Sp)* Marrow bone

hueva *(Sp)* Hard fish roe

huevos *(Sp)* Eggs

huevos duros *(Sp)* Hard boiled eggs

huevos escalfados *(Sp)* Shirred eggs

huevos a la flamenco *(Sp)* Eggs baked with chopped tomatoes, onions and ham and garnished with asparagus tips, red sweet peppers and slices of pork sausage

huevos al horno *(Sp)* Baked eggs

huevos medio cocidos *(Sp)* Poached eggs

huevos al nido *(Sp)* Egg yolks cooked in small bread rolls and covered with white of egg. Lit. eggs in a nest

huevos pasados por agua *(Sp)* Soft boiled eggs

huevos al plato *(Sp)* Shirred eggs

huevos revueltos *(Sp)* Scrambled eggs

huevos al trote *(Sp)* Hard boiled eggs, halved lengthways, egg yolks mixed with tuna fish and mayonnaise and replaced

huff juffs *(USA) see* Baptist cake

huffkin *(UK)* As Kentish huffkin but formed in large oval flat loaves weighing about 750 g

Huhn *(Ge)* Chicken

Huhn mit Käsesauce *(He)* Boiled chicken with cheese sauce

Hühnerbein *(Ge)* Chicken leg

Hühnerbraten *(Ge)* Roast chicken

Hühnerbrühe *(Ge)* Chicken broth

Hühnerbrust *(Ge)* Chicken breast

Hühnerklein *(Ge)* Chicken giblets

hui *(Ch)* Lengthy simmering of tough foods to tenderize them

huile *(Fr) fem.* Oil

huile, à l' *(Fr)* Served with olive oil or other oil or with a dressing made from the same

huile blanche *(Fr) fem.* Poppy seed oil

huile de colza *(Fr) fem.* Rapeseed oil

huile de coton *(Fr) fem.* Cottonseed oil

huile de noix *(Fr)* Walnut oil

huile d'olive *(Fr) fem.* Olive oil

huile de tournesol *(Fr) fem.* Sunflower seed oil

huile vierge *(Fr) fem.* First pressing of oil bearing berries or seeds

huitlacoche *(Me)* An edible fungus *Ustilago maydis* which infects green maize cobs causing the kernels to grow large, black and deformed but with a pleasant taste.

huître *(Fr) fem.* Oyster, originally the European flat oyster

huître de claire *(Fr) fem. see* claire

huître portugaise *(Fr) fem.* Portuguese oyster

huîtres Dubarry *(Fr) fem.* Oysters served in potato cases

huîtres, sauce aux *(Fr) fem.* Sauce normande with the addition of poached and bearded oysters. Used for poached fish

hu jiao miar *(Ch)* Pepper

hull, to To remove the outer inedible covering of

a fruit or seed or the remains of the flower calyx and stalk from berry fruits

hulled corn *see* hominy

Hülsenfrüchte *(Ge)* Pulses

hu luo bo *(Ch)* Carrots

hu ma *(Ch)* Sesame seed

humba *(Ph)* A type of Spanish estofado q.v. but with vinegar and possibly bean curd

humble pie *(UK)* A meat pie made from offal. The name is derived from the old French "nombles" meaning edible entrails of a deer [also called **umble pie**]

Humbolt dressing *(USA)* A seasoned mixture of crab butter and mayonnaise used with crab meat

Hummer *(Ge)* Lobster

hummer *(De, No & Sw)* Lobster

hummer-kotletter *(Sw)* Lobster cutlets made from hen lobster meat, coral, egg yolk and a little egg white, anchovy essence, seasoning, sugar and nutmeg, processed, formed into cutlet shape, panéed and shallow fried in butter. Served with melted butter and lobster coral

Hummerkrabben *(Ge)* Large prawns

hummerstuvning *(Sw)* Lobster stew sometimes translated as lobster Newburg. Cream and the water from making lobster butter made into a velouté and cooked out. Cut up lobster meat, seasoning, ground cloves and a little brandy added and the whole warmed but not boiled. Served as soon as the lobster meat is cooked through. Excessive cooking toughens the meat

hummus *(ME)* **1** A purée of cooked chick peas **2** An appetizer, dip or hors d'oeuvre made from cooked chick peas puréed with olive oil mixed with tahini, garlic paste and lemon juice, dressed with olive oil and garnished with chopped parsley. Often accompanied by black olives and pitta bread; *see also* hummus-bi-tahina [also called **homos, houmus, houmous, humus**]

hummus-bi-tahina *(ME)* The classic hummus of Syria made from soaked chick peas boiled and skimmed until tender with a little bicarbonate of soda added to the water, puréed with garlic and mixed with tahina paste equal to two thirds of the weight of the dry chick peas, chilli powder, ground cumin, lemon juice and salt. Garnished with olive oil, lemon juice, chopped parsley and cumin and a few whole cooked chick peas

humpback salmon *see* pink salmon

Humulus lupulus *Bot.* Hop

humus *see* hummus

Hunan Chinese province north of Kwantung, with a similar style of cuisine to Cantonese

hundred year egg *see* Chinese preserved eggs

hundreds and thousands Fine (to 1mm dia) multicoloured strands or balls of sugar, used as a cake decoration [also called **nonpareille** (Fr)]

hundredweight A measure of weight used for large quantities of goods. Now obsolete in the UK but still used in the USA. In the UK it is equal to 112 lb and in the USA to 100 lb. Abbreviated to cwt

Hundshai *(Ge)* Larger spotted dogfish

hung *(Vi)* A type of mint

Hungarian butter *see* beurre de paprika

Hungarian goulash An authentic Hungarian stew containing cubed beef, fried onions, green sweet peppers, tomatoes, garlic, pasta, stock and caraway seeds. Not thickened [also called **borgrács gulyas**]

Hungarian millet *see* foxtail millet

Hungarian salami A well spiced lightly smoked salami made from fatty pork. It keeps well and the flavour improves with age

Hungarian sauce *see* sauce hongroise

hung jo *(Ch)* Jujube

hung liu *(Ch)* Five spice powder

hung que *(Vi)* Mint

hungry rice A variety of millet *Digitaria exilis* important as a staple in the dry areas of West Africa

hung zao *(Ch)* Jujube

hunter's sauce *see* sauce chasseur

hunter's sausage *see* Jagdwurst

Huntingdon fidget pie *(UK) see* fidget pie

Huntsman *(UK)* A speciality cheese from Melton Mowbray consisting of a layer of blue Stilton between two layers of double Gloucester

hun tun *(Ch)* Won ton wrappers

hunyadi töltöt *(Hu)* An escalope of sirloin steak covered with a mixture of butter creamed with egg yolk, chopped ham, sliced macaroni and stiffly beaten egg white, rolled and tied, seasoned, browned in lard then stewed with a little brown stock, fried onion slices, thinly sliced sweet green peppers and plenty of paprika with sour cream added at the half cooked stage

hunza Small wild apricots from the Himalayas

with a delicious flavour. Usually traded in the dried form when they are pale brown and wrinkled. Ideal soaked and poached

huo tui *(Ch)* Ham

hure *(Fr) fem.* Head of pig or boar

hure de sanglier *(Fr) fem.* Boar's head

hús *(Hu)* Meat

hush puppies *(USA)* Deep fried dumplings from the southern states of the USA made from a cornmeal batter flavoured with onions and served with fried fish. Used to be thrown to dogs to keep them quiet

Hushållsost *(Sw)* A semi-soft, scalded-curd, pale and mild creamy cows' milk cheese shaped like a cylinder. It has a slightly open texture and some holes. Sometimes flavoured with cloves and cumin and covered in wax or plastic

husk 1 The outer bran layer of cereals and seeds **2** The empty shell of a nut

huss *see* dogfish

hussaini kabab *(In)* Nuts and raisins formed into cylinders and coated with a bound minced beef, then pan fried or grilled

hussarde, à la *(Fr)* In the style of the hussar, i.e. garnished with aubergines, stuffed potatoes, grated horseradish and possibly mushrooms, esp. applied to joints of meat

hussarde, sauce *(Fr) fem.* Finely sliced onions and shallots, browned in butter, white wine added and reduced by half, demi-glace sauce, tomato purée, white stock, garlic, a BG and a piece of raw ham added and all simmered 30 minutes, strained, ham reserved and the sauce finished with finely chopped reserved ham, a little grated horseradish and chopped parsley. Served with grilled or spit roasted meat

hustlers *(USA) see* Baptist cake

hu tieu *(Vi) see* banh pho

hutspot *(Ho)* A type of Irish stew or hotpot of meat with carrots, onions and mashed potatoes

Hüttenkäse *(Ge)* Cottage cheese

Hutzelbrot *(Ge)* Fruit bread

huzarensla *(Ho)* Russian salad, a mayonnaise bound salad of diced meat, apples, beetroot and potatoes with pickles. Lit. Hussar's salad

hvalk kjøtt *(No)* Whale meat

hveteboller *(No)* Sweet bread rolls

hvid *(De)* White

hvide bønner *(De)* Kidney beans

hvidløg *(De)* Garlic

hvidløgssmør *(De)* Garlic butter

hvidvinssovs *(De)* White wine sauce

hvit *(No)* White

hvitkålsalat *(No)* Coleslaw

hvitløk *(No)* Garlic

hvitting *(No)* Whiting, the fish

hyacinth bean A warm climate legume *Lablab purpureus* from India now cultivated worldwide. The whole pods which range in colour from green to purple may be treated as French beans when young or the dried beans which are brown with a white hilum may be used as a pulse. The beans must be well boiled before eating. They may also be sprouted in the dark for bean sprouts [also called **Egyptian bean, lablab bean, dolichos bean, bonavist bean, black bean**]

hydrochloric acid The acid secreted in the stomach which maintains the pH of the contents around 2, thus inhibiting or killing bacteria and helping with the breakdown of food. A permitted food additive, (E)507, in the UK

hydrogen A highly inflammable light gas occasionally used in sealed packaging, more often for hydrogenating vegetable and fish oils in order to harden them

hydrogen sulphites Salts similar to the sulphites but containing a higher proportion of sulphur dioxide, used as food preservatives in the food industry. Those permitted are sodium hydrogen sulphite, E222, and calcium hydrogen sulphite, E227.

hydrogenated glucose syrup A modified glucose syrup used in sugar free confectionery

hydrogenation The process of chemically combining hydrogen with unsaturated oils and soft fats to make them more saturated and harder. Used to make margarine and lard substitutes from oils. Doubts are being cast on the wholesomeness of the resulting hard fats many of which have no natural analogs

hydrolysed protein Protein which has been broken down into smaller sub units *(peptides)* by treatment with water at high temperature and pressure or other hydrolysing agents. This produces highly-flavoured compounds as in yeast and meat extracts amd also occurs during fermentation of proteins (soya sauce, miso, tempeh, etc.) and to a limited extent when cooking proteins

hydrolysis The reaction of water molecules with other compounds, usually to break them down into smaller sub units and requiring the action of acids, enzymes or long heating. It is used for example to convert starch into simpler sugars and is the process which occurs when starch solutions and sauces are thinned by boiling them too long

hydrometer A short stubby cylinder surmounted with a long graduated tube. The whole is sealed and weighted so that it floats upright in a liquid always displacing its own mass of liquid thus indicating by the depth to which it sinks the density or specific gravity of the liquid. Used for measuring alcohol, salt and sugar concentrations in solution

hygiene The general term for those procedures and practices which prevent the transmission of disease between and to humans, the multiplication of harmful microorganisms in the body or environment and the accumulation of dirt, poisons and toxins where they could be harmful to living creatures

hylderbærsuppe *(De)* Elderberry soup

hyoshi-giri *(Ja)* Baton cut for root vegetables [also called **clapper cut**]

hyse *(No)* Haddock

hysope *(Fr) fem.* Hyssop

hyssop A hardy semi-evergreen shrub *Hyssopus officinalis* whose leaves can be used in small amounts to flavour game, pâtés, soups, lamb stews and fruits

Hyssopus officinalis *Bot.* Hyssop

Ii

i'a lawalu Fish baked in taro leaves, a speciality of Hawaii

iahnie de ciuperce *(Ro)* Chopped onions fried lightly in oil followed by sliced mushrooms until all browned, tomato concassée or purée, seasoning and chopped dill added and all served cold

iahnie de fasole *(Ro)* Cooked navy or haricot beans mixed whilst hot with sliced fried onions, oil, lemon juice, seasoning and chopped dill and served cold

ibu roti *(Ma)* Khamir

iç pilav *(Tu)* A pilaf made from round short grain rice, fried onions and pine nuts, chopped lamb's liver, currants, tomato, cinnamon and seasoning, braised in water in the oven in a covered dish [also called **Turkish pilaf**]

ice Frozen water sometimes used in place of water where intense agitation or prolonged processing might overheat a mixture. The energy necessary to melt ice would heat the same mass of water by 80°C. Also used for cooling

ice, to To cover or decorate cakes, biscuits, buns, etc. with icing

ice cream A flavoured, sweetened and coloured mixture of (egg) custard and cream (substitute) rapidly frozen to a stiff paste to avoid the formation of large detectable ice crystals. Used as a dessert and for many made up desserts

ice cream sundae Individual portions of ice cream topped with canned or fresh fruit, whipped cream, chocolate or other sweet sauce and chopped nuts. Used for a dessert

ice glaze, to To add a thin layer of ice to frozen food by spraying with or dipping in water. It is said to preserve freshness and flavour but is usually used to increase apparent weight. Common with frozen prawns

iceberg lettuce A crisphead, tightly packed ball lettuce with the outer leaves removed and with little flavour. Ideal for shredding or for a chiffonade

icebox pie *(USA)* A pie with a filling which is chilled or frozen to make it firm

iced fancies Small sponge cakes completely covered with flavoured fondant icing and decorated

Iceland moss An edible lichen *Cetraria islandica* resembling a dark carragheen from mountainous and arctic regions. It grows to 1.2 m in length and is prepared by soaking it in boiling water with sodium bicarbonate to remove the bitter flavour, then soaking in water overnight. Used like carragheen or may be dried and ground to make a flour

Iceland scallop A small species of scallop *Chlamys islandica* fished in the northern Atlantic

iceplant A sprawling succulent plant *Mesambryanthemum crystallinum* whose fleshy leaves and young stems may be used raw in salads or cooked like spinach

ichiban dashi *(Ja) see* dashi

ichigo *(Ja)* Strawberries

ichimi *(Ja)* Flaked red peppers

icho giri *(Ja)* A quarter round cut of vegetables, esp. large and tapering root vegetables [also called **ginkgo leaf cut**]

icing A paste formed from icing sugar and water with possible additions of lemon juice, egg white, glycerine, colouring and flavouring, used to coat cakes and buns, etc. for decorative purposes; *see also* American frosting, glacé icing, fondant, royal icing, transparent icing

icing bag *see* piping bag

icing sugar Very finely ground sugar with no particles larger than 0.1 mm (100 microns) used to make icing, to dredge desserts and cakes, etc. for decoration, and to make some confectionery items

ICMSF The International Commission on Microbiological Standards for Foods which sets standards for assigning foods to various classes of health hazard ranging from case 1, no health hazard and low incidence of spoilage, to case 15, severe and direct health hazard possibly influenced by conditions of handling

Idiazabal *(Sp)* A smoked ewes' milk cheese from the Basque country. It is firm with a few holes and has a mild smoky flavour [also called **aralar, urbasa, urbia**]

idli *(In)* Small steamed cakes served with spices, coconut or other flavourings as an accompaniment to a main dish. Made from a batter of rice flour and urad dhal which has been left to ferment overnight

iets vooraf *(Ho)* Appetizer

igat *(Ph)* Eel

igname *(It & Fr) fem.* Yam

Igny *(Fr)* A mild cows' milk cheese made in the shape of a disc, from the abbey of the same name in Champagne

iguana A large lizard *Iguana iguana* up to 2 m long from Central and South America with white tender mild-flavoured meat generally more expensive than beef or fish

ijs *(Ho)* Ice cream, ice

ika *(Ja)* Cuttlefish and squid, used raw in sushi

ikan alu-alu *(Id)* Barracuda

ikan bawal hitam *(Id)* Black pomfret, the fish

ikan bawal putih *(Id)* White pomfret, the fish

ikan berinti *(Ma)* Stuffed fish

ikan bilis *(Ma)* Small fish such as anchovy and similar, cooked, dried in the sun then deep fried. Used as an addition to other dishes [also called **ikan teri**]

ikan karau *(Id)* A fish similar to salmon

ikan kembung *(Id)* A fish similar to a small bonito

ikan merah *(Id)* Snapper or bream

ikan merah puchat *(Id & Ma)* Snapper or bream

ikan teri *(Id & Ma) see* ikan bilis

ikan terubuk *(Id)* Herring

ikra *(Ru)* Caviar

ikura *(Ja)* The large (0.5 cm dia) orange-red eggs of salmon. Often used in sushi [also called **caviar pearls, keta caviar, salmon caviar**]

ilama A custard apple *Anona diversifolia* growing in lowland tropics and similar to the cherimoya

Ilchester *(UK)* A beer and garlic-flavoured Cheddar cheese

îles flottantes *(En & Fr) fem.* A thin egg custard topped with spoonfuls of poached meringue mixture and finished with a sprinkling of crushed praline or caramel. Served cold

Ilha *(Po)* A Cheddar type cows' milk cheese from the Azores. Lit. island

Illicium verum *Bot.* Star anise

illipe butter *(In) see* mowra butter

illustrierte Salatgurke *(Ge)* A compound salad of sliced pickled cucumbers alternated with slices of Emmenthal and anchovy fillets garnished with ham cornets filled with capers and halved hard boiled eggs.

imam bayaldi *(ME) see* abou ganouje

imamdusta *(In)* A ceramic mortar used for grinding soft grains and spices using a matching pestle *(daanti)*

imbiancare *(It)* To blanch

Imbiss *(Ge)* Snack

imbottini delizia *(It)* Paupiettes of veal stuffed with ham, cheese and truffle shavings

imbottito *(It)* Stuffed

imbrecciata *(It)* A chick pea, bean and lentil soup from Umbria

imbriaco *(Sp)* Red mullet *Mullus barbatus*

imitation caviar A product made from the hard female roe of some types of fish just before spawning. It is washed, sieved to remove fibre, salted (1:6 or less on roe), kept 2 to 3 days, drained, surface dried and pressed into jars. It goes under names such as lumpfish caviar, German caviar, etc.

imli *(In)* Tamarind

impanato *(It)* Panéed or coated with bread crumbs

impastare *(It)* To knead

impastoiata *(It)* A mixture of polenta and beans from Umbria served with a tomato sauce

impératrice, à l' *(Fr)* The name given to enriched dishes and cakes see e.g. riz à l'impératrice

imperial agaric *see* ovoli

impériale, à l' *(Fr)* In the imperial style, i.e. chicken garnished with foie gras, mushrooms and cockscombs or kidneys

inaka-miso *(Ja)* A red coloured miso usually made with barley as the added grain. May be sweet or salty. Used in soups and stews [also called **sendai-miso, red miso**]

inari *(Ja)* A sushi product, see age

inari-zushi *(Ja)* A sushi packed into an aburage (deep fried bean curd pouch)

incanestrato *see* canestrato

incasciata *(It)* A mixture of noodles, chopped hard boiled eggs and shredded meat

incassettato *(It)* Encased, e.g. in pastry

incir *(Tu)* Figs

incise, to To cut deep slits in raw food, e.g. to aid penetration of a marinade or tenderizer or to insert garlic, herbs or spices

inconnu *(Cn & USA)* A white fleshed oily freshwater fish *Leucichthys mackenzii* with a protruding lower jaw, from the great lakes of Canada. It has a silver grey back and white underside and weighs up to 4 kg. Use as salmon

Indian bread *(USA)* Cornmeal bread

Indian butter tree A tree *Madhuca indica* and *M. longifolia* from central India. The dried flowers are used as food and the seeds are the source of mowra butter

Indian corn *(USA)* An alternative name for the maize which is generally known in the USA as corn

Indian cress *see* nasturtium

Indian date *see* tamarind

Indian dill A plant *Anethum sowa* similar to the European dill but with longer and narrower seeds and a slightly different flavour

Indian fig *see* prickly pear

Indian jujube *see* jujube

Indian lotus *see* lotus

Indian millet *see* common millet

Indian mustard *see* brown mustard seed

Indian nut Pine nut

Indian oyster A small rectangular-shaped oyster *Crassostrea cucullata* with a pink margin on its black shell, found throughout the coasts of SEA and Japan. Usually cooked by simmering, see e.g. kaki-miso, or quick frying and using in filled omelettes

Indian pear *see* prickly pear

Indian pudding *(USA)* A traditional pudding made from cornmeal, milk, butter, treacle, eggs and spices. Similar to hasty pudding

Indian rice *see* wild rice

Indian spinach *see* amaranths and Ceylon spinach

Indian sweet lime *see* sweet lime

Indianerkrapfen *(Au)* A light pastry dipped in chocolate and filled with whipped cream

indienne, à l' *(Fr)* In the Indian style, i.e. Indian style cooking, highly spiced, etc.

indienne, sauce *(Fr) fem. see* sauce currie à l'indienne

indigo carmine E132, a synthetic blue food colouring [also called **indigotine**]

indigotine *see* indigo carmine

indisches Ragoutpulver *(Ge)* Curry powder

indivia belga *(It)* Belgium chicory

indmad *(De)* Giblets, offal

indring *(Id)* Hairy basil

indyeika *(Ru)* Turkey

infarinata *(It)* A Tuscan dish of polenta cooked with beans, bacon and cabbage, cooled and eaten cold or sliced and fried

infiammato *(It)* Flambéed

infra-red That portion of the electromagnetic spectrum which is used in cooking to transfer heat by radiation from a hot surface to the food as in a grill, barbecue, electric or halogen hob

infuse, to To bring a liquid into contact with some food, herb or spice so as to transfer aroma, taste and soluble components to the liquid from which the solid material is strained. e.g. brewing of coffee or tea, extraction of vanilla from a pod and of aromatics from a BG

infuser A small perforated closed container which allows boiling water to come into contact with tea, herbs, spices, etc. thus extracting flavour from the solid

ingee *(In)* Ginger

ingefaer brød *(De)* Gingerbread

ingefära *(Sw)* Ginger

ingemaakte vruchten *(Ho)* Canned fruit

ingen *(Ja)* Runner beans

inguru *(Sr)* Ginger

Ingwer *(Ge)* Ginger

Ingwerbrot *(Ge)* Gingerbread

Ingwerkuche *(USA)* A ginger cake introduced by Dutch immigrants to Pennsylvania

inhame *(Po)* Yam

inihaw *(Ph)* A description of fish, poultry or meat grilled on skewers over the heat source

injera *(Af)* A round, sour-tasting flat bread from East Africa resembling pitta bread, made from millet flour, yeast and water using the sourdough method. It has the texture of tripe and is eaten with stews

ink cap *see* shaggy ink cap

inkfish *see* squid

inkokt ål *(Sw)* Boiled eel often served cold at

the smörgåsbord. Made from pieces of skinned eel simmered in a white wine court bouillon for 25 minutes

inlagd gurka *(Sw)* Thinly sliced cucumber marinated in vinegar, sugar and water, drained and served with a garnish of chopped dill and parsley

inlagd sill *(Sw)* Salt herring soaked in water for at least 12 hours, washed and drained, cleaned, boned and filleted and marinated in vinegar and water (5:2), sugar, white pepper, bay leaves and sliced shallots. Served with the marinade coloured with betroot juice

innards Internal organs of an animal esp. in the abdominal cavity [also called **guts, viscera**]

inosine 5'-disodium phosphate *see* (E)631

inositol A water-soluble carbohydrate which is found in fruits and cereals either free or combined. It has a role in fat metabolism and also appears to be essential for the transmission of nerve impulses as the concentration in nerves is much higher than in the blood and is correlated with the speed of response, since both decline with age. It is also a major constituent of human semen. It has no known toxicity

insaccati *(It) coll.* Sausages. Lit. in a bag

insalata *(It)* Salad

insalata alla moda d'alba *(It)* A salad of asparagus, celery and truffles

insalata capricciosa *(It)* A salad made from a julienne of celeriac, ham, tongue and mushrooms bound with mayonnaise

insalata composta *(It)* Salade composée

insalata cotta e cruda *(It)* A salad of mixed cooked vegetables and raw salad greens

insalata di mare *(It)* Seafood salad

insalata mista *(It)* Mixed salad.

insalata paesana *(It)* A peasant salad of potatoes, eggs and vegetables, all cooked and cooled

insalata di rinforzo *(It)* A salad of anchovies, capers and olives, topped up daily with the same or similar items as part is consumed

insalata russa *(It)* Russian salad

insalata siciliana *(It)* Stuffed tomatoes with anchovies

insalata verde *(It)* Green salad, usually of only one type of leaf

insalatine *(It)* Salad greens

insalato *(It)* Salted

insalatone *(It)* A mixed salad of cooked vegetables

insolation A method of drying food by exposing it to the sun. Used for meat, fish and fruit

instant food Food which has been prepared and dehydrated in such a way that it is immediately useable on adding (boiling) water. Coffee, tea, soup and noodles are typical examples

instant rice *see* precooked rice

integrale *(It)* Wholemeal, bread, flour, etc.

integument The barrier around natural food items such as egg shell and vegetable or fruit peel, which provides a barrier to microbial invasion of the food

intercosta *(It)* A small entrecôte steak

interiora *(It)* Offal, innards

interlard, to *(USA) see* lard, to

international kidney *see* Jersey royal, the potato

International Library of Gastronomy A library of over 3,500 rare books related to cooking and gastronomy from the 14th to the 19th century assembled by Arazio Bagnasco in Lugano Switzerland. Address: Bibliothèque Internationale de Gastronomie, Casella Postale 33, 6924 Soprengo (Lugano) Switzerland

intestines That part of an animal's digestive system between the last stomach and the rectum which forms a tube or in some cases a blind sac. After cleaning they may be used as sausage casings, eaten after preparation or incorporated into manufactured foods. See chitterlings, andouille, casings, etc.

intingolo *(It)* Sauce, gravy, tasty dish, sometimes stew

in umido *(It)* Braised, stewed

invernengo *(It) see* Parmigiano Reggiano

invert sugar Simple sugars *(monosaccharides)* whose configuration has been changed by heat, enzyme or acid treatment so that they will not crystallize and will prevent other sugars from crystallizing

invertase An enzyme obtained from *Saccharomyces cerevisiae* that is used to prevent granulation in thick sugar syrups and fondants

involtini *(It)* Slices of meat, ham and cheese rolled together and served in broth

involtini di vitello *(It)* Paupiettes of veal stuffed and cooked as beef olives

involtino *(It)* A roll or roulade (not bread)

iodine A trace element required for health esp. of the thyroid gland, now included in iodized salt but available particularly from shell fish, seawater fish and seaweed

iodized salt Salt to which potassium iodide or iodate (a source of iodine) is added in order to overcome any deficiencies of iodine in the diet, esp. in certain parts of the country where iodine is not present in the soil or drinking water

ionizing radiation Electromagnetic radiation which causes chemical changes in materials through which it passes, in particular ionization of compounds and production of short-lived free radicals which cause the death of living organisms. It is used for the sterilization of food in hermetically sealed packs, for the reduction in amount of spoilage flora on perishable foods, for the elimination of pathogens in foods, for the control of infestation in stored cereals, for the prevention of sprouting of root vegetables in storage and for retardation of the development of picked mushrooms (e.g. opening of the caps). Unfortunately there is no current legislation requiring the labelling of foods so treated

iota *(It) see* jota

Ipomoea aquatica *Bot.* Swamp cabbage

Ipomoea batatas *Bot.* The sweet potato plant

Ipomoea reptans *Bot.* Swamp cabbage

ippoglosso *(It)* Flounder

Iraty *(Fr)* A strong cheese from the Basque county made from a mixture of cows' and ewes' milk. The flavour depends on the proportions of each milk which in turn depends on the season

Iraty brebis pyrénées *(Fr)* A semi-hard ewes' milk cheese from the Basque region, made in 4 to 5 kg cylinders. It is matured for 3 months and has a golden mellow tasting paste with small holes. Farm produced cheeses have AOC status

iri dori *(Ja)* A chicken casserole made from pieces of skinned chicken breast, reconstituted shiitake mushroom caps, carrot and bamboo shoot browned in oil then simmered in dashi, mirin and sugar for 10 minutes. Soya sauce is added and the cooking liquor reduced to a quarter. Peas, sliced onions, cauliflower or any other quickly cooked vegetables are added and cooked a further 3 minutes

irio *(Af)* Seasoned mashed potatoes mixed with sweet corn kernels, green peas and cooked green bananas or plantains. A speciality from East Africa

Irish moss *see* carragheen

Irish potato cake *(UK)* A paste of mashed potatoes, flour, butter and salt rolled out to 8 - 10 mm, cut into triangles and fried until brown on both sides [also called **fadge**]

Irish soda bread *see* soda bread

Irish stew *(UK)* A stew or casserole of cheap cuts of lamb on the bone with waxy potatoes, onions and seasoning, once popular in the North of England and Northern Ireland

Irish Swiss cheese *see* Blarney

irlandaise, à l' *(Fr)* In the Irish style, i.e. with potatoes

irlandisches Moos *(Ge)* Carragheen

iron A trace element vital for many body processes esp. formation of haemoglobin in the blood. Available in meat, offal, fish, cereals, pulses and vegetables. Vitamin C ingested at the same time as iron-containing foods facilitates absorption in the gut

iron hydroxide E172, various hydrated iron oxides of which ordinary rust is the common example. When finely ground they can be used as a brown food colouring

iron oxide E172, various combinations of iron and oxygen which when finely ground have colours ranging from yellow through brown to black and are used as a food colouring and source of iron

iron rations Emergency food of high calorific value for a given weight, esp. high fat, high protein, chocolate, etc. Often dehydrated or tinned so that they will keep for years for use in emergencies

irradiate, to To treat food with ionizing radiation in order to kill all microorganisms and insects in fruits, cereals, pulses, dried fruits and the like. It also prevents sprouting of roots and tubers. It does not destroy toxins or viruses and may cause chemical changes in the food. Often used to preserve sealed packs of food and to increase the shelf life of perishables. Since no laws govern the labelling of irradiated food it is impossible to know whether it has been treated in this way. Some authorities consider it a dangerous practice

is *(De, No & Sw)* Ice

is longus *(It)* A Sardinian dish of the grilled or spit roasted intestines of cattle

iscas *(Po)* Casserole, a typical one might be tripe with white beans and sausages in a cream sauce

iscas de figado *(Po)* Thinly sliced calves' liver marinated in oil, wine, chopped onion and garlic overnight, drained, dried and fried in small batches in oil for 2 minutes, reserved, then served with the pan residues deglazed with the marinade and reduced by half.

ischiana, all' *(It)* In the style of Ischia, i.e. stewed in oil and white wine with tomatoes and herbs

Ischler biscuits *(Au)* Rich round buttery

biscuits made with a mixture of ground almonds and flour sandwiched in pairs with red jam and covered with chocolate icing

Ischlertörtchen *(Ge)* As Ischler biscuits

ise ebi *(Ja)* Lobster

isinglass **1** An extract from the buoyancy bladders of fish used to clarify liquids esp. wine. Can be used as a gelling agent **2** A solution of sodium silicate in water used to preserve eggs by its reaction with the shell which makes it impervious to air

iskembe çorbasi *(Tu)* Tripe soup flavoured with lemon juice, garlic and vinegar and thickened with a liaison of egg yolks and cream

Islay *(UK)* A miniature Dunlop cheese suitable for melting. When mature eaten for dessert

isleta bread *(USA)* A bread shaped like a bear's paw made by Pueblo Indians

isomalt A modified malt sugar used in sugar-free confectionery and as an extender in some foods

isopropyl alcohol A solvent used for food colours and flavourings and in glass cleaners

issopo *(It)* Hyssop

isterband *(Sw)* A skinless sausage made with minced beef and pork mixed with parboiled barley and possibly mashed potato, salt cured and air dried. May be hot smoked. Split and fried or grilled and served with fried onion and pickled beetroot

ita-kamaboko *(Ja)* A Japanese fish cake *(see* kamaboko), formed on a small rectangle of wood and often grilled or coloured brown

Italian bread sticks *see* grissini

Italian brine A sausage curing solution consisting of equal parts of water and white wine, fully saturated with salt and with 17 g of saltpetre and 8 g of bicarbonate of soda per litre

Italian broccoli *see* calabrese

Italian meringue mixture Sugar syrup boiled to the soft ball stage (115°C) then beaten into egg whites until soft and peaky

Italian millet *see* foxtail millet

Italian parsley *see* parsley *Petroselinum crispum 'Neapolitanum'*

Italian red onion An oval shaped onion somewhat smaller then the globe with a red tinge to the flesh and a mild almost sweet flavour. It makes an attractive garnish when cut in rings. Whitens on cooking. [also called **red onion**]

Italian sandwich *(USA) see* hoagie

Italian sauce *see* sauce italienne

Italian sausage *(USA)* A type of pork sausage which may be hot (peppery) or sweet

Italian white truffle A smooth beige-pink truffle *(Tuber magnatum)* with a stronger aroma than the French black truffle. Best left uncooked

italico *(It)* A generic term for a variety of quick ripening cheeses started with *Streptococcus thermophilus* and ripened for 20 to 30 days. Bel Paese is a well known example. Usually contain 51% water, 25% fat and 21% protein

italienne, à l' *(Fr)* In the Italian style, i.e. with pasta, cheese, mushrooms, tomatoes and sometimes artichokes

italienne, sauce *(Fr) fem.* **1** A mixture of demi-glace, duxelles, chopped lean ham and tomato concassée simmered and finished with chopped parsley, chervil and tarragon. Served with fried lamb or veal **2** A cold sauce of poached brains, puréed, strained and mixed with a lemon juice mayonnaise, seasoning and finely chopped parsley. Served with cold meats

itami udon *(Ja)* Soft fried noodles made from udon noodles boiled in salted water until al dente, drained, refreshed, redrained and oiled, mixed in the frying pan with grated carrot, shredded Chinese cabbage and diced sweet pepper which have all been fried in oil flavoured with chopped garlic and ginger and all fried gently whilst being stirred. Seasoned and sprinkled with soya sauce before serving

itik *(Ma)* Duck

ito *(Ja)* A prefix meaning cut in fine strips

ito-kezuri-katsuo *(Ja)* Fine pink thread-like shavings of dried Pacific bonito flesh used as a garnish

ito konnyaku *(Ja)* A type of konnyaku made by extruding shiritaki noodle mix through multiple holes so that the noodles come together in blocks

ito-zukuri *(Ja)* A type of cut for small fish used for sashimi rather like a julienne, 5 cm by 3 mm square

ivoire, sauce *(Fr) fem.* Suprême sauce with meat glaze added to give an ivory colour. Used with boiled chicken [also called **ivory sauce**]

ivory egg A rare variety of plum tomato with a pale golden yellow skin which contains no lycopeine. This may make it suitable for those allergic to the red fruit. Available in the USA but rare in Europe due to EU regulations

ivory sauce *see* sauce ivoire

ivy gourd *see* tindoori

iwashi *(Ja)* Sardines

iwashi no tsumire jiru *(Ja)* Sardine balls made with fresh, skinned sardine fillets processed with miso, ginger and flour. These are poached in water until they rise then reserved, the cooking liquor strained, salted, flavoured with soya sauce, the cooked sardine balls and cooked turnip slices added and the soup served at once with a lemon peel garnish

iyokan *(Ja)* A naturally occurring hybrid of *Citrus* spp. as yet relatively unknown outside Japan

izer cookie *(USA)* A biscuit baked in a mould with various figures and designs embossed in it

izmir köftesi *(Tu)* A mixture of chopped raw mutton, soaked white breadcrumbs, eggs, onion juice, seasoning and nutmeg, shaped into long rolls, fried in butter then simmered in tomato purée and water

Jj

ja *(Ch)* Deep frying

jääpalanen *(Fi)* (Piece of) ice

jäätellö *(Fi)* Ice cream

jabalí *(Sp)* Wild boar

jabuke u rumo *(Bk)* Apples poached in syrup, chilled and topped with whipped cream, glacé cherries and a little rum. From Slovenia

jachtschotel *(Ho)* A casserole of meat, potatoes and onions, a hunter's dish.

jack 1 *see* crevalle jack **2** *see* Monterey jack

jack bean A perennial legume *Canavalia ensiformis* from tropical America and grown in the southern USA. It has edible white beans which require boiling to destroy toxins and the immature pods can be eaten as a vegetable [also called **horse bean**]

jack-by-the-hedge *see* garlic mustard

jacket potato Washed, cleaned and dried potatoes with skin on, pricked with a fork and baked in an oven, in hot ashes or on a barbecue with or without a covering of aluminium foil until the flesh is soft. Often served cut open with some kind of filling

jackfish *see* pike

jackfruit The Malaysian fruit of a tree *Artocarpus heterophyllus* and *A. integrifolia* which can take up to six months to ripen from picking. The fruit is large (to 32 kg) with a yellow to brown spiky skin and yellow fibrous flesh. The juicy pulp surrounding the large white seeds is eaten and tastes like a mixture of banana and pineapple, the seeds may be dried and roasted or ground and the fibrous flesh is sometimes boiled or baked as a vegetable. The flowers and young leaf shoots are used in salads and as a vegetable [also called **jakfruit**]

Jacobean potatoes Potatoes roasted in their skins

Jacobsmuschel *(Ge)* Coquille Saint-Jacques (scallop) [also called **Pilgermuschel**]

Jaffa orange *see* shamouti

jagaimo *(Ja)* Potato

Jagdwurst *(Ge)* Hunter's sausage. A large Brühwurst of diced pork fat and finely minced lean pork [also called **German garlic sausage, hunter's sausage**]

Jägerart *(Ge)* In the hunter's style, i.e. with mushrooms and wine

jägert *(Ge)* Sautéed with onions.

jaggery 1 *(In)* A crude brown sugar made from the sap of coconut or palmyrah palm trees, sold in round cakes or lumps [also called **gur, palm sugar**] **2** Brown cane sugar, often sold in round sticky balls

jagri *(In)* Jaggery

jagung *(Id & Ma)* Miniature corn

jahe *(Id)* Ginger

jaiba *(Me)* A small crab with a hard shell

jaiphal *(In)* Mace and nutmeg

jajka minsky *(Ru)* Halved hard boiled eggs filled with the yolks mashed with mayonnaise, double cream, chopped dill and parsley and paprika and mixed with chopped white of egg, the filled eggs sprinkled with breadcrumbs and grated cheese, decorated with crossed anchovy fillets and baked for 10 minutes at 200°C and served warm. A traditional Ukrainian dish at Christmas and Easter

jakfruit *see* jackfruit

jalapeño chile *(Me)* A variety of gently tapering hot green Mexican chilli about 6 cm long. Used fresh in curries or pickled for use as a snack food

jalea *(Sp)* Jelly

jalea, en *(Sp)* Jellied.

jalebi *see* jelabi

jälkiruokaa *(Fi)* Sweet, dessert

jalousie *(En & Fr) fem.* A medieval tart consisting of a rectangular puff pastry sheet covered in a sweet filling held in by a thin strip of puff pastry around the sides, this covered with a further sheet of puff pastry cut horizontally to resemble a slatted blind. The French word for slatted blind comes from the name of this tart

Jamaica flower The red flower of a mallow bush *Hibiscus sabdariffa* which originated in Mexico and is now grown in the Caribbean and India, used as a flavouring, as a vegetable and as the basis of sauces. The fruit of the plant can be used to make jam and jelly [also called **Flor de Jamaica, Jamaica sorrel, red sorrel, rosella**]

Jamaica plum *see* hog plum

Jamaica sorrel *see* Jamaica flower

Jamaican pepper *see* allspice

Jamaika Pfeffer *(Ge)* Allspice

jam A fruit preserve made by mixing fruit or boiling it with sugar and water and adding extra gelling agent if required, usually pectin. The high sugar concentration inhibits but does not totally prevent proliferation of microorganisms, so jam is usually bottled hot in sterile jars with a seal, or sterilized after bottling

jam puffs Puff pastry, cut into shapes, cooked, slit in half and filled with jam and whipped cream

jam roly-poly *(UK)* Suet-crust pastry spread with jam, rolled up, wrapped in a cloth or placed in a mould and steamed, boiled or baked.

jam sauce *(UK)* Jam boiled with lemon juice and water, thickened with arrowroot or cornflour if required, cooked out and strained. Traditionally used with steamed or baked puddings

jam sugar Granulated sugar mixed with citric acid and pectin, used for making jam with those fruits that need extra acid and pectin

jam tart A small or large open tart made with sweet pastry filled with jam let down with a little water

jam turnover A diamond shaped piece of pastry, half covered with jam leaving the edges free, the other half folded over, sealed at the edges, pricked and glazed with milk and caster sugar prior to baking

jambalaya *(USA)* A Creole rice dish similar to the Spanish paella including any of chicken, ham, sausage, prawns and crayfish together with fried onions, celery, green pepper cooked with long grain rice, mounded onto a plate and served with tabasco sauce

jambalaya aux chaurices *(USA)* A jambalaya with chopped sausages as the principal meat

jamberry *see* tomate verde

jambon *(Fr) masc.* Ham

jambon des Ardennes *(Fr) masc. see* Ardennes ham

jambon de Bayonne *(Fr) masc. see* Bayonne ham

jambon blanc *(Fr) masc.* An unsmoked or lightly smoked French cooking ham usually boiled [also called **jambon glacé, jambon de Paris**]

jambon de campagne *(Fr) masc.* A locally produced ham for cooking, usually sweet cured and smoked

jambon cru *(Fr) masc.* Raw, air dried ham

jambon cuit de Prague *(Fr) masc. see* Prague ham

jambon fumé *(Fr) masc.* Smoked ham

jambon glacé *(Fr) masc. see* jambon blanc

jambon de Paris *(Fr) masc. see* jambon blanc

jambon persillé *(Fr) masc.* The raw, lean meat from cured shoulder and leg of pork, mixed with a wine-flavoured jelly and chopped parsley, cooked in a mould, cooled until set and turned out [also called **parsley ham**]

jambon de Toulouse *(Fr) masc.* An unsmoked ham that is salted and dried. Eaten raw or cooked

jambonneau *(Fr) masc.* **1** Pork hock or knuckle from either the front or hind leg **2** A small knuckle of ham

jambonnette *(Fr) fem.* A saucisson sec from Vivarais shaped to look like a ham

jambos *see* Surinam cherry

jambu air *(Id & Ma)* Water apple

jamón *(Sp)* Ham

jamón serrano *(Sp)* A high quality salted and air dried ham, matured for 18 months. Eaten raw. It should be made from free range lean black Iberian pigs and weigh between 6 and 8 kg. Fakes weigh less. It is salted for 10 days, lightly brined and hung for a least a year [also called **mountain ham**]

Jamswurzel *(Ge)* Yam

jamu *(Ja)* Jam

jamur *(Id & Ma)* Straw mushroom

jamur hitam *(Id)* Shiitake mushroom

jamur tiram *(Id & Ma)* Oyster mushroom

jan coude mai marge *(Ca)* A stew of salt beef, salt pork, red kidney beans, yellow yams and other vegetables flavoured with thyme and coconut oil. From St Lucia

jan hagel *(Ho)* Finger biscuits flavoured with cinnamon and topped with flaked almonds and sugar

jan in de zak *(Ho)* A steamed pudding with currants and raisins

jang yau see yau *(Ch)* Dark soya sauce

janis *(Fi)* Hare

Janssons frestelse *(Sw)* *see* Jansson's temptation

Jansson's temptation *(Sw)* A traditional casserole of grated raw potatoes, chopped onions, butter, anchovy fillets or strips of matjes herring and cream baked to a golden crust. Reputed to have tempted a religious fanatic from his vow to give up earthly pleasures of the flesh. Often served at the end of a party when it is supposed to tempt guests to stay longer

jantar *(Po)* Dinner

jao lei *(Ch)* A wire mesh strainer or spider used to manipulate food in water or oil

Japanese artichoke *see* Chinese artichoke

Japanese aubergine A small (to 7 cm long) cylindrical or pear shaped aubergine often cooked as tempura

Japanese black mushroom *see* hoshi-shiitake mushroom

Japanese broiled vegetables Vegetables such as leeks, courgettes, sweet peppers, aubergines and mushrooms, threaded on skewers, oiled, grilled until brown, brushed with a mixture of miso, sugar and mirin and reheated under the grill for a further 2 minutes. Served immediately

Japanese bunching onion *see* oriental bunching onion

Japanese chestnut A large but inferior chestnut *Castanea crenata* which has replaced the native American chestnut which was lost to the blight

Japanese cucumber A small ridge cucumber with the characteristic skin. Most varieties are quite small (to 5 cm) with very thin skin and small seeds. Slices are used as a garnish for sushi and sashimi

Japanese fish balls *see* kamaboko

Japanese fish sausage *see* kamaboko

Japanese gelatine *see* agar agar

Japanese ginger sauce Chicken glace de viande, soya sauce, grated ginger root, minced spring onions and soft brown sugar combined to give a thickish sauce adding water if necessary. Used with sukiyaki

Japanese horse radish *see* wasabi

Japanese meat balls Finely minced or double minced beef, mixed with minced spring onions, grated ginger root, flour, soya sauce and egg to make a thick paste, formed into balls and normally deep fried

Japanese medlar *see* loquat

Japanese millet An Asian coarse grass *Echinocloa frumentacea* grown for its seeds which are eaten as porridge or with rice

Japanese omelette Eggs beaten with a little dashi and salt, cooked in a rectangular omelette pan *(maki yakinabe)*, rolled up, and this repeated 2 more times each time rolling the omelette around the previous roll. It is then sliced. Often the egg is layered with some contrasting coloured ingredient before rolling

Japanese oyster *see* Pacific oyster

Japanese parsley *see* mitsuba

Japanese pear *see* Asian pear

Japanese pepper *see* anise pepper

Japanese plum A small round yellow, orange or red plum from China *Prunus salicina* or *P. triflora* [also called **salicine plum**]

Japanese quince *see* japonica

Japanese radish *see* mooli or daikon

Japanese red prawn One of the famous large prawns *Penaeus nipponensis* of Japan, up to 20 cm long

Japanese rice *(USA)* A variety of hard short grain rice which is greyish white and translucent with a dark mark in the centre

Japanese rice vinegar A mild clear rice vinegar which is not very strong. The aroma is pleasant but quickly disappears on exposure to the air. Used as a dressing for the salads sunomono and aemono

Japanese rice wine *see* sake

Japanese sherry *see* mirin

Japanese vegetable cuts The mundane and decorative cuts and garnishes of vegetables which have been brought to a high art by Japanese chefs. See e.g. hana giri, hangetsu giri, hyoshigi giri, icho giri, katsura muki, matsuba, matsuka nani, mijin giri, ogi giri, roppo muki, sainome giri and sen giri

Japanese wineberry *see* wineberry

japonais *(He)* Small round almond macaroons filled with butter cream

japonaise, à la *(Fr)* Garnished with Japanese artichokes

japonica The fruit of the ornamental quince *Chaenomeles speciosa* which sometimes ripen on the tree but can be ripened indoors. Must not be eaten raw. Used in pies or stewed or made into a jelly [also called **Japanese quince**]

japonica rice A short grained rice shorter and thicker than Carolina rice but with similar characteristics and uses

japuta *(Sp)* Pomfret, the fish

jardinière *(Fr)* A garnish of mixed spring vegetables

Jarlsberg *(No)* A hard scalded-curd cheese similar to but softer and sweeter than Emmental, shaped in a large round and coated with wax. Made from pasteurized cows' milk

jarret *(Fr) masc.* Shin and shank of beef or knuckle of veal

jarrete *(Sp)* Knuckle

jasmine Various climbing shrubs *Jasminum sambac* and other *Jasminum* spp. of the olive family whose leaves and flowers are used to flavour Chinese and SEA dishes. The unopened buds are used as table decoration and jasmine oil and essence are extracted from the flowers

jasmine essence An alcoholic extract of jasmine flowers used to flavour desserts, rice and other dishes esp. in Thailand

jasmine fragrant rice An aromatic long grain rice with a more subtle flavour than basmati and slightly sticky when cooked. Best cooked for 10 minutes without salt. Used in Chinese and SEA cookery [also called **Thai fragrant rice, Thai jasmine rice**]

jasmine oil The essential oil from jasmine flowers

Jasminum sambac *Bot.* Jasmine

jätkän lohipotti *(Fi)* Laxgryta (Sw)

jaune d'oeuf *(Fr) masc.* Egg yolk

Jausenwurst *(Au)* A snack sausage made with beef, lean pork and bacon fat, seasoned, flavoured and bound with fécule

Java coffee A mature coffee from Indonesia with a subtle mellow flavour

Java rice A short grained variety of rice particularly suitable for rice pudding as 80 g will absorb a litre of milk

Java sugar *see* palm sugar

Javaanse sla *(Ho)* A salad based on Indonesian ingredients.

javali *(Po)* Wild boar

Javanese winged cardamom A cheap cardamom substitute from a variety of *Amomum* spp. available in South East Asia

javitri *(In)* Nutmeg and mace

jbane *(NA)* A Moroccan goats' milk cheese eaten fresh or after maturing on straw

jean-doré *(Fr) masc.* John dory

jeera *(In)* Cumin

jeera sali *(In)* A delicate long grain rice shaped in a crescent rather like cumin seeds. Sold in the west as basmati or pilau rice. Always cooked by the absorption method

jelabi *(In)* Spirals of batter formed and fried in a deep frying pan by dribbling batter out of a funnel. Served as a dessert with rose water-flavoured sugar syrup

jelita *(Cz)* A small blood sausage which is boiled or fried

jellied eels *(UK)* Portions of fresh skinned eel, simmered in water or flavoured fish stock with vinegar, allowed to cool and served as a snack

jellied mayonnaise *see* mayonnaise collée

Jello *(USA)* A proprietary jelly, i.e. the gelatine based product as opposed to the clear jam

jelly 1 The name given to any sweet or savoury liquid which is converted to a solid with a small amount of a gelling agent such as gelatine or agar agar **2** *(USA)* Jam

jelly bag A cloth bag used to strain fruit juice prior to making jelly from it

jelly crystals *(Aus)* Flavoured gelatine used to make jelly

jelly cube A concentrated jelly made from gelatine, sugar and flavouring in water, set in a rectangular shape and partially divided into cubes to be used by adding to hot water to make fruit-flavoured jelly.

jelly mould A plastic or metal container with various shapes in which jelly is set then demoulded and turned out onto a plate or dish

jelly mushroom *see* straw mushroom

jelly noodles *see* cellophane noodles

jelly roll *(USA)* Swiss roll

jellyfish The salted and sun dried skin of the jellyfish *Rhopilema esculenta* is used in Chinese cooking. It is rather tasteless and either shredded or sold in a piece. It should be reconstituted, shredded if necessary and marinated but not cooked and has a crunchy texture

jemuju *(Ma)* Caraway seed

jengibre *(Sp)* Ginger

jerked beef *see* charqui

jerked meat *see* charqui

jerky *see* charqui

Jerome *(Ge & Au)* A semi-hard cows' milk cheese with a mild to slightly sharp paste

Jersey milk *see* Channel Islands milk

Jersey royal One of the earliest well-flavoured new potatoes harvested in the UK on the island of Jersey and commanding a premium price [also called **international kidney**]

Jersey wonder *(UK)* A deep fried twist or ring of a light dough mixture, dusted with sugar and eaten warm. From the Channel Islands.

jeruk asem *(Ma)* Citron

jeruk bodong *(Id)* Citron

jeruk nipis *(Id)* Lime, the fruit

jeruk purut *(Id)* Kaffir lime

jeruk sekade *(Id & Ma)* Citron

Jerusalem artichoke A knobbly brown root of a plant *Helianthus tuberosus,* which is a relative of the sunflower with a flavour similar to the artichoke. Jerusalem is a corruption of the Italian girasole meaning sunflower [also called **winter artichoke**]

Jesuit's cress *see* nasturtium

Jesuit's nut *see* caltrops

jésus *(Fr) masc.* A large cured dry sausage (to 3 kg) made with coarsely chopped pork meat and pork fat and matured for a long time

jets de houblon *(Fr) masc.* Hop shoots

jeung *(Ch)* Ginger

jewfish *(USA)* Giant sea bream

Jewish chicken soup *see* gildeneh yoich

Jewish salami A kosher salami made from beef with garlic and seasonings

Jewish sausage Small sausages made of minced beef, onion and carrot extended with matzo meal and bound with egg. Served at Passover

jew's ear A fungus *Auricularia auriculajudae* similar to and related to cloud ear fungus and available dried. This is a mistranslation from the latin for Judas's ear and is so called because it grows on the elder tree on which he is reputed to have hanged himself [also called **Judas's ear**]

jhanna *(In)* A perforated spoon with small holes used for producing small droplets of batter to be deep fried or boiled

jhingli *(In)* Angled loofah

jhol *(Ne)* Soup

ji *(Ch)* Shallow frying

jian *(Ch)* Shallow frying

jiang *(Ch)* Ginger root

jiang niu rou *(Ch)* Marinated beef

jiang you *(Ch)* Soya sauce

jiao zi *(Ch)* Dumpling

jibia *(Sp)* Cuttlefish

jicama The large turnip-like root (25 cm in diameter) of a leguminous plant *Pachyrrhizus erosus* from Central and South America, with a brown inedible easily separated skin and juicy white flesh which can be eaten raw or cooked. The root contains little or no protein and may be lobed. The pods and seeds of the plant are edible when young but can be poisonous when mature. Popular in Mexico and California [also called **yam bean, jicana, Mexican yam bean**]

jicana *see* jicama

ji dan *(Ch)* Hen egg

jiemo *(Ch)* Mustard

ji gan *(Ch)* Chicken liver

jin dan *(Ch)* Meiwa kumquat

jinga *(In)* Shrimp or prawn

jing lung *(Ch)* The round bamboo nesting steamers used for dim sum and other steamed foods

jintan manis *(Ma)* Aniseed or fennel seed

jinten *(Id)* Cumin

jinten putih *(Ma)* Cumin

jiraa *(Ne)* Cumin seed

ji rou *(Ch)* Chicken meat

ji tang *(Ch)* Chicken soup

jit choh *(Ch)* Red vinegar

jit gwa *(Ch)* Fuzzy melon

jitrnice *(Cz)* A fresh offal (liver and lungs) sausage for boiling or frying

jiu la choy *(Ch)* One of the oriental mustards with thick white stems and pointed green leaves growing to 45 cm. It has a strong bitter flavour and is parboiled before stir frying [also called **Chinese green cabbage, sow cabbage**]

ji you *(Ch)* Chicken fat

Job's tears A warm climate plant *Coix lachryma-jobi* with large seeds, eaten mainly in SEA and the Phillipines as a source of protein. The fruits are used for necklaces and it is grown as a garden plant in southern Europe

Jochburg *(Au)* A Tyrolean cheese made from

cows' and goats' milk with a distinctive flavour and shaped into large thin discs

jocoque *(Sp)* Sour cream

jodda *(It)* The local Sicilian name for yoghurt

Joe Mazetti *(USA)* A split round bread bun (balm cake) with a filling of cooked minced beef, oregano, basil, tomato sauce and seasoning

joetkal *(Ko)* Dried and salted fish similar to Bombay duck. Used for flavouring or as a snack food or side dish

Joghurt *(Ge)* Yoghurt

joghurt *(Hu)* Yoghurt

Johannisbeer Kaltschale *(Ge)* Red currants cooked in sugar syrup, sieved and mixed with white wine. Served cold garnished with whole red currants and crushed macaroons

Johannisbeer Sosse *(Ge)* A jus roti or similar with added red currant jelly

Johannisbeere *(Ge)* Red currant

Johannisbrot *(Ge)* Carob bean

John Dory A seawater flat fish *Zeus faber* with olive brown skin, two distinguishing black thumb marks *(St Peter's thumb)* on each side below the head and very sharp spines, found in the Atlantic and Mediterranean. It is similar to sole, has firm white fillets and the bones make excellent stock

Johnny cake *(USA)* A cornmeal batter pancake similar to hoecake made from the less starchy flint corn [also called **Rhode Island johnny cake**]

joint A large thick portion of animal flesh often including some bone. Names of the same joint vary considerably from place to place even within one country

joint, to To divide a carcase into manageable portions by severing a joint in the skeleton, by chopping, or by removing whole muscles or muscle groups

Joinville, sauce (Fr) *fem.* Sauce normande finished with crayfish and shrimp butters instead of cream and butter. Used with fish

jojutla rice A type of long grain rice

Jókai bableves *(Hu)* A fresh or dried butter bean soup with smoked pig knuckle and carrots, flavoured with garlic, paprika and parsley. Named after the author.

jollof *(Af)* A stew or casserole from West Africa made of of beef, chicken or mutton simmered with fried onions, tomatoes, rice and seasonings

jolly boy *(USA)* A fried flat cake made with cornmeal dough, split in half, buttered and served with maple syrup

Jonagold apple A hybrid of the Jonathan and Golden Delicious apples with a sweet, slightly tart, flavour used both for dessert and cooking

Jonah crab A close relative *Cancer borealis* of the rock crab but a little heavier (to 500 g). It has a brick red shell and like the rock crab is not particularly well-flavoured although quite edible

jonc odorant *(Fr) masc.* Lemon grass

jonchée *(Fr) fem.* **1** A fresh cream cheese from Poitou-Charentes **2** A type of junket

jong eendje *(Ho)* Duckling

jook *(Ch)* Congee

Jordan almond *see* sugared almond

jordärtskockor *(Sw)* Jerusalem artichoke

jordbær *(De & No)* Strawberry

jordgubbar *(Sw)* Strawberries

jordnötter *(Sw)* Peanuts

joshinko *(Ja)* Rice flour

jota *(It)* A slowly cooked soup from the north east of potatoes, beans or polenta, turnips, bacon and sauerkraut [also called **iota**]

joue *(Fr) fem.* Cheek (of pork)

jou kuei *(Ch)* Cinnamon

joule The scientific unit of energy too small to be of use in nutrition, hence the kilojoule q.v. equal to one thousand joules is used. Named after the Manchester, UK, scientist who investigated the equivalence of heat and other forms of energy

jour, du *(Fr)* Of the day as in soupe du jour, soup of the day

jowar *(In)* Great millet, sorghum, usually the white grained seed ground for making unleavened bread

ju *(Ch)* Blanching and quick boiling for 5 minutes in plain water to release blood from meats

juan canary melon *(USA)* An oval melon with sweet white flesh tinged with pink near the seeds and a bright yellow skin

jubna *(ME) see* Haloumi

judas's ear *see* jew's ear

judd mat gaardebou'nen *(Lu)* Smoked collar of pork cooked with broad beans and flavoured with summer savory. The national dish of Luxembourg

judias *(Sp)* Kidney beans, butter beans

judias blancas *(Sp)* Haricot beans

judias verdes *(Sp)* Runner beans

judias verdes a la andaluza *(Sp)* Boiled green beens sautéed with chopped tomatoes and julienne of ham

judic, à la *(Fr)* Garnished with stuffed tomatoes, braised lettuce, potatoes and sometimes truffles and kidney

judru *(Fr) masc.* A type of salami from Beaune made with pork only

jug, to An old fashioned term for cooking in a heavy earthenware casserole or jug

jug-jug *(Ca)* A stew containing fresh or salted beef and pork and a purée of pigeon peas

jugged hare *(UK)* A jointed hare tossed in seasoned flour, browned with bacon and butter, then beef stock, port, onion clouté, marjoram and redcurrant jelly added, boiled then casseroled for 3 hours or until tender, onions removed and cooking liquor thickened with the reserved blood of the hare. Garnished with chopped parsley

Juglans cinerea *Bot.* Butternut tree

Juglans nigra *Bot.* Walnut tree

Juglans regia *Bot.* Walnut tree

jugo *(Sp)* Juice or gravy

jugo de naranja *(Sp)* Orange juice

jugurttia *(Fi)* Yoghurt

juhla *(Fi)* A sharp-flavoured Cheddar type cheese made from cows' milk

juice The liquid expressed or released from fruits, vegetables or even meats by any or several of squeezing, pressing, liquidizing, freezing and thawing, heating, etc. Usually strained to remove solids

juice extractor An implement for manually or mechanically extracting juice from fruits. For citrus fruits usually consists of a ribbed convex cone above a slotted base on which half the citrus fruit is turned. Other fruits are generally liquidized and strained

jujube The red, wrinkled fruit of a shrub *Zizyphus jujuba* of the buckthorn family which grows in the East and Provence and is partially dried, candied or made into a stiff jelly. It is the shape of an olive, green when unripe and red to dark brown when ripe with a single stone and a sweet and sticky white flesh, rather like a small date. Other shrubs of the genus *Zisyphus* have similar fruits. The name is now applied to confectionery made from jellied and sweetened fruit juices; *see also* Mauritian, Argentinian and lotus jujube [also called **Chinese red date, Indian jujube, red date, jujube nuts**]

jujube nuts *see* jujube

juk *(Ch)* Congee

julefrokest *(De)* A Christmas cold table with a whole cooked gammon as centrepiece

julekake *(No)* Christmas cake

julienne *(En & Fr) fem.* A cut of vegetables, fruit or citrus rind measuring roughly 25 by 3 by 3 mm (smaller in the case of citrus rind). Usually used either raw, blanched or cooked as a garnish

julskinka *(Sw)* A hot or cold ham sometimes used as a centrepiece of a Christmas cold table. If cold piped with Happy Christmas ('God Jul') in white chaud-froid sauce. The ham is prepared by simmering a whole gammon with a BG, nutmeg and an onion clouté until the internal temperature reaches 80°C. It is then cooled in the cooking liquor, removed, dried, skin stripped off, coated with a mixture of mustard and ginger followed by breadcrumbs, egg yolk and sugar and browned in the oven. Nowadays, often baked in the oven

jumble **1** A small lemon or almond-flavoured biscuit baked in a tiny heap or an 'S', shape **2** *(USA)* A biscuit flavoured with rose water and containing chopped walnuts and desiccated coconut

jumbo The term descriptive of foods larger than normal or expected, e.g. jumbo oats, jumbo burger

jumeau *(Fr) masc.* A cut of the forequarter of beef extending down from the end of the côtes couvertes including the leaner parts of the leg of mutton cut and the brisket immediately in front of the foreleg. Used for braising

jump baarn *(Ch)* A chopping block usually made from soapwood cut across the grain so as not to take the edge off the cleaver

juneberry *(USA)* The fruit of a decorative shrub *Amelanchier canadensis* with a red to black fruit similar to a blackcurrant. Eaten raw or cooked [also called **serviceberry**]

junges Hammelfleisch *(Ge)* Lamb

junges Huhn *(Ge)* Spring chicken

Jungeszwiebeln *(Ge)* Spring onions

juniper The dried berries of a shrub *Juniperus communis* from temperate Northern regions used to flavour gin, for marinades and as a pickling spice. The piney flavour also goes well with game and pork

juniper spice mix A mixture of ground spices suitable for flavouring dense textured fish, beef and lamb before barbecueing made from juniper berries, black peppercorns, allspice, cloves, dried bay leaves and salt

junípero *(Sp)* Juniper

Juniperus communis *Bot.* Juniper

junk food Food with plenty of Calories, generally in the form of cheap sugar, fat, starch and recovered protein, highly seasoned and flavoured if savoury, but with few or no vitamins or trace elements, and if the major source of energy will lead to suboptimal health

junket *(UK)* Sweetened and flavoured milk mixed at blood heat (37°C) with rennet to cause it to set. Once set it must not be disturbed or it will separate into curds and whey

Jurawurst *(He) see* saucisses d'Ajoie

jus *(Fr) masc.* Juice, either from fruit, vegetables or from meat

jus, au *(Fr)* A description of roasted food served only with its own juices

jus lié *(Fr) masc.* Espagnole sauce made from veal or chicken bones without flour, thickened with arrowroot or cornflour, simmered briefly, seasoned and strained [also called **thickened gravy**]

jus (de) rôti *(Fr) masc.* Roast gravy

jus de viande *(Fr) masc.* Gravy; *see also* jus lié and jus (de) rôti

Jussière, garnish *(Fr)* Onions, braised lettuce, potatoes and sometimes carrots

juusto *(Fi)* Cheese

juustoleipä *(Fi)* A hand made low fat cows' milk slicing cheese in the form of a loaf. Often sliced and toasted or dunked in coffee [also called **leipäjuusto**]

ju zi *(Ch)* Orange

juzi *(Ch)* Tangerine

Kk

kaagati *(Ne)* Lemon

kaali *(Fi)* Cabbage

kaalikääryle *(Fi)* Blanched cabbage leaves wrapped around a stuffing and baked

kaalipiiras *(Fi)* A cabbage filled pie served hot or cold

kaankro *(Ne)* Cucumber

kaas *(Ho)* Cheese

kaassaus *(Ho)* Cheese sauce

kabab *(In)* Kebab, usually on a wooden skewer or on iron if cooked in a tandoori oven

kabachok *(Ru)* Squash, marrow

kabak dolmasi *(Tu)* A young marrow or large courgette filled with a mixture of onions, raisins, pine nuts, chopped parsley or dill and seasoning, baked in the oven and served cold

kabak tathsi *(Tu)* A dessert made from cooked pumpkin flesh, soaked in sugar syrup and sprinkled with chopped walnuts

kabanosy *(Pl)* A thin and hard smoked pork sausage made into links about 30 cm long

kabaragh *(In)* Lamb chops cooked in milk with ginger and fennel

Kabeljau *(Ge)* Codfish

kabeljauw *(Ho)* Codfish

kabocha *(Ja)* A small winter squash similar to a small green pumpkin. Cooked like swede or marrow

kabosu *(Ja)* A very acid citrus fruit *Citrus sphaerocarpa* grown in Japan for use as a garnish or flavouring. It has a very dark green rind which is thin and smooth and juicy flesh with several seeds

kabu *(Ja)* Turnip

kabuli channa *(In)* Yellow chick peas

kabu no tsukemono *(Ja)* A salad pickle made from thinly sliced turnip mixed with a little crumbled kombu, sliced ginger, chopped dry red chillis, chopped lemon rind, julienned carrot and salt, all pressed under a weighted board for 12 hours or more, wrung out and dressed with equal parts of soya sauce and mirin

kacang djong *(Ma)* Bean sprouts

kacang eeris *(Ma)* Pigeon pea

kacang goode *(Id)* Pigeon pea

kacang ijo *(Ma)* Bean sprouts

kacang-kacang *(Id & Ma)* Barracuda

kacang kedele *(Id)* Soya bean

kacang merah *(Id)* Black-eyed pea

kacang mete *(Id)* Cashew nut

kacang monyet *(Id)* Cashew nut

kacang padi *(Ma)* Bean sprouts

kacang panjang **1** *(Id)* Black-eyed pea **2** *(Ma)* Long bean

kacang tanah *(Id & Ma)* Peanut

kachauri *(In)* A type of pitta bread made into a pocket and stuffed with a spiced bean mixture

Kachkaval *see* Kashkaval

kachkeiss *(Lu)* A matured and hardened curd cheese cooked with butter, sour cream, seasoning and sometimes yolk of egg, served on bread

kachoomar *(In)* A side dish of sliced onions, tomatoes and sweet peppers dressed with lemon juice. often served before a meal as the menu choice is being made

kachur *(In)* Zedoary

kacsa *(Hu)* Duck

kadhai *(In & Ne) see* karahi

kadin budu köfte *(Tu)* Chopped raw beef mixed with boiled rice, chopped parsley and salt, shaped into oval cakes, steamed or boiled, cooled, dipped in beaten egg and fried

kadin göbegi *(Tu)* Small fried biscuits soaked in syrup and eaten as a dessert. Lit. lady's navel

kadju *(In)* Cashew nut

kadu *(In)* Winter squash

Kaempferia galanga *Bot.* Kempferia galangal

Kaempferia pandurata *Bot.* Kempferia galangal

kaeng *(Th) see* gaeng

kærnemælk *(De)* Buttermilk

kærnemælkskoldskaal *(De)* Cold buttermilk soup

kærnemælksuppe *(De)* A cold soup made from eggs, buttermilk, sugar, vanilla and lemon sprinkled with crushed cornflakes and chopped almonds

kaffe *(De, No & Sw)* Coffee

kaffebröd *(Sw)* Coffee cake

Kaffeekuchen *(Ge)* Coffee cake

kaffir corn A variety of millet *Sorghum vulgare* var. *caffrorum* from South Africa used as millet or sorghum

kaffir lime *see* makrut lime

kaga *(Ja)* A variety of Japanese cucumber

kage *(De)* Cake

Kaggost *(Sw)* A medium soft and mild, yellow coloured cheese made from cows' milk and sometimes flavoured with cumin

kaha bath *(Sr)* Turmeric coloured spiced rice used on festive occasions

kahve *(Tu)* Turkish coffee

kai *(Th)* Egg or chicken

kai kem *(Th)* Salted duck eggs

kail *see* kale

kaimak *(Ru)* A type of clotted cream from Armenia made by simmering a mixture of double cream and milk (5:3) for 15 minutes whilst repeatedly incorporating air with a ladle. It is then cooled slowly for 4 hours and refrigerated for 24 hours all without agitation. The solidified cream from the top is cut in squares and lifted out with a slotted spoon. It will keep up to a week in a refrigerator

kai pad bai krapow *(Th)* Diced chicken meat stir fried with fresh basil leaves and bird's eye chillis, moistened with a little fish sauce and served as a side dish

kaiseki ryori *(Ja)* A succession of small dishes served in a formal style, ingredients change with the seasons but do not included red meat

Kaiser Koch *(Ge)* Rice pudding with almonds

Kaiserfleisch 1 *(Ge)* Smoked sucking pig **2** Boiled bacon

kaiserfleish *(It)* Kaiserfleisch

Kaisergranat *(Ge)* Dublin bay prawn

Kaiserschmarren *(Au)* A thick sweet batter containing sultanas or raisins, shallow fried in long strips until crisp, drained and served in a heap dredged with sugar. Eaten as a dessert with stewed fruit [also called **emperor's omelette**]

kajiki *(Ja)* Swordfish

kajmak *(Bk)* Feta and cream cheeses beaten with butter until fluffy and served as an appetizer

kaju *(In)* Cashew nut

kaka *(Sw)* Cake

Kakao *(Ge)* Cocoa

kakao *(Ru & Sw)* Cocoa

kakavia *(Gr)* A fish soup similar to bouillabaisse; *see* psarosoupa

kakda *(In)* Cucumber

kake *(No)* Cake

kakee *see* persimmon

kakejiru soup *(Ja)* Dashi, soya sauce and mirin (10:1:1) with a little salt and sliced spring onions simmered for about 10 minutes

kaki 1 *see* persimmon **2** *(Ja)* Oyster

kaki-miso *(Ja)* Oysters simmered in a miso and sake broth

kakitama-jiru *(Ja)* A soup made from dashi flavoured with a little salt and soya sauce, slightly thickened with cornflour. After cooking out it is brought to a very gentle simmer and beaten egg mixed with a little dashi is dribbled in from a moving ladle and allowed to set. The soup is removed from the heat and finished with juice squeezed from freshly grated ginger root and garnished with lemon rind shapes. Lit. egg drop soup

kakku *(Fi)* Cake

kakukfú *(Hu)* Thyme

kaku-zukuri *(Ja)* A type of cut for large thick fillets of fish used in sashimi consisting of 1 cm dice

kål *(De, No & Sw)* Cabbage

kala *(Fi)* Fish

kalács *(Hu)* A well raised white milk-bread available as rolls or in slices

kala jeera *(In)* **1** Black cumin, a variety of cumin found in Kashmir, Pakistan and Iran. Used in Moghul cooking **2** Caraway seed

kalakakot *(Fi)* Fish cakes

kalakeitto *(Fi)* A fish, onion and potato soup with a milk and water base thickened with ryebread and cornflour and garnished with chopped fresh dill leaf

kalakukko *(Fi)* A hollowed out rye loaf filled with small white fish *(muikko)*, fat pork and seasoning, baked slowly until filling is cooked, then sliced and served hot

kalamansi *(Ph)* The local lemon which is about the size of a small lime and has a bright green skin. Generally used as a lemon. The rind is crystallized for use as a garnish or snack

kalamarakia tiganita *(Gr)* Young squid, cleaned, sliced and floured then browned in hot oil for 3 minutes. Served as an appetizer on cocktail sticks

kalamarossoupa me domata *(Gr)* A thin stew or thick soup made from sliced squid, sweated onions and garlic, tomato concassée, sliced mushrooms, red wine and water (1:4), all simmered for 10 minutes only, seasoned and finished with chopped parsley

kala namak *(In)* Salt

kalassås *(Sw)* A festive sauce for fish used at parties, made with double cream with 10% of uncooked egg yolk mixed in and flavoured with wine vinegar, caster sugar, French mustard and freshly ground white pepper

Kalb *(Ge)* Veal

kalbashira *(Ja)* Scallops

Kalberwurst *(He)* Veal sausage

Kalbfleisch *(Ge)* Veal

Kalbfüsse *(Ge)* Calves' feet

Kalbsbeuschel *(Au)* A ragout of calves' lights and hearts, once a dish of the poor but now fashionable

Kalbsbraten *(Ge)* Roast veal

Kalbsbratwurst *(He)* A white bratwurst made from a mixture of veal, bacon and milk, seasoned and flavoured with spices

Kalbsbries *(Ge)* Calves' sweetbreads

Kalbsbrust *(Ge)* Breast of veal

Kalbshaxen *(Au & Ge)* A speciality of the Austrian Bavarian border region consisting of a well roasted or fried pork or veal leg joint which is crisp, brown and tender, served with boiled potatoes and salad

Kalbsleber *(Ge)* Calves' liver

Kalbsleberwurst *(Ge)* A spreading sausage made from calves' liver

Kalbslende *(Ge)* Fillet of veal

Kalbsmilch *(He)* Calves' sweetbreads

Kalbsnierenbraten *(Ge)* Boned loin of veal with some flank, stuffed with halved, skinned and cored calves' kidneys, seasoned and sprinkled with dried thyme, rolled, tied and roasted on a mirepoix of vegetables at 175°C in the usual way

Kalbsrippchen *(Ge)* Veal chop

Kalbsrolle *(Ge)* Boned breast of veal covered with a stuffing containing minced beef and sausage with breadcrumbs soaked in milk, sweated chopped onion, parsley, nutmeg, lemon zest and seasoning bound with egg, rolled up, tied, browned in lard and braised in stock for about 2 hours. Served hot with the reduced cooking liquor thickened with beurre manié or cold with clarified and jellied cooking liquor

Kalbsroulade *(Ge)* A type of meat loaf made with a pork and veal mixture containing diced pork fat and pistachio nuts

kald *(No)* Cold

Kaldaune *(Ge)* Tripe

kåldolmar *(Sw)* Blanched cabbage leaves wrapped around a filling of minced beef or pork, butter, rice cooked in milk until very soft and seasonings, lightly fried then baked in a covered dish with a sweetened stock. Served with the cooking liquor thickened with cornflour and soured cream, boiled potatoes and cranberry sauce

kåldolmer *(De)* Stuffed cabbage

kaldt kjøtt *(No)* Cold sliced meats, assiette anglaise

kale A member of the *Brassica* family *Brassica oleracea* Acephala Group with a tall thick stem from which spring large curly leaves and, later, tender flower stalks. It will stand through the winter and both the leaves and the flowering stalks (in spring) can be eaten. It has a stronger flavour than cabbage and is known in North Europe as peasant's cabbage. When shredded and fried in oil it resembles fried seaweed; *see also* borecole [also called **curly kale, kail**]

kale brose *(UK)* A Scottish peasant dish of cow's heel simmered and skimmed for 4 hours, finely shredded kale and toasted oatmeal added and boiled until cooked. A more up-market version uses beef broth with beef cheek

kalfsgehakt *(Ho)* Minced veal

kalfskotelet *(Ho)* Veal cutlet

kalfslapje *(Ho)* Veal steak

kalfsoester *(Ho)* Grenadin, of veal

kalfsvlees *(Ho)* Veal

kalfszwezerik *(Ho)* Calves' sweetbreads

kali *(In)* Loofah

kalia *(Pl)* Chicken broth flavoured with the juice of pickled cucumbers and garnished with diced chicken meat, celeriac, carrots and Hamburg parsley

kali mirch *(In)* Black peppercorn

kali mirich *(In)* Black peppercorn

kalkkuna *(Fi)* Turkey

kalkkunapaisti *(Fi)* Roast turkey

kalkoen *(Ho)* Turkey

kalkon *(Sw)* Turkey

kalkun *(De & No)* Turkey

kalkunragout *(De)* Casserole of turkey in a sweet and sour sauce, served with mashed potatoes or chestnut purée

kall *(Sw)* Cold

kall citron-kyckling *(Sw)* Cold lemon chicken made from boiled, skinned and deboned chicken meat covered with a sauce made from cream, egg yolk and sherry (12:1:1) stirred over heat until thick, and the whole topped with shredded lemon zest

kall tomatsoppa *(Sw)* Tomatoes boiled in just sufficient water to cover them for 15 minutes, passed hot through a chinois onto grated or processed onion, seasoned and flavoured with sugar, lemon juice and Worcestershire sauce. Served cold as a soup

kallaloo *see* callaloo soup

kalmar *(Ge)* Squid

kalocsai halászlé *(Hu)* A fish soup based on red wine

kalonji *(In)* Nigella

kalops *(Sw)* Beef stewed in the old fashioned way with onions, peppercorns, bay leaf and possibly allspice

kalt *(Ge)* Cold

kalte pikante Sosse *(Ge)* Ketchup

kalte Speisen *(Ge)* Cold dishes

Kalteschale *(Ge)* Cold fruit soup

kalua puaa *(USA)* A Hawaiian speciality of seasoned shredded roast pork, wrapped in taro leaves and briefly roasted or barbecued

kalv med fänkål *(Sw)* Lightly browned veal escalopes simmered in white wine or stock in a closed dish over a bed of chopped bulb fennel for about 20 minutes and served with the reduced cooking liquor thickened with a liaison of egg and cream

kalvbräss-stuvning *(Sw)* Creamed calves' sweetbreads made from cleaned and blanched whole sweetbreads, sweated in butter with sliced onion and carrot and boiled 10 minutes with flavoured veal stock. The sweetbreads are then reserved, cooled, chopped and combined with a cream sauce [also called **stuvad kalvbräss**]

kalvebrisler *(De)* Calves' sweetbreads

kalvekjøtt *(No)* Veal

kalvekød *(De)* Veal

kalvemedaljong *(No)* Roast veal

kalvenyrestek *(No)* Loin of veal

kalvfilé pandora *(Sw)* Seasoned escalopes of veal, fried in butter, arranged in an oven-proof dish and covered with strips of ham, sweet green pepper and sliced mushroom. This covered with the pan juices which have been deglazed with cream, topped with slices of Gruyère cheese and browned under the grill

kalvfilet Oscar *(Sw)* Flattened medallions of veal passed through seasoned flour, browned in butter, napped with choron or béarnaise sauce and garnished with lobster and asparagus tips. Named after King Oscar II of Sweden

kalvkött *(Sw)* Veal

kalvkyckling *(Sw)* Paupiettes of veal, veal birds, veal olives

kalvrulad med bacon *(Sw)* Escalopes of veal covered with bacon, rolled and tied, dusted with flour and browned with chopped bacon, onions and shallots, covered with stock and a BG, seasoned and then braised with a cover for 1 to 1.5 hours, untied and served with the strained braising liquor

kalvstek på grönsaksbädd *(Sw)* Veal shoulder rubbed with seasoning and powdered rosemary, roasted on a mirepoix of onions, carrots, leeks and celeriac and basted with stock from time to time. When cooked (1 to 2 hours) the veal is sliced, laid over the vegetables and served from the dish

kalvsteck i öl *(Sw)* Leg or shoulder veal browned with carrots and onions in butter then simmered in brown ale with bay, cloves and seasoning until tender

kama *(Ja)* A heavy metal pan used for cooking rice by the absorption method

kamaboko *(Ja)* Cooked fish cakes made with ground up white fish flesh bound with starch, egg white, mirin and sugar. Either steamed or dusted with cornflour and shallow fried. They have a slightly rubbery texture and are either sliced and added to soups, noodles, etc. or served as a hors d'oeuvres with a sauce. The surface is often coloured to give an attractive appearance when sliced; *see also* the variations chikuwa, hanpen, ita-kamaboko and natuto [also called **Japanese fish balls, Japanese fish sausage**]

kamano lomi *(USA)* An appetizer from Hawaii made with chopped smoked or desalted salted salmon, chopped onions and salt to taste

kamasu *(Ja)* Saury pike

kambing *(Id)* Goat

kamias *(Ph)* Belimbing (1), the fruit

kami-jio *(Ja)* A method of lightly salting food esp. raw fish by wrapping the food in paper and allowing it to stand for an hour immersed in salt

kamin *(Th)* Turmeric

kaminari-jiru *(Ja)* A soup containing bean curd and vegetables

kammar *(Sw)* Cinnamon-flavoured butter cream placed over the central 10 by 32 cm strip of a rolled 32 cm square of Danish pastry, the sides folded over to give a 10 by 32 cm rectangle, cut in 4 cm pieces, each piece having 4 cuts to the centre along the long side, brushed with water, rolled in coarse sugar and almond knibs, bent to open out the cuts, proved 30 minutes and baked at 230°C for 8 minutes. Lit. combs

kammuschel *(Ge)* Scallop, the shellfish

kampyo *(Ja)* Thin dried strips of the flesh of bottle gourd. When softened by blanching in weak brine they are used as edible strings for tying and wrapping food or as a filling for sushi [also called **kanpyo, dried gourd strips**]

kamrakh *(In)* Carambola, the fruit

kana *(Fi)* Hen

kana gushi *(Ja)* Short metal skewers for grilling whole or sliced fish and other foods

kananpoika *(Fi)* Chicken

kanari fruit The small sour fruit of a Chinese tree *Canarium album*. The kernels from the stone are known as Chinese olive seeds

kandierte Früchte *(Ge)* Candied fruit

kaneel *(Ho)* Cinnamon

kanel *(Sw)* Cinnamon

kanewala choona *(In)* Lime (calcium hydroxide)

kangaroo tail *(Aus)* The tail of a kangaroo cooked as oxtail

kangaroo tail soup *(Aus)* As oxtail soup with kangaroo tail substituted for oxtail

kangkong *(Ph)* Swamp cabbage

kani *(Ja)* Crab, used both generally and in sushi

kaniini *(Fi)* Rabbit

kanin *(De, No & Sw)* Rabbit

kanin i flødepeberrod *(De)* Jugged rabbit served with a horseradish and cream dressing, mushrooms and onions

Kaninchen *(Ge)* Rabbit

kan lan *(Ch)* Kanari fruit

kanom *(Th)* Cake, dessert

kanom bang *(Th)* Bread

kanoon *(Th)* Jackfruit

kan phoo *(Th)* Cloves

kanpyo *(Ja) see* kampyo

kanten *(Ja)* Agar-agar

Kanter *(Ho) see* Kanterkaas

Kanterkaas *(Ho)* As Nagelkaas but without the cumin and cloves [also called **Kanter, Friese Kanterkaas**]

kantola A small bitter gourd *Momordica muricata* used in the cooking of India and the Far East. It is similar to a courgette with a thick green knobbly skin. The young seeds are edible but harden with age like a marrow. It should be blanched and degorged before cooking and hard seeds removed [also called **balsam apple, ucche**]

Kantwurst *(Au)* A rectangular shaped Rohwurst made with lean pork and pork fat (2:1)

kao 1 *(Ch)* Roasting **2** *(Th)* Rice

kao liang *(Ch)* Millet

kaolin *see* (E)559

kao mao *(Th)* Young unhusked rice, flattened and roasted. Used as a coating for fried food

kao mian bao *(Ch)* Toast

kaong *(Ph)* Palm nut

kao pan *(Th)* A variety of Thai pummelo with a sweetish flavour and with less acid than a grapefruit

kapama *(Bu)* A ragoût of floured pieces of boneless lamb, sautéed in oil with sliced onions and then simmered with paprika, seasoning and a little water until nearly cooked, mixed with plenty of chopped spring onions, simmered until all cooked, covered with blanched spinach leaves and served

Kapaun *(Ge)* Capon

Kapern *(Ge)* Capers

kaperssaus *(Ho)* Caper sauce

kapi *(Th)* Blachan, a moist shrimp paste which becomes very pungent and dark brown as it matures

kapor *(Ma)* Lime (Calcium hydroxide)

kapormártás *(Hu)* Dill sauce

káposzta *(Hu)* Cabbage

kappan *(Hu)* Capon

kapulaga *(Id)* Cardamom

kapúsniak *(Pl)* A soup of sauerkraut cooked in water with marrow bones, pork and bacon pieces, pork sausage, carrots, celeriac, Hamburg parsley and onions, then strained, the liquid thickened with a roux and served with a garnish of diced pork, bacon and sausage

kapusta *(Ru)* Cabbage

kapustny rulet *(Ru)* Cabbage rolls stuffed with a mixture of sweated chopped onions, seasoned minced pork and veal, boiled barley, chopped gherkins and sweet peppers and meat stock, placed in a baking dish with a thickened tomato sauce mixed with sour cream, covered with a yeast-raised rye dough, proved and baked at 180°C until brown

Kapuzinerkresse *(Ge)* Nasturtium

kara-age *(Ja)* A description of food which has been dusted with flour and deep fried

karabu nati *(Sr)* Cloves

karahi *(In)* A small wok used in Northern Pakistan for one dish cooking. Used to serve food in Balti q.v. restaurants [also called **kadhai, kurhai**]

Karamel *(Ge)* Caramel

karamelrand *(De)* Caramel custard

karapincha *(Sr)* Curry leaf

karashi *(In)* English style mustard condiment without adulterants

karashina *(Ja)* A mild version of mustard greens

karasumi *(Ja)* The salted roe of mullet similar to caviar

karaya gum *see* (E)416

karbonader 1 *(De)* Fried pork and veal rissoles **2** *(Ho)* A spiced rolled meat ready for roasting

Kardamome *(Ge)* Cardamom

kardemommerkoekje *(Ho)* Cardamom-flavoured biscuits

kardi *(In)* A spicy yoghurt based sauce

Kardone *(Ge)* Cardoon

karee *(Th)* Curry

karei *(Ja)* Flounder or sole

kare kare *(Ph)* A meat and vegetable stew thickened with ground peanuts and coloured red with burong-mustaza. The meat is usually oxtail, shin beef or tripe. Served with fried bagoong [also called **kari kari**]

karela *(In)* Bitter gourd

Karelian hotpot *see* karjalanpaisti

Karelian open pasties *(Fi)* Rye dough formed into an oval boat shape, filled with a cooked savoury rice mixture, baked in the oven and served warm with a topping of chopped hard boiled eggs and butter

karella *(In)* Bitter gourd

Karfiol *(Au)* Cauliflower

karhu *(Fi)* Bear

karhunkinkku *(Fi)* Smoked leg of bear

karhunliha *(Fi)* Bear meat

kari *(Sr)* Curry; *see also* red curry and white curry

karicollen *(Be)* Tiny steamed snails served as street food

karides güveç *(Tu)* Prawns cooked in a tomato sauce and gratinated with cheese

kari kari *(Ph)* *see* kare kare

kari patty *(In)* Curry leaves

kari phulia *(In)* Sweet nim leaves

karjalanpaisti *(Fi)* A casserole of cubed lamb, pork or beef with onions and carrots, seasoned and flavoured with bay, cooked very slowly in the oven and served with boiled potatoes and mashed swede [also called **Karelian hotpot**]

karljohanssvamp *(Sw)* The boletus fungus

karlovska lukanka *(Bu)* A large sausage made with pork, beef and bacon (4:2:1), chopped and mixed with sugar, seasoning, caraway seeds and oregano, filled into wide casings, tied in 25 cm links, pricked, air dried, wrapped and stored in wood ash for up to a year

Karlssons frestelse *(Sw)* As Jansson's temptation but using buckling instead of anchovies or matjes herring

karnemelk *(Ho)* Buttermilk

karni yarik *(Tu)* Aubergine flesh removed via a single incision, chopped and fried in butter with onions and minced lamb or mutton, placed back in the skin, buttered and baked in the oven until browned

kärnmjölk *(Sw)* Buttermilk

Karotten *(Ge)* Carrots

karp *(Ru)* Carp

karpalo *(Fi)* Cranberry

karpalo kiisseli *(Fi)* A cranberry pudding made from the juice thickened with fécule or similar

karper *(Ho)* Carp

Karpfen *(Ge)* Carp

karry *(De)* Curry

Kartano *(Fi)* A cow's milk cheese similar to Gouda

kartofel *(Ru)* Potato

kartofelnye piroshki z barabinoy *(Ru)* Lamb patties from Kazakhstan made with grated potatoes, squeezed dry in a towel, mixed with grated onion and minced lamb, seasoned and flavoured with chopped parsley, coriander and ground cumin and brought together with flour and egg, made into round patties and fried in clarified butter

kartofelnye vareniky *(Ru)* Potato dumplings made from mashed potatoes, flour and lard (11:3:1) bound with egg yolk and kneaded to a silky dough, stuffed with sweetened chopped prunes and walnuts, poached until they float, drained and rolled in toasted breadcrumbs mixed with cinnamon and sugar. Served immediately with sour cream

kartofelny salat *(Ru)* Potato salad, potatoes usually sliced with radishes, spring onions, gherkins and dill and dressed with Russian dressing

Kartoffel *(Ge)* Potato

Kartoffelbrei *(Ge)* Mashed potatoes

Kartoffelklösse *(Ge)* Potato dumplings made with riced cooked potatoes, semolina and flour (8:1:1), seasoned, flavoured with nutmeg and brought together with beaten egg until the dough holds its shape in a spoon. Made into balls about 5 to 7 cm in dia. and poached in simmering water until they float and a further minute after they float. Served with butter and fried or toasted breadcrumbs. Usually stuffed with e.g. croûtons, meat or plum jam

Kartoffelklösse mit Fleisch gefüllte *(Ge)* Potato dumplings filled with meat

kartoffelmos *(De)* Mashed potato used as a stuffing, potato puffs

Kartoffelpuffer *(Ge)* Large potato pancakes made from grated raw potato fried in a flour and egg batter served very hot with cold apple purée as accompaniment

Kartoffelspatzen *(Ge)* Cold boiled potatoes on the raw side, grated and mixed with hot milk, butter, breadcrumbs and seasoning and bound with egg, made into small dumplings and poached in water. Drained and served with melted butter

Kartoffelsuppe *(Ge)* Potato soup made with diced potatoes, stock or water and cream (5:3:1) cooked in the stock or seasoned water, rubbed through a sieve (not liquidized), and mixed with cream, some milk and grated onion, and simmered 5 minutes

kartoffler *(De)* Potato

kartofi sus sirene *(Bu)* Sliced potatoes and cheese baked in milk

karupillam *(Ma)* Curry leaf

karvaviza *(Bu)* A black pudding including pork from the neck and belly minced with lungs, heart and kidneys, mixed with pigs' blood, seasoned, flavoured with allspice, caraway and oregano, packed in casings, linked, dried and smoked

karvaviza po banski *(Bu)* As karvaviza but including pigs' melt (spleen)

karvaviza drug vid *(Bu)* A karvaviza which is boiled rather than air dried

kasar peyniri *(Tu)* A hard, cooked-curd ewes' milk cheese with a strong, pungent-flavoured and dense paste, dry salted for 15 days and ripened for 3 months

kascher *(Fr)* Kosher

Käse *(Ge)* Cheese

Käsefladen *(Ge)* Cheese omelette

Käsefläled *(Ge)* Cheesecake

Käsekuchen *(Ge)* A flat cheesecake

Käserösti 1 *(Ge)* Same as potatiskaka med ost **2** *(He)* Sliced crustless white bread soaked in milk in a baking dish, topped with Swiss cheese and baked until brown. Served with a sprinkling of chopped fried onions

Käsestangen *(Ge)* Cheese wafers or twists

Käseteller *(Ge)* Cheese plate

Käsetorte *(Ge)* Cheesecake

Käsewurst *(Au)* A sausage made from a pork sausage mix containing an additional 15 to 35% diced Gruyère, Emmental or similar cheese

kasha *(Ru)* **1** Whole buckwheat groats **2** The dish made by dry frying the buckwheat groats until they pop, then adding 1.5 to 2 times their weight in water and cooking in the oven (180°C) or in a steamer for about 45 minutes until soft

kashia keihi *(Ja)* Cassia

Kashkaval A hard, scalded ewe or ewes' and cows' milk cheese made from spun curd in the Balkans with an aromatic salty flavour and which has been ripened for 2 to 3 months. Similar to Caciocavallo [also called **kaskaval, kachkaval**]

Kashmir masala A mild Indian spice mix containing black cumin seeds, green cardamoms, black peppercorns, cloves, cinnamon, mace and nutmeg

Kashmiri chilli *(In)* A large deep red chilli from Kashmir used throughout India for its colour and flavour rather than for its hotness. Treat as sweet red pepper

Kashmiri mirich *(In)* Kashmiri chilli

kashrut *see* kashruth

kashruth Orthodox Jewish dietary laws and a description of the state of a food being kosher [also called **kashrut**]

kashubha *(Ph)* Saffron

kas kas *(Ma)* Poppy seeds

Kaskaval *see* Kashkaval

Kasseler Leberwurst *(Ge)* A dark coloured Westphalian sausage made from pigs' liver and diced lean pork

Kasseler Rippchen *(Ge)* Smoked loin and spare rib of pork usually roasted and served with potatoes and braised red cabbage or sauerkraut

Kasseri *(Gr)* A hard, scalded-curd, mild and white ewes' milk cheese similar to Provolone. Often panéed and deep fried as a hors d'oeuvres but also used for dessert or as a melting cheese on Greek pizza

Kassie *(Ge)* Cassia

Kassler *(Ge)* A lightly salted loin of pork, mildly smoked with the smoke from juniper berries. Eaten raw, fried or roasted. Served cold in thin slices as a hors d'oeuvre or hot with creamed potatoes or noodles and pease pudding

Kastanie *(Ge)* Chestnut

Kastanienreis *(Au)* A dessert made from puréed chestnuts and whipped cream

kastanier *(De)* Chestnut

kastaniesovs *(De)* A chestnut sauce flavoured with Madeira

kastanja *(Fi)* Chestnuts

kastanje *(Ho)* Chestnut

kastanjepuré *(Sw)* Chestnut purée

kastanjer *(Sw)* Chestnuts

Kastlerribchen *(Be)* Smoked pork loin cooked in white wine with sauerkraut and juniper berries

kasutado *(Ja)* Custard

kaszanka *(Pl)* A popular soft sausage or black pudding made with a well spiced mixture of pork, pigs' liver, lungs and blood, extended with boiled buckwheat, packed in casings and knotted

kaszinótojás *(Hu)* Egg mayonnaise

katai *(In)* Whitebait

katakuri-ko *(Ja)* A starch thickener, once obtained from the roots of the dog tooth violet *Erythronium dencanis* but now usually fécule which is much cheaper

katalou *(Tu)* A type of vegetable stew made with coarsely chopped French beans, aubergines, sweet green peppers, tomatoes and okra simmered in oil with garlic and chopped parsley

katch *(In)* Lamb

kateh *(ME)* Plain boiled rice dried off in the oven to form a crust on the surface of the rice

Katenrauchwurst *(Ge)* A country style, very large (45 cm by 10 cm) Rohwurst made from coarsely chopped pork containing chunks of smoked pork slowly smoked over aromatic woods such as juniper, pine, heather or beech until very dark and strongly-flavoured. Often served with beer and black bread

Katenschinken *(Ge)* A smoked ham baked in a rye flour dough

Katenspeck *(Ge)* A speciality pork product made from cured, smoked and cooked belly pork. It has a dark brown rind and may be eaten cold or used to flavour stews and soups

Katerfisch *(Ge)* Fillets of sole marinated for 10 minutes with salt and lemon juice, laid in a buttered baking dish, covered with a layer of tomato purée mixed with vinegar and horseradish, scattered with sweated onion rings, dotted with butter and baked at 190°C until firm. Served from the dish

kathal *(In)* Jackfruit

kathal ke beej *(In)* Jackfruit

katiem *(Th)* Garlic

katkarapu *(Fi)* Shrimp or prawn

katnim *(In)* Curry leaf

katora The small metal or earthenware bowls in

which individual portions of food are served at an Indian meal. The different components of a meal are served separately and not on one plate as in the West [also called **katori**]

katori *(In) see* katora

katrinplommen *(Sw)* Prunes

katsuo *(Ja)* Skipjack tuna, usually referred to as bonito, strictly Pacific bonito

katsuobushi *(Ja)* Blocks of boned and dried Pacific bonito (skipjack tuna) flesh used to make bonito flakes

katsuo dashi *(Ja)* A liquid concentrate of dashi, instant dashi

katsuo-kezuriki *(Ja)* A special implement for making Pacific bonito flakes from blocks

katsura-muki *(Ja)* A long very thin sheet of mooli or carrot cut from a cylinder of the vegetable in one continuous motion. The sheet is as wide as the cylinder is long and can be up to 40 cm long. When rolled it is used to make very fine shreds

katushki *(Ru)* Fish quenelles made from white fish flesh and softened white bread processed with egg, seasoning and chopped dill, consistency adjusted with flour, formed into balls (2cm dia.), chilled, then poached in fish stock, broth or consommé

Katzenjammer *(Ge)* Sliced cold beef and cucumber in mayonnaise

Katzenkopt *(Ho) see* Edam

Katzenminze *(Ge)* Catmint

kau fu *(Ch)* A type of half cooked spongy gluten dough added to braised dishes

kaviaarib (Fi) Caviar

Kaviar *(Ge)* Caviar

kaviar *(De, No & Sw)* Caviar

kaviár *(Hu)* Caviar

kavurma *(Tu)* A dish of boiled, drained and chopped spinach mixed with chopped onions and minced mutton, fried in butter and served with a poached egg on top

käx *(Sw)* Biscuit

kayla *see* plantain

kayu manis *(Id & Ma)* Cinnamon

kaz *(Tu)* Goose

kazuno kon agemono *(Ja)* Soft herring roes, blanched in salted water for 2 minutes, dried, coated in batter and deep fried. The batter is made from flour, salt and warm water rested and, at the last minute, stiffly beaten egg white folded in

kazy *(Ru)* A horsemeat sausage from Kirghistan and Kazakhstan

kebab *(ME & In)* Any cubed or sliced food esp. meat and vegetables impaled on a skewer or brochette and cooked under the grill, over a barbecue or in a tandoori oven until lightly charred on the outside. If meat, often tenderized by marinating with an acid based marinade and basted whilst cooking. Usually served on or off the skewer with rice and salad [also called **kebob, shashlik**]

kebabchés *(Bu)* Meat balls

kebap *(Tu)* Kebab

kebob *see* kebab

kecap asin *(Id)* A thick, salty and dark coloured soya sauce used for colouring and flavour

kecap bentang manis *(Id) see* kecap manis

kecap ikan *(Id)* A fermented fish sauce

kecap manis *(Id)* A sweet, thick dark aromatic soya sauce used as a seasoning and condiment and for satay [also called **ketjap sauce, kecap bentang manis, sweet soya sauce**]

kecipir *(Id)* Goa bean

kecombrang *(Id)* Ginger buds

kecsege *(Hu)* Sterlet, a small sturgeon from the Caspian sea

kecskeméti barackpuding *(Hu)* Apricot pudding with vanilla cream

kedgeree *(UK)* A dish of flaked smoked haddock mixed with cooked rice, curry powder and hard boiled egg usually served at breakfast. Adapted from the Indian dish khichhari (fish with rice and lentils) during the British occupation of India

keem *(Ko)* Nori

keema *(In)* Minced meat

Kefalotir *(Bk)* A cheese similar to Kefalotiri

Kefalotiri *(Gr & Cy)* A very hard scalded-curd ewes'or ewes' and goats' milk cheese similar to Parmesan and made in a cylindrical shape with a rounded top [also called **Kefalotyri**]

Kefalotyri *see* Kefalotiri

kefir *(Ru & Sa)* A slightly alcoholic and sour drink made originally from mare's milk, now from cow's milk and cultured with mixed microorganisms in the form of kefir grains.

Contains 0.6 to 0.9% lactic acid and 0.2 to 0.8% alcohol. It is used to treat gastro-intestinal problems in Russia

kefir grains A dried agglomeration of lactic Streptoccocci, Leuconostocs, yeasts and dried milk, broken into small pieces, To use, they are soaked in 2 changes of water at 20 to 30°C until swollen to 3 or 4 times their original size. They are then used to ferment milk or whey for 1 day to make kefir. They may be reused until they disintegrate if washed after each use and kept in the refrigerator

kefta *see* kefteji

keftedakia *(Gr)* Small keftedes eaten as an appetizer [also called **keftethakia**]

keftedes *(Gr) see* keftethes

kefteji *(NA)* Fried meat balls usually of mutton or offal flavoured with coriander and cumin. Often served in a rich pepper sauce with an egg [also called **kefta**]

keftethakia *(Gr) see* keftedakia

keftethes *(Gr)* Large meat balls made from seasoned minced lamb, beef or veal, mixed with white breadcrumbs, sweated chopped onions and garlic and flavoured with ouzo and mint, floured and fried. Served with salad and bread. [also called **keftedes**]

keitto *(Fi)* Soup

kekada *(In)* Crab

kekererwten *(Ho)* Chick peas

Keks *(Ge)* Biscuit

keksi *(Fi)* Biscuit

kela *(In)* Banana

keladi *(Ma)* Yam

kelapa *(Id & Ma)* Coconut

kelapa muda *(Id)* A young coconut about 10 months old. It has a soft gelatinous sweet flesh which is easily scraped from the shell. Used in desserts and drinks

kelapa sayur *(Ma)* Chopped mixed vegetables cooked in coconut milk

kelapa setengah tua *(Ma)* Young coconut; *see* kelapa muda

kelapa tua santan *(Ma)* Coconut milk

kelbimbó *(Hu)* Brussel sprouts

keledek *(Ma)* Sweet potato

kelp A general name for varieties of brown seaweed *Laminaria* spp. common on the European coasts. Can be eaten raw or cooked

kelt A salmon which has spawned and is thin and useless for eating

kem *(Th)* Salty

kemangi *(Id & Ma)* A mild basil native to Indonesia and Malaysia

kembang kol *(Id)* Cauliflower

kembang pala *(Ma)* Mace

kemiri *(Id)* Candlenut

kempferia galangal Long thin roots of a plant *Kaempferia galangal* or *K. pandurata* which resemble dahlia tubers. Normally dried and sliced for use in East Asian dishes. It has a stronger flavour than lesser galangal q.v. and should be used sparingly [also called **lesser ginger**]

kencur *(Id)* **1** Powdered lesser galangal root **2** Zedoary

keng *(Th) see* gaeng

kenkey *(Af)* A kind of porridge from Ghana made with fermented maize

Kent lent pie *(UK)* Short crust pastry baked blind in a flan case, filled with milk thickened with ground rice which is added into a creamed butter, sugar and egg mix flavoured with grated lemon zest, salt and nutmeg, currants sprinkled on top and the whole baked at 190°C until browned

Kentish cob *see* filbert

Kentish huffkin *(UK)* A small oval flat yeast-raised loaf or roll with a deep indentation in the centre and a soft crust. The dough is enriched with a little sugar and butter and they weigh about 60 g each

Kentish pudding pie *(UK) see* Kent lent pie

Kentish sausage *(UK)* A coarse textured sausage containing lean pork and pork fat (2:1), seasoned and flavoured with sage, mace and nutmeg

kentjoer *(Ho)* Zedoary

Kentucky ham *(USA)* Ham made from pigs traditionally fattened on acorns, beans and clover. The ham is dry salted and smoked over apple and hickory wood and matured for up to a year. The name refers to the method of curing

Kenya coffee A sharp, aromatic coffee from Kenya

kenyér *(Hu)* Bread

kepong beras boh *(Id)* Galapong

kepro knedlo zelo *(Cz)* A traditional Czech dish of roast pork with dumplings and sauerkraut

képviselófánk *(Hu)* Cream puff

keraa *(Ne)* Banana

keran ka achar *(In)* Pickled venison meat

kerapu bara *(Ma)* Garoupa, the fish

kerapu lodi *(Id)* Garoupa, the fish

kerbau *(Id)* Buffalo

kere *(Id)* Ridged sand clam

kerma *(Fi)* Cream

kerma kastike *(Fi)* Cream sauce

kermakakku *(Fi)* Cream cake

kermes A red dye similar to cochineal from an insect *Coccus ilicis* which lives on the kermes oak. Referred to by Chaucer as grains of Portugal

kern milk *(UK)* The Scottish term for buttermilk

kernel The edible, usually central part of a nut or stone of a fruit

Kernhem *(Ho)* A soft sticky cows' milk cheese with 60% butterfat. Initially rindless, it can be ripened for 30 days in a cool damp atmosphere to give a rich full flavour and an orange-brown rind

kerrie *(Ho)* Curry

kerrierijst *(Ho)* Curried rice

kers *(Ho)* Cherry

kerupuk *(Id) see* krupek

kerupuk singkong *(Id)* A type of poppadom made from tapioca starch and cassava chips

kesäkeitto *(Fi)* Summer vegetable soup. Lit. summer soup

kesar *(In)* Saffron

keshar *(Ne)* Saffron

keshy yena *(Ca)* Edam cheese stuffed and baked with various mixtures of poultry, fish, shellfish, meat, etc. From the Dutch East Indies

keskülü fukara *(Tu)* A sweetened milk pudding thickened with rice flour and flavoured with liquidized almonds or almond essence and chopped almonds and topped with chopped pistachio nuts and desiccated coconut. Served chilled

kesong puti *(Ph)* Cottage cheese made from water buffalo milk [also called **quesong puti**]

kesram *(In)* Saffron

kesti *(Fi)* A cheese similar to Tilsit, flavoured with caraway seeds

keta *(Ru)* Siberian salmon

keta caviar *see* ikura and ketovaia

ketan *(Id)* A glutinous rice served as a dessert with desiccated coconut and a brown sugar syrup

ketchup A commercially produced sauce sold in bottles to be used cold as a condiment. Usually of one particular flavour, e.g. tomato, mushroom, etc. The name is derived from the SEA word for sauce i.e. kecap; *see also* pontac ketchup [also called **catsup, catchup**]

ketela pohon *(Id)* Cassava

ketelkoek *(Ho)* Steamed pudding

ketimun *(Id)* Cucumber

ketjap *(Ho)* Ketchup

ketjap sauce *see* kecap manis

ketola *(Ma)* Angled loofah

ketola ular *(Ma)* Snake gourd

ketovaia *(Ru)* The large red and almost transparent eggs of Siberian salmon. It is more salty then true caviar and has a different flavour [also called **red caviar, keta caviar**]

ketumbar *(Id & Ma)* Coriander seeds

ketumbar jinten *(Id & Ma)* A mixture of ground cumin and coriander seeds

Keule *(Ge)* Saddle, haunch or leg (of meat)

Keulenrochen *(Ge)* Thornback ray

kevada *(Ne)* Screwpine

kewra *see* screwpine

kewra essence An extract of the flowers of screwpine used in India to flavour meat, poultry and rice dishes

kex *(Sw)* An unsweetened cracker biscuit

key lime *see* West Indian lime

key lime pie A blind baked pastry or Graham cracker case filled with a mixture of sweetened condensed milk, lime juice and egg yolks which have been cooked out over a bain marie. Served cold or topped with meringue and browned in the oven

kezuri-bushi *(Ja)* Flakes or shavings of dried Pacific bonito

kg The abbreviation for kilogram in any language

kha *(Th)* Greater galangal

khachapuri *(Ru)* A Georgian yeasted flour water dough incorporating melted butter (25% of flour), kneaded and allowed to rise, rolled out, cut into squares, grated Haloumi cheese mixed with egg piled in the middle of each square and the corners pulled into the centre, egg washed, filling sprinkled with chopped herbs and the breads baked at 190°C for 25 minutes or until the cheese is browned.

khajur *(In)* Date

kha kho *(Vi)* Shallots

khal *(Ne)* A stone mortar used for grinding grains and spices

khalia *(In)* A brass or cast iron mortar used for grinding hard grains and spices using a matching pestle *(musaria)*

kha mar *(Bm)* Oyster

kha-min *(Th)* Turmeric

kha min khao *(Th)* Zedoary

khamir *(In)* A natural yeast used for making soft bread. It is propagated in sourdough fashion with flour and yoghurt

khanom chine *(Th)* Small bundles of cooked rice noodles sold as instant food. Usually resteamed and served with a savoury sauce or curry

khanom jeen *(Th)* Fast food, instant food

khao *(Th)* Rice

khao chair *(Th)* Ice cold cooked long grain rice served with a selection of small snacks and appetizers

khao niew *(Th)* Sticky rice

khao pad *(Th)* Fried rice

khao phod *(Th)* Sweet corn

khao phoune *(La)* Cooked rice vermicelli topped with bean sprouts, salad leaves, chopped banana heart and flower and covered with a creamy coconut milk sauce flavoured with chillis and peanuts and containing chopped fish, meat or poultry. Often served for breakfast

khao tom gung *(Th)* Congee flavoured with fish sauce. Eaten for breakfast

khas khas 1 *(In)* Poppy seeds **2** An aromatic grass *Vetiveria zizanioides* used as a flavouring in Indian cooking. Grown in India and the south of the USA [also called **vetiver**]

khas syrup A sweetened extract of the aromatic grass khas khas

khas water An extract of the aromatic grass khas khas

kha-wel *(Bm)* Cuttlefish

kha-ya-nyo *(Bm)* Asian mussel

kheer *(In)* A sweet made from rice cooked in milk until it is completely disintegrated, then sugar, raisins, chopped dried apricots, bruised cardamom seeds and cinnamon stick added and the whole cooked for 1.5 hours, almond slivers added towards the end, cooled and thinned with a little rose water until a thick pouring consistency, put in individual bowls, chilled and decorated

kheera *(In)* Cucumber

khesari *(In)* Lath

khichhari *(In)* A dish of cooked rice mixed with a variety of ingredients from a few sprouted seeds or lentils to an elaborate mixture of spices, nuts and raisins. The origin of kedgeree [also called **kichardi, kitcheri, khichri**]

khichri *(In)* *see* khichhari

khing *(Th)* Ginger

khing dong *(Th)* Chow chow preserve

khleb *(Ru)* Bread

khleb i sol *(Ru)* Bread and salt, the traditional words of welcome in Russia. The two commodities are often offered to guests when arriving for a celebratory meal

khli *(NA)* Dried meat sometimes used in tagine

khnehey *(Cm)* Ginger

khoa *(In)* *see* khoya

khoai mon *(Vi)* Taro

khobz *(NA)* Bread

khobz bishemar *(NA)* A savoury turnover or similar made from pastry wrapped around a filling or from a stuffed pitta-type bread

khoobani *(In)* Apricot

khoresh *(Pe)* A thin stew of meat, fruit and nuts served with rice

khoya *(In)* Milk dehydrated by stirring over a low heat until it becomes a thick paste which is pressed into cakes. It is used for making sweetmeats and Indian cakes and to enrich sweet or savoury dishes. A different texture is obtained by coagulating the milk with lemon juice before dehydrating [also called **khoa**]

khren *(Ru)* Horseradish

khtim baraing *(Cm)* Onion

khtim kraham *(Cm)* Shallots

khtim slek *(Cm)* Spring onion or scallion

khubz-tanou *(ME)* A very thin bread from the Lebanon

khum *(In)* Cloud ear fungus

khurma po-samarkandski *(Ru)* Blanched persimmons, skinned, cut in sections and fanned on a plate, covered with a sauce made with cornflour thickened orange juice, flavoured with lemon juice and zest, and scattered with pomegranate seeds

khus-khus *(In)* Poppy seeds

khuwa *(Ne)* Khoya

khvorost *(Ru)* Deep fried biscuits made from egg yolk, egg and icing sugar, creamed, flavoured with rum and vanilla and mixed with salted plain flour to make a stiff paste, kneaded 10 minutes, rolled out very thin and cut into 12 by 5 cm rectangles, a longitudinal slit made at one end and the other end threaded through this, deep fried in hot oil, drained and sprinkled with cinnamon and icing sugar. A very traditional biscuit.

kibbeh *(ME)* **1** Description of dishes made with burghul **2** Burghul and lean lamb (1:2), the burghul washed and water squeezed out, the lamb double minced, mixed with finely chopped onion and seasoning and kneaded for 10 to 15 minutes with wet hands until a smooth cohering paste results. Strict Muslims are not allowed to eat raw meat

kibbeh nayeh *(ME)* *see* kibbeh niya

kibbeh niya *(ME)* Kibbeh made with fine burghul, spread on a plate, covered with olive oil amd sprinkled with chilli powder and pine nuts. Served with lettuce and raw onion [also called **kibbeh nayeh**]

kibbeh tarablousieh *(ME)* Minced lamb fried in oil for 15 minutes, chopped onion, seasoning and allspice added and fried 20 minutes, then roasted or fried pine nuts and parsley added to form a stuffing. Kibbeh in egg sized balls made into long oval purses between the index finger and thumb, stuffing added, the package closed, rolled into an oval shape and deep fried. Served with lemon wedges.

kibble, to To grind or chop coarsely

kibbled wheat *see* cracked wheat

kicap cair *(Ma)* Light soya sauce

kicap hitam *(Ma)* A sweet dark soya sauce similar to kecap manis

kicap pekat *(Ma)* Dark soya sauce

kichardi *(In)* *see* khichhari

Kichererbsen *(Ge)* Chick peas

kickshaw *(UK)* An old fashioned term for a food delicacy or fancy dish

kid A young goat, popular in Mediterranean countries

kidney The internal organ of an animal which filters out breakdown products of metabolism from the blood and delivers them in water solution to the bladder. Their main bulk is a uniform brownish red tender tissue arranged around blood vessels and tubes. Generally prized as tender and tasty offal. The kidneys of smaller animals are grilled or fried after coring and removing the outer membrane and fat. The kidneys of larger animals are generally stewed

kidney bean A type of kidney-shaped dried French bean q.v. ranging in colour from white to black; *see also* red kidney bean

kidney fat *see* suet

kidney soup A brown roux and tomato purée boiled with brown stock, chopped ox kidney, carrot and onion lightly browned in fat and a BG added, simmered and skimmed for 2 hours, BG removed, liquidized, strained, seasoned, consistency adjusted and garnished with diced cooked kidney [also called **soupe aux rognons** (Fr)]

kiebasa *(Pl)* A boiling sausage formed in a ring containing beef, pork, garlic, seasoning and spices

Kieler Sprotten *(Ge)* Salted and smoked sprats

kieli *(Fi)* Tongue

kiev A method of pocketing, stuffing and cooking chicken breasts; *see* chicken kiev

kikka-kabu *(Ja)* Baby turnips, peeled and trimmed top and bottom, cut with a chrysanthemum cut, stood in salted water for 30 minutes to soften, dried and sprinkled with a mixture of caster sugar and salt and garnished with sweet pepper rings or with grated lemon to resemble red or yellow chrysanthemums. Stood in individual bowls lined with chrysanthemum leaves

kiku *(Ja)* Chrysanthemum flowers and leaves used as a garnish [also called **kikuna**]

kikuna *(Ja)* *see* kiku

kikurage *(Ja)* Cloud ear fungus

kilawin *(Ph)* A method of preparing fish for consumption without heating it by marinating in coconut vinegar, lime juice or kalamansi juice until it becomes translucent

kilic kebap *(Tu)* A kebab of swordfish pieces, onion, tomatoes and bay leaves dressed with lemon and grilled over charcoal

kilkis *(Sc)* *see* anchois de Norvège

Killarney *(Ir)* Irish Cheddar cheese

Kilner jar *(UK)* A strong glass jar with a separate glass lid sealed to the jar with a rubber ring and held on by a metal closure. Used for preserving fruit and vegetables. Named after Kilner's Bridge, a village in South Yorkshire

kilocalorie The old unit of energy being one thousand scientific calories. Often referred to as Calorie with a capital C. It is the energy necessary to heat 1 kg of water by 1°C

kilogram The common measure of weight approximately equal to 2.2 pounds, abbreviated kg in all languages, and divided in grams (g) (1000 g per kg). 1lb is approximately 454 g and 1 oz approximately 28 g

kilogramme *(Fr) masc.* kilogram, abbreviated kg

kilojoule The unit of energy used in nutrition which has replaced the kilocalorie or Calorie. 4.2 kilojoules equals 1 Calorie. Written kJ

kim *(Ko)* Toasted nori or laver eaten as a snack or crumbled over food

kim cham *(Vi)* Lily buds

kimchi *(Ko)* Fermented cabbage (usually Chinese leaves) or other vegetables, flavoured with salt, garlic and chillis. An aquired taste which provides most of the vegetable nutrients in the Korean diet. A western substitute can be obtained by mixing chopped Chinese leaves which have been salted to remove excess liquid, with minced spring onions, garlic, ginger, chillis, a little sugar, soya sauce and vinegar and storing in a closed jar in the refrigerator for at least 24 hours [also called **Korean pickled cabbage**]

kimini *(Ja)* Glazed shrimps made from large prawns with the tail shell left on, passed through cornflour, boiled 10 seconds in water then placed in a samll amount of boiling dashi, sake, sugar and salt, brought back to the boil, beaten egg yolk poured slowly over the prawns, simmered 2 minutes without stirring, removed from the heat and rested for a further 2 minutes

kinako *(Ja)* Soya bean flour

kinchay *(Ph)* Chinese celery

king *(Th)* Ginger

king, à la *(En & Fr)* Used of a dish served in a rich cream sauce with mushrooms and green sweet peppers

king crab A large light brown crab *Paralithodes camtschatica* with long legs and weighing to 3.5 kg, found on the coasts of Alaska

king mandarin An important mandarin *Citrus nobilis*, probably a mandarin/orange cross, from SEA and Japan. The Japanese variety is smaller and has a smoother rind than that from SEA but is slightly bitter

king prawn A large prawn of the *Penaeidae* family, found in the Mediterranean, off the Spanish and Portuguese coasts and elsewhere in the world. Generally a dirty greyish brown when raw and pink to red when cooked. See under crevette rose, crevette royale, crevette rouge, eastern king prawn, western king prawn, banana prawn and tiger prawn

king salmon *see* chinook salmon

king scallop *see* great scallop

kings acre berry A hybrid blackberry *Rubus* spp.

kinkan *(Ja)* Kumquat

kinkku *(Fi)* Ham

kinoko *(Ja)* Mushrooms

kinome *(Ja)* Young shoots of the anise pepper tree *Xanthoxylum piperitum* used as a garnish

kinugoshi tofu *(Ja)* Silk bean curd

kip *(Ho)* Chicken

kip aan't spit *(Ho)* Grilled chicken

kippelever *(Ho)* Chicken liver

kipper A degutted herring, split and flattened from the belly side, lightly brined and then cold smoked

kipper, to To preserve fish by salting then smoking

kipper sausage *(UK)* A Scottish sausage made with kipper flesh without bones or skin, probably mixed with suet and breadcrumbs

kippesoep *(Ho)* Chicken broth

kiri bath *(Sr)* A thick mixture of cooked soft rice and coconut cream, shaped into flat diamonds and served with jaggery at festivals

kiriboshi daikon Sun dried strips of mooli. Added to soups and stews

kirkeen *(Ir)* Carpet shell clam

kirsch A strong alcoholic infusion of cherry and cherry kernels used as a flavouring in e.g. black forest gateau

Kirschen *(Ge)* Cherries

Kirschenkaltschale *(Ge)* Morello cherries and the cracked kernels cooked in sugar syrup, strained, mixed with white wine and served cold, garnished with whole pitted cherries

Kirschwasser *(Ge)* Kirsch, the liqueur

kirsebær *(De)* Cherries

kirsikka *(Fi)* Cherries

kisel *(Ru)* Kissel

kishk *(ME)* A fermented mixture of bulgar, milk and yoghurt, dried, powdered and used to make a kind of porridge

kishka *(Ru & Hu)* A sausage rather like haggis made from chopped beef suet, onion, flour or rice and seasonings, stuffed in beef intestines, tied and simmered over a low heat with onions. Served hot with horseradish sauce as an appetizer [also called **stuffed derma**]

kissel An East European dessert of puréed red berries and/or fruit juice, thickened with gelatine, cornflour or arrowroot and served with cream. Sometimes used in the same way as redcurrant jelly in savoury sauces

kissela dahorp *(Bk)* Diced mutton simmered with herbs, separated and mixed with half cooked rice, fried chopped onions, paprika, a little vinegar and sufficient of the cooking liquor to be absorbed by the rice and all baked in the oven until the rice is cooked

kisu *(Ja)* A small white fish

kiszka kaszana *(Pl)* A cooked sausage made with blood and dehusked buckwheat

kitcheri *(In) see* khichhari

kited fillet *(USA)* A boned and filleted round fish in which a cut is made along the top of the fish to expose the main bones and viscera which are removed leaving the two halves joined by the abdominal flesh at the bottom of the fish

kitha neem *(In)* Curry leaf

kitsune donburi *(Ja)* Udon noodles cooked until al dente, topped with aburage, simmered in dashi, soya sauce, mirin and sugar until they have absorbed most of the liquid and served with kakejiru soup

kiwano A large egg shaped fruit with a reddish yellow warty skin enclosing a sweet green watery and rather insipid flesh and large cucumber like seeds. Eaten like passion fruit. Grown in Africa and New Zealand [also called **horned melon**]

kiwi fruit A small egg-shaped fruit from a trailing climber *Actinidia chinensis* and *A. deliciosa*, to 10 cm long, with a light brown hairy skin containing a sweet bright green flesh tasting of melons and strawberries and with symmetrically arranged black seeds. Often peeled and sliced for decoration or used in tarts and salads. As the fruit contains proteases it can be used to tenderize meat but will degrade gelatine and prevent jellies from setting. Originally from China but now mainly grown and exported from New Zealand [also called **Chinese gooseberry**]

kjeks *(No)* Dry crackers, biscuits

kjøtt *(No)* Meat

kjøttbolle *(No)* Meat ball

kjøttedeig *(No)* Minced meat

kjøttfarse *(No)* Hamburger meat, minced meat

kjøttpudding *(No)* Meat loaf

kjøttsuppe *(No)* Meat broth, bouillon

Klaben *(Ge)* A white fruit bread with nuts and dried vine fruits

klarbär *(Sw)* Amarelles, the sour cherry

klare Fleischbrühe *(Ge)* Clear beef broth, consommé

klare Rindsuppe *(Au)* Clear beef broth

klatkager *(De)* Rice fritters

Kleie *(Ge)* Bran

kleine gevlekte hondshaai *(Ho)* Dogfish

kleingefleckter Katzenhai *(Ge)* Dogfish

Kleist *(Ge)* Brill

klejner *(De)* Crullers

kletskoppen *(Ho)* Gingersnaps

Kliesche *(Ge)* Dab, the fish

klimatofilla *(Gr)* Vine leaves

klimp *(Sw)* A traditional product of dumplings made from a very thick roux-based white sauce with added egg yolk and variously flavoured with grated bitter almonds, crushed cardamom seeds, or grated cheese, poured into moulds, chilled, turned out and nowadays usually sliced for use as a consommé garnish

klippfisk *(No)* Cod that is salted and spread out on stones and rocks to dry [also called **clipfish**]

klobas *(Cz & Hu)* A juicy sausage made from smoked pork or veal mixed with wine, filled into casings and formed into a continuous spiral like a Cumberland sausage

Kloepfer *(He)* A cervelas sausage from Basle made of beef, pork, bacon and pork rind, seasoned and lightly spiced, packed in medium or narrow hog casings, tied into 10 cm lengths and lightly smoked [also called **Klöpfer**]

Klöpfer *(He) see* Kloepfer

Klopse *(Ge)* Meat balls made with a mixture of meats

Klösse *(Ge)* Dumplings made from potatoes and flour mixed with milk, fat and sometimes bacon. Breadcrumbs and semolina may be incorporated. Boiled and served as an accompaniment to sweet or savoury dishes [also called **knödel**]

Klosterkäse *(Ge)* A soft, surface ripened

cheese made in block form from semi-skimmed cows' milk. Similar to Romadur. Contains 52% water, 19% fat and 24% protein

kluay *(Th)* Banana

klyukva *(Ru)* Cranberries

Knackerli *(He)* A spiced sausage from Appenzell made from beef, pork and veal [also called **Appenzellerli**]

Knackwurst *(Ge)* A short fat variety of Frankfurter made from a seasoned mixture of lean pork, beef, pork fat and saltpetre, flavoured with garlic and cumin, filled into beef runners, dried and smoked. Served hot after boiling

knaidlech Very popular Jewish dumplings made with crushed unleavened matzos, eggs, water, salt and molten fat or oil, boiled and served with soup. Suitable for passover since made with matzo meal [also called **knedlach**]

knakworst *(Ho)* Sausage, Frankfurter

Knaost *see* pultost

knead, to To mix a stiff dough by repeatedly compressing it and folding in or over, this may be done manually or mechanically by using a dough hook at slow speed. In the case of bread doughs made from strong flour it is used to develop sheets of gluten in the mixture and to incorporate air. The air acts as nuclei for the formation of bubbles of carbon dioxide during rising and proving, the gluten sheets facilitate their retention in the cooking dough

kneaded butter Beurre manié

knedelach *see* knaidlech

knedlíky *(Cz)* Huge soft dumplings made from flour and/or semolina, eggs, fat and water, boiled and served with soup or if sweetened as a dessert

Knepfle Small dumplings from Alsace made with semolina or mashed potatoes and flour, mixed with chopped parsley, chopped leek and egg yolks

kneten *(Ge)* To knead

knickerbocker glory Alternate layers of jelly, fruit, ice cream and whipped cream assembled in a tall sundae glass

Kniestück *(Ge)* Knuckle of veal

knife A thin steel blade one edge of which is sharpened, the whole fitted with a handle. They come in various thicknesses and profiles and sometimes with a serrated or saw edge, for various types of work. See under office, turning, cooks, filleting, boning, slicing and bread knife

knishes Semicircular Jewish pastry turnovers with a variety of fillings, some specific to particular festivals

kniv *(De, No, Sw)* Knife

knob celery *see* celeriac

Knoblauch *(Ge)* Garlic

Knoblauchwurst *(Ge)* A sausage made from a seasoned mixture of lean pork and pork fat, spiced and heavily flavoured with garlic and formed in a ring [also called **knoblaugh** (USA)]

knoblaugh *(USA)* *see* Knoblauchwurst

Knochen *(Ge)* Bones

knock back, to To lightly knead a yeast-raised dough which has risen once in order to eliminate large gas bubbles and help further develop the gluten. This is done prior to shaping the dough [also called **to knock down**]

knock down, to *see* to knock back

knockpølse *(De)* A Danish version of knackwurst made from a mixture of finely chopped beef, pork and veal with about 10% diced pork back fat, seasoning and saltpetre, flavoured with nutmeg, cinnamon, ginger and garlic, packed into hog casings, linked (12 cm), air-dried and hot smoked

knockwurst *(USA)* A version of Knackwurst made with smoked beef and pork

Knödel *(Ge & It)* Dumpling

knödel alla tirolese in brodo *(It)* Bread and bacon dumplings served in beef broth

knoflook *(Ho)* Garlic

knol *(Ho)* Turnip

knol-kohl *(In)* Kohlrabi

knolle *(It)* Large boiled dumplings from the north west

Knollensellerie *(Ge)* Celeriac

knotted marjoram *see* marjoram

knuckle The lower parts (shin) of a leg of veal, pork or lamb, extending down to the hock

knuckle of lamb *see* shank end of leg of lamb

knuckle of veal The lower part of a leg of veal below the thick part of the muscle usually cut into rounds for osso buco q.v.

knusprige Kruste *(Ge)* Pork crackling

kobe *(Ja)* Steaks from a type of beef cattle reared or finished on beer and brewer's grains and massaged daily to produce tender back meat marbled with fat. The technique has now been introduced into France; *see* boeuf de Constance

Koblenz sausage *(Ge)* A thin sausage made

from veal and pork which has been pickled in brine for several days, minced with onions and garlic, flavoured with pepper, packed loosely in narrow hog casings, linked, air dried and smoked over oak and beech. Served hot [also called **Coblenz sausage**]

koblihy *(Cz)* Jam doughnut

kochujang *(Ko)* Chilli bean paste

Kochwurst *(Ge)* A group of German/Austrian slicing or spreading sausages such as Leberwurst, Zungenwurst and Berliner Rotwurst which are steamed or boiled for a considerable time. They do not keep

kød *(De)* Meat

kødboller *(De)* Meat balls

kødfars *(De)* Meat stuffing, forcemeat

koek *(Ho)* Cake or biscuit, plural koekjes

kofta 1 *(ME)* Cylinders of a spiced minced meat mix formed around skewers brushed with oil, and grilled over charcoal. A typical mix might contain double minced lamb, chopped onion, chopped parsley, ground allspice, fenugreek, red pepper and salt [also called **kofte, kufta**] **2** *(In)* Finely ground meat sometimes blended with finely chopped aromatics, seasoning and herbs, bound with egg and formed into balls, sometimes over sweet-sour plums or a paste of dried apricots and herbs. May be braised, curried or grilled on skewers; *see also* nargisi

kofte *see* kofta

köfte *(Tu)* Meat balls shaped like small rolls and fried in mutton fat. Usually made from chopped raw lamb or mutton, mixed with water, soaked breadcrumbs, eggs, garlic, cinnamon and salt

kogt *(De)* Cooked or boiled

kohana fu *(Ja)* Fully cooked, dried and crushed gluten dough rather like breadcrumbs which is sprinkled directly over food [also called **flower fu**]

kohitsuji *(Ja)* Lamb

Kohl *(Ge)* Cabbage

Kohl und Pinkel *(Ge)* Cabbage and sausage

Kohlehydrate *(Ge)* Starch

Kohlrabi *(Ge)* Kohlrabi

kohlrabi The thickened turnip-like lower stem of a member of the *Brassica* family *Brassica oleraceae* Gongylodes Group from which the rather sparse leaves spring, generally green to red, and grows above ground. The flesh is crisp, has a mild flavour and is eaten raw or cooked. Popular in Germany

Kohlroulade *(Ge)* Blanched cabbage leaves wrapped around minced meat, fried then braised.

koi-kuchi shoyu *(Ja)* Dark soya sauce

kokoska u unaku od slacice *(Bk)* A Croatian speciality of roast chicken coated with a thick sauce made from seasoned chicken stock and vinegar thickened with egg yolks and soured cream. Served with dumplings

kokosnoot *(Ho)* Coconut

kokosnøtt *(No)* Coconut

koksalt *(No)* Salt

kokt *(No & Sw)* Boiled

kokt torsk *(Sw)* Thick slices of poached cod served with egg sauce or melted butter and accompanied by boiled potatoes

kokum The fruit of an Indian tree *Garcinia indica* of the same family as the mangosteen. The flesh is dried and used as a souring agent. A semisolid fat, kokum butter, is extracted from the large seeds. The dried fruits resemble sour prunes [also called **cocum**]

kola nut *see* cola bean

koláce *(Cz)* A fruit-filled bun

kolbasa *(Ru)* Smoked ham sausage common in Poland and the western Russian republics

kolbász *(Hu)* Sausage

kol-bee *see* colbi

kolcannon *see* colcannon

koldt kød *(De)* Cold sliced cooked meats

koldtbord *(No)* Fork supper (buffet), cold collation, similar to smörgåsbord

kolja *(Sw)* Haddock

kolje *(No)* Haddock

Kölle *(Ge)* Savory, the herb

kolokythaki *(Gr)* Courgettes

kolska *(Pl)* A firm pork sausage form Poznan and Lublin

komatsuna A diverse group of oriental brassicas *Brassica rapa* var. *perviridis.* The loose leaves which form a plant up to 30 cm by 18 cm have a flavour between cabbage and spinach. They are eaten cooked as a vegetable or sliced raw in salads [also called **spinach mustard**]

kombu *(Ja)* A type of broad leafed kelp *Laminaria* spp. which is available as dried thick dark green strips (30 cm long and folded) or in powdered form. Used to make stock, to make a tea or eaten as a vegetable after boiling for 30 minutes. On storage it develops a white surface covering which should be wiped off before use. It is soaked to soften and then scored with a knife to release the flavour and may be used twice or more before before all the flavour is extracted; *see also* oboru-, tororo- and shiraita-kombu [also called **sea kelp, tangle kelp**]

kome *(Ja)* Uncooked rice

Komijnekass *(Ho)* A hard cheese flavoured with caraway seeds and cloves

komkommer *(Ho)* Cucumber

komló *(Hu)* Hops

kompot *(Ru)* Compote, often made with a mixture of diced fruit and nuts, sweetened with honey

Kompott *(Ge)* Fruit stewed in a sugar syrup

kong syin tsai *(Ch)* Swamp cabbage

Königinpastete *(Ge)* A savoury filled pasty, usually meat and mushrooms

Königinsuppe *(Ge)* A chicken soup thickened with a liaison of cream and eggs

Königsberger Klopse *(Ge)* Meat balls simmered in good stock and served with the thickened cooking liquor flavoured with capers and boiled rice

Königskuchen *(Ge)* A rum-flavoured cake made by the creaming method from flour, sugar, butter, separated eggs and ground almonds (2:3:2:4:1) with 8 teaspoonfuls (6 g) of baking powder per kg of flour, creaming with egg yolks and folding in the stiffly beaten egg whites after the flour. The cake is flavoured with lemon zest and rum-soaked dried vine fruits and baked at roughly 175°C

Königwurst *(Ge)* King's sausage. Made from equal parts of chicken and partridge meat mixed with chopped mushrooms, truffle shavings, seasoning and mace, moistened with wine, packed into casings, tied and braised. Eaten cold

konijn *(Ho)* Rabbit

koning inne groente *(Ho)* Literally queen of vegetables, used of the thick white asparagus much liked by the Dutch and in season during May and June

konjak *(Sw)* Brandy

konjakk *(No)* Brandy

konnyaku *(Ja)* Black bean curd q.v. which may be unrefined (black) or refined by bleaching and filtering (white); *see also* ito konnyaku

konservirovannye tomaty po-bakinsky *(Ru)* A Georgian tomato chutney made with chopped red and yellow sweet peppers, chillis, chopped onions and tomatoes all combined in their raw state with sugar, salt and a little wine vinegar and left for at least 24 hours before using

konservirovannye yabloki *(Ru)* Apple preserve made from peeled, cored and chopped dessert apples stewed in dry cider with light brown sugar, finely chopped onion, garlic, peeled ginger and sweet red pepper, flavoured with lemon zest, lemon juice and cayenne pepper and matured for at least 3 days. Served with pork

kookoo *see* eggah

kool *(Ho)* Cabbage

koolraap *(Ho)* Turnip

koosmali *(In)* A side dish made with grated raw carrots and fried black mustard seeds

kop *(De)* Cup

Kopanisti *(Gr)* A semi-hard creamy strong tasting blue cheese from the Aegean islands. It is salted and placed in pots to ripen for 1 to 2 months

Kopenhagener *(Ge)* Danish pastries

Kopfsalat *(Ge)* Lettuce

Kopfsalatherzen *(Ge)* Lettuce hearts

Kopfsalatsuppe *(Ge)* Lettuce soup

kopp *(No & Sw)* Cup

koprivstenska lukanka *(Bu)* A keeping sausage made from neck or spare rib of pork and leg of beef (2:1), chopped, drained, minced, seasoned, mixed with sugar and caraway seeds, allowed to mature for 12 hours then packed in ox casings, made into long links and air dried for 3 months

kopvoorn *(Ho)* Chub, the fish

kop yop *(Id)* Makapuno

Korbkäse *(Ge)* A soft acid-curdled cows' milk cheese with a smooth texture and thin rind weighing to 125 g

Korean cabbage *see* Chinese leaves

Korean pickled cabbage *see* kimchi

koriandr *(Ru)* Coriander

korinkake *(No)* Currant cake

Korinthen *(Ge)* Currants, from grapes

koritsa *(Ru)* Cinnamon

korma *(In)* Indian braising of meat or vegetables with some or all of water, stock, yoghurt or cream. Styles vary with some cooked to a thick sauce, some almost dry and others to a flaky crust. Only the best young meat is used. The early parts of the braising process often involve dry cooking, i.e. using a heavy pan over a fierce heat, searing the meat, then adding cooking liquor gradually so as to maintain dry but not burnt conditions. See e.g. shikar korma and shahar korma; *see also* doh peeazah

korma powder *(In)* A mild spice mix used in korma cooking with white pepper instead of chilli powder

Korn *(Ge)* Cereals, grain

körsbär *(Sw)* Cherries

körte *(Hu)* Pear

korv *(Sw)* Sausage

korv och bröd *(Sw)* Sausage in a roll

korv Stroganoff *(Sw)* A sausage stroganoff made with strips of skinned Vienna type sausage (Frankfurter, Falukorv, etc.), fried in butter with chopped onions until brown then simmered in a closed pan for 10 minutes with acidulated cream and tomato purée

Koscher *(Ge)* Kosher

kosher Food slaughtered and/or prepared according to the strict Jewish dietary laws

kosher salt *(USA)* Sea salt

koshi-an *(Ja)* A smooth sweet red bean paste q.v.

kosho *(Ja)* Peppercorn

Kossuth cake *(USA)* Iced sponge cake filled with whipped cream or ice cream

Kostromskoi *(Ru)* A cows' milk cheese similar to Gouda

kota kapama *(Gr)* Portioned chicken, browned in olive oil and butter, reserved, chopped onions, garlic and celery browned in the same fat, then all combined with tomato purée, chopped or canned tomatoes and red wine, flavoured with a cinnamon stick and simmered 45 minutes, cinnamon removed and the chicken served with the reduced cooking sauce

kotduny *(Pl)* A type of ravioli

kotelet *(De & Ho)* Cutlet, chop

Kotelett *(Ge)* Cutlet, chop

kotelett *(No)* Chop

kotlett *(Sw)* Chop, cutlet

kotlety *(Ru)* Minced beef and pork, milk-soaked breadcrumbs, egg and seasoning formed into round or oval patties, panéed and fried. Served with a Béchamel or tomato sauce and vegetables

kotlety po-kievsky *(Ru)* Chicken kiev, the stuffing is traditionally unsalted butter, lemon juice, lemon zest and chopped tarragon. Deep fried at 190°C

kotlety pojarski *(Ru)* Minced chicken, veal or pork processed with breadcrumbs, butter and cream and flavoured with nutmeg, chilled, panéed, rechilled then fried and served with an appropriate sauce

kotlety iz rybi *(Ru)* As kotlety but made with minced cod or pike flesh and butter. Served coated with melted butter and with vegetables in a Béchamel sauce

kotopitta *(Gr)* A double crust chicken pie using layers of buttered filo pastry as the container filled with diced cooked chicken bound with a chicken velouté flavoured with chopped coriander and walnuts and enriched with egg

kött *(Sw)* Meat

köttbullar *(Sw)* Minced beef meat balls fried and served with creamed potatoes and cranberry sauce

köttfärs *(Sw)* Minced meat, meat loaf

koud *(Ho)* Cold

koud vlees *(Ho)* Assorted sliced cold cooked meats

koulibiac *see* coulibiac

koumiss A thick slightly alcoholic and sour drink originally made from ass or camel's milk now made from fresh mare's milk. It is similar to but more alcoholic than kefir and rather like a gassy alcoholic yoghurt. Used to treat gastro-intestinal problems in Russia [also called **kumiss, kumyis**]

kou mou *(Ch)* A white irregular shaped mushroom similar to an oyster mushroom. Grown and use in northern China. Possibly the same species as St George's mushroom

kouneli *(Gr)* Rabbit

kourabi *(Sw)* A sweet biscuit served with coffee

kourabiedes *(Gr)* A crisp crescent-shaped biscuit flavoured with almond and aniseed

koya tofu *(Ja)* Freeze dried bean curd

koyendoro *(Ja)* Coriander leaves

koyun *(Tu)* Mutton

krab *(Ru)* Crab

krabba *(Sw)* Crab

Krabbe *(Ge)* Crab

krabbe *(No)* Crab

krabbesalat *(No)* Crab meat on lettuce, celery and dill with a mustard dressing

krabbetjes *(Ho)* Pork spareribs

krachai Kempferia galangal

kra dook *(Th)* Spare ribs

kräfta *(Sw)* Crayfish

Kraftbrühe *(Ge)* Beef consommé

kraftor *(Sw)* Crayfish

Kraftsuppe *(Ge)* Beef and vegetable soup

Kraine *(Au)* A sausage similar to Burgenländische Hauswürstel

krajana *(Pl)* A firm smoked sausage from Poznan knotted in links

Krakauer *(Au)* A sausage similar to Polish krakowska but containing visible chunks of lean meat

Krake *(Ge)* Octopus

krakelingen *(Ho)* Crackers, pretzels

krakowska *(Pl)* A slicing sausage made from a very firmly consolidated mixture of seasoned chopped lean beef, lean pork and pork fat packed in beef middles and smoked. Common throughout the country

kranjska kobasica *(Bk)* A smoked sausage made from diced pork and bacon (6:1), kneaded with sodium nitrate, garlic and seasoning for about 30 minutes, filled into small casings, linked in pairs and smoked for 3 days if to be eaten immediately or longer if to be kept

kransekage *(De)* Almond pastry ring

Kranzkuchen *(Ge)* A braided sweet cake

Krapfen 1 *(Ge & It)* Sweet fritters **2** *(He)* A rich fruit cake with pears, nuts and marzipan

Krapfenchen *(Ge)* Special doughnuts or fritters served on Shrove Tuesday *(Mardi Gras)*

krapivnie shchi *(Ru)* A soup made from seasoned meat or vegetable stock, with young nettles, sorrel, sausages and chopped onions. Served with soured cream

krapow *(Th)* *see* bai krapow

krappe *(De)* Crab

krasny perets *(Ru)* Paprika

kra-thin *(Th)* Cassia

kratiem *(Th)* Garlic

kratiem dong *(Th)* Pickled garlic

krauch soeuch *(Cm)* Kaffir lime

Krauskohl *(Ge)* Kale

Kraut *(Ge)* *coll.* Sauerkraut

Kraut mit Eisbein und Erbensuppe *(Ge)* A national dish of pigs' knuckles with cabbage and pea soup

Kraut Fleckerl *(Ge)* A dish of boiled cabbage mixed with noodles

Kräuter *(Ge)* Herbs

Kräuterkäse *(He)* *see* Sapsago

Kräuterklösse *(Ge)* Dumplings coloured green with spinach or herbs

Kräuterleberwurst *(Ge & He)* A well seasoned liver sausage flavoured with herbs and with large pieces of liver embedded in it [also called **Krauterwurst**]

Kräuterwurst *(Ge & He)* *see* Kräuterleberwurst

Kräuterwurst à la Montreux *(He)* Kräuterwurst (liver sausage) laid on a bed of baked leeks, napped with a rich brown gravy and heated through

Krautkräpfli *(He)* A type of ravioli filled with spinach

Krautwürsteln *(Au)* Cabbage rolls stuffed with minced beef and onions

krawaan *(Th)* Cardamom

Krebs *(Ge)* Crayfish

krebs *(De)* Crayfish

Krebstieren *(Ge)* Crustaceans

kreeft *(Ho)* Crayfish

Kreivi *(Fi)* A loaf shaped cheese resembling Tilsit but not flavoured with caraway seeds

krem *(No)* Whipped cream, custard

Kren *(Ge)* Horseradish

krendel *(Ru)* An egg and butter enriched yeasted dough formed after raising into a long cylinder (5 cm dia.) and tied like a pretzel, proved, egg washed, sprinkled with almond flakes and baked at 200°C, initially covered with foil then uncovered and dusted with icing sugar

Krenfleisch *(Ge)* Sliced hot boiled beef served with horseradish sauce

krenfleish *(It)* Pork, boiled in vinegar and wine and served with horseradish and potatoes

krenten *(Ho)* Currants (dried vine fruit)

krentenbrood *(Ho)* Currant bread

krentenbroodjes *(Ho)* Currant buns

kreplach A type of Jewish ravioli with a variety of fillings. Meat or chicken are served in chicken consommé. Fillings based on cheese, soured cream and eggs are served with melted butter and either salt or sugar

kreps *(No)* Small crayfish

Kreuzkümmel *(Ge)* Cumin

Krevetten *(Ge)* Shrimps

kroepoek *(Ho)* Krupek

Krokette *(Ge)* Croquette

kromeski *see* cromesquis

kromesky *see* cromesquis

krona *(Mee)* A mild red pepper

kronärtskocka *(Sw)* Artichoke

Kronsbeere *(Ge)* Cranberry

kroppkakor *(Sw)* Potato dumplings made with minced raw potatoes mixed with egg, flour and seasoning to a give a light mixture. Formed into dumplings around a filling of sweated chopped gammon and onions, boiled in water until they float plus a further 5 minutes. Served with melted butter and cranberry sauce

kropsla *(Ho)* Lettuce

kropsua *(Fi)* A thick pancake

krøsesuppe *(De)* A soup made from a mixture of dried fruits, apples and chicken giblets

kruiden *(Ho)* Herbs

kruiden azn *(Ho)* Herb-flavoured vinegar

kruidenagel *(Ho)* Clove, the spice

kruisbes *(Ho)* Gooseberry

krumpli *(Hu)* **1** Potato **2** A stew of mainly vegetables, onions, potatoes, tomatoes, green sweet peppers, etc. with bacon and sausage, seasoned and flavoured with paprika

krung gaeng *(Th)* The general term for curry pastes

krung gaeng kao wan *(Th)* A very hot green curry paste made hot by the fresh green chillis which give it its colour

krung gaeng kare leung *(Th)* A mild yellow curry paste coloured using fresh turmeric root

krung gaeng ped daeng *(Th)* A medium to hot commercial and very aromatic curry paste coloured red. A typical formulation contains chopped seeded New Mexico chillis, minced greater galangal root, coriander root and shallots, chopped kaffir lime rind and lemon grass root and shrimp paste

krung gaeng som An orange coloured curry paste used in seafood soups and dishes

krupek *see* krupuk

krupek tempeh A krupuk chip flavoured with tempeh

krupek udang A shelled. deveined and flattened shrimp, dried and resembling a crisp. Alternatively, a rice flour batter flavoured with powdered dried shrimp, dried and deep fried

krupuk *(Id)* A large deep fried crisp pancake flavoured with dried prawns similar to the Indian poppadom or Chinese prawn cracker. Smaller varieties are made with fresh ingredients, e.g. shrimps and tapioca chips, by rolling out and drying; *see also* krupek udang, krupek ikan, singkong, emping melinjo and krupek tempe [also called **krupek, kerupuk**]

krupuk ikan *(Id)* A rice flour batter flavoured with fish, dried and deep fried rather like an Indian poppadom or Chinese prawn cracker

krusbär *(Sw)* Gooseberries

Krustentieren *(Ge)* Crustaceans

kryddersild *(No)* Spiced herring

kryddor *(Sw)* Condiments, spices

Kryddost *(Sw)* A cows' milk cheese flavoured with caraway seeds and cloves

kryddpeppar *(Sw)* Allspice

Kryddsvecia *(Sw)* Sveciaost cheese flavoured with various spices

kuali *(Ma)* Wok

kubis bunga *(Ma)* Cauliflower

ku cai *(Ma)* Garlic chive

Kuchen *(Ge)* Cake or pastry

Küchenragout *(Ge)* A rich stew of chicken, sweetbreads, veal meat balls, clams, asparagus and peas

kudamono *(Ja)* Fruit, served at the end of a meal in small portions and decorative shapes

kudzu *see* kuzu

kuei *(Ch)* Cassia

kugel A Jewish baked pudding consisting of rice or noodles with dried vine fruits, fresh fruit, chopped nuts, eggs, sugar, spices and margarine or molten chicken fat

Kugelhopf *(Ge & He)* Sponge cake or large choux pastry balls filled with whipped cream [also called **Kugelhoph**]

Kugelhoph *(Ge & He) see* Kugelhopf

kugelhumf tin A tubular cake tin hinged along the length for cooking long cylindrical cakes

kugelis *(Li)* A famous dish of grated raw potatoes, salted and drained for 10 minutes, dried, combined with a little flour, baking powder, bacon fat, egg, grated onion, caraway seed and pepper, placed in a baking dish, dotted with butter and baked at 180°C for 35 minutes then at 200°C until browned. Served with fried onions

ku gua *(Ch)* Bitter melon

kühl *(Ge)* Cool

kuha *(Fi)* Pike-perch

kui *(Ko)* Grilled or cooked on the griddle

kuiken *(Ho)* Squab, young chicken, young pigeon

kukhura ka phul *(Ne)* Hen egg

kukorica *(Hu)* Sweetcorn

kukuruza *(Ru)* Maize

kulchas *(In)* A yeast or other leaven raised white flour dough made into rounds and deep fried. May be filled with cheese or vegetables before cooking

kulfi *(In)* A type of ice cream made from sweetened full cream milk thickened with cornstarch, mixed with chopped almonds and pistachio nuts and flavoured with rose water

kulfi mould A small conical metal mould used for shaping kulfi

kulibyaka *(Ru)* The original Russian coulibiac q.v.

kulich *(Ru)* A traditional yeast-raised Easter cake made with flour, milk, sugar and butter (11:5:4:2) mixed with eggs and egg yolks to make a firm well kneaded dough, after allowing a thin batter made with some of the flour, the milk and the yeast to rise, mixed after the first proving with sultanas, rum, powdered saffron, crushed cardomom seeds, chopped mixed peel and almond slivers, knocked back, proved and baked at 200°C for 15 minutes then at 180°C until cooked

kulitis *(Ph)* Amaranth

kulthi bean *see* horse gram

kumara *(NZ)* The Maori term for sweet potato

kumin *(Ja)* Cumin

kumiss *see* koumiss

kumler *(No)* Potato dumplings

kummel *(Sw)* Hake

Kümmel **1** *(Ge)* Caraway seed **2** *(Ho)* A caraway-flavoured liqueur sometimes used for flavouring

Kümmelkase *(Ge)* A soft surface ripened caraway-flavoured cows' milk cheese. Contains 58% water, 21% fat and 19% protein

Kümmelsuppe *(Ge)* Caraway-flavoured soup

kumquat One of the three principal varieties of citrus *Fortunella* spp. esp. *F. japonica* & *F. margarita* with oval shaped fruits about 2 to 4 cm in diameter with an edible skin and an unusual bitter sweet flavour. Introduced to the UK in 1846 and thence worldwide. Crystallized, made into marmalade, often sliced for decoration and used in sweet and savoury dishes; *see also* marumi, nagami and meiwa kumquat [also called **cumquat**]

kumys *(Ru)* *see* koumiss

kun choi *(Ch)* (Chinese) celery

kunchor *(Ma)* Lesser galangal

kung haeng *(Th)* Dried shrimp

kung yue *(Ch)* A small fish similar to an anchovy prepared like ikan bilis

kunyit *(Id & Ma)* Turmeric

kunyit basah *(Ma)* Turmeric

kunyit kering *(Ma)* Saffron

kupang *(Ma)* Asian mussel

kura *(Ru)* Chicken

Kürbis *(Ge)* Squash, pumpkin, gourd

kure po plzensku *(Cz)* Chicken cooked in beer with sultanas

kurhai *(In & Ne)* *see* karahi

kuri *(Ja)* Chestnut

kuri am-ni *(Ja)* Candied chestnuts similar to marrons glacés

kurista *(Ru)* A boiling fowl, old hen

kurnik **1** *(Pl)* A double crust puff pastry pie filled with four thin unsweetened pancakes interspersed with 3 separate layers, the first, chicken in a cream sauce, then sautéed mushrooms in a sour cream sauce and finally boiled rice mixed with chopped hard boiled eggs and onions bound in a cream sauce. The pie is egg washed, baked and served with a suprême sauce **2** *(Ru)* A simpler version of the Polish kurnik using a shortcrust pastry and a creamy filling of hard boiled eggs, cooked rice and chopped roast chicken meat

kuro goma *(Ja)* Black sesame seeds

Kurt *(Ru)* A hard pungent sun-dried ewes' milk cheese from Kazakhstan

kurundu *(Sr)* Cinnamon

kurzemes *(Lv)* Patties made with a duxelle of onions and mushrooms mixed with minced pork, veal or ham and breadcrumbs, seasoned and flavoured with chopped parsley and dried thyme, bound with egg, fried both sides and served with a sauce made from the reduced deglazed pan juices and sour cream

kushikatsu *(Ja)* Skewers of pork, chicken, seafood and vegetables, panéed and deep fried and eaten with a variety of sauces and relishes

Kuttelflech *(Au)* Tripe

Kutteln *(Ge)* Tripe

kuzu A pale gray starch rather like arrowroot made from the roots of a vine related to jicama. Used in Chinese and Japanese cooking to thicken sauces and make translucent glazes and it is excellent as a coating for fried foods

kvæder *(De)* Quince

kvarg *see* quark

kvas *(Ru)* A slightly alcoholic drink made from stale rye bread and water (1:6), the bread is dried and powdered, steeped for 8 hours, sieved, yeasted and fermented with mint and sugar (1:30 on water) for 8 hours, strained, a few sultanas added and the whole left for about 3 days until the sediment settles and the sultanas float. Decanted and strained before use. Juniper is occasionally used in place of mint

kveite *(No)* Halibut

kwabaal *(Ho)* Eel pout, the fish

kwali *(Ma)* A Chinese style wok used by the Malaysian Chinese (Straits Chinese) for cooking rempah

kwark *(Ho)* Quark, curds

kway tio *(Ma)* Rice ribbon noodles

kyabetsu *(Ja)* Cabbage

kyainthee *(Bm)* Candlenut

kyauk kyaw *(Bm)* Agar agar

kyauk-nga *(Bm)* Garoupa, the fish

kyckling *(Sw)* Baby chicken or poussin

kyet-thun-ni *(Bm)* Shallots

kylling *(De & No)* Chicken

kyodo ryori *(Ja)* Specialities of a region, either single dishes or a complete meal

kypsäksi paiste *(Fi)* Well done, of meat, steaks, etc.

kyringa *(Ru)* A central Asian fermented milk similar to koumiss made in wooden vessels which become impregnated with the starter culture and are not sterilized

kyufte *(Bu)* Meat balls

kyuri *(Ja)* Cucumber

Ll

la *(Ch)* Hot and peppery

laab *(Th)* A mixture of lightly stir fried meat and onions with herbs and other salad ingredients

la bai cal *(Ch)* Peppery pickled cabbage

labelling *see* food labelling, organic labelling or nutritional labelling

lablab bean *see* hyacinth bean

Lablab purpureus *Bot.* Hyacinth bean

labna *(ME)* A cream cheese made from the solids remaining when goats' milk yoghurt is strained through muslin.It is formed into 3 cm balls which are coated with olive oil and chopped herbs or paprika. Eaten with bread and keeps well [also called **labneh**]

labneh *see* labna

labong *(Ph)* Bamboo shoot

Labquark *(Ge)* *see* quark

Labskaus *(Ge)* A northern dish of mashed potatoes, fried chopped onion, chopped corned beef and seasoning, served hot topped with a fried egg and accompanied by pickled beetroot and gherkins. Sometimes well soaked, filleted and chopped salt herrings are added

labu air *(Ma)* Bottle gourd

labu merah *(Id & Ma)* Winter squash

labu siam *(Id)* Choko

la cari *(Vi)* Curry leaves

lace, to To add alcohol, condiments or spices to a dish to make it more tasty or interesting

laccetto *(It)* Mackerel

lacerto *(It)* Mackerel

la chang *(Ch)* *see* lap cheong

Lachs *(Ge)* Salmon

Lachsforelle *(Ge)* Salmon trout

Lachsschinken *(Ge)* The main muscle of pork loin, lightly smoked and wrapped in a sheet of raw bacon fat and tied into a neat cylinder with string. Eaten raw and thinly sliced as a hors d'oeuvre or sandwich filling [also called **Laxschinken**]

Läckerli *(He)* Sweet biscuits containing chopped nuts and candied peel [also called **Leckerli**]

lacón con grelos *(Sp)* Boiled cured shoulder of pork with turnip tops

lactalbumin One of the proteins in milk

Lactarius deliciosus *Bot.* Saffron milk cap

lactates Salts of lactic acid used as buffers i.e. to maintain near constant pH in foods and as firming agents. Sodium-, E325, potassium-, E326 and calcium lactate, E327 are used in the food industry

lactic acid E270, an important food acid which is the end product of anaerobic fermentation of sugars by *Lactobacillus* spp. Added as a preservative (to reduce pH) or made naturally in the production of yoghurt, sauerkraut, some cheeses, olives, other varieties of pickles and in continental sausages

lactic butter Butter made from a cream treated with *Lactobacillus* spp. to give it a slightly sour flavour

lactitol A modified lactose used in sugar-free confectionery

Lactobacillus bulgaricus One of the microorganisms used in starter cultures for yoghurt and continental cheeses

Lactobacillus caseii A microorganism associated with the ripening of Cheddar cheese

Lactobacillus helveticus One of the microorganisms in starter cultures for yoghurt and Swiss cheeses

Lactobacillus plantarum One of the microorganisms included in starter cultures for the fermentation of cucumbers and olives

Lactobacillus sanfrancisco Bacteria used for the leavening of sour dough bread

***Lactobacillus* spp.** Bacteria used for the production of lactic acid in cheese and other milk products and in sauerkraut production

Lactococcus lactis A microorganism which can ferment traditional foods made from rice to prevent transmission of infection to weaning children in underdeveloped countries. It has the advantage of producing a safe form of lactic acid, the laevo isomer (L-lactic acid) which cannot harm children. Other lactic fermenters produce both the L and D forms of the acid which are easily tolerated by adults

lactofil *(Sw)* A cultured milk concentrated by removing whey equal to half its volume. It is then enriched with cream to give 5% butterfat and homogenized

lactoglobulin One of the proteins in milk

lacto-ovo-vegetarian A person who will not eat the flesh of animals and former living creatures but will eat eggs and milk products

lactose The main sugar in milk. It is a disaccharide composed of a glucose and a galactose unit. Less sweet than sucrose [also called **milk sugar**]

lactose intolerance An inability to absorb and metabolize the galactose component of lactose hence the cause of many bowel complaints due to fermentation in the lower gut. Common in persons of Chinese origin

lacto-vegetarian A person who will not eat animal flesh, fish or eggs but will eat milk and milk products

Lactuca sativa *Bot.* Lettuce

låda *(Sw)* Casserole

lada cabai *(Id)* Black pepper

lada hijau *(Ma)* Green chilli

lada hitam *(Ma)* Peppercorn

lada merah *(Ma)* Green chilli

la de *(Ch)* Spicy

ladies' cheese *see* Butterkäse

ladies' fingers *see* okra

ladies' mustard An old fashioned French name for tarragon

ladle A cooking implement for transferring liquids or skimming liquids, consisting of a hemispherical metal scoop attached at an angle to a long handle hooked at the other end. Usually sized in fluid measure

la dua *(Vi)* Screwpine

Lady Baltimore cake *(USA)* A white layer cake, layers separated with a meringue like icing mixed with dried fruits and nuts, the whole covered with white icing

lady finger *(USA)* Sponge finger

lady fingers *see* langues de chat

lady's bedstraw A wild plant *Galium verum* of the madder family whose small yellow flowers were once used to curdle milk

lady's fingers A short variety of banana not to be confused with ladies' fingers which is okra

lady's mantle A low growing hardy perennial *Alchemilla vulgaris* whose mildly bitter young leaves may be used sparingly in salads [also called **dewcup**]

lady's smock A common wild plant *Cardamine pratensis* tasting like cress which can be eaten young as a salad vegetable [also called **cuckoo flower**]

laevulose *see* fructose

Lafayette gingerbread *(USA)* A spiced gingerbread with added orange juice and zest

Lageneria siceraria *Bot.* The bottle gourd and hairy gourd plant

lagerblad *(Sw)* Bayleaf

lagopède *(Fr) masc.* Ptarmigan

lagopède d'Écosse *(Fr) masc.* Grouse

lagópodo escocés *(Sp)* Grouse

lagos *(Gr)* Hare

lagôsta *(Po)* Spiny lobster

lagostim *(Po)* Prawn, small lobster, Dublin bay prawn

lagostino *(Sp) see* caramote (Fr)

Laguiole *(Fr)* A semi-hard pressed cows' milk cheese from the mountains of Aquitaine, with a soft dry rind and a supple homogeneous paste whose herby flavour comes from the pasture on which the cows feed, resembling Cantal. Protected by an appellation d'origine. Contains 37% water, 28% fat, and 26% protein [also called **forme de Cantal, Laguiole-Aubrac**]

Laguiole-Aubrac *see* Laguiole

laguipierre, sauce *(Fr) fem.* Butter sauce with the addition of the juice of one lemon and 60 ml of fish glaze per litre. Used for boiled fish

lahana dolmasi *(Tu)* Blanched cabbage leaves wrapped around a mixture of cooked rice, chopped onions, raisins, pine nuts, seasoning and chopped parsley or dill, baked in the oven and served cold

la he *(Vi)* Garlic chive

lait *(Fr) masc.* Milk

lait, au *(Fr)* Cooked or mixed with milk

lait aigre *(Fr) masc.* Sour milk

lait d'amande *(Fr) masc.* Almond oil

lait caillé *(Fr) masc.* Milk curds, sour milk

lait de coco *(Fr) masc.* Coconut milk

lait écrémé *(Fr) masc.* Skimmed milk

lait en poudre *(Fr) masc.* Dried or powdered milk

laitance *(Fr) fem.* Soft roe

laitances d'alose *(Fr) fem.* Shad roe

laiterie *(Fr) fem.* Dairy

laitue *(Fr) fem.* Lettuce

laitue beurrée *(Fr) fem.* Round lettuce

laitue romaine *(Fr) fem.* Cos lettuce (UK), romaine lettuce (USA)

la jiao fen *(Ch)* Chilli pepper

la jiao jiang *(Ch)* Chilli sauce

la jiao xiang you *(Ch)* Sesame chilli oil

lake bass A freshwater game fish *Micropterus* spp. caught throughout North America (except Alaska), with firm white lean flesh up to 1.5 kg in weight which is also farmed. Baked or fried

lake herring A freshwater fish *Leucichthys* spp. from the great lakes of North America. Similar in shape and colour to a herring but only medium oily with white flesh. It weighs up to 1 kg and may be poached or fried [also called **cisco**]

lake trout *(Cn & USA)* A large trout *Salvelinus namaycush,* light green to near black with oily pink flesh weighing on average 2 kg. Caught all the year round in North American lakes and rivers. Cook as trout [also called **great lakes trout**]

lake whitefish *(Cn & USA)* A fish *Coregonus clupeaformis* from the trout and salmon family with a light brown back and white, medium oily, delicate flesh which cooks in flakes like cod. Found in North American lakes. Cook as trout

Lakeland A variety of limequat q.v.

lakka *(Fi)* Cloudberry

laks *(De & No)* Salmon

laksa **1** *(Id & Ma)* A stew of fish, shrimp or chicken in a well-flavoured and possibly soured, curry type sauce based on coconut milk. Served with rice noodles **2** *(Ph)* A stew containing a wide variety of vegetables, shrimp and pork, served with fine bean flour vermicelli (sotanghon). Lit. 10,000 referring to the number of ingredients

laksa ikan *(Ma)* A fish soup containing noodles

lala mirich *(In)* Red chilli

lal mirch *(In)* Cayenne pepper, chilli powder

lal sarsu *(In)* Brown mustard seed

lam *(De & Ho)* Lamb [also called **lamsvlees** (Ho)]

la Mancha saffron Reputed to be the best saffron from Spain. It contains the white styles as well as the red stamens

lamb A young sheep under one year old but preferably 3 to 4 months old and weighing about 10 kg. The meat is tender and suitable for grilling, frying and roasting

lamb cutlet A transverse slice cut from a skinned and chined best end of lamb containing one rib the rib sometimes scraped to the bone for 5 to 7 cm

lamb cutlets Reform *(UK)* Lamb cutlets panéed with a mixture of breadcrumbs and finely chopped ham, grilled or fried, garnished à la réforme and served with Reform sauce.

lamb flank *(UK)* The Scottish term for breast of lamb

lamb herbs The principal herbs used with lamb are basil, chervil, cumin, dill, lemon balm, lovage, marjoram, mint, parsley, rosemary, savory and thyme

lamb's fry **1** The liver, kidney, sweetbreads, heart and sometimes the brains and some of the internal abdominal fat of a lamb. Generally cut in pieces, panéed and fried **2** The testicles of sheep, very rare since most are now castrated by a bloodless method

lamb's kidneys Small kidneys which are skinned and cored in the usual way and cooked whole or halved in kebabs, mixed grills or other dishes

lamb's lettuce A slow growing hardy annual *Valerianella locusta* grown for its leaves which will stand the winter and are used in winter salads. The growing plant may be blanched to reduce the slight bitterness. There are two varieties, a floppy large leaved version and a smaller more hardy upright type [also called **corn salad, marche, field lettuce** (USA)]

lamb's liver A delicate light brown liver very popular in the UK. Should not be cooked too long or it becomes tough

lamb's quarters *(Cn)* A wild vegetable which is a cross between Swiss chard and spinach and cooked in the same way. Said to have a faint flavour of lamb. Grows profusely in New Brunswick

lamb's tongues Small pink tongues weighing about 200 g with a good flavour. May be stewed and jellied as other tongues

lamb's tongue Ste Menehould *(Fr)* Lamb's tongues braised. panéed and grilled

lamballe, crème *(Fr) fem.* Crème St Germain garnished with cooked and washed tapioca

lambascioni *(It) see* copollotto

lam chiak *(Th)* Screwpine

Lamellibranchiata The scientific name for bivalves. Shellfish with two hinged shells including oysters, clams, scallops, mussels, razor shells, abalone, etc.

Lamington *(Aus)* A small square cake made from sponge coated with chocolate icing and sprinkled with desiccated coconut

lam keong *(Ch)* Greater galangal

Lamm *(Ge)* Lamb

lamm *(Sw)* Lamb

lammasta *(Fi)* Mutton, lamb

lamme *(De)* Lamb, mutton

lamme kotelet *(De)* Lamb chop

lammesteg *(De)* Roast lamb

Lammkeule *(Ge)* Leg of lamb

Lammkotelett *(Ge)* Lamb chop

lammkotlett *(Sw)* Lamb chop

lammstek *(Sw)* Roast lamb

Lammzunge *(Ge)* Scald, the fish

la mocetta *(It)* A large salami

lampaankyljys *(Fi)* Mutton or lamb chop

lampaanliha *(Fi)* Mutton, lamb

lampaanpaisti *(Fi)* Roast leg of lamb or mutton

lampada, alla Cooked at the table over a portable heat source

lampari *(Sr)* Curried rice baked in banana leaves

lampern A fish resembling a small lamprey. Cooked like an eel

lampone *(It)* Raspberry

lampreda *(It)* Lamprey

lamprey Various small round anadromous sea fish rather like eels, with sucking mouthparts and rough tongues. Popular in Spain, Portugal and Southern France. Require longer cooking than eels

lampries *(Sr)* A mixture of several types of food separately wrapped in banana leaves and baked. From the Dutch lomprijst. Typical dishes might be frikkadels, buttered rice, various curries and sambals. Very much party food in which the guests make and bake the parcels

lamproie *(Fr) fem.* Lamprey, the fish

lampuga *(It)* Dolphin fish

lamsbout *(Ho)* Leg of lamb

lamsvlees *(Ho)* Lamb [also called **lam**]

Lanark blue *(UK)* A blue-veined ewes' milk cheese from Strathclyde Scotland, similar to Roquefort

Lancashire cheese *(UK)* An excellent white melting cheese with a crumbly texture. When new it has a mild flavour but this develops as it matures esp. if made with unpasteurized milk

Lancashire hot pot *(UK)* A casserole of lamb chops from the neck end and kidneys with onions, carrots and potatoes, topped with a layer of sliced potatoes which become brown and crisp in the oven

Lancashire parkin *(UK)* A gingerbread containing oatmeal, chopped candied peel, demerara sugar and caraway seeds

lançon *(Fr) masc.* Sand eel

land cress A slightly peppery leafy plant *Barbarea verna* found wild but also cultivated in Europe and North America to provide green leaves for salads in winter [also called **early flowering yellow rocket, American cress**]

landaise, à la *(Fr)* In the style of Landes, i.e. cooked in goose fat with garlic and pine nuts

Landes chicken Chickens from Landes in south west France. Usually free range and maize fed with a dark well-flavoured leg meat, slightly firmer than normal

Ländjäger *(Ge)* A small smoked and scalded sausage made from up to 40% pork, beef, garlic, caraway seeds and red wine pressed into a square mould and cold smoked or air dried

landlady's loaf *see* barrel bread

Landmettwurst *(Ge)* A Mettwurst made in the countryside

landrail *see* corncrake

ländstycke *(Sw)* Sirloin steak

Lane cake *(USA)* A layered cake containing chopped nuts, dried fruit and coconut and covered with a fluffy icing

lange japanische Auster *(Ge)* Pacific oyster

Langermannia gigantea *Bot.* Giant puffball

langka *(Ph)* Jackfruit

lángos *(Hu)* Fried doughnuts

langosta *(Sp)* Spiny lobster

langostino *(Sp)* General term for crayfish or large prawn

langostino moruno *(Sp)* Crevette rouge (Fr)

langouste *(Fr) fem.* Spiny lobster

langoustine *(Fr) fem.* Dublin bay prawn

Langres A soft, surface ripened and washed curd cows' milk cheese with a tangy flavour and shaped like a squat cylinder (300 g). The salted curd is ripened for 2 to 3 months

langsam kochen *(Ge)* To simmer

langsat A round or oval fruit of a tree *Lansium domesticum* from Malaysia which is about 4 cm dia. and grows in clusters. The flesh is white, juicy and fragrant, contains one or two large inedible seeds and is enclosed in a tough brown mottled skin. Eaten raw

Langskaill *(UK)* A cows' milk cheese from Scotland which resembles Gouda

Languas galanga *Bot.* Greater galangal

Languas officinarum *Bot.* Lesser galangal

langue *(Fr) fem.* Tongue

languedocienne, à la *(Fr)* In the style of Languedoc, i.e. with a garnish of aubergine, mushrooms, tomatoes and parsley

langues de chat *(Fr) fem.* Small sweet flat biscuits made by the sugar batter method with butter, icing sugar, egg white, flour and vanilla essence. Can be moulded when hot. Lit. cat's tongues [also called **lady fingers**]

languier *(Fr) masc.* Smoked pigs' tongue

Languste *(Ge)* Spiny lobster

Lansium domesticum *Bot.* Langsat

lansur *(Af)* A leaf vegetable from Nigeria rather like a cross between parsley and watercress

lanttu *(Fi)* Kohlrabi

lanzado *(It)* Mackerel

laos *(Id)* Greater galangal

laos ginger *see* greater galangal

laos powder The dried and ground root of greater galangal, rather like ginger

Laotian caviar *see* som khay

Laotian coriander *see* dill weed

Laotian rice A rice grown on the dry hillsides and not in paddy fields. It is soaked before being steamed in a luang prabang (woven cane basket)

lap *(Ko)* Finely ground raw water buffalo meat or venison, flavoured with chilli and herbs and served wrapped in bite size rolls using blanched lettuce leaves

lap of lamb *(UK) coll. (north of England)* Breast of lamb

lapa *(Sp)* Limpet

lap cheong *(Ch)* The standard pork sausage made from chopped lean pork and pork fat, mixed with sugar, salt, saltpetre and softened grain, flavoured with paprika and soya sauce, moistened with rice wine, filled into casings and air dried. Usually steamed to soften before use. [also called **la chang, lap xuong, lop cheeng**]

lapereau *(Fr) masc.* Young rabbit

lapin *(Fr) masc.* Rabbit

lapin à l'aigre doux *(Be)* masc. Jointed rabbit marinated for 24 hours in white wine and vinegar with sliced onion and herbs, dried off, browned in butter and stewed with demi-glace sauce, stock and a little of the marinade until tender, reserved and mixed with pickled cherries and the reduced cooking liquor flavoured with melted dark chocolate

lapin aux pruneaux *(Be) masc.* Jointed rabbit, marinated, dried, browned in butter then simmered in equal parts of water and the strained marinade with destoned prunes plumped in water and white wine until tender. Served with the cooking liquor thickened with red currant jelly

lapjes *(Ho)* Small slices of meat

lap ngup *(Ch)* Pressed duck

lapocka *(Hu)* A cut of meat from the shoulder

Lapskaus *(Ge)* Lobscouse; *see also* Labskaus

lapskaus *(No)* A thick stew of meat and potatoes

lapskojs *(Sw)* A modern version of lobscouse made with corned beef

lapskous *(Ho)* Lobscouse

lapu lapu *(Ph)* Garoupa, the fish

lapwing *see* plover

lap xuong *(Vi)* Lap cheong, Chinese sausage

lap yoke *(Ch)* Dried and smoked belly pork, rather like smoked streaky bacon

laranja *(Po)* Orange

laranja cravo *(Br)* A variety of mandarin grown extensively in Brazil. It is medium large and has a rather thick skin. The flavour whilst being appreciated in Brazil is too insipid for European and North American tastes

laranja lima *(Br)* A variety of acidless orange

q.v. very popular in Brazil where over half a million tonnes are grown annually [also called **lima orange**]

lard 1 *(En & Fr) masc.* The rendered down fat of the pig which is white, soft and has a distinctive flavour. The best lard comes from leaf fat. Often used with equal parts of butter or margarine for pastry making **2** *(Fr) masc.* Bacon

lard, to To thread small strips of fat or fat bacon through the lean flesh of game birds, poultry and other meat to keep it succulent during roasting using a needle with a large eye

lard maigre *(Fr) masc.* Streaky bacon

lard net Caul

larder *(Fr)* To lard (meat)

larding needle A large needle with a wide eye used for larding

lardo *(It)* Bacon or salt pork

lardo affumicato *(It)* Bacon

lardoire *(Fr) masc.* Larding needle used for large cuts of meat

lardon *(En & Fr) masc.* Small strips of pork or bacon fat, square in cross section used for larding lean meat, or similar strips of bacon used for flavouring or after cooking as a component of a salad

lardoncini *(It)* Fried cubes or strips of salt pork, lardons

lardy cake *(UK)* A south Midlands cake made from bread dough enriched with lard, sugar and dried vine fruits, baked in small square tins with rounded corners and the tops scored in diamonds. Eaten warm with butter

large calorie *see* kilocalorie

large round kumquat *see* meiwa kumquat

large thread stage *see* sugar cooking

largemouth black bass A bass-like freshwater game fish *Micropterus salmoides* with a silvery skin and a dark tail and mouth parts, found in Europe and North America and weighing up to 10 kg

larger argentine *see* argentine

larger spotted dogfish The most common British dogfish *Scyliorhinus stellaris* up to 1.2 m long and with rather coarse tasteless flesh [also called **nurse hound**]

largo *(Me)* A long thin variety of chilli pepper which is fairly hot.

lark A small wild bird almost hunted to extinction. Eaten in France and Italy but will soon be protected

larm yum *(Ch)* Chinese olive seeds

Laruns *(Fr)* A ewes' milk cheese from the Basque country

lasagna *(En & It)* A wide flat pasta which comes in a strip, rectangle or square about 1 to 2 mm thick. Poached in salted water before incorporation in a made up dish. The plural is lasagne [also called **lazagne** (It)]

lasagna verde *(En & It)* Lasagna made with a paste coloured green with spinach purée

lasagne all bolognese *(It)* Poached lasagne layered with a meat sauce and topped with Béchamel sauce and grated Parmesan cheese

lasagne all fiorentina *(It)* Poached lasagne with a meat sauce and cheese

lasagne da fornel *(It)* Poached lasagne with a sauce of nuts, raisins, apples and figs

lasagne pasticciate alla napoletana *(It)* Cooked lasagne layered with cooked cheese and Bolognaise sauces, topped with a final layer of cheese sauce and gratinated. Finished in the oven until crisp on top

lasagnette *(It)* Wide ribbons of flat pasta intermediate in size between lasagne and tagliatelle

lasca *(It)* Roach, the fish

lassan *(In)* Garlic

lassi *(In)* Yoghurt diluted with water or mineral water (1 part yoghurt to 1 to 2 parts water), used as a refreshing drink either with sugar or flavoured with e.g. cumin and mint. Sometimes made from salted and sweetened buttermilk

lasun *(In)* Garlic

lat chu jeung *(Ch)* Chilli bean paste

lath A legume *Lathyrus sativus* grown as a fodder plant and, in poor areas, for its seeds which are used like other pulses [also called **chickling vetch, grass pea**]

latholemono *(Gr)* An olive oil and lemon juice (3:1) salad dressing with chopped marjoram and parsley, seasoning and possibly a little sugar

Lathyrus sativus *Bot.* Lath

latik *(Ph)* The brown curds produced by heating coconut milk to separate the oil. Used on desserts and snack foods

lat jiu jiang *(Ch)* A medium to hot, orange red thickish chilli sauce

lat jiu keung yau *(Ch)* A ground garlic and chilli paste

latkes The Jewish term for Rösti [also called **potato latka**]

lato *(Ph)* An edible seaweed with clusters of small bladders rather like a bunch of grapes

latour *(Fr)* Porbeagle shark

latte *(It)* Milk

latte acido *(It)* Sour milk

latte di mandorla *(It)* Almond milk. Whole almonds blended with water until creamy, separated from the solid residue, sweetened to taste and possibly flavoured with lemon zest and cinnamon. Served chilled

latte de pesce *(It)* Soft fish roe

latte scremato *(It)* Skimmed milk

latteria *(It)* **1** Dairy, dairy farm **2** The name generally used for cheeses from the Friule region

latterino *(It)* Smelt, the fish

Lattich *(Ge)* Lettuce

lattuga *(It)* Lettuce

lattuga a cappuccio *(It)* Round lettuce

lattuga romana *(It)* Cos lettuce

Latviiski *(Ru)* A cows' milk cheese with a strong smell and pungent taste [also called **Latviysky**]

Latviysky *(Ru)* *see* Latviiski

lat you *(Ch)* Chilli oil

Laubfrösche *(He)* A type of cabbage roll made with spinach leaves with a filling of fresh white breadcrumbs, sweated chopped onion, scrambled eggs, seasoning and nutmeg, moistened with water if necessary and cooked in the usual way. Lit. tree frogs

Lauch *(Ge)* Leek

lauki *(In)* Wax gourd

laulau *(USA)* A Hawaiian speciality consisting of taro leaves wrapped around a filling of salt pork and either butterfish, mackerel or salmon, steamed and served hot

Laums *(Fr)* A cows' milk cheese from Burgundy made in a brick shape and often soaked in coffee

laung *(In)* Cloves

laurel *see* bay *Laurus nobilis,* the only edible member of the laurel family

laurie *(Fr)* Porbeagle shark

laurier *(Fr) masc.* Bay *Laurus nobilis,* but also used of several other toxic members of the laurel family

laurier, feuille de *(Fr) fem* Bayleaf

lauro *(It)* Bay *Laurus nobilis,* but also used of several other toxic members of the laurel family

Laurus nobilis *Bot.* Bay

lavagante *(Po)* Large American or European lobster

Lavandula angustifolia *Bot.* Lavender

Lavarel *(Au & He)* Lake trout

la Varenne The founder of French classical cooking (1618 - 1678)

lavaret de bourget *(Fr) masc.* Pollan, the fish

lavender The bitter leaves of lavender *Lavandula angustifolia* are used in South European cooking

laver 1 A red seaweed *Porphyra umbilicus* found round the coasts of South Wales and Ireland, similar to the Japanese nori. Prepared by cleaning, soaking in sodium bicarbonate solution, then washing and stewing until tender when it resembles spinach purée [also called **sloke, stoke, stake, slouk, slokum**] **2** *(Fr)* To wash

laver bread *(UK)* Cooked laver mixed with porridge oats and fried in bacon fat as a breakfast dish. Popular in south Wales

laverello *(It)* Lake trout from the northern lakes

lawalu, i'a *see* i'a lawalu

lax *(Ic & Sw)* Salmon

laxforell *(Sw)* River trout

laxgryta *(Sw)* Salmon slices sprinkled with salt and dried dill weed, layered in a pan, covered with equal parts of butter and boiling water and simmered until most of the water has evaporated. Served with new potatoes

laxpudding *(Sw)* Layers of seasoned salmon and raw sliced potatoes alternated in a greased oven-proof dish starting and finishing with potato, covered in an egg custard mix to leave the potatoes showing and baked in a moderate oven for about 1 hour [also called **salmon pie**]

laxschinken *see* lachsschinken

layer cake A sponge cake baked in several tins then assembled together when cold with various fillings between the layers and finally decorated [also called **sandwich cake**]

lazagne *(It)* *see* lasagna

lb Abbreviation for pound weight

L-cysteine hydrochloride *see* (E)920. The L- refers to the naturally occurring laevo form

LDL Low density lipoprotein

Lea and Perrins' sauce *see* Worcestershire sauce

leaf beet *see* Swiss chard

leaf fat A sheet of soft fat from the lower part of the abdominal cavity of the pig

leaf gelatine Rectangular shapes of purified gelatine rather like stiff cellophane. Each sheet weighs 2 g and will set 100 ml of water on average, but dependent on temperature and stiffness of gel required. Should be softened in water for 5 minutes prior to using

leaf lard A very fine quality lard made from leaf fat

leather *(USA) see* fruit leather

leaven **1** A piece of dough reserved from yeast-based bread making, placed in water possibly with a little sugar and allowed to rise when it can be used in place of yeast for the next batch of dough and is the basis of the sour dough production method. This process may continue indefinitely **2** Any yeast or other raising agent used in dough to make leavened bread

leavened bread Any bread using yeast or other raising agent to lighten it and incorporate carbon dioxide or air

leban *(ME)* Yoghurt

Lebanon bologno *(USA)* A hardwood smoked Bologna sausage from Lebanon, Pennsylvania made with coarsely ground precured meat

leben *(ME)* Yoghurt

leben raib *(ME)* The Saudi Arabian term for yoghurt

Leber *(Ge)* Liver

Leberkäse *(Ge)* A precooked meat loaf from Bavaria made from a mixture of finely minced liver and sausage meat. Usually sliced and grilled or fried

Leberklösse *(Ge)* Liver dumplings

Leberknödel *(Ge & It)* Liver dumplings made with a processed and seasoned mixture of beef liver, onions, chopped parsley and soaked bread brought together with a little flour and egg, formed into small balls and simmered in beef stock until they rise to the surface

Leberknödelsuppe *(Au & Ge)* A clear consommé containing small dumplings made from ground liver, breadcrumbs, herbs and seasonings, garnished with chopped parsley or chives

Lebersalsiz *(He)* A rohwurst containing pork meat, pork fat, pigs' liver and beef, air dried and smoked

Leberspätzle *(Ge)* Liver dumplings

Leberspiessli *(He)* A kebab of pieces of liver wrapped in sage leaves and bacon and grilled over charcoal

Leberstreichwurst *(Au)* A small coarse-textured spreading sausage made with pork and pigs' liver

Leberwurst *(Ge & Au)* Liver sausage made from boiled pig meat, pig's liver, salted pork fat, onions fried in lard and seasoning, all pounded to a fine paste and cased, the whole boiled, air dried and smoked

Lebkuchen *(Ge)* Highly spiced soft brown ginger cakes with a hard white icing or chocolate covering. Eaten over the Christmas season

lebonnet rice A type of long grain rice

lebre *(Po)* Hare

leccia *(It)* Pompano, the fish

lechas *(Sp)* Soft fish roe

leche *(Sp)* Milk

leche desnatada *(Sp)* Skimmed milk

leche de manteca *(Sp)* Buttermilk

lechecillas *(Sp)* Sweetbreads

lechón *(Sp)* Sucking pig

lechón de leche *(Ph)* A whole barbecued sucking pig

lechón sarsa *(Ph)* A thick sauce made from ground pig's liver, brown sugar, vinegar, garlic, spices and seasoning, thickened with biscocho. Served with roast pork

lechoncillo *(Sp)* Small sucking pig

lechuga *(Sp)* Lettuce

lecithin E322, a natural substance found in egg yolk used as an emulsifier and antioxidant

Leckerli *(He) see* Läckerli

le colombo *(Ca)* A meat or fish and tropical vegetable curry flavoured with rum, coconut and lime

lecsó *(Hu)* A sauce used for flavouring made by sweating green sweet peppers with chopped bacon, onions, paprika, tomatoes and salt in lard until soft, purééing and straining. Used cold, may be frozen

lectins Types of proteins found mainly in legume seeds, some of which are highly poisonous and believed to act as a protection for the seed against insect and animal attack. They attack differing human populations differently depending on their blood type. They are inactivated by boiling at 100°C for at least ten minutes. It has been reported that the lower boiling point of water at high altitude can prevent inactivation [also called **haemagglutinin**]

Lecythis sabucajo *Bot.* Paradise nut

Lederzucker *(Ge)* Marshmallow

ledvinková polévka *(Cz)* Kidney soup made from sliced onions and potatoes sweated in lard, flour added to make a roux and all simmered with white stock, paprika, caraway seeds and garlic, sieved and garnished with sliced and sautéed calves' kidneys

Lee cake *(USA)* A white sponge cake flavoured with citrus juice and zest

leek A mild-tasting member of the onion family *Allium porrum* with a thick multilayered stem which is the part eaten. The stems are white in the centre but may be fully blanched if planted deep in the soil or protected from light with a collar. The edible part is cylindrical up to 30 cm long and 5 cm in diameter

leek and potato soup Paysanne cut leek sweated in butter without colour, white stock, a BG and paysanne cut potatoes added, seasoned and simmered until all cooked

leek soup Basic soup with leeks, garnished with a fine cooked julienne of leek

leen chee *(Th)* Lychee

leen ngau *(Ch)* Lotus

leg of beef *(UK)* The English term for the lower part of the hind leg of beef. It is tougher and has more gristle than other cuts and is braised, stewed or casseroled

leg chops of lamb *(UK)* A Midlands term for chump chops of lamb and generally used for slices cut from the top end of a leg of lamb

leg of lamb A prime roasting joint being the rear leg cut from the carcase at the cocyx and pelvis. Often divided into two, the fillet end nearest the loin and the knuckle or leg end

leg of mutton As lamb but from an older sheep

leg of mutton cut A part of the beef carcase which resembles a leg of mutton from just above the shank of the foreleg, below the chuck and in front of the brisket. Used for braising and stewing.

leg of pork A prime roasting joint being the hind leg cut from the carcase at the cocyx and pelvis. Often cut into two joints the fillet and knuckle

leg of veal A prime roasting joint being the rear leg cut from the carcase at the coccyx and pelvis. Can be roasted whole but is more often divided into knuckle, thick flank, cushion and under cushion

legumbres *(Sp)* Vegetables

legumbres secas *(Sp)* Pulses

legume The general name for plants whose seeds are enclosed in two sided pods attached along one join. Sometimes the whole pod is eaten but more often the seeds only, either in the green or dried state, are consumed. When dried they are known as pulses and are an important source of protein. Well over 10,000 varieties are known, most of which are edible; *see also* bean, pea, etc.

légume *(Fr) masc.* Vegetable

legume soups Soups made from pulses, usually puréed and possibly creamed

legumes *(Po)* Vegetables

légumes, crème de *(Fr) fem.* Vegetable soup with added cream, milk or thin Béchamel sauce

légumes, purée de *(Fr) fem. see* vegetable soup

légumes secs *(Fr) masc.* Pulses

legumi *(It)* Vegetables

leguminous A description of plants which are legumes

Leicester cheese *(UK)* A mild-flavoured hard cheese coloured orange red with annatto and made from pasteurized cows' milk [also called **red Leicester**]

leichte Kraftsuppe *(Ge)* Chicken and veal broth

Leiden *see* Leyden

Leinsamenbrot *(Ge)* A yeast-raised bread made from wholemeal flour and unground linseeds. Said to aid digestion [also called **linseed bread** (UK)]

leipä *(Fi)* Bread

leipajuustö *see* juustöleipa

Leipziger Allerlei *(Ge)* Diced root vegetables, green beans and morels all cooked separately and drained, mixed with cooked green peas and steamed and sliced asparagus tips, buttered and bound with crayfish sauce. Served garnished with crayfish tails, fleurons and small semolina gnocchi

leitão assado *(Po)* Roast sucking pig

leite *(Po)* Milk

leivokslet *(Fi)* Pastries, tarts, pies

leivos *(Fi)* Pastry, pie, tart

lei yu *(Ch)* Rock carp

lekach A Jewish New Year cake sweetened with honey and flavoured with spice, raisins and chopped mixed candied peel [also called **haniglekach**]

Le Moine *(Cn)* A cheese resembling Port-Salut made by monks in Quebec

lemon One of the most important of the *Citrus* family from a tree *Citrus limon* which grows in Mediterranean climates and is probably a hybrid of Indian lime and pummelo. It originated in the Punjab, was further developed in the Middle East and taken to Spain by the Arabs around 1150 A.D. Although there are many varieties they differ very little more between varieties than a single variety does at different times of the year. The fruit is shaped like a rugby ball with usually a thick yellow skin. The juice is used extensively for flavouring, for souring and to add bite to sauces. Segments and slices are used as garnishes and for decoration and the zest is an important flavouring ingredient

lemon balm A clump forming perennial plant *Melissa officinalis* with lemon-scented oval leaves used as flavouring herb with fish, poultry and ham. Also used in fruit drinks, salads, mayonnaise and sauerkraut [also called **melissa**]

lemon barley water The strained cooking liquor from barley mixed with sugar and lemon juice, used as a high calorie drink

lemon basil A variety of basil *Ocimum basilicum* var. *citriodorum* with lemon-scented green leaves

lemon butter sauces *see* meunière butter sauce

lemon curd The commonest of the smooth fruit curds made from butter and sugar emulsified and thickened with egg yolks and flavoured with the juice and zest of lemons

lemon essence An alcoholic extract of lemon zest used for flavouring

lemon grass The fresh or dried stalks and leaves of a perennial grass *Cymbopogon citratus* and *C. flexuesus* native to South Asia but widely grown in hot climates. It has a lemony flavour and is common in South East Asian dishes particularly in Thai cooking [also called **citronella**]

lemon juice The juice of lemons used for flavouring, souring and to prevent cut fruit and vegetables from browning or to whiten fish and fish bones for stock. The juice of 1 lemon amounts to between 50 and 100 ml, say 60 ml or 4 tablespoons

lemon meringue pie *(UK)* A blind baked pastry case or base filled or topped with a thick setting lemon-flavoured sauce, topped with meringue and baked until browned. Served cold. Although of UK origin very popular in the USA

lemon mint A type of mint *Mentha aquatica* var. *citrata)* with smooth lemon-scented green leaves. Used for flavouring

lemon pudding *(UK)* A pudding made from basic steamed pudding mixture flavoured with grated lemon zest

lemon sauce As orange sauce but with lemon zest and juice substituted for orange

lemon scented verbena *see* lemon verbena

lemon sole A North Atlantic dextral flat fish *Microstomus kitt* similar to plaice with a brownish-yellow upper skin covered with spots and with a faint lemon scent when freshly caught. It has a very small head and can grow to 60 cm long. The flesh is white and lean but not considered as fine as Dover sole [also called **long flounder**]

lemon soufflé A cold soufflé flavoured with finely grated lemon zest [also called **Milanese soufflé**]

lemon squeezer *see* juice extractor

lemon thyme A hardy low-growing thyme *Thymus x citriodorus* with lemon-scented leaves used in stuffings, fresh fruit salads and dips

lemon verbena A half hardy shrub *Aloysia triphylla* with pointed crinkly leaves which have a sharp lemony fragrance. The chopped young leaves can be used to flavour desserts, cakes, ice cream and the fresh or dried leaves are used in white meat and fish dishes. Can be used as a substitute for lemon grass [also called **lemon scented verbena, verbena** (USA)]

lemon zester *see* zester

lencse *(Hu)* Lentils

Lende *(Ge)* Loin or sirloin (of meat)

Lendenbraten *(Ge)* Roast sirloin of beef

Lendenschnitte am Grill *(Ge)* Grilled fillet of beef

Lendenstück *(Ge)* Fillet or loin (of meat)

lengkuas *(Ma)* Greater galangal

lengua *(Sp)* Tongue

lenguado *(Sp)* Dover sole, dab

lenguado a la vasca *(Sp)* Boiled Dover sole with potatoes and mushrooms

lenkuas *(Ma)* Greater galangal

lenrimmad lax *(Sw)* Home salted salmon

prepared as gravlax but with twice as much salt as sugar. Cut in very thin slices and served with potatoes mashed with chopped parsley and dill

Lens culinaris *Bot.* Lentil

Lens esculenta *Bot.* Lentil

lentejas *(Sp)* Lentils

lenticchie *(It)* Lentils

lentil The seed of the oldest documented leguminous plant *Lens culinaris* and *L. esculenta* originating in the Middle East but now common throughout the world. It is about 5 mm in diameter and usually dehusked and split in two. Red, green and brown (orange when dehusked) varieties exist, the latter keeping their shape on cooking. None require soaking prior to cooking. Other seeds are incorrectly called lentils see e.g. black lentil (black gram) and green lentil (mung bean)

lentil soup Washed lentils, chopped carrot and onion, a BG, knuckle of ham and tomato purée simmered and skimmed with white stock until all cooked, ham removed and the whole liquidized and passed through a chinois, seasoned and served hot with croûtons [also called **purée de lentilles** (Fr)]

lentilhas *(Po)* Lentils

lentille *(Fr) fem.* Lentil

lentilles, purée de *(Fr) fem. see* lentil soup

lentilles vertes du Puy *(Fr) fem.* Very tiny green and expensive lentils regarded as a delicacy

Lentinus edodes *Bot.* Shiitake mushroom

lentischio *(It)* Mastic

lentisco *(Sp)* Mastic

lentisk A straggly bush *Pistacia lentiscus* with red berries which grows wild on arid Mediterranean hillsides. If cut it exudes the aromatic resin, mastic

León *(Sp)* A hard cows' milk cheese, dry salted and ripened for about 20 days. It is made in small cylinders (500 to 800 g) and has a close textured paste with a hard, yellow and rough rind

Leoni *(Ge)* A sausage made from a mixture of coarsely ground beef, pork and pork back fat, with seasoning, sugar, ginger, coriander and nutmeg, packed into beef middles and tied

Lepidium sativum *Bot.* Cress

Lepiota rhacodes *Bot.* Shaggy parasol

lepre *(It)* Hare

lepre agrodolce *(It)* Hare cooked in sweet and sour sauce and topped with shredded chocolate, almonds and raisins

lepre crostata *(It)* Spit-roasted hare, baked with cream and covered in almond paste

lepre in salmi *(It)* Hare marinated in vinegar and cooked in red wine

lepudrida *(It)* A rich meat and vegetable stew from Sardinia

le rouge royal *(USA)* A very large, brilliant red and thick-walled sweet pepper

lesch *(Ru)* Bream

lesch v pergamente *(Ru)* Fillets of bream, soaked in hot water then cooked en papillote with grated carrot, onions and butter with lemon juice and herbs. Served with boiled potatoes and Béchamel or fish velouté with pickled cucumbers

Les Orrys *(Fr) see* Orrys, the cheese

Les Riceys *(Fr)* A soft cows' milk cheese from Troyes made in discs and covered in wood ash

lessato *(It) see* lesso

lesser argentine *see* argentine

lesser galangal The root of a Chinese plant *Languas officinarum* or *Alpinia officinarum* with a reddish brown skin resembling a smaller version of ginger root. It has a pungent flavour of cardamom and ginger with a hint of eucalyptus. Used extensively in South East Asian cooking

lesser ginger *see* kempferia galangal

lesser spotted dogfish A common British dogfish *Scyliorhinus caniculus*, up to 75 cm long and slightly better tasting than the larger variety

lesso *(It)* Boiled, boiled meat, boiled beef [also called **lessato**]

lesso valdestano *(It)* Meat and sausage boiled in a sealed pot

letsprængt oksebryst *(De)* Corned beef

letterato *(It)* A small tuna fish

letterbanket *(Ho)* Marzipan

lettuce The most common salad vegetable which is occasionally braised or stir fried. It is an annual low growing plant *Lactuca sativa* varying from a 10 to a 30 cm spread, usually green leaved but some varieties are red or brown. They may be loose leafed, curly or form tight compact heads. The principal types are cos (romaine), semi-cos, butterhead, crisphead and loose leaf. Typical named varieties are Webb, Great Lakes, little gem, sugar cos, oak leaf, lollo rosso and lollo biondo

lettuce laver *see* sea lettuce

lettuce leaf basil A variety of basil with a fruity scent

Leuconostoc mesenteroides One of the microorganisms included in starter cultures for the fermentation of cabbage, cucumbers and olives and the production of cottage cheeses

***Leuconostoc* spp.** Bacteria used for the production of lactic acid in cheese and other milk products and in sauerkraut production

leudar *(Sp)* To leaven or raise with yeast or a chemical raising agent

leuqkuas *(Ma)* Greater galangal

levadura *(Sp)* Leavening agent such as baking powder, sourdough starter, yeast

levain *(Fr) masc.* Leaven, sourdough starter

lever *(De, No & Sw)* Liver

leveret A young hare up to 1 year old

leverkorv *(Sw)* A liver sausage made with pigs' liver, fat bacon and veal, separately minced, combined with seasoning, chopped onion and marjoram, moistened with milk, packed loosely into casings and simmered for 30 minutes

leverpastej *(Sw)* Liver pâté

leverpølse *(De)* A firmer version of the liver sausage leverpostej

leverpostej *(De)* A liver sausage made with pigs' liver, lean pork and flare fat, seasoned, flavoured with anchovies, nutmeg and cinnamon, bound with egg, packed into beef runners and simmered for 2 hours

leves *(Hu)* Soup

levistico *(It)* Lovage

Levisticum officinale *Bot.* Lovage

levraut *(Fr) masc.* Young hare, leveret

levreteau *(Fr)* Young hare

Levroux *(Fr)* A soft goats' milk cheese similar to Valençay, shaped like a pyramid (300 g)

levulose *see* fructose

levure *(Fr) fem.* Yeast, leavening agent

levure chimique *(Fr) fem.* Baking powder

Leyden cheese *(Ho)* A highly-flavoured yellow, semi-hard scalded-curd cheese made from cows' milk with a hard rind and red wax coating. Often flavoured with cumin seed, caraway seed or cloves

ley nyin bwint *(Bm)* Cloves

L-glutamic acid *see* (E)620

liaise, to To thicken with a liaison

liaison *(En & Fr) fem.* A combination of ingredients used to thicken and bind soups, sauces, stews, etc. Egg yolks and cream, beurre manié and all the starch-based mixtures are typical liaisons

liba *(Hu)* Goose

libamáj pástétom *(Hu)* A hot puff pastry bouchée or vol-au-vent filled with a mixture of goose liver paté, butter, Béchamel sauce, brandy and spices

lichee *see* lychee

lichene d'Irlanda *(It)* Carragheen

li chi *(Ch)* Lychee

licki kupus *(Bk)* A Croatian dish made from three or more different cuts of pork simmered with sauerkraut and served with boiled potatoes

licorice *see* liquorice

Liebig beef extract The original concentrated beef extract named after the German chemist Leibig who developed it for production in South America before refrigerated ships could bring their beef to Europe

liebre *(Sp)* Hare

Liebstöckel *(Ge)* Lovage

Liederkranz *(USA)* A soft golden yellow cheese with an orange rind somewhat milder than Limburger, made in Ohio from cows' milk

liemi *(Fi)* Soup

lien jee *(Ch)* Lotus seeds

lien ngow *(Ch)* Lotus root

lier *(Fr)* To blend or bring together, to thicken or to bind, hence jus lié

lievero *(It)* Leveret, a small hare

lievitare *(It)* To leaven or raise with yeast or a chemical raising agent

lievito *(It)* Yeast

lievito chimico *(It)* Baking powder

lievito naturale *(It)* Sourdough starter

lièvre *(Fr) masc.* Hare

lièvre en civet *(Fr) masc.* Jugged hare [also called **civet de lièvre**]

liégeoise, à la *(Fr)* In the style of Liège, i.e. including gin or juniper berries

lifrarpylsa *see* blodmor

lift A description of the rising of puff pastry when

cooked due to the generation of steam which separates the layers of dough as they are cooked. Also used for the rising of any cooked mixtures such as cakes and soufflés

light brown sugar *(USA)* A refined pale brown sugar which looks like damp sand [also called **soft sugar, sand sugar, pieces, yellows**]

light corn syrup *(USA) see* corn syrup

light cream *(USA) see* coffee cream

light muscavado A semi-refined soft brown sugar about the same crystal size as granulated or caster sugar

light soya sauce A thin, light coloured and salty soya sauce used where colouring is not required as e.g. with seafood [also called **thin soya sauce**]

light syrup 1 *(USA) see* corn syrup **2** *see* syrup

light whipping cream *(USA)* Cream with 30 to 40% butterfat

lights Lungs of animals used in manufactured meat preparation but rarely eaten in meals in the UK

Ligueil *(Fr)* A strong-flavoured goats' milk cheese from the Loire valley made in a cylindrical shape

ligurienne, à la *(Fr)* In the style of Liguria, Italy, i.e. with a garnish of stuffed tomatoes, risotto flavoured with saffron and duchesse potatoes

ligústico *(Sp)* Lovage

Ligusticum scoticum *Bot.* Scottish lovage

ligzdinas *(Lv)* A type of scotch egg

liha *(Fi)* Meat

lihakääryle *(Fi)* Beef olive

lihaliemi *(Fi)* Consommé

lihamureke *(Fi)* Forcemeat

lihamurekepiiras *(Fi)* Meat pie with a sour cream crust

lihapallero *(Fi)* Meat balls, croquettes

lihapiirakka *(Fi)* Meat pie or pasty

lihapyörykkä *(Fi)* Meat ball, croquette

liiaksi paiste *(Fi)* Overdone, overcooked, of meat, baked goods, etc.

li jiang *(Ch)* Oyster sauce

li ju *(Ch)* Carp

likky pie *(UK)* A West country dish of sliced parboiled leeks and cubed lean pork cooked in milk for about an hour, mixed with cream and eggs, placed in a pie dish, covered with puff pastry and baked at 220°C until brown

Lilium tigrinum *Bot.* Lily bulb

lily buds The 5 cm long, furry, slim unopened flower buds of a day lily *Hemerocallis fulva* with a woody scent, used in Chinese cooking. They are light brown in colour and are soaked in water prior to use. Usually tied up when cooked in simmering dishes to avoid them falling apart [also called **golden needles**]

lily bulb The bulbs of a tiger lily *Lilium tigrinum* resembling a head of garlic. Used fresh in Japan and Korea or dried in China. Must be parboiled before use to remove bitterness

lima *(It & Sp)* Lime, the fruit

lima bean *(USA)* Butter bean

lima orange *see* laranja lima

limanda *(It)* Dab, the fish

limande *(Fr) fem.* Dab, the fish

limão *(Po)* Lemon

limão galego *(Br) see* West Indian lime [also called **galego lime**]

limau *(Id)* Pummelo

limau kesturi *(Ma)* A small lime (1.5 cm dia) used as a souring agent

limau nipis *(Ma)* Lime, the fruit

Limburger A very strong smelling, soft, surface ripened cheese originally from Belgium then adopted in Germany and now made worldwide. It is made from pasteurized full cream cows' milk started with *Streptococcus lactis* and *S. thermophilus* to develop acidity, coagulated with rennet, the curd formed into small bricks, dry salted, ripened at high humidity for about 10 days until the surface develops a red colour, then further ripened at lower temperatures until finished. It has a very strong aroma and a cream coloured close textured paste

lime 1 *(En & Fr) fem.* A small round citrus fruit of which there are four principal species. *Citrus aurantifolia,* the West Indian lime, requires very hot conditions and is not usually exported; *Citrus latifolia,* the Persian or Tahiti lime, is rather larger and is seedless; *Citrus limettiodes,* the Indian or sweet lime, is grown extensively in the Middle East, India, the Caribbean and South America, and *Citrus limetta,* the Tunisian sweet limetta. Limes generally have a thin green skin and few pips; they are sharper and more acid than lemons, but are used in the same way. They are also available dried and as such frequently used in Middle and Far Eastern cooking. Often pickled with spices, salted and/or dried or preserved in soya sauce **2** Calcium hydroxide, the hydrated form of calcium oxide, (E)529, used in SEA to add crispness to batter, to reduce the acidity of fruits in desserts and as a component of pan. It is an important source of calcium in these diets; *see also* tortilla flour for another application [also called **slaked lime**]

lime leaves The leaves of the makrut (kaffir) lime, q.v.

lime sauce As orange sauce but with lime juice and zest substituted for orange

limequat A hybrid of the lime and kumquat *Citrus aurantifolia x Fortunella japonica.* The principal varieties are eustis and Lakeland which are both small and green with a thin edible skin and very sour flesh. Used as a garnish

limon *(Ru)* Lemon or lime, the citrus fruit

limón *(Sp)* Lemon

limoncello *(It)* The zest of Amalfi lemons macerated in alcohol and sugar

limoncillo *(Sp)* Lemon grass

limone *(It)* Lemon

limone, al *(It)* Description of meat, sautéed and finished with lemon juice

limone Amalfitano *(It) see* Amalfi lemon

limone di mare *(It)* Violet (2)

Limousin tart clafoutis *see* tarte limousine clafoutis

limousine, à la *(Fr)* In the style of Limousin, i.e. with red cabbage, ceps and chestnuts

limpa bread *(Sw)* A dark yeast-raised bread made with milk, brown sugar and/or treacle and a mixture of wheat and rye flour, flavoured with caraway seed, fennel seed and grated orange zest which has been covered with boiling water then cooled

limpet A single-shelled mollusc *Paletta vulgaris,* with a shell shaped like a flat cone up to 5 cm dia. and which is commonly seen clinging to rocks. It is found in the Atlantic and the Mediterranean and is prepared and served like cockles. They are not traded and not particularly good to eat on their own but may be used in sauces and stews

limpin' susan *(USA)* A dish of rice and red beans

limun helou *(Ey)* Sweet lime

limun succari *(Ey)* Sweet lime

line, to To cover the inside of a cooking utensil e.g. a cake tin, pudding bowl or terrine dish, with edible matter, e.g. bacon, or non-edible matter, e.g. greaseproof paper, for protection, decoration or to prevent the enclosed food sticking to the container

ling A round seawater fish *Molva molva* with a brownish black top, a member of the cod family but longer (to 2 m) and thinner than cod. Often salted or smoked. Cooked as cod [also called **sea burbot, common ling**]

ling fun *(Ch)* Tapioca starch

ling gok *(Ch)* Water caltrop

lingon *(Sw)* Cowberries

lingonberry *see* cowberry

lingua *(It & Po)* Tongue

lingua alla borghese *(It)* Ox tongue, braised with wine, brandy and salt pork

linguado *(Po)* Sole, the fish

linguado com bananas *(Po)* Baked fillets of sole topped with bananas, served with boiled potatoes and salad

linguattola *(It)* General name for small flat seawater fish, dabs

lingue *(Fr) fem.* Ling, the fish

lingue di gatto *(It)* Langue de chat

lingue di passero *(It)* Thin strips of noodle-like pasta. Lit. sparrow's tongues

linguica *(Po)* A coarse textured pungent small sausage, usually grilled or barbecued

linguine *(It)* Small tongue-shaped pieces of flat pasta

link sausages Frying or grilling sausages made in a long chain with one casing and formed into links by taking them three at a time with a twist between each group of three

Linköping *(Sw)* A spreading sausage made from pork and beef and salt cured

linquisa *(Po)* A brine-cured pork-based sausage, flavoured with garlic, cumin and cinnamon. Requires cooking

linseed bread *see* Leinsamenbrot

linseed oil Cold pressed oil from the seeds of the flax plant which can be used in food and as a nutritional supplement being rich in EFAs

Linsen *(Ge)* Lentils

Linsensuppe *(Ge)* Lentil soup with chopped sausage

linser 1 *(De)* Cream tarts **2** *(No)* Lentils

Linz cake *see* Linzertorte

Linz tart *see* Linzertorte

Linzer Delicatesse A small pleasant-tasting salad potato

Linzer Torte *(Ge)* *see* Linzertorte

Linzertorte *(Au)* A flan made with a base of almond-flavoured pastry filled with raspberry jam and topped with latticework pastry. Eaten warm or cold with slagsahne [also called **Linz cake, Linz tart**]

lipeäkala *(Fi)* Lutefisk

lipid *see* fat

lipoic acid This acid is an essential growth factor for many microorganisms. Whether it has any function in human metabolism is not known

Liptauer *(Ge)* A soft strong tasting ewes' milk cheese with no rind. It is made by ripening the curd for 10 days, removing the rind, blending with salt and ripening for a few more days. Contains 50% water, 22% fat and 21% protein.

Liptauer cheese spread Liptauer cheese mixed at the blending stage with cream and flavourings such as anchovies, onions, capers, caraway seed, chives, paprika, etc.

Liptói *(Hu)* A soft creamy ewes' milk cheese, similar to Liptauer

liqueur A sweetened alcoholic extract of various herb, spice and fruit based flavourings, used as a drink but also as a flavouring in many dishes, e.g. cointreau, Kümmel, kirsch

liquid measure *see* volume measure

liquid paraffin *see* mineral hydrocarbon

liquid smoke *see* pyroligneous acid

liquidize, to To pulverize fruits and vegetables or mixtures of liquids and the same into a soft purée by breaking down the cell walls and releasing their contents

liquidizer *see* blender

liquirizia *(It)* Liquorice

liquor *see* cooking liquor

liquorice A Mediterranean plant *Glycyrrhiza glabra* which probably originated in China. It is grown for the rhizomes and roots from which, after 3 to 5 years growth, the flavouring is extracted in water and boiled down to a black tarry substance. The roots used to be chewed by children as a sweet [also called **licorice, Spanish**]

liscio *(It)* Smooth

lisette *(Fr) fem.* A small mackerel

lissamine green E142, a synthetic green food colouring

lista *(It)* Menu

Listeria monocytogenes A bacterium which grows in soft ripened cheeses (unpasteurized milk has been wrongly implicated), patés, shop-prepared salads, etc. It will grow in these foods at less than 4°C with a doubling time of 18 hours. Samples cultured at 37°C normally have a doubling time of 7.4 hours but after subjecting them to cold shock at 4°C the doubling time drops to 2.5 hours, at the same time refrigeration appears to select for more virulent strains. The incubation period is up to 4 weeks and the resulting illness can range from a general feeling of malaise to meningitis and septicaemia. It is more likely to cause stillbirths and miscarriages and for this reason pregnant women are recommended to refrain from the food items mentioned unless home cooked. It does not grow in raw milk farmhouse cheeses due to the low pH (less than 5), and better hygienic practices. Subsequent pasteurization cannot be used as a letout, and there is more rapid transfer of the milk from cow to cheese making.

listeriosis The disease caused by the bacterium *Listeria monocytogenes* q.v.

litchee *see* lychee

litchi *see* lychee

Litchi chinensis *Bot.* Lychee

litekokt *(No)* Soft boiled, as of eggs

Liter *(Ge)* Litre, unit of volume

liter *(USA)* Litre

lithol rubine BK *see* E180

litre *(En & Fr) masc.* The normal measure of volume approximately equal to 1.75 imperial pints or 2.1 US pints, abbreviated l, or divided into decilitres (dl) (10 per litre), centilitres (cl) (100 per litre) or millilitres (ml) (1000 per litre). A teaspoon is 5 ml, a dessertspoon 10 ml, a tablespoon 15 ml and an imperial pint 568 ml

litro *(It & Sp)* Litre, unit of volume

little cuttlefish A very small cuttlefish *Sepiola rondeleti* with a maximum length of 4 cm. Usually cleaned and eaten whole

little gem A semi-cos type lettuce with soft leaves, usually harvested when up to 15 cm high

little neck clam A small (to 6 cm) and slightly oblong clam *Venerupis japonica* found in the Pacific ocean. May be eaten raw or cooked

little tuna *see* little tunny

little tunny A tropical seawater fish *Euthynnus alletteratus* resembling a small albacore and also related to the tuna. It has a firm oily flesh and dark blue to green striped skin on top. Weighs up to 7 kg. Baked or grilled [also called **bonito, little tuna**]

liu *(Ch)* A method of cooking involving coating with cornflour, frying or steaming then simmering in sauce

lívance *(Cz)* A mixture of flour, milk, butter, sugar and egg yolks, lightened with stiffly beaten egg whites, shaped into small balls and baked until brown on both sides in the oven. Served coated with plum jam and sprinkled with cinnamon and sugar

Livarot *(Fr)* A soft cows' milk cheese from Normandy cast in small discs (500 g) with a brownish shiny rind and a strong flavour and smell. It is protected by appellation d'origine status and the label should contain the words Pays d'Auge. Contains 51% water, 20% fat and 24% protein

live yoghurt Yoghurt which still contains live microorganisms and hence can be used to inoculate further batches. It is kept at a low temperature to slow down the growth

livèche *(Fr) fem.* Lovage

liver A large internal organ in all vertebrates consisting of pink to dark brown soft uniform tissue interspersed with veins, etc. all enclosed in a membrane. It functions as a detoxifying organ for poisons such as alcohol and plant alkaloids, as an energy store (glycogen) and as a source of fat emulsifiers for the bowel. The flavour depends on the age and type of animal. The most commonly used are lamb's, pig's, and calf's which are grilled, fried or braised, goose, duck, pig and chicken which are made into pâtés and pig and ox which are braised and stewed

liver herbs The principal herbs used with liver are basil, dill, marjoram, sage and tarragon

liver pudding *see* maksalaatikko

liver sausage A very common sausage made in many countries from a fine paste of cooked liver, sometimes with meat, and with flavourings and seasonings. Can be sliced or spread; *see also* Leberwurst

livonienne, sauce *(Fr) fem.* A fine julienne of carrots, celery, mushrooms and onions sweated in butter, added to a fish velouté and finished with julienned truffle and chopped parsley. Served with fish

livornaise, à la *(Fr)* In the style of Livorno, Italy, i.e. accompanied with shallots, tomatoes and truffles, particularly poached fish

livornese, alla *(It)* In the style of Livorno, Tuscany, i.e. with tomato sauce, esp. fish and shellfish

livre *(Fr) fem.* Pound, 500 g, unit of weight

li yi *(Ch)* Carp

li yu *(Ch)* Rock carp

li zhi *(Ch) see* lychee

llantén *(Sp)* Plantain

lliseria *(Sp)* Megrim, the fish

loach One of three types of small European freshwater fish of the carp family *Cobitidea* spp. They have a good flavour but lots of small bones and when fried are popular in France. Treat as smelt

loaf **1** A standard quantity of bread dough usually baked in a rectangular loaf tin to give a characteristic shape **2** Any type of food baked in a loaf tin, e.g. meat loaf, fruit loaf, etc.

loaf cheese *see* Edamer

loaf sugar *(USA)* Cube sugar or sugar cubes, not the same as sugar loaf

loaf tin A rectangular tin, of length approximately twice, and width equal to, the depth, with slightly outward sloping sides to allow for easy removal of whatever is cooked in it

lo baak *(Ch)* Mooli [also called **lo bok**]

lo baak gor *(Ch)* A solid steamed savoury pudding or dumpling made with grated mooli and rice flour, then sliced and fried

lobak *(Id & Ma)* Mooli

lobe leaf seaweed *see* wakame

lobhia *(In)* Cow pea

lobia *(In)* Cow pea

lo bok *(Ch)* Mooli [also called **lo baak**]

lobscouse *(UK & USA)* A meat and vegetable stew thickened with ships biscuit, once popular on sailing vessels where it could easily be prepared. Variants on the name occur in all north Atlantic seafaring nations. In the UK it is associated with Liverpool, hence the name scouse or scouser for inhabitants of that city. In the USA it is associated with New England. Nowadays it is made without the ship's biscuit [also called **scouse** (UK)]

lobskovs *(De)* Lobscouse served with rye bread

lobster The largest sea crustacean *Homarus gammarus (Eu)* and *H. americanus (USA)* with eight legs, two forward facing strong crushing claws, several antennae and a muscular tail. they are blue grey when alive and pink when cooked. They are caught on both sides of the Atlantic and in Europe weigh up to 2 kg. The North American variety is larger. Female lobsters which are more tender may contain orange eggs called coral. They should feel heavy for their size, generally yield half their weight in edible meat and are normally bought alive. To kill them they can either be suffocated for 30 minutes in deaerated water (water which has been vigorously boiled and cooled), be dropped in boiling water and held under for 2 minutes or be severed along the centre line of the whole body using a cleaver or heavy knife and starting at the head end. The RSPCA recommend placing them in cold salted water (35 g salt per litre) which is gradually brought to the boil

lobster bisque *see* bisque de homard

lobster butter **1** Lobster shell pounded with unsalted butter to a smooth paste, sweated in a pan, a little water added and all boiled for 15 minutes, strained and cooled until the butter fat sets. Used quickly. The water may also be used for its flavour **2** A compound butter made with the creamy parts, eggs and coral of lobster pounded together with an equal amount of butter and sieved

lobster mayonnaise Half a cold boiled lobster served in its shell with mayonnaise and salad

lobster Newburg *(USA)* Cubed cooked lobster meat, sautéed in butter, sherry added, the juices thickened with a liaison of egg yolks and cream and all served on a paprika-flavoured rice

lobster sauce *see* sauce homard

lobster thermidor *see* homard thermidor

lobya *(In)* Cow pea

Loch Fyne kipper *(UK)* An excellent fat and plump kipper from Loch Fyne in Scotland

Loch Fyne oysters *(UK)* Farmed Pacific oysters from Loch Fyne in Scotland

lochshen A Jewish term for noodles, traditionally made by cutting thinly rolled pasta dough into strips, now usually commercial vermicelli [also called **lokshen**]

locro *(SA)* An Ecuadorian potato soup with cheese, garnished with pieces of avocado

locust bean *see* carob

locust bean gum E410, A plant gum extracted from carob, used as a thickener or gelling agent

lodger's loaf *see* barrel bread

lodole *(It)* Larks, the birds

lofschotel *(Ho)* Chicory

løg *(De)* Onion

loganberry A hybrid of a raspberry and blackberry or dewberry looking like a large dark raspberry about 5 cm long, with a sweet sour taste and fragrant aroma. Use as raspberry

lohi *(Fi)* Salmon

lohikeitto *(Fi)* Salmon soup with potatoes and leeks

lohilaatikko *(Fi)* As laxpudding but with the addition of chopped onions and breadcrumbs to the layers and gratinated with breadcrumbs

lohipiirakka *(Fi)* Salmon pie

lohipiiras *(Fi)* Salmon pie, similar to koulibiac

loin The general name for the joint of an animal consisting of the ribless vertebrae up to the pelvis plus up to 4 vertebrae with ribs, cut through the centre of the backbone to include all the longitudinal muscles plus a small portion of the ribs and the abdominal cavity muscles

loin end of lamb The front half of a loin of lamb

loin of lamb *(UK)* Term used in Scotland for a best end of lamb [also called **single loin of lamb**]

loin of veal *(UK)* That part of the back between the ribs and leg. May be stuffed, rolled and roasted or cut into chops

lök *(Sw)* Onion

løk *(No)* Onion

lok dow *(Ch)* Mung beans

lokhi *see* bottle gourd

löksås *(Sw)* Onion sauce made from finely chopped onions sweated in butter, flour added to make a blond roux and let down to a thin sauce with milk, cooked out and seasoned. Often served with baked potatoes

lokshen *see* lochshen

lokshyna *(Ru)* Egg noodles

löksoppa *(Sw)* Onion soup

lökströmming *(Sw)* Uncleaned sprats marinated in equal parts of white vinegar and water for 12 hours, drained, then layered with sliced onions and a mixture of sugar, black pepper, crushed white peppercorns, cloves and salt in a pot and kept in the refrigerator for 5 days Served with potatoes boiled in their skins

lollo biondo *(It)* A non-hearting loose leaf lettuce with well-flavoured green frilly leaves. May be harvested over a long period by picking individual leaves or cutting and leaving to resprout [also called **green lollo lettuce**]

lollo rosso *(En & It)* As lollo biondo but with frilly leaves tinged with red/bronze and of excellent flavour [also called **red lollo**]

lombarda *(Sp)* Red cabbage

lombata *(It)* Loin (of meat)

lombatina *(It)* Entrecôte steak of beef, loin chop

lombo *(It & Po)* Loin (of meat)

lombo di maiale al latte *(It)* A pork loin, piquéed with cloves and cinnamon bark and braised in milk

lombok chilli A deep red pointed chilli from Indonesia and used in its cuisine

lo mein *(Ch)* Fresh egg noodles

lomi-lomi salmon *(USA)* A Hawaiian dish of salted salmon cooked with chopped tomatoes, sweet mild onions and spring onions

lomo *(Sp)* **1** Saddle, loin or back (of meat) **2** The eye of a loin of pork, cured and packed without further treatment into a close fitting casing. Usually eaten raw

lon *(Th)* Various cooked sauces made with ingredients such as shellfish, fish and meat with flavouring agents and seasoning and simmered in coconut milk until thick

lonac *(Bk)* A deep earthenware casserole dish

London broil *(USA)* Boneless flank of beef, marinated and grilled then cut on the slant

London particular *(UK)* A bacon and green split pea soup made with a chicken or ham stock with aromatic vegetables, puréed, strained, seasoned and finished with cream or yoghurt and garnished with chopped grilled bacon and croûtons. Named after a particularly nasty London fog whose colour it resembled

long back bacon Long rashers of bacon from that part of a side of bacon without ribs

long bean A relative *Vigna sesquipedalis* of the cow pea grown extensively in India, China and SEA both for the mature yellow beans which are harvested from pods (up to 1 m long) or for the young pods (to 35 cm) which are cooked whole. The plants need high supports [also called **yard long bean, long-podded cow pea, snake bean**]

long cucumber Indoor grown cucumbers 25 to 65 cm in length with usually smooth skins. They do not require fertilization. If fertilized they produce bitter fruits and it is for this reason that they must be grown in the absence of insects

long fin tuna *see* albacore

long flounder *see* lemon sole

long grain rice Rice which releases little starch when boiled thus remaining in separated grains. See brown and white long grain rice

Long Island duck *(USA)* An intensively raised duck killed at 1.5 to 2.5 kg, 7 to 8 weeks old

long life A description of foods, usually milk, cream and other liquid dairy products, which have been heated to 132°C for 1 to 2 seconds (occasionally up to 6 minutes depending on the foodstuff) rapidly cooled and aseptically packaged [also called **UHT, ultra heat-treated**]

long-neck clam *see* soft-shell clam

long pepper A plant *Piper longum* (In), *P. retrofractum* (Id), related to the pepper vine whose berries are harvested green and sun dried. Its flavour resembles a milder black pepper. It is grown only in India and Indonesia and is used in Far Eastern cooking [also called **pippali**]

long-podded cow pea *see* long bean

longan A small round tropical fruit *Nephelium longana* from SEA and China resembling a lychee. It has a brown and brittle skin, a central inedible stone and a sweet aromatic white flesh [also called **dragon's eye, lungan**]

longaniza *(Po)* A large sausage similar to chorizo

Longchamp, crème *(Fr) fem.* Crème St Germain garnished with cooked and washed vermicelli and a julienne of sorrel cooked in butter

longe *(Fr) fem.* Loin (of veal or pork)

longeole *(He) fem.* A sausage from Geneva made with chopped pork filled into a casing, air dried for 2 days and cooked for 2 hours. Served hot

longnose *see* garfish

longsong *(La)* A type of fondue Chinoise in which thin strips of buffalo meat or venison are cooked at the table in a pot of simmering flavoured stock and dipped in a peanut sauce

long xia *(Ch)* Lobster

long xu niu rou *(Ch)* Thin sliced beef and asparagus shallow fried

lontong *(Id)* Boiled short grain white rice pressed into a greased square dish, covered with banana leaf, cooled and cut into cubes. Served with satay

lonza *(It)* The eye of a loin of pork, salted and air dried. Eaten raw in very thin slices

loofah The slightly bitter gourd from a plant *Luffa cylindrica,* which looks like a cucumber when young and can be used as a vegetable after soaking in salted water to remove the bitter flavour. When old it is made into a rough bath sponge. Grown in China and the Caribbean; *see also* angled loofah [also called **sponge gourd, luffa**]

loose leaf lettuce A type of lettuce with leaves often indented and very decorative but not forming a heart. The most nutritious type of lettuce

lop cheeng *(Ch) see* lap cheong

loquat The fruit of a tree *Eriobotrya japonica* once from Japan but now grown in

Mediterranean and similar climates. It looks like a small golden yellow plum and has a sweet slightly tart flesh with a fruity aroma and a large central stone. Use as plums [also called **Japanese medlar**]

Lorbeer *(Ge)* Bay *Laurus nobilis* but also used of several other toxic members of the laurel family

lorgnettes *(Fr) fem.* **1** Fried onion rings **2** Small dessert biscuits **3** Candied fruit

Lormes *(Fr)* A goats' milk cheese shaped like a cone from Nivernais

Lorraine *(Fr)* A whitish cows' milk cheese with a distinct lactic flavour formed into stubby cylinders. Similar to Munster and Géromé cheeses [also called **Gérardmer, Gros Lorraine**]

lorraine, à la *(Fr)* In the style of Lorraine, i.e. garnished with small potatoes sautéed in butter and balls of red cabbage

losh kibbehskiye kebaby *(Ru)* Azerbaijani kebabs made from a processed mixture of soaked bulgar, minced lamb, chopped onion, tomato purée, parsley, allspice, cayenne pepper, lemon zest and seasoning, formed into cylinders around skewers, brushed with oil and grilled for 10 to 15 minutes. Served with chopped sweet red peppers and parsley

löskokt *(Sw)* Soft boiled (egg)

losos *(Ru)* Salmon

lota *(Sp)* Eel pout

lote *see* eelpout

loto *(It & Sp)* Lotus

Lotos *(Ge)* Lotus

Lotosblume *(Ge)* Lotus flower

lotte *(Fr) fem.* Burbot, the freshwater fish

lotte de mer *(Fr) fem.* Monkfish [also called **baudroie, diable de mer**]

lotte de rivière *(Fr) fem.* Eel pout

loture *(It)* A type of bread from Sardinia

lotus *(En & Fr) masc.* A water plant *Nelubium nuciferum* related to the water lily and used in Chinese and Indian cooking. The leaves are used for wrapping food, the tuberous roots which have internal holes are used as a vegetable and the black seeds are used like a nut when ripe and after removing the bitter germ. The young stems are eaten as a vegetable in SEA; *see also* lotus root flowers [also called **Chinese water lily, Indian lotus**]

lotus flowers The petals of the lotus flower are used as a garnish in Chinese and Thai cuisines and the open flower is used to contain food

lotus jujube A species of jujube *Zizyphus lotus* from North Africa, only noted because its fruits were mentioned by Homer as the food of the lotus eaters

lotus root The tuberous roots of the lotus with many longitudinal internal holes are eaten young and taste rather like artichokes. The Japanese value them for their appearance. They are often stuffed and deep fried or braised before slicing

lotus root starch A gray coloured and slightly granular starch made from lotus' roots and used for soft cakes and sweet dishes

lotus seeds *see* ds of the lotus used in desserts and stews or roasted as a snack

Lotus tetragonolobus *Bot.* The asparagus pea

lou-kenkas *(Fr)* A small spicy garlic-flavoured sausage from the Basque country. Sometimes eaten hot with cold oysters [also called **loukinka**]

Lou Palou *(Fr)* A hard scalded-curd ewes' and/or cows' milk cheese with a thick black, dry rind and a dense paste whose flavour depends on the milks used varying from strong and aromatic to mild and nutty

Louis sauce *(USA)* Mayonnaise incorporating whipped cream, flavoured with chilli sauce, finely chopped green sweet peppers and spring onions, and lemon juice. Served with seafood

Louisiana yam *see* sweet potato

loukanika *(Gr)* A sausage made with seasoned pork belly marinated with red wine, salt and some or all of cinnamon, coriander, allspice, herbs and orange for a week, packed into hog casings and air dried for a week

loukinka *(Fr)* *see* lou-kenkas

loukoum *(NA)* Turkish delight

loup de mer *(Fr) masc.* Sea bass

loup marin *(Fr) masc.* Catfish

lovage **1** A perennial herb *Levisticum officinale* with a sharp peppery flavour rather like celery. Used in strong tasting dishes and soups. The seeds can also be used in bread and pastries and sprinkled on salads, rice and mashed potatoes. The stems are occasionally candied like angelica **2** An Indian name for ajowan

lövbiff *(Sw)* Sliced beef with Béarnaise sauce

love apple *(UK)* The original name given to the tomato when it was introduced, probably as a marketing ploy

love in disguise *(UK)* Calf's heart stuffed and baked in the oven, served with gravy and bacon

love and tangle *(USA)* Deep fried twisted and tangled doughnuts

low calorie Term used to describe foods with low energy value. The guidelines used in the EU (not law) require such foods to have less than 40 Kcal per 100 g of food

low density lipoprotein A specific complex of a lipid (fat) and a protein that transports cholesterol in the blood. High levels appear to increase the risk of heart and vascular disease; *see also* cholesterol and high density lipoprotein

low fat Term used to describe any food which contains less fat than normally expected or a low fat substitute for a fatty food. Examples are milk, cheese, yoghurt, substitute butter spreads, etc. Guidelines in the EU (not law) require foods so labelled to have less than 5 g of fat per 100 g of food

low fat milk *(USA)* Milk with no more than 2% butterfat

low mull *(USA)* A vegetable and meat stew related to the Irish Mulligan stew

low starch flour Flour from which most of the starch has been removed. Used for diabetics and makes a bread rather like an open foam or sponge

lox *(USA)* Smoked salmon

loza de barro *(Sp)* Earthenware

lsanat matabbli *(ME)* A salad from Syria and the Lebanon of lambs' tongues boiled in water with aromatic vegetables and a BG until tender, cooled, skinned, sliced and arranged decoratively, chilled, dressed with olive oil and lemon juice and garnished with paprika, chopped parsley and lemon wedges.

lua *(Th)* Blanched

luang prabang *(La)* A round hand woven basket in which rice is steamed and served. The rice is normally formed into small balls with the fingers and eaten by hand

luau soup *(USA)* A cream soup from Hawaii made with puréed taro leaves, stock and seasonings

lubia *(ME)* Hyacinth bean

lubina *(Sp)* Bass, the fish

lucanica *(It) see* luganeghe

luccio *(It)* Pike, the fish

luccio marino *(It)* Barracuda, the fish

luccio del trasimeno arrostito *(It)* Pike, larded with bacon and anchovies, roasted and served with a sharp mayonnaise

luccioperca *(It)* Pike-perch

lucines *(Fr)* Clams or mussels

lucio *(Sp)* Pike, the fish

luciperca *(Sp)* Pike-perch

luffa *see* angled loofah and loofah

Luffa acutangula *Bot.* Angled loofah

Luffa cylindrica *Bot.* The loofah plant

lufttrockene Mettwurst *(Ge)* An air dried Mettwurst from Westphalia

luganeaga *(It) see* luganega

luganega *(It)* A small pure pork based sausage flavoured with Parmesan cheese from Northern Italy looking rather like a Cumberland sausage [also called **lucanica, luganeghe, luganiga** and many other spellings]

luganeghe *see* luganega

luganiga *(It) see* luganega

lukanka *(Bu)* A slightly salted and spiced pork sausage eaten raw or cooked

luk chand *(Th)* Nutmeg

lukewarm A description of temperatures around 37°C [also called **blood heat**]

luki *(Ru)* Onion

luk jun *(Th)* Nutmeg

luk kra waan *(Th)* Cardamom

luk mangkak *(Th)* Hairy basil

luk taan *(Th)* Palm nut

lumache *(It)* Snail-shaped pasta

lumachi 1 *(It)* Snails **2** *(He)* Snails served with walnut paste

lumberjack pie *(USA)* Venison and vegetable pie

lumi *(Ma)* Bummaloe, the fish

lump sucker *see* lumpfish

lump sugar 1 *see* cube sugar **2** Irregular shaped pieces of sugar made by crushing a sugar loaf **3** A semi-refined sugar from SEA and China compressed into flat slabs and cut into 15 x 3 x 3 cm fingers [also called **brown slab sugar, rock sugar, yellow rock**]

lumpfish A grey or green seawater fish *Cyclopterus lumpus* with a humped back and knobbly skin, found in the North Atlantic and Baltic and growing to about 60 cm. The male is oily but can be poached. The female is not eaten but caught for the lumpfish roe [also called **lump sucker, sea owl, cock paddle**]

lumpfish roe The eggs of the lumpfish used as a substitute for caviar esp. as a garnish. Coloured white, black, orange or red; *see also* imitation caviar

lumpia *(SEA)* A type of spring roll in which the wrapping is a thin sheet of cooked beaten egg

lunch *(En & Sw)* A meal taken between around 12 noon to 1.30 p.m. (13.30 hrs.)

luncheon A more formal lunch

luncheon meat A mixture of pork, ham, cereal, fat, colouring and seasoning usually cooked in deep rectangular cans to form a solid pink mass which can be sliced and eaten cold or hot. A superior version known as spam (spiced ham) was shipped in great quantities during World War II from the USA to the UK

luncheon sausage A slicing sausage made with ground beef and salt pork mixed with saltpetre, sugar and flour or starch, seasoned, spiced and coloured pink, filled into ox bungs, simmered at 75 to 80°C for 3 hours, smoked and oiled

lungan *see* longan

lungfish *see* barramunda

lungs The soft spongy tissue used in vertebrates to transfer oxygen from air to blood and carbon dioxide from blood to air. Known normally as lights. Used in manufactured meat products, not normally eaten in the UK except by pets (the animal kind). Sometimes eaten as a part of a cooked dish in other cuisines

lunsj *(No)* Lunch

luo bo gao *(Ch)* A dim sum made from a type of turnip cake

luo han zhai *(Ch)* Bamboo shoots, nuts and mushrooms, stir fried with soya sauce and rice wine or sherry. Lit. Budhha's vegetables

Luostari *(Fi)* A cows' milk cheese resembling Port-Salut

luppoli *(It)* Hops

lúpulo *(Sp)* Hops

lu rou *(Ch)* Deer

lu shui *(Ch)* *see* lu soy

Lusignan *(Fr)* A fresh goats' milk cheese from Poitou

lu soy *(Ch)* A mixture of soya sauce with sugar, ginger and five spices used as a basic flavouring for cooking liquors used for simmering meat and poultry

lustrer *(Fr)* To glaze with aspic

lustro *(It)* Grey mullet *(Calabria)*

lute A flour and water paste used to seal the lids of casseroles, terrines and other cooking pots for baking in the oven

lute, to 1 To seal the gap between the lid and body of a cooking dish with a flour and water paste which bakes hard in the oven. Used for slow cooking casseroles, etc. **2** To place a strip of pastry around the rim of a pie dish to seal on the pastry cover

lutefisk *(No)* Air dried cod, cut into pieces, soaked in water for 12 to 14 days, then in dilute caustic soda solution for 2 days, resoaked in water for 3 to 4 days, boiled and served with fried bacon and its fat. An acquired taste

lutein *see* E161(b)

lutfisk *(Sw)* As lutefisk (No)

lut tzee *(Ch)* Chestnut

luumu *(Fi)* Plum

luumut *(Fi)* Plums

luvasu *(It)* *(Sicily)* Pandora and sea bream

luxerna *(It)* *(Italian Riviera)* Grouper, the fish

luya *(Ph)* Ginger

Luzener Allebei *(He)* A vegetable and mushroom salad

lychee The fruit of a Chinese sub-tropical evergreen tree *Litchi chinensis,* now grown worldwide. They are about 4 cm long with a central stone, sweet juicy white grape-like flesh and a hard rough pink to brown skin and grow in bunches. May be eaten raw or cooked after peeling and destoning. Available canned [also called **Chinese cherry, lichee, litchee, litchi, lizhi**]

lycopene E160(d), an extract from ripe fruit, esp. tomatoes, used as a natural red food colour

Lycoperdon perlatum *Bot.* Common puffball

Lycopersicon esculentum *Bot.* Tomato

lye A dilute solution of sodium hydroxide

Lymeswold *(UK)* A so called designer cheese deliberately developed and marketed commercially in 1982 as the UK answer to soft blue cheeses. It did not survive

Lyoner *(Ge)* The German version of the French saucisson de Lyon made with beef, pork and veal and containing pistachio nuts

lyonnaise, à la *(Fr)* Containing fried chopped onion

lyonnaise, sauce *(En & Fr)* *fem.* Onion sweated to a light colour in butter, vinegar added and reduced completely, demi-glace added, simmered, skimmed and seasoned. Served with Vienna steak or fried liver [also called **brown onion sauce**]

lyre of beef *(UK)* The term used in the east of Scotland for clod of beef

lys saus *(No)* Light sauce, e.g. thin Béchamel, etc.

lysosyme An enzyme found in egg white which protects the egg from bacterial contamination by destroying the cell walls of any invading bacteria

Mm

maanz *(In)* Meat

Maasdam *(Ho)* A yellow wax-coated cows' milk cheese resembling Emmental

maatjes haring *(Ho)* Lightly cured young herrings which have not yet developed roe. Eaten as a snack or as a main course with boiled potatoes and salad (not to be confused with matjes herring q.v.)

maayi *(ME)* A popular Iraqi mezze dish of turnips peeled, diced and simmered in salted water for 30 to 45 minutes with beetroot cut in quarters. The beetroot is discarded and the turnips drained and served hot, sprinkled with salt

mabalo A variety of persimmon *Diospyros discolor* grown in the Phillipines, Malaysia and Sri Lanka [also called **velvet apple**]

maçã *(Po)* Apple

maçã do pieto *(Po)* Brisket of beef

Macadamia integrifolia *Bot.* Macadamia nut

macadamia nut The fruit of a tree *Macadamia ternifolia* (hard shell) and *M. integrifolia* (softer shell) originally from Australia, developed in Hawaii and now grown worldwide. Rather like a a large hazelnut with a very hard shell. Usually sold shelled. Use as hazelnuts [also called **Queensland nut**]

Macadamia ternifolia *Bot.* Macadamia nut

maçapão *(Po)* Marzipan

macaron *(Fr) masc.* Macaroon

macaroni *(En & Fr) masc.* Thick hollow tubes of pasta, often cut into short lengths

macaroni cheese *(UK)* Cooked macaroni mixed with cheese sauce, gratinated with cheese and browned under the grill

macaroni alla veronese *(It)* Potato gnocchi served with butter and grated Parmesan cheese

macaroon A small light crisp cake or biscuit made from ground almonds, sugar and egg white (6:5:1), the egg white being whisked to a stiff peak with the sugar and baked at 150°C after resting on rice paper. Used as petit fours or crushed for use in desserts. The mixture may be cooked in a pastry tartlet

macarrão *(Po)* Macaroni

macarrones *(Sp)* Macaroni

maccarello *(It)* Mackerel

maccheroncini *(It)* A thinner version of macaroni

maccheroni *(It)* Macaroni, sometimes used as a general description of all types of dried pasta

macco *(It)* Mashed boiled beans mixed with oil and fennel, from Sicily [also called **maccu**]

maccu *(It) see* macco

mace The lace like covering or aril that surrounds the stone (nutmeg) in the apricot-like fruit of an evergreen tree *Myristica fragrans,* originally from the Moluccas but now grown extensively in maritime tropical areas. It has a slightly bitter aromatic flavour and is widely used in both sweet and savoury dishes. Sold as blades (whole mace), chips or powder

macédoine *(En & Fr) fem.* **1** A cut for vegetables and fruit consisting of small cubical dice **2** A mixture of diced fruit or vegetables

macédoine de fruits *(Fr) fem.* Fruit salad

macedone *(It)* Macedoine

macedonia di frutta *(It)* Fruit salad, usually with a liqueur

macelleria *(It)* Butcher's shop

macerate, to To leave a solid in contact with a liquid either to soften the solid, to reconstitute it, to extract flavour from it or to add flavour to it [also called **to steep**]

macérer *(Fr)* To macerate, steep or soak

mach *(It) see* al macc

machado *(Sp)* Bread fried in olive oil until crisp, pounded or blended with white wine and used as a thickening agent for stews and soups, etc.

mâche *(Fr) fem.* Lamb's lettuce, corn salad

machi *(In)* Fish

ma chin *(Ch)* Cumin

macia *(Sp)* Mace

macinare *(It)* To grind

macinato *(It)* Ground, pounded or minced

macis *(It, Sp & Fr) masc.* Mace

mackerel A round seawater fish *Scomber scombrus* up to 55 cm long with blue black stripes on its back and an off white, firm, well-flavoured oily flesh. Available fresh or smoked. Cooked whole in fillets or in steaks and often served with gooseberry sauce [also called **Atlantic mackerel**]

mackerel shark *see* porbeagle shark

mâconnaise, à la *(Fr)* In the style of Mâcon, i.e. garnished with croûtons, braised button onions or shallots and button mushrooms, esp. of poached freshwater fish

macque choix *(USA)* A Cajun Christmas dish of tomatoes stewed with sweetcorn, hominy, green sweet peppers, celery, lemon juice, and seasoning. Served as an accompaniment to duck

macquée *(Be)* A soft, mild, brick-shaped cheese made from skimmed cows' milk

macreuse *(Fr) fem.* Scoter duck

macrobiotic The description of a philosophy of eating or diet developed by Japanese Zen Buddhists. Each person's diet seeks to complement their Yin and Yang components or tendencies. The diet is very restrictive but adherents claim it promotes health and spiritual harmony

Madagascar bean *see* butter bean

Madagascar green peppercorns *see* green peppercorns

madarina *(Sp)* Mandarin orange

maddalene *(It)* Madeleine, the cake baked in a madeleine mould

made *(Fi)* Burbot, the fish

Madeira A fortified and heat-treated wine from Madeira used to flavour foods esp. sauces and once popular as the drink to be taken with the Victorian madeira cake

Madeira cake A rich yellow sponge cake flavoured with lemon juice and zest and decorated with candied citron peel during the baking process

Madeira sauce 1 part Madeira to 10 parts demi-glace, seasoned, passed through a chinois and butter added. Served with braised ox tongue

madeirense, à *(Po)* In the style of Madeira, i.e. with tomatoes, onions and garlic

madeleine **1** *(UK)* A small cake made from Victoria or Genoese sponge, baked in a dariole mould, coated with jam, dredged with desiccated coconut and decorated with a glacé cherry and angelica [also called **madeline**] **2** *(Fr) fem.* A small sponge cake baked in a madeleine mould

madeleine mould A hinged scallop shaped mould which completely encloses the cake baked in it

madeline *see* madeleine

madère, sauce *(Fr) fem. see* Madeira sauce

Madras curry powder A fragrant, fairly hot, ground spice mixture made from deseeded and dried red chillis, coriander seeds, cumin seeds, mustard seeds, black peppercorns, curry leaves, all dry roasted, plus dry ginger and turmeric

Madras gram *see* horse gram

madrilène, à la *(Fr)* In the style of Madrid, i.e. garnished with or incorporating tomatoes

madun *(Th)* **1** Belimbing, the fruit **2** A small juicy sour fruit from the the tree *Gardinia schomburgiana,* similar to a small star fruit. Used as a souring agent

maduru *(Sr)* Fennel

mÜlk *(De)* Milk

mafalde *(It)* Long flat ribbons of pasta with crinkly edges

magdalenas *(Sp)* A popular breakfast food often dunked in coffee. The traditional recipe uses equal weights of eggs in the shell, sugar, flour and aniseed-flavoured olive oil. The ingredients are vigorously beaten into the oil to incorporate as much air as possible. They are then spooned into paper cases with flavourings and baked at 180°C for about 20 minutes. Nowadays egg whites may be whisked separately before folding them in and baking powder is usually added

Magenbrot *(He)* A bitter-sweet cake flavoured with cinnamon. Lit. stomach bread

Magerquark *(Ge)* Fat free quark, i.e. containing less than 1 % butterfat [also called **skimmed milk quark**]

maggengo *(It) see* Parmigiano Reggiano

maggiorana *(It)* Marjoram

magnesium An essential element required for health and a constituent of many enzymes, necessary for bone and teeth growth and repair. Available from all seeds but often taken as a supplement in the form of Epsom salts

magnesium carbonate *see* (E)504

magnesium hydroxide *see* (E)528

magnesium oxide *see* (E)530

magnesium silicate *see* (E)553(a)

magnesium stearate *see* (E)572

magnesium sulphate *see* (E)518

magnesium trisilicate *see* (E)553(a)

Magnifera indica *Bot.* Mango

magnonese *(It)* Warm mayonnaise served with fish or boiled meat

magnosa *(It) see* cigarra (Sp) [also called **cicala**]

Magnum *(Fr)* **1** A rich creamy cows' milk cheese from Normandy made in the shape of a disc and similar to Brillat-Savarin **2** *(Fr) masc.* A large bottle of about 1.5 litre capacity

magoro *(It)* Tuna

magret *(Fr) masc.* Grilled and sliced underdone breast of duck or goose taken from a force-fed bird [also called **maigret, maigret de canard**]

magro *(It)* The description of a dish without meat

magrut *(Th)* Makrut lime

maguro *(It & Ja)* Tuna

magyar gulyás leves *(Hu)* Soup made like a thin goulash from sweated onions and diced beef simmered in water with seasoning, paprika, marjoram and crushed caraway seeds. Strips of sweet red pepper, diced tomatoes and czipetkes are added at intervals so that all are cooked at the same time

magyar halleves *(Hu)* A fish soup made from sweated onions sprinkled with flour and simmered with fish stock, seasoned and flavoured with paprika. Towards the end blended with sour cream and garnished with small pieces of fish roe and czipetkes and all cooked out

ma-gyi-thi *(Bm)* Tamarind

mahallebi *(Tu)* A dessert of sweetened milk thickened with rice starch, flavoured with rose water, poured into a mould and chilled

mahlab Small beige oval kernels of the black cherry tree *Prunus mahaleb* with a bitter, rather sour taste used when dried and ground to flavour breads and pastries in Turkey and the Middle East

mahlen *(Ge)* To grind

mah mee *(SEA)* A soup from Singapore consisting of a clear stock with noodles, shellfish, pork, vegetables and seasoning

Mahón *(Sp)* A semi-hard cows' and ewes' milk cheese from the Balearic islands, white, soft and creamy when young but becomes harder, darker and more tasty as it matures. It is cast in a rounded brick shape and normally brined, matured for 3 weeks, then coated with olive oil

mahonesa *(Sp)* Mayonnaise

Mährische *(Au)* A sausage made from lean pork, beef and bacon fat (2:1:1) plus seasoning

mah tai *(Ch)* Water chestnut

maiale *(It)* Pig or pork

maiale ubriaco *(It)* Pork chops cooked in red wine. Lit. tipsy pork

maialino *(It)* Sucking pig

maid of honour *(UK)* A small puff pastry tartlet with a filling made from milk curds or curd cheese, egg yolks and butter or clotted cream (5:3:5), with sugar to taste and flavoured with lemon zest and possibly cinnamon and nutmeg. Other additions to the filling include coconut, flour or ground almonds and some recipes give orange flower water as a flavouring. It is said to have been invented by Anne Boleyn when she was a maid of honour to King Henry VIII's first wife, Catharine of Aragon

maida flour A soft white flour for making naan, from the north of India

maidenhair fern A feathery fern *Adiantum capillus-veneris* which can be used for decoration or when extracted with water is used to make capillaire syrup

maidenhair tree The tree *Ginkgo biloba* from which ginkgo nuts are obtained

Maidstone biscuit *(UK)* A light crisp biscuit made with plain flour, caster sugar and butter (5:4:4), using the creaming method and flavoured with rose water and chopped blanched almonds. Baked at 180°C

Maifisch *(Ge)* Shad

maigre *(Fr)* Lean, low fat, clear, of soup

maigre, au *(Fr)* A description of a dish not containing meat

Maigrelet *(Cn)* A medium soft cheese made from skimmed cows' milk in Quebec

maigret *(Fr) masc. see* magret

maigret de canard *(Fr) masc. see* magret

maik yu *(Ch)* Cuttlefish

maillard reaction The reaction, responsible for the browning of meat, bread, chocolate, coffee and other roasted food, between a sugar and an amino acid, both of which are usually part of a carbohydrate and a protein respectively

maillot, à la *(Fr)* Garnished with turnips, carrots, French beans, braised lettuce and peas

main course The central and most substantial dish of a meal usually containing a fair amount of meat, fish or pulse protein

Mainauerkäse *(Ge & He)* A semi-hard, surface ripened, scalded-curd cows' milk cheese with a smooth texture and slightly acid pleasantly aromatic taste. Contains 43% water, 25% fat and 24% protein

maintenon, à la *(Fr)* Garnished with an onion sauce containing puréed onions and chopped mushrooms

Mainz *(Ge)* A hand moulded cheese similar to Harzerkäse and often flavoured with cumin. An acquired taste

Mainzer Rippchen *(Ge)* Pork chops

maionese *(It)* Mayonnaise

maioran *(Ru)* Marjoram

Mais *(Ge)* Maize, corn on the cob

maïs *(Fr) masc.* Maize, sweetcorn

maïs en épi *(Fr) masc.* Corn on the cob

Maismehl *(Ge)* Cornflour

maison *(Fr) fem.* House. Used as an adjective to indicate that the food was made on the premises, e.g. pâté maison

maison, de la *(Fr)* Of the house, made on the premises

Maistorta *(Ge)* A type of pudding made with cornmeal

maito *(Fi)* Milk

maitoporsas *(Fi)* Sucking pig

maître d' *(USA) coll.* Maître d'hôtel. Pronounced maître dee

maître d'hôtel *(Fr) masc.* The person in charge of a dining room in a restaurant or hotel, the head waiter or waitress; *see also* beurre à la maître d'hôtel

maíz *(Sp)* Maize, corn on the cob

maize A Central American cereal *Zea mays* now grown worldwide, consisting of a large number of individual white, yellow, red or blue seeds packed in a single layer around a central wide stalk tapering to a point called a cob, the whole enclosed in several papery leaves with a tassel emerging from the point. Several of these cobs which are about 6 to 8 cm diameter and up to 30 cm long sprout from the leaf bases of a tall large leaved grass. The individual seeds (kernels) are stripped from the cob for further processing, the white and yellow being used for human consumption. Maize is an important source of carbohydrate for both humans and animals. There are various types. Dent, var. *indentata* is soft and has a depression in the seeds, this is used for flour. A hard type, flint var. *indurata* is used for popcorn and a sweet sugary type var. *saccharata* is for use as a vegetable; *see also* sweet corn, miniature corn, popcorn, hominy, corn syrup, etc. [also called **corn** (USA)**, Indian corn, mealies**]

maize meal *(USA)* Coarsely ground dehusked maize

maize oil *see* corn oil

majonnäs *(Sw)* Mayonnaise

Majoran *(Ge)* Marjoram

majorana *(Sp)* Sweet marjoram

makapuno *(Ph)* A mutant coconut which cannot mature and in which the fruits are full of a soft gelatinous meat instead of separate liquid and flesh. Used as a dessert and for making ice cream

makaronilaatikko *(Fi)* Macaroni baked in milk and cream thickened with egg yolks

ma kham *(Th)* Tamarind

makhan *(In)* Butter

maki-su *(Ja)* A flexible mat made of strips of bamboo used for rolling up suki

maki yakinabe *(Ja)* A rectangular omelette pan the same shape as a Swiss roll tin used for making rectangular egg or batter sheets which are rolled up or used as a wrapping [also called **tamago-yakiki**]

maki zushi *(Ja)* A sushi wrapped in nori with the filling in the centre of the sushi-meshi rice. Rolled up using a bamboo mat (maki-su). The roll is cut in 3 cm pieces to show the decoratively arranged filling [also called **nori-maki**]

makkara *(Fi)* Sausage

Makkaroni *(Ge)* Macaroni

makki ki roti *(In)* A thin bread from the Punjab made from fine cornmeal. It is soft on the inside and crisp on the outside

mak mo *(Ch)* Cuttlefish

mako *(Ja)* Shark

mako shark A member *Isurus oxyrhynchus* of the shark family which makes good eating

makreel *(Ho)* Mackerel

makrel *(De)* Mackerel

Makrele *(Ge)* Mackerel

makrell *(No)* Mackerel

makrill *(Sw)* Mackerel

makrillgryta *(Sw)* Pieces of seasoned mackerel fillet, layered with thin slices of lemon and peeled tomatoes in a pot, a little stock and butter added and simmered with a tight fitting lid for 20 minutes. Finished with chopped parsley or dill

makrilli *(Fi)* Mackerel

Makrone *(Ge)* Macaroon

makroner *(De)* Macaroons

makrut lime This citrus fruit from SEA *Citrus hystrix* is not a true lime but is picked in the immature state and used as such. The rind is irregular and very bumpy with a pronounced smaller stem end. There is very little juice. The rind and leaves are used to flavour curries, soup, salads and vinegar. They are known in Paris as combavas [also called **kaffir lime**]

maksa *(Fi)* Liver

maksalaatikko *(Fi)* A liver pudding made with liver, rice, onions, milk, water, golden syrup, raisins, eggs, marjoram and seasoning. Served with melted butter, boiled potatoes and cranberry sauce

makua *(Th)* Aubergine

makua phuong *(Th)* Pea aubergine

mal passado *(Sp)* Rare (of meat, steaks, etc.)

malácz kovesonya *(Hu)* Brawn made from pig's head boiled with a minimum of water with garlic, carrots, onion, Hamburg parsley, seasoning and spices

maladi *(ME)* Common orange

Málaga *(Sp)* A soft cream-coloured cheese made from goat's milk, covered with a yellow rind, with a mild goaty flavour and many fine holes. Eaten fresh within a few days of manufacture

malagliata *(It)* Roughly cut elongated diamonds of pasta. Lit. badly cut

malai *(In)* Cream used in Indian cooking, similar to clotted cream q.v. but made by repeatedly boiling the milk and removing the skin from the top until it is all reduced to a crumbly texture

Malakoff, tarte *(Fr) fem.* A cake made from layers of rum-soaked sponge fingers in a rich cream mixture made from butter, sugar, ground almonds and cream, flavoured with coffee or vanilla essence. Named after the suburb of Paris.

malanga *see* eddoe

malasado *(Po)* An egg enriched puff pastry deep fried and dredged with sugar Lit. unlucky

Malay apple *(USA)* A crisp red bland-flavoured and pear-shaped fruit

Maldive fish *(Sr)* Various fish species local to Sri Lanka, dried and crumbled or powdered for use in cooking; *see also* bummaloe

malet kött *(Sw)* Minced beef

malfatta *(It)* Home made balls of pasta dough. Lit. badly made

malfatti *(It)* A gnocchi coloured with spinach and flavoured with ricotta cheese

malfattina *(It)* Finely chopped sheets of pasta dough

mali *(Th)* Jasmine flowers and jasmine essence used as flavouring

malic acid A fruit acid (E)296 found in underripe apples, rhubarb and some berries. It is not suitable for setting jams. Used as a flavouring in soft drinks, dessert mixes and pie fillings

malinovyi sup *(Ru)* A cold soup from the Baltic region made from the strained juice of summer fruits sweetened with brown sugar and flavoured with cinnamon, lemon juice and lemon zest and slightly thickened with cornflour

malka sabat *(In)* Dehusked and split red lentils

mallard A wild duck, suitable for one or two servings depending on size. Brushed with oil and roasted at 200°C for approximately 50 minutes and then treated as duck. Shooting season 1st September until the 31st of January or until the 21st of February if shot below the high water mark of spring tides. Hanging time 2 to 3 days

mallow A family of plants many of which are edible, e.g. abelmusk, Jamaica flower, abutilon, marshmallow, okra, and meloukhia

malong *(Ma)* Eel

malosol *(Ru)* Fresh caviar prepared with only a little salt

malosolni *(Ru)* Lightly salted, a description of some Russian caviar

Malpighia glabra *Bot.* Barbados cherry

malpuri *(In)* Puri bread flavoured with crushed fennel seed

malt *(En & Fr) masc.* Barley which has been germinated and allowed to sprout under warm humid conditions. The sprouting liberates enzymes which convert the starch into a variety of sugars and polysaccharides of which maltose is the most important. Heat is used to denature the enzymes and the malt is then dried and crushed. The soluble sugars are extracted with water either for brewing or for concentration into malt extract, a thick brown sweetish syrup

malt bread A yeasted bread dough enriched with malt extract, black treacle and dried vine fruits prior to baking to a soft moist loaf

malt extract A concentrated solution of the soluble sugars extracted from malt. Used in cakes, bread and puddings in the West and as a constituent of sauces and meat glazes in China

malt sugar *see* maltose

malt vinegar A brown vinegar made by partial

oxidation of the alcoholic liquor (ale) made from the water extract of malt. Contains about 5% acetic acid

malta *(Sp)* Malt

maltaise, à la *(Fr)* In the Maltese style, i.e. with the addition of orange zest and juice

maltaise, sauce *(En & Fr) fem.* Hollandaise sauce flavoured with the strained juice of blood oranges and orange zest [also called **Maltese sauce**]

malted milk A mixture of dried milk powder and ground malted barley reconstituted with milk. Served hot or cold

Maltese sauce *see* sauce maltaise

malto *(It)* Malt

maltose A disaccharide consisting of two glucose units. The principal sugar in malt [also called **malt sugar**]

Malus pumila *Bot.* Crab apple

Malus sylvestris* var. *domestica *Bot.* Apple

Malva moschata *Bot.* Muskmallow

malvavisco *(Sp)* Marshmallow

Malz *(Ge)* Malt

mămăligă *(Ro)* Cornmeal cooked slowly in salted water with butter until thick and served with melted butter. A national dish of Romania

mămăligă cu ochiuri romănesti *(Ro)* Mamaliga topped with poached eggs and melted butter with sour cream served separately

mamalyga *(Ru)* The Russian Moldavian version of mamaliga made from polenta, butter and melting cheese (3:1:4 based on cornmeal), flavoured with marjoram and pepper, put in a buttered dish and baked at 190°C until skinned over, cooled, divided in squares and served gratinated with cheese and grilled

mamelle *(Fr) fem.* Udder

mamey The spherical fruit of a tree *Mammea americana* from the Carribean and South America, up to 15 cm in dia. with a brown to grey rough outer skin, a thin bitter, yellow, inner skin and yellowish flesh tasting of raspberries and apricots, surrounding up to 4 inedible seeds. May be eaten raw [also called **mammee**]

Mamirolle *(Fr)* A semi-hard washed-rind cows' milk cheese made in the same way as Limburger but not as pungent. Usually brick-shaped (600 g)

Mammea americana *Bot.* Mamey

mammee *see* mamey

mammella *(It)* Udder

mämmi *(Fi)* A pudding made from rye meal sweetened with molasses and flavoured with Seville oranges. Usually baked in the oven in birch bark baskets for Easter and served with cream

Mamsell Babette *(Ge)* A firm, loaf shaped mild-flavoured cows' milk cheese from Bavaria which contains small pieces of smoked ham

mam tom *(Vi)* Shrimp paste

manaita *(Ja)* A chopping board

ma-nao *(Th)* Lime, the fruit

manapua *(USA)* A dough bun from Hawaii filled with various savoury fillings and steamed

manbollen *(Ho) see* Edam

mâncare cu bame *(Ro)* Diced pork and fried onions stewed in tomato juice with herbs and seasonings. Served with bread

manche *(Fr) masc.* The scraped bone end of a cutlet or the knuckle of a leg of lamb. Lit. handle

Manchego *(Sp)* A strong tasting, pale coloured, hard scalded-curd cheese with a sprinkling of small holes, made from ewes' milk. It uses a lactic starter and the yellow paste is covered with a greenish black mould. Very popular and eaten both fresh and matured to varying degrees of hardness and dryness. The mature varieties are washed and oiled

Manchester pudding *(UK)* Soft white breadcrumbs mixed with egg yolks, sugar and lemon peel infused milk, cooked until set in a bain marie in individual dishes. Cooled, covered with raspberry jam, piped with meringue, coloured under the grill and dredged with icing sugar

manchette *(Fr) fem.* Cutlet frill

manchon, en *(Fr)* A method of presenting panéed and deep fried small fish by cutting off the head and tail after cooking so that they appear to be served in sleeves

mancu A black colouring used in black puddings

mandaliya *(In)* An almost vegetarian sausage consisting of marrow and spices stuffed into a casing

mandarin The general name of a group of citrus fruits *Citrus reticulata* which are all generally sweet and have very easily separable thin orange skins and segments. Generally classified as Satsuma or Unshui mandarin *Citrus unshui,* Mediterranean mandarin *C. deliciosa,* King mandarin *C. nobilis* and Common mandarin *C. reticulata.* The zest is not usually used except dried and ground as a spice [also called **tangerine**]

mandarin cooking The haute cuisine of Chinese cooking originating in the royal court and combining Peking (Beijing) and Shanghai styles

mandarin pancake The pancake in which Peking duck is wrapped made from a flour and boiling water dough (5:3) which is kneaded until silky with a further part of cold water. It is rolled out, cut in squares, one side of each coated in sesame seed oil and sandwiched in pairs with the oiled sides together. These are rolled out again, fried in an oiled pan until browned on each side, separated and folded in triangles

mandarin peel *see* tangerine peel

Mandarine *(Ge)* Mandarin, the fruit

mandarine *(Fr) fem.* Mandarin, the fruit

mandarino *(It)* Mandarin.

Mandel *(Ge)* Almond

Mandel Halbmonde *(Ge)* Almond crescent biscuits made by the creaming method from flour, butter, sugar and egg yolks (6:4:3:1) in which two thirds of the egg yolks are hard boiled and sieved before incorporation. Formed into crescents from bent and flattened cylinders of paste, dipped in egg white and coated with a mixture of almond nibs, sugar and cinnamon, then baked at 160°C until firm

mandelbiskvier *(Sw)* Almond biscuit

Mandeltorte *(Ge)* An almond layer cake with a filling of jam or crème patissière and covered with a royal icing flavoured with rum or butter icing or the like. The cake mixture is a type of fatless cake mixture with mainly ground skinned and dry roasted almonds mixed into an egg yolk, egg and sugar batter with a little flour and stiffly whisked egg whites folded in at the end. The baking tins are coated with melted butter and dredged with fine dried breadcrumbs before filling

mandioca *(Sp)* Cassava

mandlar *(Sw)* Almonds

mandler *(De & No)* Almonds

mandolin An implement for slicing any firm vegetable or fruit or making it into batons or julienne strips. It consists of a strong rectangular metal frame supported at an angle to the bench top with various transverse cutting blades and attachments. The food to be sliced is moved by hand downwards across the blade and the slices, etc. fall beneath

mandora *(Cy) see* ortanique

mandorla *(It)* Almond

mandorlato *(It)* Almond cake, nougat

mandur *(Bk)* A hard grating cheese made from a mixture of cows' and ewes' milk and the whey from cheese making

maneira de, à *(Po)* In the style of, in the manner of

mangetout *(En & Fr) masc.* A variety of pea *Pisum sativum* var. *macrocarpum,* which has a delicate skin and is eaten whole when young. Lit. eat all [also called **snow pea, sugar pea, sugar-snap pea, Chinese pea**]

manggis *(Id & Ma)* Mangosteen

mang guo *(Ch)* Mango

mangkut *(Th)* Mangosteen

Mango *(Ge)* Mango

mango *(En, It & Sp)* A large round to pear- or kidney-shaped tropical fruit weighing between 0.25 and 1 kg, from a tree *Magnifera indica* which is widely distributed. The fruit when ripe has a juicy, slightly fibrous orange flesh with a distinctive flavour, a large central stone and a thickish green through yellow to red inedible skin. Sold whole or skinned and destoned in canned or dried form

mango pickle An Indian pickle made from chopped very underripe raw mango, destoned but not peeled mixed with turmeric, ground cinnamon, nigella, fennel seed, soaked fenugreek seed, salt and chilli powder, left for two days then covered with warm oil flavoured with dried chillis and allowed to mature

mango powder *see* amchoor

mango squash *see* choko

Mangold *(Ge)* Spinach beet

mangostan *see* mangosteen

mangosteen The fruit of a Malaysian evergreen tree *Garcinia mangostana* which grows in wet tropical regions. It has a deep purple fibrous outer casing enclosing segments of juicy, creamy white flesh containing an inedible seed. The flesh has a sweet-sour flavour reminiscent of molasses. The skin contains an indelible dye; *see also* kokum [also called **mangostan**]

mang tre *(Vi)* Bamboo shoot

mangue *(Fr) fem.* Mango

maniche *(It)* Wide tubes of pasta resembling short cannelloni

manicotti *(It)* Large cannelloni often stuffed with a Ricotta cheese mixture and baked in a sauce. Lit. muff

maniera di, alla *(It)* In the style of

manina ferrarese *(It)* A crisp bread roll in the shape of a double horseshoe

manioc *(En & Fr) masc.* Cassava

manioca *(It)* Cassava

manjar blanco *see* arequipe

manju *(Ja)* A cake eaten with tea

mannagrynspudding *(Sw)* Semolina pudding

mannaya kasha *(Ru)* A type of slightly sweetened gruel made from semolina with milk and salt

mannitol E421, a compound similar to sorbitol found in many plants, now synthesized from sucrose for use as a humectant

mano *(Me)* A stone ball-like roller used on a metate to grind grains and spices

manoa *(USA)* A variety of butterhead lettuce from Hawaii

Manoori *(Gr)* A ewes' milk cheese from Crete eaten with honey as a dessert [also called **Manouri**]

Manouri *see* manoori

mansikkasoppa *(Fi)* Strawberries with cream and sugar

mansikkat *(Fi)* Strawberries

mansikkatorttu *(Fi)* Strawberry tart

mantar *(Tu)* Grilled mushroom caps with a garlic filling

man tau *(Ch)* Steamed buns

manteca 1 *(It) see* burrino **2** *(Me)* Lard

manteca de cerdo *(Sp)* Pig's lard

mantecado *(Sp)* Ice cream with added whipped cream

mantecare *(It)* To whip or whisk

mantecato *(It)* **1** Softened, pounded **2** Soft ice cream made by adding whipped cream to ice cream

manteenmäti *(Fi)* The roe of the burbot processed like caviar and very expensive

mantega bean A bean from Chile which does not cause flatulence and which is being used to breed more popular varieties with the same properties

manteiga *(Po)* Butter

manteli *(Fi)* Almond

mantelimassa *(Fi)* Marzipan

mantequilla *(Sp)* Butter

manti *(Tu)* Fresh ravioli, poached, drained and coated with a sauce made from yoghurt, melted butter, chopped garlic and paprika

mantis shrimp A large crustacean *Squilla empusa (USA)* and *S. mantis (Eu)* from the eastern coast of the USA and the Mediterranean somewhat larger than a prawn and when eating resembles a praying mantis. It is related to the crab but looks more like a prawn. Usually only found where landed. Cooked like prawns

manty *(Ru)* Steamed filled dumplings from Uzbekistan made with a flour and water dough, rolled out, cut in 10 cm circles each of which is wrapped around a teaspoonful of filling and some butter. Usually served with yoghurt or vinegar as a dipping sauce

man yu *(Ch)* Eel

manzana *(Sp)* Apple

manzo *(It)* Beef from cattle under 4 years old

manzo arrosto *(It)* Roast beef

manzo brassiato *(It)* Braised beef

manzo alla certosina *(It)* Beef stewed with bacon, anchovies and herbs

manzo lesso *(It)* Boiled beef

manzo salato *(It)* Corned beef

manzo stuffato *(It)* Stewed beef

manzo uso *(It)* Pot roasted beef

maple sugar *(Cn & USA)* A solid sugar (saccharose) with a characteristic flavour crystallized from the sap of the sugar maple tree *Acer saccharum*

maple syrup *(Cn & USA)* A sweet sugar syrup prepared from the sap of the sugar maple tree *Acer saccharum* which is collected by boring a hole into the trunk during March. Used as a sweetening agent esp. to produce a sauce for waffles and hot cakes

maple syrup pie *(Cn)* A double crust pie filled with a mixture made from maple syrup, cornflour, butter and chopped nuts

maprao *(Th)* Young coconut, see kelapa

maque choux *(USA)* A sweet, highly seasoned Cajun dish of maize

maquereau *(Fr) masc.* Mackerel

maquereaux au vin blanc *(Fr) masc.* Mackerel fillets poached in white wine and served cold as a starter

maracuya *(SA)* Purple passion fruit grown in Columbia

maraîchère, (à la) *(Fr)* In the style of a

market gardener, a description of joints of meat garnished with salsify, Brussels sprouts, potatoes, onions and carrots

maräng *(Sw)* Meringue

maranta *(It)* Arrowroot

Maranta arundinacea *Bot.* Arrowroot

marasche *(It)* Morello cherries

maraschino A colourless liqueur flavoured with maraschino cherries and their crushed kernels. Used for flavouring

maraschino cherry Cherries preserved in a red coloured sugar syrup flavoured with almond oil, or in maraschino liqueur

Marasmius oreades *Bot.* Fairy ring mushroom

maratello rice *(It)* A moderately priced semi-fino, oval, slightly sticky rice suitable for minestrone

marbled 1 The description of lean meat when it is is interspersed with long visible flecks of fat, usually a sign of high quality beef. The fat helps to prevent the meat drying out **2** A description of pastry or cake made from two contrasting coloured pastes mixed together to resemble marble when cooked

marbrade *(Fr) fem.* A dish from the south west consisting of a cooked pig's head in aspic

marbré *(Fr)* Striped bream

marc An alcoholic spirit distilled from the fermented skins and pips of pressed grapes. Used as a cheap substitute for brandy

marcassin *(Fr) masc.* A young wild boar

marchand de vin *(Fr)* Cooked with red wine and shallots, esp. steak

marchand de vin, sauce *(En & Fr) fem.* A chasseur sauce based on red wine as well as stock

marche *see* lamb's lettuce

marchepain *see* marzipan

Maredsous *(Be)* A rectangular shaped cows' milk cheese similar to Saint-Paulin

Marengo *see* poulet sauté Marengo

marennes *(Fr) fem.* A variety of small oysters

maréchal, à la *(Fr)* In the style of the marshal, i.e. garnished with asparagus tips, truffles, cockscombs and peas

marée *(Fr) fem.* Fresh seawater fish and shellfish

margarine *(En & Fr) fem.* A butter substitute made by hydrogenating liquid vegetable and deodorized fish oils to give a fat solid at room temperature. Once thought to be healthier than butter due to its lower proportion of saturated fat. Unfortunately the chemical processes produce fats which do not occur in nature (trans- as opposed to cis- forms) which, although they do appear in butter at a lower concentration, may be deleterious to health in some as yet unknown way. One of the more successful examples of persuading the public to substitute a factory product for a farm-produced equivalent

margarita *(Sp)* Golden carpet shell clam

marge *(UK) coll.* Margarine

Margotin *(Fr)* A soft buttery cows' milk cheese from Périgord, flavoured with pepper or herbs

Marguery, fish As for fish Bercy but garnishing the fish with cooked prawns and mussels before coating it with sauce and glazing

marha gulyás *(Hu)* A goulash of diced beef heart, ox liver and cow's udder with chopped onions and garlic sweated in lard, flavoured with paprika, crushed caraway seeds and marjoram, seasoned and stewed with tomato purée and water with diced potatoes and csipetkes

marhahús *(Hu)* Beef

Maribo *(De)* A semi-hard, scalded curd open-textured cows' milk cheese, cream coloured with a slightly lactic flavour and many small holes. The curd which is cast in large rounds (to 14 kg) is salted and ripened for 3 to 5 weeks and covered in yellow wax. The white paste has a mild to strong aromatic flavour depending on age

Marie-Louise, (à la) *(Fr)* In the style of Marie-Louise, i.e. garnished with onion purée, artichoke hearts, mushrooms and potatoes

Marienhofer *(Au)* A cheese from the Austrian Tyrol resembling Limburger

Marienkraut *(Ge)* Sweet marjoram

marignan *(Fr)* A type of rum baba with an apricot glaze and filled with crème chantilly

marigold A hardy annual *Calendula officinalis* grown as a garden plant. The petals can be used to colour and flavour a variety of dishes and as a garnish. The leaves can be used sparingly in salads [also called **calendula, pot marigold**]

Marille *(Au)* Apricot

marinade *(En & Fr) fem.* A mixture of various tenderizing and flavouring agents, usually including an oil, an acid such as vinegar or lemon juice and a selection from wine, sherry, yoghurt, coconut milk, fruit juices and similar liquids, herbs, spices, seasonings and flavour enhancers such as soya sauce. Used to treat raw meat and fish for periods from an hour upwards to tenderize, flavour and add moisture. Sometimes the strained marinade is used in the resulting dish. The classic marinade contains 1 litre of wine, 0.5 litres of vinegar and 0.2 litres of oil to 200 g of chopped aromatic vegetables plus garlic, parsley stalks, bay leaf, peppercorns and cloves and may be cooked or uncooked

marinades *(Cn)* Pickles

marinar *(Sp)* To marinate

marinara *(It)* A rich tomato sauce prepared very quickly from ripe tomatoes.

marinara, alla *(It)* In the sailor's style, e.g. with seafood, or, of shellfish, simmered with oil, wine, parsley and garlic

marinare *(It)* To marinate

marinate, to To treat raw meat, poultry, game or fish with a marinade

marinato *(It)* Pickled, marinated

mariné(e) *(Fr)* Pickled, marinated or soused

mariner *(Fr)* To marinate

marinerad böckling *(Sw)* Cleaned, filleted and deboned (as far as possible) buckling, marinated for 2 hours in oil, vinegar and seasoning, drained and garnished with chopped dill or chives

marinière, à la *(Fr)* In the style of a boatman, i.e. garnished with mussels; *see also* moules marinière

marinière, sauce *(Fr) fem.* Sauce Bercy with 100 ml of reduced mussel cooking liquor per litre and finished with 6 egg yolks per litre

marinieren *(Ge)* To marinate

mariniert *(Ge)* Pickled, marinated

Marinierter Hering *(Ge)* Soused herring

marinovannya arbuznaya korka *(Ru)* Pickled watermelon rind from which all the pink flesh and the green skin has been removed. It is brined (50 g per litre) overnight, drained and rinsed, boiled until soft in vinegar and water (2:1), sugar equal in weight to the rind added plus cinnamon, cloves, root ginger and allspice in a muslin bag and all boiled until the rind is transparent. The rind is then bottled with the reduced syrup and served on the zakuska (hors d'oeuvre) table

marinovannye griby *(Ru)* A type of mushroom à la grecque made with a variety of fungi cooked in wine vinegar and water (3:2) with garlic, cloves, bay, salt, sugar and peppercorns, bottled in the cooking liquor, covered with oil and refrigerated for at least 10 days before use

mariscos *(Sp)* Shellfish

maritozzo *(It)* A currant bun

marjolaine *(Fr) fem.* **1** Marjoram **2** A pie case made of meringue mixed with almonds and filberts, layered with chocolate, praline and butter cream

marjoram The name given to species of the origanum group in particular *Origanum majorana* - sweet or knotted marjoram, *Origanum onites* - pot or French marjoram, and *Origanum heracleoticum* - winter marjoram. See under the above names, *Oreganum* spp. and oregano

Mark *(Ge)* Bone marrow

market crab *see* Dungeness crab

market measure The system of volume measures used for large quantities of goods, now in hectolitres (100 litres). In the pre-metric system the most common were the bushel (equal to 8 gallons, either imperial or US), the quarter (equal to 8 bushels), the bag, sack, chest, hogshead and barrel. Because many dry goods were originally sold by volume, the weights of a bushel and other volume measures were standardized, e.g. a bushel of wheat equals 60 lb, of maize, 56 lb, of oats, 39 lb in the UK and 32 lb in the USA and so on

Markklössen *(Ge)* Bread dumplings mixed with beef marrow. Served with consommé

Markknochen *(Ge)* Marrow bone

mark yang tong *(Ch)* Malt extract or maltose

Marlborough pie *(USA)* A blind cooked pie case filled with a mixture of sweetened apple purée and cream flavoured with nutmeg and sherry and thickened with eggs. The whole baked until the filling sets

marlin A seawater game fish *Makaira nigricans* (blue) and *M. albida* (white) with a long pointed upper jaw similar to the swordfish but with not so good a flavour

marmalade A jam made from citrus fruit esp. Seville oranges, by boiling the juice with water, shredded peel and a muslin bag containing all the pips, pith and excess peel for several hours to extract pectin. The muslin bag is removed, sugar added and the whole boiled for a short time until it reaches setting point

marmalade pudding *(UK)* A pudding made from the basic steamed pudding mixture poured into a greased basin whose base is covered with marmalade

marmalade sauce As apricot sauce but using marmalade in place of apricot jam. Served with steamed and baked sponge puddings

marmande farcie *(Fr) fem.* A marmande tomato stuffed with e.g. tuna, onion and olive oil or minced lamb and onion. Served as a starter

marmande tomato A large ribbed tomato up to 10 cm in dia.

marmelad *(Sw)* Marmalade

Marmelade *(Ge)* Marmalade, jam

marmelade *(Fr) fem.* A thick purée of fruit made by stewing until well reduced

marmellata *(It)* Marmalade, jam

marmelo *(Po)* Quince

marmite 1 *(Fr) fem.* A special metal or earthenware pot with a lid and handles used for long slow cooking **2** *(UK)* Marmite, the proprietary name for a thick dark brown extract of hydrolysed yeast protein used for spreading on bread or to flavour soups, sauces and vegetarian dishes

marmite dieppoise A fish soup made of sole, turbot and red mullet cooked in mussel liquor, white wine or cider and vegetables, garnished with mussels, shrimps and finished with cream

marmitta *(It)* A cooking pot similar to a marmite

marmora *(It)* Striped sea bream

Marmorgugelhopf *(Au)* A chocolate and vanilla-flavoured cake

Marmorkuchen *(Ge)* Marbled cake

maro *(It)* Pounded and sieved cooked beans mixed with chopped mint, garlic, cheese and oil [also called **pestun de fave**]

marocaine, à la *(Fr)* In the Moroccan style, i.e. garnished with courgettes, sweet peppers, saffron-flavoured rice and tomatoes

Maroilles *(Fr & Be)* A soft, thick, square cheese from the French/Belgian border region (Aisne and Nord), pale yellow and slightly elastic with a strong taste and smell. It is started with a mixed culture of *Streptococcus cremoris, S. lactis, S. diacetilactis* and *Leuconostoc citrovorum*, the curd is drained, moulded and brined and kept so as to allow surface moulds and yeasts to develop when the rind becomes rough and red. It is ripened for 6 months and brine washed regularly. Contains 50% water, 25% fat and 23% protein and has appellation d'origine status in France. Sold as a quart (180 g), mignon (360 g), sorbais (540 g) and the full Maroilles (720 g) [also called **Marolles**]

Marolles *see* Maroilles

Maronen *(Ge)* Chestnuts

marquise *(Fr) fem.* A frozen dessert made from a fruit sorbet mixed with a liqueur and whipped cream

Marrajo *(Ge)* Porbeagle shark

marron 1 *(Fr) masc.* Chestnut **2** *(Aus)* A fine tasting crayfish *Cherax tenuimanus* from Western Australia which weighs up to 2 kg

marrona *(Sp)* Chestnut

marroni *(It)* Chestnuts

marrons glacés *(En & Fr) masc.* Shelled chestnuts boiled in sugar syrup and drained for use as a dessert, as a decoration, or, when puréed and sieved, as a flavouring and bulking agent for meringue and whipped cream

marrons Mont Blanc *(Fr) masc.* Chestnut purée heaped into a cone and topped with whipped cream to resemble the mountain

marrons plombières *(Fr) masc.* Iced custard with chestnuts, rum, vanilla and kirsch

marrons, purée de *(Fr) fem.* Chestnut purée with or without vanilla and sugar

marrow 1 A vegetable, see vegetable marrow **2** The blood forming tissue of the body which takes the form of pink pulpy material in the hollow centres of some of the larger skeletal bones esp. thigh and leg bones. Beef marrow is often poached in the bone wrapped in a cloth for an hour, for use as a garnish and sometimes served in the bone with a special metal scoop to extract it

marrow bone The large hollow bones of the skeleton which contain marrow esp. the thigh bone of beef

marrowfat pea The original European pea now grown mainly for canning, drying or to make mushy peas

Marsala *(It)* A sweet fortified wine from Sicily used to make zabaglione and for general flavouring uses

marseillaise, à la *(Fr)* In the style of Marseilles, i.e. garnished with tomatoes, anchovies and olives, used esp. of steaks

marsepein *(Ho)* Marzipan

marsh samphire *see* samphire *Salicornia europaea*

marsh seedless The commonest variety of grapefruit grown worldwide since it keeps well and is easily processed for juice and segments

marshmallow 1 A tall hardy perennial *Althaea officinalis* from whose roots and leaves a thickening agent used to be extracted which with sugar made the original marshmallow confection. The seeds and flowers are edible and the young leaves can be used in salads or steamed and served as a vegetable and were used as such by the ancient Romans **2** A soft, sweet, opaque jelly-like confection cut in 2 to 3 cm cubes and rolled in icing sugar. Sometimes used in desserts

marula The light yellow, 3.5 cm dia. fruit of a South African tree *Scelerocarya birrea* with an intense fragrance and a white fibrous flesh enclosed in a leathery skin with one central stone. The stone contains 2 or 3 kernels (marula nuts) slightly bigger than a peanut and similar in shape to a pinenut. The flesh is a good source of vitamin

C and the nut of protein. Not yet marketed commercially

marumi kumquat *(Ja)* A round kumquat *Fortunella japonica* weighing about 12 g and grown mainly in the Far East. The rind is thinner and sweeter than the nagami and has slightly more segments and seeds but is otherwise similar [also called **oval kumquat**]

Maryland *(USA)* A description of food served in a butter and cream sauce. See chicken Maryland

Maryland cookies *see* chocolate chip cookies

marzapane *(It)* Marzipan

Marzipan *(Ge)* Marzipan

marzipan A kneaded paste of ground almonds and sugar bound with sugar syrup (hard crack) or white of egg or whole egg, used for covering cakes or producing various sweetmeats [also called **marchpane, almond paste**]

masa 1 *(Sp)* Dough **2** *(Me)* A corn meal dough used for making tortillas, tamales and enchilladas

masa harina *(Me)* A heavy type of white flour made from maize with a much larger particle size than cornflour, treated with lime water and used for making masa; *see also* nixtamal [also called **tamale flour**]

masala *(In)* A general term for a blended mixture of ground spices, either produced commercially or in the home. See e.g. garam masala, chaat masala, dhansak masala

masala dosa *(In)* A South Indian pancake made from a lentil flour and water batter which is allowed to ferment overnight. After frying, it is stuffed with mashed potato and spices

masar dal *(In) see* masoor dal

Mascarpone *(It)* A rich unsalted cream-cheese-like confection made from cows' cream heated to 90°C, curdled with citric or tartaric acid, drained then beaten or whipped and eaten freshly made. Sometimes-flavoured with chocolate, coffee, liqueur, brandy, etc. for use as a dessert. Contains around 45% water, 45% fat, 7% protein and 2 to 3% lactose [also called **Maschepone, Mascherpone**]

Maschepone *see* Mascarpone

Mascherpone *see* Mascarpone

mascotte, à la *(Fr)* A description of chicken and roast joints garnished with artichoke hearts, truffles and potatoes

masculini *(It)* Tiny anchovies from Sicily, served with spaghetti

mash 1 *(UK) coll.* Seasoned boiled potatoes formed into a stiff purée with margarine or butter and milk. See bangers and mash **2** *(In) see* black gram

mash, to To pound or process a soft fruit or vegetable to a smooth paste

mashed potatoes Floury potatoes cooked in their jackets, skinned, dried over heat and mashed with milk, butter (5:2:1) and seasoning until smooth and creamy

mask, to To cover or coat a piece of cooked meat, fish or similar item with a savoury sauce, glaze or jelly or to coat the inside of a mould with the same

maslina *(Ru)* Olive

maslo *(Ru)* Butter or oil

Masnor *(Bk)* A semi-hard cooked-curd pear shaped goats' milk cheese made in the same way as Ricotta, dry salted and ripened for 1 to 2 months

masoor *(In)* Lentils either whole or dehusked and split; *see also* saabat masoor and masoor dal [also called **Egyptian lentils**]

masoor dal *(In)* Split dehusked lentils which are pink and easy to cook

masquer *(Fr)* To mask or nap

massa *(Po)* Noodles and other similar pasta products, dough, paste

massa folhada *(Po)* Puff pastry

massa de pimentão *(Po)* A chilli pepper paste

Masséna, à la *(Fr)* A description of steaks garnished with artichoke hearts, Béarnaise sauce and bone marrow

massepain *(Fr) masc.* **1** Marzipan **2** A cake made with marzipan

mast *(Pe)* Yoghurt

Mastgeflugel *(Ge)* Corn fed poultry of high quality

mastic The resin exuded by the Mediterranean plant lentesk and other similar plants used as a flavouring in some Greek dishes and in Turkish delight

mastice *(It)* Mastic

mastique *(Sp)* Mastic

Mastix *(Ge)* Mastic

mastokhiar *(Pe)* A light Iranian version of tsatsiki containing sultanas and chopped cucumber combined with yoghurt and garnished with dry mint

mastuerzo de jardin *(Sp)* Cress

masuka nani *(Ja)* A decorative carrot garnish made from a flat rectangle of carrot part cut through from each of the two short ends and twisted so that one length is trapped between the two remaining

ma taai *(Ch)* Water chestnut

matafan aux pommes *(Fr) masc.* Sliced, peeled and cored dessert apples mixed into a baking powder raised batter flavoured with brandy, cooked in a frying pan over a low heat for 30 minutes, turned, cooked a further 15 minutes and served dredged with icing sugar. Other fruit can be used [also called **matefaim**]

matambre *(Ar)* A long thin slice of meat rolled round a filling of spinach, onion rings, sliced carrots and quarters of hard boiled eggs, simmered in stock until tender, drained, cooled and sliced for use as an appetizer

matar dal *(In)* Yellow dal

matefaim *(Fr) masc. see* matafan aux pommes

matelote *(Fr) fem.* A rich freshwater fish stew made with wine, onions and mushrooms

matelote d'anguilles *(Fr) fem.* Eels stewed in a wine sauce

matelote blanche, sauce *(Fr) fem.* Sauce canotière with the addition of button onions glazed in butter and blanched button mushrooms

matha *(In)* Buttermilk

matie herring *see* matjes herrings

matière grasse *(Fr) fem.* Fat; also indicating the fat content on a product. See fat content of cheese

matignon *(Fr) masc.* Minced or finely chopped aromatic vegetables used in the same way as a mirepoix

matisha mesla *(NA)* A Moroccan dish of chicken cooked in a sauce of tomatoes, honey, ginger and cinnamon

matjes herrings Gutted herrings if small or gutted and filleted if large, lightly cured in salt, sugar and saltpetre used in made up dishes or served with raw onion and boiled potatoes. Not to be confused with maatjes haring q.v.

Matjeshering *(Ge)* Lightly cured young virgin herrings which have not yet developed roe

matjessill *(Sw)* Rinsed and wiped but not cleaned salt herring, layered in a pot with brown or granulated sugar and saltpetre (140:1) and covered with milk for 3 weeks in a cool place, then filleted as required. Traditionally served on Midsummer's day

matjessill à la Russe *(Sw)* Fillets of matjessill covered with a sauce of mayonnaise mixed with French mustard, wine vinegar, sugar and cream and decorated with diced hard boiled eggs, chives, beetroot and capers

matoke *(EA)* Mashed boiled plantains with butter and seasoning

matrimony vine Various shrubs *Lycium* spp. related to the boxthorn, whose minty-flavoured leaves are used for tea and to flavour soup. All parts of the plant are used in Chinese medicine

matsedeln *(Sw)* Menu

matsoon *(Ru)* The Armenian term for yoghurt

matsuba *(Ja)* The pine needle garnish made from an 8 cm long halved piece of thin cucumber with many 0.5 cm deep longitudinal cuts made on the skin side followed by a series of oblique 2 cm slashes across the length, the slashes being pushed to alternate sides to give what looks like a series of rows of pine needles

matsutake *(Ja)* A dark brown thick capped mushroom *Armillaria edodes* which grows under red pine. They are very expensive and are eaten fresh and cooked very simply as a single dish [also called **pine mushroom**]

matsutake fu *(Ja)* Baked gluten dough cut to resemble mushroom slices and flavoured and aromatized with an extract of matsutake or shiitake mushrooms. Used in sukiyaki

Matteuccia struthiopteris *Bot.* The fiddlehead fern

mattha *(In)* Seasoned yoghurt flavoured with dry roasted cumin and chopped fresh mint. May be let down as a drink

mature Description of food kept for a considerable time to develop flavour esp. of fermented and cured products such as cheese, salami, etc.

matzo A large thin piece of very dry unleavened Jewish bread eaten during Passover. The bread is rather like a water biscuit or cream cracker. Crushed matzos are used in Jewish cooking [also called **Passover bread**]

matzo meal Finely powdered matzos often used as a flour substitute in Jewish cooking

matzo mel Matzo bread crushed and sieved to give a uniform meal, the equivalent of dried breadcrumbs

maui onion *(USA)* A very mild sweet onion from Hawaii which may be eaten raw without treatment

ma uk *(Th)* Hairy aubergine

mau lai *(Ch)* Oyster

Maultasche *(Ge)* A filling of minced pork,

veal, brains, spinach, spices, etc. wrapped in a thin sheet of noodle dough and braised in gravy

maund *(In)* A unit of weight equal to 40 seers, approximately 36 kg, 80 lb

Mauritian jujube A species of jujube *Zizyphus mauritiana* [also called **Chinese date**]

Maximillian sauce Mayonnaise flavoured with tomato purée and chopped gherkins, capers and parsley, served with fish

ma yau *(Ch)* Sesame seed oil

Mayence red sausage A type of fat sausage or pudding from Germany consisting of the chopped neck meat, rind and tongue of pig moistened with pigs blood, flavoured with white pepper, peppermint, cloves, marjoram and mace, stuffed into a pig's stomach and boiled until cooked

mayonesa *(Sp)* Mayonnaise

mayonnaise *see* sauce mayonnaise

mayonnaise chantilly *(Fr) fem. see* chantilly, sauce

mayonnaise collée *(En & Fr) fem.* Mayonnaise mixed with melted aspic jelly (7:3), used to bind vegetable salads or to coat à la russe, chaud-froid dishes. [also called **jellied mayonnaise**]

mayonnaise à la russe *(Fr) fem.* Mayonnaise whisked over ice with a little melted aspic jelly, tarragon vinegar and grated horseradish until frothy. Used for binding Russian salad, etc.

mayonnaise, sauce *(En & Fr) fem.* Egg yolks, vinegar, French mustard and seasoning combined, oil poured in slowly with vigorous whisking until the consistency of the resulting emulsion is as desired. More oil makes it thicker and stiffer, more vinegar less so. Generally nowadays made with a blender. Served cold and used as a base for many other cold sauces

mayonnaise verte *(Fr) fem.* Mayonnaise coloured with a raw green purée of spinach, watercress, parsley or tarragon or any combination

Maytag Blue *(USA)* A local speciality blue cows' milk cheese from Newton, Iowa

mazamorra *(SA)* A sweet dessert made from chuño blanco, fruit and molasses

mazapán *(Sp)* Marzipan

mazoon *(Ru) (Armenia)* Yoghurt

mazurek *(Pl)* A Polish cake made from a flat pastry base spread with jam or vanilla cream and sprinkled with dried fruit and nuts

mazzacuogni *(It)* Caramote (Fr)

mazzafegati *(It)* A pork liver and pine kernel sausage from Umbria flavoured with fennel and garlic

mazzancolla *(It)* Caramote (Fr)

m'choui *(NA) see* mechoui

mchuzi *(EA)* A beef and vegetable stew lightly flavoured with curry powder

me *(Vi)* Tamarind

meadowsweet A hardy perennial herb *Filipendula ulmaria* up to 1 m high, whose flowers give a slight almond flavour to jams and fruit. Leaves may be added to soups. Once used for flavouring mead and called meadsweet, hence the current name

meal 1 Any combination of foods which is eaten at a single sitting **2** The ground edible parts of any grain, seed, nut, etc. usually coarser than flour. The word is often tacked on to the end of the seed's name as wheatmeal, oatmeal, cornmeal, etc.

mealie pudding *(UK) see* white pudding

mealies *(SA & Ca)* Maize

mealy endosperm An endosperm with an open structure containing voids and which is not very tough

mean see jiang *(Ch)* Soya bean paste

measuring cup The standard volume measure used in North America and Australasia equal to 236 ml and used in recipes for both free flowing solids and liquids. Referred to as a cup. See cup measure

measuring jug A toughened glass, metal or plastic jug inscribed on the side with volume measure usually in ml, litres, fluid ounces and pints. The ideal shape tapers towards the base so that small quantities can be measured accurately

measuring spoon Plastic or metal, usually hemispherical spoons used for measuring small quantities of liquid or powder, graded one quarter, one half or one teaspoon (1.25, 2.5 or 5 ml), dessertspoon (10 ml) and tablespoon (15 ml)

meat The edible muscle of any animal including vertebrates, invertebrates, molluscs, crustaceans, etc. Sometimes used of soft tissues not necessarily muscular as in molluscs or of the central edible part of a fruit or nut

meat birds Any paupiette of meat with a savoury stuffing, usually browned then braised. Also often called olives

meat cleaver A heavy chopping implement which can cut through bone

meat extract The soluble components of meat extracted by heating with water sometimes under pressure above its normal boiling point, filtering off the debris and reducing the solution to a thick dark syrupy paste. Used for spreading, making drinks and as a flavouring

meat glaze White or brown beef stock, reduced by boiling until a sticky consistency. Used as a base for sauces or to improve their flavour [also called **glace de viande** (Fr)]

meat grading *(USA)* Beef is graded in the USA as prime, choice, good, standard and commercial or utility. See under each name. There are no official gradings in the UK

meat loaf Minced raw meat mixed with flavourings, seasoning and extenders, bound with egg or flour, baked in a tin, demoulded and sliced. Served hot or cold

meat pie A pie filled with precooked meat, gravy, flavouring and seasoning prior to baking

meat safe A well ventilated cupboard in a cool place with wire mesh or perforated metal over all ventilation holes. Used to keep meat or other food in a relatively uncontaminated state before refrigerators were in common use [also called **food safe**]

meat tenderizer Some form of proteinase, often from papaya or pineapple, which in a water solution is used to break down the muscle fibres in meat. Care must be taken not to use for too long as the enzymes are not used up and the meat may be reduced to soft slush. The enzymes can be deactivated by heat or alcohol

meat thermometer A metal thermometer with the measuring element in a sharp point and a circular indicating dial, placed with its point in the thick part of a joint so as to indicate its internal temperature. Beef and lamb temperatures are 51°C, 60°C and 70°C for rare, medium and well done, pork and veal are 75°C, chicken, ducks and turkey 80°and goose 85°C

mechanically recovered meat The waste meat, etc. left on animal carcases and bones after trimming, removed as a soft pink slurry by subjecting the bones to very high pressure under a piston. All the soft tissues and marrow are squeezed out leaving bone fragments behind [also called **MRM**]

mechoui *(NA)* A lamb, or occasionally a young camel, roasted on a spit or baked in a special oven and served whole to be carved at the table. Accompanied by ground cumin seed and bread

mechouia *(NA)* A Tunisian salad of assorted vegetables

Mecklenberg *(Ge)* A hard cheese made from skimmed cows' milk

Mecklenburger Bratwurst *(Ge)* A Bratwurst q.v. made of equal parts of lean and fat pork, seasoned, spiced and moistened with brandy

Mecklenburger Leberwurst *(Ge)* A liver sausage of coarsely minced pig's liver mixed with chopped boiled breast of pork, pork kidney, tongue and back fat, pepper, allspice and powdered sage, filled into casings, boiled in the cooking liquor, refreshed then dried and smoked

medaglioni *(It)* Small slices of fillet steak or slices of veal, medallions

medallion A small round piece of tender meat easily cooked by frying or grilling, esp. of beef or veal [also called **médaillon** (Fr)]

médaillon *(Fr) masc. see* medallion

Médici, à la *(Fr)* A description of steak garnished with artichoke hearts, peas, carrots, turnips and sometimes tomatoes, named after Catherine de Médici

medio *(Po)* Medium cooked (of steaks, meat, etc.)

medister pølse *(De)* A sausage made with pork and pork fat with the possible addition of beef, seasoned, packed into 4 cm dia. casings and hot smoked. May be fried, grilled or boiled

Mediterranean grouper A grouper *Epinephelus caninus* with a grey-green to reddish-brown skin, weighing normally around 2 kg. Often baked whole at 200°C from 30 minutes to 1 hour if stuffed [also called **rock bass**]

Mediterranean hare A strong-coloured small hare *Lepus capensis* found in Spain and Mediterranean islands

Mediterranean mandarin The first mandarin *Citrus deliciosa* introduced to England from China in 1805 from where it spread to the Mediterranean and throughout the western world. The fruit is small to medium with a small, heavily furrowed neck and sometimes a navel. It peels very easily, the segment walls are fairly tough but the flesh is very juicy with an aromatic and sweet taste. It does not ship or store very well. Essential oils are produced from the rind and the leaves and twigs (pettigrain) [also called **willowleaf mandarin** (USA), **thorny mandarin** (Aus)]

Mediterranean medlar *see* azarole

Mediterranean mussel A mussel *Mytilus gallaprovincialis* very similar to the common variety with an overlapping range

Mediterranean rocket *see* rocket

Mediterranean squid The common squid *Loligo vulgaris* traded in Europe and up to 50 cm in length

Mediterranean sweet lime *see* Tunisian sweet limetta

Mediterranean sweet limetta *see* Tunisian sweet limetta

Mediterrnean sturgeon *see* common sturgeon

medium fat Description of foods, esp. cheese, yoghurt, etc. containing between 10% and 20% butterfat according to type

medium oily Description of fish flesh containing between 2% and 6% fat or oil

medium rare A description of meat, usually a steak or a chop, cooked so that the centre of the meat is just pink but set

medium syrup *see* syrup

medium white sauce *(USA)* A sauce made with a blond roux and with a liquid to flour ratio of 14:1

medivnyk *(Ru)* A rich, heavily spiced and fruited, chemically raised honey cake for Christmas made with creamed butter, brown sugar and egg yolks mixed with a molten honey, spice and baking soda mixture then flour, yoghurt and cottage cheese with orange zest are alternately folded in followed by the fruit and stiffly beaten egg whites, all baked in a tube tin, cooled, brushed with honey and matured for several days

med-kha-noon *(Th)* A kind of dessert which looks like jackfruit seeds

medlar A small brown fruit about the size of an apple from a deciduous tree *Mespilus germanica* which grows in temperate climates. The sharp-flavoured flesh can be eaten raw if very overripe (bletted), i.e. after the first frost; otherwise they are used to make jam

medvurst *(Sw)* A Rohwurst similar to Mettwurst usually moistened with stock and brandy.and either hot or cool-smoked. May be eaten raw or cooked in any way

mee krob *(Th)* Deep fried puffed up rice noodles mixed with stir-fried fish, pork and vegetables flavoured with lemon juice, vinegar and sugar and garnished with strips of egg omelette, chopped spring onions and coriander leaves [also called **mi krob**]

mee noodles Chinese egg noodles

meenchi *(Sr)* Mint

Meer *(Ge)* Bass, the fish

Meeraal *(Ge)* Conger eel

Meerbarbe *(Ge)* Red mullet

Meerengel *(Ge)* Angel fish

Meerfenchel *(Ge)* Samphire *Crithmum maritimum*

Meerpolyp *(Ge)* Octopus

Meerrettich *(Ge)* Horseradish

Meersalz *(Ge)* Sea salt

Meerschildkröte *(Ge)* Turtle

mee siam *(Ma)* A noodle dish made by frying a pounded mixture of spring onions, red chillis and shrimp paste in oil, adding mashed soya beans, sugar, fried onions and coconut milk, simmering then adding rice vermicelli, dried shrimp powder, fried bean curd and peeled and fried shrimps. The whole is heated through, seasoning corrected and finished with lime juice and garnished with sliced hard boiled eggs and shredded spring onions

meggyleves *(Hu)* A cold summer soup based on cherries

megrim A rather dry sinistral flat fish *Lepidorhombus whiffiagonis* lacking in any distinctive flavour of its own. Requires a strong-tasting sauce [also called **whiff**]

mehemalou *(Pe)* Cubed lamb or mutton, marinated in lemon juice with chopped onions, bay leaf, garlic, cloves and peppercorns, drained, floured and browned then simmered in stock with salt, sugar and saffron, stoned prunes and raisins added at the half cooked stage and the sauce finished with grape juice syrup. Served with a topping of dry roasted almond slivers

Mehl *(Ge)* Flour

Mehlpüt *(Au)* Stewed pears with sweet dumplings

Mehlspeise *(Au)* A sweet pastry dish or pudding

mei fun *(Ch)* Rice vermicelli

mei gee *(Ch)* Rice paper

mei jing *(Ch)* Monosodium glutamate

mein jin pau *(Ch)* Small balls of cooked gluten dough which are deep fried and may be added to soups and stews

mein noodles Chinese egg noodles

meiwa kumquat A hybrid kumquat *Fortunella margarita x F. japonica* grown in China and Japan. It is larger than either of the parent species, has a thicker peel and fewer seeds, is the sweetest of the three and is considered to be the best eating variety [also called **large round kumquat**]

mei zi *(Ch)* Prunes

mejillones *(Sp)* Mussels

mejillones rellenos *(Sp)* Stuffed and baked mussels

mejiso *(Ja)* Shiso seed sprouts used as a garnish

mejorana *(Sp)* Marjoram

mekabu *(Ja)* The root or thickened base of

wakame q.v. used whole or shredded in stews or as a separate vegetable

mel *(Po)* Honey

mela *(It)* Apple

melaço *(Po)* Molasses

melacotogna *(It)* Quince

melagrana *(It)* Pomegranate

melancia *(Po)* Watermelon

mélange *(Fr) masc.* Blend or mixture

melanger *(Fr)* To mix or blend

melanzana *(It)* Aubergine

melanzane alla finitese *(It)* A Calabrian dish of aubergines stuffed with cheese, basil and peppers and deep fried

melão *(Po)* **1** Melon **2** Bread roll

melassa *(It)* Treacle, molasses

Melasse *(Ge)* Treacle, molasses

mélasse *(Fr) fem.* Treacle, molasses

melaza *(Sp)* Treacle, molasses

Melba sauce A sweet sauce made from puréed and sieved fresh raspberries. Used on fruit sundaes and similar desserts

Melba toast Very thin (3 mm) slices of bread, dried and browned in the oven or under the grill. Served with soup or as a base for hors d'oeuvre and appetizers

melboller *(De)* Dumplings

Melbury *(UK)* A soft mild white mould-ripened cheese with a mellow taste and formed in the shape of a loaf

mele alla certosa *(It)* Baked stuffed apples

mele in gabbia *(It)* Apple dumplings Lit. apples in a cage

melegueta pepper *see* grains of paradise

meli *(Gr)* Honey

melilot A hardy biennial *Melilotus officinalis* whose faintly aromatic leaves are used to flavour the Swiss cheeses Gruyère and Sapsago. It may also be used in small amounts in sausages, stuffings and marinades [also called **sweet clover**]

Melilotus coeruleus *Bot.* Blue melilot

Melilotus officinalis *Bot.* Melilot

melindres de Yepes *(Sp)* Dessert fritters

melinjo *(Id)* The small red fruit of a tree *Gnetum gnemon.* The kernel and its covering are used to make emping q.v. and the young flowers and leaves are used as a vegetable, raw or cooked. The ripe peel is fried in oil and served with rice as a side dish. The immature nuts can be added to soup [also called **belinjo, blindjo**]

melissa *see* lemon balm

Melissa officinalis *Bot.* Lemon balm

melitzanes *(Gr)* Aubergine

melitzanes me domata *(Gr)* A type of ratatouille made from chopped onions softened in olive oil mixed with chopped tomatoes and peeled garlic cloves, simmered 15 minutes, diced grilled aubergine which has previously been salted and drained added and the whole simmered over a low heat until all tender

melitzano salata *(Gr)* **1** A salad made from chopped cooked aubergine, onions, garlic and tomatoes, garnished with black olives, parsley and rings of sweet green pepper and dressed with oil, vinegar, lemon juice and seasoning **2** Roasted aubergine flesh puréed to a fine paste with chopped onions, garlic, skinned tomatoes, oil, lemon juice and fresh herbs, spread over a flat dish, covered with olive oil and garnished with olives. Served as a starter with pitta bread

melk *(Ho & No)* Milk

melkbrood *(Ho)* Milk bread, i.e. made with milk instead of water

melkchocolade *(Ho)* Milk chocolate

melktert *(Saf)* A custard tart lightly flavoured with cinnamon

melocotón *(Sp)* Peach

melocotón en almibar *(Sp)* Peach in syrup

meloen *(Ho)* Melon

melokhia *see* meloukhia

melon *(De, En, No, Sp Sw & Fr) masc.* The fruit of a climbing annual vine (*Cucumis melo*) related to the cucumber. It is round or oval with a hard thick skin enclosing a thick layer of sweet (when ripe) juicy flesh with a mass of inedible seeds at the centre. The three principal types are cantaloupe, winter and musk, q.v.; *see also* water melon [also called **sweet melon**]

melón de agua *(Sp)* Watermelon

melon baller A parisienne cutter used to make melon balls

melon pear *see* pepino

melón de verano *(Sp)* Cantaloupe melon

Melone *(Ge)* Melon

melone *(It)* Melon

meloukhia *(ME)* A plant *Corchorus olitorius* related to the okra and hibiscus. The leaves which are used in cooking and soup-making release a gelatinous thickening agent similar to that from okra [also called **melokhia, molokhia**]

melt The spleen of an animal sometimes classed as offal [also called **milt**]

melt, to To convert a solid to a liquid by heating

melted butter sauce *see* beurre fondu

melting cake method A method of making cakes by melting and mixing together all liquid, liquefiable and soluble ingredients such as fat, sugar, milk, etc., but not eggs, then folding in the sieved dry ingredients and beaten eggs if any. e.g. parkin

melting moments Small crisp round biscuits covered with oats which melt in the mouth

Melton Mowbray pie *(UK)* A raised pork pie from Leicestershire, with a ground mace and ground ginger flavoured chopped (not minced) pork filling

melu *(It)* Blue whiting, the fish

membrillo *(Sp)* Quince

men *(Ch)* Red cooking

mendo limon *(Sp)* Lemon sole

mendoan *(Id)* A fermented paste similar to tempe made from the residual solids after making bean curd and from peanuts. It has a finer texture than tempeh and is usually fried

menestra *(Sp)* Stew

menestra a la castellana *(Sp)* Meat and vegetable stew in a wine and tomato sauce

menestras de legumbres frescas *(Sp)* Mixed cooked vegetables with a poached egg

mennola *(It)* Picarel, a type of sea bream

menrui *(Ja)* Noodles

men-ryori *(Ja)* Noodles

menta *(It & Sp)* Mint, the herb

menta peperina *(It)* Peppermint

Mentha aquatica* var. *citrata *Bot.* Lemon mint

Mentha x gentilis 'variegata' *Bot.* Ginger mint

Mentha x piperita *Bot.* Peppermint

Mentha x piperita* var. *citrata *Bot.* Eau-de-cologne mint

Mentha pulegium *Bot.* Pennyroyal

Mentha raripila rubra *Bot.* Red raripila spearmint

Mentha requiena *Bot.* Corsican mint

Mentha spicata *Bot.* Spearmint

***Mentha* spp.** *Bot.* Mint

Mentha suaveolens *Bot.* Applemint

Mentha x villosa 'Alopecuroides' *Bot.* Bowles' mint

menthe *(Fr) fem.* Mint

menthe poivrée *(Fr) fem.* Peppermint

menthe verte *(Fr) fem.* Spearmint, garden mint

mentonnaise, à la *(Fr)* In the style of Menton, i.e. garnished, esp. joints of meat, with vegetable marrow or courgette, potatoes and artichokes

menu **1** *(Fr) masc.* Meal or diet **2** *(En & Fr) masc.* A list of foods available at a restaurant or eating establishment with the prices of individual dishes or of whole meals and the conditions of sale, or the list of items at a meal without prices if a formal meal where the participants do not pay at the time

Menü *(Ge)* Menu

menudillos *(Sp)* Giblets, offal

menudo *(Sp)* A maize and tripe stew

menukort *(De)* Menu

merca *(It)* Grey mullet boiled in a court bouillon then rolled into a cylindrical shape with a coating of herbs

merenda *(It)* Snack, light meal

merendeiras *(Po)* Small fresh 50 g ewes' milk cheeses kept in olive oil prior to sale Lit. Intended for lunch

merguez *(NA & Fr) fem.* A highly spiced short stumpy beef or lamb sausage from Algeria, now popular in France and generally in NA. Usually grilled

merica cabai *(Id)* White pepper

merica hitam *(Id)* Peppercorn

meriendas *(Sp)* Snack, the term used in the Phillipines for tapas-like dishes

meringato *(It)* With meringue

meringue *(En & Fr) fem.* A whisked mixture of egg white and caster sugar in which a large amount of air is incorporated. The mixture is dried in a slow oven. The principal types are meringue suisse (often known simply as meringue), meringue cuite, Italian meringue and American meringue. All are shaped before drying and all use about 50 g of sugar per egg white

meringue cuite *(Fr) fem.* Professional meringue made by whisking the egg whites over a boiling bain marie whilst incorporating the sugar. It is harder, whiter and more powdery than meringue suisse and requires more care and intenser mixing, but keeps better

meringue suisse *(Fr) fem.* Meringue in which half the sugar is incorporated during whisking, the remainder being folded in. The mixture is firm and glossy [also called **Swiss meringue, meringue**]

merinhe *(It)* Meringues

merise *(Fr) fem.* Wild cherry

merlan *(Sp & Fr) masc.* Whiting

merlano *(It)* Whiting

merlo marino *(It)* Wrasse, the fish

merlu *(Fr) masc.* Hake [also called **colin**]

merluche *(Fr) fem.* **1** Dried cod or stock fish **2** Hake

merluza *(Sp)* Haddock, cod or hake

merluzzo *(It)* Hake

merluzzo comune *(It)* Cod

mermelada *(Sp)* Jam

mermez *(NA)* A mutton stew from Tunisia

mero *(Sp)* Mediterranean grouper

mérou *(Fr) masc.* Mediterranean grouper

mersin *(Tu)* Smoked swordfish

Mesambryanthemum crystallinum *Bot.* Iceplant

mesclun *(Fr) masc.* A mixed green salad from Provence

mesentery A deep frilly fold in the interior lining of the abdominal cavity (the peritoneum) which is used to keep the intestines in position and attach a part of them to the back wall [also called **mudgeon, frill, crow**]

Meshanger *(Ho)* A soft cows' milk cheese with a delicate tasting and smooth paste covered with a thin natural rind. Contains 53% water, 23% fat and 21% protein

mesi *(Fi)* Honey

mesimarja *(Fi)* The honey berry or arctic bramble, found in the Arctic and used for flavouring

Mesost *(Sw)* A cows' milk whey cheese made in the same way as Gjetost

Mespilus germanica *Bot.* Medlar

mesquite *(USA)* A tree whose wood is used as part of barbecue fuel to add a strong flavour to the food cooked over it

mesquite bean The seeds of various spiny shrubs *Prosopis glandulosa, P. juliflora* and other spp. mainly used as cattle fodder but also ground for pinole

mess A portion of food for 2 to 4 persons served on a trencher in medieval times

messina cob *see* Turkish hazelnut

messicani *(It)* Stuffed paupiettes of veal

mesticanza *(It)* A dressed mixture of tender salad leaves

metabisulphites Salts similar to the sulphites and hydrogen sulphites used both as sterilants and food preservatives. Sodium-, E223 and potassium-, E224 are used in the food industry

metabolize, to To convert food, which has been broken down in the gut and transported in the blood to the cells of the body, into new or repaired cell material and tissues and energy

metabolism The process of converting circulating blood components derived from food or the breakdown of body tissues, principally fats, sugars and amino acids, into new or repaired body tissues and into energy by chemical reaction and conversion in the body's cells. The end products of these reactions are transported by the blood and excreted via the lungs, skin or kidneys

metatartaric acid *see* (E)353

metate *(Me)* A large stone with a dished upper surface used for grinding grains and spices using a mano

metchnikoff *(Ru)* A soured milk product named after the Russian bacteriologist who isolated the important bacterium *Lactobacillus bulgaricus* used for yoghurt and similar products

methai *(In) see* mithai

methe *(In)* Fenugreek

methi ka beej *(In)* Fenugreek seeds

methi ka saag *(In)* The leaves of fenugreek q.v. with a bitter taste and strong aroma. Often cooked with starchy root vegetables. The bitter taste disappears on cooking

methis *(Id)* Fenugreek

methods of cookery *see* under particular

class of items to be cooked such as biscuit, cake, fish, meat, etc.

metre The normal measure of length approximately 3 feet 3 inches, abbreviated m, divided into centimetres (cm) (100 per metre) and millimetres (mm) (1000 per metre). One inch is approximately 2.5 cm, one foot 30 cm and one yard 91 cm

Metroxylon sagu *Bot.* Sago palm

metso *(Fi)* Capercaillie, the game bird

metton *(Fr)* A spread made from evaporated whey similar to a soft gjetöst. Made in the Jura

mettre en boîte *(Fr)* To can

Mettwurst *(Ge)* A Rohwurst of equal parts of lean pork, lean beef, and fine diced fat bacon, seasoning, spices such as cloves, paprika and nutmeg and a little sugar and saltpetre, filled into casings, cooled and dried then dry cured with salt, sugar and saltpetre for 2 days, retied and cool smoked. It may be coarse textured (grosse Mettwurst) or smooth and fine textured (feine Mettwurst). Cooked in any way [also called **Metwurst**]

Metwurst *(Ge) see* Mettwurst

Metzithra *(Gr)* A Cretan cheese

meunière, à la *(Fr)* Cooked in butter and finished with beurre noisette or lemon juice and chopped parsley. Applied esp. to shallow fried fish

meunière butter sauce Clarified butter heated until it just starts to brown then cooled with lemon juice and finished with parsley and ground white pepper. Used with fish [also called **meunière butter, beurre noisette** (Fr)]

meunière, fish Shallow fried fish cooked à la meunière; *see also* fish aux amandes, belle meunière, doria, grenobloise, bretonne, etc. for variations on this style

meurette *(Fr)* A mixture of fish stewed in red wine from Burgundy

Mexi-bell pepper *(USA)* A mildly hot sweet pepper-sized capsicum

Mexicaine, à la *(Fr)* In the Mexican style, i.e. garnished with tomatoes, mushrooms, sweet peppers, rice and sometimes aubergine

Mexican bean *see* red kidney bean

Mexican black bean *see* black bean

Mexican lime *see* West Indian lime

Mexican saffron *see* safflower

Mexican tea *see* epazote

Mexican yam bean *see* jicama

mexikansk vårkyckling *(Sw)* Mexican spring chicken made from pot roasted and boned poussins laid on a sort of risotto made with half and half wild rice and short grain rice, separately cooked with chopped fried onion, mushrooms and green and red sweet peppers plus petit pois and chopped parsley. Served with a red wine sauce

mexilhãos *(Po)* Mussels

meyve *(Tu)* Fruit

mezclar *(Sp)* To mix or blend

meze *see* mezze

mezes *see* mezze

mézeskalacs *(Hu)* Honey cake

mezethes *(Gr)* Appetizers

mezzaluna *(It)* A two handled crescent shaped chopping knife which is rocked back and forth over the food to be chopped. Two and more bladed version are available [also called **hachoir** (Fr)]

mezzani *(It)* Pasta tubes

mezze *(Gr & Tu)* A selection of small dishes of food similar to hors d'oeuvres, appetizers or tapas served as starters or as a main meal. Both hot and cold dishes are served with pitta bread [also called **mezes, meze**]

mezze penne *(It)* Short pasta quills

mezze ziti *(It) see* ziti mezze

mezzefegati *(It) see* mazzafegati

mezzi rigatoni *(It)* Ridged pasta tubes

mezzo *(It)* Half, semi-

mhaans turrcarri khasta *(In)* A piquant mutton curry made by cubing and piquéing mutton, rubbing in a pounded paste of minced onion, black pepper, paprika, dry roasted mustard seeds and ground cinnamon with oil, leaving 2 hours then layering the meat in a buttered pan with onion rings, ground fenugreek, chopped ginger and garlic, finishing with onion rings and chopped mint. This is covered with mutton stock and simmered until the meat is tender skimming and adding stock to keep the level high *(see* turcarri). Finally it is mixed, a little asafoetida added and the whole kept warm for 15 minutes before serving

mhaans turrcarri sadah *(In)* A simple mutton curry made by browning chopped onion in ghee and reserving, browning the trimmed and cubed shoulder of mutton in the same ghee for 10 minutes, turmeric and ground coriander added, cooked briefly, reserved onion and cayenne pepper added and cooked briefly, seasoned, a little water added to deglaze the pan, covered with water *(see* turcarri) and simmered until the meat tender. Finished with chopped parsley or coriander leaf and kept warm for 15 minutes before serving. Potatoes may be added towards the end

mhon-la-u *(Bm)* Mooli

mi *(Vi)* Wheat flour noodles

miascia *(It)* A baked bread pudding from Lombardy containing apples, pears, raisins and herbs

Michaelmas *(UK)* The feast of St Michael on the 29th of September regarded as being the end of the harvest, used as an adjective to describe particular food served to celebrate the occasion such as Michaelmas goose.

miche *(Fr) fem.* A cob or round loaf

Michelin guide *(UK)* One of the restaurant guides to whom complaints and experiences may be sent. Address: Michelin Tyre plc, Tourism dept., 38 Clarendon Rd., Watford, Herts WD1 1SX. Others are Egon Ronay and Good Food Guide

mi-chèvre *(Fr) fem.* Cheese made from a mixture of goats' and cows' milk containing at least 25% goats' milk

Michigan banana *see* papaw

microcrystalline cellulose E460(i), a very finely divided form of cellulose used to add bulk and fibre to slimming food, convenience foods, desserts and the like

microcrystalline wax *see* (E)907

microwave cooker A small oven fitted fitted with a timer, power variation and sometimes elaborate programmers, which cooks by subjecting the food to very high frequency electromagnetic radiation (microwaves) similar to radio waves, generated in a magnetron and piped to the oven through a wave guide. The microwaves are contained within the cooking chamber by the reflective walls but are absorbed by the food which should be contained in materials such as ceramics, glass and plastics which do not absorb microwaves and so do not themselves get hot; *see also* microwaves

microwave thermometer A thermometer without any metal parts which can be used inside a miocrowave cooker

microwaves Very high frequency electromagnetic radiation used to heat up and cook foods. Microwaves transfer their energy to food by causing certain types of molecules to vibrate at their frequency. They are generally absorbed in the first cm of the surface and hence solid food to be cooked should be less than 2 cm thick or well stirred from time to time if contained in a deep container. Microwaves are reflected off metal surfaces but isolated metal within an enclosure will heat up and sometimes cause sparking

middag *(De, No & Sw)* Dinner

middellandse-zeetapijtschelp *(Ho)* Carpet shell clam

middle *see* ox casings. Used for salami. knackwurst, Cervelat, etc.

middle bacon Bacon from the centre of the pig combining streaky and back bacon. May be sliced for rashers or stuffed, boiled or baked

middle gammon A lean cut of bacon from between the corner gammon and the hock

middle neck of lamb *(UK)* The cutlets, rib bones, vertebrae and longitudinal muscles which lie between the best end and the scrag end (neck) behind the shoulder. Used for stewing or sometimes passed off as cutlets

middle rib of beef *(UK)* The 3rd to the 6th ribs of beef counting from the head end. Used as a second class roasting joint or for braising, e.g. beef olives

midolla *(It)* Crumb of a loaf, flesh of a fruit

midollo *(It)* Bone marrow

mie *(Fr) fem.* The soft crustless interior of white bread

miel *(Sp & Fr) masc.* Honey

miele *(It)* Honey

mien bao *(Ch)* Bread

mien see *(Ch)* Yellow bean sauce

mien tiao *(Ch)* Noodles

Miesmuschel *(Ge)* Mussel

miette *(Fr) fem.* Crumb

mi fan *(Ch)* Rice

miga *(Sp)* Crumb

migas **1** *(Sp)* A Spanish breakfast dish consisting of fried breadcrumbs, flavoured with garlic, bacon and peppers **2** *(Po)* Tender cubed lean pork and beef, coated with massa de pimentão overnight and each sautéed separately in olive oil and bacon fat until brown. The pan juices deglazed with water, mixed with fried diced bacon, sweated garlic and chunks of moistened stale bread, seasoned as required, beaten until fluffy and served with the beef and pork **3** *(Po)* Panada

migliaccio *(It)* Pig's blood mixed with a variety of nuts, spices, dried vine fruits, honey, etc. and baked in a tart or fried as a flat cake. From central Italy [also called **sanguinaccio alla fiorentina**]

miglio *(It)* Millet

mignardise *(Fr) fem.* Small and dainty made up dishes

mignon *(Fr)* **1** A description of something small and dainty esp. when applied to cuts of meat, e.g. the small muscle in a chicken breast or the small end of a fillet of beef. Lit. dainty **2** *see* Maroilles (cheese)

mignonette *(Fr) fem.* Small round fillets of lamb

mignonette pepper Coarsely crushed white peppercorns [also called **shot pepper**]

Mignot *(Fr)* A cheese from Normandy similar to Livarot

mignuic *(It) see* cavatieddi

mignule *(It) see* cavatieddi

mihun *(Id & Ma)* Rice vermicelli

mi-iro gohan *(Ja)* Boiled rice dressed with the cooking liquor from the meat served in individual dishes with petit pois, seasoned egg scrambled with a little sugar and minced topside of beef, lightly cooked with soya sauce, salt, sugar and dashi, all arranged decoratively on top of the rice

mijin giri *(Ja)* Finely shredded or brunoise vegetable

mi jiu *(Ch)* Yellow rice wine

mijo *(Sp)* Millet

mijoter *(Fr)* To simmer or cook very slowly

mikan *(Ja)* Mandarin orange, often hollowed out and used as a dish e.g. for orange-flavoured jelly or seafood

mike cho *(Ch)* Rice vinegar

mi krob *see* mee krob

mil folhas *(Po)* Flaky pastry, millefeuille

milagia podi *(In)* A condiment from the south made from dry roasted sesame and coriander seeds, red chillis and black gram, dehusked chick peas or similar and all coarsely ground. Used on bread or vegetarian snacks

milanaise, à la *(Fr)* In the style of Milan, i.e. garnished with spaghetti or macaroni, tomato sauce and ham or tongue or panéed with breadcrumbs and grated cheese prior to frying

milanese, alla *(It)* In the style of Milan, i.e. panéed, fried in butter and finished with lemon, esp. of escalopes and liver

Milanese soufflé *see* lemon soufflé

Milch *(Ge)* Milk

Milchrahm strudel *(Au)* Strudel pastry wrapped round a light curd cheese and baked in a cream sauce

mild cure A term used to describe foods cured by the quick method using a solution of salt, saltpetre, flavourings and sometimes polyphosphates, which is either injected into the food or in which the food is immersed.

mildew A fungus which grows on the surface of food exposed to a warm humid atmosphere, usually in the form of green furry blotches, each of which has grown from a single organism

milho *(Po)* Maize

milk The liquid food provided by all mammals for new-born young, consisting of a water solution of sugars and proteins with emulsified fats, various minerals, vitamins and health protective substances. The most important milk in cooking is from the cow, but milk from sheep, goats, buffalo, camels and horses, etc. is used in various cultures esp. for cheese and yoghurt manufacture. Cows' milk is available with various fat contents and in various forms. The first milk drawn at a particular time from a mammal is usually high in sugar and low in fat and becomes progressively less sugary and more fatty as the glands are emptied, thus allowing some control over quality

milk bread A white yeast-raised bread containing about 6% of dried milk by weight of the dry ingredients

milk chocolate A high sugar content (greater than 48%) chocolate confectionery with added milk solids

milk fed lamb 3 to 4 week old, unweaned lamb weighing 4 to 5 kg. Usually born in winter and raised indoors on milk only. Should be eaten fresh not more than 3 days after slaughter [also called **house lamb**]

milk pudding Grain, either whole or ground, and other starch products cooked in sweetened milk, e.g. rice pudding, semolina, sago, tapioca

milk substitute *see* creamer

milk sugar *see* lactose

milkfish *see* bangus

mill An implement used to reduce a solid to a fine powder, as with pepper, salt crystals, coffee, spices, etc.

mill, to To reduce foods to a powder or paste, generally by grinding or squeezing the material through close, counter-rotating or moving metal, stone or other hard solid plates, rollers or discs

millassata *(It)* A cheese omelette from Sicily filled with artichokes and asparagus

mille foglie *(It)* Puff pastry

millefeuille *(Fr) masc.* Cream slice. Lit. a thousand leaves or a thousand sheets [also called **Napoléon**]

millet *(En & Fr) masc.* The general name for a variety of small seeds produced by grasses used as food sources for both humans and animals. Millets tend to be drought and waterlogging resistant and hence important food sources in drought prone or marshy areas. Millet has a delicate bland flavour and is cooked as any other grain. See common millet, sorghum, finger millet, kaffir corn, bulrush millet, hungry rice, etc.

milo maize *(USA)* A variety of sorghum *Sorghum vulgare* subsp. *glabrescens* used to make sorghum flour

milt 1 *see* soft roe **2** *see* melt

milza *(It)* Spleen, occasionally fried with herbs and anchovies

milzschnittensuppe *(It)* Beef broth served with fried bread spread with a mixture of minced spleen with eggs and garlic

Milzwurst *(Ge)* A Bavarian veal sausage usually fried in butter, probably contains spleen

Mimolette *(Fr)* An Edam-type cows' milk cheese coloured a dark orange

mimosa A garnish or decoration made by forcing hard boiled egg yolk through a sieve to resemble the petals of the mimosa flower

mince The name given to any foodstuff processed by a combination of chopping and crushing as in a mincer, esp. for meat and dried vine fruits. See minced meat, mincemeat

mince, to To reduce the size of solid or semi-solid foodstuffs by a combination of chopping and crushing usually in a mincer or food processor

mince pie A small round pastry tartlet with a pastry top, filled with mincemeat, baked and sprinkled with icing sugar [also called **mynce pie, shred pie**]

minced meat Meat which has been finely divided by being chopped or passed through a mincer. Used to convert tough meat into a more palatable and tender form. Used in stews, hamburger, pies, etc. [also called **ground meat** (USA)]

mincemeat A mixture of dried vine fruits, chopped mixed peel, apples and suet, with sugar, nutmeg, cinnamon, grated lemon zest, lemon juice and sometimes spirits all passed through a mincer, allowed to mature and used as a filling for mince tarts and other sweets, cakes and puddings

mincer A culinary implement used for mincing, consisting of a barrel with a hopper above possibly tapering towards one end, into which fits a well-fitting scroll feeder with a pitch which reduces towards the output end. When the scroll is turned either manually or mechanically it forces food towards the output end slightly crushing it. A three or four bladed knife rotates with the scroll and cuts the crushed food as it is forced through a stationary circular disc containing a number of holes. The holes in the stationary disc may be of various sizes to give varying degrees of size reduction

Mineiro Frescal *(Br) see* queijo Minas frescal

mineola See tangelo

mineral hydrocarbons (E)905, highly purified oils derived from crude oils with high boiling points and usually colourless and transparent. Technical white oils come in a range of viscosities. The highest viscosity oil is called liquid paraffin. Once used as fat or oil substitutes in slimming foods since they are not metabolized. Used as release agents to prevent dried vine fruits sticking together.

mineral water *see* carbonated water

minerals The name given to various metals and other elements usually in the form of salts, oxides or organic compounds which are necessary for health. See under individual names e.g. calcium, chromium, copper, iodine, iron, magnesium, potassium, selenium. Those required in very small amounts are called trace elements q.v.

miner's lettuce *see* winter purslane

minestra *(It)* The first course of a meal after the antipasto either soup, pasta, rice, gnocchi or similar

minestra asciutta *(It)* Dry minestra, i.e. pasta, rice, etc. eaten with a fork, not a spoon

minestra col battuto alla romana *(It)* Soup with pasta containing ham fat, onions and garlic

minestra in brodo *(It)* Pasta or rice cooked in broth

minestra di riso alla cappuccina *(It)* Thick rice soup with pounded anchovies

minestrina *(It)* A light broth

minestrina tricolore *(It)* Potato soup garnished with diced cooked carrots and chopped parsley

minestrone *(It)* A substantial thick, mixed vegetable soup with the addition of some of pasta, rice, beans amd potatoes in many local variations. The UK version is given in the next entry

minestrone *(UK)* A soup made from paysanne cut mixed vegetables sweated in oil without colour, white stock, a BG and seasoning added and simmered 20 minutes, peas and diamond cut green beans added and simmered 10 minutes, paysanne cut potatoes, short lengths of spaghetti, tomato purée and diced, skinned and deseeded tomatoes added and simmered until all cooked. A processed mixture of fat bacon, garlic and parsley formed into pea sized balls dropped into the boiling soup, the BG removed and all served with grated Parmesan cheese and toasted slices of French bread

minestrone alla milanese *(It)* The classic minestrone with tomatoes, peas, beans, courgettes, potatoes, cabbage, bacon and rice, often served at room temperature or chilled

minestrone alla sarda *(It)* A minestrone with beans, chick peas, potatoes, cabbage, fennel, pasta and pork

Ming dynasty egg *see* Chinese preserved eggs

minhota, à *(Po)* In the style of Minho, i.e. with chopped ham and vinho verde

miniature corn Small (to 10 cm long) cobs of sweet corn used as a vegetable and eaten whole [also called **baby corn**]

Minneola *see* tangelo

Minnesota slim *(USA)* A moist, open-textured cows' milk cheese coloured orange which easily melts

mint A large group of hardy herbaceous perennials *Mentha* spp. which interbreed readily to form hybrids. Generally to 1 m high with oval pointed aromatic leaves deep veined and set in pairs up a square green to purple stalk. Some varieties are variegated (two colours). All are edible save that penny royal should only be used in small quantities. For details of some individual species see under *Mentha* spp.

mint sauce *(UK)* Chopped mint leaves, macerated with boiling water and sugar and combined with an equal amount of vinegar. Served with roast lamb

minute *(Fr) fem.* Description of food which has been cooked quickly

minute steak Lean pieces of beef which have been passed through rollers covered with sharp projections. These have the effect of breaking down the fibres in the steak so that it cooks quickly when grilled or fried [also called **flash fry steak**]

miñyak kelapa *(Id & Ma)* Coconut oil

Minze *(Ge)* Mint, the herb

miolos *(Po)* **1** Brains **2** The soft crumb inside a loaf of bread

Mirabeau, à la *(Fr)* Garnished, esp. of grilled meats, with anchovies, olives and pats of anchovy butter

mirabelle *(Fr) fem.* A small, golden, cherry-sized variety of plum *Prunus insititia,* very popular as a dessert fruit in Europe, also the alcoholic liqueur made from the same [also called **golden gage**]

mirasol *(Sp)* Sunflower

mirchi *(In)* Chilli peppers

mirepoix *(En & Fr) masc.* A mixture of rough cut aromatic vegetables used as a bed on which to braise meats and to flavour sauces. Often browned in fat in the oven before use

mirin *(Ja)* A sweet rice wine used almost exclusively for cooking and not classed as an alcoholic drink. Used in basting sauces to give food a translucent glaze. A well-flavoured sweet sherry with a little extra sugar may be substituted [also called **hon mirin, Japanese sherry, sweet sake**]

mirliton **1** *see* choko **2** *(Fr) masc.* Small almond-flavoured pastry cake from Normandy

miroton *(Fr) masc.* A dish of boiled beef warmed up with an onion and mustard sauce [also called **boeuf miroton**]

mirride odoroso *(It)* Sweet cicely

mirtilli *(It)* Bilberries

mirto *(It & Sp))* Myrtle

mirto holandés *(Sp)* Bog myrtle

mischen *(Ge)* To mix or blend

mischiare *(It)* To mix or blend

Mischling *(Au)* A hard scalded-curd strong-flavoured mountain cheese made from cows' milk coagulated with a natural lactic starter. The paste contains a few irregular shaped holes and cracks but the rind is dry, hard and unbroken

mise en place *(En & Fr) fem.* The collection, weighing and preparation of all ingredients for a recipe before it is assembled and cooked. Lit. putting into place. It is an essential in a commercial kitchen and will save time in a domestic situation

Mish *(Ey)* A soft buffalo milk cheese which is kept for up to a year in salted buttermilk

mishikaki *(EA)* Charcoal grilled meat

miso *(Ja)* Fermented tofu and grains left to mature and gradually darken in colour from cream through red to dark brown finally becoming a dark brown salty paste tasting rather like soya sauce. Used as a flavouring and condiment. A good source of B vitamins; *see also* hatcho-miso inaka-miso, shinshu-miso and shiro-miso [also called **bean paste, bean sauce**]

misoltini *(It)* Salted and dried agoni [also called **missoltitti**]

miso ramen *(Ja)* A white curly noodle containing the cream coloured miso

miso-shiru *(Ja)* A traditional soup made from kombu and shiitake mushrooms simmered in dashi and finished with shredded spring onions, diced bean curd and red miso. It must not be boiled at the finishing stage

Mispel *(Ge)* Medlar

missoltitti *(It)* *see* misoltini

misticanza *(It)* Mixed salad

misto *(It)* Mixed

misto griglia *(It)* Mixed grill

misto mare *(It)* Mixed fried seafood

mistol jujube *see* Argentinian jujube

miswa *(Ph)* Fine white wheat flour noodles similar to hiyamugi noodles. Sold in bundles and should be cooked carefully to avoid breaking up

mithai *(In)* Indian sweetmeats made in various ways but often based on evaporated or condensed milk (khoya) and nuts. Usually bought in [also called **methai**]

mitha nimboo *(In)* Sweet lime

mithia tiganita *(Gr)* Cooked mussels, battered and deep fried at 180°C. Served with lemon wedges

mitili *(It)* Mussels

mititei *(Ro)* Skinless sausages flavoured with garlic and ground caraway seed and containing bicarbonate of soda which gives them an unusual texture and flavour

mitsuba *(Ja)* A herb resembling Italian parsley whose leaves are used as a garnish either chopped or whole [also called **Japanese parsley, trefoil** (USA)]

mitsuna *(Ja)* A bitter leaf used as a herb

Mittagessen *(Ge)* Lunch

miúdos *(Po)* Giblets

mix A mixture of dry ingredients to which water, milk, eggs or a combination of these is added and the result may be eaten as is, left to set, or further cooked, e.g. bread mix, soup mix, cake mix

mix, to To combine two or more ingredients so that they are intimately and irrevocably mingled

mixed grill A mixture of small portions of various grilled meats, offal, bacon, ham, sausage together with grilled mushrooms and tomatoes, served as a main meal or breakfast dish

mixed herbs Mixtures of dried herbs supplied for flavouring, often proprietary brands formulated for different applications such as sausages and the like

mixed salad An assortment of raw or cooked vegetables, leaves, fruit, cheese, sometimes with cooked fish, shellfish, meat, offal or egg assembled together as a single dish of attractive appearance and treated or served with a suitable dressing. Served warm or cool

mixed spice Mixtures of ground spices supplied for flavouring, often proprietary brands formulated for various cakes, biscuits, desserts, etc.

mixed vegetable soup *see* potage paysanne

mixer Any hand operated or machine operated implement used for mixing ingredients ranging from a simple spoon to a complex food processor. See e.g. whisk, food processor, blender, etc.

Mizithra *(Gr)* A Ricotta-like cheese made from the whey remaining after conventional cheese making with ewes' milk

mizu *(Ja)* Water

mizuna greens An annual or biennial oriental brassica *Brassica rapa* var. *nipposinica* with dark green, glossy, almost feathery leaves with white stems which form large rosettes rather like endive but not bitter. They may be eaten at any stage of growth up to 10 weeks and are cooked as a vegetable or the young tender leaves used in salads

m'jadarah *(ME)* Sliced onions fried until crisp in olive oil, most removed and drained and reserved, cooked lentils and rice added to the leftover oil and onions with cinnamon, allspice and pepper and cooked until dry. Served covered with the reserved crisp fried onions

mjölk *(Sw)* Milk

mjuka småfranska *(Sw)* Soft bread rolls

moa luau *(USA)* A Hawaiian dish of diced boiled chicken mixed with cooked taro leaves, butter and seasoning

moa niu *(USA)* A Hawaiian dish of boiled chicken in a white sauce placed in a halved coconut shell still containing coconut flesh, covered in cooking foil and baked in a bain marie in the oven

mocetta, la *(It)* **1** *see* la mocetta **2** Dried salted chamois or goat flesh served in very thin slices as an antipasto

Mocha A strong-flavoured coffee. The word is also used to describe a mixture of coffee and chocolate flavours used for cakes and puddings and sometimes the cake itself

mochi *(Ja)* Steamed glutinous rice pounded to

a smooth paste and made into small sweet or savoury cakes or dumplings. May be grilled and served with soya sauce

mochi-gome *(Ja)* A very small grain glutinous rice. Used to make mochi cakes

mochiko *(Ja)* Ground mochi-gome used as a thickening agent

mochomos *(Me)* Cooked, shredded and crisply fried meat.

mock crab *(UK)* Chopped hard boiled egg and egg yolk mixed with grated red Leicester cheese and shredded cooked chicken breast bound with a mixture of cooked egg yolk, mustard, anchovy essence, butter and pepper. Rested, then presented on crab shell and garnished as for dressed crab

mock cream A creamed mixture of fat and sugar, mixed with a cornflour thickened milk-based white sauce. Used as a cake filling esp. in the UK during World War II

mock hollandaise *see* Dutch sauce

mock turtle soup *(UK)* Soup made from stock derived from calf's head, aromatic vegetables and turtle herbs, strained, thickened and coloured brown, garnished with diced lean meat from the calf's head

moda, à *(Po)* In the style of

moda di, alla *(It)* In the style of

mode, à la 1 *(Fr)* In the fashion **2** *(USA)* Served with a scoop of ice cream e.g. a cake or a fruit pie **3** *(Fr)* A description of a dish of beef with carrots, onions and a calf's foot braised in wine, i.e. boeuf à la mode

mode de, à la *(Fr)* In the style of

moderne, à la *(Fr)* In the modern style, i.e. garnished with cauliflower sprigs coated with cheese sauce, tomatoes and duchesse potatoes

moelle *(Fr) fem.* Bone marrow

moelle, sauce *(Fr) fem.* Bordelaise sauce finished with poached and diced bone marrow and chopped parsley

moeum spey sar *(Cm)* Mooli

Moghul masala A mild Indian spice blend containing green cardamoms, cinnamon, black peppercorns, mace and cloves

mo gwa *(Ch)* Bitter gourd

mohali mandarin *see* ponkan mandarin

mohingha *(Bm)* A spicy fish soup based on coconut milk with local vegetables, served with noodles, hard-boiled eggs, raw onions, chillis and lemon. The national dish of Burma

moh lung ye baw *(Bm)* Small flour and grated coconut dumplings filled with jaggery and cooked in a coconut milk based sauce. Eaten to celebrate the cutting of a baby's first tooth, which meant it had survived the first hazardous months of life [also called **teething cake**]

Mohnbrötchen *(Ge)* Poppy seed rolls

Mohnkipfel *(Ge)* Poppy seed crescent rolls

Mohnkuchen *(Ge & Au)* A cake made from a base of white yeast-raised dough topped with a sweet rich mixture containing poppy seeds. Served in pieces dredged with icing sugar

Mohnsamen *(Ge)* Poppy seed

Mohnspielen *(Ge)* Christmas bread soaked in milk and sprinkled with poppy seeds, currants and sugar

Mohnstriezel *(Ge)* Poppy seed cake made from a yeasted egg and butter enriched stiff dough, rolled in a ball, submerged 5 to 8 cm below cold water and left until it rises above the surface, dried, punched down and kneaded and allowed to prove, rolled into a 6 mm thick rectangle about 25 by 40 cm amd covered with a filling of ground poppy seeds, raisins and almond nibs (5:3:1), mixed with an egg yolk-enriched and sweetened Béchamel with stiffly beaten egg whites folded in at the end and brushed with melted butter. The rectangle is rolled from either short side like palmiers and baked seam side down at 190°C until golden brown and crusty

Mohr im Hemd *(Au)* A chocolate pudding topped with ice cold whipped cream and covered with hot chocolate sauce. Lit. Moor in a shirt

Möhre *(Ge)* Carrot

Mohrenkopf *(Ge)* A Genoese sponge cooked in hemispherical moulds. Two placed together with a chocolate filling and covered with whipped cream. Lit. Moor's head

Mohrrüben *(Ge)* Carrots

moilee *(In) see* molee

moist sugar *(USA) see* muscovado sugar

moisten, to To add a little liquid to a dry mixture of foods so as to soften or flavour it, but not so as to be able to see free liquid

mojettes *(Fr) fem.* White cooked haricot beans, eaten warm or cold as a salad

moka *(Fr) masc.* Mocha

moke-kaung *(Bm)* Ridged sand clam

Mokka *(Ge)* Mocha

molasses The thick brown drainings from raw and recrystallized sugars which is a complex mixture of sugar, invert sugar and other plant derived components and minerals. Cane sugar molasses are used to produce treacle. Beet sugar molasses contains too many bitter and astringent beet compounds to be palatable

molasses sugar A fine grained unrefined sugar containing a large admixture of molasses so that it is very soft. Used in cakes and puddings

Molbo *(De)* An Edam-type cows' milk cheese covered in red wax

mold *(USA)* Mould

Moldavia *(Ru)* A hard smoked scalded-curd ewes' milk cheese made in the form of a cylinder (to 25 kg). Contains 42% water, 31% fat and 25% protein

moleas de vitela *(Po)* Veal sweetbreads

mole *(Me)* As mole poblano but with added tomatoes, thickened with tortillas and sweetened with raisins [also called **molli**]

mole poblano *(Me)* A sauce made from deseeded chile poblano puréed and fried with onion, coriander and garlic and combined with a small amount of unsweetened chocolate. Individual cooks may add other chillis for their own special flavour

mole poblana con guajalote *(Me)* Boiled turkey served with mole or mole poblano sauce

moleche *(It)* Small shore crabs cultivated in the Venice lagoon and eaten just after they have shed their shells and before the new shells have hardened

moleche alla muranese *(It)* Moleche floured, egged and fried

moleche ripiene *(It)* Moleche, killed by being left in beaten egg for 2 hours, then floured and fried

molee *(In)* A dish of fish or meat containing thick coconut milk in the sauce which is usually made from sweated onions, garlic, chillis and fresh ginger with spices to which the coconut milk is added. The fish or meat are then cooked in this sauce without boiling [also called **moilee**]

moler *(Sp)* To grind

molho *(Po)* A bunch

môlho *(Po)* Gravy, sauce

môlho branco *(Po)* White sauce

môlho de maças *(Po)* Apple sauce

mølja *(No)* Cod steaks boiled in water and served with sliced, cold, boiled cod's roe and a sauce made from boiled cod's liver heated with onion and water and the oil which floats on the top of the water in which the liver is boiled

moll de roca *(Sp)* Red mullet *Mullus surmuletus*

molle *(It)* Soft, soft-boiled. [also called **molletto**]

mollejas *(Sp)* Sweetbreads

mollet *(Fr)* Soft or soft-boiled, esp. of eggs

molletto *(It)* *see* molle

molli *see* mole

mollica *(It)* Crumb

mollusc The general term for creatures with soft bodies and hard either external or internal shells, but not segmented, many of which live in the sea. They are divided into gastropods (univalves) with a single solid external shell, bivalves which have a hinged two part external shell and the cephalopods some of which have an internal shell

molluschi *(It)* Molluscs

mollusk *(USA)* Mollusc

molokhia *see* meloukhia

moloko *(Ru)* Milk

molto cotto *(It)* Well done, cooked through

molva occhiona *(It)* Ling, the fish

momen tofu *(Ja)* Bean curd which has been strained through cloth, slightly pressed and presented in cubes or similar [also called **cotton bean curd**]

momiji-oroshi *(Ja)* A mixture of finely grated mooli and red chillis served wet as a condiment or dry after expelling the juice through a cloth. The juice may be used for flavouring other dishes. The grating of the chillis is achieved by inserting the long red variety into holes pierced in the mooli then grating the combination

Momordica charantia *Bot.* The bitter gourd

Momordica cochiniensis *Bot.* The spiny bitter gourd

Momordica muricata *Bot.* Kantola

Monarda didyma *Bot.* The herb bergamot

Monascus purpureus A fungus used in addition to the alcohol producing microorganism to impart a purplish red colour to the rice which is used to make ang-kak or rice wine; *see also* red rice

mondé(e) *(Fr)* **1** Past participle of monder, to hull **2** Formed into a round ball shape e.g. when a tomato is cored and skinned

mondeghili *(It)* Meatballs from Lombardy made with minced beef and cheese then panéed and fried

Mondseer *(Au)* A semi-hard, cooked-curd

cows' milk cheese made with a lactic starter. The cheeses are brined then ripened for up to 8 weeks. The supple yellow paste contains small irregular holes and is enclosed in a thin dry rind. The taste varies from mild to piquant depending on age

mongo-ika *(Ja)* Cuttlefish strips used for flavouring stocks and soups

Mongolian barbecue An upwardly convex domed steel plate set over a fierce heat source and usually with a gutter round the edge. Finely chopped foods (often self selected by the guest) are cooked rapidly on the plate in small quantities. Said to be derived from the upturned shield on which Mongolian horsemen cooked their food [also called **Genghis Khan griddle**]

Mongolian fire-pot *see* Mongolian hot pot

Mongolian hot pot A large pot with a funnel through the middle somewhat like a ring mould, and with a burner below which uses the funnel as a flue. Food is cooked at the table, possibly a stew or a stock into which finely sliced raw meat is briefly dipped as in flying lamb slices q.v. [also called **Mongolian hot-pot**]

monguete *(Sp)* A Spanish variety of French bean

mong yau *(Ch)* Caul

monkey bread **1** *see* baobab **2** *(USA)* A sweet bread made by placing separate pieces of dough at random into a bread tin and baking. The bread may be enriched and flavoured.

monkey nut *see* peanut

monkfish **1** A round seawater fish *Lophius piscatorius* with a large ugly head and very fine tasting white tail flesh often used as a substitute for scampi. The whole tail can be roasted like a leg of lamb. The fish can grow up to 2 m in length and 30 kg, but is usually sold smaller. It is found in the Mediterranean and the Atlantic [also called **anglerfish, goosefish** (USA)] **2** A name sometimes given to the angel fish q.v., a type of shark

monk's hotchpotch *see* ghiveci calugaresc

monoacetin *see* glycerol monoacetate

Mononatriumglutamat *(Ge)* Monosodium glutamate

monopotassium glutamate *see* (E)622

monosaccharide A simple sugar consisting of a 6 membered ring structure. The important monosaccharides in food are glucose, fructose and galactose which in various combinations form most of the sugars, starches and carbohydrates found in food

monosodium glutamate. The white crystalline sodium salt of the amino acid, glutamic acid, a constituent of proteins now produced by fermentation. It has a distinctive meaty taste in itself but is used to enhance the flavour of other foods esp. in Chinese cooking and in convenience foods; *see also* (E)621 [also called **MSG, aji-no-moto, taste powder, gourmet powder, ve tsin**]

monounsaturated As polyunsaturated but only one carbon atom has less than two hydrogen atoms or other groups attached

monounsaturated fat A fat or oil which contains a single unsaturated (i.e. double) bond in the chain of carbon atoms which make up the fatty acid part. Olive oil is the commonest example

monsieur *(Fr) masc. see* monsieur fromage

monsieur fromage *(Fr) masc.* A small double cream cows' milk cheese from Normandy with a strong flavour and in the shape of a tall cylinder [also called **monsieur**]

monstera deliciosa The fruit of a tropical tree *Monstera deliciosa* with a green scaly skin about the size of a large maize cob. The ripe pulpy flesh is white and has a strong pineapple/banana like flavour [also called **ceriman**]

Mont Blanc *(Fr) masc.* A dessert of sweetened chestnut purée topped with whipped cream

Montasio *(It)* A hard, cooked-curd wheel shaped (to 15 kg) cows' milk cheese made with a whey starter, pressed, salted 10 days, brined for 7 days and ripened for 6 to 12 months and varies from a dessert cheese to a grating cheese as it ages. Resembles Asiago

montata *(It)* Whipped

Monte Bianco *(It)* As Mont Blanc with chocolate and rum

monté, to The shortened anglicization of monter au beurre, meaning to add butter to a sauce before service to enrich, thicken and gloss it

Montecenisio *(Fr & It)* A soft blue cheese made with cows' milk possibly mixed with goats' milk from the region west of Turin

monter *(Fr)* To increase the volume of an ingredient by whipping to incorporate air

monter au beurre *(En & Fr)* To add butter to a sauce at the last moment to give it a sheen

Monterey Jack *(USA)* A scalded-curd bland Cheddar-like cows' milk cheese made in dessert, semi-hard or grating textures depending on the ripening time. The grating version is known as Dry Jack. Originally from Monterey, California

Montia perfoliata *Bot.* Winter purslane

Montmorency, à la *(Fr)* **1** Dishes dedicated to the Montmorency family esp. various cakes and sweet and savoury dishes containing Montmorency cherries **2** Garnished, esp. steaks, with artichokes, carrots, potatoes and sometimes with Madeira sauce

Montmorency cherry A particularly prized variety of cherry used in many sweet and savoury dishes

Montoire *(Fr)* A mild, pleasant tasting goats' milk cheese from the Loire

montone *(It)* Mutton

Montpellier butter *see* beurre de Montpellier. This butter without the oil and egg yolks is sometimes chilled and cut into decorative shapes for cold buffets

Montpensier, garnish *(Fr)* A steak garnish of artichokes, asparagus, truffles and potatoes

Montrachet *(Fr)* A small, delicate and creamy goats' milk cheese made in the shape of a small cylinder and wrapped in grape or chestnut leaves

Montreuil *(Ge)* Fish poached in white wine and served with potatoes and shrimp sauce

montreuil *(Fr)* With peaches

Montségur *(Fr)* A bland cows' milk cheese from Languedoc-Roussillon

monzittas *(It)* *(Sardinia)* Snails

moo *(Th)* Pork

moolee *(In)* Cooked in a coconut sauce

mooli *(In & Ca)* The long white tubers of a species of radish (*Raphanus sativus*), with a similar and sometimes hotter taste. Up to 40 cm long and eaten raw, pickled or cooked [also called **Japanese radish, white radish, giant white radish, mouli, muli, daikon**]

moong dal *see* mung bean

moong ke dal *(In)* Dehusked and split mung beans

moongphali *(In)* Peanut

moon sin *(Ch)* Eel

moorcock *see* grouse and black grouse

moorfowl *see* grouse and black grouse

moorkoppen *(Ho)* Moors' heads, filled tarts piled high with whipped cream

Moor's head *see* Edam

Moors' heads *(USA)* As Mohrenköpfe but with various fillings and coverings

Moosbeere *(Ge)* Cranberry

moose A large wild herbivore *Alces americana* from the north of Canada. The membrane around the muscles gives the flesh a gamey flavour and should be removed before cooking. Marinating is recommended

moo shu zoh *(Ch)* A pancake rolled around a filling of chopped pork stir fried with spring onions, cloud ear fungus and eggs

mo qua *(Ch)* Fuzzy melon

mora *(It & Sp)* Blackberry

mora di gelso *(It)* Mulberry

morangos *(Po)* Strawberries

Moravsky bochník syr *(Cz)* A cows' milk cheese similar to Emmental

Moray eel A warm seawater fish *Muraena helena* with a brown and fawn mottled skin. It is up to 1.5 m in length, has excellent flesh although with many bones and is suitable for poaching or boiling

morbidelle *(It)* Tiny dumplings used to garnish soup

Morbier A hard cows' milk cheese from Franche-Comté with a delicate flavour. The milk is treated with a lactic starter, coagulated with rennet and the curd, drained, pressed, brined and ripened for 2 to 3 months. Before brining, the cylinder of immature cheese is cut in half horizontally with a knife dipped in soot to give a characteristic black line when it is finally cut in wedges

mørbrad *(De)* Tenderloin of pork, i.e. that muscle corresponding to the fillet of beef

morceau *(Fr)* *masc.* A small portion

morcela *(Po)* The Portuguese version of boudin noir

Morchel *(Ge)* Morel

morchella *(It)* Morel

Morchella esculenta *Bot.* Morel

morcilla *(Sp)* The Spanish version of boudin noir from Asturia [also called **boudin Asturien** (Fr)]

morcilla blanca *(Sp)* A boudin blanc made with chicken meat and hard boiled eggs

morcilla negra *(Sp)* A boudin noir from Andalusia made from pig's blood, minced almonds, sweet peppers and parsley

more *(It)* Blackberries

morel The fruiting body of a highly prized wild fungus *Morchella esculenta* the commonest of the *Morchellaceae,* all of which are edible. It has an erect brownish fruit body with deep pits surrounded by irregular ridges 3 to 10 cm high and 3 to 7 cm in diameter, attached to a whitish stem which thickens towards the base. It must be washed carefully to remove grit and dirt from the pits. Available dried, fresh or canned [also called **common morel**]

morello cherry The best cooking variety of cherry, almost black in colour and slightly tart when ripe

morena *(Sp)* Moray eel

Moreton Bay bug *(Aus) see* sand lobster

morgen complet *(De)* Full breakfast

morgenmad *(De)* Breakfast

Morgenrot *(Ge)* A chicken broth with tomato purée and pieces of chicken meat. Lit. dawn

moriawase *(Ja)* A celebratory display of sashimi arranged artistically on a wooden platter and garnished

moriglione *(It)* Pochard, a red headed diving duck

morille *(Fr) fem.* Morel, the fungus

Moringa oleifera *Bot.* The drumstick bean

Moringa pterygosperma *Bot.* Drumstick vegetable

morkov *(Ru)* Carrots

mörkt rågbröd *(Sw)* Toast

Morlacco *(It)* A semi-hard, scalded-curd cows' milk cheese similar to Montasio with a smooth rind and a firm paste with a few holes

mormora *(It)* Striped bream

Mornay, à la *(Fr)* Description of dishes which include Mornay sauce

Mornay, fish White fish poached in fish stock, drained and kept warm, reduced cooking liquor added to boiling Béchamel sauce, egg yolk whisked in, removed from heat, grated cheese added, seasoned, strained, butter and cream added, fish coated with sauce and gratinated with grated cheese

Mornay, sauce *(En & Fr) fem. see* cheese sauce

Moroccan spearmint *see* spearmint

Morón *(Sp)* A mild and delicate white cheese made from a variety of milks in the Seville region and often consumed within 24 hours of production. If kept longer it is steeped in olive oil and rubbed with paprika

morötter *(Sw)* Carrots

morozhenoye *(Ru)* Ice cream

Mortadella *(It)* The original Bologna sausage, noted for its size and dating from the 12th century if not before. The composition is variable but the best contain only pork, garlic and seasoning. Cheaper ones may contain in addition, veal, tripe, donkey and spices, etc. All are ground to a fine paste and stuffed into pig's or beef bladders, boiled and hung up to dry for a few days

mortadella di campotosta *(It)* A type of mortadella with a cylinder of bacon through the centre

Mortadelle *(Fr) fem.* A version of Mortadella made from pork, salt pork fat and fresh pork fat, soaked in wine and smoked

mortar The round ceramic, stone or steel bowl in which food is placed to be broken down by the pestle. See pestle and mortar

mortella *(It)* Myrtle

mortella di palude *(It)* Cranberry

mortifier *(Fr)* To hang meat or game

mortpølse *(No)* A sausage made from a mixture of beef, mutton and reindeer meat

morue *(Fr) fem.* Cod, also used for salt cod

morue salée *(Fr) fem.* Salt cod

Morus nigra *Bot.* Mulberry

Morven *(UK)* A soft cows' milk cheese with a yellow rind from Scotland made into square blocks. It is similar to Butterkäse and like that cheese is flavoured with caraway seeds

moscardino bianco *(It)* Curled octopus

moscovita *(It)* A rich dessert mousse

moscovite, sauce *(En & Fr) fem.* Poivrade sauce made with venison stock and finished at the last minute with a sweet fortified wine infused with juniper berries, soaked and plump currants and toasted pinenuts or chopped almonds

mosede kartofler *(De)* Mashed potatoes

moskovitaeg *(De)* Egg mayonnaise

Moskovski *(Ru)* A hard cows' milk cheese with a good flavour matured for 3 to 4 months

moss curled endive *see* endive

moss curled parsley *see* parsley *Petroselinum crispum*

mossel *(Ho)* Mussel (blue)

mostacciolo *(It)* A rich fruit cake with almonds, chocolate and candied fruit

mostarda *(It & Po)* Mustard

mostarda di Cremona *(It)* A mixture of

fruits preserved in a mustard-flavoured sugar syrup served with boiled meats [also called **mostarda di frutta**]

mostarda di frutta *(It) see* mostarda di Cremona

mostaza *(Sp)* Mustard

mostelle *(Fr) fem.* Three-bearded rockling, the fish

mosterd *(Ho)* Mustard

mosto *(It)* Unfermented grape juice, must

Motal *(Ru)* A salty ewes' or cows' milk cheese from the Caucasus matured in brine for 3 to 4 months

motella *(It)* Three-bearded rockling, the fish

moth bean One of the most recently domesticated legumes *Phaseolus aconitifolius* which is very drought-resistant and is grown in India for its green or black seeds

mother The name often given to a undefined mass of microorganisms, yeasts, bacteria, etc. which are used to start a fermentation

mother of vinegar The whitish flora which grows on the surface of naturally brewed vinegar used as a starter for vinegar

moti sonf *(In)* Fennel

mouclade *(Fr) fem.* A mussel stew with a white wine and cream sauce thickened with egg yolks

moudre *(Fr)* To grind

moufflon *see* mouflon

mouflon *(En & Fr) masc.* A wild sheep originally from Corsica but now the name applies to all large horned wild sheep [also called **moufflon** (En), **muflon** (En)]

mould 1 A hollow container of metal, ceramic, glass or plastic in which liquids are placed so as to set and take up the shape of the mould. Used for jellies, blanc-mange and a variety of solid foods set in aspic **2** The fungi which grow on the surface of food left exposed to ambient conditions. Often moulds are not noticed until the fruiting bodies appear. These are usually either a white coating or a furry white, grey or green growth, both of which grow outwards from the original inoculating spore. Some moulds are deliberately encouraged as on the surface of Camembert and in blue cheeses where they are deliberately introduced into the centre by needling. Mould growth is also important in many fermented foods such as soya sauce and tempeh. Very few moulds are toxic and many have antibiotic (anti-bacterial) properties

mould, to To form into a desired shape either by hand or in a mould

moule 1 *(Fr) masc.* Mould for jellies, etc. **2** *(Fr) fem.* Mussel

moule à gateaux *(Fr) masc.* Cake tin

moule à manqué *(Fr) masc.* A deep cake tin with outward sloping sides. This facilitates icing or coating the sides of cakes baked in it

moule à tarte *(Fr) masc.* Pie plate, flan dish

moules à l'escargot *(Be)* Mussels, stuffed and prepared to look like snails

moules marinière *(En & Fr) fem.* Cleaned and debearded mussels cooked in a deep closed pan with dry white wine, chopped onion, chopped parsley and seasoning. When the mussels open they are served with the cooking liquor. Any which do not open must be discarded [also called **moules à la marinière**]

moules à la marinière *(Fr) fem. see* moules marinière

moules poulettes *(Fr) fem.* Mussels presented in timbales with creamed mushrooms, parsley and lemon sauce

mouli 1 *(Fr) masc.* A hand operated food mill for puréeing soft food or slicing raw vegetables consisting of various perforated discs over and through which food is forced by rotating blades operated via a cranked handle **2** *see* mooli

mountain ash 1 *see* rowanberry **2** *(USA)* Various trees *Sorbus americana* and *S. scopulina* with larger fruit similar to the rowan, with berries used in the same way

mountain cheese *see* Bergkäse

mountain chicken *(Ca)* **1** *see* crapaud **2** Frog's legs

mountain cranberry *see* cowberry

mountain grouse *see* ptarmigan

mountain ham *see* jamón serrano

mountain hollyhock *see* wasabi

mountain oysters *see* prairie oysters

mountain spinach *see* orach

mountain yam A temperate climate variety of yam *Dioscorea japonica* which grows in Japan. It has a gluey texture and is often grated and used as a binder

mousaka *(Gr) see* moussaka

mousetrap cheese *(UK) coll.* Various types of bland tasteless Cheddar-type cheese imported from different countries and occasionally from British commercial cheesemakers. Only suitable for baiting mousetraps

mousquetaire, sauce *(Fr) fem.* Mayonnaise flavoured with chopped onion or shallot which has been simmered in dry white wine. Served cold

moussaka *(En & Gr)* Alternating layers of partially cooked and flavoured minced lamb and fried aubergine slices in a deep dish, topped with a Béchamel sauce or a yoghurt, eggs and cheese mixture, flavoured with nutmeg, gratinated with breadcrumbs and cheese and baked in the oven. Served with salad and pitta bread [also called **mousaka**]

mousse *(En & Fr) fem.* A flavoured egg mixture or purée of fruit, vegetables, fish or shellfish into which whisked egg whites and whipped cream are folded to make a stiff foam, this poured into a mould, set and demoulded. Gelatine may be used in the base mix as a setting agent or the mousse may be frozen. Served as a cold dessert, as a starter or sometimes used as a filling for fish paupiettes, etc.

mousse de foie gras *(Fr) fem.* As pâté de foie gras but need contain only 55% or more of goose liver, almost as good as the pâté but will melt if heated

mousse perlée d'Irlande *(Fr) fem.* Carragheen

mousseline *(Fr) fem.* A small individually served sweet or savoury mousse

mousseline, sauce *(En & Fr) fem.* Hollandaise sauce mixed with whipped double cream prior to serving. Used with asparagus, broccoli and poached fish, chicken and egg dishes. Sometimes called sauce chantilly

mousseron *(Fr) masc.* St George's mushroom, meadow mushroom

mousseuse, sauce *(Fr) fem.* A type of compound butter made by whisking the juice of half a lemon, 16 g of salt and 800 ml of cream into a litre of softened butter which is then chilled and sliced for use with boiled fish

moutabel *see* mutabbal

moutarde *(Fr) fem.* Mustard

moutarde extra-forte *(Fr) fem.* English mustard

moutarde forte *(Fr) fem.* English mustard

moutarde de Meaux *(Fr) fem.* A whole grain mustard made from a mixture of mustard seeds with their husks

moutarde, sauce *(Fr) fem. see* mustard sauce

mouton *(Fr) masc.* Sheep, mutton

mowra butter *(In)* A soft yellow oil extracted from the seeds of the Indian butter tree. Used locally for cooking and exported for margarine manufacture [also called **bassia fat, illipe butter**]

moyashi *(Ja)* Bean sprouts

Mozzarella *(It)* A soft pale spun-curd cheese made from buffalo or cow's milk eaten very fresh. Formed into a round or pear shape and often stored in brine. Used for pizzas, lasagne and in salads. It becomes characteristically stringy when cooked. Contains 55 to 65% water, 18 to 20% fat and 16 to 21% protein.

Mozzarella affumicata *(It)* A smoked Mozzarella cheese

Mozzarella di bufala *(It)* A Mozzarella cheese made with pure buffalo milk and given legal protection [also called **Trecce di bufala**]

mozzarella in carrozza *(It)* A fried sandwich filled with Mozzarella cheese

MRM *see* mechanically recovered meat

mrouziya *(NA)* A Moroccan tagine made from middle neck of lamb rubbed with ras el hanout, powdered saffron, cinnamon and seasoning, simmered with blanched almonds, onions, butter and a little water and finished with raisins and honey about 30 minutes before serving

MSG *see* monosodium glutamate

mucca *(It)* Cow

Mucor pusillus A microorganism used for the production of a protease used in curdling milk for cheese production. Acceptable to vegetarians

mud crab A dull green crab *Scylla serrata* growing up to 2 kg in weight and found throughout SEA in shallow muddy water. The claw meat is especially prized

mudgeon *see* mesentery

mudjemeri *(Tu)* Very similar to kadin budu köfte but finely minced and made into small balls fried in mutton fat

mu er *(Ch)* Cloud ear fungus

muesli A mixture of raw or semi-processed and dry cereals with dried vine fruits, chopped nuts, bran, sugar and chopped dried fruit, used as a breakfast cereal and eaten uncooked. Typical cereals used are wheat, rye, barley and oat flakes as well as others less common

muffin 1 *(UK)* A yeast-raised dough made with strong flour, milk, a little semolina and salt, rolled out and cut in 8 cm rounds, proven and cooked on a griddle or hot plate for about 7 minutes each side until golden brown **2** *(USA)* A baking powder raised sweet sponge mix baked in deep patty tins to a soft doughy consistency. Sometimes flavoured with fresh or dried fruit, glacé cherries, honey or maple syrup

muflon *see* mouflon

mugwort A wild perennial herb *Artemesia vulgaris,* originally used in place of hops. The crushed dried leaves may be sprinkled on fatty meats and poultry prior to roasting; *see also* white mugwort

muhamara *(ME)* Red chilli pepper blended with a little water, olive oil, ground walnuts and a few stale breadcrumbs, allspice, ground cumin, salt and pomegranate (or lemon) juice until a smooth paste. Chilled and garnished with chopped parsley and served as a mezze dish [also called **Garmerong in Armenia**]

muhennettu *(Fi)* Stewed

muhennos *(Fi)* Stew

muik *(Ko)* Kombu

muikku *(Fi)* A tiny white fish similar to whitebait

mui kwai cheung *(Ch)* A sausage from Hongkong made from a mixture of lean and fat pork, soya sauce, rosé wine, salt and sugar

mújol *(Sp)* Grey mullet

muk bampound *(Cm)* Squid

muki goma *(Ja)* Hulled sesame seeds

muktuk *(Cn)* The tough outer flesh of whales used by the Inuit people (Eskimos) of Canada as food

mulard *(Fr) masc.* A modern crossbred duck bred for the table and its liver. It is fleshier and leaner than the standard French breeds

mulato *(Me)* A large brown chilli pepper, usually dried

mulberry The soft very perishable blackberry-like fruit of a tree *Morus nigra* which grows to about 10 m. Treat as blackberries

mulet doré *(Fr) masc.* Golden grey mullet

mulet gris *(Fr) masc.* Grey mullet

muli *see* mooli

mull, to To heat wine or beer with or without spices and sugar

mulled wine Red wine heated with a sugar syrup flavoured with cinnamon stick, bruised dried ginger, cloves and orange zest. Traditionally heated by immersing a red hot poker in the mixture

mullet *see* grey mullet and red mullet, two different species

mulligan stew *(USA) see* burgoo

mulligatawny soup *(UK)* A Victorian soup made from pre-browned chopped onions fried in oil with curry powder and flour, stock, tomato purée, chopped apple, chutney and desiccated coconut added, simmered and skimmed for 1 hour, liquidized, strained, seasoned and consistency corrected and served with a garnish of boiled rice. An alternative uses only chicken stock, fried curry powder (mixed Indian spices) and yoghurt. Adapted from the Tamil milakutanni (pepper water) during the British occupation of India

multer *(No)* Cloudberry

mum bar *(ME)* A highly spiced sausage from Iraq containing lamb and rice

muna *(Fi)* Egg

muna kova *(Fi)* Hard boiled eggs

muna pehmeä *(Fi)* Soft boiled eggs

muna ja pekoni *(Fi)* Eggs and bacon

munakas *(Fi)* Omelette

munakokkeli *(Fi)* Scrambled eggs

Munchener Weisswurst *(Ge)* A Brühworst made from veal and possibly beef with parsley, filled into a light coloured casing. Served steamed or grilled with sauerkraut, puréed potatoes and sweet Bavarian mustard

munchies *(UK & USA) coll.* **1** Snack foods **2** The state of being peckish, hungry, e.g. to have the munchies

mung bean A small spherical green bean *Phaseolus aureus* with a white hilum, used as a source of bean sprouts q.v., but may eaten as a vegetable when the pod is young. Its principal use is as a pulse which is also made into a flour used in Indian cooking. If used as a pulse requires 8 hours soaking and long cooking. It may also be candied as a snack food or used to make a type of bean curd [also called **golden gram, moong dal, green gram, green lentil**]

mung bean flour Flour made from mung beans, sold natural colour or pink or green for use in making SEA sweetmeats

mung dal *(In)* Dehusked and split mung beans

mungerela *(In)* Nigella

munk *(Sw)* Doughnut

munkar *(Sw)* Dumplings

munna juusto *(Fi)* A delicately-flavoured golden coloured cheese made from cows' milk mixed with eggs

Münster *(Ge & Fr) masc.* A soft yellow, surface-ripened cows' milk cheese with an orange-red rind from Alsace. It uses a lactic starter and has an open textured delicately-flavoured paste with some cracks. It has a recorded history going back to the 7th century. The German variety is milder than the French. Traditionally served with Gewürztraminer and a bowl of cumin seeds. The French version has appellation d'origine status

mun sum palung *(Th)* Cassava

Murazzano *(It)* A soft cheese made from a mixture of 60% ewes' milk and 40% cows' milk. It is formed into small cylinders (to 400 g), dry salted, and then washed daily for 7 days. It has no rind and a dense texture

Mürbeteig *(Ge)* Short pastry

Murbodner *(Au)* A large (to 15 kg) hard, cooked-curd cows' milk cheese resembling Emmental which is ripened for 2 months. It contains 39% water, 28% fat and 26% protein

murcott *see* honey tangerine

mûre *(Fr) fem.* Mulberry

mûre de ronce *(Fr) fem.* Blackberry

mûre sauvage *(Fr) fem.* Blackberry

murena *(It)* Moray eel

murène *(Fr) fem.* Moray eel

murex A small gastropod mollusc from the Mediterranean, the original source of the Roman imperial purple dye

murgh *(In)* Chicken

murgh musallam *(In)* A Pakistani dish of chicken roasted with spices.

muriche *(It)* Murex, the shellfish

murlins *see* alaria

Murol *(Fr)* A semi-hard washed-rind pressed cows' milk cheese from the Auvergne made in 500 g discs with a hole in the centre. It has a red rind and the flavour of the paste starts off mild but gradually becomes strongly aromatic over the 7 week ripening period

Murray river crayfish *(Aus)* A crayfish *Euastacus armatus* with a spiny blue shell and weighing up to 2 kg

Murraya koenigii *Bot.* Curry leaf

murseddu *(It)* A flat bread from Calabria filled with a mixture of tripe, offal, tomatoes and spices

mursiellu alla cantanzarese *(It)* Pork stewed in wine

murtabah *(In)* A southern dish consisting of a very large pancake filled with curried meat and onions

murtabak *(SEA)* Pasties with a savoury meat and vegetable filling, fried and eaten as a snack

mus *(It) see* farinata alla contadina

Musa paradisica *Bot.* The plantain

Musa sapientum *Bot.* The banana

musaca *(Ro)* Moussaka topped with soured cream instead of the customary cheese sauce

musakka *(Tu)* A type of moussaka made with layers of fried sliced aubergine, fried onions, minced lamb or beef, sliced tomatoes and halved green peppers, baked or simmered very slowly

musaman curry *see* gaeng mussaman

musaria *(In)* A brass or cast iron pestle used with a matching mortar (khalia). Used for hard grains and spices

muscade *(Fr) fem.* Nutmeg

muscadine *(USA)* A white grape used for the table and for making raisins

muscat grape *see* dessert grape

muscatel raisins Dried muscat grapes sometimes still in the original bunch

muscatny oreckh *(Ru)* Nutmeg

Muscheln *(Ge)* Shellfish

muscle *(Sp)* Mussels

muscoletti *(It) see* muscolo

muscoli *(It)* Mussels

muscolo *(It)* Beef or veal shank [also called **muscoletti**]

muscovado sugar A soft and sticky partially refined cane sugar with fine crystals. Both light and dark varieties are available [also called **Barbados sugar, moist sugar** (USA)]

muscovy duck *see* barbary duck

musgo de Irlanda *(Sp)* Carragheen

mush *(USA)* A cooked porridge made from maize meal similar to polenta

mushi-ki *(Ja)* A steamer, usually 2 or 3 tiered dishes with a topmost lid which fit over a pan of boiling water. The steamer dishes may be in metal or bamboo [also called **seiro**]

mushimono *(Ja)* Steamed or steaming as applied to cooking methods. Abbreviated in recipes to mushi

mushizakana to daikon to tamago tsuke awase *(Ja)* Pieces of white fish placed in individual bowls, moistened with sake, covered with a mixture of egg, sake, sugar and grated mooli, garnished with a spinach leaf, steamed until set, sprinkled with grated ginger and served immediately

mushroom A general name given to various edible fungi but in the UK the name is generally applied to the common mushroom *Agaricus bisporus* which is widely cultivated and the field mushroom *Agaricus campestris.* Common mushrooms are sold as buttons (completely closed caps to 2 cm dia.), closed cup (skin still closed below cup to 4 cm dia.), open cup (pink gills visible) and flat (fully open with dark brown gills). Other common types of cultivated mushroom in the UK are oyster, chestnut and shiitake. For a complete listing, see under fungi

mushroom essence The juices extracted from mushrooms. This is best done by freezing them, thawing them and squeezing out the liquid. The tissue remaining may be chopped and added to duxelles before preparation

mushroom ketchup A dark brown salty cold condiment sauce made with mushrooms

mushroom sauce 1 For meat: A suprême sauce but with sliced and sweated button mushrooms added after the velouté sauce has been strained. Used for boiled chicken, sweetbreads, etc. [also called **sauce aux champignons** (Fr)] **2** For fish: See sauce aux champignons

mushroom sausage *(UK)* An English link sausage containing about 5% chopped fresh mushrooms in the usual rusk/meat mixture

mushroom soup A mirepoix of onions, leek and celery sweated in butter, flour added and cooked out without colour, white stock, a BG and chopped mushrooms added, simmered and skimmed for 1 hour, BG removed, liquidized, strained, seasoned and consistency adjusted. Finished with cream [also called **crème de champignons** (Fr)]

mushroom soya sauce Soya sauce flavoured with an extract of straw mushrooms

mushy peas Marrowfat peas, cooked until soft and mashed. May be forced through a sieve to remove the skins. Served as an accompaniment

musillo *(It)* The thick central cut of salt cod

musk mallow A bushy perennial *Malva moschata* growing to 60 cm. The leaves can be boiled and eaten as a vegetable

musk melon A variety of sweet melon *Cucumis melo,* smaller than cantaloupe or winter melons but variable in size and with fine reticulate markings (a raised network) on smooth or ribbed yellowish or green skins. The aromatic flesh is green to salmon orange. It was the common variety grown in UK hothouses. When ripe the skin at the stalk end will give slightly when pressed [also called **netted melon, nutmeg melon, cantaloupe** (USA)]

muska börek *(Tu)* A borek (deep fried puff pastry pasty) filled with feta cheese and chopped parsley

Muskatblüte *(Ge)* Mace

Muskatnuss *(Ge)* Nutmeg

Muslim curry *see* gaeng mussaman

muslin A relatively open simple woven cotton used for straining liquids or to wrap up a BG, dried herbs, spices, etc. from which the flavour is to be extracted in a simmering liquid

muslinger *(De)* Mussels

muslo *(Sp)* Leg (of meat)

muso *(It)* Beef muzzle and nose

musola *(Sp)* Smooth hound, the fish

mussel A very common bivalve mollusc (various spp.) found worldwide usually attached to rocks near the water line, but some bury themselves in the sand. Most have dark blue to black shells to 8 cm long but some from New Zealand have blue and green shells. Generally sold live in their shells or removed, cooked and preserved in brine, sauce or by canning. Sometimes sold smoked. Cooked as any other mollusc. The mussel is a highly productive shellfish producing up to 10000 kg of meat per hectare per year. See in particular, common mussel, green-lipped mussel, horse mussel and fan mussel

mustard 1 The name of a range of seeds with a generally hot taste native to Europe and India. None have any smell. See under black mustard, brown mustard, white mustard, oriental mustard **2** A mixture of various ground or whole mustard seeds and other spices, etc. often moistened with vinegar, wine, verjuice or water, used as a condiment or for flavouring other dishes **3** A fast growing brassica *Brassica hirta* usually grown as sprouted seed for the sharply-flavoured seedling leaves and stems which are used in salads or as a garnish. If allowed to grow on, the young leaves may also be used in salads; *see also* mustard and cress

mustard butter A compound butter made with 120 g of French mustard per kg of softened butter. It is shaped into a 2.5 cm roll, refrigerated and cut in 6 mm slices for use as a garnish on grilled meats, mackerel and herrings

mustard and cream sauce Double cream whipped into English mustard let down with lemon juice as when making mayonnaise. Used on hors d'oeuvres and canapés

mustard and cress Seeds of mustard and cress laid thickly on a water saturated substrate and root support, allowed to grow to the the two leaf stage and a height of 5 to 7 cm and sold in this form for cutting to use as a garnish. The mustard is sown 2 days after the cress so that both are of equal height

mustard greens *see* oriental mustard

mustard oil A deep yellow highly-flavoured oil extracted from mustard seeds. Used in Indian cooking and in pickles and chutneys. Usually diluted with a blander oil

mustard pickle *see* piccalilli

mustard sauce Béchamel sauce with the addition of English or French mustard and possibly vinegar. Used with pork, ham or cheese dishes, with fried or grilled herring or mackerel and with hot boiled tongue [also called **sauce moutarde** (Fr)]

mustard seeds Small (to 1.5 mm dia.) seeds used extensively in Indian cooking. Usually fried before use to bring out the pungent flavour; *see also* mustard

mustella *(It)* Forkbeard, a fish similar to whiting

Musteweck *(Ge)* A bread roll with chopped pork

mustikka *(Fi)* Blueberry, bilberry

mustikkakeito *(Fi)* A dessert made from cornflour thickened blueberry juice

mustikkapiiras *(Fi)* Blueberry tart

mutabbal *(ME)* A purée dip or mezze similar to hummus-bi-tahina but substituting the flesh of grilled aubergines for the chick peas [also called **moutabel**]

mutton The meat of sheep older than one year but nowadays over two years. The meat is darker and stronger-flavoured than lamb and was preferred in Victorian times. Most mutton sold today is from old breeding ewes killed at 3 to 5 years and is generally tough and only suitable for boiling. The best mutton, now difficult to find, is killed at 18 months and is more expensive than lamb

mutton broth Blanched neck or scrag end of mutton simmered with water or stock and washed barley, skimmed, brunoise carrot, leek, turnip, celery and onion and a BG added, simmered and skimmed, meat removed, diced lean meat returned, BG removed, seasoned and served with chopped parsley

mutton fat A hard highly saturated fat from lamb and mutton used for cooking in the Middle East. Contains 50% saturated, 45% monounsaturated and 5% saturated fat

mutton fish **1** A type of abalone *Haliotis naevosa* from Australian waters **2** *see* ocean pout **3** *see* mutton snapper

mutton ham Cured leg of mutton. Used in Muslim cooking

mutton sausage *(UK)* An English type sausage made with lean mutton, mutton suet, breadcrumbs, chopped boiled bacon and seasoning, moistened with mutton stock

mutton snapper An olive-green snapper *Lutjanus analis* fished for sport in the warm western waters of the Atlantic

muy hechos *(Sp)* Well done (of meat, steak, etc.)

myaso *(Ru)* Meat

myaso po-tatarsky *(Ru)* Steak tartare made with triple minced seasoned fillet steak mixed with egg yolks, chopped spring onions and capers, horseradish sauce, Worcestershire sauce, oil and pepper vodka

myata *(Ru)* Mint

mycella *(De)* A semi-hard full fat cows' milk cheese shaped in cylinders and with a creamy yellow blue veined paste. Milder than Danish blue

mylta med grädde *(Sw)* A compote of cloudberries with cream

mynce pie *(UK)* *see* mince pie

myoga *(Ja)* Ginger buds

Myristica fragrans *Bot.* Mace and nutmeg

myrobalans *see* cherry plum

myrrh *see* sweet cicely

Myrrhis odorata *Bot.* Sweet cicely

Myrte *(Ge)* Myrtle

myrte *(Fr) masc.* Myrtle

myrte des marais *(Fr) masc.* Bog myrtle

myrtille *(Fr) fem.* Bilberry, blueberry

myrtle A half-hardy evergreen shrub *Myrtus communis* growing to 3 m with small shiny leathery leaves which have a spicy orange fragrance used for stuffings and with pork or lamb. The small white flowers excluding the green calyx may be used in fruit salads and the dried black berries have a mild juniper flavour and may be used as juniper berries. Grows in Mediterranean climates and is common in Corsican and Sardinian cooking. An oil is extracted from the ripe berries

myrtle pepper *see* allspice

Myrtus communis *Bot.* Myrtle

mysliwska *(Pl)* An expensive smoked and linked pork sausage in a natural casing

Mysore coffee A rich full-flavoured coffee from Mysore in Southern India

Mysost *(No)* A fawn, slightly sweet caramel-flavoured cheese made from the whey from a mixture of cows' and goats' milk in a similar manner to Ricotta. The whey is boiled and reduced to a brown sticky mass containing whey proteins, lactose and caramelized sugars. It is stirred whilst cooling to a solid to prevent crystallization of the sugars. Usually cut or shaved in very thin slices and served on crispbread, but also used in cooking [also called **Gjetost, Norwegian whey cheese**]

Mysuostur *(Ic)* A cheese very similar to Mysost made from the whey of cows' milk

Nn

naam gwa *(Ch)* Winter squash

naan *(In) see* nan bread

naartjie *(Saf)* A variety of tangerine

naawr mai *(Ch)* Glutinous rice

naba *(Sp)* Kohlrabi

nabemo *(Ja)* A single pot meal cooked at the table using sliced raw prepared ingredients and usually a central casserole of simmering stock. Sukiyaki and shabu shabu are the two most famous

nabo sueco *(Sp)* Swede

nabos *(Po & Sp)* Turnips

nachos *(Me)* Pieces of fried tortilla topped with grated cheese, browned under the grill and garnished with green chillis. Served as a snack

Nachspeise *(Ge)* Dessert, sweet

Nachtisch *(Ge)* Dessert, sweet

nadru *(In)* Lotus

nagami kumquat *Fortunella margarita*, the commonest kumquat in Europe and the USA, grown mainly in Morocco, Palestine, Brazil and the USA. It is an oval fruit with a smooth rind and a pronounced spicy citrus flavour. The flesh is acidic with a few seeds [also called **oval kumquat**]

naganegi *(Ja)* Asian leek

nagashi-bako *(Ja)* A small square mould used for making jellies and jellied (e.g. aspic coated) food

nage, à la *(Fr)* Shellfish cooked in white wine with aromatic vegetables and herbs

nagelkaas *(Ho)* A pale strong-flavoured and very hard and dense cows' milk cheese made with a lactic starter, flavoured with cumin and cloves and matured for six months. The hard yellow rind is usually oiled. The unspiced version is Kanterkaas [also called **Friese nagelkaas, Friese**]

Nagelrochen *(Ge)* Thornback ray

nagerecht *(Ho)* Dessert

nagkesar *(In)* Cassia buds

näkinkenka *(Fi)* Mussel

nakiri bocho *(Ja)* A vegetable knife rather like a very sharp diminutive chopper. Used for peeling and the production of the characteristic vegetable cuts of Japan

näkkileipä *(Fi)* Crispbread, hard ryebread, hardtack

naky pliak *(Ru)* A cabbage soufflé considered to be a good test of a Ukrainian cook. It is made from shredded cabbage which has been lightly salted and pressed then covered in boiling water and left for 3 to 4 days to partially ferment. The drained, rinsed and dried cabbage is mixed into an onion, garlic and milk based roux sauce, flavoured with cheese, thickened with egg yolks and lightened by folding in stiffly beaten egg whites (cabbage to eggs 2:1), placed in a buttered soufflé dish, dotted with butter sprinkled with breadcrumbs and baked at 190°C

nalesniki *(Pl)* Fritters made from cottage cheese mixed with egg yolks and butter sandwiched between thin pancakes, cut into squares, dipped in batter and deep fried

nama-age *(Ja)* Lightly fried bean curd

nama fu *(Ja)* Fresh gluten cake

namagashi *(Ja)* Soft cakes usually including adzuki bean paste *(anko)*

namasu *(Ja)* Julienned mooli and carrot salted in a bowl for 30 minutes, wrung out and dressed with a rice vinegar flavoured with soya sauce, chopped ginger root and sugar. Best left to mature for 8 hours

nama-wuni *(Ja)* Sea urchin ovaries

nam dong ca *(Vi)* Shiitake mushroom

ñame *(Sp)* Yam

nameko *(Ja)* A small gelatinous mushroom native to Japan, used in soups and sunomono. Usually sold preserved in a light brine

nameshi *(Ja)* Green rice made by mixing salted plain boiled rice with shredded spinach that has been cooked 5 minutes and wrung out

namida *(Ja)* Wasabi. Lit. tears

nam jim kratiem *(Th)* A sweet and sour garlic sauce with chillis, made by slowly cooking the ingredients with a little water until soft and reduced to a sauce, then salting to taste

na mool *(Ko)* Accompaniments and side dishes at Korean meals, often marinated or cold cooked vegetables

nam pa *(La)* A thin straw coloured fish sauce similar to nuoc mam

nam pla *(Th)* The salty brown liquid which drains from salted and fermented fish used as a flavouring in the same way as soya sauce [also called **fish sauce**]

nam pla ra *(Th)* A thin sauce made by boiling nam pla with lemon grass and kaffir lime leaves and straining

nam prik *(Th)* The general name for Thai relishes made from a mixture of spices, herbs and other flavouring agents such as red chillis, dried shrimps, garlic, trassi, fish sauce, brown sugar, shallots, tamarind, lime juice, peanuts, sour fruits, etc. all processed together

nam prik pao *(Th)* A hot chilli sauce made from roasted red deseeded chillis fried in oil with garlic, onions and shrimp paste, then all processed with brown sugar and tamarind to a thin paste [also called **roasted chilli paste, roasted curry paste**]

nam som *(Th)* Rice vinegar

nan (bread) 1 *(In)* A yeast-raised bread made from white flour and yoghurt, cooked very quickly as a large flat pear shaped bread on the side of a tandoori oven. The shaped dough is moistened so that it sticks to the side of the oven and is hooked off when cooked. Served with Indian meals **2** *(Pe)* bread

nangka *(Id & Ma)* Jackfruit

nangpur suntara *(In)* Ponkan mandarin

nan nan bin *(Bm)* Coriander leaves

nan nan zee *(Bm)* Coriander seeds

nannee *(Ca)* Anise seeds

Nantais *(Fr)* **1** A semi-hard smooth textured, washed-rind cheese made from cows' milk. The rind is light brown and the smooth paste has a strong flavour and smell [also called **Véritable Nantais**] **2** A small almond cake

Nantais duck *see* Nantes duck

nantaise, à la *(Fr)* In the style of Nantes, i.e. garnished, esp. roasts, with peas, potatoes and turnips

Nantes duck One of the two main breeds of French domesticated duck, similar to the Aylesbury and less plump than the Rouen duck.It is usually killed at about 2 kg and provides 4 portions It may be braised or poéléed as well as being roasted

Nantua, à la *(Fr)* In the style of Nantua, i.e. garnished with crayfish tails and truffles, esp. of fish

Nantua, sauce *(En & Fr) fem.* 200 ml of cream per litre of Béchamel sauce, reduced by one third, consistency adjusted with more cream and finished with crayfish butter and a few small cooked and shelled crayfish tails

nap, to To cover a food item, usually a piece of meat or fish on a plate or dish, with sauce

Napfkuchen *(Ge)* A yeast-raised sweet bun with raisins

Napfschnecke *(Ge)* Limpet

Naples biscuit *(USA)* A light dessert or tea biscuit similar to a sponge finger

Naples medlar *see* azarole

Napoléon *(Fr) masc.* Cream slice made with layers of puff pastry

Napoléon biscuits Two biscuits sandwiched together with a filling of jam and dusted with icing sugar

napolitaine, à la *(Fr)* In the Neapolitan style, i.e. garnished with spaghetti in tomato sauce, grated cheese and chopped tomatoes, or a description of spaghetti served with a tomato sauce and grated cheese

nappa cabbage *(USA)* Chinese leaves

napper *(Fr)* To nap

nara nut The seed of a gourd from a spiny shrub *Acanthosicyos horrida* that grows in South West Africa and is about the size of a large melon seed [also called **butternut, butter pit**]

naranja *(Sp)* Orange, the fruit

naranja amargo *(Sp)* Seville orange

narbonnaise, à la *(Fr)* In the style of Narbonne, i.e. garnished with haricot beans, aubergine and tomatoes

nargisi *(In)* A forcemeat of finely ground meat blended with aromatics and herbs, moulded around a hard boiled egg rather like a Scotch egg and baked or fried. Lit. narcissus

narial *(In)* Coconut

narijal *(In)* Young coconut, see kelapa

narm yu *(Ch)* Bean curd cheese

narrow headed softshell turtle A species of turtle from Thailand now endangered due to over exploitation

narrow leaf sage *see* Spanish sage

naseberry *see* sapodilla

nasello *(It)* Hake, the fish

nashi *see* Asian pear

nasi *(Id & Ma)* Rice

nasi goreng *(Id)* Fried rice with chopped pork, ham, onion, garlic, seafood and vegetables. Served with acar, krupek and strips of cooked egg omelette

nasi padang *(Id)* A very hot-flavoured and spicy rice dishes from Padang, Sumatra

nässelkål *(Sw)* Nettle soup made from fresh young nettles cooked like spinach, chopped and added to a seasoned beef stock thickened with a blond roux, the whole finished with chopped chives and served with one poached egg per portion

nasturtium A trailing plant *Tropaeolum majus* with bright red to yellow trumpet shaped flowers and round green leaves. The leaves and flower buds may be used in salads, the flowers as decoration and the young green seeds may be pickled in vinegar and resemble capers [also called **Indian cress, Jesuits' cress**]

Nasturtium officinale *Bot.* Watercress

nasturzio *(It)* Nasturtium

nasu *(Ja)* Japanese aubergine

nata 1 *(Sp)* Cream **2** *(Ph)* A translucent degraded starch, probably a dextran, which appears on the surface of fruits after they are inoculated with a dextranase producing bacteria. It is scraped off, washed and boiled and used as a flavouring for desserts

nata batida *(Sp)* Whipped cream

nata de coco *(Ph)* A nata q.v. produced on coconut flesh

nata de pina *(Ph)* A nata q.v. produced on pineapple flesh

natillas *(Sp)* A soft custard dessert made with ewes' milk and flavoured with cinnamon and lemon

natillas piuranas *see* arequipe

native oyster A smaller variety of oyster *Ostrea edulis* with a smooth flat shell famous for its flavour. Can grow to 12 cm but normally sold somewhat smaller

natsudaidai *(Ja)* A naturally occurring hybrid of *Citrus* spp. relatively unknown outside Japan

Natterkopf *(Ge)* Viper's bugloss

nattmat *(Sw) see* vickning

natur *(Ge)* Plain, not garnished or decorated

naturale *(It)* Plain, not garnished or decorated

nature *(Fr)* Plain as in omelette nature, or a description of tea or coffee without the addition of milk

naturel, au *(Fr)* Plainly cooked without sauces or garnish or served in its plain uncooked state as e.g. huîtres au naturel

Naturschnitzel *(Ge)* Plain veal cutlet or escalope not panéed

natuto *(Ja)* A Japanese fish cake *(see* kamaboko) formed into a cylinder and the surface decorated with red colouring after steaming to give an attractive garnish when sliced

naudanliha *(Fi)* Beef

naudanpaisti *(Fi)* Beefsteak

nauris *(Fi)* Turnip

navaja *(Sp)* Razor shell

navarin *(Fr) masc.* A lamb or mutton stew with onions and potatoes

navarin à la printanière *(Fr) masc.* A lamb or mutton stew with onions, garlic, root vegetables, peas, green beans, herbs and seasoning

navel orange A type of sweet orange q.v. which has a small secondary fruit embedded in the apex of the primary fruit. They are seedless, with deep orange, easily peeled rinds and with a rich sweet flavour. One of the best dessert fruits. They are unsuitable for processing as the juice develops bitterness on standing. The two common varieties are the Washington and the Bahia

navet 1 *(Fr) masc.* Any type of turnip **2** *(En)* Small immature and tender white turnips tinged with red, generally require no peeling

navets, purée de *see* turnip soup

navone *(It)* Swede

navy bean *(USA)* A variety of haricot bean used for making the ubiquitous canned baked beans [also called **American navy bean, Boston bean, great northern bean, pea bean, yankee bean**]

'ncapriata *(It)* A bean purée flavoured with chillis and other spices. From Puglia

ndizi na nyama *(EA)* A beef or mutton stew containing plantains, onions, tomatoes, coconut, spices and seasoning

neapolitan A description of sweets, cakes and ice creams made in multicoloured layers

Neapolitan ice cream *see* cassata

Neapolitan parsley A type of parsley grown for its leaf stalks used in the same way as celery

Neapolitan sauce A tomato sauce from Naples flavoured with onion, basil and parsley

nebu *(In)* Lemon

necares *(Sp)* The blue velvet swimming crab most favoured by Spanish gourmets

neck of beef *(UK) see* clod

neck end of pork A joint of meat from the shoulder of the pig near the neck. Usually boned and rolled

neck end of veal The ribs and muscles behind the shoulder and in front of the best end. Used for stewing and sautéing after boning out

neck fillet *(UK) see* scrag end of lamb

nectar **1** The sugary liquid extracted from flowers by bees which after ingestion is chemically transformed and regurgitated as honey **2** Any thick sweetened fruit juice

nectarine The fruit of a deciduous tree *Prunus persica* var. *nectarina,* with a worldwide distribution. The fruit is a variant of the peach with a smooth shiny orange red skin and white to red firm flesh surrounding a rough central stone. Use as peach

needle A thin steel rod, sharpened at one end and pierced with a flattened hole at the other, used for trussing or larding a bird or piece of meat

needle, to To pierce food singly or repeatedly with single or multiple needles either to make it more absorptive, to introduce microorganisms as e.g. in making blue cheeses, or to inject fluids through hypodermic needles (hollow needles) as in quick curing or tenderizing of meats

needle cut *see* sen giri (Ja)

needlefish A fish similar to the garfish found in the Atlantic and Pacific oceans

neep *(UK) coll.* Scottish for turnip. e.g. bashit neeps, mashed turnips

neeseberry *see* sapodilla

nèfle *(Fr) fem.* Medlar

nèfle d'Amérique *(Fr) fem.* Sapodilla

negi *(Ja)* Asian leek

negi shigi-yaki *(Ja)* Broiled leeks. See Japanese broiled vegetables for method

négresse en chemise *(Fr) fem.* A sweet made of a chocolate ice cream or mousse, heaped up in the centre of a plate with cream over and surrounding it

negretti *(It)* Individual square chocolate coated almond cakes

negritas *(Sp)* Chocolate mousse topped with whipped cream

neguilla *(Sp)* Nigella

neige *(Fr) fem.* White of egg beaten to a froth. Lit. snow, as in oeufs à la neige (= floating islands)

neige de Florence *(Fr) fem.* Very small thin flakes of pasta

neige, monter en *(Fr)* To whisk egg whites to a stiff peak

neiha kinkan *(Ja)* Meiwa kumquat

Nelke *(Ge)* Clove, the spice [also called **Gewürznelke**]

Nelubium nucifera *Bot.* The lotus plant

nenna *(In)* Loofah

neohesperidin The compound responsible for the bitterness of the Seville orange

nep *(Vi)* Uncooked glutinous rice; *see also* xoi

Nepal cardamom A cheap cardamom substitute from a perennial plant *Amomum subulatum* which has ribbed and deep red pods becoming black or brown when dried and resembling a small coconut (to 2.5 cm long). The seeds have a distinctly camphorous flavour

nepaul pepper *(USA)* A chilli pepper similar to cayenne with a sweet pungent flavour

Nepeta cataria *Bot.* Catmint

Nephelium lappaceum *Bot.* Rambutan

Nephelium longana *Bot.* Longan

Nephelium mutabile *Bot.* Pulasan

nero *(It)* Black

neslesuppe *(No)* Nettle soup

nespola *(It)* Medlar

nespola del Giappone *(It)* Loquat, Japanese medlar

Nessel *(Ge)* Nettle

Nesselrode *(Fr)* A description of sweet or savoury dishes containing chestnut purée

Nesselrode pudding A dessert made from chestnut purée, egg yolks, cream and possibly candied fruits, cooked without curdling then frozen in a mould; *see also* pouding Nesselrode for the French version

nesting frying baskets Two wire mesh baskets one slightly smaller than the other, used to make edible bowls by trapping finely shredded or precooked ingredients between the two baskets before deep frying them

netted melon *see* musk melon

nettle A wild plant *Urtica dioica,* which grows in clusters on well manured ground with leaves that sting the exposed skin. The young leaves may be used as spinach or to make soup and lose their stinging capacity on boiling [also called **stinging nettle**]

nettoyer *(Fr)* To clean

Neufchâtel *(Fr)* A soft white creamy cows' milk cheese from Normandy with a rind like Camembert and a salty lactic taste. It is produced in various small shapes and eaten young; *see also* the similar Bondon and Carré de Bray [also called **Coeur, Briquette**]

New Bedford pudding *(USA)* A molasses-sweetened pudding made with cornmeal, flour, milk and eggs

new cheese *see* Caerphilly

new cocoyam *see* tannia

New England boiled dinner *(USA)* A one pot dinner of corned beef or chicken cooked with cabbage, potatoes, carrots, etc. and served with horseradish sauce or mustard

New Mexico chilli A variety of red and hot chilli pepper about 8 cm by 0.5 cm from Mexico and the southern USA. They are used in curries and sauces and are often dried and ground. In New Mexico green chillis are included in this category

New Zealand grapefruit A citrus hybrid with characteristics similar to grapefruit but not directly related. Taken from Shanghai to Australia in 1820. It has a straw coloured coarse flesh which is tender and far more juicy than most grapefruit. The flavour combines that of grapefruit with a trace of lime and lemon. Usually used as a breakfast fruit [also called **poorman orange**]

New Zealand spinach A half-hardy creeping perennial *Tetragonia tetragonioides* or *T. expansa* grown as an annual. The thick triangular leaves are used in the same way as spinach It is at its best eaten young and the water should be changed during the cooking

Newburg, sauce *(En & Fr) fem.* Diced lobster meat cooked in court bouillon or oil and butter, drained, covered with Madeira wine and reduced, seasoned with cayenne pepper, cream and fish stock added, simmered then thickened with egg yolks. The lobster may be flamed with brandy and the pounded coral and creamy parts may be added towards the end

newrex rice A type of long grain rice

newspaper cooking *(UK)* A method of cooking cleaned whole fish by wrapping in 8 or 9 layers of newspaper, thoroughly soaking in water then cooking in a moderate oven until the paper is completely dry (approximately 1 hour for a 1.5 kg fish)

nga *(Th)* Sesame seed

nga choy *(Ch)* Mung bean sprouts

nga hnap *(Bm)* Bummaloe, the fish

nga-man-gyaung *(Bm)* Small fish similar to anchovy prepared like ikan bilis

nga-mote-phyu *(Bm)* Pomfret, the fish

ngan pye ye *(Bm)* Fish sauce similar to nuoc mam

ngan pye ye chet *(Bm)* A strong-flavoured sauce made from ngan pye ye (fish sauce), lemon grass, garlic and chilli powder

ngapi *(Bm)* A dark grey paste made from fermented fish commonly used as a flavouring in Burmese cooking. Lit. rotten fish

ngapi htaung *(Bm)* A pungent dipping paste made from a finely ground mixture of ngapi, onions, garlic and dried shrimps

ngapi nut The seed of a Burmese jungle tree *Pithecolobium lobatum* with a smell similar to ngapi. Used raw or cooked

nga-youk-kuan *(Bm)* Peppercorn

nga yut thee *(Bm)* Chilli pepper

ng he *(Vi)* Turmeric

ng heung fun *(Ch)* Five spice powder

ngun jump fun *(Ch)* Wheat starch

ngun nga choy *(Ch)* Silver sprouts

ngup jern *(Ch)* Duck feet

ngup yu *(Ch)* Cuttlefish

ngu vi huong *(Vi)* Five spice powder

niacinamide *see* vitamin B3

niacin *see* vitamin B3

niban dashi *(Ja) see* dashi

niboshi *(Ja)* Dried and salted fish similar to Bombay duck. Used for flavouring or fried as a snack food or side dish

niçoise, à la *(Fr)* In the style of Nice, i.e. garnished with olives, tomatoes, garlic, French beans, etc.

niçoise, salade *(Fr) see* salade niçoise

niçoise, sauce *(En & Fr) fem.* Vinaigrette with French mustard, diced anchovies and chopped capers, olives and parsley. Served with meat salads and hard boiled eggs

nicotinic acid *see* vitamin B3 and (E)375

nidi *(It)* Tangles of thin pasta. Lit. nests

nido, al *(It)* In a nest, i.e. one ingredient in another

Nieheimer *(Ge)* A soft cheese made with skimmed cows' milk coagulated with lactic acid. The curd is salted and flavoured with caraway seeds, formed into 40 g cheeses, ripened for a short time and wrapped in hop leaves [also called **Hopfenkäse**]

Nieren *(Ge)* Kidneys

Nierenfett *(Ge)* Suet

nigella *(En & It)* The small black seeds of an annual plant *Nigella sativa* related to love-in-a-mist and resembling onion seeds. They have a delicate, slightly peppery flavour and are used in Indian spice mixtures and to flavour bread in India and the Middle East. Not to be confused with black cumin

Nigella sativa *Bot.* Nigella

nigelle *(Fr) fem.* Nigella

niger oil A highly-flavoured oil extracted from the seeds of a plant *Guizotia abyssinica* which grows in Africa and India. It has a pleasant nutty flavour

nigiri *(Ja)* Crude sea salt (sodium chloride)

nigiri-zushi *(Ja)* A hand moulded sushi made in a rugby ball shape with the fillings placed on top after smearing the ball with a little wasabi

nihai-zu *(Ja)* A vinegar based dressing for sunomono consisting of a mixture of rice vinegar, soya sauce and dashi

nihura *(Ne)* Drumstick vegetable

nijuseki *(Ja)* Asian pear

niku-ryori *(Ja)* Meat

nikuzuku *(Ja)* Nutmeg

nimbu *(Ja)* Lemon

nimono *(Ja)* Simmered, e.g. of meats or vegetables in a well-flavoured stock using an otoshi buta. The solids are usually served with a little of the stock

ninfea *(It)* Lotus

Niolo *(Fr)* A soft, washed-rind cheese from Corsica made in a brick shape (600 g) from a mixture of ewes' and goats' milk. It is dry salted and ripened for 15 days

nishin *(Ja)* Herring

nisin *see* (E)234

níspola *(Sp)* Medlar

nitrate of potash *see* saltpetre

nitrites Salts of nitrous acid which are involved in producing the pleasant pink colour of cured meat. They are formed by reduction of nitrates (saltpetre) by bacterial action in the meat or can be included in the curing liquor. Because of the method of production sal prunella contains a little nitrite as impurity

nitrogen The inert gas which forms 79% of air, used to fill sealed packaging so as to displace air and prevent oxidation

nitrous oxide Laughing gas, once used as an anaesthetic, now used as a propellant in aerosol packs of whipped cream

nitsuke *(Ja)* Simmered, in clear liquid or thin sauce

Niva *(Cz & Ru)* A soft blue-veined cheese similar to Roquefort, made from a mixture of ewes' and cows' milk and surface ripened. Contains 47% water, 23% fat and 22 % protein

nixtamal *(Me)* Maize kernels treated with water and lime (15:30:1) until the skins can be rubbed off, washed until white in clean water then used for making masa or masa harina

nizakana *(Ja)* Oily fish such as herring, mackerel, sardine, etc. cleaned and gutted, slashed and placed in a boiling mixture of equal parts of dashi, soya sauce and sake with a little sugar, and simmered until cooked on a very low heat. Served immediatley with some of the cooking liquor

Njeguski *(Bk)* A hard, scalded-curd, pressed ewes' milk cheese made in a drum shape (to 3 kg). It is dry salted and ripened for up to 4 months. Contains 33% water, 33% fat and 31% protein

njure *(Sw)* Kidney

njursauté *(Sw)* Cleaned and blanched calves' or lambs' kidneys diced or sliced and sautéed with mushrooms in butter. Flour, stock, mushroom juices and cream added, seasoned and simmered 10 minutes and finished with Madeira wine

njursoppa *(Sw)* Kidney soup made from diced kidney flesh sweated with chopped onion and parsley, flour added to make a roux and let down with beef stock, boiled 10 minutes and finished with a whisked mixture of eggs and sour cream. Served over toast

nocciola *(It)* **1** Hazelnut **2** Noisette of meat

nocciolina *(It)* Peanut

noce *(It)* **1** Nut, walnut **2** Rump (of meat) **3** Knob (of butter)

noce di acagiu *(It)* Cashew nut

noce di areca *(It)* Betel nut

noce de Brazile *(It)* Brazil nut

noce di coco *(It)* Coconut

noce moscata *(It)* Nutmeg

noce del para *(It)* Brazil nut

nødder *(De)* Nuts

nodino *(It)* Meat chop

nodsolnechnoye maslo *(Ru)* Sunflower oil

noisette *(Fr) fem.* **1** Hazelnut **2** A neatly trimmed and tied boneless piece of meat at least 1.5 cm thick, cut from the eye of the loin of lamb, the filet mignon of beef or a small grenadin of veal, usually surrounded on its edge with a thin layer of fat **3** Knob (of butter)

noisette, beurre *(Fr) masc. see* beurre noisette

noisette, beurre de *(Fr) masc. see* beurre de noisette

noisette cutter A larger version of the Parisienne or Paris cutter used for scooping balls out of raw vegetables and fruit, etc.

noisette, sauce *(Fr) fem.* Hollandaise sauce finished at the last moment with 150 g of beurre de noisette per kg of butter used in making the Hollandaise. Used with poached salmon and trout

noix *(Fr) fem.* **1** Walnut **2** Eye of a chop or cutlet, i.e. a round piece of lean meat cut from across a long circular muscle **3** Knob (of butter) **4** Cushion of veal

noix d'arec *(Fr) fem.* Betel nut

noix du Brésil *(Fr) fem.* Brazil nut

noix de cajou *(Fr) fem.* Cashew nut

noix de coco *(Fr) fem.* Coconut

noix de muscade *(Fr) fem.* Nutmeg

noix pâtissière *(Fr) see* gîte à la noix

noix de pecan *(Fr) fem.* Pecan nut

noix de veau *(Fr) fem.* Cushion of veal

Nøkke *(No) see* Nøkkelost

Nøkkelost *(No)* A hard scalded-curd cheese made in wheels (to 15 kg) from semi-skimmed cows' milk and flavoured with cumin and caraway. It contains 43% water, 20% fat and 33% protein [also called **Nøkke**]

non *(Ru)* A flat onion-flavoured bread from Asiatic Russia, similar to the Indian paratha

non-dairy creamer *see* creamer

nonats *(Fr)* Gobies, Mediterranean fish similar to whitebait

nonna, alla *(It)* In the style of grandmother, i.e. home cooked

nonnati *(It)* Goby, the fish

nonnette *(Fr) fem.* Spiced bun

nonnette de Dijon *(Fr) fem.* Iced gingerbread cake

nonpareille *(Fr) fem.* Hundreds and thousands

nonya cuisine The distinctive cuisine of the Chinese Malaysians and Singaporeans (Straits Chinese), which marries Chinese and Malaysian ingredients

noodle basket A container made by lining a wire mesh frying basket with softened and drained noodles, placing a slightly smaller basket inside to hold the noodles in place and deep frying until the noodles are crisp and adhering together. The noodle basket is used to serve some stir fried Chinese dishes [also called **noodle nest**]

noodle nest *see* noodle basket

noodles A mixture of grain or pulse flour or other starch product with egg and/or water and salt formed into a long flat ribbons of various thicknesses and cross sections. Available in most cuisines. Cooked by boiling, stir frying or deep frying and may be soft or dried. Typical names are listed under egg, rice, cellophane, soba, cha-soba, udon, somen, shiritaki, bean thread, e-fu, miswa, Shanghai and all the Italian pasta types

Noorse kreeft *(Ho)* Dublin bay prawn

nopales *(Sp)* The young leaves of the prickly pear cactus *Opuntia vulgaris* which are always sold skinned, trimmed and chopped and are used after cooking in stews and salads. Common in Mexico and southern USA [also called **nopalitos**]

nopalitos *see* nopales

noques *(Fr) fem.* Gnocchi

ñora A round red chilli from Spain, not particularly hot, almost a sweet pepper. Usually dried

norbixin *see* annatto

nordische Meerbrassen *(Ge)* Bream (1)

Norfolk apple cake *(UK)* A shortcrust pastry case with a pastry top filled with a mixture of stewed apples, orange marmalade and currants [also called **apple cake**]

Norfolk black *(UK)* A breed of turkey similar to the bronze but with a slightly less plump breast

Norfolk dumpling *(UK)* A dumpling made of flour, eggs and milk sometimes with added yeast to cause it to rise before boiling

Norfolk knobs *(UK)* Hollow biscuits made with a sweetened and butter enriched yeast-raised soft dough, kneaded, rolled, docked to remove all air, cut in 3 cm discs, proved until doubled in size and baked at 220°C then completely dried in the oven at 90°C. Eaten with cheese or jam, or the like. Introduced by the Flemish weavers

nori *(Ja)* A marine algae *Porphyra tenera* and *P. umbilicalis* found on the surface of the sea off Japan, China and Korea. It is formed into paper-like sheets, compressed and dried and has a colour ranging from green through purple. It is used in Japan to wrap around rice and various fillings to make sushi. It may also be shredded for use as a condiment or flavouring or may be formed into baskets by deep frying [also called **green laver, purple laver, sea laver**]

noriega *(Sp)* Common skate

nori maki *(Ja) see* maki sushi

normande, à la *(Fr)* In the Normandy style, i.e. descriptive of dishes containing cream, apples, cider, calvados or seafood, or of fish served with sauce normande and garnished with truffles, shrimps and crayfish or mussels

normande, sauce *(Fr) fem.* A fish velouté sauce enriched with cream, egg yolks and butter and served with fish and shellfish [also called **Normandy sauce**]

Normandy sauce *see* sauce Normande

Normanna *(No)* A semi-hard cows' milk cheese made with a lactic starter. The cylindrical cheeses (to 3kg) are ripened for 2 months and develop a sharp flavour and patches of greenish blue colouration in the white paste

North American lobster A larger variety of lobster *Homarus americanus* than the European *Homarus vulgaris*

North Staffordshire black pudding *(UK)* Black pudding flavoured with thyme, allspice, marjoram, pennyroyal and coriander

northern fluke *see* summer flounder

northern prawn *see* deepwater prawn

Norvegia *(No)* A semi-hard cows' milk cheese resembling Gouda. The paste contains small holes

norvégienne, sauce A type of mayonnaise made from pounded hard boiled egg yolk with vinegar and mustard into which oil is beaten to give a thick sauce.

Norway haddock *see* redfish

Norway lobster Dublin bay prawn

Norwegian omelette *see* baked alaska

Norwegian whey cheese *see* mysöst

nosh *(UK) coll.* Food, from the Yiddish for titbits or appetizers

nostrano *(It)* Home grown

noten *(Ho)* Nuts

nötkött *(Sw)* Beef

nötter *(Sw)* Nuts

nøtter *(No)* Nuts

nøtteterte *(No)* Nut cake

nougat *(En & Fr) masc.* Any sweetmeat made with a mixture of nuts and sugar, syrup or honey with possibly white of egg and glacé fruits. The white French version is common in the UK. In Germany it is light brown and smooth

nougatine *(En & Fr) fem.* A confection similar to praline made from a light caramel mixed with crushed almonds or hazelnuts, poured onto a flat sheet and cut into small decorative shapes, or moulded when warm into baskets and the like to contain other foods, or cut in a large circle to be used as a base for a gateau or dessert

nouilles *(Fr) fem.* Pasta, noodles

nouvelle cuisine *(En & Fr) fem.* A fashionable 1980's style of cooking using small amounts of very fresh food artistically arranged on the plate together with purées and reduced cooking liquors without cream, flour, egg or butter thickening, as sauces. Portions and sauces have now reverted to normal although much of the artistic merit has persisted. This type of cuisine tends to arise in history at favourable economic times

nova *(USA)* Cold-smoked salmon. Eaten with cream cheese and bagels

noyau *(Fr) masc.* Kernel, stone or pit of a fruit

noyau, liqueur de 1 *(Fr) fem.* A liqueur flavoured with kernels of cherry and apricot stones used as a flavouring

noz *(Po)* Walnut

nozzle An open ended hollow metal or plastic cone in varying sizes used in the end of a piping bag. The smaller end may be a plain circle, star shaped or other shapes to give different decorative effects

Nudeln *(Au & Ge)* Egg noodles not made with durum wheat flour

Nudelschöberl *(Au)* Noodle pie, served as an accompaniment to meat

nudlar *(Sw)* Dumplings

nuea *(Th)* Beef

nueces *(Sp)* Walnuts, nuts

nueng *(Th)* Steamed

nuez *(Sp)* Walnut, nut

nuez americana *(Sp)* Hickory nut

nuez de anacardo *(Sp)* Cashew nut

nuez de areca *(Sp)* Betel nut

nuez de Brasil *(Sp)* Brazil nut

nuez moscada *(Sp)* Nutmeg

nuez nogal *(Sp)* Walnut

nuka *(Ja)* Rice bran; *see also* nuka-zuke and nukamiso-zuke

nukamiso-zuke *(Ja)* A mixture of rice bran, salt, beer and mustard made into a paste with water. Salted vegetables are immersed in the mixture and left for from 1 to 30 days to mature and become preserved

nuka-zuke *(Ja)* Dry rice bran in which salted vegetables are immersed while they are being preserved

num krathi *(Th)* Coconut

num taan *(Th)* Sugar

num taan peep *(Th)* Palm sugar

num taan sai *(Th)* Sugar

nun's toast *(USA)* Hard boiled eggs in thickened milk, served over toast

nuoc cham *(Vi)* A condiment and dipping sauce made from dried red chillis, garlic and sugar, processed with water, fish sauce and lime juice. Will keep fresh for 3 days in the refrigerator

nuoc cham tuong gung *(Vi)* Tuong sweetened with sugar and processed with ginger and chillis. Served with roast meats

nuoc cot dua *(Vi)* Coconut milk (1)

nuoc dua tuoi *(Vi)* Coconut water

nuoc mam *(Vi & Th)* A thin fish sauce made from the liquid which drains from salted and fermented anchovies or other small fish [also called **nuoc-nam**]

nuoc mau *(Vi)* Caramelized sugar used as a colouring and for glazing grilled food. Sometimes used of brown sugar

nuoc-nam *see* nuoc-mam

nuoc tuong *(Vi)* Soya sauce

nuoc tuong hot *(Vi)* Bean paste

nuo mi zong zi *(Ch)* Lotus leaves stuffed with sweet rice and meat

Nur Hier *(Ge)* A solid black bread only available in Hamburg. Lit. only here

Nürnberger *(Ge) see* Nürnbergerwurst

Nürnbergerwurst *(Ge)* A sausage made from minced lean pork mixed with diced bacon fat, seasoned, flavoured with kirsch, thyme and marjoram, packed into casings and linked. Fried in butter and served with horseradish sauce and sauerkraut [also called **Nürnberger**]

nurse hound *see* larger spotted dogfish

Nuss *(Ge)* Nut

Nuss und Mohnstrudel *(Au)* A walnut and poppy seed strudel with a filling made from ground walnuts, sugar, butter, raisins, cinnamon, lemon zest, rum and biscuit crumbs. Sprinkled with poppy seeds

Nusstorte *(CE)* A speciality cake containing ground almonds or walnuts filled and coated with whipped or butter cream

nut *see* nuts

nut brittle *see* praline

nut cracker An implement used to crack the hard outer shell of nuts using a lever or screw thread action

nut meal Ground nuts used to substitute for some of the flour in biscuit and cake mixes and in fillings

nut oil Any oil expressed or extracted from a nut, usually carrying the particular flavour of the nut

nut of veal *(UK) see* cushion of veal

nutmeg The hard, dried, oval, shelled seed (to 2 cm long) of which the outer covering is mace, from the fruit of an evergreen tree *Myristica fragrans.* It has a warm sweetish aromatic flavour and is used when grated to a fine powder to flavour both sweet and savoury dishes, vegetables and cakes, etc. especially by the Dutch. Also used as a condiment. It is hallucinogenic if taken in large quantities (1 - 3 whole nutmegs) and can be poisonous; *see also* mace

nutmeg melon *see* musk melon

nutria A small rat-like herbivore from Louisiana, USA, considered to be a luxury. Generally stewed in a tomato sauce [also called **nutria rat**]

nutria rat *see* nutria

nutrient Any substance in food which is utilized in the body for energy production, for the growth, reproduction and repair of tissues or for other physiological functions such as providing bulk or a substrate for micro-organism growth in the bowel

nutrition The study of the food requirements of humans and animals in terms of quantity, quality and the content of protein, fat, carbohydrate, fibre, vitamins, mineral, and trace elements, etc.

nutritional labelling In the EU, nutritional labelling is optional, but if given, must contain the energy value and the amounts of protein, carbohydrate and fat. It may also show, sugar, saturated fats, fibre and sodium

nutritional needs The amounts of the various components of food required to be eaten for health and well being; *see also* RDI

nutritionist A person who makes a study of and is an expert in nutrition and nutritional needs. Often works with the kitchens and chefs of hospitals, schools and other institutional food providers

nuts The seeds of plants usually enclosed in a fruit and edible when ripe without further cooking or processing, or some underground seed-like tubers. Most, apart from chestnuts, contain large amounts of protein and oil or fat. The most important in commerce are almonds, brazils, cashews, chestnuts, cobnuts, filberts, macadamia nuts, peanuts, pecans, pine nuts, pistachios and walnuts. The coconut is an unusual hollow nut and there are many others of regional interest

NVQ National vocational qualification. The UK craft training qualification which consists, for cooking, of on-the-job training with agreed competencies but no formal externally marked examinations or time limits for completion. Exact details of certificated competencies should always be examined if this qualification is offered and the reputation of the training school or workplace is important. The question of formal examinations is under consideration

nyana creole *(WA)* A stew from Ghana made from oysters, onions, green sweet peppers, tomatoes, garlic, chilli pepper, oil and seasoning. Served with rice or bread

Nymphaea lotus *Bot.* The Egyptian lotus

nymphes à l'aurore *(Fr) fem.* Frogs' legs poached in white wine and covered with pink chaud-froid sauce and garnished with chopped aspic

nypon *(Sw)* Rose hips

nyponsoppa *(Sw)* Rose hip soup

nyre *(De & No)* Kidney

nyrøket laks *(No)* Smoked salmon

Oo

oak leaf lettuce A loose leaf lettuce with deep bronze serrated leaves and a mild flavour [also called **red oak leaf lettuce, red salad bowl lettuce**]

oak mushroom *see* shiitake mushroom

oast cake *(UK)* A type of thin chemically raised scone containing currants, not baked but fried in oil and butter until golden brown.

oat bran The fibrous outer layer of the whole oat grain separated during the process of making oat flour. Usually mixed with oat germ q.v.

oat flakes *see* porridge oats

oat flour Flour ground from oats. Does not contain much gluten and must be combined with wheat flour to make a bread which rises

oat germ The germ of the oat grain separated during the process of making oat flour. Usually mixed with oat bran to a brown powder which can be used to make a thin porridge or added to other flours for use in bread making

oatcake *(UK)* An unsweetened Scottish and Northern English unleavened bread or biscuit made with oatmeal, water, fat and salt. Some are relatively thick and baked in the oven or on a griddle, others are made like a pancake batter, cooked and sometimes dried

oatmeal Coarsely ground or cracked dehusked oats separated by sieving into various particle sizes, usually fine, medium and coarse, but superfine and pinhead can be found

oats The seeds of a cereal grass *Avena sativa* extensively grown in cool wet climates on poor soils. Once considered a herbal medicine now known to be an excellent source of dietary and soluble fibre. Used extensively in cooking esp. as a breakfast cereal and for cakes, biscuits and scones and for coating herring

Oaxaca *(Me)* A fresh spun-curd cows' milk cheese similar to Provolone

ob cheuy *(Th)* Cinnamon

obed *(Ru)* The main meal of the day taken any time between 13.00 and 17.00 hours

obeni-mikan *(Ja) see* Dancy tangerine

Oberland Leberwurst *(Ge)* A liver sausage made from a boiled skinned and boned shoulder of pork, drained and the pork flesh minced with half its weight of pigs' liver, mixed with diced, boiled and drained pork fat, chopped onion, seasoning and nutmeg, packed into casings, boiled 45 minutes, refreshed and air dried

Obers *(Au) coll.* Whipped cream

oblada *(Sp)* Saddled bream

oblade *(Fr) fem.* Saddled bream

oboro *(Ja)* A chicken and rice dish made from chicken breasts and petit pois, simmered in soya sauce, sake and sugar until cooked, the chicken sliced and arranged with the peas over the top of boiled rice and in turn covered with sliced, reconstituted and cooked shiitake mushroom caps and strips of Japanese omelette

oboro ebi *(Ja)* Shrimp paste

oboru kombu *(Ja)* Shavings from soaked kombu cut across the grain leaving the tough membrane

O'Brien *(USA)* A garnish of crisp fried bacon pieces with fried chopped onions and red and green sweet peppers. Often served with potatoes

Obst *(Ge)* Fruit

Obst Traubensaft *(Ge)* Verjuice

Obstkuchen *(Ge)* Fruit cake

Obstsosse *(Ge)* A sweet and sour fruit sauce such as apple or redcurrant, served with roast meat

Obstsuppe *(Ge)* A puréed fruit soup

Obsttorte *(Ge)* A glazed open mixed fruit tart. The pastry is made with flour, sugar, raw egg yolks, sieved hard boiled egg yolk and melted butter (25:4:2:1:25) kneaded and rested before baking blind at 165°C until slightly brown. The filling is mixed fresh or tinned fruit set in jelly

oca 1 *(It)* Goose **2** *see* occa

oca farcita alla borghese *(It)* Roast goose stuffed with chopped pork, apples, chestnuts and the goose liver

oca di guerra *(It)* Goose poached in water and the flesh cooled in molten goose fat like confit

occa An important white to brown tuber *Oxalis tuberosa* from the south American Andes region. It is said to have gone wild in parts of France. Requires careful cooking to rid it of oxalates [also called **oca, oka**]

occhi di lupo *(It)* Short pasta tubes

occhialone *(It)* Bream (1)

occhiata *(It)* Saddled bream

ocean perch *see* redfish

Ocean pout A seawater fish *Macrozoarces americanus* found in coastal waters off the north east coast of North America. It has a sweet white flesh with few bones [also called **mutton fish**]

ocean quahog A bivalve mollusc *Arctica islandica* similar in appearance to the quahog clam but with a dark shell and flesh which sometimes has a strong taste. Found in the North Atlantic but only fished in the USA where it is used in manufactured clam products

oceanic bonito *see* skipjack tuna

ochazuke *(Ja)* Boiled rice served with crumbled crisp nori and hot green tea poured over it. Eaten as a snack

ochro *see* okra

Ochse *(Ge)* Ox, beef

Ochsenauge *(Ge) coll.* Fried egg. Lit. ox eye

Ochsenbraten *(Ge)* Roast beef

Ochsenfleisch *(Ge)* Beef

Ochsenlende *(Ge)* Fillet of beef

Ochsenmausalat *(Ge)* A salad of sliced cold beef with onions and vinegar

Ochsenniere *(Ge)* Beef kidney

Ochsenschwanz *(Ge)* Oxtail

Ochsenschwanzsuppe *(Ge)* Oxtail soup

Ochsenzunge *(Ge)* Ox tongue

Ocimum basilicum *Bot.* Basil

octadecyl ammonium acetate An anti-caking agent for yeast foods used in bread making. Aids dispersion throughout the mix

octopus An eight armed cephalopod *Octopus vulgaris* found worldwide in warm seawater and usually in the range 30 cm to 1 m long (head and tentacles), although they can reach 3 m. They vary in colour from transparent to blue-black. The tentacles and head flesh of larger animals are usually cooked after pounding to soften the tissues. To cook, put a cork in the head and place in boiling unsalted water and boil for 10 to 20 minutes depending on size, alternatively smaller ones are tender if cooked very quickly e.g by deep frying or stir frying; *see also* warm water octopus, red octopus and curled octopus

Odelsostur *(Ic)* A cows' milk cheese which resembles Emmental

oden *(Ja) see* Tokyo hotchpot

Oderberger *(Au)* A sausage similar to the German Brunswick sausage

odour The property of a substance which causes the sensation of smell. It is caused by molecules from the substance binding to receptors in the nasal cavity which send specific signals to the brain. The six main odour qualities are fruity, flowery, resinous, spicy, foul and burnt; *see also* flavour [also called **smell**]

oeil d'anchois *(Fr) masc.* A raw egg yolk surrounded by chopped onion and anchovies served as a hors d'oeuvre

Oelenberg *(Fr)* A mild-flavoured, cows' milk cheese from Oelenberg monastery, suitable for cooking as well as dessert uses [also called **Trappiste d'Oelenberg**]

Oenothera biennis *Bot.* Evening primrose

oester *(Ho)* Oyster, originally the European flat oyster

oeuf *(Fr) masc.* Egg

oeuf dur *(Fr) masc.* Hard boiled egg

oeuf frit *(Fr) masc.* Fried egg

oeuf mollet *(Fr) masc.* A shelled soft boiled egg

oeuf poché *(Fr) masc.* Poached egg

oeuf à la poêle *(Fr) masc.* Fried egg

oeufs à l'agenaise *(Fr) masc.* Eggs fried in goose fat with aubergines and onions

oeufs à la bénédictine *(Fr) masc.* Poached eggs served on a base of creamed salt cod

oeufs brouillés *(Fr) masc.* Scrambled eggs

oeufs bûcheronés *(Fr) masc.* Beaten eggs poured over slices of ham on toast and baked in the oven

oeufs à la causalade *(Fr) masc.* Fried eggs and bacon

oeufs au chasseur *(Fr) masc.* Scrambled eggs with chicken livers

oeufs en cocotte *see* cocotte, en

oeufs à la coque *(Fr) masc.* Eggs in their shell, generally soft-boiled

oeufs farcis *(Fr) masc.* Stuffed eggs

oeufs florentine Freshly poached eggs laid on a bed of spinach, topped with cheese sauce, gratinated with cheese and breadcrumbs and browned under the grill

oeufs en gelée *(Fr) masc.* Poached eggs in aspic

oeufs en gelée Stendhal *(Fr) masc.* Poached eggs in aspic flecked with ham

oeufs Justine *(Fr) masc.* Hard boiled eggs stuffed with mushrooms in a thick cream sauce, reassembled, panéed and fried in butter

oeufs au lait *(Fr) masc.* Egg custard

oeufs de lump *(Fr)* masc, Lumpfish roe

oeufs en meurettes *(Fr) masc.* Eggs poached in red wine with lardons

oeufs montés (en neige) *(Fr) masc.* Egg whites beaten to a peak

oeufs à la neige *(Fr) masc. see* îles flottantes

oeufs sur le plat *(Fr) masc.* Eggs baked in a shallow, greased, oven-proof dish [also called **shirred eggs**]

oeufs de poisson *(Fr) masc.* Hard fish roe

oeufs Rossini *(Fr) masc.* An elaborate shirred egg dish in which the egg yolks are baked in depressions in a stiffly beaten egg white base

oeufs, sauce aux *(Fr) fem. see* egg sauce

oeufs à la tripe *(Fr) masc.* A Normandy dish of chopped hard boiled eggs with onions

Ofentori *(He)* Mashed potatoes mixed with fried finely diced bacon

offal The edible internal parts of an animal including brains, chitterlings, heart, kidneys, liver, lungs, spleen, sweetbreads (pancreas and thymus gland) and tripe. Tongues, heads, tails, trotters and testicles are sometimes included in this classification

Öffelkes *(Ge)* Small cakes

office knife A small knife with a 10 cm blade shaped like a cook's knife. Used for fine cutting and paring and for testing food to see if it is cooked

ogen melon A variety of cantaloupe melon bred on an Israeli kibbutz. The fruit is about 15 cm across with a bright orange/yellow green ribbed skin and a pale green, sweet, juicy and fragrant flesh

oggy *(UK) coll.* Cornish pasty

ogi giri *(Ja)* A fan cut of circular soft vegetables such as cucumber or thin aubergine made from a quarter of the cylinder cut lengthwise with close evenly spaced cuts to within 1 cm of the end and then pressed flat to make the fan.

ögle yemegi *(Tu)* Lunch

ogonowa *(Pl)* A skinless spicy smoked pork sausage common throughout the country

ogopogo apple dumpling *(Cn)* A rectangular baked apple turnover made from a square of pastry folded over the apple filling, sealed, coated with syrup and baked in the oven. From British Columbia

Ohio pudding *(USA)* Sweet potatoes, carrots and squash, all cooked, mashed and mixed with brown sugar, breadcrumbs and single (light) cream, then baked until firm. Served with an uncooked sweet sauce made from butter, cream, icing sugar and lemon juice

Ohrmuschel *(Ge)* Abalone

ohukas *(Fi)* A small thin crèpe

oie *(Fr) fem.* Goose

oie cendrée *(Fr) fem.* Greylag goose

oie à l'instar de Visé *(Be)* Roast goose in a rich cream and garlic sauce

oie sauvage *(Fr) fem.* Wild goose

oi gimchi *(Ko)* Cucumbers stuffed with radish and pickled with ginger, garlic, chillis and salt.

oignon *(Fr) masc.* Onion

oignon clouté *(Fr) masc. see* onion clouté

oignons, purée d' *(Fr) fem. see* white onion soup

oignons, sauce aux *(Fr) fem. see* onion sauce

oil Fat, which is liquid at ambient temperatures, comprising glycerol esters of a variety of mainly unsaturated, fatty acids. They are extracted from seeds, nuts, fruit, fish and other cold blooded animals. Most natural oils contain complex flavouring compounds some of which are essential oils. q.v. The common seed, nut and fruit oils are almond, coconut, corn, cottonseed, grapeseed, hazelnut, mustard, olive, palm, peanut, poppy seed, rape seed, safflower, sesame, soya, sunflower and walnut. The animal oils are cod liver, halibut liver, whale and snake; *see also* essential oil, essential fatty acids, cold pressing, virgin oil, solvent extraction, hydrogenation

oil pastry A short crust pastry made with oil instead of hard fat. Because of its fragility it is rolled out between sheets of non-stick paper

oil sardine A small fish *Sardinella longiceps* similar to the sardine

oily fish Fish whose flesh contains more than 6% of fat by weight

oiseau *(Fr) masc.* Bird

oiseaux sans têtes *(Fr, Be & Ho)* masc. Beef olives. Lit. birds without heads

oison *(Fr) masc.* Gosling, young goose

oka 1 *(Cn)* A semi-hard cows' milk cheese resembling Port-Salut from the village of Oka near Montreal **2** *see* occa

Okanagan savoury tomato *(Cn)* Tomato stuffed with a filling made from fried chopped onions, flour, milk, breadcrumbs, herbs, spices and grated Cheddar cheese. From British Columbia

okashi *(Ja)* Sweets and desserts, usually served with tea to visitors but not at formal meals

okayu *(Ja)* A rice gruel

okorok v rzhanom teste *(Ru)* Canned or cooked ham with the jelly removed coated with a mixture of dark brown sugar, dry English mustard, ground cloves and cinnamon and baked en croûte at 180°C for 45 minutes per kg. The pastry crust is traditionally a yeast-raised rye flour and water dough flavoured with caraway seeds and molasses and may be eaten

okra The seed pod of a plant *Abelmoschus esculentus,* used when young as a vegetable or when mature, dried and powdered as a flavouring. Generally about 5 to 10 cm long (but see Chinese okra), green, deeply ridged and full of seeds. They liberate a gelatinous material when cooked unless treated with lemon juice and salt prior to frying. In the Middle East great care is taken not to cut the pod if the release of gelatinous material is not wanted. Grown in most hot areas of the world [also called **gumbo, gombo, lady's fingers, ochro, bhindi, bindi, bamiya**]

ok-rong *(Th)* A pale yellow mango considered to be the best dessert variety

okroshka *(Ru)* A cold uncooked soup made from cooked egg yolks mashed with dry English mustard and sour cream and let down with kvas (or flat beer or semi-sweet cider) and mixed with chopped white of egg, cooked potatoes, spring onions and cold roast meat all diced, flavoured with cayenne pepper and garnished with chopped dill

oksebryst *(De)* Brisket of beef

oksefilet *(De)* Fillet steak

oksekjøtt *(No)* Beef

oksekød *(De)* Beef

oksekødsuppe *(De)* Beef broth

oksesteg *(De)* Roast beef

oksestek *(No)* Roast beef

oksetunge *(De)* Ox tongue

Öl *(Ge)* Oil

olallieberry *(USA)* A hybrid of the loganberry and the youngberry, grown in the South Western states of the USA

olandese, all' *(It)* With Hollandaise sauce

olandese, salsa *(It)* Hollandaise sauce

Old Heidelberg A small cows' milk cheese from Illinois, USA, resembling Liederkranz

old wife *see* black bream

Oldbury tart *(UK)* A raised fruit pie from Gloucestershire filled with gooseberries and eaten hot

Olea europa *Bot.* Olive

olean The commercial name for olestra q.v.

oleic acid A monounsaturated fatty acid which when esterified with glycerol produces a low melting point fat which is a constituent of lard making it soft and of many vegetable oils including olive oil

Olenda *(It)* A cheese similar to Edam

óleo *(Po)* Oil, fat

Oléron *(Fr)* A mild creamy ewes' milk cheese from the Ile d'Oléron on the Atlantic coast

olestra An ester of fatty acids and sugar, which behaves in cooking like oil or fat but which is not absorbed by the human body. Thus it can be used as a non-fattening fat. It has been licensed in the USA for cooked snack foods such as crisps. Because of its ability to sequester vitamins A, D, E and K plus carotenes and possibly other nutrients, foods cooked with it carry a health warning. Extra vitamins are required to be added back to the food which uses olestra

olie *(De & Ho)* Oil

oliebollen *(Ho)* Deep fried doughnuts

olijfolie *(Ho)* Olive oil

olijven *(Ho)* Olives

olio *(It)* Oil

olio, all' *(It)* Cooked in oil

olio, sott' *(It)* Preserved in oil

oliva *(It & Sp)* Olive

Olive *(Ge)* Olive

olive *(En & Fr) fem.* The oval fruit of a long-living evergreen tree *Olea europa* which grows in areas with hot summers and cool winters. The fruits, up to 4 cm long, are green when unripe and turn black when fully ripe. Both green and black olives are eaten raw, the green after treatment *(see* green olive). Both kinds may be fermented (lactic fermentation) in a 10% brine. The black are often partially dried and stored in oil. The fully ripe black olives are the source of olive oil

olive all' anconetana *(It)* Large green olives,

pitted, stuffed with meat, ham or chicken and deep fried

olive oil The monounsaturated oil obtained from the ripe fruit of the olive tree. The first cold pressing of the hand picked, destoned and skinned ripe fruit from a single producer is usually the finest flavoured and most expensive and treated with the respect accorded to fine wines. Most olive oil is hot pressed or solvent extracted from the whole fruit. Olive oils are classified according to the method of production and the acidity (free oleic acid) of the oil. The Italian grades are *afiorato*, extra virgin *(extra vergine)*, superfine *(sopraffino)*, fine *(fino)*, virgin *(vergine)*, and finally the pure or 100% pure commercially blended oils. See under each heading for details

oliven *(De & No)* Olives

oliver *(Sw)* Olives

Olivet *(Fr) masc.* A soft cows' milk cheese made in the same way as Camembert in Loiret. It is eaten after 2 days ripening or left to ripen for a month in damp cellars when it develops a stronger flavour due to the growth of mould on its surface. It is then known as Olivet bleu

Olivet bleu *(Fr) masc. see* Olivet

Olivet cendré *(Fr) masc.* As Olivet bleu but the rind dried off in wood ashes

olivette 1 *(Fr) fem.* Plum tomato **2** *(It)* Beef or veal olive, paupiette

olivette cutter A sharp edged scoop shaped implement for cutting out oval shapes (olive-shaped) of potato or other vegetables or fruit.

olivette de vitello *(It)* Stuffed paupiettes of veal, veal olives

olivkovoye maslo *(Ru)* Olive oil

olja *(Sw)* Oil

olje *(No)* Oil

olla *(Sp)* Cooking pot or stew

olla gitana *(Sp)* A vegetable stew

olla podrida *(Sp)* Beef brisket, rolled rib of beef, soaked chick peas or other beans, hard sausage and salt pork or bacon (roughly 8:6:3:2:1) simmered in seasoned water with a BG until tender, aromatic vegetables and any other solid vegetables to hand added and cooked until tender and finished with chopped parsley. A traditional Spanish dish named after the pot in which it is cooked [also called **cocido, puchero**]

olla de San Antón *(Sp)* Pork with rice, beans and fennel. A traditional Andalusian dish for the feast of San Anton on the 19th of January

øllebrød *(De)* A soup made from black bread and a non-alcoholic malt liquor

Olmützer *(Au)* A strong-flavoured cow's milk cheese similar to Handkäse, sometimes flavoured with caraway seeds

Olmützer quargel *(Ge)* Very small (to 20 g) soft low fat cows' milk cheeses with a strong flavour made by coagulating the milk with acid. The paste has no holes and there is no rind save for the soft skin

Olomoucké syrecky *(Cz)* A strong cows' milk cheese similar to Handkäse [also called **Syrecky, Tvarvzky**]

Olomoucky *see* Olomouc

Olympia oyster A small delicate oyster *Ostrea lurida* found off the Pacific coast of the USA

ombre chevalier *(Fr) masc.* Arctic char [also called **omble chevalier**]

ombrina *(It)* Arctic char

omeleta *(Gr)* Omelette

omelet *(De, Ho & USA)* Omelette

omelett *(No & Sw)* Omelette

omeletta *(It)* Omelette

omelette *(En & Fr) fem.* Whole shelled eggs, lightly stirred to mix the white and the yolk, seasoned, then poured into a hot frying or omelette pan greased with butter. As the egg sets, the unset egg is run underneath so that the whole of the egg mixture cooks rapidly with a slightly brown lower surface. The omelette my be turned over to harden the upper surface or folded in half or thirds with or without a precooked filling or topping and served immediately. Generally served slightly runny *(baveuse)* in the centre; *see also* soufflé omelette

omelette landaise *(Fr) fem.* Pine nuts fried gently in the butter before adding the eggs in the usual way

omelette (à la) norvégienne *(Fr) fem.* Baked alaska

omelette pan A heavy based frying pan with rounded sloping sides usually kept exclusively for omelettes and never washed after use but cleaned with absorbent paper. Omelette pans are proved before first use by heating salt in them

omelette soufflée en surprise *(Fr) fem.* Baked alaska

omelette Stéphanie *(Au)* A light and fluffy soufflé omelette from Vienna

omena *(Fi)* Apple

omenahilloke *(Fi)* Compote of apples

omenalumi *(Fi)* Apple snow, the dessert

omenasose *(Fi)* Apple sauce

omnivore A person or animal who will eat anything edible, either of animal or vegetable origin

omul *(Ru) (Siberia)* A relative of the salmon found in lake Baikal

omum *(In)* Ajowan

omuretsu *(Ja)* Omelette

oncom *(Id)* A fermented paste made from peanuts and subsequently fried. Similar to tempe

ong choi *(Ch)* Swamp cabbage

onglet *(Fr) masc.* Thin flank of beef [also called **hampe**]

onigiri *(Ja)* Cooked rice moulded around a sweet or savoury filling and possibly wrapped in sheets of seaweed. The Japanese equivalent of the sandwich

onion A white pungent bulb from a plant *Allium cepa,* originating in Asia but now grown all over the world. It is the most important culinary vegetable and comes in many varieties. See globe, Spanish, Italian red, white, button, silverskin and spring onion. Scallions and spring onions are immature forms of onion harvested before the bulb has swollen

onion clouté *(En)* A peeled onion studded with cloves some of which may hold a piece of bay leaf, most commonly used to flavour the milk used for Béchamel sauce. Lit. nailed onion

onion kachumber *(In)* Sliced onions salted and drained for an hour, mixed with a mixture of equal proportions of water, brown sugar and tamarind then combined with chopped tomato, minced ginger, chopped coriander leaves and chopped and deseeded green chillis

onion and liver sausage *(UK)* A sausage made with minced pigs' liver and lean pork mixed with chopped onions and sliced lights, all fried in lard, mixed with seasoning, nutmeg and marjoram, packed into hog fat ends or bungs, simmered for 30 minutes, refreshed and air dried

onion rings Onions sliced across the root stem axis and the large outer rings battered and deep fried

onion sauce Finely diced onions, boiled or sweated in butter added to Béchamel sauce. Used for roast mutton [also called **sauce aux oignons** (Fr)]

onion seeds Used in India as a spice, often fried with vegetables

Onopordum acanthum *Bot.* Cotton thistle

ontbijt *(Ho)* Breakfast

ontbijtkoek *(Ho)* A spiced breakfast bun, honey cake

opal basil A variety of basil with a heavy perfumed scent

open sandwich A Scandinavian speciality consisting of a single slice of buttered bread on which food and garnishes are arranged in a decorative and artistic manner. Eaten with a knife and fork

opéra, à l' *(Fr)* In the opera style, i.e. garnished with chicken livers, duchesse potatoes and asparagus tips

Opera dell'arte del cucinare *(It)* One of the most influential early Italian cookery books by Bartalomeo Scappi, cook to Pope Pius V, 1566 to 1572 A.D. See Scappi's spice mix

operatårta *(Sw)* A cream filled layer cake

opgerolde koek *(Ho)* A Swiss roll

opisthorchis A species of fluke common in Russia and parts of SEA which is transmitted by carp and other fresh water fish. Causes liver damage

oplet A sea anemone *Anemonia sulcata* q.v., eaten in France [also called **snakelocks**]

opossum A small marsupial from the USA eaten as food in Louisiana [also called **possum**]

Opuntia ficus-indica *Bot.* Prickly pear cactus

orach A hardy annual *Atriplex hortensis* growing to 1.5 m with large indented leaves also available in gold and purple varieties. The young leaves may be used in salads, older leaves are cooked as spinach. Used in France for soups [also called **garden orach, mountain spinach**]

Orange *(Ge)* Orange, the fruit

orange *see* sweet orange

orange amère *(Fr) fem.* Seville orange [also called **orange bigarade**]

orange essence A strong extract of orange zest used as a flavouring

orange flower water An alcoholic extract from Seville orange flowers used as a flavouring

orange marmalade *(De & En)* Marmalade made with oranges

orange passion fruit *see* sweet granadilla

orange pudding *(UK)* A pudding made from basic steamed pudding mixture flavoured with grated orange zest

orange roughy *(NZ)* A seawater fish from the South Pacific with firm white, tasteless flesh, exported as boneless fillets

orange sauce 1 A 20% sugar syrup thickened

with cornflour or arrowroot, cooked out, strained then strained orange juice and blanched julienne of orange zest added **2** *see* bigarade sauce

orangeboom *(Ho)* Orange, the fruit

orata *(It)* Gilt head bream

Orbignija martinana *Bot.* Babassu

Orbignija speciosa *Bot.* Babassu

ördek *(Tu)* Duck

ordinaire *(Fr)* Ordinary, not distinguished in any way or none claimed

Orduña *(Sp)* A hard cylindrical (to 1.5 kg) ewes' milk cheese with no holes, ripened for 30 to 40 days

orecchia marina *(It)* Abalone

orecchia di San Pietro *(It)* Abalone

orecchiette *(It)* Small ear shaped or shell-like pasta shapes

orecchio *(It)* Ear, e.g. of a pig

Oregano *(Ge)* Oregano

oregano A more aromatic and strongly-flavoured herb *Oregano vulgare* than the marjorams. It has a slightly sprawling habit and white or pink flowers. Available dried or fresh and used with meat, sausages, in salads and in many Italian dishes [also called **common marjoram, wild marjoram**]

orégano *(Sp)* Oregano

Oregon grape *(USA)* Barberry

oreille *(Fr) fem.* Ear, esp. of a pig

oreille de mer *(Fr) fem.* Abalone

oreja de mar *(Sp)* Abalone

organ meat *(USA)* Offal

organic food Food which has been grown or reared without synthetic or chemically produced fertilizers, pesticides and herbicides on land which itself has been organic for 2 years

organic labelling In the EU, any food product with organic claims on the label must have been produced according to the rules on organic agricultural production. No irradiated or genetically engineered ingredients can be included

orge *(Fr) fem.* Barley

orge perlé *(Fr)* masc.. Pearl barley

oriental brassicas Brassicas cultivated mainly for their leaves, stems and young flowering shoots. They tend to grow faster and have a wider range of uses than the western varieties

oriental bunching onion A bunching onion developed from the Welsh onion with thickened white leaf bases up to 15 cm long. Usually grown as an annual or biennial plant. All parts are edible and are used at all stages of growth. Often used as a substitute for spring onions

oriental mustard The name of a variety of annual and biennial, often coarse leaved plants *Brassica juncea* with seeds the same colour as white mustard, grown in Japan for use in cooking and as a condiment. The leaves which come in various colours and textures are cooked as a vegetable or eaten raw in salads when young and are becoming popular in the west. The flavour of the leaves becomes stronger as they age [also called **mustard greens**]

oriental sesame oil Sesame seed oil

orientale, à l' *(Fr)* Description of dishes in the Eastern Mediterranean style and the Balkan style, i.e. with tomatoes, garlic and saffron

orientale, sauce *(Fr) fem.* Sauce américaine flavoured with curry powder, reduced and let down with cream

origan *(Fr) masc.* Oregano

origano *(It)* Oregano

Origanum heracleoticum *Bot.* Winter marjoram

Origanum majorana *Bot.* Sweet marjoram, knotted marjoram

Origanum onites *Bot.* Pot marjoram, French marjoram

Origanum vulgare *Bot.* Oregano

Orkney *(UK)* A firm cows' milk cheese from Orkney, resembling Dunlop

Orlando *see* tangelo

orléanaise. à l' *(Fr)* In the style of Orleans, i.e. garnished with braised chicory and potatoes

Orly, fish à l' Fish, usually fillets of white fish marinated in oil and lemon juice, passed through seasoned flour, coated in a frying batter, deep fried at 175°C, drained, garnished with lemon and picked or deep fried parsley and served with separate tomato sauce

ormer The European version of the Pacific abalone q.v., found in the Mediterranean and around the Channel Islands. Up to 10 cm long

ornato *(Sp)* A decorative bread from Estramadura with chorizo sausage inside

oronge *(Fr) fem.* Orange agaric, an edible fungus

Oropesa *(Sp)* A hard ewes' milk cheese from Toledo cast in cylinders (to 2 kg). It has a dark paste containing small holes and a hard thick rind after ripening for 2 to 3 months. Similar to Manchego

oroshigame *(Ja)* A long thin grater resembling a wood rasp or surform with one sharpened edge used for peeling and grating ginger root

orozuz *(Sp)* Liquorice

orphie *(Fr) fem. see* aiguille, the fish (garfish)

orre *(Sw)* Black grouse

ørred *(De)* Trout

ørret *(No)* Trout

Orrys *(Fr)* A hard strong tasting cows' milk cheese from Languedoc-Roussillon made in the shape of a large flat disc. May be used for grating

ort *see* orts

ortaggi *(It)* Vegetables, greens

ortanique *(Ca)* A naturally occurring hybrid of *Citrus* spp. from Jamaica grown in many semi-tropical climates under other names e.g. australique (Aus), mandora (Cy), topaz and tangor (ME) and tambor (Saf), because the original name is a trademark (from ORange, TANgerine unIQUE). The flesh is extremely tender with a very sweet aromatic juice, few if any pips and a thin easily peelable skin. It does not develop off flavours

ortega *(Sp)* Grouse

orthophenyl phenol *see* E231, 2-hydroxy phenol

orthophosphates, ammonium Ammonium dihydrogen and diammonium hydrogen orthophosphate, used as buffers and as yeast food

orthophosphates, calcium Calcium salts of orthophosphoric acid used as firming agents, anti-caking agents and raising agents in cake mixes, baking powder and dessert mixes. E341 covers calcium tetrahydrogen diorthophosphate, calcium hydrogen orthophosphate and tricalcium diorthophosphate

orthophosphates, sodium and potassium Sodium and potassium salts of orthophosphoric acid used as buffers, sequestrants and emulsifiers in dessert mixes, non-dairy creamers, processed cheese and the like. E339 covers sodium dihydrogen-, disodium hydrogen- and trisodium orthophosphate, E340 covers the equivalent potassium salts

orthophosphoric acid E338, an inorganic acid used as a buffering agent, and in the form of its salts (orthophosphates) as buffers, sequestrants, anti-caking agents, emulsifiers and firming agents in cake and dessert mixes, creamers and processed cheese

ortiche *(It)* Nettles

ortie *(Fr) fem.* Nettle

ortie de mer *(Fr) fem.* Sea anemone

ortiga *(Sp)* Nettles

ortolan A small wild bird *Emberiza hortulana* up to 15 cm long, once popular in France, now a protected species due to over-hunting

orts *(UK) coll.* Remains of food left over from a meal often eaten as a snack or at a subsequent meal

oruga *(Sp)* Rocket, the plant

Oryza glaberrima *Bot.* Red rice (2)

Oryza sativa *Bot.* Rice

orzo *(It)* **1** Barley **2** Rice shaped pasta used in soups

orzo perlato *(It)* Pearl barley

os *(Fr) masc.* Bone

os, à l' *(Fr)* Garnished or flavoured with bone marrow

os à moelle *(Fr) masc.* Marrow bone

Osborne pudding *(UK)* A bread and butter pudding made with brown bread and butter spread with marmalade but without dried fruit

oscetrova *see* osyotrina sturgeon

oseille *(Fr) fem.* Sorrel

oshi-zushi *(Ja)* Sushi-meshi rice packed into a square wooden mould, covered with filling which is pressed into place. The mould sides are removed and the rice cake cut into squares

Osmanli kebabi *(Tu)* A kebab of cubed fatty mutton or lamb marinated in vinegar with chopped onions and seasoning and grilled

osmanthus flower A tiny scented white flower from China used as a garnish. They may be fresh, candied or preserved in sweetened alcohol

oss buss *(It) see* osso buco

ossehaas *(Ho)* Fillet of beef

ossestaartsoep *(Ho)* Oxtail soup

ossetra *see* osyotrina sturgeon

ossibuchi *(It) see* osso buco

osso *(It)* Bone

osso bucco *see* ossobuco (2)

ossobuchi *(It) see* ossobuco

ossobuco *(It)* **1** Marrow bone **2** Knuckle or shin of veal cut in steaks across the bone, sautéed on the bone and then simmered with garlic, onions and tomatoes, sprinkled with a mixture of chopped parsley, garlic and grated lemon zest and served with spaghetti or rice, esp. risotto alla Milanese [also called **osso bucco, ossibuchi, ossobuchi, oss buss**]

ost *(De, No & Sw)* Cheese

østers *(De & No)* Oysters

ostia *(It)* Wafer

ostkaka *(Sw)* A type of cheesecake baked in a mould

ostra de Portugal *(Sp)* Portuguese oysters

ostras *(Po & Sp)* Oysters, originally the European flat oyster

ostrica giapponese *(It)* Pacific oyster

ostrica piatta *(It)* European flat oyster

ostrica portoghese *(It)* Portuguese oyster

ostrich A very large flightless bird *Struthio camelus* with a long bare neck, small head and two toed feet. It is now being farmed for its flesh which is very lean, its feathers and its skin which makes good leather. The meat is best with little cooking

ostrich fern *see* fiddlehead fern

ostriche *(It)* Oysters

ostron *(Sw)* Oyster

ostsås *(Sw)* A type of cheese or rarebit sauce made from diced cheddar cheese melted with butter and cream over a low heat, seasoned with salt and cayenne pepper, flavoured with a little dry mustard and diced gherkin and finished with beaten egg. Used with fish.

ostsoppa med åggkulor *(Sw)* Veal or chicken stock, thickened with a blond roux, flavoured with salt, paprika and white wine, boiled and whisked into a frothy but not too thick mixture of double cream, egg yolks and grated cheese. Served hot, garnished with chopped parsley, chervil and åggkulor (egg balls)

osyotrina sturgeon *(Ru)* A somewhat larger sturgeon *Acipenser guldenstädti* than the sevruga. It weighs up to 18 kg and yields about 4 to 7 kg of caviar. The caviar known variously as osciotre, ossetra, osetrova in the west is considered to be one of the finest [also called **white sturgeon**]

ot *(Vi)* Chillis

otaheite apple A very sweet variety of hog plum q.v. from a tree *Spondias dulcis*

otak-otak *(Ma)* A mixture of chopped raw fish, chopped onions, grated coconut, herbs and spices, bound with egg and wrapped in banana leaf or aluminium foil prior to steaming

o'teano *(It)* A Neapolitan vegetable pie made with steamed potatoes, zucchini and aubergines, flavoured with oregano. Lit. saucepan, in local dialect

otochi-buta *(Ja)* A circular piece of wood with a central handle placed directly on simmering food to prevent too much turbulence and the food breaking up

ottarde *(It)* Bustard, the bird

ou *(Ch)* Lotus root

ouaouaron *(USA & Cn)* Bullfrog in the Cajun patois

ouillade *(Fr) masc.* A bean and vegetable soup from Languedoc, well flavoured with garlic

oukha *(Ru)* Fish consommé made with white fish bones, aromatic vegetables, a BG, cloves and fresh dill

oukrop *(Ru)* Dill

ounce A unit of weight equal to one sixteenth of a pound. Still in use in the USA. Abbreviated oz

oursin *(Fr) masc.* Sea urchin

outlaw soup *see* bakonyi betyárleves

ouvrir *(Fr)* To open

ouzhin *(Ru)* Supper, a late evening meal varying in style from zakuski with unlimited vodka to a more Western 3 course meal

ouzo *(Gr)* An aniseed-flavoured liqueur also useful as a culinary flavouring

oval kumquat *see* nagami kumquat

ovalbumin The main protein comprising about 70% of egg white protein. It is partially coagulated by fast beating esp. at higher temperatures and is responsible for the stability of whipped egg white. It starts to coagulate with heat at around 60°C

Ovár *(Hu)* A supple textured, yellow cows' milk cheese with a reddish-brown rind resembling Tilsit

Ovcí Hrudkovy syr *(Cz)* A semi-hard unpressed ewes' milk cheese made in spheres or brick shapes (to 10 kg) and ripened in brine for a week

oven An insulated enclosed space, usually rectangular but may be other shapes, heated by any type of fuel including solar radiation, either directly or indirectly, with a door or opening and in which food is baked, roasted or cooked

oven fry, to *(USA)* To pass meat through seasoned flour, brush with molten fat or oil and bake in the oven on a flat sheet or dish until brown and cooked through

oven-ready A description of foods sold in a state ready to be put in the oven for heating or cooking after removing any unwanted packaging, usually descriptive of chickens, potato chips or prepared meals

oven temperature Oven temperature is set according to four different scales, three quantitative, viz. Fahrenheit °F, Centigrade °C, or gas mark GM, and one qualitative viz. cool <120°C, slow 120°C, moderate 180°C, hot 220°C and very hot 250°C. As a rule of thumb °F are twice °C. This is exactly so at 144 °C, above this °F are slightly less than double and below slightly more than double. For gas mark equivalents see entry under gas mark

oven toast Bread lightly buttered on each side and baked in the oven until golden brown

ovini *(It)* Sheep

ovo *(Po)* Egg

ovoli *(It)* **1** A small ball-shaped Mozzarella cheese sometimes eaten with Parma ham **2** An egg-shaped mushroom with a bright orange cap which is highly prized and eaten raw [also called **Caesar's mushroom, imperial agaric**]

ovos duros *(Po)* Hard boiled eggs

ovos escalados *(Po)* Poached eggs

ovos estrelados *(Po)* Fried eggs

ovos mexidos *(Po)* Scrambled eggs

ovos moles *(Po)* Egg yolks mixed with sugar and used as a sauce or filling or poached in spoonfuls and dusted with cinnamon

ovos quentes *(Po)* Soft boiled eggs

ovotarica *(It)* Botargo

ox 1 A general name for the male or female of common domestic cattle (bulls and cows), esp. a castrated male, the original Anglo Saxon name. The name is still used as a prefix for some items of offal e.g. liver, kidney, heart, etc. **2** *(Sw)* Prefix indicating beef which cannot occur alone, see below

ox brains The brains of older cattle, not now used in the UK because of BSE

ox casings The trade term for casings (cleaned intestines) of cattle, known as runners to 48 mm dia., middles 45 to 55 mm dia. and bungs 75 to 150 mm dia

ox cheek Very gelatinous and tasty meat from the cheek of cattle generally classed as offal. Requires long slow cooking and is used in soups, stews and casseroles

ox kidney The large dark red kidney from mature cattle. It has a core of fat and requires long slow cooking. Often soaked in warm salted water with a little vinegar prior to cooking to reduce the strong flavour. Used in steak and kidney puddings and pies

ox liver The deep brown coloured and strong-flavoured liver from mature cattle. It requires long cooking and is suitable for stewing, braising and for casseroles and coarse patés. The flavour may be reduced by soaking in milk

ox tongue The large tongue of mature cattle weighing about 3 kg. Sold fresh or brined and often cooked, jellied and pressed as a slicing meat and sandwich filling. When cooked it has a rich flavour and may be served hot with mustard sauce or Madeira sauce

oxalic acid The acid found in spinach, rhubarb and some other leaves, stems and tubers which serves to prevent insect attack. It has no known benefit to humans and may be deleterious esp. for certain health conditions

Oxalis tuberosa *Bot.* Occa

oxbringa *(Sw)* Brisket of beef

oxfilé *(Sw)* Fillet of beef

Oxford cheese *(UK)* A cheese intermediate in flavour and texture between Cheddar and Cheshire. May be smoked

Oxford John steak *(UK)* A speciality of Oxfordshire, consisting of leg steaks of lamb including the bone, fried with onion, thyme and parsley and served with a brown gravy flavoured with port and lemon juice

Oxford pudding *(UK)* A pastry tart lined with apricot jam and filled with meringue

Oxford Sauce As Cumberland sauce but finished with chopped blanched orange and lemon zest instead of julienne of orange

Oxford sausages *(UK)* Sausages made from minced pork, minced pork fat and fresh white breadcrumbs (2:1:1), mixed, seasoned and flavoured with sage, winter savory and marjoram and grated lemon zest, moistened with water and may be packed into casings and linked or left skinless. Fried and served hot. A 19th century version substituted veal for half the pork, suet for pork fat and reduced the breadcrumbs by half

oxidation In cooking, the reaction of a food with the oxygen of the air which usually produces off flavours. Oxidation reactions are often promoted by light and high temperature increases the rate of reaction (approximate doubling for every 10°C rise). Anti-oxidants are used to inhibit the reaction

oxkött *(Sw)* Beef

oxstek *(Sw)* Roast beef

oxsvans *(Sw)* Oxtail

oxsvanssoppa *(Sw)* Oxtail soup

oxtail The tails of beef cattle usually weighing about 1.4 kg when skinned. There is a fair amount of lean meat with a good meaty flavour and a thin layer of firm white fat. Usually braised or made into soup

oxtail soup *see* thick or clear oxtail soup

oxtunga *(Sw)* Ox tongue

oxygen The gas which is necessary for most animal life and which forms about 20% of the air. At high temperatures it causes oxidation and deterioration of food. The rate of oxidation doubles for every 10°C increase in temperature. Occasionally used as a packaging gas

oxymel A mixture of 4 parts honey to 1 part vinegar which may be used as a marinade or, after diluting with water, as a drink

oxystearin A sequestering agent and inhibitor of fat crystallization used in salad creams and similar foodstuffs

oyakonabe *(Ja)* A small round frying pan

oyster **1** A seawater bivalve *Ostrea* spp., *Crassostrea* spp. and *Saccostrea commercialis,* once the food of the poor but now a gourmet delicacy. May be wild or farmed, sold alive or in dried or other preserved form and since they are static feeders are influenced by sea conditions and hence known by the name of a district, e.g. Whitstable and Colchester in the UK, Galway in Ireland, Belon and Armoricaine in France. Not at their best when spawning hence traditionally eaten in the Northern Hemisphere in months with an 'R' in them, i.e. September to April; *see also* native, Pacific, Portuguese, American, Indian, Australian, South American and Olympia oyster **2** A prized small muscle in poultry which sits in an indentation in the carcase just in front of where the thigh bone is attached

oyster bacon A round cut of bacon from the end of the back containing a fair amount of fat

oyster crab A very small (1 cm) crab which lives in the shells of live oysters. May be eaten raw or fried [also called **pea crab**]

oyster fungus *see* oyster mushroom

oyster meat *see* oyster (2)

oyster mushroom An edible wild mushroom *Pleurotus ostreatus* with a short stalk on one side of the smooth bare oyster-like cap which is up to 15 cm in dia. and blue-grey when young. It grows on the trunks of deciduous trees and has a rather tough, juicy flesh with no smell but a slightly fishy flavour. Now cultivated [also called **oyster fungus, abalone mushroom, tree oyster mushroom**]

oyster plant *see* salsify

oyster sauce **1** *(Ch)* A condiment and flavouring sauce consisting of soya sauce combined with dried oysters. It has a strong shellfish flavour **2** See sauce aux huîtres **3** *(UK)* A Béchamel sauce with cream, a little cayenne pepper, oyster juice and poached and bearded oysters

oyster sausage *(UK)* A traditional sausage made when oysters were the food of the poor. Made from pounded veal, chopped or minced oysters and breadcrumbs soaked in oyster liquor, seasoned and bound with egg before being packed in casings. Not made commercially nowadays but almost certain to be taken up by expensive restaurants specializing in traditional English cooking

oyster of veal A prime roasting cut of veal from the forequarter, generally boned and rolled

oysters Bienville *(USA)* Oysters on the half shell covered with a Béchamel sauce containing chopped and sweated green sweet peppers and onion, gratinated with breadcrumbs and cheese and grilled.

oysters Rockefeller *(USA)* A New Orleans speciality of oysters topped with a Pernod-flavoured savoury breadcrumb mixture and baked quickly on the half shell

oz Abbreviation for ounce

Pp

pa amb olli *(Sp)* A snack from Catalonia made from a thick slice of crusty bread rubbed with a vine-ripened cut tomato, sprinkled with good oil and salted

paahdeleipää *(Fi)* Toast

paahdepaisti *(Fi)* Roast beef

paak cheong *(Ch)* White pomfret, the fish.

paan *(In)* A breath freshener taken after a meal usually consisting of a mixture of aromatic seeds, often garishly coloured; *see also* pan (2)

paayap *(Ph)* Long bean

PABA This constituent of sunscreen agents appears to maintain hair colour and skin conditions in rodents, but its function in humans is obscure. It is found in whole grains and wheat germ and is an essential growth factor for many microorganisms [also called **para-amino-benzoic acid**]

pabellon caroqueno *(Ve)* A national dish consisting of a mixture of steak, rice, black beans and plantains or bananas topped with a fried egg

pa boeuk *(La)* A very large fish (to 2 m) caught in the Mekong river. Its roe alone can weigh up to 10 kg. The flesh may be eaten fresh, but because of the amount is usually preserved by fermentation

pabulum An archaic term for food of any kind esp. of animals and plants

paca *(SA)* An edible rodent from the north of South America with a white spotted brown coat

pachadi *(In)* Chopped vegetables bound with yoghurt and flavoured with mustard seeds

Pachyrrhizus erosus *Bot.* The jacama plant

Pacific bonito *see* skipjack tuna

Pacific cod A relative *Gadus macrocephalus* of the Atlantic cod with a brown to grey back weighing 2 to 4 kg and up to 60 cm long. Treat as cod

Pacific dogfish *see* rock salmon

Pacific hake A variety of hake caught in the Pacific ocean mainly used for processed fish products

Pacific halibut The halibut *Hippoglossus stenolepsis* found in the northern Pacific ocean

Pacific mackerel The mackerel *Scomber japonicus* found off Japan and California

Pacific oyster A variety of disease-resistant oyster *Crassostrea gigas* used to restock many European farmed oyster beds wiped out by disease in the 1970's. Has a craggier and deeper shell than the Portuguese oyster and can grow to 30 cm but normally sold at 6 to 12 cm [also called **Japanese oyster**]

Pacific thread herring A relative of the thread herring found off the west coast of North America

packet *(Ir)* A black pudding from Limerick similar to Drisheen. Eaten with tripe. See Drisheen for more details

Pacrasma excelsa *Bot.* Bitter ash from which quassia is extracted

pad *(Th)* Stir fried

paddestoel *(Ho)* Mushroom

paddy rice Freshly harvested rice still with its husk

paddy straw mushroom *see* straw mushroom

pa-de-gaw-gyi *(Bm)* Greater galangal

padeira, à *(Po)* Baked in an oven proof dish in a hot oven. From padeiro, baker

padek *(La)* A fish paste made by salting fish or fermenting it with rice bran

padella *(It)* Frying pan

padrushka *(Pl)* Hamburg parsley

paella A savoury mixture of rice, vegetables, chicken and shellfish cooked in a large pan called a paellera in the same way as risotto but with a less starch-releasing rice such as Valencia. Shellfish are normally added about 5 to 10 minutes after adding stock so that they are not overcooked and paella is finished with liquidized garlic and decorated before service from the pan

paella de campiña *(Sp)* Paella with ham, bacon, chicken and sausage

paella powder A colouring agent, usually synthetic tartrazine, used to colour paellas instead of saffron. Not recommended

paella Valenciana *(Sp)* Paella with chicken, shellfish, peas, beans and artichokes

paellera *(Sp)* A wide, round, shallow, 3 to 5 cm

deep pan with 2 handles. The diameter, which can be up to a metre, depends upon the number of servings required. Used for cooking paella which is served direct from the pan

pære *(De & No)* Pear

paesana, alla *(It)* In country style, i.e with bacon, mushrooms and tomatoes, esp. of pasta

paeta *(It)* Turkey

pagello *(It)* Sea bream, the fish [also called **fragolino**]

pageot rouge *(Fr)* Pandora, the fish

Paglia *(He)* A soft cheese similar to Gorgonzola from Ticino

paglia e fieno *(It)* Thin green and yellow dried noodles sold mixed in the packet. Lit. straw and hay

pagnotta *(It)* A round loaf of bread

pagnotta Santa Chiara *(It)* A potato bread from Naples filled with tomatoes, anchovies and herbs

Pago *(Au)* A ewes' milk cheese

pagre *(Fr) masc.* Sea bream

pagro comune *(It)* Sea bream

paguro *(It)* Hermit crab

pahari mirich *(In)* Sweet peppers

pähkinäkakku *(Fi)* A rich cake containing ground walnuts and smothered in whipped cream

pähkinäpaisti *(Fi)* A vegetarian patty made from ground nuts and cream

pai chi *(Ch) see* dang gui

paillard 1 *(Fr) masc.* A thin escalope or slice of meat or fish **2** *(It)* Grilled sirloin steak

paillard di vitelle A grilled veal cutlet served with lemon juice

paillettes *(Fr) fem.* Thin slivers or rings, e.g. of potatoes, pastry, onions, etc. Lit. spangles, flakes

paillettes dorées *(Fr) fem.* Cheese straws

paillettes d'oignons frits *(Fr) fem.* Fried onion rings

paimi *see* conkies

pain *(Fr) masc.* Bread, also used for the long 400 g baguette type of loaf

pain bis *(Fr) masc.* Wholemeal or brown bread

pain blanc *(Fr) masc.* White bread

pain à cacheter *(Fr) masc.* Wafer

pain au chocolat *(Fr) masc.* A rectangular shaped croissant-type pastry with chocolate in the centre. Eaten warm

pain complet *(Fr) masc.* Wholemeal, wholewheat or granary bread

pain doré *(Fr) masc. see* pain perdu

pain entier *(Fr) masc.* Wholemeal bread

pain épi *(Fr) masc.* A large French bread stick, shaped like an ear of corn, weighing about 250 g

pain d'épices *(Fr) masc.* Well spiced gingerbread

pain fig banane *(Ca)* A speciality of St Lucia consisting of banana bread flavoured with cinnamon, nutmeg, ginger and cloves eaten like cake [also called **Caribbean banana cake**]

pain de Gênes *(Fr) masc.* Genoa cake

pain à la grecque *(Be)* Small cakes made from a rich cake mixture

pain grillé *(Fr) masc.* Toast

pain intégral *(Fr) masc.* Wholemeal bread

pain de la Mecque *(Fr) masc.* A cream filled puff pastry

pain de ménage *(Fr) masc.* Home made bread

pain de mie *(Fr) masc.* Soft crusted English-style white bread for sandwiches

pain noir *(Fr) masc.* Wholemeal bread or brown bread

pain parisien A long loaf of bread rather like a large baguette

pain des paysans *(Fr) masc.* Chestnut flour

pain perdu *(Fr) masc.* Stale bread slices dipped in an egg and milk mixture, sweetened and flavoured with vanilla for the dessert version, then fried in (clarified) butter until crisp and golden [also called **pain doré, French toast** (USA)]

pain pistolet *(Fr) masc. see* pistolet

pain rôti *(Fr) masc.* Toast

pain de seigle *(Fr) masc.* Rye bread

pain de son *(Fr) masc.* Wholemeal bread

pain au sucre *(Cn)* masc. A French Canadian speciality of bread toasted on one side, the untoasted side covered with maple sugar, grilled until the sugar melts then served with cream

pain trouvé *(Be)* masc. Pain perdu topped

with a mixture of Béchamel sauce and chopped ham and sprinkled with grated Parmesan cheese

pain de veau *(Be)* masc. A meat loaf made with veal

pain de volaille *(Fr) masc.* A finely processed chicken meat loaf or mould

Painswick chop *(UK)* A bacon chop from the West country often baked in the oven with cider, brown sugar and mustard

paio *(Po)* A thick garlic-flavoured pork sausage

paistettu *(Fi)* Roasted, fried

paistettu kana *(Fi)* Fried chicken

paistettut sienet *(Fi)* Fried mushrooms

paisti *(Fi)* Steak, roast (as of meat)

paistinperunat *(Fi)* Fried potatoes

paj *(Sw)* Pie

pak *(Th)* Vegetables

pak bung *(Th)* Swamp cabbage

pak chai *(Ch)* Pak choy

pak chee *(Th)* Coriander seed and leaves

pak chee lao *(Th)* Dill seed

pak chi met *(Th)* Coriander

pak choi *see* pak choy

pak choy A loose leaved Chinese brassica *Brassica rapa* var. *chinensis* with white leaf stems and dark, succulent mild leaves, very fast growing and cooked when young with at most 12 opened leaves [also called **pak choi, pak soi, bok choy, bok choi, celery cabbage**]

pak hom ho *(Vi)* Mint

pak kard hom *(Th)* Lettuce

pak kok *(Ch)* Star anise

pakode *(In)* Fritters

pakoras *(In)* Bite sized fritters made with a batter containing besan or chickpea flour. Deep fried and served hot with chutney. Usually vegetables, but can be made with shellfish, fish, cooked rice, cheese or meat. The north Indian equivalent of bhajias

paksiw *(Ph)* Large pieces of fish simmered until cooked in a clay pot with vinegar, salt and possibly ginger and sugar. Allowed to cool in the liquid and served cold with some of the pickling liquid

pak soi *see* pak choy

pala *(Id)* Nutmeg

palabok *(Ph)* Garnishes, usually to give added flavour, such as dried fish flakes, pork crackling, chopped scallions, dried shrimps, chopped hard boiled eggs, etc.

palacinky *(Cz)* Light batter pancakes filled with grated chocolate, apricot jam or a sweetened mixture of cream cheese and sultanas

palacsinta *(Hu)* Small pancake, crêpe

pålæg *(De)* The filling on open topped Danish sandwiches

palak *(In)* Spinach

palamita *(It)* Bonito, the fish

Palatschinken *(Au)* Thin pancakes filled with marmalade, chocolate, chopped nuts and/or sweetened cheese

palayok *(Ph)* A terracotta cooking pot similar to the Indian chatty

paleron *(Fr) masc.* A cut of beef including part of the chuck and clod used for stewing or braising; parts are sometimes marinated in the piece and roasted

Palestine, crème *(Fr) fem.* Artichoke soup finished with cream, milk or thin Béchamel sauce [also called **cream of artichoke soup**]

Palestine sweet lime *see* sweet lime

palette *(Fr) fem.* Blade of pork or lamb from the shoulder

palette knife A 2 to 3 cm wide, flexible handled blade with a round blunt end and not sharpened. Used for manipulating food, e.g. fish fillets, and for smoothing icings and toppings

palm An important family *Palmae* of plants of which there are over 4000 species, generally tropical or sub-tropical and mostly trees with the characteristic tuft of fan like leaves, although a few are climbers, e.g. the rattan palm. They supply edible vegetable matter, fruit, nuts, oil and sap as well as building materials

palm butter *see* palm kernel oil

palm cabbage The growing tip of the coconut palm considered to be a delicacy and eaten as a vegetable in tropical Asia

palm heart *see* heart of palm

palm kernel oil A white oil extracted from the kernels of the fruits of the oil palm (*Elaeis guineensis*) mainly used for margarine manufacture; *see also* palm oil [also called **palm butter**]

palm nut The fruit of the palmyra palm q.v. about 9 cm long and containing 3 kernels in each.

The immature kernels are used in desserts and have a taste of coconut. The mature kernels are a source of palm kernel oil but may be germinated to give an enlarged fleshy embryo used as a vegetable [also called **palmyra fruit**]

palm oil The oil extracted from the fruits of the oil palm *Elaeis guineensis* which originated in Africa but is now grown in Malaysia, Indonesia and other high rainfall tropical areas. About half the African production is used as cooking oil, the remainder is used for soap and industrial purposes and after treatment for margarine. The oil sets to a soft solid after extraction. It contains 40% saturated, 40% monounsaturated and 10% polyunsaturated fat; *see also* palm kernel oil

palm sugar A sugary substance obtained by boiling down the sap from the palmyra palm or sugar palm [also called **jaggery, java sugar, coconut sugar**]

palm tree *see* palm

palma *(It & Sp)* Palm

Palme *(Ge)* Palm

palme *(Fr) fem.* Palm

palmetto A palm tree *Sabal palmetto* which grows in the south east of the USA and in Mexico. Its main use is for brushes but the growing tips are boiled as heart of palm and eaten hot as a vegetable or cold as a salad [also called **cabbage palm**]

palmiers *(En & Fr) masc.* A square of sugared puff pastry rolled like a scroll from opposite sides to meet in the middle, egg washed, cut into 2 cm slices, one side sugared and baked sugar side down for about 10 min. in a hot oven, turned and sugar caramelized

palmitic acid A saturated fatty acid found in its glycerol ester form in beef and lamb fat and other hard fats

palmito *(Po & Sp)* Heart of palm

palmyra fruit *see* palm nut

palmyra palm A palm tree *Borassus flabellifer* from India, Africa and Asia. Sap is extracted by tapping the unopened male or female flower stalks and immediately boiled down to produce palm sugar or fermented to toddy. Alternatively the fruits (palm nuts) are allowed to grow. Their sap is used as a drink, the soft kernel is also eaten and the germinated nuts produce an enlarged fleshy embryo which is used as a vegetable [also called **Borassus palm**]

paloise, sauce *(En & Fr) fem.* As Hollandaise sauce but with chopped mint in the initial reduction and finished after straining with chopped fresh mint

paloma *(Sp)* Pigeon

palomba *(It)* Wood pigeon

palombacce *(It)* Wood pigeon

palombe *(Fr) fem.* Woodpigeon

palombo *(It)* **1** Smooth hound, the fish **2** Ring dove

palometa *(Sp)* Pomfret, the fish

palourde *(Fr) fem.* Cockle, clam, carpet shell or similar bivalve mollusc

palwal *(In) see* tindori

pámpano *(Sp)* Vine leaf

Pampelmuse *(Ge)* Grapefruit

pamplemousse *(Fr) masc.* Grapefruit or pummelo

pan 1 A metal, glass or ceramic vessel usually deep and round but may be other shapes, fitted with one long handle or two small handles **2** *(It & Sp)* Bread, cake **3** *(In)* A betel leaf folded into a parcel containing a betel nut, spices and a little lime paste. Chewed to extract the flavours and considered by some to be an aid to digestion to be taken after a meal. The lime provides much needed calcium. The fibrous mass left after all the flavour has been extracted is not swallowed. Sometimes spelled paan but this refers to another mix

pan, to *(USA)* To cook vegetables without water in a tightly closed pan with a little fat.

pan bagnat *(Fr) masc.* A sandwich from Provence containing salade niçoise ingredients. A hollowed out loaf or roll is often used as the bread base

pan blanco *(Sp)* White bread

pan broil, to *(USA)* To cook meat in a very hot iron (non-stick) frying pan with no fat by rapidly browning all sides to seal in the juices

pan dolce *(It)* A tall octagonal sweet yeast-raised and enriched bread from Verona. Served at Christmas [also called **pandoro**]

pan dressed *(USA)* Description of gutted and scaled fish with the head and fins removed ready for baking, grilling or frying

pan drippings *(USA)* Residues in the pan left after roasting or frying meat or vegetables used as a basis for gravy

pan de frizze *(It)* A bread containing pork scratchings

pan fry, to To cook in a frying pan with a small quantity of fat or oil

pan di Genova *(It)* Genoa cake

pan haggerty *(UK)* A Northern dish made in a wide shallow pan with heated butter and oil, layered with sliced raw waxy potatoes, onions and grated Cheddar or Lancashire cheese and seasoning, topped with cheese and cooked in the oven on a low heat for 30 minutes uncovered, then grilled to brown the top. Served from the pan

pan moreno *(Sp)* Brown bread

pan di natale *(It)* A soft yeast-raised enriched dough mixed with a variety of candied fuits, nuts, raisins, pine nuts, etc. and formed into various shapes. Lit. Christmas bread

pan d'oro *(It)* A round sweet yeasted bun

pan pepato *(It)* A nutmeg and pepper flavoured cake containing raisins, almonds, hazelnuts and chocolate

pan di Spagna *(It)* A liqueur soaked sponge cake filled with cream or jam

panaché(e) *(Fr)* **1** A term descriptive of multicoloured mixtures or layered foods, desserts, salads, ice creams, etc. **2** Garnished with a mixture of flageolet and French beans

panada 1 *(Sp & En)* A stiff pounded and boiled mixture of stale bread and water with possibly oil, used for thickening and binding **2** *(En & Fr)* A double thickness Béchamel sauce used as a binding agent **3** *(It)* A broth thickened with breadcrumbs and egg and finished with grated Parmesan cheese

panade *(Fr) fem.* **1** As panada (Sp) **2** A peasant soup based on water, stock or milk and thickened with bread

panafracchi *(It) see* ciambelle

panais *(Fr) masc.* Parsnip

Panama orange *see* calamondin

panarda *(It)* A celebratory feast of 20 or more dishes traditional in the Abruzzo region

panato *(It)* Panéed, breaded

pancake A thin flat cake cooked on both sides with oil or fat in a pancake or frying pan, made from a thin pouring batter of milk, egg, flour and possibly sugar, normally served with a sweet or savoury filling or sauce. In the UK served with lemon juice and sugar on Shrove Tuesday.

pancake pan A pan similar to an omelette pan reserved for pancakes and crêpes

pancake roll *see* spring roll

pancetta *(It)* Belly of pork cured with salt and spices, rolled up and eaten either raw in thin slices or cooked in thicker slices [also called **panchetta**]

panchetta *(It) see* pancetta

panch foran *(In)* A Bengali spice mix consisting of cumin, nigella, aniseed, fenugreek and brown mustard seeds ground to a well mixed powder. Used to flavour oils as well as in made up dishes [also called **panchphoran, panch poran**]

panchphoran *(In) see* panch foran

panchporan *(In) see* panch foran

pancit canton *(Ph)* E-fu noodles made with duck eggs

pancotto *(It)* A soup thickened with stale bread, containing seasonal vegetables and finished with oil and cheese [also called **pappa**]

pancreas An abdominal gland which supplies insulin to the blood and digestive juices to the small intestine. Together with the thymus it comprises the sweetbreads

pancreatin A protease produced by various microorganisms and used to convert proteins into emulsifying agents

Pandanus amaryllifolius *Bot.* The more aromatically flavoured variety of screwpine

pandanus leaf The leaf of the screwpine used both for its colouring and flavour

Pandanus odoratissimus *Bot.* Screwpine

pandekager *(De)* Pancakes

pandora A pink seawater fish *Pagellus erythrinus* similar in size and appearance to the sea bream

pandorato *(It)* Pain perdu, French toast, often with Mozzarella cheese and anchovies spread on the bread before egging

pandoro *(It) see* pan dolce

pandowdy *(USA)* A type of apple pie made from stewed sliced apples layered in an ovenproof dish with butter, brown sugar and spice, moistened with cider, covered with biscuit dough then baked until golden brown

pane *(It)* Bread

pané, to An anglicization of the French paner, meaning to coat foods with seasoned flour, beaten egg and breadcrumbs in that order, prior to frying them

pane bianco *(It)* White bread

pane bigio *(It)* Brown bread

pane bolognese *(It)* A sweet bread made from cornmeal and containing candied fruit and nuts

pane carasau *(It)* A very thin bread from Sardinia

pane di frumento *(It)* Whole wheat bread

pane grattugiato *(It) see* pangrattato

pane scuro *(It)* Dark bread

pane de segala *(It)* Rye bread

pane tostato *(It)* Toast

panée à l'anglaise *(Fr)* Panéed

paneer *(In)* Curds made from boiling milk acidified with lemon juice. Used for making desserts and as an accompaniment to vegetarian meals. May be fried [also called **panir, chenna, chhena, channa**]

paneermeel *(Ho)* Breadcrumbs

panela *(SA)* A hard dark sugar from Colombia formed into loaves

panelle *(It)* Fritters made in Sardinia from chick pea flour

paner *(Fr)* To pané

panetière *(Fr)* A baked pastry case filled with precooked food or a small precooked bird and served hot

panettone *see* pannetone

Panfisch *(Ge)* A mixture of cooked minced fish and onions served on mashed potatoes

panforte *(It)* A rich cake from Sienna containing glacé fruits and nuts

panggang *(Id)* Spit roasted. The food is usually marinated

pang kao niew *(Th)* Glutinous rice flour

pang khao chao *(Th)* Rice flour

pang khao phod *(Th)* Cornflour

pang mun *(Th)* Tapioca starch

pangrattato *(It)* Dried stale bread reduced to fine breadcrumbs

pang tao yai mom *(Th)* Arrowroot

pang xie *(Ch)* Crab

paniccia *(It) see* panissa

panicia *(It)* A barley soup from the Dolomite region

Panicum miliaceum *Bot.* Common millet

panini imbottini *(It)* Sandwiches

panino *(It)* Bread roll

panir *(In) see* paneer

paniscia *(It)* Rice, beans and sausage cooked in broth

panissa *(It)* A dough made from boiled chick pea flour and finely chopped and sweated onions, sliced and fried

panitsa *(Ph)* Palm sugar

panko *(Ja)* Large sized toasted dry breadcrumbs used for coating fried foods

panna *(It)* Cream

panna cotta *(It)* **1** A type of crème caramel **2** Coffee-flavoured cream custard

panna fermentata *(It)* Sour cream

panna montata *(It)* Whipped cream, usually sweetened

Pannarone *(It)* A rich, soft, quick ripening cheese from south Lombardy, made from whole milk, the curds not salted but gathered in cheese cloths, drained, kept at 28°C for 7 days and ripened for a further 8 to 19 days at a lower temperature. It has a thin yellow rind and a white to fawn, mild and slightly bitter paste with lots of small holes [also called **Pannerone**]

pannbiff med lök *(Sw)* Chopped beef steak and onions

pannekoeken *(Ho)* Pancakes

pannequet *(Fr)* A small crêpe filled with a sweet or savoury mixture and folded into quarters

Pannerone *(It) see* Pannarone

pannetone *(It)* A tall yeast-raised cake from Milan containing nuts, spices, sultanas and candied peel often associated with Christmas and New Year's eve [also called **panettone**]

pannkakor *(Sw)* Pancakes

pannkoogid A large soufflé type of pancake from Estonia made from a flour, egg, milk and sugar batter (4:4:8:1) flavoured with vanilla essence. The egg whites are reserved whilst the batter matures for 12 hours, beaten to a stiff peak and folded into the batter just before it is fried in 100 ml lots. Filled with a thickened soft fruit compote

pannocchia *(It)* Mantis shrimp

Pannonia *(Hu)* A hard cows' milk cheese similar to Gruyère and made in cylinders (to 40 kg). The paste has a few holes and a pleasant flavour. Contains 38% water, 31% fat and 30% protein

pannukakku *(Fi)* An oven baked sweet pancake

panocha *(Me) see* piloncillo

panoche *(Me) see* piloncillo

pansit *(Ph)* Noodles fried with various ingredients such as garlic, onions, vegetables, shrimps, meat, etc.

pansoti *(It) see* pansotti

pansotti *(It)* Triangular shaped ravioli filled with meat, offal or cheese [also called **pansoti, panzerotti**]

pansy A plant *Viola tricolor* with edible flowers used for decoration and to add a subtle flavour to salads

panthe kaukswe *(Bu)* A mild chicken curry flavoured with onions, garlic, chillis, coconut milk and turmeric, served with noodles, hard boiled eggs, raw onion slices, lemon quarters and prawn crackers

pantosta *(It)* Toast [also called **pane tostata**]

pantothenic acid *see* vitamin B5

pantserkreeft *(Ho)* Spiny lobster

panucha *(Ph)* Palm sugar

panucho *(Me)* A small tortilla from the south west, part fried to make it puff up, partially split, filled with a savoury filling then fried until crisp.

panunto *(It) (Tuscany)* Bruschetta

panure *(Fr) fem.* Breadcrumbs or the coating of flour, beaten egg and breadcrumbs See to pané

panurette *(Fr) fem.* Finely grated rusks used as a lining in moulds

panvis *(Ho)* Fried fish, also a casserole made with dried codfish, onions and potatoes

panzanella *(It)* A bread salad from Tuscany made from coarse bread soaked in water and squeezed dry, mixed with chopped tomatoes, basil and other salad vegetables, dressed with oil and vinegar and left to develop the flavours for a few hours before serving

panzarotti *(It)* Deep fried pastry turnovers filled with a chopped ham, cheese, parsley and egg filling or as an alternative, anchovies, basil and egg

panzerotti *(It) see* pansotti

pão *(Po)* Bread

pao yu *(Ch)* Dried abalone, requires soaking for 4 days

pap 1 Soft mushy foods served to weaning infants and persons with eating or swallowing difficulties **2** *(Ho)* Porridge

papa *(Me)* Potato

papa seca *(SA)* Boiled and peeled non-bitter potatoes from Peru, dried in the sun and then ground. Used for the preparation of carapulca

papadam *(In) see* poppadom

papads *(In) see* poppadom

papadum *(In) see* poppadom

papaia *(It)* Papaya

papain A protease derived from papaya latex, used to remove protein hazes from beer, in bread dough modification, for yeast autolysis and for tenderizing meat for manufacturing purposes. It is also present in pineapples and figs

Papaja *(Ge)* Papaya

papalina *(It)* Sprat [also called **spratto**]

papalina, alla *(It)* In the style of the pope (strictly of the pope's skullcap), i.e. with ham, cream, eggs and Parmesan cheese

papanasi cu smantană *(Ro)* Sieved cottage cheese mixed with butter, eggs, egg yolks, double cream and a little sugar, seasoned and flavoured with grated lemon zest, made into small patties, fried and served with sour cream

papanasi fierti *(Ro)* Curd cheese dumplings, poached in water, drained and coated with melted butter, breadcrumbs and caster sugar

papas rellenos *(SA)* A type of cottage pie with a base of meat, vegetables, hard boiled eggs, olives, raisins and spices topped with mashed potatoes

papatzul *(Me)* Tortilla filled with egg and pumpkin seeds

Papaver rhoeas *Bot.* Field poppy, corn poppy, a source of poppy seed

Papaver somniferum *Bot.* Opium poppy, a source of poppy seed

papavero, al *(It)* With poppy seeds

papaw A variety of green custard apple *Asimina triloba* which grows in temperate regions of the USA. It is kidney shaped with smooth yellow skin and large brown seeds surrounded by a sweet yellow pulp tasting of bananas and pears. Not to be confused with pawpaw, the alternative name for papaya

papaya *(En & Sp)* A large pear- or melon-shaped fruit to 20 cm long, from a tree *Carica papaya* which grows in most tropical and sub-tropical regions and is second only in importance to the banana amongst tropical fruit. When ripe it has a yellow/orange skin and a juicy pink/orange flesh tasting like a mixture of roses, peaches and strawberries with many black seeds in a central cavity. The unripe fruit can be boiled and used as a vegetable in the same way as a marrow. The juice contains the protease papain and the seeds may be used as a condiment [also called **pawpaw**]

papaye *(Fr) fem.* Papaya

papaz yahnisi *(Tu)* Thick slices of mutton or lamb stewed in mutton fat with sliced onions, garlic, seasoning, cinnamon and a little vinegar

papel de paja de arroz *(Sp)* Rice paper

paper frill *see* cutlet frill

paperino *(It)* Gosling

Paphos sausage *(Cy)* Seasoned minced lean leg of pork mixed with chopped pork fat, flavoured with ground coriander and herbs, marinated with red wine for 2 days, filled into pricked casings and air dried for 5 to 10 days, fried or grilled. May be preserved after drying in rendered pork fat

papier de riz *(Fr) masc.* Rice paper

papillon *(Fr) masc.* A butterfly shaped small cake of flaky pastry dredged and possibly glazed with sugar

papillote *(Fr) fem.* Cutlet frill or the paper frill on the bone of a leg of lamb

papillote, en *(En & Fr)* Term for food baked in a buttered greaseproof paper or aluminium foil packet. Usually a piece of meat or fish with flavourings, served from the packet

papo de anjo *(Po)* Small spherical cakes made with mostly egg yolks and served with syrup, alternatively a frothy dessert made with egg white

papo seco *(Po)* Bread roll or ordinary bread without butter

pappa *(It) see* pancotto

pappa al pomodoro *(It)* A Tuscan bread soup with tomatoes cooked in oil, garlic and basil

pappadam *(In) see* poppadom

pappadum *(In) see* poppadom

pappardelle *(It)* Wide egg noodles with crinkly edges

paprica dolce *(It)* Paprika

paprika *(En & Fr) masc.* A variety of sweet red pepper *Capsicum annuum* from Hungary, used fresh or more commonly dried and ground as the flavouring of the same name

paprika butter *see* beurre de paprika

paprika spice mix A pungent blend of flavouring agents used to coat chicken prior to barbecueing, consisting of fresh ginger, fresh garlic, paprika and ground cumin pounded into a paste

Paprikapfeffer *(Ge)* Powdered paprika

paprikas *(Ho)* Sweet peppers, capsicums

paprikás borjúszelet *(Hu)* Veal escalopes seasoned and sprinkled with paprika, floured and fried in lard with chopped onions, simmered in white stock with sliced sweet green peppers and served with the reduced cooking liquor and sour cream as a sauce

paprikás csirke *(Hu)* A chicken stew flavoured with onions, sweet peppers, tomatoes, paprika, soured cream and seasonings. Served with pasta or tarhonya

Paprikaskrumpli *(Au)* A type of goulash made from sliced onions and garlic sweated in oil, sliced potatoes and sausages (debrecen or chorizo), paprika and chilli powder added and cooked, peeled and diced tomatoes, stock, sliced green sweet peppers and dried Hungarian peppers and seasoning added and the whole simmered until cooked

papu *(Fi)* Bean

Păpuşi de caş *(Ro)* A hard spun-curd and smoked ewes' milk cheese with a sharp salty taste made in 500 g cylinders or bricks

paquette *(Fr) fem.* The dark green mature lobster roe about to be laid or the lobster carrying such roe.

para-amino-benzoic acid *see* PABA

paradicsommártás *(Hu)* Ketchup

Paradiesapfel *(Ge)* Tomato

Paradieser *(Au & Ge)* Tomato

paradise cake *see* carrot cake

paradise nut *(SA)* A nut from a tree *Lecythis sabucajo* which resembles the Brazil nut but has a more delicate flavour and a thinner shell [also called **sapucaya nut**]

paragonimus A species of fluke endemic in Asia and parts of Africa, transmitted mainly in freshwater crabs and crayfish, causes tuberculosis-like symptoms since it lives in the lungs; can also affect the brain. Easily cured with 1 dose of praziquantel

Paranuss *(Ge)* Brazil nut

parasol mushroom An edible fungus *Lepiota procera* found in grassy areas and resembling a light brown umbrella. The cap which has a scaly surface which should be removed can be up to 15 cm in dia. Best eaten when young [also called **umbrella mushroom**]

paratha *(In)* Flaky unleavened bread made from a mixture of white and brown flour, water and salt, the dough formed into rounds coated with ghee and fried until crisp on the outside

parboil, to To boil foods until they are about half cooked

parboiled rice *see* converted rice

parch, to To dry roast until slightly brown

parched corn Maize kernels which have been cooked or dry roasted slightly

pare *(Id)* Bitter gourd

pare, to To peel thinly, e.g. skins from potatoes, apples, etc.

párek v rohlíku *(Cz)* Hot dog, boiled or steamed sausage in a roll

parenica *(Cz, Hu & Ru)* A soft spun-curd ewes' milk cheese cut into long strips, rolled up and smoked [also called **ribbon cheese**]

pareve A Jewish term descriptive of food made without milk or meat or derivatives of them, so that it may be eaten with either type

parfait *(Fr) masc.* A frozen, flavoured cooked egg custard mixture in which the eggs have been well beaten to incorporate air, served as a dessert. Flavourings included coffee (traditional), chocolate, fruit, vanilla, liqueurs and praline

parfum *(Fr) masc.* Flavour, aroma

pargo 1 *(Po)* Barbel, the fish **2** *(Sp)* Sea bream

paria *(Id)* Bitter gourd

Paris-Brest A cake consisting of three concentric baked rings of choux pastry, split in half and filled with whipped cream or crème patissière mixed with a fine praline and decorated with icing sugar and flaked almonds. It is named after a famous 19th century bicycle race

Pariser Schnitzel *(Au)* Veal escalope, dipped in flour and lightly beaten egg and fried in butter

parisersmörgås *(Sw)* An open sandwich consisting of a thick slice of bread and butter topped with a forcemeat of minced beef, egg yolk, breadcrumbs, grated onions, finely chopped pickled beetroot and seasoning. The whole fried both sides, meat side first

Parisian spice *(USA)* A mixture of dried thyme, bay, basil and sage ground with coriander seed, mace and black peppercorns used for flavouring

parisien *(Fr) masc. see* gros pain

parisienne, à la *(Fr)* Garnished with parisienne potatoes and artichoke hearts, and sometimes other vegetables

parisienne cutter A sharp edged scoop-shaped implement for cutting out balls of potato or other vegetables or fruit

parisienne potatoes Potatoes scooped out with a parisienne cutter, browned in a frying pan, finished in the oven at 240°C and coated with meat glaze just before serving

parisienne, sauce *(En & Fr) fem. see* sauce allemande

Parker House Roll *(USA)* A yeast-raised dough formed into a roll and folded in two before proving and baking.

parkia A medium sized leguminous tree *Parkia speciosa* from Thailand and Indonesia which produces flat seed pods about the size of broad beans with a peculiar smell. The pods are eaten as a vegetable and the sun dried and peeled beans are fried in oil or softened in water and eaten as a snack [also called **stink bean, twisted cluster bean**]

Parkia speciosa *Bot.* Parkia

parkin *(UK)* A moist and dense dark brown ginger cake from Yorkshire made with oatmeal and sweetened with black treacle. Usually served in squares after maturing for a week

párky *(Cz)* Frankfurter type sausages often boiled or steamed in pairs. Popular as a street snack in Prague

Parma ham A dry cured ham eaten raw as prosciutto. It must come from around the town of Parma in Italy, have been air dried for at least 8 months and be branded on the skin

Parmentier *(Fr)* A description of dishes containing potatoes

Parmentier, purée *(En & Fr) fem.* Sliced onion and leek sweated in butter, BG, stock and sliced peeled potatoes added, simmered, skimmed, BG removed, passed through a sieve or liquidized, seasoned, consistency adjusted and served hot with croûtons

Parmesan A very hard Italian grating cheese with a strong and distinctive flavour made from unpasteurized skimmed cows' milk. The curds are heated and packed into very large circular moulds and matured for well over 2 years, ending up with a pale straw colour and a black rind. When grated it is used on a wide variety of Italian dishes; *see also* Parmigiano Reggiano. The composition depends on age, at 18 months it is 27% water, 37% fat and 31% protein

parmesane, à la *(Fr)* Descriptive of dishes containing or sprinkled with Parmesan cheese

parmigiana, alla *(It)* Description of boiled vegetables finished with butter and grated Parmesan or an escalope panéed with a mixture of grated Parmesan cheese and breadcrumbs

Parmigiano Reggiano *(It)* The finest and authentic Parmesan cheese made in squat barrel shapes (to 35 kg) which are salted in brine and turned and brushed regularly. It is unique to its particular region and although it may be made at any time it has special names according to the date of manufacture, 'maggengo' April to November and 'invernengo' December to March. The non-winter period can also be split, 'ditesta' April to June, 'agostano' or 'di centro' July and August and 'tardno' September to November. One year old cheeses are called 'vecchio' and two year old 'stravecchio'. Always stamped with the name. It may be eaten young as a dessert

päron *(Sw)* Pear

parr A young river salmon in its second or third year before it leaves for the sea. Protected from fishing [also called **samlet**]

parrilla *(Sp)* Grill

parrillada *(Ar)* Barbecue

parrillada de pescado *(Sp)* A mixed seafood grill

parsa *(Fi)* Parsley

parsi dhansak masala *(In)* A hot spice mix containing in addition to those listed under garam masala, fenugreek seeds, mustard seeds, chillis and turmeric

parsley A hardy biennial plant with either bright green very curly leaves *Petroselinum crispum* or flat duller leaves *P. crispum 'Neapolitanum'*. The flat-leaved variety which is common outside the UK has a stronger flavour. It is very widely used as a culinary herb, as a decoration or garnish either in sprigs or chopped, and as an essential part (esp. the stalks) of a BG. The flat-leaved variety is also called **French parsley, Italian parsley**

parsley butter *see* beurre à la maître d'hôtel

parsley ham *see* jambon persillé

parsley root Hamburg parsley

parsley sauce **1** Béchamel sauce with finely chopped parsley. Used for poached and boiled fish and vegetables **2** A fish velouté mixed with a strong infusion of parsley, chopped parsley and a little lemon juice

parsnip A biennial plant *Pastinaca sativa* whose long (up to 25 cm) conical tap root is harvested as a winter root vegetable in the first year. The roots have a cream sweetish flesh with a distinctive flavour and are best after being frosted. Served boiled, roasted, fried or puréed, etc.

parson's nose The small projecting fatty tissue growth at the rear of a chicken which carries the tail feathers and, in the case of the male, the sexual organs and glands. It has a strong flavour and is not usually eaten except by those who wish to draw attention to themselves

parson's venison *(UK)* A skinned and boned leg of lamb, stuffed with a duxelle mixed with chopped ham and chives, marinated for 24 hours in port, red wine, red wine vinegar, juniper, allspice, bay leaf and grated nutmeg, drained, dried, seared then braised in the marinade in a covered dish at 180°C for up to 2 hours until cooked and served with the reduced strained cooking liquor

partan bree *(UK)* Puréed soup from Scotland containing crab meat and rice

partridge **1** *(UK)* A greyish-brown game bird widespread in Europe and the Middle East weighing about 450 g at 2 to 4 months and serving 1 person. Barded and roasted at 200°C for 1 to 2 hours. They come in two varieties:grey legged *Perdrix perdrix* and red legged *Alectoris rufa*. The shooting season is the 1st September to 1st February, and the hanging time 3 to 5 days **2** *(USA)* The general name for various game birds including the American ruffed grouse, quail, pheasant and bobwhite

parut *(Id & Ma)* Coconut grater

parwal *(In)* *see* tindori

pasa *(Me & Sp)* Raisin

pasha *(Fi)* A type of cheesecake introduced from Russia

pashka *see* paskha

pashtet iz tielyatiny *(Ru)* A veal and liver pâté from the Ukraine made with fried calves' liver, veal, bacon and vegetables simmered with chicken stock and dried mushrooms, strained, processed with softened bread, bound with egg, seasoned and flavoured with allspice then baked in the oven at 180°C

Pasiego prensado *(Sp)* A soft mild white smooth cream cheese from Santander made from ewes' and semi-skimmed cows' milk. Eaten after 2 weeks maturation. The white paste contains small holes and has a decided flavour

Pasiego sin prensar *(Sp)* A cheese similar to Pasiego prensado but hand moulded into various shapes

pasilla chile *(Me)* A variety of long, hot and dark brown chilli, commonly dried

pasionara *(Sp)* Nigella

paskha *(Ru)* A rich dessert made from a mixture of curd cheese, cream, almonds and dried fruits placed in a muslin lined sieve or unglazed earthenware (flower)pot, weighted and left to drain for 24 hours, then turned out, muslin removed, and decorated. Traditionally served at Easter [also called **pashka**]

pass, to **1** To pass a food item through an excess of flour, beaten egg, oil or similar so as to completely coat it with the material **2** To make something pass through a sieve or strainer as in making a purée or coulis

passa de Corinto *(Sp)* Currants, from grapes

passas *(Po)* Raisins

passata *(It)* Purée, in the UK usually of raw tomatoes

passato *(It)* **1** Purée soup **2** Well done, overcooked **3** Skinned and deseeded tomatoes simmered with chopped onions (10:1) with garlic, basil, bay and celery until reduced by half, then seasoned and passed through a sieve. May be frozen

passé l'an *(Fr)* **1** A hard cooked-curd cows' milk cheese from Languedoc weighing to 40 kg. Similar to Parmesan but with a more mellow flavour. Lit. passed the year, i.e. more than 1 year old **2** Ripened, of cheese

Passendale *(Be)* A semi-hard loaf shaped cows' milk cheese weighing up to 7 kg. The moist and supple paste has many small holes

passer *(Fr)* **1** To pass (food through flour, beaten egg, etc.) **2** To quickly seal the surface of food in a hot frying pan prior to cooking by another method

passera *(It)* Plaice

passera pianuzza *(It)* Flounder

passerino *(It)* Plaice

Passiflora edulis *Bot.* Purple passion fruit

Passiflora edulis var. flavicarpa *Bot.* Yellow passion fruit

Passiflora laurifolia *Bot.* Yellow granadilla

Passiflora ligularis *Bot.* Sweet granadilla

Passiflora maliformis *Bot.* Curuba

Passiflora quadrangularis *Bot.* Giant granadilla

passion cake *see* carrot cake

passion fruit The globular fruit of climbing plants *Passiflora edulis, P. edulis* v. *flavicarpa* and *P. ligularis* which grow in warm, humid, frost-free climates. See purple passion fruit, yellow passion fruit and sweet granadilla. Passion fruit on its own generally refers to the purple variety

passoire *(Fr) fem.* Colander, strainer, sieve

passover bread *see* matzo

pasta 1 *(It)* Dough, paste **2** *(En & It)* A variety of extruded, cut or pressed shapes and sheets of pasta dough made either fresh and soft, or dried, from a basic dough of water and/or eggs, salt and hard durum wheat flour and sometimes oil. The simplest pasta is made from strong flour and eggs only (9:5), kneading up to 10 minutes until small blisters appear. There are innumerable names and shapes but the main types are spaghetti, macaroni, noodles, vermicelli, lasagne, canneloni and ravioli. Most pastas are cooked and served with a sauce **3** *(Sp)* Pasta or pastry **4** *(It & Sp)* Noodle

pasta d'acciughe *(It)* Anchovy paste

pasta asciutta *(It)* Pasta in a sauce

pasta in brodo *(It)* Pasta cooked and served in broth

pasta callo acciughe *(It)* Pasta with tomato sauce, anchovies and clams

pasta cresciuta *(It)* Vegetable, etc. fritters made with a yeast-raised flour, water and salt batter

pasta e fagioli *(It)* A traditional soup made with pasta, white beans and salt pork

pasta fatta in casa *(It)* Fresh pasta usually made in the place where it is cooked

pasta filata *(It)* The term for scalded milk curds that are kneaded until they become an elastic dough and easy to shape

pasta frolla *(It)* Shortcrust pastry

pasta de hojaldre *(Sp)* A patty made from puff pastry

pasta italiana *(Sp)* Spaghetti

pasta liscia *(It)* Smooth pasta

pasta reale *(It)* Small pasta grains for soup

pasta rigata *(It)* Ridged pasta which traps more sauce than smooth

pasta rosso *(It)* A red or pink pasta coloured with tomatoes

pasta alla sarde *(It)* Alternate layers of macaroni, fennel and fresh sardines, cooked in a pie dish and served cold

pasta secca *(It)* Dried pasta usually manufactured and sold through retail outlets

pasta sfoglia *(It)* Puff pastry

pasta trinata *(It)* Flat pieces of pasta with frilly or lacy edges wedges

pasta all'uovo *(It)* Pasta made from flour and eggs only without water or oil. Available in various shapes and usually made on the premises where cooked or sold. By law it must contain at least 4 eggs per kg of flour

pasta verde *(It)* A green pasta coloured with spinach

paste The name given to any thick relatively smooth semi-solid which is spreadable, such as a flour water paste or pastry but more specifically to cooked and pounded meat and fish mixed with flavourings and extenders

pastei *(Ho)* A pie or pasty usually containing meat in a thick sauce

pasteijes *(Ho)* Blind cooked pastry shells

pastéis *(Po)* A round patty shaped food item, may be a sweet cake or a savoury item such as a fish cake or rissole

pastéis de bacalhau *(Po)* Dried salt cod, cooked and then recooked en croûte

pastej *(Sw)* Pie

pastel *(Sp)* Pastry, cake, pie or pâté

pastel, en *(Sp)* In batter

pastél *(Po)* Pie, tart or pastry

pastela *(Sp)* An Andalusian speciality consisting of shredded beef cooked with cumin, nutmeg and honey in a pastry case

pastelería *(Po & Sp)* Pastry

pastelillos *(Ca)* Small deep-fried pasties containing meat or cheese served as a hors d'oeuvre or appetizer

pastélinho *(Po)* Small pie

pastelito de almendra *(Sp)* Almond cake

pastelitos *(Me)* Biscuits or small cakes

pastella *(It)* Batter

pastèque *(Fr) fem.* Watermelon

Pastete *(Ge)* Pie

pastetice od sira-skute *(Bk)* Turnovers from Serbia filled with ham and using a pastry made from flour, butter and cottage cheese

pasteurize, to To heat a substance, usually a liquid, to a temperature between 60 and 100°C to kill particular pathogenic organisms, e.g. milk may be pasteurized at 62.8°C for 30 minutes or at 72°C for 15 seconds, shelled eggs at 64.4°C for 2 to 5 minutes, etc. This process does not completely sterilize the substance

pasteurized milk Milk pasteurized at 72°C for 15 seconds and then rapidly cooled. This does not affect the flavour of the milk but causes the cream to rise unless it is homogenized

pasticceria *(It)* Pastry, pastry making, cakes, cake shop

pasticciata *(It)* Baked pasta with a savoury sauce, cheese and cream

pasticcino *(It)* Fancy cake or pastry

pasticcio *(It)* **1** A savoury pie of meat, pasta, vegetables or cheese or a combination of these **2** Pâté, meat loaf, any mould of processed fish, meat, etc.

pasticcio di maccheroni *(It)* A large double crust deep pie made in a cake tin with a removable base, lined with a sweet egg and butter enriched pastry filled with a mixture of cooked pasta, meatballs, peas, rich tomato sauce and diced Mozarella cheese heaped up in the centre and filled with a sweetened egg custard (5 eggs per litre of milk), covered with a pastry lid, decorated and glazed, then baked at 190°C for 45 minutes. Rested 10 minutes in the tin

pastiera *(It)* A tart filled with ricotta cheese

pastiera Napoletana *(It)* A puff pastry case filled with fruit

pasties *see* pasty

pastilla *see* bastilla

pastillage A dough-like mixture of icing sugar, water and gum tragacanth which can be coloured and moulded or shaped to make cake coverings and decorations

Pastinaca sativa *Bot.* Parsnip

Pastinake *(Ge)* Parsnip

pastine *(It)* Tiny pasta shapes for soup

pastitsio *(Gr)* Cooked pasta layered with a cooked meat sauce, usually lamb, an egg enriched and cinnamon-flavoured Béchamel and grated cheese, finishing with a final layer of grated cheese and fresh breadcrumbs then baked at 190°C until the top is golden brown (40 minutes)

Pastorella *(It)* A small version of Bel Paese cheese

pastrami *(USA)* Dry cured and smoked brisket or other similar cut of meat usually boiled then thinly sliced for use as a sandwich filling

pastries Various types of small cakes, often iced, filled or decorated and made of pastry or various sponge or cake mixtures

pastry A mixture of flour, fat, possibly egg and sugar, the fat usually dispersed as small solid globules coated with flour and the whole brought together with liquid prior to shaping and baking. There are many types of pastry. See under shortcrust, flan, sweet, flaky, puff, rough puff, hot water crust, suet crust, choux and filo pastry

pastry board A square or oblong board preferably marble but usually wood on which pastry is rolled out

pastry brake Opposed and contra-rotating rollers with a variable gap through which pastry can be worked and reduced in thickness for commercial production. A very small version is used domestically for pasta production

pastry case An uncooked or blind baked pastry container used to hold savoury or sweet mixtures

pastry cream *see* crème pâtissière

pastry cutters Various metal or plastic outlines of shapes, e.g. circles, fluted circles, diamonds, gingerbread men, etc. sharpened on one edge and used to cut out corresponding shapes from biscuit, scone, pastry or cake mixtures, etc.

pasty A doubled over sheet of pastry containing a savoury filling, sealed around the edges and baked flat on a baking tray without support. Usually a half circle

pasztetowa *(Pl)* Seasoned pigs' liver and veal processed and packed into casings

pat A small shaped amount of solid or semi-solid such as a butter pat

pat, to To shape a solid or semi-solid into a pat by using two flat wooden paddles, by forming into a roll, refrigerating and slicing, or by use of a mould

pata de mulo Lit. mules foot or shoe. Villalon cheese q.v. made in this shape

pataca *(Sp)* Jerusalem artichoke

patagras *(SA)* A semi-hard cows' milk cheese resembling Edam and Gouda

patakukko *(Fi)* A double crust pie from Karelia made with rye flour and filled with muikko fish, fat pork and seasoning, cooked very slowly to completely soften the filling

patata *(It & Sp)* Potato

patata arrostita *(It)* Roast potato

patata asada *(It)* Baked potato

patata bollita *(It)* Boiled potato

patata dolce *(It)* Sweet potato

patata fritte *(It)* Potato crisps, game chips

patata lesso *(It)* Boiled potatoes

patata purea *(It)* Mashed potato

patata sfogliata *(It)* Deep fat fried potato, chips, French fries

patata stacciato *(It)* Mashed potato

patatas fritas *(Sp)* Chips, fried potatoes

patate alla borghese *(It)* Potatoes with butter and lemon

patate (douce) *(Fr) fem.* Sweet potato

patate sabbiose *(It)* Sauté potatoes

patate tenere *(It)* New potatoes

patate alla veneziana *(It)* Diced potatoes fried with onions and herbs

patates *(Tu)* Potato

pâte *(Fr) fem.* **1** Pastry (note the unaccented e) **2** A softish mixture such as batter, etc. **3** Paste (e.g. of cheese)

pâte d'amandes *(Fr) fem.* Marzipan

pâte d'anchois *(Fr) fem.* Anchovy paste

pâte brisée *(Fr) fem.* Shortcrust pastry

pâte à choux *(Fr) fem.* Choux pastry

pâte à crêpes *(Fr) fem.* Pancake batter

pâte croquante *(Fr) fem.* A crisp ground almond and sugar pastry

pâte feuilletée *(Fr) fem.* Flaky or puff pastry

pâte à foncé *(Fr) fem.* Shortcrust pastry

pâte à frire *(Fr) fem.* Batter

pâte de fruit, en *(Fr)* Fruit jelly as in framboise en pâte de fruit, raspberry jelly

pâte frollée *(Fr) fem.* Almond-flavoured pastry

pâte sablée *(Fr) fem.* Sugar pastry (UK), sugar crust pastry (USA)

pâte à sucre *(Fr) fem.* Sugar pastry

pâte sucrée *(Fr) fem.* A sweetened shortcrust pastry (pâte brisée) used extensively for patisserie. Quite fragile and requires careful handling

pâté 1 *(Fr) masc.* A raised pie with a meat filling completely enclosed in pastry. Eaten hot **2** *(En & Fr) masc.* A cooked, smooth or coarse meat paste made from a variety of meats, often liver and belly pork or bacon plus flavourings and seasoning. Allowed to cool in the mould then turned out and eaten cold, usually as a hors d'oeuvres. As a rule of thumb there should be equal amounts of lean meat and fat to which are added binders such as eggs, flour, choux pastry or white sauces. Sometimes vegetarian pastes with a similar texture are so called

pâté de campagne *(Fr) masc.* Farmhouse pâté, usually made from coarely chopped pork with garlic and herbs

pâté en croûte *(Fr) masc.* Meat pie

pâté de foie gras *(En & Fr) masc.* An expensive gourmet pâté made with the enlarged livers (foie gras) of force-fed geese, seasoned and flavoured with truffles. The best pâté is made from livers trimmed of any yellow gall stains, rested or soaked overnight, trimmed of connective tissue, seasoned, possibly marinated, piquéed with truffle slivers, squashed into a terrine, sealed with a flour and water paste and cooked in the oven in a bain-marie. By law, pâté de foie gras must contain 80% goose liver

pâté maison *(Fr) masc.* A cold pâté produced on the premises usually cut in slices as a hors d'oeuvre and served with a garnish and fingers of hot toast

pâté de Pâques *(Fr) masc.* Veal and pork pie

pâté de Pâques au biquion *(Fr) masc.* An elaborate Easter pie made with puff pastry which uses a mixture of butter and goat's cheese (3:2) instead of all butter. The filling is a mixture of diced pork, veal and kid, fried in butter and mixed with finely chopped onion, parsley and egg yolk, seasoning and nutmeg. The pie is assembled on a baking sheet from a circle of puff pastry with the filling heaped in the centre, halved hard boiled eggs on the top and all covered with another circle of puff pastry sealed around the edges and crimped. Baked at 200°C for 20 minutes, then at 170°C until cooked

pâtée *(Fr) fem.* The mash that is force fed to geese and chickens

pâtes *(Fr) fem.* Pasta, noodles

pâtes alimentaires *(Fr) fem.* Pasta, noodles

pâtes de fruits *(Fr) fem.* Pieces of crystallized fruits

patella *(It)* Limpet

patelle **1** *(Fr) fem.* Limpet **2** *(It)* Limpets, the shellfish

patent blue V E131, a synthetic blue food colouring

paternostri *(It)* Small squares of flat pasta

patience A sorrel-like herb *Rumex patientia* with a slightly acidic taste. Used like sorrel or spinach

patila *(In) see* degchi

patinho *(Po)* Duckling

patis *(Ph)* A fermented fish sauce

pâtisserie *(Fr) fem.* **1** Cake shop **2** Sweet items generally made of pastry, filled and decorated. The filling is often crème pâtissière overlaid with glazed fruit or cream, chocolate, jam and the like **3** The art of cake and pastry making and baking

pâtissier,-ière *(Fr)* masc./fem. confectioner or pastrycook

patlican dolmasi *(Tu)* Aubergine halves, filled with a mixture of minced beef, chopped onions, tomatoes, rice and seasonings, baked in the oven and served hot

patlican salatasi *(Tu)* Cooked aubergine flesh puréed with lemon juice and olive oil, served cold garnished with tomato wedges, strips of green sweet pepper and black olives

Patna rice A north Indian long grain rice which stays separate during cooking. Similar to Basmati but not so fragrant. Excellent for rice salads

pato *(Po & Sp)* Duck

pato bravo *(Po)* Wild duck

patola *(Ph)* Angled loofah

patra Dasheen leaves used as a vegetable

patrijs *(Ho)* Partridge

pattegris *(Sw)* Sucking pig

patty A small pie or pasty

patty pan squash A summer squash *Curcubita pepo* common in the USA, so called because of its dish shape with scalloped edges. The creamy white skin and flesh and the seeds are eaten as a vegetable when it is very young [also called **scallop squash, custard marrow, cymling**]

patty shell *(USA)* A puff or short pastry shell for serving hors d'oeuvres, bouchées, vol-au-vents, barquettes, etc.

patty tin *see* bun tin

pau *(In) see* powa

paua *(NZ)* A type of abalone *Haliotis iris* with a rainbow coloured shell which is often used as an ornament

Pauillac lamb Milk-fed lamb from Pauillac, France

paunce bourré *(USA)* A Cajun dish of stuffed pork stomach

paunch, to To remove the entrails, heart and lungs of an animal, esp. a hare

paupiette **1** *(En & Fr) fem.* A stuffed and rolled thin fillet of fish **2** *(Fr) fem.* Beef or veal olive

paupiettes d'anchois *(Fr) fem. see* anchovy paupiettes

pau ts'ai *(Ch)* Pak choy

pav *(In) see* powa

pava *(Sp)* Hen turkey

pavé *(Fr) masc.* A thickish square or rectangle e.g. of steak, cheese, cake or mousse. Lit. cobblestone, paving stone

pavé d'Auge *(Fr) see* Pont l'Evêque

pavé de Moyaux *(Fr) see* Pont l'Evêque

Pavlova *(Aus)* Meringue piped into a shallow basket, dried, filled with whipped cream and decorated with fresh fruit. Named in honour of the famous Russian ballet dancer

pavo *(Sp)* Turkey

pavo relleno a la catalana *(Sp)* Stuffed and roasted turkey

pavot *(Fr) masc.* Poppy seed

pawpaw *see* papaya

payasam *(In)* A paste made from various ingredients but always containing coconut milk, eaten as a sweet snack or accompaniment to a meal. Typical ingredients are cooked and mashed pulses, cooked rice, cooked sago, cashew nuts, jaggery or sugar

pay darn *(Ch)* Chinese preserved eggs

payousnaya *(Ru)* The less mature eggs of sturgeon treated with hot brine to coagulate them and packed into small wooden tubs [also called **pressed caviar**]

pays *(Fr) masc.* Country or region, as in vin de pays, locally produced wine

paysanne A vegetable cut in thin slices and small (1 cm) triangular, square or round shapes

paysanne, à la *(Fr)* In the peasant style, i.e. a simple dish containing onions, carrots and bacon

pazlache *(It) see* agnoletti

pazon ng api *(Bm)* Shrimp paste

pazun nga-pi *(Bm)* A pungent fermented fish sauce made from shrimps

pea The fruit of a climbing legume *Pisum sativum* grown extensively in temperate climates, consisting of a green pod to 10 cm long containing a row of soft, round green seeds which become brown and hard when ripe. Some varieties (e.g. mangetout) have edible pods which are eaten whole before the seeds begin to swell, but most have inedible pods and the green underripe seeds are eaten either raw if very young or cooked. Most peas are frozen in the developed world. Some are dried, possibly dehusked and split or further processed. The fully ripe seed is brown and used as animal and bird food in developed countries but may also be used as a pulse; *see also* pea leaf [also called **garden pea**]

pea aubergine Tiny pale green, white/yellow or purple/brown relatives of the aubergine *Solanum torvum,* grown in the Seychelles, Thailand and the Caribbean, which look like a rather straggly bunch of grapes. They are picked while unripe and used raw in hot sauces and chutney. Used in nam prik [also called **susumber, gully bean**]

pea bean *see* navy bean

pea crab A very small crab from New England, USA which lives in empty oyster shells and is eaten whole after stewing in cream [also called **oyster crab**]

pea flour Flour produced from fully mature dried peas used for soups and thickening sauces [also called **pea starch**]

pea leaf The young leaves and shoots of the garden pea which have been prevented from flowering. Used as a gourmet vegetable in stir fries and soups [also called **pea sprout**]

pea man *(Ja)* Green sweet peppers

pea sausage *(UK)* A vegetarian sausage made from mashed cooked yellow peas with a little grated carrot, onion, nutmeg and seasoning, possibly bound with a little fat and flour, packed in non-animal casings

pea sprout *see* pea leaf

pea starch *see* pea flour

peaberry A mutant arabica coffee which is a single round bean instead of the two matching hemispheres as is normal

peach The fruit of a deciduous tree *Prunus persica* originally from China but now cultivated worldwide in temperate climates. Most fruits are spherical up to 7.5 cm dia. with a single longitudinal indentation from the stalk to the calyx end. The sweet juicy flesh may be white, yellow or orange, surrounds a large rough central stone and is enclosed in a downy skin ranging in colour from cream to orange/pink. Used both raw and poached as a dessert and for jam

peach Melba An individual dessert made with vanilla ice cream plus poached skinned and destoned peaches with a topping of fresh raspberry sauce. Served in a coupe dish

peanut A plant *Arachis hypogaea* from South America whose fertilized flowers send shoot-like structures into the soil where the immature fruits develop as two to four nuts in a light brown, dry and soft shell or pod, each nut being covered by a thin papery skin. The Spanish type has 2 light brown seeds per pod, the Valencia type up to 4 dark red seeds per pod and the Virginia type 2 dark brown seeds per pod. They are eaten raw or roasted as a snack food and are a major source of oil and protein. Peanuts are made into peanut butter and are used to thicken and flavour many sauces and stews [also called **groundnut, monkeynut**]

peanut butter Ground peanuts sometimes with added peanut oil, salt or sugar with a buttery consistency. Sold as smooth or crunchy, the latter containing chopped peanuts. Used as a sandwich spread or to flavour some dishes

peanut flour *(USA)* Ground peanuts sometimes used to enrich baking flours

peanut oil Oil extracted from peanuts containing 20% saturated, 50% monounsaturated and 30% polyunsaturated fat. It has a rather high melting point (freezing point) and a high smoke point. Used for deep frying [also called **groundnut oil, arachis oil**]

pear The fruit of a deciduous tree *Pyrus communis* var. *sativa* native to Europe and western Asia which requires cool winters to fruit. The thin, usually smooth, green through yellow to brown and often mottled skin encloses a firm, juicy, delicately-flavoured flesh surrounding a core of seed somewhat smaller than an apple. The fruit is narrow at the stalk end widening towards the calyx. There are both cooking and dessert varieties and they may be eaten raw, poached, baked, etc.

pear apple *see* Asian pear

pear Condé A Condé dessert, possibly made with a short grain rice, topped with a fanned poached pear [also called **poire Condé**]

pearks sakhoo *(Th)* Tapioca

pearl barley Pot barley which has been steamed and tumbled in a revolving cylinder to remove the outer coating. Softens more quickly than pot barley

pearl millet A white seeded variety of bulrush millet

pearl moss *see* carragheen

pearl onion *see* button onion

pearl rice *(USA)* A short grain soft sticky rice

pearl sago *see* sago

peasant's cabbage *see* kale

pease pudding Split dehusked dried green peas, soaked, boiled, drained and mashed with butter, egg yolks and seasoning. Reheated in the oven before serving

peau blanche *(Fr) fem. see* ziste

peber *(De)* Pepper

pebernødder *(De)* A spiced Christmas biscuit

pecan nut The central stone of the fruit of a large hickory (pecan) tree *Carya illinoensis* from central and southern USA. It has walnut-like wrinkled flesh enclosed in a smooth oval brown outer shell (to 2.5 cm long). Eaten raw or cooked

pecan pie *(USA)* A sweet open-topped pie filled with pecan nuts often served at Thanksgiving

pecc ed vaca *(It)* Elder, usually served sliced as antipasto

pechay *(Ph)* Chinese leaves

pêche *(Fr) fem.* Peach (Note - also means fishing)

pechena tikva *(Bu)* Pumpkin slices baked with honey, walnuts, cinnamon and lemon zest

pêches Melba *(Fr) fem.* Peach Melba

pecho de ternera *(Sp)* Breast of veal

pechuga *(Sp)* Chicken breast

pechuga de ave a la Sarasate *(Sp)* Chicken breast filled with chopped veal

pecora *(It)* Sheep, ewe, mutton

Pecorino *see* Canestrato

Pecorino canestrato *see* Canestrato

Pecorino foggiano *(It)* A hard ewes' milk cheese made in cylinders (to 7 kg), dry salted and cured for 6 months. It has a sharp flavour and a hard rind. Contains 40% water, 29% fat and 25% protein

Pecorino Romano *(It)* A hard cooked-curd ewes' milk cheese made around Rome and in Sardinia and shaped into cylinders (to 20 kg). The curds are tapped and pierced in their moulds to promote drainage of whey and the cheeses are dry salted and needled to allow salt to penetrate over a period of 3 months. They are then ripened for a further 5 months. It has a dense white to yellow paste with a sharp ewes' milk cheese flavour and a brown oiled rind. Used as a dessert cheese since Roman times. Contains 31% water, 33% fat, 28% protein and 4 to 5 % salt

Pecorino Siciliano *(It)* A hard ewes' milk cheese made between October and June and formed in a basket mould. The cheeses are dry salted and ripened for 8 months. They have a pale yellow oiled rind and the pale paste which contains a few peppercorns has a sharp flavour and a few holes

Pecorino Siciliano bianco *(It)* Pecorino Siciliano without peppercorns [also called **Pecorino Siciliano calcagno**]

Pecorino Siciliano calcagno *(It) see* Pecorino Siciliano bianco

pectin E440(a), a natural hemicellulosic carbohydrate gelling agent which in acid conditions (less than 3.46 pH) causes jam and marmalades to set. If the acidity is too low, less than 3.2 pH, then the jelly will weep, boiling also reduces the gelling power. Citrus fruits, apples, currants and some plums are rich in pectin and acids. Other fruits require added pectin and acid to make a satisfactory jam

pectinase An enzyme obtained from *Aspergillus niger*, used for the clarification of wines and beers and for the extraction of fruit juices by breaking down pectin

peda *(In)* Milk fudge formed into small rounded blocks and garnished with pistachio nuts

pedas *(In)* Hot-flavoured as from chillis

Pediococcus cerevisiae Bacteria used as a starter culture for lactic fementation in meat products e.g. salami and in vegetables, e.g. cucumbers

Pediococcus halophilus Bacteria use for the second phase acidification of soya sauce

Pedroches *(Sp)* A hard ewes' milk cheese with holes in the paste, ripened for 1 to 2 months. Contains 40% water, 30% fat and 24% protein

peel 1 The outer skin or rind of fruits and some,

principally root, vegetables **2** The long handled paddle used to move bread, baked goods, pizzas, etc. in and out of ovens

peel, to To remove the skin or rind from fruit or vegetables or to remove any outer covering, e.g. paper from a cake or rind from a cheese

peeler An implement used for peeling, consisting of a handled steel blade in which a longish slot with a raised sharp edge has been formed. This is used to remove a uniformly thick continuous slice from the surface of the object being peeled [also called **potato peeler, vegetable peeler**]

peelings The lengths of peel produced by a peeler

peertjes *(Ho)* Cooking pears

pee tee *(Th)* A deep saucer shaped mould on the end of a long handle which is dipped in oil, then in batter, and deep fried to produce a thin crisp case for filling with appetizers and the like

pei sooli *(Ch)* Asian pear

peixe *(Po)* Fish

peixelua *(Po)* Sunfish, a type of basking shark

pejerrey *(Sp)* Smelt

pekin duck *(UK)* One of the two standard duck breeds, Aylesbury is the other. It matures in about 7 weeks from hatching and contains a lot of fat

Peking cooking The style of cooking practised in the north east of China around Beijin. It is suited to a colder climate and includes carp, crab and giant prawns, roasts, hotpots, wheaten bread and noodles. Typical flavourings included garlic, ginger, onions, chives and leeks

Peking duck A renowned Chinese speciality of crisp, marinated and roasted duck, pieces of which are wrapped up in a small pancake with spring onions, strips of cucumber, and a soya based sauce prior to eating with the fingers. The ducks are specially bred with a meaty breast and an even layer of fat between the skin and the carcase so that the skin separates when roasted and becomes crisp [also called **Beijing duck**]

Peking pear *see* Asian pear

pekoni *(Fi)* Bacon

pelagic A description of fish which move about in large shoals in the open sea

Pelardon *(Fr)* A mild, smooth, close textured, white goats' milk cheese from Languedoc, formed into small rounds and often cured in the local brandy

pelargonium *see* scented geranium

Pelargonium capitatum *Bot.* A rose-scented geranium used as an infusion to flavour sauces, custards, jellies, etc.

***Pelargonium crispum* 'Prince of Orange'** *Bot.* An orange scented geranium used as an infusion for general flavouring

Pelargonium x fragrans *Bot.* A pine scented geranium used in soup and Welsh rarebit

Pelargonium graveolens x tomentosum *Bot.* A rose-peppermint scented geranium used to flavour liver pâté

Pelargonium odoratissimum *Bot.* An apple scented geranium used with fish baked in cider

Pelargonium quercifolium *Bot.* An oak-leaved incense scented geranium

Pelargonium radens *Bot.* A rose-lemon scented geranium. An infusion of the leaves is used for general flavouring

pelato *(It)* Peeled, skinned

pelau *(Ca)* A version of rice pilaff including boiling fowl meat, salt beef, almonds, sugar, butter, chopped onions, tomatoes, herbs, spices and seasoning

pelle di porco *(It)* Pork crackling

pelli-pelli *see* piri-piri (2)

Pellkartoffeln *(Ge)* Potatoes boiled in their skins

pelmeni *(Ru)* A type of ravioli made in the same fashion and filled with three different freshly minced meats mixed with just enough water to keep them juicy and carefully sealed in an envelope of extra thick dough. Traditionally made at the beginning of winter, left frozen outside in the snow and used as required

pelota *(Sp)* Meat ball

peltopyy *(Fi)* Greylegged partridge

pemican *see* pemmican

pemmican *(USA)* Lean dried meat pounded to a paste with molten fat and used by the native Indians as an easily transportable energy source. It will keep for some time. Occasionally used with an admixture of dried vine fruits as iron rations [also called **pemican**]

pen shell *see* fan mussel

Peña Santa *(Sp)* **1** A baked Alaska type dessert **2** An Asturian cheese

Penang sugar A crude unrefined sugar containing a high proportion of molasses

Pencarreg *(UK)* A Welsh cheese made from pasteurized cows' milk resembling Brie in appearance but softer and with a stronger flavour

peng *(Ch)* A method of cooking in which ingredients are first deep fried to seal the surface quickly and then stir fried

Penicillium camembertii One of the penicillium moulds associated with the ripening of soft Camembert type cheeses

Penicillium candidum A strain of the penicillium mould used to give the characteristic skin and flavour to Camembert cheese

Penicillium glaucum A strain of the penicillium mold used for the production of bleu d'Auvergne cheese

Penicillium roquefortii A strain of the penicillium mould used to produce the veining in Roquefort and Stilton cheese

penne *(It)* Short tubes of pasta about 4 cm long and cut on the diagonal to resemble quill pens

penne rigate *(It)* A finely ribbed penne

pennette *(It)* Thin penne

Pennisetum typhoideum *Bot.* Bulrush millet

pennone *(It)* Large penne

penny bun *see* cep

pennyroyal A type of mint *Mentha pulegium* with bright green peppermint scented leaves. There are two main varieties 'creeping' which grows to a height of 15 cm and 'upright' with upright stems to 30 cm. Should only be used in small quantities and not when pregnant or suffering from kidney problems [also called **pudding grass**]

pensées brouillées *(Fr) fem.* Crisply fried pastries

Penteleu *(Ro)* A ewes' milk cheese very similar to kashkaval [also called **dobrogea**]

penyu *(Id & Ma)* Turtle

peoci *(It)* Oven browned mussels

pepato *(It)* A Pecorino type of cheese containing crushed peppercorns

pepe *(It)* Pepper

pepe di caienna *(It)* Cayenne pepper

pepe forte *(It)* Chilli pepper

pepe nero *(It)* Black pepper

peper *(Ho)* Pepper

peperata *(It)* A peppery sauce served with roasts [also called **peverada**]

peperkoek *(Ho)* Gingerbread

pepermunt *(Ho)* Peppermint

pepernoten *(Ho)* Tiny cubes of spiced ginger cake served on the 5th of December, the eve of St Nicholas' day when the Dutch give presents

peperonata *(It)* A type of ratatouille q.v., made with sweet onions, red and yellow sweet peppers, tomatoes and a little garlic finished with chopped fresh parsley. Often served cold as antipasta

peperoncino *(It)* **1** Hot chilli pepper **2** Paprika

peperone *(It)* Sweet pepper, capsicum, occasionally used for chilli peppers and grains of paradise

peperoni gialli *(It)* Sweet yellow peppers

pepinillo **1** *(Sp)* Gherkin **2** *see* choko

pepino **1** A large round or oval fruit of a plant related to the tomato. It has a yellow to green, smooth, shiny and bitter skin streaked with purple, a sweet, slightly acid, yellow flesh and a central mass of white seeds. Eaten fresh or in cooked sweet or savoury dishes [also called **melon pear**] **2** *(Po & Sp)* Cucumber

pepinos de mar *(Sp)* Sea cucumber

pepita *(Sp)* Pumpkin seed

pepitoria *(Sp)* Meat hash or stew

pepitoria de gallina a la española *(Sp)* A chicken fricassé with peas, flavoured with nutmeg and saffron

pepo A type of marrow with a hard rind and many seeds [also called **pepos**]

pepos *see* pepo

peppar *(Sw)* Pepper

pepparkakor *(Sw)* A traditional crisp biscuit, variously flavoured with powdered cinnamon, cloves and cardomom seeds, served especially at Christmas

pepparrot *(Sw)* Horseradish

pepparrotskött *(Sw)* Brisket of beef boiled with vegetables and herbs and served with a velouté sauce made from the skimmed and strained cooking liquor flavoured with grated horseradish and finished with cream

pepparrotskött Sacher *(Sw)* Boiled beef with Sacher sauce

pepper **1** Refers either to the capsicum, sweet or hot, or the spice *Piper nigrum,* which latter see under peppercorn **2** *(No)* Pepper, the spice

pepper, to To sprinkle or season with ground pepper

pepper dulse A seaweed *Laurencia pinnatifida* with a strong flavour once used as a condiment and chewed like tobacco in Iceland

pepper jelly *(USA)* A Cajun condiment from Louisiana made with chillis, sweet peppers, sugar, vinegar and pectin and coloured red or green. It has a very hot taste

pepper mill A hand operated implement for grinding dried peppercorns to a powder as required

pepper salami A salami covered in crushed peppercorns instead of a casing

pepper sauce *see* sauce poivrade

pepper steak A beef steak coated with crushed peppercorns before frying and served with a sauce made from the deglazed pan juices and cream [also called **steak au poivre**]

pepper tree Various evergreen trees *Schinus* spp. esp. *S. molle* found in South America and from which a commercial food flavouring oil is obtained

peppercorn The berries from a perennial vine *Piper nigrum* harvested at different stages of maturity with a pungent taste. Unripe green peppercorns can be preserved in brine or vinegar and are used whole or crushed. If the green berries are allowed to ferment and then dried they become black peppercorns. White peppercorns are the dried, dehusked ripe berries. All forms are used whole for flavouring. Black and white are also ground for use as a flavouring agent or as a condiment; *see also* long pepper

peppercress *see* cress

peppergrass *see* cress

peppermint A strongly scented plant of the mint family *Mentha x piperita* with dark green pointed leaves and small pink or purple flowers. Mainly cultivated for its oil which is used as a flavouring, but may be used as a culinary herb

peppermint cream A peppermint-flavoured fondant very popular in chocolates served with coffee at the end of a meal

peppermint oil The essential oil extracted from peppermint used as a flavouring

pepperoncini *(USA)* A small, mild, green chilli pepper used sparingly in salads

pepperone *(It)* A sausage made from beef and pork with chopped sweet red peppers and fennel. Cannot be kept

pepperpot *(USA)* A highly seasoned thick soup or thin stew made with tripe

pepperpot soup *(Ca)* A rich soup made from beef, oxtail, pig's trotters, chicken and mixed vegetables including okra, pumpkins and yams, flavoured with chillis and often containing cassava juice

pepperrotsaus *(Ho & No)* Horseradish sauce

pepsin One of the proteases found in the human digestive system and also extracted from pigs' stomachs for use in cheese making

pera *(It & Sp)* Pear

pêra *(Po)* Pear

perca *(Sp)* Perch

percebes *(Sp)* Goose barnacles which grow along the northern Galician coast of north west Spain. Cannot be frozen or canned and are eaten after boiling for 10 minutes. Very expensive

perch A round freshwater fish *Perca* spp. esp. *P. fluviatilis* with a fine delicate flesh but many bones; found in the northern hemisphere. It has a greenish yellow back and is usually up to 30 cm long (500 g). Cooked in any way

perche *(Fr) fem.* Perch, the freshwater fish (Note - also means pole, stick)

perche-soleil *(Fr) fem.* Butterfish (3)

perche-truite *(Fr) fem.* Largemouth black bass

perchia *(It)* Comber, the fish

perciatelli *(It) see* bucatini

perciatelloni *(It) see* bucatini

perdigón *(Sp)* Partridge

perdikes *(Gr)* Partridge

perdiz *(Po & Sp)* Partridge

perdiz a la moda de Alcántara *(Sp)* Stuffed and roasted partridge

perdiz blanca *(Sp)* Ptarmigan

perdiz en chocolate *(Sp)* Partridge baked in a casserole with onions, garlic, parsley and vinegar and topped with chocolate

perdiz estofada a la catalana *(Sp)* Partridge stuffed with sausage and served with a wine and vinegar sauce with chocolate

perdreau *(Fr) masc.* Young partridge

perdrix *(Fr) fem.* Partridge

pere *(It)* Pears

perejil *(Me & Sp)* Parsley

peren *(Ho)* Pears

perets *(Ru)* Pepper

perets farshirovanny *(Ru)* *see* farshirovannye pertsy

Perifollo oloroso *(Sp)* Sweet cicely

périgord, à la *see* périgourdine, à la

Périgord black truffle An edible truffle *Tuber melanosporum* from Périgord, France, which has a wrinkled warty appearance amd a strong distinctive fragrance but with a somewhat mild flavour. Very rare and expensive; *see also* truffle

périgourdine, à la *(Fr)* In the style of Périgord, i.e. sometimes including truffles and/or foie gras

périgourdine, sauce *(Fr) fem.* As sauce Périgueux but with parisienne cut balls or thick slices of truffle instead of chopped truffle

Périgueux, à la *see* périgourdine, à la

Périgueux, sauce *(En & Fr) fem.* An espagnole sauce to which port and finely chopped truffles are added. Served with meat and omelettes

perilla **1** *see* shiso, the herb **2** *see* tetilla, the cheese

Perilla arguts *Bot.* Shiso

perilla oil Oil from the roasted seeds of a variety of perilla *Perilla frutescens* grown in north India, China and Japan and used in Asian cooking

peri-peri *see* piri-piri (2)

perişoare cu verdeaţă *(Ro)* Meatballs made of a mixture of minced beef and fat pork (1:3) with plenty of chopped and fried onions and seasoning, shaped into small balls, rolled in a mixture of chopped green herbs and fried very slowly in butter. Served with demi-glace sauce

periwinkle *see* winkle

perlé(e) *(Fr)* Polished or pearl shaped

perleløge *(De)* Silverskin onions

perles du Japon *(Fr) fem.* Tapioca pearls

Perlhuhn *(Ge)* Guinea fowl

perline *(It)* Tiny balls of pasta used in soup

Perlmoos *(Ge)* Carragheen

perna de carne *(Po)* Leg of meat

pernice *(It)* Grey-legged partridge

pernice di montagna *(It)* Ptarmigan

pernice rosa *(It)* Red-legged partridge

perpetual spinach *see* spinach beet

Persea americana *Bot.* Avocado

Pershore egg plum *(UK)* A yellow, almost pear shaped plum used in cooking and jam making

Persian leek A small variety of leek about the size of a spring onion used as a flavouring

Persian lime A lime *Citrus latifolia* with a very thin skin and a distinctive aroma, usually picked when dark green. It has a very juicy and acid flesh with no seeds and is unsuitable for manufacturing purposes. It is produced in the USA, Israel and Australia [also called **Tahiti lime, bearss lime**]

Persian melon *(USA)* A large spherical dark green netted melon with a bright pink-orange flesh. It has finer netting than the musk melon

Persian style rice *(USA)* Plain boiled rice with a crust similar to kateh

persicata *(It)* A paste made from peaches which is dried and cut into squares

persico comune *(It)* Perch

persico sole *(It)* Butterfish (3)

persico trota *(It)* Largemouth black bass

persika *(Sw)* Peach

persil *(Fr) masc.* Parsley

persil, sauce *(Fr) fem. see* parsley sauce

persilja *(Sw)* Parsley

persiljespäckad kalv *(Sw)* Fillet or cushion of veal stuffed with chopped parsley and chervil, browned in butter then pot roasted with tomato concassé and stuffed olives. The meat is cut in thick slices and served over the reduced cooking liquor

persillade *(Fr) fem.* A mixture of chopped garlic or shallots and chopped parsley used as a flavouring

persillade, sauce *(Fr) fem.* A vinaigrette dressing flavoured with persillade

persille *(De)* Parsley

persillé(e) *(Fr)* **1** Sprinkled with parsley **2** The name of many local goats' milk cheeses from the Savoie, each named after a village as e.g. Persillé de Thônes, meaning veined **3** *(of beef)* Marbled

persimmon A large tomato-like fruit from a large group of tropical trees *Diospyros* spp. but normally *D. kaki.* The green inedible skin turns a glossy yellow-orange as the fruit matures and has a central core of seeds like an apple and a large calyx. Found in three principal varieties viz. kaki (Ja & Ch), apple of the orient, Sharon fruit (Israel) and mabalo, q.v. Eaten as a dessert in fruit salads or other dishes. May be used as a decoration, in jam making or may be dried [also called **kaki**]

peru *(Po)* Turkey

peru paulistano *(Br)* Turkey stuffed with a mixture of bread, tapioca and chopped ham, braised and served with thickened cooking liquor

peruna *(Fi)* Potato

perzik *(Ho & Ru)* Peach

pesca *(It)* Peach (Note - also means fishing)

pesca nettarina *(It)* Nectarine

pescada *(Po)* Haddock, cod and similar fish

pescadilla *(Sp)* Whiting

pescado 1 *(Po)* Any food fish **2** *(Sp)* Fish

pescado a la asturiana *(Sp)* Fish cooked in wine with onions and chocolate and served with mushrooms

pescado blanco a la malagueña *(Sp)* Cold skinned and deboned whitefish served with a covering of mayonnaise

pescado frito a la andaluza *(Sp)* Fish coated in an egg and flour batter and fried in olive oil

pescado a la sal *(Sp)* Whole unskinned fish baked in hot rock salt

pesce *(It)* Fish

pesce cane *(It)* Dogfish

pesce cappone *(It)* Scorpion fish

pesce al cartoccio *(It)* Fish baked en papillote

pesce castagna *(It)* Pomfret, the fish

pesce di castagna *(It)* Fish baked with chestnuts and served with mint sauce

pesce forca *(It)* Gurnard, the fish

pesce gatto *(It)* Channel catfish

pesce martello *(It)* Hammerhead shark

pesce persico *(It)* Perch

pesce San Pietro *(It)* John Dory

pesce sciabola *(It)* Scabbard fish

pesce spada *(It)* Swordfish

pesce stocco *(It)* Stockfish, dried cod

pesce da taglio *(It)* Halibut

pesce turcino *(It)* Mackerel

pesce violino *(It)* Guitar fish

pesce volante *(It)* Flying fish

pesche *(It)* Peaches

pesche noce *(It)* Nectarines

pesciolini *(It)* Young fish similar to whitebait but of the local fish varieties, mainly sardines. Cooked as whitebait

pêssego *(Po)* Peach

pestiño *(Sp)* A sweet honey fritter

pestle A heavy and short stumpy stick-like implement with a rounded end of ceramic, glass, metal or other hard material for use with a mortar. See pestle and mortar

pestle and mortar The pestle and mortar are used in combination to crush and/or to grind by hand foods, spices and the like to a fine powder or paste

pesto *(En & It)* A mixture of basil, parsley, pine kernels and olive oil pounded together or processed. Used to flavour pasta and as a general flavouring. Sometimes contains grated Parmesan cheese. So called because once prepared in a pestle and mortar

pestun de fave *(It) see* maro

pet de nonne *(Fr) masc.* A light deep fried sweet fritter similar to a beignet from Burgundy. Lit. nun's fart

petacciuola *(It)* Plantain

petai *(Id)* Parkia

petcha A Jewish appetizer made from calf's foot jelly flavoured with garlic and vinegar, seasoned and studded with wedges of hard boiled egg [also called **cholodyetz, fisnoga, pilsa, putcha**]

pétéram *(Fr)* A rich offal stew containing sheep's trotters and tripe from Languedoc

Petersilie *(Ge)* Parsley

petha *(In)* Strips of wax gourd softened with lime water (Calcium hydroxide), then boiled in sugar syrup to form a candied confection

petis *(Id)* A fermented fish sauce

petit beurre *(Fr) masc.* A small biscuit made with butter. Butter cookie (USA)

petit déjeuner *(Fr) masc.* Breakfast. Lit. small lunch

petit-duc, au *(Fr)* In the style of the small duke, i.e. garnished with asparagus tips, truffles, creamed chicken in small pastry cases and possibly mushrooms

petit four *see* petits fours

petit gris *(Fr) masc.* A small dark brown snail from the North of France

petit lait *(Fr) masc.* Milk whey

petit pain *(Fr) masc.* A quarter sized baguette weighing about 50 g

petit pain fourré *(Fr) masc.* A filled roll or bridge roll

petit pâté *(Fr) masc.* A small pork pie or meat patty

petit salé *(Fr) masc.* Small pieces of salt pork

petit-suisse *(He & Fr) masc.* A 30 g Suisse cheese [also called **Demi-suisse**]

petite marmite 1 *(En & Fr) fem.* Double strength consommé in which are simmered progressively diced lean beef, blanched pieces of chicken winglets, turned carrots, pieces of celery, leek and cabbage and turned turnip so that all are cooked at the same time, the whole seasoned, degreased and served in a marmite dish garnished with slices of beef bone marrow and accompanied by a slice of toasted French bread and grated cheese **2** *(Fr) fem.* A small earthenware bulbous dish with two moulded handles used to serve consommé.

petite roussette *(Fr) fem.* Lesser spotted dogfish

petites *(Fr) masc.* Sheep's or calves' tripe

petits fours *(En & Fr) masc.* Small sweetmeats, chocolates and tiny decorated cakes served with the coffee at the end of a meal

petits pois *(En & Fr) masc.* A small variety of a very tender pea with a delicate flavour

petits secs *(Fr) masc.* Small cream biscuits

petonchio *(It)* Variegated scallop

pétoncle *(Fr) masc.* Variegated scallop

pétrir *(Fr)* To knead

Petroselinum crispum *Bot.* Curly parsley

Petroselinum crispum 'Neapolitanum' *Bot.* Flat leaved (Italian or French) parsley

Petroselinum crispum 'tuberosam' *Bot.* Hamburg parsley

Petrus *(Be)* A pale yellow, supple textured, strong smelling but mild-flavoured cows' milk cheese from Loo with an orange rind. The cheese contains many small holes

petruska kudryavana *(Ru)* Flat leaved parsley

pe tsai *(Ch) see* Chinese leaves

petti di pollo *(It)* Chicken breasts

petti tachino a la milanese *(It)* Panéed and fried breast of turkey

petticoat tails *(UK)* Skirt-shaped shortbread biscuits from Scotland

pettine *(It)* Small scallops

pettitoes Young sucking pig's trotters which may be braised or grilled or used for their gelatine content

petto *(It)* Breast of an animal, brisket, etc.

peultjes *(Ho)* Small young peas or mangetout

peverada *(It) see* peperata

peynir *(Tu)* Cheese

pez *(Sp)* Fish

pez cinto *(Sp)* Scabbard fish

pez espada *(Sp)* Swordfish

pez de limón *(Sp)* Amberjack

pez martillo *(Sp)* Hammerhead shark

pez de San Pedro *(Sp)* John Dory

pezzo *(It)* A piece (of cake, etc.)

Pfahlmuschel *(Ge)* Farmed mussel

pfälzer Leberwurst *(Ge)* Smooth liver sausage containing coarse pieces of offal

Pfannkuchen *(Ge)* Pancake. The German variety tend to be thicker than in the UK or France

Pfeffer *(Ge)* Pepper

Pfeffergurke *(Ge)* Gherkin

Pfefferkuchen *(Ge)* A spice cake similar to gingerbread eaten at Christmas

Pfefferlinge *(Ge)* Chanterelle

Pfefferminz *(Ge)* Peppermint

Pfeffernüsse *(Ge)* Spiced ginger biscuits made by the blending method e.g from self-raising flour, golden syrup, honey, sugar and butter (12:8:6:4:1) well-flavoured with spices and baked at 205°C

Pfefferpotthast *(Ge)* Boned and trimmed stewing steak cut in large pieces, simmered with sliced onions, a BG and seasoning until cooked, BG removed and all thickened with breadcrumbs and flavoured with plenty of pepper and lemon

Pfeilwurz *(Ge)* Arrowroot

Pfirsich *(Ge)* Peach

Pflaume *(Ge)* Plum

Pflaumenschlehe *(Ge)* Bullace, the fruit

Pfnutli *(He)* Apple fritters

pH A measure of acidity or alkalinity related to the concentration of hydrogen ions (positively charged hydrogen atoms) in solution. Values range from 1 the most acid through 7, neutral, to 14 the most alkaline. Some typical pH values are: gastric juice 1.3 to 3.0, lemon juice 2.1, cranberry sauce 2.6, orange juice 3.0, apples 3.4, tomatoes 4.4, black coffee 5.0, egg yolk 6.0 to 6.6, milk 6.9, baking soda solution 8.4, egg white 9.6 to 10.0, household ammonia 11.9

phai tong *(Th)* Bamboo shoot

phak hom pom *(La)* Coriander leaves

phak si *(La)* Dill seed

phalazee *(Bm)* Cardamom

phase A physical state of matter such as gas, vapour, liquid or solid. Two or more phases are common in many foods, e.g. milk and cream contain two liquid phases, water and butterfat, whipped eggs contain liquid and gas phases, cooked meringue contains a solid and gas phase and some cake mixtures are very complex mixtures of phases; *see also* dispersed phase, continuous phase

Phaseolus aconitifolius *Bot.* Moth bean

Phaseolus acutifolius *Bot.* Tepary bean

Phaseolus aureus *Bot.* Mung bean

Phaseolus canceratus *Bot.* Rice bean

Phaseolus coccineus *Bot.* Runner bean

Phaseolus limensis *Bot.* Butter bean

Phaseolus lunatus *Bot.* Butter bean

Phaseolus mungo *Bot.* Mung bean

Phaseolus vulgaris *Bot.* French bean, kidney bean, etc.

pheasant The most widespread of all game birds *Phasianus colchicus* weighing about 1 to 1.5 kg and suitable for two persons. Hen birds are less tough than the cock but the cock has a better flavour. The feathered birds should be hung by the feet for 3 to 10 days until blood begins to drip from the beak. The young birds are barded, not larded, with fatty bacon and roasted at 190°C for 45 to 60 minutes. Shooting season in the UK 1st October to the 1st of February. Hanging time 3 to 10 days, some say 12 to 15 days at 6°C

phen *(Vi)* Alum

phenyl benzene *see* E230, diphenyl

Philadelphia cheese steak *(USA)* A crisp roll covered with thin slices of beef and/or cheese, with relishes, etc.

Philadelphia cream cheese A heavily promoted and well-known brand of processed cream cheese q.v.

Philadelphia eggs *(USA)* A split muffin covered with cooked sliced breast of chicken, a poached egg and Hollandaise sauce

phil noi *(La)* Peppercorn

philpy *(USA)* A rice bread from South Carolina

pho *(Vi)* A rice noodle soup made with beef stock

phong jau *(Ch)* Chicken feet

phool gobi *(In)* Cauliflower

phooti *(In)* A variety of melon which burst open when ripe. Used in the unripe state as a vegetable

phosphated flour *(USA)* Flour with added salt, yeast and yeast nutrients which only needs mixing with water to make dough. Does not keep well

phosphates Salts of phosphoric acid used for flavouring and as stabilizers. The important ones used in the food industry are disodium dihydrogen, tetrasodium, tetrapotassium and trisodium diphosphate all classified as E450(a) and pentasodium triphosphate and pentapotassium triphosphate classified as E450(b); *see also* polyphosphates

phosphoric acid *see* orthophosphoric acid, E338

phosphorus An essential inorganic element necessary for health. Usually in the form of phosphates which are essential for cellular processes as well as for the construction of bones and teeth

phul *(Ne)* Egg

phulka *(In)* A small chapati

phyllo pastry *see* filo pastry

Phyllostachys pubescens *Bot.* One of the cultivated bamboo shoots

physalis *see* cape gooseberry

Physalis alkekengi *Bot.* Chinese lantern

Physalis ixocarpa *Bot.* Tomatillo

Physalis peruviana *Bot.* Cape gooseberry

Physalis pruinosa *Bot.* Dwarf cape gooseberry

phytic acid A plant acid which tends to bind iron and zinc in the plants and to carry these trace elements through the human gut without absorption. The amino acids methionine and cysteine present in animal products but not in plant-derived protein promote the release of these trace elements and hence their absorption.

Phytolacca americana *Bot.* Pokeweed

phytomenadion *see* vitamin K

piacere, a *(It)* At choice, free choice of menu items

piada *(It) see* piadina

piadina *(It)* A soft flat bread usually served warm filled with sausage, ham or spinach and/or Ricotta cheese [also called **piada, pie**]

piantaggine *(It)* Plantain

pianuzza *(It)* Dab, the fish

piatti *(It)* Dishes, plates (of food)

piatto, al *(It)* A description of eggs shirred or gently cooked in a dish

piatto del giorno *(It)* Dish of the day

piaz *(In)* Onion

pibil pork *(Me) see* cochinita pibil

picada *(Me) see* garnacha

picadillo 1 *(Sp)* Minced meat **2** *(Me)* A cooked savoury mixture of minced pork and beef with onions, oil, tomatoes, garlic, vinegar, raisins, chopped almonds, spices, herbs and seasonings, used as a filling or served with rice **3** A salad of orange, onion, sweet peppers and cooked shredded salt codfish

picadinho *(Br)* Minced beef simmered in stock with chopped onions and tomatoes. Served with the addition of chopped hard-boiled eggs and olives, accompanied by rice or mashed potatoes

picado *(Po)* A type of meat hash

Picadon *(Fr)* A soft goats' milk cheese from the Rhône valley cast in 100 g discs. The white paste has a sharp nutty-flavoured taste after maturing for 1 to 4 weeks. It has AOC status. Contains 45% fat

picante *(Sp)* Piquant, hot and spicy

picatostes *(Sp)* Deep fried bread slices

piccalilli A bright yellow mustard-flavoured pickle made from brined pieces of cauliflower, marrow, green beans, pickling onions and cucumber in a sauce made from white vinegar, flour, sugar, mustard, ginger and turmeric [also called **mustard pickle**]

piccante *(It)* Piquant, hot and spicy

piccata *(It)* A small medallion or escalope of meat, usually a thin fried escalope of veal served in a sour lemon sauce and garnished with lemon wedges

piccioncello *(It)* Pigeon

piccioncino *(It)* Pigeon

piccione *(It)* Pigeon [also called **piccioncello, piccioncino**]

piccolo *(It)* Small

Pichelsteiner *(Ge) see* Pichelsteinerfleisch

Pichelsteinerfleisch *(Ge)* A flame proof earthenware dish filled with alternate layers of meat (sliced marrow, beef, pork, veal and mutton mixed together) and vegetables (sliced onions, carrots, celeriac, potatoes and savoy cabbage), seasoned, moistened with water, covered and baked in the oven. Served from the pot [also called **Pichelsteiner**]

pichón *(Sp)* Pigeon, squab

pickerel A young pike also a small relative of the pike found in North America

Pickert *(Ge)* A type of peasant bread made from potato flour or grated potatoes and wheat flour or buckwheat meal, fried or baked

pickle Food, usually chopped vegetables and fruits, preserved in a flavoured sauce or solution which prevents the growth of microorganisms. Usually used as a condiment or accompaniment and appreciated for its salty or sharp acidic flavour

pickle, to To preserve food by placing it in brine, vinegar or other acid solutions together with flavourings. The low pH or high salt concentration prevents the growth of microorganisms

pickled bean curd *see* bean curd cheese

pickled cucumber Cucumbers or cucumber pieces or slices pickled in spiced brine or vinegar

pickled eggs Shelled hard-boiled eggs pickled in spiced and seasoned vinegar. Usually eaten between 1 and 4 months after pickling

pickled fish *see* caveach

pickled garlic Peeled garlic cloves pickled in vinegar, possibly with the addition of sugar. Eaten as a snack or side dish

pickled limes Limes are preserved by immersing in soya sauce with sugar, salt and vinegar (SEA), by salting and drying (Ch), or by slitting, filling with spices and immersing in oil (In)

pickled shallots Shallots pickled in a vinegar and sugar mixture, used as a snack or side dish in China and Japan

pickled testicles *(Ic)* Testicles pickled in whey

pickling brine A mixture of 500 g salt, 40g of saltpetre and 20 g of brown sugar per litre of water. This mixture is oversaturated and will contain solid salt but this will disappear as pickling progresses. Various spices and herbs may be added. Joints of meat are normally pickled for about 8 days and if weighing over 4 kg should be injected with the brine

pickling onion *see* button onion

pickling salt *(USA)* Pure salt without additives such as anti-caking agents which are often insoluble and would cloud the pickle

pickling spice *(UK)* A mixture of whole spices used to flavour vinegar for preparation of pickles and chutney, consisting of a selection from dried ginger, mustard seed, cloves, black peppercorns, small chilli peppers, mace, coriander seed and allspice berries

picnic A meal taken in the open air usually from food laid out on a cloth on the ground or on collapsible tables

picnic ham *(USA)* A cured and smoked front leg of pork, similar in taste to ham

Picodon *(Fr)* The name of various goats' milk cheeses from the Drôme-Rhône valley

Picón *(Sp) see* Cabrales

pi dan *(Ch)* Salted duck eggs

pie 1 A sweet or savoury mixture enclosed totally in pastry and cooked in a container or placed in a pie dish and covered with pastry prior to cooking **2** *(It)* Foot **3** *(It) see* piadina

pie, à la *(Fr)* black and white like a magpie. See e.g. fromage à la pie

pie d'asino *(It)* Dog cockle

pie cherry *see* acid cherry

pie dish A round or oval dish with a rim on which the pastry crust is supported, sometimes with a projection rising from the centre to also support the pie crust

pie veal *(UK)* Diced meat from cheap secondary cuts of veal e.g. neck, scrag and breast

pièce de boeuf *(Fr) fem.* A prime cut of beef

pièce montée *(Fr) fem.* The centrepiece of a cold or hot buffet or other display of food; alternatively a French wedding cake of profiteroles built up into a cone and held together with caramel

pieces *see* light brown sugar

piecrust pastry *(USA)* Shortcrust pastry

pied *(Fr) masc.* Foot or trotter

pied de cochon *(Fr) masc.* Pig's trotter

pied de porc *(Fr) masc.* Pig's trotter

piedini *(It)* Feet, trotters, e.g. of a pig

piedini di maiale alla piemontese *(It)* Pig's trotters, panéed and deep fried

Piedmontese truffle *see* Italian white truffle *(Tuber magnatum)*

Piedrafita *(Sp) see* Cebrero

pieds cendrillons *(Fr) masc.* A mixture of seasoned meat from pigs' trotters minced with mushrooms and truffles either made as a crépinette, wrapped in pastry and baked in the oven or wrapped in greased paper and cooked in hot ashes

pieds et paquets *(Fr) masc.* A Provençal dish of sheep's tripe folded into packets filled with a savoury mixture and cooked slowly with trotters, skinned tomatoes, herbs and seasoning [also called **pieds-paquets, pieds-en-paquets**]

piémontaise, à la *(Fr)* In the style of Piedmont, Italy, i.e. garnished with polenta or risotto, white truffles and sometimes tomato sauce

pierna *(Sp)* Leg of meat

pierna de cordero *(Sp)* Leg of lamb

piernik *(Pl)* A Christmas gingerbread cake made by the melting method sweetened with sugar and honey, raised with baking powder and flavoured with ground ginger, cinnamon and nutmeg

pierog *(Ru, Pl & Hu)* Potato dough stuffed with potato and onion, served fried with sour cream

pierogi *(Pl)* A type of ravioli usually filled with either curd cheese, sauerkraut or mushrooms. Larger than Italian ravioli

pierozki *(Ru & Pl)* Small savoury semi-circular pasties made from 10 cm rounds of choux, sour or puff pastry with a variety of fillings, baked at 200°C or deep fried. Often served as an accompaniment to soup or as a snack [also called **pirozhki**]

pieterman *(Ho)* Weever fish

pieuvre *(Fr) fem.* Octopus

pig 1 *(UK)* Any member of the *Suidae* family, intelligent animals with a bristly skin and long snouts with which they can root about in earth and leaf litter looking for food; esp. *Sus scrofa*, the domesticated pig, and European wild boar [also called **porker**] **2** *(USA)* A sucking pig or young immature pig

pig-in-a-blanket *(USA)* Sausage roll

pig weed *see* summer purslane

pigeon *(En & Fr) masc.* A rather tough wild bird or more tender domesticated bird weighing about 450 to 700 g. Part roast at 200°C for 15 minutes, remove breasts and poach in stock made from the remainder of the carcase, using reduced cooking liquor as sauce. The domesticated bird is treated like chicken. There are no restrictions on shooting; *see also* wood pigeon [also called **wood dove**]

pigeon pea The peas from a short lived perennial shrub *Cajanus cajan,* which are a staple food and grown in Africa, India and the Caribbean. The peas may be red to white, brown, mottled or black and the green pods can be used as a vegetable. [also called **cajan pea, red gram, gunga pea, toor dal, red chick pea, tuware, tur, tuvaran, rarhar, arhar**]

pigeonneau *(Fr) masc.* Squab or young pigeon

piggvar *(No & Sw)* Turbot

pigment rubine *see* E180

pigmented grapefruit A comparatively recent development of grapefruit, some varieties having occurred naturally and other having been produced by irradiating seed (e.g. rio red). All are characterized by a red pigmentation of the flesh and in some varieties, of the rind. The pigment is lycopene (as in tomatoes) and is produced by prolonged high temperature. The common variety is ruby but many new varieties are in the process of development

pigmented orange A type of sweet orange which develops red pigmentation (anthocyanins) in the flesh adjacent to segment walls and near the flower end. The flavour is distinctive and is sometimes said to resemble that of a raspberry or cherry. As they require low night temperatures to develop the red colour they tend only to be grown in the Mediterranean and similar climates [also called **blood orange**]

pignatta *(It)* Earthenware cooking pot

pignola *(USA)* Pine nut

pignoli *(It)* Pine nuts

pignolia *see* pine nut

pignons *(Fr) masc.* Pine nuts

pignut *see* tiger nut

Pigouille *(Fr)* A creamy cheese from Charente made from any milk and usually sold wrapped in straw

pigs in blankets *(UK)* Cabbage rolls

pig's cheek Half the lower part of the pig's cheek including the jaw bone, and half the tongue and snout, pickled, boiled, boned and coated with breadcrumbs, sliced and served cold or for frying. Alternatively dried and cured [also called **Bath chap**]

pig's ear Pig's ears may be cooked together with pig's trotters but are generally used for manufactured meat products

pig's fry **1** *see* haslet **2** Heart, liver and sweetbreads of a pig, cut in pieces, boiled until tender, drained, coated with a mixture of seasoned flour and rubbed sage and fried. Served with fried potatoes, greens and gravy

pig's head The major source of meat for brawn q.v., occasionally used as a source of meat for pie fillings and sometimes roasted whole, glazed and an apple placed in its mouth for use as a table decoration esp. at theme banquets

pig's kidney Small but elongated kidneys with a good flavour which may be cooked in any way. Allow one per person

pig's liver A strong-flavoured liver which should be soaked in milk for at least 1 hour. Generally stewed or casseroled, made into pâté or used in stuffings

pig's trotters Pig's feet used like calves' feet as a source of gelatine or may be boned, stuffed and roasted or the meat used in brawn. Boiled pig's trotters used to be eaten dressed with vinegar as a northern UK delicacy

pihvi *(Fi)* Beef steak

piimä *(Fi)* Curdled milk, junket, clabbered milk, buttermilk

piirakka *(Fi)* Meat or fish and rice cooked in a pasty

pijlinktvis *(Ho)* Squid

pikant *(Ge)* Piquant, spiced, often denotes coated with a hot prepared mustard

Pikantesosse *(Ge)* Piquant sauce

Pikantwurst *(Au)* A spicy sausage similar to Csaba

Pikatinij *(Ru)* A semi-hard surface ripened cows' milk cheese with scattered holes. Contains 45% water, 25% fat and 23% protein

pike A large (up to 4 kg commercially but can be 20 kg) freshwater fish *Esox* spp. with a long pointed nose, greenish yellow back and lighter underside found in temperate waters of the northern hemisphere. The flesh is lean, white and dry with an excellent flavour but very bony. Usually soaked before cooking in any way [also called **jackfish, freshwater shark, waterwolf**]

pike-perch A temperate freshwater fish from the northern hemisphere *Stizostedion* or *Lucioperca* spp. which has the body of a perch but a pike's nose and a brown striped back. Cooked like pike or perch

pikefleisch *(Fr & Ge) see* boeuf salé

pikelet *(UK)* A name used for a variety of teacakes, in particular the crumpet *(Yorkshire)* and the Scottish pancake, either the yeasted or non-yeasted types. Usually eaten warm

pilaf *(Tu) see* pilav

pilaff A rice dish made from finely chopped onions sweated in butter, rice added and sweated 2 minutes, twice the volume of boiling seasoned white or fish stock added with a BG and all cooked under a cartouche in a 240°C oven for 15 to 20 minutes until cooked. The BG is removed, the dish seasoned and butter stirred in. Often served with cooked meat, fish or vegetables; *see also* pilaw (Pl) and pilau (In)

pilafi *(Gr)* **1** Grains of pasta resembling rice **2** Rice fried to a cream colour in butter then simmered in stock until tender

pilaki *(Tu)* Fish cutlets or steaks braised with vegetables and garlic then served cold, dressed with lemon juice and garnished with chopped parsley

pilao *(In) see* pilau

pilau *(In)* A savoury rice dish made from spices, garlic and chilli fried in butter or ghee, meat added and fried 5 minutes, yoghurt progressively added until no more is absorbed, soaked and drained Basmati rice added with saffron and salt and fried. The whole is then covered with stock, brought to the boil and cooked on a very low heat until the rice is tender adding more stock if too dry. Garnished with crisply fried onions before service. Fruits and vegetables may be added with the rice [also called **pilao, pulao, pullao**]

pilav *(Tu)* Round grain rice or bulgar wheat cooked until tender then mixed with butter or oil [also called **pilaf**]

pilaw *(Pl)* A type of pilaff with lamb and tomato purée

pilchard A small round oily seafish *Sardina pilchardus* and *Clupea pilchardus* which when immature is called a sardine. Often canned in brine or tomato sauce, but can be cooked whole. Found off the south west coast of the UK. Fresh pilchards can be distinguished from small herring by raised lines that run back from the eyes and from sprats by their lack of the line of spiny scales along the centre line of the belly

Pilgermuschel *(Ge)* Pilgrim scallop [also called **Jacobsmuschel**]

pilgrim scallop The Mediterranean scallop *Pecten jacobaeus,* slightly smaller than the great scallop [also called **coquille Saint Jacques**]

piliç *(Tu)* Chicken

pili pili *(Af)* Chilli pepper

pillau *see* pilau

pilon de cuisse *(Fr) masc.* Chicken drumstick

piloncillo *(Me)* A dark unrefined sugar similar to muscovado, formed into small cylinders and sometimes wrapped in raffia [also called **panoche, panocha**]

pilot biscuit *see* hardtack

pilsa *see* petcha

Pilz *(Ge)* **1** A crumbly, yellowish, blue-veined semi-soft cows' milk cheese (to 5 kg) with a strong distinctive flavour and a soft or dry rind. Usually served as a dessert cheese. Contains 49% water, 27% fat and 18% protein [also called **Edelpilzkäse**] **2** Mushroom

Pilzschnitzel *(Au)* A vegetarian cutlet made from mushrooms, carrots and peas

piman *(Ja)* Sweet pepper

pimen *(Ja)* Sweet pepper

piment *(Fr) masc.* Capsicum

piment doux *(Fr) masc.* Sweet pepper

piment fort *(Fr) masc.* Chilli or cayenne pepper

piment rouge *(Fr) masc.* Chilli pepper

pimenta-da-caiena *(Po)* Cayenne pepper

Pimenta dioica *Bot.* Allspice

Pimenta officinalis *Bot.* Allspice

pimentão-doce *(Po)* Sweet red or green pepper

pimento **1** *(It)* Allspice **2** *see* pimiento **3** A very mild chilli pepper

pimento butter Red peppers pounded with butter and sieved

pimento-do-reino *(Po)* Black pepper

pimentón *(Sp)* Dried and ground red pepper, generally bright red and with a strong aroma, similar to paprika

pimient *(Ru)* Allspice

pimienta **1** *(Po & Sp)* Pepper, capsicum **2** *(Sp)* Pepper *P. nigrum*

pimienta inglesa *(Sp)* Allspice

pimienta negra *(Sp)* Black pepper

pimiento **1** *(Sp)* A variety of red, yellow or green sweet pepper with a good flavour often sold canned or bottled [also called **pimento**] **2** *(USA)* Sweet pepper

pimiento de Jamaica *(Sp)* Allspice

pimpinela *(Sp)* Salad burnet

pimpinella *(It)* Salad burnet

Pimpinella anisum *Bot.* Anise

Pimpinelle *(Ge)* Salad burnet

pimprenelle *(Fr) fem.* Salad burnet

pin bone of beef *(UK)* Welsh and west country term for rump of beef

pin cherry *(USA) see* bird cherry

piña *(Sp)* Pineapple

pinaattiohukaiset *(Fi)* Spinach-flavoured pancakes

pinaksiw *(Ph)* Sardines or similar fish layered in a pot with banana leaves, salt and coconut vinegar and simmered for 20 minutes

pinaroli *(It)* A small fungus found in pine woods

pinbone steak *(USA)* A steak cut from the sirloin. See sirloin steak

pinch A dry measure often used in recipes for a small quantity of powder. The amount of powder held between the thumb and forefinger, roughly equal to one quarter of a gram. 15 pinches per teaspoon

pincisgrassi *(It) see* vincisgrassi maceratese

pinda *(Ho)* Peanuts

pindakaas *(Ho)* Peanut butter

pindangga *(Ph)* Eel

Pindos *(Gr)* A cheese similar to Kefalotiri

pine kernel *see* pine nut

pine mushroom *see* matsutake (Ja)

pine nut The seed of the Mediterranean stone pine tree *Pinus pinea* from the Mediterranean and North Africa. They are sold shelled, are cream coloured with a slightly resinous flavour and oily texture and about the size of a lemon pip. Popular in Middle Eastern and Italian cooking and used to make pesto. The seeds of various other pine trees are eaten worldwide e.g. *P. koraiensis* (Ko), *P. gerardiana* (Himalayas), *P. cembra* (He), *P. cembroides* (Me and southwest USA). In fact most pine tree seeds if sufficiently large are eaten somewhere [also called **Indian nut, pignola, pine kernel**]

pine nut oil An expensive fine oil extracted from pine nuts. Used for salad dressings

pineapple The fruit (to 30 cm long and 15 cm dia.) of a tropical plant *Ananas comosus* which is the result of the coalescence of the fruits of a hundred or more flowers. It grows at the top of a thick stalk which springs from the centre of a rosette of long spiky leaves. The golden-yellow flesh is firm, juicy and fibrous with a central inedible core. The skin varies from green to yellow or red as it matures. Sold whole or tinned with the skin and central core removed. Used as a dessert fruit or in savoury dishes, e.g. with pork. The uncooked juice which contains active proteases may be used to tenderize meat and will prevent gelatine based jellies from setting

pineapple cheese *(USA)* A pink coloured soft textured Cheddar-like cheese from Connecticut

pineapple fritter A slice of pineapple, skinned, cored, floured, coated with a batter and deep fried

pineapple guava *see* feijoa

pineapple melon A Japanese melon rather like a water melon with a green striped skin and a crisp, sweet, golden flesh tasting slightly of pineapple. now grown in Israel

ping *(Th)* Dry cooking of food in the oven or over a source of heat such as charcoal [also called **bing**]

ping guo *(Ch)* Apple

pinhead oatmeal Dehusked whole oats cut into 3 or 4 pieces per individual grain [also called **steel cut oatmeal**]

Pinienkern *(He)* Pine nut

Piniennuss *(Ge)* Pine nut

pinion The wing of a bird (poultry or game)

pinipig *(Ph)* Toasted and flattened glutinous rice used in cakes and desserts and after deep frying used as a crisp topping for sweets and ice cream

pink bean *(USA)* Pinto bean

pink fir apple An irregularly shaped potato with a pink skin, a smooth waxy flesh and a fine nutty flavour. Used for potato salad

pink gingerbuds *see* ginger buds

pink peppercorn *see* schinus molle

pink salmon The smallest of the Pacific salmon *Oncorhynchus gorbuscha* with a dark blue spotted back and silvery underside weighing to 2.5 kg. The flesh is pink, oily and firm textured and it may be cooked in any way [also called **humpback salmon**]

pink sauce *(USA)* Marie-rose sauce

pink shrimp One of the common British varieties (*Pandalus montagui*) of shallow water shrimps, not as good tasting as the brown shrimp

pink trout *see* salmon trout

Pinkel *(Ge)* A type of sausage from Bremen made from beef and/or pork, onions, oats and seasonings and sometimes lightly smoked. Boiled or cooked with other foods [also called **Pinkelwurst**]

Pinkelwurst *(Ge) see* Pinkel

pinne *(It)* Fan mussels

pinnekjøtt *(No)* Salt cured mutton chops steamed over peeled birch twigs

pinocchio *(It)* Pine nut

pinole A mixture of finely ground maize or wheat flour made from the parched grain and mesquite beans sometimes used to make a sweet drink. Used in Mexico and south western USA

pinoli *(It)* Pine nuts

pinolli *(SA)* A mixture of powdered vanilla, spices and ground and toasted chocolate beans

pinolo *(It)* Pine nut

piñón *(Me & Sp)* Pine nut

pint A non-metric fluid measure still in use in the USA and still seen in English recipes. The UK measure is divided into 20 fluid ounces and is 567.5 ml (0.57 litres). The USA measure is divided into 16 fluid ounces and is 0.8 times the UK measure i.e. 473 millilitres. Both are abbreviated pt; *see also* gallon, cup measure, liquid measure, volume measure, dry measure

pintada *(Sp)* Guinea hen

pintade *(Fr) fem.* Guinea fowl

pintadeau *(Fr) masc.* Young guinea fowl

pintail duck A wild duck *Anas acuta* shot for the table

pintarroja *(Sp)* Dogfish [also called **gato marino**]

pinto bean A variety of pale kidney bean *Phaseolus vulgaris* with bright red markings, popular in Spain, Mexico and North America

pin tong *(Ch)* Lump sugar (3)

***Pinus* spp.** *Bot.* Pine trees, the source of pine nuts q.v.

Pinzgauer Bier *(Au)* A distinctive, full-flavoured cows' milk cheese from the district around Salzburg

pinzimonio *(It)* A mixture of olive oil, salt and pepper used as a dressing for raw vegetables

Piora *(He)* A hard scalded-curd cows' milk cheese shaped like a cylinder (to 12 kg). The cheeses are salted and ripened for up to 6 months

pip The small seed of which several are usually found in fruits such as apples, citrus, grapes and melons

pip, to To remove seeds or pips from fruit or vegetables

pipe, to To force a semi-solid mixture through the nozzle of a piping bag and lay it down on some surface; *see also* piping bag

Piper betle *Bot.* The betel pepper vine from which betel leaf is obtained

Piper cubeba *Bot.* Cubeb

Piper longum *Bot.* Long pepper (In)

Piper nigrum *Bot.* Pepper

Piper retrofractum *Bot.* Long pepper (Id)

piperade *(Fr) fem.* Tomatoes, sweet peppers, onions and garlic cooked in olive oil or goose fat until soft, then chopped herbs and beaten eggs added to the mixture and lightly scrambled. Served with fried or grilled ham and garnished with triangular pieces of fried bread

pipi Smooth shelled seawater bivalves found in New Zealand *Mesodesma nova-zelandiae* and Australia *Plebidonax deltoides*

pipián *(Me)* A sauce served with chicken made from ground sesame and pumpkin seeds, spices and ground peanuts or almonds and coloured red

pipikaula *(USA)* A Hawaiian dish of dried beef cooked with soya sauce

piping The decorative lines of icing piped onto a cake

piping bag A triangular shaped bag made of a flexible impervious material with a hole at the pointed end into which a metal or plastic cone with a plain circular or star shaped hole may be fitted. Used for piping any soft but self supporting mixture such as whipped cream, icing, mashed potatoes, meringue mix, etc. into various patterns prior to cooking or for decoration [also called **forcing bag, icing bag**]

Pipo crem' *(Fr)* A log shaped blue-veined cows' milk cheese from Grièges with a similar flavour to Bleu de Bresse [also called **Grièges**]

pippali *(In)* Long pepper

pippuri *(Fi)* Pepper

piquant sauce Chopped shallots and vinegar, reduced by half, demi-glace added, simmered and seasoned. Finished with chopped gherkins, capers, chervil, tarragon and parsley. Served with made up dishes and grilled meats [also called **sauce piquante** (Fr)]

piquante *(Fr)* Highly seasoned, sharp

piquante, sauce *(Fr) fem. see* piquant sauce

piquer *(Fr)* To pierce a joint of meat at various points on its surface with the point of an office knife so as to be able to insert slivers or cloves of garlic or sprigs of herbs

piquín *(Me)* A very small, hot and dark green chilli pepper

piri piri *(Af & Po)* **1** A hot chilli pepper **2** Meat or fish dishes served with a sauce made from piri piri chillis, originally from Portuguese Africa [also called **peri-peri, pilli-pilli**]

piri-piri sauce A simple sauce made from hot chillis in various ways, e.g. by simmering red sweet peppers and red chilli peppers in lemon juice for 5 minutes, passing through a sieve, salting and simmering further or by infusing small red chillis in warm oil

pirinç *(Tu)* Rice

pirog c limonem *(Ru)* Lemon tart

pirogen Semicircular Jewish turnovers similar to piroshki, made with a kneaded dough and a variety of fillings, some specific to particular festivals [also called **knishes**]

pirozhki *(Ru)* Small semicircular pasties made from 10 cm rounds of choux, sour or puff pastry with a variety of fillings, baked at 200°C or deep fried. Often served as an accompaniment to soup or as a snack

pirurutung *(Ph)* A dark purple coloured rice grown around Luzon

pisang *(Id & Ma)* Banana

pisang goreng *(Ho)* Indonesian style fried or baked bananas

pisang-pisang *(Ma)* Bangus, the fish

pisang starch *see* banana flour

piselli *(It)* Peas

piselli all'antica *(It)* Peas cooked with lettuce and finished with cream

piselli alla romana *(It)* Peas cooked in butter with chopped onions and ham

piselli secchi *(It)* Split peas

Pishingertorte *(Au)* A cake made from circular wafers sandwiched with chocolate hazelnut cream and covered with chocolate

pisi hui lal mirich *(In)* Chilli powder

pismo clam A very large hard shell clam *Tivela stultorum* up to 500 g in weight from the coasts of southern California, USA. It makes excellent chowder

pissaladière *(Fr) fem.* A savoury open tart filled with cooked tomatoes and onions, black olives and anchovy fillets from Provence. Eaten hot or cold

pissaldeira *(It)* A flat bread covered with onions, black olives, tomatoes, cheese and anchovies similar to pissaladière

pissenlit *(Fr) masc.* Dandelion

pista *(In)* Pistachio nut

pistacchio *(It)* Pistachio nut

pistache *(Fr) fem.* Pistachio nut

pistachio nut The fruit of a small tree *Pistacia vera* from the Middle East and Central Asia, with bright green kernels in a beige shell which splits but does not detach itself when ripe. Often soaked in brine and dried. Used as a snack, flavouring, garnish or in nougat, halva, ice cream and mortadella [also called **green almond**]

pistacho *(Sp)* Pistachio nut

Pistacia lentiscus *Bot.* Lentisk

Pistacia vera *Bot.* Pistachio nut tree

Pistazie *(Ge)* Pistachio nut

pisto *(Sp)* Chopped tomatoes, courgettes, onions and sweet peppers, fried and stewed together [also called **samfaina, frito de verduras**]

pistocco *(It) see* carta di musica

pistol *see* barrel bread

pistoles *(Fr) fem.* Peeled, stoned and flattened prunes

pistolet *(Fr) masc.* A third sized baguette used for sandwiches [also called **pain pistolet**]

piston *see* barrel bread

pistou *(Fr) masc.* **1** A dip or accompaniment similar to pesto made from basil, garlic and Gruyère cheese processed to a soft paste with olive oil **2** A rich soup containing green beans, potatoes, tomatoes, garlic and vermicelli

Pisum sativum *Bot.* Pea

Pisum sativum* var. *microcarpum *Bot.* The mangetout pea

pit *(USA)* The stone of a fruit

pit, to *see* to stone

pita bread *see* pitta bread

pitahaya The fruit of a cactus from Central and South America with a scaly reddish purple skin and sweet pink but bland flesh containing embedded tiny black edible seeds

Pitcaithly bannock *(UK)* Scottish

shortbread containing chopped mixed peel and topped with flaked almonds before baking

pitepalt *(Sw)* Potato dumplings stuffed with pork

pith The soft white tissue found beneath the zest of citrus fruits and in the centre of some stalks. Citrus pith is usually bitter and is removed in all dishes except marmalade where its pectin content is required

Pithecolobium lobatum *Bot.* Ngapi nut

Pithiviers *(Fr) masc.* A puff or flaky pastry tart or cake filled with almond paste or Pithiviers cream. From the town of the same name

Pithiviers cream A French cake filling made from butter, sugar, eggs, ground almonds and flavourings

Pithiviers au foin *(Fr) masc.* A soft cheese shaped like a disc and covered with dried grass

pito-ja-joulupuuro *(Fi)* A pudding made from pearl barley cooked in milk and served with rosehip or raisin purée

pi-tsi *(Ch)* Water chestnut

pitta *(It)* A flat bread or pizza from Calabria with various toppings

pitta bread *(ME)* Yeast-raised dough formed into thin flat ovals and baked in the oven. Allowed to cool in a humid atmosphere or wrapped in a damp cloth to make the surface leathery. Often opened along one side to make a pocket which can be filled with cooked meat, salad, etc. Known as khubz in Arabic [also called **pita bread**]

pitta maniata *(It)* A sandwich of pitta filled with eggs, cheese, sausages and peppers

pitta 'nchiusa *(It)* A sandwich of pitta filled with nuts and raisins moistened with grape juice

pitulle *(It)* A yeasted plain flour dough with a little olive oil and coarse sea salt, proved until doubled, mixed with a selection of chopped onions, sun dried tomatoes, olive, capers, anchovies, mushrooms, etc. proved again, then fried in small teaspoonfuls until golden and puffed up.

piviere *(It)* Plover

pizza *(It)* A popular and cheap meal which was once used for leftover dough from bread baking. The yeast-raised dough is rolled out into a thin circle, covered with sieved tomatoes, oregano and pieces of mozarella cheese together with various toppings such as ham, salami, hard boiled eggs, tuna, anchovies, olives, etc. all in small pieces. This is cooked quickly in the oven on a flat sheet or in a shallow dish until the cheese melts and bubbles

pizza cheese *(USA)* A soft spun-curd cheese similar to Mozzarella made from cows' milk using either a starter of *Lactobacillus bulgaricus* and *Streptococcus thermophilus* or citric acid to curdle the milk. Used particularly for pizzas and contains somewhat less water than real Mozzarella, roughly 47% water, 24% fat and 25% protein

pizza dough A typical yeasted dough made of strong flour and tepid water with 30 to 60 ml of olive oil, 10 to 30 ml of active dried yeast and 10 ml of salt per kg of flour. Proved, knocked back and proved again. Exact proportions of flour and water depend on the flour. This dough will keep for 7 days in the refrigerator if oiled and covered with film

pizza oven The traditional pizza oven was brick with a stone floor and a wood fire to one side radiating heat from the brick roof onto the pizza. Modern ovens mimic these characteristics by having a large hot mass of metal

pizza di ricotta *(It)* Cheesecake

pizzaiola *(It)* A sauce made from skinned and deseeded tomatoes, garlic, parsley, oregano and seasoning. The word is also used to describe dishes served with this sauce

pizzelle *(It)* **1** Deep fried pizza dough served with tomato sauce and a variety of fillings **2** A thin circular biscuit baked on a patterned griddle and bent when hot to form a cone or similar for filling with various creams

pizzette *(It)* A dough made from flour, eggs, gorgonzola or similar cheese and butter (4:2:2:1) plus seasoning, rested, rolled out, cut in shapes, glazed with egg white and baked at 200°C. Eaten as a snack

pizzoccheri *(It)* Short stubbly noodles made from buckwheat flour

pkhala *(Ru)* A Georgian dish made from a purée of cooked and wrung out spinach with sweated chopped onion and garlic and chopped parsley and coriander leaves mixed with soaked saffron, vinegar and lemon juice, finely chopped walnuts and sufficient chicken stock to make a stiff paste. Served after standing 3 hours as a hors d'oeuvre scattered with chopped walnuts and/or toasted pinenuts

pla *(Th)* Fish

pla chalard *(Th)* Dried fish used for flavouring

pla chalarm *(Th)* Shark

plăcinte moldovenesti *(Ro)* Puff pastry turnovers filled with a mixture of sieved cottage cheese, egg yolks, butter, sugar and salt, egg washed and baked at 210°C

pla duk *(Th)* Catfish

pla haeng *(Th)* Dried fish

pla hai ling *(Th)* Bangus, the fish

plaice A flat seawater fish *Pleuronectes platessa* with orange or red spots on a brown upper skin weighing up to 1.5 kg. Found throughout the Atlantic and North Sea. Cooked as any white fish

plain bacon *see* green bacon

plain cakes Cakes made by the rubbing in method with a low ratio of fat to flour (1 or less to 2)

plain chocolate Chocolate confectionery with a low percentage of sugar (less than 30%) and no milk solids

plain court bouillon A cooking liquor for deep poached or boiled fish consisting of water, milk, salt and lemon juice, used for large cuts of turbot and brill

plain flour Wheat flour made from any type of soft wheat with between 9 and 10% protein with no added raising agents. Used mainly for cakes and pastries where less rise and a finer texture than bread is required. Not used for puff pastry [also called **household flour**]

plain leaved escarole *see* Batavian endive

plain omelette An omelette made with no filling or addition to the eggs except seasoning and possibly water

plain tripe *see* blanket tripe

pla in-see *(Th)* Mackerel

pla jalamed *(Th)* Pomfret, the fish

pla jara met khao *(Th)* Pomfret, the fish

pla jien *(Th)* Steamed filleted fish in a light soya sauce

pla kapong *(Th)* Sea bass

pla karang *(Th & Ph)* Garoupa, the fish

pla karang daeng jutfa *(Th)* Garoupa, the fish

pla lai *(Th)* Eel

pla mangkor *(Th)* Eel

pla muk *(Th)* Squid

planche de charcuterie *(Fr) fem.* A platter of cold meats

plank A well seasoned hardwood board usually with a groove or gutter to catch juices cut into the surface around the outer edge. The plank is warmed, oiled and used to serve and sometimes to grill and serve meat or fish dishes

plank, to *(USA)* To bake or grill meat or fish on a plank

plantain *(En & Fr) masc.* A type of banana, genus *Musa,* sometimes named *M. paradisica,* with firm and starchy flesh cooked either in the green (if dessert types) or ripe (if non-sweet types) state; used as a staple food in Africa, the Caribbean and South America [also called **Adam's fig, green banana**]

plantain flour *see* banana flour

plantation shortcake *(USA)* Hot cornbread topped with chopped chicken or ham in a cream sauce

pla o *(Th)* Tuna

pla pak khom *(Th)* Bummaloe, the fish

plastic icing *(Aus)* A thick icing resembling fondant icing made from a mixture of granulated and icing sugar with water, gelatine, lemon juice and butter which after resting can be rolled out or moulded [also called **Australian fondant icing**]

plat *(Bk)* Turbot

plátano *(Sp)* Banana

plat-de-côte *(Fr) masc.* A cut of beef from the lower centre of the animal including the plate and parts of the rib bones which would be included with the ribs in English butchery. It is either boned or left on the bone and used for braising, pot roasts or boiled beef

plat-de-côtes *(Fr) masc.* The front of the pork belly containing the ribs. Used for braising, pot roasting or casseroles

plat du jour *(Fr) masc.* The special dish for the day in a restaurant. Normally changed daily and cheaper or better value than other menu dishes

plat à sauter *(Fr) masc.* A large diameter shallow copper pan with straight vertical sides, tinned on the inside and used professionally for sautéing and shallow frying. The sides are almost as hot as the base and are used to cook the sides of steaks chops, etc.

plátano manzano *(Me)* A stubby banana with a hint of strawberry and apple in its flavour

plate 1 A flat oval or round piece of crockery on which food is served **2** *(UK)* The rear part of the lower half of the ribs of beef behind the brisket, usually used for stewing and manufacturing

plate, to To place food and garnishes on a plate preparatory to serving it to a customer

plate of beef *(UK)* The Scottish name of a tough lean cut from the shoulder

plate ring A metal ring used for stacking plates with food on them so as to prevent the food on one plate touching the base of the one above. Commonly used in restaurants and at banquets

Plateau *(Be)* masc. A soft cows' milk cheese similar to Saint-Paulin and Herve. It has a smooth pungent taste and a yellow crusty rind

plateau de fromages *(Fr) masc.* Cheeseboard

plateau de fruits de mer *(Fr) masc.* A speciality of Brittany and northern France consisting of a mixture of shellfish and crustaceans served cold on a plate

platija *(Sp)* Flat fish, plaice, flounder or dab

pla too *(Th)* Fried fish such as salted mackerel, trout and herring. Served with nam prik

plat siew *(Th)* Dried fish, fried with dried noodles and a black bean sauce

plättar *(Sw)* Small pancakes made with a butter and egg enriched sweet batter, flavoured with brandy and served with a jam or fresh fruit and cream stuffing

Plättchen *(Ge)* Pretzels

plattekaas *(Be)* A curd cheese usually made from cows' milk

platter A large plate generally used for serving food to several people or for serving several foods on the same plate, e.g. seafood platter

Plattfisch *(Ge)* Plaice

plava A fatless sponge cake made with matzo meal and flavoured with almonds for use at the Jewish Passover meal

plegonero *(Sp)* Whiting, the fish

pletzlach Squares of pastry with an apricot or plum filling served at the Jewish Passover feast

pleurote *(Fr) masc.* Oyster mushroom

pleurotis mushroom *(USA)* Oyster mushroom

Pleurotus ostreatus *Bot.* Oyster mushroom

plie *(Fr) fem.* Plaice

Plinz *(Ge)* Fritter or pancake

ploat, to *see* pluck, to

Plockwurst *(Ge)* An air dried, smoked slicing sausage with a deep red colour, made from a variety of meats e.g. beef, pork, ham, pickled pork, etc.

Ploderkäse *(He)* A soft scalded-curd surface ripened cows' milk cheese coagulated with a lactic starter, formed into blocks (to 10 kg), dry salted and ripened. The paste is smooth with a slightly bitter taste

plombières *(Fr) fem.* Tutti frutti ice cream

plomme *(No)* Plum

plommegrøt med fløtemelk *(No)* A milk and cream pudding thickened with groats and mixed with plums

plommon *(Sw)* Plum

plommonspäckard fläskkarré *(Sw)* Loin of pork with a prune stuffing

plot toffee *(UK)* A treacle toffee served on Guy Fawkes night (5th of November)

ploughman's lunch *(UK)* A typical public house lunch of cheese, crusty bread, butter and pickles

plov *(Ru)* Rice pilaf

plov iz rybi *(Ru)* A risotto made from rice, fish, tomatoes, onions and butter

plover A small wild wading bird common in Norfolk but now rarely hunted for the table. There are several varieties of which the lapwing *Vanellus vanellus,* [also called **bustard plover or green plover**], the golden plover *Pluvialis apricaria* and the grey plover *Pluvialis squatarola* are the most well known. The golden plover is the most sought after. Usually roasted with or without the innards at 220°C and served on buttered toast with lemon and watercress garnish

plover's eggs The eggs of plovers considered to be a delicacy, generally cream or buff coloured with dark brown spots or blotches, generally replaced by eggs of various species of gull (black-headed, lesser black-backed, great black-backed, etc.), which are similar in colour. In the UK they can only be gathered up to April the 14th and for home consumption only. Their sale is prohibited

pluches *(Fr) fem.* A spray of chervil or other fresh herb used as a garnish

pluck The liver, lungs and heart of an animal

pluck, to To remove the feathers from poultry and birds [also called **to ploat**]

plum The fruit of deciduous trees *Prunus domestica* and other *Prunus* spp. with yellow through purple skin usually with a fine bloom of wild yeast, a central stone and a generally sweet flesh. All need cool winters to fruit. There are many varieties, see e.g. greengage, damson, cherry plum, mirabelle, quetsch plum, bullace, Japanese or salicine and Victoria. Dried plums are known as prunes

plum duff Suet pudding containing currants, raisins, spices and brown sugar. Boiled in a cloth and served hot with English custard or cream

plum pudding **1** *see* Christmas pudding **2** A porridge-like mixture of raisins (otherwise called plumbs), dried fruits, spices, oranges, lemons, sugar, minced veal or beef and sherry, thickened with bread. Once popular in the UK but since evolved into Christmas pudding

plum sauce A Chinese condiment made from

dark red plums, sugar and water [also called **Chinese plum sauce**]

plum tomato A bright red elongated Italian tomato with a good flavour. The principal variety used for canning

plumb o.e. raisin

plumcot A rediscovered eighteenth century fruit. The taste is intermediate between plum and apricot [also called **violet apricot, pope's apricot**]

pluvier *(Fr) masc.* Plover

plyskavice *(Bk)* Grilled hamburgers from Serbia

po boy *(USA) see* poor boy

poach, to To cook food, usually eggs or fish, in a cooking liquor at the simmer, i.e. at around 96/7°C in an open or closed pan on the stove or in the oven. Coddling is a kind of poaching and is as equally successful with fish and small pieces of tender meat as with eggs

poached eggs Shelled eggs, yolk intact, placed in acidulated water just below simmering point for about 3 minutes until set then carefully removed. May be poached in other cooking liquors.

poached white fish Fillets of white fish or whole, skinned and trimmed sole, shallow poached and served with a sauce usually derived from the cooking liquor. See under headings: Bercy, bonne femme, Bréval, Dugléré, florentine, Marguery, Mornay, Véronique, vin blanc, Walewska. Listed as Walewska, fish, etc.

poacher's pie *(UK)* A pie made from alternate layers of boned rabbit, bacon, potatoes and leeks in a pie dish, seasoned, flavoured with herbs, half filled with stock and topped with shortcrust pastry. Baked covered at 190°C for 30 minutes and finished uncovered at 180°C until brown and cooked

pochade *(Fr) fem.* A freshwater fish stew from Savoie containing raisins and carrots

pochard A wild duck *Aythya fernia* shot for the table in the UK

poche *(Fr) fem. see* caecum

poché(e) *(Fr)* Poached

pocher *(Fr)* To poach

pocheret *(De)* Poached

pocheteau *(Fr) masc.* Common skate

po chio *(Ch)* Aniseed

pochouse *(Fr) fem.* A mixture of various freshwater fishes, esp. eel, stewed in white wine from Burgundy

pochty nichevo *(Ru)* Soup made from equal quantities of mixed bones and water (1.5 kg of each) simmered with a cleaned but unpeeled onion until the liquid has reduced by half, strained, chopped onion and clean potato peelings, sautéed in bacon fat, simmered with the strained stock, puréed, seasoning and consistency adjusted and the whole finished with cream and chopped chives. Lit. almost nothing (soup)

poco hecho *(Sp)* Rare, underdone, of meat, steak, etc.

poco pasado *(Sp)* Rare, of meat, steak, etc.

pod The elongated seed capsule of leguminous plants which contains a row of seeds and splits lengthways into two halves to release the seeds when ripe. Usually picked before maturing unless ripe seeds are to be harvested as pulses. Sometimes eaten whole, otherwise immature seeds are removed

pod, to To remove seeds from a pod

podina *(In)* Mint [also called **pudeena**]

poêle *(Fr) fem.* Frying pan

poêle *(Fr) masc.* Stove

poêlé(e) **1** *(En)* Braised or pot roasted **2** *(Fr)* Fried

poêlon *(Fr) masc.* A casserole, a small tight lidded heavy pan with a long handle used for slow cooking

poem card cut *see* tanzako giri

poffertjes *(Ho)* Puffed up fritters made with a chemically raised batter

poffertjies *(Saf)* Apple fritters made from sieved apple purée, milk, flour, sugar, egg and raisins (12:3:2:2:1:1), beaten together into a stiff batter then deep fried in small quantities, drained and served with cinnamon and sugar

po gwa *(Ch)* Hairy gourd

poha The wild dwarf cape gooseberry found in Hawaii

poh pia *(Ch)* Spring roll

poi A staple food of the Pacific islands made from the boiled and mashed tubers of taro or sweet potato with possibly banana and breadfruit

point, à *see* à point

point steak *(UK)* The thin end of a slice of beef rump steak

pointe *(Fr) fem.* **1** Tip, as in pointes d'asperge, asparagus tips **2** A small amount as in pointe d'ail; a small amount of any ingredient that can be held on the tip of a knife

pointe de filet *(Fr) fem.* Pork fillet (tenderloin)

poire *(Fr) fem.* Pear

poire condé *(Fr) fem. see* pear condé

poireau *(Fr) masc.* Leek

poireaux, purée de *(Fr) fem. see* leek soup

poirée *(Fr) fem.* Chinese leaves; *see also* bette

poires Alma *(Fr) fem.* Pears poached in port

poires Belle Hélène *(Fr) fem.* Pear halves, poached in sugar syrup and served with vanilla ice cream and chocolate sauce

pois *(Fr) masc.* Peas

pois cassés *(Fr) masc.* Split peas

pois chiches *(Fr) masc.* Chickpeas

pois à la française *(Fr) masc.* Peas braised with lettuce, a little sugar, chopped spring onions and parsley and a small amount of water

poisson *(Fr) masc.* Fish

poisson brun *(Be)* masc. Browned fish with a wine and herb sauce

poisson-chat *(Fr) masc.* Channel catfish

poisson fumé *(Fr) masc.* Smoked fish

poisson meunière aux amandes *(Fr) masc. see* amandes, fish aux

poisson volant *(Fr) masc.* Flying fish [also called **Exocet**]

poissonnière *(Fr) fem.* Fish kettle

poitrine *(Fr) fem.* **1** Breast (of lamb or veal), stewed or boned out and stuffed rolled and roasted **2** The abdominal part of pork belly **3** A cut of lean beef from the shoulder immediately in front of the jumeau, used for braising, pot roasting and boiled beef

poitrine de porc *(Fr) fem.* Pork belly

poitrine fumée *(Fr) fem.* Smoked streaky bacon

poivrade *(Fr) fem.* Vinaigrette sauce with pepper

poivrade, à la *(Fr)* Description of dishes containing freshly ground pepper or dried green peppercorns

poivrade, sauce *(En & Fr) fem.* A mirepoix of onion, carrot, celery, bay leaves and thyme, sweated in butter, fat removed, reduced with wine, vinegar and mignonette pepper, simmered with demi-glace for 30 minutes, strained and seasoned. Served with venison [also called **pepper sauce**]

poivre *(Fr) masc.* Pepper

poivre, au *(Fr)* A description of any dish with pepper, usually coarsely crushed peppercorns

poivre d'âne *(Fr) masc.* **1** A goats' milk cheese from the Alpes Maritime with a distinctive flavour of herbs, probably savory **2** *coll. Provence* Savory, the herb

poivre de la Jamaïque *(Fr) masc.* Allspice

poivron *(Fr) masc.* Sweet pepper, capsicum

poke *(USA)* A Hawaiian dish of fish marinated in a highly spiced sauce

Pokel *(Ge)* Pickle

pokeweed A shrub *Phytolacca americana* from North America with poisonous roots but whose young leaves (to 15 cm) may be boiled and treated like asparagus. The red berry may be used as a food colouring. The whole plant is classified as poisonous in the UK

pok kak bua *(Th)* Star anise

pole dab *(USA) see* witch sole

Poledwica sopocka *(Pl)* As Poledwica tososiowa but not packed in casings

Poledwica tososiowa *(Pl)* A hard smoked sausage from Gdansk made of pork and pork back fat packed in casings and knotted

Polei *(Ge)* Pennyroyal

polenta *(En & It)* Fine yellow cornmeal, dry fried until it loses its colour It is used as a thick porridge, and to make some types of bread and gnocchi. This porridge, also known as polenta, is made by mixing the cornmeal with salted water (150 g per litre). This is brought to the boil then simmered with stirring until thick and the paste leaves the side of the pan. It is a major source of carbohydrate in Italy and is often left to cool then sliced and fried as an accompaniment to meat dishes

polenta alla bergamasca *(It)* Polenta baked with tomatoes, sausage and cheese

polenta al forno *(It)* Polenta casseroled with sausages in a meat sauce covered with cheese

polenta d'ivrea *(It)* A cake resembling polenta made with buckwheat flour flavoured with vanilla

polenta taragna *(It)* Polenta liberally sprinkled with grated Bitto cheese and covered with melted butter

polentagrøt *(No)* Cornmeal pudding

poleo *(Sp)* Pennyroyal

polewka *(Pl)* A very simple soup of seasoned water thickened with rye flour and blended with cream

pólipo *(Sp)* Octopus

poliporo *(It)* A fungus which grows on trees

Polish sausage A generic term for a variety of sausages using the usual pork, beef and pork fat with flavourings, saltpetre and sometimes dextrose to facilitate lactic fermentation, normally cased, air dried and smoked until hard

polished rice Rice from which the vitamin B-rich outer coating has been removed during processing. Prized because of its whiteness

polla *(Sp)* Young chicken

pollack A coastal seawater fish *Pollachius pollachius* of the cod family with a protruding lower jaw and a dark green upper skin, found throughout the North Atlantic. It does not have as fine a flavour as cod but is otherwise similar and cooked in the same way. Generally sold at 50 cm in length [also called **green cod, pollock**]

pollame *(It)* Poultry

pollan *see* pullan

pollanca *(It)* Young chicken

pollastre *(Sp)* Young chicken

pollastro *(It)* Young chicken

pollito *(Sp)* Pigeon or squab

pollo *(Sp & It)* Chicken

pollo all'arentina *(It)* Chicken stewed in wine

pollo alla cacciatora *(It)* Chicken stewed in stock with mushrooms and seasoning and flavoured with Marsala. Served with fresh pasta

pollo en chanfaina a la catalana *(Sp)* Chicken sautéed with sweet peppers, aubergine and tomato sauce

pollo a la chilindrón *(Sp)* Sautéed chicken

pollo alla contadina *(It)* Portioned chicken fried in oil for 20 minutes, mixed with potatoes cut in 2 cm slices and fried separately, then, both stewed in chopped deseeded tomatoes with seasoning and a little wine until all tender. Lit. peasant woman's chicken

pollo a la extremeña *(Sp)* Chicken with sausages and baked tomato

pollo fandango *(Sp)* Chicken cooked in a creamed sauce and served with braised celery

pollo alla marengo *(It)* Chicken stewed in stock and white wine with tomatoes, mushrooms, parsley, black olives and seasoning; *see also* poulet sauté marengo

pollo de naranja *(Sp)* Chicken pieces marinated in sherry and orange juice and shallow fried in butter

pollo a la navarra *(Sp)* Chicken casseroled in wine with carrots, onions and strips of ham

pollo alla padovana *(It)* Chicken browned, then braised in the oven with onions and finished with egg and lemon

pollo rebozado *(SA)* A Bolivian speciality of chicken joints coated in an egg, milk and polenta batter, fried, then simmered in a sauce made from wine, tomatoes, spices and seasoning

pollo ripiena alla trentina *(It)* Chicken stuffed with a mixture of chopped nuts, breadcrumbs, beef marrow and chopped liver, then boiled

pollo alla romano *(It)* Chicken simmered with white wine, tomato, ham, sweet pepper and herbs

pollo salteado *(Sp)* Chicken sautéed with onion and served with artichoke hearts and tomato sauce

pollock 1 *see* pollack **2** *see* coley

polmone *(It)* Calves' lungs

polo *(Pe)* Cooked rice

polonaise, à la *(Fr)* In the Polish style, i.e. containing soured cream, red cabbage or beetroot, or vegetables topped with a mixture of chopped hard-boiled eggs and parsley with fried breadcrumbs

poloney The name of a sausage common in English-speaking countries, probably a corruption of Bologna or Polonia since it has the characteristics of both Italian and Polish sausages. All are coloured red. See Bologna sausage

polony *see* poloney

polpa *(It)* Lean meat, flesh of fruits

polpessa *(It)* Warm water octopus

polpetiello *(It) see* polpo

polpetta *(It)* Croquette, meat ball, rissole

polpettine *(It)* Meat balls

polpettine di spinaci *(It)* Spinach-flavoured and coloured dumplings

polpettone *(It)* **1** Meat or fish loaf **2** A baked mixture of vegetables bound with egg

polpettone alla genovese *(It)* A mixture of chopped cooked potatoes and French beans bound with grated cheese and eggs and baked in a loaf tin

polpettone alla toscana *(It)* A minced meat and cheese loaf bound with egg and braised, fried or poached

polpo *(It)* Octopus [also called **polpetiello**]

pølser *(De & No)* Sausages

Polsterzipfel *(Au)* A jam filled turnover

polvere di curry *(It)* Curry powder

polydextrose A bulking agent used in reduced and low calorie foods

polygonum A herb *Polygonum* spp. with long slender deep green leaves and with an intense flavour of basil and mint. Used to flavour fish and noodle dishes in Malaysia and salads in Vietnam [also called **Vietnamese mint**]

polyoxyethylene (20) sorbitan esters *see* (E)432 to (E)436 [also called **polysorbate**]

polyphenol oxidase The enzyme in plants which causes browning of fruits and vegetables on exposure to air by oxidation of phenolic compounds to melanin pigments. Its effects are being eliminated by genetic engineering of plant varieties

polyphosphates E450(c), complex phosphates of sodium and potassium used mainly to retain added water without exudation in frozen chickens, ham, bacon and other similar meat products, and also as stabilizers and emulsifiers

polysaccharide Long chains or branched chains of simple sugars which make up starch, dextrins, cellulose and other carbohydrates of natural origin

Polyscias scutellarium *Bot.* Daun mangkok

polysorbate ( ) The alternative names for polyoxyethylene (20) sorbitan esters. For polysorbate 20 see (E)432, polysorbate 40 see (E)434, polysorbate 60 see (E)435, polysorbate 65 see (E)436 and for polysorbate 80 see (E)433

polyunsaturated A description of long chains of carbon atoms that occur in fats, oils and fatty acids in which several of the carbon atoms do not have as many hydrogen atoms attached as they could and are therefore connected to neighbouring carbon atoms by double or triple bonds. Hence polyunsaturated fats

pomace The residue after juice or oil has been physically crushed out of fruit. The pomace from oil bearing fruits is often treated by solvent extraction to produce inferior oils

pomegranate The beige to red fruit of the pomegranate tree *Punica granatum,* up to 8 cm in dia. with a hard skin filled with numerous seeds each in a red, juicy, fleshy sac. Sweet varieties are eaten (rather messily) as a dessert. Seeds of the sour pomegranate have a sweet-sour taste and are used as a garnish in the Middle East. The dried, ground seeds, known as anardana, are used as a souring agent and with bread, vegetables and pulses in North India [also called **Chinese apple**]

pomelo 1 *see* pummelo **2** *(Sp)* Grapefruit

pomfret A tropical seawater fish *Pampus argenteus* with a silvery skin and tiny black spots, found around and used in India, China and SEA. It has white flesh similar to, but not as tasty as, that of turbot or sole and is cooked in the same ways. There is also a darker variety with a brownish-gray skin found in Indonesia and the Phillipines with an inferior flavour. The Chinese smoke pomfret over tea leaves. [also called **Ray's bream, white butter fish**]

pomfret cake *see* Pontefract cake

pomme *(Fr) fem.* Apple; also used as an abbreviation of pomme de terre

pomme de terre *(Fr) fem.* Potato, often abbreviated to pomme esp. with potato dishes

Pommel *(Fr)* An unsalted double cream cows' milk cheese similar to Petit-Suisse

pommes allumettes *(Fr) fem.* Very thin potato chips

pommes amandine *(Fr) fem.* Potatoes made in the same way as croquette potatoes but panéed with flour, egg and nibbed almonds instead of breadcrumbs

pommes à l'anglaise *(Fr) fem.* Plain boiled potatoes

pommes Anna *(Fr) fem.* Layers of thinly sliced potatoes, melted butter and seasoning, baked in a straight sided metal dish in the oven in a dish until browned, inverted on a plate and served in slices or wedges. Note that the dish for pommes Anna should not be washed

pommes boulangère *(Fr) fem.* Roast potatoes

pommes en copeaux *(Fr) fem.* Grated potatoes or potato shavings

pommes dauphine *(Fr) masc.* A mixture of potato croquette mixture and choux pastry (3:1) formed into small cylinders, panéed and deep fried

pommes dauphinoises *(Fr) fem.* Sliced potatoes layered in a dish with milk, grated cheese, garlic and butter and cooked in the oven. Egg and cream may be added but the egg tends to scramble [also called **gratin dauphinois**]

pommes duchesses *(Fr) fem.* *see* duchesse potatoes

pommes frites *(Fr) fem.* Potato chips, thinner and crisper than the UK variety

pommes mousselines *(Fr) fem.* Mashed potatoes

pommes pailles *(Fr) fem. see* straw potatoes

pommes en robe de chambre *(Fr) fem.*

Potatoes boiled or steamed in their skins [also called **pommes de terre en robe des champs**]

pommes sauvages *(Fr) fem.* Crab apples

pommes savoyarde *(Fr) fem.* As gratin dauphinois but substituting stock for cream [also called **gratin savoyard**]

pommes vapeur *(Fr)* Boiled or steamed potatoes

pomodori di magro alla sarda *(It)* Tomatoes stuffed with anchovies, tuna and aubergine flesh and baked

pomodori ripieni alla novarese *(It)* Tomatoes stuffed with rice, onions and cheese, panéed and deep fried

pomodorini *(It)* Small tomatoes

pomodoro *(It)* Tomato

pompano A small, oily, round seawater fish *Trachinotus* spp. with a high yellow to green-blue back, a deep belly and deeply forked tail fin from the Mediterranean, Caribbean and south east USA. They can weigh up to 3 kg but are better at 1 kg and have a sweet-flavoured, rather dry, white flesh. Often cooked en papillote. Prepared like perch

pompano rellena *(Me)* Pompano stuffed with a mixture of chopped onions and tomatoes sweated in oil, chopped hard boiled eggs, parsley and spices then poached and served with a fish velouté

pompelmo *(It)* Grapefruit or pummelo

pompelmoes *(Ho)* Grapefruit

pompoen *(Ho)* Pumpkin

pomtannia *see* tannia

ponceau 4R E124, a synthetic red food colouring banned in the USA [also called **cochineal red**]

poncirus One of the three important genera of Citrus [also called **trifoliate orange**]

pondah *(Id)* Ubod, palm pith

ponkan mandarin The most widely grown mandarin in the world found in Japan, the Phillipines, India, south China and Brazil. The rind is moderately thick and very loose, the juice content whilst sweet and pleasant tasting is rather low in quantity and the segment walls are somewhat tough [also called **Chinese honey orange, mohali mandarin**]

Pont l'Evêque *(Fr) masc.* A soft orange coloured cows' milk cheese from Normandy, made in a square about 10 cm on the side and 4 cm deep with a thick brown rind mottled with thin smears of mould. The paste contains a few round holes and has a strong smell and a less strong taste. It has AOC status. Contains 47% water, 27% fat and 20% protein

Pont Moutier *(Fr) masc.* A soft square shaped cows' milk cheese weighing to 2.5 kg. The brown rind had a white bloom and the smooth fragrant and aromatic tasting paste has a few cracks and holes

Pontac ketchup *(UK)* Ripe elderberries covered with warm boiling vinegar and kept hot in the oven for 3 hours. Juice strained off without pressure and boiled with mace, peppercorns, shallots and salted anchovies (250 g per litre of juice) until the anchovies have disintegrated, strained and bottled [also called **Pontac sauce**]

Pontac sauce *(UK)* A sharp condiment sauce based on elderberries, invented by a Monsieur Pontac of Lombard St. London

Pontefract cake A small flat round (to 2 cm dia) liquorice-based sweet usually embossed as though by a seal [also called **Pomfret cake**]

ponzu sauce *(Ja)* A dipping sauce for sashimi and condiment use made from lemon juice, soya sauce, mirin, sake and dried bonito flakes (20:20:3:3:1 by volume) with a piece of kombu all macerated for 24 hours then strained

poong dang *(Th)* **1** Alum **2** A paste of lime (Calcium hydroxide)

poor boy *(USA)* A Cajun sandwich from Louisiana consisting of a French bread stick split lengthwise and filled with a savoury mixture of foods, salads, etc. similar to casse-croute. It originated in New Orleans in the 19th century when oyster sandwiches were given as charity to the poor; *see also* hoagie [also called **po boy**]

poor knights of Windsor *(UK)* Fingers of bread dipped in egg and milk mixture sometimes flavoured with liqueur or spirits, deep fried and eaten hot sprinkled with cinnamon and caster sugar; *see also* pain perdu

poor man's beefsteak *see* beefsteak fungus

poor man's caviar A dip made from the flesh of roasted aubergines processed with garlic and olive oil to a thick purée, seasoned, let down with a little lemon juice and garnished with chopped parsley

poor man's goose *(UK) see* faggot

poori *(In) see* puri

poorman orange *see* New Zealand grapefruit

pop tart *(USA)* A thin pastry turnover with various fillings which can be heated in a pop-up toaster or in the oven

popara *(Bu)* A porridge made from bread, butter, cheese and milk, eaten at breakfast

popcorn A variety of maize kernels *indurata* which when heated in a closed container are blown up into a soft foamed starch as the bound water turns to steam. Eaten as a snack with salt, sugar or butter

pope A freshwater fish similar to the perch [also called **ruffe**]

pope's apricot *see* plumcot

pope's eye *(UK)* **1** The small circle of fat in the centre of a leg of lamb or pork **2** The Scottish name for prime rump steak

pope's nose The equivalent of the parson's nose q.v. on a duck or goose

popone *(It)* Melon

popover 1 *(UK)* A small individual Yorkshire pudding, often flavoured with grated cheese, chopped onions, bacon and herbs or in a sweet version with chopped fruit and sugar **2** *(USA)* A quickly made type of muffin using a Yorkshire pudding batter baked in the oven

poppa *(It)* Udder

poppadom *(In)* A thin round pancake made from a lentil flour batter which is occasionally spiced, deep fried until crisp and served as an appetizer or accompaniment to Indian food. Sometimes the lentil flour is mixed with or substituted by rice or potato flour [also called **papadum, papadam, pappadam, pappadum, puppadom, papads**]

popper *(USA)* A type of pan used to prepare popcorn

poppy seed The ripe seeds of an annual poppy (*Papaver somniferum* and *P. rhoeas*) which vary in colour from cream through to almost black according to origin. They have a slightly nutty aroma and flavour and are often sprinkled on bread and cakes or crushed with honey or sugar to make pastry fillings. Used with other spices in Indian cooking

poppy seed oil A light odourless oil with a faint almond taste from the first cold pressing of poppy seeds. Used for salads

poppy seed paste Roasted and ground poppy seeds formed into a paste much used in Turkish cooking

porbeagle shark A member *Lamna nasus* of the shark family which grows to 4 m and is common in the Atlantic. It makes good eating and is often larded and grilled as steaks

porc *(Fr) masc.* Pig or pork

porc salé *(Fr) masc.* Salt pork

porcella *(Sp)* Catalan for sucking pig

porché *(Fr)* A Breton dish of stewed pigs' ears and trotters

porchetta *(It)* Sucking pig

porcini *(It) Boletus edulis* or ceps, usually sliced and dried

porco *(Po)* Pork

porgy Various deep-bodied seawater fishes *Calamus* spp. esp. *Pagrus pagrus* with long spiny dorsal fins chiefly found in the Mediterranean and the Atlantic ocean and similar to bream. They have delicate, moist sweet flesh but many bones; *see also* red porgy

pork The flesh of the pig

pork belly Meat from the underside of the abdominal and chest cavity of the pig equivalent to breast of lamb and consisting of alternating layers of fat and lean muscle. Used in sausages, patés and terrines or may be cooked as a dish in its own right [also called **belly pork**]

pork chop A transverse slice from a loin of pork

pork crackling *see* crackling

pork fat Fat from the pig is graded according to hardness and has many uses in sausages, terrines, pâtés and other items. Back fat tends to be the hardest and belly fat the softest. Lard is rendered pork fat and is traditionally used in pastry and in the cooking of eastern France. It contains about 49% saturated, 42% monounsaturated and 9% polyunsaturated fat

pork fillet *see* tenderloin of pork

pork herbs The principal herbs used with pork are chervil, coriander, fennel, lovage, marjoram, rosemary, sage, savory and thyme

pork pie *(UK)* A raised pork pie similar to a Melton Mowbray pie but the cooked pork is in cubes and/or minced and whole hard boiled eggs are sometimes included in the filling of the larger ones

pork sausage The most common sausage of English-speaking countries made from ground pork, flavourings, extenders and binders filled into casings and linked. Quantities of extenders depend on the price and local laws. In the UK many suspect extenders which legally count as meat such as drinde, MRM, etc. are incorporated in the cheaper versions, together with a high proportion of rusk and cereal fillers. UK sausages are usually flavoured with sage, cayenne pepper and possibly cloves, ginger, nutmeg or mace. USA sausages are normally flavoured with cardamom, coriander and nutmeg

pork scratchings *see* scratchings

pork vindaloo A dish of lean pork, cubed, piquéed, rubbed with a paste of dry roasted coriander and cumin seeds plus cardomom seeds, cinnamon, cloves, black peppercorns, turmeric, onion salt, ground ginger and cayenne pepper to taste, all well pounded, then marinated in vinegar or vinegar and water (1:1) with bay leaves for 24 hours. The meat and its marinade are then simmered slowly with mustard seeds fried in ghee until tender, adding water as required

porker *see* pig

porkkana *(Fi)* Carrot

pörkölt *(Hu)* **1** Roasted **2** A thick braised stew with very little added water made with fried meat, poultry or game pieces, tomatoes, green sweet peppers, onions, paprika and seasoning, served with boiled potatoes or rice, green salad and/or pickled cucumbers

poron *(Fi)* Reindeer

poronkäristys *(Fi)* Very thin slices of braised reindeer

poronkieli *(Fi)* Reindeer tongue

poronliha *(Fi)* Reindeer meat

poronpaisti *(Fi)* Reindeer steak

Porphyra tenera *Bot.* Nori

Porphyra umbilicalis *Bot.* Nori

porpore *(It)* Murex, the shellfish

porridge A kind of gruel made by boiling porridge oats with water or milk or mixtures of both and salt until the desired consistency is reached. Eaten as a breakfast dish with sweetening and milk or cream. The name is also used for oatmeal, maize, etc. boiled to the same consistency with water

porridge oats The breakfast cereal produced by heating either pinhead oatmeal or whole oats with steam as they are passed through rollers to flatten them. The pinhead oatmeal produces the normal porridge oats, whilst the whole oats produce oat flakes which can be used in muesli [also called **rolled oats**]

porro *(It)* Leek

porsaankyljys *(Fi)* Pork chops

port A fortified wine from Portugal made by stopping the fermentation of full bodied grape juice with brandy before all the sugar has been fermented to alcohol. Used as a flavouring in sauces and served with melon

Port-Salut *(Fr) masc.* A semi-hard mild-flavoured cows' milk cheese from the west of France. Made in large rounds (to 2 kg) with an orange rind. Used as a dessert cheese

Port-du-Salut *(Fr) masc.* The original Port-Salut cheese made by the Trappist monks of Port du Salut monastery at Entrammes. The name was sold to commercial cheesemakers in the late 1940's

port-wine jelly *(UK)* A gelatine-based sweetened jelly flavoured with port and spices, moulded, cooled, demoulded and served with whipped cream

port-wine sauce As Madeira sauce but substituting port

porter cake *(UK)* A chemically raised basic cake mixture flavoured with mixed spice and grated lemon zest with 3 parts dried vine fruits to 2 parts flour, brought together with a dark stout and all ingredients whisked together for a few minutes and baked at 170°C until cooked. From Northern Ireland

porterhouse steak A steak without bone cut from the large end of the short loin of beef possibly including some of the sirloin and including the fillet. It is usually about 5 cm thick and will easily feed 2 people. Grilled or fried

portmanteau lamb chops *(UK)* Lamb loin chops pocketed from the skin side to the bone and filled with a cooled and seasoned cooked mixture of finely chopped chicken liver and mushrooms, sealed with a stick, panéed and baked in melted butter at 200°C until brown on both sides

porto, sauce *(Fr) fem. see* port-wine sauce

portugaise, à la *(Fr)* **1** A method of cooking vegetables similar to à la grecque, q.v., using a cooking medium consisting of water, olive oil, skinned and deseeded tomatoes, chopped onion, tomato purée, garlic, parsley, bay leaf, thyme and seasoning, served hot or cold **2** In the Portuguese style, i.e. including onions, tomatoes and garlic

portugaise, crème *(Fr) fem.* Crème de tomate, cream of tomato soup, garnished with plain boiled rice

portugaise, sauce *(Fr) fem.* A type of espagnole sauce made with fresh tomatoes instead of tomato purée

Portugiesische Auster *(Ge)* Portuguese oyster

Portuguese boiled dinner *see* cozido à Portuguesa

Portuguese cabbage A smooth-leaved, blue-green cabbage *Brassica oleracea* var. *tronchuda* from Portugal used in their national dish caldo verde. Kale or Savoy cabbage may be substituted [also called **Braganza cabbage, Galician cabbage, couve gallego, couve tronchuda**]

Portuguese oyster A variety of oyster *Crassostrea angulata* once popular as the farmed European oyster now displaced by the Pacific or Japanese variety. It is elongated in shape and up to 17 cm long. It is best used in cooked dishes

portulaca *see* summer purslane

Portulaca oleracea *Bot.* Summer purslane

poshekhonskij *(Ru)* A hard scalded-curd cows' milk cheese with a hard dry rind and containing small irregular holes. Contains 41% water, 26% fat and 26% protein

posset *(UK)* **1** An old English dessert made from a rich egg custard flavoured with sherry, lemon and sometimes almonds **2** A hot, spiced and sweetened milk drink mixed with ale or wine

possum *see* opossum

posta de carne *(Po)* A slice, not a steak, of beef

postej *(De)* Pâté or paste

postny farshirovoni baklazhana *(Ru)* Pulped aubergine flesh mixed with fried onions and tomatoes, chopped hard-boiled eggs, parsley and seasoning, stuffed into aubergine skins, two sandwiched together and baked in a little water and lard

postre *(Sp)* Dessert course

pot **1** A deep ceramic or metal cylindrical container with a lid and two handles used on the stove for slow cooking of stews, etc. **2** A cylindrical container usually of ceramic or glass in which food is placed for serving or storage as in potted meat or jams, etc. **3** General term for crockery when used in the plural form pots

pot, to To put food into jars or ramekins and seal with molten butter, fat, greased paper, etc. for presentation at the table or so as to preserve it for a long or short time

pot barley Dehusked whole grain barley with no other treatment. Requires long soaking and cooking to soften. Used for soups and stews [also called **Scotch barley**]

pot cheese *(USA)* Cottage cheese

pot au feu *(Fr) masc.* A traditional French stew of meat or poultry sealed in fat and braised or simmered in stock with a variety of vegetables. The broth and the meat are often served separately

pot herbs Leaves or stems of green plants used as vegetables or culinary herbs

pot liquor *(USA)* The liquid in which vegetables have been cooked or blanched. May be used as a basis for vegetarian soups esp. if not salted and the same water used for several batches [also called **potlikker**]

pot luck Whatever food is available for eating when arriving somewhere unannounced, thus to take pot luck

pot marigold *see* marigold

pot marjoram A type of marjoram *Origanum onites* which originated in Sicily and has a much stronger flavour than sweet marjoram [also called **French marjoram**]

pot roast, to To cook meat which has been sealed in hot fat in a covered pan or casserole with a little fat and a small amount of liquid or vegetables over a low heat for a considerable time

potage **1** *(Fr) masc.* A light soup or broth **2** *(En)* A meat or vegetable stock with added paysanne cut vegetables, e.g. minestrone

potage à l'albigeoise *(Fr) masc.* A soup from Albi based on beef stock with a selection from preserved goose, calves' feet, ham, sausage and various vegetables

potage bonne femme *(Fr) masc.* Leek and potato soup finished with cream and butter

potage à la bressane *(Fr) masc.* Pumpkin soup

potage paysanne *(Fr) masc.* Paysanne cut mixed vegetables sweated in butter without colour until tender, white stock and a BG added, seasoned, simmered and skimmed for 20 minutes, peas and diamond cut green beans added and the whole simmered until all cooked [also called **mixed vegetable soup**]

potage de tomates *(Fr) masc. see* tomato soup

potaje *(Sp)* A thick soup or stew

potassium An important mineral essential for health, esp. to maintain the fluid balance in the body and the correct working of muscles and nerves. Found in all plant and animal cells

potassium acetate E261, the potassium salt of acetic acid used as a preservative and firming agent

potassium bisulphite *see* E228

potassium bromate A flour improver and bleaching agent

potassium carbonate *see* (E)501

potassium chloride *see* (E)508

potassium gluconate *see* (E)577

potassium hydrogen carbonate *see* (E)501

potassium hydrogen L-glutamate *see* (E)622

potassium hydrogen tartrate *see* cream of tartar

potassium hydroxide *see* (E)525

potassium lactate *see* E326

potassium nitrate *see* saltpetre

potassium nitrite E249, the potassium salt of nitrous acid used in curing mixtures to preserve meat and maintain the pink colour

potassium sulphate *see* (E)515

potassium tartrate *see* cream of tartar

potatis *(Sw)* Potatoes

potatis och purjolöksoppa *(Sw)* Potato and leek soup, the same as potage bonne-femme

potatiskaka med ost *(Sw)* Cheese potato cakes made from a mixture of grated potatoes and onions, half fried in butter, mixed with grated Gruyère cheese, brought together in the frying pan and fried until browned, turned over, refried and topped with slices of Gruyère cheese which should just melt [also called **Käserösti** (Ge)]

potatismos *(Sw)* Mashed potatoes

potato One of the commonest and most versatile of vegetables which is the swollen tip of an underground stem of the plant *Solanum tuberosum,* used as a store of starch to support the growth of new stems from the eyes. The two main types are floury and waxy, distinguished by the cohesivenes of the tissues. Waxy potatoes are less dense than floury and will float in a brine of 1 part salt to 11 parts water. Stem end blackening due to the reaction of compounds in the potato with iron during cooking can be minimized by boiling with acidulated water (0.5 tsp of cream of tartar per pint). Common varieties of waxy potatoes in the UK are Arran Comet, Ulster Sceptre, Maris Bard, Pentland Javelin, Alcmaria and Romano and of floury potatoes, Desirée, Estima, Home Guard, Kerrs Pink, King Edward, Maris Peer, Maris Piper, Pentland Dell, and Pentland Squire

potato cakes *(UK)* A northern speciality of floury potatoes, mashed with salt and butter and enough plain flour worked in to make a stiff dough, rolled, cut in shapes, floured, fried on a griddle and served hot with butter [also called **potato scones**]

potato chips *see* chips

potato crisps *see* crisps

potato croquettes Mashed potato with butter, milk, seasoning and possibly eggs, formed into small cylinders and deep fried

potato dumplings *see* e.g. Kartoffelklosse

potato flour *see* fécule

potato latka Latkes or Rösti

potato latkes Jewish potato pancakes made with grated raw potatoes, chopped onions, eggs, flour and seasoning, fried until crisp

potato masher A flat perforated metal or plastic circle or oval with an upright handle used to mash cooked potatoes by forcing them through the perforations with an up and down movement

potato peeler *see* peeler

potato ricer A two part potato masher consisting of a receptacle for the boiled potatoes with a fine perforated plate at the base and a solid plate on a lever which forces the potatoes through the perforations. Rather like an oversize garlic press

potato salad Cooked waxy potatoes, diced and bound together with mayonnaise and sometimes with a little chopped onion and parsley or other herb

potato sausage *(Sw)* Beef, fat pork, cold cooked potatoes and onions, all minced, seasoned, and flavoured with mace, ginger and sage, packed into thin hog casings and cooked by boiling

potato scone *(UK) see* potato cakes

potato skins The skins of baked potatoes after the cooked potato has been removed for e.g. duchesse potatoes. They are often served with a filling or deep fried until crisp

potato snow *(USA)* Riced cooked potato, not mixed or treated in any way

potato soup *see* purée parmentier

potato starch *see* fécule

potato and turnip soup *see* purée Freneuse

potato yam *see* aerial yam

pote gallego *(Sp)* A thick broth of pork, bacon, beans and cabbage

potée *(Fr) fem.* A thick soup containing sausage, salt pork or streaky bacon, cabbage, potatoes, onions and possibly beans, lentils and other vegetables, seasoned and flavoured with nutmeg and bay. Sometimes reduced to a stew or hotpot

potée champenoise *(Fr) fem.* A thick soup or stew made with salt belly of pork, ham, haricot beans and vegetables. The liquid is served as soup and the meat and vegetables as a main course dish

Poterium sanguisorba *Bot.* Salad burnet

poteter *(No)* Potatoes

poteter stappe *(No)* Mashed potatoes

potetkaker *(No)* Potato cakes made from fried mashed potatoes

potetstappe *(No)* Mashed potatoes

potica *(Bk)* A walnut strudel from Slovenia known as povitica in Croatia

potiron *(Fr) masc.* Pumpkin

potje *(Fr & Be)* Pâté

potlikker *(USA) see* pot liquor

potli samosa *(In)* An Indian pasty filled with shrimps in a cumin and cardomom-flavoured yoghurt sauce

potpie *(USA)* A dish of meat and vegetables in a rich gravy baked in a deep dish and covered with pie crust to finish

pottage Broth containing mashed vegetables and chopped up pieces of meat to make a thick substantial meal in itself. Originally any food served in a pottager, a kind of medieval dish

pottager The dish in which pottage was served made of metal, earthenware or wood

potted char An old English delicacy made from char, a freshwater fish still available in the Lake District. Popular as a breakfast dish in the 19th century. It is made from unwashed skinned and bone fillets of char, rubbed with a mixture of ground pepper, allspice, mace, cloves and nutmeg (2:1:4:1:2), baked with butter for 5 hours at 120°C, drained, pressed into pots and covered with some of the melted butter

potted fish As potted meat with fish substituted for meat

potted hough *(UK)* A Scottish brawn made from shin and knuckle of beef, peppercorns and seasoning, simmered until tender, bones removed and the liquid reduced until setting consistency

potted meat **1** Cooked meat either reduced to a paste or chopped into pieces, placed in a container and sealed with molten fat or clarified butter. Commercial varieties contain preservatives **2** Shin beef, cooked until tender with calves foot, herbs and seasonings, bones removed, meat coarsely chopped, mixed with reduced cooking liquor and allowed to set in a pot

potted shrimps *(UK)* Cooked and peeled whole shrimps placed in a container and covered with molten clarified butter. Popular in the north of England

potwarak *(Bk)* Duck, browned then braised on a bed of sweated sliced onions, mixed with chopped sauerkraut, peppercorns and a little of the liquid from the sauerkraut. When cooked, sliced and served on the sauerkraut

pouce pied *(Fr) masc.* Barnacle

pouding *(Fr) masc.* Pudding

pouding de cabinet *(Fr) masc. see* cabinet pudding

pouding diplomate *(Fr) masc. see* diplomat pudding

pouding Nesselrode *(Fr) masc.* Sweetened chestnut purée, combined with egg custard, raisins and currants, flavoured with maraschino liqueur, half frozen, cream folded in then placed in a mould, cooled, demoulded and served with maraschino-flavoured custard

pouding de Noël *(Fr) masc.* Christmas pudding (UK)

pouding au pain *(Fr) masc.* Bread pudding

poudre de colombo *(Ca & Fr) fem.* A mixture of garlic, deseeded red chillis, turmeric, coriander seeds and mustard pounded together to make a paste. It originated in the French Caribbean and is used to make colombo, a type of curry

poudre de curry *(Fr) fem.* Curry powder

pouile dudon *(Ca)* Chicken stew with garlic, onions, sweet peppers, caramelized sugar, coconut oil, spices and seasoning. Served with rice and pigeon peas

poularde *(Fr) fem.* A large fattened chicken between 1.5 and 2 kg

poularde demi-deuil *(Fr) fem.* Poached chicken masked with suprême sauce and surrounded with tartlets containing a salpicon of braised calves' or lambs' sweetbreads bound with suprême sauce each topped with a slice of truffle

poule *(Fr) fem.* A boiling fowl suitable for stewing, slow braising or stock

poule-au-pot *(Fr) fem.* Stewed chicken and vegetables served with the reduced cooking liquor

poulet *(Fr) masc.* Chicken usually between 3 and 8 months old. Suitable for 2 to 4 portions depending on size. Roasted, grilled or sautéed

poulet à la crapaudine *(Fr) masc.* Spatchcock

poulet de grain *(Fr) masc.* Corn fed and free range chicken

poulet noir *(Fr) masc.* A superior variety of chicken with black feathers and a delicious slightly gamey flavour

poulet sauté Marengo *(Fr) masc.* A classic dish reputed to have been cooked by Napoleon's chef after the battle of Marengo from what could be found quickly, viz. a rooster, wild mushrooms, crayfish, eggs, garlic and brandy [also called **chicken Marengo**]

poulet au vinaigre *(Fr) masc.* A Lyonnaise dish of chicken and shallots cooked in wine vinegar and finished with cream.

poulette *(Fr) fem.* Pullet, immature chicken

poulette, à la *(Fr)* A description of dishes served with sauce poulette or garnished with onions and garlic

poulette, sauce *(Fr) fem.* A sauce made from white stock combined with lemon juice, butter and chopped parsley thickened with egg yolks

Pouligny-Saint-Pierre *(Fr)* A soft goats'

milk cheese shaped like a pyramid (250 g), which is dry-cured for a month. It is protected by an appellation d'origine

pouliot *(Fr) masc.* Pennyroyal

poulpe *(Fr) masc.* Octopus

poultry The name given to all domesticated birds bred for the table or for their eggs, as opposed to game birds which are wild. Includes chickens, hens, turkeys, ducks, ducklings, geese, and guinea fowl

poultry herbs The principal herbs used with domesticated poultry are bay, chervil, chives, fennel, lemon balm, marjoram, mint, parsley, sage, savory, tarragon and thyme

poultry shears Heavy scissors or secateurs with a serrated edge and a good hand grip used for cutting through the bones of poultry

pound The original unit of weight in the British system still in use in the USA and equal to 453.6 g. Divided into 16 ounces. Abbreviated lb. It still lingers on in mainland Europe, e.g. the French livre, but is taken as being 500 g

pound, to **1** To bruise, break up and crush any hard food item to reduce it to a smooth consistency or a fine powder. Once done in a pestle and mortar but now usually done by mechanical means, e.g. food processor, grinder or powder mill **2** To beat meat with a bat or specially shaped hammer in order to tenderize it or flatten it into e.g an escalope

pound cake A fruit cake originally made from pound (454 g) quantities of the main ingredients, fat, flour, sugar and eggs, using the creaming method to make two 20 cm. dia. round cakes

poupeton *(Fr) masc.* Veal slices with minced meat

pour batter *(USA) see* thin batter

pour-on cheese *(USA)* A bottled processed coating consistency cheese topping

pourgouri *see* bulgar

pouring batter *(UK)* A thin batter made from flour, egg, milk, salt and sometimes sugar, used for pancakes, Yorkshire puddings, etc.

pouring sauce Any flowing sauce used to cover foods usually on the plate, thickened with approximately 50 g of flour or starch per litre

Pourly *(Fr)* A white creamy and mild goats' milk cheese from Burgundy with a greyish blue rind

pousse de bambou *(Fr) fem.* Bamboo shoot

pousser *(Fr)* To rise, as of dough

poussin *(En & Fr) masc.* A single portion, small and tender chicken 4 to 6 weeks old. Usually grilled or roasted [also called **broiler chicken** (USA)]

poussin double *(Fr) masc.* A double portion 10 to 12 week old chicken, usually grilled or roasted

poutargue *(Fr) fem.* A relish made from botargo [also called **boutargue**]

Pouteria caimito *Bot.* Abiu

povitica *(Bk) see* potica

powa *(In)* A unit of weight in the old system equal to 4 challack, approximately 225 g, 8 oz [also called **pau, pav**]

powdered cellulose E460(ii), finely divided cellulose used to add bulk and fibre to slimming foods, convenience foods, etc.

powdered eggs Spray-dried mixed eggs used for manufacturing purposes. During World War 2 large quantities of eggs dried on heated revolving cylinders were imported into the UK from the USA for domestic consumption

powdered sugar *(USA)* Icing sugar

pozole *(Me)* A thick soup made with sweet corn and chicken or pork, flavoured with chilli powder, oregano and pepper and served with chiffonade of lettuce and fried tortilla strips

praakes *see* holishkes

pragerschinken *see* prazskasunka

Prague ham *see* prazskasunka

Prague powder *see* saltpetre

prahok *(Cm)* A fish paste prepared using the residue from preserved cleaned fish which have been used to make a fish sauce

praio *(It)* Sea bream

praire *(Fr) fem.* Warty venus clam

prairie chicken *(USA)* A type of wild grouse with mottled brown plumage *Tympanuchus cupido* or *T. pallidicinctus* found on the great plains of western North America

prairie oyster **1** *(USA)* Ox, pig or lamb testicles usually panéed and fried [also called **mountain oyster, rocky mountain oyster**] **2** A hangover cure consisting of a shelled egg with an intact yolk, flavoured with Worcestershire sauce, lemon juice and salt

praline *(En & Fr) fem.* Nut brittle made from toasted (dry fry, roast or grill) or boiled nuts, skins removed, retoasted, mixed with an equal weight of sugar and some water, caramelized to a rich golden brown, allowed to cool and broken down to a coarse powder

praline cream *(UK)* Praline folded into softly whipped cream, used to accompany apple tart

praliné(e) *(Fr)* Caramelised or covered with praline

pranzo *(It)* Dinner

Prästost *(Sw)* A semi-hard, creamy cows' milk cheese with an open texture and some scattered holes. Sometimes covered in wax. Contains 40% water, 30% fat and 25% protein. Lit. priest's cheese

prataiolo *(It)* Of the field, e.g. mushrooms

pratie *(Ir) coll.* Potato from the Irish práta, potato

pratos de carne *(Po)* Meat dishes

prawn The name given to various species of small clawless crustaceans with long curved tails and large heads varying in colour from white translucent to red and brown and from 7 to 20 cm long found all over the world's oceans. Available raw or cooked, shelled or unshelled and fresh, frozen or dried. The tails only are eaten. See under common prawn, spot prawn, northern prawn, deepwater prawn and king prawn

prawn cocktail A stemmed glass containing a base of chiffonade of lettuce topped with prawns bound in a cocktail or marie-rose sauce. It should be assembled just before serving

prawn crackers A Chinese snack food made from a dried, prawn-flavoured rice flour batter which when deep fried, puffs up to a light crunchy hard white foam-like biscuit or crisp

prawn pudding *see* shrimp pudding

prazheni filii *(Bu)* French toast *(pain perdu)* flavoured with cinnamon and served with honey

prazská sunka *(Cz)* A small ham on the bone cured for several months in mild brine, smoked over beech wood, then baked or boiled whole. Considered to be the best ham for serving hot [also called **jambon cuit de Prague** (Fr), **Pragerschinken** (Ge), **Prague ham**]

precio fijo, a *(Sp)* Fixed price

precipitated chalk *see* calcium carbonate

preço fixo, a *(Po)* Fixed price

pre-cook, to To cook one or more ingredients in advance of their use in another dish, e.g. a duxelle, or of their assembly into a finished dish, e.g. for a salad

precooked rice Rice that had been completely cooked then dehydrated [also called **quick cooking rice, instant rice**]

Preiselbeere *(Ge)* Cranberry

prepared mustard Various mustard seeds finely or coarsely ground and mixed with a selection of vinegars, spices, herbs and seasoning for use as a condiment or as a flavouring for other dishes

pré-salé *(Fr) masc.* Lamb or sheep raised on salt marshes

presame *(It)* Rennet

preservation *see* food preservation science

preservative Any substance added to food capable of inhibiting, retarding or arresting the growth of microorganisms or of any deterioration of food caused by microorganisms or capable of masking the evidence of any such deterioration. Traditional preservatives included salt, sugar, saltpetre, acids or alcohol. Numbers of synthetic substances and derivatives of natural substances are also used. These are identified by E numbers between 200 and 299

preserve A jam or marmalade preserved by cooking or boiling the fruit with a high concentration of sugar

preserve, to To make food suitable for long term storage by preventing growth of microorganisms or enzyme attack using a variety of techniques such as freezing, canning, bottling, drying, curing, salting, pickling, fermenting or preserving with sugar, chemical preservatives or alcohol

preserved fruit *see* candied fruit

preserved ginger Ginger rhizomes from young plants, skinned, soaked in brine for several days, refreshed in water, boiled in water then in sugar syrup. Used for decoration of cakes, in jam and as a sweetmeat

preserves *(USA)* Large pieces of fruit or whole fruit preserved in a heavy sugar syrup which may be slightly jellied with pectin

preserving pan A large deep, wide pan with outwardly sloping sides, a thick base and a large handle, once made of brass or untinned copper, now usually aluminium or stainless steel. Used for making jam and marmalade

preserving sugar A refined white sugar in large crystals used for jam-making, supposed to minimize scum formation and reduce caramelization when being dissolved

press, to 1 To shape food, usually meat but sometimes fruit, by compacting it in a bowl or basin with a weight so that when turned out it forms a solid mass which can be easily sliced **2** To squeeze juice out of fruit **3** To squeeze milk curds so as to remove excess whey thus making a harder cheese

press-sylta *(Sw)* Brawn

Pressburger Beugel *(Au)* A rich pastry with a ground walnut filling

pressé(e) *(Fr)* Pressed

pressed bean curd Bean curd wrapped in cheese cloth and pressed to reduce the water and increase the solids content. Used as a cheese substitute

pressed caviar *see* payousnaya

pressed duck Deboned duck with wing and drumstick bones left in, seasoned with salt and spices, pressed flat and dried. Used as a flavouring agent in Chinese cooking [also called **dried duck**]

pressgurka *(Sw)* Cucumber salad or relish

Presskopf *(Ge & Au)* A sausage similar to the German Presswurst but with larger pieces of meat

pressure cook, to To cook food in the presence of water or steam in a pressure cooker at a temperature above the normal boiling point of water by allowing the pressure to rise to some predetermined value. Food cooks much quicker than normal under these conditions

pressure cooker A vessel which can be completely sealed with a tight fitting lid, fitted with a pressure regulator and a pressure relief valve so that when heated with water inside, the internal pressure rises to some predetermined value above atmospheric pressure with a consequent increase in temperature above the normal boiling point; *see also* pressure-temperature relationship

pressure-temperature relationship The boiling point of water depends on the pressure exerted on its surface and is 100°C at sea level in an open vessel. This rises to 120.5°C at a pressure of 15 psi (pounds per square inch, equivalent to 1 bar) above atmospheric pressure and decreases by approximately 2.7°C for every 1000 m above sea level

Presswurst *(Ge)* A pig's stomach loosely filled with a mixture of diced pickled pork shoulder, pigs' head meat and salted pigs' tongue, salted pork rind, calves' feet and chopped shallots, all chopped until individual pieces are no bigger than a pea, bound with meat glaze, seasoned and flavoured with nutmeg and coriander, simmered for up to 2 hours and pressed in a mould until cool

presswurst *(Hu)* The Hungarian version of the German presswurst made from pigs' trotters, neck and head boiled with onions, garlic, seasoning, bay, marjoram and paprika, bones removed and when cool pigs' blood added, filled into casings simmered for 2 hours and pressed under a weight

presunto *(Po)* Smoked ham

presunto de lamego *(Po)* Salted, smoked and air dried ham made from pigs fed on acorns from the cork oak forests

présure *(Fr) fem.* Rennet

prêtre *(Fr) masc.* Smelt

pretzel A glossy brittle non-sweet snack biscuit sprinkled with coarse salt resembling a capital B, figure of 8 or lover's knot. Made by poaching the shaped dough then baking it hard in the oven [also called **bretzel, salt stick**]

preziosini al pomodoro *(It)* Fried bread dumplings with cheese and tomato sauce

prezzemolo *(It)* Parsley

prezzo fisso *(It)* Fixed price

prickly cockle A variety of cockle *Acanthocardia echinata* with raised projections on the shell

prickly custard apple *see* sour sop

prickly pear A small greenish-orange fruit from a large cactus *Opuntia ficus-indica* shaped like a 4 to 7 cm long flattened pear. The sweet juicy flesh contains edible seeds which become hard on cooking. It should be handled with leather gloves when skinning although they can be bought with the spines removed [also called **barbary pear, cactus pear, Indian pear, Indian fig, tuna fig**]

prik *(Th)* Chilli pepper

prik bod Chilli paste

prik chee far *(Th)* Cayenne pepper

prik khee noo *(Th)* Bird's eye chilli

prik khee noo kaset *(Th)* Serrano chilli

prik khee noo luang *(Th)* A small very hot chilli

prik khee noo suan *(Th)* Bird's eye chilli

prik leung A mild yellow chilli

prik pon *(Th)* Red chilli powder

prik thai *(Th)* Peppercorn

prik yuah *(Th)* Sweet pepper

prik yuak *(Th)* Medium to large, green to red mild chillis, usually stuffed and fried

prima colazione *(It)* Breakfast

primavera *(It)* A garnish of raw or blanched spring vegetables

prime beef *(USA)* The best quality beef from young specially fed cattle. It is tender, with an excellent flavour and texture and is well marbled and usually well hung

prime cut A top quality cut of meat or fish

primeurs *(Fr) fem.* Early forced fruit and vegetables. Also used as an adjective esp. of wines

primizie *(It)* First early vegetables

Primost *(Sa)* A soft form of Gjetost

Primula veris *Bot.* Cowslip

Prince Albert pudding *(UK)* A Victoria sponge sandwich mixture in which half the flour may be replaced by breadcrumbs, steamed in a basin lined with precooked prunes

Prince Jean *(Be)* A soft surface-ripened cows' milk cheese made in the shape of a cylinder (to 450 g) with an even-textured aromatic paste

princesse, à la *(Fr)* In the style of a princess, i.e. garnished with asparagus tips and truffles or noisette potatoes, and sometimes with Béchamel sauce

pringar *(Sp)* To baste or sprinkle with liquid

pringue *(Sp)* Dripping

prinskorv *(Sw)* Small sausages

printanière, à la *(Fr)* In a spring-like fashion, i.e. garnished with a mixture of spring vegetables coated with melted butter

Printen *(Ge)* Honey biscuits with nuts

prix fixe *(Fr) masc.* A fixed price menu

probecho *(Sp)* Violet (2)

process, to To grind to a fine or coarse consistency in a food processor

processed cheese Fairly bland cheese compounded with flavourings, emulsifiers, preservatives, extenders and stabilizers, then formed into blocks, portions, wedges, slices, etc. or filled into squeezy tubes or sausage casings

processed peas Marrowfat peas, cooked in their cans and coloured a particularly bright green

profiterole *(En & Fr) fem.* A light cake filled with cream or custard usually served with chocolate sauce, now restricted to choux pastry balls about 3 to 5 cm dia. with the centre hollow filled with whipped cream, Chantilly cream, ice cream or crème pâtissière

profumata, al *(It)* Flavoured with

prolamin One of the proteins in seeds and grains. It is soluble in the water-ethanol mixtures formed during dough proving and affects the texture of wheat dough during proving and baking

propan-1,2-diol A solvent used for food colours and flavourings [also called **propylene glycol**]

propan-1,2-diol alginate E405, an ester of alginic acid which is partially soluble in fats

propan-2-ol *see* isopropyl alcohol

proprionates Salts of proprionic acid used as flour improvers and food preservatives. The sodium- E281, calcium- E282 and potassium proprionates E283 are used.

***Proprionibacterium* spp.** Microorganisms associated with the ripening of Swiss cheese and the development of the holes.

proprionic acid E280, a simple fatty acid which occurs naturally in dairy products, now synthesized for use as a flour improver and preservative

propylene glycol *see* propan-1,2-diol

prosciutto *(It)* Fresh uncooked ham preserved by curing and/or air drying. Usually served in very thin slices as antipasto

prosciutto cotto *(It)* Cooked ham often boned and pressed into shape

prosciutto crudo *(It)* Raw smoked ham

prosciutto di montagna *(It)* A type of Parma ham but with a more powerful flavour and darker colour

prosciutto di Parma *(It)* *see* Parma ham

proso *see* common millet

Prosopis glandulosa *Bot.* Mesquite bean

Prosopis juliflora *Bot.* Mesquite bean

prosso *(Ru)* Millet

prostokvash *(Ru)* Milk soured at around 30°C

protease A specialized group of enzymes which attack the peptide links (i.e. between the amino acids) in proteins causing a variety of changes including complete digestion of proteins to amino acids. Used in brewing, baking, cheese making and for flavour enhancement and meat tenderization

protein Long chains of amino acids which arrange themselves in many different shapes, some for use as muscle fibres, others to act as structural building blocks of body tissue and others as the enzymes which mediate most body processes. Of the 20 amino acids required 8 (9 in the case of infants) cannot be synthesized by the body and must be supplied in the diet. These are known as essential amino acids q.v. Proteins in food are broken down into amino acids in the gut, these are absorbed into the blood and reassembled as required or burnt to provide energy

protein bodies These are roughly spherical structures consisting of protein encapsulated in a membrane which occur in all seeds including cereals. They cannot be broken mechanically but water causes them to swell and break open, this being the process occurring in germination and also in dough production; *see also* gluten, glutenin, gliadin, prolamin and lectin

protose steak *(USA)* A type of textured vegetable protein made to resemble steak

prove, to 1 To allow a yeast dough to rize both before and after shaping. Even rising depends on the incorporation and dispersion of the correct amount of air in the dough by the mixing and kneading processes **2** To heat a new frying pan to a high temperature with oil or salt prior to using it so as to fill in minute imperfections in the surface. This prevents certain mixtures containing eggs or other proteins from sticking to it. Such pans should not be washed in detergents

provençale, (à la) *(Fr)* In the style of Provence, i.e. with olive oil, garlic, olives and tomatoes, and sometimes mushrooms or anchovies

provençale, sauce *(Fr) fem.* A fondue of concassée tomatoes fried briefly in hot oil then cooked very slowly in a covered pan with crushed garlic, chopped parsley, seasoning and a little sugar

provision, to To purchase or acquire all the foods necessary for a particular task, usually for a voyage or expedition

provisions Foodstuffs acquired for use or storage

provitamin A *see* carotenes

Provola *(It)* A soft spun-curd cheese made with buffalo or cows' milk in the same way as Mozzarella but ending up rather more firm. It is formed into 500 g pear shapes and a string tied around the top leaves a small sphere where the stalk of the pear would be

Provolone *(It)* A hard, scalded and spun-curd smooth textured, pale yellow cheese made from unpasteurized cows' milk. It is started with fermented whey and rennet and the curd is warmed and washed to reduce calcium which makes it more pliable. It is then cheddared and drained, moulded by hand into a variety of shapes, cooled, brined and ripened at high humidity and strung in pairs when moulds develop on the surface. It is brushed and washed before sale. Used for dessert and cooking, as it matures the flavour increases in intensity. The mature form contains 33% water, 35% fat, 28% protein and 4% salt

Provolone affumicata *(It)* A smoked Provolone cheese

Provolone piccante *(It)* A type of grating provolone in which the milk is coagulated with kid's rennet and the cheese is left to mature for up to 2 years when it becomes dark, hard and strong

prugna *(It)* Plum

prugna secca *(It)* Prune

prugna selvatica *(It)* Sloe

prugnolo *(It)* Sloe

prugnuoli *(It)* St George's mushrooms

pruim *(Ho)* Plum

prune 1 A whole plum with or without the stone dried to a black colour **2** *(Fr) fem.* Plum

prune d'Agen *(Fr) fem.* One of the best French plums, used for making prunes

prune de Damas *(Fr) fem.* Damson

pruneau *(Fr)* Prune

prunelle *(Fr) fem.* Sloe

Prunus armeniaca *Bot.* Apricot

Prunus avium *Bot.* Sweet cherry

Prunus cerasifera *Bot.* Cherry plum

Prunus cerasus *Bot.* Acid or sour cherry

Prunus communis* var. *sativa *Bot.* Pear

Prunus domestica *Bot.* Plum and gage

Prunus dulcis* var. *amara *Bot.* Bitter almond

Prunus dulcis* var. *dulcis *Bot.* Sweet almond

Prunus insititia *Bot.* Damson, gage, mirabelle and bullace

Prunus mahaleb *Bot.* Mahlab

Prunus pennsylvanica *Bot.* Bird cherry

Prunus persica *Bot.* Peach

Prunus persica* var. *nectarina *Bot.* Nectarine

Prunus salicina *Bot.* Japanese or salicine plum

Prunus spinosa *Bot.* Sloe

Prunus triflora *Bot.* Japanese or salicine plum

Prunus virginiana *Bot.* Chokecherry

psarassoupa *(Gr)* A thick fish soup made from fish stock simmered for 30 minutes with sliced onions, celery, carrots, potato and garlic all sweated in olive oil, plus tomato concassée and bay leaf. Skinned boned and portioned white fish (about 1:2 on the original stock) and white wine added, simmered 10 minutes then seasoned and finished with lemon juice and simmered a further 2 minutes. Served with chopped parsley [also called **kakavia**]

psari *(Gr)* fish

pshennaya kasha *(Ru)* A porridge made from millet and milk with salt and sugar

Psidium guajava *Bot.* Guava

psiti crema *(Gr)* A baked custard made from plain yoghurt, sugar and egg yolks (15:3:2) flavoured with cinnamon. The yoghurt is whisked into the creamed egg and sugar and all cooked in a bain-marie

psito arni *(Gr)* Roast lamb

Psophocarpus tetragonolobus *Bot.* Goa bean

ptaquiloside The compound in bracken *Pteridium aquilinum* which is broken down in the body into dienone, a potent carcinogen. This may explain the high incidence of throat cancer amongst the Japanese who eat bracken shoots

ptarmigan A small rarely seen wild bird *Lagopus mutus* of the grouse family from northern Europe and North America, which goes white in winter. It is generally cooked in the same way as grouse. Shooting season 12th of August to the 10th of December. Hanging time 2 to 4 days [also called **willow partridge, rock partridge, mountain grouse**]

puak *(Th)* Taro

Pucheria campechiana *Bot.* Canistel

puchero 1 *(Sp) see* olla podrida **2** *(Ar)* An olla podrida containing diced pumpkin and quarters of corn on the cob

puchero argentina *(Ar)* A complex stew of cubed brisket of beef, lamb's and pig's heads, portioned chicken and chick peas, simmered slowly with diced bacon, chorizo sausage, cabbage, potatoes, rice and tomatoes added towards the end

puchero mexicana *(Me)* A one pot meal of beef, veal, pickled pork and goose giblets cooked in plenty of water with carrots, turnips, onions, Hamburg parsley and chick peas in a special earthenware pot and served as both soup and main course

puddenskins *(UK)* A Cornish sausage of slightly salted pork, potatoes, turnips and onions, seasoned and baked in the oven in a covered dish, chopped and mixed with flour, suet, oatmeal and raisins, bound with egg and filled into large casings, tied and baked or fried until coloured

pudding 1 The general term for sweet or savoury dishes cooked or assembled and set in a pudding basin or other type of mould **2** The general term for hot sweet dishes served at the end of a meal **3** o.e. Minced meat or offal and cereal packed into a casing and boiled. Haggis and black pudding are the two common survivors of this once common practice **4** *(Ho)* Pudding

pudding grass *see* pennyroyal

pudding iz kartophelya i yablok *(Ru)* A Baltic dish of equal parts of mashed potatoes mixed with mashed cooking apples sautéed in butter, flavoured with sugar and nutmeg and mixed with a little cream, placed in a baking dish covered with breadcrumbs and butter and baked at 200°C until golden

pudding rice A short grain rice, chalky when raw and sticky when cooked. Requires 40 minutes to cook

pudding spice *(UK)* An English blend of ground spices used in cakes, biscuits and puddings selected from cinnamon, cloves, mace, nutmeg, coriander seeds and allspice

pudeena *(In)* Mint

pudim *(Po)* Pudding

pudim flan *(Po)* Crème caramel

pudim de nozes *(Po)* Custard with cinnamon and walnuts

pudim de ovos *(Po)* Caramel custard flavoured with lemon and cinnamon

pudim portugués *(Po)* Orange custard

pudín *(Sp)* Pudding

pudina ki patti *(In)* Mint

puerco *(Sp)* Pig or pork

puerros *(Sp)* Leeks

puff pastry Pastry made from 700 to 1500 interleaved layers of a very short flour dough and fat formed by rolling out a rectangular layer of the short flour dough, coating or sandwiching with fat, folding in 3 (3-fold turn) or folding the ends to the centre and then together like a book (book turn), rotating a quarter turn and repeating this, resting for 20 minutes in the refrigerator between turns. 5 book folds and 6 3-fold turns are required. The fat used must be of the same consistency as the dough. Margarine or pastry fat requires a strong flour, butter a softer flour. The ratio of fat to flour in the dough is roughly 1:8 whilst overall, the fat flour ratio is 1:1. See French puff pastry method and English puff pastry method for forming the initial layers; *see also* rough puff pastry, puff pastry fat, virgin pastry

puff pastry fat A high melting point fat which can be used to make puff pastry in warm conditions and which will withstand rough handling. Usually free of water. If it contains water the amount of fat in the puff pastry must be increased to give the correct ratio of pure fat to flour.

puffball An edible pear-shaped or spherical fungus of two distinct types called the common puffball and the giant puffball, q.v.

Puffer *(Ge)* Fritter, potato pancake

puffer fish A yellow and black fish *Fugu rubripes* with a white underside whose raw flesh is prized by Japanese gourmands for use in sashimi. It contains a powerful toxin which kills several consumers each year; *see also* fugu

puffs Small cakes or tarts made with a casing of puff pastry filled with jam, custard, whipped cream, etc.

pui la ceaun cu mujdei *(Ro)* Roast chicken served with a sauce made from chicken stock and garlic

puila A sweet bread from Finland flavoured with cardamom

puits d'amour *(Fr) masc.* A small round pastry filled with cream, jelly or fruit. Lit. well of love

pulao *(In) see* pilau

pulasan The fruit of a small tree *Nephelium mutabile* covered with red to yellow warts, similar to the lychee and used in the same way

puleggio *(It)* Penny royal

puli *(Id)* Blade mace

pulla *(Fi)* A roll or bun esp. an enriched and sweetened yeast-raised dough formed into a braid or plats before proving

pullan *(Ir)* A white-fleshed fish *Coregonus lavaretus* similar to vendace found in freshwater lakes esp. in Ireland [also called **whitefish**]

pullao *(In) see* pilau

pullet A young hen or laying fowl

pullet eggs The small eggs laid by pullets when they first start to lay. Not normally sold through other than producer outlets

pulp 1 The soft, somewhat formless, interior of a fruit or vegetable **2** A thick or coarse purée of fruit or vegetables **3** The residue of cooked or uncooked fruit or vegetables after sieving or pressing out the juice. Citrus pulp is sometimes used in manufactured orange drinks

pulp wash The liquid containing sugars, acids and minerals obtained by washing the pith and cell walls left when orange juice is separated from whole oranges. It is illegal to add it to pure orange juice in the UK but not in the USA

pulpeta *(Sp)* Slice of meat

pulpo *(Sp)* Octopus or squid

pulse The general name for most dried leguminous seeds used for their protein content, such as beans, peas, lentils, etc.

Pultost *(No)* A soft cooked-curd naturally curdled cheese made from very low fat cows' milk. The curds are salted and often flavoured with caraway seeds to give a very tasty paste. Contains 60% water, 3% fat and 30% protein [also called **knaost, ramost**]

pummelo The fruit of a tree *Citrus grandis* which looks like a large pale green grapefruit and has a firm sharp tasting white or pink flesh and a very thick skin. It probably originated in southern China but is now grown throughout SEA. There are 3 main groups: the Thai which is relatively small and of high quality, the Chinese which is medium sized with a coarse juicy flesh and the Indonesian which is the largest and is perfectly spherical. They are usually eaten by removing a segment and peeling away the walls on two sides [also called **pomelo, shaddock**]

pumpa *(Sw)* Pumpkin

pumpernickel A dark brown slightly sticky dense German-style bread made from coarse rye flour and steamed for up to 20 hours. Usually eaten in very thin slices [also called **black bread**]

pumpkin The various yellow to orange fruits of a vine *Cucurbita pepo,* a member of the *Cucurbitaceae* family native to America. Pumpkins are usually used for decoration e.g. jack o' lantern and Connecticut field cultivars. Pumpkin pie is usually made from squash which have better cooking qualities; New England sugar however is a small pie pumpkin

pumpkin pie *(USA)* A dessert served with whipped cream consisting of a cooked pumpkin or squash purée mixed with eggs, sugar, cream, black treacle or molasses and spices, baked in a precooked open pastry case until set

pumpkin seeds Large flat green seeds from pumpkins and squashes eaten raw or cooked, in sweet or savoury dishes or as a snack food. Can be sprouted

punajuuri *(Fi)* Beetroot

punajuurikeitto *(Fi)* Borsch

punchero *(Me)* A one pot meat, bean and vegetable stew. The broth is served first, then the meat and vegetables

Punica granatum *Bot.* Pomegranate

Punkersdorker *(Ge)* A strong juicy salami-style sausage

punnet A small square, rectangular or oval basket originally of woven wood or leaves but now plastic or card, used to hold soft fruit, mushrooms and the like for sale

Punschtorte *(Ge)* A rum-flavoured cake

punta di vitello *(It)* Breast of veal

puntarelle *(It)* A winter salad green with thin serrated leaves on long stalks

puntina *(It)* Pinch, e.g. of salt

puntine *(It)* Tiny pasta seeds, smaller than semini

puntino, a *(It)* Medium well done as applied to meat

puntitas Paco alcade *(Sp)* An Andalusian speciality of beef sautéed with fresh tomatoes, black olives and garlic

punto, en su *(Sp)* Medium cooked, of meat steaks, etc; *see also* à point

puppadom *(In) see* poppadom

pur chèvre *(Fr) masc.* Cheese made only from goats' milk

pure olive oil Blended olive oil made by larger companies from a mixture of refined oils from various sources [also called **100% pure olive oil**]

puré de patata *(Sp)* Mashed potato

purea *(It)* Purée

Püree *(Ge)* Purée

purée *(En & Fr) fem.* **1** A type of soup in which fresh vegetables and pulses are simmered in stock with flavouring then forced through a sieve or liquidized to give a smooth consistency. Usually served accompanied with croûtons in a separate dish **2** Any food processed or pounded to a smooth consistency, somewhere between coating and pouring

puri *(In)* A deep fried chapati which puffs and swells as it is cooked. Served hot, often with a hot spicy filling for use as a snack [also called **poori, bhatura, bhatoora**]

purjo *(Sw)* Leeks

purple basil A type of basil from SEA with red to purple tinged leaves and red stalks. The flavour and aroma become intense when it is cooked

purple granadilla *see* purple passion fruit

purple guava *see* strawberry guava

purple laver *see* nori

purple passion fruit A large (to 7.5 cm dia) globular fruit *Passiflora edulis* with a hard wrinkled purple to black skin containing a deliciously-flavoured mucilaginous yellow pulp full of small edible seeds. The pulp is scooped out for eating or use in desserts or it may be sieved to use as a flavouring [also called **maracuya, purple granadilla**]

purple sage A variety of sage *Salvia officinale 'Purpurascens'* with very strong-flavoured purple leaves, good for tea

purple sprouting broccoli *see* sprouting broccoli

purslane A plant of two distinct types, summer purslane which is a half hardy annual and winter purslane which is fully hardy. See under the separate entries

pusit calmar *(Ph)* Squid

puso no saging *(Ph)* Banana flower

pu tao *(Ch)* Grapes

pu tao gan *(Ch)* Raisins

pu tao jiu *(Ch)* Wine made from grapes

putcha *see* petcha

Pute *(Ge)* Hen turkey

Puter *(Ge)* Cock turkey

puttanesca, alla *(It)* In the style of the harlot, a description of pasta with tomatoes, garlic, capers, olives and anchovies

puuro *(Fi)* Porridge

Puzol *(Sp)* A soft ewes' milk cheese eaten very fresh. Contains 61% water, 21% fat and 18% protein

pwdin gwaed *(UK)* A Welsh black pudding made of salted fresh pig's blood mixed with a little water, allowed to stand overnight, chopped onions and a little fat coated with oatmeal, herbs and seasoning added, this then mixed with the blood, all packed into hog casings, boiled 30 minutes then dried. Served sliced and fried

pwdin gwaed gwyddau *(UK)* As pwdin gwaed but using goose blood instead of pig's blood

pyaaj *(In & Ne)* Onion

pyechenye *(Ru)* Tart

pyechyen-grill *(Ru)* Liver and onion kebabs basted with mutton fat from Asiatic Russia. The liver can be wrapped in bacon for non-Muslims

pyechyen kur v madere *(Ru)* Floured chicken liver pieces sautéed with sweated onions, stewed in chicken stock and Madeira until cooked and served with the reduced cooking liquor blended with sour cream and garnished with chopped parsley

pyechyenka *(Ru)* Liver

pyin daw thein *(Bm)* Curry leaf

pyin tha-leik *(Bm)* Turtle

p'yogo *(Ko)* Shiitake mushroom

pyramide *(Fr) fem.* A soft surface ripened goats milk cheese with a sweet flavour which becomes stronger as it ripens. It is formed in the shape of a truncated pyramid and sometimes coated with ashes to dry it out

pyridoxal *see* vitamin B6

pyridoxamine *see* vitamin B6

pyridoxine *see* vitamin B6

pyridoxol *see* vitamin B6

pyroligneous acid A yellow liquid obtained by condensing the vapours obtained by heating sawdust in a closed metal retort. Used to impart a smoky flavour to some foods

Pyrus communis *Bot.* Pear tree

Pyrus pyrofolia *Bot.* Asian pear

Pyrus ussuriensis *Bot.* Asian pear

pytt i panna *(Sw)* Fried cubes of potato, ham and beef, mixed with fried onions and chopped parsley, the whole topped with a raw egg yolk which is stirred into the mixture at the table [also called **Swedish hash**]

pyy *(Fi)* Hazel hen

Qq

qâlat daqqa *(ME & NA)* An Arabian spice blend of ground black peppercorns, cloves, grains of paradise, nutmeg and cinnamon used in vegetable dishes and with lamb

qataif *(ME)* A pancake made from flour, water and yeast, dipped after cooking in lemon-flavoured syrup scented with orange flower water. Can be stuffed, folded and deep fried

qawwrama *(ME)* Lebanese preserved meat made from the rendered fat of specially fattened sheep in which cubes of lean mutton which have been pressed to remove moisture are fried and the fried meat and fat to cover, packed in earthenware pots. Will keep for several months

quadrello *(It)* Rack of lamb or loin of pork

quadretti di riso alla piemontese *(It)* Rice fritters with meat sauce and cheese

quadrucci *(It)* Small squares of egg pasta used in soups

quaggiaridda *(It)* A mixture of sheep's offal, sausage and cheese wrapped in a pig's caul and baked

quaglia *(It)* Quail

quaglie alla borghese *(It)* Quails wrapped in vine leaves and roasted on a bed of puréed peas and lettuce

quaglie rincartate *(It)* An Umbrian dish of quails wrapped in bread dough and baked

quagliette *(It)* Cabbage rolls and similar

quagliette di vitello *(It)* Paupiettes of veal stuffed with ham and grilled on a skewer

quahog clam An Atlantic ocean clam *Mercenaria mercenaria* up to about 13 cm in dia. with a dull grey to brown exterior and purple interior shell. Eaten raw or cooked [also called **hard clam** (USA), **hard shell clam** (USA), **hard-neck clam, cherrystone**]

quaietta *(It)* A dish from Turin of veal cutlets stuffed with meat, cheese and truffles

quail A small game bird *Coturnix coturnix* now protected in the wild but farmed for table use. The English version is usually more tasteless than the French which has a yellow flesh from being corn fed. Usually barded and roasted at 220°C for 25 minutes and served one per person on buttered toast garnished with watercress

quails' eggs Small eggs regarded as a delicacy, boiled for 1 minute or hard boiled and served with a dip as an appetizer or used as a garnish for cold buffets

quaking custard *(USA)* A New England demoulded egg custard garnished with egg white which tends to shake easily on the plate

quarg *see* quark

quark *(En, Ge & CE)* A soft, slightly sour, curd cheese sometimes flavoured with fruit or herbs, made from skimmed, whole or buttermilk possibly with added cream. Eaten as a dessert. Contains 70 to 80% water, and less than 3 % fat [also called **kvarg, quarg, Buttermilchquark, Labquark, Speisequark**]

Quarkklösse *(Ge)* Dumplings made with quark

Quarktorte *(Ge)* A type of cheesecake with a short pastry base. The filling is strained quark creamed with butter, sugar and egg yolk flavoured with lemon zest and cinnamon and with currants and stiffly beaten egg whites folded in. The base and fillings are baked in a very slow oven and served cold dusted with icing sugar

quart 1 2 pints in either imperial or USA volume measure **2** *(Fr) masc.* A quarter, one fourth part

quarter A volume measure equal to 8 bushels or 64 gallons in either imperial or USA measure

quarter of meat *see* hindquarter or forequarter

quartier *(Fr) masc.* Fore or hindquarter of an animal carcase

Quartirolo *(It)* A soft, cows' milk cheese similar to Taleggio made with a lactic starter and having a distinctive mushroom flavour

quarto *(It)* **1** A quarter, one fourth part **2** Leg, haunch or hindquarter of meat

quasi *(Fr) masc.* The top of the leg of veal cut from the English cushion and undercushion and the rear of the loin

quasi de veau bourgeoise *(Fr) masc.* Boneless quasi of veal casseroled with pork, calf's foot and vegetables

quassia A bitter flavouring extracted from the wood and bark of a South American tree *Quassia amara* or West-Indian tree *Pacrasma excelsa* mainly used for drinks and tonics

Quassia amara *Bot.* Quassia

quatre-épices *(Fr) fem.* The classic French spice blend used in charcuterie and stews, consisting of 5 parts black peppercorns, 2 parts nutmeg, 1 part cloves and 1 part dried ginger ground to a fine powder. Cinnamon is substituted for black pepper if used in sweet dishes and the proportions vary from place to place

quatre-quarts *(Fr) masc.* The French version of pound cake q.v.

quattro spezie *(It)* A spice mix of pepper, nutmeg, juniper and cloves Lit. four spices

quattro stagioni *(It)* **1** A butterhead lettuce with dimpled soft and glossy leaves tipped with red **2** A type of pizza in which the four quarters have different additions to the tomato and cheese base to represent the four seasons

que *(Vi)* A type of mint

queen cake A small individual cake made from the basic cake mixture using the creaming method with a final addition of washed and dried mixed dried vine fruits

queen crab *see* snow crab

queen of puddings *(UK)* Bread or cake crumbs covered with a sweetened and flavoured egg custard mixture baked in the oven in a bain-marie until set, cooled, spread with warmed jam or fruit, topped with a meringue mixture and browned in the oven

queen scallop A small variety of scallop *Pecten opercularis* or *Chlamys opercularis* with an almost circular shell up to 10 cm dia. and a vivid red roe. Found in deeper waters than the great scallop. The flesh weighs about 12 g [also called **queenie, quin scallop**]

queenie *see* queen scallop

Queensland nut *see* macadamia nut

queijadas de sintra *(Po)* Unsweetened patties made with eggs, almonds and cheese served with French beans

queijo *(Po)* Cheese

queijo arreganhado *(Po)* A mild and mellow cheese made from the first milk drawn from the ewe which doesn't contain much fat

queijo do ceu *(Po)* A cheese dessert

queijo da Ilha *(Po)* A hard cows' milk cheese from the Azores resembling a mature Cheddar, used mainly for cooking [also called **queijo da Terra**]

queijo Minas *(Br)* A white scalded-curd cheese made from cows' milk eaten fresh as a dessert or allowed to mature and become yellow

queijo Minas curado *(Br)* The mature, semi-hard version of Minas with a thin rind and paste containing scattered holes. Contains 45% water, 20% fat and 28% protein

queijo Minas frescal *(Br)* A soft fresh cows' milk cheese with a pleasant acid taste. Contains 60% water, 16% fat and 17% protein [also called **Mineiro Frescal**]

queijo da Serra *(Po)* The famous semi-hard high fat cheese made from the milk of ewes pastured on the high meadows of the north east. It resembles a well-flavoured Brie and is eaten either runny or ripened until firm and pungent. Its origin and method of production are controlled by the government [also called **Serra**]

queijo da Terra *(Po)* *see* queijo da Ilha

queijos frescos *(Po)* Fresh cheeses made from ewes' or goats' milk sometimes allowed to ripen

quemada *(Me)* Milk which has been boiled until it turns a caramel colour

quenelle *(En & Fr) fem.* Fish, meat or poultry meat processed to a very fine forcemeat, bound with eggs or fat, shaped with two spoons into small round or oval dumplings and poached in a cooking liquor. Served as a garnish or as a main course with a sauce

quenelles de brochet *(Fr) fem.* Quenelles or dumplings made with the flesh of pike

quente *(Po)* Warm, hot

queso *(Sp)* Cheese

queso de los Bellos *(Sp)* *see* Bellos

queso blanco *(SA)* A soft cheese made from cows' milk curdled with acetic acid, the curds kneaded, pressed and salted. Eaten fresh or after ripening for up to 3 months. Contains 50% water, 19% fat and 25% protein

queso de bola *(Sp)* A round ball Dutch style cheese

queso de cabra *(SA)* A soft cylindrical (to 1 kg) goats' milk cheese from Chile with a sharp flavour

queso de cerdo *(Sp)* Brawn made from pig's head

queso Ciudad Real *(Sp)* A smoked goats' milk cheese

queso helado *(Sp)* An ice cream brick

queso manchego *(Sp)* A hard sheep's milk cheese

queso de nata *(Sp)* Cream cheese

quesong puti *(Ph)* *see* kesong puti

quetsche *(Fr) fem.* A variety of dark purple plum

queue *(Fr) fem.* Tail, of an animal; handle of a pan

queue de boeuf *(Fr) fem.* Oxtail

queue de boeuf claire *(Fr) fem. see* clear oxtail soup

queue de boeuf liée *(Fr) fem. see* thick oxtail soup

queues d'écrevisses *(Fr) fem.* Crayfish tails

quiche A savoury custard tart made from a shortcrust or puff pastry-lined quiche dish or flan ring, possibly precooked, filled with various solid savoury and raw salad or vegetable items which are then covered with a seasoned mixture of eggs and milk and/or cream, possibly gratinated and/or decorated, then baked in the oven at 200 to 230°C until cooked and browned

quiche dish A shallow (about 3 cm deep), round, glazed ceramic dish used for cooking quiches

quiche lorraine *(En & Fr) fem.* A quiche made with a filling of chopped ham or bacon and grated cheese or slices of Gruyère

quick bread *(USA)* Bread made with chemical raising agents

quick cooking rice *see* precooked rice

quick freeze, to To freeze food so that it spends a minimum of time between 0°C and −4°C, the region where ice crystals would, if given the time, grow to such a size as to rupture cell walls releasing their contents on thawing. Usually done by blasting with liquefied gases. Quick frozen food is usually stored at around - 30°C

quiejo do Reino *(Br)* A cows' or goats' milk cheese similar to the Portuguese Serra cheese

quiejo Prato *(Br)* A flat semi-hard Edam-like cows' milk cheese with a few small holes and a tender rind

quignon *(Fr) masc.* Crust or hunk (of bread)

quill Cinnamon bark rolled up into a cigar-like tube

quillaia The compound extracted from the bark of the soap bark tree from SA used as a foaming agent in soft drinks. Permitted for use in the UK

quillings Small broken pieces of cinnamon bark often rolled up within larger quills

quin scallop *see* queen scallop

quince The apple or pear-shaped fruit of a temperate climate bush *Cydonia oblonga* with a green skin which turns to gold when ripe and is covered by a greyish-white down. The ripe flesh is sweet, juicy and yellow with a pronounced scent and is alway cooked. Used as apples or made into jam without the need of added pectin. They originated in western Asia but are now grown worldwide esp. in Uruguay

quin choy *(Ch)* Winter rape

quing dou *(Ch)* Fresh soya beans

quing suan *(Ch)* Asian leek

quinoa A tiny golden seed from South America cultivated since 3000 BC. It is rather like rice but has a higher protein content. Requires 10 to 15 minutes boiling. Can be grown in temperate climates

quinoline yellow E104, a synthetic yellow food colouring

quire of paper *(UK)* An old English cake made from very thin pancakes cooked on one side only, sprinkled with sugar and built up into a cake. The pancake mixture is rich in eggs, cream and melted butter and flavoured with sherry, rose water and nutmeg

quisquilla *(Sp)* Shrimp

quisquilla gris *(Sp)* Brown shrimp

Quitte *(Ge)* Quince

Quittengelee *(Ge)* Quince jam

quorn The thread like mycelium of a fungus grown industrially in a medium made principally from the starch content of field beans. It contains about 45% protein and 13% fat together with dietary fibre and after drying and compounding, is used as a high class protein in vegetarian meals, both made up and home cooked

Rr

rã *(Po)* Frog finished with cream and chopped dill

rabaçal *(Po)* A mild, white and soft curd cheese made from a mixture of ewe's and goat's milk. Eaten young but the taste intensifies as it ripens. Often cured in the sun

rabadi *(In)* Condensed milk

rabanadas *(Po)* A dessert made from sweetened fried bread

rabanetes *(Po)* Radishes

rábano *(Sp)* Radish

rábano picante *(Sp)* Horseradish

rabarbaro *(It)* Rhubarb

rabarber *(De & Sw)* Rhubarb

rabarbra *(No)* Rhubarb

rabbit A small furry burrowing game animal *Oryctolagus caniculius* of the hare family sometimes farmed and weighing when dressed around 1.2 kg to 4 kg for some of the farmed animals. The farmed animal's flesh resembles chicken, the wild animals are more gamey but this may be reduced by soaking in salted water and briefly blanching. They are not hung. Cooked in any way, traditionally served with onion sauce.

rabbit Latrobe *(Aus)* Marinated pieces of rabbit stewed in a sour cream sauce

rabbit sausage *(UK)* Meat from cooked rabbit, shredded and mixed with one third its weight of coarsely chopped bacon, seasoned, flavoured with ground cloves and mace, packed into casings and boiled or fried. Eaten hot or cold

rabbit-eye blueberry *see* blueberry

råbiff *(Sw)* Raw beef, steak tartare

râble *(Fr) masc.* Saddle of hare or rabbit

rabo de buey *(Sp)* Oxtail

rabotte *(Fr) fem.* An apple cooked in pastry as a dessert. From Champagne

raccoon *(USA)* A small furry carnivorous animal sometimes used in Cajun cuisine

rachel, à la *(Fr)* In Rachel's style, i.e. steaks garnished with artichokes, bone marrow and parsley

racine *(Fr) fem.* Root vegetable

rack of lamb One half of the vertebrae and first six rib bones counting from the rear end of the lamb equivalent to the best end. Usually chined, skinned and roasted

raclette *(He)* **1** An unpasteurized cow's milk cheese similar to Gruyère and made in small rounds; *see also* Valais raclette **2** A dish made by halving a raclette cheese, toasting it in front of the fire or grilling it and serving the molten centre with boiled potatoes and pickles

radappertization The production of food free from spoilage microorganisms using ionizing radiation

radicchio *see* red chicory

radici *((It)* Radishes

radicidation The elimination of pathogens in food using ionizing radiation

Radieschen *(Ge)* Radishes

radijs *(Ho)* Radish

radis *(Fr) masc.* Radish, radishes

radis noir *(Fr) masc.* Horseradish

radish The root of a plant *Raphanus sativus* and *R. sativus* Longipinnus Group of the mustard family grown in many forms and colours from 1 cm dia. spheres to 30 cm long carrot-like roots and with colours from white through red to black. The crisp white flesh has a slightly peppery flavour of varying degrees of strength. Generally used raw in salads and for decoration in many sculpted shapes. The larger varieties, e.g. mooli, may be eaten raw, cooked or pickled. The young leaves are also edible

radisor *(Sw)* Radish

radisser *(It)* Radishes

rådjurssadel *(Sw)* Roasted saddle of venison

rådjursstek *(Sw)* Venison steak

radurization The reduction of the content of spoilage organisms in perishable food using ionizing radiation

rådyr *(No)* Venison

rafano *(It)* Radish

rafano tedesco *(It)* Horseradish

raffreddato *(It)* Chilled

rafinat *(Fr)* A refined product

rafraîchi(e) *(Fr)* Refreshed or chilled, the past participle of rafraîchir, to refresh or cool down

ragee *see* ragi

raggee *see* ragi

raggmunkar *(Sw)* Potato (pan)cakes

raggy *see* ragi

ragi 1 The seeds of an East Indian grass *Eleusine caracana* used as a cereal grain in Africa and India and used for bread and beer [also called **ragee, raggee, raggy, finger millet**] **2** *(SEA)* A rice cake, widely sold as street food

ragno di mare *(It)* Spider crab

ragoo *(UK)* An English spelling of ragoût used as a description of a rich meat and vegetable casserole

ragoût *(Fr) masc.* A thick stew with a high proportion of meat or poultry sometimes including offal and sausages

Ragoût fin *(Ge)* Sweetbreads, brains and other fine offal cooked with mushrooms in a cream and wine sauce

ragú *(It)* **1** Ragoût **2** A sauce made from olive oil, butter, cooked meat and garlic **3** *(De, No & Sw)* Stew

Ragusano *(It)* A hard, scalded and spun curd cheese from Sicily made in rectangular blocks (to 12 kg). It is matured for 3 months for dessert use or up to 12 months for grating. The dessert cheese has a mild delicate flavour, the grating cheese which had an oiled dark brown rind is sharp and savoury

rahat lokum *(Tu)* A type of turkish delight mixed with almond slivers, pistachios and hazelnuts after it is cooked but before setting

Rahm *(Ge)* Cream

Rahmfrischkäse *(Ge)* A soft fresh cheese made with acid curdled cows' milk. Contains 70% water, 18% fat and 9% protein

Rahmkäse *(Ge)* Cream cheese

Rahmschnitzel *(He)* Veal escalopes in a cream sauce

Rahmsosse *(Ge)* Cream sauce

rai *(In)* Black mustard seeds

raia blanca *(Po)* White skate

raie *(Fr) fem.* Ray or skate, the fish

raie blanche *(Fr) fem.* White skate

raie bouclée *(Fr) fem.* Thornback ray

raifort *(Fr) masc.* Horseradish

raifort, sauce *(Fr) fem. see* horseradish sauce

rainbow sardine A small fish *Dussumiera acuta* similar to the sardine. It is fished off the south west coast of India and canned in the same way

rainbow smelt *see* smelt

rainbow trout A generally freshwater trout *Salmo gairdnerii* occasionally found in the sea, with a silvery green back, banded with pink and weighing about 500 g, now usually farmed. The flesh may be white or pink depending upon the diet. Grilled, poached, shallow fried or baked en papillote

Rainfarn *(Ge)* Tansy

Rainha Claudia *(Po)* A type of greengage; *see also* Reine Claude

raise, to To lighten baked doughs and cake mixtures by the addition of raising agents or by fermentation with yeast prior to cooking

raised pie A pie made with a very stiff pastry (hot water pastry) which is self-supporting, will hold the filling without support and can be moulded by hand sometimes around a tin or more commonly in a fluted oval mould which separates into pieces. See e.g. Melton Mowbray pie and pork pie

raisin 1 Dried white grapes made from either the naturally seedless Thompson type or the muscatel grape **2** *(Fr) masc.* grape

raising agent Any chemical mixture which liberates carbon dioxide on heating so as to form small bubbles and hence lighten the mixture it is in. Bicarbonate of soda and baking powder are typical examples

raisins de Corinthe *(Fr) masc.* Currants (the dried vine fruits)

raisins de Smyrne *(Fr) masc.* Sultanas

raisins secs *(Fr) masc.* Raisins

raisu *(Ja)* Cooked rice served in a Japanese style bowl

raita *(In)* A combination of chopped vegetables and fruit, usually cucumber, onion and bananas mixed with thick yoghurt and flavoured with cumin, coriander and seasoning, served as an accompaniment to other foods

rajas *(Me)* Strips of chile poblano fried with onion, potatoes and/or tomatoes and garnished with melted cheese

rajma *(In)* Red kidney beans

rakkyo *(Ja)* Pickled shallots

räkor *(Sw)* Prawns, shrimps

rakørret *(No)* Salted and cured trout

rakott káposzt *(Hu)* Sauerkraut layered in a dish with slices of smoked bacon covered with chopped lean pork which has been browned in lard with garlic and paprika, slices of debreszin sausage and with a final layer of sauerkraut, then covered with sour cream and baked in the oven

räksås *(Sw)* Shrimp sauce. Chopped and cooked shrimps, sweated with butter and flour, combined with fish stock

rambutan *(En & Id)* The oval fruit of a tropical tree *Nephelium lappaceum* about 5 cm long with a central inedible stone, a delicate sweet white flesh tasting of raisins and a green skin turning to red when ripe, covered with soft spines. Eaten raw [also called **hairy lychee**]

ramekin 1 A small individual circular, usually white, porcelain, glass or earthenware oven-proof dish from 4 to 15 cm in dia. used for pâtés, mousses, egg custards, baked eggs and soufflés, etc. **2** A mixture of cheese, eggs and bread crumbs or unsweetened puff pastry baked in an individual dish

ramen *(Ja)* The common noodle of Japan, thin, yellow and made from wheat flour and egg

ramequin *(Fr) masc.* **1** Ramekin **2** A type of cheese fritter

ramequin au fromage *(Fr & He)* masc. A cheese tart or fritter served hot or cold

ramereau *(Fr) masc.* Young woodpigeon

ramerino *(It)* Rosemary

ramier *(Fr) masc.* Woodpigeon

ramo de cheiras *(Po)* Flavourings wrapped in muslin like a BG always containing garlic, parsley and bay leaf plus other herbs according to the dish

ramolaccio *(It)* Horseradish

ramost *see* pultost

ramp *(USA)* A wild leek with a strong flavour

rampe *(In & Sr)* Screwpine

ramphal *see* bullock's heart

rampion A European flowering plant *Campanula rapunculus* of the harebell family. The leaves and roots are eaten

ram's head pea *see* chickpea

ram tulsi *(In)* White basil

rana comune *(It)* Edible frog

rana pescatrice *(It)* Monkfish

ranchero *(Sp)* In a country style

rancid The description of the smell of oxidized stale fats which is due to liberated free fatty acids and other oxidation compounds

rane fritte *(It)* Fried frogs' legs

ranghi *see* abutilon

rango ko maasu *(Ne)* Water buffalo meat

rankins *(USA)* A type of light cheese pudding or soufflée containing stiffly beaten egg whites

ranocchio *(It)* Edible frog

rapa *(It)* Turnip

rapa svedese *(It)* Swede

raparperi *(Fi)* Rhubarb

rapata *(It)* A rice and turnip soup from Lombardy

rape 1 The plant *Brassica napus* from which rapeseed is obtained. Some varieties known as salad rape are used in the west as a source of salad leaves. It is used as a vegetable in northern China where 3 types, broccoli rape (probably the same as broccoli raab), heart of rape and winter rape are used [also called **cole, coleweed, coleseed**] **2** *(Sp)* Monkfish

rape rosse *(It)* Beetroot

râpe *(Fr) fem.* Grater

râpé(e) *(Fr)* **1** Grated, past participle of râper, to grate **2** *masc.* Grated cheese (from fromage râpé)

rapeseed The seed of a yellow flowered plant *Brassica napus* closely related to the swede, now commonly grown for its oil, but can also be sprouted as a substitute for mustard in mustard and cress [also called **canola**]

rapeseed oil The oil from the rapeseed, grown in great quantities in the EU. Used as a cooking oil and for margarine manufacture. Low erucic acid strains of rape are now normal [also called **colza oil**]

Raphanus sativus *Bot.* Mooli

***Raphanus sativus* Longipinnatus Group** *Bot.* Radish

raphøne *(De)* Pheasant

rapini *(It)* Broccoli raab

rapphöna *(Sw)* Partridge

rapphøne *(No)* Partridge

Raps *(Ge)* Rape *Brassica napus*

Rapsöl *(Ge)* Rapeseed oil

rårakor *(Sw)* A type of crêpe made from grated or processed raw potato and onion, seasoned, bound with egg and fried as very thin pancakes in hot butter

rare The description of meat cooked so that the inside is still red or pink

rarebit *see* Welsh rarebit and buck rarebit

rarhar *(In) see* pigeon pea

rarrah *(In)* Saddle, usually of lamb

rasam *(In)* A lentil broth soured with tamarind

rascasse *(Fr) fem.* Scorpion fish, used in bouillabaisse [also called **rascasse rouge**]

rascasse de fond *(Fr) fem.* Bluemouth, the fish

rascasse rouge *(Fr) fem. see* rascasse

Raschera *(It)* A semi-hard cows' milk cheese sometimes with ewes' or goats' milk added. It is made in squares (to 8 kg) and has a yellow, supple paste with a delicate taste and containing a few holes [also called **Raschiera**]

Raschiera *(It) see* Raschera

rasedar *(In)* Vegetables in a thin sauce

ras el hanout *(NA)* A mixture of many spices, herbs and other items, up to 20 or more in number including so-called aphrodisiacs such as cantharides (Spanish fly), ash berries and monk's pepper. Sold whole by the merchants who each have their own recipe and grind as required. Used in sweet and savoury dishes

rasher *see* bacon rasher

rasp *see* barrel bread

rasp, to To grate or break up into raspings

raspberry A fruit similar to the blackberry q.v. but softer, light red, occasionally white or black, with a covering of fine down and a sweet, slightly acid, fruity, perfumed flavour. The wild variety are small to 5 mm but domesticated varieties can grow to 2.5 cm long. It is grown on a cool climate rambling plant *Rubus idaeus* which is cultivated so as to produce new, relatively short canes each year. The fruit tend to soften and go mouldy quickly and must be used when fresh, canned or deep frozen. Used raw or cooked and often puréed to form a coulis or sauce. One of the fruits in summer pudding

raspberry sauce As apricot sauce but made with raspberries

raspings Breadcrumbs

Rässkäse *(He)* A hard cooked-curd cows' milk cheese similar to but stronger tasting and less supple than Appenzell and with more holes. It is slightly bitter

rassolnik *(Ru)* A soup based on beef stock simmered with presweated aromatic vegetables, wilted sorrel or spinach, bay leaf and seasoning until cooked, bay leaf removed, all puréed, finely chopped gherkins, pickling juice and prefried, floured pieces of lambs' kidney added and simmered 5 minutes then thickened with egg yolk and served hot or chilled with sour cream

råstekt potatiskaka *(Sw)* A type of Rösti made from grated potatoes, seasoned and fried in butter in a closed pan as a solid cake. Butter is put on top and the pan is left on a very low heat until the base of the cake is browned. Served browned side up

rat *see* grenadier, the fish

raţă pe varză *(Ro)* Duck browned in fat then braised in the oven on a deep bed of sauerkraut mixed with chopped onions browned in lard and moistened with sauerkraut juice, defatted and the duck carved and served on the sauerkraut and onion mixture

ratafia 1 A liqueur flavoured with the kernels of cherries, almonds, peaches and other stone fruits **2** A small sweet macaroon-like biscuit flavoured with ratafia essence. Once eaten with the liqueur but now used for decoration, as a base for cold desserts or, when crushed, as a constituent of various dessert creams; *see also* macaroon

ratafia essence An alcoholic extract of the kernels of cherries, peaches, almonds and other stone fruits used as a flavouring

ratalu *(In)* White yam

ratatouille 1 *(En & Fr) fem.* A Provençal dish made from a mixture of tomatoes, aubergines, green and red sweet peppers, onions, garlic and olive oil seasoned and flavoured with marjoram or oregano. Courgettes and stoned olives are sometimes included. Traditionally each vegetable is fried or grilled separately and then combined. In the UK and commercially all tend to be stewed together **2** *(Fr)* Bad stew, lousy food

rathu miris *(Sr)* Chilli pepper

raton *(Fr) masc.* A type of cheesecake

rat's ear Cloud ear fungus

rattan palm A climbing palm *Calamus rotang* whose shoots and seeds are edible but whose main use is as a source of cane for weaving furniture and baskets

rattatuia di frutti di mare alla marchigiana *(It)* A stew of seafood and tomatoes in wine, served with rice

rattle A variety of salad potato

Raubreif *(Ge)* A dessert of chilled Chantilly

cream blended at the last moment with peeled and cored dessert apples which have been coarsely grated into a mixture of orange juice, lemon juice and sugar (6:3:4) previously prepared and chilled

rau cai tau *(Vi)* Chinese cabbage

rau can *(Vi)* Celery leaves

Räucherall *(Ge)* Smoked eel

Räucherkäse *(Ge)* Naturally smoked cheese, often of the processed kind and with various flavourings and additives

Räucherlachs *(Ge)* Smoked salmon

räuchern *(Ge)* To smoke

räuchfleisch *(Ge)* Smoked meat

rau hun cay *(Vi)* Mint

Rauke *(Ge)* Rocket, the plant

Raukenkohl *(Ge)* Rocket, the plant

rau la tia to *(Vi)* Caraway mint

rau muong *(Vi)* Swamp cabbage

rau ngo *(Vi)* Coriander leaves

rau que *(Vi)* Basil

rau ram *(Vi)* Polygonum

Raute *(Ge)* Rue, the herb

rau thom *(Vi)* Mint

rava *(In)* Semolina

ravanelli *(It)* Radishes

ravier *(En & Fr) masc.* A dish in which compound hors d'oeuvres are presented, usually rectangular (10 by 20 cm) in shape

ravigote butter A compound butter made by mixing butter with blanched, refreshed and dried chopped shallots, parsley, chervil, tarragon, chives and salad burnet which have been pounded to a paste, the whole passed through a sieve [also called **beurre Chivry, beurre ravigote, beurre vert** (Fr), **green butter**]

ravigote, sauce *(En & Fr) fem.* **1** A reduction of white wine and vinegar mixed with a velouté sauce and finished off the heat with shallot butter and chopped chervil, tarragon and chives. Served hot **2** A vinaigrette made with oil and vinegar, small dried capers, chopped parsley, tarragon, chervil, chives, onion and seasoning

ravioli *(En & It)* A filling made from cheese, spinach, ground meat or similar items piped gridwise on to a sheet of pasta, egg washed, a similar sized sheet laid over and small squares or circles cut out with a filling in the centre of each, poached and served with a sauce.

ravioli alla calabrese *(It)* Ravioli with a filling of sausage, cheese and egg and served with a sauce sprinkled with cheese

ravioli caprese *(It)* Ravioli stuffed with cheese, eggs and herbs

ravioli dolci *(It)* Ravioli from Liguria stuffed with beef marrow and candied fruit, fried and dredged with sugar

ravioli alla napoletana *(It)* Ravioli filled with a mixture of ham, ricotta, Mozarella and Parmesan cheese

ravioli trentini *(It)* Ravioli stuffed with a mixture of meat and chicken

ravioli della val pusteria *(It)* Ravioli made with rye flour, filled with spinach, cheese or sauerkraut and poached or fried

raviolini *(It)* Very small ravioli

ravo *(In)* Semolina

raw Not cooked

raya de clavos *(Sp)* Thornback ray

rayed-trough shell clam A cream coloured clam with purple markings about 13 cm in dia

ray's bream *see* pomfret

raznjici *(Bk)* Grilled meat kebabs from Serbia

razor shell A cut-throat razor shaped mollusc *Solen vagina* about 6 cm long. Treat as mussels

razor shell clam A long thin bivalve mollusc *Ensis ensis* resembling a cut-throat razor up to 13 cm long and found on sandy beaches. Not traded commercially but may be eaten raw or cooked like mussels if gathered in unpolluted water. Toughens with overcooking

razza *(It)* Common skate, the fish

razza chiodata *(It)* Thornback ray

rBST Recombinant BST made by genetic engineering not involving the cow

RDI *see* recommended daily intake

ready basted poultry Poultry, usually turkeys, which have fat, emulsifiers, flavourings, etc. injected and massaged into the flesh to improve the apparent quality of intensively reared birds

rebenblatt *(Ge)* Vine leaf

Rebhuhn *(Ge)* Partridge

Reblochon *(Fr) masc.* One of the oldest mild French cheeses from Haute Savoie made with the later part of the cows' milking which has the higher fat content. It is shaped like a wider and thinner Camembert with a soft supple centre and a deep orange to red coloured washed rind. It is packed between very thin wooden discs and does not go runny like Camembert. It has a pleasant buttery flavour with a fruit finish when young but becomes bitter when old. Protected by an appellation d'origine

rebong *(Id & Ma)* Bamboo shoot

receipt o.e. Recipe

reçel *(Tu)* Jam

recette *(Fr) fem.* Recipe

réchaud *(Fr) masc.* Hot plate or small stove used at the table

rechauffé(e) *(Fr)* The description of dishes made of already cooked food and reheated such as rissoles, croquettes, hash, cottage pie, etc.

rechauffer *(Fr)* To reheat, to warm up

recheado *(Po)* Stuffed, stuffing

recheio *(Po)* Stuffing, filling

recipe The list of ingredients with quantities and the instructions for making a dish

recommended daily intake The amounts of vitamins, minerals and other micro-nutrients (sometimes fat, fibre, carbohydrate and protein) that the government recommends people take in their food or otherwise every day. They tend to be set so as to avoid ill health rather than to promote optimum health and are not related to body weight, age, physical activity, type of work, state of health, etc. Most can be exceeded with safety. The amount of vitamins and some micro-nutrients that remain in food depends on its age, storage conditions and cooking methods [also called **RDI**]

reconstitute, to To add back liquid, usually water, to dried foods so as to restore them to some semblance of their original state

recovery time The time it takes for a cooking appliance (deep fat fryer, oven, blanching liquor, etc.) to return to the required temperature for another batch of food after a batch of cooked food has been removed from it

rectifier (l'assaisonnement) *(Fr)* To adjust the seasoning according to taste

red 2G A synthetic red food dye (E)128 used for sausages. Licensed for use in the UK but not generally in the EU

red banana *(USA)* A short stumpy banana with a purplish red skin and a very sweet tasting flesh

red bean curd *see* bean curd cheese

red bean sauce A Chinese paste made from fermented soya beans used as a condiment or flavouring

red beans and rice *(USA)* A Louisiana dish of red kidney beans cooked with a ham hock and served over rice

red braising *see* red cooking

red bream *see* bream

red cabbage One of the cabbages *Brassica oleracea* Capitata Group with red to purple leaves and a round firm head, generally available in autumn and winter, often casseroled with sugar, sultanas and vinegar, or pickled

red caviar *see* ketovaia

Red Cheshire A deep orange coloured Cheshire cheese dyed with annatto

red chick pea *see* pigeon pea

red chicory A low growing perennial chicory *Cichorium intybus* var. *foliosum* grown as an annual. It has slightly bitter red leaves with white veins and a compact heart rather like a loose red cabbage. Used in salads and as a garnish [also called **radicchio, red-leaved chicory**]

red cooking A Chinese technique of cooking meat by first browning it then slow cooking it in a tightly sealed casserole with dark soy sauce, sherry, sugar and spices which turns the meat a dark reddish brown colour [also called **red braising, red stewing**]

red crab *(USA)* A bright red crab *Geryon quinquedens* up to 15 cm across found in deep water along the eastern coast of North America. It has thin legs and a good flavour

red curry *(Sr)* An intensely hot curry coloured a deep red from the number of red chillis used

red curry paste *(Th)* A paste used for beef and similar curries made from dry fried shallots and garlic, lemon grass, coriander seeds and cumin seeds, blended with black peppercorns, dried red chillis, coriander root, galangal, lime peel, trassi and salt

red date *see* jujube

red deer A species of deer *Cervus elaphus* found in Scotland, UK. The meat is inferior to that from roe deer

red flannel hash *(USA)* Chopped onions, bacon, corned beef and cooked beetroot, often the leftovers from New England boiled dinner seasoned and mixed with mashed potatoes, shallow fried on both sides and served in wedges with fried or poached eggs

red garoupa *see* garoupa

red girl wine *(Ch) see* Shaohsing rice wine. So called because a bottle would be laid down on the birth of a girl in anticipation of her marriage

red gram *see* pigeon pea

red grouse The finest flavoured of the grouse family *Lagopus lagopus scoticus* is found only in the UK and Ireland. It is a sub species of the willow grouse, which is ruddy brown and does not go white in winter. See grouse [also called **Scottish grouse**]

red gurnard A variety of gurnard *Trigla pini* sometimes confused with red mullet. Red gurnard does not have long barbels hanging from the underside of the mouth as does the red mullet; *see also* gurnard

red herring Whole herring cured in brine for several weeks then smoked until a mahogany colour. Must be desalted by soaking before eating. Usually used as part of a mixed hors d'oeuvres or as decoration for egg-based canapés [also called **hard smoked herring**]

red kidney bean The reddish brown French bean shaped like a kidney used in chilli con carne and other dishes. Must be boiled vigorously to destroy toxins. Often sold precooked in cans [also called **Mexican bean, chilli bean**]

red-leaved chicory *see* red chicory

red-legged partridge The French native partridge *Alectoris rufa,* distributed from central UK to Spain. It is plumper but less tasty than the grey-legged. Roast as grey-legged

Red Leicester *see* Leicester cheese

red lollo lettuce *see* lollo rosso

red mash *see* fermented red rice

red meat Meat which is red in appearance in its raw state as opposed to the paler types such as chicken, veal, rabbit, etc.

red miso *see* inaka-miso

red mullet A small crimson to dull pink seawater fish *Mullidae* spp. esp. *Mullus surmuletus* (red) and *M. barbatus* (pink), not related to the grey mullet. It has a delicate flavour and is generally cooked whole with its liver which is considered a prized delicacy. It can be hung for 24 hours to give it a gamey flavour. It can weigh up to 1 kg but is usually caught much smaller [also called **goatfish, golden mullet**]

red mustard A prepared mustard made with a mixture of whole mustard seeds and crushed dried red chillis

red octopus A small octopus *Eledone moschata* more tender than the curled octopus but with a musky flavour

red onion 1 *see* Italian red onion **2** A small red skinned onion similar to a shallot used in Asian cooking and pickled in China

red pepper 1 A general term for dried and ground red capsicums such as cayenne and chilli peppers or paprika **2** Red sweet peppers

red perch *see* redfish

red porgy *see* porgy

red pork *see* char siu

red prawn *see* crevette rose du large

red raripila spearmint A type of spearmint *Mentha raripila rubra* with pointed dark green leaves, a sweet spearmint flavour and purple stems

red rice 1 *see* fermented red rice **2** An inferior dull reddish strain of rice *Oryza glaberrima,* grown in many parts of Asia for processing. Not generally used in cooking

red salad bowl lettuce *see* oak leaf lettuce

red salmon The flesh of the sockeye salmon, usually canned

red sauce *(USA)* Any Italian type of tomato sauce

red sea bream A type of sea bream q.v. eaten raw in Japan as sushi [also called **tai, dai**]

red seedless watermelon *(USA)* A spherical (dia. 30 cm) water melon with no seeds

red shiso The leaves of the red variety of shiso used to colour and flavour umeboshi as well as being used as a vegetable

red snapper A seawater fish *Lutjanus campechanis* of the snapper family with a distinctive red skin and fine white flesh, weighing between 0.5 and 2 kg. Baked, grilled, deep fried or stir fried. Often used in Eastern dishes

red sorrel *see* Jamaica flower

red stewing *see* red cooking

red top milk *(UK)* Homogenized whole milk containing 3.8% butterfat on average. The cream does not separate out

red vinegar A slightly salty clear pale red vinegar made in China. Used as a condiment and added to soups to give them a lift

red wine court bouillon Equal quantities of red wine and water with 120g each of onion and carrot and 12 g of salt per litre together with parsley stalks, a little thyme and bay leaf and peppercorns added. Used for trout and carp

red wine sauce *see* sauce au vin rouge

redcurrant A small red fruit similar to the black currant but more acid and from a more hardy bush *Ribes sativum.* Usually cooked for jams, jellies and sauces

redcurrant and horseradish sauce *(UK)*

Port wine reduced with seasoning, ground nutmeg and cinnamon, mixed with redcurrant jelly and finely grated horseradish. Served cold

redcurrant jelly This jelly used in many sauces is made from red currants, boiled with a little water until the skins break, strained, sugar equal in weight to the juice added and all boiled for 3 to 4 minutes to produce a setting jelly

redcurrant sauce As apricot sauce but made with redcurrants

reddiker *(No)* Radishes

redeye gravy *(USA)* The gravy made by deglazing the dish in which ham is baked or roasted with water or coffee plus a little brown sugar

redfish A short thick bodied orange/red deep-sea fish *Sebastes* spp. esp. *S marinus* and *S. viviparus* up to 25 cm long and found in the North Atlantic. The delicately flavoured flesh is white and flaky and they may be cooked in any way [also called **ocean perch, Norway haddock, red perch**]

redhead duck *(USA)* A highly prized wild duck *Nyroca americana* shot for the table

reduce, to To boil a liquid so as to remove water and thus thicken the liquid and intensify the flavour. Often done during sauce making with wine and stock

reduced fat EU guidelines (which do not have the force of law) state that this means the foodstuff contains less than 25% of the fat normally found in the product

reduction milling The stage in the conversion of grain to flour where the endosperm is ground from semolina size particles to flour after the preceding bran separation

reduction sauce Any sauce based on vinegar, wine or stock concentrated by boiling to give an intense flavour and sometimes a pouring consistency

réduire *(Fr)* To reduce a liquid by boiling

ree *(Ho)* Roe deer

reebout *(Ho)* Haunch of venison

reedmace *see* bulrush millet

refined microcrystalline wax *see* (E)907

refined oil Culinary oil which has been treated to remove flavouring and other compounds which oxidize easily, which would reduce its shelf life and would depress the maximum temperature at which it could be used

refogado *(Po)* An onion and tomato sauce

Réforme, à la *(Fr)* In the style of the Reform club, i.e. garnished with strips of carrot, ham and gherkin and white of egg, and slices of mushrooms and truffles

Réforme, sauce *(En & Fr) fem.* A mirepoix of carrot, onion, celery, bay leaf and thyme, fried in butter, fat drained off, vinegar and crushed peppercorns added and reduced, demi-glace added, simmered and skimmed, red currant jelly added, strained through a chinois and garnished with a julienne of cooked beetroot, hard boiled egg white, gherkin, mushroom, truffle and tongue. Served with lamb cutlets

refresh, to 1 To immerse blanched vegetables in fast running cold water so as to cool them quickly and prevent further cooking **2** To freshen up herbs, leaves and vegetables by immersing them in cold water. Any plant cells which have lost water and crispness will replace some of it

refreshments Light food and drink taken between meals or on some informal occasions

refried beans *(USA) see* frijoles refritos

refrigerator A cooled sealed storage box, usually with shelves and a front opening door which maintains food at a preset temperature between 1 and 6°C

refrigerator cookies *(USA)* Biscuits prepared and baked as needed by slicing them from an uncooked roll of thick biscuit dough usually wrapped or cased in plastic and kept in the refrigerator

refroidir *(Fr)* To refresh, cool, chill

regaliz *(Sp)* Liquorice

regattakotlett *(Sw)* Pork chops rubbed with seasoning and paprika, browned in butter, reserved, chopped onion fried in the same pan until golden, tomato concassé, a bayleaf and thyme added, all reduced, chops added back and simmered until cooked. Lit. yachtsman's chop

Regenbogenforelle *(Ge)* Rainbow trout

regenboog forel *(Ho)* Rainbow trout

régence, sauce *(Fr) fem.* For meat, a mirepoix sweated in butter with a reduction of white wine mixed with demi-glace sauce and truffle essence, simmered and strained. For fish and poultry, sauce normande with a reduction of white wine, mushroom and truffle trimmings, strained and finished with truffle essence

Regenpfeifer *(Ge)* Plover

Regensburger *(Ge)* Short sausages from Bavaria rather like Frankfurters, made from ground pork and beef with embedded small pieces of bacon. Boiled before consumption. May be eaten hot or cold

regina in porchetta *(It)* Carp from Umbria, stuffed and baked in a wood burning stove

réglisse *(Fr)* masc./fem. Liquorice

regular milled white rice *(USA) see* American long grain rice

regulo *see* gas mark

Reh *(Ge)* Deer

Rehbraten *(Ge)* Roast venison

Rehrücken *(Ge)* **1** Saddle of venison **2** A long thin chocolate cake made with egg yolks, sugar, ground hazelnuts and breadcrumbs by the creaming method, flavoured with vanilla and grated chocolate and into which the stiffly beaten egg whites are folded and all baked at 175°C. So called because of it resemblance to a loin of venison

Rehrücken mit Rahmsauce *(Ge)* Saddle of venison, larded, marinated in wine, cloves, juniper berries, bay leaves, peppercorns and grated nutmeg for a day, browned in lard with aromatic vegetables, covered with reduced marinade and baked in the oven. Served with noodles, cranberry sauce and poached pears with a sauce of reduced cooking liquor and cream

Rehrücken mit Schlag *(Ge)* A pastry (resembling a saddle of venison) with almonds, chocolate and whipped cream

Rehschnitzel *(Ge)* Venison cutlets

rehydrate, to To add back the water lost by dehydration either by soaking or cooking in water

Reibeküchen *(Ge)* Grated potato pancakes

reindeer meat *(Sc)* The meat of reindeer, usually smoked and salted

reine, à la *(Fr)* The description of dishes made from chicken esp. coated with an allemande or chicken velouté sauce and garnished with mushrooms and sliced truffles

reine, crème *(Fr) fem. see* chicken soup

reine-claude *(Fr) fem.* A variety of greengage very popular in France

reinette grise *(Fr) fem.* Russet apple

reinsdyr *(No)* Reindeer

reinsdyrpølse *(No)* A spiced reindeer meat sausage

reinsdyrstek *(No)* Reindeer steak

Reis *(Ge)* Rice

Reisauflauf *(Ge)* Rice pudding

Reispapier *(Ge)* Rice paper

Reiswurstchen *(Au)* A forcemeat of minced and cooked veal mixed with cold boiled rice, bound with egg, wrapped in rice paper, panéed and fried. Used in soups

rejemad *(De)* The piles of tiny shrimps put on Danish open sandwiches

rejer *(De)* Shrimps

rekening *(Ho)* The bill

reker *(No)* Shrimps

relative density *see* specific gravity

relevé *(Fr) masc.* Originally the second meat course of a formal dinner in the days when there were many courses, usually a large joint or bird. Nowadays the course between the fish and entrée or the soup and entrée if no fish course, in a formal meal

relevée, sauce *(Fr) fem.* Ketchup

religieuse *(Fr) fem.* A cooked choux pastry sphere filled with whipped cream, topped with a smaller choux pastry sphere and coated with coffee or chocolate icing so as to resemble the rear view of a nun

religious food laws Some religions have particular food prohibitions in particular; Buddhist, usually vegetarian; Hindu, complex laws depending on caste but generally no beef; Jain, strict vegetarian with no eggs but dairy products allowed; Jew, no horse or pig, seafood must have fins and scales, unfertilized eggs only, dairy products and meat must not be mixed and animals are examined for blemishes, slaughtered and prepared by licensed persons; Muslim, no pork or alcohol, special slaughter of animal and no gold or silver plate; Sikh, Muslim or Jewish slaughter not allowed

relish *(USA)* Pickles and highly seasoned sauce-like condiments

rellenos *(Sp)* Stuffed or stuffing

remis *(Ma)* Surf clam

remolacha *(Sp)* Beetroot

Remoudou *(Be)* A strong-flavoured, soft, cow's milk cheese matured for 3 months and made in 200 g loaves. The brownish orange rind has a stronger smell than the centre

remoulade, sauce *(En & Fr) fem.* Tartare sauce plus anchovy essence. Served with fried fish

remouladsås *(Sw)* Remoulade sauce usually served with panéed and fried plaice

rempah *(Id & Ma)* A spicy paste made by grinding, pounding or processing shallots, garlic and some or all of lemon grass, coriander, cumin, turmeric, candlenut, cinnamon, ginger, galangal, chillis, peppercorns, sugar and salt. Sometimes fried in oil. Used for flavouring curries or to season meat for satays

rendang *(Id)* A coconut based highly-flavoured curry cooked until all the liquid is absorbed

rendang chicken Seasoned and browned chicken pieces mixed with a cooking liquor made from thick coconut milk simmered with a fried paste of spring onions, garlic and chillis together with lemon grass, lime leaves, tamarind, turmeric and seasoning and simmered until tender

render, to To heat animal fat tissues so that the fat content is released and can be separated from the remaining tissue. Usually done in a heavy pan over a low heat or in the oven at 150°C

rene *(It)* Kidney

Reneklode *(Ge)* A type of greengage; *see also* Reine-Claude

Renette *(Ge)* Rennet

renkon *(Ja)* Lotus

renne *(Fr) masc.* Reindeer

rennet A mixture of enzymes extracted from the stomachs of suckling animals such as calves, kids and lambs, but usually from the fourth stomach of the unweaned calf. Is is used to curdle milk as the first stage in cheese making. Vegetarian rennets are now made using microorganisms. Some extracts of plants, esp. cardoon, are used for the same purpose

rennin The main protease enzyme in rennet

renstek *(Sw)* Roast reindeer

renversé(e) *(Fr)* Past participle of renverser, to turn out or demould

repápalos *(Sp)* Sweet bread fritters. Eggs mixed with soft breadcrumbs fried in spoonfuls in olive oil, then placed in a pan with orange peel, cinnamon, sugar and milk, simmered for 15 minutes and allowed to rest for 15 hours. Served chilled

repas *(Fr) masc.* Meal

repasser *(Fr)* To strain or pass through a sieve a second time

repast o.e. meal

repollo *(Sp)* Cabbage

repollo relleno *(SA)* A speciality of Bolivia consisting of a hollowed out cabbage stuffed with a meat mixture and simmered in stock. Served with rice

requeijão 1 *(Po)* A cheese similar to Ricotta made from the whey of ewe's milk, often enriched with butter and cream. It is white, smooth and has a fresh taste. Sold in straw baskets and served on fig or cabbage leaves **2** *(Br)* A soft cooked-curd cows' milk cheese made with a lactic starter. The hot, washed and salted curd is placed in oblong or cylindrical moulds to make 500 g cheeses

requin marteau *(Fr) masc.* Hammerhead shark

réserver *(Fr)* To put aside to be used later in the same recipe

resin Solid exudate from plants and trees used to seal wounds in the bark or skin and prevent infection. Some such as asafoetida, mastic and pine resin are used as flavourings

restaurant A place where complete meals are sold for consumption on the premises

rete *(It)* Pig's caul

reticella *(It)* Pig's caul

retinol *see* vitamin A

retort, to To treat food by heating to 121°C in order to kill all microorgansisms. Usually used for canned foods

Rettich *(Ge)* Radish

reuben *(USA)* A corned beef and Swiss cheese sandwich dressed with mayonnaise topped with sauerkraut and grilled

revbensspjäll *(Sw)* Spare ribs

Réveillon *(Fr) masc.* The festive meal held in France after midnight mass on Christmas Eve and on New Year's Eve. Usually includes traditional foods according to region, often boudin noir

revenir, faire *(Fr) see* faire revenir, to brown

revuelto de triguero *(Sp)* An Estramaduran dish consisting of wild asparagus tips mixed with ham, garlic, cumin and bay, fried in olive oil then beaten eggs added and gently scrambled

revythia soupa *(Gr)* A meatless chick pea soup made from chick peas parboiled for 15 minutes and drained, boiled in water until tender and a few reserved, a sauté of onions, carrots, garlic, tomato purée and tomato concassée added to the chick peas and water, all puréed, seasoned and finished with lemon juice, chopped parsley and the reserved chick peas.

Rhabarber *(Ge)* Rhubarb

Rheinlachs *(Ge)* Rhine salmon

Rheinsalm *(Ge)* Rhine salmon

Rheum x cultorum *Bot.* Rhubarb

Rhizopus oligosporus The fungal organism used in the manufacture of tempeh. It also has the beneficial effect of removing the bean flavour

Rhode Island johnny cake *(USA) see* johnny cake

rhodoxanthin *see* E161(f)

rhubarb A deep-rooted perennial plant *Rheum x cultorum* which produces thick pink to red stems at ground level each topped with a large green leaf. The stems are stewed with sugar and used as a dessert, in pies, crumbles, fools, etc. and for jam making. Early rhubarb is forced by excluding light and is the most tender. The leaves are poisonous

rhubarbe *(Fr) fem.* Rhubarb

rhum *(Fr) masc.* Rum

Rhus coriaria *Bot.* Sumac

riatto *(It)* Reheated

rib That part of the carcase of an animal comprising the vertebrae and associated muscles plus a length of attached rib bone equal in length to twice the diameter of the main muscle or less in the case of large animals. It is usually divided along the spinal column and may be cut into single rib portions (cutlets, etc.) or 3 or more ribs (rib roasts)

rib of beef *(USA)* The wing, fore and middle ribs of beef extending about half way down the animal to the short plate. Often cut into steaks, each including one rib bone; *see also* ribs of beef

rib steak *(USA)* A steak cut from the rib one rib thick and including the outer layer of fat. May be on or off the bone

ribbe *(No)* Pork chops from the rib

ribbon cheese *see* Parenyica

ribes *(It)* Red currants

ribes comune *(It)* Red currant

ribes nero *(It)* Black currant

Ribes nigrum *Bot.* Blackcurrant

Ribes sativum *Bot.* Redcurrants and whitecurrants

Ribes uva-crispa *Bot.* Gooseberry

riboflavin Vitamin B2, essential for health, also used as an orange food colouring E101

riboflavin-5' phosphate *see* E101

ribollita *(It)* A cabbage and bean soup from Tuscany which is reboiled *(ribollita)* each day and thickened with bread

ribs of beef Half of the ribs and the vertebrae together with associated muscle from a side of beef. In total there are 13 which are numbered from the head end. The English cuts are 1 and 2 chuck ribs, 3 to 6 middle ribs, 7 to 10 fore ribs and 11 to 13 wing ribs. See under each term

ricciarelli *(It)* Almond biscuits

riccio di mare *(It)* Sea urchin

ricciola *(It)* Amberjack, the fish

ricciolina *(It)* Curly endive

ricciolini *(It)* Pasta curls

ricco *(It) (of food)* Rich

rice A cereal grain *Oryza sativa* cultivated in China since 6000 BC, grown extensively in warm moist climates and forming the principal energy source for a major part of the world's population. There are thousands of different varieties but all have a high starch content and are between 3 and 6 mm long and about 2 mm in dia. See long grain, short grain, brown, white, glutinous, pudding, polished, prefluffed, Arborio, Basmati, Carolina, fragrant, jasmine, Patna, Thai, etc.

rice, to To force a semi-solid through a perforated plate or mesh so as to form thin fragile strands. See e.g. entry under potato ricer

rice bean A small yellow to deep red dried bean *Phaseolus canceratus* from SEA, grown in the Nepal and Assam and similar in size to the adzuki bean but less rounded, with a larger hilum running the length of the bean and crinkly edges. Said to taste like rice when cooked and reputed to have the highest calcium content of all beans

rice dough Rice flour mixed with boiling or cold water to make a dough which is used for wrappers, cakes or dumplings. Boiling water makes a translucent wrapper for wonton

rice flakes Rice grain steamed or softened by partial cooking and flattened through rollers, may be cooked or eaten uncooked in e.g. muesli [also called **flaked rice**]

rice flour Ground polished rice which is mainly starch with very little gluten. Used in the same way as cornflour and for noodles, sweets and short pastry

rice gruel *see* congee

rice noodles Noodles made with rice flour in very long strands and of varying thicknesses and widths. Very common in Vietnam. Usually folded into a compact bundle. When deep fried they puff up [also called **rice stick noodles**]

rice paper A very thin edible white paper made from the pith of a small tree *Tetrapanax papyriferum* grown in Taiwan. It is used to line baking trays used for sticky baked goods such as macaroons and similar, and does not need greasing. Usually sticks to the base of the biscuit or cake

rice pudding *(UK)* Short grain rice covered with sweetened milk and baked slowly in the oven in a covered dish. Sultanas or other dried fruit may be added and the top is usually sprinkled with grated nutmeg. Proportions may be adjusted to give thin or stiff finished results and the lid left off towards the end to give a crisp top

rice ribbon noodles Flat noodles about 1 cm wide made from a thin rice flour and water dough which is cooked in thin sheets to a firm jelly-like texture, brushed with oil and cut into strips to be sold as fresh noodles in most Chinese communities in SEA. The same dough cut in 20 cm squares is used when filled with meat or shrimps as dim sum

rice soup *see* congee

rice stick noodles *see* rice noodles

rice vermicelli Very thin rice noodles which only require softening in hot water, or they may be deep fried in the dried state

rice vinegar Vinegar made by oxidizing the alcoholic beer or wine made from fermented rice starch. There are several varieties in use in Asia; *see also* black, red and sweet vinegar

rice wine An alcoholic liquid made by fermenting a cooked ground rice mash. It has a sherry-like taste and is both used as a drink and as a cooking liquid. Clear and amber coloured varieties are available; *see also* Shaohsing rice wine and sake

rich A description of food that is very sweet, high in fat, oil or cream content or highly seasoned

rich cakes *see* creamed cakes

riche, sauce *(Fr) fem.* Sauce diplomate finished with truffle essence and finely diced black truffles

richelieu *(Fr) masc.* A layer cake with apricot glaze and frangipane cream between the layers, the whole iced with a maraschino-flavoured fondant and decorated with angelica strips

richelieu, à la *(Fr)* In the style of the Duc de Richelieu, i.e. garnished with stuffed tomatoes, mushrooms, potatoes and braised lettuce, esp. of roasts

Ricotta *(It)* A soft cow's or ewe's milk cheese made from whey which may be enriched with milk or cream. The whey is heated with citric or tartaric acid to cause the proteins to coagulate. These are separated off, drained, usually in basin shaped baskets and demoulded. Used widely in Italian cooking or may be eaten as a dessert with fruit, chopped nuts, chocolate or instant coffee. May be matured and hardened for grating. Contains 50 to 60% water, 15% fat, 23 to 26% protein, mainly albumen, and 3% lactose. Not usually salted

Ricotta Piemontese *(It)* Ricotta made from cows milk whey enriched with 10 to 20% milk

Ricotta Romana *(It)* Ricotta made with the whey left over from making Pecorino Romano

Ricotta salata moliterna *(It)* A semi-hard cooked curd cheese made from the whey of ewes' milk heated to 90°C to precipitate soluble proteins. The filtered curd is salted and formed into cylinders. It may be eaten young as a dessert cheese or ripened for grating

Ridderost *(No & Sw)* A semi-hard, deep yellow, cow's milk cheese similar to St Paulin with an orange rind and slightly nutty flavour, surface ripened for 5 to 6 weeks. Suitable for dessert and as a melting cheese

ridge cucumber An outdoor cucumber often with a grooved, indented or knobbly skin, usually smaller than long cucumbers. They require fertilization. So called because they used to be planted on ridges in the open field

ridged sand clam A clam which is found in SEA on beaches with surf and strong tidal currents

Riebisel *(Ge)* Red currant

riekko *(Fi)* Ptarmigan (white or willow)

rigaglie *(It)* Giblets

Rigatello *(It)* A hard scalded-curd cows' milk cheese made in cylinders (to 3 kg). The paste is hard, dense with a few cracks and strong tasting. Eaten for dessert or used for cooking; *see also* Canestrato

rigato *(It)* **1** *see* Canestrato **2** Ridged as applied to pasta shapes

rigatoni A large ridged macaroni cut in pieces about 5 cm long and 1 cm in dia.

rigg *see* dogfish

Rigottes *(Fr)* A soft surface ripened goats' milk cheese from the Ardèche with a delicately flavoured velvety paste made in 60 g cylinders. Contains 45% water, 22% fat ad 24% protein

riisi *(Fi)* Rice

riisivanukas *(Fi)* Rice pudding

rijst *(Ho)* Rice

rijsttafel *(Ho)* An Indonesian inspired meal of many contrasting savoury dishes each accompanied by rice or noodles

riklingur *(Ic)* An air dried fish *(hardfiskur)* made from halibut or catfish

rillettes *(Fr) fem.* A rich meat paste made by simmering herbs and pork or goose meat in its own fat until tender then pounding it to a smooth texture

rillons Crisply fried or grilled pieces of cooked pork or goose preserved in fat

rimestato *(It)* Stirred or scrambled

rimmad skinka *(Sw)* Salted ham

rimmat kött *(Sw)* Salt meat

rims *(Po)* Kidneys

Rind *(Ge)* Beef

rind The outer skin of bacon, ham, pork, cheese, and some fruits and vegetables

Rinderbraten *(Ge)* Roast beef

Rinderbrust *(Ge)* Brisket of beef

Rinderleber *(Ge)* Ox liver

Rindermark *(Ge)* Beef marrow

Rindfleisch *(Ge)* Beef

Rindfleisch Kochwurst *(Ge)* A sausage made from a mixture of 75% lean beef and 25% pork fat with saltpetre and seasoning, packed into casings, linked in pairs and air dried for 2 days. Boiled before serving

Rindfleischwurst *(Ge)* A sausage filled with a mixture of minced lean beef, lean pork, bacon fat, saltpetre and seasoning, flavoured with garlic and ground cloves. Simmered for an hour before serving

Rindkraftfleisch *(Ge)* Corned beef

Rindsrouladen *(Ge)* Beef olives

ring doughnut The ring form of the doughnut q.v.

ring mould A round mould in the shape of a half torus so that when the food is demoulded it forms a round ring on the plate. Used for cakes, desserts, jellies, savoury custards, etc. [also called **border mould**]

ring-neck dove *(USA)* A highly prized wild duck *Aythya collaris* shot for the table

Ringelblume *(Ge)* Marigold

riñones *(Sp)* Kidneys

riñones a la española *(Sp)* Kidneys sautéed with onions, tomatoes and sweet peppers

Rio red A highly pigmented grapefruit variety which was produced by inducing mutations using ionizing radiation

ripa *(Sw)* Grouse

ripe Fully developed or matured and ready for eating, usually used of fruits, vegetables and cheese

ripe tart *(UK)* A butter-based shortcrust pastry brought together with egg yolk and water, baked blind in a flan tin, lined with stoned cherries, filled with an egg, icing sugar and ground almond mixture and baked at 170°C until golden brown

ripen, to To allow time for fruit, vegetables and cheese to become ripe. Fruit may be ripened more quickly by putting it in a plastic bag with a ripe tomato

Ripennstück *(Ge)* Beef ribs

ripiddu nivicatu *(It)* A Sicilian dish of rice cooked with cuttlefish and their ink, put in a heap and topped with Ricotta cheese and tomato sauce so as to resemble Mount Etna

ripieno *(It)* Stuffed with or stuffing

Rippchen *(Ge)* Rib chops, cutlets usually of smoked pork

Rippe *(Ge)* Rib of meat

Rippenbraten *(Ge)* Roast loin

Rippenspeer *(Ge)* Spareribs of pork

ris 1 *(Fr) masc.* Sweetbreads, esp of veal, ris de veau or lamb, ris d'agneau **2** *(De, No & Sw)* Rice

ris à l'amande *(De)* Rice pudding mixed with whipped cream and chopped almonds served with cherry sauce

ris d'agneau *(Fr) masc.* Lamb sweetbreads

ris de veau *(Fr) masc.* Veal sweetbreads

rise, to To allow a yeast dough to increase in size by the production of bubbles of carbon dioxide within it or a baked dish or cake to similarly increase in size by the action of heat on air bubbles entrapped in the mix, e.g. soufflés, or the production of carbon dioxide by reactions of chemical raising agents; *see also* to prove, lift

risengrød *(De)* A sweetened rice soup or porridge sprinkled with cinnamon and topped with butter served at Christmas before the main course of the meal. The person who receives the one almond in the mixture receives a present

risengrynsklatter *(De)* Rice fritters

risengrynslapper *(No)* Rice flour pancakes

risetto *(It)* Croquettes made with tiny anchovies and sardines

risgrøt *(No)* Rice pudding

risgryn *(Sw)* Rice

risgrynsgröt *(Sw)* Rice pudding

risi e bisi *(It)* A mixture of cooked rice and peas in a small amount of thick stock sprinkled with grated Parmesan cheese

riso *(It)* Rice

riso alla canavesana *(It)* Rice boiled in meat broth and finished with Fontina, Grana and Emmental cheeses

riso commune *(It)* The cheapest rice

riso al forno *(It)* A meat sauce with rice baked in the oven

riso al forno in peverada alla rovigina *(It)* Rice baked with chicken livers, mushrooms and anchovies

riso alla milanese *(It)* Rice boiled in meat broth with saffron and served with butter and cheese

riso alla piemontese *(It)* Rice with a chicken or meat sauce

riso ricco *(It)* Boiled rice with a cream and cheese sauce

riso alla ristori *(It)* Rice with cabbage, bacon and sausage

riso alla siciliana *(It)* Rice with aubergines, tomato, parsley and basil, gratinated with cheese and baked.

risoles *(Me)* Fritters

risotto *(It)* A classic Italian dish best made with arborio or carnaroli rice fried in butter and/or olive oil with chopped onion and any other flavouring elements (cooked chicken, shellfish, vegetables, etc.), a splash of white wine added over the heat until absorbed, then hot stock added progressively with stirring until no more can be absorbed and the dish is moist and creamy. May be finished with grated Parmesan cheese and butter

risotto alla certosina *(It)* Risotto with prawns, mushrooms, peas and frogs' legs

risotto alla chioggiotta *(It)* A risotto from Chioggia with gobies (fish), white wine and Parmesan cheese

risotto kalamara *(Bk)* A risotto flavoured with chopped squid, coloured with the ink from the squid and sprinkled with grated Parmesan cheese

risotto alla milanese *(It)* A risotto made with chopped onions, flavoured with saffron and grated Parmesan cheese only. Served by itself or as an accompaniment to osso bucco

risotto alla monzese *(It)* Risotto with sausages and tomato sauce

risotto polesano *(It)* Risotto with eel, mullet and bass

risotto in salto *(It)* Cooked risotto formed into a thick round and fried

risotto alla toscano *(It)* Risotto with beef, calves' kidney and liver and tomatoes

rissole 1 *(UK)* A small shaped patty or roll of minced meat bound with mashed potatoes or similar vegetarian mixtures, panéed and fried **2** *(Fr) fem.* A small sweet or savoury filled (puff) pastry turnover usually deep fried and served with a sauce

rissolé(e) *(Fr)* **1** Baked or fried until brown, past participle of rissoler, to brown **2** Pork crackling

ristet *(No)* Grilled, fried or roasted

ristet brød *(De & No)* Toast

ristet loff *(No)* Toast

ristretto *(It)* Reduced, concentrated, of stock, sauce and soup

river trout *see* brown trout

rivierkreeft *(Ho)* Freshwater crayfish

riz *(Fr) masc.* Rice

riz, au *(Fr)* Description of dishes served with rice

riz au blanc *(Fr) masc.* Plain boiled rice

riz complet *(Fr) masc.* Brown rice

riz au gras *(Fr) masc.* Fried rice

riz à l'imperatrice *(Fr) masc.* A cold dessert made from a layer of set red jelly in the base of a charlotte mould. Short grain rice cooked in milk until tender is mixed with sugar, vanilla essence, gelatine, diced angelica and glacé cherries and when near the setting point has stiffly beaten egg whites and whipped cream folded in. This is poured over the jelly and when all set, the dessert is demoulded and turned out on a plate. Created for Empress Eugénie

riz sauvage *(Fr) masc.* Wild rice

rizi pilafi me garithes *(Gr)* A pilaff of rice fried with chopped onions and garlic previously sweated in olive oil, simmered with water, tomato concassée, sugar, chopped herbs and lemon juice until 5 minutes before the rice is cooked and all liquid absorbed, cooked and peeled prawns added and then all cooked 5 minutes. Feta cheese is added off the heat until melted, and the dish is finished with chopped parsley

rizi pilafi me mithia As moules marinière but with the chopped onions sweated in olive oil and the shelled mussels mixed with long grain rice boiled in the mussel cooking liquor for about 12 minutes

rízek *(Cz)* Schnitzel, pork cutlet

roach A small red freshwater fish *Rutilis rutilis* similar to carp. Rarely eaten because of the numerous bones but if to be eaten then best fried after soaking in salted water.

roast A joint of piece of meat cooked in the oven on a trivet without any cover at around 230 to 250°C.

roast, to To cook food in the oven by a combination of convected and radiated heat with good air circulation around it and usually with fat. The object is to brown the surface of the food, to make it crisp and tasty and to just cook the interior to the right degree. Generally used for meats and root vegetables; *see also* to spit roast

roast beef *(UK)* A classic dish ideally of sirloin, wing rib, fore rib or fillet, but often nowadays of topside or middle rib. Traditionally cooked slightly underdone and served with Yorkshire pudding, horseradish sauce and roast gravy and garnished with watercress

roast gravy All fat poured off the roasting pan, deglazed with the appropriate brown stock, simmered, skimmed, strained and seasoned. Served with roast meat [also called **jus de rôti**]

roast pork spice A spice mix containing five spice powder, sugar, salt, dried soya sauce and ground annatto seed. Rubbed over pork before roasting to give the characteristic Chinese colour and flavour [also called **char siu powder**]

roast potatoes Parboiled potatoes roasted in the oven at a temperature of 230 to 250°C in a tray containing hot fat which is used to baste the potatoes until the surface is crisp and brown

roasted cheese canapés *(Ca)* A seasoned cheese and breadcrumb mixture spread over slices of toast, grilled and cut into fancy shapes and served hot

roasted chilli paste *see* nam prik pao

roasted curry paste *see* nam prik pao

robalo **1** The general name for various pike-like fish, esp. *Centropomus undecimalis* which has a particularly fine-flavoured flesh, caught in tropical seas [also called **snook**] **2** *(Sp)* Bass, the fish

Robbiola *(It) see* Robiola

Robert, sauce *(En & Fr) fem.* Chopped onion sweated in butter, vinegar added and reduced completely, demi-glace added, simmered, mustard diluted with water and castor sugar added, skimmed and seasoned. Served with fried pork chop

Robiola *(It)* A soft surface ripened cows' milk cheese from Lombardy and Piedmont made using a natural or cultured lactic starter and rennet coagulation. The curd is cast in square moulds (20 by 20 cm) to drain, demoulded, cut in 4 pieces, dry salted or brined and ripened at high humidity [also called **Robbiola**]

Robiolini *(It)* Very small (to 70 g) soft raw cows' milk cheeses curdled with acid whey and rennet and ripened for 10 to 15 days at high humidity [also called **Formaggini**]

robusta coffee A high yielding variety of coffee but with a flavour inferior to that of the arabica variety

rocambole *see* giant garlic

rocciata di Assisi *(It)* Pastry filled with a mixture of nuts, raisins, chopped dried figs and prunes

rochambeau *(Fr)* A garnish for large cuts of meat of carrots in duchesse potato baskets, stuffed lettuce, cauliflower florets à la polonaise and pommes Anna

Rochen *(Ge)* Skate, the fish

rock bass *see* Mediterranean grouper

rock cakes Small individual cakes made from the basic cake mixture with dried fruit using the rubbing in method. Baked in rough irregular shaped mounds

rock carp A variety of carp with a large head, a thick body, small bones and a delicious rich meat. Popular with the Chinese

rock cornish A breed of table chicken with a finer flavour than standard breeds. It thrives in free range and is popular in the USA

rock crab A crab *Cancer irroratus,* Atlantic or *C. autannarius,* Pacific with a yellowish shell marked with purple or brown spots and up to 10 cm wide. They are not particularly well-flavoured and are often eaten after they have shed their shell

rock dove A wild pigeon *Columba livia* treated as wood pigeon

rock eel *see* dogfish

rock herring *see* shad

rock lobster *(USA)* The name given for legal reasons to the spiny lobsters which are caught in Australia and shipped in large quantitites to the USA. See under western, southern and eastern rock lobster

rock melon *see* cantaloupe melon

rock partridge *see* ptarmigan

rock salmon A small shark *Squalus acanthias* 2 to 3 kg in weight and up to 60 cm long with a medium oily delicate white flesh. Very widely distributed and commonly served as deep fried battered fish where the type is not otherwise named. Cooked in any way [also called **spurdog, Pacific dogfish, spiny dogfish**]

rock salt Unrefined salt as mined, used as a heat transfer medium e.g. in baking potatoes and heating oysters, or as a freezing mixture with ice

rock samphire *see* samphire *Crithmum maritimum*

rock sole A flat seawater fish *Lepidopsetta bilineata* about 20 cm with a brown to grey skin and a non-oily white flesh. Caught off the west coast of Canada [also called **roughback**]

rock sugar Large brown transparent irregular shaped crystals of sugar; *see also* lump sugar (3)

rocket A slightly bitter, peppery-flavoured plant *Eruca vesicaria* which grows wild in cold climates and is cultivated in Italy and Cyprus. The dandelion shaped leaves are used in salads [also called **arugula, rokko, salad rocket, Mediterranean rocket, erugala, roquette**]

rockfish A large group of seawater fish *Sebastodes* spp. found off rocky coasts in most parts of the world. Generally 30 to 90 cm long weighing 1 to 2.5 kg. The flesh is white to pink turning to white when cooked, and is firm, flaky and mid-oily. May be poached, baked or grilled. One of the more common in the USA is the striped bass q.v.

Rocky Mountain oysters *(USA) see* prairie oysters

röd *(Sw)* Red

rød *(De & No)* Red

rodaballo *(Sp)* Turbot

rodaballo menor *(Sp)* Brill, the fish

rødbeter *(No)* Beetroot

rödbetor *(Sw)* Beetroot

rode kool *(Ho)* Red cabbage

rødgrot *(No)* A dessert made from thickened and sweetened purée of redcurrants and raspberries

rødgrød med fløde *(De)* Stewed and sweetened summer fruits (berries and currants) thickened with arrowroot. Served cold when set in individual dishes topped with Chantilly cream

rødkål *(De)* Red cabbage cooked with chopped apple and flavoured with caraway seeds. Served with poultry, pork and meatballs

rødkål *(No)* Red cabbage

rödkål *(Sw)* Red cabbage

rodovalho *(Po)* Turbot

rødspætte *(De)* Plaice

rödspätta *(Sw)* Plaice

rödspätta i sardellsås *(Sw)* Skinned and gutted whole plaice simmered in a little water with salt and lemon juice until cooked (to 20 minutes), fish removed and flesh reserved, the cooking liquor made into a velouté sauce and finished with cream and diced fillets of anchovy. The sauce is poured over the fish, gratinated with breadcrumbs and all put into a medium oven and browned

rödtunga *(Sw)* Lemon sole

rödvinssås *(Sw)* Red wine sauce made by simmering a well cleaned cod's head in red wine with a BG for 30 minutes, then straining, seasoning and thickening it with beurre manié

roe The egg or sperm of fish or the eggs of shellfish. See hard roe and soft roe

roe deer A species of deer *Capreolus capreolus* which is very common in the UK and Northern Europe. The meat is known as venison and is considered to be the best of its type

roebuck The male roe deer

roebuck sauce A reduction of vinegar with a BG and a brunoise of onion and raw ham browned in butter, espagnole sauce added and simmered 15 minutes, BG removed and the sauce finished with port and red currant jelly. Used for venison

roereieren *(Ho)* Scrambled egg

rogan josh *(In)* Lamb or beef cooked in a yoghurt based sauce with sweet peppers, tomatoes and aromatic spices including chilli powder and paprika to give a red colour

Rogen *(Ge)* Fish roe

Rogeret de Cévennes *(Fr)* A goats' milk cheese similar to Pélardon

røget *(De)* Smoked

røget sild *(De)* Smoked herring

roggebrood *(Ho)* Rye bread

Roggen *(Ge)* Rye

Roggenbrot *(Ge)* Rye bread

rognon *(Fr) masc.* Kidney

rognone *(It)* Kidney

rognons blancs *(Fr) masc.* Veal testicles, usually floured and shallow fried

rognons en chemise *(Fr)* Veal kidneys still surrounded with suet, seasoned, laid on rosemary or thyme sprigs on a rack and roasted at 180°C for about 25 to 30 minutes until all the suet has melted, rested 10 minutes and served with the pan residues, defatted and deglazed with wine

rognons turbigo *(Fr) masc.* Skinned split kidneys, sautéed in butter, presented around a centre garnish of grilled mushrooms and chipolata sausages and napped with a sauce made from the white wine deglazed pan juices mixed with a tomato flavoured and seasoned demi-glace sauce.

rognures *(Fr) fem.* Trimmings

roh *(Ge)* Raw

roher Schinken *(Ge)* Raw ham

Rohkost *(Ge)* Crudités, raw vegetables used as a hors d'oeuvre

Rohkostplatte *(Ge)* A salad of raw vegetables

Rohwurst *(Ge & Au)* A group of German/Austrian slicing or spreading sausages such as salami, Mettwurst, Ländjäger, Plockwurst and Teewurst, which are made of raw meat then cured, air dried and/or smoked. All can be kept

rokko *see* rocket

rökt *(Sw)* Smoked

rökt ål *(Sw)* Smoked eel

rökt lax *(Sw)* Smoked salmon

røkt *(No)* Smoked

roll **1** A small bread separately cooked from about 50 to 60 g of raw dough **2** Any food item shaped like a cylinder e.g. Swiss roll, meat roll, etc.

roll, to **1** To thin out, e.g. pastry or dough, with a rolling pin by compressing it between the rolling pin and a flat surface with a to and fro rolling motion. More accurately, to roll out **2** To form in to a cylinder. More accurately, to roll up

roll mac *(UK)* Mackerel fillets filled with fruit chutney and rolled up, laid on a bed of chopped onions and mushrooms, moistened with white wine, topped with more chutney and cooked in a 200°C oven until a crust forms on top. Served with soured cream

rolle *(It)* Roll of veal or beef

rolled bean curd *see* bean curd sticks

rolled cutlets *(USA)* Beef and veal olives *(paupiettes)*

rolled oats *see* porridge oats

rolled rump *(USA)* The top of the round of beef without bone used for roasting

roller milled flour Flour produced from cereal grains by passing the larger pieces or whole grains though rollers set close together and rotating at slighltly different speeds so as to shear the grain

rolling pin A wooden or ceramic cylinder about 5 cm in dia. and 25 to 50 cm long used for rolling out pastes and doughs or crushing brittle foods such as nuts, praline, etc. Some rolling pins, e.g. for making pasta, are longer and thinner

rollmop herring Fillets of herring rolled with chopped onions, gherkins and peppercorns, secured with a sliver of wood and marinated in spiced vinegar for 7 to 10 days

Rollmöps *(Ge)* Rollmop herring

roly-poly pudding *(UK)* Suet pastry rolled out into an oblong, spread with jam, mincemeat or any sweet filling, rolled up, wrapped in a cloth or foil and steamed or baked for 1.5 to 2 hours. Served with English custard

Romadur A soft, smooth textured and surface ripened block shaped cow's milk cheese with a yellowish brown washed rind. It tastes like a milder and sweeter version of Limburger cheese. Made in central Europe

romaine, à la In the Roman style, i.e. roasts garnished with tomatoes, or tomato sauce, spinach and occasionally, potatoes

romaine lettuce *see* cos lettuce

romaine, sauce *(Fr) fem.* Caramel dissolved in vinegar as soon as it is made, espagnole sauce and game or brown stock added, reduced by one quarter, strained and finished with pine nuts and a few currants and raisins soaked in water until plump

roman pot *see* chicken brick

roman snail An edible European snail *Helix pomatia*

romanesco A pale green very decorative variety of cauliflower in which each floret rises to a peak and can be seen individually although they are all bunched together like a true cauliflower

Romano *(USA)* A hard, cooked-curd drum-shaped cow's milk cheese made in the Pecorino Romano manner. It is close textured with a strong taste and thin rind. Contains 32% water, 26% fat and 33% protein

romarin *(Fr) masc.* Rosemary

rombo *(It)* Turbot

rombo chiodato *(It)* Turbot

rombo giallo *(It)* Megrim, the fish

rombo liscio *(It)* Brill, the fish

romdeng *(Cm)* Greater galangal

romero *(Sp)* Rosemary

Römertopf *(Ge)* Chicken brick

romesco chilli A mildly piquant smoky-flavoured dried chilli from Spain used to make romesco sauce. No other should be substituted

romesco sauce *(Sp)* Romesco chilli, blistered in the oven and peeled, blended with oven softened garlic and skinned tomatoes, roasted hazelnuts and almonds, chopped parsley, wine vinegar, olive oil and seasoning to form a smooth paste. Sweet red pepper and cayenne pepper may be substituted for the romesco chilli

romiet *(Cm)* Turmeric

Romorantin *(Fr) see* Selles-sur-Cher

ron *(Sp)* Rum

Roncal *(Sp)* A hard ewe's milk cheese made in 2 kg rounds and matured for 4 months. It has a yellowish white, hard but open textured paste with a pungent taste. The rind is light brown and slightly greasy. Used as a dessert cheese or for cooking

rond de gigot *(Fr) masc.* A thick leg steak of lamb or mutton

rondelle *(Fr) fem.* A round thin slice of carrot, lemon. salami, etc.

rondinella *(It)* Flying fish

rondino *(It)* Pomfret, the fish

rookworst *(Ho)* A spiced and smoked sausage

roomali roti *(In)* A very thin bread somewhat like a pancake

root celery *see* celeriac

root ginger The solid root form of ginger q.v., either fresh or dried

root vegetables The general name for vegetables consisting of the swollen roots of plants from which the leaves and flowers spring. Common examples are carrots, turnips, swedes, beetroot, parsnips, salsify and radish [also called **roots**]

roots A general name for the common root vegetables as in bed of roots which is a mirepoix of carrots, turnips and swedes

rôti *(Fr)* **1** Roasted, past participle of rôtir, to roast **2** masc. Roast of beef, pork, etc.

rôtir *(Fr)* To roast

rôtisserie **1** *(En)* A rotating spit within a conventional oven on which joints of meat or poultry may be turned as they are roasting. Used to give more even cooking and browning **2** *(Fr) fem.* Steak house type of restaurant, shop selling roast meat.

roppo muki *(Ja)* A cut for small vegetables such as baby turnips in which the top and base are trimmed flat and they are cut into hexagons

Roquefort *(Fr) masc.* A soft, virtually rindless blue cheese made from unpasteurized ewe's milk, the curds of which are sprinkled with *Penicillium roquefortii* mould spores as they are being formed into 2.5 kg rounds. The cheeses are matured for 3 months in underground caves in currents of air at a constant temperature and humidity. The cheeses are needled to assist mould growth. It has a delicate and subtle tangy flavour and production is strictly controlled. It has AOC status

roquette Rocket

röra *(Sw)* Scrambled as in ägg röra, scrambled egg

røræg *(De)* Scrambled egg

rörd smörsås *(Sw)* A stirred butter sauce made by creaming butter and egg yolk (3:1), seasoning and whisking in lemon juice

Rorippa nasturtium-aquaticum *Bot.* Watercress

Rosa canina *Bot.* Wild rose, dog rose

Rosa eglanteria *Bot.* Eglantine, sweet brier

rosa Krebse *(Ge)* Prawn

***Rosa* spp.** *Bot.* Rose

rosbif *(It, Sp & Fr) masc.* Roast beef, usually very rare

rose A hardy shrub with pink to red fragrant flowers *Rosa* spp. The wild rose or dog rose *R. canina* and the eglantine or sweet brier *R. eglanteria* have large red seed capsules known as hips or rose hips. The flower petals with the bitter white heel removed may be crystallized or used for decoration, in salads, in fruit pies or as a general flavouring. The bright red rose hips, after dehairing, may be used in jams or puréed for use in sauces or to make a sweet syrup high in vitamin C; *see also* rosewater

rose apple A fruit which grows in clusters on a tree *Syzygium malaccensis* from the Far East. They are small, pink and white, pear shaped and have an apple flavour, but are rather soft and full of seeds

rose cocoa bean *see* borlotto bean

rose coco bean *see* borlotto bean

rose hip The orange to dark red fruit of the rose *Rosa* spp. esp. *R. canina* and *R. eglantina* with an edible fleshy casing up to 2.5 cm long containing a mass of inedible seeds. Usually used to make syrups and jams and valued for their high vitamin C content

rose hip catsup *(Cn)* A cold sauce or ketchup made in Alberta from rose hips, onions, garlic, sugar, spices, vinegar and water

rose hip syrup A sweetened extract of rose hips used for flavouring and colouring (pink) drinks and desserts and as a source of vitamin C

rose oil The essential oil extracted from rose petals used as a flavouring and perfume

rose water Diluted essence of rose petals used as a flavouring in confectionery and desserts esp. in Middle Eastern, Indian and SEA cooking

rosella *see* Jamaica flower

rosemary An evergreen perennial shrub *Rosmarinus officinalis)* with woody upright stems and thin pointed aromatic leaves which grows in temperate and Mediterranean climates. Used to flavour meat dishes esp. lamb and strong-flavoured soups. A twig of rosemary is often laid on fish or meat as it is being cooked

Rosenkohl *(Ge)* Brussel sprouts

roseroot A perennial rock plant *Sedum rosea* whose thick succulent leaves are eaten in salads in Greenland

rosette de Lyon *(Fr) fem.* A large coarse textured salami-like dried pork sausage made with chopped pork shoulder and matured very slowly. Eaten raw

roşii umplute cu castraveţi *(Ro)* Tomatoes stuffed with a mixture of seasoned tomato concassée, chopped onions, cucumber and parsley

Rosinen *(Ge)* Raisins

Rosmarein *(Ge)* Rosemary

Rosmarin *(Ge)* Rosemary

rosmarino *(It)* Rosemary

Rosmarinus officinalis *Bot.* Rosemary

roso *(Pl)* A mixed beef and chicken broth thickened with buckwheat groats and garnished with diced chicken, diced bacon and chopped parsley and fennel

rospa *(It)* Monkfish

rossetti *(It)* Goby, the fish

rosso *(It)* Red

rossolye *(Ru)* A traditional Baltic salad of diced cooked beetroot, cooking apples, boiled potatoes, gherkins, pickled herring and cold cooked meat dressed with cream lightly whipped with dry English mustard and caster sugar, all chilled and served on lettuce decorated with chopped hard boiled egg and some of the dressing

rosta *(It)* Roasted

rostat bröd *(Sw)* Toast

Rostbratwurst *(Ge)* A sausage made from a seasoned mixture of mainly lean pork with one half its weight of fat pork and veal all finely chopped, packed into narrow hog casings and linked

rösten To grill, roast or fry

Rösti *(He)* A mixture of grated parboiled potatoes, chopped onion and seasoning, formed into pancakes or patties and shallow fried

rosticceria *(It)* Rotisserie, delicatessen

Röstkartoffeln *(Ge)* Fried potatoes

rotary beater A hand-held and hand-operated mechanical whisk or beater consisting of two counter rotating intermeshed metal loops, now generally superceded by electrically powered mixers, beaters or whisks [also called **rotary whisk**]

rotary whisk *see* rotary beater

Rotbarbe *(Ge)* Red mullet *Mullus barbatus*

rote Johannisbeere *(Ge)* Red currant

Rotegrütze *(Ge)* Strained and sweetened fruit juice thickened with corn flour or potato flour, cooled and set in individual dishes and served with cold milk or cream

rotelli *see* fusilli

Roterübe *(Ge)* Beetroot

Rotforelle *(Ge)* Arctic char, the fish

Rothbart *(Ge)* Red mullet *Mullus barbatus*

roti **1** *(In)* Bread, of any kind **2** *(Sr)* An unleavened flat bread made from wheat flour and grated coconut

roti jala *(In)* A thick pouring batter made with flour, eggs, salt and thin coconut milk dripped in a continuous stream through a perforated cup into a hot greased frying pan to form a lacy pattern. Cooked both sides and then rolled up

roti jala cup A metal vessel with four spouts issuing from the base each with a fine hole. Used for making roti jala and string hoppers

rotini *(It) see* ruoti

Rotkohl *(Ge)* Red cabbage

Rotkraut *(Ge)* Red cabbage cooked with apples and vinegar

rotmos *(Sw)* Mashed boiled turnips

rotolo alla marmellata *(It)* Swiss roll

rotolo *(It)* Roll

rött *(Sw)* Red

Rotwurst *(Ge)* A well seasoned blood sausage containing large chunks of meat

Rotzunge *(Ge)* Witch sole

rou *(Ch)* Meat

rouelle *(Fr) fem.* Leg of veal excluding the jarret and the very top of the cushions or a thick slice cut across same

Rouen duck One of the two main types of French domesticated duck. It is usually killed by suffocation or strangulation and eviscerated carefully so that no blood escapes. Usually roasted slightly underdone and used e.g. for canard à la presse

rouennaise, sauce *(Fr) fem.* Hot bordelaise sauce mixed with processed raw duck liver, heated very gently so as not to harden the liver then strained and seasoned

rougail *(USA)* A highly spiced Creole condiment served with rice dishes

rouget *(Fr) masc.* Mullet, the fish

rouget barbet *(Fr) masc.* Red mullet *Mullus barbatus*

rouget grondin *(Fr) masc.* Gurnard

rouget de roche *(Fr) masc.* Red mullet *Mullus surmuletus*

rough puff pastry A puff pastry made with the conventional turns to build up layers but the fat is mixed with the flour in the form of solid cubes 1 to 2 cm on the side and water added to make the dough, keeping the cubes as intact as possible. The flour fat ratio is 4:3. Used only where scrap puff pastry would be used e.g. pies, palmiers

roughage *see* dietary fibre

roughback *see* rock sole

rouille *(Fr) fem.* A processed sauce of water softened and squeezed bread, garlic, salt, deskinned red peppers, and olive oil with possibly cayenne pepper or paprika. It is not cooked. Spread on bread and served with bouillabaisse and other fish soups in Provence.

roulade A type of presentation of sweet cakes, savoury mixtures, cheeses, layered meats or fish, cooked egg mixtures, etc. by taking a rectangle of one item, covering it with a filling or layer in contrasting colour or texture, then rolling up into a spiral which may be served as is, sliced or further cooked. Examples are Swiss rolls, salmon and turbot roulades, nut and vegetable roulades and similar

Rouladen *(Ge)* Beef olives

roulé *(Fr) masc.* **1** Swiss roll, rolled meat or similar **2** A fresh soft cow's milk cheese made into a roulade with layers of flavourings such as garlic, herbs and peppercorns [also called **roulette**]

rouler *(Fr)* To roll

roulette *(Fr) fem.* **1** *See* roulé **2** A pastry or pasta cutting wheel

round of beef *(USA)* The whole of the rear leg of beef excluding the shin but including the rump, topside, silverside and part of the thick flank. It is cut into a number of joints and steaks ranging from rump at the top to round steak at the bottom

round of bread A single slice of bread

round fish Fish which may be round or elliptical in cross section and have an eye on each side of the head

round gourd *see* tinda

round kumquat *see* marumi kumquat

round lettuce *see* butterhead lettuce

round steak *(USA)* Steak cut form the lower part of round of beef. It may be fried but is not very tender. When tenderized it is called Swiss steak

round yam *(Aus)* A ball shaped yam from the Burdekin vine

roux *(En & Fr) masc.* A combination of fat and flour cooked together to varying degrees of colour, i.e. white roux, blond roux or brown roux q.v. Used to thicken liquids to make sauces of various kinds; *see also* block roux

roux blond *(Fr) masc. see* blond roux

Rouy *(Fr)* A soft strong-smelling cows' milk cheese from Dijon, packed in square boxes

rova *(Sw)* Turnip

rovello *(It)* Blue-spotted sea bream

roventini alla toscana *(It)* Fried pigs' blood and Parmesan cheese

rowanberry The small red berries of the mountain ash or rowan tree *Sorbus aucuparia* which grows in temperate climates. The soft, orange to red berries grow in clusters and although too bitter to eat on their own, their high pectin content is useful when combined with other fruits to make jams [also called **sorb**]

rowanberry jelly *(UK)* A condiment jelly made in Scotland from rowanberries, apples, sugar and water

royal *see* royale

royal chinook *see* chinook salmon

royal custard *see* royale

royal glaze *(USA) see* royal icing

royal icing A hard white icing made from lightly beaten egg whites into which is beaten icing sugar, lemon juice and at the end a little glycerine [also called **royal glaze *et al*** (USA)]

royal icing praline Egg whites and icing sugar whipped to the ribbon stage and mixed with finely chopped almonds to the required consistency

royale *(Fr) fem.* A savoury egg custard made from equal parts of egg and stock or milk, seasoned, strained and poached in a buttered mould in a bain-marie. Cut into neat shapes and used as a garnish esp. for consommé [also called **royal, royal custard**]

royale, à la In the royal style, i.e. coated with a rich white sauce and garnished with truffles and button mushrooms. Also used of a consommé garnished with a royale

royale cherry *see* duke cherry

Royalp *(He)* A mild, semi-hard cheese made from unpasteurized cow's milk cast in large rounds (to 5 kg), similar to Tilsit with a buttery paste and moist reddish brown rind. Contains 39% water, 28% fat and 27% protein

royan *(Fr) masc.* Pilchard

roz bil habib *(NA)* A sweetened rice dessert cooked in milk, flavoured with almonds, vanilla and orange-flower water

rozijnen *(Ho)* Raisins

rub in, to To combine hard fat with flour and other dry ingredients using the tips of the fingers or a food processor so as to end up with a dry flowable mixture resembling breadcrumbs in which small particles of solid fat are coated with the dry ingredients

rubanné(e) *(Fr)* The description of a moulded dish made up of well defined layers of different colours and flavours

rubbing in biscuit method A method of making biscuits by rubbing the fat into the flour as in short pastry making, then adding the liquid ingredients and sugar and mixing as little as possible e.g. shortbread and ginger biscuits

rubbing in cake method A method of making cakes by combining fat and sieved flour and raising agent to a sandy (breadcrumb) texture, mixing in other dry ingredients then adding liquid to make a dough, e.g. rock cakes, raspberry buns

Rübe *(Ge)* Turnip

Rubens, sauce *(Fr) fem.* A slow reduction (25 minutes) of white wine, fish stock and a fine brunoise of aromatic vegetables, thickened with yolk of egg and finished with Madeira wine, crayfish butter and anchovy essence

rubixanthin *see* E161(d)

Rubus idaeus *Bot.* Raspberry

Rubus phoenicolasius *Bot.* Wineberry

***Rubus* spp.** Hybrids of the wild blackberry, raspberry and other similar soft fruits

ruby *see* pigmented grapefruit

ruchetta *(It)* Rocket

rucola *(It)* Rocket

ruda *(Sp)* Rue, the herb

rudder-nosed lobster *see* sand lobster

rue A hardy evergreen shrub *Ruta graveolens* with small lobed bluish green leaves which have a strong bitter flavour and pungent aroma. Used in small quantities as a garnish and in egg, cheese and fish dishes. The seeds are infused together with with lovage and mint in marinades for partridge. It is said to be poisonous in large quantities [also called **garden rue**]

rue odorante *(Fr) fem.* Rue, the herb

Ruegenwalder Teewurst *(Ge)* A smooth spreading sausage made with pork and collar bacon, smoked over beechwood

rue kewra *(In)* Screwpine

ruffe *see* pope

Ruffec *(Fr)* A strong tasting goats' milk cheese from Charentais

rugbrød *(De)* Dark rye bread

rugde *(No)* Woodcock

rughetta *(It)* Rocket

rugola *(It)* Rocket

Rühreier *(Ge)* Scrambled egg

ruibarbo *(Sp)* Rhubarb

ruladă de nuci *(Ro)* A Swiss roll filled with a mixture of ground walnuts, sugar, milk, rum and grated lemon zest

rulader *(Sw)* Beef roll, beef olive

rullepølse *(De)* A type of roulade made with the belly meat of any animal spread with a mixture of minced onion, spices and herbs, tightly rolled, tied then either dry salted with salt and saltpetre for a week and simmered in water or braised as is

rullesild *(No)* Rollmop herring

Rum *(Ge)* Rum

rum *(En & It)* An alcoholic spirit distilled from a fermented molasses solution, used as a flavouring

rum baba A baba cake soaked in rum-flavoured sugar syrup and decorated with whipped cream, glacé cherries and angelica strips. It was created for the King of Poland when living in Alsace Lorraine and is based on the recipe for Kougelhopf; *see also* baba

rum butter A mixture of softened butter, brown sugar and rum and sometimes cinnamon. When cool used as an accompaniment to hot puddings

rum sauce *(UK)* A sweet white sauce flavoured with rum, usually served with Christmas pudding or mince pies

rumaki *(USA)* A cocktail snack consisting of chicken liver and water chestnuts, wrapped in bacon, grilled and dipped in a savoury sauce

Rumex acetosa *Bot.* Sorrel

Rumex patientia *Bot.* Patience

Rumex scutatus *Bot.* Buckler leaf sorrel

rump *(UK)* A cut of beef from the hindquarter, being a vertical slice from the coccyx (fused vertebrae near the tail) behind the sirloin and extending down to the thick flank. It is a prime joint which can be roasted, fried or grilled. A rump and sirloin of beef joined together is called a choice

rump steak *(UK)* A slice of beef cut from the rump

rundergehakt *(Ho)* Minced beef

runderlapje *(Ho)* Beefsteak

rundstycke *(Sw)* Bread roll [also called **franksbröd**]

rundstykke *(De & No)* Bread roll

rundvlees *(Ho)* Beef

runner *see* ox casings. Used for black and white puddings, Bologna sausage, etc.

runner bean The pods and beans from a climbing legume *Phaseolus coccineus* which was introduced into Europe from South America as a flowering plant in the 18th century. The long narrow green pods are generally cooked and eaten whole when young since the pods tend to become stringy with age. The unripe beans may also be used at a later stage and the ripe beans may be dried [also called **scarlet runner, string bean, stick bean**]

runny *see* baveuse

ruoka *(Fi)* Food, meat, dish or course

ruokalista *(Fi)* Menu

ruoti *(It)* Small cartwheel shaped pieces of pasta [also called **rotini**]

ruotini *(It)* Small ruoti

rushnut *see* tiger nut

rusinakakku *(Fi)* Fruit cake

rusinat *(Fi)* Raisins and sultanas

rusk Ground rusks made from unleavened bread used as an extender in sausages and sausage meat. Yeast-raised bread rusk can cause off flavours in the sausage

rusks Small pieces of bread, dried and baked until golden brown

russe, à la *(Fr)* In the Russian style, i.e.garnished with beetroot, soured cream, hard boiled egg and sometimes salt herring

russet apple A reddish brown apple with a dull non-shiny skin and crisp sweet/sour flesh

Russian dressing **1** *(Ru)* Mayonnaise combined with a little dry white wine, horseradish and Worcestershire sauces and tomato ketchup **2** *(USA)* Mayonnaise combined with tarragon vinegar or lemon juice, parsley and chopped hard boiled egg

Russian fish pie *(UK)* As coulibiac but with any suitable cooked fish and using puff pastry only

Russian salad A mixture of cooked diced potatoes and carrots with peas and sliced green beans bound together with mayonnaise. Usually served on lettuce garnished with sliced hard-boiled egg, sliced gherkins and diced beetroot

Russian tarragon A milder tarragon *Artemesia dracunculoides* than the French variety. It may be distinguished from the French by its ability to set seed

russin *(Sw)* Raisin

russische Eier *(Ge)* Sliced hard boiled egg dressed with mayonnaise, served with salad

russole *(It)* A type of fungus

rustica, alla *(It)* In the rustic style, e.g. used of spaghetti served with an anchovy and cheese sauce flavoured with garlic and oregano

ruta *(It)* Rue, the herb

Ruta graveolens *Bot.* Rue

rutabaga **1** A variety of swede *Brassica campestris* var. *rutabaga* with yellow flesh **2** *(USA)* Swede, kohl rabi **3** *(Fr) masc.* Swede

rutin One of the bioflavonoids q.v. found in high concentration in buckwheat

Rutland *(UK)* Cheddar cheese flavoured with beer, chopped parsley and garlic

ryba *(Ru)* Fish

rybia polewka *(Pl)* A fish soup made from fish stock simmered with carrots, celeriac, onions, cabbage, parsley and cauliflower until all tender, sieved, finished with egg yolks and milk and garnished with sliced hard carps' roes poached in fish stock

rye A cereal grain *Secale cereale* which grows mainly in Baltic areas. Used for dense breads and crispbreads. A fungus *Claviceps purpurea* which grows on the seed heads, esp. during wet harvesting weather, is responsible for a sickness St Anthony's fire, characterized by hallucinations and mental derangement. An extract of the fungus is used to induce labour and as an illegal abortifacient

rye bread A bread usually shaped like a baton and flavoured with caraway seeds, made from a mixture of rye and wheat flour

rye flakes Flakes made by rolling steamed or softened rye grains. Used in muesli and for a cooked breakfast cereal

rye flour Flour made from rye which has a more sticky and less elastic gluten than wheat and is thus usually mixed with wheat flour to make bread. Used on its own for unleavened bread and crispbreads

rye meal Coarsely ground rye

rygeost *(De)* Smoked cream cheese

rype *(De & No)* Grouse or ptarmigan

rype i fløtesaus *(No)* A famous dish of ptarmigan in a cream sauce

rysk kolja *(Sw)* Haddock à la Russe

Ss

saabat masoor *(In)* Lentils with a dark brown or pale green skin which when dehusked are a pale pink-orange. They take a considerable time to cook

saabat moong *(In)* Whole mung beans

saabat urad *(In)* Whole seeds of black gram

saag *(In)* A general term for green vegetables

saa got *(Ch)* Yam bean

Saanenkäse *(He)* A hard, cooked-curd cow's milk cheese similar to Sbrinz, suitable for slicing or grating. The cheeses are dry salted and matured in cool damp conditions for up to 5 years [also called **Walliskäse**]

saang choy *(Ch)* Cos lettuce

saba 1 *(Ja)* Mackerel **2** *(Ph)* Banana

Sabal palmetto *Bot.* Palmetto

sábalo *(Sp)* Shad

sabayon A mixture of egg yolk and a little water whisked to the ribbon stage over gentle heat. Added to sauces to assist glazing under the grill

sabayon sauce A French, thinner, lighter and frothier version of zabaglione made from egg yolks, sherry or rum and sugar, sometimes with whipped cream folded into the mixture. Served with fruit desserts and rich sponge puddings

sablé biscuits A rich sandy-textured biscuit made from a buttery paste containing granulated sugar, formed into a roll, chilled, sliced and the round slices baked in the oven [also called **sand biscuits**]

saboga *(Sp)* Twaite shad

sabor *(Sp)* Flavour

sabre *(Fr) masc.* Scabbard fish

sabre bean *see* sword bean

sabroso *(Sp)* Savoury, tasty

sabzi *(In)* Vegetables

sac *(Fr) masc. see* caecum

saccharin A synthetic chemical which weight for weight is 400 times sweeter than sugar. It is approved for use in the UK for soft drinks, cider and diet products. It does not have an E number and is therefore not universally approved in the EU

saccharometer A hydrometer q.v. which is directly calibrated with the percentage of sugar in the sugar/water solution

Saccharomyces cerevisiae The most common yeast used for converting sugars into alcohol or water and carbon dioxide, for breadmaking and as a source of some enzymes, e.g. invertase

Saccharomyces exiguus A yeast used for the leavening of sour dough bread

Saccharomyces inusitatus A yeast used for the leavening of sour dough bread

Saccharomyces rouxii A yeast used in the third phase of the production of soya sauce

saccharose *see* sucrose

sacchetto *(It)* Sea perch

sacher sauce A blond roux made into a thin sauce with equal parts of consommé and cream, flavoured with Worcestershire sauce, thickened with egg yolks and finished with chopped chives

Sachertorte *(Au)* Vienna's most famous torte created by Franz Sacher in 1832 made from a butter, sugar and egg yolk creamed batter into which rum or Madeira-flavoured molten chocolate is beaten, this followed by folding in flour and stiffly beaten egg whites and baking at 180°C. The cake is rested and covered with chocolate icing to make a rather dry torte which is best served with whipped cream

Sacherwürstel *(Au)* A bratwurst containing mainly beef and bacon fat

sacristain *(Fr) masc.* A spiral shaped puff pastry with almonds and sugar or cheese

sad A description of a cake or loaf which is heavy, sunken or has not risen as required

saddle A large joint of meat from smaller animals, consisting of two joined loins and sometimes including ribs

saddle of lamb The two joined loins of a lamb before cutting through the backbone. Normally skinned and roasted, garnished with water cress, carved longitudinally in thick slices and served with gravy, mint sauce, and red currant jelly

saddled bream A small seawater bream

Oblada melanura. The grey-blue skin has longitudinal stripes

sadikka *(Sr)* Nutmeg

safardjaliyya *(NA)* A beef stew with quince

safflower A thistle like plant *Carthamus tinctorius* with large orange red flowers cultivated in India, China and the Middle East. The flowers are used as a yellow colouring and oil is extracted from the seeds. The styles are sometimes sold as true saffron to unsuspecting customers [also called **saffron thistle, Mexican saffron**]

safflower oil A mild-flavoured, high polyunsaturated oil from the seeds of the safflower, which is a good source of vitamin E. Not suitable for deep frying. Used for margarine manufacture and in salad dressings. Contains about 10% saturated, 15% monounsaturated and 75% polyunsaturated fat

safflower styles The style of the safflower is often used to replace or adulterate saffron by unscrupulous traders, but it is yellow as opposed to the red of real saffron. Will colour dishes orange but has no flavour [also called **bastard saffron**]

saffransbröd *(Sw)* A yeast-raised fruit bread flavoured and coloured with saffron. Served on St Lucia's feast day, the 13th of December

saffron The red/orange thread-like 3 branched styles of the perennial crocus *Crocus sativus* about 2.5 cm long with a penetrating aromatic flavour that is medicinal in high concentration. Cultivated from the Mediterranean to Kashmir. It is the most expensive spice known but a small amount (0.1 g) will both flavour a dish and colour it a brilliant gold. Sold either as strands which should be infused in hot water for at least 8 hours or as a red powder which gives a fast release of aroma. Used with fish and rice dishes and in buns. Often adulterated, and should only be purchased from reputable merchants; *see also* safflower stigmas

saffron cake *see* Cornish saffron cake

saffron milk cap An edible mushroom *Lactarius deliciosus* with an irregular orange circular cap containing a central depression. The yellow sap turns green on drying and is a positive identification of the species. Pickled and used in cooking

saffron sauce Finely chopped shallots or onions cooked in white wine, the volume reduced to about one sixth of the original, double cream, equal in amount to the original wine, whisked in off the heat and saffron powder added to colour and flavour

saffron thistle *see* safflower

Saflor *(Ge)* Safflower

safran *(Fr) masc.* Saffron

safran d'Inde *(Fr) masc.* Turmeric

Safrangewürz *(Ge)* Saffron

Saft *(Ge)* Juice, gravy

saft *(De & No)* Juice

Saftbraten *(Ge)* A thin beef stew or braised beef

Saftig *(Ge)* Juicy, spicy

safuran *(Ja)* Saffron

sag *see* amaranth. Usually spinach in Europe

sagaloo *see* amaranth. Usually spinach in Europe

saganaki *(Gr)* Thick slices of Kessari or Kefalotiri cheese, floured, deep fried and served with lemon wedges as an appetizer

sage A perennial bush herb *Salvia officinalis* of the mint family which grows worldwide. It has silvery leaves, a highly aromatic flavour and aroma and is used as a flavouring esp. in Italian cooking. It goes well with fatty meats and liver and is used to flavour sausages, vinegar, and compound butters [also called **broad leaved sage**]. It is also available in a prostrate form *S. officianils 'Prostratus'* which has a very balsamic flavour.

Sage Derby *(UK)* A hard, mild cheese with a slightly flaky texture and marbled appearance made by adding the juice of sage leaves mixed with chlorophyll to the curds

sage grouse *(USA)* A species of grouse *Centrocerus urophasianus* which feeds on sagebrush buds. The crop must be removed as soon as it is shot, otherwise it would give the bird an objectionable flavour

Sage Lancashire *(UK)* Lancashire cheese flavoured with chopped sage

sage and onion stuffing *(UK)* Onions baked in the oven, the inner soft flesh mixed with white bread which has been soaked in milk and squeezed out, seasoning and chopped sage. Chopped beef suet may be added. Used as a stuffing for poultry or may be diluted with gravy for use as a sauce

Sägegarnele *(Ge)* Common prawn

saging *(Ph)* Plantain

Sagittaria sagittifolia *Bot.* Arrowhead

Sago *(Ge)* Sago

sago A starch extracted mainly from the pith of the sago palm *Metroxylon sagu* using water. The starch is then dried and granulated into small balls known as pearl sago. Used for milk puddings. Many palm trees which grow in India and SEA, the cabbage palm from the American tropics and cyclads which grow in Sri Lanka, India and Japan all have a starchy pith at a certain phase in their life cycle and are used as a source of starch

sago palm A palm tree *Metroxylon sagu* which grows wild in fresh water swamps in SEA. Just before flowering at about 15 years, starch reserves build up in the pith and the palm is felled to extract the starch from which sago is produced

sagú *(It & Sp)* Sago

Sahne *(Ge)* Cream

Sahnequark *(Ge)* Cream cheese

Sahnetorte *(Ge)* Cream cake

saiblinge *(Fr)* A fish of the salmon family

sai dau naga choy *(Ch)* Mung bean sprouts

saignant(e) *(Fr) adj.* Rare or underdone esp. as a description of meat. Lit. bleeding

saigneux, bout *(Fr)* Neck of lamb or veal

sai gwa *(Ch)* Water melon

sai jar *(Id)* Drumstick vegetable

sailor's beef *see* sjömansbiff

saín *(Sp)* Suet

saindoux *(Fr) masc.* Pig's lard

saingorlon *(Fr)* A soft blue-veined cows' milk cheese similar to Gorgonzola and cast in 5 to 10 kg cylinders. Contains 55% water, 21% fat and 20% protein

sainomo-giri *(Ja)* Dice cut food (1 cm)

Saint Albray A semi-soft, mellow and delicate cow's milk cheese from Béarn produced in a 2 kg flower shape. It has a pale orange bloomed rind with a pale yellow paste containing small holes. Suitable for dessert and sandwiches

Saint-Benoît *(Fr)* A round cows' milk cheese from the Loire with a fruity flavour

Saint Chevrier A mild and creamy goat's milk cheese covered with ash

Saint-Florentin *(Fr)* A washed rind, full-flavoured cows' milk cheese from Burgundy

Saint-Gildas-des-bois *(Fr)* A triple cream cows' milk cheese from Brittany with a rather mouldy smell

Saint Honoré The patron saint of pastry cooks; *see also* Gateau Saint Honoré

Saint-Jacques *(Fr) see* coquilles Saint-Jacques

Saint Laurence The patron saint of cooks

Saint-Malo, sauce *(Fr) fem.* Sauce vin blanc with mustard, chopped shallots cooked in white wine and a little anchovy essence

Saint-Marcellin *(Fr) see* Tomme de Saint Marcellin

Saint-Nectaire *(Fr)* A semi-hard cows' milk cheese from the Dordogne cast in large discs (to 2 kg). It is salted and ripened in caves for 60 days. The smooth paste has an aromatic flavour and a slight smell of mildew. It has appellation d'origine status. Contains 45% water, 25% fat and 23% protein

Saint-Paulin *(Fr)* A semi-hard creamy yellow round cheese with a mild delicate flavour made from cow's milk and cast in discs (to 2 kg). It is made with a lactic starter, is washed in weak brine, salted in brine and cured at high humidity. Sometimes sold as Port Salut

Saint-Pierre *(Fr) masc. see* John dory

Saint-Rémy *(Fr)* A soft, washed rind cows' milk cheese from Lorraine with a strong smelling paste and a reddish brown rind. Made in squares

Sainte-Maure *(Fr)* A soft creamy goat's milk cheese from the Loire made in long cylinders often moulded around a straw

Sainte-Menehould *(Fr)* A description, originating in the Champagne region, of cooked food coated with mustard, dipped in melted butter, covered with breadcrumbs and grilled. In France, pigs trotters are traditionally treated in this way

saisir *(Fr)* To sear

Saiten *(Ge)* A juicy sausage often served with lentils

saithe *see* coley

saka-mushi *(Ja)* A method of steaming food over sake and water or steaming food which has been marinated in sake

sakana-ryori *(Ja)* Seafood

sakana shioyaki *(Ja)* Cleaned and gutted herring, dried, sprinkled with salt and allowed to rest for 30 minutes, sprinkled with more salt especially on the tail and grilled or barbecued for 15 to 20 minutes, turning as required

sake *(Ja)* **1** A rice wine used principally for drinking but can be used as a substitute for mirin in cooking. It is brewed from steamed rice using the mould *Aspergillus oryzae* as the fermentation agent. Lactic acid is added to reduce the pH and prevent contamination with a yeast. It is filtered and used immediately [also called **saki, Japanese rice wine**] **2** Salmon (note - stress on first syllable)

sake kasu *(Ja)* Red rice

saki *(Ja) see* sake

sakizuke *(Ja) see* aemono

saku *(Th)* Sago

sal *(Po & Sp)* Salt

sal prunella Saltpetre cast in cakes. Because of the method of manufacture it contains potassium nitrite as an impurity and thus imparts a pink colour to meat products. Used for curing meat

salaatti *(Fi)* Salad

salaattikastike *(Fi)* Salad dressing

Salacca edulis *Bot.* Snake fruit

salad A mixture of raw leaves, vegetables, fruit, warm or cold cooked vegetables, sausages, ham, cheese, fish, shellfish, cereal grains, pasta, etc. Virtually any edible foodstuff may be incorporated in a salad but, save for pure fruit salads, all are dressed with some kind of acid-based sauce or dressing and seasoned. Served as a course or meal in its own right or as an accompaniment to other food. See e.g. Russian salad, green salad, fruit salad, salade niçoise

salad burnet A perennial hardy evergreen herb *Sanguisorba minor* with tiny green/red spherical flowers. The lacy leaves have a slightly nutty flavour with a hint of cucumber. Used in salads, sauces, soups and stews

salad cream A commercial emulsion sauce made to resemble mayonnaise but deriving its texture more from thickeners than from emulsified oil

salad dressing A sauce usually based on oil and an acid such as vinegar, lemon juice or possibly yoghurt, either a stable or unstable emulsion, seasoned and flavoured with herbs, spices, garlic, etc. Generally used to coat very lightly the components of a salad esp. leaves, but occasionally to bind the ingredients together

salad flowers The principal flowers used in salads are bergamot, borage, calendula, chives, nasturtium, primrose, rose petals, sweet rocket and violet

salad herbs The principal herbs used in salads are (leaves only): alexanders, angelica, basil, bistort, borage, caraway, chervil, chicory, Chinese chives, coriander, corn salad, dill, fennel, lemon balm, lovage, marjoram, mint, mustard, nasturtium, orach, parsley, salad burnet, salad rocket, savory, sorrel, summer purslane, sweet cicely, tarragon, thyme, watercress, wild celery and winter purslane; *see also* salad flowers

salad onion *see* spring onion

salad patta *(In)* Lettuce

salad rape The light green leaves of a small annual plant *Brassica napus* of the rape and swede family used as a salad leaf, or when older, may be cooked as a vegetable

salad rocket *see* rocket

salada *(Po)* Salad

salade *(Fr) fem.* Lettuce, green salad

salade composée *(Fr) fem.* A substantial mixed salad with a selection of bacon, poached egg, offal, deep fried cheese and the like. See e.g. salade niçoise

salade des fruits *(Fr) fem.* Fruit salad

salade niçoise *(Fr) fem.* A typical Provençal salad made of a selection of most of tomatoes, cucumbers, skinned raw broad beans, cooked French beans, hard-boiled eggs, anchovy fillets, tuna, black olives, basil and parsley dressed with a garlic-flavoured vinaigrette

salade panachée *(Fr) fem.* Mixed or layered salad

salade russe *(Fr) fem.* Russian salad

salade simple *(Fr) fem.* Plain salad

salade tiède *(Fr) fem.* A lukewarm salad achieved by using a relatively hot salad dressing

salade verte *(Fr) fem.* Green salad

saladier *(Fr) masc.* Salad bowl

salado *(Sp)* Salted or salty

salaison *(Fr) fem.* **1** The process of salting meats, cheeses, etc. **2** Salted meat or fish used as a hors d'oeuvres

salak *(Id & Ma)* Snake fruit

salam *(He)* A type of cervelas or Brühwurst

salamander **1** A commercial high intensity grill used in restaurant kitchens **2** A small circular metal block on the end of a metal rod with a wooden handle, heated to red heat on a fire or stove then held over the food surface to have the same effect as an overhead grill, nowadays a gas operated blow torch is often used for the same effect

salamandre *(Fr) fem.* Salamander

salambo *(Fr)* An open topped tart filled with a kirsch-flavoured pastry cream and topped with caramel

salame *(It)* A type of cased sausage named after Salamis which was a city of the Roman empire in Cyprus. The plural of the Italian is salami which is the English word for the sausage of that name. Salame is variable in composition and texture although with few exceptions it is 100% meat and flavourings and is usually known by a district name in Italy. A selection are described [also called **salami** (En & Fr)]

salame calabrese *(It)* A short thick salami made of pure pork embedded with chunks of white fat weighing about 250 g. It has a strong peppery flavour and is linked and tied with string

salame casalingo *(It)* Home made salami

salame cotto *(It) see* cotto

salame di Cremone *(It)* A large coarse textured salami similar in composition to salame milanese

salame fabriano *(It)* A salami made of equal parts of pork and vittelone

salame di fegato *(It)* Liver sausage

salame di felino *(It)* A succulent salami of pure pork meat moistened with white wine, flavoured with garlic and whole peppercorns in a rather uneven shape

salame finocchuona *(It)* A large salami made with pork containing some large chunks of lean meat as well as fat and flavoured with fennel

salame fiorentino *(It)* The most famous of the Tuscan salami made of pork containing chunks of fat and lean which give them a mottled appearance when cut. About 10 cm in dia

salame alla friulana *(It)* Sautéed slices of salami with vinegar eaten with polenta

salame genovese *(It)* A salami made of roughly equal parts of vitellone and fatty pork. Very popular in the USA

salame iola *(It)* A pure pork salami from Sicily flavoured with garlic

salame milanese *(It)* A salami made in large quantities containing 50% lean pork, 20% fat pork and 30% beef or vitellone, all coarsely chopped, seasoned and flavoured with garlic and whole white peppercorns. Dextrose is added to encourage lactic fermentation and it is air dried and matured for 2 to 3 months

salame napoletano *(It)* A long thin salami from Naples made of pork and beef seasoned with a lot of ground pepper and with a very strong flavour

salame di porco *(It)* Brawn

salame sardo *(It)* A salami from Sardinia highly-flavoured and with red pepper

salame di Sorrento *(It)* A garlic free salami from Sorrento containing 80% pork and 20% beef

salame ungherese *(It)* A Hungarian salami made in Italy from finely chopped pork, pork fat, beef and garlic, seasoned, moistened with white wine and flavoured with paprika

salame Val d'Ostana *(It)* A small soft sausage made of pork and beef and flavoured with garlic

salamella di cinghiale *(It)* Wild boar sausage

salami 1 *(En & Fr) masc.* A hard sausage with excellent keeping qualities, variously made from fine or coarse chopped pork, beef or veal and mild or spicy often with peppercorns. Normally brined and smoked. Used for antipasto, hors d'oeuvres and sandwiches **2** *(Pl)* A hard cows' milk cheese with a close textured paste containing many small holes

salamin d'la duja *(It)* A soft mild type of salami preserved in fat in a special pot called a duja

salamini *(It)* pl. Small salami

salamini di cinghiale *(It)* A strong-flavoured sausage made of wild boar meat and preserved in brine or oil

salamoia *(It)* Pickling liquid, brine

Salat *(Ge)* Salad, lettuce

salat *(De, No & Ru)* Salad

salat olivier *(Ru)* A salad of julienned chicken meat with chopped hard boiled eggs, slices of waxy new potatoes, peas and chopped gherkins mounded on a serving dish decorated with slices of hard boiled egg each with half an olive and topped with a mixture of mayonnaise and sour cream flavoured with Worcestershire sauce

salat po-karabakhsky *(Ru)* A salad from the Caucasus made from sliced radishes, deseeded and peeled cucumber and spring onions, dressed with olive oil, lemon juice, chopped fresh mint and served with a feta type of cheese

salata *(Gr)* Salad of raw fresh vegetables

salată di vinete *(Ro)* The flesh of baked aubergines, finely chopped, seasoned and mixed with lemon juice and grated onion then blended with oil to form a purée which is served cold as an appetizer

salatagurker *(No)* Dill pickles

salatah arabiyeh *(ME)* Arabic salad generally of chopped or sliced sweet green pepper, onion, tomato, radish and garlic with crushed coriander seeds, dried mint, chopped parsley and seasoning and usually dressed with olive oil and vinegar

salatah-bi-laban *(ME)* Salad ingredients as salad arabiyeh with a yoghurt salad dressing

salatah-bi-taheenah *(ME)* Salad ingredients as salatah arabiyeh with a tahini salad dressing

salatina *(It)* Fresh salad leaves

salato *(It)* Salted, savoury, esp. of meats

Salatsosse *(Ge)* Salad dressing

Salbei *(Ge)* Sage

Salber *(Ge)* Salt pork

salceson woski *(Pl)* A hard unsmoked pork sausage in a natural casing popular throughout the country

salchichas *(Sp)* Dark coarse-textured fresh sausages with a delicate flavour made from various meats. May be eaten raw or cooked

salchichas estremeñas *(Sp)* A salchichas containing equal parts of pork belly, lean pork meat and liver

salchichón *(Sp)* A large sausage made from lean pork meat and pork belly, seasoned, spiced, dry salted and lightly smoked

salciccia napoletana *(It)* A pork and beef sausage strongly spiced with powdered sweet red pepper

salcraute *(It)* Sauerkraut

sale *(It)* Salt

salé(e) *(Fr)* Salted, also corned, as of beef

sale grosso *(It)* Coarse salt

sale marino *(It)* Sea salt

saleem *(Th)* *see* salim

salema *(En & Sp)* A small round seawater fish *Boops salpa* with a grey skin and regularly spaced yellow horizontal lines weighing to around 1 kg. Treat as sea bream

salep *(En & Fr) masc.* A starch preparation from the dried tubers of various Middle Eastern orchids used as a thickening agent

saleratus *(USA)* Potassium and/or sodium bicarbonate used as a raising agent or as an ingredient of baking powder. From the Latin, sal aeratus

salers *see* Cantal

sa leung geung *(Ch)* Lesser galangal

salgado *(Po)* Salted

salgam *(In & Ne)* Turnip

salicine plum *see* Japanese plum

Salicornia europaea *Bot.* Samphire (marsh samphire or glasswort)

salim *(Th)* A dessert made from thin tapioca noodles in a coconut milk and jaggery sauce [also called **saleem**]

Salisbury steak *(USA)* A grilled seasoned beef patty rather like a hamburger without the bun

sallad *(Sw)* Mixed salads made with a variety of salad ingredients including preserved fish, shellfish, pickled beetroot, apples and cold potato

salladsås *(Sw)* Salad dressing

Sally Lunn A plain teacake made from a white yeast dough enriched with eggs and butter and baked in various size tins. Served hot, split and buttered, or cold, topped with glacé icing

Salm *(Ge)* Salmon

salmagundi *(UK)* A type of old English salad consisting of diced meats, hard boiled eggs, anchovies, pickles and beetroot, all diced and arranged in a pleasing pattern on a bed of salad leaves [also called **salmagundy**]

salmagundy *see* salmagundi

salmi, in *(It)* In a rich wine sauce, esp. game

salmigondis *(Fr) masc.* Hotchpotch

salmis *(En & Fr) masc.* A dish made from game birds by roasting in the usual way for about half the usual time, removing and reserving the breasts and finishing these off in a salmis sauce made with the remains of the bird, e.g. salmis of grouse, salmis de canard

salmis, sauce *(En & Fr) fem.* A mirepoix of vegetables browned in butter, chopped game carcases and white wine added and reduced, demi-glace sauce and stock added, simmered and skimmed until reduced to a thick consistency, then strained and finished with mushroom essence and truffle essence. Served with game

salmistrato *(It)* Pickled, cured in brine

salmon A large round oily seawater fish *Salmo salar* with a silvery skin and pink flesh which spends the first two years of its life in a river and returns to the same river to spawn. Found throughout the north Pacific and Atlantic oceans. Now extensively farmed in Scotland and Norway. The farmed variety may be distinguished from the wild by their intact tails and fins. They normally weight from 3 to 13 kg and are often cooked whole and served cold and decorated at buffets and banquets. May be cooked in any way and smoked

salmón *(Sp)* Salmon

salmón ahumado *(Sp)* Smoked salmon

salmon bass *see* bass

salmon caviar *see* ikura

salmon dace *see* bass

salmon pie *see* laxgryta

salmon trout 1 A variety of trout *Salmo trutta* which spends a season or more in the open sea, where the diet of small crustaceans gives its flesh a pink colour. The flesh is coarser and less succulent than salmon. The salmon trout can be distinguished from the salmon by the jaw line which extends beyond the eye [also called **pink trout, sea trout**] **2** Name given to various similar fishes in Australia and North America

salmone *(It)* Salmon

salmone affumicato *(It)* Smoked salmon

Salmonella enteritidis A food poisoning bacterium found in up to 75% of chickens

***Salmonella* spp.** A large group of food poisoning bacteria found in meat, milk, cream and eggs. The incubation time is 6 to 48 hours but usually in the range 12 to 36 hours and the duration is 1 to 7 days. The symptoms are diarrhoea, abdominal pain, vomiting and fever.

salmonete *(Po & Sp)* Red mullet *Mullus surmuletus*

salmorejo *(Sp)* A thick, smoothly blended sauce of tomato concassée, garlic, oil, vinegar and salt in which charcoal-grilled fresh chicken, rabbit or fish is placed when hot and left to cool and marinate for at least 6 hours

salmuera *(Sp)* Pickling brine

saloio *(Po)* A fresh and creamy cow's milk cheese from the countryside near Lisbon Lit. Peasant

salpa *(It)* Salema, the fish

salpicão *(Po)* A fine sausage made with pork fillet, seasoned, spiced and smoked

salpicon *(En & Fr) masc.* A mixture of chopped (traditionally 0.5 cm dice) or minced fish, meat or vegetables with flavourings and bound with a sauce. Used for stuffings, canapés, croquettes, vol-au-vents, etc. or similar mixtures of chopped raw or cooked fruits sweetened and flavoured as appropriate for use as fillings

salsa 1 *(It, Po & Sp)* Sauce, gravy, ketchup **2** *(Po)* Parsley

salsa borracha *(Me)* A cold sauce made from a processed mixture of raw onions, pasilla chillis, orange juice and tequila or pulque

salsa de chile chilpotle *(Me)* A sauce made from smoked green chillis (chilpotles), garlic, oil, water and salsa para enchiladas (tomato sauce); used in Mexican cooking

salsa comun *(It)* One of the earliest known recipes for a spice mixture from Ruperto de Nola, cook to the King of Naples, consisting of 3 parts cinnamon, 2 parts cloves, 1 part pepper and 1 part ginger with a little ground coriander seed and saffron if so wished

salsa francesa *(Sp)* French dressing

salsa inglesa *(Sp)* Worcestershire sauce

salsa di noci *(It)* Skinned walnuts, processed with moistened bread, parsley, salt, oil and a little garlic, let down with cream or curds and served with ravioli

salsa alla pizzaiola *(It)* A tomato sauce well-flavoured with garlic, basil or oregano and chopped parsley. Served with meat, poultry and pasta

salsa rossa *(It)* A thick sauce made from chopped shallots sweated in butter and olive oil, tomato concassée, finely chopped carrots, roasted, skinned and chopped sweet red peppers, seasoning and a little chilli powder, simmered until all tender and amalgamated

salsa di soia *(It)* Soya sauce

salsa de tomate *(Sp)* Tomato ketchup or sauce

salsa verde *(It)* An oil and vinegar mixture flavoured with crushed garlic, anchovy essence or chopped salted anchovies, chopped parsley and capers. Served with salads, cold meats and hard boiled eggs [also called **green sauce**]

salsetta *(It)* Salad dressing, light sauce

salsicce e fagioli *(It)* A Tuscan dish of cannellino beans and coarse-textured sausage with garlic, tomatoes, olive oil and sage

salsicce alla romagnola *(It)* Sausages fried with sage and tomato sauce

salsiccia *(It)* A small fresh or dried sausage

salsiccia di Bologna *(It)* Bologna sausage

salsiccia bolognese *(It)* A sausage containing minced heart and lungs

salsiccia di fegato *(It)* A sausage made with liver and flavoured with pepper and fennel seeds

salsiccia fresca *(It) see* luganeghe

salsiccia matta *(It)* A sausage made with giblets and spleen

salsiccia di nicosia *(It)* A pork and rabbit meat sausage mixture

salsiccie alla romagna *(It)* Poached sausages, dried, fried until brown in butter and oil, covered with half their weight of tomato concassé and simmered for 15 minutes

salsiccia salamella *(It)* A thicker fresh sausage divided into links with looped string

salsiccia salamella vaniglia *(It)* A sausage flavoured with vanilla

salsiccia secca *(It)* Dried salsiccia

salsiccia toscana *(It)* A salsiccia flavoured with garlic, pepper and aniseed

salsifí *(Sp)* Salsify

salsichas *(Po)* The Portuguese version of salchichas

salsifis *(Fr) masc.* Salsify

salsify A long narrow root of a hardy biennial plant *Tragopogon porrifolius,* originating from Spain with an oyster-like flavour. Can be boiled, fried or eaten raw. Similar to scorzonera [also called **oyster plant, vegetable oyster**]

Salsiz *(He)* A Rohwurst made from a mixture of lean pork meat, beef and pork fat, air dried and smoked

salt The general chemical name for the compound formed when an acid reacts with a base (usually an alkali) as for example sodium acetate, which is formed by the reaction of acetic acid with the corrosive alkali sodium hydroxide or with sodium bicarbonate which is itself the salt of a weaker acid. The common example is sodium chloride, formed from the highly corrosive hydrochloric acid and it has appropriated the name salt to itself (see next entry); *see also* acid, base, alkali

salt *(De, En, No & Sw) (sodium chloride)* Sodium chloride is used extensively in food processing and cooking as a taste item, to extract plant juices in fermented vegetables, e.g. sauerkraut, to solubilize proteins in meat, to assist emulsification, e.g. frankfurters, and to act as a preservative in e.g. salted fish and meat

salt, to To preserve food by immersing it in brine or covering it with dry salt. This replaces the water in the tissues with salt or a strong solution of salt, in which bacteria and other food degrading organisms cannot grow; *see also* to cure

salt beef A joint of beef, usually brisket, cured in a spiced brine. Usually boiled and served hot or cold, usually in rye bread to make a sandwich

salt cod Filleted cod layered in coarse salt and allowed to dry out. Used throughout southern Europe and the Caribbean as a cheap source of fish protein

salt herrings Gutted herrings preserved between layers of salt, often in wooden casks

salt pork Fat pork cured and preserved in salt or brine

salt potato *(USA)* A small new potato which has been soaked in brine, from Syracuse N.Y.

salt stick *see* pretzel

saltato *(It)* Sautéed

salted almonds *see* amigdala alatismena

salted duck eggs Duck eggs packed in tubs and covered with a mixture of finely ground charcoal in brine. After 6 weeks to 3 months, the yolk becomes firm and the white becomes salty as the salt diffuses in. They are cooked by cleaning and boiling for 10 minutes. Used in curries and as hors d'oeuvres. The yolks are used in Chinese moon cakes. Common in China and SEA; *see also* Chinese preserved egg

salted water A cooking liquor for poached and boiled fish consisting of 15 g of salt per litre of water used for sea perch, mullet, etc.

saltfish and akee *(Ca)* A mixture of diced salt pork fried in its own fat and reserved, chopped onion, sweet peppers, chillis, spring onions and tomatoes fried in the same fat with a sprig of thyme and all combined and heated with deskinned, deboned and flaked poached saltfish plus the creamy parts of akee which have been boiled in the saltfish poaching liquor for 15 minutes

saltfiskur *(Ic)* Salted and dried cod

saltimbocca *(It)* A meat dish made from thin slices of veal and ham sandwiched together with sage and seasoning, formed into rolls, fried in butter and simmered in wine for 15 minutes

saltimbocca alla marchigiana *(It)* As saltimbocca but made with beef, bacon and ham

saltimbocca alla partenopea *(It)* As saltimbocca but with veal, ham and cheese and cooked in a tomato sauce

saltine biscuits Thin cracker biscuits sprinkled with coarse salt crystals before baking

salto, in *(It)* Turned over and fried as in sautéing

saltpetre E252, potassium nitrate, a chemical used in mixtures for curing meat and fish. Also a constituent of gunpowder [also called **nitrate of potash, Prague powder, sal prunella**]

salts of hartshorn Ammonium bicarbonate, once obtained from the antlers of deer, now produced synthetically for use as a raising agent

saltsa avgolemono *(Gr) see* avgolemono

saltsa domata *(Gr)* Tomato sauce

saltspring lamb *(Cn)* Baby lamb raised on salt marshes in British Columbia, similar to the French pré-salé lamb

saltwater fish Fish which live in the open sea

salume *(It)* Salt pork

salumeria *(It)* Delicatessen, grocer's shop

salumi *(It)* Salted meats

salva *(Po)* Sage

salvado *(Sp)* Bran

salvastrella *(Sp)* Salad burnet

salvia *(It & Sp)* Sage

Salvia lavandulifolia *Bot.* Spanish sage

Salvia officinalis *Bot.* Sage

Salvia officinalis 'Purpurascens' *Bot.* Purple sage

Salvia sclarea *Bot.* Clary sage

Salz *(Ge)* Salt

Salzburger Nockerln *(Au)* Soufflé omelettes baked in three's on a large dish and served with sweetened strawberry flavoured cream or jam sauce [also called **Austrian pancakes**]

Salzburgerwurst *(Au)* A non-keeping sausage made with a mixture of beef, pork and bacon, lightly smoked and scalded. Grilled or fried

Salzgebäck *(Ge)* Pretzels or crackers sprinkled with coarse salt before baking

Salzgurken *(Ge)* Dill pickles

Salzkartoffeln *(Ge)* Plain boiled parsley potatoes

Salzlake *(Ge)* Pickling brine

Salzwasser *(Ge)* Brine

samak mahshi beroz *(NA & ME)* A dish of Syrian origin consisting of whole white fish, stuffed with rice, pine nuts and almonds, baked and served with a tamarind sauce

sambaar *(In)* A highly-flavoured split pea and vegetable stew containing a lot of chillis, too hot for most western tastes

sambal 1 *(Id)* Paste like mixtures of various flavouring agents served separately in small dishes at the table **2** *(In)* Various cold vegetables and fruits such as chopped tomatoes, sliced sweet peppers, sliced bananas, etc. often sprinkled with grated coconut and served in individual dishes as accompaniments to Indian food, esp. curries **3** Side dishes of various meats, vegetables, etc. served with South East Asian meals

sambal asem A spice paste similar to sambal trassi with added sugar and tamarind concentrate

sambal bajak *(Id)* A paste of red chillis, onions, garlic, trassi, candlenuts, tamarind, galangal, oil, salt, soft brown sugar, kaffir lime leaves and coconut cream ground together. Used as a relish

sambal goreng sotong *(Ma)* A side dish of fried squid flavoured with chilli

sambal kemiri A spice paste similar to sambal trassi with added ground dry roasted candlenuts

sambal manis *(Id)* A fairly mild dark brown condiment sambal made from mixed herbs, onions and brown sugar

sambal oelek *(Id)* Dry roasted fresh red chillis, salt and soft brown sugar processed together to make a paste which is used as a relish and served at the table in a separate dish [also called **sambal ulek**]

sambal trassi A spiced highly-flavoured paste made from cooked trassi (180°C for a few minutes), red and green chillis, salt, lemon juice and soft brown sugar pounded together. Widely used in the Far East

sambal ulek *(Id) see* sambal oelek

sambar masala *(In)* A spice mix used in the south with a thin vegetable curry comprising urad dal, coriander, cumin and fenugreek seeds and black peppercorns, all dry roasted and ground. Sometimes contains in addition mustard seeds, dried curry leaves and dried chillis

sambola *(Sr)* Sambal-like side dishes

samfaina *(Sp) see* pisto

samla mchou banle *(Cm)* Seafood, grilled and served with, or poached in, an aromatic herby stock with lemon juice and lemon grass

samlet *see* parr

samna *(ME)* Clarified butter

samong-saba *(Bm)* Fennel

samoosa *(In) see* samosa

samosa *(In)* A triangular pastry turnover containing a savoury filling, deep fried and eaten as a snack [also called **samoosa**]

sam palok *(Ph)* Tamarind

samphire 1 The annual salt marsh plant *Salicornia europaea,* whose fleshy stems are cooked like asparagus. The fleshy part is stripped away from the hard core using the teeth. Because of its high proportion of silica it was once used in glassmaking. The succulent young leaves and shoots may be used in salads [also called **glasswort, marsh samphire**] **2** A bushy member of the carrot family with fleshy green leaves which grows on sea cliffs and in rocky coastal districts. The fleshy leaves and stems have a strong flavour and may be cooked as a vegetable or pickled [also called **rock samphire, sea fennel** (USA)]

samsa *(Ru)* Pasties made with an unleavened dough of creamed greek style yoghurt and butter with flour, rolled out and cut into 10 cm circles and each filled with a spiced and flavoured meat mixture, sealed, egg washed and baked at 200°C for 15 minutes until golden

Samsø *(De)* A semi-hard, scalded curd cow's milk cheese cast in 15 kg cylinders. The paste has a few irregular holes and a delicate nutty flavour which develops as it matures. Not normally cooked

San Maurin *(It)* A soft cheese from Piedmont with a lactic goaty flavour made from naturally soured goats' milk and cast in small elongated cylinders

San Pedro *(Sp)* John Dory, the fish

San Simón *(Sp)* A pear-shaped (to 2 kg) cow's milk cheese from Galicia. It is ripened in hot whey and often smoked

sanbai-zu *(Ja)* A vinegar based dressing for sunomono consisting of a mixture of rice vinegar, soya sauce and a little mirin

sanbusak *(Tu)* A turnover made with a yeasted dough filled with a mixture of minced meat and onions with pine nuts and cinnamon

sancele *(It)* A black pudding from Sicily made with pig's blood, raisins, sugar and spices. Usually sliced and fried with onions

sanchal *(In)* A blackish rock salt with a good flavour due to other mineral contaminants

sancoche *(Ca)* A thick broth made from salt pork, salt beef, fresh meat, tropical vegetables, green figs, yellow split peas and coconut. Served with dumplings

sancocho *(SA)* A meat and vegetable stew similar to cocido from Columbia

sand biscuits *see* sablé biscuits

sand cake A rich sponge cake made with cornflour, ground rice or fécule [also called **sandkage** (De)]

sand crab *see* blue crab

sand dab *see* American plaice

sand eel Various small thin long fishes *Ammodytidae* or *Hypotychidae* family which bury themselves in the sand at low tide. Used as bait and an important food for sea birds, They may be substituted for elvers in the appropriate dishes. Referred to and used as whitebait in the USA [also called **sand lance** (USA)]

sand lance *(USA) see* sand eel

sand lobster A general name for various species of small lobster-like crustaceans with similar quality meat known variously as bay lobster, bay bug, shovel-nosed lobster, rudder-nosed lobster, similar to slipper lobsters. Some bay bugs *(Moreton Bay bug and Balmain bug)* are fished commercially in Australia

sand smelt A thin round oily seawater fish *Atherina presbyter* up to 15 cm long found in the Mediterranean. It has a translucent green skin and a silver line along each side. Fried or grilled [also called **silverside, European sand smelt**]

sand sole A flatfish *Pegusa lascarisk* smaller than the Dover sole with a speckled brown upper surface, found in shallow waters around the Mediterranean and the English channel. The flesh is not as fine as Dover sole but may be cooked in the same way

sand sugar *(USA) see* light brown sugar

Sandaal *(Ge)* Sand eel

sandía *(Sp)* Water melon

sandkage *(De)* Sand cake

sandre *(Fr) masc.* Pike-perch

Sandspierling *(Ge)* Sand eel

sanduiche *(Po)* Sandwich

sandwich Two slices of bread enclosing a filling. The bread is coated on the inside with butter or similar to prevent the filling soaking into the bread; *see also* open sandwich, smørrebrød, double-decker sandwich, cassecroûte

sandwich cake *see* layer cake or sponge sandwich

sang *(Fr) masc.* Blood

sang chau *(Ch)* Light soya sauce

sang chow bow *(Ch)* A stir fry of diced pigeon meat, lap cheong and spices wrapped in bite sized parcels of lettuce leaf

sang keong *(Ch)* Ginger

sanglier *(Fr) masc.* Wild boar

sangrando *(Sp)* Rare, underdone, as of meat

sangre *(Sp)* Blood

sangre, con *(Sp)* Rare, underdone, as of meat

sangre con cebolla *(Sp)* A fried mixture of sliced onions, garlic, finely chopped fennel, cooked potatoes and pieces of baked coagulated blood

sangre con pimientos *(Sp)* As sangre con cebolla, but including sweet pepper and less onion

sangue *(It & Po)* Blood

sangue, al *(It)* Rare, underdone, as of meat

sangue, em *(Po)* Rare, underdone, as of meat

sanguinaccio *(It)* The Italian version of black pudding (boudin noir)

sanguinaccio alla fiorentina *(It) see* migliaccio

Sanguisorba minor *Bot.* Salad burnet

Sanroch *(It)* A somewhat sharp soft goats' milk cheese made in small elongated cylinders

sansho One of the few spices used in Japanese cooking. It is the berry corresponding to anise pepper from the variety of *Xanthoxylum piperitum* cultivated in Japan. Used as a condiment

sansho sauce *(Ja)* Equal quantities of soya sauce and sake mixed with soft brown sugar, thinly sliced spring onions and a small amount of ground sansho. Used with sukiyaki

Santa Claus melon *(USA) see* Christmas melon

santan *(Id & Ma)* Coconut milk

santara *(In)* Mandarin orange

santola *(Po)* Edible crab

santoreggia *(It)* Savory

sanwa *(Ja)* Japanese millet

sa-nwin *(Bm)* Turmeric

saor, in *(It)* Soused, pickled

sap *(Ho)* Juice

saparot *(Ph)* Pineapple

sapin-sapin *(Ph)* A layered dessert made from galapong or rice flour mixed with sweetened coconut milk. Each layer is separately coloured and the whole is steamed

sapodilla The fruit of the evergreen tree *Achras sapota* from Central America now grown in SEA and Sri Lanka, which is also the source of chewing gum base. The fruits are 5 to 7.5 cm in dia. and when ripe, the skin is brown, rough and sticky, the seeds are inedible and the flesh is pasty, sweet and tastes of burnt sugar. Used as a dessert [also called **chiko, chiku, chikku, naseberry, neeseberry, tree potato, zapote, sapodilla plum**]

sapodilla plum *see* sapodilla

saponins Chemical compounds found in many plants and esp. in legumes such as chick peas, soya beans and navy beans thought to have important blood cholesterol lowering effects

sapore *(It)* Taste, flavour

saporoso *(It)* A relish

sapota *(It)* Sapodilla

sapote The fruit of a deciduous Central American tree *Calocarpum mammosum*. It is oval, up to 15 cm long and has a brown rough skin enclosing a sweet spicy flesh with a large central seed. May be eaten as a dessert, used in fruit salads or made into jam

sapotiglia *(It)* Sapodilla

Sapotiglis *(Ge)* Sapodilla

sapotille *(Fr) fem.* Sapodilla

SAPP Sodium acid pyrophosphate, used to prevent blackening in potatoes

Sapsago A very hard grating cheese from Switzerland made from cow's milk and shaped like a truncated cone, weighing from 50 to 200 g. It is flavoured with a local herb *Melilotus caerulea* which gives it a green tinge. Contains 37% water, 15% fat and 41% protein [also called **Schabzieger** (USA), **Ziger** (He), **Glarnerschabziger** (He), **Krauterkäse, green cheese**]

sapsis *(USA)* A type of porridge made from beans

sapucaya nut *see* paradise nut

saracen corn *see* buckwheat

saraceno *(It)* Buckwheat

sarago *(It)* Sea bream

sarang burung *(Ma)* Bird's nest

sarapatel *(Po)* A type of haggis, hodgepodge

sarashi-an *(Ja)* Ground adzuki bean flour used for making desserts

Saratoga potatoes *(USA)* Potato chips, named after the town where they were first introduced

sar bo *(Ch)* A terracotta cooking pot glazed or unglazed on the inside that can be placed directly on a heat source. The clay from which it is made contains a high proportion of sand

sarcelle *(Fr) fem.* Teal, the wild duck

sarda *(It)* Sardine

sarde à la In the Sardinian style, i.e. roasts garnished with rice, tomatoes, stuffed cucumber and possibly mushrooms

sardeles sto fourno *(Gr)* Cleaned and prepared sardines baked in a shallow dish at 190°C for 15 minutes with a dressing of latholemono. Served with chopped marjoram

sardella *(It)* Sardine

Sardelle *(Ge)* Sardine

sardenaira *(It) see* pissaladeira

sardin *(Sw)* Sardine

sardina *(It & Sp)* Sardine

Sardine *(Ge)* Sardine

sardine *(En & Fr) fem.* A young pilchard q.v. Also used for the young of other oily fish such as sprats and herring. Grilled or available in cans

sardiner *(De, No & Sw)* Sardines

sardineta *(Sp)* Sprat

sárgarépa *(Hu)* Carrot

sargo *(It)* Sea bream

sarma *(Bk) see* sarmale (Ro)

sarmale *(Ro)* Cabbage rolls filled with a mixture of minced beef and pork, chopped onion, boiled rice, garlic and seasoning, placed in a baking dish between 2 layers of sauerkraut with a layer of fried sliced onions at the base, covered with tomato sauce mixed with juice from the sauerkraut and braised in the oven until cooked through. Served with thick sour cream

sarmale în foi de spanac *(Ro)* As sarmale but in spinach leaves and without the sauerkraut

sarmale în foi de viţă *(Ro)* As sarmale but in vine leaves and without the sauerkraut

sarnie *(UK) coll. (North West)* Sandwich

sarpa *(It)* Sea bream

sarrasin *(Fr) masc.* Buckwheat

sarriette *(Fr) fem.* Savory, the herb

sarsaparilla A flavouring made from the dried roots of a tropical climbing plant *Smilax officinalis,* used mainly for soft drinks [also called **sarsparilla**]

sarson *(In)* Mustard greens

sarson ka tel *(In)* Mustard oil

sarsparilla *see* sarsaparilla

Sarusø *(De)* A semi-hard cows' milk cheese made in squat cylinders to 14 kg. It has a dry golden brown rind and a firm, mild and sweet paste with pea sized holes

sås *(Sw)* Sauce

sås till grönsaker *(Sw)* Mousseline sauce

sasafrás *(Sp)* Sassafras

sasami *(Ja)* The two small muscles in a chicken breast closest to the carcase and breast bone, often called the mignons. They are readily detached from the complete chicken breasts

sashimi *(Ja)* Raw, very fresh seafood of contrasting textures and colour, sliced very thin and arranged decoratively on a bed of salad or grated mooli or rolled with contrasting colours, etc. Served with wasabi and a dipping sauce based on flavoured soya sauce; *see also* alto-zukuri, hira-zukuri, kaku-zukuri and usu-zukuri for types of cut

sashimi bocho *(Ja)* A long thin bladed knife for cutting fish fillets

saslik *(Tu)* Kebab

Sassafras *(Ge)* Sassafras

sassafras The tree *Sassafras albidum* whose dried leaves are used to make filé powder. A spicy, lemon-scented oil used as a flavouring for confectionery and ice cream is extracted from the leaves, bark and roots

Sassafras albidum *Bot.* Sassafras

sassage *(Ja)* Asparagus bean

sassefrica *(It)* Salsify

Sassenage *(Fr) see* Bleu de Sassenage

sassofrasso *(It)* Sassafras

saster *(UK)* A sausage made with pork shoulder meat containing about 25% fat, seasoned, flavoured with cloves, packed into casings, linked and air dried

sa-taw *(Th) see* parkia

satay *(SEA)* Cubes of meat, poultry or seafood marinated in a highly spiced mixture threaded on skewers and grilled until cooked. Usually served with a sweet or peppery hot peanut sauce [also called **saté**]

saté *see* satay

sato imo *(Ja)* Field yam

sa tong *(Ch)* Granulated sugar

satsivi *(Ru)* A classic Georgian sauce of shelled walnuts processed with garlic and chopped onions sweated in chicken fat, simmered in chicken stock with a bay leaf for 15 minutes until a thick sauce, bay leaf removed, flavoured with vinegar, ground coriander, turmeric, cloves, cayenne pepper and seasoning, finished with chopped tarragon and parsley and chilled for 2 hours. Served with chicken [also called **Circassian sauce**]

satsuma A variety of mandarin *Citrus unshui* which arose as a sport fairly recently. It is slightly flattened and seedless with a well developed orange colour and sweet flavour, sometimes with a navel at the tip. It is grown extensively in Japan and Spain since both have cold winters [also called **unshui, mikan**]

satsuma-imo *(Ja)* Sweet potato

saturated fat Hard fats in which all the carbon atoms are attached to the maximum number of other atoms, usually two carbon and two hydrogen atoms. Unsaturated soft fats and oils are converted to harder fats by hydrogenation, a process which can produce the trans fatty acids which some suspect to be harmful for pregnant and nursing mothers. Saturated fats are said to be unhealthy but fashions in health change from time to time. Small amounts of natural saturated fats (suet, lard, butter, etc.) are probably beneficial

saturated solution A solution containing the maximum amount of solid (solute) that can be dissolved in and remain in solution in a liquid solvent at a particular temperature. The amount of solute dissolved depends upon and usually increases with temperature. A supersaturated solution may be obtained by cooling a saturated solution but this is unstable and any shock will cause solid to crystallize out

Satureja hortensis *Bot.* Summer savory

Satureja montana *Bot.* Winter savory

Saubohnen *(Ge)* Broad beans

sauce *(En & Fr) fem.* A liquid thickened by a roux, starch, beurre manié, egg yolks, blood, by adding cream and/or butter or oil to a reduced cooking liquor or other liquid, or with puréed vegetables or fruit. The sauce should have a smooth glossy appearance in most cases and a definite taste and light texture. It is used to flavour, coat or accompany a dish or to bind ingredients together. Savoury sauces are usually based on stock, milk, wine or juices extracted from vegetables; sweet sauces on milk, fruit juice or puréed fruits. Emulsion sauces are emulsions of fat or oil with vinegar or acid, and a few sauces are made by compounding butter with flavourings, by combining herbs and spices with vinegar and/or oil or from a variety of puréed beans, fermented products, nuts and the like. For particular sauces see under the second word, e.g. sauce normande is listed under, normande, sauce

sauce, to To nap with sauce, to place sauce on a plate either to stop food sticking to the plate and/or to contribute to the decorative effect

sauce boat An oval shallow wide mouthed jug standing on an oval plate. Used to serve sauces usually with a small ladle

sauce soja *(Fr) fem.* Soya sauce

saucepan Once restricted to a small pan for making sauces, now used for cylindrical pans q.v. of all sizes

saucer scallop A large variety of scallop *Amusium balloti* common in Australia

saucière *(Fr) fem.* Sauce boat, gravy boat

saucijzebroodje *(Ho)* Sausage roll, a pastry roll filled with sausage meat

saucijzen *(Ho)* Sausages

saucisse *(Fr) fem.* Sausage, esp. the smaller types of fresh sausage made with chopped lean pork shoulder, seasoned and minced, packed into 2 to 3 cm casings and linked. Normally grilled or fried; *see also* entries under saucisses and saucisson

saucisse d'Ajoie *(He)* A smoked sausage from the Jura made with seasoned chopped pork. It can be boiled and eaten hot, or air-dried and eaten cold [also called **Jurawurst**]

saucisse d'Alsace-Lorraine *(Fr) fem.* A sausage made from 2 parts of lean pork to 1 part pork fat mixed with saltpetre, seasoning and flavoured with quatre-épices and ginger, packed into hog casings and linked. Sometimes decorated for the Christmas season and eaten at the Réveillon celebratory meal either fried or heated in stock

saucisse d'Auvergne *(Fr) fem.* A small saucisson sec

saucisse bretonne *(Fr) fem.* Chopped fat pork meat mixed with chopped parsley, chives, quatre-épices and seasoning, packed into casings and linked

saucisse en brioche *(Fr) fem.* A good quality sausage baked in a brioche paste rather like a large sausage roll. Served warm and sliced as a starter

saucisse à la catalane *(Fr) fem.* A ring of sausage (e.g. Cumberland) fried in fat until brown then simmered for 30 minutes in a sauce consisting of a roux made with pan residues, white wine, stock, tomato purée, a BG, orange peel and a large number of garlic cloves

saucisse de campagne *(Fr) fem.* A common air dried sausage made from a mixture of seasoned lean pork and fat bacon, moistened with red wine and flavoured with any of allspice, savory, marjoram, thyme, bay or coriander, packed into beef runners and sometimes lightly smoked

saucisse au champagne *(Fr) fem.* A gourmet sausage made from very fresh, preferably just killed, trimmed meat from a leg of pork and back fat, chopped and mixed with egg, sugar, quatre-épices and seasoning, moistened with Champagne and left to marinate for 12 hours, chopped truffles mixed in and all packed into sheep casings and linked, allowed to mature for a further 12 hours and deep fried before serving

saucisse de Dole *(Fr) fem. see* saucisse de Montbéliard

saucisse espagnole *(Fr) fem.* A sausage made of equal parts of seasoned lean pork and pork back fat mixed with raisins and flavoured with quatre-épices and allspice

saucisse au fenouil *(Fr) fem.* Very small sausages flavoured with fennel and poached then grilled as a kebab

saucisse juives *(Fr) fem.* A sausage similar to the merguez but whose meat content is entirely calves' liver

saucisse madrilène *(Fr) fem.* A sausage made from chopped veal, pork fat and filleted sardines in oil, seasoned, packed into beef runners and tied in rings, poached in veal stock, cooled and fried in butter

saucisse de Montbéliard *(Fr)* A lightly

smoked sausage made of pork only. It is cooked by placing in cold water, bringing to the simmering point. Served with lentil purée or sauerkraut [also called **saucisse de Dole, saucisse de Thann**]

saucisse au paprika *(Fr) fem.* A kind of short Frankfurter flavoured with paprika and cooked in the same way

saucisse du Périgord *(Fr) fem.* A sausage made from lean pork plus three quarters as much pork back fat, minced, mixed with a little saltpetre, flavoured with shaved truffles and quatre-épices, seasoned, moistened with white wine and left to mature for a day before being packed in casings

saucisse sèche *(Fr) fem.* Small coarse-textured sausage, partially dried and sometimes lightly smoked and usually cooked further before consumption

saucisse soudjouk *(ME)* A highly spiced beef sausage served as a hors d'oeuvre

saucisse de Strasbourg *(Fr) fem.* A thin sausage made of lean pork, possibly salted, and two thirds its weight of pork back fat, seasoned and flavoured with coriander and mace or similar, mixed with a little saltpetre, all minced at least twice to make a fine paste, packed into thin casings, tied off into 15 to 20 cm lengths, air dried and then cold smoked for 8 hours

saucisse de Thann *(Fr) fem. see* saucisse de Montbéliard

saucisse de Toulouse *(Fr) fem.* A sausage made from 3 parts coarsely chopped lean pork to 1 part pork back fat with sugar and saltpetre, seasoned and packed into 3 to 4 cm casings and either linked or left as a continuous length

saucisse viennoise *(Fr) fem.* An expensive sausage from Vienne made of equal parts of finely minced lean pork, veal and fillet steak with saltpetre, seasoning, cayenne pepper and coriander, moistened with a little water, packed in casings and lightly smoked

saucisses d'Arosa *(He)* Sausages made from 2 parts of chopped pork to 1 part viande de boeuf blitzée. Eaten hot [also called **Aroserli, saucisses de Davos, saucisses de Schaffhouse**]

saucisses de Davos *(He) see* saucisses d'Arosa

saucisses de Francfort *(Fr) fem.* Frankfurter

saucisses au gruau *(Fr) fem. see* Grützewurst

saucisses à la languedocienne *(Fr) fem.* Sausage (e.g. saucisse de Toulouse) sweated in goose fat with chopped garlic and a BG for 20 minutes and served with a sauce made with the pan residues, demi-glace sauce, tomato purée, wine vinegar and capers and finished with chopped parsley.

saucisses de Schaffhouse *(He) see* saucisses d'Arosa

saucisson *(Fr) masc.* A normally large sausage, either boiled like Cervelas, dried to make saucisson sec or smoked to make saucisson fumé. Named after either a district or some component of the contents

saucisson d'Arles *(Fr) masc.* A mixture of coarsely chopped seasoned pork, pork fat and ground lean beef, flavoured with garlic, paprika, peppercorns and quatre-épices. May have saltpetre, sugar (for lactic fermentation) and red wine added, then packed into large casings and air dried for some considerable time.

saucisson de Bourgogne *(Fr) masc.* 2 parts of finely minced seasoned pork mixed with 1 part of coarsely chopped pork back fat and some sugar, flavoured with quatre-épices and brandy or kirsch, packed into beef middles and air dried for at least 6 months

saucisson de campagne *(Fr) masc.* A sausage made in the same way as saucisson de Bourgogne but with the addition of garlic and with the brandy or kirsch left out. May be smoked [also called **saucisson de ménage**]

saucisson-cervelas *(Fr) masc.* A sausage filled with various mixtures of meat and bacon, sometimes pork only together with saltpetre, garlic, shallots and other spices, packed into beef runners, linked or looped, possibly brined and lightly smoked

saucisson chasseur *(Fr) masc.* A small air dried sausage consisting mainly of pork, for snacking

saucisson de cheval *(Fr) masc.* A pork sausage containing approximately 25% horse meat

saucisson cuit au madère *(Fr) masc.* A sausage made with 2 parts of seasoned pork fillet and 1 part pork back fat, flavoured with quatre-épices and Madeira wine, mixed with truffle shavings and/or blanched pistachio nuts, packed in 5 cm dia. casings and simmered until cooked

saucisson au foie de porc *(Fr) masc.* Equal parts of pork liver, pork back fat and lean pork, separately chopped and combined with chopped onions sweated in lard, seasoning, quatre-épices, cayenne pepper and Kirsch, rechopped, packed into hog casings, tied or knotted to make 10 to 15 cm lengths, air dried for a day, simmered in water until cooked and served cold

saucisson gris *(Fr) masc. see* saucisson lorrain

saucisson d'Italie *(Fr) masc.* Minced seasoned lean pork and veal with about one fifth of the combined weight of pork back fat, flavoured with nutmeg, cinnamon and ginger, moistened with pigs' blood and white wine, packed into a pig's bladder, air dried, smoked with juniper berries added to the wood, and coated with olive oil

saucisson de jambon *(Fr) masc.* A ham sausage from Strasbourg

saucisson de lièvre *(Fr) masc.* A sausage from Savoie made with hare meat

saucisson lorrain *(Fr) masc.* A saucisson sec made of 2 parts of lean pork, 1 part of soft pork fat and 1 part lean beef, all chopped finely and mixed with saltpetre, quatre-épices and chopped and crushed garlic, packed tightly into hog casings, tied and strung in 40 to 50 cm links, air dried for up to 6 months, packing down the filling as needed and keeping the sausage straight [also called **saucisson gris**]

saucisson de Lyon *(Fr) masc.* A saucisson sec made as saucisson lorrain but with 4 parts of lean pork leg meat to 1 part of pork back fat (salted pork or bacon)

saucisson de ménage *(Fr) masc. see* saucisson de campagne

saucisson de montagne *(Fr) masc.* A coarsely chopped pork sausage, air dried

saucisson de Paris *(Fr) masc.* A small sausage made of coarsely chopped lean pork with little fat, seasoned, flavoured and packed in casings. Normally boiled

saucisson au poivre vert *(Fr) masc.* A sausage made of 100% pork flavoured with green peppercorns

saucisson provençal *(Fr) masc.* A sausage made from pork from the leg or shoulder with little fat, containing saltpetre, peppercorns, quatre-épices and seasoning. Air dried for several days and lightly smoked

saucisson sec *(Fr) masc.* Cured and dried sausages similar to some salami, normally eaten without further cooking

saucisson sec aux herbes *(Fr)* Coarse textured dried pork sausage coated with herbs from Provence

saucisson vaudois *(Fr) masc.* An air dried and smoked sausage made with chopped pork and cured pork back fat

Sauerampfer *(Ge)* Sorrel

Sauerbraten *(Ge)* Beef, marinated in boiling red wine vinegar and water (1:2) with chopped onion, herbs and spices for 2 days, dried, browned and baked in a covered dish with the onions and half the marinade at 250°C for 1.5 hours. Served with the strained thickened pan juices. Sometimes ginger biscuits or ginger cakes are added to the cooking liquor.

Sauerkraut *(Ge)* Salted cabbage which has been subjected to a lactic fementation. Widely used in central European cooking. Available canned. It may be made from cleaned, washed and finely shredded white cabbage mixed with 1.5% by weight of salt, placed in a straight sided, sterilized tub and covered with a sterilized muslin cloth, droplid and weight. After a day liquid should cover the lid and the sauerkraut is ready in 3 weeks, The liquid is skimmed off and the sauerkraut is used from the tub as required, always covering it with a sterilized cloth

Sauermilch *(Ge)* Sour milk

säuern *(Ge)* To leaven or raise with yeast or a chemical raising agent

Sauerteig *(Ge)* Sourdough starter

sauge *(Fr) fem.* Sage

saumon *(Fr) masc.* Salmon

saumon blanc *(Fr) masc.* Hake, the fish

saumon fumé *(Fr) masc.* Smoked salmon

saumure *(Fr) fem.* Pickling brine

saumuré Pickled or marinated in brine

saunf *(In)* Aniseed or fennel

saupe *(Fr)* Salema, the fish

saupiquet *(Fr) masc.* A sharp spicy wine-based sauce or stew. The sauce sometimes served with roast hare.

saur *(Fr)* A description of herring that have been salted and smoked

saure Kartoffeln *(Ge)* Sliced peeled potatoes boiled until tender and served in a sauce which is made from a brunoise of bacon fried until crisp, flour added and cooked to a roux, potato cooking liquor added, seasoned and soured with vinegar at 65 ml per litre

saure Rahmsauce *(Ge)* Sour cream, salad dressing

saure Sahne *(Ge)* Sour cream

Sauremilchkäse *(Ge) see* Handkäse

saurer Sahnensosse *(Ge)* Sour cream sauce

sauro *(It)* Sorrel

saursuppe *(It)* Tripe soup from the north

saury pike A long beaked seawater fish *Scomberesox saurus* found in temperate waters

sausage Chopped or minced meat, seasoned, possibly mixed with spices, herbs, flavouring agents, extenders and binders, all stuffed into a casing usually of cleaned intestines, may then be boiled, scalded, cured, dried, smoked or any combination of these before sale. The name probably derived from the Latin salsisium, meaning salted, i.e. preserved

sausage maker A hollow long tapered cylinder that fits over the outlet of a mincing machine. The casing with one end tied in a knot is placed over the cylinder like a wrinkled stocking and as it is filled with the mixture extruded from the machine is allowed to slip off the cylinder. The long sausage may then be linked or divided as required

sausage meat A meat mixture similar to that for stuffing sausages, used for pies, rolls, turnovers, meat loaf, etc. In the UK, a revolting paste of ground meat scraps, drinde, MRM, rusk, etc.; *see also* English sausage

sausage roll Sausage meat or similar meat mixture wrapped in puff or shortcrust pastry to form a small roll, egg washed and baked in the oven

saus *(Ho & No)* Sauce

sauté, to To shallow fry food in hot fat or oil whilst shaking or tossing the ingredients so as to cook it and/or brown the surface. From the French sauter, to jump, from the jumping of the food as it is tossed around the pan

sauté de boeuf et rognons en croûte *(Fr) masc.* Steak and kidney pudding

sauté pan *see* plat à sauter

sauter, faire *(Fr)* To sauté or to fry

sautoir *(Fr) fem.* Sauté pan, plat à sauter

sauvage *(Fr)* Wild, undomesticated, usually of animals

savarin *(En & Fr) masc.* A rich yeast mixture similar to a baba, baked in a ring mould and demoulded. Sometimes soaked in spirit or liqueur-flavoured sugar syrup and may be filled or decorated, sometimes cut in slices as a basis for other desserts such as croûte aux fruits. Named after Brillat-Savarin. Often incorrectly used to describe a sweet or savoury mousse set in a ring mould, demoulded and garnished or sauced

savarino *(It)* Savarin

Savaron *(Fr)* A semi-hard mild-flavoured cows' milk cheese from the Auvergene with a thick covering of mould on the rind. Similar to Saint Paulin

savelha *(Po)* Shad, the fish

saveloy *see* cervelas

savenna *(Sp)* Venus shell clam

savijaca od jabuka *(Bk)* The original apple strudel from Croatia which eventually found its way to Hungary and Austria

savoiardi *(It)* Sponge fingers

savore *(It)* Savory, the herb

savory A perennial herb similar to thyme which comes in two main forms, summer savory and winter savory, q.v. Traditionally used to flavour beans

savoureux *(Fr)* Tasty, flavoursome

savoury **1** *adj.* With a pleasant meaty, salty, piquant, herby or spiced flavour, the opposite of sweet **2** A small savoury item of food usually presented on a small piece of toast for eating with the fingers **3** A savoury tasting dish, once served in small quantities after the sweet at very formal multi-course dinners. Nowadays a substantial savoury-tasting dish used as a main course at a lunch, supper or snack meal

savoury butter A compound butter with a savoury flavour, e.g. anchovy butter

savoury duck *(UK) see* faggot

savoy biscuit A small dry sponge finger biscuit made by the creaming method with whipped egg whites folded in at the end. Used for lining moulds or as the base of desserts made from setting mixtures such as charlottes; *see also* sponge finger

savoy cabbage A winter ball type cabbage with dark green crinkly leaves surrounding a tight ball of similar but light green leaves. Excellent boiled, braised or steamed, then wrung out, chopped, buttered, seasoned and reheated. The finest cabbage commonly available

savoyarde, à la In the style of Savoie, i.e. dishes containing potatoes and a local cheese

savu *(Fi)* Smoked

savulohi *(Fi)* Smoked salmon

saw A serrated-edge steel blade with sharp, ground, alternately offset to right and left, teeth used for cutting bones and frozen food, shaped like a hacksaw or conventional saw or made as a continuous power driven loop (bandsaw) for cutting up animal carcases

saw knife *see* breadknife

sawara *(Ja)* Mackerel

saya endo *(Ja)* Mangetout peas

sayote *(Ph)* Choko

sayur *(Id)* A dish of crisp cooked vegetables in a thin coconut milk sauce

sayur salat *(Ma)* Lettuce

sayyadiya *(ME)* A fish, onion and rice stew popular in the Arabian gulf, esp. Kuwait.

sbattere *(It)* To whip or whisk

Sbrinz *(He)* A hard, dark-yellow grating cheese made from unpasteurized cows' milk. A lactic whey starter is used and the curd is hard cooked, gathered in cheesecloths, moulded in up to 25 kg lots, pressed and brined for 3 weeks then matured for 6 to 12 months. It is also made in Germany, France and Italy [also called **Spalenkäse**]

sbrisolona *(It)* A flat crisp cake made with a mixture of wheat flour and cornmeal and incorporating chopped almonds

scabbard fish A long thin edible seawater fish *Lepidopus caudatus* with a smooth silvery skin

scad *see* horse mackerel

scads *(UK) coll. (Scilly isles)* Fish

scalcione *(It) see* focaccia del Venerdi Santo

scald A sinistral flat fish *Arnoglossus laterna* similar to the lemon sole but of inferior quality

scald, to 1 To pour boiling water over something or immerse in steam for a few moments so as to cook a thin outer layer without affecting the inner part. Used to remove skin from tomatoes or to loosen hair on animal skin **2** To heat milk to just below boiling point and then immediately cool **3** To clean cooking utensils by immersing in boiling water **4** To seal in flavour by bringing food in water to a temperature which coagulates surface proteins, usually 80°C

scalded cheese Cheese which has been made from curds which have been heated to between 40 and 48°C, soft cheeses at the lower temperature

scalded curd Curd for cheesemaking which has been heated to a temperature between 40 and 48°C

scalded sausages *see* brühwurst

scale, to To remove the scales q.v. from fish

scales 1 A device for measuring weight **2** The outer protective coat of fish consisting of overlapping tile-like sheets of chitin about 3 to 6 mm in dia. attached at one edge. Removed by scraping against the free side with the back of a knife or similar

scallion 1 *see* spring onion **2** The name often given in Chinese and SEA cooking to the Welsh onion q.v.

scallop A bivalve mollusc of the *Pectinidae* family with an almost circular white to brown shell with a distinctive straight hinge varying in dia. from 7.5 to 20 cm. After scrubbing and washing they are baked at 150°C for 10 minutes to open the shell. After opening and detaching from the rounded upper shell, the beard is removed, the scallop separated from the lower shell and the black intestinal sac removed. The shell and flesh with the orange roe are well washed to remove all traces of sand. Usually served on the shell and have a delectable flavour and soft texture. They must not be overcooked. There are over 400 species worldwide; *see also* great, queen, bay, saucer, pilgrim, Atlantic deep sea, Iceland and variegated scallop [also called **scollop, coquille St- Jacques** (Fr)]

scallop, to 1 *(UK)* To decorate and seal the edge of a double crust pastry pie by making small radial incisions in from the edge and half turning over the pastry with the back edge of the knife to give a scalloped effect. A similar effect may be obtained with the forefinger of the left hand and the thumb and forefinger of the right hand or vice versa **2** *(USA)* To cover with sauce and breadcrumbs and bake in a casserole

scallop squash *see* patty pan squash

scalloped Description of food, usually savoury, cooked in a scallop shell

scalloped potatoes *(USA)* Raw sliced potatoes, baked in a dish with butter, milk and seasoning

scallops 1 The pieces of meat and hard tissue left after rendering down fat into lard [also called **greaves**] **2** *(UK) coll.* Slices of potato fried like potato chips

scalogni *(It)* Shallots

scalopine *(It)* A schnitzel of veal or pork fillet, either panéed and fried or floured and fried, often finished with Marsala and/or cream and served with tomato sauce

scalopine milanese *(It)* A plain Wiener Schnitzel garnished only with lemon wedges

scaly custard apple *see* sweet sop

Scamorza *(It)* A soft spun-curd cows' milk cheese similar to but somewhat firmer than Mozarella. A lactic starter is used followed by rennet and the curds are hot kneaded and shaped into tear drops (up to 250 g) which are tied with raffia at the top. They are then cooled, briefly brined and sold young. Contains 51% water, 24% fat and 23% protein

scampi 1 *(UK)* The tail meat of the Dublin bay prawn. Many restaurants substitute pieces of monkfish tail if they can get away with it **2** *(It)* Dublin bay prawns (singular scampo), strictly only those caught in the Bay of Naples

Scandinavian sweet mustard sauce *see* gravlaxsås

scapece, a *(It)* A description of soused fish which has been fried then marinated in oil and vinegar with garlic and herbs

Scappi's spice mix A mixture of cloves, dried ginger, nutmeg, grains of paradise, saffron and soft brown sugar from Bartolomeo Scappi's cook book Opera dell' Arte del Cucinare

scarlet runner bean *see* runner bean

Scarlett O'Hara herb *(USA)* Lemon verbena

scarola *(It)* Batavian endive

scarole *(Fr) fem.* Batavian endive

scaup A wild duck *Aythya marlo* shot for the table in the UK

scaveccio alla grossetana *(It)* Eel, marinated in oil, vinegar and pepper

scelta, a *(It)* According to choice, as preferred

scented geraniums Tender evergreen perennials *Pelargonium* spp. growing to 1 m with various scented leaves which may be used for flavouring or crystallized for decoration. The flowers may be used in salads. See under *Pelargonium* spp. for particular scents and uses

schaaldieren *(Ho)* Shellfish

Schabzieger *(USA) see* sapsago

Schafmilckkäse *(Ge)* A slicing cheese made from ewe's milk

Schafsragout Emmentaler Art *(He)* A blanquette of lamb or mutton, coloured with saffron and containing diced root vegetables

Schalotten *(Ge)* Shallots

Schaltiere *(Ge)* Shellfish

schapevlees *(Ho)* Mutton

Schaum *(Ge)* Mousse or foam

schaum torte *(De)* A dessert made with almonds and egg white, sometimes incorporating crushed fruit

Schaumrollen *(Ge)* Puff pastry rolls filled with whipped cream

schav A Jewish soup made from spinach or sorrel, lemon juice, eggs, sugar and soured cream. Served chilled

Schellfisch *(Ge)* Haddock

schelvis *(Ho)* Haddock

Schenkeli *(He)* Small oval rolls, fried in butter. Lit. little thigh

schiacciata *(It)* A very thin flattened yeast-raised bread incororating olive oil and sometimes herbs, chopped onions or olives

schiacciato *(It)* Crushed, flattened

schidionata *(It)* Spit roasted

Schildkröte *(Ge)* Turtle

Schildkrötensuppe *(Ge)* Turtle soup

Schinken *(Ge)* Ham

Schinkenbrötchen *(Ge)* Ham sandwich

Schinkenkipferl *(Au)* A yeasted dough made from mashed potatoes, flour, eggs, egg yolks and milk, proved, rolled out thinly, filled with a mixture of chopped boiled ham, butter, egg yolks and grated Parmesan cheese, formed into croissants, proved, egg washed and baked. Served hot or cold

Schinkenkipper *(Au)* A croissant with a ham filling

Schinkenplockwurst *(Ge)* A somewhat firmer sausage than Schinkenwurst containing large pieces of fat

Schinkenwurst *(Ge)* A speciality slicing sausage from Westphalia made with flaked ham and smoked over beech and ash with juniper berries. Best chilled before slicing to prevent it disintegrating

schinus molle The aromatic dried red berries of a tree *Schinus molle* often sold as a pink peppercorn. They have a brittle outer shell enclosing a small seed

schiumare *(It)* To skim

Schlachtplatte *(Ge)* A plate of sliced cold meat and sausages

Schlackwurst *(Ge)* A dark red coloured beef and pork sausage similar to cervelat

Schlag *(Ge)* With cream

schlagen *(Ge)* To whip or whisk

Schlagobers *(Au)* Whipped cream

Schlagsahne *(Ge)* Whipped cream

Schlegel *(Ge)* Drumstick (of poultry), leg (of veal)

Schlehe *(Ge)* Sloe

Schleie *(Ge)* Tench, the fish.

Schlemmer Topf *(Ge)* Chicken brick

Schlesisches Himmelreich *(Ge)* A dish from Silesia of pork chops cooked with dried apples, pears, apricots and prunes, alternatively roast pork or goose with potato dumplings or with sauerkraut and purée of peas

Schlosskäse *(Au)* A cow's milk cheese similar to, but milder than Limburger

Schlumperweck *(Ge)* A pie filled with grated apple and baked

Schlupfkuchen *(Ge)* A chemically raised sponge cake flavoured with lemon zest made by the creaming method, 3 mm slices of apple inserted in to the dough and all sprinkled with a cinnamon and sugar mixture before baking at 175°C

Schmalz *(Ge)* Melted or rendered down fat, dripping, lard, etc., more specifically a description of chicken fat rendered down with onion; *see also* chicken fat

Schmalzgebackenes *(Ge)* Fried food

Schmand *(Ge)* Sour cream

Schmankertorte *(Au)* Pastry

Schmelz *(Ge)* Processed cheese

Schmorbraten *(Ge)* A pot roast of beef with mushrooms, gherkins and vegetables

schmoren *(Ge)* To braise or stew

Schmorfleisch *(Ge)* Spiced meat, meat for pot-roasting or stewing

Schmorgurken *(Ge)* Peeled and seeded cucumbers, halved and cut into 3 cm pieces, poached in a type of Béchamel made with browned chopped onion and a brown roux, served with sour cream and chopped dill

Schnäpel *(Ge)* Houting, the fish

Schnecken *(Ge)* **1** Snails **2** Sweet cinnamon-flavoured rolls

Schneeballen *(Au)* Strips of sugared pastry twisted into large constructions

Schneeklosschen *(Au)* A wine and egg based soup

Schnepfe *(Ge)* Woodcock

Schnitt *(Ge)* Slice or description of of a food which can easily be cut into slices

Schnitte *(Ge)* Chop, steak, slice of meat, fillet of fish, etc.

Schnittlauch *(Ge)* Chives

Schnittlauchsoss *(Au)* Chive sauce. An emulsion sauce made with milk soaked white bread, hard boiled and raw egg yolks pounded together with oil added as for mayonnaise, finished with vinegar, seasoning and chopped chives

Schnitzel *(En & Au)* A piece of tender meat beaten out to a large thin sheet using a cutlet bat, then panéed, shallow fried and garnished. Usually pork or veal

Schöbrunner Lunch *(Ge)* Ham and vegetable pie

Schokolade *(Ge)* Chocolate

Schokoladeneis *(Ge)* Chocolate ice cream

Schokoladenpudding *(Ge)* A type of chocolate mousse made from plain chocolate, butter. separated eggs and blanched almonds (2:2:5:2) and a little strong coffee. The chocolate is melted with the coffee (6:1), the butter and sugar are creamed, the egg yolks whisked in followed by the cooled chocolate and almonds and finally the whipped egg white (soft peak) are folded in. The mixture is cooked in a covered mould in a simmering bain-marie for 1 hour, demoulded and served with Chantilly cream whilst still hot

schol *(Ho)* Plaice

Scholle *(Ge)* Plaice.

school prawn *(Aus)* A type of prawn *Metapenaeus macleayi* intermediate in size between the deepwater and king prawn found in river estuaries and bays

Schöpsenschlegel *(Ge)* Roast leg of lamb

schorseneer *(Ho)* Scorzonera

Schotensuppe *(Ge)* Fresh green pea soup

schotisches Moorhuhn *(Ge)* Grouse

schrod *(USA)* Baby halibut under 1 kg, popular on the north east coast of North America; *see also* scrod

Schrotbrot *(Ge)* Wholewheat bread

Schübling *(He & Au)* A small smoked sausage containing beef, pork, bacon, diced bacon, seasoning and spices. Eaten hot

Schulter *(Ge)* Shoulder

Schupfnudeln *(Ge)* Thick and heavy noodles

Schutzauf *(Au)* A cream cheese cake

Schwäbischewurst *(Ge)* A mixture of two thirds lean pork and one third fat pork, seasoned, flavoured with garlic, packed into casings, boiled then smoked

Schwamm *(Ge)* Mushroom

Schwärtelbraten *(Ge)* Roast leg of pork usually accompanied with sauerkraut, dumplings and sour cream

schwartenmagen *(Fr)* A type of short black pudding from Alsace made with minced lean pork and pigs' blood [also called **blut schwartenmagen**]

Schwarzbrot *(Ge)* Brown or rye bread, coloured with molasses or treacle

schwarze Johannisbeere *(Ge)* Black currant

Schwarzkümmel *(Ge)* Nigella

Schwarzsauer *(Ge)* Goose giblets stewed with dried apples, pears and prunes and thickened with goose blood

Schwarzwälder Eierküchlein *(Ge)* Pancake batter flavoured with kirsch, cooked very thin. rolled around a filling of butter cream with sugar mixed with chopped and drained morello cherries flavoured with kirsch. Flamed with kirsch when served

Schwarzwälder Kirschtorte *(Ge)* Black Forest gateau

Schwarzwurst *(Fr & Ge)* A highly spiced black pudding from Alsace and adjoining Germany, made from minced lean pork, fat, breadcrumbs and garlic, mixed with pig's blood, seasoned, flavoured with cloves, packed into casings, linked, boiled, air dried and smoked. Sometimes flavoured with onions

Schwarzwurzeln *(Ge)* Salsify

Schwein *(Ge)* Pig

Schweinebauch *(Ge)* Belly pork

Schweinebraten *(Ge)* Roast pork, often browned and then covered and baked at 250°C

Schweinefett *(Ge)* Lard

Schweinekeule *(Ge)* Hind leg of pork

Schweinekotelett *(Ge)* Pork chop

Schweineohren *(Ge)* Crisp and very thin sweet pastry. Lit. pigs' ears

Schweinepfeffer *(Ge)* Highly seasoned cooked pork with pepper

Schweinepökelfleisch *(Ge)* Salt pork

Schweinerippchen *(Ge)* Pork spare ribs or cutlets

Schweinerucken *(Ge)* Pork fillet (tenderloin)

Schweineschenkel *(Ge)* Leg of pork

Schweinesülze *(Ge)* Jellied pork, brawn

Schweinfleisch *(Ge)* Pork

Schweinshaxe *(Ge)* Leg of pork

Schweinsjungfernsbraten *(Ge)* The back meat of the pig after removing the eye of the loin and fillet, roasted until the skin is crisp

Schweinskarre *(Ge)* Smoked pork chops

Schweinskopfwurst *(Au)* A sausage made from 4 parts of pork head meat mixed with 1 part of beef, all minced, seasoned, moistened with water, bound with fécule and packed into casings

Schweinswurst *(Ge)* Pork sausage from Bavaria flavoured with marjoram and scalded before sale

Schweizer Leberspiessli *(He)* Bacon wrapped liver kebabs, brushed with molten butter, seasoned, flavoured with chopped sage and wrapped in pig's caul before grilling

Schweizerkäse *(Ge)* Swiss cheese

Schwertfisch *(Ge)* Swordfish

sciarrano *(It)* Sea perch

sciatti *(It)* Pancakes filled with a mixture of molten Bitto cheese and grappa and served hot. Lit. sloppy

sciroppato *(It)* Sweetened in syrup

sciroppo *(It)* Syrup

sciroppo d'acera *(It)* Maple syrup

sciroppo di zucchero *(It)* Treacle

scissors Two pivoted opposing blades with handles arranged to close together and overlap. Used for a variety of cutting tasks in the kitchen. The two blades are differently ground and sharpened, one being the cutter with the oblong finger hold and rounded tip, the other being the anvil blade with the round finger hole and the sharp tip. The cutter blade is usually on top of the work and does the actual cutting

scoiattolo *(It)* Squirrel

scollop *see* scallop

Scolymus ardunculus *Bot.* Cardoon

scone An eggless plain cake made with self-raising flour, butter and sugar (4:1:1) and added baking powder (50g per kg flour) using the rubbing in method, gathered into a paste with milk possibly with added sultanas, cut into small rounds or a quartered larger circle and baked at 200°C for 15 to 20 minutes. Must be eaten fresh, usually split and buttered or with jam and whipped cream [also called **English scone, hot biscuit** (USA)]

scone round A large round scone scored in wedges before baking. The separate wedges are usually split open and eaten with a savoury or sweet filling

score, to To make shallow cuts (1 to 4 mm) in the surface of food using the point of an office knife, to assist marinating, or skinning, or in the case of skin on the surface of meat to assist the rendering of the subcutaneous fat and to prevent the shrinking of the skin from distorting the shape of the meat, or to make indentations in a cake, biscuit or scone, etc. to assist portioning

scorfano di fondale *(It)* Bluemouth, the fish

scorfano roso *(It)* Scorpion fish

scorpion fish A very ugly fish *Scorpaena scrofa* with a rough red mottled skin and weighing up to 1 kg. Used in bouillabaisse and similar soups and stews. Found in Mediterranean and similar climates

scorthalia *see* skorthalia

scorza *(It)* Skin, rind or peel, e.g. of citrus fruit

scorzonera *(En & It)* The long black root of a member of the daisy family *Scorzonera hispanica,* originating from Spain and used as a vegetable or in salads. Lit. black serpent [also called **black salsify**]

Scorzonera hispanica *Bot.* The scorzonera plant

Scotch barley *see* pot barley

Scotch bean *see* broad bean

Scotch black bun *see* black bun

Scotch bonnets The common Caribbean name for a rounded version of the sweet pepper which comes in a wide range of colours

Scotch broth Washed barley simmered in white beef stock until tender, brunoise of carrot turnip, leek, celery and onion and a BG added, simmered until tender, skimmed, BG removed, seasoned and served with chopped parsley

Scotch bun *see* black bun

Scotch egg A hard boiled egg completely covered in sausage meat, panéed and deep fried at 185°C, halved and served hot with tomato sauce or cold with salad

Scotch egg sauce *(UK)* As egg sauce but the yolks of the hard boiled eggs passed through a coarse sieve and the whites diced. Served with salt cod

Scotch grouse See grouse

Scotch kale *(UK)* A thick broth from Scotland containing shredded cabbage similar to the soup part of pot-au-feu

Scotch pancake *see* drop scone

Scotch woodcock A savoury made of buttered toast variously covered with a thick butter sauce containing anchovy purée and capers then gratinated and grilled or lightly scrambled eggs decorated with fillets of anchovy and capers or similar, served hot

scoter duck A large dark coloured diving duck genus *Melanitta* or *Oidemia* which lives in coastal seas

scottadito *(It)* Small cutlets eaten with the fingers whilst hot. Lit. burning fingers

scottare *(It)* To scald

scottiglia *(It)* A rich stew from Tuscany made with veal, poultry, pork and game

Scottish black pudding *(UK)* Salted and sieved fresh pig's blood mixed with milk (4:1), one third the combined weight of suet, minced onions, seasoning and a small quantity of lightly toasted oatmeal, filled into beef runners leaving room for expansion, tied, simmered for 2 hours pricking to prevent splitting, then dried. Served hot either boiled or fried

Scottish ginger cake *(UK)* As gingerbread with a little oatmeal, sultanas, chopped stem ginger and mixed peel

Scottish grouse *see* red grouse

Scottish hare A hare *Lepus timidus scoticus* found in the Alps, Scotland, Ireland and Scandinavia. It has a smaller body, shorter ears, a larger head and longer legs than the common hare and its fur turns white in winter; *see also* hare [also called **varying hare, blue hare, Alpine hare**]

Scottish lovage A plant *Ligusticum scoticum* very similar to lovage which grows wild on rocky coasts. Used in salads and as a pot herb

Scottish pancake *see* drop scone

Scottish shortbread *see* shortbread

scouse *see* lobscouse

scrag end of lamb *(UK)* The neck of the lamb extending to the ribs from the head end. Used for stewing. Occasionally the longitudinal muscle is dissected out and sold as neck fillet

scrag of veal *(UK)* The neck and neck vertebrae of veal used for stewing and stock. Usually boned out for stewing

scram *(UK) coll. (navy)* Food in its cooked form

scramble, to To stir beaten eggs continuously over heat scraping solid egg off the base of the pan until all is set to the required consistency

scrambled eggs Seasoned beaten eggs mixed with milk or cream and scrambled with a little butter in the pan. It should look moist and creamy and not be overcooked

Scrapple 1 *(Ge)* Pork scraps and offal, boiled and chopped, seasoned, mixed with cornmeal or other cereal and flavoured with sage, cooked like a meat loaf, cooled, sliced and fried **2** *(USA)* As the German Scrapple but made with better quality meat

scratchings *(UK)* Crisp fried pieces of pork skin, eaten as a bar snack [also called **pork scratchings**]

screwpine The fragrant leaves of the palm-like screwpine *Pandanus odaratissimus* and *P. amaryllifolius* from tropical swamps in SEA, used as a flavouring in Malay, Thai and Indonesian dishes, and as a source of kewra essence [also called **pandanus leaf**]

scrigno di venere *(It)* Large stuffed pasta shells

scrod *(USA)* Young cod under 1 kg in weight, popular on the north east coast of North America; *see also* schrod

scum The layers of greyish, foamy, coagulated protein and dirt which rise to the top of a simmering liquid. Must be skimmed off or the liquid will lack clarity

scungilli *(It)* Conches, the gastropod mollusc

scup *(USA)* Sea bream

sea anemone A primitive flower-like polyp consisting of a digestive sac with a ring of tentacles around the opening and attached to the rocks at the base by a foot, common in European waters. They are prepared by removing the tentacles, turning inside out and cleaning thoroughly. The beadlet (tomate de mer) and oplet are eaten in France

sea bass A seawater bass *Centropristus* spp. which feeds mainly on shellfish and crustaceans and has a delicately-flavoured firm white flesh. Found off the coast of North America

sea beet A species of wild beet *Beta vulgaris* subsp. *maritima* with a sprawling habit which grows on the seashore and sea walls. The leaves are cooked like spinach [also called **sea spinach**]

sea biscuit *see* hardtack

sea bream Various blunt-nosed medium oily seawater fish of the *Pagellus* and *Spondyliosoma* families, principally *Pagrus pagrus* and *P. vulgaris,* with deep, red to pink bodies ranging in length from 20 cm to 1 m. The flesh is pink or white and may be cooked in any way [also called **porgy** (USA), **red porgy** (USA), **scup** (USA)] *see also* bream

sea burbot *see* ling

sea cat *see* catfish

sea cucumber A slow moving worm-like sea grub *Isostichopus fuscus* related to the star fish, between 3 and 9 cm in length, which processes sea sediments to extract nutrients. The dried flesh is much prized in Asia and is used to thicken and flavour soups. The flesh is firm and gelatinous with a slight fishy flavour. The dried variety most commonly available must be soaked for several days before cooking. To prepare from fresh, wash and clean, soak overnight, blanch 5 minutes, cut open and gut, then simmer for 4 hours [also called **bêche de mer, sea slug, sea rat**]

sea date A tiny bivalve mollusc *Lithophaga lithophaga* from the Mediterranean which is the same shape, colour and size as a date, usually eaten raw [also called **date shell, date mussel**]

sea drum A deep bodied seawater fish *Pogonias cromis* of the drum group up to 4 kg in weight and 1 m long. The lean flesh may be cooked in any way [also called **black drum**]

sea ear *see* abalone

sea fennel *(USA)* Samphire

sea girdle A variety of brown kelp *Laminaria digitata* similar to kombu and found in shallow water of the North Atlantic [also called **tangle, sea tangle** (UK) **finger kombu** (USA)]

sea kail *see* seakale

sea laver 1 *see* sea lettuce **2** *see* nori

sea lettuce 1 A pale green seaweed *Ulva lactuca* resembling lettuce leaves, found around the shores of the UK and sometimes used as a vegetable [also called **sea laver, green laver, lettuce laver, ulva**] **2** *see* carragheen

sea oak *(USA) see* arame

sea ormer *see* abalone

sea owl *see* lumpfish

sea perch *see* comber, the fish

sea pie 1 *(UK)* A beef stew partially cooked in a casserole, a layer of suet crust pastry rested on top of the stew, the lid replaced and cooking continued until the meat is tender. Served from the casserole **2** *(USA)* A veal, pork or chicken stew with dried dessert apples, molasses and dumplings from New England

sea rat *see* sea cucumber

sea robin *see* gurnard

sea salt Salt produced by the artificial evaporation of cleaned and filtered seawater. Usually large crystals up to 5 mm

sea slug *see* sea cucumber

sea spinach *see* sea beet

sea tangle *(UK) see* sea girdle

sea trout *see* salmon trout

sea urchin A spherical-spine covered animal *Paracentrotus lividus* and other spp. up to 8 cm in dia. which lives on rocky coasts in all oceans and seas. The spines require careful handling. They are opened when alive and the orange coloured ovaries are removed and either eaten raw or used as a garnish. Must be live when purchased and consumed as soon as possible; *see also* edible sea urchin and green sea urchin

sea vegetables Edible seaweed, i.e. plants of the algae family which grow in seawater and may be green (shallow water), brown, or red (deep water). Usually dried; *see also* sea lettuce, laver, dulse, kombu, nori and wakame [also called **seaweed**]

sea wing *see* fan mussel

sea wolf *see* catfish

Seabutt *(Ge)* Brill, the fish

seafood Any edible marine animal, fish, shellfish, and various other species which inhabit the sea bottom or are free floating or swimming

seafood in puff pastry *see* bouchées de fruits de mer

seakale A seashore plant *Crambe maritima* of the cabbage family prevalent in northern Europe whose stems are blanched and served like asparagus with melted butter [also called **sea kail**]

seakale beet *see* Swiss chard

seal, to To briefly expose the surface of meat to intense heat which is supposed to form an impermeable seal to prevent loss of juices on further cooking

sear, to To brown food, esp. meat, in a very little hot fat or oil before grilling, roasting, braising or stewing

season, to To add salt and ground pepper to taste

seasoned flour Flour mixed with salt and ground pepper used for coating food (esp. surface damp food) before frying

seasoned salt *(USA)* A mixture of salt, MSG, spices and vegetable salts, used as a general seasoning

seasoning Salt and ground pepper

seawater This contains 35 g of salt per litre. Fish and shellfish should be boiled in a similar concentration of salt in water to avoid making the flesh soft and watery

seaweed *see* sea vegetables

seaweed gelatine *see* agar-agar

seaweed jelly *see* agar-agar

sebo *(Sp)* Suet

sec *(Fr) adj.* Dry or dried, the feminine form is sèche

secchielli *(It)* Dried chestnuts

secco *(It)* Dry, dried

sèche *see* sec

séco *(Po)* Dried, dry

second bamboo *see* bean curd sticks

second feather duck A duck which is not killed until it has replaced its first set of feathers at about 3 months of age. Usually free range and with a fuller and more mature flavour

seconda portata *(It)* The main dish or course of a meal

secondi *(It)* The main courses of a meal as displayed on a menu

secondo grandezza *(It) see* S.G.

section waiter *see* station waiter

sedani *(It)* Ridged macaroni. Lit. sticks of celery

sedani corti Short pieces of sedani, the classical pasta for minestrone

sedano *(It)* Celery

sedano rapa *(It)* Celeriac

sedano di verona *(It)* Celeriac

Sedgemoor Easter cake *(UK)* A thin crisp biscuit from the south west containing currants and flavoured with brandy

sediment Unwanted solid particles which settle out at the bottom of liquids

sedlo olenya *(Ru)* Saddle of venison marinated 24 hours, barded with bacon and roasted with the marinade at 230°C for 30 minutes, reducing to 180°C until tender. Served with reduced pan juices mixed with cream and horseradish.

Sedum rosea *Bot.* Roseroot

Seeanemone *(Ge)* Sea anemone

Seebarsch *(Ge)* Bass, the fish

see byan *(Bm)* The stage in making a curry at which the oil or fat separates. This occurs when most of the water has evaporated and the dish is then considered to be correctly cooked

seed The structure containing an embryo, stored food and a seed coat derived from the fertilized ovule of a flowering plant or tree from which a new plant will arise if it germinates successfully. Variously known as grains, cereals, pips, nuts, stones, kernels, etc.

seed cake A type of Madeira cake flavoured with caraway seeds and possibly lemon and/or vanilla

Seedattel *(Ge)* Sea date

seedless A term descriptive of fruits or vegetables without seeds, some varieties of which have seeds

Seehecht *(Ge)* Hake

Seeigel *(Ge)* Sea urchin

Seekarpfen *(Ge)* Black bream

seek kabab *(In)* Minced meat croquettes shaped with the hand over a steel or iron skewer the thickness of a pencil and grilled over or under a fierce heat. The meat should be free of fat and gristle and may contain aromatics and herbs and is bound with an egg

Seekrabben *(Ge)* Crabs

seeng *(In)* Drumstick vegetable

Seeohr *(Ge)* Abalone

Seepolyp *(Ge)* Octopus

seer *(In)* A unit of weight equal to 4 powas or 20 chattaks, approximately 900 g or 2 lb

Seespinne *(Ge)* Spider crab

Seeteufel *(Ge)* Monkfish

seet gnee *(Ch)* White fungus

seethe, to To simmer

see yau *(Ch)* Light soya sauce

Seezunge *(Ge)* Dover sole

segala *(It)* Rye, rye bread

segedínsky gulás *(Cz)* *see* selny gulás

seiche *(Fr) fem.* Cuttlefish

seigle *(Fr) masc.* Rye

seiro *(Ja)* *see* mushi-ki

seiron-nikkei *(Ja)* Cinnamon

seitan Wheat gluten obtained by washing the starch out of flour dough. It is marinated in soya sauce with various flavourings and used in vegetarian meals as a protein source and flavouring agent

sekar pala *(Id)* Mace

seker geker *(Tu)* Sugar

seki han *(Ja)* Boiled rice mixed towards the end of the cooking with cooked adzuki beans and cooked a further 5 minutes, then flavoured with a little sake and soya sauce. The rice is cooked in the liquor from the cooked adzuki beans made up with extra water as required

sel *(Fr) masc.* Salt

sel de mer *(Fr) masc.* Sea salt

selasih *(Id)* A wild basil with a very mild flavour

Selchfleisch *(Ge)* Smoked pork

Selchwurst *(Au)* A sausage similar to Burgenländische Hauswürstel

sel'd *(Ru)* Herring

selderie *(Ho)* Celery

self-raising flour A wheat flour which incorporates a chemical raising agent, usually sodium bicarbonate plus an acid salt for reaction and completed liberation of all the available carbon dioxide. 30 g of baking powder per kg of plain flour may be substituted (9 teaspoons per kg or 4 teaspoons per lb)

self rising flour *(USA)* Self-raising flour

self-service A type of service of food where the customers go to a counter where food is laid out and usually help themselves to cold items and sometimes to hot items. The food is then taken to a cash receiving point, if to be paid for, where the cost is computed and paid. Cutlery, napkins, seasonings and condiments are usually collected after payment

selha chawal *(In)* Converted rice

selino *(Gr)* Celery

Selkirk bannock *(UK)* A yeast-raised sweetened dough enriched with butter and sultanas, baked and glazed to a golden brown. From the Scottish border country and traditionally served at Hogmanay. It weighs about 0.5 kg

sell-by date Date shown on packaged food to aid stock control, usually for food with a short shelf life. Food may well remain edible after this date but should be consumed quickly or stored appropriately

sella *(It)* Saddle (of lamb or veal)

selle *(Fr) fem.* Saddle, e.g. of lamb or venison

selleri 1 *(De)* Celery **2** *(Sw)* Celeriac, not celery

Sellerie *(Ge)* Celery

Selles-sur-Cher *(Fr)* A soft, mild-flavoured goats' milk cheese from Loire et Cher, whose rind is dusted with powdered charcoal. Protected by appellation d' origine status [also called **Romorantin**]

sellou *(NA)* A dryish sweet made with sugar, butter and ground almonds

selon grandeur *(Fr)* *see* S.G.

selshcaree Trimmed loin of pork cured in spiced brine and lightly smoked. Popular in Northern Europe boiled with sauerkraut

Selva *(Sp)* A soft cows' milk cheese made in small cylinders (to 2 kg) with a delicate slightly salty taste which develops after ripening for 3 to 6 weeks

selvaggina *(It)* Game, venison

selvatico *(It)* Wild, uncultivated

sem *(In)* Green beans

semangka *(Id & Ma)* Water melon

sembei *(Ja)* A small crisp rice cracker

sementare *(It)* Very small eels, elvers

semi *(It)* **1** Seeds **2** Half

semi-cos lettuce A type of lettuce with sweet crunchy leaves shorter than the cos

semi-fino *(It)* A grade of rice requiring about 15 minutes cooking time. See e.g. ardizone and maratello

semi-hard cheese A fairly rigid cheese with normally a moisture content between 40 and 45%

semi di papavero *(It)* Poppy seeds

semi-skimmed milk *(UK)* Milk with a butterfat content between 1.5 and 1.8%. Sold in bottles with a silver and red striped top

semi-soft A description of food which holds its shape but is easily cut with a knife

semi-sweet A description of food which is lightly sweetened

semidure *(It)* Soft boiled, of eggs

semifreddo *(It)* A chilled mousse type dessert or ice cream on a crushed biscuit base

semifrío *(Sp)* A chilled dessert

semini *(It)* Small seed-shaped pasta

semlor *(Sw)* Light sweetened yeast-raised buns flavoured with spice and filled with almond paste. Served as a dessert floating in bowls of hot milk on Shrove Tuesday [also called **Shrove Tuesday bun**]

semmel *(USA)* A breakfast roll introduced by German immigrants (i.e. the Pennsylvania Dutch from Deutsch)

Semmelkloss *(Ge)* Bread dumpling

sémola *(Sp)* Semolina

semolina 1 A technical term for the large pieces of endosperm from wheat which are made by the fluted rolls used to separate the bran from the semolina **2** The culinary term for a particular type of semolina made from durum wheat. The particle size varies according to the use to which it is going to be put. Fine semolina is used for pasta, coarser varieties are used to make a boiled milk pudding.

Semolino *(It)* Semolina, from durum wheat

semoule *(Fr) fem.* Semolina

Sempervivum tectorum *Bot.* House leek

semplice, alla *(It)* Simply cooked

senap *(Sw)* Mustard

senape *(It)* Mustard

senape di digione *(It)* Dijon mustard

senapssås *(Sw)* Mustard sauce made with a fish velouté with dry mustard added equal in weight to one sixth of the flour used in the roux. Finished with cream

sendai-miso *(Ja) see* inaka-miso

Senf *(Ge)* Mustard

Senf Kartoffeln *(Ge)* Sliced cooked potatoes in a mustard sauce

Senfkohl *(Ge)* Rocket, the plant

sen giri *(Ja)* A very fine julienne vegetable cut [also called **needle cut**]

sen leck *(Th)* Medium sized rice noodles

sen mee *(Th)* Small rice noodles similar to vermicelli

senmen-giri *(Ja)* A cucumber fan used as a garnish

sennep *(De & No)* Mustard

sen yai *(Th)* Rice sticks

separate, to To take one part of a substance away from the whole, as for instance in separating egg yolks from whole eggs or cream from whole milk

sepia *(Sp)* Cuttlefish

seppia *(It)* Cuttlefish

sera *(In)* Lemon grass

serai *(Ma)* Lemon grass

serai powder *see* sereh powder

serbal *(Sp)* Rowanberry

serbuk perasa *(Ma)* Monosodium glutamate

sereh *(Id & Ma)* Lemon grass

sereh powder Dried and ground lemon grass used for flavouring [also called **serai powder**]

Serena *(Sp)* A hard vegetarian cows' milk cheese with a dry rind and dense hole-free yellow paste cast in cylinders (to 1.5 kg). The curd is moulded in esparto grass containers and is ripened for 50 days. Contains 40% water, 30% fat and 26% protein

sériole *(Fr)* Amberjack

Serpa *(Po)* A ewes' milk cheese eaten fresh

when soft and buttery or ripened for 1 to 2 years in caves where it is regularly cleaned and wiped with a paste of olive oil and paprika. It has a dry texture and nutty flavour

serpenyös rostélyos *(Hu)* Sirloin steak flattened and browned in lard with chopped onions and garlic, well dusted with paprika and flour, and braised in water with crushed caraway seeds, marjoram, tomato purée and chopped sweet green peppers, adding thick slices of parboiled potatoes towards the end

Serra *(Po) see* Queijo da Serra

serrano chilli A variety of hot chilli pepper from Mexico, usually sold green. They are plumpish (4 cm by 1.5 cm) with a strong rich flavour

serrated knife *see* bread knife

seru ndeng *(Id)* A condiment made from fried shredded coconut mixed with peanuts and brown sugar. Served with rice

service 1 A full set of crockery for a specific meal for several persons (usually 4, 6 or 12), as in tea service, dinner service **2** The attendance given to customers in a restaurant by waiters and staff

service charge The charge added to a restaurant bill, usually as a percentage of the total to cover the cost of providing waiters. It originated in the times when waiters were paid only this percentage for their labour. This archaic and demeaning practice dies out as society develops

service compris *(Fr) masc.* Service included (on a restaurant bill)

serviceberry *see* juneberry

serviço incluido *(Po)* Service included

Serviettenklösse *(Ge)* Bread dumplings cooked in a cloth to hold their shape. Usually served with cooked pears, bacon and French beans in a sweet and sour sauce

serving A single portion of food or drink; *see also* serving - fish and shell fish, serving - healthy eating, serving - meat, servings soup and sauce, serving - vegetables, grains and pulses

serving - fish and shell fish Main course servings are 300 g fish per portion on the bone, 125 g fish boned and skinned, 250 g or half lobster in the shell, half a litre of mussels in the shell

serving - healthy eating Nutritionists state that an adequate diet should contain 5 servings per day of fruit or vegetables each approximately 80 g (3 oz). Typical servings are, a medium sized apple or orange, half a grapefruit, 2 to 3 tablespoons (50 ml) of peas or beans or other vegetables, 200 ml of salad, 100 ml of fruit juice

serving - meat Main course servings are meat off a piece, 100 g off the bone, 150 g on the bone, individual steak or chop, 2 to 3 lamb cutlets or two lamb kidneys

serving - soups and sauces Soup as starter 100 to 150 ml, sauce with meat or fish 50 to 75 ml, sauce as accompaniment e.g. mint, cranberry, apple, 20 to 40 ml

serving - vegetables, grains and pulses Cooked vegetables 80 to 100 g, mushrooms 50 g, old potatoes in skin 170 g, new potatoes in skin 125 g, rice and other dried starch staples 25 to 50 g, pulses and beans as main course 60 g

servizio *(It)* Service charge in a restaurant

sésame *(Fr) masc.* Sesame

sesame butter *see* tahini

sesame chilli oil Red chillis fried in sesame seed oil to give the oil a red colour and hot flavour. Used as a seasoning and condiment

sesame salt *see* gomasio

sesame seed Cream to black oval seeds from the seed pods of an annual plant *Sesamum indicum* mainly grown in China, Central America and South West USA. After dry roasting they have a pleasant nutty taste and contain about 50% oil. Used in bread and cakes, to make tahini and to add texture to other foods; *see also* black and white sesame seed and tahini [also called **benne seed**]

sesame seed oil Oil extracted from sesame seeds, sometimes toasted, with a pronounced flavour and good colour. Used for stir frying, to add flavour to other dishes and added to deep frying oil (1 part in 10) [also called **oriental sesame oil**]

sesame seed paste *see* tahini

sesamo *(It)* Sesame

sésamo *(Sp)* Sesame

Sesamum indicum *Bot.* Sesame

sesos *(Sp)* Brains

set, to 1 To lay out crockery, cutlery and glassware on a table **2** To leave jellies and other thickened mixtures to go solid usually by cooling **3** To freeze ice cream, sorbets, etc.

Setaria italica *Bot.* Foxtail millet

setas *(Sp)* Mushrooms

seui gwa *(Ch)* Loofah

sevastopolskoye pyechenye *(Ru)* An almond tart from the Crimea made in a square blind-baked case, the pastry made from flour, sugar, butter and eggs (8:3:5:3), filled with a mixture of egg white and light brown sugar (7:10) mixed with flaked almonds and flavoured with cinnamon and lemon zest, the mixture slightly thickened over a low heat, then baked until brown. Served cut in 5 cm squares

seven minute frosting *(USA)* Egg whites, granulated sugar, boiling water, cream of tartar and flavouring beaten briskly for 7 minutes over hot water until of a meringue-like consistency. Used for icing and as a cake filling

sevian *(In)* Baked vermicelli-type noodles in a creamy sugar syrup flavoured with rosewater

seviche *see* ceviche

Seville orange The round orange-coloured fruit of the original orange tree of the Mediterranean *Citrus aurantium* about 7 cm in dia. which is now only cultivated around Seville and Malaga. It is harvested in January and used for marmalade manufacture and as a substitute for lemon [also called **sour orange, bitter orange**]

sevruga sturgeon The smallest of the sturgeon *Acipenser stellatus* up to 10 kg in weight, which produces about 1.5 to 2 kg of fine-flavoured, dark grey to black caviar which has the same name

sew, to To close a pocket of meat or the abdominal cavity of a bird or fish by sewing with thick thread so as to prevent a stuffing from leaking out during cooking

sfenj *(NA)* Doughnuts

sfilatino *(It)* A bread from Tuscany

sfilato *(It)* A description of the state of being boned or jointed as applied to small game animals. Lit. unthreaded

sfincione *(It)* A Sicilian pizza with a thick soft base topped with tomato, cheese, anchovies and olives

sfingi *(It)* Sweet biscuits

sfoglia *(It)* A sheet of pasta dough

sfogliata *(It)* **1** Flaky pastry **2** A type of Napoleon cake possibly filled with ricotta cheese, spices and candied fruit

sfogliatelle *(It)* A Neapolitan speciality cake

sformata *(It)* Moulded food, timbales, etc.

S.G. 1 *(Fr & It)* Selon grandeur (Fr) or secondo grandezza (It), i.e. according to size, used e.g. for pricing fish in restaurants according to the weight of the fresh fish to be cooked **2** *see* specific gravity

S-Gebäck *(G)* S shaped biscuits flavoured with lemon zest made from flour, butter sugar and egg yolk (4:2:2:1) by the creaming method. The dough is refrigerated, rolled out into 1 cm by 10 cm sticks, formed into flattened S shapes on the baking tray, brushed with egg white, sprinkled with crushed sugar lumps and baked at 200°C until firm

sgombro *(It)* Mackerel

shabu shabu *(Ja)* A one pot meat and vegetables dish cooked at the table in boiling stock. Served with sesame-flavoured sauce. Similar to sukiyaki

sha cha jiang *(Ch)* A slightly coarse textured sauce made from peanuts, dried fish, dried shrimp, chillis, garlic and various spices such as five spices and coriander. Used in Cantonese cooking [also called **sha zha chiang**]

shad A group of white, seawater fish *Alosa* spp. belonging to the herring family, which migrate from the sea to rivers to spawn. There are several varieties, e.g. Allis shad *Alosa alosa* and the slightly smaller twaite shad *Alosa fallax* [also called **gizzard shad**], ranging from 30 cm to 1 m in length. Their oily delicate flesh is often marinated in acid or cooked with acidic leaves to loosen or dissolve the bones and is used raw in sushi. Generally grilled, fried or baked [also called **alose shad, gizzard shad**]

shaddock *see* pummelo

shaggy cap *see* shaggy ink cap

shaggy ink cap An edible fungus *Coprinus comatus* with a dark shaggy cap on top of a short stem, paler when young [also called **ink cap, shaggy cap**]

shaggy parasol An edible mushroom *Lepiota rhacodes* similar to the parasol mushroom with a rough light brown cap on an off-white stem. Skinned before cooking

sha gou dou fu *(Ch)* Casseroled bean curd stew

sha he *(Ch)* A noodle made from rice flour which puffs up when deep fried

sha jeera *(In)* Caraway seed

sha jen *(Ch)* Cardamom

shakarkandi *(In)* Sweet potato

shake *(USA) see* milk shake

shallot 1 A small hard onion *Allium cepa* Aggregatum Group which grows in clusters, usually stronger flavoured than the onion. The green leaves may be harvested for use as a flavouring **2** *(Aus)* Spring onion q.v.

shallot butter *see* beurre d'echalote

shallow fry, to To cook food in a small amount of hot oil and/or fat in a frying pan or plat à sauter, the aim being to complete the cooking of the centre of the food at the same time as the outside is brown and crisp

shallow frying, fish Skinned and filleted or whole fish washed and drained, passed through seasoned flour, fried in a small amount of hot clarified butter presentation side first, placed on a dish, covered with beurre noisette and garnished with a slice of lemon

shallow poaching, fish A method of cooking cuts of fish by placing presentation side up on sweated chopped onions or shallots in a pan, adding cooking liquor to half way up the fish, bringing to the boil, placing a cartouche over then placing the pan in the oven at 160°C to 180°C for 3 to 10 minutes. The fish is removed and kept warm while the cooking liquor is made into a sauce; *see also* poached white fish

shama millet A slightly smaller seed than normal from a millet *Echinochloa colona* used in the same way as Japanese millet

shami kebab *(In)* Deep-fried meat balls made from lamb, onion, garlic, yellow split peas, ground black cumin, chilli powder, cashew nuts, garam masala, salt and chopped coriander leaves blended together and bound with egg and lemon juice

shamouti *(ME)* A variety of common orange which occurred by mutation in a Palestinian orchard in 1844. It is easily peeled without releasing much oil and is virtually seedless and has a good flavour. It is not suitable for processing owing to delayed bitterness (like the navel orange). Grown in Cyprus, Turkey and Swaziland [also called **Jaffa, Cyprus oval**]

Shanghai cooking A cosmopolitan style of Chinese cooking influenced by many of the provinces of China

Shanghai hairy crab A small square-bodied crab with a covering of dark hair on the legs and edge of the top shell. It is found on the Chinese coast around Shanghai and the meat and the roe are highly prized

Shanghai noodles Round fresh egg or white wheat flour noodles from Shanghai which are thicker than Italian spaghetti. Generally served with sauce in the same way as spaghetti

Shanghai nuts Roasted peanuts with a crisp savoury coating. Eaten as a snack

shank **1** Part of the leg of any animal, usually including the knuckle **2** *(UK)* Beef from the lower muscular part of the foreleg, with more gristle than shin beef and generally used for consommé and stock **3** The Welsh term for leg of lamb

shank end of lamb *(UK)* The lower half of a hind leg of lamb

shan na *(Ch)* Lily bulb

Shantung cabbage *see* Chinese leaves

shan yao *(Ch)* Chinese yam

shao *(Ch)* Braising

Shaohsing rice wine The classic Chinese rice wine made from a cooked glutinous rice and millet mash fermented with yeast, often aged for up to 10 years and possibly to 100 years. The younger wines are used in Chinese cooking in the same way that wines, fortified wines and brandy are used in the west [also called **red girl wine, rice wine, yellow wine, yellow rice wine**]

shao mai *(Ch)* Steamed pork dumplings

shark A group of fish ranging from 70 g to 20 tonnes characterized by their lack of mineralized bones, the skeleton being of very flexible cartilage-like material. Many of the smaller varieties are edible and traded. Because of their unusual physiology they tend to smell of ammonia but this can be counteracted by cooking at high temperatures e.g. deep fat frying. See e.g. tope, guitar fish, angel fish, dogfish, skate, porbeagle, hammerhead, mako

shark-ray *see* angel fish

shark's fin The fin of a species of shark found in the Indian ocean. It requires lengthy preparation to clean and soften it and it may be converted into chips or strands. It is always cooked in a rich stock of poultry bones and pork shank possibly supplemented with dried oyster and conpoy. Whole cleaned fins are slow cooked and eaten for their taste and texture usually without any accompaniment save perhaps a little vinegar.

shark's fin soup A soup made with prepared shark's fin (chips or strands) cooked in clarified and seasoned chicken stock with strips of chicken meat and Chinese mushrooms. May be thickened with cornflour and garnished with a julienne of ham

shark's skin Dried shark's skin is used as a flavouring agent. It has to be softened by repeated long simmering and refreshing

shark's stomach The dried stomachs of sharks are treated in the same way as shark's fin

sharlottka *(Ru)* Charlotte Russe

sharon fruit A seedless variety of persimmon, not as astringent as the true persimmon with a thin edible orange skin grown in and exported from Israel. It should be eaten when hard and may be used in fruit salads, stuffed or sliced as a decoration or garnish

sharp **1** With a pungent, tart or acid flavour **2** Descriptive of a knife or cutting implement with a finely ground and honed edge. A really sharp knife should easily cut a ripe tomato without deformation using only a slight downward pressure

shashlik *(Ru)* The Georgian term for kebabs, usually cubes of lamb marinated in wine and lemon juice with garlic, parsley, dill and seasonings, skewered with sweet red pepper and button onions and grilled

shauk-nu *(Bm)* Kaffir lime

shauk-waing *(Bm)* Kaffir lime

sha zha chiang *(Ch) see* sha cha jiang

shchi *(Ru)* Cabbage soup made with beef stock, tomatoes, onions, butter and herbs accompanied by soured cream [also called **shtchi**]

she-crab soup *(USA)* A soup from South Carolina made from the roe and the meat of the female blue crab flavoured with Worcestershire sauce and sherry and finished with cream

shea butter An edible solid fat obtained from the shea nut. Also used for soap and candle making

shea nuts The seeds of the tropical shea tree *Butyrospermum parkii* used for their fat content

shebbakia *(NA)* Pastry formed into knots, deep fried and dipped in honey

sheep casings The cleaned and scraped intestines of sheep ranging from 16 to 24 mm in dia. Classified as narrow, medium, wide and extra wide. Used for thin sausages such as chipolatas and frankfurters

sheepshead fish *(USA)* **1** A deep-bodied seawater fish *Archosargus probatocephalus* caught off the south-east coast with white firm flesh similar to the sea bream. It weighs from 2.5 to 4.5 kg and its back is silvery blue with seven dark vertical bars on the back and each side. Poach, bake or grill [also called **fathead**] **2** *see* freshwater drum

sheftalia *(Cy)* A crepinette with a filling of seasoned fatty pork mixed with an equal quantity of veal or lamb, all minced with grated onion

sheh paan *(Ch)* Garoupa, the fish

shelf life The length of time a foodstuff will stay fresh and palatable when stored as indicated by the supplier or manufacturer

shell bean *see* broad bean

shell mould *see* pee tee

shell steak *(USA)* A boneless steak cut from the fleshy part of the sirloin of beef

shellac (E)904, the strained resin exuded by various lac insects which live on the bark of some eastern trees. Used to coat apples to give them a glossy appearance

shellfish The collective name for a group of generally sea dwelling creatures comprising molluscs, cephalopods and crustaceans. Oysters, squid and lobsters are typical examples The only freshwater shellfish is the crayfish which is a crustacean. See under the different names for more detail

sheng tsai *(Ch)* Lettuce

shepherd's pie *(UK)* A dish made in the same way as cottage pie and often confused with it. However the meat used is lamb or mutton. See cottage pie

shepherd's purse A common weed *Capsella bursa-pastoris* which was once eaten as a green vegetable. So called from the shape of the seed capsule

sherbert *(USA)* A frozen dessert made from sweetened fruit juice or purée or other flavoured syrups with added beaten egg white and/or cream

sherry sauce As Madeira sauce but substituting dry sherry [also called **sauce xérès** (Fr)]

Sherwood A double Gloucester cheese flavoured with chives and onions

Shetland sheep *(UK)* A breed of sheep from the Shetland Isles which feed on grass, heather and seaweed to produce a tender lamb with a gamey flavour

Shetland sparls *(UK)* A Scottish pudding of seasoned minced beef flavoured with allspice, cloves, mace, ginger and cinnamon, wrapped in wide sheep casings and smoked

sheung moy cheung *(Ch)* Plum sauce

shia jeera *(In)* Caraway seed

shiba kuri *(Ja)* Small firm sweet chestnuts

shichcheta *(Bu)* Spicy lamb kebabs

shichimi *(Ja) see* shichimi togarishi

shichimi togarashi *(Ja)* A blend of seven flavouring agents, white and black sesame seeds, sansho, nori, dried tangerine peel, togarashi and white poppy seeds, ground together and used as a condiment and to flavour soups, noodles and grilled meats. Some formulations include black hemp seeds [also called **shichimi**]

shiitake mushroom A variety of fungus fruiting body *Lentinus edodes* from the Far East where it is grown on tree trunks, now grown in Europe on wheat straw. They have a white stem, a brown flattish cap and white ruffled gills. They are high in protein and keep their shape when cooked. The flavour intensifies on drying and they become darker. Often sold dried in Chinese shops as winter mushrooms. Lit. tree mushroom [also called **Chinese dried black mushroom, black forest mushroom, fragrant mushroom, oak mushroom**]

shikar korma *(In)* A pork korma made with loin of pork cut in pieces, fried with honey and ghee until browned, salted water added and all simmered until cooked and dry. Grated shallots, turmeric, black pepper, orange and lemon peel are added and the whole cooked until the butter fat separates, yoghurt added and again cooked until the fat separates, crushed garlic, ground cardamom and cinnamon added and cooked 1 minute, a little mace added and all left in a slow oven with a tight fitting lid on the dish for 15 minutes

shiltong *(Ne)* Rice bean

shimeji *(Id & Ma)* Oyster mushroom

shin beef *(UK)* The lower muscular part of the rear leg of beef. It contains a lot of connective tissue and being well used is tough but of excellent flavour. Used for making consommé, beef tea and for long stewing

shina-nabe *(Ja)* Wok

shingala *(In)* Catfish

shinmai rice *(Ja)* Freshly harvested rice with moist, tender and sweet grains which do not require as much water for cooking as most rice types

shinshu-miso *(Ja)* A light thin yellowish miso in which rice is the added grain

shio *(Ja)* Salt

shiogame *(Ja)* A heavy earthenware platter used for grilling or roasting food. Usually covered with a layer of coarse salt on which the food rests

ship biscuit *(USA)* Hardtack

ship caviar *(USA)* The caviar from a hybrid of the osciotre and sevruga sturgeon

shiraita kombu The thin membrane left after shaving off the fleshy part of kombu to make oboru and tororo kombu. Used as a food wrapping

shirano *(Ja)* Whitebait

shirasu ae *(Ja)* Cooked vegetables, e.g. dried beans, mushrooms, aubergines, courgettes containing as little moisture as possible, combined with a sesame seed sauce made from dry roasted white sesame seeds pounded with sugar, vinegar, mirin, salt and bean curd which has been boiled for 3 minutes and wrung out in a cloth. The sauce should be smooth and sticky

shirataki noodle A very fine noodle made from the glutinous tuber of the snake palm plant. They soften immediately on contact with hot food and require no other cooking. Often stored in cold water in the same way as cooked spaghetti is stored in commercial kitchens

shiratamako *(Ja)* Glutinous rice flour

shirazi *(Pe)* West Indian lime [also called **torsh**]

shirini polo *see* shirin polo

shirin polo *(ME)* A rice and chicken dish flavoured with almonds, saffron and candied orange peel [also called **shirini polo**]

shiro goma *(Ja)* White unhulled sesame seeds

shiro kikurage *(Ja)* White fungus

shiro-miso *(Ja)* A very light coloured, almost sweet, miso suitable for making salad dressings

shiromono *(Ja) see* shirumono

shirona *(Ja)* Chinese leaves

shirr, to To bake food, esp. eggs, in small shallow containers or dishes in the oven

shirred eggs Shelled eggs baked in a shallow tray in the oven. Alternatively stiffly beaten egg white spread in a buttered shallow tray, depressions made for individual yolks and all baked in the oven at 180°C for 10 minutes; *see also* oeufs sur le plat

shirumono *(Ja)* Technically a thick soup but the thickness is only relative when compared with suimono and usually comes from the higher proportion of vegetables, tofu, mushrooms, etc. in the soup [also called **shiromono**]

shish kebab A kebab made with cubes of lamb and possibly pieces of tomato, onion and sweet pepper

shishi-to *(Ja)* Sweet pepper

shishi-togarashi *(Ja)* Sweet pepper

shiso *(Ja)* A member of the mint family *Perilla arguts* which comes in both green and red leaved forms and is used as a garnish or a vegetable; *see also* green shiso, red shiso, hojiso and mejiso [also called **perilla, beefsteak plant**]

shi zi *(Ch)* Persimmon

shi zi tou *(Ch)* Large meatballs of minced pork

shizuoka no ume shiso zuke *(Ja)* Tiny pickled plums with sushoga and shiso

shoestring potatoes *(USA)* Very thin deep-fried strips of potatoes like pommes pailles

shoga *(Ja)* Ginger

shoga sembei *(Ja)* Small crisp rice crackers coated with a mixture of ground ginger and sugar

shole zard *(Pe)* An Iranian dessert made from soft cooked rice, sugar and crushed almonds, flavoured with rosewater, saffron and cinnamon

shoofly pie *(USA)* A sweet treacle or molasses pie with a crumble topping. Served cold or warm with cream or ice cream

shoppe kebab *(Bu)* A beef stew with tomatoes, onions, paprika, butter, marjoram and chillis thickened with eggs, yoghurt and flour, finished with vinegar and garnished with chopped parsley

shopska *(Bu)* A salad of cucumber, dried

tomatoes and ewe's milk cheese dressed with vinaigrette and garnished with chopped parsley

shore crab A small green shelled crab *Carcinus maenus* and *C. mediterraneus* sometimes with yellow spots and up to 7 cm across. Popular in Venice just after they have shed their shell where they are known as moleche. If the shell has hardened they are used in soups and stocks [also called **green crab, green swimming crab**]

shore dinner *(USA)* A seafood dinner

short grain rice A rice with a low length to dia. ratio, generally sticky when cooked

short loin *(USA)* The front half of a sirloin of beef including the fillet

short pastry *see* shortcrust pastry

short plate *(USA)* The lower part of the centre of the beef animal extending from halfway down the body including the the ends of the ribs, the English plate and part of the thin flank. Used for braising

short ribs *(USA)* Part of the ribs of beef excluding the large longitudinal muscles beside the vertebrae, i.e. between the rib roast and the plate

shortbread *(UK)* A Scottish crisp biscuit made of butter, caster sugar and flour or flour plus fine semolina mixed (2:1:3), baked at 150°C, usually prescored in thick rectangles [also called **Scottish shortbread**]

shortcake *(USA)* Two rounds of a baked rich scone mixture sandwiched together with a filling of fruit and cream

shortcrust pastry The commonest pastry made of soft flour, lard or vegetable shortening and butter (4:1:1). It is mixed by the rubbing in method and brought together with sufficient chilled water. The paste should not be kneaded, rolling will compact the mixture. It improves if rested for 30 minutes after forming. Baked at 200 to 220°C until light brown [also called **short pastry, pâte à foncer** (lining pastry) (Fr), **pâte brisée** (Fr), **piecrust pastry** (USA)]

shortening The fat used in pastry, biscuit and cake making; *see also* shortening power

shortening power The ability of a fat to allow air bubbles to become trapped in a mixture and therefore lighten the texture of the resulting baked item. This is achieved by adding soft unsaturated fats or oils to harder ones to increase their plasticity or by adding emulsifying agents such as glycerol monostearate to the fat. Such a superglycerinated fat prevents the development of gluten network structures in the dough and also aids the incorporation of more liquid and hence sugar in the mix

shortnin' bread *(USA)* A chemically raised sweet bread from the southern states made with butter or lard

shorva *(In)* Soup

shot pepper *see* mignonette pepper

shou de *(Ch)* Lean, as of meat, without fat

shoulder The top of the foreleg of an animal including the shoulder blade and surrounding muscles but not the vertebrae and ribs and the longitudinal muscles associated with them. The methods of cooking depend upon the amount of work the muscles have done, e.g. lamb, pork and veal may be roasted, older beef and mutton shoulder is usually stewed or braised

shoulder of veal *(UK & USA)* The shoulder blade, the upper bone of the leg and the surrounding tissues excluding the rib sheet. Similar to shoulder of lamb and used for braising and stewing

shovel-nosed lobster *see* sand lobster

shoyu *(Ja)* A naturally fermented light soya sauce made from soya beans and grains such as wheat or barley

shpinatnie shchi *(Ru)* Spinach and sorrel soup made with beef stock with added onions and root vegetables, served with hard boiled eggs and soured cream [also called **zelonye shchi**]

shproti *(Ru)* Sprats

shred, to To cut food into very thin pieces or strips

shred pie *see* mince pie

shredded wheat A crisp breakfast cereal made from a cooked wheat flour paste extruded in a rectangular multitude of fine (0.5 to 1 mm) threads, partly dried, chopped transversally into rectangular biscuits, dried and browned

Shrewsbury biscuit *(UK)* A traditional English biscuit about 13 cm dia., made from a basic biscuit paste flavoured variously with citrus rind, mixed spice, dried vine fruits or cocoa, rolled and cut into shape

Shrewsbury Eastertide biscuit *(UK)* A rich crisp biscuit made with brown sugar and flavoured with caraway seeds, vanilla and sherry [also called **Shrewsbury Eastertide cake**]

Shrewsbury Eastertide cake *(UK) see* Shrewsbury Eastertide biscuit

shrimp 1 Small white transparent to grey brown crustaceans generally much smaller than prawns and cooked as soon as caught. Used fresh cooked and shelled in potted shrimps and shrimp salads and also either shelled or unshelled as a snack food. They are also salted and dried for use in Chinese cooking; *see also* brown, pink and deepwater shrimp **2** *(USA)* A general term used for assorted species of prawns and shrimps

shrimp butter Beurre de crevette

shrimp eggs The roe of shrimps and prawns usually dried and salted. They are very expensive and used as a garnish in Chinese cuisine

shrimp floss *see* dried shrimp

shrimp paste A paste of ground, salted and partially fermented shrimps, dried and compressed into blocks. See e.g. blachan and bagoong

shrimp powder Dried shrimps ground to a fluffy powder and used as a condiment on salads, vegetables, rice dishes, etc.

shrimp pudding *(UK)* Equal parts of minced shrimp or prawn meat and chopped cold chicken, veal or sweetbreads, bound with egg yolks, breadcrumbs and cream, packed into casings and served fried in butter

shrimp sauce *see* sauce aux crevettes

shrinkage The reduction in size of baked items or roast meat and poultry due to loss of water. Generally less when cooked at lower temperatures

Shropshire blue *see* blue Shropshire

Shrove Tuesday bun *see* semlor

shtchi *(Ru) see* shchi

shuan yan grou *(Ch)* Mongolian firepot with lamb. See flying lamb slices

shuck, to *(USA)* To open and prepare bivalve shellfish or to remove husks, shells or pods from seeds and nuts, etc.

shui dian fen The suspension of cornflour or other starch in water (1:2) always kept together with oil and stock beside the wok where the Chinese restaurant cook prepares food

shui dou fu *(Ch)* Silk bean curd

shui guo *(Ch)* Fruit

shui guo zhi *(Ch)* Fruit juice

shui jiao *(Ch)* Boiled dumpling

shungiku *(Ja)* Leaves of the garland chrysanthemum which impart a subtle flavour to soups and other dishes

Siamese ginger *see* greater galangal

sianliha *(Fi)* Pork

siba *(Po)* Cuttlefish

Siberian millet *see* foxtail millet

Siberian salmon A salmon *Oncorhynchus keta* found in the Siberian and western Canadian rivers which drain into the Pacific. The source of ketovaia and ikura [also called **dog salmon, chum salmon**]

Siberian sturgeon A variety of sturgeon *Acipenser baeri* found in the Siberian rivers that drain into the Pacific ocean

Sichuan *(Ch)* A province of China famous for its cooking [also called **Szechuan** q.v.] The words tend to be interchanged at random

Sichuan dumplings *(Ch)* Ground seasoned pork fillet mixed with finely chopped pork fat, chopped garlic or garlic chives, bound with a little sesame seed oil, cornflour and egg white, divided amongst wonton wrappers, formed into purses, poached in simmering water for 5 minutes and served with a spicy sauce

Sichuan hot bean paste *see* chilli bean paste

Sichuan pepper *see* anise pepper

Sichuan pepper oil Vegetable oil flavoured with finely ground anise pepper

siciliana, alla *(It)* In the Sicilian style, i.e. with anchovies, pine nuts, sultanas and vinegar, esp. fish and vegetables

Siciliano *see* canestrato

side dish An accompaniment to a main food dish such as a salad, a bowl of rice or pasta or vegetables

side of meat One half of an animal carcase split lengthways along the centre of the backbone, generally without the head

Siebling *(Ge)* Arctic char

sieden *(Ge)* To boil or simmer

sieni *(Fi)* Mushroom

sienimunakas *(Fi)* Mushroom omelette

sienisalaatti *(Fi)* Mushroom salad

sien ts'ai *(Ch)* Kale

siero di latte *(It)* Buttermilk or whey

sierra The local name for snoek caught off the coast of Chile

sieva bean A variety of butter bean q.v.

sieve A fine stainless steel wire, plastic or other stranded fine mesh either stretched in a flat circle on a metal or wooden former or made into the shape of a half sphere or inverted cone. Used for separating large from fine particles, for straining liquids or for reducing soft foods to a purée

sieve, to To pass dry powder, e.g. flour or icing sugar, through a sieve to remove large particles or foreign bodies and to aerate it, or to pass a liquid through it to remove solid particles

si-ew *(Th)* Light soya sauce

sift, to To pass dry ingredients through a sieve either to clean or aerate them or to spread them evenly over a food

sifter A closed cylindrical container with a sieve or perforated top at one end for sprinkling flour, sugar or other powders over food items

sigarilla *(Ph)* Goa bean

sigir *(Tu)* Beef

signal crayfish A large fast growing crayfish farmed in the UK for the restaurant trade. It has now escaped into the wild where it is supplanting the native species

sigtebrød *(De)* Light ryebread

sigui A fish found in the Baltic with flesh similar to the shad

siikas ja munakokkelia *(Fi)* White fish with scrambled egg

sik *(Sw)* Whitefish

sikbadj *(NA)* A lamb stew with dates and apricots from Morocco

si-klok *(Th)* A sausage made of 3 parts of minced pork mixed with 2 parts of crabmeat, chopped onion, coriander leaves and roasted peanuts, flavoured with red curry paste, moistened with equal parts of nuoc mam and coconut milk, filled into casings and coiled like a Cumberland sausage

silakka *(Fi)* Baltic herring

silba *(Bk)* A cow's milk cheese resembling Port-Salut

sild 1 *(En & No)* A small type of herring once found in huge quantities off the Norwegian coast and canned in the same way as sardines **2** *(De)* Baltic herring

sildeboller *(No)* Herring fish balls

sildesalat *(No)* Herring salad

silgochu *(Ko)* Finely shredded dried chillis used as a seasoning and condiment instead of powdered or whole chillis

silicon dioxide *see* (E)551

silk bean curd A very smooth soft bean curd made by straining the coagulated bean curd through fine mesh and allowing the strained curds to settle under gravity without pressing

silke cepts *(Li)* A Lithuanian dish of herring fillets in a mustard and onion sauce

sill *(Sw)* Herring

sill med brynt smör *(Sw)* Herrings in brown butter made from matjes herrings or soaked cleaned and filleted salt herrings covered with a mixture of dried dill weed and equal parts of diced hard boiled egg and chopped onion and served covered with beurre noisette

sill med gräslök och gräddfil *(Sw)* Herring with sour cream and finely chopped chives

sillabub *see* syllabub

sillgratäng *(Sw)* Gratinated herrings made with sliced matjes herring fillets, sliced boiled potatoes and sweated onion rings layered alternately in a greased dish with potatoes on top, gratinated with toasted breadcrumbs and possibly cheese, heated in the oven or under the grill and buttered

silli *(Fi)* Herring

sillpudding *(Sw)* As laxpudding but using salt herring or matjes herring fillets instead of salmon

sillsalad *(Sw)* Finely chopped salt herrings mixed with chopped cooked potatoes, pickled beetroot, pickled cucumber, chopped dessert apple and onion, bound with a little of the beetroot vinegar, packed in a mould, chilled, demoulded, garnished with hard boiled eggs and picked parsley and served with soured cream which can be coloured pink with beetroot vinegar.

silotakia tiganita *(Gr)* Small pieces of fried chicken liver or calf liver dipped in lemon juice and speared on cocktail sticks for use as a snack or appetizer

Silter *(It)* A hard, scalded-curd skimmed cows' milk cheese from Brescia. It has a close textured curd with a few cracks and holes

silvano *(It)* Chocolate meringue tart

silver E174, a precious metal sometimes used in very thin films as a food decoration

silver balls Small silver-coloured sugar balls, 2 to 4 mm in dia. used for cake decoration

silver beet *(Aus & USA)* Swiss chard

silver fungus *see* white fungus

silver hake A seawater fish *Merluccius bilinearis* of the cod family with a silvery skin, weighing about 400 g found off the North American Atlantic coast. It has a white moist flesh which softens rapidly if not frozen and it may be cooked in any way [also called **whiting** (USA)]

silver leaf E174 as gold leaf but made with silver. Used for decorating Indian festive dishes [also called **varak**]

silver salmon *see* coho salmon

silver smelt *see* smelt

silver sprouts Mung bean sprouts which have had the root and leaf removed to leave a thin white stalk. Used as a garnish or vegetable in expensive Chinese dishes

silver threads *(USA)* Cellophane noodles

silver top *see* full cream milk

silverbeet *(USA)* Swiss chard

silverside *(UK)* The inside cut from the top of the rear leg of beef. It is virtually fat free and traditionally is pickled in brine and boiled, but now sometimes sold, wrapped in a layer of fat, as a cheap roasting joint.

silverside (fish) **1** *see* Atlantic silverside **2** *see* sand smelt

silversides *(USA)* Any small silver coloured fish such as whitebait, anchovies, sardines, etc.

silverskin onions A very small variety of onion, less than 2 cm in dia., with a silver skin and white flesh. Used for pickling, or, in a sweet pickle, as a cocktail onion for use with drinks and snacks, etc.

simi *(Ne)* French bean

simla mirich *(In)* Sweet pepper

simmer, to To keep a liquid at a temperature just below boiling point around 95 to 97°C for pure water, but around 87°C for meat. The heat input necessary to maintain this temperature with a heat source under the pan will cause slight movement of the surface of the liquid but no evolution of steam bubbles. The lower temperature is best for extracting the maximum flavour from meat, bones and vegetables as in making stock, but speed of extraction is increased with temperature [also called **to seethe**]

simmuledda alla foggiana *(It)* Potato and fennel soup thickened with buckwheat flour

simnel cake *(UK)* A spiced Easter fruit cake with a layer of marzipan baked in the centre. Sometimes covered with marzipan and decorated

sinaasappel *(Ho)* Orange, the fruit

sinaasappelen *(Ho)* Oranges

sinappi *(Fi)* Mustard

sindootan *(Id)* *see* parkia

sin gaun *(Bm)* Sea urchin

singe, to To use a flame (blow torch or lighted taper) to remove hairs from pork skin or pin feathers, etc. from poultry and game birds

singhara nut *(In)* The fruit of an aquatic plant *Trapa bispinosa* similar to the water caltrop, but it may have either 1 or 2 projecting horns. It is extensively grown in Kashmir and either eaten raw or cooked as a kind of porridge

singing hinny *(UK)* A Northumberland cake, made from a currant scone mix, cooked on a griddle and eaten hot. The name comes from the sound of the steam being released when it is cooked on the griddle

singkong *(Id)* Cassava

single cream Cream with a minimum butterfat content of 18%. Not suitable for whipping

Single Gloucester A hard, mild Cheddar-like white farmhouse cheese made in the form of a squat cylinder from the skimmed cow's milk of an early season day's milking [also called **haymaking cheese**]

single loin of lamb *see* loin of lamb (UK)

sinigang *(Ph)* A thin stew of meat or fish with vegetables, simmered in a cooking liquor soured with some of lime, lemon, tamarind or unripe tomatoes, seasoned and flavoured with fish sauce or soya sauce

sinistral Term used of a flat fish in which the eye on the right of the juvenile form moves to join that on the left which becomes the uppermost side of the adult fish

sink tidy A triangular metal or plastic dish with perforations in the base and sides used to strain off vegetable peelings and the like

sinn *(Ch)* Eel

Sint Jakobsschelp *(Ho)* Coquille Saint-Jacques (scallop)

sipoli merce *(Lv)* A dish of herring fillets coated in a mixture of German mustard, French mustard, egg yolks and cream, covered and left overnight in the refrigerator, passed through rye flour and pan fried in butter. Served with onion rings and lemon wedges

sippet A small right-angled isosceles triangle of toast about 2 cm on the side (12 per slice of English bread). Several are served in a sauce boat as an accompaniment to soup; *see also* croûton

sipuli *(Fi)* Onion and the onion family generally

sipulipihvi *(Fi)* Steak and onions

sir The generic name for cheese in Balkan and some Slav countries

siracha *(Th)* A thin red chilli sauce in which individual flakes of chilli pepper can be seen

sirap *(Sw)* Syrup

Sirene *(Bu)* A firm white salty and crumbly white cheese similar to Greek feta

sirka *(In)* Vinegar

sirloin *(USA)* A cut of beef from the upper part

of the loin just in front of the round, including some of the English rump and the rear part of the English sirloin, the rear half of the whole loin

sirloin of beef Part of a loin of beef, comprising about 6 full vertebrae. Sometimes roasted on the bone, boned out and reassembled on the bone or boned and rolled. Also used as steaks

sirloin steak **1** *(UK)* A slice about 1.5 to 2 cm thick cut from a boned out sirloin of beef [also called **entrecôte steak**] **2** Steak cut from the USA sirloin usually including bone and the outer layer of fat. They are designated by the shape of the vertebra and its extension as pinbone, flatbone and wedgebone or if without bone as boneless.

sirop *(Fr) masc.* Syrup

sirop d'érable *(Fr) masc.* Maple syrup

sirsak *(Id & Ma)* Soursop

Sirup *(Ge)* Treacle

sis kebap *(Tu)* A shish kebab consisting of cubes of meat, pieces of tomato and pieces of sweet pepper grilled on separate skewers, removed from the skewers on to the plate and served with a rice pilav

sis köfte *(Tu)* Meatballs of lamb threaded on and/or formed around a skewer as a flattened rectangle, grilled and served off the skewer with a rice pilav

sishi salad *(Ho)* A dark bluish brown sprouted seed grown like mustard and cress as a decoration

sissay yassa *(WA)* Joints of chicken marinated in lemon juice and oil with onions, garlic, ginger and chilli, fried and served with rice. A Gambian speciality

sitaw *(Ph)* Long bean

sitron *(No)* Lemon

sitruuna *(Fi)* Lemon

sitruunakohokas *(Fi)* Lemon soufflé

sitruunankuori *(Fi)* Lemon zest

sitsaro *(Ph)* Mangetout peas

sitsaron *(Ph)* A dry snack made from pork crackling or fried chitterlings [also called **chitcharon**]

siu choy *(Ch)* Chinese leaves

siu mai *(Ch)* Dumplings made from wonton wrappers filled with a paste made from lean pork and prawn meat, chopped water chestnuts, reconstituted black mushrooms, spring onions, fresh ginger, salt, sugar and soya sauce. The wrappers are circular and made into a cup shape as they are filled, left open at the top, sprinkled with grated carrots and the dumplings placed in an oiled steamer basket and steamed for 12 minutes

Sium sisarum *Bot.* Skirret

siwalan *(Id)* Palm nut

sjokolade *(No)* Chocolate

sjokoladefarget *(No)* Covered in chocolate

sjömansbiff *(Sw)* A casserole of alternate layers of fried slices of rump or sirloin beef, sliced onions with seasoning and thyme and sliced potatoes, starting and finishing with potatoes, simmered in water, lager or stout. Lit. seaman's beef

sjøørret *(No)* Sea trout

sjötunga *(Sw)* Dover sole

sjøtunge *(No)* Dover sole

skaba puta *(Lv)* A cold soup made from a duxelle of mushrooms and onions brought to the boil with tomato purée, lemon juice and chicken stock, barley added and simmered until tender, cooled, mixed with 10% buttermilk and 10% sour cream and chopped dill. Served cold garnished with chopped hard boiled eggs and gherkins

skalddyr *(De)* Shellfish

skaldjur *(Sw)* Shellfish

skalldyr *(No)* Shellfish

skånsk kålsoppa *(Sw)* Cabbage soup from Skåne, made from diced lean pork simmered in water, skimmed, sliced cabbage, swede, carrots and potatoes added with salt, peppercorns and a bay leaf, simmered until all tender, seasoning adjusted and served with a chopped parsley garnish

skånsk potatis *(Sw)* Diced potatoes browned in butter and reserved. Chopped onion fried in the same fat, potatoes added back, seasoned and the whole mixed with double cream. Served with a chopped parsley garnish

skärbönor *(Sw)* French beans

skarpsås *(Sw)* A sharp sauce made with equal parts of mashed hard boiled and raw egg yolk, with a little vinegar and French mustard into which oil is emulsified as in mayonnaise production, seasoned with salt and cayenne pepper, mixed with an amount of double cream equal to the oil and finished with chopped dill. Often served with baked fish

skate A flat triangular shaped seawater fish *Rajus batis* of the shark family, with eyes on the upper side and mouth and gills on the lower side. The upper surface is greenish brown with spots and they can be up to 2 m wide. The white medium oily flesh from the skinned sides (wings) cut into pieces and nuggets of flesh cut from under the body are cooked in any way; *see also* common skate, thornback ray and guitar fish [also called **ray**]

skewer Variously sized wooden or metal rods resembling knitting needles with a handle, loop or enlargement at one end. Used for trussing joints of meat, birds and poultry or for holding meat, fish or pieces of vegetables for grilling

skewer, to To hold the edges of joints of meat together, to hold the limbs of poultry and birds against the body using skewers or to thread pieces of meat or vegetable on a skewer

skillet *(USA)* Frying pan, sometimes with a lid

skim, to To remove surface layers of fat, froth and scum from a simmering stock, sauce, soup, stew or jam, using a ladle, spoon or skimmer. Occasionally adsorbent kitchen paper is used esp. to remove the last traces of fat from a consommé

skimmed milk Milk with a butterfat content of 0.3% or less. Tends to burn on heating. Sold in bottles with a silver and blue checked top

skimmed milk quark *see* magerquark

skin **1** The outer protective covering of an animal, fruit or vegetable **2** The hard dryish film which forms on top of soups, sauces and jams when cooled and left. Prevented by using a cartouche or other means to avoid evaporation

skin, to To remove the skin from food items such as fish, fruit, meat, vegetables, etc.

skink of beef *(UK)* A Scottish term used for leg or shin of beef [also called **hough of beef**]

skinka *(Sw)* Ham

skinkbullar *(Sw)* Ham and potato balls

skinke *(De & No)* Ham

skinkestek *(No)* Roast ham

skinkfärs *(Sw)* A mousse made with finely ground ham

skinklåda *(Sw)* Ham omelette cooked in the oven

skipjack tuna A cheap species of tuna fish *Katsuwonus pelamis* often substituted for the more expensive yellow fin or the rare blue fin [also called **Pacific bonito, California bonito, oceanic bonito**]

skirlie *(UK)* A Scottish accompaniment to grouse consisting of finely chopped onion fried slowly until coloured in butter or pork dripping, then enough medium oatmeal added to absorb the fat, crisped and seasoned

skirret A hardy herbaceous perennial *Sium sisarum* growing to 1 m with small clusters of tiny fragrant flowers, narrow leaves and aromatic tuberous roots. The young shoots may be steamed or stir fried. The roots, which should be cooked in their skins to preserve the flavour, are steamed, boiled or pickled and are eaten in Germany with new potatoes. The hard inner core of the root is removed

skirt *(UK)* A fairly tough cut of beef from the extreme bottom of the belly of the animal and the diaphragm, divided into thick, thin and body skirt. Thick skirt is part of the inner muscle of the belly wall attached to the rump, whilst thin skirt and body skirt are part of the diaphragm. It must either be braised very slowly or cooked fast on a high heat and served rare [also called **thin flank**]

sköldpadda *(Sw)* Turtle

sköldpaddsoppa *(Sw)* Turtle soup

skordalia *see* skorthalia

skorpor *(Sw)* Rusks

skorthalia *(Gr)* Mayonnaise flavoured with raw garlic, ground almonds and lemon juice or vinegar, thickened with pounded bread and sometimes with the addition of chopped walnuts or pine nuts. Used as a general cold sauce or condiment [also called **skordalia**]

skull cap Preformed cooked pieces of puff pastry used to cover sweet or savoury dishes of food. The pastry is rolled to 3 mm, cut to the shape of the bowl, edges dampened and placed on bowls full of warm water and baked in the oven at 220°C for 12 minutes

skyr *(Ic)* **1** Curds **2** A soft cultured and very smooth cheese made from rennet-curdled skimmed milk similar to fromage frais or a strong-flavoured yoghurt

Skyros *(Gr)* A cheese from the island of the same name similar to Kefalotiri

sla *(Ho)* Salad, lettuce

sladkoye pyechenye iz gryetskikh orekhov po-uzbeksky *(Ru)* Uzbekistan walnut brittle

slagroom *(Ho)* Whipped cream

Slagsahne *(Au)* A Chantilly cream combined with whisked egg whites, served with cakes and pastries

slake, to To mix a powder with a small amount of water or other liquid to a creamy lump-free consistency

slaked lime *see* lime (calcium hydroxide)

släpärter *(Sw)* Peas in the pod

slapjack *(USA)* A large flat pancake

slatka *(Bk)* Preserved fruits from Serbia served

as an afternoon snack with strong coffee and cold water

slatur *(Ic)* **1** Butcher's meat **2** Sheep's pluck **3** A version of haggis

slätvar *(Sw)* Brill, the fish

slaughterhouse *see* abattoir

slaw *see* coleslaw

slice, to To cut into thin sheets

sliced beef *(USA)* *see* dried beef

slicing knife A knife with a long thin blade (30 cm by 2 to 3 cm) with a rounded end used for slicing, usually cooked food

slip *(Aus)* Baking tray

Slipcote *(UK)* A small soft cheese produced in Kent which is placed between cabbage leaves to ripen for 1 to 2 weeks. When ripe its skin becomes loose

slipper lobster A small lobster *Scyllarus arctus* or *Scyllarides squammosis* with a flat slipper-shaped tail which is the part used. The Mediterranean variety *S. arctus* (to 13 cm) has little meat and is usually used in soups. The tail of the larger variety *S. squammosis* which is fished off the coast of Queensland in Australia, is eaten as a dish in its own right [also called **flat lobster**]

sliver A thin narrow strip of a foodstuff, e.g. of almonds, cheese and the like

sloe The small black sour fruit of the blackthorn bush *Prunus spinosa* about 1 cm in dia. and with a central stone. May be used in jam, as a souring agent or to make sloe gin

sloke *see* laver

slokum *see* laver

sloppy joe *(USA)* A split bread bun filled with a thinnish mixture of seasoned and cooked minced beef mixed with tomato sauce

slotted spoon A large long-handled spoon with holes in the bowl end used for removing large solids from a liquid

slottsstek *(Sw)* Roast sirloin of beef generally served with braised onions, roast potatoes and jus rôti, More traditionally a boned sirloin was seasoned, browned then braised in a covered dish with stock, onion, anchovy, bay, white vinegar, sugar and peppercorns. Served with a jus lié thickened with beurre manié and finished with cream, accompanied with boiled potatoes, cucumber salad and red currant or cranberry jelly

slouk *see* laver

slow cook, to To cook at a low temperature in the range 80 to 95°C

slow cooker A thermostatically controlled electrically heated deep metal container into which a lidded earthenware or glass, deep and well fitting pot is placed. Used for slow cooking food at or below simmering temperature for long periods of time

Slow Food Society *(It)* The Arcigola slow food society of Cuneo, Italy was formed in 1986 to promote slow eating and has since flourished. Their logo is a snail shape and appears in restaurant guides, the most well known of which is the Osteria d'Italia, a guide to Italy's family run restaurants

slumgullion *(USA)* *coll.* Disgusting food

slump *(USA)* A dessert made of stewed fruit topped with a dumpling-like pastry and served with cream

sly cake *see* Cornish sly cake

små köttbullar *(Sw)* Small meat balls

småbröd *(Sw)* Small cakes and biscuits

småkage *(De)* Biscuits

småkakor *(Sw)* Biscuit

småländsk ostkaka *(Sw)* A type of cheesecake from Småland

small calorie The scientific calorie written with a lower case c, equal to the one thousandth part of the calorie (kilocalorie) used in nutrition; *see also* calorie

small eats *(UK)* *coll.* *(navy)* Savouries, canapés, etc. served with drinks

small thread stage *see* sugar cooking

smallage *see* wild celery

Smältost *(Sw)* A mild runny cooking cheese

småsill *(Sw)* Pilchards

smatana *see* smetana

småvarmt *(Sw)* Hot dishes served at the smörgåsbord, traditionally filled omelette, sautéed kidneys, chipolata sausages or items in a thick cream sauce

smedovska lukanka *(Bu)* A smoked sausage made with two thirds pork and one third beef, chopped, mixed with sugar, seasoning and carraway seed and packed into ox middles

smell *see* odour

smelt Various small round oily silver coloured seawater fish *Osmerus* spp. with a flavour similar to trout. Gutted by squeezing out the entrails through an incision made below the gills and deep fried or baked

smeriglio *(It)* Porbeagle shark

smetana A soured low-fat cream (12% butterfat) originating in Russia and Eastern Europe, now made in the west from a mixture of skimmed milk and single cream. The original Russian version was made by mixing sweet double cream and sour cream and had a much higher fat content than nowadays [also called **smatana, smitane, smytana**]

Smilax officinalis *Bot.* Sarsaparilla

sminuzzato *(It)* Brawn

smitaine sauce *see* sauce smitane

smitane *see* smetana

smitane, sauce *(En & Fr) fem.* Chopped onions, sweated in butter, white wine added and reduced, sour cream added and reduced, strained, seasoned and finished with lemon juice [also called **smitaine sauce**]

Smith tangerine *see* honey tangerine

Smithfield ham *(USA)* Ham from pigs traditionally fattened in the woods on hickory nuts, beechnuts and acorns, finished before slaughter on peanuts, obtained by rooting in the fields after the peanut harvest, followed by maize. The hams are dry salt cured, spiced and smoked. From the town of the same name [also called **Virginia ham**]

smoke, to To expose food, usually hung on racks, to the dense smoke from slowly smouldering sawdust or wood chips. Usually fish, meat and occasionally cheese are smoked but most of the latter so described is flavoured with a synthetic mix of chemicals which mimic the real thing. Meat and fish will be partially cooked and dried which helps to preserve them and the flavour will be improved; *see also* to cold smoke, and to hot smoke

smoke roast, to *(USA)* To smoke meat such as spare ribs or steaks at a temperature between 97 and 107°C without prior salting or cold smoking. Such meat requires cooking

smoked bacon Bacon which is smoked after curing

smoked beef *(USA) see* dried beef

smoked cheese *see* Raucherkäse

smoked cod Brined cod fillets, naturally smoked to a pale straw colour or more often dyed a deep yellow and then smoked or sprayed with a smoke flavour

smoked cod's roe Salted and smoked cod roes usually separated from the tough enclosing membrane and used for savouries, canapés and hors d'oeuvres

smoked eel Lightly brined eel, smoked then cut in slices. Served in the same manner as smoked salmon and equally regarded as a delicacy

smoked egg Shelled hard boiled eggs marinated then smoked and served as a hors d'oeuvre

smoked fillets *see* golden fillets

smoked haddock Unskinned haddock fillets or small whole haddock, brined then smoked as cod. Sometimes dyed. Finnan haddock is the superior version

smoked haddock creams *(UK)* A processed mixture of smoked haddock, egg and egg yolk, curd cheese or yoghurt with seasoning and Tabasco sauce, filled into ramekins, cooked in a bain-marie, cooled and demoulded

smoked mackerel A popular prepared fish usually filleted and cold or hot smoked. Often coated with crushed peppercorns. Eaten cold as purchased or hot

smoked mussels Cooked mussels, brined (250 g salt per litre) for 5 minutes, oiled, smoked at 82°C for 30 minutes packed in jars with oil and retorted at 121°C for about 15 minutes

smoked oysters Oysters removed from the shell, steamed to set them, brined, smoked and generally canned or packed in oil. Used for savouries, canapés or as an appetizer

smoked salmon Fillets of salmon still on the skin, cold smoked for a long period of time and considered by some to be a delicacy. Usually cut very thin on the slant and served with brown bread and butter and garnished with lemon slices or wedges

smoked salmon butter A compound butter made from smoked salmon pounded with 2.5 times its weight in butter and sieved

smoked sprats Lightly brined and smoked sprats which keep their silvery appearance. Eaten without further cooking as a savoury or as a hors d'oeuvre. Sometimes canned in oil

smokehouse A well sealed chamber in which food is hung on racks for smoking with provision for the generation of smoke from smouldering wood, for temperature control and for the removal of smoke. Such a chamber may range in size from a small box up to a large room

smokie *(UK)* Hot smoked, gutted and deheaded haddock or whiting tied together in pairs by the tails; *see also* Arbroath smokie

smolt A 2 to 3 year old salmon about 12 to 14 cm long which is leaving the river where it hatched for the open sea. Not caught or eaten at this stage

smooth hound A large, long and thin, edible sea fish *Mustelus mustelus* with a brown skin, very prominent fins and a fairly well-flavoured flesh

smooth venus clam *see* venus shell clam

smör *(Sw)* Butter

smør *(De & No)* Butter

smørbrød *(No)* Open sandwiches similar to smörrebröd

smörgås *(Sw)* Sandwich

smörgåsbord *(Sw)* A buffet meal of various hot and cold fish, meat and egg dishes with vegetables, salads, etc., always starting with herring, bread and butter and boiled potatoes followed by a succession of more or less elaborately presented foods and finally cheese and coffee, all eaten separately in small portions

smørrebrød *(De)* Open sandwiches consisting of a rectangular slice of buttered bread topped with cold savoury items, meats, fish, salads, etc. usually eaten with a knife and fork at informal or snack meals [also called **Danish open sandwich**]

smother, to *(USA)* To braise in a covered pot with gravy or sauce

smothered beef *(USA) see* étouffe of beef

smultringer *(No)* Doughnuts

smultron *(Sw)* Wild strawberry

Smyrnium olusatrum *Bot.* Alexanders

smytana *see* smetana

snack A small amount of food, often savoury, usually eaten between meals, but sometimes as a replacement for a meal

snail Various edible gastropod molluscs *Helix* spp. found in the wild on land and in both fresh and seawater and sometimes cultivated. Prepared by starving for at least 24 hours, cleaning and boiling or frying for 5 minutes. The flesh is then removed from the shells, degutted and cooked as appropriate. Sometimes returned to the shell for service

snail butter Butter mixed with finely chopped shallots, garlic paste, chopped parsley and seasoning. Put in an empty snail shell before inserting the cooked snail

snake bean *see* long bean

snake fruit *(Id & Ma)* The small fruit of a low palm with little or no trunk *Salacea edulis.* The fruit is triangular with a coarse red peel like snakeskin and the flesh is firm and crunchy with a slightly sweet flavour [also called **snakeskin fruit**]

snake gourd The narrow cylindrical fruit of an annual climber from Africa, Asia, Australia, and India *Trichosanthes anguina* and *T. cucumerina* which can grow to 2 m long in a spiral shape. Picked when immature and treated like a courgette save that the central core of seeds should be discarded and the skin rubbed with salt to remove the down

snake palm plant A plant *Amorphophallus konjac* with a glutinous starchy tuber used to make shiritaki noodles and black bean curd [also called **devil's tongue, arum root**]

snakelocks *see* oplet, the sea anemone

snakeskin fruit *see* snake fruit

snap *(UK) coll.* Food taken to work in a lunchbox, esp. by the once numerous coal miners

snap, to To break a brittle foodstuff with a clean break

snap bean *(USA) see* French bean

snapdoodle *(USA)* A New England chocolate-coated cake

snapper An inshore fish *Chrysophrys auratus* of the red snapper type found in New Zealand and the Arabian gulf

sneeuwballen *(Ho)* A cream puff pastry

snickerdoodle *(USA)* A New England sweet biscuit flavoured with cinnamon and possibly containing dried vine fruits and nuts

snijbonen *(Ho)* Haricot or kidney beans

snip, to To cut into small pieces or cut a small portion off something with scissors

snipe A game bird *Gallinago gallinago* with a long bill and striped plumage weighing about 110 g and requiring two per person. Cooked as plover by roasting at 190°C for 15 to 20 minutes. Shooting season in the UK is 12th August to the 31st of January. Young ones can be eaten fresh but skinned if they smell fishy, older ones can be hung for 3 to 4 days

Snir *(ME)* A semi-soft cow's milk cheese from Israel similar to Bel Paese

snitbønner *(De)* French beans

snoek 1 A seawater fish *Thyristes atun* related to the mackerel, tuna and swordfish found in the southern hemisphere warm waters only. It may weigh up to 8 kg and be up to 1.2 m long and has a delicious flesh [also called **Australian barracuda, sierra, barracouta) 2** *(Ho)* Pike

snoekbaars *(Ho)* Pike-perch

snook *see* robalo

snöripa *(Sw)* Ptarmigan

snow A mixture of sweetened puréed fruit and egg white whisked to a peak. Used as a dessert either as a topping or served on its own with biscuits or sponge fingers

snow crab *(Cn)* A cold water crab *Chionoecetes opilio* from the coast of Canada, with long thin claws which contain a fine tasting meat

snow eggs *(USA)* Iles flottantes

snow fungus *see* white fungus

snow pea *see* mangetout

snow pear *see* Asian pear

so' o-yosopy *(SA)* *see* sopa de carne

soak, to To immerse a foodstuff in water either to rehydrate it or to dissolve out excessive salt used in its preservation, or undesireable constituents e.g. alkaloids, prussic acid, etc. so as to make it suitable for cooking

Soay lamb *(UK)* Lambs from sheep raised on the Scottish islands with an excellent flavour

soba *(Ja)* A thin brown noodle with a square cross section made from buckwheat flour or a mixture of buckwheat and wheat flour. Popular in Tokyo

Sobado *see* Armada

sobbollire *(It)* To simmer

sobrasada *(Sp)* Chorizo sausage mix but minced much finer and with extra red peppers

sobrasada mallorquina *(Sp)* A milder version of sobresada from Majorca with the filling ground to a paste-like consistency

sobremesa *(Po)* Dessert

sobretto al frutto *(It)* Fruit sherbert

socker *(Sw)* Sugar

sockerkaka *(Sw)* Sponge cake

sockeye salmon One of the Pacific salmon *Oncorhynchus nerka* caught off the north west coast of North America weighing up to 2.5 kg. The deep red flesh is oily with small flakes. Cooked in any way but usually available in Europe as canned red salmon [also called **red salmon**]

sock mai jai *(Ch)* Miniature corn

socle A bed of rice, vegetables or similar on which the main component of a dish is raised above a flat for presentation to the customer, alternatively a base or ornamental stand on which a food item is raised above the rest esp. in buffet presentation

sød *(De)* Sweet

sød frugtsuppe *(De)* A sweet fruit soup

soda **1** A general name for alkaline sodium compounds such as caustic soda, bicarbonate of soda, washing soda and soda ash. They are not interchangeable **2** *(USA)* Bicarbonate of soda

soda ash The dry powdered anhydrous form of sodium carbonate used for cleaning floors and absorbing dangerous spilt, esp. acid, liquids

soda bread *(Ir)* A bread made with soured milk or buttermilk and using bicarbonate of soda instead of yeast as the raising agent. It may be made with white or brown flour, if brown, cream of tartar is also added [also called **Irish soda bread**]

soda cake *(UK)* A light spicy fruit cake from Somerset raised with bicarbonate of soda and an acid, usually sour milk (lactic acid) or vinegar [also called **Somerset soda cake**]

soda water *see* carbonated water

sode *(It)* Hard boiled, of eggs

sodium 5'-ribonucleotide *see* (E)627

sodium acid pyrophosphate A compound used in 2% water solution in the USA to treat potato chips before deep frying to prevent blackening

sodium aluminium phosphate *see* (E)541

sodium bicarbonate *see* bicarbonate of soda and (E)500

sodium carbonate A mild alkali used for cleaning purposes; *see also* (E)500 [also called **washing soda, soda ash**]

sodium carboxymethyl cellulose E466, the sodium salt of a derivative of cellulose used as a thickener and bulking agent

sodium caseinate A food additive made from milk protein used to maintain colour in sausages and other processed meats

sodium chloride The common salt used as a seasoning and preservative

sodium diphenyl-2yl-oxide E232, a synthetic derivative of diphenyl (E230) used in the same way as a fungicide

sodium ferrocyanide *see* (E)535

sodium formate E237, the sodium salt of formic acid used in the same way as the acid

sodium gluconate *see* (E)576

sodium glutamate *see* monosodium glutamate

sodium guanylate *see* (E)627

sodium heptonate A sequestering agent used in edible oils

sodium hydrogen diacetate E262, a sodium salt of acetic acid used as a preservative and firming agent

sodium hydrogen L-glutamate *see* (E)621

sodium hydroxide (E)524, the strongest alkali available for domestic or general industrial use. It should be handled with extreme care with all bare skin and eyes protected. Used for dissolving fats from drains, etc. by converting them to soaps and for removing the bitterness from unripe olives [also called **caustic soda**]

sodium inosinate *see* (E)631

sodium lactate *see* E325

sodium nitrate E251, the sodium salt of nitric acid used for curing and preserving meat

sodium nitrite E250, the sodium salt of nitrous acid which is used in curing salts to preserve meat and maintain a pink colour by its reaction with haemoglobin. Banned in some countries because of fears that it might induce stomach cancers

sodium orthophenylphenate *see* E232

sodium phosphate An emulsifier used to assist in the incorporation of water into various processed foods such as sausage, luncheon meats, etc.

sodium polyphosphate A chemical used to increase the water uptake of poultry and of other meats and bacon so as to increase their weight. All of this water is lost on cooking and can cause problems e.g. when frying bacon.

sodium saccharin A sodium salt of saccharin used in the same way as saccharin

sodium sesquicarbonate *see* (E)501

sodium stearoyl-2-lactate E481, the sodium salt of a stearic acid ester with the lactate of lactic acid used to stabilize doughs and emulsions and to improve the mixing properties of flour and the whipping and baking properties of dried egg white

sodium sulphate *see* (E)514

soep *(Ho)* Soup

soezen *(Ho)* A large cream puff

soffiato *(It)* Soufflé

soffrito *see* sofrito

soffrito calabrese *(It)* Lamb's offal cooked to a paste with tomatoes, herbs and seasoning and spread on bread [also called **suffritu**]

sofrito 1 *(It & Sp)* A condiment and flavouring made by slowly cooking until tender a mixture of chopped onions, garlic, green sweet peppers, ham, salt pork, tomatoes, herbs and seasoning. Also popular in the Caribbean, Central and South America [also called **soffrito**] **2** Floured and seasoned stewing steak, browned in oil then simmered in equal parts of vinegar and water with garlic, herbs and tomato purée until tender, seasoned and finished with chopped parsley

soft ball stage *see* sugar cooking

soft boil, to To boil an egg in the shell for roughly 3 to 4 minutes so that the white is just set but the yolk remains runny

soft cheese A cheese made with the retention of much of the whey so it has a high water content. The limits of water content are 80% for low fat (2 to 10% butterfat), 70% for medium fat (10 to 20% butterfat) and 60% for full fat (greater than 20% butterfat) soft cheeses

soft corn *see* squaw corn

soft dough *(USA)* A thick flour water mixture suitable for biscuits and bread, roughly 1.5 parts of flour per part of water. The proportions depend on the flour

soft drop batter *(USA)* A soft flour water mixture suitable for cakes and muffins with roughly equal parts of flour and water. The proportions depend on the flour

soft flour Flour made from soft wheat consisting of unbroken starch granules, mostly used for cakes, biscuits and general thickening and coating. Much cheaper than strong flour

soft fruit Summer fruits such as berries and currants which are easily damaged

soft red winter wheat flour *(USA)* A good low gluten pastry flour

soft roe The sperm of male fish which is soft and creamy and forms a long packet within the abdominal cavity. Usually floured and fried, steamed or poached [also called **milt**]

soft roe butter Beurre de laitance (Fr)

soft-shell clam A large, grey to fawn coloured clam *Mya arenaria* up to 15 cm dia. with a thin brittle shell. They are often gritty and need thorough cleaning. Found throughout the Atlantic ocean [also called **long neck clam, steamer clam**]

soft-shelled crab A crab eaten just after it has shed the hard shell it has grown out of before its new shell has had time to harden. Usually applied to the American blue crab

soft sugar *see* light brown sugar

soft wheat A wheat in which the starch granules are loosely bound with voids between. This is thought to be caused by the protein triabolin which is only found in soft wheats. The endosperm is brittle and when ground tends to give intact granules since the cracks pass around them. Not necessarily, but often with a low protein content

soften, to 1 To allow hard fats or frozen foods to become soft by raising their temperature **2** To sweat chopped vegetables in a little oil or fat to make them soft

so fun *(Ch)* Rice vermicelli

soggy A description of baked goods which are damp and heavy in the centre due to excess of moisture, lack of raising agent or incorrect baking temperature

sogi giri *(Ja)* A diagonal cut of long thin vegetables such as leeks, carrots, etc.

sogliola *(It)* Dover sole

sogliola limanda *(It)* Lemon sole

soia *(It)* Soya

soissonaise, à la *(Fr)* Garnished with or including white cooked haricot beans

soissonaise, purée *(Fr) fem.* As purée St Germain but with soaked haricot beans substituted for the peas [also called **haricot bean soup**]

soja *(Sp & Fr) masc.* Soya

Sojabohne *(Ge)* Soya bean

sokeri *(Fi)* Sugar

Solanum x Burbankii *Bot.* Wonderberry

Solanum melongena *Bot.* Aubergine

Solanum torvum *Bot.* Pea aubergine

Solanum tuberosum *Bot.* Potato

sole *(En & Fr) fem.* The name given to several types of flatfish, see in particular Dover sole, lemon sole and witch or Torbay sole. In French also flounder

sole Albert Whole soles skinned and cleaned, one side dipped in melted butter and stale white breadcrumbs, put crumb side up in a buttered baking tin with the base covered with 3 parts dry vermouth to 1 part water, seasoned and sprinkled with chopped shallots and parsley and baked in a hot oven so that the bottom is steamed and the top browned. The fish is removed carefully and served with the strained and reduced cooking liquor with butter *(monté au beurre)*

sole Bercy *(En & Fr) fem. see* fish Bercy

sole bonne femme *(En & Fr) fem. see* fish bonne femme

sole Colbert *(En & Fr) fem.* Whole sole skinned, gutted, eyes and gills removed, fins trimmed, fillets on one side cut from centre to within 1 cm of the edge and folded back, back bone broken in 3 places, the whole panéed and deep fried with fillets open, bone removed exposing white flesh in the centre which is piped with parsley butter. The whole served with lemon wedges or pigtails

sole dieppoise *(Fr) fem.* Sole poached in white wine and mussel liquor, garnished à la dieppoise and napped with sauce vin blanc made with the poaching liquor

sole Dugléré *(En & Fr) fem. see* fish Dugléré

sole limande *(Fr) fem.* Lemon sole

sole normande *(Fr) fem.* Poached sole coated with a truffle-scented cream sauce and garnished with oysters, mussels and other seafood

sole Walewska *(En & Fr) fem. see* fish Walewska

soles in coffins *(UK)* Baked potatoes with a lid cut off, scooped out, filled with poached paupiettes of sole napped with a suitable sauce, lids replaced and the coffins baked at 200°C for 10 minutes

Solferino, crème *(Fr) fem.* Equal parts of crème de tomates and purée parmentier

solferino cutter A sharp edged scoop shaped implement for cutting out small pea shaped balls of e.g. carrot, turnip, cucumber

Solferino, sauce *(En & Fr) fem.* The juice from very ripe tomatoes reduced, mixed with meat glaze, lemon juice and a little cayenne pepper, finished with maître d'hôtel butter, pounded shallots and chopped tarragon

sôlha *(Po)* Plaice

solidified cooking oil Decolorized and deodorized vegetable oil, hardened by hydrogenation and used for frying and baking

sollo *(Sp)* Pike

solöga *(Sw)* Lit. eye of the sun, consisting of concentric rings starting from the centre of chopped anchovies, chopped onions, capers and chopped pickled beetroot. A raw egg yolk is placed in the centre just before serving and the ingredients are mixed at the table and either fried in butter and spread on toast or spread on buttered bread and grilled

solomillo *(Sp)* **1** Loin of pork **2** Sirloin

solomillo a la sevillana *(Sp)* Loin of pork with boiled potatoes, artichoke hearts, stuffed olives and tomato sauce

solomon gundy *(Cn)* Chopped salt herrings and onions pickled in spiced vinegar with sugar for several days and served as an appetizer. From Nova Scotia

soluble fibre Various non-metabolizeable soluble polysaccharides such as pectin, gums and related compounds found in vegetable matter, seeds, nuts, grains, etc. said to reduce blood cholesterol and low density lipoprotein levels and to be essential for good health

sølvkake *(No)* A light coconut and lemon-flavoured cake

solyanka *(Ru)* A thick fish soup or thin stew made with salmon, chopped pickled cucumbers, olives, capers, onions, etc., butter and seasoning

som *(Th)* Orange

somen *(Ja)* A thin white noodle resembling vermicelli, made from wheat flour

Somerset apple cake *(UK) see* apple sauce cake

Somerset cider Cheddar *(UK)* A mild Cheddar cheese flavoured with cider

Somerset fish casserole *(UK)* Deboned and skinned white fish cut in chunks, passed through seasoned flour, briefly fried with previously sweated chopped onion and mixed with a sauce made from pan residues, butter, flour, cider, anchovy essence, lemon juice and seasoning then baked at 180°C for 20 minutes. Garnished with apple rings fried in butter and chopped parsley

Somerset soda cake *(UK) see* soda cake

som khay *(La)* A delicate coloured dip made from the roe of the pa boeuk [also called **Laotian caviar**]

sommacco *(It)* Sumac

sommargryta med korv *(Sw)* A summer casserole of fresh spring vegetables simmered with good quality pork sausages

sommelier *(Fr) masc.* Wine waiter

som mu *(La)* A pungent flavouring ingredient made from powdered pork and fermented rice

som-o *(Th)* Pummelo

som pa *(La)* A pungent flavouring ingredient made from pounded fish and fermented rice

som saa *(Th)* Citron

son *(Fr) masc.* Bran

soncaya A particularly large custard apple *Anona purpurea* from Mexico and Central America

sone ka warq *(In)* Gold leaf used for decorating food

song tse *(Ch)* Mulberry

song zi huang yu *(Ch)* Yellow croaker fish garnished with pine nuts

Sonnenbarsch *(Ge)* Butterfish (3)

Sonnenblume *(Ge)* Sunflower

sonth *(In) see* soondth

soo hoon *(Ma)* Cellophane noodles

soojo *(In)* Semolina

sookha dhania *(In)* Coriander seeds

soondth *(In)* Dried powdered ginger root [also called **sonth**]

soonf *(In)* Fennel seed

soon geung *(Ch)* Pickled ginger

soong hwa dan *(Ch)* Chinese preserved eggs

sop Hard bread soaked in a hot liquid such as milk or soup

sopa 1 *(Po & Sp)* Soup **2** *(Sp)* A breakfast dish of hot coffee and milk poured over toasted bread from the previous day

sopa de aguacate *(Me)* Soup made from defatted seasoned chicken stock with mashed avocado and chopped parsley and coriander leaf. Served lukewarm or chilled [also called **avocado soup**]

sopa de almejas *(SA)* A clam and white fish soup with vegetables (from Colombia)

sopa de batata e agrião *(Po)* Potato and watercress soup

sopa blanca *(Sp)* A cold soup from Andalusia made from equal parts of blanched and skinned almonds and cooked broad beans processed with garlic and oil and let down with lemon juice and water, seasoned, chilled and served over cubes of bread

sopa burgalesa *(Sp)* Lamb and crayfish soup

sopa coada *(It)* A bread-thickened soup made from roast pigeon flesh

sopa cuarto de hora *(Sp)* Quick soup made by adding leftovers to stock

sopa de camarão e mexhilhao *(Po)* A soup of mussels and shrimps

sopa de carne *(SA)* A beef and vegetable soup with rice or vermicelli (from Paraguay). Served with grated Parmesan cheese [also called **so' o-yosopy**]

sopa de feijão *(Po)* Bean soup

sopa de legumbres *(Sp)* Vegetable soup

sopa a la mallorquina *(Sp)* A fish soup with tomatoes and onions

sopa de moni *(SA)* A peanut and potato soup finished with cream (from Ecuador)

sopa de pescado *(Sp)* Fish soup

sopa seca *(Po)* Shredded left-over meat layered in a large oven-proof pot with sliced boiled potatoes and carrots, bread and chopped mint, covered with boiling stock and dried in a hot oven. Lit. dry soup

sopaipilla *(M)* A flat bread which is fried and puffs up

sopari *(In)* Betel nut

sope *(Me) see* garnacha

sopp *(No)* Mushroom [also called **sjampinjong**]

soppa *(Sw)* Soup

soppressa *(It)* A Veronese salami made from pork and beef

soppressa del pasubio *(It)* A firm textured pork sausage with potatoes and chestnuts

soppressate *(It)* A large sausage from the southwest, oval in cross-section, well seasoned and flavoured with ginger, sometimes preserved in olive oil

soprafino *(It) see* superfine olive oil

sopressa *(It) see* coppa

sorb *see* rowanberry

sorb apple A close relative *Sorbus domestica* of the rowanberry, native to southern Europe. It is cultivated for the small green apple- or pear-shaped fruit which may be eaten as a fruit or used to make a type of cider

Sorbais (Maroilles cheese) *(Fr) see* Maroilles

sorbates Salts of sorbic acid used as permitted food preservatives, the sodium salt is E201, the potassium E202 and calcium sorbate is E203

sorbet A soft, water ice rather like a soft snow made by freezing a sweetened fruit juice or liqueur-flavoured light syrup mixed with whipped egg white, whisking vigorously at intervals to inhibit ice crystal formation and to incorporate air. Used as a dessert.

sorbet colonel *(In)* An Anglo-Indian dessert of lemon sorbet with a sprig of mint floating in a coupe of spirituous liquor, e.g. vodka

sorbetto *(It)* Sorbet

sorbic acid A permitted preservative, E200, for use in baked and fruit products. May be obtained from berries of the mountain ash but is now synthesized and is a mould and yeast inhibitor

sorbier des oiseaux *(Fr) masc.* Rowanberry

sorbitol E420(i), a compound found in many fruits and berries but now synthesized from glucose for use as a humectant and as a sweetening agent for diabetics. Available as a water solution E420(ii)

Sorbus americana *Bot.* Mountain ash (2)

Sorbus aucuparia *Bot.* Rowan tree (rowanberries)

Sorbus domestica *Bot.* Sorb apple

Sorbus scopulina *Bot.* Mountain ash (2)

sorgho *(Fr) masc.* Sorghum

sorghum A very important plant *Sorghum vulgare* which grows in semi-arid tropical and sub-tropical regions. It has the general appearance of the maize plant with thinner leaves and a top terminal spike of small seeds. Some varieties produce white seeds which are preferred for eating, the red seeded type is more bitter and used for brewing beer. There is also a variety whose stems are crushed like sugar cane to produce a syrup used for sweetening, mainly in the USA. Sorghum grain is used for human consumption where grown and is only traded for compounding animal feeds; *see also* sweet sorghum, great millet and Kaffir corn [also called **Guinea corn** (WA)]

sorghum flour Ground sorghum or milo maize occasionally used to thicken soups

sorghum syrup The juice of the sweet sorghum evaporated to produce a slightly acid molasses-like syrup

Sorghum vulgare *Bot.* Sorghum, great millet

sorpresine *(It)* Tiny pasta shapes used in soups

sorrel A hardy perennial plant *Rumex acetosa* with pointed oval, sour leaves used in salads, soups, etc., cooked with fish or used as a spinach-like vegetable. The variety grown in France is less acid than that which grows wild in the UK. The leaves may be blanched before final cooking to reduce the acidity [also called **broad leaf sorrel, sourgrass**]

sorsa *(Fi)* Wild duck

sorsapaisti *(Fi)* Roast wild duck

sorvete *(Po)* Ice cream

sosaties *(Saf)* Mutton kebabs

sose *(Fi)* Purée, sauce, stewed and mashed, mash

sosiska *(Ru)* Sausage, usually pork and smoked. May be cooked or eaten as a snack

sospiri *(It)* Small custards with a cheese and egg filling

Sosse *(Ge)* Sauce, gravy

Sosse von Soja *(Ge)* Soya sauce

søt *(No)* Sweet

söt, sött *(Sw)* Sweet

sot-l'y-laisse *(Fr) masc.* Oyster (2), part of chicken

sotánghon *(Ph)* Cellophane noodles

sotong *(Ma)* Squid

sotong karang *(Ma)* Cuttlefish

søtsuppe *(No)* A sweet fruit soup

sottaceti *(It)* Pickles, pickled vegetables

sottaceto *(It)* Pickled

sotto *(It)* Under, as in sottaceto, under vinegar

søtunge *(De)* Sole, the fish

Soubise, sauce *(En & Fr) fem.* An onion sauce boiled with more onion to extract the onion flavour or a Béchamel with a large quantity of onion purée added, passed through a chinois, seasoned and flavoured with nutmeg. Used for roast meats

souchet *(Fr) masc.* A type of wild duck

souchet, sauce *(Fr) fem.* The poaching liquor from fish, reduced, mixed with sauce aux vin blanc, consistency corrected if necessary with beurre manié and garnished with julienned carrot, leek and celery which has been sweated in butter and drained

souci *(Fr) masc.* Marigold

soudzoukakia *(ME & Gr)* A variety of frying sausage made from seasoned and minced pork or veal, breadcrumbs and onions, flavoured with garlic, salt, parsley and ground cumin and bound with egg

soufflé *(En & Fr) masc.* An air-raised fluffy sweet or savoury baked dish made from a flavoured starch-based mixture (a thick white panada or crème patissière) into which stiffly beaten egg whites are folded, this poured into a buttered and floured soufflé dish and baked for about 25 minutes at 200°C. The soufflé should rise well above the rim of the dish and be served immediately; *see also* cold soufflé.

soufflé dish A straight sided oven proof dish in which soufflés are baked

soufflé omelette Whisked sweetened or seasoned egg whites, folded into slightly stirred egg yolks, a little water added, rewhisked then cooked as an omelette, often with a sweet filling

soulie *(Ir)* Sugar dissolved in hot vinegar used as a salad dressing

Soumaintrain *(Fr)* A strong-flavoured surface-ripened cows' milk cheese from Burgundy cast in the form of a disc. The rind is reddish brown and the paste has a slightly spicy flavour

so-un *(Id)* Cellophane noodles

soup A flavoured liquid based on meat and/or vegetable extracts in water, milk or occasionally water only, with added ingredients. Derived from the old English 'sop' a term applied to hard bread dipped into water or wine to make it palatable. There are 7 classical types of soup: consommé, potage, broth, purée, cream, velouté and bisque plus a few specials, often cold, based on fruit or tomato juice, wine and the like. See under individual names and basic soup

soup herbs The principal herbs used in soup are basil, bay, borage, caraway, chervil, chives, dill, juniper, lemon balm, lovage, marjoram, mint, parsley, rosemary, summer savory, sorrel, tarragon, thyme, wild celery and winter savory

soupa *(Gr)* Soup

soupa faki *(Gr)* A brown lentil soup made from blanched and refreshed lentils simmered in water (1:3 on dried lentils) for 45 minutes in a closed pan with finely sliced onions, garlic, celery and carrots, olive oil, tomato purée, tomato concassée and a faggot of herbs, the herbs removed and the soup finished with a little vinegar and chopped thyme or parsley

soupe *(Fr) fem.* Soup, tends to be more substantial than potage q.v.

soupe à l'ail *(Fr) fem.* Garlic soup

soupe germou *(Ca)* A vegetable soup with pumpkin, onions, celery and garlic thickened with a roux and served hot or cold

soupe aux légumes *(Fr) fem.* Vegetable soup

soupe à l'oignon *(Fr) fem. see* brown onion soup

soupe au pistou *(Fr) fem.* A country style vegetable soup accompanied with a pistou q.v. The soup is made from shredded white of leek and brunoise-cut carrots and turnips sweated in butter, mixed with cooked haricot beans, chopped green beans, broad beans, tomato concassé, tomato purée, macaroni, seasoning and vegetable stock simmered until all tender

soupe de poisson *(Fr) fem.* Saffron-flavoured and coloured fish soup, usually passed through a chinois to remove all large pieces of fish and bones. Served in the south of France with rouille, toast and grated cheese

soupe aux rognons *(Fr) fem.* Kidney soup

sour, to To add a souring agent such as acid or acid fruits to a foodstuff to give it a sour taste

sour cherry *see* acid cherry

sour cream Cream allowed to sour by a lactic fermentation either naturally or more usually with the addition of a starter culture which may be cottage cheese; *see also* acidulated cream

sour cream sauce A chicken or game velouté flavoured with vinegar, sweated chopped shallots, white wine and soured cream. A simple version of smitane sauce

sour finger carambola *see* belimbing (1)

sour milk Milk which has naturally curdled or been deliberately exposed to some acid-producing organism and thus curdled at around 30 to 35°C. UHT milk should not be soured

sour milk cheese 1 *see* Handkäse **2** The curd separated from naturally soured milk by straining through muslin. Commonly made in the home before refrigerators

sour orange *see* Seville orange

sour sop A type of custard apple from a tree *Anona muricata* which has large 15 to 23 cm long heart-shaped fruits with a green spiny skin. They are more acid-tasting than most custard apples and the texture of the juicy flesh is not as good. Suitable for drinks and desserts [also called **prickly custard apple**]

sourdough bread Bread which uses in place of yeast, dough from a previous batch which has been allowed to ferment with a little warm water and sugar overnight or longer. About 10% of a batch is reserved as starter for the next equal sized batch. Less will require a longer time to prove. The method is simple and the taste of the bread is thought by some to be superior

soured cream Made by adding a souring culture *Lactobacillus* spp. to homogenized single cream

sourgrass *see* sorrel

souring agent Any edible substance containing a reasonable concentration of acid such as vinegar, lemon juice, tamarind, etc.

sous-chef *(Fr) masc.* Under chef, assistant chef

sous-noix *(Fr) fem.* Undercushion of veal

souse, to To pickle in vinegar or brine esp. of herrings

soused herrings *(UK)* Herring fillets, rolled and secured with a sliver of wood, briefly cooked in a non-metallic covered dish with vinegar, water, onions, sugar, herbs, spices and seasoning and allowed to cool in the cooking liquor. Eaten cold

soused mackerel *(UK)* As soused herring but substituting small mackerel fillets for the herring

South American oyster An oyster *Crassostrea chilensis* found off the coasts of central and south America

southern bean *(USA)* Cow pea

southern blue whiting A deep water fish from New Zealand

southern bluefin tuna A common variety of tuna *Thunnus macoyii* from the southern hemisphere. The catch is worth half a billion pounds a year but is in danger of being fished out

southern cornpone *(USA) see* cornpone

southern fried chicken *(USA)* Jointed portions of chicken passed through seasoned flour and fried until crisp on the outside and just cooked through. Sometimes served with a Béchamel based sauce and mashed potatoes

southern lobster *see* spiny lobster

southern rock lobster A type of spiny lobster *Jasus novahollandiae* coloured yellow, orange and purple, found in Southern Australia and shipped to the USA as rock lobster [also called **crayfish (seawater)**]

southern stone crab *(USA)* A greyish crab *Menippe mercenaria* up to 12 cm across and with very large claws, one of which is bigger than the other. It lives in deep holes in mud or rock piles around the coast from Texas to the Carolinas. Only the claw meat is edible and often only the claws are traded

soutribbetjie *(Saf)* Ribs of lamb or mutton lightly brined, hung up to dry then cooked on a barbecue

Souvaroff, à la *(Fr)* The description of a casserole of poultry or game birds containing brandy, foie gras and truffles

souvlakia *(Gr)* Kebabs of lamb, veal or pork, cooked on a griddle or over a barbecue and sprinkled with lemon juice during cooking. Served with lemon wedges, onions and sliced tomatoes

sovs *(De)* Sauce

sow cabbage *see* jiu la choy

sowa *(In)* Dill

sowbelly *(USA)* Salted fat belly pork or streaky bacon

soy bean *see* soya bean

soy bean oil *see* soya oil

soy sauce *see* soya sauce

soya batter *(Ja)* A batter sometimes used for tempura made from water, egg and soya sauce (13:3:1) whisked together lightly then mixed with half its combined weight of flour to give a lumpy consistency

soya bean The seeds of an erect bushy plant *Glycine max* of the pea family, originating in China but now a major crop grown worldwide in frost-free, warm summer climates and containing about 20% oil and 35% protein on a dry weight basis. The pods contain between 2 and 4 seeds which may be green, brown, yellow or black. A common food in China and SEA and an important animal feed. Used as a source of bean sprouts, oil, flour, milk, protein curds, vegetable protein and meat analogues and sauce as well as being an important food pulse in its whole state. The beans, esp. the oil, are rich in compounds which behave like weak oestrogens and dilute the effect of the body's own oestrogens, thus reducing the risk of breast cancer, but evidence has been reported that raw soya flour fed to rats produced pancreatic cancer. See also, black soya bean, yellow soya bean and entries under bean curd

soya bean cheese *see* bean curd cheese

soya bean condiment *see* yellow bean sauce

soya bean curd *see* bean curd

soya bean flour Ground lightly-roasted soya beans containing a high percentage of fat from the beans

soya bean oil *see* soya oil

soya bean paste Ground fermented black soya beans mixed with flour, salt and water to give a thick paste used in Chinese cooking

soya bean sprouts Long (to 13 cm) yellow sprouts from soya beans, used as a vegetable

soya flour Flour produced from soya beans with a high fat and protein content, used together with wheat flour in baking and in ice creams and other manufactured foods

soya milk A substitute for cow's milk used by vegetarians and vegans made by boiling ground soya beans with water for long periods of time and filtering off the sediment

soya noodles *see* bean curd noodles

soya oil Oil extracted from soya beans used as a cooking oil, for salad dressings and for the manufacture of margarine containing only about 10% of saturated fat. Said to have protective effects against breast cancer [also called **soy bean oil**]

soya sauce A highly-flavoured liquid which is obtained by long fermentation of soya beans and various cereal grains. It is produced in 3 stages. In the first, polished rice is fermented with *Aspergillus oryzae*. This is then mashed with boiled soya beans and crushed roasted grains of wheat, incubated at 30°C for 3 days, diluted with brine then fermented with *Pediococcus halophilus* to reduce the pH. In the third stage the mixture is fermented slowly for between 1 and 3 years with *Saccharomyces rouxii*. Both light and dark varieties are produced with varying amounts of salt added [also called **soy sauce**]

soya vermicelli *see* bean curd noodles

Spaetzle *(Ge) see* Spätzle (1)

spag bol *(UK) coll.* Spaghetti Bolognese

spagetti *(Sw)* Spaghetti

Spaghetti *(Ge)* Spaghetti

spaghetti *(En & It)* Thin solid pasta made by extruding a pasta paste though circular holes about 2 to 3 mm in dia., either cooked immediately or cut into lengths (up to 40 cm) and dried for future use

spaghetti al aglio e olio The basic dish of spaghetti with chopped garlic and olive oil

spaghetti all'amatriciana *(It)* Spaghetti with a tomato sauce flavoured with chopped onions and pieces of salt pork or bacon and sprinkled with grated Pecorino cheese

spaghetti alla Bellini *(It)* Spaghetti with tomatoes, aubergines and ricotta cheese named after the composer

spaghetti bolognese *(It)* Spaghetti with a tomato and minced meat (Bolognaise) sauce

spaghetti al burro *(It)* Spaghetti with butter

spaghetti alla carbonara *(It)* Freshly cooked spaghetti tossed with crisply fried bacon chopped in small pieces, cream and sometimes beaten egg. Served with a sprinkling of grated Parmesan

spaghetti carrettiera *(It)* Spaghetti with tuna fish, mushrooms and tomato concassée or purée

spaghetti marinara *(It)* Spaghetti with clams, mussels, garlic, tomatoes and onions

spaghetti marrow *see* vegetable spaghetti

spaghetti alla napoletana *(It)* Spaghetti with mushrooms, tongue and tomatoes

spaghetti pesto *(It)* Spaghetti with a pesto sauce

spaghetti pommarola *(It)* Spaghetti with tomatoes, garlic and basil

spaghetti puttanesca *(It)* Spaghetti with capers, black olives, parsley, garlic and olive oil

spaghetti squash *see* vegetable spaghetti

spaghetti alle vongole *(It)* A classic spaghetti dish with a sauce made from chopped tomatoes and courgettes, sweated in olive oil, warty venus clams put in a minimum of cold water and heated until all the clams open, clams reserved, cooking liquor added to the vegetables and all reduced, the reserved clams added just before serving

spaghettini *(It)* a thin version of spaghetti

spalla *(It)* **1** Shoulder of lamb, veal, etc. **2** Cured and pressed shoulder of pork forced into a rectangular mould

spam *(USA)* A canned pork and ham meat loaf imported in large quantities into the UK during world War II (from Spiced Pork And Ham)

spanakopita *(Gr)* Cheese and spinach pie

spandauer *(De & Sw)* A cake made from squares of unproved Danish pastry each with a blob of apple purée, almond paste, conserve, crème pâtissière or similar in the centre, the four corners folded in towards the centre and pressed down, proved 30 minutes then baked at 230°C for 10 minutes and glazed with icing after cooking

Spanferkel *(Ge)* Sucking pig

spanische Pfeffer *(Ge)* Sweet pepper, capsicum

spanische Windtorte *(Ge)* A decorative meringue shell filled with cooked berry fruit and topped with whipped cream

Spanish *(UK) see* liquorice

Spanish bayonet *(USA) see* yucca (2)

Spanish black radish A round radish the size of an orange with a black skin, eaten raw or cooked

Spanish chestnut *see* chestnut

Spanish dagger *(USA) see* yucca (2)

Spanish garlic *see* giant garlic

Spanish lime *see* genip

Spanish ling A fish related to the ling found in the Western Mediterranean and the Bay of Biscay

Spanish omelette *see* tortilla

Spanish onion A large delicately-flavoured onion with a brown or red skin favoured by professional chefs for its ease of handling and suitability for frying. Grown in most countries. May be served raw

Spanish peanut A variety of peanut with an upright habit and 2 light brown seeds per pod

Spanish pepper *see* sweet pepper

Spanish rice *(USA)* A mixture of rice, chopped onion, chopped green sweet pepper and chopped tomatoes all cooked separately with herbs and seasoning. Served as an accompaniment to a meat course

Spanish sage A narrow-leaved sage *Salvia lavandulifolia* with a slightly balsamic flavour [also called **narrow leaf sage**]

Spanish salami A salami very similar to the Italian but with a milder flavour

Spanish sauce *see* espagnole sauce

spanner crab *(Aus)* A deep red-coloured frog-like crab *Ranina ranina* with claws that resemble spanners. It is found along the coasts of Queensland and northern New South Wales. The white meat is particularly fine

spanocchi *(It)* Large prawns

sparaglione *(It)* Small sea bream

spare rib of pork *(UK)* The cutlets, i.e. rib bones, vertebrae and longitudinal muscles equivalent to middle neck of lamb, which are hidden behind the shoulder. They may be roasted whole, chopped into cutlets for grilling or the meat used for pies, etc.

spare ribs *(UK)* A sheet of skinned and partially defatted lower part of the rib bones of pork cooked either as a whole sheet or in separate ribs, often marinated in a spicy sauce, and barbecued or fried. Served as a starter or appetizer. Not to be confused with spare rib

Spargel *(Ge)* Asparagus

Spargelfest *(Ge)* A country festival held annually in the spring for the sole purpose of eating white asparagus

Spargelkohl *(Ge)* Broccoli

sparl *(UK)* A broad sheep casing

sparling *(USA) see* smelt

sparris *(Sw)* Asparagus

sparrow grass *see* asparagus

spatchcock A chicken prepared by removing the wish bone, severing the leg sinews, cutting horizontally from below the rear point of the breast over the tops of the legs down to the wing joints without removing the breasts, bending the breasts towards the neck end and snapping the backbone so that the point of the breast extends forward, flattening and neatening the whole chicken. When placed skin side up it should resemble a toad. It is then seasoned, brushed with oil and cooked under the grill for approximately 15 minutes per side. So called because it can be cooked in a hurry, i.e. with dispatch [also called **chicken spatchcock, poulet à la crapaudine** (Fr)]

spatula 1 A flexible plastic or rubber scraper, rectangular in shape with a curve on one side, used for removing all the contents of bowls and pans which would otherwise stick to the sides. Some have a handle **2** A long thin flexible rectangular metal blade on a handle used for spreading and smoothing icing and fillings and for handling long fillets of fish

spatule *(Fr) fem.* Spatula

Spätze *(Ge)* A type of gnocchi made with seasoned flour and beaten eggs (2:1) made into a soft dough with water if necessary, teaspoonfuls poached in boiling salted water for 6 to 10 minutes, drained and served with molten butter and fried bread crumbs

spätzele *(Fr)* Short lengths of cooked pasta lightly browned in the oven or fried until golden. From the Alsace region of France [also called **spetzli**]

Spätzle *(Ge)* **1** A batter of flour, milk, eggs, salt and nutmeg made into noodles by pouring through one or more small holes into fiercely boiling water. Served tossed or fried in butter. From the southern and Alsace regions **2** A type of gnocchi made with seasoned flour and beaten eggs (2:1), made into a soft dough with water if necessary, teaspoonfuls poached in boiling salted water for 6 to 10 minutes, drained and served with molten butter and fried bread crumbs

spaul of beef *(UK)* A Scottish term for chuck and blade steak of beef

spear A young pointed cylindrical plant sprout, esp. of asparagus

spearmint A type of mint *Mentha spicata* with closely set toothed leaves and a clean spearmint flavour. Used for drinks and for flavouring and can be crystallized for decoration [also called **Moroccan spearmint**]

specialité *(Fr) fem.* Speciality e.g of the house, de la maison, etc.

specific gravity The ratio of the density of a substance to the density of water at the same temperature. It has no units and substances with a specific gravity greater than 1 will sink in water, whilst if less than 1 they will float. Sugar solutions and brines have a specific gravity greater than 1, oils and fats less than 1 [also called **SG, relative density**]

Speck *(Ge)* Bacon or the mildly cured and smoked pork fat used in traditional cooking

Speckblutwurst *(Ge)* A large diameter sausage made with seasoned and minced lean pork mixed with diced speck and pigs' blood

Speckknödel *(Au)* Bread and onion dumplings mixed with diced bacon and Speck from the Tyrol

Speckkuchen *(Ge)* A flat cake containing diced bacon

Specklinsen *(Ge)* Lentils cooked with a piece of bacon, a whole onion and root vegetables until soft, bacon and vegetables removed, strained and the lentils bound with a demi-glace sauce and sprinkled with crisply fried finely diced bacon

speculaas *(Ho)* Spiced biscuits made for the feast of St Nicholas and the rest of the Christmas season

spegepølse *(De)* A type of salami made with a mixture of various minced or chopped meats, seasoned. sugar and saltpetre added, packed into ox runners, dry salted then air dried and smoked

speilegg *(No)* Fried egg

Speiseeis *(Ge)* Ice cream

Speisekarte *(Ge)* Menu

Speisequark *(Ge) see* quark

spejleæg *(De)* Fried egg

spekemat *(No)* Cured meat

spekepølse *(No)* A mutton sausage, lightly smoked

spekeskinke *(No)* Cured ham eaten raw

Spekulatius *(Ge)* A sweet almond biscuit

spelt flour Flour made from an ancient variety of wheat which has a hard husk making it difficult to mill. It has a high gluten content which makes it very suitable for breadmaking

spenat *(Sw)* Spinach

spenatsoppa *(Sw)* Spinach soup based on roux-thickened beef stock finished with double cream

spencer *see* Ulster roll

spencer steak *see* Delmonico steak

sperm oil The oil rendered from the blubber of the sperm whale used as a releasing agent

spermaceti A low melting point wax obtained from the whale's buoyancy aid, used as a releasing agent

spettekaka *(Sw)* A tall cake baked on a spit

spetzli *(Fr) see* Spätzele

spezie *(It)* Spices

spezzatino *(It)* A light stew usually of tender meat, sautéed and finished with a sauce [also called **spezzato**]

spezzato *(It) see* spezzatino

spicchi, in *(It)* In segments or sections

spicchio *(It)* Clove, e.g. of garlic

spice One or other of various strongly-flavoured aromatic substances of vegetable origin obtained from tropical plants, particularly dried roots, seeds, buds, berries, fruits and bark

spice bread *see* Yorkshire spice bread

spice Parisienne *(USA) see* épices composés

spiced beef *(UK)* Salted and rolled silverside, soaked, simmered with onions, carrots and turnips for 4 hours, left to cool in the cooking liquor, drained, stuck with cloves, covered with dark muscovado sugar, mustard powder, ground cinnamon and lemon juice and baked at 180°C for one hour

spiced salt *(Ch)* A mixture of salt and anise pepper heated in a heavy frying pan until the anise pepper darkens, cooled and ground. Used in China as a dip for raw or deep fried vegetables, roast meat and poultry

spicken sill *(Sw)* Top quality plain salt herrings, soaked 12 hours, rinsed, dried, deboned and skinned. Two fillets formed into a whole herring and cut into 2 cm slices, garnished with fresh dill and accompanied by potatoes boiled in their skins, chives and soured cream

spicken sill med sur grädde *(Sw)* Pieces of pickled herring dressed with a mixture of soured cream and mayonnaise flavoured with chopped dill weed or chives

Spickgans *(Ge)* Smoked breast of goose

spider A shallow circle of steel mesh with the appearance of a spider's web about 20 cm in dia. with a metal handle used for collecting deep fried food, esp. fritters and any food in batter, from the oil or fat

spider crab A round-bodied leggy crustacean *Maia squinado* from Spain also found in the English channel. It has an oval shell to 20 cm across and is brown to reddish-orange with prickly spines. It has a fine flavour and is usually poached and served in its shell [also called **spiny crab**]

spiedino *(It)* Skewered or spitted, usually meat or prawns

spiedo, alla *(It)* Grilled over charcoal

Spiegelei *(Ge)* Fried egg

Spiessbraten *(Ge)* Spit roasted meat

spigola *(It)* Bass

spijskaart *(Ho)* Menu

spinace *(It)* Spinach

spinach A fast-growing annual plant *Spinacia oleracea* which grows as a loose cluster of leaves to a height of 15 to 20 cm and a spread of 15 cm. Used as a vegetable and puréed as a base for other food. Very popular in Italian cooking as a colouring for pasta and as a constituent of fillings

spinach beet A variety of beet *Beta vulgaris* Cicla Group grown for its leaves which resemble spinach. Grows well in northern climates

spinach mustard *see* komatsuna

spinaci *(It)* Spinach, the vegetable

spinaci alla milanese *(It)* Spinach finished with pine nuts and butter and served with scrambled eggs

spinaci in padella alla trasteverina *(It)* Spinach cooked in fat in a frying pan with raisins and pine nuts

spinaci alla piemontese *(It)* Spinach finished with garlic and anchovies

spinaci alla romana *(It)* Spinach finished with garlic, ham, pine nuts and raisins

Spinacia oleracea *Bot.* Spinach

spinacio *(It)* Spinach, the plant

spinarola *(It)* Rock salmon

Spinat *(Ge)* Spinach

spinat *(De & No)* Spinach

spinazie *(Ho)* Spinach

spineless amaranth *see* Chinese spinach

spinkrab *(Ho)* Spider crab

spinola *(It)* Sea bass

spiny bitter gourd A close relative *Momordica cochiniensis* of the bitter gourd but more rounded in shape with pointed warts on the skin

spiny cockle A large variety of cockle *Acanthocardia aculeata* to 10 cm dia.

spiny crab *see* spider crab

spiny dogfish *see* rock salmon

spiny lobster A seawater crustacean *Palinurus elephas* var. *vulgaris* resembling a lobster in taste and texture but without the large claws. They are reddish brown with yellow and white markings and may be up to 50 cm long, but taste better when smaller. They are found around the coasts of Britain, Spain, France and the Mediterranean, but now rare. Often called crayfish esp. in Australia and the USA. Cooked as lobster [also called **crawfish** (UK), **rock lobster** (USA), **southern lobster**]

spisekart *(No)* Menu

spit A substantial metal rod on which meat is impaled for roasting in front of, over, or under a source of radiant heat, or in an oven. It usually has attachments which clamp to the rod and engage the meat so that it turns as the rod is turned giving even cooking on all sides. The term often includes the supporting structure and the mechanism for turning the spit

spit roast, to To roast meat whilst it is being turned on a spit

spitchcock A split eel, grilled or fried

spitskool *(Ho)* Chinese cabbage

spleen A soft red pulpy organ near the stomach of an animal which is used for recycling the iron from dead or damaged red blood cells. Used in offal-based dishes or for stuffings

split almonds Blanched and dehusked almonds split into their two halves

split pea Dehusked dried peas split into two equal hemispheres along the natural dividing line

split tin loaf *(UK)* A bread loaf baked in a tin in which the top of the dough has been cut along the centre to allow outward expansion as the dough rises and more crust area

spongada *(It)* A type of sherbert made with stiffly beaten egg whites

sponge cake A light chemical or air raised cake generally made by the creaming or whisking methods. See for example Genoese or Victoria sponge

sponge finger biscuits *see* sponge fingers

sponge fingers Thin fingers of sponge made from creamed egg yolks and caster sugar (3 per 100 g of sugar) mixed with sifted flour equal in weight to the sugar, the stiffly beaten egg whites and salt folded in to the mixture progressively and then baked for 12 minutes at 160°C either in sponge finger tins or after piping onto a baking tray.

sponge flan A circular flan case made with a sponge cake mixture in place of pastry. After baking and cooling, the centre is filled with fruit, whipped cream, mousse or the like and decorated

sponge gourd *see* loofah

sponge pudding A hot, baked or steamed pudding made from a Victoria sponge mixture possibly with added fruits which is cooked in a pudding basin, sometimes with jam, golden syrup or treacle in the base. Served hot with a sweet sauce

sponge sandwich A Victoria sponge or Genoese sponge sliced horizontally in half using a serrated knife, and filled with jam and/or whipped cream or butter cream, the top dusted with icing sugar [also called **sandwich cake**]

spoom *(Fr)* A dessert made from fruit juice, champagne or fortified wine, frozen then mixed with Italian meringue

spoon An implement with a shallow, oval or round bowl at one end of a handle, constructed of metal, plastic, ceramic, wood or other natural materials or a combination of these. Wooden spoons are often used in mixing and stirring so as not to abrade the utensil. Spoons used for eating are either small (around 5 ml capacity) called teaspoons, medium (around 10 ml capacity) called dessert spoons or large (around 15 ml capacity) called tablespoons. Larger ones may be used for serving. The Chinese ceramic spoon is around 20 ml capacity; *see also* measuring spoon, slotted spoon, ladle, etc.

spoon bread *(USA)* *see* batter bread

sport coconut *see* makapuno

sposi *(It)* A small soft cream cheese

spot prawn *(Cn)* The most important prawn *Pandalus platyceros* found on the west coast of Canada

spotted dick *(UK)* A steamed pudding made from a sweetened, egg-enriched suet pastry mix with dried vine fruits and a raising agent cooked in a pudding basin or cloth for several hours and served with cream or English custard. An alternative uses fresh breadcrumbs, self raising flour, shredded suet, caster sugar and currants in the proportions 4:3:3:2:6, flavoured with grated lemon zest and brought together with milk [also called **spotted dog**]

spotted dog *(UK)* *see* spotted dick

sprængt oksekød *(De)* Corned beef

sprag *(USA)* A large codfish

sprängd *(De & Sw)* Salt cured e.g. of meat

sprat *(En & Fr)* *masc.* A small, round-bodied member of the herring family *Sprattus sprattus* up to 14 cm long and with a bluish-green back. Found on the north eastern shores of the Atlantic. Baked, fried or grilled [also called **brisling, Swedish anchovy**]

spratto *(It)* Sprat [also called **papalina**]

spray drying A method of drying solutions of foods or other soluble materials in liquid by spraying the liquid into a warm atmosphere and collecting the solid powder. Used for coffee extracts, milk and egg white

spread A semi-solid savoury paste spread on bread for sandwiches or on toast for canapés, also any soft food item which can easily be spread

spread, to To smear out a semi-solid food to form a uniform thin layer using a knife or a spatula as with butter on bread, whipped cream or icing on a cake or a savoury spread on toast

spremuto *(It)* Squeezed, of citrus fruit, etc.

spring cabbage An early season cabbage, mainly leaf with no heart, planted in the autumn, overwintered and harvested in spring; *see also* spring greens

spring chicken A chicken weighing a round 1.5 kg and 3 to 4 months old

spring greens Individual leaves of the brassicas esp. cabbage picked early in the season before the plants have hearted

spring onion A variety of onion *Allium cepa* which initially grows with a long white leek-like stem (to 1 cm dia.) before forming a bulb. When young has a mild flavour and the whole stem including part of the green leaves is used in salads, as a garnish, and in many Chinese dishes [also called **salad onion, shallot** (Aus)]

spring roll A thin rectangle of pastry made with eggs instead of water, wrapped securely around a cylinder of filling and deep-fried until crisp and golden. The filling consists of various mixtures of cooked chopped meat, poultry, shellfish or vegetables [also called **pancake roll**]

spring salmon *see* chinook salmon

Springerle *(Ge)* Aniseed-flavoured biscuits stamped with various designs before cooking for the Christmas season

sprinkle, to To scatter small or large particles or liquid drops over the surface of food as e.g. icing sugar over cakes, grated cheese over soup or a fish dish, flour over bread or vinegar over a salad; *see also* to drizzle

spritärter *(Sw)* Green peas

spritsar *(Sw)* Almond butter biscuits

spritz biscuits Biscuits made by piping or squirting a biscuit mixture in zig zag shapes onto a tray then baking at 175°C until crisp and brown. A typical mixture might be flour, butter, sugar, ground nuts and eggs (2:2:2:1:1) made by the creaming method. Popular in Holland and Belgium

Spritzgebäck *(Ge)* Spritz biscuits

Sprotten *(Ge)* Sprats, whitebait

sprout 1 The initial growth from a seed, usually very delicate and crisp, see e.g. bean sprouts **2** *see* Brussel sprouts

sprout, to To keep seeds, beans or grains in warm damp conditions after soaking in water so that they germinate and begin to grow and generally convert starch and protein into sugars and plant tissue. Many seeds become more palatable and digestible after this process

sprouting broccoli Large, very hardy biennial plants *Brassica oleracea* Italica Group growing to 90 cm, with many flowering shoots which develop in spring and are cooked as a vegetable. Both purple and white forms are available

sprue Thin shoots of asparagus

spruitjes *(Ho)* Brussel sprouts

spruzzare *(It)* To baste or sprinkle with a liquid

spuma *(It)* Mousse

spun curd cheese Cheese in which the curd had been extruded through small holes or otherwise drawn and kneaded to make cheeses like Mozzarella

spun sugar Sugar syrup cooked to the hard ball stage (121°C) which is spun or pulled into fine threads when sufficiently cool and used to make cake and dessert decorations

spur dog *see* rock salmon

spurtle *(UK)* A carved wooden stick used in Scotland to stir porridge

squab 1 *(UK)* A young pigeon **2** *(USA)* A small single portion chicken

squab pie *see* Devonshire squab pie

squadro *(It)* Angel fish

squash The American Indian derived name for various members of the *Cucurbitaceae* family, a vine crop originating in North America now grown worldwide. See under winter squash or summer squash

squash blossom *see* courgette flowers

squash melon *see* tinda

squaw corn A soft mealy variety of maize preferred by Amerindians and South Americans [also called **soft corn, flour corn**]

squid A widely distributed member *Loligo* spp. of the cephalopod group of molluscs varying from small to over 60 cm in length with a torpedo shaped body, eight arms and two long tentacles growing from around the central mouth parts at the rear of the body. It is semi-transparent with a reddish spot but can change colour and is opaque when cooked. May be cooked in any way. It has an inner shell; *see also* flying squid [also called **inkfish**]

squidgy chocolate roll *(UK)* A fatless, flourless type of Swiss roll made from eggs, caster sugar, milk and cocoa powder (8:4:5:1). The egg yolk and sugar are creamed and mixed with milk and cocoa powder, the stiffly beaten egg whites folded in, all baked in a Swiss roll tin at 180°C, rolled, cooled, filled with whipped cream and decorated

squille *(Fr) fem.* Mantis shrimp

squirrel A bushy tailed tree climbing rodent of the family *Sciuridae,* eaten in many parts of the world. Well known in Cajun cookery, probably the grey squirrel *Sciurus carolinensis*

squirrel cut A method of preparing fish for frying by cutting at an angle to the vertical in a cross hatch pattern from skin to bone for whole fish or from fish to skin for fillets so that it looks like a pine cone. The cuts are opened out with the fingers and dusted with cornflour to prevent them closing up

srikhand *(In)* A dessert made from drained yoghurt with sugar, nuts and saffron

srpska proja *(Bk)* Serbian bread made from maize flour

stabburpølse *(No)* Black pudding

stabilizers Food additives used to prevent food constituents separating out from a mixture. Emulsifiers are usually considered to be under this classification. See under E numbers E400 onwards

Stachelbeere *(Ge)* Gooseberry

stachys *see* Chinese artichoke

Stachys sieboldii *Bot.* Chinese artichoke plant

stag chicken *(USA)* An old male chicken with a good strong flavour

staghorn endive *see* endive

staghorn fungus *see* bamboo fungus

stagionata *(It)* Ripe or mature, of cheese

stagione *(It)* Season, of the year, as in pizza quattro stagione

stainless steel A high chromium and nickel iron alloy which is corrosion proof and does not tarnish. Used for basins and cooking utensils

stake *see* laver

stalker's pie A type of shepherd's pie made with finely diced cooked venison and chopped onion bound with gravy, topped with mashed potatoes and root vegetables, coated with butter and baked at 200°C, covered whilst warming through then uncovered to brown the top

stallina, alla *(It)* In the style of the stable, i.e. pasta with bacon and garlic

stambecco *(It)* Wild goat

stamp and go *(Ca)* Small pieces of salt cod coated in a batter flavoured with chillis, spring onions and thyme, deep fried and eaten as a hot snack

stampinjong *(No)* Mushroom [also called **sopp, champignon**]

stamppot *(Ho)* Hotpot

standard beef *(USA)* A tough grade of beef from low quality young animals with no marbling and a bland flavour

standing rib of beef *(UK & USA)* The fore rib of beef, term used in the north west of England and North America

standing rump *(USA)* The top of the round of beef including the bone. Used for roasting

Stangen *(Ge)* Long rectangular sweet or savoury pastries

Stangenkäse *(Au)* A soft cows' milk cheese cast in bricks and resembling Tilsit

stångkorv *(Sw)* A sausage packed with beef, pork, liver, kidney and boiled pearl barley. Usually fried

stanislas *(Fr) masc.* A cake filled with almond cream

Staphylococcus aureus A food poisoning bacterium whose toxins are not destroyed by cooking. It is found in meat pies and meat products containing salt and in confectionery. The incubation period is 2 to 6 hours and the duration of the illness 6 to 24 hours. The symptoms are nausea, vomiting, diarrhoea, and abdominal pain without fever. Their may be collapse amd dehydration in severe cases

Staphylococcus carnosus Bacteria used as a starter culture for lactic fermentation in meat products such as salami and in vegetables such as cucumbers

staple crops Food plants which provide the major source of energy and/or protein for most of the world's population. The five most important are rice, wheat, corn (maize), cassava (energy only) and beans

star anise The dried fruit of a Chinese tree *Illicium verum* which has the appearance of an eight pointed star, each point containing one seed. It has a sweetish aniseed/liquorice flavour and is used in Chinese and Vietnamese cooking

star apple The fruit of a sub-tropical tree *Chrysophyllum cainito* about 7.5 cm dia. with a white to purple, sticky, inedible skin, a white sweet pulp containing inedible black seeds in a star shaped core rather like an apple core. Eaten on its own or in fruit salad

star fruit *see* carambola and babaco

star gazey pie *(UK)* A fish pie from Cornwall made with whole pilchards cooked beneath a crust of pastry with their heads poking up through the pastry around the rim of the dish. The pie also contains a sauce flavoured with onion, bacon, parsley, vinegar or cider and seasoning, which is thickened with breadcrumbs and eggs

star ruby A highly pigmented grapefruit variety developed by an artifically induced mutation using ionizing radiation

starjerska kisela corba *(Bk)* A soup from Slovenia made with pigs' tails and trotters, vegetables, garlic, seasoning and a little vinegar and thickened with flour

stark senap *(Sw)* Hot (English) mustard

starna *(It)* Grey partridge

starna di montagna *(It)* Grouse

starter **1** The first course of a meal **2** A bacterial or fungal culture used to initiate fermentation and thus flavour development in fermented foods as e.g. *Lactobacillus* spp. in milk to make yoghurt, *Rhizopus oligosporus* in tempeh or the lactic cultures used to replace the microorganisms and enzymes lost during milk pasteurization preparatory to cheesemaking

station waiter A waiter in charge of a certain number of tables in a restaurant

steak 1 *(En & Fr) masc.* A piece or slice of meat or fish up to 2.5 cm thick usually cut across the muscle fibres and sufficiently tender to be grilled or fried **2** A general name for lean muscle from animals used for braising, stewing, grilling or frying depending on the muscle concerned

steak diane Tail end of fillet of beef, batted out, sautéed in butter, flambéed with brandy and served with a sauce made from pan juices, sliced mushrooms, Dijon mustard, double cream and demi-glace

steak haché *(Fr) masc.* Hamburger steak

steak and kidney pie *(UK)* Pieces of cheek of beef marinated in red wine, dried, fried in oil and butter, dusted with flour, simmered until tender in clarified marinade and beef stock, lightly fried pieces of veal or beef kidney added, poached oysters and mushrooms added if required, cooking liquor reduced and all combined in a bowl and precooked tops (skullcaps) of puff pastry placed over. Served piping hot. A simpler version is made from precooked steak and kidney stew baked quickly between a top and bottom crust of pastry

steak and kidney pudding *(UK)* A pudding basin lined with suet crust pastry, filled with diced stewing beef and kidney, onions, seasoning and thickened stock, covered and sealed with more pastry, vents cut in the top, covered with cooking foil and boiled or steamed for 3 to 3.5 hours. Served from the basin or, less formally, turned out on a plate

steak au poivre *(Fr) masc. see* pepper steak

steak tartare Chopped (not minced) tail end of fillet of beef, mixed with chopped onions, gherkins and capers, shaped on the plate like a steak and served with a raw egg in a depression on top of the steak. Mixed at the table by the customer and eaten raw

steam, to To cook in the vapour from boiling water; *see also* steamer, atmospheric steamer, pressure steamer

steam table A stainless steel table or counter with openings to take food containers heated by steam or hot water. Used to keep food hot prior to service; *see also* bain-marie

steamboat *(SEA)* An implement for cooking at the table consisting of an annular vessel containing cooking liquor (stock) around a circular chimney at the base of which is a source of heat. Prepared food is cooked by diners using fondue forks, chop sticks or wire mesh baskets. Various dips are usually supplied and the stock is often consumed after all the solid food has been cooked and eaten; *see also* Mongolian firepot

steamed pudding Puddings based on sweetened suet pastry or a cake sponge mixture with additions and flavourings, cooked in a pudding basin, in a cloth or in a special hinged closed container using either steam or boiling water. Usually served with a sweet sauce which may be cooked as an integral part of the pudding

steamed pudding mixture *(UK)* Made from self-raising flour, shredded beef suet or softened butter, caster sugar and beaten egg (6:3:2:2), the flour, fat and sugar combined with a little salt, then brought together with the beaten egg and sufficient milk to produce a soft dropping consistency

steamed rice *see* absorption method

steamer A double or triple saucepan with a top lid in which the compartments above the bottom pan are perforated so that steam generated at the bottom can circulate around the food items in the upper compartments

steamer clam *see* soft-shell clam

stearic acid One of the main saturated fatty acids in hard beef and lamb fats, responsible when esterified with glycerine for the hardness of the fat

stearyl tartrate An ester of stearyl alcohol and tartaric acid with the same uses as sodium stearoyl-2-lactylate

stecche, al *(It)* On a skewer

stecchi *(It)* Attereaux

Steckerfisch *(Ge)* Fish on a stick

steel A tapering rod either of hardened steel with very small longitudinal sharp edged grooves, carborundum stone or diamond dust coated metal, used to put a sharp edge on knife blades. The knife blade is stroked across and down the steel at an angle of about 45° or less on either side removing a small amount of metal from the edge. After considerable sharpening on a steel a knife needs to be reground professionally

steel-cut oatmeal *see* pinhead oatmeal

steep, to *see* to macerate

steer A castrated male of the bovine spp. 2 to 4 years old

steg *(De)* Steak

stegt *(De)* Roasted [also called **stægt**]

stegt kylling *(De)* Braised chicken

stegt svinekam *(De)* Roast pork with red cabbage

stegtgås gylat med svedsker *(De)* Roast goose stuffed with prunes

Steinbuscher *(Ge)* A soft cheese made with whole or partially skimmed cows' milk. It is brick-shaped and has a smooth buttery paste with a few holes. It comes from from the east of the country and is similar to Romadur. Contains 52% water, 21% fat and 24% protein

Steinbutt *(Ge)* Turbot

Steingut *(Ge)* Earthenware

Steinpilz *(Ge)* Cep

stekt *(No & Sw)* Fried or roasted

stekt ägg *(Sw)* Fried egg

stekt and *(Sw)* Roast duck, usually stuffed with apple, prunes and the chopped up liver and heart

stekt fläsk med löksås *(Sw)* Fried strips of fresh or salt pork served with onion sauce *(löksås)*

stekt gås *(Sw)* Roast goose, the cavity stuffed with parboiled prunes and cored, peeled and sliced apples sprinkled with ground ginger, basted with stock from time to time and accompanied with jus lié made from the defatted pan juices. Served with roast potatoes, chestnut purée and red cabbage

stekt kalvbräss *(Sw)* Calves' sweetbreads prepared as for kalvbräss-stuvning, sliced, panéed and fried in oil and butter. Served with petit pois

stekt potatis *(Sw)* Fried potato slices

stekt rödspätta *(Sw)* Fried plaice usually skinned whole, panéed and fried slowly in butter

stekt salt sill med lök *(Sw)* Fried salt herring which have been soaked, filleted and coated with flour and toasted breadcrumbs. Served with sliced onions which have been fried until brown in the butter in which the fish is later fried and the pan residues deglazed with thin cream. A traditional Monday lunch

stekt salt sill papper *(Sw)* Filleted salt herrings soaked, dried and baked or fried en papillote with the usual additions (butter, dill, parsley, chives, etc.)

stekt sjötunga *(Sw)* Fried sole usually prepared as stekt rödspätta

stekt vildand *(Sw)* Wild duck usually pot roasted for 45 minutes with soured cream and milk after seasoning and browning the bird and its liver. Served with a jus lié made from the roux thickened cooking liquor finished with double cream and a little blackcurrant jelly

Stellaria media *Bot.* Chickweed

stellette *(It)* Very small pasta stars used in soup [also called **stelline**]

stellina odorosa *(It)* Sweet woodruff

stelline *(It) see* stellette

stem ginger Peeled ginger rhizome, macerated and preserved in a sugar syrup to give a soft translucent confection

stem lettuce *(USA) see* celtuce

Stephanie Cremetorte *(Au)* An over-the-top sweet dessert invented for Crown Princess Stephanie who complained of the 'coarseness' of Viennese cooking, consisting of chocolate and hazelnuts plus layers of raspberry, hazelnut and chocolate cream

Stepnoi *(Ru) see* Steppe

Stepnoj *see* Steppe

Stepnoy *see* Steppe

Steppe A strong-flavoured cow's milk cheese similar to Tilsit and sometimes flavoured with caraway made in Germany, Austria, Scandinavia, Russia and Canada [also called **Stepnoi** (Ru) **Stepnoj, Steppen, Stepnoy**]

Steppen *see* Steppe

sterilize, to To heat food to between 115 and 140°C depending on the type of food and the time at the high temperature. This kills all pathogenic organisms and most microorganisms and spores; *see also* UHT

sterilized cream Tinned cream sterilized at about 120°C. It has a slight caramel flavour and cannot be whipped

sterilized milk Milk heated to 120°C for a few minutes or to just over 100°C for 20 to 30 minutes and aseptically sealed in a narrow necked bottle with a crown cork. This process kills all pathogenic and most other microorganisms and spores and the milk will keep for 1 to 2 years. The milk is off white in colour and has a characteristic caramel, boiled milk taste which is not to everyone's liking; *see also* UHT milk

sterlet A small and very rare sturgeon *Acipenser ruthenus* found in the Volga river and Caspian sea and famed for its golden caviar, the caviar of the Tsar. The fish which is ugly and eel-like is served baked with vegetables

sterlyad *(Ru)* Sterlet

steur *(Ho)* Sturgeon

stew A mixture of meat, usually tough and cut into small pieces, cooked slowly with vegetables, cooking liquor and flavourings on top of the heat source until tender, a process which can take many hours

stew, to To simmer meat and poultry with

cooking liquor and vegetables in a heavy pan with a tight fitting lid or to cook fruit in water until soft, possibly with the addition of a sweetening agent

stewed fruit Fruit simmered in sweetened water until soft

St. George's mushroom An edible mushroom *Tricholoma gambosum* with a cream coloured irregular cap on a thick stem found in grassland in spring and early summer. Used as a flavouring for soups and stews

St. Germain, à la *(Fr)* In the style of St. Germain near Paris, i.e. including peas

St. Germain, crème *(Fr) fem.* Onion, leek and celery sweated in butter, white stock, mint, a BG and shelled green peas added, boiled 5 minutes, BG removed, an equal quantity of Béchamel added, boiled, consistency adjusted, liquidized, seasoned and passed through a chinois and finished with cream [also called **cream of green pea soup**]

St. Germain, fish Fillets of fish passed through seasoned flour, melted butter containing English mustard, and breadcrumbs. Breadcrumbs neatened on the presentation side with a palette knife and marked with a diamond pattern, grilled and served with Béarnaise sauce

St. Germain, purée *(Fr) fem.* Soaked dried or washed fresh peas, whole carrot, chopped green leek and onion, a BG and a knuckle of ham added to white stock, simmered and skimmed until all tender, carrot and ham removed, the remainder liquidized or passed through a sieve, strained, seasoned, consistency adjusted and served hot acompanied with croûtons [also called **green pea soup**]

St. Honoré The patron saint of pastry cooks; *see also* gateau St.Honoré

St. John's bread *see* carob powder

St. Peter's fish *see* tilapia

stick bean *see* runner bean

sticking piece *(UK) see* clod (of beef)

sticky bun *(UK)* A sweet yeast-raised bun often flavoured with cinnamon and coated with a soft icing

sticky rice *see* glutinous rice

stifado *(Gr)* A stew based on meat, poultry, octopus or squid with oil, onions, garlic, tomatoes, shaliots, wine, wine vinegar, herbs and seasoning

stiff dough *(USA)* A very stiff mixture of 2 parts flour to one part water. The exact proportions depend on the flour used

stiffen, to To briefly cook flesh in water or fat until it stiffens but is not coloured

stifle *(USA)* A salt pork and vegetable stew from New England

Stilton *(UK)* An uncooked curd, blue veined, semi-soft cow's milk cheese with a creamy yellow paste made only in Leicestershire, Derbyshire, Nottinghamshire and Rutlandshire. The blue variety is inoculated with *Penicillium roquefortii* spores and the edges of the cheese are hand rubbed to exclude air, slow down development and give the characteristic hard greyish brown rind. The cheeses are needled after 10 weeks to encourage veining and may be sold after 12 weeks. Often sold in small earthenware pots and prized as a dessert cheese

Stilton pears *(UK)* A starter made from cored but not skinned Comice pears stuffed with a mixture of Stilton and curd cheese, refrigerated, halved and fanned on individual plates, covered in seasoned mayonnaise thinned with oil and lemon juice and flavoured with mustard

stinco *(It)* Shank of veal

stinging nettle *see* nettle

stink bean *see* parkia

Stint *(Ge)* Smelt, the fish

stir, to To agitate a liquid, semi-solid, or powder mixture with a spoon or spatula to bring to a uniform consistency or a liquid mixture to prevent sticking or burning during heating.

stir-fry, to To cook small thin pieces of meat or vegetables very rapidly using hot oil in a wok by continuously moving them and turning them over. Used extensively in preparing Chinese food

stirabout An oatmeal or maize porridge made with water or milk, originally from Ireland

stivaletti *(It)* Small pasta shapes Lit. small boots

stoccafisso *(It)* Stockfish

stock Water flavoured with extracts from herbs, spices, vegetables and/or bones by long simmering. See under white or brown followed by the appropriate terms such as beef, fish, etc.

stock cube A mixture of salt, MSG, vegetable and/or meat extracts and various flavourings pressed into soft crumbly cubes or blocks each individually wrapped. One stock cube will usually make 0.4 litres (0.75 pints) of stock. The salt and fat content and their flavour make them unsuitable for the finest cooking; *see also* bouillon [also called **bouillon cube**]

stock pot A large cylindrical vessel with a draw off tap between 2 and 5 cm from the base in which stock is prepared and into which all the suitable trimmings of a professional kitchen together with the usual stock ingredients are put, and stock drawn off as required. It is usually kept simmering all the time and cleaned out and replenished on a regular basis

stock syrup A basic sugar solution with many uses containing 0.3 kg of granulated sugar and 0.1 kg of glucose per litre of water. Often 0.4 kg of granulated sugar with no glucose is used, but it may tend to cause crystallization

Stockfisch *(Ge)* Stockfish

stockfish Air dried cod from Norway which is very popular in Italy. Requires prolonged soaking in water

stodge *coll.* Heavy starchy solid food such as overcooked stews, suet puddings and the like

stoemp *(Be)* A dish similar to colcannon made with mashed potatoes and vegetables

stoke *see* laver

Stokenchurch pie *(UK)* A Buckinghamshire baked pie filled with minced meat in a sauce mixed with macaroni

stokkfisk *(No)* Stockfish [also called **tørrfisk**]

Stollen *(Ge)* A sweetened enriched yeast dough rolled in a rectangle, filled with dried vine fruits, nuts and sometimes marzipan, folded or rolled, baked, brushed with molten butter and dredged with icing sugar. Eaten during the Christmas season [also called **Christollen**]

stomna kebab *(Bu)* A lamb stew with butter, tomatoes, spring onions, herbs and seasonings, thickened with flour and cooked in an earthenware pot

stone The hard central seed of fruits such as cherry, peach, mango, plum, olive, etc., usually with a hard woody shell enclosing a soft kernel [also called **pit** (USA)]

stone, to To remove the central stone from a fruit [also called **to pit (USA), to destone**]

stone crab *(USA)* A large edible crab *Menippe mercenaria* with very large claws, from the coast of Florida

stone plover *see* plover

stoneground flour Flour which has been ground between a stationary and a rotating stone as opposed to rollers which are used to grind most flour nowadays. The slight frictional heating modifies the flavour of the flour

Stör *(Ge)* Sturgeon

stör *(Sw)* Sturgeon

storage temperatures Recommended storage temperatures for food are precooked, −3°C for up to 5 days; chilled, less than 5°C; eggs in shell, −10 to-16°C for up to 1 month; bakery produce, −18 to −40°C, blanched vegetables, less than −18°C; apples and pears, −1 to +4°C

store A designated room, cupboard, refrigerator or freezer where foods are kept in their purchased or partially processed condition prior to use

store to To keep foods and articles for future use, either in a dry store, vegetable store, refrigerator or freezer

Störe *(Ge)* Sturgeon

storione *(It)* Sturgeon

stortini *(It)* Small pasta crescents used in soup

stove, to *(UK)* A Scottish term dating from the 17th century derived from the French étouffer, meaning to cook in a closed pot, generally in the oven at around 150°C, e.g. stoved chicken

stoved chicken *(UK)* A Scottish dish of chicken pieces sealed and casseroled in a closed pot with bacon, potatoes, onions, thyme, seasoning and chicken stock at 150°C in the oven

stovies *(UK) coll.* (Scotland). Boiled potatoes

stoviglie *(It)* Earthenware

straccetti *(It)* Thin slices

Stracchino *(It)* A soft cow's milk cheese from the north cultured with *Streptococcus thermophilus,* coagulated with rennet, the curd then heated to 80°C for 6 to 10 hours in square 20 cm moulds, salted in brine and matured for 7 to 10 days. Originally made in the autumn from the milk of cow's brought down from Alpine pasture, from stracche meaning tired [also called **Crescenza**]

Stracchino di Gorgonzola *(It)* The original Gorgonzola made from an evening's and the following morning's milking of cows being brought down from mountain pasture and resting at the town of Gorgonzola. The evening curd which cooled overnight was mixed with the next morning's curd and gave a heterogeneous mixture which encouraged mould growth

stracci di antrodoco *(It)* Pancakes layered with cheese, meat and vegetables

stracciata *(It)* Chiffonade of e.g. lettuce

stracciate *(It)* A flat cake

stracciatella *(It)* A beef or chicken broth into which a mixture of beaten eggs, semolina and grated Parmesan is whisked to give solid ragged looking strands

stracciato *(It)* Scrambled, of eggs

stracotto *(It)* A very slowly cooked pot roast or meat stew

straight neck squash A summer squash common in the US

strain, to To pass a mixture of solid particles

and liquid through a strainer, colander, sieve, chinois, muslin cloth, etc. to separate the solid and liquid either of which may be the desired product

strainer General name for colander, sieve or chinois

Strandkohl *(Ge)* Sea kale

Strandkrabbe *(Ge)* Shore crab

strangolapreti *(It)* Small dumplings similar to strozzapreti and for the same purpose, i.e. to strangle, figuratively, the priest. There are many local spellings all beginning with strang- for what was obviously a widespread problem

strapazzato *(It)* Scrambled, e.g. of eggs

strasbourgeoise, à la *(Fr)* In the style of Strasbourg, i.e. cooked with sauerkraut, bacon and foie gras

strascinati *(It)* Baked ravioli with sauce

Strassburger Truffelleberwurst *(Ge)* A liver sausage flavoured with truffles

stravecchio *(It)* Very old, mature, used of cheese or other food items which might improve with age

straw chips *see* straw potatoes

straw mushroom A globular, stemless edible mushroom *Volvariella volvacea* grown on beds of straw in China. Available canned, but not dried, for use in Chinese and Japanese dishes. It is fawn when young but becomes gray-black and gelatinous as it matures [also called **grass mushroom, yellow mushroom, paddy straw mushroom**]

straw potatoes Well washed and drained julienne potatoes deep fried at 185°C until golden brown and crisp, drained and lightly salted and used as a garnish for grilled meat [also called **pommes pailles** (Fr), **straw chips**]

strawberries Romanoff *(USA)* Strawberries steeped in an orange-flavoured liqueur and served with crème chantilly

strawberry The sweet, flavoursome and decorative fruit of a ground creeping perennial plant *Fragaria x ananasa* generally conical, to 5 cm long and consisting of a cluster of small fleshy globules, each of which has a single seed on the outer surface, around a central fleshy stem, with the remains of the calyx at the broad end. Eaten on their own with cream and possibly caster sugar or in made up desserts, tarts, cakes and jams; *see also* wild strawberry, Alpine strawberry

strawberry guava A smaller and sweeter version of the guava *Psidium cattleianum* from Brazil with small reddish purple fruit [also called **cattley**]

strawberry shortcake *(USA)* A large scone-like cake split whilst warm, buttered and made into a sandwich with whipped cream and sliced strawberries as a filling

straws *see* cheese straws

streaky bacon Bacon from the rib cage and belly of the pig which when sliced shows alternate strips of lean and fat. Often used to line terrines and pâté dishes

Streckrübe *(Ge)* Swede

Streichwurst *(Ge)* The generic name for any paste-like spreading sausage

Streptococcus lactis* subsp. *cremoris One of the microorganisms used in the starter cultures for soured cream, buttermilk and English cheeses

Streptococcus lactis* subsp. *diacetilicos As *S. lactis* subsp. *cremoris*

Streptococcus lactis* subsp. *lactis As *S. lactis* subsp. *cremoris*

***Streptococcus* spp.** Bacteria used for the production of lactic acid in the manufacture of cheese and sauerkraut. Some of the species are pathogenic

Streptococcus thermophilus One of the microorganisms used in starter cultures for yoghurt and continental cheeses

Stretford black pudding *(UK)* Black pudding flavoured with ground marjoram, mint and penny royal

streusel *(USA)* A mixture of flour or breadcrumbs with sugar, butter and spices used as a crumble topping on baked goods

streusel cake A slightly sweet yeasted cake with a crumble topping of sugar flavoured with cinnamon or mixed spice from Central and Northern Europe

Streuselkuchen *(Ge)* Streusel cake

string bean 1 *(USA) see* French bean **2** *(UK) see* runner bean

string cheese *(USA)* A cow's milk cheese similar to Mozarella which originated in Armenia and Georgia and is shaped as a small cylinder. Sometimes flavoured with caraway [also called **braid cheese**]

string hoppers *(Sr)* A thin pouring appa q.v. batter poured into hot fat through a moving funnel to give long threads of cooked dough [also called **hoppers**]

strip loin *(USA)* The round longitudinal muscle from the back of the beef equivalent to the eye of a lamb loin, boneless and trimmed and usually cut in steaks

strip steak *(USA)* A beef steak cut from a

boneless short loin and sirloin after the fillet has been removed. Popular in New York

striped bass A medium-oily seawater fish *Morone saxatilus* and *Roccus saxatilus* which spawns in fresh water and is found off the coasts of North America. It has a deep olive-green body with longitudinal stripes and weighs up to 2.5 kg. The flesh is white and flaky and it may be cooked in any way [also called **rockfish**]

striped bream A small seawater bream *Lithognathus mormyrus* with transverse dark grey stripes on a silvery background

striped mullet *(USA)* A species of mullet *Mugil cephalus* with longitudinal lines of dark grey on a silvery grey background

stroganoff *see* beef stroganoff or bef stroganov

strömming *(Sw)* High quality herring and sprats found only in the Baltic and commanding a premium price

strömming à la Operakällaren *(Sw)* Cleaned and rinsed herrings and sprats with fins and tails removed, salted, marinated in a mixture of whipped egg and double cream (2:5) for at least an hour, removed, coated in wholemeal flour and shallow fried in butter until well browned. Served with a simple parsley and lemon wedge garnish

strömmingslada *(Sw)* Young herrings filleted kipper style (from the back), bones removed as far as possible, seasoned, placed in a buttered baking dish and gratinated with grated Parmesan cheese and breadcrumbs in the oven until browned

strong flour Flour of any type made from a hard wheat, usually containing between 11 and 12% protein which is mostly gluten. Used mainly for bread and puff and choux pastry

stroop *(Ho)* Syrup or molasses

strozzapreti *(It)* Flour and egg based dumplings or gnocchi flavoured with spinach, basil, nutmeg and grated cheese, poached and served with a tomato sauce. Lit. choke the priest, allegedly to fill up the priest when he called on his parishioners

struccoli *(It)* Sweet pastry rolls filled with fruit or cream cheese

strudel *(Au & It)* A generic name for a rectangle of strudel pastry spread with a sweet or savoury filling, layered or rolled up like a Swiss roll and after further proving and egg washing baked at 190°C for approximately 1 hour

strudel pastry A wafer-thin pastry common in Austria and Hungary but originating in the ME and brought to Europe in the Ottoman invasions of the 15th century. Made from strong white bread flour, beaten egg, melted butter (4:1:1), vinegar and salt, all mixed to a silky dough, rested, rolled out and stretched until thin, then layered to build up thickness. Other formulations omit the vinegar and include milk, sugar and lemon zest and use yeast to raise the dough as in bread dough production; *see also* filo pastry

struffoli *(It)* A pasty filled with cooked sliced onion

strutto *(It)* Lard

stucolo *(It)* A north Italian version of strudel usually layered rather than rolled

stud, to To insert small items such as cloves, sprigs of herbs or slivers of garlic or the like regularly at intervals over the surface of a food item such as an onion or a joint of meat [also called **to piqué**]

stuet *(No)* Creamed

stufatino *(It)* *see* stufato

stufato *(It)* Beef braised in red wine with onions, tomatoes, celery, garlic and ham [also called **stufatino**]

stuff, to To fill the central abdominal cavity of animals or fish or of hollowed out vegetables or fruit with a sweet or savoury stuffing or forcemeat

stuffau *(It)* *see* ghisau

stuffed derma *see* kishka

stuffed olive A green preserved olive which has been destoned and the central cavity filled with a small piece of anchovy, a piece of sweet red pepper, a caper or the like

stuffing A sweet or savoury mixture or forcemeat used to fill the cavity of animals, fish or hollowed out vegetables or of fruits prior to cooking; *see also* forcemeat

stump *(UK)* A Northern vegetable purée made from a combination of carrots, swedes and potatoes mashed with milk, butter and seasoning

sturgeon A medium to large anadromous fish found in the rivers that flow into the the Caspian sea, Black sea, the Western Pacific and the Eastern Atlantic oceans with a firm white to pink flesh, which may be baked, fried, grilled or smoked. They have armour-plated bodies and an elongated snout with a dark grey-green back. The females which are caught in the estuaries of the rivers to which they return to spawn are the source of caviar which may amount to 22 kg from a single fish. There are about 24 species but the important ones in order of size are the sterlet and the sevruga, osciotre, common and beluga sturgeon

stuvad *(Sw)* Creamed

stuvad kalvbräss *(Sw)* *see* kalvbräss-stuvning

stuvas potatis *(Sw)* Diced potatoes, sweated

in butter, boiled with minimum milk and salt until tender, seasoning adjusted and flavoured with chopped herbs

stuvet *(De)* Creamed

stuvet oksekød *(De)* Stewed beef

stuvning *(Sw)* Stew [also called **ragu**]

Stück *(Ge)* **1** Steak **2** A piece

su 1 *(Ja)* Rice vinegar **2** *(Tu)* Water

sua *(Vi)* Jellyfish

sua bhati *(In)* Dill seed

suacia *(It)* Scald, the fish

su-age *(Ja)* Deep frying of food without any coating

suan *(Ch)* Preliminary boiling of large cuts of meat prior to other forms of cooking

suan la tang *(Ch)* Hot and sour soup from Canton

suan mei jiang *(Ch)* Hoisin sauce

suan niu nai *(Ch)* Yoghurt

suave *(Me)* A description of a mildly and subtly flavoured dish

sub *(USA)* Hoagie

sub gum geung *(Ch) see* chow chow preserve

submarine *(USA)* Hoagie

subo benachin *(WA)* A stew from Gambia made with beef, lamb or fish together with onions, chillis, tomatoes, rice and seasoning

subrics *(Fr) masc.* Croquettes sautéed without being panéed or coated

subtilisin A protease obtained from various Bacillus strains *(bacteria)* used for flavour production from soya bean and milk protein *(casein)*

succari orange *(Ey)* A variety of acidless orange q.v. with a highly adhering skin and a large number of seeds, very sweet but without the familiar orange flavour

succinic acid *see* (E)363

succo *(It)* Juice

succory *see* Belgian chicory

succotash *(USA)* A native American Indian dish taken over and adapted by the Pilgrim Fathers, consisting of cooked lima beans and sweet corn kernels heated together with cream and seasoning. Often served at Thanksgiving

succu tundu *(It) see* fregula

sucker *(USA)* Various freshwater fishes of the *Catostomidae* family, with a thick-lipped mouth adapted for sucking, most with sweet white flesh

sucking pig A small unweaned baby pig 3 to 6 weeks old which is usually roasted

suckling A young unweaned animal

suco *(Po)* Juice

suco de laranja *(Po)* Orange juice

sucre *(Fr) masc.* Sugar

sucre cristallisé *(Fr) masc.* Granulated or castor sugar; *see also* sucre en poudre and sucre semoule

sucre filé *(Fr) masc.* Spun sugar

sucre glace *(Fr) masc.* Icing sugar

sucre en morceaux *(Fr) masc.* Lump or cube sugar

sucre d'orge *(Fr) masc.* Barley sugar

sucre en poudre *(Fr) masc.* Castor sugar

sucre semoule *(Fr)* Granulated sugar

sucrose A disaccharide composed of a glucose and a fructose unit which is the normal commercial variety found in cane and beet sugar

sucuk *(Tu)* Sausage flavoured with garlic and herbs

sudachi *(Ja)* A small citrus fruit *Citrus sudachi* similar to kabosu q.v. but only about one third of its weight. Used in the same way

sudako *(Ja)* Octopus pickled in vinegar

Sudanese pepper A dried and ground hot chilli pepper from the Middle East

sudare *(Ja) see* maki-su

sudulunu *(Sr)* Garlic

suduru *(Sr)* Cumin

suédoise *(Fr) fem.* A dessert of sugared fruit and jelly

suédoise, sauce *(Fr) fem.* Mayonnaise mixed with apple purée and grated horseradish

suen *(Ch)* Bamboo shoots

suen tau *(Ch)* Garlic

suer, faire *(Fr)* To sweat

suero *(Sp)* Whey

suet The hard fat surrounding kidneys which

has very good cooking properties. Used for suet pastry and puddings and in sweet mincemeat fillings. Commercial suet is granulated and coated with up to 15% flour or starch to prevent sticking

suet crust pastry *see* suet pastry

suet pastry Self-raising flour and shredded beef suet (2:1) with a little salt brought together with water, kneaded slightly and rested [also called **suet crust pastry**]

suet pudding *(UK)* A traditional pudding made from chopped or granulated suet, breadcrumbs, flour, sugar, eggs, milk and flavourings, steamed or boiled in a covered pudding basin and served with a sweet sauce

sufed kaddu *(In)* Wax gourd

suffle *(It)* Soufflé

Suffolk ham *(UK)* Ham cured in beer and sugar or molasses. It has a deep golden skin and a rich red-brown meat with a blue bloom

Suffolk sausage *(UK)* A meaty pork sausage flavoured with herbs

suffritu *(It) see* soffrito calabrese

sugar The sweet-tasting water-soluble, monosaccharides and disaccharides crystallized from plant juices *(sucrose, fructose)* or obtained, usually as syrups, by breaking down starch *(glucose, maltose) see also* jaggery, palm sugar, brown sugar, lump sugar

sugar apple *see* sweet sop

sugar batter biscuit method A method of making biscuits by creaming butter and sugar, mixing in eggs to form a stable emulsion, then blending in the dry ingredients, e.g. langues des chats

sugar beet A variety of beet *Beta vulgaris* whose roots when mature contain a high concentration of sucrose which is extracted using water and crystallized from the solution

sugar cane The thick bamboo-like canes of a tropical grass *Saccharum officinarum* about 2 m long by 4 to 5 cm dia. Sometimes sold in pieces as a sweet for children to chew, but usually chopped and crushed to a give a liquid from which sucrose is crystallized

sugar cooking The process of modifying sugar (pure granulated sucrose) by dissolving it in a little water then heating it without stirring to various temperatures to produce various non-crystalline consistencies until finally there is caramelization which changes its flavour and chemical composition. The stages are: small thread (103°C), large thread (107°C), soft ball (115°C), hard ball (121°C), hard crack (157°C), and caramel (182°C). With practice these stages can be judged by the behaviour of the sugar between the fingers or when dropped into cold water or on a cold plate. In the USA the stages recognized are thread (110°C), soft ball (112°C), firm ball (118°C), soft crack (132°C), hard crack (149°C) and caramel (154 to 170°C). The differences may be due to differences in the sugar. In France and Europe generally, the density of the sugar water mixture in °Be is often used but is rather inconvenient. Many names for the various stages exist and the above are not exclusive [also called **sugar boiling**]

sugar crust pastry *(USA)* Sugar pastry

sugar loaf A brick or cone shaped mass of refined sugar made by pouring wet sugar crystals into moulds to dry. Sugar used to be sold in this form

sugar loaf chicory A green leaved chicory *Cichorium intybus* which forms a conical head rather like cos lettuce. The leaves may be harvested separately or the whole head cut when mature. The inner leaves are naturally blanched and are less bitter than the outer leaves

sugar lump *see* cube sugar

sugar maple tree A variety of maple *Acer saccharum* found in North America. The spring sap obtained by boring a hole in the trunk contains 1% to 4% saccharose and is used to prepare maple syrup and maple sugar

sugar orange *see* acidless orange

sugar palm A large palm tree *Arenga saccharifera* or *A. pinnata* which grows to over 15 m. The sugary sap is obtained by beating the feathery immature male flower spike for 14 days, then as soon as the flowers open the spike is cut off at the base of the flowers and the sap collected. The beating and slicing off of a little more of the flower stem continues until the flow of sap stops

sugar pastry Pastry made from soft flour, butter, eggs and sugar (8:5:2:2) with a little salt using the creaming or rubbing in method. Used for flans and fruit tartlets [also called **sugar crust pastry** (USA)]

sugar pea *see* mangetout

sugar-snap pea *see* mangetout

sugar sorghum *see* sweet sorghum

sugar substitutes *see* artificial sweeteners

sugar syrup A solution of sugar in water; *see also* syrup, light sugar syrup, heavy sugar syrup

sugar thermometer A thermometer used to measure the temperature of boiling sugar syrups, usually calibrated from 50 to 200°C, sometimes marked with the stages of sugar cooking q.v.

sugared almond A large Spanish almond coated with a layer of amorphous, coloured and flavoured sugar [also called **Jordan almond**]

sugna *(It)* Lard

sugo *(It)* Gravy, juice, sauce

sugo, al *(It)* Served with any sauce

sugo de carne *(It)* Meat gravy

suif *(Fr) masc.* Mutton fat or suet

suiker *(Ho)* Sugar

suimono *(Ja)* A delicate clear soup served in a fine lacquered bowl with traditionally three additional ingredients, a few pieces of fish, shellfish or chicken, a few decorative vegetables, mushrooms or pieces of seaweed and a piquant or fragrant addition such as ginger juice, lemon peel or yuzu. Often accompanied by sashimi

suino *(It)* Pig, pork

suisse *(Fr) masc.* An unsalted soft fresh cheese made from cows' milk enriched with cream. The mixture is curdled with a small quantity of rennet and left to stand for 1 to 2 days. The soft curd is then collected and packed into 60 g pots for immediate consumption. Served with fruit, desserts, etc.; *see also* petit-suisse, demi-suisse

suji *(In)* Semolina

suka *(Ph)* A low acidity (1 to 3% acetic acid) vinegar with a pleasant aroma made from coconut sap

sukade *(Ho)* Candied peel

sukat *(No)* Candied lemon peel

sukiyaki *(Ja)* Very thin slices of beef fried at the table in oil, soya sauce, rice wine, sugar and water added followed by squares of bean curd and sliced vegetables, the whole cooked for a few minutes, then taken by guests, dipped in beaten raw egg followed by a dipping sauce and eaten with rice. Lit. broiled on a plough share

sukiyakinabe *(Ja)* A shallow iron pan used for cooking sukiyaki

sukker *(De & No)* Sugar

sukkererter *(No)* Petit pois, sugar peas

sukkerkavring *(No)* Sweet biscuit

suklaa *(Fi)* Chocolate

suklaakuorrute *(Fi)* Chocolate icing

Sulperknochen *(Ge)* Pickled pork boiled with sauerkraut

sulphites Salts of sulphurous acid which is formed when sulphur dioxide is dissolved in excess water, used as food preservative. Common in the food industry are sodium sulphite E221 and calcium sulphite E226

sulphur dioxide E220, a pungent and irritating gas which dissolves in water to form sulphurous acid or its salts the sulphites, hydrogen sulphites and metabisulphites, all of which liberate the gas in solution. It is one of the most common preservatives used in foods

sulphuric acid *see* (E)513

sultanas Dried seedless white grapes kept light-coloured by treatment with sulphur dioxide

sultanina *(It)* Sultana

Sultanine *(Ge)* Sultana

Sültzwurst *(Ge)* A type of brawn made with large pieces of cooked pork from the head and leg, sometimes with sliced mushrooms, in a wine-flavoured aspic jelly. Usually sliced and served with French dressing

süri rüewe *(Fr)* Smoked bladebone and knuckle of beef stewed with turnips and onions in white wine. From the Alsace region of France

Suluguni *(Ru)* A Georgian cheese rather like haloumi

sülün *(Tu)* Pheasant

sülze *(Ge)* In aspic

sumac *(En & Fr) masc.* The dried red berries of a Middle Eastern bush *Rhus coriaria* containing several small brown seeds with a sour flavour. Commonly used in Middle Eastern cooking

Sumach *(Ge)* Sumac

suman *(Ph)* Glutinous rice or other starchy material possibly mixed with coconut cream and sweetened, wrapped in young banana leaves, boiled and served with grated coconut as a dessert

summer flounder *(USA)* A large flatfish *Paralichthys dentatus* related to plaice but up to 1 m long with a dark grey to brown spotted skin, found all along the east coast of North America. It is mainly caught in summer when it moves to shallow waters. The flesh is firm, white and non-oily and may be cooked in any way [also called **northern fluke**]

summer melon *see* fuzzy melon

summer pudding *(UK)* A uncooked pudding of soft fruits and bread made from a sauce of sieved raspberries, icing sugar and liqueur, which after warming slightly is mixed with a variety of soft fruits. White crustless bread soaked in the juice from this mixture is used to line a mould, the fruits are packed into the lined mould which is covered with more sauce-soaked bread and the whole left under pressure and chilled. When firm the pudding is demoulded onto a plate and garnished as appropriate

summer purslane A half-hardy low-growing plant *Portulaca oleracea* with slightly succulent leaves used in salads or as a vegetable. There are two varieties, green leaved with the better flavour and the yellow or garden type which looks better in salads. The leaves may be cut regularly during the summer [also called **pigweed, portulaca, common purslane, green purslane**]

summer sausage *(USA)* The general term for keeping sausages made with cured pork and beef, similar to cervelat. Sometimes dried and smoked

summer savory An annual herb *Satureja hortensis* with a taste like a mixture of rosemary and thyme with a hint of pepper. It has slightly larger and more rounded leaves than the winter variety and a sparser habit. Used in the same way as winter savory

summer squash Various fruits of *Cucurbita* spp. which are normally harvested when immature before the skin hardens, and the whole fruit used as a vegetable. The most common is the vegetable marrow, the juvenile version of which is the courgette. Examples of USA squashes are crookneck, straight neck, scallop or patty pan, cocozelle, beinz and vegetable spaghetti

sumo domoda *(WA)* A meat or fish stew from Gambia containing fried onions, tomato purée, peanut butter, chillis and seasoning

Sumpfmyrte *(Ge)* Bog myrtle

su mui jeong *(Ch)* Plum sauce

sunberry 1 *see* wonderberry **2** A hybrid blackberry *Rubus* spp.

sunchoke *(USA)* Jerusalem artichoke

sundae An elaborate decorated dessert made with ice cream, whipped cream, fruit or chocolate sauces and chopped nuts

sunflower A tender annual *Helianthus annuus* which grows up to 3 m high with a large yellow daisy type of flower. The seeds are a major source of vegetable oil and are often eaten raw or roasted esp. as a snack. The flower buds may be steamed and served like globe artichokes

sunflower (seed) oil One of the commonest European vegetable oils extracted from sunflower seeds. Suitable for all culinary uses and used to make margarine. Can be heated to high temperatures without burning

sunflower seeds The seeds of the sunflower q.v. eaten raw or roasted as a snack or used in salads

sunfruit A citrus hybrid grown in Swaziland which is very similar to the New Zealand grapefruit

sung kha ya *(Th)* An egg custard made with sweetened coconut milk flavoured with jasmine essence or orange-flower water and baked in the shells of young coconuts

sunnyside up *(USA)* Description of a fried egg with the yolk uppermost on a plate and which has not been turned over in the frying pan to set the yolk

sunomono *(Ja)* A variety of salad-type dishes (poultry, seafood, vegetables, etc.) dressed with variously flavoured vinegar-based sauces and served in tiny portions as an appetizer or served as a separate course in a formal meal

sunset yellow FCF E110, a synthetic yellow food colouring

sun tsui *(Ch)* Sweet pepper

suola *(Fi)* Salt

suomalainen lammamuhennos *(Fi)* A mutton stew with potatoes, onions, carrots and turnips. Lit. Finnish lamb stew

suomolaisleipä *(Fi)* Yeasted bread Lit. Finnish bread

sup *(Ru)* Soup

sup iz syra i kartophelya *(Ru)* A potato and cheese soup from Moldavia made from chopped onions and carrots sautéed in butter until golden, simmered with chopped potatoes, seasoning, paprika, cayenne pepper and parsley in chicken stock, puréed, consistency adjusted and hard ewes' milk cheese (Brynza, Ektori or equivalent, 50 to 100 g per litre) dissolved in over a low heat.

sup iz yogurta *(Ru)* A cold soup made from Greek style yoghurt and soda water (2:1), seasoned and flavoured with chopped tarragon and dill. Chopped walnuts, dried apricots or other ingredients may be added

supa kangya *(WA)* A Gambian dish of fried fish and onions simmered in stock with tomato purée, garlic, spinach, okra and palm oil

supa khlebova *(Ru)* A Ukrainian black bread soup made from mixed vegetables e.g. carrot, leek, celery, onion, parsnip and broad beans, a little stale black bread and beef stock, simmered until tender, puréed, seasoned, thickened with egg yolk and finished with 10% buttermilk and 10% milk. Served with croûtons fried in bacon fat

super chill storage Storage of food at −5°C

superfine olive oil The second cold pressing (higher pressure) of the olives with a 1.5% maximum oleic acid content

superfine sugar *(USA)* Icing sugar

superfino *(It)* The finest grade of rice with large long grains of which arborio is the well known example. It requires 18 minutes cooking time and is used for the best quality risotto

supparod *(Th)* Pineapple

Suppe *(Ge)* Soup

suppe *(De & No)* Soup

Suppenbrühe *(Ge)* Stock

supper Either a light meal or snack taken after the main evening meal before retiring or an alternative name for the main evening meal

suppli *(It)* Croquettes made from a mixture of boiled risotto rice mixed with butter, Parmesan, eggs and pepper wrapped around a filling of ham and cheese or tomato and chicken liver, panéed and deep fried. Eaten as a snack

suprême *see* suprême de volaille, alternatively the best or most delicate cut

Suprême des Ducs *(Fr) masc.* A soft surface ripened cheese made from whole cows' milk and cast in small ovals. The smooth creamy paste becomes stronger tasting as it ages

suprême of fish A piece of fish cut diagonally from a fillet of fish

suprême de volaille *(Fr) masc.* The breast and wing to the first joint from one side of a chicken, turkey or other bird.

suprême, sauce *(En & Fr) fem.* A velouté sauce made from chicken stock flavoured with mushroom trimmings, strained, reboiled, a liaison added to the sauce off the heat and finished with lemon juice.

sur 1 *(No)* Milk several months old **2** *(No & Sw)* Sour

sur grädde *(Sw)* Sour cream

suram *see* elephant's foot

surati panir *(In)* A white cheese produced in Gujarat from buffalo milk. It develops a sharp pungent flavour as it is matured in whey

surf clam *(USA & SEA)* A very abundant clam *Spisula solidissima* up to 15 cm across found in deep water off the eastern coasts. It is triangular in shape with dark brown zig zag markings on a yellowish shell. The flesh is usually cooked in other made-up dishes [also called **bar clam, eastern surf clam**]

surf 'n' turf *(USA)* Seafood and meat served together

surface ripened cheese Cheeses ripened by the growth of moulds (Camembert or Brie types) or bacteria (Pont l'Evêque, Munster types) on the surface of the cheese

surgelato *(It)* Deep frozen

surgelé(e) *(Fr)* Deep frozen

suribashi *(Ja)* A ceramic mortar with a rough sandy surface used with a wooden pestle *(surikogi)*

surikogi *(Ja)* A wooden pestle used with a ceramic mortar *(suribashi)*

surimi *(Fr & Ja)* Imitation crab meat made from processed white fish flavoured and coloured. Similar to crab sticks

surimi soup An unthickened fish soup based on fish stock simmered with surimi, sliced mushrooms and cucumber and finished with soya sauce and chopped celery leaves

Surinam amaranth *see* amaranths

Surinam cherry The fruit of a shrub *Eugenia uniflora* of the myrtle family which grows in tropical or sub-tropical areas. The fruit is like a large red, turning to black, cherry with eight clefts starting at the stem end. The red flesh is soft and juicy and may be eaten raw or cooked [also called **jambos**]

surkål *(No & Sw)* Sauerkraut

suro *(It)* Horse mackerel

surstek *(Sw)* Sirloin, marinated for 5 to 10 days in red wine, vinegar and oil with chopped sweated shallots, thyme, cloves, bay, crushed peppercorns and juniper berries, sugar and salt. It is then dried, larded, seasoned, browned and roasted at a low temperature until tender. Lit. sour roast

surströmming *(Sw)* Fermented strömming (Baltic herring) from the north of Sweden

surtidos *(Sp)* An assortment

surumi-ika *(Ja)* A type of squid

sushi *(Ja)* Small rolls of cooked rice flavoured with rice vinegar, sugar and salt, topped with a variety of sliced or shaved raw seafood, pieces of sweet omelette or shredded vegetables, wrapped in nori and sliced, or alternatively moulded to form a decorative bite-sized package. Served with wasabi, beni-shoga and a soya sauce dip. Sushi was invented to fulfil the same need as the sandwich, i.e. for keen gamblers who wished to eat whilst playing; *see also* sushi meshi, chirashi-zushi, fukasa-zushi, maki-zushi, nigiri-zushi and oshi-zushi

sushi meshi *(Ja)* The rice used in sushi made by cooking short grain rice in water with kombu, draining, removing the kombu and tossing with a mixture of rice vinegar, salt and sugar whilst still hot. Prepared as needed

sushi-su *(Ja)* Seasoned rice wine vinegar

sushoga *(Ja)* Pink coloured, wafer-thin slices of pickled ginger rhizome used as an accompaniment to Japanese dishes esp. sushi

susina damaschina *(It)* Damson

susine *(It)* Plums

susino selvatico *(It)* Bullace, the fruit

süss-saure *(Ge)* Sweet and sour

süsse *(Ge)* Sweet

Süssespiesen *(Ge)* Sweet desserts

sütlaç *(Tu)* Rice pudding made on top of the stove and served with ice cream

Sussex dumpling *(UK)* A dumpling made only of flour, salt and water [also called **hard dumpling, Sussex swimmer**]

Sussex heavies *(UK)* Scones

Sussex pond pudding A suet pudding made by lining a pudding basin with suet pastry and filling with brown sugar, currants and butter with a pricked lemon in the centre, covering the top with pastry and foil, boiling for 3 hours and turning out on a plate when a pond is formed around the pudding.

Sussex swimmer *(UK) see* Sussex dumpling or swimmers

Süssholz *(Ge)* Liquorice

Süssigkeiten *(Ge)* Sweet desserts

susumber 1 *see* pea aubergine **2** *see* drumstick pod

süt *(Tu)* Milk

su tang *(Ch)* A rectangle of gluten dough rolled up like a Swiss roll then cut across in slices and cooked in stir fried and braised dishes

sutari *(In)* Rice bean

suyo *(Ja)* A variety of Japanese cucumber

Suzette *see* crêpes Suzette

suzuki *(Ja)* Sea bass

svamp *(Sw)* Mushrooms [also called **champinjoner**]

svampfylld kalkon *(Sw)* Turkey, seasoned and rubbed with lemon, stuffed with cold creamed mushrooms *(svampstuvning)* mixed with the chopped heart and liver plus butter, barded with bacon and roasted whilst basting with water. Served with jus rôti and red currant jelly

svampstuvning *(Sw)* Creamed mushrooms made from seasoned and chopped onions and mushrooms sweated in butter, to which flour is added, cooked and followed by cream, then all boiled for about 20 minutes

svariati *(It)* Assorted, varied

svarta vinbär *(Sw)* Black currant

svartsoppa *(Sw)* A very elaborate soup garnished with slices of apple and prunes boiled in water, goose liver sausage and giblets, served at the goose feast on the 11th of November. It is made from a strained veal and goose giblet stock, thickened with flour, cooked out and removed from the heat to which 20% of strained goose blood is added with vigorous stirring whilst the soup is brought back to boiling point. It is again removed from the heat and 3% red wine, 2% Madeira, 1% brandy and 1% sugar syrup (all percentages on original stock) added plus water from cooking the apples and prunes. The whole is seasoned and flavoured with cinnamon, ginger and cloves. The flavour improves with aging up to 24 hours

Sveciaost *(Sw)* A hard cow's milk cheese made in very large blocks and varying in taste from mild to strong depending on maturity. It has a few medium sized holes

svedsker *(De)* Prunes

Svenbo *(De)* A semi-hard cooked-curd cows' milk cheese with a mild flavour and a few large holes. Contains 43% water, 25% fat and 24% protein

Svensk panna *(Sw)* Slices of veal and pork fillet and calf's kidney blanched, refreshed and boiled in stock with a BG and sliced onions until half cooked. Sliced potatoes are added and all cooked until just done. Lit. Swedish pot

svestkové knedliky *(Cz)* A plum dumpling formed round a prune, possibly with cottage cheese

svieza desra *(Ru)* A highly prized pork and beef sausage

svin *(De)* Pig

svine kotelette *(De)* Pork chops

svine mørbrad *(De)* Pork fillet

svinekød *(De)* Pork [also called **flæsk**]

svinekjøtt *(No)* Pork

svinekotelett *(No)* Pork chop

svinestek *(No)* Roast pork

svinina *(Ru)* Pork

svinoye filye *(Ru)* Pork loin

svisker *(No)* Prunes

sviskon *(Sw)* Prunes

swäbischer Kalbsvogel *(Ge)* Paupiettes of veal filled with veal forcemeat and bacon, braised on a mirepoix with stock and white wine. Served with the reduced cooking liquor mixed with capers and chopped anchovies

Swaledale *(UK)* A semi-soft, creamy and moist cheese matured for 3 weeks to give it a mild distinctive flavour. It is made from whole Jersey cow's milk in Swaledale, Yorkshire

swamp cabbage A relative of the sweet potato *Ipomoea aquatica* and *I. reptans* which grows in water, hence the botanical name. Grown for its delicate leaves and stems which are used as a vegetable and eaten raw in salads. Originated in Africa but now grown in Australia, USA and SEA [also called **water spinach, Chinese water spinach, swamp spinach, water convolvulus**]

swamp spinach *see* swamp cabbage

Swatow mustard cabbage *see* daai gaai choy

sweat, to To cook without colouring in fat over a low heat in a pan with a tightly-fitting lid

swede The large swollen spinning-top shaped root of a brassica *Brassica napus* Napobrassica Group, with purple skin and dense yellow flesh weighing up to 1.5 kg. Used as a vegetable in the same way as carrots and turnips and also as animal feed [also called **Swedish turnip**]

Swedish anchovies *see* brisling and sprat

Swedish blood sausage *(Sw)* A black pudding made with pig's blood, rye meal and raisins

Swedish hash *see* pytt i panna

Swedish sauce Mayonnaise mixed with apple purée and grated horseradish served with cold meats, etc.

Swedish turnip *see* swede

sweet One of the four fundamental tastes, sweet, sour, bitter and dry; *see also* sweets

sweet almond *see* almond

sweet anise *(USA) see* Florence fennel

sweet apple *see* sweet sop

sweet basil *see* basil

sweet bay *see* bay

sweet bean paste A thick brown sauce made from ground fermented soya beans mixed with sugar and brine. Popular in Taiwan as a condiment or seasoning

sweet brier *see* rose

sweet cherry The dessert cherry *Prunus avium* used for eating raw or cooking and varying in colour from pale yellow to deep red

sweet chestnut *see* chestnut

sweet cicely A hardy herbaceous perennial *Myrrhis odorata* with feathery leaves and long (to 20 mm) ridged black seeds. The leaves have a pleasant myrrh-like scent and flavour with a hint of aniseed. Both the unripe and ripe seeds have a stronger aniseed flavour. Unripe seeds may be used in salads, ripe seeds as a spice. The leaves may be added to soups, stews, or used to flavour omelettes, salad dressing and cabbage [also called **myrrh**]

sweet clover *see* melilot

sweet corn A variety of maize *Zea mays saccharata* with a higher proportion of sugars in the maturing kernels. Usually boiled or roasted and eaten directly from the cob after being buttered and salted. The kernels are often sold separately either canned or frozen. Unscrupulous suppliers will often sell maize cobs *Zea mays* which are less sweet and more chewy [also called **corn on the cob**]

sweet cream butter *(USA)* Unsalted butter containing at least 80% butterfat

sweet crust pastry *see* flan pastry

sweet cumin Fennel seed

sweet cure A quick curing fluid containing a high proportion of sugar

sweet flag *see* calamus

sweet gale *see* bog myrtle

sweet granadilla The fruit of a variety of passion flower *Passiflora ligularis* which has a typical orange-coloured passion fruit skin enclosing a loose packet of grey seeds in a gelatinous pulp, which taste rather like a sweet gooseberry [also called **orange passion fruit**]

sweet laurel *see* bay

sweet lime A low acid rather insipid lime *Citrus limettiodes.* It has a smooth yellow rind with a distinctive aroma and a tender flesh with a few seeds. Popular in India and the Middle East [also called **Indian sweet lime, Palestine sweet lime**]

sweet marjoram A herb *Origanum majorana* with aromatic grey-green leaves from the Mediterranean and western Asia now grown in France, Chile, Peru and California. Used in Italian cooking and with lamb, chicken and oily fish. Since it has a delicate flavour which is destroyed by cooking it should be added at the last moment; *see also* marjoram [also called **knotted marjoram**]

sweet melon *see* melon

sweet milk *(USA)* Cow's milk

sweet nim Leaves of a bush similar in appearance to bay but smaller and thinner

sweet orange The common orange of commerce *Citrus sinensis* with an easily removed skin, and an excellent, sometimes slightly acid, flavour and few or no seeds. Classified in four groups, Navel, Common (e.g. Valencia), Pigmented (blood orange) and Acidless. It has been cultivated in southern China for several thousand years and was first grown in the Mediterranean around 1450. Modern varieties were introduced by the Portuguese [also called **orange**]

sweet pepper The fruit of an annual bush *Capsicum annuum* Grossum Group which is green when unripe and passes through yellow to red as it becomes riper. Some can be purple or brown. They are generally about 8 - 15 cm long, 6 - 10 cm in diameter, possible tapering with a fleshy outer covered with a tough shiny skin and with small seeds in the mainly hollow interior. Known by their colour (i.e. green, red peppers) or as paprika or bell peppers. Their flavour is due to the compound capsaicin which is an irritant in high concentrations [also called **Spanish pepper**]

sweet pickle *see* chutney

sweet potato A starchy tuber similar to an elongated potato which grows on a tender perennial *Ipomoea batatus,* with trailing stems usually grown as an annual in tropical and subtropical climates (24 to 26°C). It has a white to purple skin and a dense white to orange flesh with a sweetish perfumed taste. Used as a staple food and cooked like potatoes. The leaves may also be eaten as spinach [also called **kumara, Louisiana yam, yam, yellow yam**]

sweet red bean paste Boiled adzuki beans mashed into a paste with oil and sugar and cooked until fairly thick and dry. Used in cakes and desserts; *see also* koshi-an and tsubushi-an

sweet rocket A hardy biennial cottage flower *Hesperis matronalis* with white to purple four-petalled flowers, now a wild garden escape. The young leaves are more bitter than rocket q.v. but may be used sparingly in salads

sweet sake *(Ja) see* mirin

sweet sop A type of custard apple q.v. from a tree *Anona squamosa* cultivated in the tropics. It is about 5 to 7.5 cm in dia. with a green scaly skin and a white flesh with the texture of thick custard containing embedded black inedible seeds. Eaten raw or in made-up dishes and drinks [also called **sugar apple, sweet apple, scaly custard apple**]

sweet sorghum A variety of sorghum *Sorghum vulgare* var. *saccharatum* which is grown for the sugary sap pressed from the stems esp. in the USA. This is evaporated to make sorghum syrup which is like a thin and slightly acidic molasses [also called **sugar sorghum**]

sweet and sour A method of cooking or preserving food in a mixture of vinegar and sugar

sweet and sour pork A typical Chinese dish served in Europe of floured pork, deep fried and served in sweet and sour sauce possibly mixed with stir-fried vegetables and fruit

sweet and sour sauce A cornflour thickened sauce based on vinegar and sugar with soya sauce, flavourings and rice wine or sherry, possibly with the addition of white stock, chopped pineapple and vegetables

sweet soya sauce A dark soya sauce sweetened with sugar and maltose which gives it a malty taste. Used extensively in the eastern coastal provinces of China

sweet vinegar *(Ch)* A dark, mild rice vinegar containing sugar and caramel and flavoured with cassia and star anise. Used in relatively large quantities in braised meat dishes

sweet violet The most highly scented of the violets *Viola odorata* is a hardy, spreading, perennial growing to 15 cm. The flowers are crystallized for use as a decoration and also used to flavour syrups and vinegar

sweet woodruff A white flowered herb *Galium odoratum* with the scent of new mown hay found growing wild in woodland. Used to flavour some wines, apple juice, liqueurs and German white beer as well as the young German wine known as Maibowle

sweetbreads The pancreas and thymus glands from beef cattle, calves and lambs. Usually prepared by washing, blanching, refreshing and trimming then braising with stock on a bed of roots until tender. Served with some of the cooking liquor.

sweeten, to To add sugar or artificial sweetener to a dish

sweetgrass buffalo and beer pie *(Cn)* A stew of buffalo meat with vegetables, sago, herbs, spices, beer and seasoning, cooked then put in a pie dish, covered with pastry and baked. From Alberta

sweetheart melon A type of canteloup melon with a bright scarlet flesh

sweetie *(ME)* A pummelo/grapefruit cross extensively grown in Israel. It has a greenish thick rind, a high sugar content and low acidity. As it matures, the rind becomes yellow orange and it is marketed as golden sweetie

sweets **1** Confections based mainly on flavoured sugar, caramel and chocolate with sometimes butter, cream and/or milk. Made in small individual bite-sized pieces as comfort food **2** A common name for desserts, puddings, etc. being a variety of fruit, cake, pastry, sugar, eggs and cream confections served at or near the end of a meal, before the cheese in the UK and after the cheese in France

sweetwater grape *see* dessert grape

swimmers *(UK) coll. (Norfolk)* Suet and self-raising flour dumplings flavoured with chopped chives and cooked on top of soups or stews [also called **Sussex swimmers**]

swimming crab A small crab *Macropipus puber* to 10 cm across found in the Mediterranean and Atlantic. Eaten in France

swirl, to To mix one liquid with another or a soluble solid in a liquid by a gentle circular, figure-of-eight or to-and-fro motion

Swiss bun A plain white yeast-raised dough shaped into a long soft roll (to 15 cm), cooled and covered with glacé icing

Swiss chard A variety of beet *Beta vulgaris* Cicla Group grown for its dark crinkly glossy leaves with thick white or red stems which grow in a cluster from the base. The leaves and stems are generally cooked as separate vegetables usually by steaming. Common in the Mediterranean countries and similar to spinach [also called **chard, silver beet** (Aus & USA), **white beetleaf beet, seakale beet**]

Swiss cheese *(USA)* A hard cooked-curd cows' milk cheese made in large cylinders or blocks (to 100 kg) to resemble Emmental. The starter culture contains *Lactobacillus bulgaricus, Streptococcus thermophylus* and *Propionibacter shermanii* and the milk is curdled with rennet. The pressed curd is brined, stored at high temperature and humidity for 3 to 6 weeks and ripened at low temperatures for 4 to 12 months

Swiss fondue *see* fondue

Swiss meringue *see* meringue Suisse

Swiss omelette *see* Eierhaber

Swiss roll A Genoese sponge baked in a shallow rectangular tray about 1.5 cm final thickness on greased paper, turned out onto sugared paper, spread with jam and rolled up whilst still hot leaving the paper to hold its shape until cooled. If to be filled with cream, first rolled hot then unrolled to fill. May be eaten cold as a cake or hot with a suitable sweet sauce

Swiss steak *(USA)* **1** Rump steak, seasoned and stewed with onions, tomatoes, sweet peppers and possibly garlic and flavoured with herbs and spices **2** Round steak tenderized by breaking down the fibres mechanically with a mallet faced with many points at the same time forcing flour and seasoning into the meat then treating as (1)

sword bean A perennial legume *Canavalia gladiata* similar to the jack bean but with curved pods and pink to brown seeds. Used both for the ripe beans which should be boiled and for the green pods [also called **sabre bean**]

swordfish A seawater fish *Xiphias gladius* which grows to 3 m long with a snout or sword one third its length. It can weigh up to 100 kg and travel at 100 km per hour. It has a dryish firm pink flesh usually sold in steaks and grilled or fried esp. in Mediterranean countries. May be smoked and served as smoked salmon

syau *(Ne)* Apple

Sydney rock oyster *(Aus)* A comparitively cheap and popular variety of farmed oyster *Saccostrea commercialis*

syllabub *(UK)* An old English dessert originally either the froth from a whisked mixture of cream, wine, sugar and lemon zest, or a frothy mixture of milk with wine, cider or ale and sugar, spices and spirits. Nowadays made by mixing whisked egg whites with sweetened whipped cream flavoured with lemon juice and wine or spirits [also called **sillabub**]

sylt *(Sw)* Jam

syltede rødbeder *(De)* Pickled beetroot

syltetøj *(De)* Jam

syltetøy *(No)* Jam

syltlök *(Sw)* Button onion

Symphytum officinale *Bot.* Comfrey

symposium The second part of a formal meal in ancient Greece given over to drinking and entertainment; *see also* deipnon

synthetic fats E471, E472(a to e), E473, E474, E475 and E477, various esters of fatty acids all derived from natural products for use in place of natural fats and oils in baked goods, desserts, etc. to improve their keeping qualities and to soften and stabilize them

syr *(Ru)* Cheese

Syrecky *(Cz)* *see* Olomoucké syrecky

syrniki *(Ru)* Curd cheese fritters

syrup A concentrated solution of sugar (sucrose or sucrose with a third its weight of glucose) in water used as an ingredient in many sweet dishes and drinks. Concentrations can be measured in °Beaumé, kg of sugar per litre of solution or kg of sugar per litre of water, the last named being the most convenient. In these last units, a light syrup has between 0.1 and 0.4 kg, a medium syrup between 0.4 and 0.8 kg and a heavy syrup between 0.8 and 3.0 kg of sugar per litre of water. Stock syrup has 0.4 kg of sugar per litre of water

syrup pudding *(UK)* **1** A roly-poly pudding q.v. sweetened with golden syrup [also called **syrup roly-poly**] **2** A pudding made from the basic steamed pudding mixture poured into a greased basin whose base has been covered with golden syrup

syrup roly-poly *(UK)* *see* syrup pudding

syrup sauce Stock syrup and lemon juice, thickened with cornflour or arrowroot, cooked out and strained

Syzygium malaccensis *Bot.* Rose apple

Szechuan *(Ch)* A province of China [also called **Sichuan**]. The two names are interchanged at random

Szechuan pepper *see* anise pepper

Szechuanese cooking The style of cooking from the Chinese province of Szechuan which is in the west next to the Tibetan border. It is renowned for its peasant based hot and spicy dishes with a strong emphasis on preserved foods

sze gwa *(Ch)* Angled loofah

székelygulyás *(Hu)* A seasoned pork stew with onions fried in lard, sauerkraut and flavoured with caraway, garlic, paprika and chopped dill. Served with soured cream

szynka sznurowana *(Pl)* A hard smoked ham sausage available throughout the country

Tt

taai goo choy *(Ch)* Chinese flat cabbage

ta'amia *(Ey)* Soaked and cooked chickpeas or broad beans minced, mixed with water, egg, seasoning, turmeric, ground cumin, cayenne pepper, chopped garlic and coriander leaves, breadcrumbs and tahini or olive oil to form a soft but firm paste, formed into 2 to 3 cm balls and shallow fried until golden brown. Traditionally a Coptic Lenten dish but now served throughout the ME; *see also* falafel

taapke *(Ne)* Frying pan

taart *(Ho)* Layer cake, fancy cake

Tabasco sauce A hot, red- coloured sauce made from particular red chillis grown in Louisiana, USA, ground with vinegar and matured for 3 years in oak barrels

tabbouleh *(ME) see* tabouleh

tabbuli *(ME) see* tabouleh

tabil *(NA)* A Tunisian mixture of coriander seeds, caraway seed, garlic and chilli flakes, dried in a slow oven and ground

table cream *(USA) see* coffee cream

table d'hôte *(En & Fr) fem.* A fixed price menu with a fixed number of courses with possibly some choice of dishes in each course. Sometimes supplements for more expensive dishes are charged

table queen squash A winter squash common in the USA which varies in colour from pale green to deep orange. It is round with a tough green skin [also called **acorn squash**]

table salt A fine-grained, free-flowing salt suitable for being dispensed at the table from a salt shaker. It is pure sodium chloride with the addition of anti-caking agents, a function which was performed before additives by a few grains of dry rice

table water *see* mineral water

tablier de sapeur *(Fr) masc.* Panéed pieces of tripe, fried or grilled and served with snail butter. Lit sapper's apron

tabouleh *(ME)* A salad made with fine bulgar which has ben well washed and drained, mixed with peeled and chopped tomatoes, cucumber, sweet green pepper and onion, chopped mint and parsley, seasoned then dressed with olive oil and lemon juice. Eaten with lettuce or pitta bread [also called **tabbouleh, tabbuli**]

tacchina *(It)* Turkey hen

taccula *(It)* Blackbirds trussed and defeathered but not drawn, wrapped in myrtle leaves and braised

taco *(Me)* A small tortilla either fried crisp and eaten immediately or cooked like a pancake, rolled around a stuffing and eaten hot. Served as a snack or a light meal

tadka *(In)* A spice-flavoured butter used in cooking

taeng ka *(Th)* Cucumber

Tafelsenf *(Ge)* Common table mustard

Tafelspitz *(Au)* Top rump or other good cut of beef simmered with blanched beef bones, aromatic vegetables, BG, leeks, onion clouté, garlic, tomato and dried ceps. Served with Apfelkren and Schnittlauchsoss

Taffel *(Au)* A semi-hard cooked-curd cows' milk cheese with a close textured paste containing a few holes. Contains 45% water, 24% fat and 23% protein

Tageskarte *(Ge)* Dish of the day

Tagessuppe *(Ge)* Soup of the day

tagine *(NA) see* tajine

tagliarine *(It) see* tagliatelle

tagliatelle *(It)* 5 mm wide noodles made from an egg based pasta dough, available fresh or dried [also called **tagliarine**]

tagliatelle alla biellese *(It)* Tagliatelle with milk or cream, butter and grated Parmesan cheese

tagliatelle della duchessa *(It)* Tagliatelle with chicken livers, egg yolk and grated Parmesan cheese

tagliatelle verde *(It)* Green tagliatelle made from egg-based pasta dough coloured with spinach purée

tagliato *(It)* Cut or sliced

tagliolini *(It)* A thin linguine

tahari *(In)* A dish of rice and peas flavoured with spices and herbs

taheena *see* tahini

tahina *see* tahini

tahini A thick paste made from ground, husked or unhusked white sesame seeds mixed with sesame seed oil and of the same texture as peanut butter. The unhusked seeds give a darker and more bitter paste. Used in savoury dishes and as a constituent of hummus. In Asia usually made from toasted seeds [also called **taheena, tahini, sesame butter, sesame seed paste**]

tahini salad dressing Tahini paste, lemon juice and water (2:2:5) mixed until smooth

tahinyeh *(ME)* Tahini paste mixed with lemon juice, milk, finely chopped parsley, crushed garlic, salt, chilli powder and white breadcrumbs to form a thick creamy paste and sprinkled with parsley and cumin. May be used as a dip or in place of mayonnaise

Tahiti lime *see* Persian lime

taho *(Ph)* Bean curd brains or silk bean curd

tahong *(Ph)* Asian mussel

tahu 1 *(Ch)* Tofu or bean curd **2** *(Id & Ma)* Bean curd or bean curd cheese

tahure *(Ph)* Bean curd

tai *(Ja)* Sea bream

taikina *(Fi)* Dough, batter, pastry

tail The tails of animals or fish. Of the animal tails only oxtail is commonly used. Pigs' tails are occasionally used in some cuisines

tail cut The tail end of a fillet from a large round fish

tailed pepper *see* cubeb

tailler *(Fr)* To cut

taingang daga *(Ph)* Cloud ear fungus

tai tai *(Ch)* Seville orange

tai tempura *(Ja)* Fried fish cakes

tajadas *(Sp)* Slices, of e.g. roast meat

tajine *(NA)* **1** A slowly simmered stew of meat or fish with appropriate vegetables, pulses and fruits, cooked in its own juices in an earthenware pot with a conical lid. Almost anything can go in a tajine. See further entries for types **2** The pot in which tajine is cooked

tajine bel hout *(NA)* A fish tajine containing tomatoes, sweet red pepper, chillis, ginger and saffron

tajine de lapin *(NA)* A tajine of rabbit with vegetables

tajine de poisson *(NA)* A tajine of fish, usually bream or sardines, with tomatoes and herbs

tajine de poulet *(NA)* A tajine of chicken cooked with lemon and olives

tajine slaoui *(NA)* A tajine of meat balls with vegetables

tajine de viande *(NA)* A mutton tajine with vegetables or prunes

take-away 1 A food shop or restaurant which supplies hot food, generally cooked to order, in containers or wrappings for taking away and consuming elsewhere, e.g. fish and chips, Indian and Chinese dishes **2** The general name for the hot package of food supplied by a take-away.

takegushi *(Ja)* Bamboo skewers used for grilling chicken and tofu

takenoko *(Ja)* Bamboo shoots

takiawase *(Ja)* A mixture of firm vegetable pieces (e.g. potatoes, carrots, courgettes, aubergines), each fried separately in separate oil until al dente, mixed with fried cubes of tofu and flavoured with a light soya sauce

taklia *(Ey)* A spice mix of ground coriander fried with either crushed garlic or cumin

tako *(Ja)* Octopus

tako kushisashi *(Ja)* Octopus kebabs

ta krai *(Th)* Lemon grass

takuan *(Ja)* A pickle made of mooli, air dried for 2 to 3 weeks, salted and immersed in dry rice bran *(muka-zuke method)*

talaba *(Ph)* Oyster

talas *(Id)* Taro

talattouri *(Gr) see* tsatsiki

talawa *(In)* Deep frying in exactly the same way as in the West

talc *see* (E)553(b)

Taleggio *(It)* A semi-soft, mild cow's milk cheese from Lombardy resembling Camembert. It is produced in 2 kg squares and has a white paste with a few small holes and a pinkish-grey surface mould on the rind. It develops flavour as it matures [also called **Talfino**]

Talfino *(It) see* Taleggio

tal ha'emek *(ME)* An Emmental type cheese from Israel

taliány *(Cz)* A sausage similar to vurty but with diced fat bacon in the mix

talim num *(Ph)* Spinach

tallarines *(Sp)* Noodles

Talleyrand, à la *(Fr)* In the style of Prince

Talleyrand, i.e. garnished, esp. poultry, with macaroni, cheese, truffle, foie gras and possibly button mushrooms

tallow A hard coarse fat originally rendered from mutton and used for lighting

talmouse *(Fr) fem.* Cheesecake

talong *(Ph)* Aubergine

tamaater *(Ne)* Tomato

tamago *(Ja)* Eggs

tamago-hanjuku *(Ja)* Soft-boiled eggs

tamago-medamayak *(Ja)* Fried eggs

tamago-pochi *(Ja)* Poached eggs

tamago-yakiki *(Ja) see* maki yakinabe

tamago-yude *(Ja)* Hard-boiled eggs

tamakibi *(Ja)* Winkle, the shellfish

tamale flour *see* masa harina

tamale pie *(USA)* Cornmeal porridge with a filling of chopped meats and hot chilli sauce

tamales *(Me)* A thick porridge made from masa harina, one serving placed on a banana leaf, maize leaves or foil and topped with a cooked meat and chilli mixture or with cheese, rolled up, steamed and served hot with chilli sauce

tâmaras *(Po)* Dates

tamari *(Ja)* A naturally fermented dark soya sauce

tamarillo A large yellow to red, hard, egg-shaped fruit of an evergreen shrub *Cyphomandra betacea* related to the tomato and kiwi fruit and resembling a giant rosehip, grown in tropical and sub-tropical climates. The flesh is somewhat acid but high in vitamin C and the seeds are edible. It is blanched and peeled before eating and may be used in fruit salads, for jam making and has been used for flavouring yoghurt and cheesecake [also called **tomarillo, tree tomato**]

tamarin *(Fr) masc.* Tamarind

tamarind The long (10 cm) dark brown pods of a tropical tree *Tamarindus indica,* usually sold as blocks of mashed pods and pulp or as a concentrated juice. The former is soaked in hot water and the juice squeezed out and used for souring in the same way as lemon juice [also called **Indian date**]

Tamarinde *(Ge)* Tamarind

Tamarindicus indica *Bot.* Tamarind

tamarindo *(It)* Tamarind

tamatar *(In)* Tomato

tambak merah *(Ma)* Snapper or bream

tamba kuri *(Ja)* Large mealy chestnuts

tambor *(Saf) see* ortanique

tambusa *(In)* Red snapper

Tamié *(Fr)* A smooth round cows' milk cheese from Annecy [also called **Trappiste de Tamié**]

tamis *(Fr) masc.* Sieve or sifter

tamiser *(Fr)* To rub through a tammy cloth, to sieve

tammy cloth A fine woven woollen cloth used for straining very fine particles from stocks, sauces, juices, etc. Best used after an initial straining through muslin

tampala *(In)* Chinese spinach

tanaceto *(It & Sp)* Tansy

Tanacetum balsamica *Bot.* Costmary

Tanacetum vulgare *Bot.* Tansy

tanaisie *(Fr) fem.* Tansy

tanche *(Fr) fem.* Tench

tandoor *(In)* An unglazed barrel-shaped, deep clay pot with a top opening, used as an oven in India. It is heated by charcoal in the base or gas. The food is either stuck on the side, e.g. nan bread, or put on long skewers which are either rested over the opening or stood with their points at the base propped up against the rim

tandoori *(In)* A method of cooking on a greased spit in a clay oven. The oven is often a deep pot and the spits stand vertical from the bottom resting on the rim. It gives a crisp dry finish. See tandoor

tandoori colouring A special food colouring powder formulated to give the orange red colour required in tandoori cooked food. Added to marinades

tandoori spice mix A selection from cinnamon bark, nutmeg, dried ginger, dried red chillis, paprika, cardamom, dried garlic, cumin and coriander seeds, ground to a fine powder, the colour adjusted to a bright orange with food colourings and used for marinating and coating meat prior to tandoori cooking

tang *(Ch)* Soup

tang chi Preserved radish, whole or in slices, usually vacuum packed in the West. Used to add texture and flavour to SEA dishes

tang cu li ji *(Ch)* Sweet and sour boneless pork

tangelo A naturally occurring hybrid of *Citrus* spp. *mandarin x grapefruit)* which occurs as two varieties Minneola and Orlando

tangerina *(Po)* Tangerine

tangerine *see* mandarin

tangerine peel The dried peel of mandarins (tangerines) which is ground and used as a flavouring in Chinese and Vietnamese food

tangia *(NA)* A casserole of lamb or beef cooked with spices

tang kuei *(Ch) see* dang gui

tangle *see* sea girdle

tangleberry A dark blue berry with a sweet sharp flavour which grows in the USA. Similar to the blueberry or huckleberry

tang mien *(Ch)* Noodles in soup

tangor *(ME) see* ortanique

tang ya suan tou *(Ch)* Pickled shallots

tanmen *(Ja)* A white instant noodle for soup

tannia A plant *Xanthosoma sagittifolium* which yields heavy (3-5 kg) yam-like tubers and arrow-shaped leaves which are used as a leaf vegetable. Cultivated throughout the tropics [also called **new cocoyam, pomtannia, yantia, yautia**]

tannic acid One of the acids in tannin, used for flavouring and as a clarifying agent in beer, wine and cider and other natural brewed drinks

tannin A mixture of strong astringent acids found in plants, particularly tea leaves, red grape skins and the bark of trees, with the ability to coagulate proteins. Responsible for the keeping qualities of fine red wines

tanrogan *(UK)* The local name in the Isle of Man for great and queen scallops which are found around its coasts

tansy 1 A hardy perennial and very invasive herb *Tanacetum vulgare* with green leaves and yellow flowers and a very strong flavour. Used by the Victorians for flavouring baked goods, sausages, stuffings and some desserts **2** A soufflé omelette mixture with fried tart fruit originally flavoured with tansy, nowadays with cloves and cinnamon. See e.g. damson and apple tansy

tanuki soba *(Ja)* Brown buckwheat noodles

tanuta *(It)* Black sea bream

tanyet *(Bm)* Palm sugar

tanzaku giri *(Ja)* Thin slender rectangles cut from root vegetables [also called **poem card cut**]

taoco *(Id)* Yellow bean sauce

tao do *(Vi)* Dried Chinese plums

tao hu *(Th)* Bean curd

tao hu kon *(Th)* Bean curd

tao tanu *(Th)* Turtle

tao zi *(Ch)* Peach

tapa *(Ph)* Thinly sliced dried and/or cured meat used as a snack. From the Spanish tapas q.v.

tapas *(Sp)* Originally a slice of ham or chorizo sausage placed over the mouth of a wine glass, from tapa to cover, some say to keep out flies, others to increase thirst. Now consists of small portions of any kind of made-up dish or individual snack served in bars with wine

tapénade A Provençale purée of capers, black olives and anchovies in olive oil. Sometimes other ingredients are added. Used as a dip or spread or to fill hard boiled eggs or hollowed out cucumber

tapéno *(Fr) masc.* Caper

ta pin *(Ma)* Steamboat

tapioca *(En, It, Sp & Fr) masc.* An alternative name for cassava but also used for the processed starch produced from cassava by cooking, drying and then flaking the starch. It is a useful thickener as it holds its consistency better than cornflour and arrowroot. Sometimes added to other flours to strengthen the dough

tapioca starch *see* tapioca

Tapioka *(Ge)* Tapioca

tapulon alla burgomanerese *(It)* Stewed donkey with red wine and cabbage

taquitos *(Me)* Small tacos filled with picadillo (2), folded, secured with a skewer and deep fried,

tara *(Ja)* Cod

tarako *(Ja)* Codfish roe, salted and dyed red to resemble caviar

tarama *(Gr)* The orange-coloured salted and dried roe of the grey mullet, an expensive delicacy used for hors d'oeuvres or in the preparation of authentic taramasalata

taramasalata *see* taramossalata

taramossalata *(Gr)* A pounded mixture of tarama, or more usually, smoked cod's roe, soft white breadcrumbs or mashed potatoes, crushed garlic, olive oil and lemon juice, used as a dip or served with bread as part of a mezze. More commercial versions, known as taramasalata in the West, are smoother and contain excessive amounts of extenders and fish flavouring, besides being a rather strange pink colour

tarator *(Bu & Hu)* A chilled, dill-flavoured yoghurt and cucumber sauce thickened with ground walnuts; alternatively a chilled soup made with grated cucumber, yoghurt, milk, lemon juice, garlic and parsley

tarator od krastavaca *(Bk)* A Macedonian salad of grated cucumber, green chillis, yoghurt and garlic

Taraxacum officinale *Bot.* Dandelion

tarbot *(Ho)* Turbot, the fish

tarbujaa *(Ne)* Watermelon

tardno *(It) see* Parmigiano Reggiano

targone *(It)* Tarragon

tarhonya *(Hu)* Small dried barley-shaped pellets of egg noodle dough. They are fried in lard then cooked in bouillon like a risotto and served with goulash, etc.

tari *(In)* Gravy

tarkaari *(Ne)* Vegetable

tarka *(In)* A style of finishing in Indian cookery involving the fierce searing of precooked food in ghee and seasonings to flavour and coat the surface of the food [also called **chamak**]

tarkari *(In)* A description of dishes containing vegetables which have been fried in ghee then gently cooked in their own juices

taro A tropical and sub-tropical tuber of a plant, *Colocassia antiquorum* var. *esculenta,* brought from SEA to the Caribbean as a staple food for slaves, hence the alternative name dasheen *(= de Chine)*. The tubers are boiled baked or roasted and the leaves are also edible [also called **dasheen (leaves), coco yam (tubers)**]

taro starch A greyish flour made by grinding taro chips. Used as a thickener and for making desserts

tarragon A half hardy perennial herb *Artemesia dracunculus* (Fr) and *A. dracunculoides* (Ru) growing to 1 m, whose narrow leaves have a warm, peppery bitter-sweet scent with a note of anise. The Russian variety is milder than the French. It has a wide variety of uses, as a flavouring for vinegar, emulsion sauces and dips, soups, omelettes, chicken, compound butters, etc. One of the constituents of fines herbes. Unlike the Russian, French tarragon does not set seeds and is propagated from cuttings; *see also* Russian tarragon [also called **French tarragon, Russian tarragon**]

tarragon butter A compound butter made from blanched and drained tarragon leaves squeezed dry, pounded with twice their weight of butter and sieved

tarragon vinegar A white wine vinegar flavoured with tarragon leaves

tart A shallow dish-shaped open pastry case usually shortcrust or flan pastry with a filling which may either be baked with the case e.g. Bakewell tart, or added later to a case which has been baked blind e.g. custard tart and most French fruit tarts; *see also* flan, patisserie

tarta *(Sp)* A small, single crust, open top tart

tårta *(Sw)* Layer cake

tartafin *(Fr)* A potato dish made from slices of waxy potatoes laid over sweated garlic with seasoning, covered with sliced Gruyère cheese and cooked in a closed container over a low heat until done

tartaleta *(Sp)* Small tart

tartar med æg *(De)* Steak tartare used as a topping for smørrebrød

tartar sauce *(USA)* Tartare sauce

tartara, alla *(It)* With tartare sauce

tartare 1 *(Fr)* A fresh cream cheese made from cow's milk and flavoured with chopped herbs **2** *(En) see* steak tartare

tartare, sauce *(En & Fr) fem.* **1** Chopped capers, gherkins and parsley, dried and mixed well with mayonnaise. Served with fried fish **2** Mashed hard boiled egg yolks, seasoned and mixed with vinegar, oil whisked in as in making mayonnaise and finished with a sieved purée of raw spring onions mixed with a little mayonnaise

tartaric acid E334, an acid present in many fruits which is precipitated as crystals in old wine. See E334 for uses

tartaruga aquatica *(It)* Terrapin

tartaruga *(It)* Turtle

tarte *(Fr) fem.* A single crust, open top tart

tarte au citron *(Fr) fem.* A pâte sablée pastry case filled with a whisked egg and sugar mixture to which has been added melted butter, lemon juice and grated lemon zest

tarte à la crème *(Fr) fem.* Custard tart on thin pastry

tarte limousine clafoutis *(Fr) fem.* A clafoutis q.v. baked in a blind pastry case

tarte lorraine *(Fr) fem.* A tart similar to a quiche filled with well spiced pork or veal and onions

tarte normande *(Fr) fem.* An apple flan

tarte à l'oignon *(Fr) fem.* An open tart filled with onions in a rich cream sauce

tarte Tatin *(Fr) fem.* An upside down apple pie made from sliced dessert apples fried in a baking dish with butter and flavourings, possibly with sugar so as to caramelize, covered with pastry, baked in the oven and turned out on a serving dish with the apple slices uppermost, hopefully with an attractive appearance

tarte au riz *(Be)* An open pastry case filled with a creamy dessert rice mixed with raisins or sultanas, chopped almonds and flavoured with nutmeg

tarteletta *(It)* Tartlet

tartelette *(Fr) fem.* Tartlet, small tart

tartina *(It)* Canapé, tartine

tartine *(Fr) fem.* A slice of bread and butter, sometimes a small tart or slice of fruit loaf

tartine suisse *(Fr) fem.* Puff pastry filled with vanilla-flavoured crème patissière

tartrates Salts of tartaric acid used as stabilizers, the principal ones being sodium- E335, potassium- E336 and the potassium sodium mixed salt E337

tartrazine E102, a synthetic dye used as a yellow food colouring, suspected of causing hyperactivity and allergies in some children

tartufato *(It)* With truffles

tartufi di cioccolati *(It)* Chocolate truffles

tartufi tre scalini *(It)* A ball shaped dessert of chocolate ice cream, cake and whipped cream

tartufo *(It)* Truffle

tartufo di mare *(It)* Warty venus clam

tarwebrood *(Ho)* Wholewheat bread

tasala The traditional cooking pot of Nepal and Kashmir with a round base and a flared neck and rim

Taschenkrebs *(Ge)* Common crab

Tascherin *(Au)* A type of ravioli with either a jam or savoury filling

Tasmanian crayfish *(Aus)* A large crayfish *Astacopsis gouldi* which can grow up to 6 kg in weight

tasse *(Fr) fem.* Cup

tasse, en *(Fr)* Served in a cup, esp. of soups

taste powder *see* monosodium glutamate

ta suan li *(Ch)* Asian pear

tate-jio *(Ja)* A method of treating food with a low concentration brine (30 g per litre) containing some kombu flavouring

tatties *(UK)* coll; *(Scotland)* Potatoes

Taube *(Ge)* Pigeon

taucheo *(Ma)* Yellow bean sauce

tauge *(Id)* Bean sprouts

tauhu tod *(Th)* Fried bean curd

tau kau *(Ch)* Nutmeg

tau ngok *(Th)* Mung bean or bean sprouts

taupe *(Fr) fem.* Porbeagle shark

tau sa *(Ma)* Yellow bean sauce

tausi *(Ph)* Bean curd cheese

tavola calda *(It)* Snack bar

tavola fredda *(It)* Cold buffet, cold table

tavsan *(Tu)* Hare

tawa *(In)* A circular, slightly dished steel or iron griddle with a handle, used for making Indian breads or, when placed below another dish, to reduce the heat esp. on a difficult to control heat source

tawas *(Ph)* Alum

tayberry A cross between a blackberry and raspberry *Rubus* spp. It is large and conical, a bright deep purple in colour and with a rich flavour

tay vi *(Vi)* Star anise

tazza *(It)* Cup or small bowl

tazzina Small cup, coffee cup

tazzine, nella *(It)* Coddled, of eggs

T-bone steak *(USA)* A steak cut from between the sirloin and short loin of beef (the centre of the sirloin (UK)) including a piece of vertebra in the shape of a capital T and about 5 cm thick. It will feed 2 persons

tea cake A flat, slightly sweetened yeast-raised round bread bun with currants and mixed peel about 10 cm in diameter. Usually split, toasted and buttered

tea cream *(UK)* Milk infused with an aromatic tea, thickened with egg yolks, cream and gelatine, whipped egg whites folded in, set in a mould, turned out and decorated

tea leaf egg Egg boiled for 2 to 3 hours in water with tea leaves, star anise and other flavourings. After 20 minutes the shells are cracked to allow penetration of the flavours and to produce marbling. Served as hors d'oeuvres

tea smoking A method of smoking meat or fish using a domestic steamer. The base is lined with foil and equal volumes of brown sugar, uncooked rice and an aromatic tea (e.g. lapsang souchong) are put on the foil; the food is placed on the steaming rack with a tight fitting lid. It is then placed over a high heat for 2 minutes to generate smoke, on a low heat for 10 minutes and then let stand

teal A small wild duck *Anas crecca* weighing about 400 g and served 1 per person. Roasted at 180 to 190°C for 25 to 30 minutes and served garnished with watercress and lemon wedges. Shooting season 1st September to 31st of January, hanging time 2 to 3 days

teaterskinka *(Sw)* A supper dish of slices of ham marinated in sherry, removed, dried, covered with a mixture of double cream and tomato purée and warmed in the oven. Lit. theatre ham

tebrød *(No)* Teacake

technical white oil *see* mineral hydrocarbons

Teegebäck *(Ge)* Tea cake

tee ma yau *(Ch)* Sesame seed oil

teeri *(Fi)* Black grouse

teething cake *see* moh loung ye baw

Teewurst *(Ge)* A smooth, pink, spreading sausage made from the finest of pork, beef and spices

teff *(Af)* One of the indigenous cereals of Ethiopia *Eragrostis teff.* The pinhead sized grain is part of the Ethiopian staple diet and used to make the bread indura [also called **teff grass**]

teff grass *see* teff

teg *see* hogget

tegame *(It)* A heavy frying pan or casserole

tegame, al *(It)* Fried or pot roasted

tegamino, al *(It)* Coddled, of eggs

teglia *(It)* A wide and shallow baking dish or pie dish

Teifi *(UK)* A Gouda-like cheese from Wales

Teiggemüse *(Ge)* Macaroni dishes

teisen lap *(UK)* An oblong fruit and spice cake from Wales eaten when cold as buttered slices

teishoku sakura denbu *(Ja)* A mixture of dried and ground codfish and sugar coloured pink and used as a garnish

tej pat In) The leaves of cassia used as a flavouring agent in Indian cooking

tej patta *(In)* Bay leaf

tekaka *(Sw)* Teacake, crumpet

tel *(In)* Oil

tel kadayif *(Tu)* Noodles cooked in sweetened milk and served with raisin syrup

Teleme Jack *(USA)* A cooking cheese from California resembling Mozarella

Telemea *(Ro)* A soft rindless ewe's milk cheese resembling Feta made from uncooked curd which is dried, pressed in square blocks, dry salted and matured for 30 days in a salted acid whey. It can be stored for a long period in the same whey at 5°C. Contains 50% water, 25% fat and 20% protein

tellina *(It)* Wedge shell clam

Teltower Rübchen *(Ge)* A small and well-flavoured variety of turnip grown around Berlin

telur *(Id & Ma)* Egg

telur asin *(Id & Ma)* Salted duck egg

telyatina *(Ru)* Veal

tembikai *(Ma)* Water melon

tempe *(Id)* A cheesy substance made by soaking and boiling soya beans, inoculating them with a fungus *Rhizopus oligosporus,* packing them into thin slabs wrapped in polythene or banana leaves pierced with holes and leaving to ferment. It is an easily digestible and well-flavoured source of protein and is usually shallow fried; *see also* oncom [also called **tempeh**]

tempeh *(Id)* *see* tempe

temper, to To bring to a desired consistency, texture, temperature or other physical condition by blending, mixing, kneading or standing, etc. as in to temper a pancake batter

temperature A measure of the intensity of heat such that heat always flows from a high intensity to a low one. Measured in cooking on the Fahrenheit or Centigrade scales q.v.

temperature probe A small pointed rod about 3 to 4 mm dia. which measures the internal temperature of food in which it is inserted. Used to determine the degree of roasting of meats and for checking that microwaved food is heated through

tempestine *(It)* Tiny pasta shells used in soup

temple *(Ca)* A naturally occurring hybrid of *Citrus* spp.

tempura Pieces of fish, shellfish, bundles of noodles and firm vegetables, covered with a thinnish coating of tempura batter, deep fried and served with a dipping sauce made from dashi, mirin and light soy sauce, with added grated daikon (mooli) and fresh ginger. The technique was introduced to Japan by the Spanish and Portuguese in the late 16th century

tempura batter *(Ja)* A lumpy batter made with iced water, sifted flour and egg yolk (12:6:1). The egg yolk and iced water are beaten together and poured over the flour which is stirred lightly

tempura dipping sauce *(Ja)* A mixture of dashi, light soya sauce and mirin (8:3:2), served with separate bowls of minced ginger and daikon oroshi

temu putih *(Id & Ma)* Zedoary

tenca *(Sp)* Tench

tench A small dark-skinned freshwater fish *Tinca tinca* of the carp family found in European rivers. It has rather a muddy flavour and is generally soaked in salted water for several hours before frying or grilling

tender cure, to *see* to quick cure

tenderize, to To break down the connective tissue of meat, octopus tentacles and the like by beating with a spiked mallet, by chemical treatment with acids, proteases or marinades, by hanging meat to allow natural enzymes to break down the fibres and by the correct application of heat at the right temperature

tenderloin *(USA)* Fillet steak (of beef), pork fillet and occasionally a corresponding muscle in lamb

tenderloin of pork The long inner back muscles equivalent to the fillet of beef, grilled, fried, used for kebabs, stir fries or batted out as escalopes [also called **pork fillet**]

tendon **1** The sinew or strand of strong connective tissue which attaches a muscle to bone. It contains a high proportion of elastin and does not liberate much gelatine on boiling. Usually excised and discarded **2** *(Ja)* Boiled rice with pieces of tempura (deep fried battered fish, shellfish and vegetables) arranged decoratively on top and dressed with a sauce made from dashi, sake, soya sauce, sugar and grated ginger root, then garnished with chopped spring onions

tenero *(It)* Tender, fresh, soft

teneroni di vitello *(It)* Ribs of veal (equivalent to spare ribs of pork or breast of lamb)

tengericsuka *(Hu)* Hake

tenok *(Ma)* Barracuda

tentsuya *(Ja)* A dipping sauce for tempura

tepary bean A drought resistant bean *Phaseolus acutifolius* grown in Mexico and the southern USA for local use

tepeh *(Ma)* Ridged sand clam

tepid The term applied to water at about 50 to 60°C; *see also* lukewarm

tepong pulot *(Id & Ma)* Glutinous rice flour

teppan *(Ja)* A griddle used to cook food at the table

teppan yaki *(Ja)* A method of cooking food, usually in front of the diner, either on a hot griddle or over burning charcoal

Teppichmuschel *(Ge)* Carpet shell

tepung beras *(Id & Ma)* Rice flour

tepung hoen kwe *(Id & Ma)* Mung bean flour

terasi *(Id & Ma)* Shrimp paste, blachan [also called **trasi**]

terbiye *(Tu)* A sauce used on vegetables, made from vegetable stock thickened with an egg, water and flour mixture and finished with lemon juice

terbiyéli köfte *(Tu)* Flat cakes made from a mixture of minced beef and onions, soaked breadcrumbs, eggs, chopped parsley and seasoning, fried in butter then simmered in stock and served with a sauce made from flour and water enriched with egg yolks and lemon juice, seasoned and flavoured with paprika

tereyagi *(Tu)* Butter

teri *(Ja)* A glaze for meat, vegetables, etc.

teriyaki *(Ja)* Kebabs, marinated in a soya sauce, sugar, and/or mirin mixture and grilled whilst being repeatedly basted with the marinade to give a rich, brown glaze. Alternatively escalopes, tender steaks, chicken breasts, fish, etc. browned then gently cooked in simmering teriyaki sauce until the sauce is reduced to a glaze. Served with a decorative garnish

teriyaki sauce *(Ja)* Equal quantities of sake, mirin and dark soya sauce with about one twelfth ot the combined weight of sugar and all boiled until the sugar dissolves

Terlaner Weinsuppe *(Au)* A South Tyrolean soup made from beef stock and white wine with egg yolk and whipped double cream

termites akoumba *(Af)* Pounded fresh termites mixed with palm oil and used as a dip in Malawi and Zaire

ternera *(Sp)* A rose coloured veal from calves which have been raised outdoors and are slaughtered between 8 and 12 months

terong *(Ma)* Aubergine

terraglie *(It)* Earthenware

terrapin *(USA)* A small fresh or brackish water turtle whose flesh is considered a delicacy. Available canned in Europe

terre cuite *(Fr) fem.* Earthenware

terrina *(It)* Terrine

terrine *(En & Fr) fem.* **1** A meat or fish loaf made from coarsely chopped or finely processed meat, chicken or game flesh, liver, fish or shellfish and fat with herbs, spices and flavourings, placed in an oblong earthenware dish lined with streaky bacon, blanched leek leaves or similar, covered and baked in the oven, cooled, demoulded and sliced for use as a hors d'oeuvre **2** A heat proof earthenware dish with a lid used for baking a terrine

terrine, en *(Fr)* potted

terung *(Id)* Aubergine

testa *(It)* Head of an animal or cap of a mushroom

testicles The sperm producing organs of male animals shaped like elongated balls, often cooked as a delicacy; *see also* mountain oysters, lamb's fry

testicoli *(It)* Testicles, lamb's fry

testina *(It) see* testa

testuggine marina *(It)* Turtle

tête *(Fr) fem.* Head

Tête de Moine *(He)* An alpine semi-hard unpasteurized cow's milk cheese with a pale yellow, mild and creamy paste enclosed in a rough slightly greasy rind. It is made in 0.5 to 2 kg rounds and is cured for 3 to 5 months. Traditionally served in thinly sliced curls with ground pepper and cumin

tête de nègre *(Fr) fem. see* cèpe de vendage

Tetilla *(Sp)* A soft white cheese made from cow's milk, the salted curd being placed in pear-shaped moulds and cured for 2 months. It has a slightly sour salty flavour. Contains 50% water, 22% fat and 21% protein [also called **Perilla**]

tétine *(Fr) fem.* Udder

Tetragonia expansa *Bot.* New Zealand spinach

Tetragonia tetragonioides *Bot.* New Zealand spinach

Tetrapanax papyriferum *Bot.* The tree from which rice paper is made

tétras *(Fr) masc.* Grouse

tetrazzini *(It)* Pasta with a creamy cheese sauce and seafood or poultry meat

tette melk *(No)* Cultured milk preserved and flavoured with tette leaves

Teviot Dale pie *(UK)* Lean minced beef browned in its own fat, chopped onion added and sweated, the whole simmered in seasoned beef stock and Worcestershire sauce for 20 minutes, covered with a thick batter made from self raising flour, suet, a little cornflour and milk and baked at 180°C until risen and browned

Tewkesbury mustard *(UK)* A pale smooth blend of mustard seed, horseradish, wine vinegar and salt. Used with sausages

Texas ruby red *(USA)* A red fleshed grapefruit

Texel *(Ho)* A green ewes' milk cheese

textured vegetable protein Protein extracted from vegetable sources, usually soya beans which is flavoured, solubilized and forced through a multitude of fine holes into a coagulating medium. The numerous fibres are brought together into a thick rope which is then chopped into pieces and dried. Used as a meat substitute; *see also* quorn [also called **TVP**]

Thai fragrant rice *see* jasmine fragrant rice

Thai ginger *see* greater galangal

Thai jasmine rice *see* jasmine fragrant rice

Thai yellow chilli A pale yellow green chilli with a mild flavour, often stuffed and cooked as a snack

thal *(In)* A large brass, copper, silver or stainless steel platter with raised edges on which Indian food is served

thala *(Sr)* Sesame seed

thali *(In)* A smaller version of the thal

thambili *(Sr)* Milk from the king coconut which is drunk directly from the shell

thaumatin A protein extract from berries *Thaumatococcus danielli* which is 3 to 4000 times as sweet as sucrose, used in table top sugar substitutes and yoghurts

thee complet *(Ho)* Afternoon tea with biscuits and cakes

Theobroma cacao *Bot.* Cocoa bean tree

thermidor *see* homard thermidor (lobster thermidor). The method of preparation is only used with lobster

thermometer An instrument for measuring temperature, essential for cooking esp. for determining when meat is cooked, for oven, freezer, refrigerator, fat and sugar temperatures and for ensuring adequate defrosting and cooking in microwave ovens

thermos flask A double-walled vessel made from silvered glass or stainless steel in which the space between the inner and outer wall is a vacuum, mounted in a protective case and fitted with a closure. The vacuum reduces transfer of heat by convection and the silvering reduces transfer by radiation, thus the contents may be kept hot or cold for a considerable period of time (heat is eventually transferred by conduction). Other types of insulation, e.g. foamed polystyrene or polyurethane, are used for the same purpose esp. in larger rectangular containers [also called **vacuum flask**]

thermostat An electrically or mechanically operated instrument which monitors the temperature in an enclosure and if it deviates from a preset value increases or reduces the energy input to or abstracts more or less energy from the space to maintain the preset temperature. Commonly used in gas or electric ovens, refrigerators and freezers, deep fat fryers, slow cookers and the like

thiabendazole *see* E233

thiamine Vitamin B1

thick batter *(USA)* *see* soft drop batter

thick flank *(UK)* A cut of beef from the front of the rear thigh. It is lean and used for braising and pot roasting. Often sold as cheap frying steak [also called **top rump**]

thick flank of veal *(UK)* The muscle at the front of the thigh bone of the rear leg of veal, equivalent to thick flank of beef. Used in the same way as cushion of veal

thick oxtail soup Disjointed oxtail and a mirepoix of onion, garlic, carrot and turnip browned in fat, flour added to make a brown roux, tomato purée, a BG and brown stock added, simmered and skimmed for 4 hours, oxtail and BG removed, flesh returned, liquidized, strained, seasoned and consistency corrected, finished with sherry and garnished with diced or balled carrots and turnips and the tip of the oxtail cut in rounds [also called **queue de boeuf lié**]

thick seam tripe Tripe from the third stomach of the cow or ox. It has the same flavour as blanket tripe or honeycomb tripe

thick skirt *(UK)* That part of the inner muscles of the belly wall attached to the rump [also called **goose skirt**]

thicken, to To increase the viscosity or consistency of a liquid by a variety of techniques including reduction, addition of cooked starches, gums, proteins such as white of egg or yolk or gelatine, by emulsifying a discontinuous phase into the liquid or by adding finely ground solids; *see also* roux, liaison, beurre manié, purée, coulis, sabayon, emulsions, etc.

thickened gravy *see* jus lié

thickeners Substances, usually carbohydrates or proteins which may have been chemically modified, used to increase the viscosity or consistency of liquids

thiebou diene *(WA)* Braised fish and vegetables served with rice

thin *(Vi)* *see* thinh

thin batter *(USA)* A thin flour liquid mixture (1:2) suitable for crêpes, pancakes, dipping, popovers, cream puffs, etc. The proportions depend upon the flour [also called **pour batter**]

thin flank *(UK)* The better cut of beef from the abdominal cavity equivalent to pork belly. Contains a lot of fat and is used for stewing and manufacturing

thin skirt *(UK)* The muscular part of the diaphragm of beef cattle

thin soya sauce *see* light soya sauce

thinh *(Vi)* Rice dry-fried to a deep golden brown then ground into a coarse powder and used as a flavouring and binder [also called **thin**]

thit-ja-bo-gauk *(Bm)* Cinnamon

thon *(Fr)* *masc.* Tuna fish

thon rouge *(Fr)* *masc.* Blue fin tuna fish

thonine *(Fr)* *fem.* Bonito (2), the fish

thornback ray A type of skate *Raja clavata* found in European and Mediterranean waters which grown to about 1 m long

thorny mandarin *see* Mediterranean mandarin

Thousand Island dressing Olives, onion, hard boiled egg, green sweet pepper and parsley all chopped and combined with mayonnaise and tarragon vinegar or lemon juice

thousand year egg *see* Chinese preserved egg

thread herring A species of herring *Opisthonema oglinum* up to 15 cm long and with a distinctive thread-like ray at the end of the dorsal fin. It is found in the Gulf of Mexico and off the southeast coast of the USA. Used mainly for canning [also called **Atlantic thread herring**]

three-bearded rockling A small, round, pink skinned seawater fish *Gaidropsarus mediterraneus* found in the Mediterranean sea

throughcut bacon A complete rasher of bacon including the back and the streaky from the middle portion of the pig

thrumenty *see* frumenty

thrush A small brown songbird *Turdidae* family caught in France and Italy for use in patés, pies or terrines.

Thunfisch *(Ge)* Tuna fish

Thüringer Blutwurst *(Ge)* A blood sausage made with diced parboiled pork belly and finely chopped pork rind, liver and lights plus occasionally other cooked offal. This is mixed with warm pigs' blood, seasoned, flavoured with marjoram, caraway and ground cloves, loosely filled into large casings, boiled, refreshed, dyed red and cold smoked with juniper berries and sawdust

Thüringer Rostbratwurst *(Ge)* A Bratwust made of pork or veal from Thuringia

Thüringer Rotwurst *(Ge)* A cooked, red-coloured blood sausage from Thuringia

thym *(Fr) masc.* Thyme

thyme A hardy evergreen low growing sub shrub *Thymus vulgaris* with tiny aromatic leaves and pale lilac flowers. The stalks with leaves attached are used in BG's or bundled up with other herbs to make a faggot of herbs. Alternatively the leaves alone are used fresh or dried in stuffings, sauces, soups, stocks and meat dishes. Fresh sprigs may be used to flavour oil or vinegar [also called **garden thyme**]

Thymian *(Ge)* Thyme

thymus A large gland from the neck of vertebrates important in the immune response. It, together with the pancreas, comprises the sweetbreads

Thymus x citriodorus *Bot.* Lemon thyme

Thymus pulegioides *Bot.* Broad leaf thyme

Thymus vulgaris *Bot.* Thyme

tian *(Fr) masc.* A shallow dish used in Provence, in which food is baked or grilled; alternatively a dish of food made in a tian

tian ya *(Ch)* Peking duck

tidbid *(De)* Light snack

tiède *(Fr)* Warm, tepid

tiefgefroren *(Ge)* Deep frozen

Tiefseegarnele *(Ge)* Deepwater prawn

tiella *(It)* A large baking dish or the food cooked in it, usually a mixture of vegetables with offal, shellfish, cheese or ham, possibly in pastry case

Tientsin pear A smooth, almost round, yellow fruit with a sweet crisp pear-like texture. Eaten raw after peeling and coring

tieo *(La)* Chilli paste

tiffin *(In)* Lunch, light repast from o.e. tiff, to drink or to lunch

tiffin box *(In)* Stackable stainless steel boxes or tins with lids in which lunch and snacks are delivered to office workers in India

tiganita *(Gr)* Fried or deep fried

tiganito sikoti *(Gr)* Calves' liver cut in 2.5 cm cubes, passed through seasoned flour mixed with powdered dried herbs, fried in hot butter for 1.5 to 2 minutes until brown and served as a starter with salad and bread

tiger lily bulb *see* lily bulb

tiger melon A variety of cantaloupe melon from Turkey with an orange-yellow and black striped skin and a fragrant orange flesh

tiger nut A small wrinkled brown tuber which forms on the roots of a plant *Cyperus esculantus* that grows around the Mediterranean. It has a crisp, sweet, nutty-flavoured white flesh and is eaten as is, in ice cream or is ground to make the Spanish drink horchata (de chufa) [also called **chufa** (Sp), **galingale, earth almond, pignut, rushnut**]

tiger prawn A type of king prawn *Penaeus esculentus* with a brown and orange striped shell and a dark coloured head and tail. It retains the stripes on cooking

tigerella tomato A decorative tomato streaked with green

tikka *(In)* Small pieces of meat or poultry marinated in yoghurt and tandoori spice mix, grilled or roasted and served with Indian bread and salad

til *(In)* Sesame seed

tilapia A perch-like member of the *Cichlid* family originating in Africa but now the most widely farmed fish in the tropics. An all-male variety has been genetically developed which grows to 2 kg in 1 year. It is also farmed in temperate climates, where supplies of warm fresh water are available from industrial processes [also called **St Peter's fish**]

tilefish A reddish blue seawater fish *Lopholatilus chamaeleonticeps* with small yellow spots on the upper side and fins, found in deep waters off the North American coast. The flesh is very firm and tender and may be substituted for lobster or scallops

til ka tel *(In)* Sesame seed oil

Tillamook *(USA)* A Cheddar-type cow's milk cheese from Oregon

Tilsit *(Ge)* A semi-hard, cooked curd, slicing cheese made from raw or pasteurized cow's milk inoculated with a *Lactobacillus* spp. and curdled with rennet. They are cast in large rounds or loaf shapes, dry salted and ripened for a month whilst being regularly washed with brine, then matured for 5 months. The paste is creamy-yellow with a mild and delicate flavour and numerous small holes. It is suitable for cooking and melting as well as for slicing. Made in many CE countries. Contains 45 to 50% water, and 10 to 30% fat [also called **Tollenser, Tilsiter**]

Tilsiter *(Ge) see* Tilsit

timbale *(En & Fr) fem.* **1** A cup-shaped mould **2**

A light creamy puréed mixture, baked in a timbale, demoulded and served with a sauce

timballa e'latte *(It)* A baked almond custard from Sardinia [also called **tumbada**]

timballo *(It)* A hot pie or mould much more robust than the English timbale

timballo al abbruzzese *(It)* Pancakes layered in a dish with meat balls, chicken livers, cheese and tomato sauce and baked in the oven

timballo di riso alla piemontese *(It)* A mould of rice with chicken livers, kidneys and a meat sauce

tim cheon *(Ch & Ma)* Plum sauce

tim cheong *(Ma)* A sweet and very dark soya sauce similar to the Chinese sweet soya sauce

timo *(It)* **1** Thyme **2** The thymus gland

timpana *(Ml)* A covered pie made with puff pastry filled with cooked al dente macaroni, fried chicken livers, grated cheese and chopped hard boiled eggs in a Bolognaise sauce prior to baking at 190°C for 40 minutes

timun *(Ma)* Cucumber

timum balu *(Ma)* Fuzzy melon

timur *(Ne)* Anise pepper

tin **1** Any metal container used for baking, e.g. cake tin, loaf tin, bun tin, etc. or for storing or preserving food **2** The relatively inert metal used to coat the inside of copper cooking utensils to prevent corrosion in acid solutions

tinamou *(SA)* A game bird of the *Tinamidae* family resembling a partridge. Sold in France

tinca *(It)* Tench

tinda *(In)* A type of squash *Citrullus vulgaris* var. *fistulosus* resembling a small green, apple-sized water melon with cream flesh and light coloured seeds. Used as a summer vegetable [also called **round gourd, squash melon**]

tindola *see* tindoori

tindoori *(In)* A small elongated oval green squash from a vine *Trichosanthes dioica* rather like a cucumber. Important in Indian cooking and may be eaten cooked or raw [also called **ivy gourd, parwal, palwal, tindola, tindori**]

tindori *see* tindoori

ting hsian *(Ch)* Cloves

tinker *see* common skate

tinned food Food preserved and sterilized in sealed, tinned or coated steel or aluminium cans

Tintenfisch *(Ge)* Cuttlefish

tippaleipä *(Fi)* A spiral shaped sweetened pastry similar to crullers. Traditionally eaten on May day

Tippenhaas *(Ge)* A type of jugged hare

tipsy cake *(UK)* A dome shaped cake moistened with sherry, studded with dehusked almonds and coated with an egg custard sauce. Served cold as a dessert

tipsy pudding *(USA)* An English-style trifle without fruit but well laced with liqueur or sherry

tirakia tiganita *(Gr)* Stiffly beaten egg whites seasoned with pepper, mixed with finely grated Parmesan or Kefalotiri cheese until firm, deep fried at 190°C in teaspoonfuls until puffy and brown, drained and served hot on cocktail sticks as an appetizer

tiram *(Id)* Oyster

tiram batu *(Ma)* Oyster

tiramisú *(It)* A rich dessert from Venice made with sponge fingers dipped in coffee and spirit or liqueur and layered with a creamed egg yolk, sugar and Mascarpone cheese (1:1:5) mixture sprinkled with chopped chocolate, finished with chopped nuts and refrigerated. Lit. pick me up

Tirggel *(He)* A heavily spiced Christmas gingerbread biscuit baked in a wooden mould carved with a relief of some ancient or modern design; *see also* Basler Leckerli

Tirolen Eierspeise *(Au)* A casserole of hard boiled eggs, potatoes and anchovies

Tiroler *(Au)* An extrawurst type sausage containing mainly lean cured pork with a little veal and/or beef

Tirolerknödel *(Au)* Meat ball

Tirolersuppe *(Au)* Soup with dumplings

tiropita *(Gr)* A triangular filo pastry pasty filled with cheese mashed with egg, seasoned and flavoured with nutmeg and chopped parsley [also called **tiropitakia**]

tiropitakia *(Gr)* *see* tiropita

tit-bits Small items of savoury food, appetizers

titanium dioxide E171, an inert white pigment permitted for use in food. It has no known health benefits

Tivoli, à la *(Fr)* In the style of the Tivoli, i.e. garnished, of meat dishes, with asparagus tips and mushrooms

tjobek *(Id)* *see* cobek

tlacenka *(Cz)* A large sausage filled with a kind of brawn

tlanochtle *(Me)* A sweet, green skinned fruit

with a very high vitamin C content about the size of a tomato from a plant *Lycianthes moziniana*, once widely cultivated by the Aztecs but now rare, suitable for steep marginal land

t'meen *(Ru)* Caraway seed

toad in the hole *(UK)* Cooked English sausage placed in a shallow tin with a Yorkshire pudding mix and baked

toast Slices of bread browned on both sides either under the grill or in a toaster; *see also* French toast

toast, to To brown bread, marshmallows, cheese and similar items under the grill or in front of a fire, or to brown bread in a toaster

toasted almonds *see* toasted seeds

toasted seeds Seeds, e.g. buckwheat, sesame seeds, almond pieces, which are baked in the oven on an ungreased tray until they are brown

toaster An implement consisting of a spring loaded carrier for a slice of bread moving in a vertical slot with electrically heated elements on either side. The bread is placed in the carrier which when depressed, automatically switches on the elements and a timer which after a preset time releases the catch which holds the carrier down thus releasing the toast and switching off the elements

toastie A sandwich which has been fried or toasted between two electrically heated grill plates which are pressed together. Depressions moulded in the grill plates hold the sandwich and give it a distinctive cushion shape

tobiko *(Ja)* Orange/red flying fish roe with a crisp crunchy texture. Used with sushi and as a garnish

tocană cu mămăligă *(Ro)* Boned and cubed shoulder pork, browned in lard and braised with sliced onions browned in the same fat, stock and white wine flavoured with thyme. Served with mamaliga

tocino *(Sp)* Salted pork belly or other fat pork often covered in crystalline salt

tocino de cielo *(Sp)* A thick crème caramel (Note - not bacon)

tocmchams *(Pe)* Apricots

tocopherols E306, a group of natural substances with vitamin E activity used as anti-oxidants. Individual tocopherols now synthesized are alpha-tocopherol E307, gamma-tocopherol E308 and delta-tocopherol E309

tod *(Th)* Deep fried

toddy *see* coconut wine

toespijs *(Ho)* Sweet, dessert, side dish

toey *(Th)* Screwpine

tofeja canavesana *(It)* A stew of pork offal, sausages and beans

tofu *see* bean curd

tofu no jiru *(Ja)* A tofu soup made with dashi flavoured with a little soya sauce, mirin and reconstituted shiitake mushroom caps, boiled and thickened with cornflour, simmered for 15 minutes, diced tofu added, simmered a further 5 minutes and served

tofu no miso shiru *(Ja)* A very simple soup made from dashi mixed with diced bean curd and miso (20:5:1 by volume) and garnished with chopped spring onions

togan *(Ja)* Wax gourd

togarishi *(Ja)* A small intensely hot chilli, usually flaked, used as a flavouring and in shichimi, also used of the dried chilli powder made from the same

Toggenburger *(He)* A semi-hard white cheese made from naturally soured skimmed cow's milk which is shaped into cubes and matured for 6 months

Toggenburger Ploderkäse *(He)* *see* Ploderkäse

togue *(Ph)* Bean sprouts

toheroa *(NZ)* A rare shellfish *Amphidesma ventricosum* found on only a few beaches and used to make a highly prized green soup. Lit. long tongue

toi *(Vi)* Garlic

tokány *(Hu)* A thick beef stew with tomatoes, green peppers, onions, garlic, sliced mushrooms and paprika. Served with soured cream and accompanied with rice or pasta

Tokyo hotchpot *(Ja)* A stew of squid, turnips, carrots, potatoes, konnyaku, aburage, hard boiled eggs and deep fried Japanese meat balls all simmered in dashi with soya sauce and sugar for 2 to 3 hours. Bean curd is added towards the end and the stew is served with wasabi. The ingredients are normally cut in decorative shapes

tola *(In)* A unit of weight based on the old rupee coin equal to 0.4 oz or approximately 11 g

tolee molee *(Bm)* Condiments including fish sauces and other pungent mixtures and pastes

Toll House cookie *(USA)* A biscuit made with brown sugar, nuts and chocolate chips in the paste. named after the Toll House inn in Massachusetts

Tollenser *see* Tilsit

töltött káposzta *(Hu)* Cabbage rolls filled

with a mixture of chopped onions, boiled rice, eggs, garlic, marjoram, paprika and seasonings, braised in a covered dish, between two layers of sauerkraut which have been sprinkled with flour and paprika. Sour cream is added when the dish is half cooked

tom *(Th)* Boiled or simmered in water

Toma *(It)* A hard cheese made from whole or partially skimmed cows' milk and cast in thick discs (to 4kg). The curd is moulded, dry salted or brined and ripened for at least 30 days. The rind is rough and the dense paste has a sharp salty taste

tomaat *(Ho)* Tomato

tomalley The liver of the lobster which is yellow green in colour and a delicacy. Used like the coral in sauces. Also used of crab eggs and ovaries

Tomar *(Po)* A very small ewes' milk cheese from Tomar north of Lisbon. It may be smoked

tomarillo *see* tamarillo

tomat *(De, No & Sw)* Tomato

Tomate *(Ge)* Tomato

tomate *(Po, Sp & Fr) fem.* Tomato

tomate con cáscara *(Me) see* tomate verde. Lit. tomato with a husk

tomate de mer *(Fr) fem.* Beadlet, a sea anemone

tomate, sauce *(Fr) fem. see* tomato sauce

tomate verde *(Me & Fr) fem.* The fruit of a plant *Physalis ixocarpa,* a relative of the cape gooseberry, resembling a green tomato with a papery husk. Used extensively in Mexican cookery and in the production of salsa verde. It develops flavour when boiled and is an essential ingredient of genuine guacamole [also called **tomate con cáscara, jamberry, ground tomato, tomatillo**]

tomates, crème de *(Fr) fem.* Tomato soup finished with milk or cream in the proportions of 1 to 4 [also called **cream of tomato soup**]

tomates farcies *(Be)* fem. Skinned tomatoes, stuffed with shrimps in mayonnaise

tomatillo *see* tomate verde

tomato The fruit of an annual plant (in temperate climates) or short-lived perennial (in warm climates) *Lycopersicon esculentum* of which some varieties grow to over 2.5 m high whilst others are low bushes. Although technically a fruit they are used exclusively as a salad or cooking vegetable or as a flavouring and thickener for a range of soups, sauces and other cooked dishes. The fruits are from 1 cm to over 10 cm in dia., slighltly flattened spheres with a yellow to red fleshy pulp divided internally in hollow segments each containing a slack pulp with embedded seeds. They are easily skinned by blanching for 10 to 20 seconds in boiling water and are used skinned and unskinned, raw, cooked and sometimes deseeded in a wide variety of dishes. Most tomatoes of commerce are picked green and ripened in the box. Vine ripened tomatoes found in warmer climates generally have a superior flavour; *see also* cherry tomato, plum tomato, beef tomato, marmande tomato, tigerella tomato, and yellow pear tomato

tomato concassé Finely chopped skinned and deseeded tomato pulp used in a variety of sauces and soups. The juice from the seeds may be strained off and added to the chopped pulp

tomato paste *see* tomato purée

tomato purée Partially dehydrated sieved tomato pulp with a deep red colour and spreadable consistency used for flavouring. Sold in collapsible tubes, tins and jars [also called **tomato paste**]

tomato sauce A mirepoix of onion, carrot, celery, bay leaf and thyme browned with bacon scraps in butter, flour added and cooked to a slight colour, tomato purée and white stock added, boiled than simmered with garlic, strained and seasoned [also called **sauce tomate** (Fr)]

tomato sausage *(UK)* An English sausage containing about 10% tomato, popular in the Midlands

tomato soup A mirepoix of bacon, onion and carrot browned in butter, flour added and cooked out, tomato purée or fresh tomatoes, stock and a BG added off heat, simmered and skimmed for 1 hour, passed through a chinois, seasoned, consistency adjusted and served hot with croûtons [also called **potage de tomates** (Fr)]

tomatsaft *(No)* Tomato juice

tomatsoppa *(Sw)* Tomato soup

tom bac ga *(Vi)* Shrimp or prawn

tombarello *(It)* Bonito (1)

tomber à glace *(Fr)* To reduce a stock to a thick sticky glaze

tomillo *(Sp)* Thyme

Tomino *(It)* A soft cows' milk cheese shaped in 2 to 3 cm elongated cylinders which are consumed as soon as they have been salted. A lactic starter is used which gives the fresh white paste its characteristic flavour. Used for dessert or as a hors d'oeuvre

Tomme *(Fr) fem.* The general name of a variety of small cheeses produced in Savoie, being the name for the container in which the cheese is made

Tomme d'Annot *(Fr) fem.* A goats' or ewes' milk cheese from the Haut-Alpes

Tomme de Cantal *(Fr) fem.* A cooking cheese from the Dordogne made from cows' milk or occasionally from goats' milk

Tomme du Mont-Ventoux *(Fr) fem.* A fresh and slightly salty ewes' milk cheese from Provence

Tomme de Saint Marcellin *(Fr) fem.* A soft cows' milk cheese from Savoie made from various milks and formed into thin discs (to 80 g) which are ripened for 2 weeks to give a hole free paste and a delicate rind covered in greenish blue mould

Tomme de Savoie *(Fr & It)* fem. A semi-hard skimmed cow's milk cheese formed into a squat cylinder (to 1.5 kg). It has a pleasant aromatic and lactic flavour and a firm texture resembling Saint Paulin

Tomme au raisin *(Fr) fem.* A small round cheese made from skimmed milk and ripened in a coating of grape pips [also called **fondu au marc, fromage fondu, fondu au raisin, grape cheese**]

Tomme vaudoise *(He)* A soft surface ripened cows' milk cheese made in small cylinders or oblongs (to 100 g). The taste varies from mild to savoury and fragrant after 10 days ripening

tom su *(Vi)* Shrimp or prawn

tom yam gung *(Th)* A spicy prawn soup flavoured with herbs and lemon juice

tom yam kung *(Th)* A spicy brown soup

Tonbridge biscuit *(UK)* A thin sweet biscuit glazed with egg white and sprinkled with caraway seeds before baking

tonfisk *(Sw)* Tuna fish

tonfisksallad *(Sw)* Tuna salad, normally tinned tuna, mixed with diced hard boiled eggs, chopped onions and celery and arranged on lettuce. Generally served on the smörgåsbord

tong *(Ho)* Dover sole

tongs A scissor shaped implement made of metal or wood, with blunt ends and no cutting edges used for handling hot or delicate foods

tongue The tongues of cattle and lambs usually soaked, cleaned, simmered with a BG and aromatic vegetables until tender, skinned and the meat pressed in a basin to cool and set in the natural jelly. Sliced and eaten as a cold meat or julienned for use as a garnish

ton hom *(Th)* Scallion

tonijn *(Ho)* Tuna fish

tonka bean The leguminous seeds of various trees of the *Dipteryx* spp. They contain coumarin, a chemical responsible for the smell of new mown hay and are used as a flavouring

tonkatsu *(Ja)* Thin slices of pork fillet, panéed with panko (large toasted breadcrumbs), deep fried, sliced in strips and served on a chiffonade of lettuce garnished with lemon wedges and served with tonkatsu sauce

tonkatsu sauce *(Ja)* A type of barbecue sauce served with tonkatsu. A typical recipe might contain tomato ketchup, dark soya sauce, sake, Worcestershire sauce and mustard

tonnato *(It)* With tuna fish or a tuna fish sauce

tonnetto *(It)* Little tunny, the fish

tonnino *(It)* Tuna fish

tonno *(It)* Tuna fish

tonyina *(Sp)* Little tunny, the fish

tooa lisong *(Th)* Peanut

toon *(Th)* To steam or steaming

toonhaai *(Ho)* Smooth hound, the fish [also called **gladde hai**]

toor dal *see* pigeon pea

top round steak *(USA)* Steak cut from the the upper part of a round of beef below the rump. It is more tender than round steak

top rump *(UK) see* thick flank

top shell Winkle, the shellfish

top and tail, to To remove either end of a fruit or vegetable, as in removing the stalk and tip of a French bean

topaz *(ME) see* ortanique

tope A type of shark *Galeorhinus galeus* taken as a game fish in the Atlantic. The fresh fish has a strong smell of ammonia which disappears on cooking

Topf *(Ge)* Pot

Topfen *(Au)* Curd or cottage cheese made from skimmed milk

Topfenknödel *(Au)* A sweet dumpling flavoured with curd cheese

topfenpalatschinken *(Hu)* Large thin pancakes spread with a mixture of strained cottage cheese, sugar, egg yolks, currants and grated lemon zest into which the stiffly beaten egg whites are folded. These are rolled, cut in pieces, placed in a greased dish, filled with a sweet egg custard, baked in the oven and finished with a dusting of icing sugar glazed under the grill

Töpferware *(Ge)* Earthenware, crockery

topinambour *(Fr) masc.* Jerusalem artichoke, said to be named after a group of Brazilian natives of the Topinambous tribe brought to Paris at the same time as the tuber was introduced

topinambur *(It)* Jerusalem artichoke

topinky *(Cz)* Fried bread with garlic

topping Any covering such as breadcrumbs, grated cheese, sweet or savoury sauces, cream, etc. placed on the surface of a prepared dish as a garnish or decoration or as an integral part of the dish

topside *(UK)* A lean boneless beef joint from the rear inside of the hind leg. It is inclined to be dry and fine grained with no marbling and is used for braising, stewing and second class roasting

toranja *(Po)* Grapefruit

Torbay sole *see* witch sole

torch ginger The pink tinged ginger bud q.v. and the tender part of the pink stem

torciolo *(It)* Pancreas gland of veal or beef. Together with the thymus makes up the sweetbreads

tordi *(It)* **1** Thrushes, the birds **2** Wrasse, the fish

tordi allo spiedo *(It)* Small birds (thrushes), skewered and grilled or barbecued

tori 1 *(Ja)* Chicken **2** Loofah and angled loofah

torigai *(Ja)* A type of cockle

torigan no miso-ni *(Ja)* Deep fried chicken meat balls made from minced chicken meat and onion with finely diced bamboo shoot bound with flour, egg and miso. Served with wasabi

torinese *(It)* *see* grissini

toriniku *(Ja)* Chicken meat

torkad frukt *(Sw)* Dried fruits

tørkage *(De)* Plain cake

torlo *(It)* Yolk, of an egg

toronja *(Sp)* Pummelo, grapefruit

tororo kombu *(Ja)* Shavings from soaked kombu cut with the grain leaving the tough membrane

torrada *(Po)* Toast

tørret fruktsuppe *(No)* A soup made from dried fruits, served hot or cold

tørrfisk *(No)* Stockfish

torrone *(It)* Nougat

torsh *(Pe)* West Indian lime. Lit. acid

torshi *(ME)* Pickles

torshi betingan *(ME)* Long thin aubergines, incised to a depth of 2 cm down the long side, simmered in water for 10 minutes, drained, the aubergines filled with a mixture of chopped garlic, chilli pepper, celery leaves and stalks and walnuts, then pickled in water and vinegar (4:3) plus salt. Left for 3 weeks before eating after rinsing in cold water.

torshi khiar *(ME)* Gherkins pickled in water and vinegar (3:1) with salt, dill seeds, coriander seeds, black peppercorns and garlic cloves

torsk *(De, No & Sw)* Cod; *see also* tusk

torsk-filé à Willy *(Sw)* Seasoned cod fillets put in a buttered oven proof dish with a little water, coated with French mustard and sprinkled with sliced leek, covered and cooked for about 20 minutes in a moderate oven until tender

torsk på Norsk *(Sw)* Cod slices, 2.5 to 3 cm thick, boiled vigorously for 5 minutes in a 10% brine, removed immediately and kept warm

tort iz sushyonykh fruktov i orekhov *(Ru)* A sweet pastry single crust tart with a filling of dried apricots and peaches boiled in sweet white wine and honey (3:1) until the liquid is absorbed, mixed to a sloppy consistency with blanched almonds, walnuts, egg, honey, butter and wine and baked at 180°C for 45 minutes. Served with cream whipped with cinnamon and sugar

torta 1 *(It)* Cake, tart or pie **2** *(Me)* Cake or loaf **3** *(Po)* A rolled and filled cake similar to a Swiss roll **4** *(Sp)* Pie or tart

torta del Casar *(Sp)* A soft ewes' milk cheese with a thin soft rind and a white paste with a few small holes. The milk is curdled with vegetable rennet, drained, pressed in flat discs, then salted and ripened for 30 days at low humidity

torta Gorgonzola *(It)* *see* torta San Gaudenzio

torta margherita *(It)* A basic sponge cake usually dusted with cocoa powder

torta pasqualina *(It)* An Easter dish of boiled eggs, beetroot and cottage cheese layered with pasta and baked

torta San Gaudenzio *(It)* A cheese built up from alternate layers of Mascarpone and blue-veined Gorgonzola to give a layered effect. Sometimes flavoured with anchovy and caraway seeds [also called **torta Gorgonzola**]

Törtchen *(Ge)* Small tarts

torte *(Ge & Au)* An open tart or flan with a pastry or rich, dry cake type of lining filled with a variety of sweet ingredients

torteau *(Fr)* A sweet cornmeal pancake from Bordeaux

tortellata alla crema *(It)* Cream tart

tortelli *(It)* Variously shaped ravioli often with unusual fillings

tortelli alla cremasca *(It)* Bow shaped tortelli filled with a processed mixture of macaroons, sultanas, nutmeg and cheese and served with butter

tortelli sguazzarotti *(It)* Tortelli filled with a mixture of beans, vegetable marrow and nuts. Served cold with a wine sauce

tortelli di zucca *(It)* Tortelli filled with a mixture of macaroons, vegetable marrow, pickled fruit and cheese

tortellini *(It)* **1** Small parcels of pasta with a cheese or meat filling available fresh or dried. The meat should be chopped rather than minced and lightly browned in oil before mixing with breadcrumbs and egg **2** Small versions of the tortello fritter from the Bologna region

tortellini in brodo *(It)* Tortellini cooked in a well-flavoured broth

tortello *(It)* **1** A type of doughnut or sweet fritter **2** A kind of pie

tortelloni Large versions of tortellini (1)

tortera *(Sp)* Pastry

tortiera *(It)* Cake tin

tortiglione *(It)* **1** *see* fusilli **2** Almond cake

tortilha de mariscos *(Po)* An omelette filled with chopped cooked shellfish

tortilla 1 *(Sp)* A Spanish omelette usually consisting of fried sweet onion and potatoes bound together with egg and shallow fried on both sides [also called **Spanish omelette**] **2** *(Me)* A thin pancake made from a dough of masa harina or tortilla flour, shaped and flattened by hand and cooked on both sides on a griddle until dry. May be salted and eaten after rolling in place of bread or filled and rolled as tacos or enchilladas. Not to be confused with the Spanish tortilla

tortilla chips Small triangles (2 to 4 cm on the side) cut from the Mexican tortilla and deep fried until crisp. Used as potato chips [also called **corn chips, totopos [also called** (Me), **tostaditas** (Me)]

tortilla flour Flour made from maize kernels by soaking them in lime water (calcium hydroxide solution) until they are soft enough to pound into flour. This process imparts a special tortilla flavour by breaking down the amino acid tryptophan in the corn to 2-amino acetophenone, and also makes the B vitamin niacin available. Those who use the untreated flour may suffer from vitamin deficiency

tortilla de huevo *(Me & Sp)* Omelette

tortilla de pimientos *(Sp)* The standard Spanish tortilla with the addition of sliced green sweet pepper

tortina *(It)* Tartlet

tortino *(It)* **1** Pie **2** A frittata (Spanish tortilla) baked in the oven and drier than normal

tortoni *(It)* Ice cream made from cream and sugar flavoured with Maraschino cherries, chopped almonds and rum

torttu *(Fi)* French or Danish pastry, cake, tart

torttutaikina *(Fi)* Pastry or cake dough

tortue *(Fr) fem.* Turtle

tortue claire, soupe *(Fr) fem.* Clear turtle soup

tortue d'eau douce *(Fr) fem.* Terrapin

tortue, sauce *(Fr) fem.* Boiling veal stock infused with mixed herbs, mushroom trimmings and crushed peppercorns off the heat, strained and mixed with demi-glace and tomato sauce, reduced, strained and finished with Madeira wine, truffle essence and a little cayenne pepper. It should have a definite herby flavour

tortuga *(Sp)* Turtle

tortuga de agua dulce *(Sp)* Terrapin

tor yau yu *(Ch)* Squid

tosa soya sauce *(Ja)* A mixture of light and dark soya sauces with a little mirin flavoured with Pacific bonito flakes and kombu, both of which are removed by straining before the sauce is served with sashimi

toscane, à la *(Fr)* In the style of Tuscany, i.e. garnished with pasta, foie gras and truffles esp. of panéed and fried chicken or sweetbreads

toscanello *(It)* A semi-hard scalded-curd ewes' milk cheese from Tuscany and Sardinia made in cylinders (to 3 kg). The drained and moulded cheeses are brined and ripened for 3 to 4 months to give a yellow to white rind and a dense white, mild to sharp-flavoured paste with a few holes

toscatårta *(Sw)* An almond topped cake

toss, to 1 To turn over food, usually with two spoons, so that it becomes coated with a dressing, e.g. melted butter on vegetables or vinaigrette dressing on salads **2** To coat pieces of food with a powder such as flour by shaking them together in a bag **3** To turn over something being cooked in a frying pan by throwing it into the air with a flicking motion of the pan and catching it

tostada *(Sp)* Toast, rusk

tostadas *(Me)* Medium sized tortillas, fried until crisp and served with a topping of salad, meat, poultry, fish or cheese with chilli sauce and served as a light meal or snack

tostaditas *(Me) see* tortilla chips

tostato *(It)* Toast, toasted

tostones *(Ca)* Fried plantain chips flavoured with garlic. Served as an appetizer

tôt-fait *(Fr) masc.* A quickly made sponge cake. Lit. soon made

totano *(It)* Flying squid

totopos *(Me) see* tortilla chips

toucinho defumado *(Po)* Smoked bacon in a piece

toulonnaise, à la *(Fr)* In the style of Toulon, i.e. with a tomato, aubergine and garlic sauce

toulousaine, à la *(Fr)* In the style of Toulouse, i.e. chicken garnished with kidneys, cockscombs, mushrooms, truffles and sauce suprême

Toulouse sausage A fresh French sausage made from pork or chicken

tourangelle, à la *(Fr)* In the style of Touraine, i.e. garnished with a mixture of flageolet beans and chopped French beans in a velouté sauce

tourin *(Fr) masc.* Cream of onion soup thickened with egg yolks and sprinkled with grated cheese

tourné(e) *(Fr)* Turned in the sense of shaped like a barrel. See to turn (3)

tournedos *(En & Fr) masc.* Individual steaks cut from the middle part of a trimmed fillet of beef and grilled or shallow fried. Usually tied before cooking to preserve a round shape

tournedos Oscar *(USA)* A tournedos shallow fried and served on an equal sized croûton of fried bread garnished with crab meat and asparagus tips or artichoke hearts topped with Béarnaise sauce

tournedos Rossini A tournedos shallow fried in clarified butter and served on an equal sized croûton of bread, topped with a slice of lightly fried foie gras and a slice of truffle. Served with a Madeira sauce

tournesol *(Fr) masc.* Sunflower

Tournon Saint Pierre *(Fr)* A soft strong smelling cows' milk cheese from Poitou-Charente made in the shape of a cone

touron *(Fr) masc.* A type of nougat or almond pastry covered with nuts

tourrée de l'Aubier *(Fr)* A large cow's milk cheese with a thin rind and a sweet, nutty-flavoured, velvety paste. Suitable for cooking and as a dessert cheese

tourte *(Fr) fem.* A shallow tart or flan made with puff pastry and with a savoury or sweet filling

tourteau *(Fr) masc.* Common crab

tourtière **1** *(Fr) fem.* Pie dish, tin or plate **2** *(Cn)* A topped pastry pie from Quebec filled with seasoned minced pork and onion flavoured with herbs

toute-épice *(Fr) fem.* Allspice

tovaglia *(It)* Tablecloth

tovagliolo *(It)* Napkin, serviette

towel gourd A type of gourd

toyo *(Ph)* Light soya sauce

trace elements Mineral elements, usually metals in various chemical forms, which are needed by the body for optimum health in quantities of less than 50 mg per day. Those currently identified as necessary are, in alphabetical order, chromium, cobalt, copper, fluorine, iodine, iron, manganese, molybdenum, nickel, selenium, silicon, vanadium and zinc. Other minerals required in greater daily quantities and not classed as trace elements are calcium, chlorine, magnesium, phosphorus, potassium and sodium; *see also* essential minerals

tragacanth *see* gum tragacanth

Tragopogon porrifolius *Bot.* The salsify plant

trail **1** The name given to the entrails of birds and fish which are cooked with the item and considered a delicacy, esp. the heart and liver of a woodcock served with the roast bird **B2** The long somewhat ragged piece of muscle which runs the length of fillet steak as it is cut in the UK. Usually removed from the muscle before slicing it into tournedos, filet mignon and chateaubriand steaks **3** A stage in the whipping of cream when the cream poured from a spoon onto the whipped cream leaves a distinct trail which persists for several seconds

traiteur *(Fr) masc.* An establishment which prepares and sells food for consumption off the premises, both in a shop and as an outside caterer; *see also* chef traiteur

tranche *(Fr) fem.* Slice or rasher

tranche de boeuf *(Fr) fem.* A beef steak [also called **bifteck**]

tranche grasse *(Fr) fem.* Silverside, of beef

tranche napolitaine *(Fr) fem.* Multiflavoured and layered ice cream

tranche plombières *(Fr) fem.* A slice of tutti frutti ice cream

tranchelard *(Fr) masc.* A long thin carving knife

trancher *(Fr)* To slice

trancia *(It)* Slice

transmontana, à *(Po)* In the style of Tràs-os-Montes, i.e. with chopped sausage, beans, garlic and onions

transparent icing A very thin icing used to give a professional finish to royal icing after it has been sanded or scraped down until quite smooth

transparent noodles *see* cellophane noodles

transparent vermicelli *see* cellophane noodles

Trapa bicornis *Bot.* Water caltrop

Trapa bispinosa *Bot.* Singhara nut

Trapa natans *Bot.* Caltrops

Trappiste *(Fr) masc.* A semi-hard cows' milk cheese closely associated with the Trappist monks and made in most countries where they had monasteries. It resembles Port Salut with a smooth close-textured paste containing a few holes covered with a soft rind. Usually cast in 3 kg discs. Contains about 45% water, 25% fat and 22% protein [also called **Trappisten** (Ge & Au)]

Trappiste de Chambarand *(Fr) masc. see* Chambarand

Trappiste d'Oelenberg *(Fr) masc. see* Oelenberg

Trappiste de Tamié *(Fr) masc. see* Tamié

Trappisten *(Ge & Au) see* Trappiste

trasi *(Id & Ma) see* terasi and blachan

trattoria *(It)* A family-run style of restaurant

Traube *(Ge)* grapes

travailler *(Fr)* To work in the sense of beating or blending

treacle The non crystallizeable impurities in sugar cane juice which remain in liquid form after processing to separate the pure sucrose. It is thick, black, sticky and sweet with a distinctive flavour and used in cakes, tarts and toffees. The similar substance from sugar beet juice is too bitter for human consumption; *see also* black treacle

treacle pudding *(UK)* A pudding made from basic steamed pudding mixture poured into a greased basin whose base is covered with treacle or golden syrup, before steaming or baking

treacle tart An open tart made from shortcrust pastry with a filling of golden syrup (not black treacle) and breadcrumbs flavoured with grated lemon zest and mixed spice and covered with a lattice of pastry strips before baking

Trebizond nuts *see* Turkish hazelnuts

Trecce di bufala *(It) see* Mozzarella di bufala

tree ear *see* cloud ear fungus

tree fungus *see* cloud ear fungus

tree onion *see* Egyptian onion

tree oyster mushroom *see* oyster mushroom

tree potato *see* sapodilla

tree tomato *see* tamarillo

trefoil *(USA)* Mitsuba

trelleborgsgryta *(Sw)* Herring and tomato stew made from rolled herring fillets packed lightly in a greased dish covered with salted water with lemon juice, parboiled small onions and peeled sliced tomatoes placed on top and the whole sprinkled with chopped dill, parsley and ground pepper and small pieces of butter. Simmered for 20 minutes

trelough duck A modern breed of duck similar to the Gressingham

tremadodes *see* flukes

tremella *see* white fungus

Tremella fuciformis *Bot.* White fungus

trencher 1 A squared up plate made from coarse wholemeal bread four days old, 60 to 75 mm thick, used in medieval times to hold food. Lower classes of person known as trenchermen also ate the trencher. Upper classes didn't **2** A wooden serving dish

trencherman A hearty eater and drinker

trenette A small noodle from Genoa similar to tagliatelle and usually eaten with a pesto sauce

Trenton cracker *(USA)* A light, round, puffy cracker

trepang Sea cucumber

Tresterbrantwein Ge) The German equivalent of marc or grappa

trey andeg *(Cm)* Catfish

trey pek chhieu *(Ch)* Pomfret, the fish

trey reach *(Cm) see* pa boeuk, the fish

triabolin A protein found only on the starch

granules of soft wheats and which may be responsible for reducing the adhesion between them

triacetin *see* glycerol tri-acetate

triammonium citrate *see* (E)380

trianon *(Fr)* A garnish of 3 colours

trichinosis A disease of humans caused by eating fresh pork infested with the eggs or cysts of a parasitic worm *Tricinella spiralis* which can also reproduce in the human body. It is for this reason that pork is always well cooked and never eaten raw. Curing and smoking raw meat kills any infestation so that hams, bacon, salamis and smoked pork sausages are safe. They are also killed at 75°C and at −15°C for 3 weeks

Tricholoma gambosum *Bot.* St. George's mushroom

Tricholoma matsutake *Bot.* Matsutake

Tricholoma nuda *Bot.* Wood blewit

Tricholoma saevum *Bot.* Blewit

Trichosanthes anguina *Bot.* Snake gourd

Trichosanthes cucumerina *Bot.* Snake gourd

Trichosanthes dioica *Bot.* The tindoori plant

trid *(NA)* A chicken stew with ribbons of warkha pastry

trifle *(UK)* A cold dessert made with sherry, fruit juice or liqueur-soaked sponge cake in the base of a large or individual dish, covered with layers of fruit, jelly, custard and whipped cream in various combinations and usually elaborately decorated

trifle sponge Fatless sponge cake or plain Madeira cake used as a base for English trifles

trifolato *(It)* Thinly sliced and sautéed in oil with garlic and parsley and possibly mushrooms and lemon

trifoliate orange *see* poncirus

triglia *(It)* Red mullet

triglia di fango *(It)* Plain red mullet *Mullus barbatus*

triglia di scoglio *(It)* Striped red mullet *Mullus surmuletus*

triglyceride The medical term for fats and oils containing three fatty acid molecules esterified with a glyerol molecule. Often measured in blood analysis

trigo *(Me & Sp)* Wheat

trigo negro *(Sp)* Buckwheat

Trigonella foenum-graecum *Bot.* Fenugreek

trim, to 1 To removed unwanted bits such as fat, gristle, tendons, blood vessels, feet, etc. from meat or poultry or fins from fish **2** To cut to a pleasing shape

trimmings 1 The discarded parts resulting from trimming food, e.g. small pieces of pastry, bread crusts and the like **2** Traditional garnishes and accompaniments to a dish as in the phrase 'steak and all the trimmings'

tripa *(Po)* Tripe

tripailles *(Fr) fem.* Guts or innards, sometimes tripe

tripe *(En & Fr) fem.* The stomach lining of animals, usually cattle (first 3 stomachs), which are cleaned, and in the UK, bleached and parboiled before sale. Various types are available depending on the animal and which stomach it comes from. Normally boiled in salted water until tender then stewed, braised or fried or in the north of England, served cold with vinegar; *see also* blanket tripe, honeycomb tripe and thick seam tripe

tripe and onions *(UK)* Pieces of prepared tripe simmered with onions in seasoned and flavoured milk, thickened with flour and simmered a further 10 minutes

tripes à la mode de Caen *(Fr) fem.* Pieces of prepared tripe simmered or casseroled until tender with calf's foot, belly pork, carrots, onions, garlic cloves and a BG in either cider and calvados or dry white wine. The casserole may be covered with thin strips of bacon. Thickened if necessary with cornflour

tripes à l'Djotte *(Be)* A traditional Christmas season sausage made from equal parts of chopped borecole sweated in fat, scallops (from lard making) and finely chopped raw pork, mixed with chopped onion and seasoning, flavoured with grated nutmeg and whole cloves and packed into fat ends prior to tying and cooking

tripoux *(Fr) masc.* A dish of sheep's trotters and veal tripe flavoured with herbs and cloves

trippa *(It)* Tripe

trippa alla fiorentina *(It)* Thinly sliced tripe casseroled with meat, tomatoes and stock and served with white beans and grated cheese

trippa alla romana *(It)* Tripe with a cheese sauce

tritato *(It)* Finely chopped or minced

tritello d'avena *(It)* Oat grits, coarse oatmeal

triticale A cross between wheat and rye with a

higher protein content than wheat. Not in common use because of poor agricultural yields

Triticum aestivum *Bot.* Common wheat

Triticum durum *Bot.* Durum wheat

Triticum monococcum *Bot.* Einkorn

Triticum spelta *Bot.* Spelt

Trockenmilch *(Ge)* Dried milk

Troldkrabbe *(Ge)* Spider crab

Tronchón *see* Aragón

tronçon *(En & Fr) masc.* A slice of fish at right angles to the backbone of a large flat fish and including the bone; *see also* fish steak

tronçonner *(Fr)* To cut into steaks

Tropaeolum majus *Bot.* Nasturtium

Tropaeolum tuberosum *Bot.* Ysaño

trota *(It)* Trout

trota iridea *(It)* Rainbow trout

trota salmonata *(It)* Salmon trout

trota di torrente *(It)* Brown trout

trotters *see* pig's trotters and calf's foot

Trou de Sottai *(Be)* A soft buttery cows' milk cheese made in cylinders (to 400 g) with a smooth paste and yellow rind

trousser *(Fr)* To truss

trout A round, oily fish *Salmo trutta* of the salmon family which is found in both fresh and salt water in a variety of forms varying from a few hundred grams to 35 kg (the American lake trout). The flesh is cream to pink depending on diet and the fish may be cooked in any way although they are generally shallow fried or grilled in Europe. Nowadays extensively farmed as well as being an important game fish

trout caviar Cured trout eggs which are orange in colour and similar to sturgeon caviar in taste and texture

Troyes *(Fr) see* Barberey

trucha *(Sp)* River trout

truckle *(UK)* The name of a smaller version of farmhouse Cheddar to 7 kg

truelle à poisson *(Fr) fem.* Fish slice for cutting and serving fish

trufas *(Po & Sp)* Truffles

truffade *(Fr) fem.* A dish from the Auvergne of potatoes fried with bacon, garlic and cheese

truffe *(Fr) fem.* **1** Truffle **2** Chocolate truffle

truffé(e) *(Fr)* Garnished with truffle

Trüffel *(Ge)* Truffle

Trüffel Leberwurst *(Ge)* A liver sausage flavoured with truffles

truffiat *(Fr) masc.* A potato cake from the Loire

truffle 1 A fungus whose fruiting body grows underground as an irregular roundish mass without a distinct stalk. They are always associated with the roots of trees and may have a symbiotic relationship with the tree. The two most highly prized are the French black and the Italian white. See main entries under French black truffle, Italian white truffle, English truffle, and Chinese truffle **2** A round soft chocolate-based sweet or confection usually rolled in grated chocolate, cocoa powder or chopped nuts or dipped in chocolate couverture and served with a selection of small cakes or as an after dinner sweet with coffee

truffle butter A compound butter made from diced black truffles with a little Béchamel sauce, pounded with twice their weight of butter and sieved

truite *(Fr) fem.* Trout

truite arc-en-ciel *(Fr) fem.* Rainbow trout

truite à la hussarde *(Fr) fem.* Trout slit open sideways and stuffed with aubergine

truite de mer *(Fr) fem.* Sea trout, salmon trout

truite de rivière *(Fr) fem.* River trout

truite saumonée *(Fr) fem.* Salmon trout

trumpet gourd *see* bottle gourd

trumpeter *see* agami

trung den *(Ch)* Chinese preserved egg

trunza di fera *(It)* Red cabbage stewed in oil with vinegar, capers amd olives

truss, to To tie or skewer into shape before cooking. Usually applied to poultry, game birds or boned joints of meat

truta *(Po)* Trout

Truthahn *(Ge)* Male turkey

Truthenne *(Ge)* Female turkey

trypsin One of the proteases in the human digestive system which is made in the pancreas. Seeds of some legumes contain trypsin inhibitors which prevent its digestive action

tsarine, à la *(Fr)* In the style of the Tsarina, i.e. chicken breasts garnished with cucumber cooked in butter and mixed with cream

tsatsiki *(Gr)* Finely chopped or grated, deseeded cucumber, salted and drained, washed, dried and mixed with yoghurt, chopped garlic and mint, seasoning and possibly oil and vinegar. Used as a dip or constituent of mezze and eaten with pitta bread [also called **talattouri, tzajiki, zatziki, tzatsiki**]

tseet gwa *(Ch)* Fuzzy melon

tseng dau gok *(Ch)* A dark green variety of long bean

tseng gwa *(Ch)* Cucumber

tseng loh baak *(Ch)* Green oriental radish

tsimmes **1** A thickened Jewish New Year dish of brisket of beef simmered with carrots, onions and potatoes, sweetened with sugar and honey [also called **tzimmes**] **2** The vegetables of tsimmes without the meat often supplied as the vegetable accompaniment to salt beef in a Jewish restaurant

tsim tau sha *(Ch)* Shark

tsing kaau *(Ch)* Mackerel

tso gwoo *(Ch)* Straw mushroom [also called **cha gwoo**]

tsubushi-an *(Ja)* A crunchy sweet red bean paste in which the beans are only partially crushed

tsukemono *(Ja)* Pickles, generally served at the end of a meal with rice to clean the palate. Pickling may be in salt or vinegar or in rice bran. See nuka-zuke and nukamiso-zuke

tsukemono-ki *(Ja)* A large wooden or earthenware vessel used for the production of preserved vegetables

tsuki dashi *(Ja) see* aemono

tsuma *(Ja)* The general name for a wide variety of attractively constructed garnishes of vegetable origin

ts'ung *(Ch)* Scallion

ts'ung tau *(Ch)* Shallots

tsu ts'ai *(Ch)* Nori

tsut sing paan *(Ch)* Garoupa, the fish

tua *(Th)* Bean or nut

tua ngak *(Th)* Bean sprouts

tua poo *(Th)* Goa bean

tub fish *see* tub gurnard

tub gurnard A small round seawater fish *Trigla lucerna* with a medium brown skin and two characteristic gill whiskers on either side. Similar to the gurnard [also called **tub fish**]

tubellini *(It) see* tubetti

tuber The fleshy swollen underground root or root tip of a plant used as a store of carbohydrate for the next generation of the plant which usually sprouts from the tuber. An important source of energy in human nutrition

Tuber aestivum *Bot.* English truffle

Tuber himalayense *Bot.* Chinese truffle

Tuber magnatum *Bot.* Italian white truffle

Tuber melanosporum *Bot.* French black truffle

tubero edule *(It)* Arrowroot [also called **maranta**]

tubetti *(It)* Very small pasta tubes used in soup [also called **tubellini, tubettini**]

tubettini *(It) see* tubetti

tuchowska *(Pl)* A regional sausage

tuck shop A shop, usually in a school, which sells snacks to the pupils

tucker *(Aus) coll.* Food, usually informally presented

tuiles *(Fr) fem.* Thin sweet biscuits sometimes covered in almond flakes slightly rounded when still hot to resemble continental tiles

tule potato *see* arrowhead

tulingan *(Ph)* Tuna, bonito

tulipe *(Fr) fem.* A circular brandy snap type of biscuit, draped when hot over a cup to cool so as to make an edible bowl in which fruit or desserts might be served

tulsi *(In)* Hairy or purple basil seeds

tumbada *(It) see* timballa e'latte

tumbet *(Sp)* A vegetarian dish made from alternate layers of sliced potatoes and salted, drained, washed and dried aubergines brushed with oil and browned on both sides, the layers separated by thinly sliced sweet peppers fried in olive oil and a tomato sauce made from finely chopped onions sweated in olive oil to a golden brown, combined with oregano and tomatoes and simmered to a purée. The whole built up in an ovenproof dish and baked at 180°C until cooked through

tumbler A flat bottomed tall cylindrical drinking glass

tummelberry A hybrid blackberry *Rubus* spp.

tumpaeng *(Cm)* Bamboo shoot

tuna A large round fish *Thunnus* spp. esp.

Thunnus thynnus weighing up to 600 kg which comes in various forms. The flesh looks almost like beef, some is light and lean and some dark and oily. Baked or grilled when fresh but most consumption in Europe is in canned form; *see also* bluefin tuna, yellow fin tuna, skipjack tuna and albacore [also called **tunny**]

tuna fig *see* prickly pear

Tunbridge Wells sausage *(UK)* An English sausage from the town of the same name made to a 100 year old recipe comprising coarsely chopped lean pork, chopped pork fat and yeastless bread rusk (10:5:2), seasoned, flavoured with sage, mace and other herbs, filled into casings and linked

tunfisk *(De & No)* Tuna fish

tunga *(Sw)* Tongue

tunge *(De & No)* Tongue

tung sum *see* bamboo shoots

tung ts'ao *(Ch)* Rice paper

Tunisian sweet limetta A small North African lime *Citrus limetta* only of local importance [also called **Mediterranean sweet limetta, Mediterranean sweet lime**]

Tunke *(Ge)* Sauce or gravy

tunny *see* tuna

tuong *(Vi)* A very strong-tasting fermented sauce probably including soya sauce and fermented fish [also called **Vietnamese soya sauce**]

tuong ngot *(Vi)* Hoisin sauce

tuong ot *(Vi)* Yellow bean sauce

tuoni e lampo *(It)* Bits of cooked pasta mixed with cooked chick peas. Lit. thunder and lightning

tuorlo d'uovo *(It)* Egg yolk

tupí *(Sp)* A spread or flavouring made from finely grated old cheese blended with oil and wine or brandy and left to mature in jars for 2 to 3 months

tur *(In)* Pigeon pea

turban *(Fr) masc.* A ring mould or a method of presenting food in a circle on the plate usually by using a ring mould

turban gourd A type of gourd

turban squash *see* Turk's cap squash

turbante *(It)* A ring mould of food, e.g. rice, presented in a demoulded ring with a filling in the centre

turbinado sugar *(USA)* A coarse grained partially refined sugar which is light beige in colour and contains a little adhering molasses

turbo *(Ja)* Abalone

turbot 1 *(En & Fr) masc.* A diamond shaped flatfish *Psetta maxima* up to 1 m in length and 15 kg with a spotted sandy back covered in small bumps. Found in the North Atlantic, the Mediterranean and the Black Sea. The fine white flesh is firm and medium oily and can be cooked in any way. The head and bones are a rich source of gelatine and make excellent stock. The turbot found in the East Atlantic is a different species *Scophthalmus maximus* but otherwise is similar **2** *(Cn) see* Greenland halibut [also called **bannock fluke**]

turbotière *(Fr) masc.* A large fish kettle for poaching whole turbot and similar large fish

turbotin A small turbot weighing 1 to 2 kg

turcarri *(In) see* turrcarri

tureen A large dish with a lid and ladle from which soup is served at the table

turian *(Th)* Durian

turkey A large (to 15 kg) flightless bird *Meleagris galopavo,* native to North America but now farmed worldwide for its high-yielding flesh. Popular in the UK at Christmas and in the USA at Thanksgiving but now available throughout the year as one of the cheapest forms of animal protein. Cooked like chicken

turkey cock A male turkey

turkey roll Boned and cooked turkey meat formed in a tight roll and encased in plastic, sold for slicing

Turkish delight A confection made from sugar boiled with water to the large thread (107°C) stage and thickened with cornflour, lemon juice and gum arabic, cooled until thick, flavoured with rosewater and poured into a flat cake moulds which have been liberally dusted with icing sugar or chopped pistachio nuts. When set cut into cubes and rolled and stored in icing sugar

Turkish hazel nut A smaller and cheaper hazel type of nut *Corylus colurna* than hazel nuts or filberts [also called **Messina cob, Trebizond nut**]

Turkish pilaf *see* Iç pilav

Turk's cap gourd A type of gourd

Turk's cap squash A decorative thick-skinned winter squash *Cucurbita maxima* with a flattened circular base surmounted by a smaller grooved top resembling a turban. It has a firm, slightly sweet orange yellow flesh with a green and white streaked orange skin. Boiled or baked as a vegetable [also called **turban squash**]

türlü *(Tu)* A mixed vegetable stew including a selection from onions, sweet peppers, tomatoes, green beans, courgettes, aubergines, okra, squash, chillis and the like

turmeric The boiled and skinned root of a perennial plant *Curcuma longa* which is dried and ground. It originated in India but is now also grown in the Far East and South America. It has a slightly aromatic peppery and musky taste and imparts a deep yellow colour to food. Used in Indian and Asian cooking and as a colouring agent in the west

Turmerikwurzel *(Ge)* Turmeric

turn, to **1** To become sour or start to ferment usually by adventitious microorganisms **2** To rotate some item of food so as to promote even cooking or browning of the surface **3** To shape solid root vegetables in a barrel or rugby ball shape, or button mushrooms with a series of swirling radial V-shaped cuts. Used to present an attractive appearance

turn, to cook to a To cook a food so that it is correctly cooked to the degree expected by the consumer

turnedo *(It)* Fillet of beef *(= tournedos)*

turning knife A small pointed knife with a concave shaped cutting edge used for turning vegetables

turnip **1** A temperate climate biennial plant *Brassic rapa* Rapifera Group grown as an annual for the swollen underground roots which are 2.5 to 7 cm in dia and round, flat or long and tapering. The hard flesh is white or yellow and the skin white, pink, red or yellow. Young turnips may be eaten raw or pickled, the mature ones are used as a root vegetable. The young leaves are known as turnip tops **2** *(UK, Scotland and USA)* Swede

turnip greens The green leaves from the top of turnips used as a vegetable

turnip rape *see* broccoli raab

turnip rooted parsley *see* Hamburg parsley

turnip soup Basic soup with turnips [also called **purée de navets** (Fr)]

turnip tops The young leaves and flower heads of the turnip plant *Brassica rapa* Rapifera Group eaten as spring greens or raw in salads

turnover A circular or square piece of pastry folded over into a sealed half circle or triangle and containing a sweet or savoury filling. See e.g. apple turnover, jam turnover, Cornish pasty

turntable **1** A rotating circular platform on a stand onto which a cake may be placed to assist in its icing and decoration **2** A rotating circular platform on the base of a microwave oven on which the dish of food being cooked is placed to ensure even penetration of microwaves

turrcarri *(In)* A style of curry making with meat simmered in excess of water (at least 5 cm over the top of the meat) until the meat falls apart; *See e.g.* mhaans turrcarri, gurdakupura turrcarri and other turrcarris

turrcarri molee *(In)* A meat curry with coconut. The meat is cut in strips, simmered in coconut milk with chopped ginger, coriander, garlic and sliced onion for 45 minutes. The solids are strained and fried in ghee adding ground fenugreek and poppy seed until all dry and golden, the liquid plus more coconut milk if required added back and all simmered with lemon or lime leaves until tender, leaves removed and lime juice and seasoning added before serving

turrón *(Sp)* Praline or a sweetmeat made with almonds resembling halva or sometimes nougat

turtle The aquatic version *Chelonia mydas* of the tortoise found worldwide in warm seas. Most varieties have edible flesh. The green turtle was once famed as the basis of turtle soup but has now been hunted almost to extinction. Turtles have long been exploited in SEA for their meat and as medicine. Turtle eggs are considered an aphrodisiac, the blood is believed to increase a person's energy and the ground up shells are considered to have medicinal properties. To prepare and cook, decapitate the live turtle, drain the blood, blanch for 3 minutes, scrape off the skin, cut the body from the shell, disembowel, rinse and cut the meat into strips

turtle herbs A blend of basil, sage, thyme, coriander leaves, marjoram, rosemary, bay leaf and peppercorns used to flavour turtle soup

turtle soup **1** Basic consommé simmered with turtle herbs in muslin for 10 minutes, thickened with arrowroot, seasoned, strained and finished with dry sherry and cooked and diced reconstituted turtle meat. Served with cheese straws and lemon wedges [also called **tortue claire** (Fr)] **2** Genuine turtle soup for the London Lord Mayor's banqyuet was made from 80 kg of cleaned female turtles simmered with their shell for 2 days in 450 litres of veal stock flavoured with thyme, marjoram, basil, parsley, 9 litres of sherry and 4.5 litres of sweet white wine, settled, clarified, reduced to 225 litres and finished with sherry and diced gelatinous turtle meat

tuscarora rice *see* wild rice

tusk A North Atlantic fish *Bromse bromse* which resembles hake but is of the cod family. It has lean white flesh and may be cooked in any way. Often substituted for cod in Scandinavian cooking

tusli *(In)* Basil

Tussilago farfara *Bot.* Coltsfoot

tutti frutti *(En & It)* Ice cream containing chopped dried or glacé fruits

tuvaram *(In)* Pigeon pea

tuware *see* pigeon pea

tu ya ts'ai *(Ch)* Bean sprouts

tuyo *(Ph)* Small fish, salted and dried then fried or grilled. Served with sliced tomatoes

tuz *(Tu)* Salt

Tvarvsky *(Cz) see* Olomoucké syrecky

Tvorog *(Ru) see* Twarog

tvorozhinka *(Ru)* Cheese dumplings

tvorozhniki *(Ru)* Thin patties made from sieved curd cheese, flour and egg (9:1:1) with a little sugar, salt, vanilla essence and lemon zest, chilled and rested, floured then fried, with some difficulty, in butter until brown on each side. Served at breakfast

TVP *see* textured vegetable protein

twaalfuurtje *(Ho)* Lunch

twaite shad *see* shad

Twarog *(Pl)* A soft acid curdled cows' milk cheese without rind eaten young. Contains approximately 70% water, 10% fat and 20% protein [also called **Tvorog** (Ru)]

Twelfth night cake A rich fruit cake sweetened with brown sugar and black treacle and flavoured with cinnamon and mixed spice eaten on the twelfth night after Christmas. Traditionally some silver charms are baked in it

twisted cluster bean *see* parkia

twists napolitani *(USA)* Gemelli pasta

txangurro al horno A dish of baked spider crabs with tomato, chilli and brandy from the Basque country of northern Spain

Tybo *(De)* A hard scalded-curd cow's milk cheese with a supple paste containing a few scattered holes and a thin yellow rind cast in bricks (to 4 kg). Similar to Samsø

tykmælk *(De)* Junket dessert

tykvenny sup z pryanostyami *(Ru)* An Armenian soup made from sweated pumpkin flesh, chopped leeks, carrots and currants, puréed with chicken stock and milk flavoured with allspice and simmered until cooked. Finished with yoghurt and dry roasted pumpkin seeds

Tyroler Alpenkäse *(Au & He)* A hard cooked-curd cows' milk cheese made in large wheels to 14 kg. It is ripened for 3 months and the paste is mild and slightly sweet and contains a few large holes

Tyroler Graukäse *(Au & He)* A soft surface ripened cooked-curd cows' milk cheese curdled with a lactic ferment. It is formed into discs and ripened for 10 to 20 days at high temperatures and humidity

tyrolienne, à la *(Fr)* In the style of the Tyrol, i.e. garnished with tomatoes and fried onions

tyrolienne à l'ancienne, sauce *(Fr) fem.* Finely chopped onion sweated in butter mixed with an equal weight of tomato concassé and twice its weight of sauce poivrade and all simmered until cooked

tyrolienne, sauce *(En & Fr) fem.* Finely chopped shallots cooked with colour in oil, tomato concassé added and cooked until dry, all passed through a fine sieve, cooled and mixed with mayonnaise, chopped parsley, chervil and tarragon. Served with fried fish and cold meats

tyttebær *(De)* Lingonberry

tzatsiki *(Gr) see* tsatsiki

tzimmes *see* tsimmes

Uu

ube *(Ph)* Yam

ubi *(Ph)* Yam

ubi jalar *(Id)* Sweet potato

ubi manis *(Id)* Sweet potato

ubod *(Ph)* The central pith of trunks of the coconut and other palms. Eaten raw or cooked as a vegetable or salad ingredient

ubre *(Sp)* Udder

ubriaco *(It)* Drunk, i.e. cooked in wine

uccelletti *(It)* Small birds

uccelletti alla maremmano *(It)* Small birds, browned in oil then cooked in a vinegar and tomato sauce with anchovies, olives and garlic

uccelletti scappati *(It)* Paupiettes of veal with bacon cooked on a skewer

uccelli *(Id)* Birds

ucche *see* kantola

uchepos *(Me)* Fresh corn tamales from Michoácan

udang *(Id & Ma)* Shrimp or prawn

udang kering *(Id & Ma)* Dried shrimp

udder The fatty white meat of the mammary glands of milking animals such as cows, sheep and goats which is cooked and sliced. Once popular but now rarely available. Occasionally used as a pasta stuffing [also called **elder**]

udo *(Ja)* A stalk vegetable with a flavour similar to fennel used raw or blanched and sliced in salads

udon *(Ja)* A wheat flour noodle from the south of Japan. It is thicker than the soba noodle, is either round or flat and is usually served in soup

Uferschnecke *(Ge)* Winkle

ugali *(EA)* A cooked cornmeal porridge eaten as the carbohydrate filler with stew

ugli fruit A naturally occurring hybrid of the grapefruit and mandarin found growing wild in Jamaica in 1914. It has a very rough, uneven and thick peel usually with blemishes. The orange flesh has a soft texture and is very juicy. Usually eaten with a spoon like a grapefruit

ugnsångad fisk *(Sw)* Oven steamed fish. Cleaned whole fish put in an oven-proof dish which has been rinsed out with water and cooked in the oven at 95°C for between 1 and 4 hours. No other treatment is necessary

ugnspannkaka *(Sw)* A thick pancake baked in the oven

ugnstekt *(Sw)* Oven baked

ugnstekt blomkål med tomat *(Sw)* Parboiled cauliflower surrounded with halved tomatoes in a buttered dish, gratinated with cheese and butter and baked in a hot oven until browned

UHT *see* ultra-heat treated

uien *(Ho)* Onions

uitsmijter *(Ho)* An open sandwich with a slice of ham or roast beef topped with two fried eggs and garnished with lettuce, tomato and sliced gherkin, eaten as a snack

ukad *(In)* Unpolished rice, slightly dusty with a reddish colour and thick grain

ukoy *(Ph)* A fritter of peeled shrimps mixed with chopped spring onions, in a rice or wheat flour batter. Fried and served with vinegar and minced garlic

Ukraine eggs *(Ru)* Very intricately decorated hard-boiled eggs. A peasant art form in the Ukraine dating back to 1000 BC at least

uleg-uleg *(Id)* A ceramic pestle that goes with a matching mortar *(cobek)*

ulekan *(Id)* A small deep granite or other hard rock mortar and pestle

uliva *(It)* Olive

Ulloa *(Sp)* A semi-hard cows' milk cheese similar to Tetilla cast in 1 kg discs

ulluco The pink or yellow tubers of a half hardy perennial yam *Ullucus tuberosus* from South America. It can be grown in the UK

Ullucus tuberosus *Bot.* Ulluco

Ulster roll *(UK)* A boned bacon joint from Northern Ireland which is cured, dry salted, soaked in water then dried and smoked [also called **spencer**]

ultracongelado *(Sp)* Deep frozen

ultra-heat treated The description applied to

any liquid which has been rapidly heated to 132°C, held at this temperature for 1 to 2 seconds (up to 6 minutes for some products), then rapidly cooled, generally in a stainless steel plate heat exchanger through which the liquid flows as a very thin film. This treatment sterilizes the liquid without too much change in its flavour. However the process does not necessarily destroy enzymes which may induce rancidity after several months [also called **UHT, long life, extended life**]

uluhaal *(Sr)* Fenugreek

ulutham *(In)* Black gram

ulva *see* sea laver

Ulzama *(Sp)* A semi-hard ewes' milk cheese from Navarra made in cylinders to 2 kg. The white dense paste has a strong flavour and a few holes and is covered in a brown rind

umani *(Ja)* Vegetables simmered in dashi flavoured with soya sauce, mirin, sugar and salt, added to the broth in order of cooking times. Garnished with very fine strands of mooli

umble pie *see* humble pie.

umbles The edible entrails of deer or other game animals

umbra *(Sp)* Arctic char

umbra, all' *(It)* In the style of Umbria, i.e. with an anchovy, tomato and truffle sauce

umbrella mushroom *see* parasol mushroom

ume *(Ja)* Plum

umeboshi plum A Japanese apricot, coloured with red shiso leaves and pickled in salt. It has a tart salty flavour and is served at the end of a meal as a digestive and is also used in cooking. It may be puréed for use as the souring agent bainiku

umido *(It)* Stew

umido, in *(It)* Braised, stewed

unagi *(Ja)* Freshwater eel

unbleached flour Flour which has not been treated with a bleaching agent to whiten the colour

unchun *(Th)* A natural blue colour obtained from the petals of a local plant. Often used to colour jicama and water chestnuts for dessert use

uncooked curd Curd for cheese making which has not been heated to more than 40°C

Undaria pinnatifida *Bot.* Wakame

undercushion of veal *(UK)* The thick longitudinal muscle at the rear outside of a leg of veal equivalent to silverside of beef with the same uses as cushion of veal [also called **undernut of veal**]

underdone Description of meat which is still red or pink in the centre after cooking [also called **rare**]

undernut of veal *(UK) see* undercushion of veal

Ungarische Art *(Ge)* In the Hungarian style, i.e. with paprika

ung choi *(Ch)* Swamp cabbage

ung choy Swamp cabbage

uni *(Ja)* Sea urchin, the eggs are often presented in a nori basket as sushi

univalve *see* gastropod

unleavened Without any natural or chemical raising agent

unleavened bread Bread made from flour, water and salt without using a raising agent or incorporating air

unpolished rice Rice from which the bran and most of the germ has been removed; *see also* brown rice

unshui mikan *(Ja) see* satsuma

unsweetened chocolate Chocolate containing no sugar, used for baking

uova alla Bela Rosin *(It)* Egg mayonnaise

uova di bufala *(It) see* Mozzarella di bufala

uova con pancetta *(It)* Bacon and eggs

uova di pesce *(It)* Hard fish roe

uova strapazzate *(It)* Scrambled eggs

uovo *(It)* Egg

uovo affogato *(It)* Poached egg

uovo bazzotto *(It)* Lightly boiled (3 minutes) egg

uovo al burro *(It)* Fried egg

uovo di mare *(It)* Violet (2)

uovo molle *(It)* Soft boiled egg

uovo sodo *(It)* Hard boiled egg

uovo al tegamino *(It)* Shirred egg

upotettu muna *(Fi)* Poached egg

upside down cake A cake baked in a tin with a decorative layer of fruit on the bottom so that when it is turned out the fruit will be on top

upside down pudding A Victoria sponge pudding made in the same way as upside down cake

urad dal *(In)* Black gram

urad dal chilke wali *(In)* Split but unskinned black gram

urad dal dhuli *(In)* Polished black gram

Urbasa *see* Idiazabal

Urbia *see* Idiazabal

urd bean *(In) see* black gram bean

urda A Balkan cheese similar to Ricotta

Urtica dioica *Bot.* Nettle

use-by-date Date mark used on packaged food which is intended to be consumed within 6 weeks. Under UK regulations this date may be changed by the manufacturer after the first date has expired

usli ghee *(In) see* ghee

uso di, all' *(It)* In the style of

usuage *(Ja) see* aburage

usu-kuchi shoyu *(Ja)* A particularly light, clear and salty soya sauce

usu-zukuri *(Ja)* A diagonal cut of thin slices of firm fish fillets for use in sashimi

utaw *(Ph)* Soya beans

utility beef *(USA) see* commercial beef

uunipuuru *(Fi)* A baked barley or rice porridge

uunissa paistettu hauki *(Fi)* Baked stuffed pike

uva *(It, Po & Sp)* Grape

uva fragola *(It)* Strawberry grape

uva passa *(It)* Raisins and currants

uva secca *(It)* Raisins and currants

uva spina *(It)* Gooseberry

Uzbekistan walnut brittle *(Ru)* Light brown sugar and evaporated milk (3:1) flavoured with allspice, ginger and cinnamon, cooked to the soft ball stage (115°C) then mixed with halved walnuts and vanilla essence, cooled and broken up

uzura no tomago *(Ja)* Quail egg

Vv

vaca *(Po & Sp)* Meat from old cows, rather tough

vaca cozida *(Po)* Boiled beef

vaca guisada *(Po)* Beef stew

Vaccinium ashei *Bot.* Blueberry (rabbit eye blueberry)

Vaccinium corymbosum *Bot.* Blueberry (highbush blueberry)

Vaccinium macrocarpum *Bot.* Cranberry

Vaccinium vitis-idaea *Bot.* Cowberry

Vachard *(Fr)* A strong-flavoured cows' milk cheese from the Massif Central similar to Saint Nectaire

vacherin *(Fr) masc.* **1** Meringue formed in a large or small shell or disc filled with whipped cream, ice cream or fruited ice cream. Served as a dessert or cake **2** A soft runny cheese from the Jura usually served with cream

Vacherin des Beauges *(Fr) masc.* Soft cows' milk cheese cast in large flat discs to 2 kg and wrapped in a strip of spruce bark to give it a resinous flavour. The rind becomes soft and grey or brown after it is ripened in cool damp conditions

Vacherin fribourgeoise *(Fr) masc.* A smaller (to 12 kg) soft version of Gruyère cheese with golden yellow paste and holes of varying shapes. It is started with a lactic culture, pressed, salted and surface ripened in high humidity. Considered as a cheese for special occasions [also called **Freiburger Vacherin**]

Vacherin Mont d'Or *(He)* masc. A winter cheese made from unpasteurized cow's milk which is sold in thin wooden boxes. The paste is very soft and runny and eaten with a spoon. The rind is rust coloured

Vacherol du Port-du-Salut de la Trappe *(Fr)* A semi-hard cows' milk cheese made in squat cylinders (to 5 kg) and similar to Saint Paulin. The paste is yellow with a reddish rind

vacuum drying A method of drying foods by subjecting them to a vacuum so that the water evaporates at ambient temperatures. May be used with frozen food

vacuum flask *see* thermos flask

vacuum pack A long-life pack in which food is sealed under vacuum in polythene or other clear plastic pouches. Also known as sous-vide when the contents are cooked or partially cooked food or meals for use in restaurants

vadelmat *(Fi)* Raspberries

våfflor *(Sw)* Waffles

vafler *(No)* Waffles

vagem *(Po) see* feijão verde

vainilla *(Sp)* Vanilla

vaktel *(Sw)* Quail

val *(In)* Hyacinth bean

Val di Muggio *(He)* A cows' milk cheese with a delicate taste and smooth rind

Valais raclette *(Fr)* A semi-hard scalded-curd cows' milk cheese made in 6 to 7 kg wheels from full cream milk. The paste is pale and creamy and very suitable for melting as a raclette q.v.

Valdeteja *(Sp)* A semi-hard goats' milk cheese shaped into long cylinders with a white paste containing a few holes. It is ripened for up to 15 days and the rind is rubbed with olive oil

Valençay *(Fr)* A pyramid-shaped soft goat's milk cheese from the Loire valley, matured for 4 to 5 weeks and coated in wood ash

Valencia orange The most well known of the common (sweet) oranges and probably the most important world orange. Its history can be traced back to the Portuguese but it was popularized by a British nurseryman who recognized its good qualities and shipped it around the world. It has medium to large fruits with a thin and leathery peel, about 2 to 4 seeds per fruit and an excellent flavour, though slightly acid if immature. The rind is often greenish especially if grown in tropical regions

Valencia peanut A variety of peanut with an upright habit and up to four dark red seeds per pod

Valencia rice A Spanish rice similar to Carolina which swells and becomes tender without releasing starch. Ideal for paella

valenciano *(Me)* A type of chilli pepper

valeriana cultivado *(Sp)* Lamb's lettuce

Valerianella locusta *Bot.* Lamb's lettuce

valérianelle *(Fr) fem.* Lamb's lettuce

valigini mantovani *(It)* Cabbage rolls filled with chicken and potato and cooked in tomato sauce in the usual way

välikyljys *(Fi)* Entrecôte of beef

valkokaalisalaatti *(Fi)* Cabbage salad, coleslaw

valnødkage *(De)* Walnut cake

valnødromkager *(De)* Walnut and rum-flavoured biscuit

valois, sauce *(Fr) fem. see* sauce foyot

valor *(In)* Hyacinth bean

vanaspati *(In)* Hydrogenated vegetable oil used as a butter substitute and for cooking

vand *(De)* Water

vand melon *(De)* Watermelon

vaniglia *(It)* Vanilla

vanigliato *(It)* Vanilla-flavoured

vanilje *(No)* Vanilla

vaniljglass *(Sw)* Vanilla ice cream

vaniljsås *(Sw)* English custard

vanilla The seed pod of a vine *Vanilla planifolia* which can grow up to a height of 15 m. The pods are picked when unripe and go through a complex curing process which leaves the best pods narrow, dark brown, supple and long, coated with white crystals of vanillin, but this frosting can be faked. The flavour is mellow and the aroma fragrant and unmistakeable. It is used to flavour desserts and chocolate. Synthetic vanillin is widely available and is used in most manufactured goods. It has a heavier odour and a disagreeable aftertaste

vanilla bean *see* vanilla pod

vanilla essence An alcoholic extract of the vanilla pod used for flavouring

vanilla flavouring The name usually given to an aqueous solution of artificial vanilla made from the eugenol in clove oil

Vanilla planifolia *Bot.* Vanilla

vanilla pod The fruit of the vanilla vine [also called **vanilla bean**]

vanilla sugar Sugar flavoured by being kept in contact with a vanilla pod in a closed jar. Used for flavouring other dishes

Vanille *(Ge)* Vanilla

vanille *(Ho & Fr) fem.* Vanilla

Vanille Rahmeis *(Ge)* Vanilla ice cream

vanillin One of the flavouring components of natural vanilla, now synthesized chemically and used in artificial vanilla flavourings

vann *(No)* Water

vanneau *(Fr) masc.* Queen scallop

vannmelon *(No)* Watermelon

vanukas *(Fi)* Pudding

vapeur, (à la) *(Fr)* Steamed, esp. of potatoes

vapor, à *(Po)* Steamed

varak *(In)* Silver leaf

varaq *(In)* Silver leaf

varié(e) *(Fr)* Assorted, as in hors d'oeuvres variés, mixed hors d'oeuvres

variegated scallop A small variety of scallop *Chlamys varia* with a firmer and less white muscle than the queen or great scallop

variety meats *(USA)* Offal

varkenskarbonaden *(Ho)* Fried pork chops

varkenvlees *(Ho)* Pork

värmlandskorv *(Sw)* A sausage made from equal parts of finely minced pork, finely minced beef and chopped raw potatoes all reminced with onion, seasoned, flavoured with allspice, moistened with ham stock, packed loosely into casings, linked, dry salted for a day then cooked and refreshed

varmrätt *(Sw)* A hot dish (of food)

vår-primör *(Sw)* Smoked salmon served with creamed spinach and poached eggs as an early spring delicacy

varske *(Ru)* Cottage cheese

vårsoppa *(Sw)* Spring vegetable soup based on beef stock with new carrots, cauliflower, asparagus, fresh peas and fresh spinach, chopped as appropriate, boiled in turn until tender and reserved, the stock thickened with a liaison of egg yolks and double cream and the vegetables added back together with chopped parsley and dill and sliced radish. Served hot

varying hare *see* Scottish hare

vasikanliha *(Fi)* Veal

vasikanpaisti *(Fi)* Roast veal

vassoio *(It)* Tray or cheese board

Västerbottenost *(Sw)* A hard scalded-curd cow's milk cheese made with a lactic starter followed by rennet. The scalded curds are pressed in moulds, salted and ripened for up to 8 months to give a strong flavoured firm paste with small holes [also called **Västergota**]

Västergota *see* Västerbottenost

västkustsallad *(Sw)* A mixed salad of prawns, lobster meat, cooked and shelled mussels, cooked peas and asparagus, sliced raw mushrooms and tomatoes dressed with a dill-flavoured vinaigrette. Served in individual dishes garnished with dill weed

vat A large tub used for large-scale processing of cheese, pickles, etc. and for fermenting and ageing wine

vatruschki s tvorogom *(Ru)* Turnovers made with an unsweetened yeast-raised dough filled with a mixture of cottage cheese, butter, eggs and salt, egg washed, proved and baked in a hot oven. Served with sour cream

vatrushki *(Ru)* Savoury tartlets made from an egg and sour cream enriched short pastry raised with baking powder and filled with an egg, cottage cheese, sugar, butter and lemon zest filling

vatten *(Sw)* Water

vattenmelon *(Sw)* Watermelon

vaxbönor *(Sw)* Wax beans

veado *(Po)* Deer

veal The meat of a young calf. Rearing methods range from calves run with their mothers on grass which gives a good textured, dark pink meat, to those which are removed from their mothers at birth, crated and fed with an iron deficient reconstituted milk to give an anaemic animal with very pale flesh. This latter was once highly prized but is now gradually going out of fashion

veal axoa A veal hash from the Basque country of France made with chopped onions and sweet red peppers fried in olive oil, diced veal added to the frying pan followed by tomato concassé, all cooked briskly for 5 minutes then simmered with dry white wine until tender

veal chops Chops cut from the loin of veal

veal cordon bleu An escalope cordon bleu made with veal

veal cuts *(USA)* Cuts of veal generally correspond to beef cuts but because of European, especially Italian influence, there are many separate cuts such as neck slices, riblets, foreshanks, brisket pieces, etc. confined to particular localities

veal and ham pie *(UK)* A raised pie with a filling of diced ham, pork and veal, usually surrounding a hard-boiled egg

veal Oscar *(USA)* A veal cutlet, sautéed, garnished with asparagus tips and crayfish tails and accompanied with a Béarnaise sauce

veal Parmigiana *(USA)* Veal chops panéed using breadcrumbs mixed with grated Parmesan cheese as the final coating, baked or fried and served with a tomato sauce

veau *(Fr) masc.* Calf or veal

veau de mer *(Fr) masc.* Porbeagle shark

veau sous la mère *(Fr) masc.* Veal from calves which have been reared outdoors with their mothers until ready for slaughter

vecchio *(It)* Old, used of cheese or other food items which might improve with age

vecchio maniera, alla *(It)* In an old fashioned style

vegan A person who will not eat the meat or products derived from any animal or once living creature including eggs, milk, fish, etc. Honey is excluded by some

vegetable carbon *see* carbon black

vegetable extract A dark brown paste made from hydrolysed vegetable protein and vegetable flavourings, possibly mixed with yeast extract. Used as a flavouring agent esp. by vegetarians and vegans

vegetable gelatine *see* agar-agar

vegetable marrow The large cylindrical green to yellow fruits of the *Curcubita* spp. known as summer squashes which are harvested in summer. Cooked whole or stuffed or their flesh made into jams or used as a vegetable. Very young vegetable marrows up to 15 cm in length are known as courgettes or zucchini

vegetable oyster *see* salsify

vegetable pear *see* choko

vegetable peeler *see* peeler

vegetable soup A mirepoix of mixed vegetables sweated in butter, flour added and cooked out without colour, white stock, a BG and sliced potatoes added, simmered and skimmed for 1 hour, BG removed, the remainder liquidized, seasoned, consistency adjusted and served accompanied by croûtons [also called **purée de légumes** (Fr)]

vegetable spaghetti A yellow summer squash whose flesh separates into spaghetti-like strands when it is cooked [also called **spaghetti marrow**]

vegetais *(Po)* Vegetables

vegetale *(It)* Vegetable

vegetarian A person who avoids eating the

flesh of once living creatures although some will eat animal products such as eggs, milk and milk products and fish; *see also* vegan, lacto-vegetarian and lacto-ovo-vegetarian

vegetarian cheese Cheese made with a curdling agent not derived from animals

veggieburger *(UK) coll.* A vegetarian patty shaped like a hamburger, made with a savoury mixture of vegetables and vegetable protein

veggies *(UK & USA) coll.* Vegetables as in veggieburger

Veilchen *(Ge)* Violet, the flower

veitchberry A hybrid blackberry *Rubus* spp.

vellay poondoo *(In)* Garlic

vells The lining of the fourth stomach of an unweaned calf used as a source of rennet

velösleves *(Hu)* A soup made from calves' brains and sliced mushrooms sweated in butter with parsley, sprinkled with flour and simmered with seasoned beef stock flavoured with mace until all cooked. Passed through a sieve, reheated and served with croûtons

velouté *(En & Fr) masc.* A type of soup in which a blond roux is combined with stock and vegetables, possibly sweated, herbs and seasonings, simmered and skimmed, then forced through a sieve or liquidized and finished with a liaison of egg yolk and cream. Lit. velvety

velouté sauce A basic white sauce made from a blond roux and a white stock, simmered and skimmed for one hour and strained. (100 g flour per litre)

velutato *(It)* Thickened with egg yolks, Lit. velvety

velvet apple *see* mabalo

Venaco *(Fr)* A soft surface ripened goats' milk cheese from Corsica made in cylinders (to 400 g) and ripened for up to 50 days in cool damp caves to give a greyish rind. Only made at certain times of the year

venado 1 *(Sp)* Venison **2** *(Me)* Deer, venison

venaison *(Fr) fem.* Venison

venaison, sauce *(Fr) fem.* Venison sauce

vendace A small, medium oily, freshwater fish *Coregonus albula,* smaller than the related lake whitefish. Found in European waters and may be baked or fried

vendace roe *(Fi)* The highly prized roe of the local vendace served as caviar, e.g. with chopped onion, smetana and blinis

Vendôme *(Fr) masc.* An unpasteurized cows' milk cheese from the Loire valley cast in 250 g discs. The cheeses are ripened for 1 month either in humid caves so as to blue externally *(Vendôme bleu)* or covered in wood ash from vine shoots to give a brown ashy crust *(Vendôme cendré).* Contains 50% fat based on dry matter

venison The meat of deer either farmed or caught in the wild. That from the wild is in season from July to the end of February. The meat tends to be tough and is usually hung for 1 to 2 weeks and marinated before use. It has a low proportion of fat and requires special care in cooking. Popular in Germany

venison salami Lean venison and one quarter its weight of lean pork finely minced and mixed with coarsely minced pork belly and diced pork back fat each equal in weight to the lean pork, seasoned, mixed with saltpetre and brown sugar and flavoured with nutmeg, ginger, peppercorns, garlic and juniper berries, packed tightly into ox middles or bungs and air dried until mature

venison sauce Poivrade sauce made with game stock and finished with molten red currant jelly and cream

venison sausage *(UK & USA)* A sausage of variable composition, roughly 2 parts lean venison to 1 part fatty pork, minced, extended with soaked pinhead oatmeal in Scotland, seasoned and mixed with any of saltpetre, sage, garlic, juniper berries, brown sugar, lemon zest, spices and brandy, moistened with red wine, stock or lemon juice, packed into casings, linked and dried

vénitienne, sauce *(Fr) fem.* A reduction of tarragon vinegar, chopped shallots and chopped chervil, strained, mixed with twice the original vinegar volume of sauce vin blanc and finished with green butter, chopped tarragon and vinegar

venkel *(Ho)* Fennel

ventaglio *(It)* Scallop, the shellfish

ventaglio, a *(It)* Scallop or fan shaped

ventresca *(It)* Belly of pork or tuna fish

ventresca bollita *(It)* Boiled belly of tuna fish, considered to be the tastiest part

Venushaar *(Ge)* Maidenhair fern

venus shell clam A shiny red or pink clam *Callista chione* up to 9 cm in dia. Found from southern England through to the Mediterranean. It can be cooked or eaten raw [also called **smooth venus clam**]

verace *(It)* Authentic, fresh, not tinned

Verbena *(Ge)* Lemon verbena

verbena *(It, Sp & USA)* Lemon verbena [also called **Scarlett O'Hara herb** (USA)]

verde *(It)* Green

verdesca *(It)* A type of shark

verdura *(It & Sp)* Vegetables, greens

vergine *(It) see* virgin olive oil

verigüeto *(Sp)* Warty venus clam

Veritable Nantais *(Fr) see* Nantais

verivanukas *(Fi)* Black pudding

verjuice In England the juice of crab apples, in France the juice of unripe grapes. Used as a souring agent in place of vinegar

verjus *(Fr) masc.* Verjuice

vermicelli *(It)* A very fine thin pasta usually bundled up like a bird's nest and used in soups

vermicellini *(It) see* angel's hair

Vermont *(USA)* A Cheddar-type cheese from the state of the same name

vermouth A spice, herb and essential oil flavoured wine used as an aperitif and as a flavouring agent

verni *(Fr)* Venus shell clam

vero *(It)* Real, authentic

Véron, sauce *(Fr) fem.* 3 parts of sauce normande mixed with 1 part of sauce tyrolienne and finished with a pale meat glaze and anchovy essence

Véronique *(Fr)* A description of any savoury dish garnished with white seedless grapes

Véronique, fish As for fish Bercy, glazed and garnished with white grapes, blanched, skinned and depipped

verseworst *(Ho)* Fresh sausage

vert galant *(Fr) masc.* A jam made from blueberries, honey and spices from Béarn. Lit. ladies's man after the French king Henri IV

vert-pré, au *(Fr)* Garnished with water cress and straw potatoes or coated with green mayonnaise or a sauce suprême coloured with a green beurre printanier and garnished with bouquets of green vegetables. Lit. like a green meadow

verte, sauce *(En & Fr) fem.* Mayonnaise flavoured and coloured with chopped tarragon or chervil, chives and watercress. Lit. green sauce

verveine *(Fr) fem.* Lemon verbena

Verwurrelt gedanken *(Lu)* Crisply fried pastries

verza *(It)* Savoy cabbage

verzelata *(It)* Grey mullet

verzini *(It)* Small cooking sausages

Vescheperle *(Ge)* Snack

vescica *(It)* Bladder, used as a sausage casing

vesi *(Fi)* Water

vésiga *(Fr)* The dried spinal cord of the sturgeon

vesigha *(Ru)* Dried sturgeon marrow

vesop A concentrated vegetable extract used in Eastern cooking

vetchina *(Ru)* Ham

vetiver *see* khas khas

Vetiveria zizanioides *Bot.* Khas khas

ve tsin *(Vi)* Monosodium glutamate

Vézelay *(Fr)* A strong-flavoured goats' milk cheese from Burgundy, shaped like a cone

Vezzena *(It)* A hard scalded-curd cheese made from skimmed cows' milk, curdled with rennet and formed into cylinders (to 40 kg). These are dry salted and ripened for 6 months to give a slicing cheese or for 12 months to give a grating cheese

vialone rice *(It)* A fino grade rice with long tapering grains able to absorb large quantities of liquid without losing its structure. Used for risotto

viande *(Fr) fem.* Meat

viande de boeuf blitzée *(He)* Beef reduced to a very fine paste or cream using a bowl chopper or possibly a high powered food processor

viande faisandée *(Fr) fem.* Meat kept until it is high, well hung

viande des grisons *(Fr) fem.* Bundnerfleisch

viande hachée *(Fr) fem.* Minced meat

viandes froides *(Fr)* Fem. Sliced cold meats

viands o.e. A formal term for food and provisions [also called **victuals, vittals**]

Vibrio parahaemolyticus An infective type of food poisoning bacteria found in shellfish and seafoods generally. The incubation period is 2 to 48 hours, usually 12 to 18 hours and the duration of the illness is 2 to 5 days. The symptoms are diarrhoeas often leading to dehydration, abdominal pain and fever.

Vichy, à la *(Fr)* Garnished with Vichy carrots, or with a sauce containing the red of carrots which has been sweated and puréed

Vichy carrots Young carrots turned or

scraped, cooked in (Vichy) water, butter, a little sugar and seasoning until all the liquid has evaporated and the carrots are tender and glazed

Vichyssoise A cold version of the homely French leek and potato soup, potage bonne femme which has been finished with cream. Invented by Louis Diat, chef at the New York Ritz Carlton in a fit of nostalgia for his Vichy boyhood

Vichy water A natural mineral water bottled in Vichy, France

Vicia faba *Bot.* Broad bean

vickning *(Sw)* Food offered to guests just before they are about to leave, e.g. Jansson's temptation. Sometimes called nattmat, night food, but this refers more to solitary midnight snacks

Victoria, à la *(Fr)* In the style of Victoria, i.e. garnished with tomatoes, macaroni, lettuce, potatoes and sometimes artichokes

Victoria plum *(UK)* A large oval red skinned dessert plum with sweet juicy flesh. Often eaten raw but may be cooked

victoria sandwich A victoria sponge mixture baked in two shallow cake tins, turned out, cooled, trimmed and sandwiched together with a filling of whipped cream and/or jam and the tops dusted with icing sugar

victoria sponge mixture Equal parts by weight of flour, butter, castor sugar, and eggs with 2 level teaspoons of baking powder per 4 oz of flour (60 g per kg flour) made up using the creaming method

victuals *see* viands

Vidalia onion *(USA)* A particularly sweet onion which may only be grown in a limited area near Glenville, South Georgia. One of the few restricted area foods in the USA

vider *(Fr)* To empty, to draw poultry, to disembowel or eviscerate

Vienna bread *see* Vienna loaf

Vienna coffee A particular blend of coffee beans favoured in Vienna

Vienna loaf A short oval-shaped white bread about 30 cm long often with several diagonal slashes and with a fairly crisp brown crust. The inspiration for French baguettes and other similar breads [also called **Vienna bread**]

Vienna sausage **1** A small Frankfurter **2** *(USA)* Frankfurter sausage

Viennese coffee *(Au)* **1** A mocha coffee **2** Ground coffee mixed with dried figs

viennois, pain *(Fr) masc.* An oval soft-crumbed crusty loaf of bread

viennoise, à la *(Fr)* In the Viennese style, i.e. roasts garnished with noodles, spinach, celery and potatoes or escalope garnished with a lemon slice plus some of anchovy fillets, chopped hard-boiled egg white and yolk, chopped capers or chopped parsley arranged in a pleasing pattern

viennoiserie *(Fr) fem.* The generic name for French pastries, croissants, pain au chocolate, Danish pastries, brioche, pain au raisins, etc.

vierge, beurre *(Fr) masc.* Softened butter whipped with seasoning and lemon juice, used to dress boiled vegetables

Vietnamese mint *see* polygonum. So called because of its introduction into Australia by Vietnamese migrants

Vietnamese peanut sauce Roasted peanuts, deseeded red chillis, garlic, mint and lemon juice, processed to a fine paste then thinned down with a 4:1 mixture of thin coconut milk and fish sauce

Vietnamese soya sauce *see* tuong

Vigna catjang *Bot.* Black-eyed pea

vignarola *(It)* Chopped leeks, quartered artichokes, mint, seasoning, shelled broad beans and peas added progressively to heated olive oil and cooked until soft and all liquid disappeared

Vigna sesquipedalis *Bot.* Long bean

Vigna unguiculata *Bot.* Cow pea

vigneronne, à la *(Fr)* In the style of the wine grower, i.e. with a wine sauce and garnished with grapes

viili *(Fi)* A soured milk, curds, junket, yoghurt

viinimarjakiisseli *(Fi)* Red currant sauce

viinirypäle *(Fi)* Grape

vijg *(Ho)* Fig

vild hönsfågel *(Sw)* Grouse [also called **ripa**]

villageoise, sauce *(Fr) fem.* A mixture of veal stock, mushroom essence, velouté sauce and soubise sauce, reduced, strained and thickened with egg yolks and cream and finished with butter. Used for white meat

Villalón *(Sp)* An even textured, soft, mild and rindless ewe's milk cheese from Valladolid. The paste is made from scalded curds and has lots of small holes. It is moulded in the shape of a long cylinder with rounded ends and an oval cross section [also called **Pata de Mulo**]

Villeroi, sauce *(Fr) fem.* Sauce allemande mixed with ham fumet and truffle essence, reduced until very thick. Used for coating items of food which are then panéed and deep fried

Villeroi Soubise, sauce *(Fr) fem.* Villeroy

sauce with one part soubise sauce added to 2.5 parts of sauce allemande at the initial stage

Villeroi tomatée, sauce *(Fr) fem.* Villeroi sauce with 1 part fresh tomato purée added to 3 parts of sauce allemande at the initial stage

viltfågel *(Sw)* Game

viltsuppe *(No)* Game or venison soup

vin *(De, No, Sw & Fr) masc.* Wine

vin blanc, au *(Fr)* With white wine

vin blanc, fish As for fish Bercy but sauce finished only with butter and cream and not glazed. Garnished with fleurons

vin blanc, sauce *(Fr) fem.* Boiling fish velouté mixed with white wine, cooled, butter and cream added, seasoned, lemon juice added then strained through a tammy cloth. Used for fish [also called **white wine sauce**]

vin rouge, au *(Fr)* With red wine

vin rouge, sauce *(Fr) fem.* A fine mirepoix of vegetables lightly browned in butter, red wine added and reduced by half, crushed garlic and espagnole sauce added, simmered, skimmed, strained and finished with butter, anchovy essence and a little cayenne pepper. Served with fish

vinäger *(Sw)* Vinegar [also called **vinättika**]

vinagre *(Po & Sp)* Vinegar

vinaigre *(Fr) masc.* Vinegar. Lit. sour wine

vinaigrette *(En & Fr) fem.* **1** A mixture of oil and vinegar seasoned with salt and pepper, possibly with mustard and sugar, then shaken together but not so as to make a stable emulsion. Used to dress salads or as a dip **2** *see* ravigote sauce [also called **French dressing**]

vinbär *(Sw)* Currant

Vincent, sauce *(Fr) fem.* Equal parts of green sauce and tartare sauce well mixed

vincisgrassi maceratese *(It)* An 18th century pasta dish consisting of lasagne layered with ceps, cream and parma ham, topped with Parmesan cheese and white truffle shavings, named after the Austrian Prince Windischgratz [also called **pincisgrassi**]

vindaloo *(In)* A particularly hot Indian stew (from chillis). The name is a corruption of vinho de alhos (wine and garlic marinade) introduced to the Portuguese colony of Goa. Other authorities derive the name from vinegar and aloo the Indian word for potato. See pork vindaloo for the traditional dish

vindaloo paste A spice paste used to make vindaloo consisting of dried red chillis, coriander, cumin and fenugreek seeds and peppercorns, all dry roasted then processed with turmeric, salt, vinegar, tamarind, garlic, fresh ginger root and plenty of raw onion

vindrue *(No)* Grape

vindruvor *(Sw)* Grapes

vine fruits *see* dried vine fruits

vine leaves The young leaves of grape vines sold fresh, canned or pickled in brine. Served in salads or used as a wrapping for various stuffings, see e.g. dolmades

vine spinach *see* Ceylon spinach

vinegar A dilute solution (4 to 6%) of acetic acid made by biological oxidation of alcoholic liquids such as ale, cider or wine. Known by its source i.e. malt vinegar (from ale), cider vinegar or red or white wine vinegar. Occasionally a cheap solution is made from chemically produced acetic acid which is known as spirit vinegar. Many flavourings are added to vinegar e.g. tarragon or garlic. Extensively used as a preservative and flavouring agent in all cuisines. Vinegar can be made by allowing a 15% sugar solution to ferment, open to the air, for about 6 months using yeast and/or bread as a starter if mother of vinegar is not available

vinegar cake *(UK)* An eggless fruit cake made with plain flour, mixed dried fruit, butter and soft brown sugar (2:2:1:1) using the rubbing in method and brought together with a foaming mixture of milk with bicarbonate of soda and vinegar (60:1:9), baked at 200°C for 30 minutes then at 170°C until cooked

vinegar herbs The principal herbs used for flavouring vinegars are basil, bay, chervil, dill, fennel, lemon balm, marjoram, mint, rosemary, savory, tarragon and thyme

vinha d'alhos *(Po)* Fish fillets or pork steaks marinated in wine with garlic, cloves, pepper and bay leaf, then fried, alternatively, the marinade

vino *(It & Sp)* Wine

vinous grape *see* dessert grape

vinsuppe *(No)* Wine soup

viola mammola *(It)* Sweet violet

Viola odorata *Bot.* Sweet violet

Viola tricolor *Bot.* Pansy

violaxanthin *see* E161(e)

violet **1** A small wild flower *Viola* spp. which looks like a very small pansy whose mauve flowers are crystallized for use as cake or dessert decoration. The petals of the sweet violet *V. odorata* are used for their flavour by steeping them in vinegar; *see also* sweet violet **2** *(En & Fr)* *masc.* A Mediterranean sea creature *Microcosmus sulcatus* like a soft sac enclosed in a rubbery skin similar to the sea squirt and attached to deep rocks. The raw soft insides are relished by some who like the sour iodine taste. An acquired taste

violet apricot *see* plumcot

violetta, alla *(It)* With crystallized violets

violette odorante *(Fr) fem.* Sweet violet

violon *(Fr) masc.* Guitar fish

vipérine *(Fr) fem.* Viper's bugloss

viperino *(It)* Viper's bugloss

viper's bugloss A hairy biennial plant *Echium vulgare* similar to borage which grows on chalky and sandy soils to a height of 60 cm to 1 m. The flowers are edible and can be crystallized and used for decoration or in salads

virgin oil Oil which has not been treated after being pressed from the fruit or seed and thus has a more distinctive flavour and higher vitamin content. Not to be confused with extra virgin or virgin as applied to olive oil

virgin olive oil Oil produced by the next pressing of the heated olive pulp after fine olive oil has been removed. The free oleic acid content must not exceed 4%. This oil is referred to as refined

virgin pastry Puff pastry after it is first made, which must be used for vol-au-vents, bouchées and items which require an even rise or lift. Cuttings which are rerolled are only suitable for pies, palmiers, etc.

Virginia ham *(USA) see* Smithfield ham

Virginia peanut A less common variety of peanut with two dark brown seeds per pod

Viroflay, à la *(Fr)* In the style of Viroflay, near Paris, i.e. garnished with spinach, artichokes, potatoes, parsley and occasionally mornay sauce, esp. roast lamb

vis *(Ho)* Fish

viscera *see* innards

viskoekjes *(Ho)* Fish cakes

visniski *(Ru)* A chopped fish ball seasoned with fennel, covered with dough and deep fried

vispgrädde *(Sw)* Whipping cream

vispi puuro *(Fi)* The juice from summer berries cooked with sugar and semolina to a paste then whipped off the heat until light and frothy. Served cold with milk and sugar. Lit. whipped porridge

vit, vitt *(Sw)* White

vit sås *(Sw)* Béchamel sauce

vitamin A naturally occurring substance required by the human body for optimum health usually in small milligram quantities but sometimes gram quantities may be beneficial. Complete lack of any vitamin usually causes disease or birth defects in foetuses. Recommended daily amounts (RDAs) avoid these diseases but some advocate taking greater amounts esp. of antioxidants. All vitamins are listed under either alphabetical names e.g. Vitamin A, B, C, etc or under their chemical name. These latter include, bioflavanoids, biotin, choline, folic acid, inositol, lipoic acid, orotic acid, PABA. Whether all the chemical names listed are true vitamins is constantly being reassessed and new vitamins are discovered at intervals; *see also* trace elements

vitamin A A long-chain fat-soluble alcohol which exist in various forms of which the most active is retinol which is found in animal tissues. Precursors of the vitamin are widely distributed in vegetables as carotenes q.v. which are transformed in the intestinal wall into Vitamin A. It is concerned with the integrity of epithelial tissues (skin and mucous membranes) and of the retina esp. for low light conditions and is also needed for the correct functioning of many body cells. Major food sources are fish and animal livers, eggs and milk. It is possible to overdose

vitamin B1 A water-soluble vitamin which must be taken daily. It maintains normal carbohydrate metabolism and nervous system function and is found in high concentration in yeast and the outer layers and germ of cereals. Other major sources are beef, pork and pulses. It has no known toxicity but colours the urine a bright yellow. Lack of vitamin B1 causes beri-beri, the first deficiency disease to be recognized which led to the discovery of vitamins [also called **aneurin, thiamine**]

vitamin B2 A water-soluble vitamin (riboflavin), essential for metabolic processes and for cell maintenance and repair. It is stored in the liver, kidneys and heart muscles. It is widely distributed in all leafy vegetables, in eggs, milk and the flesh of warm blooded animals. Lack of vitamin B2 causes soreness of the lips, mouth, tongue and eyelids. It has no known toxicity

vitamin B3 A water-soluble vitamin which occurs in three forms, niacin, nicotinic acid and nicotinamide. The first two can cause skin flushing and should only be taken by diabetics and persons with peptic ulcers under strict medical supervision. Both niacin and nicotinamide forms are essential for bodily health. They are widely distributed in foodstuffs. Meat, fish, wholemeal flour and peanuts are major sources. Maize contains the vitamin in a non-absorbable form and it is for this reason that it is treated with lime which makes the vitamin available as well as improving the taste. Lack of the vitamin causes pellagra summarized as diarrhoea, dermatitis and dementia. It can also cause severe lesions when the skin is exposed to light

vitamin B5 A water soluble vitamin (pantothenic acid) destroyed by boiling, found in all animal and plant tissues esp. poultry, liver, fish, eggs, potatoes and whole grains. It is converted to co-enzyme A in the body and as such is involved in all metabolic processes. There is no known toxicity. Lack of the vitamin can cause headaches, fatigue, impaired motor coordination, muscle cramps and gastrointestinal disturbance. Severe deficiency cause the burning feet syndrome observed in prisoners of war in the the Far East during World War 2

vitamin B6 A water-soluble vitamin which consists of three compounds, pyridoxal, pyridoxol (also called pyridoxine) and pyridoxamine, each with a different function. They are found in low concentration in all animal and plant tissues esp. fish, eggs and wholemeal flour. They are involved in protein, fat and carbohydrate metabolism and in brain function. Lack of the vitamin can cause lesions around the eyes, nose and mouth, peripheral neuritis and, in infants, convulsions. It is not recommended that supplements exceed 300 mg per day

vitamin B12 A cobalt containing water-soluble vitamin (cobalamin) which together with folic acid has a vital role in metabolic processes and in the formation of red blood cells. It is responsible for the general feeling of well-being in healthy individuals. It is normally found only in animal products, particularly ox kidney and liver and oily fish. Vegetarians and vegans should take supplements which are produced by a fermentation process. Lack of vitamin B12 which may be due to its absence in the diet or poor absorption in the gut can cause a form of anaemia (Addison's pernicious anaemia). It is normally prescribed together with folic acid

vitamin Bc *see* folic acid

vitamin B complex The whole complement of B vitamins plus biotin and folic acid. They are all water-soluble and tend to be found together in natural foodstuffs. Most are prone to destruction by excessive temperatures and sunlight. Some authorities include choline, inositol and PABA in this grouping

vitamin C A water-soluble vitamin (ascorbic acid) which is synthesized in the bodies of most animals except humans, primates and guinea pigs who have to obtain it from vegetables and fruit. It is essential for good health, wound repair, the effectiveness of the immune system and is thought by some to play a role in the prevention of cancer. Vitamin C deficiency results in scurvy, a disease still found in the poor and the old. Large amounts (up to 8 g daily) are recommended by some doctors and more famously by Linus Pauling, the chemistry Nobel prize winner. It has no known toxicity

vitamin D A fat-soluble vitamin (calciferol) whose main function is regulating calcium and phosphate metabolism (bone formation and repair). It is not normally present in nature but its precursors or provitamins, vitamin D2 and D3 are found in milk, cheese, eggs, butter, margarine (fortified) and esp. oily sea fish. These provitamins are converted in the body to vitamin D by the action of sunlight. Lack of vitamin D causes rickets (deformation of the bones) in children and liability to fracture in adults. The vitamin is toxic in excess, 30,000 IU for adults and 2,000 IU for children

vitamin D2 A precursor of vitamin D [also called **ergocalciferol**]

vitamin D3 A precursor of vitamin D [also called **cholecalciferol**]

vitamin E A fat-soluble vitamin (tocopherol) found in small quantities in soya beans, other seeds, butter, margarine (fortified), vegetables, whole grains, eggs and liver. It exists in several forms indicated by a Greek prefix, the alpha form being the most potent. It is a very powerful antioxidant and is vital for normal procreation and for cell processes. There is some evidence that it has anti-cancer activity. Natural sources are the best and though it has no known toxicity it may affect some medical conditions and supplements should only be taken on medical advice. Deficiency diseases in otherwise normal humans have not been reported

vitamin F An obsolete term for essential fatty acids

vitamin H *see* biotin

vitamin K This vitamin relates to a group of chemical quinones, some fat-soluble and others water-soluble, which are synthesized by human gut microorganisms and are found in abundance in brassicas and spinach and in moderate concentration in tomatoes and pig's liver. Lack of the vitamin causes haemorrhages esp. in new born infants. It is usually only administered under medical supervision

vitamin M *see* folic acid

vitela *(Po)* Veal

vitello *(It)* Veal from milk fed calves, calf

vitello alla genovese *(It)* Thin slices of veal cooked with wine and artichokes

vitello di lette *(It)* Sucking calf

vitello di mare *(It)* Dogfish

vitello alla sarda *(It)* Veal, larded with anchovies and braised with tomato and olives

vitello tonnato *(It)* Cold roast veal coated with a sauce made from canned tuna, mayonnaise and lemon juice processed to a smooth mixture, the whole garnished with lemon wedges

vitellone *(It)* Meat from up to 3 year old beef cattle, darker than normal veal but lighter than beef

vitelotte *(Fr)* A firm waxy variety of potato

Vitis labrusca *Bot.* American fox grape

Vitis rotundifolia *Bot.* American muscadine grape

Vitis vinifera *Bot.* European grape

vitkålsoppa med kroppkakor Cabbage soup with dumplings

vitling *(Sw)* Whiting, the fish

vitlök *(Sw)* Garlic

vitreous endosperm A wheat endosperm with a very dense structure

vitt bröd *(Sw)* White bread

vittals *coll. see* viands

Vivaro *(It)* A semi-hard scalded-curd cows' milk cheese very similar to Montasio. The pale yellow paste has a few holes, a mild pleasant taste and is covered with a hard smooth brown rind

viveiro de mariscos *(Po)* A shellfish stew

viveur en tasse *(Fr) masc.* A strong-flavoured bouillon or consommé, often with cayenne pepper, served in a cup

vla *(Ho)* Custard, flan, tart

vlees *(Ho)* Meat

vleesnat *(Ho)* Gravy

voi *(Fi)* Butter

vol-au-vent *(En & Fr) masc.* A round or oval puff pastry case filled with a cooked savoury mixture. It is made by rolling the pastry to 6 to 8 mm thick cutting out the shape, then half cutting a smaller shape in the centre. When baked the centre is removed and the crisp top replaced over the filling

vol-au-vent régence *(Fr) masc.* An oval vol au vent with a foie gras, mushroom, truffle and chicken quenelle filling

vol-au-vent à la toulousaine *(Fr) masc.* A vol au vent with a sweatbreads, mushroom and truffle filling

volaille *(Fr) fem.* Poultry, chicken

volaille, crème de *(Fr) fem. see* cream of chicken soup

voleipä *(Fi)* Sandwich

voleipäpöytä *(Fi)* Hors d'oeuvres, smörgåsbord

volière, en *(Fr)* Descriptive of game decorated with their own plumage

volpallière *(Fr)* Small chicken fillets, larded, braised and served with a truffle sauce

volume measure A convenient method of measuring ingredients by volume, reasonably accurate in the case of liquids but less so for solids. Volumes are measured in millilitres (ml) and litres (l) in the metric system used in most countries and in fluid ounces (fl oz), pints (pt) and gallons (gal) in the old imperial system taken over with different sizes in the USA. Other measures of volume are in use; see e.g. cup measure, can measure and market measure. The disadvantages of volume measure are the variation in density (weight per unit volume) of any solid commodity with particle size and moisture content and the inaccuracy of dispensing from common measuring jugs, etc. Volume measures also include the standard teaspoon, dessertspoon and tablespoon

Volvariella volvacea *Bot.* Straw mushroom

vongola *(It)* Clam, esp. the warty venus clam used in a pasta sauce. See e.g. spaghetti alle vongole

vongola grigia *(It)* Golden carpet shell

vongola nera *(It)* Carpet shell clam

vongola verace *(It)* Carpet shell clam

voorgerechten *(Ho)* Canapés, appetizers

voorjaarssla *(Ho)* Spring salad

vorschmack *(Fi)* Minced mutton, beef and salt herring cooked with onions and garlic

Vorspeisen *(Ge)* Hors d'oeuvres, first course, starters

vörtbröd *(Sw)* Malt bread

vørterkake *(No)* Spice cake

vrai(e) *(Fr)* True, real, as in vraie tortue, real turtle

vrilles de vigne *(Fr) fem.* Young shoots or tendrils of grape vines, usually blanched and either dressed with vinaigrette or cooked in olive oil

vrucht *(Ho)* Fruit

vruchtengelei *(Ho)* Jam

Vulscombe cheese *(UK)* A goat's milk cheese from Devon

vurty *(Cz)* A short fat sausage

Ww

Wachholder *(Ge)* Juniper

Wachsbohnen *(Ge)* Wax beans, butter beans, yellow beans

Wachtel *(Ge)* Quail

wafer A thin, crisp, unsweetened biscuit with a papery texture made by cooking a batter between hot plates, served with ice cream and sometimes sandwiched together in several layers with a sweet or savoury cream filling to form a wafer biscuit

wafer biscuit *see* wafer

Waffel *(Ge)* Waffle, wafer

waffle A crisp golden brown pancake made by cooking a batter between two metal waffle irons which have corresponding indentations and protusion so that the waffle when cooked has a series of indentations on both sides. Usually served hot with butter or maple syrup or cold with whipped cream or ice cream

waffle iron Two thick metal plates hinged along one edge with handles at the opposite edge and with heated indented mating surfaces which give waffles their characteristic appearance

wah-bho-hmyit *(Bm)* Bamboo shoot

Wähe *(He)* An open faced large pie or tart filled with fruit, vegetables or cheese

waiter, waitress A male, female person who serves the customers in a restaurant and is usually responsible for laying up and clearing the tables, making the coffee and presenting the desserts and gateaus on a trolley. In some case waiters carve meat at a side table or in expensive establishments prepare food such as tournedos, beef stroganoff or steak tartare and flambé dishes in front of the customers

wajan *(Id)* A type of wok but deeper than the Chinese and with straighter sides

wakame *(Ja)* A type of curly leaved brown algae *Undaria pinnatifida* found in coastal waters, with a mild vegetable taste and a soft texture. It is blanched in the whole leaf form and either sold undried in Japan or exported in dried form. The fresh and, after soaking, the dried form can be used in salads or as a vegetable after boiling for 10 minutes [also called **curly algae, curly seaweed, lobe leaf seaweed**]

wakegi *(Ja)* Scallion

wal *(In)* Hyacinth bean pods

Waldmeister *(Ge)* Sweet woodruff

Waldorf salad A salad of chopped apple, walnut and celeriac or celery, dressed on lettuce leaves with mayonnaise let down with lemon juice

Waldschnepfe *(Ge)* Woodcock

Walewska, à la *(Fr)* In the style of Comtesse Walewska, Napoleon's mistress, i.e. garnished with lobster, truffles and a mornay sauce

Walewska, fish As fish mornay but with a slice of cooked lobster and sliced truffles placed on the fish before coating with sauce

wallenbergare *(Sw)* Triple minced trimmed fillet of veal, seasoned, cooled, mixed with cooled egg yolks and double cream, made into egg shaped balls, rolled in breadcrumbs and fried carefully in butter. Served with petit pois, creamed potatoes and cranberry sauce. Named after the Wallenberg family

walleye pike *(USA)* A freshwater pike with a firm, fine textured flesh found in the great lakes of North America

walleye pollack *see* Alaska pollack

walleye pollock *see* Alaska pollack

wallies *(UK) coll.* Pickled cucumbers

Walliser Raclette Käse *(Ge & He)* The general name for the semi-hard scalded-curd cows' milk cheeses made in the Valais region and used as melting cheeses and for raclette

Walliskäse *(He) see* Saanenkäse

walnoot *(Ho)* Walnut

Walnuss *(Ge)* Walnut

walnut The brown nut from the fruit of the walnut tree *Juglans regia* and *J. nigra* which when ripe has a crinkly brain-like appearance and is enclosed in a hard relatively smooth brown shell up to 4 cm in dia. The nut has a distinctive flavour and is used in both savoury and sweet dishes. The unripe nuts and shells are often pickled in vinegar or preserved in syrup [also called **hickory nut** (USA), **butternut** (USA)]

walnut oil A fine nutty-flavoured oil extracted from walnuts. Used as a flavouring

walu jepan *(Id)* Choko

wan dou *(Ch)* Peas

wansuey *(Ph)* Coriander leaves

wappato *see* arrowhead

warabi *(Ja)* A fern sprout used in salads or as a vegetable

wara einab *(ME)* Salted vine leaves wrapped around a mixture of cooked rice, pine nuts and raisins and served cold as an appetizer [also called **waraq ainab**]

waraq ainab *(ME)* *see* wara einab

waribashi *(Ja)* Disposable chopsticks

wari shio *(Ja)* A blend of cornflour, salt and monosodium glutamate used as a coating for fried foods

warishita *(Ja)* The mixture of soya sauce and mirin added to sukiyaki

warkha pastry *(NA)* A type of flaky pastry

warm, to To heat slowly to around 50 to 80°C

warm water octopus A small species of octopus *Octopus macropus* up to 1.2 m maximum length with thin tentacles found in warm waters throughout the world. The quality is not as good as the common octopus

Warmbier *(Ge)* A soup made with beer

warq *(In)* Silver leaf used for decoration of foods

warsche *(UK) coll. (Scotland)* Lacking salt

Warszawski *(Pl)* A ewe's milk cheese similar to Kashkaval

warty venus clam A plump, grey to brown coloured clam *Venus verrucosa* with raised rows of wart-like projections on the shell, up to 7 cm in dia. Found from southern England to the Mediterranean. Used in vongole sauce

Wartzige venusmuschel *(Ge)* Warty venus clam

wasabi The edible root of a plant *Wasabia japonica* which only grows in Japan. The skinned, pale green root has a fierce flavour rather like horseradish. It is grated and served like this or made into a paste for use with sashimi or in sushi. It can also be dried to a pale brown powder [also called **Japanese horseradish, mountain hollyhock, wasebi**]

Wasabia japonica *Bot.* Wasabi

wasa-vasi *(Sr)* Mace

wasebi *see* wasabi

washed curd Milk curds which have been separated from the whey then steeped in cold water one or more times. This lowers the acid content of the curds and gives a coarser cheese

washed rind cheese A surface ripened cheese which relies on bacteria on the surface to develop the flavour. They are frequently washed to discourage mould growth and to encourage the growth of bacteria and usually have an orange-red rind and a pungent smell although the paste tends to be sweet to the taste. They are normally small to give a high surface to volume ratio. Pont l'Evêque and Munster are typical examples

washing soda The crystalline hydrated form of sodium carbonate

Washington The original navel orange from which most navel varieties have been developed [also called **Bahia**]

Washington, à la *(Fr)* In the Washington style, i.e. garnished with sweetcorn kernels in a cream sauce

Washington clam *see* giant west coast clam

Wasser *(Ge)* Water

Wasserkresse *(Ge)* Watercress

Wassermelone *(Ge)* Watermelon

wastle cake *(UK)* A type of griddle cake from Scotland

wat A traditional Ethiopian stew spiced with berbere or a similar mix of long pepper, black peppercorns, nutmeg and cloves, all dry roasted and ground to a fine powder with turmeric; *see also* zegeni

water activity A measure of the effective water content (from the point of view of a microorganism) of a food, not necessarily related to the actual water content (% by weight). It is defined as the ratio of the pressure exerted by water vapour in equilibrium with the food to the pressure exerted by water vapour in equilibrium with pure water at the same temperature as the food. (Both increase with temperature but the ratio remains roughly constant.) A food containing no water has a water activity of zero and pure water has a value of 1.0. Freezing reduces water activity by turning liquid water into ice

water apple A type of rose apple *Eugenia aqua* which is smaller, juicier and a deeper pink colour. It may be eaten as a fruit or the juice extracted [also called **watery rose apple**]

water biscuit A thin crisp plain biscuit made of flour, salt and water only, similar to a cream cracker and usually eaten with cheese

water caltrop The fruit of an aquatic plant *Trapa bicornis* with a shiny brown to black skin and two projecting horns. It has been used for food since neolithic times and is still grown and eaten in China, Korea and Japan. It has a semi-sweet potato-like flesh and must be boiled for an hour to destroy parasites. It is used in various dishes and preserved in honey or syrup.

Unfortunately it is often misnamed water chestnut and a flour made from it is called water chestnut starch

water chestnut The bulbous corm of a plant (*Eleocharis dulcis* and *E. tuberosa*), a type of sedge. It is used in Chinese and Thai cooking and can be purchased fresh or canned and eaten raw or cooked. It is used as a vegetable in the West but more usually to make desserts and drinks in SEA and used for its crunchy texture in Chinese cooking; *see also* caltrops and water caltrop [also called **Chinese water chestnut**]

water chestnut starch A gray starch made from the water caltrop. Considered to be very good for making crisp batters and coatings and for producing a good gloss in sauces

water concentrations The highest water concentrations (% by weight) at which microbial spoilage will not occur are approximately 13 to 15% for wheat flour, 14 to 20% for dehydrated vegetables, 10 to 11% for dehydrated whole egg and 15% for fat free meat; *see also* water activity

water convolvulus *see* swamp cabbage

water ice Fruit or liqueur-flavoured sugar syrup, frozen with continuous stirring to make a frozen dessert similar to sorbet

water icing *see* glacé icing

water lemon *see* yellow granadilla

water melon The large round or oval fruit of an annual warm climate trailing plant *Citrullus lanatus* and *C. vulgaris* with a thick dark green, possibly yellow striped, skin enclosing a watery crisp, pink/red and slightly sweet flesh with embedded black seeds. Eaten raw as a thirst quencher. The seeds which are oily and nutritious can be eaten as a snack food

water souchet *(USA)* The North American equivalent of waterzoetje

water spinach *see* swamp cabbage

water wolf *see* pike

watercress A hardy aquatic perennial *Rorippa nasturtium-aquaticum,* also called *Nasturtium officinale,* with a round, sharply-flavoured green leaf, generally grown in slightly alkaline running water. Used principally as a garnish for roasts and grills, in salads and in soups. It was introduced to Asia by the British and is used in salads in SEA, as a garnish in Japan and is boiled in soup in China [also called **winter rocket** (USA)]

waterfisch *(Ho)* **1** Freshwater fish **2** Fish sauce made from vegetables and Seville orange, cooked in fish stock, seasoned, flavoured with mustard and strained

waterless cooking *(USA)* A style of cooking using very low heat, a pot or pan with a very tight fitting lid and not more than 1 tablespoon of water

watery rose apple *see* water apple

waterzoetje *(Ho)* *see* waterzooi

waterzoie *see* waterzooi

waterzooi **1** *(Be)* A local Brussels dish of boiled chicken in a stock and white wine based cream sauce with julienned vegetables **2** *(Be & Ho)* A thin stew or thick soup made with mixed fish and julienned vegetables [also called **waterzoetje** (Ho)]

waved whelk *see* whelk

wax bean A type of French bean with yellow waxy pods [also called **waxpod bean**]

wax gourd A very large (to 45 kg) marrow type vegetable *Benincasa hispida* from China with a thin hard waxy green skin, resembling a water melon in appearance. The flesh is cooked by steaming, braising or simmering. Cubes of the flesh are slit, stuffed and steamed as dim sum. The flesh and skin may also be candied or pickled. The skin lends itself to the carving of elaborate patterns; *see also* petha and dong gwa jong [also called **winter gourd, white gourd, winter melon, Chinese vegetable marrow, ash gourd**]

wax myrtle *(USA)* Bayberry

wax palm *see* carnauba

waxpod bean *see* wax bean

weakfish *(USA)* One of the drum family of fish *Cynoscium regalis* very similar to trout. Fished both for game and food off the Atlantic coast

weasand The lining of a pigs gullet used for casing sausages. Rather rare

Webb's lettuce A common crisphead lettuce

Weckewerk *(Ge)* Pork and pigskin boiled with white bread and flavourings

wedding breakfast The celebratory meal after a marriage ceremony which has taken place in the morning, much more elaborate than a breakfast

wedding cake A celebratory cake served at a wedding feast. In the UK it is a rich fruit cake covered with almond paste and royal icing elaborately sculpted. In France it is a conical heap of profiteroles, held together with caramel

wedge A triangular cut from the the circumference to the centre point of a round cake, cheese, pie, etc. Between 4 and 12 wedges are normally cut from a circle

wedge shell clam A small white, brown or purple clam *Donax trunculus* up to 4 cm dia., which is plentiful in the Mediterranean. Related to the American bean clam

wedgebone steak *(USA)* A steak cut from the sirloin. See sirloin steak (USA)

Wedmore *(UK)* A semi-hard cheese from Somerset made with unpasteurized cows' milk and with a band of chopped chives running through the centre

weever fish Various edible seawater fish *Trachinus* spp. with upward-looking eyes and very sharp spines on the back and gill covers

Wegerich *(Ge)* Plantain

wei *(Ch) see* dun

weich Ei *(Ge)* Soft boiled egg

Weichkäse *(Ge)* The generic name for various fresh tasting soft cows' milk cheeses with high water content, close textured pastes and white bloom covered rinds

weight measure The most accurate method of measuring ingredients using the gravitational force exerted on the material to deflect a calibrated spring or by balancing the weight of the ingredient against a known weight using a lever. Weights are measured in grams (g) and kilograms (kg) and tonnes (1000 kg) in the metric system used in most countries and in ounces (oz) and pounds (lb) in the imperial system still in use in the USA. Other cultures, esp. in country districts, still use local measures; *see also* volume measure

Weihnachtsbäckerei *(Au)* Small pastries and biscuits specially baked for Christmas

Weihnachtstollen *(Ge)* An enriched almond-flavoured bread popular at Christmas

Wein *(Ge)* Wine

Weinbergschnecken *(Ge)* Snails

Weinkraut *(Ge)* **1** Sauerkraut heated with bacon fat, then simmered in reduced white wine for 10 minutes, seedless green grapes or peeled apple pieces added and simmered a further 5 minutes **2** Rue, the herb

Weinschaum sauce A German version of Zabaglione sauce often served with vanilla-flavoured blancmange

Weintrauben *(Ge)* Grapes

weiss *(Ge)* White

Weissbrot *(Ge)* White bread

weisse Bohnen *(Ge)* Butter beans

Weissfisch *(Ge)* Whiting

Weissfleisch *(G)* White meat

Weisskäse *(Ge)* Cottage cheese

Weisskohl *(Ge)* White cabbage

Weisslacher Bierkäse *(Ge) see* Weisslacker

Weisslacker *(Ge)* A rectangular shaped sharp tasting semi-hard cow's milk cheese with a very white heavily salted paste made from uncooked curd and weighing about 4 kg. The surface is covered in moulds which ripen the cheese from the outside [also called **Bierkäse, Weisslacher Bierkäse**]

Weissrüben *(Ge)* Turnips

Weisswurst *(Ge)* A mild-flavoured white sausage made from pork and veal with flavourings, similar to Münchener Weisswurst. Usually heated in water then fried and served with mustard and bread

Weizen *(Ge)* Wheat

Weizenbrot *(Ge)* Brown bread

well done *(UK)* A description of meat which is cooked so that no trace of pinkness or free juice exists in the centre

Wellhornschnecke *(Ge)* Whelk

well hung A description of meat or game which has been hung sufficiently long to develop flavour and tenderness. The classic description is - hang two pheasants by their necks, when one drops off, cook the other

wels A very large freshwater catfish *Silurus gianis* found throughout Central Asia and Central Europe

welscher Kohl *(Ge)* Savoy cabbage

Welsh blood pudding *(UK) see* pwdin gwaed or pwdin gwaed gwyddau

Welsh cake *(UK)* A drop scone mixture containing currants, cooked by shallow frying

Welsh cawl *(UK)* A mutton stew with potatoes, cabbage and carrots

Welsh faggot *(UK) see* faggot

Welsh onion A very hardy perennial *Allium fistulosum* with hollow leaves to 45 cm tall and 1 cm in dia. which grows in clumps like chives with thickened leaves below ground level. Either the leaves or parts of the clump are used, esp. as a winter vegetable. Not from Wales, the name probably derived from the German 'welsch' meaning foreign [also called **ciboule, European Welsh onion**]

Welsh rabbit *see* Welsh rarebit

Welsh rarebit *(UK)* A piece of buttered toast covered with a thick cheese sauce made from a white roux, milk, possibly ale, French mustard, Worcestershire sauce and seasoning mixed with an equal weight of grated Cheddar until smooth, and the whole browned under the grill. The sauce may be kept in a refrigerator until needed [also called **Welsh rabbit**]

Wensleydale cheese *(UK)* A hard cow's

milk cheese from Yorkshire, made from milk inoculated with a small amount of fermenting whey but not allowed to become acid. The curd is uncooked and cast in 3 to 4 kg discs. The white paste matures rapidly in 3 to 4 weeks to a mellow honey-like taste. It should not be yellow or sour. A blue veined version is produced which is matured for 4 to 6 months and is similar to Stilton

wentelteefjes *(Ho)* French toast, pain perdu

West Indian cherry *see* acerola

West Indian curry powder A ground spice mix introduced to the Caribbean by Indian migrants consisting of coriander seeds, aniseed, cumin seed, black mustard seeds, fenugreek seeds, black peppercorns and cinnamon, all dry roasted, plus dry ginger and turmeric

West Indian lime The original true lime *Citrus aurantifolia* originating in or around Malaysia, now grown worldwide. It is a small round lime picked either green or yellow and it has a very acid light greenish yellow flesh with many seeds. Used to make lime juice. [also called **Mexican lime, key lime, Galego lime** (Br)]

western *(USA) see* western sandwich

western king prawn A grayish king prawn *Penaeus latisulcatus*

western rock lobster *(Aus)* A type of spiny lobster *Panulirus cygnus* found in Western Australia. It varies in colour from pink to deep reddish brown and is of excellent quality [also called **crayfish (seawater)**]

western sandwich *(USA)* A scrambled egg or omelette sandwich with sautéed ham, sweet peppers and onions [also called **Denver sandwich, western**]

Westfälische Blindhunde *(Ge)* Soaked haricot beans simmered with pieces of bacon until nearly tender, diced peeled and cored apples, French beans, carrots and potatoes added, seasoned and simmered a further 30 minutes until all tender

Westfälische Bohnensuppe *(Ge)* Puréed kidney beans let down with white stock and garnished with blanched julienne of celeriac, carrots, leeks and potatoes and sliced Bologna sausage

Westfälische Kartoffeln *(Ge)* Mashed potatoes, mixed with mashed cooking apples and butter, covered with breadcrumbs and butter and browned under the grill

Westfälische Schinken *(Ge)* Westphalia ham

Westmorland pepper cake *(UK)* A chemically-raised basic cake mixture with added fruit and flavoured with ground ginger, cloves and black pepper but with half the normal quantity of eggs. Made by the melting method and baked at 180°C until cooked

Westphalia ham *(Ge)* A brine-cured boneless ham made from pigs fed on acorns. They are well rested before slaughter and completely desanguinated by massaging the meat. The pork is dry salted for 2 weeks, immersed in a 20% brine for a further 2 weeks and cold smoked over ash and beech wood with juniper berries for up to 5 weeks. Served raw in very thin slices

Westphalian sausage *(Ge)* A sausage made from lean pork and fat pork (3:1) from the forequarter, minced, seasoned, flavoured with ground cloves, packed in casings and air dried until yellow

wet fish Fresh uncooked fish, hopefully so fresh that it is still twitching

wet nellie *(UK) coll. (North of England)* A doughnut with jam in the centre

wetha see pyan *(Bm)* Pork curry flavoured with lemon, turmeric, garlic and ginger served with boiled rice

wether A castrated male sheep. The flesh is considered to be less fine than a comparable young ewe

wether gammon Leg of mutton

whale Animal of the largest mammal order *Cetacea* which, although it breathes air, lives in the sea. There are various species ranging in weight from 2 to 120 tonnes, although dolphins and porpoises which are the same family may be considerably smaller than this. They are hunted for their subcutaneous fat (blubber) which is further processed into whale oil, and the flesh which finds a ready sale in Japan and the Far East. Once a major food source for the inhabitants of Arctic and northern latitudes

whale oil Oil rendered from whale blubber used after deodorization for margarine and soap manufacture

wheat The seed of a plant *Triticum aestivum* which is the most important food grain of the developed world. Used, when ground into flour and processed, to make bread, pastry and cakes, as a thickening agent and for a multitude of other uses. Also used as an animal feedstuff. Alternatively it can be cooked whole, dried and cracked to form another food staple. It contains roughly 85% endosperm, 13% bran and 2% wheat germ [also called **corn**]

wheat classification Wheats are classified either as hard vitreous, hard mealy, soft vitreous or soft mealy; *see also* vitreous endosperm, soft and hard wheats

wheat composition Protein 8 to 15% and fat around 2%. It is the protein type and not the percentage composition which is the underlying cause of hardness in wheat

wheat duck *(USA)* A type of wild duck similar to widgeon

wheat flakes Partially boiled cracked wheat crushed between rollers then dried, lightly toasted and used in muesli and as a breakfast cereal

wheat germ The embryo of the wheat grain which is removed from white flour. It constitutes about 2% of the total weight of the grain, consists mainly of fat and protein and contains most of the B and E vitamins. Often sold separately as a food supplement

wheat germ flour *(USA)* The pulverized germ of wheat usually dry fried or roasted before use

wheat germ oil The oil extracted from wheat germ used as a health supplement and high in vitamin E, which is destroyed by heating

wheat hardness A measure of the ease of grinding of wheat into flour determined either by standard milling tests (time to grind to a particular size in standard apparatus), by biting the wheat seed (miller's test) or by measuring the force necessary to penetrate the wheat with a sharp point (micro penetration test)

wheat starch A gluten free wheat flour consisting mainly of starch. It is used as a thickener and is mixed with tapioca starch (2:1) to make a boiling water dough suitable, after kneading and rolling or flattening, for wrapping small parcels of food such as dim sum; *see also* wheat starch dough

wheat starch dough A dough suitable for food wrappers made from 2 parts wheat starch, 1 part tapioca starch and a little salt, briskly mixed with 4 parts of boiling water and a little oil, kept warm whilst resting then kneaded to a silky soft dough. Small chestnut-sized pieces can be rolled out or pressed out with the fingers or back of a knife.

wheatear A small buff and grey European game bird *Oenanthe oenanthe* with a white rump (Note - from 'white arse')

wheatmeal flour *see* brown flour

whelk A large (to 4 cm across) carnivorous gastropod mollusc *Buccinum undatum* with a grey/brown snail-like shell. They are usually boiled at the place of landing and checked for toxicity. They may be sold shelled or unshelled and are poached, baked or grilled. They are rather tasteless and therefore often served with vinegar [also called **waved whelk**]

whetstone cakes *(UK)* Hard round cakes made with flour, sugar and egg whites and flavoured with carroway seed. Baked in a cool oven until hard

whey The translucent liquid which is formed when coagulated milk separates into a semi-solid portion (curds) and a liquid portion (whey). It contains most of the lactose of the milk and a small amount of protein and fat. Usually a waste product but sometimes boiled or acidified to separate more solids from which a kind of cheese is made

whey of butter Buttermilk

whey cream Any cream or fat still remaining in whey after the curds have been separated in cheese making

whiff *see* megrim

whig Sour milk, whey, buttermilk

whim wham *(UK)* An 18th century dessert of sponge fingers soaked in muscatel or sweet sherry with brandy, orange juice and grated orange zest, topped with whipped cream and sprinkled with almond praline

whimberry Bilberry

whip A dessert to which whipped cream or whipped egg white is added, often containing gelatine and with a light texture

whip, to To beat one or a mixture of ingredients with a whisk, rotary beater or electrically-operated mixer to incorporate air and in some cases to form emulsions or to change the phase relationships in emulsions e.g. from oil in water to water in oil [also called **to whisk**]

whip topping *(USA)* A non milk fat substitute for whipping cream

whipped butter Softened butter whipped to incorporated air so as to make it easy to spread

whipped cream Cream containing between 35 and 40% butterfat which is whipped to incorporate air and to begin linking up the fat globules to make it a semi-solid. If whipping is carried on for too long the fat will become the continuous phase and it will turn to butter. For this reason, food processors must be carefully watched when being used to whip cream

whipping cream *(UK)* Cream containing a minimum butterfat content of 35%, but see also light and heavy whipping cream.

whisk An implement used for hand whisking, either a balloon whisk, a coiled wire whisk or a rotary whisk. See under the different headings

whisk, to *see* to whip

whisking method for cakes A method of making cakes by following the procedure for fatless whisking, then at the end folding in molten clarified or whole butter very gently (e.g by simultaneously throwing in the fat while switching the machine off), used for making e.g. Genoese sponge

whistle pig *(USA)* *see* woodchuck

white asparagus Asparagus shoots cut below ground level when the tips protrude at most 5 cm into the light

white aubergine A very light green aubergine used in central China

white beef stock Beef bones with fat and marrow removed, blanched and refreshed, simmered with aromatic vegetables and a BG for 8 hours, skimming continuously then strained. Proportions 4 bone, 1 vegetables and 10 water [also called **fond blanc** (Fr) **fond de marmite** (Fr)]

white beet *see* chard

white bordelaise sauce *see* sauce bonnefoy

white bread Bread made from a white flour dough

white butter fish *see* pomfret

white butter sauce *see* beurre blanc

white cabbage A spherical cabbage consisting of a tightly-packed ball of rather thick white leaves with a few green leaves surrounding it. Used for making coleslaw and sauerkraut and in the UK for institutional boiled cabbage

white cake *(USA)* A cake made with all white ingredients, i.e. with no egg yolk or coloured fats, etc.

white chicken stock As for white beef stock but substituting chicken bones and carcases for the defatted beef bones [also called **fond blanc de volaille** (Fr)]

white chocolate A white, chocolate-tasting confectionery item made from bleached cocoa butter and white sugar

white cinnamon The inner bark of wild cinnamon

white crystal sugar *(USA)* Granulated sugar

white cumin Cumin, the common brown variety

white currant A variety of red currant which lacks the gene for the colouring matter

white curry *(Sr)* A mild curry based on coconut milk

white of egg *see* egg and egg white

white fish 1 A general name for any type of fish with white flesh and less than 6% fat in the flesh, such as haddock, whiting, cod, plaice, etc. **2** *(USA)* A small freshwater fish related to the salmon and trout. It is often smoked and the roe processed into a caviar substitute

white flour Wheat flour from which the bran and wheat germ have been removed leaving between 72 and 74% of the original dehusked grain. Sometimes bleached chemically to enhance the white colour

white fungus A white to golden-coloured crinkly and rather tasteless fungus *Tremella fuciformis* similar to cloud ear fungus and resembling a ball of sponge, normally available in dried form [also called **snow fungus, silver fungus, tremella**]

white gourd *see* wax gourd

white long grain rice A polished long grain rice with the bran and outer coating removed giving separate fluffy grains when cooked. Requires about 15 minutes boiling to cook

white meat Term used for the breast flesh of poultry to distinguish it from the dark meat of the legs. Also used of pork and veal

white mugwort A hardy deciduous shrub *Artemesia lactiflora* whose aromatic green leaves are used in stuffings for roast goose

white mustard The pale yellow or fawn, pungent seed of an annual plant *Brassica hirta* or *Sinapsis alba* native to Southern Europe. This mild form of mustard is combined with brown mustard, a more aromatic variety, in various proportions to give the variety of mustard-based condiments available

white mutton stock As white beef stock but substituting mutton or lamb bones for beef bones [also called **fond blanc de mouton** (Fr)]

white octopus *see* curled octopus

white onion A variety of onion with a similar shape to the globe but with a silvery white skin. They have a mild sweet flavour and are usually served raw

white onion soup Basic soup with onions [also called **purée d'oignons** (Fr)]

white pepper The dried dehusked berries of a vine *Piper nigrum* sold either as whole berries or ground to a fine fawn powder. Used in white sauces where the dark specks from the husks of black peppercorns would detract from the appearance; *see also* peppercorn

white pomfret The silvery skinned variety of pomfret q.v. with the finer flavour

white pork *(USA)* The flesh of completely desanguinated young pigs

whitepot *(UK)* A Devonshire custard made with eggs, flour, milk and cream

white pudding 1 *(UK)* Skirlie, q.v. packed into hog casings [also called **mealie pudding**] **2** A general name for sausages made from light coloured offal and meats such as brains, tongue, lights, etc. mixed with whitish cooked grains such as pearl barley, oatmeal, etc., seasoned, flavoured and packed into off-white casings. Generally fried and eaten hot

white radish *see* mooli

white roux Equal quantities of plain soft flour and butter, cooked together to a sandy texture for a few minutes without colouring. Used for Béchamel sauce

white sapote *(USA)* A type of baseball-sized custard apple with a green, shading to yellow, edible skin and soft flesh

white sauce *see* Béchamel sauce

white sesame seeds The white variety of sesame seeds used to make tahini. Used as a garnish in Asia and crushed for use in sauces and coatings. In Asia they are dry fried or roasted to release flavour

white skate A variety of skate *Raja marginata* with a fawny red upper skin and white underside. Used as skate

white sprouting broccoli *see* sprouting broccoli

white stew A stew made from poultry or veal with onions in a white sauce; *see also* blanquette

white Stilton A semi-hard, crumbly, slightly acid, whitish cheese which is young Stilton before the veining has started. It is matured for about 4 weeks, has little crust and does not keep. May be used as a substitute for Feta

white sturgeon *see* osyotrina sturgeon

white sugar Fully refined sugar, either granulated, caster or icing

white tuna fish A variety of tuna with very pale flesh

white turmeric *see* zedoary

white veal stock As for white beef stock but substituting veal bones for beef bones [also called **fond blanc de veau** (Fr)]

white vegetable stock Chopped aromatic vegetables simmered in water for 1 hour and strained. Proportions 1 vegetables, 4 water

white vinegar A colourless transparent vinegar either spirit vinegar or a decolourized malt vinegar. Often used for pickling

white wine court bouillon Equal quantities of white wine and water with 120 g of onion and 12 g of salt per litre together with parsley stalks, a little thyme and bayleaf and peppercorns added. Used for trout, eel, pike and most fish

white wine sauce *see* sauce vin blanc

white yam A most important species of yam *Dioscorea rotundata* which is grown in the high rainfall zone of West Africa where it is a staple food

whitebait Young sprats, herring and possibly other fish under 5 cm long, generally deep fried whole à l'anglaise and seasoned with salt and cayenne pepper; *see also* fish à l'anglaise, sand eel

whitetail A name for various gamebirds with white tails, e.g. wheatear

whiting **1** A round bodied seawater fish *Merlangus merlangus* of the cod family found generally in the North Atlantic and weighing about 400 g. The upper skin is grey to dark green or blue and the flesh is lean, white and delicate and may be cooked in any way **2** *(USA) see* silver hake

Whitstable oyster *(UK)* A fine native oyster

whole milk **1** *(UK) see* full cream milk **2** *(USA)* Cows' milk with a least 3.25% butterfat and 8.25% non fat solids

wholegrain wheat Dehusked wheat grains

wholemeal bread Bread made from wholemeal flour [also called **Graham bread** (USA)]

wholemeal flour A flour produced from dehusked wheat grains containing both the bran and the wheat germ [also called **wholewheat flour**]

wholewheat flour *see* wholemeal flour

whortleberry *see* bilberry

wiankowa *(Pl)* A hard sausage made from lean pork and pork fat, formed into the shape of a horseshoe [also called **wiejska**]

wichity grub *see* witchetty grub

wickenin' *(UK)* Yeast

widgeon A small wild duck *Anas penelope* which is normally plucked, drawn and trussed and roasted at 220°C for 20 to 25 minutes, garnished with watercress and lemon and served with an orange salad and a jus lié flavoured with redcurrant jelly or port wine. The shooting season is the 1st of September to the 31st of January. Hanging time 2 to 3 days [also called **wigeon**]

wiejska *(Pl) see* wiankowa

wiener *(USA)* Frankfurter sausage

Wiener Backhendl *(Au)* Deep fried panéed chicken meat possibly beaten out to escalope thickness

Wiener Schnitzel *(Au)* A veal escalope or cutlet, panéed (sometimes olive oil in the egg) and fried in butter. Served with a wedge of lemon

Wiener Schnitzel Holstein *(Au)* A Wiener schnitzel topped with a fried egg

wienerbrød *(De)* Danish pastry. Lit. Vienna bread

wienerlängd *(Sw)* A cake made from a rolled out sheet of Danish pastry 40 by 15 cm. Crème patissière laid lengthways along the centre, the 2 sides folded in over part of the filling and pressed down, proved 40 minutes, baked at 230°C for 20 minutes, cooled, iced and cut across into individual pastries

Wienerwurst *(Au & USA)* A coarse sausage similar in shape to the Frankfurter made from veal or beef and pork lightly cured in sugar, salt and saltpetre, chopped separately, the pork finer than the veal or beef, mixed, seasoned, flavoured with coriander, garlic and grated shallots, filled into narrow sheep casings, lightly smoked, boiled until they rise to the surface, then air dried [also called **wienie** (USA), **Würstel** (Au)]

wienie *(USA) see* Wienerwurst

Wiesenschaumkraut *(Ge)* Lady's smock

wig *(UK)* A small one-portion cake or bun

wigeon *see* widgeon

wijen *(Id)* Sesame seeds

wijn *(Ho)* Wine

Wild *(Ge)* Game

wild boar The original ancestor of the domesticated pig, sometimes hunted but now farmed in enclosed woodland. They grow slowly and the flesh is red and tastier than ordinary pig. Generally killed at 14 to 18 months

wild celery A biennial plant *Apium graveolens* whose ground brown seeds are a constituent of celery salt. The chopped leaves may be used in salads, as a garnish or as an aromatic flavouring [also called **smallage**]

wild duck *see* mallard

wild goose Either pinkfoot or greylag. Shooting season 1st September to the 31st of January. Hanging time 2 to 9 days

wild marjoram *see* oregano

wild rice A black and white seed of a rush plant *Zizania aquatica,* which is grown in China, Japan and the USA. It is not a rice in spite of its name. It is now cultivated as well as being gathered in the wild. Cooked like rice, but requires about 45 minutes boiling [also called **Indian rice, tuscarora rice**]

wild rice shoot The young shoots of the wild rice plant *Zizania aquatica* used as a vegetable. They are up to 25 cm long and may be steamed, boiled, baked or stir fried

wild rose *see* rose

wild spinach *(USA) see* pigweed

wild strawberry A hardy evergreen plant *Fragaria vesca* whose small fruits have a very fine flavour. The cultivated strawberry was bred from imports *F. virginiana* and *F. chiloensis* in the 16th and 18th centuries [also called **wood strawberry**]

wild yeast A yeast which grows naturally on ripe fruit and will cause fermentation. Often a mixture of yeasts and bacteria esp. in hot countries

wildappel *(Ho)* Crab apple

wildbraad *(Ho)* Game

Wildbret *(Ge)* Venison, game

Wildbret Pastete *(Ge)* Venison pie

wilde eend *(Ho)* Wild duck

Wildegeflügel *(Ge)* Game birds

Wildente *(Ge)* Wild duck

wildfowl Game birds such as partridge, wild duck, etc.

Wildschwein *(Ge)* Wild boar

willick *(UK) coll.* (*Northern Ireland*). Winkle

willow grouse A member of the grouse family *Lagopus lagopus* widely spread throughout Scandinavia, northern Russia and the north of North America. It goes completely white in winter. Cooked as grouse

willow partridge *see* ptarmigan

willowleaf mandarin *see* Mediterranean mandarin

Wiltshire cure *(UK)* The principal method of curing bacon in which the curing solution is injected under pressure into a whole side of pork through multiple hollow needles. The sides are then steeped in brine for 2 to 3 days and matured in a cold room for 7 days. At this stage it is known as green bacon. The sides may then be cold smoked to give smoked bacon

Wiltshire sausage *(UK)* A sausage made from freshly killed lean pork, fat pork and rusk (7:3:1), minced, seasoned, flavoured with mace, ginger and sage, packed into hog casings and linked

wind egg An imperfectly formed egg with a soft shell

windberry *see* bilberry

Windbeutel *(Ge)* A large hollow-centred choux pastry ball filled with whipped cream

Windermere char *(UK)* The British version of the freshwater Arctic char from the lake of the same name

windfall Fruit which has fallen off trees and is usually bruised or damaged

Windsor bean *see* broad bean

Windsor red cheese *(UK)* A mature Cheddar cheese flavoured and coloured with a red fruit wine to give a veined appearance

wine **1** The juice of red or white grapes, fermented on or off the skins and matured for varying periods of time depending on quality. Used as a constituent of many sauces esp. when reduced to concentrate the flavour, as a cooking liquor and as a constituent of a marinade **2** Alcoholic drink made from various sources: palm wine, rice wine, barley wine, elderberry wine, etc.

wine ball A mixed culture of yeasts and funghi formed into small balls used for making Chinese alcoholic beverages and fermented red rice [also called **wine cube**]

wine cube *see* wine ball

wine jelly A jelly made with wine, gelatine and flavourings. May be eaten as a dessert or as an accompaniment to meat and game

wine plant *(USA) coll.* Rhubarb

wine vinegar Wine in which the alcohol has been biologically oxidized to acetic acid. The normal concentration is 3 to 4 percent of acetic acid

wineberry The sweet and juicy fruit of a prickly shrub *Rubus phoenicolasius* rather like a conical red blackberry. It may be used as blackberries or raspberries [also called **Japanese wineberry**]

wing The feathered front limbs of a bird used for flying or fast ground running. Usually only the bone nearest the body is used, the remainder going into the stockpot. If very meaty the two bones may be used and are often marinated and grilled

wing kelp *(USA)* Alaria

wing rib of beef *(UK)* The last three ribs of beef closest to the sirloin and the choicest roasting joint. The wing rib with possibly some of the fore ribs is used for the traditional roast beef of England

winged bean *see* asparagus pea

winged pea *see* asparagus pea

winged yam *see* Asiatic yam

winkle A small herbivorous gastropod mollusc (*Littorina littorea*) up to 2.5 cm long found in most coastal waters and usually sold cooked either shelled or still in its shell. They have to be extracted with a long pin or winkle pick. Rather tasteless and usually eaten with vinegar [also called **periwinkle, willick**]

winkle pick A straight pin, 4 to 5 cm in length, used for extracting winkles from their shells

winter artichoke *see* Jerusalem artichoke

Winter Bergminze *(Ge)* Winter savory

winter cress *(USA)* A wild cress *Barbarea vulgaris* with somewhat spicy bitter leaves which may be used in salads. Can be cultivated throughout the winter under protection [also called **yellow rocket**]

winter flounder A flat fish *Pseudopleuronectes americanus* similar to a large plaice. It is found off the eastern coast of Canada and northern USA and moves towards the coast in winter. It weighs about 2 to 3 kg and averages 45 cm long. The upper skin is reddish brown. Cook as plaice [also called **common flounder, George's bank flounder**]

winter frisée *see* endive

winter gourd *see* wax gourd

winter melon A variety of sweet melon (*Cucumis melo*) with smooth yellow or yellow and green striped skin, weighing up to 1 kg and with a sweet juicy white to orange and green flesh. The melon is ripe when the skin gives slightly at the stalk end when pressed. The name is also used confusingly for the wax gourd [also called **casaba melon**]

winter mushroom *see* hoshi-shiitake mushroom and shiitake mushroom

winter purslane A hardy invasive annual plant *Montia perfoliata* with mild-flavoured, heart-shaped leaves and small flowering shoots, all of which are cut continuously for use in salads [also called **miner's lettuce, claytonia**]

winter radish Varieties of radish which can be left in the ground throughout the winter

winter rape *see* rape

winter rocket *(USA)* Watercress

winter savory A perennial herb *Satureja montana* with small narrow pointed and folded leaves rather like thyme which is slightly milder than the summer variety. Used in bean and cheese dishes, on roast duck, to flavour vinegar, chopped to garnish soups and sauces and to flavour salami

winter squash Various fruits of *Curcubita* spp., e.g. *Curcubita maxima, C. moschata,* which are used when fully ripe and the rind has hardened. They are peeled and the seeds removed before cooking. Used for pumpkin pie and soup. Examples are Hubbard, table queen or acorn, golden delicious, butter cup, butternut, turk's cap, etc. They all have much the same flavour. They are often added to curries in India and used tempura style in Japan. They may also be pickled or made into chutney. The salted and dry-roasted seeds are eaten as a snack food

winter wheat Wheat planted in the autumn. The young plants overwinter and growth recommences in spring. Harvested slightly earlier than spring wheat

wintergreen *(USA)* A native evergreen plant

Gaultheria procumbens with deep green aromatic leaves and edible spicy berries used as a flavouring [also called **checkerberry**]

Winterkohl *(Ge)* Kale

wishbone A thin V-shaped bone found in birds which connects the centre of the breast bone to the wing joints, equivalent to the collar bone of humans. It should always be removed from chickens and turkeys to aid carving and jointing

witch sole A small long deepwater flatfish *Glyptocephalus cynoglossus* from north Atlantic European waters, up to 50 cm long and with a brown to grey upper skin.Somewhat thinner than the similar winter flounder. Cook as sole [also called **Torbay sole, pole dab** (USA)]

witchetty grub *(Aus)* The large white larva of an Australian insect eaten after frying by the aboriginal population and becoming more generally popular. It tastes like fish cooked in cream [also called **wichity grub**]

witherslacks *(UK) coll. (Cumbria)* Damson

witlof *(Ho)* Belgian chicory

witloof chicory *see* Belgian chicory

wittebonen *(Ho)* White butter beans

wittegoud *(Ho)* Literally white gold, the name used for the thick white asparagus much liked by the Dutch and in season during May and June

wittekool *(Ho)* Cabbage

Wittling *(Ge)* Whiting

wohlriechende Süssdolde *(Ge)* Sweet cicely

wok *(Ch)* A thin steel pan with one or two handles made in the form of a section of a sphere which is used for very fast Chinese stir-frying. The wok is placed over a very intense heat source and different ingredients may be added to hot oil in order of cooking time. Cooked and part cooked food is often kept on the shallow sloping sides of the wok. Toward the end of the cooking process stock and sauces may be added to complete the whole dish of food. The wok is also used for rapid stir-frying of a single vegetable or item of food, for deep frying and it can be used for steaming using bamboo nested steamers

wok lok wuat *(Ch)* Cardamom

wolf fish *see* catfish

Wolfbarsch *(Ge)* Bass, the fish

wolfberry The seed of the matrimony vine which turns a bright red when cooked. It is used as a flavouring and as a tonic in Chinese medicine

wolke *(UK)* o.e. Rolled or kneaded dough

Wollwurst *(Ge)* A finely minced and ground veal sausage from Bavaria. Normally fried in butter

wonderberry A tropical and sub-tropical annual plant *Solanum x Burbankii* which grows to 1 m and has oval light green leaves and clusters of purple berries each berry up to 1 cm dia. The young leaves and shoots are cooked as spinach. The ripe berries must be thoroughly cooked. Unripe berries contain a poisonous alkaloid [also called **sunberry**]

wong bok *(Ch)* Chinese leaves

wong geung *(Ch)* Turmeric

wong gwa *(Ch)* Cucumber

wong keung *(Ch)* Turmeric

wong nga baak *(Ch)* Chinese leaves

wong paan *(Ch)* Garoupa, the fish

won ton *(Ch)* A type of ravioli made with very thin 8 cm squares of noodle pastry with a small amount of a savoury mixture of meat, fish or vegetables placed in the centre, the pastry is then folded into a triangle, sealed and the two acute angles brought together and the right angle folded outwards. They are either deep fried and served as an appetizer, boiled in a soup or poached until they float

won ton skin *see* won ton wrapper

won ton wrapper Egg pasta or egg noodle dough rolled out as thinly as possible, cut into 8 cm squares and dusted with cornflour [also called **won ton skin**]

won yee *(Ch)* Cloud ear fungus

woo chak *(Ch)* Cuttlefish

wood apple An edible fruit indigenous to the Indian sub-continent about the size of an orange. It is eaten raw or mashed with sugar and water and made into jellies or sherberts. Occasionally available in cans [also called **aegletree fruit, elephant apple**]

wood blewit A variety of edible fungus *Tricholoma nudum* with a relatively long cylindrical stem and a 5 to 14 cm dia. smooth cap, deep purple to brownish purple in damp conditions and beige brown during drought and when mature. The flesh has a pleasant scent and they grow in clusters on forest floors; *see also* blewitt

wood dove *see* pigeon

wood duck *see* Carolina duck

wood ear *see* cloud ear fungus

wood fungus *see* cloud ear fungus

wood grouse *see* capercaillie

wood hedgehog *(USA)* A type of wild mushroom with a near white flesh and a bitter flavour

wood pigeon The wild pigeon *Columba palumbus* recognized by its large feet. Young ones are barded with bacon and stuffed with shallots before roasting at 200°C for 30 to 40 minutes; older birds may be casseroled or stewed. There is no close season (May to October best) and no hanging time is required, although 2 to 3 days are recommended by some authorities

wood sorrel One of the sorrel family with small heart shaped sour leaves used for flavouring and in salads and soups

wood strawberry *see* wild strawberry

woodchuck *(USA)* A North American burrowing rodent *Marmota monax* weighing around 2.5 kg in March to 4.5 kg in September prior to hibernation. The flesh when young resemble pork [also called **groundhog, whistle pig**]

woodcock 1 A small squat wild bird *Scolopax rusticola* from boggy land with mottled plumage, a long bill and large eyes. It weighs about 280 gram and forms one portion. Roasted with the head on, barded with bacon and without drawing the bird at 190°C for 20 to 30 minutes. The trail (liver and heart) is spooned onto the bread on which they are served and the whole garnished with watercress and lemon and accompanied with a jus lié and cranberry sauce. The shooting season is the 1st of October to the 31st of January in England, 1st of September to the 31st of January in Scotland. Hanging time 1 to 3 days **2** *(USA)* A slightly smaller relative *Philobela minor* of the woodcock found in Europe and Asia

woodruff *see* sweet woodruff

wooi heung *(Ch)* Fennel

woolly pyrol *(Ca)* Black gram. Sometimes grown as green manure

woo lo gwa *(Ch)* Bottle gourd

woon sen *(Ch)* Cellophane noodles

woo tau *(Ch)* Taro

wop salad *(USA)* Lettuce with olives, anchovies, oregano, capers, and garlic dressed with olive oil. A politically incorrect name and probably soon obsolete

Worcester sauce *(UK)* A misspelling of Worcestershire sauce

worcesterberry An intermediate sized blue-black hybrid of the North American gooseberry and the blackcurrant. May be used instead of blackcurrants or blueberries

Worcestershire sauce *(UK)* A thin strong-flavoured sauce usually used to add flavour to sauces and cooked dishes. Made commercially from vinegar, molasses, sugar, salt, anchovies, tamarind, shallots, garlic and spices. It is said to have originated when a barrel of vinegar and spices made up for a customer with Indian connections by the pharmacist's shop, Lea and Perrins, in the early 19th century was not collected and bottled for sale by the pharmacist [also called **Lea and Perrins' sauce, Worcester sauce**]

work, to 1 To mix or knead dough with a steady motion **2** During the process of fementation, the liquid or paste is said to work

workseed *see* epazote

wormseed Certain types of fennel used to make a herb tea

worst *(Ho)* Sausage

worteltje *(Ho)* Carrot, root vegetable

wot *(Af)* A hot curry-like meat stew from East Africa

wrasse A very bony fish usually used as bait in the UK but used in other countries to add flavour to soups and stews

wreckfish *(USA)* A name given to various different types of fish

wu kwok *(Ch)* A dim sum made by deep frying a meat filling surrounded by mashed taro. The taro beomes crisp and lacy

wun sen *(Th)* Clear transparent noodles

Würfelzucker *(Ge)* Sugar lumps, cubes

Wurmkraut *(Ge)* Tansy

Wurst *(Ge)* Sausage

Wurst von Kalbsgekrüse *(Ge)* A sausage made from finely chopped calf mesentery, seasoned, flavoured with nutmeg, bound with eggs and cream, packed into hog casings and linked

Wurst in Teig *(Ge)* A sausage wrapped in dough and baked

Würstchen *(Ge)* Small sausages made from lean pork, veal and pork from the throat, seasoned, flavoured with allspice and cardamom, moistened with wine, filled into casings, tied in bundles, boiled 3 minutes in salted water then dried and grilled

Würste *(Ge)* Cold cuts of meat

Würstel *(Au)* **1** Sausage **2** *see* Wienerwurst **3** *(It)* Frankfurter sausage

Würstelbraten *(Au)* A large joint of beef, larded with sausages, slowly braised in the oven with a little stock, sliced across the sausages and served with a sauce made from the pan juices thickened with cream

Wursteplatte *(Ge)* A plate of assorted sliced sausages

Wurstspeisen *(Ge)* Pork products *(charcuterie)*

Würze *(Ge)* Seasoning, spice or condiment

Würzfleisch *(Ge)* A spicy beef stew containing sour cream, served with dumplings or potatoes

Xx

xa *(Vi)* Lemon grass

xacutti masala *(In)* A spice mix from Goa consisting of desiccated coconut, dried Kashmiri chillis, coriander, cumin and fenugreek seeds and black peppercorns, all dry-roasted and ground

xa-lach xon *(Vi)* Watercress

xanthan gum E414. A gum produced from a bacterium *Xanthomonas campestris* by commercial fermentation used as a thickener or gelling agent

xanthophyll *see* E161(b)

Xanthosoma sagittifolium *Bot.* The tannia plant

xanthoxylum *see* anise pepper

Xanthoxylum piperitum *Bot.* Anise pepper and sansho

xarope *(Po)* Syrup

xato *(Sp)* A salad of endive and almonds flavoured with chopped red chilli peppers and garlic and dressed with a vinaigrette. Usually served in winter

Xaviersuppe *(Ge)* Consommé garnished with small cheese dumplings

xérès, sauce *(Fr) fem. see* sherry sauce

xia *(Ch)* Shrimp

xiang gu *(Ch)* Shiitake mushroom

xiang tsai *(Ch)* Coriander

xiang you *(Ch)* Sesame seed oil

xian su ya *(Ch)* Crisp roasted or grilled duck

xiao long bao Small steamed buns

xi dau *(Vi)* Light soya sauce

xie *(Ch)* Crab

xie rou dou fu *(Ch)* Fresh crab meat mixed with soya bean paste

xi gua *(Ch)* Watermelon

xi hong shi *(Ch)* Tomatoes

xing zi *(Ch)* Apricot

xin xiang de *(Ch)* Fresh

xiu *(Ch)* A method of cooking in which ingredients are first fried or steamed, then simmered and finally heated uncovered over a high heat to reduce the cooking liquor to a thick sauce

xoconostle *(Me)* Green prickly pear

xoi nep *(Vi)* Cooked glutinous rice served at breakfast or dinner in place of plain boiled white rice, but never at lunch

xoxo *see* choko

xylitol A polyhydroxy alcohol somewhat sweeter than sugar used in sugar free chewing gum

Yy

ya *(Ch)* Duck

yabbie *(Aus)* A freshwater crayfish *Cherax destructor* widely distributed in Australian waters and growing to a maximum length of 30 cm but generally caught at a smaller size. They have a slightly muddy flavour and may be brown, green or purple

yabloko *(Ru)* Apple

yachmenny khleb *(Ru)* Yeast raised barley bread made with barley flour and wheat flour (2:3), milk, a little honey and yeast, kneaded and proved in the usual way and baked at 200°C for 15 minutes reducing to 180°C until cooked

yachmyen *(Ru)* Barley

Yachtwurst *(Ge)* A coarse-textured sausage made with beef, pork and pistachio nuts

ya dan *(Ch)* Duck egg

ya gan *(Ch)* Duck liver

yahni *(Tu)* Leg of mutton on the bone, browned in mutton fat with sliced onions, then pot roasted with a little water and seasoning in a well sealed fireproof dish

yahniya ot spanak *(Bu)* Stewed lamb with spinach

yahourt *see* yoghurt

yair choy Ch) Cauliflower

yaitsa po-russki *(Ru)* Eggs à la russe. Hard boiled eggs, eggs halved, yolks blended with English and French mustard, seasoning and finely chopped gherkins and spring onion, the mixture returned to the eggs and decorated with paprika and capers

yak A domesticated animal from Tibet mainly reared for its butter

yak butter A very strong-smelling butter made from yak milk and invariably used in Tibetan tea

yakhnee *(ME) see* yakhni (2)

yakhni 1 *(In)* Stock made from meat, bones and vegetables as in the West, simmered 12 to 14 hours in a sealed pan, the vegetables being removed after 3 hours. It may be reduced to a glace de viande when it is known as garhi yakhni [also called **yakni**] **2** *(ME)* Stew, with potatoes as the main ingredient [also called **yakhnee**]

yaki *(Ja) see* yakimono and yakitori

yaki fu *(Ja)* Large cubes of gluten cake roasted until brown

yakimono *(Ja)* The term used for foods which are rapidly grilled, barbecued or fried to give a crisp exterior and only a lightly cooked interior. The food is usually supported on one or more thin skewers depending on the size of the food. Abbreviated in recipes to yaki

yaki myoban *(Ja)* Alum

yakinasu *(Ja)* Aubergine

yakitori *(Ja)* Grilled chicken, chicken livers, onion or Asian leek and sweet pepper kebabs brushed with yakitori sauce during the cooking and sprinkled with sansho or shichimi to garnish

yakitori sauce *(Ja)* Dark soya sauce, sake, mirin, rock sugar and light soya sauce (12:8:5:5:4), simmered for 15 minutes then cooled and refrigerated

yaki zakana *(Ja)* Fish wrapped in foil parcels with onion slices, quarters of sweet green pepper, sliced mushrooms, sake, seasoning and a slice of lemon, baked in a 220°C oven for 15 to 20 minutes and served immediately

yakju *(Ko)* Rice wine

yakni *(In) see* yakhni (1)

yam 1 A generally large tuberous root of one of the *Dioscorea* spp. with dense flesh, used as a starch staple and ranging from less than 0.5 kg to 25 kg in size. They must be cooked and are treated like potatoes. Varieties are found in all tropical and sub-tropical areas and a few in temperate regions. Typical are cush cush yam, Chinese yam, aerial yam, winged yam, guinea yam and Asiatic yam **2** *(Th)* The decorative salads of Thailand which are an art form in their own right **3** The name sometimes incorrectly given to the sweet potato grown in the USA

yam bean 1 *see* jicama **2** An edible tuber of a plant *Sphenostyllis stenocarpa* similar to the jicama q.v. grown in West Africa

yamabukusu *(Ja)* A sweetened vinegar used for seasoning rice as in sushi. A reasonable substitute is vinegar, sugar and salt (15:2:1) with a pinch of MSG

yamadon An oil obtained from yellow nutmeg

yamaimo *(Ja)* Yam

yamo no imo *(Ja)* Mountain yam. Lit. long potato

yang-baechu gimchi *(Ko)* Pickled cabbage leaves wrapped around a filling of white radish and spring onions flavoured with ginger, garlic, chillis, anchovies and salt

yang-hoe *(Ko)* Raw minced beef mixed with sesame seed oil, sesame seeds, ginger, garlic, onions and sugar, formed into mounds, topped with a raw egg yolk, sprinkled with chopped pine nuts and garnished with strips of peeled pear

yan grou *(Ch)* Lamb or mutton

yankee bean *see* navy bean

yan kok *(Ch)* Aniseed

yan wo *(Ch)* Bird's nest

yao dou *(Ch)* Cashew nut

yao gou ji ding *(Ch)* Diced chicken with cashew nuts

yao horn *(Cm)* A type of fondue Chinoise in which thin slices of beef, chicken and seafood are poached at the table in stock and dipped in raw egg and peanut sauce after cooking and before eating

yaourt *(Fr) masc.* Yoghurt

yaout *(Ru & Bu)* Yoghurt

ya pi *(Ch)* Duck skin

yapon *(USA)* A plant similar to holly. The leaves are used by American Indians to make the tea, yaupon

yaprak dolmasi *(Tu)* Vine leaves wrapped around a filling of rice, raisins, chopped onions, pine nuts, chopped parsley or dill and seasoning, baked in the oven and served cold

yard bean *see* asparagus bean

yard long bean *see* long bean and asparagus bean

yari-ika *(Ja)* Grilled squid

Yarmouth bloater *(UK)* A slightly salted and smoked herring from Yarmouth

yarpakh dolmasy *(Ru)* Vine leaves stuffed with a filling of soaked bulgur, fried chopped onions and minced lamb with pine nuts, currants, chopped dried apricots, lemon juice and herbs, casseroled in chicken stock for 40 minutes and served cold with cinnamon-flavoured yoghurt and lemon wedges

yarrow A hardy wild perennial *Achillea millefolium* with clusters of small flowers and feathery leaves. The slightly bitter and peppery young leaves may be chopped and used in moderation for salads, to flavour dips and as a garnish

yasai-ryori *(Ja)* Vegetables

yasawa A fried meat ball made with chicken from the South Pacific islands

yassa au poulet *(WA)* Chicken fried with onions then simmered in a marinade

yau char koay *(Ma)* Crullers

yau jaar gai *(Ch)* Crullers

yaupon *(USA)* Tea made by American Indians from yapon leaves

yautia *see* tannia

yau yu *(Ch)* Squid

ya xin *(Ch)* Duck hearts

ya you *(Ch)* Duck fat, often used to add a finish to Chinese food

ya zhang *(Ch)* Duck feet

ya zhen *(Ch)* Duck gizzards

yeaning *(USA)* A young lamb or kid

yeanling *(UK)* A young lamb or kid

yearling A year old domesticated animal. It might be any age under 2 years

yearn, to *(USA)* To coagulate or curdle milk

yearning *(USA)* Rennet

yeast A microorganism (strictly speaking a fungus) which reproduces by budding from the parent microorganism. The most important in cooking is *Saccharomyces cerevisiae* which has a multitude of variants used principally for converting sugars to alcohol or water and carbon dioxide as in beer, wine, and bread production. Yeasts can also excrete some enzymes which break down polysaccharides into simple sugars. Yeasts work best around 30 to 35°C and are killed above 60°C

yeast extract A dark brown thick glossy semi-solid made by hydrolysing disrupted yeast cells to form a complex mixture of amino acids, peptides, nucleic acids and their reaction products together with vitamins and fragments of other cell contents and concentrating the solution. It has an intense flavour and is used by vegetarians and others for flavouring savoury dishes, as a vitamin supplement and as a sandwich spread

yeasted goods Flour and starch based mixtures which are treated with yeast to produce a multitude of carbon dioxide bubbles within the mixture prior to baking

yee raa *(Th)* Cumin

ye-khu *(Bm)* Sea urchin

yellow bean paste A strong-flavoured Chinese paste made from fermented soya beans. Sold in jars as a flavouring

yellow bean sauce Fermented yellow soya beans let down with brine. Used in Sichuan and Hunan cuisines and generally in SEA [also called **brown bean sauce, soya bean condiment**]

yellow cake *(USA)* Cake in which egg yolks but not egg whites are used

yellow chilli A smooth waxy-skinned chilli slightly larger than a jalapeño and very hot [also called **yellow wax chilli**]

yellow chive Chinese chives whose leaves have been blanched by growing in the dark and which have a mild flavour

yellow crookneck squash An important commercial squash grown in south eastern USA. One of the first plants to be genetically engineered to be resistant to mosaic viruses

yellow cucumber A coarse yellow variety of cucumber grown in China. It has a rough skin and a melon like taste. It is often peeled, shredded and preserved in honey with possibly ginger. Also pickled in soya sauce

yellow dal *(In)* An Indian variety of yellow pea *Pisum sativum* allowed to mature and dry on the vine. Normally dehusked and split. Often used as a snack food after dry roasting with spices (e.g. in Bombay mix) [also called **yellow lentil, yellow split pea**]

yellow eel *(USA)* Ocean pout, one of the eelpout family with a sweet white flesh

yellow fin tuna A variety of tuna fish *Thunnus albacares* more expensive than skipjack

yellow granadilla A type of passion fruit *Passiflora laurifolia* [also called **water lemon**]

yellow gurnard *see* gurnard

yellow lentil *see* yellow dal

yellow passion fruit The fruit of a vine *Passiflora edulis* f. *flavicarpa*, with a hard smooth golden-yellow skin mottled with red and a pulpy yellow flesh with a mass of embedded seeds. Slightly larger than the standard purple passion fruit [also called **golden passion fruit, granadilla, grenadilla**]

yellow pear tomato A tiny pear-shaped yellow tomato used for garnishing and decoration

yellow pea soup *see* purée égyptienne

yellow rice wine See Shaohsing rice wine

yellow rock *see* lump sugar (3)

yellow rocket *see* winter cress

yellow soya bean The dried yellow beans are the common soya bean of commerce. Used for making soya derivatives and the variety which is sold cooked and canned in the west

yellow split pea *see* yellow dal

yellow squash *see* crookneck squash

yellow wax chilli *see* yellow chilli

yellow wine *see* Shaohsing rice wine

yellow yam *see* Guinea yam

yellows *see* light brown sugar

yellowtail dab *see* yellowtail flounder

yellowtail flounder A flat fish *Limanda ferruginea* up to 40 cm long and 500 g in weight with an olive-brown upper skin with reddish-brown spots and a yellowish tail. It is found on the North East coast of North America. Cook as flounder [also called **yellowtail dab**]

yelt *(USA)* A young sow

yemas de San Leandro *(Sp)* Egg yolk threads cooked in hot sugar syrup; *see also* golden threads

yemek listesi *(Tu)* Menu

yen wo *(Ch)* Bird's nest

yerba *(Sp)* Herb

yerba buena *(Me & USA)* A strongly aromatic wild mint used as a flavouring

Yersinia enterocolitica Food poisoning bacteria related to the plague organism. It is found in pork and raw milk and will grow at temperatures below 10°C. The incubation period is not known, the duration is 3 plus days and the symptoms are abdominal pain, fever, headache, malaise, vomiting, nausea and chills. Common in Scandinavia and the USA

yeung choy *(Ch)* Watercress

yeung chung *(Ch)* Onion

ye zi *(Ch)* Coconut

yiaourti *(Gr)* Yoghurt, traditionally made with goats' milk

yield The number of servings or portions obtained from a given recipe or amount of food

yiner *(Ch)* White fungus

ying-shu *(Ch)* Poppy seed

yin wor *(Ch)* Bird's nest

yiouvetsi *(Gr)* Pasta

yira *(Th)* Cumin or fennel

yi tong *(Ch)* Malt extract or maltose

yiu gor *(Ch)* Cashew nut

yod nam mali *(Th)* Jasmine oil

yoghoort *see* yoghurt

yoghourt *see* yoghurt

yoghurt *(De, En, Ho, It & No)* A fermented product made from any milk treated with a culture of *Lactobacillus bulgaricus* and possibly *Streptococcus thermophilus* at a temperature of 37 to 44°C. The fermentation is stopped by cooling to below 5°C after 4 to 6 hours when the liquid will have developed a lactic acid flavour and will be more or less thick, possibly even a gel. Different cultures of the microorganisms and the different milks lead to country-specific textures and flavours. The raw natural yoghurt so obtained may be further pasteurized, sweetened, flavoured, thickened with gums or starches, have fruit added or be treated in a variety of other ways to satisfy Western tastes [also called **natural yoghurt, plain yoghurt, yahourt, yoghoort, yoghourt, yogurt**]

yoghurt salad dressing Natural yoghurt mixed with ground coriander seeds, dried mint and seasoning with possibly olive oil and lemon juice

yogur *(Sp)* Yoghurt

yogurt *(USA & It)* Yoghurt

yok kai sake *(Ja)* Thinly sliced strips of fresh salmon marinated for an hour in a mixture of sake, soya sauce with chopped ginger root, garlic, spring onions, sugar and salt and served with decorative garnishes

yolk *see* egg and egg yolk

York cheese *(UK)* A rich creamy soft cheese made from raw or unpasteurized cow's milk [also called **Cambridge cheese**]

York ham *(UK)* A ham cured with dry salt, lightly oak smoked and matured for 3 to 4 months prior to being boiled. The meat is pale with a mild delicate flavour. One of the classic hams now made all over the world and considered to be the best cooked ham for serving cold

Yorkshire black pudding *(UK)* Black pudding flavoured with marjoram, thyme, lemon thyme and savory

Yorkshire cheese cake *(UK)* An open shortcrust pastry tart filled with a mixture of curd (or sieved cottage) cheese, butter, currants, eggs, sugar, grated lemon zest and nutmeg before baking [also called **Yorkshire curd tart**]

Yorkshire curd tart *see* Yorkshire cheese cake

Yorkshire parkin *(UK)* A type of gingerbread made with fine or medium oatmeal

Yorkshire pie A galantine of meat

Yorkshire pudding A savoury batter nowadays baked in the oven in a large flat tin or individual patty tins together with a roast of beef, and used as an accompaniment to it. Originally the tin of batter was placed beneath a joint of beef roasting on a spit to catch the juices. The batter would cook with the heat from the fire

Yorkshire sauce *(UK)* A julienne of orange zest cooked gently in port, reserved, the port thickened with equal parts of espagnole sauce and red currant jelly flavoured with cinnamon and cayenne pepper, reduced, strained and finished with orange juice and the julienne of orange zest. Served with braised duck or ham

Yorkshire spice bread A heavily spiced fruit loaf raised with yeast or baking powder

yosenabe *(Ja)* Poached chicken breast meat and shellfish served in dashi

you ga li *(Ch)* Curry-flavoured oil

you men sun *(Ch)* Braised bamboo shoots

youngberry A hybrid of the loganberry and dewberry from the south of the USA. Use as blackberry

you yu *(Ch)* Squid or cuttlefish

ysaño A South American knobbly yellow tuber from a perennial climbing plant *Tropaeolum tuberosum* related to the nasturtium. It is eaten in Bolivia after freezing [also called **añu**]

Ysop *(Ge)* Hyssop

yu *(Ch)* **1** Fish **2** Pummelo

yuba *(Ja)* Bean curd sticks

yuca *see* cassava

yucca 1 *see* cassava **2** A wild cactus-like plant *Yucca gloriosa* and related spp. with long fleshy leaves ending in a spike. The young stalks may be cooked like asparagus and fruits may be roasted. [also called **Spanish bayonet, Spanish dagger, Adam's needle, bear grass, Eve's darning needle**]

Yucca gloriosa *Bot.* Yucca (2)

yu chee *(Ch)* Shark's fin

yu chiap *(Ch)* A fermented fish sauce

yu choy *(Ch)* Broccoli rape

yu choy sin *(Ch)* Heart of rape

yudebutaniko no nikomo *(Ja)* Boneless pork loin simmered in water until tender and most of the water has evaporated, cooled, cut in 2 cm cubes and simmered for 10 minutes in soya sauce, sake, sugar and sliced ginger root and a little water, more soya sauce and sugar added and all evaporated to dryness. Served with minced spring onions

yueh shih huo kwo *(Ch)* Steamboat

yuen sai *(Ch)* Coriander leaves

yufka *(Tu)* Filo pastry

yule cake Christmas cake

yule log *see* chocolate log

yu lu *(Ch)* A fermented fish sauce

yum *(Th) see* yam (2) salad

yum cha *(Ch)* Sweet cakes and savouries served with tea during the late morning

yumurta *(Tu)* Egg

yun er *(Ch)* Cloud ear fungus

Yunnan A hand made goat's milk cheese from the mountainous south west province of the same name in China

yu pei *(Ch)* Shark's skin

yuri-ne *(Ja)* Lily bulb

yu ts'ai *(Ch)* Broccoli rape

yu tu *(Ch)* Fish maw

yu xian rou si *(Ch)* Shredded spiced pork

yuzu *(Ja)* A small yellow coloured citrus fruit *Citrus junos* grown mainly for its rind which is used as a garnish and flavouring for soups and vinegars

Zz

zabade *see* zabady

zabady The Arabic for yoghurt [also called **zabade, roba, rob**]

zabaglione *(It)* A warm dessert made from Marsala, egg yolks and sugar [also called **zabaione**]

zabaglione sauce A sauce made from Marsala, whipped eggs and sugar served warm with fruit desserts or from white wine and whipped eggs as a savoury sauce

zabaione *see* zabaglione

zabalin *(Bm)* Lemon grass

zachte eiren *(Ho)* Soft-boiled eggs

zádéllávané drstky *(Cz)* Thin strips of parboiled tripe sautéed in butter with chopped onions and garlic, flour added to make a roux, stock added with chopped ham and parsley and all simmered until cooked

zafferano *(It)* Saffron

zafferanone *(It)* Safflower

zaffran *(In)* Saffron

zafraan *(In)* Saffron

Zahnbrasse *(Ge)* Dentex, the fish

zahtar 1 *(NA)* A spice mixture of 2 parts dry roasted sesame seeds, 1 part sumac and 1 part dried thyme, ground together and used as a condiment, dip or mixed with olive oil and used as a bread glaze **2** *(ME)* Similar to the north African zahtar, it is dry mixture of dry roasted sesame seeds, coriander seeds, walnuts and cooked and dried chick peas, all crushed but not pulverized, with ground cumin, seasoning, cinnamon powder, dried marjoram and sumac powder. Served with a separate dish of olive oil into which bread is dipped prior to its being dipped into the zahtar [also called **dukkah** (Ey)]

zakouski *(Ru & Fr) masc.* **1** Hors d'oeuvres **2** In Russia, a table of cold meats, fish, small appetizers and hors d'oeuvres, traditionally, and in wealthy households, made available for casual guests between late afternoon and dinner but now often including hot dishes and served as a first course or like smörgåsbord

Zakoussotchnyï *(Ru)* A Camembert type cheese made from pasteurized cow's milk

zakrytye buterbrody *(Ru)* Sandwich

zalm *(Ho)* Salmon

zamia A type of palm tree from the pith of which a starch is extracted

zampe *(It)* Feet, trotters

zampetto *(It)* Pig's leg

zampone di Modena *(It)* A sausage made of a mixture of lean and fat pork, seasoned, spiced, moistened with wine and packed into a boned pigs trotter, simmered for an hour and served with potatoes and a sweet sauce. From the province of Emilia-Romagna

zanahorias *(Sp)* Carrots

Zander *(Ge)* The freshwater pike-perch caught in European rivers and lakes and considered to be a delicacy. The flesh is firm and white with a stronger flavour than cod. It was introduced into the UK in the 1970's and is in danger of wiping out native species of fish [also called **Zant**]

zanoibe *(It)* A hors d'oeuvres of stuffed pigs' trotters similar to sampone, served hot or cold

Zant *(Ge)* *see* pike-perch

zao zi *(Ch)* Dates

zapote *see* sapodilla

zarda *(In)* A sweet rice dessert

zaru *(Ja)* A bamboo strainer

zarzamora *(Sp)* Blackberry

zarzuela *(Sp)* A colourful seafood stew mainly of shellfish. A typical zarzuela might consist of cleaned, and prepared as for a stew, mussels, squid, Dublin bay prawns, spiny lobster, hake and eel, added to a mixture of onions, garlic, tomatoes and sweet peppers all chopped and sweated in oil, simmered for 20 minutes with wine, seasoning, saffron and chopped parsley in a casserole dish and finished with stoned olives

zarzuela de mariscos *(Sp)* A Catalan seafood dish. Lit. an operetta of seafood

zatore *(ME)* A herb and spice mix used in bread which usually includes sesame seeds, thyme and savory

zatziki *(Gr)* *see* tsatsiki.

zatzizi *(Ru)* A Georgian dish of chicken flavoured with herbs and served with mashed walnuts

zavtrak *(Ru)* Breakfast, traditionally tea, rolls, curd cheese and/or buckwheat porridge and buttermilk

Zea mays *Bot.* Maize

Zea mays saccharata *Bot.* Sweet corn

zebu A type of domesticated ox *Bos indicus* found throughout Africa, India and East Asia

zedoaire *(Fr)* Zedoary

zedoaria *(It)* Zedoary

zedoary The dried and ground root of a plant *Curcuma zedoaria* and *C. zerumbet* grown and used as a spice in South East Asia. It has a pungent gingery flavour with a hint of camphor. The young shoots and leaves of the plant are used in Indonesian cooking [also called **white turmeric**]

zeeduivel *(Ho)* Monkfish

zeekreeft *(Ho)* Lobster

Zeeland oysters Fine oysters from the Zeeland province of the Netherlands

zeelt *(Ho)* Tench

zeepaling *(Ho)* Conger eel

zeera *(In)* Cumin

zeevis *(Ho)* Seafood

zegeni *(NA)* A spicy meat stew [also called **wat**]

zelná polevká *(Cz)* Cabbage soup made from beef stock thickened with white roux, seasoned and flavoured with nutmeg, finished with egg yolks and cream and mixed with chopped blanched cabbage

zelny gulás *(Cz)* A beef goulash flavoured with paprika, caraway seeds and a little vinegar and mixed with shredded white cabbage [also called **segedinsky gulás**]

zelyonye shchi *(Ru) see* shpinatie shchi

zemikand *(In)* Elephant's foot

zensai *(Ja) see* aemono

zenzero *(It)* **1** Ginger **2** *(Tuscany)* Chilli pepper

zephyr 1 *(En & Fr) masc.* A very light mousse of Italian origin made with fish or other foodstuff pounded to a smooth paste, mixed with egg white and cream, refrigerated and used to fill small moulds lined with thin fish escalopes or similar, baked in a moderate oven, cooled and demoulded. **2** *(USA)* A light delicate cornmeal puff served instead of bread rolls with a meal

zeppole *(It)* Doughnut, fritter

zest The coloured outer layer of citrus fruit skin which contains the essential oil

zeste *(Fr) masc.* Zest

zesté(e) *(Fr)* Flavoured with citrus fruit zest

zeste confit *(Fr) masc.* Candied peel

zeste d'Italie *(Fr) masc.* Candied peel

zester A small very fine toothed metal grater often mounted on a wooden handle for grating the zest of citrus peel

zeytinyagli sebzeler *(Tu)* Mixed vegetables, garlic and seasoning simmered slowly with very little water until tender. Served cold with a sprinkling of chopped parsley

zha *(Ch)* Deep fried

zha cai tang *(Ch)* A spicy vegetable soup

zha ge zi *(Ch)* Deep fried pigeon

zhang cha ya *(Ch)* Duck, smoked over camphor and tea

zha yu qiu *(Ch)* Deep fried square pieces of fish in a hot and spicy sauce

zheng *(Ch)* Steamed

zhi ma yoo *(Ch)* A dark coloured sesame seed oil

zhou *(Ch)* A kind of porridge

zhou fan *(Ch)* Congee rice

zhu *(Ch)* Pig

zhug *(ME)* A typical spice mix from the Yemen used as a condiment and containing red peppers, red chillis, coriander leaves and seeds, garlic, green cardamom and lemon juice pounded into a paste

zhu jidan *(Ch)* Boiled eggs

zhum *(ME)* Cooked junket

zhu rou *(Ch)* Pork meat

zhu sun *(Ch)* Bamboo fungus

zhu you *(Ch)* Lard

zia, alla *(It)* In the aunt's style, i.e. home cooking

zibet A variety of Asian chive

zibidina *(It)* Pig's ears, chops and calves' feet cooked in chicken stock with salt and liberal pepper then cooled to form a strong jelly

Zichorien *(Ge)* Chicory

Ziebelwähe *(He)* Onion pie

Ziege *(Ge)* Goat

Ziegen *(Ge)* Goat's milk cheese

Ziegenkäse *(Ge)* Goat's milk cheese

Ziegenpfeffer *(Ge)* Sweet pepper

Ziger *(He) see* Sapsago

Zigeuner Art *(Ge)* In the gypsy style. See Zingara, à la

Zigeunerspeck *(Ge)* Lightly cured and smoked pork fat rolled in paprika and eaten raw

Zigeunerspies *(Ge)* Meat, pepper and onion kebab grilled on the barbecue or over a fire

zik de venado *(Me)* Shredded cooked venison served with onion, chilli peppers, coriander leaf and Seville orange flesh

zimino *(It)* A soup or stew of fish with white wine, tomatoes, mushrooms and herbs

ziminu *(Fr)* As zimino but from Corsica

Zimt *(Ge)* Cinnamon

Zimtplätzchen *(Ge)* Cinnamon cakes

Zingara, à la *(Fr)* In the gypsy style, i.e. with ham, tongue, mushrooms and tomatoes

Zingara, sauce *(Fr) fem.* A sauce for veal and poultry made to a variety of recipes and little used

Zingiber officinale *Bot.* Ginger

ziste *(Fr)* The white pith on the inner surface of citrus fruit peel (albedo) [also called **peau blanche**]

zita *see* ziti

ziti *(It)* Long lengths of thick macaroni

ziti mezze *(It)* Long lengths of macaroni slightly thinner than ziti

zitoni *(It)* A very thick version of ziti

zitoni rigati *(It)* A fluted or ridged zitoni

Zitroenstrauch *((Ge)* Lemon verbena

Zitronat *(Ge)* Candied peel

Zitrone *(Ge)* Lemon

Zitwerwurzel *(Ge)* Zedoary

Zizania aquatica *Bot.* Wild rice

Zizyphus lotus *Bot.* Lotus jujube

Zizyphus mauritania *Bot.* Mauritian jujube

Zizyphus mistol *Bot.* Argentinian jujube

Z'nuni *(Ge)* The second breakfast or midmorning snack in Bavaria, traditionally blackbread, raw bacon or ham and cherry liqueur

zoetwaterkreeft *(Ho)* Crayfish

zoetzuur *(Ho)* Sweet and sour, pickles

zoni *(Ja)* A New Year celebration soup of mochi, kamaboko, chicken meat and sliced vegetables in dashi garnished with yuzu

zoolak A lactic fermented milk product

zosui *(Ja)* A thick rice soup made from well washed and soaked short grain rice simmered in boiling dashi with grated ginger root until the rice disintegrates, seasoned, petit pois, crumbled crisped nori and beaten egg yolk added and all simmered for 10 minutes

zout *(Ho)* Salt

zoutevis *(Ho)* Salt cod

zrasy *(Ru)* Beef or veal olives filled with sour pickles, hard boiled eggs and/or vegetables

zrázy *(Pl)* A sirloin steak beaten flat, coated with a mixture of sweated chopped onions, bacon, breadcrumbs, egg and seasoning, rolled and tied, browned in butter then simmered in red wine with chopped onions, diced bacon and a faggot of herbs. Served with the drained cooking liquor thickened with beurre manié

Zsendice *(Hu)* A soft, smooth, creamy ewe's milk and whey cheese

zucca *(It)* Marrow, squash

zucca gialla *(It)* Pumpkin

zucchero *(It)* Sugar

zucchetti *(It)* Small courgettes

zucchini *(En & It)* Courgette

zucchini flowers *see* courgette flowers

Zucker *(Ge)* Sugar

Zuckererbsen *(Ge)* Petit pois

Zuckerrübe *(Ge)* Sugar beet

Zuckerwähe *(Ge)* A sugar tart

Zuger Kirschtorte *(He)* A sponge cake soaked in Kirsch-flavoured syrup and covered with pink icing

zulynez *(Ru)* Sour cream

zulynez gribnoy po-odessky *(Ru)* Mushrooms in sour cream made by sweating chopped onions in butter, button mushrooms added and softened, a little flour added and cooked to a roux, equal parts of sour cream and double cream added, all well mixed, placed in an oven proof dish, topped with grated cheese and butter and baked at 180°C until the top colours

zumaque *(Sp)* Sumac

zumo *(Sp)* Juice

Zunge *(Ge)* Tongue

Zungenwurst *(Ge)* A blood sausage with pieces of cooked tongue and fat embedded in it

zupa *(Pl)* Soup

zuppa *(It)* A substantial soup either thickened with bread or poured over slices of bread or other farinaceous food

zuppa acida alla bolzanese *(It)* Tripe soup containing cream, sauerkraut and lemon juice, served over polenta

zuppa alla canavesana *(It)* Cabbage, bread and cheese layered in a deep dish, soaked in broth and browned in the oven

zuppa genovese *(It)* Fish soup thickened with egg yolks and garnished with small fish quenelles

zuppa inglese *(It)* An English style trifle with a base of macaroons moistened with Marsala, covered with custard and topped with whipped cream and glacé fruit

zuppa pavese *(It)* A dish consisting of a slice of toast topped with a poached egg, sprinkled with grated Parmesan cheese and floated on a clear beef consommé

zuppa di pesce *(It)* Fish soup

zuppa rustica *(It)* A country soup containing potatoes, beans and sausages

zur *(Pl)* A plain soup made from sour rye

Zürchertopf *(He)* Beef, macaroni and tomato sauce baked in a casserole

Züritirggel *(He)* A honey-flavoured thin biscuit baked in a mould carved with a traditional relief; *see also* Basler Leckerli

zurrette *(It)* A Sardinian dish of lambs' or goats' blood mixed with cheese and steamed until solid then served cold or sliced and grilled

zurruputuna *(Sp)* Salt cod soup, thickened with bread and flavoured with garlic, paprika and sweet peppers

Zutaten *(Ge)* Condiments

zuur *(Ho)* Sour

zuurkool *(Ho)* Sauerkraut

zuwai-gani *(Ja)* Crab

zwaardvis *(Ho)* Swordfish

zweischalig Muscheln *(Ge)* Bivalve shellfish

Zwetschen *(Ge) see* Zwetschgen

Zwetschgen *(Au & Ge)* Plums or prunes [also called **Zwetschen** (Ge)]

Zwetschgendatschi *(Au)* Plum cake

Zwieback *(Ge & Fr)* A small rusk made from dried and browned breads used as a snack food

Zwiebel *(Ge)* Onion

Zwiebel rostbraten *(Au)* Fried steak and onions with gravy accompanied by fried potatoes and gherkins

Zwiebelgrün *(Ge)* Spring onion

Zwiebelkuchen *(Ge)* Onion tart

Zwiebelringe *(Ge)* Onion rings

Zwiebelsosse *(Ge)* An onion sauce made with chopped onions, slightly browned in butter, flour added to make a roux, cream whisked in and boiled, seasoned, flavoured with nutmeg, passed though a sieve and the consistency adjusted

Zwischenrippenstück *(Ge)* Rib steak of beef

zwitsers kaas *(Ho)* Swiss cheese

zwyczajna *(Pl)* A hard sausage made with coarsely chopped pork, seasoned, packed into casings and knotted in long links. Found throughout the country

zymase Various enzymes which together induce the alcoholic fementation of carbohydrates, usually obtained from living yeast but may be added apart from the yeast

zyme Yeast, the origin of the word enzyme, as the first enzymes were extracted from yeast